THE
ANNUAL REGISTER
Vol. 253

THE
ANNUAL REGISTER

World Events 2011

Edited by
D.S. LEWIS
and
WENDY SLATER

FIRST EDITED IN 1758
BY EDMUND BURKE

Colophon from 1758 volume.

The 2012 Annual Register: WORLD EVENTS, 253rd Ed.
Published by ProQuest

789 E. Eisenhower Parkway
P.O. Box 1346 Ann Arbor, MI 48106-1346, USA

The Quorum, P.O. Box 1346
Barnwell Road, Cambridge, CB5 8SW, UK

www.proquest.com

Phone: +1-734-761-4700 Toll-free +1-800-521-0600
Fax: +1-800-864-0019
Email: core_service@proquest.com

ISBN: 978-1-61540-253-3 / ISSN: 0266-6170

British Library Cataloguing in Publication Data:
The Annual Register—2012
1. History—Periodicals
909.82'8'05 D410

Library of Congress Catalog Card Number:
4-17979

Set in Times Roman by
NEW AGE GRAPHICS, Silver Spring, MD, USA

Printed in the USA by
THE SHERIDAN BOOKS, Chelsea, MI, USA

Jacket Design: JOHN C. MOSS

Printed on permanent recycled paper, acid-free.

CONTENTS

VII   CENTRAL AND SOUTHERN AFRICA

VIII   SOUTH ASIA AND INDIAN OCEAN

IX   SOUTH—EAST AND EAST ASIA

X   AUSTRALASIA AND THE PACIFIC

XI   INTERNATIONAL ORGANISATIONS

CONTRIBUTORS

	D.S. Lewis, PhD, Editor of *The Annual Register*; former Editor of *Keesing's Record of World Events*; **Wendy Slater**, MA, PhD, Editor of *The Annual Register*; former Lecturer in Contemporary Russian History, University College London
	Philip M.H. Bell, Senior Research Fellow, University of Liverpool

PART I

	Paul Rogers, PhD, Professor of Peace Studies, Bradford University; Global Security Consultant to Oxford Research Group

PART II

	Lewis Baston, BA, Senior Research Fellow of Democratic Audit
	Charlotte Lythe, MA, Honorary Research Fellow in Economic Studies, University of Dundee
	Gwyn Jenkins, MA, Director of Collection Services, The National Library of Wales, Aberystwyth
	Alan Greer, PhD, Reader in Politics and Public Policy, University of the West of England, Bristol; Co-editor, *Irish Political Studies*
	Dan Hough, PhD, Lecturer in Politics, University of Sussex
	Martin Harrison, Professor of Politics, University of Keele
	Mark Donovan, PhD, Senior Lecturer in Politics, Cardiff University; Editor, *Modern Italy*
	Martin Harrison (see France)
	Johan Strang, PhD, Centre for Nordic studies, University of Helsinki
	Martin Harrison (see France)
	William Chislett, former correspondent of *The Times*, Spain, and the *Financial Times*, Mexico
	Martin Eaton, PhD, FRGS/IBG, Reader in Human Geography, University of Ulster at Coleraine
	Dominic Fenech, DPhil, Professor of History, University of Malta
	Susannah Verney, PhD, Assistant Professor of European Integration, University of Athens; editor, *South European Society and Politics*
	Robert McDonald, Writer and broadcaster on Cyprus, Greece and Turkey
	A.J.A. Mango, PhD, Orientalist and writer on current affairs in Turkey and the Near East

PART III

POLAND
George Sanford, MPhil, PhD, Professor Emeritus of East European Politics, University of Bristol

ESTONIA, LATVIA, LITHUANIA
Allan Sikk, PhD, Lecturer in Baltic Politics, University College London

CZECH REPUBLIC, SLOVAKIA
Sharon Fisher, PhD, Analyst specialising in East European political and economic affairs, IHS Global Insight

HUNGARY
Daniel Izsak, MA, PhD candidate Central European University; former BBC World Service editor and journalist

ROMANIA
Gabriel Partos, MA, Balkan Affairs Analyst/Editor, Economist Intelligence Unit

BULGARIA, ALBANIA
Genc Lamani, MA, Journalist, BBC World Service News and Current Affairs

FORMER YUGOSLAV REPUBLICS
Marcus Tanner, MA, Author; Editor *Balkan Insight*

RUSSIA, WESTERN CIS
Wendy Slater (see Preface)

CAUCASUS
Elizabeth Fuller, Writer on developments in the Caucasus

PART IV

UNITED STATES OF AMERICA
James D. Miller, PhD, Associate Dean, Department of History, Carleton University, Ottawa

CANADA
Will Stos, MA, PhD candidate, Department of History, York University, Toronto

MEXICO, CENTRAL AMERICA
Christian E. Rieck, MSc, Research Fellow, German Institute for Global and Area Studies, Hamburg; lecturer in the History Department, Humboldt-Universität, Berlin.

CARIBBEAN
Peter Clegg, MSc, PhD, Senior Lecturer in Politics, University of the West of England

BRAZIL
Kurt Perry, freelance writer specialising in Latin America

ARGENTINA, PARAGUAY, URUGAY
Christian E. Rieck (see Mexico etc.)

SOUTH AMERICA
Kurt Perry (see Brazil etc.)

PART V

ISRAEL, PALESTINE
Darren Sagar, MA, Editor of *Keesing's Record of World Events*

EGYPT, JORDAN, SYRIA, LEBANON
David Butter, MA, Chief Energy Analyst, Economist Intelligence Unit; Editor *Business Middle East*; Editor ViewsWire Middle East

IRAQ
Darren Sagar (see Israel etc.)

SAUDI ARABIA, YEMEN, ARAB GULF STATES
Fernando Carvajal, MA, Co-Editor in Chief, *International Journal for Arab Studies*

SUDAN, SOUTH SUDAN
Richard Barltrop, DPhil, writer and consultant specialising in Sudanese and Middle Eastern affairs

LIBYA, TUNISIA, ALGERIA, MOROCCO WESTERN SAHARA
Josh Bird, MPhil candidate, St Antony's College, Oxford; D.S. Lewis and Wendy Slater (see Preface)

PART VI

HORN OF AFRICA

KENYA, TANZANIA, UGANDA

NIGERIA

GHANA, SIERRA LEONE,
THE GAMBIA, LIBERIA

FRANCOPHONE AFRICA

GUINEA BISSAU, CAPE VERDE,
SÃO TOMÉ AND PRÍNCIPE

Colin Darch, PhD, Senior Information Specialist,
African Studies Library, University of Cape Town
Gabrielle Lynch, DPhil, Associate Professor of
Comparative Politics, University of Warwick
Adam Higazi, DPhil, Research Fellow in African
Studies, King's College, Cambridge
Bronwen Everill, PhD, Assistant Professor of Global
History, University of Warwick
Kaye Whiteman, former Publisher, *West Africa*
Christopher Saunders, DPhil, Professor, Department of
Historical Studies, University of Cape Town

PART VII

DRC, BURUNDI & RWANDA, MOZAMBIQUE

ANGOLA, ZAMBIA, MALAWI

ZIMBABWE

BOTSWANA, LESOTHO, NAMIBIA,
SWAZILAND, SOUTH AFRICA

Colin Darch (see Horn of Africa)
Christopher Saunders (see Guinea Bissau etc.)
R.W. Baldock, PhD, Managing Director, Yale University
Press; writer on African affairs
Elizabeth Sidiropoulos, MA, Director of Studies,
South African Institute of International Affairs; and
Terence Corrigan, BA (Hons), Political Consultant,
Johannesburg

PART VIII

IRAN

AFGHANISTAN

CENTRAL ASIAN REPUBLICS

INDIA, PAKISTAN, SRI LANKA,
BANGLADESH, NEPAL, BHUTAN

MAURITIUS, SEYCHELLES, COMOROS,
MALDIVES, MADAGASCAR

Farideh Farhi, PhD, Researcher, and affiliate of
University of Hawaii-Manoa
D.S. Lewis (see Preface)
Shirin Akiner, PhD, Lecturer in Central Asian Studies,
School of Oriental and African Studies, University of
London
James Chiriyankandath, PhD, Senior Research
Fellow, Institute of Commonwealth Studies, School of
Advanced Study, University of London
Malyn Newitt, PhD, JP, Charles Boxer
Professor of History, Department of Portuguese,
King's College London

PART IX

BURMA (MYANMAR), THAILAND,
MALAYSIA, BRUNEI, SINGAPORE,
VIETNAM, CAMBODIA, LAOS

INDONESIA, PHILIPPINES, TIMOR LESTE

CHINA, HONG KONG, TAIWAN

JAPAN

Stephen Levine, PhD, ONZM, Professor and Head
of School of History, Philosophy, Political Science
and International Relations, Victoria University
of Wellington
MacQueen, MSc, DPhil, Head of Department of
Politics, University of Dundee
Kerry Brown, MA, PhD, Head of Asia Programme at
Chatham House, former First Secretary British
Embassy Beijing
D.S. Lewis (see Preface)

NORTH AND SOUTH KOREA

J.E. Hoare, PhD, Consultant on East Asia; former chargé d'affaires in Pyongyang

MONGOLIA

Wendy Slater (see Preface)

PART X

AUSTRALIA

Graeme Orr, Associate Professor, Law School, University of Queensland

PAPUA NEW GUINEA

Norman MacQueen (see Indonesia etc.)

NEW ZEALAND, PACIFIC
   ISLAND STATES

Stephen Levine (see Burma etc.)

PART XI

UNITED NATIONS

David Travers, former lecturer in Politics and International Relations, University of Lancaster; former Specialist Advisor on the UN to the House of Commons foreign affairs committee

NATO

Paul Cornish, PhD, Professor of International Security, University of Bath

ECONOMIC ORGANISATIONS

Paul Rayment, MA, former Director of the Economic Analysis Division of the UN Economic Commission for Europe, Geneva

THE COMMONWEALTH

Derek Ingram, Consultant Editor of *Gemini News Service*

LA FRANCOPHONIE

Kaye Whiteman (see Francophone Africa)

NON-ALIGNED MOVEMENT AND
   GROUP OF 77

Peter Willetts, PhD, Emeritus Professor of Global Politics, City University, London

EUROPEAN UNION

Rory Watson, Journalist, expert on affairs of the European Union

OSCE AND COUNCIL OF EUROPE

Martin Harrison (see France etc.)

AMERICAN AND CARIBBEAN
   ORGANISATIONS

Peter Clegg (see Caribbean)

ARAB ORGANISATIONS

Darren Sagar (see Israel etc.)

AFRICAN ORGANISATIONS AND
   MEETINGS

Christopher Saunders (see Guinea Bissau etc.)

EURASIAN ORGANISATIONS

Shirin Akiner (see Central Asia)

ASIA-PACIFIC ORGANISATIONS

Stephen Levine (see Burma etc.)

PART XII

INTERNATIONAL ECONOMY

Paul Rayment (see Economic Organisations)

PART XIII

MEDICAL, SCIENTIFIC AND
   INDUSTRIAL RESEARCH

Neil Weir, FRCS, Consultant otolaryngologist; and **Lorelly Wilson,** Honorary Teaching Fellow, University of Manchester

INFORMATION TECHNOLOGY

J. Nathan Mathias, MA, Research Assistant, MIT Media Lab

ENVIRONMENT

Michael McCarthy, Environment Editor, *The Independent*

PART XIV

INTERNATIONAL LAW	**Christine Gray,** MA, PhD, Fellow in Law, St John's College, Cambridge
EUROPEAN UNION LAW	**Neville March Hunnings,** LLM, PhD, Editor, *Encyclopaedia of European Union Law: Constitutional Texts*
LAW IN THE UK	**Jonathan Morgan,** MA, PhD, Fellow and Tutor in Law, St Catherine's College, Oxford
LAW IN THE USA	**Robert J. Spjut,** ID, LLD, Member of the State Bars of California and Florida

PART XV

RELIGION	**Mark Chapman,** PhD, Vice Principal, Ripon College Cuddesdon, Oxford; **Shaunaka Rishi Das,** Director, Oxford Centre for Hindu Studies; **Colin Shindler,** PhD, Reader in Israeli and Modern Jewish Studies, SOAS, University of London; **Timothy Winter,** MA, Sheikh Zayed Lecturer in Islamic Studies, University of Cambridge

PART XVI

OPERA	**George Hall,** UK correspondent of *Opera News*
CLASSICAL MUSIC	**Igor Toronyi-Lalic,** writer on music and the arts for *The Times* and *The Daily* and *Sunday Telegraph*; co-founder, and classical music and opera editor, of London-based culture website, www.theartsdesk.com
ROCK & POP MUSIC	**David Sinclair,** Pop music critic of *The Times*, London
BALLET & DANCE	**Jane Pritchard,** Curator of Dance, the Victoria and Albert Museum of Performing Arts, London
THEATRE	**Matt Wolf,** London theatre critic of *The International Herald Tribune* and correspondent for the Broadway.com website; co-founder, and theatre editor, of www.theartsdesk.com
CINEMA	**Derek Malcolm,** Cinema critic, *The Guardian*
TV & RADIO	**Raymond Snoddy,** Freelance journalist specialising in media issues, writing for *The Independent*
VISUAL ARTS	**Anna Somers Cocks,** Group Editorial Director, *The Art Newspaper*
ARCHITECTURE	**Oliver Wainwright,** Buildings Editor, *Building Design*
LITERATURE	**Alastair Niven,** OBE, Principal, Cumberland Lodge; formerly Director of Literature, British Council

PART XVII

SPORT	**Paul Newman,** Tennis correspondent for *The Independent*

PART XVIII

OBITUARY	**D.S. Lewis** (see Preface)

ABBREVIATIONS AND ACRONYMS

AC	Arctic Council
ACS	Association of Caribbean States
ADB	Asian Development Bank
AL	Arab League
ALADI	Latin American Integration Association
ANZUS	Australia-New Zealand-US Security Treaty
APEC	Asia-Pacific Economic Co-operation
ASEAN	Association of South-East Asian Nations
AU	African Union
Benelux	Belgium-Netherlands-Luxembourg Economic Union
BSEC	Black Sea Economic Co-operation
Ancom/CA	Andean Community of Nations
CARICOM	Caribbean Community and Common Market
CE	Council of Europe
CEEAC	Economic Community of Central African States
CEFTA	Central European Free Trade Agreement
CEI	Central European Initiative
CELAC	Community of Latin American and Caribbean States
CENSAD	Community of Sahel-Saharan States
CIA	US Central Intelligence Agency
CIS	Commonwealth of Independent States
COMESA	Common Market of Eastern and Southern Africa
CPLP	Community of Portuguese-Speaking Countries
CSTO	Collective Security Treaty Organisation
DRC	Democratic Republic of Congo
EAC	East African Community
EBRD	European Bank for Reconstruction and Development
ECO	Economic Co-operation Organisation
ECOWAS	Economic Community of West African States
ECtHR	European Court of Human Rights
EEA	European Economic Area
EFSF	European Financial Stability Facility
EFTA	European Free Trade Association
EMEs	emerging market economies
EU	European Union
EurAsEC	Eurasian Economic Community
G-8	Group of Eight
G-7	Group of Seven
G-20	Group of Twenty
G-77	Group of 77
GCC	Gulf Co-operation Council
GDP	gross domestic product

GNI	gross national income
HIPC	Heavily Indebted Poor Countries
HIV/AIDS	Human Immunodeficiency Virus/Acquired Immune Deficiency Syndrome
IBRD	International Bank for Reconstruction and Development
IAEA	International Atomic Energy Agency
IDA	International Development Association
IEA	International Energy Agency
IGAD	Inter-Governmental Authority on Development
IGO	inter-governmental organisation
IMF	International Monetary Fund
IPCC	UN Intergovernmental Panel on Climate Change
IOC	Indian Ocean Commission
ISP	Internet service provider
LDCs	least developed countries
MERCOSUR	Southern Cone Common Market
NAFTA	North American Free Trade Agreement
NAM	Non-Aligned Movement
NASA	the US National Aeronautics and Space Administration
NATO	North Atlantic Treaty Organisation
NEPAD	New Partnership for Africa's Development
NGO	non-governmental organisation
OAS	Organisation of American States
OECD	Organisation for Economic Co-operation and Development
OECS	Organisation of Eastern Caribbean States
OIC	Organisation of the Islamic Conference
OIF	International Organisation of Francophonie
OPEC	Organisation of the Petroleum Exporting Countries
OSCE	Organisation for Security and Co-operation in Europe
PACE	Parliamentary Assembly of the Council of Europe
PC	Pacific Community
PFP	Partnership for Peace
PIF	Pacific Islands Forum
PPP	purchasing power parity
PRGF	Poverty Reduction and Growth Facility
SAARC	South Asian Association for Regional Co-operation
SADC	Southern African Development Community
SCO	Shanghai Co-operation Organisation
SELA	Latin American Economic System
UAE	United Arab Emirates
UEMOA	West African Economic and Monetary Union
UNASUR	Union of South American Nations
UNESCO	United Nations Educational, Scientific and Cultural Organisation
UNHRC	United Nations Human Rights Council
WHO	World Health Organisation
WMO	UN World Meteorological Organisation
WTO	World Trade Organisation

EDITORS' NOTES

THE editors gratefully acknowledge their debt to the principal sources for the national and IGO data sections (showing the situation at end 2011 unless otherwise stated), namely the World Bank Group's *World Development Report*, the United Nations, the *Financial Times* (London), the Economist Intelligence Unit's *Democracy Index 2010*, Transparency International's *Corruption Perceptions Index 2011* and *Keesing's Record of World Events* (Keesing's Worldwide). The editors also record their thanks to the British Embassy in Pyongyang for information concerning North Korean currency rates. Whilst every effort is made to ensure accuracy, the AR advisory board and the bodies which nominate its members, the editors, and the publisher disclaim responsibility for any opinions expressed or the accuracy of facts recorded in this volume.

POPULATION: figures are mid-year estimates produced by the World Bank unless otherwise indicated, based on de facto population, meaning all residents regardless of legal status or citizenship, (except for refugees not permanently settled in the country of asylum who are generally considered part of the population of their country of origin.)

GNI: gross national income: the sum of value added by all resident producers plus any product taxes (less subsidies) not included in the valuation of output plus net receipts of primary income (compensation of employees and property income) from abroad.

GNI PER CAPITA in international dollars (Intl$ at PPP): a measure of GNI that allows a standard comparison of real price levels between countries by using purchasing power parity (PPP) rates. An international dollar has the same purchasing power over domestic GNI as a US dollar has in the United States. GNI per capita is GNI divided by mid-year population.

DEMOCRACY INDEX: rates the state of democracy based on: electoral process and pluralism, civil liberties, the functioning of government, political participation, and political culture. Scored on a scale of 1-10 (the higher the score, the more "democratic"); ranked out of 167 states or territories. Derived from Economist Intelligence Unit (see above).

CORRUPTION INDEX: rates the perceived level of public-sector corruption. Scored on a scale of 1-10 (the higher the score, the "cleaner" the country); ranked out of 183 countries or territories. Derived from Transparency International (see above).

It is with great sadness that the editors and the advisory board record the death, in February 2012, of the eminent historian M.R.D. Foot, who served as the Royal Historical Society's representative on the *Annual Register* advisory board from 1972 to 2002. After his retirement, he remained actively associated with the publication and contributed a commemorative article to the 250th edition of *The Annual Register* in 2009. His erudition and his unwavering support will be much missed.

WORLD EVENTS FROM *THE ANNUAL REGISTER* 1758-2011

Selected by Philip M.H. Bell, Senior Research Fellow, University of Liverpool, nominated to the Advisory Board of The Annual Register by the Royal Historical Society.

1758 Halley's Comet returns, as calculated by Edmond Halley in 1705

1759 British conquer Quebec from the French; death of Montcalm and Wolfe

1760 Britain: accession of George III, the first British Hanoverian monarch

1761 Transit of Venus on 6 June helps understanding of the movement of planets

1762 Russia: assassination of Tsar Peter III; accession of Catherine the Great

1763 Peace of Paris ends Seven Years' War; British control in Canada and India

1764 Stanislaus Poniatowski elected King of Poland

1765 British Parliament passes Stamp Act, to tax American colonies

1766 Repeal of Stamp Act in face of American opposition

1767 Expulsion of the Jesuits from all Spanish dominions

1768 France purchases Corsica from Genoa; conquest of island

1769 Britain imposes Tea Duties on American colonies

1770 The "Boston Massacre": casualty list 4 dead, 7 wounded

1771 Dispute between Britain and Spain over Falkland Islands

1772 First Partition of Poland by Russia, Prussia and Austria

1773 "Boston Tea Party" staged as protest against Tea Duty

1774 Continental Congress in Philadelphia draws together the American colonies

1775 American victories over British forces at battles of Lexington and Concord

1776 American Declaration of Independence, 4 July

1777 Publication of *A Voyage towards the South Pole and round the World* by James Cook

1778 Death of Voltaire, 30 May

1779 Spanish and French forces begin siege of Gibraltar

1780 Gordon Riots in London: "No Popery!"

1781 Cornwallis surrenders at Yorktown; decisive defeat for British in America

1782 Admiral Rodney's victory over the French at the Saints; British naval recovery

1783 Treaty of Versailles: Britain recognises American independence

1784 Pitt the Younger becomes British prime minister at age 24

1785 Flight of Blanchard and Jeffries by balloon from Dover to Calais

1786 Death of Frederick the Great, the creator of the new Kingdom of Prussia

1787 France: Louis XVI convenes Assembly of Notables; dissolved without result

1788 Russo-Turkish war: Potemkin besieges Ochakov

1789 Revolution in France; storming of the Bastille, 14 July

1790 Death of Benjamin Franklin, statesman and polymath

1791 France: Feast of the National Confederation to acclaim the Revolution

1792 Battle of Valmy, 20 September; victory of French revolutionary army

1793 Execution of Louis XVI of France

1794 Erasmus Darwin publishes *Zoonomia*, foreshadowing the idea of evolution

1795 Third and final partition of Poland; Poland disappears from the map

1796 Napoleon's victory at Lodi marks his emergence as a dominant figure

1797 First bank-notes issued in Britain; paper currency replaces specie

1798 Napoleon's expedition to Egypt results in conquest and scientific exploration

1799 Pitt introduces income tax in Britain

1800 Act of Union between Britain and Ireland passed; takes effect, 1 January 1801

1801 Thomas Jefferson becomes president of the USA

1802 Peace of Amiens brings war between Britain and France to temporary end

1803 Louisiana Purchase: USA buys Louisiana territories from France

1804 Napoleon crowns himself Emperor of the French

1805 Battle of Trafalgar establishes British naval dominance for a century

1806 Humphry Davy presents paper on electro-chemistry to Royal Society

1807 Abolition of slave trade in British Empire

1808 Napoleon imposes Joseph Bonaparte as King of Spain; Spanish revolt

1809 Napoleon defeats Austrians at Wagram, and imposes severe peace terms

1810 Venezuela revolts against Spain; rebellion spreads to other colonies

1811 Birth of a son to Napoleon and Marie Louise, thereby starting a dynasty

1812 Napoleon captures Moscow, but is forced into disastrous winter retreat

1813 Napoleon decisively defeated at Leipzig in the Battle of the Nations

1814 Napoleon abdicates and is exiled to Elba

1815 Napoleon returns for the "Hundred Days", is defeated at Waterloo and exiled to St Helena

1816 Declaration of Argentinian independence at Buenos Aires

1817 Discontent and disorder in Britain; Habeas Corpus suspended

1818 France: abolition of slave trade in all French territories

1819 Britain: parliamentary reform rally in Manchester ends in "Peterloo" massacre

1820 Spain ratifies treaty for purchase of Florida by USA

1821 Mexican independence declared, under Iturbide as generalissimo

1822 Declaration of Greek independence; Turkish massacre of Greeks at Chios

1823 Monroe Doctrine: American continent declared closed to European colonisation

1824 Death of Byron at Missolonghi marks the creation of a Romantic legend

1825 Russia: Decembrist rising crushed in St Petersburg

1826 Opening of Telford's suspension bridge across Menai Straits, the first of its kind

1827 Battle of Navarino: Turkish defeat assists Greek struggle for independence

1828 Frontier treaty between Brazil and Argentina; establishment of Uruguay

1829 Catholic Emancipation in Britain; extension of franchise to Catholics

1830 French expedition captures Algiers; beginning of French Algeria

1831 Five-power treaty on Belgian independence declares it to be perpetually neutral

1832 Great Reform Act in Britain provides limited but significant extension of franchise

1833 General Santanna elected President of Mexico; Texas declares independence

1834 Introduction of new Poor Law in Britain creates Poor Law Boards and houses

1835 Prussia establishes Zollverein, bringing all German states into a customs union

1836 Civil war in Spain involves intervention by British warships and volunteers

1837 Accession of Queen Victoria to British throne

1838 Insurrection in Canada; Lord Durham's enquiry into its causes

1839 Chartist movement in Britain; National Petition and People's Charter

1840 British expedition to Canton to force Chinese government to accept opium trade

1841 Union of the two Canadas (Upper and Lower) comes into effect

1842 Destruction of British army in Afghanistan

1843 South Africa: Britain annexes Natal

1844 New Zealand: Maori War

1845 USA: annexation of Texas approved by Congress

1846 Ireland: failure of potato crop; resulting famine leads to large-scale emigration

1847 Vatican: first year of Pius IX's papacy shows him to be a liberal pope

1848 Year of Revolutions in Europe; Marx and Engels issue Communist Manifesto

1849 Mazzini proclaims Roman Republic; crushed by French army

1850 USA: California admitted as a state of the Union

1851 Britain: Jews allowed to sit in Parliament

1852 France: Louis Napoleon is proclaimed Emperor Napoleon III

1853 Japan: US expedition under Commodore Perry forcibly opens Japan to US trade

1854 Crimean War begins: British and French troops lay siege to Sevastopol

1855 Henry Bessemer takes out patents, which transform steel production

1856 Treaty of Paris ends Crimean War

1857 Indian Mutiny: widespread uprising against British rule in India

1858 British Crown takes over government of India from East India Company

1859 War in Italy: Sardinia and France against Austria; Battle of Magenta

1860 Election of Lincoln, an opponent of the extension of slavery, as US president

1861 American Civil War begins after secession of Confederate States

1862 Lincoln signs Emancipation Proclamation, which frees slaves in Confederate territory

1863 Battles of Vicksburg and Gettysburg mark turning-points in Civil War

1864 Prussia and Austria defeat Denmark over Schleswig-Holstein

1865 Defeat of Confederacy marks end of American Civil War; assassination of Lincoln

1866 Prussian victory over Austria at Sadowa; Prussian predominance in Germany

1867 Dual Monarchy established in Austria-Hungary

1868 British expedition to Abyssinia; capture of Magdala, and withdrawal

1869 Opening of Suez Canal, a channel for world commerce

1870 Franco-Prussian War: crushing French defeat at Sedan leads to fall of Napoleon III

1871 Darwin's *The Descent of Man* published, amid sharp debate

1872 Britain: Ballot Act introduces voting in elections by secret ballot

1873 Russian advance into Central Asia; occupation of Khiva

1874 Britain: defeat of Gladstone; Disraeli forms Conservative government

1875 Disraeli purchases Khedive's shares in Suez Canal Company for Britain

1876 Bulgarian revolt suppressed by Turks; Gladstone denounces Bulgarian massacres

1877 Invention of "talking phonograph", a recording machine, by Thomas Edison

1878 Congress of Berlin: independence of Balkan states from Turkey

1879 Zulu War: defeat of British army at Isandlwana; defence of Rorke's Drift

1880 Ireland: ostracism of Captain Boycott by the Land League creates new word

1881 International Medical Congress: Pasteur's account of vaccination experiments

1882 Egypt: British bombard Alexandria and occupy Egypt

1883 French occupation of Madagascar and expedition to Tonkin (Indo-China)

1884 Congo Conference in Berlin on partition of Africa

1885 Death of General Gordon at Khartoum

1886 Gladstone's first Home Rule Bill for Ireland; Liberal split and defeat

1887 Indian National Congress meets at Calcutta; demands representative institutions

1888 Accession of William II as Emperor of Germany

1889 Austria-Hungary: death of Crown Prince Rudolph at Mayerling

1890 USA: McKinley Tariff to protect US industry

1891 First rail of Trans-Siberian Railway laid by the future Tsar Nicholas II

1892 Britain: Gladstone forms his fourth administration after Liberals win election

1893 Arctic exploration: Nansen sails in *Fram;* Peary sets out for North Pole

1894 France: Captain Dreyfus convicted of treason; start of Dreyfus Affair

1895 Treaty of Shimonosiki ends First Sino-Japanese War; Japan annexes Formosa

1896 Ethiopia: Battle of Adowa; defeat of Italian army by Ethiopians

1897 German Navy Bill initiates naval expansion and maritime rivalry with Britain

1898 Spanish-American War; US annexation of Hawaii, Puerto Rico and Philippines

1899 Boer War begins between Britain and Boer Republics

1900 Australian Commonwealth Act: Commonwealth of Australia established

1901 Marconi sends first trans-Atlantic wireless communication

1902 Treaty of Vereeniging ends Boer War

1903 Independence of Panama from Colombia; USA begins Panama Canal

1904 Signing of Entente Cordiale between Britain and France

1905 Russo-Japanese War: Russian fleet destroyed at Tsushima

1906 Huge earthquake destroys San Francisco

1907 Finland becomes first European country to grant female suffrage

1908 Orville Wright makes flight of 1 hour and 10 minutes

1909 Britain: House of Lords rejects Finance Bill, leading to constitutional crisis

1910 China asserts suzerainty in Tibet: expedition to Lhasa, flight of Dalai Lama

1911 Moroccan crisis: French expedition to Fez, German gunboat to Agadir

1912 *Titanic* sunk by collision with iceberg, 15-16 April

1913 Niels Bohr introduces new quantum theory of atomic structure

1914 Assassination of Archduke Franz Ferdinand leads to outbreak of World War I

1915 Dardanelles campaign; ANZAC troops in action

1916 Battles of Verdun and the Somme epitomise attritional war on Western Front

1917 USA enters war; Bolshevik Revolution in Russia

1918 Treaty of Brest-Litovsk, March; armistice in France, 11 November

1919 Paris Peace Conference and Treaty of Versailles redraw world map. Einstein's new theory of the principle of relativity changes views of the universe

1920 Britain accepts mandate for Palestine, to establish a "National Home" for the Jews

1921 Washington Conference on naval disarmament and the Pacific

1922 Mussolini assumes dictatorial power in Italy; creation of fascist regime

1923 French occupation of the Ruhr; hyper-inflation in Germany

1924 Death of Lenin; struggle for succession begins

1925 Treaties of Locarno normalise relations between Germany and former Allied Powers

1926 Britain: General Strike brings country almost to a standstill

1927 Lindbergh's journey from New York to Le Bourget marks first trans-Atlantic flight

1928 China denounces all unequal treaties imposed by outside powers

1929 The Wall Street Crash: symbol of the Great Depression

1930 India: Gandhi's salt march, to protest against tax on salt manufacture

1931 Mukden Incident: Japanese occupation of Manchuria

1932 Election of Franklin D. Roosevelt as president of the USA

1933 Hitler becomes chancellor of Germany, 30 January, with conservative support

1934 Discovery of induced radio-activity by the Joliot-Curies, Paris

1935 Italian invasion of Ethiopia; enactment of Nuremberg Laws in Germany

1936 Civil War in Spain: Franco attacks Madrid; arrival of International Brigades

1937 USA: Neutrality Act forbids export of arms to belligerent states

1938 Munich Conference marks high point of appeasement of Nazi Germany

1939 German attack on Poland initiates World War II

1940 Fall of France and creation of Vichy government; German defeat in Battle of Britain

1941 German invasion of Soviet Union; Japanese attack on Pearl Harbour

1942 Decisive defeats of German army at Stalingrad and of Japanese navy at Midway

1943 Teheran Conference cements British-US-Soviet alliance; overthrow of Mussolini

1944 Normandy Landings lead to liberation of France

1945 Surrender of Germany and discovery of Nazi death camps; surrender of Japan after atomic bombs dropped on Hiroshima and Nagasaki

1946 First Session of General Assembly of the United Nations, involving 51 member states

1947 End of British rule in India; partition between India and Pakistan

1948 Palestine: establishment of Israel; conflict with Arab states

1949 Communist victory in Chinese civil war leads to establishment of Mao's regime

1950 Communist North Korea invades South; intervention by US-led UN forces

1951 Soviet Union detonates its first atomic bomb

1952 Britain: death of George VI and accession of Queen Elizabeth II

1953 Death of Stalin

1954 Defeat of French garrison at Dien Bien Phu marks end of French rule in Indo-China

1955 Asian-African Conference at Bandung (Indonesia); emergence of "Third World"

1956 Suez Crisis: Nasser nationalises Canal, prompting British-French-Israeli attack

1957 Treaties of Rome, founding the European Economic Community. Launch of Sputnik, the first man-made earth satellite, by Soviet Union

1958 France: end of 4th Republic; de Gaulle becomes president of new 5th Republic

1959 China: disastrous consequences of "Great Leap Forward", begun in 1958

1960 CERN cyclotron in Geneva produces crucial results in particle acceleration

1961 Soviet Union puts first man into space; Yury Gagarin orbits the earth

1962 Cuban Missile Crisis brings USA and Soviet Union to the brink of nuclear war

1963 USA: assassination of President Kennedy, 22 November

1964 South Africa: Nelson Mandela is sentenced to life imprisonment

1965 Britain: death and state funeral of Winston Churchill

1966 China: Cultural Revolution, led by Red Guards

1967 Six-Day War: Israel attacks and defeats Egypt, Syria and Jordan

1968 France: establishment shaken by student revolt. Soviet invasion of Czechoslovakia

1969 USA lands first men on the moon

1970 Introduction of Boeing 747 airliner marks start of mass air travel

1971 War between India and Pakistan; independence of Bangladesh

1972 Germany: success of Brandt's Ostpolitik; treaty between West and East Germany

1973 Ceasefire agreement in Vietnam War; Arab attack on Israel starts Yom Kippur war

1974 "Oil Shock" ends many years of economic growth

1975 North Vietnam conquers South. Death of General Franco in Spain

1976 China: deaths of Chou En-lai and Mao Tse-tung lead to power struggle

1977 Czechoslovakia: publication of Charter 77 against violations of human rights

1978 Election of Karol Wojtyla as Pope John Paul II, a Polish pope

1979 Islamic revolution in Iran overthrows the Shah; Ayatollah Khomeini takes power

1980 Soviet army struggles to subdue guerrillas in Afghanistan

1981 Poland: conflict between government and Solidarity trade union; martial law imposed

1982 Falklands War: Falkland Islands invaded by Argentina and recovered by Britain

1983 Missile crisis in Europe; deployment of US Pershing and Soviet SS-20 missiles

1984 India: storming of Sikh Golden Temple; Indira Gandhi assassinated by Sikhs

1985 Mikhail Gorbachev becomes Soviet leader and embarks on reform programme

1986 Explosion at Chernobyl nuclear reactor: fallout affects much of Europe

1987 Reagan-Gorbachev summit: abolition of medium and short range missiles

1988 Geneva agreement on phased withdrawal of Soviet troops from Afghanistan

1989 Fall of Berlin Wall, symbolising collapse of communism in Eastern Europe

1990 Russia declares sovereignty, heralding the demise of the Soviet Union in 1991

1991 USA and allied powers defeat Iraq after its invasion of Kuwait in 1990

1992 Former Yugoslavia: civil war in Bosnia; Croatia declares independence

1993 South Africa: new, non-racial constitution adopted

1994 Rwanda: massacre of Tutsis by Hutu militants leaves up to 500,000 dead

1995 World Health Organisation estimates number of AIDS sufferers at over one million

1996 Comprehensive Nuclear Test Ban Treaty adopted by UN General Assembly

1997 Cloning of Dolly the sheep by researchers in Edinburgh

1998 Nuclear tests conducted by India and Pakistan

1999 Russia: resignation of Boris Yeltsin; Vladimir Putin becomes acting president

2000 Completion of mapping of the human genome, the human genetic blueprint

2001 Terrorist attacks on 11 September against World Trade Centre and Pentagon

2002 European Union: introduction of single currency (the euro) by 11 member states

2003 War by USA and allies against Iraq leads to overthrow of Saddam Hussein

2004 Indian Ocean earthquake unleashes tsunami, which kills several hundred thousand

2005 Kyoto Protocol on Climate Change comes into effect

2006 Israeli offensive against Hezbullah in Lebanon

2007 USA implements troop "surge" in attempt to achieve success in Iraq conflict

2008 Election of Barack Obama as US president

2009 Worst world economic crisis since 1930s—unemployment, banking crises, government debts

2010 Craig Venter creates the first living organism with a fully synthetic genome— a bacterium

2011 "The Arab Spring": an outbreak of popular revolts that convulse North Africa and the Middle East. Magnitude 9 earthquake off Japan's north-east coast unleashes tsunami killing 20,000 people and causing nuclear meltdown at Fukushima power plant.

EXTRACTS FROM PAST VOLUMES

250 years ago

1761. *Mr. Pitt Resigns.* In short, he revived the military genius of our people; he supported our allies; he extended our trade; he raised our reputation; he augmented our dominions; and on his departure from administration, left the nation in no other danger than that which ever must attend exorbitant power ....

225 years ago

1786. *France: the state of the peasantry.* Some indulgences have been extended to the peasantry this year in France; that most valuable order of men, who are the foundation of strength, wealth and power in every community that possesses them, and who have been too long most shamefully and unwisely despised and oppressed, not only in France, but in most other countries. They are now relieved from that intolerable bondage and continued oppression to which they had so long been subjected, under the arbitrary domination of inferior mercenary officers ....

200 years ago

1811. *Lord Stanhope's Bill on Coin and Bank Notes.* Notwithstanding the confident assertions of ministers and their friends that no depreciation had taken place in bank notes, the fact of a diminution of their relative value to bullion became at length so glaring that it could no longer be denied, and its effects excited a general alarm.

175 years ago

1836. *France: Algiers.* Burdensome and expensive as France had now found her African colony of Algiers to be, her legislators could not be brought to listen even with patience to any proposition for giving it up. The committee on the budget had recommended, to diminish the expenses of the war department, by reducing the Algerian army from 22,000 men to 19,000. This was not a good way of raising the question; for, if the colony was to be retained, it was generally admitted ... that the greatest of these numbers was far from being more than the defence of the country required.

150 years ago

1861. *Civil War in America.* The election of Mr. Abraham Lincoln as President of the United States brought the feeling of discontent on the part of the Southern States to a crisis. They had long been opposed to the commercial policy of the North, which was in direct antagonism to their own interests .... But, above all these, was the question of Slavery, the everlasting source of difficulty and danger. No other topic excited in the same degree the passions of parties. The South clung to their "domestic institution", as they called that frightful evil, as a necessity of their existence ....

125 years ago

1886. *Japan: National Dress.* Close upon the revolution in the system of government has followed a not less complete change in the national dress. The native costume of many centuries which has charmed artists and amateurs is doomed, and men and women are bringing themselves to adopt European clothes, as well as customs, in many respects wholly unsuitable. In future the Empress is to wear European dress on state occasions ....

100 years ago

1911. *Militant suffragists.* The militant suffragists announced a demonstration in Parliament Square for the evening of November 21. A deputation was sent out "to protest on the floor of the House, against the deep insult to womanhood of manhood suffrage", but it was blocked by the police, who, after advising the women "not to be foolish", broke up the column and arrested them. Hereupon a number of women, evidently by pre-arrangement, broke ... a number of windows not only of Government offices but of shops ....

75 years ago

1936. *Civil War in Spain: German intervention.* The Fascist rebellion in that country [Spain] had been welcomed in with great satisfaction by the National-Socialists, and the whole machinery of German propaganda was brought into play in the interests of General Franco. After a while, Germany, in co-operation with Italy, furnished more material aid for the Spanish rebels. German aeroplanes and munitions were shipped to Spain .... Towards the end of the year, complete battalions were sent to Spain by the German Government ....

50 years ago

1961. *The Year of the Spacemen.* For better or worse 1961 will be remembered by most laymen and many scientists as the year of the Spacemen .... Russia won the first, and propaganda-wise the most important, lap of the space race. Major Gagarin was successfully orbited on 12 April. The later and less spectacular American achievement, Commander Alan Shepard's flight up through the atmosphere and down again - he did not go into orbit - still stole some of the glory from Russia.... The only useful scientific data contributed by any of the spacemen was information about how the human organism reacted to weightlessness for prolonged periods.

25 years ago

1986. *Nuclear accident at Chernobyl.* Initially, they denied responsibility, but when the evidence became irrefutable the Soviet Union admitted that an 'accident' had occurred. Even then, for several days the official Soviet response was to minimize the scale of the disaster ... Then Soviet behaviour changed dramatically, and thereafter the event was covered with commendable candour and openness ... Nonetheless, despite the heroism, impressive organization and ingenuity, Chernobyl quickly became a word in the international lexicon that symbolized the world's worst civilian nuclear accident.

PREFACE

THE two major news stories of 2011 were the natural disaster which struck northern Japan in March, and the events of the "Arab Spring" which unfolded throughout the year. The Great East Japan Earthquake was notable because of its vast magnitude and the scale of the tsunami which it unleashed. It also caused meltdown at the Fukushima power plant—the world's worst nuclear accident since the Chernobyl explosion in 1986. The effect of this was to raise public and governmental concerns over the safety of nuclear energy in Japan and many other countries.

According to World Bank calculations the triple disaster in Japan was the most expensive natural catastrophe in human history. It was also the most recorded, as the events of 11 March were filmed by tens of thousands of ordinary people using video cameras and mobile phones. Even as the events were unfolding, they were being disseminated over the Internet via social media sites, footage that was then recycled by conventional television news broadcasts. The process highlighted an important change in the means through which news events were brought to a wider audience. It was also indicative of the increasing interconnectedness of humanity, a profound development that was too often overlooked amid the vacuous noise of "social networking"—the narcissism of Facebook and the banality of Twitter. It was a reminder of the astonishing speed and scale of modern communications in an age where not just the means to record events had been democratised but also the distribution mechanisms to convey those images to a global audience.

The same force was evident in the dynamism of the Arab Spring. The self-immolation of Mohammed Bouazizi, a Tunisian street vendor, in the final days of 2010 was a personal tragedy apparently without global significance. His hometown of Sidi Bouzid was an unremarkable rural settlement with an unemployment rate of 30 per cent and a heavy mantle of local bureaucratic and police corruption. Bouazizi, or "Basboosa" as he was known to friends, had been born into crushing poverty but worked hard selling small quantities of fruit and vegetables. He supported his family, including a sister who had made it to university, and he even dreamed of one day expanding the scale of his business by renting or buying a truck. It was a small ambition for a small life. Yet even this existence was made intolerable by harassment from the local police, who demanded bribes and frequently confiscated his wares. His final words as he doused himself with petrol were to scream, "How do you expect me to make a living?" It was a howl of frustration and despair by someone who through bitter experience had come to understand that hard work, ambition and enterprise

were not enough to achieve personal progress within a tightly-controlled society, in which the cards were not just stacked against the poor but the deck itself
was maldistributed and incomplete.

Accounts suggest that Bouazizi was a popular and kindly figure. Certainly his
desperate act of public suicide provoked local protests which intensified after his
death on 4 January. The impact of social media was instrumental in intensifying
those protests and giving them a coherence that quickly ignited a regional con-
flagration, which engulfed the corrupt dictatorships in Tunisia, Egypt and Libya
and threatened to bring down a number of others in the Arab world. After a year
of struggle, in which the online dynamic of this Arab Spring was a key element,
the process remained incomplete as the world watched—often via social media
sites—a future attempting painfully and bloodily to be born.

The struggle was significant also in that it was fuelled by economic and
political frustration rather than being driven by Islamism. So, amid these
momentous events, the killing of Osama bin Laden—whilst cathartic for those
traumatised by the events of 11 September 2001—appeared a historical foot-
note. Even as his corpse slipped into the Persian Gulf, he already seemed an old
man, marginalised by events that he could neither influence nor control. Despite
founding a terrorist franchise and provoking the West into two ill-considered
wars he appeared to have failed in his greater objective of using that conflict to
advance his intolerant vision of Islam.

By contrast, the protesters who flooded into public spaces during the Arab
Spring were often young. Educated but economically marginalised, they were
rarely ideologically inspired by religion. In this sense they were less connected
to bin Laden than to other protests that developed in 2011, such as the Occupy
Wall Street Movement. This involved ordinary people camping out in public
spaces in North America and Western Europe to draw attention to the unfairness
of a system in which they, "the 99 per cent", were suffering rising unemployment and falling incomes because of the mistakes of the wealthiest "1 per cent".
Across a range of countries the idea struck a chord with populations that were
experiencing falling living standards. This perception was reinforced by statistical evidence. For instance, the US Congressional Budget Office reported that
after-tax income for the wealthiest 1 per cent of US households had grown by
275 per cent between 1979 and 2007. For the poorest 20 per cent it grew by only
18 per cent. It was no coincidence that—unlike the three decades of immediate
post-war prosperity, les "trente glorieuses"—this latter period saw declining
overall levels of economic growth. The squeezed middle class sought to maintain its living standards through working longer hours and accruing ever greater
levels of debt. The shortcomings of this response were cruelly exposed by the
financial crisis of 2008, presaging Bouazizi's anguished cry of "How do you
expect me to make a living?"

The dynamic of the Arab Spring was reflected also in the political dimension of the chatter from China's microblogging community. This saw explosive growth, trebling during 2011 to 250 million users, and providing a conduit for information and a forum for discussion that had been hitherto the preserve of a few self-proclaimed dissidents. Similarly, in Russia at the close of the year there were mass protests prompted by the evidence—gathered and disseminated via online social media—that legislative election results had been falsified. Urban, middle-class Russians staged a carnival of protests demanding an end to the hegemony of the ruling "party of crooks and thieves".

In every case, the targets of such protests were the self-serving political and financial elites who were perceived as having amassed power and wealth at the expense of the many. Often libertarian in style and amorphous in organisation, such protest movements were co-ordinated online and drew inspiration from each other. In doing so, they showed that these new tools did not have to serve the trivial and the banal. Used differently, they could offer a means of mass contact, extraordinary not just because of its speed and scale but also because it could bypass traditional and more easily controlled channels of communication. Therein lay the potential for popular empowerment on an unprecedented scale and a fundamental shift in the relationship between the rulers and the ruled.

Thus, it might be that the historical significance of 2011 will not be found in Japanese nuclear fallout or deposed Arab dictators, but in the emergence of a new challenge to the distribution of power and wealth. Similar, coordinated challenges had arisen in the past—the revolutions of 1848, and the protests of 1968—but never before have the dispossessed been armed with smartphones.

D.S. Lewis & Wendy Slater
Editors, *The Annual Register*
Aquitaine, March 2012.

2011: THE YEAR IN REVIEW

THE year started with concern over the state of the world economy, controversy over the outcome of the Cancun climate change conference and a presumption that US President Barack Obama would oversee the large-scale withdrawal of US troops from Iraq. Within weeks all of these issues were overshadowed by an unexpected development—the rapid escalation of public protest against the autocratic Ben Ali regime in Tunisia, followed by the collapse of that regime and the spread of civil protest to a number of countries in the Middle East and North Africa, most notably Egypt. In what came to be called the "Arab Spring" or the "Arab Awakening", the sheer pace of political change in the early months of 2011 caught almost every analyst by surprise. Whether the overthrow of autocratic elite regimes across the region would lead to permanent change looked likely early in the year but less so by its end. Indeed, some of the public expectations were not to be fulfilled, with violent state repression in Bahrain and Syria succeeding, at least temporarily, in holding the protests in check.

The three issues of economic uncertainty, insecurity and environmental constraints all continued to cause concern, with the economic focus being principally on the eurozone common currency area rather than the USA and its subprime mortgage crisis of 2007-8. Security issues were affected by the killing of the al-Qaida leader, Osama bin Laden, and the related expectation that this would further limit the vitality of the movement, by uncertainty in Iraq and Afghanistan and, towards the end of the year, by an increase in tension in relations between Iran and some Western states and Israel. Scientific evidence in support of the dangers arising from climate change continued to increase. This was seen in political circles as essentially a long-term problem, but the 17th Conference of Parties (COP17) held in Durban at the end of the year saw more progress than had been expected.

The three broad issues—economy, security and environment—will be examined in this chapter in that order, with the rapid changes embodied in the Arab Awakening discussed under the heading of security.

After a period of apparently stable economic growth in the early 2000s, concerns over the global economy developed in 2007-8, initially in relation to a gross overdependence of sectors of the banking system in the USA on unsustainable subprime mortgages. By mid-2008 a number of banks in the USA and some western European countries were in danger of collapse. A few did collapse but more were bailed out by massive government support which in some cases amounted to partial or complete nationalisation. The problems had stemmed from a combination of factors such as inadequate regulation, including insufficient international regulatory cooperation, and a too heavy reliance on narrow econometric analysis of market trends. This was in the context of a degree of hubris stemming from the belief that since the free market economy had emerged as the victorious economic system after the collapse of the Soviet Union, it must be intrinsically stable and the only effective form of economic organisation.

By late 2008 there were even fears that entire countries might be close to default, as Iceland had been early in the crisis, with much of the concern being over the financial viability of Ireland, Greece and Portugal. During the course of 2009, it became clear that such wholesale collapse was unlikely, and much of the reason for this was that outside of the North Atlantic community a number of significant economies, including Brazil, India and especially China, were continuing to enjoy impressive rates of growth. By mid-2010 there was a belief that the robust state of such economies might well be sufficient to prevent a long-term worldwide economic downturn and this perception held into early 2011.

It was not a universal view and some analysts made the obvious point that the robust economic growth of countries such as China was due in part to their ability to utilise low-cost labour in producing goods for export to the North Atlantic community. If this community was in near economic stagnation then it could well follow that countries such as China would have to generate far greater domestic demand for goods if they were to avoid their own economic problems. Two factors worked against this. One was that these countries had very limited public welfare systems and this resulted in high levels of personal savings rather than personal debt as people maintained reserves to meet welfare demands. The other was that even in an era of rapid economic growth there were major problems of social unrest as the majority of the benefits of growth were being concentrated in a minority of the population. This manifested itself in social unrest in many countries including China, and even significant armed insurgencies in some cases, such as the Naxalite rebellion in India.

At the core of the financial predicament in the eurozone during 2011 was an economic situation shared by several other Western countries including the UK. This was the very high level of debt held by governments and banks. The viability of government finance was even being called into question, one result being the very high costs for some governments to finance their debt by further borrowing on financial markets. In October 2011, for example, Germany and France could still negotiate 10-year loans at under 3 per cent but for Italy it was 5.5 per cent, Ireland 7.4 per cent, Portugal 10.8 per cent and Greece an entirely unsustainable 22.1 per cent. In these circumstances there was a broad disagreement as to the appropriate response between those who argued for serious austerity focused on deep cuts in public expenditure to reduce levels of debt, and those who saw this as likely to exacerbate the risk of a serious recession and believed that debt could be reduced by promoting economic growth and thereby increasing governmental revenues.

During the course of 2011, intergovernmental organisations such as the IMF encouraged the former approach of austerity policies and in some countries, including the UK, the governments in power were themselves convinced that such policies were fully appropriate. One problem for such governments and intergovernmental organisations was that the cuts in welfare and other public spending had an impact on poorer sectors of society at a time when there was increasing bitterness over the high salaries and bonuses that continued to be paid to those in the financial sector, especially the much derided and discredited bankers.

The combination of relative marginalisation with high unemployment, especially of graduates, resulted in widespread antagonism towards governments in many countries. In Greece the antagonism was frequently violent; in Chile it started with protests at a woefully inadequate state educational system; in Israel it stemmed from a constrained middle class; and in Spain it resulted in massive and persistent nonviolent protests. In the latter part of the year, the protests in many countries took the form of what became termed the "Occupy Movement", as groups of people sought to occupy public and private space in the vicinity of financial quarters of major cities. These protests were facilitated by the widespread use of Internet-based social media tools and had, at their root, young people whose economic prospects were far worse than those that their parents had enjoyed a generation earlier. What was particularly notable was that the protesters were not seriously impoverished but saw their life prospects deteriorating while elite sectors of society appeared to go largely unscathed or even to prosper.

Protesters in the "Occupy" demonstrations did not necessarily have complete or even partial demands other than the need for economic change, and it was notable that few came from a traditional Marxist orientation. By the end of the year there was a sense among protesters, shared by far more people, that something was seriously wrong with the entire free market approach. Even if it was unclear what should be done, apart from a more equitable sharing of the burden and persistent welfare assistance for the most marginalised, there was a perception of a need for radical new approaches. This was enhanced by a belief by the end of 2011 that the austerity measures themselves were not only not working but might actually be making a serious recession more likely. The argument was that cutting public spending also cuts tax revenues while increasing unemployment and was thus self-defeating. In many countries across Western Europe this remained a substantial minority view, but it was given more credence by the belief that 2012 would see further major crises, perhaps as severe as substantial national defaults in the case of countries such as Greece. Thus, the relative optimism of 2009-10, following the financial woes of 2008-9, was being replaced by an uncomfortable and deep-seated degree of pessimism.

During 2011 the international security environment was complex, multifaceted and highly unpredictable, nowhere more so than in the rapid development of public protest across the Middle East and North Africa (MENA). Although much of the unrest stemmed from the enduring frustration with the power of autocratic elites and the extent of the suppression of individual freedom, it also had underlying demographic, economic and educational elements, with the economic context bearing some relation to the eurozone crisis. The MENA region has a particularly large proportion of its population under the age of 25, most of them high school graduates and many with university degrees. Apart from a few countries with large oil and gas export earnings and small populations, the experience of these young people had been of a marked lack of employment prospects.

Tunisia, for example, with a population of around 10 million, was reported to have 140,000 unemployed graduates.

The eruption of the "Arab Spring" was a reaction to these circumstances. It began in Tunisia at the very start of the year, following the death of a young man who had set himself on fire in deep frustration at his predicament, but it spread across the country within days and led to the rapid fall of the regime. This was followed immediately by massive public protests in Egypt against the Mubarak regime which had ruled the country for decades and, while supported by Western allies, was seen as singularly repressive and systematically successful at maintaining the well-being of a rich elite, at the expense of the great majority. Within weeks the Mubarak regime had collapsed, being replaced by the rule of a military council which promised a transition to democracy. In the weeks that followed there were public protests in Algeria, Bahrain, Oman, Jordan, Morocco and Saudi Arabia, with far more serious unrest developing in Libya and Syria.

Governments adopted different approaches. Oman suppressed public protests but also introduced some reforms, Saudi Arabia combined repression in the Shia regions in the east of the country with substantial increases in public service salaries and pensions. It also provided direct security assistance to the Bahraini Sunni-dominated government in its extended repression of protesters from within the marginalised Shia majority. Algeria increased subsidies for basic foodstuffs and brought in modest reforms. The King of Morocco remained a fairly popular monarch with some significant political reforms being introduced, whereas the pace of change in Jordan was slower, leading to fears by the end of 2011 that it was heading for serious unrest.

Protests in eastern Libya resulted in immediate repression by the Kadhafi regime and this rapidly evolved into Western intervention for humanitarian purposes authorised by an unusually open resolution from the UN Security Council. The leaders of the principal Western participants—France, the USA and the UK—quickly made it clear that repression could only be prevented by regime termination and there followed a six-month military operation to provide overt air support and covert ground operations to aid the rebels. The Kadhafi regime eventually collapsed, with its leader killed in controversial circumstances, and the process of trying to heal the wounds of war began. These were made more difficult by the existence of numerous armed militias controlling districts and by the end of 2011 there was concern that stability, let alone a move towards a functioning democracy, would be a long time coming. A further factor was that the fall of Kadhafi could readily be interpreted in Iran as a consequence of Libya having given up its Weapons of Mass Destruction programme and making the mistake of assuming that it could then maintain relations with Western states while controlling dissent.

In Syria major public protests developed around the middle of the year and the Assad regime used violent measures to suppress dissent. Several thousand people were reported killed in the second half of the year but the evolution of the rebellion was more complex than a small elite maintaining control over a dissident majority. The Assad regime, including much of the army's officer class, was drawn from the Alawi religious sect, a branch of Shia Islam that formed less than 15 per cent of the overall population, but Syria had a complex confessional makeup and the regime maintained significant support in the face of protests, especially in the capital, Damascus, and the second city, Aleppo, where protests were rare. Even so, there was determination on the part of many tens of thousands of people to maintain the protests until the regime capitulated, and many other governments across the region, not least Turkey and Saudi Arabia, sought to encourage Assad to compromise. In December these efforts included an observer force from the Arab League, but doubts quickly emerged as to its value.

After the sudden fall of Mubarak in Egypt early in the year, senior military commanders took over prior to a transition to democracy, but within months there were substantial protests at the slow pace of change. While the military in Egypt had a fairly high status in the country as a whole, and the failure of middle-ranking commanders to fire on protesters had helped seal the fate of the Mubarak regime, by the end of the year there was a widespread view among those who had demonstrated to bring down the old regime, that the most senior military were determined to retain power in some form. It would not be too strong an argument to make that the long-term success of the Arab Awakening might well depend on whether 2012 saw a clear move to a more representative democracy in Egypt.

While there was a sustained focus on the "Arab Spring" for much of the year, there were numerous developments in relation to the al-Qaida movement, Iraq and Afghanistan. During the early part of the year the USA appeared to achieve considerable success in suppressing the al-Qaida movement. Part of this came from the extensive use of armed drones in Afghanistan and especially north-western Pakistan in killing middle-ranking paramilitary commanders. This, combined with numerous Special Forces "night raids" in Afghanistan had a substantial effect on the movement and, to a lesser extent, on the activities of the Taliban and other armed opposition groups in Afghanistan. The drone attacks in Pakistan became increasingly controversial within the country, being seen as a persistent infringement of Pakistani sovereignty, but they were maintained almost to the end of the year when the killing of more than 20 Pakistani soldiers in an attack across the border from Afghanistan resulted in such an outcry that one US basing facility had to be closed and drone attacks cease.

A significant individual development was the killing of Osama bin Laden by US Special Forces at the beginning of May. He was located at a compound in a Pakistani garrison town and killed in an operation that was undertaken without the Pakistani authorities being informed. This caused considerable anger there, in marked contrast to the euphoria with which the news was received in the USA. Although bin Laden was not much more than an isolated figurehead within the diffuse al-Qaida movement, he was seen in the United States as the key person in a worldwide terror network that had been responsible for the 11 September 2001 attacks. His death, therefore, was seen as providing a large measure of closure in the decade-long US response to the attacks—what had been called the "War on Terror". Indeed it could be represented in the USA as the culmination of that war, one consequence being that it was likely to prove easier for the Obama administration to engage in a negotiated withdrawal from Afghanistan without this being seen in domestic circles as a defeat.

Prior to the death of bin Laden, the Obama administration had already come to the conclusion that the Taliban and other armed opposition groups in Afghanistan could not be defeated by conventional means and that there would have eventually to be a negotiated settlement that might well involve some Taliban involvement in the future governance of the country. Indeed, the purpose of the surge in US forces in Afghanistan in 2010 was primarily to ensure negotiations could be pursued from a position of military strength. The problem for the USA was that the military surge appeared in 2011 to be increasing armed opposition rather than suppressing it. This was shown, not least, by many substantial attacks against Western interests, including bombs and raids in the heart of Kabul. Furthermore, the extent of anti-Americanism in Pakistan suggested that there was scope for radical Islamist groups to increase their influence there.

As for the al-Qaida movement, while 2011 saw further damage being done to what remained of an hierarchically organised entity, the idea of a radical Islamist movement was taking root in further regions. In Yemen, the disorder and chaos around the Saleh government provided al-Qaida-linked groups with opportunities to gather support and even take over substantial districts in the south of the country. In Somalia, the al-Shabaab group experienced reversals during the latter part of 2011 but retained control of large parts of the country. Across North Africa, al-Qaida-linked groups were increasing their activities and, most notably, in Nigeria the Boko Haram paramilitary movement was moving to become the most significant cause of instability in the country.

Against this, the al-Qaida movement stood to lose much of its support during 2011 from a quite different source—the possible success of the Arab Awakening. For al-Qaida, the idea that reform and democratisation could come from civilian non-violent action was anathema, since the true way forward had been seen as the violent overthrow of unacceptable regimes and their replacement with Islamist governance. At the same time, the risk remained that if the Arab Spring were to fail, and autocratic rule was maintained or even re-emerged, then a movement such as al-Qaida would benefit by arguing that its way forward was the only path to be taken. That would depend on the future failure of the Arab Awakening, with 2012 being a crucial time in which this might be determined. Meanwhile, the evidence from Yemen, Somalia, Nigeria and elsewhere indicated that while al-Qaida as a movement might be in decline, the idea of radical Islamist governance that it espoused was, if anything, spreading. The movement as a structured organisation might be in retreat but the idea was not.

In the early part of 2011 the Obama administration made it clear that the USA would persist in its intention to withdraw its combat troops from Iraq. This would fulfil one of the president's key election pledges of 2008 and was popular with the American public. At the same time, the intention was to maintain considerable influence in Iraq, including the world's largest embassy, diplomatic missions elsewhere in the country and a continuing if low key military presence concerned primarily with training Iraqi armed forces. Maintaining such influence was seen as essential primarily because of the need to limit the extent to which Iran could develop a political capability in the country. For the Obama administration, the outcome of what had been an appallingly costly war should at least be a stable country that would emerge as a functioning democracy and would form part of a Western-oriented regional political system.

In the event, three developments conspired to produce a different outcome. Firstly, over a three-year period from 2008 there had initially been a substantial decrease in political violence within the country, but this had levelled out in 2010 and surged upwards in 2011. The violence included major attacks with multiple coordinated bombings in a number of cities killing over 60 people in August and bombings in Baghdad killing 68 people in December. While the level of violence was still far lower than in 2007, with several hundred people being killed every month the situation was far from stable and was most certainly not matching expectations. The second issue was that the coalition led by the prime minister, Nouri al-Maliki, became steadily more fractured during the course of the year, with politicians from the minority Sunni Muslim community claiming that the government was favouring the Shia majority as well as becoming more autocratic. This came to a head in December with the arrest of a Sunni vice-president and there were fears that the coalition would break up.

Finally, the most significant development was the Iraqi government's insistence that US troops remaining in the country would not have immunity from prosecution. This was not acceptable in Washington and, as a result, all US troops were withdrawn by early December. To compensate for a potential security vacuum, the Pentagon planned to increase the military presence in neighbouring Kuwait, but this was a largely peripheral move in the face of a concern that Iran would progressively increase its influence in Iraq.

The final substantial development in the Middle East during 2011 was a steady increase in tension between Iran and Western states, especially the USA, over its nuclear programme. Although there was little firm evidence, there was an assumption within the US and Israeli governments that Iran was seeking to develop nuclear weapons, a potential outcome that was entirely unacceptable to Israel. By the end of the year the combination of this element together with Iran's growing influence in Iraq meant that the Obama administration was becoming more forceful in leading Western states to impose harsh economic sanctions. In December, the Iranian navy held exercises designed to remind other states of its claims to be able to close the Strait of Hormuz, a key waterway for oil and gas shipments out of the Persian Gulf. The exercises passed without incident but added to a concern that 2012 might see a major crisis involving Israel, the USA and Iran.

The Copenhagen climate change conference of December 2009 (COP15) was widely regarded as a failure and COP16 in Cancun in 2010 fared little better. Prior to COP17 in Durban in December 2011 there were few expectations of success. This was partly due to a lack of commitment by key countries including the USA and China, but also down to more outright opposition by countries such as Russia and Canada that were major fossil fuel exporters and also might stand to gain in the short-term from the impact of climate change. In the event, COP17 was more successful than expected with some last minute negotiations leading to a proposed post-Kyoto agreement to be negotiated by 2015 and implemented by 2020, with details to be finalised at COP-18 in Qatar in December 2012.

While this progress was welcomed, many analysts argued that what was now being proposed was simply not radical enough in terms of the problem of climate change and its likely global impact. They were supported by data that showed that the 2010 had seen the highest release of carbon at 30.6 gigatonnes, and the highest rate of increase in a year at 5.2 per cent. What was particularly surprising was that this was at a time of a developing recession in many industrialised countries, suggesting that the trend towards increased carbon emissions transcended any slow-down in economic activity. Meanwhile, other evidence indicated that feedback mechanisms were beginning to speed up the rate of carbon release, one being the melting of paleo-arctic permafrost with the consequent thawing and decay of frozen biomass and the release of methane, a particularly potent climate change gas.

On the climate change issue as a whole, there remained a division between developed and developing states, with the latter still insistent that the problem originated primarily through the past and current actions of the former. These states therefore had a duty to lead the way towards low carbon economies while aiding developing states in combining low carbon outputs with meeting their considerable human development needs. The one positive sign in this context was that 2011 also saw useful technological developments in many areas of renewable energy, not least photovoltaics where more efficient systems and large scale mass production had a substantial effect in bringing down prices. Given the setback for nuclear power as a result of the Fukushima nuclear disaster in Japan, this was a welcome development.

Thus, in broad terms 2011 saw a slowly increasing recognition of the potentially dangerous consequences of human impacts on the global ecosystem, especially climate change, and a growing concern that the dominant economic model—the free market system—was not delivering sufficient socio-economic equity. These, coupled with strident calls for greater emancipation, especially in the Middle East, looked to be the most significant issues, not just for 2012 but quite possibly for the rest of the decade.

Paul Rogers

II WESTERN AND SOUTHERN EUROPE

UNITED KINGDOM—SCOTLAND—WALES—NORTHERN IRELAND

UNITED KINGDOM

CAPITAL: London   AREA: 243,610 sq km   POULATION: 62,218,761 ('10)
OFFICIAL LANGUAGES: English; plus Welsh in Wales, Gaelic in Scotland,
HEAD OF STATE: Queen Elizabeth II (since Feb '52)
RULING PARTIES: Conservative-Liberal Democrat coalition (since May '10)
HEAD OF GOVERNMENT: Prime Minister David Cameron (Conservative) (since May '10)
DEMOCRACY INDEX: 8.16; 19th of 167   CORRUPTION INDEX: 7.8; 16th of 183
CURRENCY: Pound Sterling (Dec '11 US$1=GBP 0.64)
GNI PER CAPITA: US$38,560, Intl$36,590 at PPP ('10)

LOOKING at 2011, it is difficult not to be reminded of Antonio Gramsci's sonorous observation in *Prison Notebooks*:

The crisis consists precisely in the fact that the old is dying and the new cannot be born; in this interregnum a great variety of morbid symptoms occur.

The year 2011 was packed with events, many of which may well count as "morbid symptoms"; in December the *Guardian* asked, "Has 2011 been the biggest year for news in living memory?" As well as a turbulent world background, the United Kingdom had its first full year of coalition government since 1944, the second national referendum in its history, the prospect of Scottish independence taking a major step towards reality, riots, economic stagnation, peers and former MPs imprisoned, and a major breach in relations within the European Union. However, few of these developments seemed to be complete in themselves. The events took place as stages of the degeneration of the political and economic structure of the last few decades (centuries in the case of the Union), but left few clear pointers to what the world in 2012, let alone 2020, might look like.

THE MEDIA AND THE "HACKING" SCANDAL.   The year 2011 was when everything changed in the British media. For decades, the newspapers owned by Rupert Murdoch had been courted by politicians, and respected and feared across the spectrum of the establishment and celebrity worlds alike.

In late December 2010 the Liberal Democrat business secretary, Vince Cable, had been secretly tape-recorded at a constituency surgery by *Telegraph* journalists and was on record boasting that he had "declared war" on Rupert Murdoch. As a result, the prime minister stripped Cable of the power to rule on the bid by Murdoch's News Corporation to take full control of the now hugely profitable BSkyB satellite broadcasting company, and gave the decision to the Conservative culture secretary, Jeremy Hunt, who was seen as friendlier to Murdoch (see AR 2010, pp. 505-06). Hunt gave provisional approval to the deal in March, and a more detailed settlement was reached in June, in which the BSkyB news channel, Sky News, would be hived off.

There were already some indications that things were unstable in the world of the press. The background of deteriorating circulation figures for all newspapers (with some, such as the *Daily Star* and the *Guardian*, suffering falls of more than 15 per cent over the year), and public demand for free online content, made 2011 a year of crisis for the press even without the damage done by the hacking scandal. In January the coverage of a murder case in Bristol demonstrated an unpleasant mentality among the press: Chris Jefferies, the victim's landlord, who was entirely innocent, was subjected to attack and innuendo. Two newspapers (the *Sun* and the *Mirror*) were fined for contempt of court, and in July eight had to pay compensation and damages to settle libel claims filed by Jefferies. As well as taking deserved punishment in the Jefferies case, the newspapers also saw the legal system adopting a more restrictive attitude to personal privacy, a long-term trend which became apparent in 2011 in the rise of the "super-injunction". It emerged in the spring that a number of celebrities had taken out injunctions which specified that not only the allegation, but the fact that an injunction even existed, were prohibited from publication.

The big media story, however, was "hacking". In context, this meant the use by newspapers of information obtained by intercepting and listening to voice-mail messages left on mobile telephones. The work was done by private detectives. In January 2007 a *News of the World* reporter, Clive Goodman, and a private detective, Glenn Mulcaire, were both imprisoned for such behaviour, but at the time News International (the UK division of News Corporation, which published the *News of the World*, as well as *The Times*, the *Sunday Times* and the *Sun*) successfully suggested that this was a matter of a "rogue reporter" and not of wider significance. Over the next few years there were indications that this may not have been true, but it was a lonely pursuit by *Guardian* journalist Nick Davies, Labour MP Tom Watson, and latterly the actor Hugh Grant, whose rise as an investigative journalist and political activist was a strange feature of 2011. Things started to shift in January, with a further arrest of a *News of the World* journalist and the resignation of Andy Coulson as director of communications for Prime Minister David Cameron. Coulson had been editor of the *News of the World* during the Goodman-Mulcaire case.

There were further revelations about the extent of hacking early in the year, but the dam burst on 4 July when the *Guardian* revealed that in 2002 Mulcaire, on behalf of the *News of the World*, had listened to the voicemails of teenaged murder victim Milly Dowler, during the months between her abduction in March 2002 and the finding of her body in September. (It was alleged at the time that messages had been deleted as a result, which in December the Metropolitan Police concluded was not the case.) In October, the Dowler family settled a legal action against News International with £2 million damages and a payment of £1 million to charity. The Dowler case aroused huge public disgust. News International announced that the closure of the *News of the World* would take place after a last edition on 10 July, ending 168 years of publishing history and terminating what was still, despite falling circulation, Britain's biggest-selling Sunday newspaper.

Public revulsion at the Dowler case, and other revelations, meant that for the first time a political will to take on the press became apparent. On 13 July, in advance of a likely near-unanimous House of Commons vote for a Labour motion opposing the BSkyB bid, News Corporation withdrew the bid. The prime minister also announced that an inquiry into the press and police behaviour revealed by the hacking scandal would take place. In the meantime, there was a parliamentary inquiry by the House of Commons Select Committee on culture, media and sport.

The select committee hearings on hacking were a minor parliamentary breakthrough, in that they were the first Commons committee proceedings to capture public imagination and to be watched by a significant number of people on television. At last, there were signs that the House of Commons could do something a bit like the scrutiny and investigation undertaken by congressional committees in the United States. The Labour MP Tom Watson, who had been on the trail of the hacking story for some time, led the grilling of the Murdoch representatives but other members such as Paul Farrelly and Louise Mensch also made an impact, in what was an unusually united and effective committee.

A particularly corrosive aspect of the hacking scandal was the collusion that it revealed between the police and the press. Paying police officers for information was, of course, illegal but it seemed to have been widespread practice for some time among the press. At a higher level, there were frequent social and other contacts between senior officers and senior media executives. The scale and competence of the original Metropolitan Police investigation into Mulcaire was called into question and two, more extensive, police inquiries began. On 17 July Sir Paul Stephenson, the commissioner of the Metropolitan Police, resigned over his retention of Neil Wallis, a former News International executive arrested on 14 July, as an adviser, although Stephenson denied any impropriety. There was also an attempt by Rupert Murdoch, and his son James Murdoch, to limit the damage and renew the organisation, with the departure in particular of Rebekah Brooks, former *News of the World* editor and chief executive of News International, on 15 July (she was arrested on 17 July).

The public hearings of the inquiry announced by the prime minister, which was chaired by Lord Justice (Brian) Leveson began in September but started in earnest in mid-November with a succession of media, political and celebrity figures giving evidence. The Leveson inquiry still had much work to do at the end of 2011, but it appeared to be unlikely that the current regime of media self-regulation could survive. The year also ended with many former editors and executives of News International, including Coulson, Brooks and Wallis, having been arrested, although criminal responsibility had not been established in any of the cases.

THE BRITISH ECONOMY. The UK's economic performance during 2011 was, to put the kindest construction possible on the matter, disappointing. GDP growth over the year from the third quarter of 2010 to the third quarter of 2011 was 0.5 per cent. Following a sharp fall at the end of 2010 (down 0.5 per cent), most of which was made up in the first quarter of 2011 (up 0.4 per cent), the economy flatlined in the second quarter (0.0 per cent) and ticked upwards in the third quarter (0.6 per cent). While not technically a recession, in that there were no two successive quarters of declining output, it certainly felt like one to most people. Inflation was falling from its peak by the end of the year (4.8 per cent from November to November) but the median salary (£26,244) rose only 1.4 per cent in nominal terms, making this a year in which people's spending power fell significantly. Directors and chief executives, however, were immune from the trend and saw their median salary rise 15 per cent to £112,157. Waiters (down 11.2 per cent) and cleaners (down 3.4 per cent) saw the biggest declines in earnings. In October 2011 unemployment increased to 2.64 million, the highest since 1994, and youth unemployment reached a record level of 1.03 million, with the trend firmly upwards.

Economic growth forecasts for the next few years were also deteriorating throughout 2011, to the extent that by November the OECD was warning that the UK was slipping back into recession. The causes were much debated, although the impact of the government's own spending cuts and gloomy economic statements since 2010 played a part: growth over the year to the third quarter of 2011 had been higher in the USA and the eurozone than in the UK. In the second half of 2011 in particular, the instability in the eurozone also cast a dark shadow over exports and confidence.

Interest rates, at least, remained constant and extremely low at 0.5 per cent all year, which benefited mortgage-holders and other borrowers but meant negative real rates of return for most savers. As well as low interest rates, an expansionist monetary policy was reflected in the Bank of England's decision in October to extend its quantitative easing (QE) programme by another £75 billion. QE involved purchasing assets (mostly government bonds) from the banks, thereby supplying them with cash that could be used to lend to individuals and businesses. When first introduced in 2009, quantitative easing was described as a "last resort" and "an admission of failure" by the then shadow chancellor, George Osborne, but he seemed to take a different view in 2011.

While monetary policy was relaxed, fiscal policy was still tightening, as outlined in the 2010 Comprehensive Spending Review (see AR 2011, p. 14). The 23 March Budget itself was a modest adjustment to taxation, with a freeze in council tax, a 2 pence cut in corporation tax, some simplification of the tax code and increased personal income tax allowances. The Autumn Statement on 29 November set out more of the public spending side of the equation, particularly the increase in the state retirement age from 66 to 67 in the year 2026. Public sector pay increases would be limited to 1 per cent after 2010's two-year freeze was over. There were a couple of modestly expansionary measures, including a credit-easing programme for small businesses (there had been widespread criticisms of the banks for failing to lend to business). But the Office of Budget Responsibility (an independent Treasury unit) outlook, published alongside the Autumn Statement, was depressing and projected that "austerity" would continue for longer than originally anticipated. Borrowing projections were also bearish.

Meanwhile, the existing cuts programme was affecting life in Britain. In the spring local authorities set their budgets, which involved painful cuts in many urban areas in particular. Local news often seemed to be a grim parade of job losses and closed libraries. Youth services seemed particularly badly affected (the education maintenance allowance, a grant for over-16s who remained in education, was scrapped and replaced by a 70 per cent smaller scheme from September), while older people did less badly. On 26 March the Trades Union Congress organised a large protest march through London, the largest march since the Iraq protests in 2003, although the media predictably concentrated on a violent fringe of the sort that had marred protests against student fees in 2010. On 30 November there was a one-day strike by many public sector workers in protest at the government's plans to cut pensions; negotiations seemed to pick up momentum after the strike and there seemed to be progress when the year ended.

The financial sector was put on notice by the government's acceptance of the Vickers Report into banking which was published on 12 September. Sir John Vickers recommended separating investment and retail banking, and requiring banks to retain a "buffer" of low-risk liquid assets to provide for future problems. Business Secretary Vince Cable expressed hope that the main legislation would be passed by 2015, although this remained uncertain; full implementation was due for 2019. Also in finance, the Northern Rock bank (nationalised in 2008) was sold at a considerable discount to Virgin operator Sir Richard Branson.

Activists in the UK participated in the global "Occupy" movement. On 15 October a protest camp was established in the City of London, outside St Paul's Cathedral. As in other countries, the demands were broad rather than specific, focusing on the growth of economic inequality, the resulting inequalities in power, and the excesses of the financial sector. A pressure group in this area, UK Uncut, campaigned against the cosy relationship between senior tax officials at Her Majesty's Revenue and Customs (HMRC) and large corporations, and the apparently forgiving attitude by HMRC to these companies' tax bills; politicians of all parties called for the resignation of the HMRC chief executive, Dave Hartnett. His—ostensibly unrelated—retirement was announced on 9 December. It was an unusual case of an individual civil servant being held publicly accountable.

POLITICS I: CONSTITUTIONAL CHANGE AND THE ALTERNATIVE VOTE REFERENDUM. In May 2011, for only the second time in history (the first being in 1975, on continued membership of the European Community) there was a national referendum across the United Kingdom. The question was whether the electoral system should be changed to the Alternative Vote (AV). This was a result of the May 2010 coalition agreement, in which the Liberal Democrats (who supported Proportional Representation—PR) and the Conservatives (who supported "first past the post"—FPTP) split the difference and adopted Labour's manifesto promise of a referendum on AV.

The referendum campaign will not be remembered fondly by many of those involved, and probably not remembered at all by the general public. Although electoral systems are important, the electorate did not understand or take much of an interest in the rather technical change from FPTP to AV that was on offer in May. It was hard for the two campaigns to gain public and media attention. The No campaign (mostly Conservative-financed, but with Labour politicians well represented among its leaders) was much criticised for its crudity, and some of the claims it made (particularly over the costs of the change) were extremely difficult to justify. However, the Yes side also had its problems, particularly in over-claiming for what AV would accomplish and for indulging in anti-politics rhetoric. It also suffered from the poisonous relations between Liberal Democrats and Labour—the two parties with the largest numbers of people who were in favour of reform—which got in the way of organisation and also meant that all the campaign's activities (such as the cross-party launch event on 29 March) were seen through the prism of Nick Clegg versus Ed Miliband.

The referendum caused tensions within the coalition, with Lib Dem ministers (Chris Huhne in particular) taking strong objection to the attacks on their party made by the No campaign. They knew that Cameron would advocate a No vote, but were disappointed at the way the Conservatives' organisation and donor network were thrown into the campaign as well as by the tone of its output.

As with many referendums, the case for the status quo made the most progress during the campaign, and by May it was clear that the result would be No. The huge size of the margin for No, however, came as a surprise. The Yes vote was 6,152,607 (32.1 per cent) while the No vote was 13,013,123 (67.9 per cent) on a 42 per cent turnout. The only counting areas to vote Yes were six London boroughs, the academic-professional areas of Glasgow and Edinburgh, plus Oxford and Cambridge.

There were other aspects of constitutional reform that were in the air, even if electoral reform was—for the time being—off the agenda after May. For a Conservative-dominated government, it was a significant programme given the party's previous lack of interest in constitutional reform, and far from all of it was a concession to the Liberal Democrats. Several other changes were enacted in 2011. The act which had provided for the AV referendum also rewrote the system by which constituency boundaries were drawn. The boundary commissions were instructed to reduce the number of MPs from 650 to 600 and (with four exceptions) to make each constituency fit within 5 per cent of the average number of electors. This was criticised by the Labour opposition, who argued that the electoral registers were too inaccurate to serve as the basis for such precise calculations, that there was insufficient scope for public participation, and that a rigid limit of 5 per cent meant that constituency boundaries would ignore local identities. The Boundary Commission for England (BCE) published its initial proposals in September; they aroused considerable disquiet in several areas, including from coalition MPs. However, the timetable to vote through the new boundaries by October 2013 for implementation in 2015 remained on track.

The 3 March referendum in Wales resulted in the Welsh Assembly's gaining powers to legislate on already devolved matters without prior consent from Westminster. Another constitutional change of 2011 was "fixed term parliaments". This legislated to transfer the power to call an election from the prime minister (on the monarch's behalf) to the House of Commons itself, and to establish only two methods for dissolving parliament before the maximum five year term was up: namely a vote by two-thirds of the House to do so, or the House voting no-confidence in a government and then failing to give a successor government confidence within 14 days. The government also legislated for a new sort of directly elected office, the police and crime commissioners, to replace local police authorities with effect from autumn 2012. These would be elected under the same electoral system as existing directly elected mayors, namely the Supplementary Vote (SV); the government also extended the mayoral model into another tranche of major local authorities in its Localism Act. At the end of the year, government proposals on two further constitutional changes had been published: a directly elected replacement for the House of Lords, and the "recall" of MPs found guilty of misconduct.

A piquant element in the hacking scandal was the revenge of politics upon the press, which had taken such delight in exposing the MPs' expenses scandal in 2009 (see AR 2010, pp. 9-10; 591-96). The year 2011 saw that scandal winding down, although even that was notable for the number of parliamentarians and former MPs sent to prison for personal enrichment. Former Labour MPs David Chaytor (7 January), Jim Devine (30 March), and Elliott Morley (20 May), plus serving MP Eric Illsley (10 February; he resigned his seat) were given custodial sentences relating to parliamentary expenses, as were Conservative peers Lord (John) Taylor of Warwick (31 May) and Lord (Paul) Hanningfield (1 July). The new regime of parliamentary expenses legislated for in 2009 saw its first full year in operation; the Independent Parliamentary Standards Authority (IPSA) was no more popular among MPs than it had been in 2010 and the system was criticised in a December report of the committee on members' expenses.

Constitutional questions which the government would rather have avoided were raised in Scotland and Wales. On 8 February the Welsh Assembly voted down the Legislative Consent Order (LCO) affecting part of the UK Parliament's legislation for police and crime commissioners (the "Sewel convention" provided that Westminster legislation affecting devolved powers would take place with the consent of the devolved (Welsh) Assembly or (Scottish) Parliament). The Welsh issue was avoided by re-designating the panels that the legislation proposed to create to advise the commissioners, in order to take them out of the devolved sphere of local government, but it was still the first LCO to be refused. On 22 December the Scottish Parliament refused consent for the aspects of the UK Welfare Reform Bill that affected devolved Scottish powers. The structure of devolution in the UK had from its origins in 1999 until 2011 worked with a considerable element of political goodwill and give-and-take. The refusal of the LCOs was an indication that devolution would in future be less harmonious and more formal. The Scottish National Party's landslide victory in May's Scottish Parliament election, and the likelihood of a referendum leading at least to "devolution max" if not outright independence, seemed scarcely to have been absorbed in Westminster and Whitehall.

POLITICS II: PUBLIC OPINION, ELECTIONS AND PARTIES. Despite all the dramatic events of the year, public opinion seemed to be in stasis. From January until December, most opinion polls showed a small Labour lead over the Conservatives (although the Conservatives were ahead in some polls immediately after Cameron's "veto" at the EU in December, see below). Nearly all polls were within sampling error of Labour having 40 per cent in voting intention, the Conservatives 36 per cent and the Liberal Democrats 11 per cent. Since the May 2010 election this represented a major swing from Liberal Democrat to Labour, with the Conservatives holding steady.

This pattern was apparent in most of the elections that took place during 2011. There were six by-elections for parliamentary seats, none of which resulted in a change of allegiance. On 13 January Labour held the very marginal seat of Oldham East and Saddleworth with an increased majority. The by-election had been called after the incumbent MP's disqualification following an election petition. On 3 March Labour held Barnsley Central, vacated by Eric Illsley (see above), but the result was mostly notable for the humiliating sixth place recorded by the Liberal Democrats. Labour went on to hold Leicester South (vacated by Sir Peter Soulsby in his successful bid to be elected mayor of Leicester) on 5 May, and Inverclyde (30 June) and Feltham & Heston (15 December) following the deaths of MPs David Cairns and Alan Keen. There was also a by-election in Belfast West (9 June) which was held by Sinn Féin, after Gerry Adams had won a seat in the February election for the Dáil, the lower house of Ireland's bicameral legislature.

In the local authority elections of 5 May, Labour made a net gain of 857 seats, the Liberal Democrats made a severe net loss of 747 seats and—to general surprise—the Conservatives ended a net 85 seats ahead. Estimates of the national share of the popular vote showed both Labour and Conservative nearly level with support a little below 40 per cent. The result was respectable rather than outstanding for Labour, given that most seats had previously been contested at a fairly low point for the party in 2007, but it could claim some significant gains including Newcastle, Sheffield, Hull, Leeds, York, and Telford & Wrekin, and there were some very large swings from Lib Dem to Labour in the northern cities. However, in smaller town areas and the south of England the Conservative vote held up well or even increased, usually at the expense of the Lib Dems. It was a bad election for the British National Party (BNP), which held two and lost 11 of its seats; the party was also in danger of going out of business because of internal splits and financial mismanagement. The Greens did well in their main target of Brighton & Hove, forming their first administration in a British local authority after becoming the largest single party there. However, given the harshness of the local government financial settlement imposed by the Department of Communities and Local Government (DCLG), control of local authorities, particularly in urban areas, would involve administering painful cuts.

The party conference season in the autumn was one of the most perfunctory such series in living memory; one commentator with a long memory thought that the Conservative conference in 1960 was the only other contender in terms of dullness. There was the occasional event worth noting: at the Liberal Democrat conference Nick Clegg urged that Labour should never be trusted with the economy again, which would somewhat limit his freedom of manoeuvre should he be in coalition talks after 2015. At the Labour conference, Ed Miliband made, although in a rather tortuous fashion, probably the intellectual and political statement of the year in arguing for reward and celebration of "productive" rather than "predatory" capitalism. While the distinction was by no means a simple matter, and he was much criticised in the media, it did address something in public attitudes (as did the understanding reception for the "Occupy" protest in surprising quarters), and even David Cameron alluded to something similar. The Conservative conference was enlivened by an open quarrel between Home Secretary Theresa May and Justice Secretary Ken Clarke, about May's use of a dubious anecdote about a person given leave to remain in the UK allegedly because of a cat; it became known to the press as "Cat-flap", a welcome alternative to "-gate".

On 14 October, not long after conference season, Liam Fox resigned as defence secretary following disclosures about his self-described unofficial "advisor", Adam Werrity. Werrity had been a frequent visitor to Fox's office, and accompanied him on foreign trips, but because he had not been taken on as an official special adviser he was not subject to the usual requirements of transparency and supervision by the civil service Private Office. Werrity's links, as a consultant and in terms of finance, with a number of private companies and ideological groups came under question. Fox was replaced by Philip Hammond, and Justine Greening joined the cabinet as the replacement for Hammond at the Department of Transport. These were the only cabinet changes to take place to date in the coalition government, other than the very early reshuffle caused by the resignation of David Laws in May 2010.

By the end of the year, Labour's failure to break the deadlock led to some criticism of the leadership of Ed Miliband. The Conservatives ended the year in reasonably high morale, with David Cameron's personal position with the party much improved by the EU "veto".

In general the coalition continued to demonstrate a high degree of internal cohesion, despite the occasional rough passage arising from events like the AV referendum or the European argument at the end of the year. While 2011 saw a large number of parliamentary rebellions from MPs (the coalition recorded its 150th rebellion in September), most were small and inconsequential. The government was also generally successful in driving its business through the House of Lords. Parliament passed 25 public acts during the year, many of them mentioned above as constitutional changes. Among the others were an Energy Act concerning energy efficiency and carbon targets, a Pensions Act equalising and raising the pension age, an Education Act dealing with a wide range of educational and education management issues, and a Public Bodies Act intended to facilitate the abolition of quangos. Some of the most significant and controversial bills in Parliament were carried over into 2012, including the Health and Social Care Bill (making extensive changes to the NHS) and the Welfare Reform Bill.

THE AUGUST 2011 RIOTS. For many international observers and journalists, 2011 was above all the year of the riots in England. Serious civil disorder suddenly erupted in early August, taking the police and commentators by surprise. It was the most serious outbreak of trouble since 1985 and the most widespread since the summer of 1981. The original cause was related to protest over the death of a Tottenham man, Mark Duggan, during an attempted arrest on 4 August; protest in Tottenham turned violent on Saturday 6 August and was accompanied by looting of super-stores and small shops alike in the area. In the next few days disorder broke out in other areas, and Monday 8 August was the peak of the violence in London. There were particularly alarming events in Croydon, where arsonists burned down large buildings including a well-established furniture store, but there was rioting and looting in many other areas including Ealing, Brixton and Enfield. On 9 August a massive police presence throughout London damped down the trouble, but serious violence and looting took place in other urban centres including Manchester, Birmingham and Nottingham. There were five fatalities, including three men in Birmingham hit by a car when defending their area from looters on 10 August, and property losses included 100 homes and numerous shops and their contents. Par-liament was summoned to discuss the crisis on 11 August and the prime minister cut short his holiday.

Political analysis of the riots tended to fall out predictably. Some on the right attributed it all to bad character and alleged moral deterioration, some on the left felt that poverty and lack of opportunities among young people were to blame. Both responses seemed inadequate to a multi-causal series of events like the riots. The government, after some pressure, established a "grassroots panel", chaired by Darra Singh, to investigate the causes of the riots, which took hearings in the affected areas in the autumn. Magistrates and judges were officially urged to hand down exemplary sentences for riot-related offences. Arrests continued for the rest of the year, with the Metropolitan Police arresting 70 people on 21 December. Footage taken from mobile telephones, and even boastful pictures and statements posted on social networking websites by rioters and looters themselves, were used in evidence.

FOREIGN POLICY: EUROPE. When the coalition agreement between the most pro-European of the main parties (the Liberal Democrats) and the most anti-Euro-pean (the Conservatives) was concluded in May 2010 it seemed possible to "park" European issues for a parliament; after all, the arduous ratification of the Lisbon Treaty had just been concluded. However, 2011 was the year that the economic and financial crisis shook EU institutions to their foundations. Although not part of the eurozone, the UK was inextricably involved as an EU member state and because of the huge economic implications for the UK of instability or depression in the eurozone.

Conservative MPs were already becoming restive about the EU. On 24 October there was the largest parliamentary rebellion ever on an EU issue, with 81 Tory MPs defying the government Whip on a motion calling for a referendum on stay-ing in or pulling out of the EU, and much Conservative criticism alleging that the prime minister ignored their views and operated in an aloof and remote fashion. In early December the agenda for the European Council meeting in Brussels involved institutional changes and policy rules to attempt to restore the euro's stability and halt the sovereign debt problems afflicting southern Europe. Cameron, to the surprise of many—not least many of his own MPs—did decide to use this opportunity to press for some new "safeguards" for the interests of the City of London. Cameron attracted no support in Brussels and returned having exercised "the veto" in a summit, something that Margaret Thatcher had never done. In terms of normal diplomatic relations, it was a very questionable outcome—no effort had been made to square other countries with the demands in advance, or even to find allies—but it was popular with Conservative MPs, the press and the public. Nick Clegg initially endorsed Cameron's position, but it was clear that his party had deep misgivings. The eurosceptic tilt to government policy was followed up later in December by refusal to contribute to European stabilisation via the IMF.

The year was, therefore, one in which continuity in European policy had been expected but which ended with a rupture that was probably more severe than previous crises such as the "beef war" of 1996 or the last months of Thatcher in 1989-90.

FOREIGN POLICY: OTHER. The most notable other development, in terms of diplomatic protocol, was the state visit to the UK of US President Barack Obama and the First Lady on 24-26 May, but there was much else. Perhaps most notable was the Durban agreement in December, in which Energy and Climate Change Secretary Huhne played a part, and which brought the USA, China and India into an international climate change agreement for the first time.

Having offended Pakistani opinion in 2010 with his comments on terrorism, made in India of all places, the prime minister paid a brief visit to Islamabad on 4-5 April to mend relations and have talks with President Asif Ali Zardari. Cameron expressed hope for "the start of a new era in the relations between our countries, our governments and our peoples", and offered co-operation in dealing with extremist ideology and in practicalities like tackling roadside bombs. On 11 September Cameron paid a fence-mending visit to Russia, with which relations had been chilly since the murder of Russian dissident Alexander Litvinenko in London in 2006 (see AR 2007, p. 108). There were talks with Prime Minister Vladimir Putin and further cultural and trade exchanges, but no breakthroughs were apparent, or expected, from the visit.

International aid remained a priority for the UK government, with resource and capital spending through the Department for International Development (DfID) increasing significantly under the 2010 Autumn Statement spending plans and confirmation of the intention to meet the UN target of 0.7 per cent of GDP in aid by the year 2014. At the G-8 summit in Deauville in May, Cameron reproached other leaders: "I don't think 0.7 per cent of our gross national income ... is too high a price to pay for trying to save lives in terms of the poorest people in the poorest countries." In December the government proposed to include debt write-offs to Sudan and other very poor countries as counting towards the target, which governments had not counted hitherto.

The UK, like many nations, was active in assisting Japan in the wake of the disastrous earthquake and tsunami of 11 March. Under the auspices of DfID, an international search and rescue team was sent from the UK to help locate survivors of the disaster, and safe drinking water was supplied to areas affected by the Fukushima nuclear accident.

DEFENCE: AFGHANISTAN AND LIBYA. British troops suffered 46 fatalities and 64 seriously wounded in Operation Herrick (the deployment in Afghanistan) in 2011. This marked a fall from the higher tolls in 2009 and 2010 back to the levels that prevailed in Afghanistan before that. British forces were deployed in Libya (Operation Ellamy) in March, in response to the events of the "Arab Spring", as part of a NATO force operating under UN Resolution 1973. Cameron and France's President Nicolas Sarkozy had led calls in February and March for the imposition of a no-fly zone over Libya to protect civilian populations in rebel-held areas from reprisals by the embattled regime of Colonel Moamar Kadhafi. At the peak of the operation there were 2,300 people, 32 aircraft and four ships involved. After the rebels took Tripoli, Cameron and Sarkozy paid a brief visit to the Libyan capital on 15 September. The NATO operation, and therefore British involvement, concluded on 31 October following the collapse of the Kadhafi regime's last stronghold in Sirte and the death of the dictator. One member of the UK forces died in an accident during Operation Ellamy.

CONCLUSION AND BROADER TRENDS. The leading cultural phenomena of 2011 can probably be classified under "morbid symptoms". The trend of "reality television" was unabated, with *Strictly Come Dancing*, *The X Factor*, *I'm A Celebrity Get Me Out of Here* and *The Apprentice* continuing to be widely watched and discussed—and in the first three formats voted on—by the general public: a sanitised form of the cruelty towards "ordinary people" and "celebrities" alike that made the *News of the World* so demonised remained popular. The death of singer Amy Winehouse on 23 July (see Obituary) produced a burst of prurient and unkind media coverage and public discussion. There was a casual violence to public discourse, to the extent that a "joke" urging Labour politician John Prescott to commit suicide was fairly easily laughed off by its author, journalist Quentin Letts. Yet the greatest fuss was occasioned by a remark by motoring journalist and energetic self-publicist Jeremy Clarkson, whose response to the public sector strikes of 30 November seemed to be that strikers should be shot in front of their families. However, the remark was at least in part a joke about "balance" in the BBC and was preceded by an expression of gratitude for the traffic-free London streets brought about by the strike. Clarkson did apologise for his comment, and in its proper context it may not even have been the most offensive thing Clarkson had said in 2011, let alone the most objectionable phenomenon.

As well as modern cruelty, British taste seemed to retreat into nostalgic comfort as it had in previous recessionary times. The royal wedding between Prince William, Duke of Cambridge, and Catherine Middleton on 29 April was attended with much pageantry and watched by perhaps 24 million people on television. The best-selling film of the first half of the year was *The King's Speech*, followed by *Pirates of the Caribbean: On Stranger Tides*, respectively a sympathetic portrait of George VI and an escapist adventure. While *Brideshead Revisited* was the television programme of 1981, and *The Darling Buds of May* popular in 1991-93, the drama series of 2011 was *Downton Abbey*, an unashamed celebration of aristocratic lifestyle and values in the period around the First World War, written by a Conservative peer. One could safely assume, however, that the future market for nostalgic productions about 2011 would be very small indeed.

Lewis Baston

SCOTLAND

CAPITAL: Edinburgh   AREA: 78,313 sq km   POULATION: 5,222,100 ('10) mid-year est. Scottish gvt
OFFICIAL LANGUAGES: English and Gaelic
HEAD OF STATE AND GOVERNMENT: Queen Elizabeth II (since Feb '52)
RULING PARTY: Scottish National Party
HEAD OF GOVERNMENT: First Minister Alex Salmond (SNP) (since May '07)

ELECTIONS to the Scottish Parliament in May changed the political landscape in Scotland for the rest of the year. In contrast to its disappointments in the previous year's UK general election, the Scottish National Party (SNP) achieved outstanding success, winning an overall majority of the seats in the Scottish Parliament. This result was even more remarkable because the arrangement of a combination of "first-past-the-post" constituency and "top-up" regional seats was designed to achieve roughly proportional representation and thus to reduce the chance that any one party would have a majority. In the event, the SNP won 53 of the 73 constituency seats and a further 16 of the 56 regional seats, giving the party a total of 69 of the 129 members of the Scottish Parliament. This result was achieved at the expense of all the other major parties—Scottish Labour lost a total of seven seats (with losses at constituency level partly compensated by gains at regional level), leaving them a total of 37 seats; the Scottish Conservatives lost five seats (leaving the party with 15 seats in total); and the Scottish Liberal Democrats were the biggest losers, down 12 seats to a total of only five. The results were sufficiently shocking to the major losing parties to trigger the resignation of all three Scottish party leaders. The Scottish Liberal Democrats quickly replaced Tavish Scott with Willie Rennie (whose candidacy was unopposed), but it was not until November that the Scottish Conservatives elected Ruth Davidson to succeed Annabel Goldie, and Johann Lamont was elected to succeed Iain Gray for Scottish Labour only in December. The consequential disarray of the opposition parties and effective party discipline within the SNP meant that Alex Salmond, who was re-elected as first minister, had the freedom to follow SNP policies almost unopposed.

The major policy of the SNP was to hold a referendum within the four-year life of the new Scottish Parliament to establish whether the Scottish people wanted independence from the UK. During the election campaign, Salmond clarified this by saying that his first priority was to win greater economic powers for Scotland than those proposed in the Scotland Bill currently before the UK Parliament, and that he intended to hold the independence referendum during the latter part of the life of the Scottish Parliament. Nevertheless, issues bearing on the referendum—such as when it would be held, whether there would be a single question about independence or whether there would also be an option for greater devolution short of independence, and how the electorate for the referendum would be defined—and on the policies that might be pursued in an independent Scotland—especially on defence, on membership of the euro and on who would be head of state—tended to dominate political discussion, within and to some extent outside Scotland. Opinion polls consistently implied that despite the SNP's electoral success majority opinion in Scotland did not favour outright independence, and it was suggested that Salmond's decision to delay the referendum was designed to give him more time to convince the electorate of the merits of independence.

In the meantime, the SNP used its majority to push through legislation. Most controversially, it introduced a minimum price for alcohol (a measure which had been defeated in the previous Parliament) and sought to outlaw the singing of sectarian songs at football matches (despite opposition protests about the difficulty of defining which chants were sectarian). It extended the council tax freeze, by paying extra to local authorities which did not raise council tax levels. The public sector expenditure cuts, which had, by agreement with the UK government, been deferred for a year, started to take effect. During the early part of the year the Scottish unemployment rate was less than UK levels, and Salmond urged the Westminster government to follow the relatively relaxed economic policy of "Plan MacB" (rather than the "Plan A" that UK Chancellor George Osborne was following), but by the end of the year Scottish unemployment rose above the UK average as public sector job cuts took place. Among the most seriously affected parts of the public sector was further education. The Scottish Funding Council, responsible for funding both further and higher education in Scotland, reacted to the pressure on its finances by leaving higher education relatively untouched but cutting the recurrent funding for further education colleges by around 10 per cent, with another 20 per cent planned for the future. As intended, this precipitated a series of merger proposals as well as some course cancellations and staff redundancies. In September, the Scottish Funding Council told the two universities in Dundee—Abertay University and the University of Dundee—to commence merger talks; this was successfully resisted after protests by staff and students at both institutions, but only on the promise of closer collaboration between the two universities and Dundee (further education) College. Also in September, the Scottish government announced its intention to move to regional, rather than individual, funding for further education colleges, a move designed to reduce course duplication but also to encourage mergers.

Events in Libya and the fall of the Kadhafi regime there revived international interest in the fate of Abdel Baset al-Megrahi, the only man to have been convicted of the 1988 Lockerbie bombing, who had been released on compassionate grounds from a Scottish prison in 2009. Despite being expected to live only three months when released, al-Megrahi was still alive in Tripoli at the end of the year. In the face of complaints, particularly from some elements of US opinion, the Scottish government continued to insist that al-Megrahi's release had been appropriate and that, despite communication difficulties with the Libyan authorities, he was still being monitored by the Scottish legal system. Pressure was renewed towards the end of the year for the release of the arguments on which his (subsequently dropped) appeal against conviction was to have been based.

Charlotte Lythe

WALES

CAPITAL: Cardiff   AREA: 20,755 sq km   POULATION: 3,006,400 ('10) mid-year est. Welsh gvt
OFFICIAL LANGUAGES: Welsh & English
HEAD OF STATE AND GOVERNMENT: Queen Elizabeth II (since Feb '52)
RULING PARTY: Labour
HEAD OF GOVERNMENT: First Minister Carwyn Jones (Labour) (since Dec '09)

WELSH voters went to the polls on two occasions in the early months of 2011. In a referendum held on 3 March, they voted by two to one in favour of granting primary legislative powers to the National Assembly in the 20 devolved policy fields, without having to seek Westminster's consent. The winning margin of 27 per cent, and the fact that all counties, save Monmouthshire, voted in favour, was seen as a vote of confidence in the Assembly and a rebuff to those who had doubted the public's support for the body. However, the turnout was low and the opposition camp was largely made up of a fragmented group of dissident Labour supporters and right-wing Conservatives, easily dealt with by mainstream politicians of all the main parties.

On 4 May, the Assembly elections saw Labour increase its support, but, by only taking 30 of the 60 seats, it failed narrowly to win an outright majority. The Conservatives became the second largest party with 14 seats, ousting Plaid Cymru which lost four of its seats. Because of the success of the Conservatives in winning seats in the south-west and mid-Wales region, the party's leader, Nick Bourne, lost his regional seat under the additional member system. In due course he was replaced as leader by Andrew R T Davies, a Vale of Glamorgan farmer and Assembly Member for the South Wales Central region. At the same time, the Plaid Cymru leader and former deputy first minister, Ieuan Wyn Jones, announced that he would stand down as party leader in 2012, allowing time for a full discussion of the party's direction following its disappointing election results.

The Liberal Democrats, suffering from the unpopularity in Wales of the Conservative-Liberal Democrat coalition at Westminster, managed to win only five seats, and this by the narrowest of margins. However, two of those elected were prevented from taking their seats, as it was alleged that they had broken electoral rules relating to the membership of public bodies. Following an investigation, John Dixon was disqualified, but Aled Roberts, considered by many to be a potential party leader, was allowed to take his seat on a technicality.

The Labour leader, Carwyn Jones, was re-appointed first minister. Despite not having a clear majority, he set about forming a minority Labour government, rather than negotiating with another party to create a coalition, as had occurred in the past. The new government's legislative programme, announced in July, was criticised for its limited ambition and its failure to seek ways of addressing the nation's deep-rooted economic problems.

In October, a new commission was set up by the secretary of state for Wales, Cheryl Gillan, to review the case for the devolution of fiscal powers to the National Assembly and to improve its financial accountability. The seven commissioners, under the chairmanship of Paul Silk, former clerk to the National Assembly, met for the first time in November, with the initial task of looking at the full range of taxes and revenue generating powers and to understand the implications and suitability of transferring them to Wales. Consideration would also be given to how to improve Wales's financial empowerment through borrowing and taxation powers. Subsequently, the commission would review the powers of the National Assembly in general, recommending modifications to improve the present constitutional arrangements. However, there was criticism regarding the decision not to allow the commission to consider the reform of the Barnett formula, the calculation by which funding is allocated to Wales and a constant bone of contention between the Assembly and Westminster.

Also in November, the first minister, not unexpectedly, was forced to negotiate with other parties to gain a majority in the Assembly to pass the government's budget for 2012-13. Following an agreement with the Liberal Democrats, whereby demands for additional funding in the field of education were conceded, the budget was eventually approved in December. In the same month much concern was expressed by the first minister, and in political circles in general, over the Westminster government's stance towards Europe. It was considered that distancing the UK from the EU could be detrimental to Wales's economic interests.

By the end of the year the economic outlook appeared gloomy, with most indicators showing Wales lagging behind other parts of the UK. In December it was reported that the unemployment rate in Wales had risen to 9.1 per cent, while the average rate for the UK as a whole was 8.3 per cent. Other government statistics showed that Wales had the largest increase in Gross Value Added (GVA) per head in 2010 (3.3 per cent). At only 74 per cent of the UK average, however, Welsh per capita GVA remained the lowest among the devolved countries and English regions.

Issues relating to higher education provision were constantly in the news throughout the year. These centred on the role of the University of Wales, a confederal degree-awarding institution founded in 1893 and made up of several university colleges. In recent years, most Welsh universities had claimed the right to award their own degrees although they retained an affiliation to the University of Wales. At the beginning of the year, the University remained the second-largest degree awarding body in Britain as a result of validating courses in colleges on a worldwide basis but a damning report, published in July, on the conduct of some of these courses led to a re-examination of the University's role. In October, it was announced that the University would give up its degree awarding powers, its royal charter and its name, and a new merged institution would be formed. However, as this required legislation, the situation remained uncertain at the end of the year.

It was a dramatic year for Welsh sport. The national rugby team performed well at the World Cup held in New Zealand in the autumn, their stylish and fluent play taking them to the semi finals for the first time in 24 years. They lost by a single point to France after the referee controversially sent off Welsh captain Sam Warburton, one of the players of the tournament, for what he deemed a dangerous tackle. In soccer, Swansea City became the first Welsh club to play in the Premier League following their promotion from the Championship in May. However, the year ended on a sad note with the death, by his own hand, of the Welsh international team's young manager, Gary Speed (see Obituary), who had overseen a marked revival in Wales's footballing fortunes, with several encouraging victories in the autumn. His death provoked public mourning thoughout the country.

Gwyn Jenkins

NORTHERN IRELAND

CAPITAL: Belfast   AREA: 18,843 sq km   POULATION: 1,799,000 ('10 mid-year est. Northern Ireland gvt)
OFFICIAL LANGUAGES: English, Irish & Ulster Scots
HEAD OF STATE: Queen Elizabeth II (since Feb '52)
RULING PARTIES: Democratic Unionist Party (DUP) and Sinn Féin (SF)
HEAD OF GOVERNMENT: First Minister Peter Robinson (DUP) (since June '08); First Deputy Minister Martin McGuinness (SF) (since May '07)

IN elections for the regional assembly and local councils on 5 May the percentages of first preference votes gained by the main political parties was little changed on the previous contests in 2007 and 2005, indicating a stability in the preferences of the electorate. In the Assembly election—the first time since 1969 that parties working in a devolved system had sought re-election—the two main parties further consolidated their dominant position. Following its relatively poor performance in the 2010 general election (see AR 2011, p. 28), the Democratic Unionist Party (DUP) rebounded to take 30 per cent of the vote, winning 38 of the 108 seats (up by two). After his *annus horribilis* in 2010, party leader Peter Robinson topped the poll in East Belfast with just over 9,000 votes and was elected on the first count. Sinn Féin won 29 seats (an increase of one) with around 27 per cent of the vote.

The decline of the Ulster Unionist Party (UUP) continued, with its vote dropping to 13.2 per cent, and the 16 seats that it won represented a net loss of two. Although it outpolled the UUP, the Social Democratic and Labour Party (SDLP) also fell back, winning 14 seats with 14.2 per cent of the vote, down two on 2007. In the wake of the result party leader Margaret Ritchie resigned and was replaced in November by Alasdair McDonnell. The centre-ground Alliance Party performed well, increasing its vote by 2.5 per cent to 7.7 per cent and winning eight seats (up by one). Independents and others won three seats with 8 per cent of the vote. In East Londonderry, ex-UUP member of the legislative assembly (MLA) David McClarty held his seat as an independent, the Green Party won in North Down, and Jim Allister gained a seat for the anti-agreement Traditional Unionist Voice (TUV) in North Antrim.

After the election the 13-member power-sharing Executive was re-constituted, comprising five ministers from the DUP, four from Sinn Féin, two from the Alliance Party (including Justice Minister David Ford), and one each from the SDLP and UUP. Peter Robinson remained first minister, with Martin McGuinness as deputy first minister. However, there was criticism of the appointment of Sinn Féin's Mary McArdle as a ministerial special adviser given her conviction in 1984 for the murder of Mary Travers as she left Mass with her father, a judge, who was the target of the attack. In a Westminster by-election for West Belfast on 9 June, occasioned by the resignation of Gerry Adams and his subsequent election as a TD in the Republic, Paul Maskey easily retained the seat for Sinn Féin.

In November the Executive published the draft Programme for Government and budget for 2011-2015. This made 76 policy commitments intended to promote private sector-led economic growth (developing tourism for example), transform society (including the expansion of affordable housing) and to address the legacy of communal division (for example to promote local agreement to reduce the number of "peace walls"). In the context of a three month consultation on a UK Treasury paper on "rebalancing" the regional economy, launched in late March by Secretary of State Owen Patterson, a core demand remained for the devolution of taxation powers from Westminster—seen as precursor to reducing the rate of corporation tax to narrow the differential with the Republic of Ireland. Difficult issues remained in areas such as health and education. While cross-party agreement was reached on the creation of a single Education and Skills Authority, grammar schools continued to organise their own major academic selection tests, despite the opposition of the minister for education. In December, the report of the Compton committee presaged major changes in the health sector, recommending the concentration of emergency services in just five hospitals rather than the existing 10.

In the elections for the 26 district councils the DUP once again topped the poll, winning 175 seats with 27.2 per cent of the vote. The UUP won 99 seats (15.2 per cent) and the SDLP 87 seats (15 per cent). For all three parties there was a decline in their total number of seats. By contrast, Sinn Féin, the Alliance Party, and independents/others gained seats and increased their vote shares to 24.8 per cent (138 seats), 7.4 per cent (44) and 10.4 per cent (39) respectively. In Belfast, Sinn Féin became the largest party on the city council with 16 of the 51 councillors, one more than the DUP, while Alliance also gained two seats, giving it the balance of power. Sinn Féin's Niall Ó Donnghaile was elected lord mayor who, at the age of 26, was the youngest person ever to hold the position. In late November he was embroiled in controversy when he refused to present a Duke of Edinburgh award to a teenage army cadet. He subsequently apologised to the council and to the girl involved.

This narrative of "normal" politics took place within a still uncertain security situation. There was a surge of activity by dissident Republicans in the spring in advance of the elections and the Queen's visit to the Republic. Police constable Ronan Kerr was killed by the Real IRA in early April when a bomb exploded under his car in Omagh, and at the end of the month Republican dissidents attempted to kill police officers in Belfast. In September a bomb exploded outside the home of another Catholic police officer in Derry and a bomb left outside the home of a retired police medical officer was defused. The Real IRA was also blamed for two attacks on the City of Culture office in Derry in January and October.

Efforts to address the legacy of the past continued amidst controversy. In February a report by Police Ombudsman Al Hutchinson on the bombing of McGurk's bar in Belfast in 1971, in which 15 people were killed, found that a presumption that it was an "own-goal" by the Provisional IRA had prevented the Royal Ulster Constabulary (RUC) from properly investigating the case. However, it found no evidence of collusion with the Ulster Volunteer Force (UVF), which had carried out the atrocity. In May the report of a public inquiry into the murder by Loyalists of Rosemary Nelson in 1999 again found no evidence of security force collusion but did raise some concerns about the actions of the RUC and the Northern Ireland Office in relation to the threats made against her.

Alan Greer

REPUBLIC OF IRELAND—GERMANY—FRANCE—ITALY—BELGIUM— THE NETHERLANDS—LUXEMBOURG

REPUBLIC OF IRELAND

CAPITAL: Dublin   AREA: 70,270 sq km   POULATION: 4,481,430 ('10)
OFFICIAL LANGUAGES: Irish & English
HEAD OF STATE: President Michael Higgins (since Nov '11)
RULING PARTIES: Fine Gael-led coalition
HEAD OF GOVERNMENT: Prime Minister/Taoiseach Enda Kenny, (since March '11)
DEMOCRACY INDEX: 8.79; 12th of 167   CORRUPTION INDEX: 7.5; 19th of 183
CURRENCY: Euro (Dec '11 £1.00=EUR 1.16, US$1.00=EUR 0.74)
GNI PER CAPITA: US$40,720, Intl$32,520 at PPP ('10)

AT the start of the year, the Fianna Fáil-Green Party coalition government disintegrated in shambolic fashion in the wake of the EU/IMF bail-out (see AR 2011, pp. 30-32). Facing questions about his links with ex-directors of the Anglo Irish Bank, Taoiseach Brian Cowen survived a leadership challenge from Minister of Foreign Affairs Michael Martin, who then resigned along with five other Fianna Fáil colleagues in advance of an expected cabinet reshuffle. However, this backfired spectacularly as the Green Party refused to support changes about which they had not been consulted just weeks before a general election, and they quit the government. Cowen first allocated "double" cabinet portfolios to the remaining ministers, then resigned as leader of Fianna Fáil on 22 January (although he remained Taoiseach). Martin was elected as the eighth leader of the party at the end of January after an easy victory over three other candidates: Mary Hanafin, Brian Lenihan, and Éamon O'Cuív (who became deputy leader).

Following the dissolution of the Dáil on 1 February the election campaign was uneventful, not least because all signs pointed to a resounding defeat for the government and to big gains for the opposition parties. The main issues were the state of the public finances, job creation, public services and welfare, although all of the parties also made proposals for restructuring the political system. Both Fine Gael and Labour committed themselves to attempting to renegotiate parts of the EU/IMF bail-out deal; Fine Gael and Fianna Fáil proposed the abolition of the Senate and measures to strengthen the Dáil, although the latter went much further in its suggestion for the introduction of single seat constituencies.

In the general election on 25 February, contested by a record 566 candidates, Fine Gael emerged as by far the largest party, winning 76 seats on a 36 per cent share of first preference votes. The Labour Party came second with its best ever result—37 seats on a 19.4 per cent share of votes. Both parties increased their vote share by around 9 per cent compared with 2007. The United Left Alliance won five seats (including four in Dublin) and Sinn Féin increased its vote by three points to just under 10 per cent, winning 14 seats including in Louth where Gerry Adams topped the poll with 15,000 votes. Fourteen independents were elected on 12.6 per cent of the vote, an increase of 6 per cent. The outgoing governing parties were decimated, with the Greens losing all six seats and winning just 1.8 per cent of the vote. While defeat for Fianna Fáil had been expected, the scale of the rout was not. The party scored its worst ever result with just 19 TDs elected (none in 25 of the 43 constituencies and just a single seat in Dublin) on 17.4 per cent of the vote, a calamitous reduction of nearly 25 per cent on 2007.

While Fine Gael's impressive result raised the possibility that it could govern with the support of independents, the weight of opinion favoured a coalition with Labour (taken together they controlled 113 of the 166 seats in the Dáil). Following negotiations a "Programme for Government" was agreed and the 31st Dáil met for the first time on 9 March. After choosing Seán Barrett as the new speaker (*Ceann Comhairle*), Fine Gael leader Enda Kenny was elected Taoiseach. Ten of the 15 cabinet posts went to Fine Gael, including Alan Shatter as minister for justice, equality and defence. The five Labour ministers included party leader Eamon Gilmore as *Tanaiste* (deputy prime minister) and minister for foreign affairs and trade.

The year's second important election, on 27 October, was for the presidency. Four of the candidates were independents—Seán Gallagher, Dana Rosemary Scallon, Mary Davis and the gay rights campaigner David Norris—and three were established political figures. While Fianna Fáil decided not to contest the election or endorse a candidate, the Labour Party opted for Michael D Higgins and Fine Gael for Gay Mitchell. In the most high profile move, Sinn Féin chose the Northern Ireland Deputy First Minister Martin McGuinness. A volatile and quirky campaign was initially dominated by Norris who then withdrew from the race (after controversy about a letter he had written to an Israeli court in 1997 requesting clemency for his former partner), only to rejoin it. Gallagher, perhaps best known as a former panellist on Irish television's *Dragons Den* programme, had a clear lead in the polls in the weeks before the election. However his support collapsed after the final of the three live televised debates when he responded inadequately to a question from McGuinness (who had himself faced awkward questions throughout the campaign about his links to the IRA) about his financial links to Fianna Fáil. This opened the way for Higgins who won 40 per cent of the first preference vote and was elected on the fourth count, followed by Gallagher (28.5 per cent) and McGuinness (13.7 per cent), with Mitchell trailing in fourth place with just 6.4 per cent.

Two referendums on proposed constitutional amendments were held on the same day as the presidential election. The 29th amendment on cutting the salaries of judges was endorsed by nearly 80 per cent of the electorate, but the 30th—which proposed giving increased powers to parliamentary committees and providing an alternative to costly judicial tribunals—was defeated by 53 to 47 per cent.

The "double budget" on 5-6 December was again one of the harshest ever. Brendan Howlin, Labour Party minister for public expenditure, announced a controversial new "household charge" of €100 and unveiled swingeing spending cuts in areas such as social protection, education and health, including child benefit, and increased fees for third level students. Minister for Finance Michael Noonan announced rises in taxes and duties, including an increase in the rate of VAT from 21 to 23 per cent. However this came as little surprise. Indeed it had generated considerable controversy several weeks earlier when the planned increase was revealed in the German parliament, leading to much open debate about the nature of Irish sovereignty in the wake of the EU/IMF bail-out.

The year also saw two high profile state visits. That by Queen Elizabeth II, the first by a reigning British monarch to independent Ireland, took place between 17 and 20 May and included highly symbolic trips to the national Garden of Remembrance and to Croke Park, home of the Gaelic Athletic Association, as well as a speech in Dublin Castle. This was quickly followed by a visit by US President Barack Obama who met the president and the taoiseach, and visited his ancestral village in County Tipperary, before making a speech to a large crowd at College Green in Dublin.

Among those who died during the year were former Taoiseach Garret FitzGerald (85) on May 19, and outgoing Finance Minister Brian Lenihan (52) in June after a brave battle against cancer.

Alan Greer

GERMANY

CAPITAL: Berlin   AREA: 357,050 sq km   POULATION: 81,702,329 ('10)
OFFICIAL LANGUAGE: German
HEAD OF STATE: President Christian Wulff (since July '10)
RULING PARTIES: Christian Democratic Union/Christian Social Union (CDU/CSU)-led coalition
HEAD OF GOVERNMENT: Chancellor Angela Merkel (CDU) (since Oct '05)
DEMOCRACY INDEX: 8.38; 14th of 167   CORRUPTION INDEX: 8.0; 14th of 183
CURRENCY: Euro (Dec '11 £1.00=EUR 1.16, US$1.00=EUR 0.74)
GNI PER CAPITA: US$43,290, Intl$38,140 at PPP ('10)

THROUGHOUT 2011 Germany, as the biggest country in the European Union and the largest economy in Europe, was at the centre of the EU's attempts to resolve the sovereign debt crisis affecting members of the eurozone. Indeed, discussion over the future of the euro dominated public life for much of the year.

Angela Merkel, the federal chancellor, had to pull off an almost impossible balancing act. On the one hand, the elite consensus in Germany remained pro-European. Politicians of Left and Right urged Merkel to act decisively to preserve the stability of the euro and to defend what they saw as the achievements of decades of European integration. Germany was, therefore, morally and economically compelled to take a lead in the EU's efforts to help countries on the periphery of the eurozone which were struggling to meet their debt repayments. On the other hand, Merkel knew that the inevitable consequence of this was that Germany would, either directly or indirectly, have to get out its chequebook and support weaker EU states financially. That the scale of this support remained a point of conjecture did not help Merkel in making her case to the German people, who became increasingly suspicious that their country was committing itself to pouring billions of euros into a potential black hole. This was encapsulated by the *Bild Zeitung*, Europe's most widely-read newspaper, in its populist campaign against lazy southern Europeans who allegedly retired early, worked fewer hours and had turned tax-evasion into an art form.

Merkel's attempts to lead the eurozone countries out of the crisis were often seen as ineffectual. An attempt in October, for example, to ensure that private investors had to take a share in any losses that would occur if (or when) Greece's debt was written off prompted investors to get out of other peripheral countries as quickly as they could in case anything similar should happen there. This particular attempt by the German government to limit its own liabilities made the crisis worse rather better. Attempts to increase the funding of the European Financial Stability Facility to €1,000 billion also failed to stabilise matters as the EU slipped ever deeper into crisis. Merkel's answer to this was to insist at the European Council meeting in December 2011 that debt reduction and a series of long-term economic adjustments—overseen by European Commission officials—was the way forward. The long-term plans for eurozone fiscal union that were announced did, indeed, see a temporary lull in the storm, but as 2011 drew to a close it was clear that the markets remained unconvinced. The fight to preserve eurozone stability would remain at the centre of German politics through 2012.

The only other story to compete with the eurozone crisis involved the uncovering of a string of murders—10 in total—that were linked to a neo-Nazi cell in eastern Germany. Nine immigrants and one police officer had been killed over the course of a decade. The arrest of three people in November did little to alleviate the shock that many Germans felt at the idea of those with Nazi sympathies again murdering people on German soil. Indeed, many German newspapers spent as much time covering the events surrounding these murders as they did discussing the federal government's attempts to save the euro.

The economic turmoil evident in southern Europe and Ireland had little effect on Germany's own economy. Growth remained strong, at 3 per cent in 2011, and unemployment fell to 6.8 per cent in December, the lowest level since 1991. German exports continued to boom—up in November by 8.3 per cent on the previous 12 months—and domestic demand remained resilient enough to ensure that Germans generally stayed positive about their own future.

Such a promising economic situation should have left Merkel in a strong position at home. Yet whilst it would be unfair to say that the Christian Democratic Union/Christian Social Union (CDU/CSU) government was unpopular, there was certainly an ambivalence towards the Christian Democrats that belied the good economic statistics. Merkel's party was not helped by the abrupt departure in March of its star figure, Karl-Theodor zu Guttenberg, the minister of defence. Guttenberg was young, energetic and charismatic, and opinion polls regularly saw him top the list of Germany's most popular politicians. But his superstar status could not save him when allegations emerged of plagiarism in his doctoral thesis. By the time Guttenberg resigned it had become clear that he had passed off a great deal of his PhD as his own when, in fact, it was the work of others. His reputation as the "Mr Teflon" of German politics was lost. He subsequently resigned, not just as minister but also from the Bundestag (legislature), and he spent the rest of 2011 in the USA. The last few days of the year, however, saw Guttenberg make tentative moves to return to the political scene, publishing a book of interviews with a well-known journalist and suggesting that he intended to return to public life in due course.

There were no national elections in Germany in 2011, but seven of Germany's 16 states (*Länder*) went to the polls in regional contests. The Social Democratic Party (SPD)—in opposition at the federal level—did well in all of these elections, returning to (or remaining in) government in all seven states, whilst Merkel's Christian Democrats' performance was more patchy. But it was two of the smaller parties that attracted most attention in German politics during 2011.

The Greens performed admirably across all the state elections, even landing their first post of minister-president (regional prime minister) in the affluent western German state of Baden-Württemberg. The Green Party's success, though, was due to external events as much as the party's own efforts. First, the nuclear disaster at Fukushima, Japan, on 11 March helped to shoot the ever-contentious issue of nuclear power back up the political agenda in Germany. This allowed the Greens to talk about an issue around which they had always been able to mobilise support: eliminating all nuclear power from Germany. Indeed, the federal government immediately responded by promising to phase out nuclear power in Germany much faster than had been planned. The issue nonetheless remained live and the Greens consequently sailed high in the opinion polls (at times pushing 25 per cent). The Greens were also able to profit in Baden-Württemberg from their opposition to the redevelopment of the main railway station in Stuttgart, the provincial capital. Ordinarily an issue of local salience at best, during 2011 it became the talk of the whole country. Although plans to re-vamp the station had been agreed years before, the "Stuttgart 21" (S21) project became a vehicle for people to express their frustration at the way that politics in Stuttgart (and beyond) was functioning. The feeling of disenfranchisement was strong, and thousands of people regularly marched and protested more generally against the planned redevelopment, leading occasionally to violent clashes with the police. The fact that the Greens were the only major party consistently to oppose the project ultimately allowed their leader, Winfried Kretschmann, to form a Green-SPD coalition after the March election. By the autumn, however, the fact that the Greens were unable to stop the project—and this despite holding a referendum in November in which 58 per cent of people voted against it but turnout was insufficient to make the poll valid—contributed to a dip in the Greens' opinion poll standings. There were reasons to believe that 2011 might eventually mark the high point for the Greens. Certainly, the failure of their high-profile candidate, Renate Künast, to win Berlin's mayoral election in September dampened many spirits.

The liberal Free Democrats—the CDU's junior coalition partner in the federal government—on the other hand, had a truly abysmal year. Guido Westerwelle, Germany's foreign minister and vice chancellor, was forced to resign as party leader and as vice chancellor in April, though not as foreign minister, leaving the health minister, Philipp Rösler, to lead the FDP and to assume the post of vice chancellor. With the FDP struggling to make an impact in the federal government, Rösler had an uneasy year. A part of his own party attempted to scupper much of the government's European policy in an internal referendum that took place in December. Ultimately, the eurosceptics in the FDP lost, but with the party having slipped from 14.6 per cent of the vote in the 2009 federal election to around 3 per cent in opinion polls by the end of 2011, it was clear that much had to be done if the FDP were going to become a potent force again.

Away from party politics, the German president ended 2011 trying to explain away a number of controversies. Christian Wulff, the Christian Democrat whom Angela Merkel had hand-picked in 2010 to succeed Horst Köhler, was accused of having been economical with the truth concerning loans he had acquired to buy a new house in his native Lower Saxony. Wulff's attempts at clarifying matters only made them worse as news of other apparently dubious financial transactions, such as obtaining another loan from a bank at suspiciously low interest rates, became public knowledge. An ill-advised rant left as a voicemail for Kai Diekmann, the editor of *Bild Zeitung*, deepened the scandal with the suspicion that Wulff had tried to block the paper from publishing the story. Wulff remained in office, but his position as the country's moral authority was very much weakened.

Dan Hough

FRANCE

CAPITAL: Paris   AREA: 551,500 sq km   POULATION: 64,876,618 ('10)
OFFICIAL LANGUAGE: French
HEAD OF STATE AND GOVERNMENT: President Nicolas Sarkozy (UMP) (since May '07)
RULING PARTY: Union for a Popular Movement (UMP)
PRIME MINISTER: François Fillon (since May '07)
DEMOCRACY INDEX: 7.77; 31st of 167   CORRUPTION INDEX: 7.0; 25th of 183
CURRENCY: Euro (Dec '11 £1.00=EUR 1.16, US$1.00=EUR 0.74)
GNI PER CAPITA: US$42,390, Intl$34,440 at PPP ('10)

PRESIDENT Nicolas Sarkozy greeted the new year 2011 with an unqualified pledge to defend the euro; failure would spell the end of Europe and with it the achievements of the past 60 years. He reaffirmed his determination to proceed with reforms, following his success over pensions, particularly mentioning care of the elderly and the long-term unemployed. In the event, the euro commanded much of his not inconsiderable energies, whether directly or in dealing with the domestic consequences of the eurozone crisis. In tackling the crisis the Franco-German axis was again the "engine" of the EU, with frequent hastily convened "summits" between President Sarkozy and the German chancellor, Angela Merkel. Although they were not personally close and their initial inclinations were often at variance, Sarkozy and Merkel usually ended by agreeing a joint position where both could claim credit for the outcome. Germany was now widely perceived as the stronger partner, but it was mutually useful to the two countries to veil the strength of the one and the weakness of the other.

Although France was in better shape than many of her partners, in January a report commissioned by exporters documented a growing loss of competitiveness compared with her principal competitor—Germany. The economy gave cause for more general concern. Unemployment was running at 9.4 per cent at the start of the year but while the economy was gauged to have emerged from recession, by mid-year it had ceased growing, and it was subsequently acknowledged to be back in recession. Consumer confidence was flagging and projections of growth had repeatedly to be revised downwards from an initial 2.5 per cent in 2012 to a mere 1.0 per cent. Meanwhile, the need to cut the public deficit to 3.0 per cent of GDP by 2013 led to two sets of belt-tightening measures totalling some €11 billion in August and €7 billion in November. The 2012 budget was hailed by Prime Minister François Fillon as the first actually to cut expenditure since World War II. The annual deficit would be reduced by 20 per cent through tax increases on high-earners, cigarettes, alcohol, sugary drinks and restaurant bills, and by closing loopholes and shedding 37,400 public sector jobs. Markets were not entirely convinced and the preservation of France's cherished AAA credit rating remained uncertain. As the year ended, unemployment had risen to 9.8 per cent. Yet, although these were hard times for many, there was much less social unrest than in 2010, when many thousands had repeatedly gone on strike and protested against pensions reform. The only big demonstrations of 2011 were in February, when some 30,000 workers in the justice system protested at the "grave dysfunctionality" of the system and Sarkozy's cavalier attitude towards legal principles.

Unlike the problems of the economy, the popular uprisings in the Arab world caught the government unaware and unprepared. The initial response to both the Tunisian and Egyptian uprisings was low-key and non-interventionist, to the point where an anonymous group of senior diplomats, writing in *Le Monde*, claimed that France's voice in the world had disappeared. The response of the foreign minister, Michèle Alliot-Marie, to the revolution in Tunisia was to offer the government there the benefit of French know-how in controlling civil unrest. The subsequent refusal to let the deposed Tunisian dictator, Zine el-Abidine Ben Ali, enter France did little to redeem the situation. It emerged that, while on holiday in Tunisia during the early stages of the revolution, Alliot-Marie had accepted free flights from a prominent Tunisian businessman. Her failure to acknowledge the extent of her family's interests in Tunisia or to grasp the conflicts of interest involved led to her dismissal. She was succeeded by the former prime minister, Alain Juppé. It also emerged that the current prime minister, François Fillon, had spent part of Christmas with his family as guests of President Hosni Mubarak of Egypt only weeks before he was overthrown. Fillon survived but President Sarkozy instructed ministers that in future they must holiday in France.

The Libyan rebellion brought a very different response from that shown to Tunisia and Egypt. Waiting for nobody, Sarkozy unilaterally recognised the rebel National Transitional Council. In company with UK Prime Minister David Cameron and invoking France's commitment to human rights and freedom, he took the lead in persuading the UN Security Council to authorise military intervention. During the ensuing campaign, French forces made 35 per cent of coalition air strikes. A poll in May recorded 63 per cent approval of Sarkozy's handling of the matter—though his personal approval rating was a dismal 20 per cent.

This was not the only military involvement in Africa. In April, 300 French troops were dispatched to Côte d'Ivoire, reinforcing 1,250 already there. Primarily tasked with safeguarding civilians, they also helped to evict Laurent Gbagbo, the former president who was refusing to accept defeat at the polls, and to install the victor, Alassane Ouattara. The action roused unease in Africa that this might signal a return to an earlier, interventionist tradition abandoned for some years now, though this was denied. French troops continued to be in action in Afghanistan. Visiting them in July, Sarkozy confirmed that some 200 troops would be withdrawn by the end of the year and the remainder would be out by late 2014. Up to 31 December, the force had suffered 78 losses.

The year ended with a spat between France and Turkey when the lower house, the National Assembly, voted to make it a crime, punishable by a year in prison and a fine of €45,000, to deny that the killing of some 1,500,000 Armenians by Turkish forces in 1915 amounted to genocide. The Turkish government, already angered by Sarkozy's hostility to its bid for EU membership, retaliated by recalling its ambassador and barring French military aircraft and warships from its ports and airfields. Prime Minister Recep Tayyip Erdogan denounced the "politics of racism, discrimination and xenophobia", accusing France in turn of genocide during the Algerian war of independence (1954-62). Sarkozy hastened to smooth over the situation and Foreign Minister Juppé declared the Assembly's vote "inopportune". Some commentators suggested a possible connection with the existence of around 500,000 voters of Armenian descent in France and the approach of elections.

Whatever the truth there, every development during the year was assessed through the prism of the approaching presidential campaign. Turnout for the cantonal elections in March was at a record low of 44 per cent, possibly reflecting a widespread disenchantment with politics and politicians. Within that, the results went badly for the government. The Socialist opposition won 35.22 per cent of the first round votes, while the governing Union for a Popular Movement (UMP) attracted only 16.99 per cent, with the far-right National Front (FN) uncomfortably close with 15.66 per cent. The Front gained only a couple of seats but emerged more widely strengthened. Partly, this reflected the change in leadership from the truculent, wilfully provocative Jean-Marie Le Pen to his daughter, Marine, who brought a measure of charm and subtlety to an essentially unchanged message. At times it seemed she might even out-poll Sarkozy in the presidential ballot. Partly, too, Sarkozy's attempts to win over NF voters may have had the opposite effect of legitimising views that had formerly been unacceptable. One such attempt resulted in the wearing of the burqa—Islamic dress for women, with the face fully veiled— in any public place becoming a criminal offence in April.

The cantonal elections also produced a crucial shift in the electorate for the Senate (the upper house), the great bulk of whom were local councillors. In consequence, when the Senate was partly renewed in September it had a left-of-centre majority for the first time since the Fifth French Republic was formed in 1958. Although the Senate had less power than the democratically elected Assembly, the change in its political complexion would inevitably have an impact on the government's legislative programme, on proposals for constitutional reform, and on membership of the Constitutional Council.

The president's opponents also experienced a year of varying fortunes. In the early months of 2011 Dominique Strauss-Kahn, a former Socialist finance minister and current managing director of the IMF, took a strong lead in the polls. Extremely able, personable and highly experienced, though disparaged by some as a "champagne socialist", DSK, as he was widely known, was increasingly seen as the Left's most formidable champion for the presidency, assuming he was prepared to resign from the IMF and take his chances in the election. But, just as he seemed about to do so, disaster struck in May. He was arrested in the USA on charges of sexually assaulting a hotel maid in New York, and resigned his IMF post. The charges were eventually dropped but, by then, too much had become known about his behaviour with women for him to be acceptable as a candidate.

The revelations about Strauss-Khan prompted much reflection about standards in French public life, but they also dealt the Socialists a shattering blow. However, the party recovered remarkably quickly and set about selecting its presidential candidate by way of a "citizens' primary", open to anyone on the electoral lists who declared their support for the Left and contributed at least a symbolic euro to the party coffers. Six would-be candidates took part in three courteous, nationally televised debates, which attracted substantial audiences.

François Hollande, the party's former first secretary, emerged the winner in a run-off second ballot, in which 2,860,000 "citizen votes" were cast. With the powerful incentive of a possible victory, his notoriously contentious party rallied behind him. An amiable "Mr Normal", Hollande had considerable popular appeal but no experience of ministerial office, and neither he nor his party were as yet offering a coherent alternative approach to the financial and economic crisis. Nevertheless, the year ended with support for Sarkozy improving slightly, reflecting his high-profile role in the eurozone crisis, but with Hollande maintaining a commanding lead.

One factor influencing the public mood, and possibly the outcome of the election, was the prominence of scandals. The longstanding case against the former president, Jacques Chirac, finally came to court after years during which he enjoyed immunity as president, followed by subsequent delaying tactics. In December he was found guilty of misappropriation of public funds, breach of trust and conflict of interest arising from when he was mayor of Paris in the 1990s and used public funds to pay people deployed in party-political work. He was sentenced to two years in prison, suspended in recognition of his age and health. Eight others found guilty with him received lesser sentences.

Another long-running scandal—the Clearstream affair—also reached a conclusion. In September the former foreign minister, Dominique de Villepin, was cleared of complicity in a plot to smear Sarkozy with involvement in a particularly murky business involving bribes arising from the sale of warships to Taiwan in 1991. Now a bitter enemy of the president, de Villepin announced his candidacy for the presidency. He had no chance of winning but he might attract just enough support to frustrate Sarkozy's chances of reaching the second round run-off ballot.

Attention also focused on the Karachi affair, an inextricably tangled matter even by French standards. Essentially, it related to a car-bomb attack that killed 11 French naval engineers in Karachi, Pakistan, in 2002, and the relationship (if any) between that attack and what had happened to "commissions" on the sale of three French submarines to Pakistan in 1994—money which may have found its way illegally to finance the unsuccessful 1995 presidential campaign of the then prime minister, Edouard Balladur, whose chief campaign spokesman and minister for the budget had been one Nicolas Sarkozy. Sarkozy furiously denied any involvement. Almost the only indisputably established fact was that the engineers had died and that their families were pursuing legal action, but the rumour mills ground furiously. There were other second-order allegations, some involving people close to the president, that further tainted the fervid pre-election political atmosphere. But while all this engaged the political class, ordinary people were probably more concerned about jobs and making ends meet in an increasingly difficult economic climate. On New Year's Eve a sombre Sarkozy offered his conviction that better days would return in time, but left no doubt that 2012 would be a hard year for all.

Martin Harrison

ITALY

CAPITAL: Rome   AREA: 301,340 sq km   POULATION: 60,483,521 ('10)
OFFICIAL LANGUAGE: Italian
HEAD OF STATE AND GOVERNMENT: President Giorgio Napolitano (since May '06)
RULING PARTY: none
HEAD OF GOVERNMENT: Prime Minister Mario Monti (ind.) (since Nov '11)
DEMOCRACY INDEX: 7.83; 29th of 167   CORRUPTION INDEX: 3.9; 69th of 183
CURRENCY: Euro (Dec '11 £1.00=EUR 1.16, US$1.00=EUR 0.74)
GNI PER CAPITA: US$35,150, Intl$31,130 at PPP ('10)

THE 150th anniversary of Italy's foundation as a modern nation-state, in 1861, was a year of some drama. In April, thrown off course by the Fukushima nuclear disaster and seeking to defuse the forthcoming referendum on the resumption of nuclear power generation, the government suspended its planned re-launch of the country's nuclear energy programme. The suspension was especially significant given that, in mid-March, the Libyan civil war had led to approximately 10 per cent of Italy's oil supplies and one-quarter of its gas supplies being cut off. From July, the European sovereign debt crisis focused on Italy. In November, the government, already weak, failed to gain a parliamentary majority in a key vote and Prime Minister Silvio Berlusconi resigned. He was replaced by Mario Monti, a financial expert and member of the secretive Bilderberg Group, sometimes seen as a near "real world" approximation to an executive committee of global capitalism. Monti's government of technocrats was sworn in on 16 November and won votes of confidence in the Senate and Chamber of Deputies on 17 and 18 November respectively. The resort to non-party government, already seen in the early 1990s, confirmed the inability of Italy's party system to provide effective economic government—at least in the eyes of key international actors. A minor resurgence of anarchist letter bombing was also seen.

The year started with both government and opposition suffering in the polls and government more or less paralysed. A 40-year-old aphorism—that Italian governments survived, but did not govern—still rang true, even in the so-called Second Republic (since 1992). The Northern League, a member of the Berlusconi government which continued to present itself as an opposition movement, exploited government weakness to undermine celebrations of the country's 150th anniversary. Late in the day, the government nevertheless declared 17 March a public holiday and it was celebrated, rather successfully. In fact, even two-thirds of League supporters thought Italian unification had been a good thing, whilst the Left discovered the virtues of national solidarity, as strenuously championed by President Giorgio Napolitano and his predecessor, Carlo Ciampi (1999-2006). The next day, a joint meeting of the foreign and defence committees approved backing UN Resolution 1973 in terms of the "responsibility to protect", so that intervention in Libya did not constitute "war", which the Italian constitution prohibited. NATO operations in Libya began on 19 March. Italy was a half-hearted member of the coalition but was quick, on 4 April, to recognise the National Provisional Council (NPC) as Libya's "only legitimate interlocutor". The Northern League voiced frequent criticism of Italy's participation, not least on grounds of cost, encouraged by the see-saw nature of the campaign. With the NPC's victory, however, oil and gas production resumed, reaching 70 per cent of pre-conflict levels by mid-December, and forecast to double by the end of the decade.

In local elections in May the opposition did not do especially well but scored some important symbolic victories, notably in Naples and Milan. However, neither of the successful mayoral candidates in those cities were representatives of the Democratic Party (PD), the main opposition party. Rather, Naples was won by Luigi De Magistris, of Italy of Principles (IDV); and Milan by Giuliano Pisapia of Left, Ecology and Freedom (SEL), which had failed to enter Parliament in 2008. On 12-13 June four referendums were held and, for the first time since 1995, the quorum of a 50 per cent turnout was reached (54.8 per cent). Of those who voted, support to repeal recent legislation was overwhelming, at 95-96 per cent. Voters rejected privatisation of, and profit-making from, the supply of water; the resumption of generating nuclear energy; and two measures clarifying the "legal impediment" of ministers, including the prime minister, to appear in court when engaged in government business. This outcome was a major blow to the government, support for which was now tumbling. By September, trust in the government was down to 19 per cent according to at least one poll.

Global attention focused on Italy when the viability of the sovereign debt of several EU member states became an issue. Whilst the debts of Greece, Ireland and Portugal were too small for their default to provoke global economic crisis, the same was not true of Italy. Italy had the eighth largest GDP in the world. Combine that with a debt-to-GDP ratio of some 120 per cent, 20 years of poor economic growth (half the EU15 average) and relative decline in productivity, and a paralysed government which consistently and emphatically denied that Italy had an economic problem, and it was not surprising that the financial markets started to require higher interest rates on their loans. The situation risked becoming a vicious circle as debt repayment, already consuming 16 per cent of government expenditure, became ever more expensive. In July, President Napolitano was widely credited with organising a rapid parliamentary response to the first attacks on Italy's financial position, confirming the growing role of the presidency in Italian public affairs. In August, the European Central Bank demanded that Italy's budget be brought into balance by 2013, a year earlier than planned for by the July budget— the government having wanted its impact postponed until after the 2013 election. A further emergency budget in September sought to achieve this, but failed to convince onlookers. Standard & Poor's, one of the major credit-rating agencies, lowered Italy's rating, as did Moody's a fortnight later. On 15 October the global "day of rage" staged in some 400 cities, including 60 capitals, by protesters known as the "indignados" (outraged), uniquely saw riots in Rome.

On 23 October Italy and its prime minister were publicly humiliated at the European Council, the EU summit convened to tackle the eurozone crisis. When asked if Italy would pull through, the affirmative, formal answers of Germany's Chancellor Angela Merkel and France's President Nicolas Sarkozy were preceded by theatrical hesitation and eloquent smirks. On 3-4 November the G-20 effectively dictated yet further emergency budget measures, including quarterly supervisory reporting by the IMF. Albeit formally, Prime Minister Berlusconi requested this unique oversight of a non-IMF-recipient country in order to convince the markets that Italy was taking appropriate action. Indeed, the government (and others) argued that market fears were not only misplaced but were themselves a major cause of the crisis. The other major cause was the repeated failure of EU summits to resolve Europe's chronic liquidity crisis. In any case, Italian bond yields continued to rise, crossing what some regarded as the threshold of unsustainability: 7 per cent. On 8 November, the government failed to obtain a parliamentary majority on a key budget vote, which was won thanks only to opposition abstention. A fourth budget was then rushed through Parliament and, on 12 November, Berlusconi resigned.

In the meantime, on 9 November, President Napolitano had nominated Mario Monti as life senator. Now, Napolitano asked Monti to seek to form a government. On 16 November a government comprising all technocrats—rather similar to that of the 1995-96 government of Lamberto Dini—was sworn in. The only party to vote against the new government was the Northern League for the Independence of Padania—to give the party its full name. A month later a further budget was passed, dubbed Italy's "life-saver" by the new prime minister. The budget was supported by the two principal parties of left and right—the Democratic Party (PD) and the People of Freedom (PDL)—and by the Centre Union (UDC) and its allies. The Northern League voted against, as did Antonio Di Pietro's Italy of Principles. Both main parties were thus flanked by populist parties threatening to undermine them electorally, just as the country entered a probable recession and with elections due by the spring of 2013 at the latest. In fact, the PDL, too, was critical of the new government's measures and its supporters were quick to argue that continuing high interest rates demonstrated that Berlusconi's credibility had evidently not, therefore, been the problem that critics had argued it to be. Such assertions encouraged doubts about the new government's survival and its ability to deliver structural reforms, promised for the new year. The year 2011 thus ended amidst political uncertainty—in contrast to the economic certainty of welfare cuts, rising taxes and increases in the retirement age.

Decline in support for Berlusconi was long-term and reflected growing disillusion with the government, though continuing scandal and conflict with the judiciary may have influenced some. In January, the Constitutional Court had overruled the automaticity of the legitimate impediment legislation and two trials had resumed against the prime minister. One related to his having allegedly bribed the British solicitor, David Mills, to give false evidence; the other to alleged fraud and embezzlement in the acquisition of television rights by his Mediaset group. A third trial began in April but made slow progress. This related to payment for the prostitution of a minor, Karima El Mahroug (aka Ruby Rubacuori), and abuse of office in trying to have her freed from police custody following her arrest for theft (see AR 2010, p. 42). Major aspects of the Mediaset charges were dropped in October 2011, whilst the Mills bribery case was expected to end in 2012 due to the statute of limitations. The El Mahroug case provoked a reawakening of the women's movement under the slogan: "If not now, when?" Major demonstrations took place in several Italian cities on 13 February and again on 11 December.

Another possible sign of a turn of the political tide was the declining audience for the state television (RAI's) flagship news programme, *Tg1*, which was widely accused of political bias. In May, AGCOM, the communications regulatory authority fined *Tg1* and *Tg4* the maximum €250,000, and *Tg2*, *Tg5* and *Studio Aperto* (Italia Uno) €100,000, all for favouring the government in their election coverage. In December AGCOM also fined Auditel, the television ratings agency, €1.8 million for actions consistently favouring RAI and Mediaset over different periods during 2008-10. Meanwhile, in July, the Milan Appeal Court confirmed that Mediaset should pay damages (reduced from €750 million to €560 million) to CIR, Carlo De Benedetti's industrial holding company, resulting from a corrupted judicial decision favouring Berlusconi's Fininvest holding company in 1991. Shortly after, the European Court of Justice ruled that the switchover to digital television in Italy had been illegally subsidised, favouring, above all, Mediaset channels which would thus be required to reimburse the Italian state significant sums of money.

Monti's appointment seemed to suggest that a new era might have begun in Italian politics. Yet Berlusconi remained leader of the centre-right, whilst the oppositions were divided, even if polls had been suggesting, from the summer, that they would win an election. The PD's decision to "put Italy first" by supporting the formation of the new government, rather than seek its own advantage by pressing for potentially destabilising early elections, left the direction of Italian politics very uncertain.

Mark Donovan

BELGIUM, THE NETHERLANDS, AND LUXEMBOURG

Belgium

CAPITAL: Brussels   AREA: 30,530 sq km   POULATION: 10,879,159 ('10)
OFFICIAL LANGUAGES: French, Flemish & German
HEAD OF STATE: King Albert II (since Aug '93)
RULING PARTIES: Socialist Party (PS)-led coalition
HEAD OF GOVERNMENT: Prime Minister Elio Di Rupo (PS) (since Dec '11)
DEMOCRACY INDEX: 8.05; 23rd of 167   CORRUPTION INDEX: 7.5; 19th of 183
CURRENCY: Euro (Dec '11 £1.00=EUR 1.16, US$1.00=EUR 0.74)
GNI PER CAPITA: US$45,360, Intl$37,800 at PPP ('10)

The Netherlands

CAPITAL: Amsterdam   AREA: 41,530 sq km   POULATION: 16,612,213 ('10)
OFFICIAL LANGUAGE: Dutch
HEAD OF STATE: Queen Beatrix (since April '80)
RULING PARTIES: People's Party for Freedom and Democracy (VVD) and Christian Democratic
    Appeal (CDA) form coalition
HEAD OF GOVERNMENT: Prime Minister Mark Rutte (VVD) (since Oct '10)
DEMOCRACY INDEX: 8.99; 10th of 167   CORRUPTION INDEX: 8.9; 7th of 183
CURRENCY: Euro (Dec '11 £1.00=EUR 1.16, US$1.00=EUR 0.74)
GNI PER CAPITA: US$49,750, Intl$42,610 at PPP ('10)

Luxembourg
CAPITAL: Luxembourg   AREA: 2,590 sq km   POULATION: 505,831 ('10)
OFFICIAL LANGUAGE: Letzeburgish
HEAD OF STATE: Grand Duke Henri (since Oct '00)
RULING PARTIES: Christian Social People's Party (CSV/PCS)-led coalition
HEAD OF GOVERNMENT: Prime Minister Jean-Claude Juncker (CSV/PCS) (since Jan '95)
DEMOCRACY INDEX: 8.88; 11th of 167   CORRUPTION INDEX: 8.5; 11th of 183
CURRENCY: Euro (Dec '11 £1.00=EUR 1.16, US$1.00=EUR 0.74)
GNI PER CAPITA: US$76,630, Intl$63,950 at PPP ('10)

FOR most of the year **Belgium** was run without a government confirmed in office, following inconclusive elections in June 2010 (see AR 2011, p. 59). The country had a well-established tradition of protracted post-election haggling over the terms of a new government but this interregnum beat all records. A succession of emissaries and intermediaries tried their hand at bringing the parties together only to retire hurt, as often as not over language and constitutional issues.

In some respects the situation appeared less damaging than might have been expected. Many matters were now in the hands of the regional administrations as a consequence of the hollowing out of central government powers in recent years, and an experienced bureaucracy kept federal business ticking over satisfactorily. The presidency of the Council of the EU during the last six months of 2010 had been handled competently and the apparent emergence from the recession early in the year also eased the pressure on negotiators. Walloons and Flemings put aside their differences to agree promptly and almost unanimously to commit F-16 strike aircraft and a minesweeper to NATO operations in Libya. The federal government also acted decisively in buying the Belgian arm of Dexia, a failed Franco-Belgian bank.

Nevertheless, King Albert II was becoming increasingly exercised about the failure to agree on a new government. On Belgium's National Day in July he warned that the way the situation was dragging on could threaten both Belgium and the EU. But what brought a deal eventually was less that warning than the deepening crisis in the eurozone and the ratings agencies' nervousness at the continuing political drift. After 541 days and with a coalition agreement running to over 70 pages, a new government took office on 6 December. It was headed by the Socialist leader, Elio Di Rupo, the first francophone prime minister for over 30 years, and supported by the Walloon and Flemish Socialist, Liberal, and Christian Democratic parties, with the largest party in Flanders, the secessionist New Flemish Alliance (N-VA), promising "ferocious" opposition. It had earlier broken the traditional consensus over policy towards the EU by opposing giving the EU powers of taxation. The new government now had to cope with the impact of the eurozone crisis, the decision by ArcelorMittal to close blast furnaces near Liege—a blow to the ailing francophone south—and nationwide strikes of public employees in December over pensions reform.

One issue on which the country was not divided was sexual abuse by members of the Roman Catholic clergy. There was near unanimity in Parliament in January in approving a report by a special commission that strongly criticised the Church's failure to create a scheme to compensate victims. Polls showed confidence in the Church's handling of the matter at its lowest ebb in both the country's main communities. In April, the Vatican ordered the Bishop of Bruges, who had admitted having abused two nephews, to leave the country and withdraw from the public ministry (see AR 2010, p. 45).

The turbulence that convulsed the eurozone did not entirely pass **Luxembourg** by. When the twice bailed-out Dexia bank failed and its Luxembourg arm was sold to Qatari investors, the government stepped in to take a 12 per cent stake. The problems of ArcelorMittal steel, the country's biggest employer, were also a concern. The Fukushima nuclear disaster cast uncertainty over the future of the country's energy policy since, with only modest generating capacity of its own, Luxembourg was highly dependent on the uncertain energy policies of its neighbours. Unemployment, though well below the EU average, reached 6.1 per cent towards the end of the year.

One of the government's prime preoccupations was the health of the public finances, though these were in a better state than in most of the eurozone. The finance minister, Luc Frieden, declared his priorities as stimulating growth and increasing competitiveness, aided by an "attractive fiscal policy". Starting from a deficit of 3.2 per cent in 2010, the aim was to reduce that to 0.7 per cent by 2012, achieve balance in 2014 and move into surplus in 2015. This march towards financial rectitude brought strains to the long-established practice of tripartite bargaining between government, unions and employers. In December the prime minister, Jean-Claude Juncker, declared the system had failed to produce a result and that customary indexed increases in salaries would be implemented with a six-month delay. Normal working would be restored in 2015. Whether this would indeed happen, or whether "tripartism" had been fatally wounded, remained to be seen.

Domestically and within the EU, the year was characterised by the determined quest for healthy public finances. **The Netherlands** was among the most wary over bailing out Greece. Mark Rutte's minority government had to contend with strong parliamentary opposition, including from some nominal allies, forcing it to look to the opposition Labour Party (PvdA) for support. The ultra-right Party for Freedom (PvdV) voted against every bailout. The government pressed for enforceable sanctions against countries that failed to keep to the rules and favoured giving the European Commission greater powers to deal with them. The Netherlands had traditionally been among the strongest supporters of the institutions of the EU, but in May MPs opposed any increase in the country's contributions to it.

At home, a principal preoccupation was the search for €18 billion in expenditure cuts in the 2012 budget to bring the deficit down to 2.9 per cent of GDP, thereby meeting the requirements of the EU Growth and Stability Pact. The main areas affected were development co-operation, child care and defence. The latter entailed shedding 12,300 civil and military posts, the closure of several bases, and the decommissioning of 60 tanks, 19 F-16 aircraft and five minesweepers.

There were also cuts in health insurance, in residential care for the elderly, and in the social affairs and employment budget. The number of public broadcasting networks would also be reduced. The savings target was met but later in the year the economy had slipped back into recession and tax receipts were below what had been forecast. The finance minister, Jan Kees de Jager, warned that even more cuts would be needed during the year ahead. Still, with one of the EU's lowest unemployment rates (5.8 per cent), the Netherlands remained in relatively good economic health.

Despite the defence cuts the government, which had withdrawn combat troops from Afghanistan only a few months earlier, decided, over strong opposition, to dispatch a 545-strong police training mission there. In March, MPs agreed more readily to contribute F-16 strike fighters, a flight-refuelling tanker and a minesweeper to NATO's action in Libya.

Parliament approved pensions reform after protracted negotiations between the government, employers and unions. The normal retirement age would rise to 66 in 2020 and, probably, to 67 in 2025. People taking early retirement would have their pensions reduced; those working for longer would receive more.

Provincial elections in March, which indirectly determined the membership of the upper house of Parliament, resulted in the governing coalition having 37 of the 75 seats in the Senate, leaving it dependent on a small Calvinist party. The anti-immigrant Party for Freedom made progress across the country. Its leader, Geert Wilders, ensured that immigration-related issues remained to the fore. His diatribes against Islam led to a charge of inciting racial hatred. After a controversial trial he was found not guilty. In September the government proposed toughening the rules on immigration and asylum. Illegal immigration was made a criminal offence, family migration rules were tightened, and it was made easier to terminate aliens' residence rights. In November measures were introduced that linked residence rights for recent arrivals to fulfilling an obligation of "civic integration". A bill backed by the small Party of the Animals (PvdV) to ban the ritual slaughter of animals was approved by the lower house in June, despite protests from Muslim and Jewish groups. However, their opposition led two of the main parties in the governing coalition to have a change of heart and further progress was blocked, at least temporarily, when the proposal came before the Senate in December.

Ruling in a matter that had caused much anguish for years, the Court of Appeal in July held, in a test case, that the Dutch government was responsible for the death of three Bosniaks (Bosnian Muslims) when Dutch troops on a UN mission had handed Bosniak men and boys to Bosnian Serb forces in 1995 at Srebrenica. Compensation would now be paid. Measures were also set in play to indemnify victims of sexual abuse by members of the Roman Catholic clergy.

Martin Harrison

DENMARK—ICELAND—NORWAY—SWEDEN—FINLAND—AUSTRIA—
SWITZERLAND—EUROPEAN MINI-STATES

NORDIC COUNTRIES

Denmark

CAPITAL: Copenhagen   AREA: 43,090 sq km   POULATION: 5,523,095 ('10)
OFFICIAL LANGUAGE: Danish
HEAD OF STATE: Queen Margrethe II (since Jan '72)
RULING PARTIES: Social Democrat-led coalition
HEAD OF GOVERNMENT: Helle Thorning-Schmidt (Social Democrats) (since Oct '11)
DEMOCRACY INDEX: 9.52; 3rd of 167   CORRUPTION INDEX: 9.4; 2nd of 183
CURRENCY: Danish Krone (Dec '11 £1.00=DKK 8.65, US$1.00=DKK 5.52)
GNI PER CAPITA: US$59,210, Intl$40,290 at PPP ('10)

Iceland

CAPITAL: Reykjavík   AREA: 103,000 sq km   POULATION: 317,398 ('10)
OFFICIAL LANGUAGE: Icelandic
HEAD OF STATE: President Olafur Ragnar Grímsson (since Aug '96)
RULING PARTIES: Social Democratic Alliance (SF)-led coalition
HEAD OF GOVERNMENT: Prime Minister Johanna Sigurdardottir (SF) (since Feb '09)
DEMOCRACY INDEX: 9.65; 2nd of 167   CORRUPTION INDEX: 8.3; 13th of 183
CURRENCY: Icelandic Krona (Dec '11 £1.00=ISK 185.92, US$1.00=ISK 118.55)
GNI PER CAPITA: US$33,990, Intl$28,720 at PPP ('10)

Norway

CAPITAL: Oslo   AREA: 323,800 sq km   POULATION: 4,885,240 ('10)
OFFICIAL LANGUAGE: Norwegian
HEAD OF STATE: King Harald V (since Jan '91)
RULING PARTIES: Labour Party (AP)-led coalition
HEAD OF GOVERNMENT: Jens Stoltenberg (AP) (since Oct '05)
DEMOCRACY INDEX: 9.08; 1st of 167   CORRUPTION INDEX: 9.0; 6th of 183
CURRENCY: Norwegian Krone (Dec '11 £1.00=NOK 9.08, US$1.00=NOK 5.79)
GNI PER CAPITA: US$85,340, Intl$57,100 at PPP ('10)

Sweden

CAPITAL: Stockholm   AREA: 450,290 sq km   POULATION: 9,379,116 ('10)
OFFICIAL LANGUAGE: Swedish
HEAD OF STATE: King Carl XVI Gustav (since Sept '73)
RULING PARTIES: Alliance for Sweden coalition
HEAD OF GOVERNMENT: Prime Minister Fredrik Reinfeldt (Moderate Unity Party) (since Oct '06)
DEMOCRACY INDEX: 9.50; 4th of 167   CORRUPTION INDEX: 9.3; 4th of 183
CURRENCY: Swedish Krona (Dec '11 £1.00=SEK 10.60, US$1.00=SEK 6.76)
GNI PER CAPITA: US$50,000, Intl$39,660 at PPP ('10)

Finland

CAPITAL: Helsinki   AREA: 338,150 sq km   POULATION: 5,363,624 ('10)
OFFICIAL LANGUAGES: Finnish & Swedish
HEAD OF STATE: President Tarja Halonen (SSDP) (since February '00)
RULING PARTIES: National Coalition Party (KOK)-led coalition
HEAD OF GOVERNMENT: Prime Minister Jyrki Katainen (KOK) (since June '11)
DEMOCRACY INDEX: 9.19; 7th of 167   CORRUPTION INDEX: 9.4; 2nd of 183
CURRENCY: Euro (Dec '11 £1.00=EUR 1.16, US$1.00=EUR 0.74)
GNI PER CAPITA: US$47,160, Intl$37,180 at PPP ('10)

THE year 2011 will be remembered in the Nordic countries for the horrific events of 22 July in **Norway**. At 3.23pm a heavy car bomb exploded in the government quarter of central Oslo killing eight people, injuring 30, and causing major damage to several official buildings. It was swiftly announced that the prime minister and key members of the government were unharmed, but the bombing understandably caused wide alarm and rigorous security measures were immediately implemented. Approximately one-and-a-half hours later, a man dressed as a policeman boarded the ferry to Utoya island in Tyrifjorden (Lake Tyri), 40 km north west of the capital, where 600 to 700 teenagers were taking part in the annual summer camp of the Workers' Youth League, the youth organisation of the Norwegian Labour Party (AP). Shortly after arriving on the island, the man started firing his weapons randomly at the panicking teenagers, who were hiding in the bushes or at the shoreline, barricading themselves inside the buildings, or trying to swim over to the mainland. In total 69 people were killed and 66 injured, before the gunman surrendered to the specialised police task force that arrived on the scene one hour and 10 minutes after the first shots were fired.

The media and most Norwegians initially assumed that the bomb was an attack by al-Qaida or another radical Islamist organisation: a reaction, perhaps, to Norway's military involvement in Afghanistan and Libya; or somehow related to the 2006 controversy in Denmark over the cartoons of the Prophet Mohammed (see AR 2007, pp. 54-56). But the police soon announced that they had arrested an "ethnic Norwegian", suspected of both the bombing and the shootings. The perpetrator turned out to be Anders Behring Breivik, a 32-year-old man with extreme right-wing and Islamophobic views. He had been a member of the populist right-wing Progress Party (FP), but parted ways with the party because he found its views on immigration insufficiently radical. In the distorted mind of Breivik, the multicultural programme of the Norwegian Labour Youth represented a "cultural Marxism" that was threatening European civilisation. Psychiatrists later concluded that Breivik was psychotic during the attacks and that he suffered from paranoid schizophrenia. Their report was subject to review, but if upheld would mean that Breivik would be placed in psychiatric care for an indefinite time. His trial was scheduled for April 2012.

This was not the first time that the Nordic countries had experienced a terror attack: in 2010 there had been a suicide bombing in central Stockholm, and in 2007 and 2008 two small Finnish communities had witnessed lethal school shooting incidents. But the events of 22 July represented a direct attack on Norway's government and society and on the social democratic movement that had been the main political force in Norwegian and Nordic politics for the previous century. Norway's prime minister, Jens Stoltenberg, himself a Social Democrat and frequent guest at Utoya, received much praise for his statements after the attacks. Both in the turmoil of the day and at the memorial service on 24 July, he took a firm stand against terrorism in all its forms, without resorting to a rhetoric of vengeance or fear. Norway received condolences from around the world, and on 25 July the Nordic countries joined Norway in a minute of silence in tribute to the victims.

In the aftermath of the attacks there was discussion in all the Nordic countries about the foundations and limitations of an open, democratic society. Particular attention was given to hate speech on the Internet and to the increasingly hostile tone in the political debate on immigration. Initially, there also seemed to be a surge in political engagement and the youth organisations of all political parties experienced a rise in membership. The Norwegian municipal elections in September were heavily marked by the events of 22 July and saw a drastic decline in support for the Progress Party (down to 11.6 per cent from 17.7 per cent in the 2007 elections). There was a rise in support for the traditional parties like the Labour Party (up from 29.7 to 31.7 per cent) and the Conservatives (up from 21.3 to 28.0 per cent). Subsequent polls, however, indicated that the relative support of the parties had returned close to pre-22 July figures.

Whether or not the attacks in Norway influenced the results of **Denmark's** legislative elections in September was difficult to assess. The two most successful parties were, however, those which unambiguously profiled themselves against the restrictive immigration policies of the Liberal-Conservative government, and particularly against the nationalist anti-immigration rhetoric of the government's informal coalition partner, the right-wing Danish People's Party (DF). Votes for the centrist Social Liberal party (RV) went up from 5.1 per cent in the 2007 elections to 9.4 per cent, while on the far left the Red-Green Alliance rose from 2.2 to 6.7 per cent. This was also the first time since its foundation in 1995 that the DF had lost support in a parliamentary election (down from 13.8 to 12.3 per cent), but analysts claimed that this was due less to the attacks in Norway than to the fact that the DF had failed to make immigration a key issue in the debate. Instead, the discussion revolved very much around Denmark's faltering economy. Ultimately, the Liberal-Conservative coalition, which had been in government since 2001, failed to convince the voters. Power shifted leftwards, with the Social Democrat Helle Thorning-Schmidt leading a three-party coalition of the Social Democrats (SD), the Social Liberal Party, and the Socialist People's Party (SF). Ironically, the Social Democrats won the prime minister's post with their worst result since 1903 (down to 24.8 per cent, from 25.5 per cent). The appointment of Thorning-Schmidt also meant that Sweden was now the only Nordic country not to have been governed at some time by a female prime minister.

Although the political debate in Denmark was marked by the global economic situation, the discussion focused primarily on national issues with the European financial crisis present only in the background. The opposite was true of the only Nordic eurozone country, **Finland**, where the European debt crisis was the main talking point throughout the year. The European Financial Stability Facility (EFSF, the EU's bailout fund) and the Portuguese bailout in particular were principal issues in the legislative elections of April. The focus was mutual, as many foreigners believed that the Finnish elections would have a decisive impact on European developments. Whereas the outgoing centre-right government had supported Finland's participation in the eurozone stability measures, the challengers were unconvinced. The most fervent opponents were the eurosceptic, anti-immigration, populist True Finns party, which grew in the opinion polls from a small party with a mere 6.1 per cent support in January to a serious contender for the title of largest party by the end of March. Led by the charismatic Timo Soini, the True Finns (who in August changed their English name to "the Finns") ended up with a staggering 19.1 per cent of the vote (up from 4.1 per cent in 2007), virtually equal to the Social Democrats (SSDP), which dropped back from 21.4 to 19.1 per cent. The largest setback was suffered by former prime minister Mari Kiviniemi's Centre Party (KESK), which dropped from 22.3 to a mere 15.8 per cent.

It was the conservative National Coalition Party (KOK) that ended up as the largest party (although down from 22.3 to 20.4 per cent), and their leader, Jyrki Katainen, was thus handed the task of forming a new government. After lengthy negotiations Katainen succeeded in forming a large coalition government consisting of the National Coalition Party, the Social Democrats, the Left Alliance (VAS), the Green League (VIHR), the Swedish People's Party (SFP), and the Christian Democrats (KD). This meant that the True Finns, despite being the only party that had actually increased its share of the vote in the election, was left in opposition. Nonetheless, the elections did mark a significant change in Finnish politics, particularly on EU issues. The previous compliant (or submissive) attitude was replaced with a more reluctant approach, and in August the Social Democratic finance minister, Jutta Urpilainen, made a name for herself in Europe by insisting on guarantees for the loan package that would bailout Greece. The idea did not get much sympathy from other EU countries.

The political discussion in **Iceland** was still very much concerned with the aftermath of the 2008 financial disaster (see AR 2009, pp. 64-65). In general it seemed that Iceland had come through in reasonable shape, but the reasons for this remained very much under debate. The question of a possible indictment of the former prime minister, Geir H. Haarde of the centre-liberal Independence Party (SD), for allegedly having made the crisis worse by letting the banks fail, had not progressed and some analysts were now claiming that his actions had actually saved Iceland from total bankruptcy. Moreover, in April there was a referendum in which the Icelanders for the second time rejected a government-approved plan to repay the UK and the Netherlands for their compensation of British and Dutch nationals who had lost savings due to the failure of the Icesave bank in 2008. This was a major setback for the Social Democrat (SF) prime minister, Johanna Sigurdardottir, and the British and Dutch authorities immediately threatened to take the issue to the European courts. The negotiations on Iceland's accession to the EU nonetheless proceeded according to schedule, even if opinion polls indicated that a majority of Icelanders did not want to join the Union.

The Constitutional Assembly, elected in a general ballot at the end of 2010 in order to review Iceland's 1944 constitution, was invalidated by the Supreme Court in January. Instead the Althing (legislature) decided to appoint the 25 people who had been elected to a Constitutional Council with essentially the same task. Their work received significant international attention because of their extensive use of social media in discussing their proposals. The final result was handed over to the Althing on 29 July.

In the light of the economic and political turmoil in southern Europe, **Sweden** received much international approbation in 2011. In November the *Financial Times* selected Anders Borg from the conservative Moderate Party (MSP) as the most successful finance minister in Europe. Domestically, however, the main talking point was the largest opposition party, the Social Democrats (SAP), which, after poor results in the 2010 elections, decided to make a change in leadership. Mona Sahlin retired in favour of the outsider Hakan Juholt who, after a nice start, plunged into a series of scandals. In October it turned out that Juholt had been receiving accommodation reimbursements since 2007 to which he was not entitled, to the tune of 160 000 SEK. As a result of this and thanks to the comparative success of Fredrik Reinfeldt's conservative government, the SAP polled record low figures during the autumn. Besides the Social Democrats, another Swedish national icon, King Carl XVI Gustav, also found himself at the centre of negative media attention. Following the publication of the book *Den motvillige monarken* (*The Reluctant Monarch*) in 2010, the Nordic tabloid press had been busy discussing the king's alleged visits to strip clubs and his extra-marital affairs.

The Swedish carmaker SAAB filed for bankruptcy in December, as its owner General Motors vetoed a Chinese investment over fears of releasing important technology licences to their competitors. Unless new investors appeared, this would surely mean the end for SAAB Automobile. The Finnish telecommunications giant, Nokia, tried to counter its decreasing share of the global market by abandoning its own operating system, Symbian, in favour of co-operation with Microsoft. Nokia's Windows-based telephone series, Lumia, was unveiled in October, but it remained to be seen whether it would present a real challenge to Apple and Samsung. If Norway had been left unharmed by the European fiscal crisis, it was not safe from the butter crisis that pervaded the Nordic countries during the autumn of 2011. The exceptionally warm summer had resulted in a reduced production of fodder, which, in combination with the rising popularity of low-carbohydrate diets, surprised the dairies. As a non-EU member, Norway was apparently hardest struck, with reports that as Christmas approached butter was being auctioned for prices reaching 1,000 NOK per kg.

The success of Nordic writers continued in 2011 as the Swedish poet Tomas Tranströmer won the Nobel Prize in literature. Meanwhile, the Copenhagen restaurant Noma was elected as the world's finest by the British magazine *Restaurant* for the second year in succession. The self-proclaimed autonomous commune, Freetown Christiania, in Copenhagen ended many years of uncertainty by reaching an agreement with the state to purchase the bulk of the land that had been claimed by the hippie movement in 1971, for 73 million DKK. In order to raise the funds, the Christianites began to sell "people's shares" for amounts starting from 20 DKK to their supporters as well as to the many tourists that visited Christiania.

In May there was another volcanic eruption on Iceland causing disruption in western European air travel. The chaos of 2010 was avoided as Griimsvotn settled after only a few days. Nature did, however, test the Nordic countries and their infrastructure during the winter of 2010-11 with persistent freezing weather and huge amounts of snow. Though the winter of 2011-12 seemed likely to be considerably milder, the year ended in hostile weather conditions with the storm Dagmar (Patrick)—allegedly the worst in a decade—causing severe damage and power failures throughout Norway, Sweden and Finland.

If the year 2011 was troublesome for EU enthusiasts, it was one of success for Nordic co-operation. In April the Nordic foreign ministers signed a declaration of solidarity in crisis situations, which received surprisingly little attention in the media.

Johan Strang

AUSTRIA

CAPITAL: Vienna   AREA: 83,870 sq km   POULATION: 8,384,745 ('10)
OFFICIAL LANGUAGE: German
HEAD OF STATE: Federal President Heinz Fischer (since July '04)
RULING PARTIES: "Grand Coalition" of Social Democratic Party (SPÖ) and People's Party (ÖVP)
HEAD OF GOVERNMENT: Federal Chancellor Werner Faymann (SPÖ) (since Dec '08)
DEMOCRACY INDEX: 8.49; 13th of 167   CORRUPTION INDEX: 7.8; 16th of 183
CURRENCY: Euro (Dec '11 £1.00=EUR 1.16, US$1.00=EUR 0.74)
GNI PER CAPITA: US$46,690, Intl$39,390 at PPP ('10)

THE economies of many European countries went through difficult times in 2011. Austria, whilst not immune from the economic troubles of states around it, managed to perform well. Unemployment remained low at around 4.5 per cent, barely above what statisticians would regard as full employment; inflation remained at acceptable levels, around 3 per cent; and growth remained passable, i.e. there was some, more than could be said for most other eurozone countries.

Austria saw no major elections in 2011, although a number of prominent faces came and went and there was a substantial number of high-profile scandals. The resignation of Josef Pröll, the head of the christian democratic Austrian People's Party (ÖVP), saw Foreign Minister Michael Spindelegger take over the party leadership and in April he set about juggling his ÖVP front bench. Johanna Mikl-Leitner became the new home affairs minister, whilst Maria Fechter vacated that post for the finance ministry. Beatrix Karl became justice minister, and Karlheinz Töchterle became science minister. There were also changes of personnel in various less prominent junior positions.

Away from the cabinet table, in September the former federal chancellor, Wolfgang Schüssel (2000-07), retired from politics under a cloud following the so-called "Telekom Affair". Schüssel claimed that his resignation was simply effected to enable him (and the authorities investigating him) to clear his name, and refused to admit to any wrongdoing. The scandal shook the Austrian republic, as three former ministers were also accused of engaging in corrupt practices thanks to the evidence provided by the most high-profile witness in the case, Gernot Schieszler, an executive at Telkom Austria. A committee of investigation under the leadership of Green Party legislator, Gabriela Moser, began trying to get to the bottom of the affair.

This was not, however, the end of the corruption scandals that hit Austria in 2011. Uwe Scheuch, the leader of the ever-controversial right-wing Freedom Party (FPÖ) in Carinthia, proclaimed his innocence when accused of being involved in what came to be known as the "part-of-the-game affair". In August a court in Klagenfurt found Scheuch guilty of trying to secure investment from a Russian businessman by offering him Austrian citizenship, as well as soliciting an illegal donation to the Freedom Party. Scheuch publicly denounced the judge and promptly lodged an appeal, whilst all the time refusing to resign. Corruption (or corruption allegations) were not limited to the world of politics: the business world was also far from immune. Wolfgang Auer-Welsbach, former head of the now bankrupt financial group AvW, was sent to prison for eight years, whilst Hans Linz, also of AvW, was sentenced to seven years behind bars, both for indulging in corrupt practices to defraud investors that had come apart in the 2008 financial crisis. A scandal of an altogether different kind enveloped 100 members of a high-flying Austrian insurance company when it became apparent that they had been invited to a sex-party in a Budapest gallery.

On a more mundane level, long-standing controversies over signs in border regions were at least partly resolved in 2011. Debates around where, and under what circumstances, Austria's non-German-speaking minorities could demand that local signs were displayed in other languages had been a part of Austrian public life for decades. Finally, on 3 February, discussions began with the aim of finding a solution to such controversies. By August negotiations were bearing fruit and by 1 October, 164 towns and villages across four local authorities were displaying bi-lingual signs.

There were also several rather odd developments during the year. Chancellor Werner Faymann's Social Democrats, for example, tried to enter the world of social media, and brought together a team to help market the chancellor via these relatively new channels. However, after spending €200,000 and employing nine people, the project descended into farce. Stories of "buying" Facebook friends contributed to the enterprise ending in embarrassment for Faymann, and led most of Austria to spend weeks laughing at the antics of a comedy-double by the name of Werner "Failman". Facebook made another appearance on the political scene in October when the Freedom Party expelled one of its legislators, Werner Koenigshofer, from the party for comments made on his own Facebook page. Koenigshofer had compared the bombings and shootings in Norway in July, in which around 100 people died, to abortion. Shortly afterwards both Freedom Party leader Heinz-Christian Strache and his deputy, Norbert Hofer, found themselves in trouble for observations made on Facebook. If nothing else, Austrian politicians could agree that this particular social medium should be avoided where possible in 2012.

Dan Hough

SWITZERLAND

CAPITAL: Berne   AREA: 41,280 sq km   POULATION: 7,825,243 ('10)
OFFICIAL LANGUAGES: German, French, Italian & Rhaeto-Romanic
HEAD OF STATE: Seven-member Federal Council
RULING PARTIES: Swiss People's Party (SVP)-led coalition
HEAD OF GOVERNMENT: Micheline Calmy-Rey ('11)
DEMOCRACY INDEX: 9.09; 8th of 167   CORRUPTION INDEX: 8.8; 8th of 183
CURRENCY: Swiss Franc (Dec '11 £1.00=CHF 1.43, US$1.00=CHF 1.91)
GNI PER CAPITA: US$70,030, Intl$48,960 at PPP ('10)

COMPARED with the performance of other European countries in 2011, Switzerland's results were better than most. Growth remained around the 2 per cent mark, whilst inflation was notable for its absence (a few decimal places above zero). Unemployment also remained as low as it could ever practically be at around 3 per cent. It was not, however, all sweetness and light as Swiss firms faced the challenge of dealing with a very strong currency. The belligerent performance of the Swiss franc—the *Economist* magazine regarded it as the most over-valued currency in the world in 2011, and the central bank in September took the radical step of capping its value against the euro—proved a particular challenge for those companies relying on export markets.

One of Switzerland's most prominent companies, UBS, the financial services group that had its headquarters in Basel and Zurich, had a particularly tough year. In September it became embroiled in a major rogue-trader scandal. Kweku Adoboli, a 31 year old trader working in the firm's investment arm, ratcheted up losses of around $2.3 billion before eventually being arrested and charged with unauthorised trading and false accounting. UBS found itself having to explain how it could allow an individual to build up such a large amount of debt without anyone apparently noticing. This was particularly galling for the Swiss authorities, which had bailed out the company during the 2008 global financial crisis and had demanded it improve its management. In September the chief executive of UBS, Oswald Grübel, resigned and Sergio Ermotti, the head of UBS's Europe, Middle East and Africa division, took over.

The Swiss National Bank—an institution that normally did its best to keep out of the news—also saw a high-profile resignation at the end of the year, as the central bank's chairman, Philipp Hildebrand, left his post following controversial currency trades by his wife. The fact that Hildebrand was widely regarded as a capable operator could not save him, particularly as Christoph Blocher, the outspoken billionaire leader of the right-wing Swiss People's Party (SVP), placed himself at the centre of the campaign to remove Hildebrand. Email exchanges between Hildebrand, his wife, and their own financial advisor revealed the central banker to have been more actively involved in the trading activities of his wife than had previously been thought, and given that she had made a substantial sum of money trading on a foreign currency exchange Hildebrand ultimately realised that his integrity was being questioned and took his leave.

The Swiss went to the polls on 23 October in a federal election. The result was a moderate strengthening of the more centrist parties, reversing the trend of previous years which had seen something of a polarisation in Swiss party politics. The centrist parties gained 10 seats in the Nationalrat (the lower house), whilst parties on the left lost three and parties on the right lost seven seats, respectively. Turnout was up on 2007, the date of the last election, although only marginally so, and at 49.1 per cent it still remained below the 50 per cent mark. The Swiss People's Party was the biggest loser, as its run of more or less continuous success, dating back to the mid-1990s, came to an end. It nonetheless remained the strongest party in Swiss politics and the 26.6 per cent of the vote that the party recorded was, by historical standards, still very high.

Dan Hough

EUROPEAN MINI-STATES

Andorra

CAPITAL: Andorra la Vella   AREA: 470 sq km   POULATION: 84,864 ('10)
OFFICIAL LANGUAGE: Catalan
HEADS OF STATE: President Nicolas Sarkozy of France & Bishop Joan Enric Vives of Urgel (co-princes)
RULING PARTY: Democrats for Andorra (DA)
HEAD OF GOVERNMENT: Antoni Marti Petit (DA) (since May '11)
CURRENCY: Euro (Dec-'11 £1.00=EUR 1.16, US$1.00=EUR 0.74)
GNI PER CAPITA: US$41,750 ('08)

Vatican City State

CAPITAL: Vatican City   AREA: 0.44 sq km   POULATION: 466 (UN de jure estimate mid-'09)
OFFICIAL LANGUAGES: Italian & Latin
HEAD OF STATE: Pope Benedict XVI (since April '05)
HEAD OF GOVERNMENT: President of the Governorate, Guiseppe Bertello (since Oct '11)
CURRENCY: Euro (Dec '11 £1.00=EUR 1.16, US$1.00=EUR 0.74)

Liechtenstein

CAPITAL: Vaduz   AREA: 160 sq km   POULATION: 36,032 ('10)
OFFICIAL LANGUAGE: German
HEAD OF STATE: Prince Hans Adam II (since Nov '89)
RULING PARTY: Patriotic Union (VU)-led coalition
HEAD OF GOVERNMENT: Prime Minister Klaus Tschütscher (VU) (since March '09)
CURRENCY: Swiss Franc (Dec '11 £1.00=CHF 1.43, US$1.00=CHF 1.91)
GNI PER CAPITA: US$137,070 ('09)

Monaco

CAPITAL: Monaco-Ville   AREA: 2 sq km   POULATION: 35,407 ('10)
OFFICIAL LANGUAGE: French
HEAD OF STATE: Prince Albert II (since April '05)
RULING PARTY: Union for Monaco (UNAM) alliance
HEAD OF GOVERNMENT: Minister of State Michel Roger (since March '10)
CURRENCY: Euro (Dec '11 £1.00=EUR 1.16, US$1.00=EUR 0.74)
GNI PER CAPITA: US$183,150 ('09)

San Marino

CAPITAL: San Marino   AREA: 60 sq km   POULATION: 31,534 ('10)
OFFICIAL LANGUAGE: Italian
HEADS OF STATE AND GOVERNMENT: Captains-Regent: Gabriel Gati and Matteo Fiorini (since Oct
  '11, for six months)
RULING PARTIES: Pact for San Marino (PSM) coalition
CURRENCY: Euro (Dec '11 £1.00=EUR 1.16, US$1.00=EUR 0.74)
GNI PER CAPITA: US$50,400 ('08)

DEADLOCKED over how to tackle an economic crisis arising from a collapse in tourism and the bursting of a housing bubble, **Andorra's** parliament, the General Council, was dissolved. Elections followed in April; on a 74 per cent turnout, the recently formed Democrats for Andorra party won 20 of the 28 seats. The outgoing Social Democrats took six seats and the Lauredian Union two. Women won 15 seats, making Andorra the first European country to have a majority of female legislators.

Among the first acts of the new government under Antoni Marti was to sign a monetary agreement with the EU under which Andorra would issue euro currency and adopt EU legislation. Another early measure extended shopping hours in the hope of expanding tourism. However, the main challenge was the economic crisis. Measures developed during the summer and autumn aimed to achieve a balanced budget by the end of the legislature. Most departmental budgets were pruned, though health, education and tourism were spared. Public employees' pay was frozen for three years, with the highest salaries being cut by up to 10 per cent. A business tax of 10 per cent would be introduced in 2012, followed by a sales tax in 2013, and then by income tax. Protectionist restrictions on foreign investment were also lifted. This was a revolution, claimed Marti—"but a controlled one".

The Vatican was as closely engaged as ever with causes as diverse as guaranteed access to healthcare, help for victims of piracy, the plight of Roma in Europe, a UN protocol strengthening children's rights, regulation of global markets, action on climate change and the protection of the rights of circus and carnival workers. It also held that there was "no room" for the death penalty in modern society.

Pope Benedict XVI made four trips outside Italy, to Croatia in April, Benin in May, Spain in August and Germany in September. The second and fourth of these attracted most attention beyond the immediate ranks of the church. Benin was notable for its party-like atmosphere, albeit with a papal message about the passage to modernity in African societies and the church as an agent of reconciliation. Visiting his home country the pope found a divided church, with the wounds over priestly sexual abuse still unhealed. Elsewhere, and especially in Ireland, the Holy See had to contend with continuing criticism of its role in tackling, or failing to tackle, abuses that were widespread and longstanding

Though less battered by economic and financial storms than most of Europe, **Liechtenstein** was not entirely immune. In October, Parliament voted to reduce pensions for workers retiring early and, while approving a 2012 budget with a projected deficit, it warned that deficit financing must be tackled. However, though fresh sources of revenue were needed, tax increases were rejected lest they provoke an exodus of foreign customers.

Parliament unanimously approved a bill to allow registered same-sex partnerships. However, opponents secured sufficient signatures to force a referendum on the issue in June. On a turnout of 74.3 per cent the change was endorsed by 9,239 (68.8 per cent) compared with 4,199 (31.2 per cent) who opposed it. The Archbishop of Vaduz, Wolfgang Haas, responded by declining to celebrate the traditional open air mass on the country's national day, giving rise to much discussion of relations between church and state. There was further controversy over proposals to allow abortions during the first 12 weeks of pregnancy. Crown Prince Alois threatened to veto the change, should it be endorsed by a referendum. However, in September, it was rejected on a turnout of 61 per cent, with 5,245 votes (47.55 per cent) in favour and 5,760 (52.34 per cent) against.

The highlight of the Monegasque year was the wedding of Prince Albert II and the South African Olympic swimmer Charlene Wittstock, in July amid lavish celebrations. The one jarring factor was press reports alleging that the bride had been minded to return to South Africa after learning details about the prince's private life.

Despite the principality's affluence it was not entirely exempt from the problems of the wider world. In February a report from the Council of Europe's Commission Against Racism and Intolerance found progress in implementing its 2007 recommendations "regrettably slow": there was a continuing absence of guarantees against racism in employment and housing.

In September Prince Albert launched a council to help strengthen **Monaco's** appeal to innovators. Also in September, Michel Roger, the minister of state, introducing the 2012 budget, reported that although the public finances were healthy, the crisis in the eurozone required belt tightening to achieve a balanced budget in three years. A demonstration by pensioners alleging inadequate indexing of pensions reflected concerns voiced elsewhere in Europe.

In 2010 the OECD cleared **San Marino** from its list of tax havens, but Italy's ministry of the economy and finance proved much harder to satisfy, unconvinced that its tiny neighbour was not a hotbed of money laundering and tax evasion infiltrated by the mafia. Such suspicions were not without foundation. A major bank was implicated in money laundering and several bank directors were arrested on suspicion of financial misdemeanours. Credit San Marino bank was liquidated, with the government having to indemnify depositors, and two other banks were placed in administration.

Banking was not the only industry experiencing problems. The fraught relationship with Italy aggravated a precarious economic and financial situation. Many companies failed; unemployment rose steadily. The government responded with a mix of expenditure cuts and higher taxes. The most resented measure was a tax affecting frontaliers—Italians working in San Marino—who were hit particularly hard by the lack of a double taxation agreement with Italy. All this, when taken with government reforms of pensions, the administration and justice, made for a year in which there was much bad temper and few solutions, closing with a downbeat report from the IMF on the state of the public finances. The year's most positive event was the visit of Pope Benedict XVI in June.

Martin Harrison

SPAIN—GIBRALTAR—PORTUGAL—MALTA—GREECE—CYPRUS—TURKEY

SPAIN

CAPITAL: Madrid   AREA: 505,370 sq km   POULATION: 46,081,574 ('10)
OFFICIAL LANGUAGE: Spanish
HEAD OF STATE: King Juan Carlos (since Nov '75)
RULING PARTY: People's Party (PP)
HEAD OF GOVERNMENT: Prime Minister Mariano Rajoy Brey (PP) (since Dec '11)
DEMOCRACY INDEX: 8.16; 19th of 167   CORRUPTION INDEX: 6.2; 31st of 183
CURRENCY: Euro (Dec '11 £1.00=EUR 1.16, US$1.00=EUR 0.74)
GNI PER CAPITA: US$31,750, Intl$31,640 at PPP ('10)

THE conservative Popular Party (PP) of Mariano Rajoy Brey trounced the Socialists in the early general election on 20 November. The PP increased its number of seats in the parliament from 154 in 2008 to 186, giving it an absolute majority in the 350-seat Congress, while the Socialists, led by Alfredo Pérez Rubalcaba, dropped from 169 to 110 seats. José Luis Rodríguez Zapatero, the prime minister since 2004, did not seek a third term. The results were the best ever for the PP and the worst for the Socialists since the return to democracy after the death of Franco in 1975. Although the Socialists lost 4.3 million votes, however, the PP gained only 560,000 as disaffected voters opted instead for the hard-line United Left, which increased its number of seats from two to 11, and the Progress and Democracy Union, which won five seats, four more than in 2008.

Also successful was Amaiur, a left-wing Basque coalition which entered parliament with seven seats, two more than the more moderate Basque Nationalist Party. Amaiur was launched in September, a month before the separatist group Basque Homeland and Freedom (ETA)—which had killed 829 people in its 52-year fight for an independent Basque nation—built on its 2010 ceasefire (made permanent in January) by announcing a cessation of armed activity. Basque independence groups had last won representation in Spain's national parliament in 1996 when Herri Batasuna (HB) captured two seats.

This was the third time that Rajoy had led the PP into an election. His victory followed the equally massive defeat of the Socialists in May's municipal and regional elections. The Socialists were left in control of only two of the country's 17 regions—Andalucia, their fiefdom, and the Basque Country—compared with seven in 2007.

The Socialists' pummelling at the polls reflected the massive discontent with Zapatero's handling of the country's economic crisis. The seasonally adjusted unemployment rate had risen to almost 23 per cent (5.4 million people), the same level as when the PP last took power in 1996 and more than double the rate (10.4 per cent) when Zapatero first took office in 2004. The jobless rate for those aged between 16 and 24 was particularly bad, running at close to 50 per cent, and the country's overall unemployment level was more than double the EU average. It varied considerably by region, underscoring a growing north-south divide. The highest level was in Andalusia (31 per cent) in the south and the lowest in Navarra (12 per cent) in the north.

Reforming what the IMF called Spain's "dysfunctional" labour market was high on Rajoy's agenda. The hiring end was flexible (more than one-quarter of employees were on temporary contracts), but the costs of firing workers on permanent contracts were relatively high. Another contributing factor to the high unemployment was an economic model excessively based on a housing sector that had collapsed in 2008 when the property bubble burst. The number of unsold new homes in 2011 was estimated to be around 750,000.

The Socialist government struggled to rein in the spending of public administrations, particularly in the case of regional governments. The overall budget deficit, which had peaked at 11.1 per cent of GDP in 2009, was close to 8 per cent. Parliament approved a constitutional amendment in September to restrict the size of budget deficits and the level of public debt in order to keep them within the EU's limits (3 per cent of GDP for the budget and 60 per cent of GDP for public debt). Public debt as a proportion of GDP was close to 70 per cent, lower than Germany. However, as the reform was not due to come into force until 2020 the gesture did not assuage market concerns about Spain. The country's risk premium over Germany's 10-year government bonds reached close to 500 basis points and the yield hovered around 7 per cent, an unsustainable level, at certain points in the autumn.

Other measures included reinstating for two years the wealth tax—applied to taxpayers' net worth (assets minus debts) above €700,000—that had been abolished in 2008. Cuts in healthcare and education spending, both of which had been devolved to regional governments, were also made, sparking protests, particularly in Madrid and Barcelona. The global movement of "indignados" (the indignant ones) was born in Spain in May when tens of thousands of people, mainly young adults, staged sit-ins in public places to protest at the impact of the economic crisis and the failure of the political class to respond adequately. This heterogeneous movement, mobilised through mobile phones and the Internet, included the unemployed, students, pensioners and almost anyone with a grievance.

Agreement was reached with trade unions and employers to increase the legal retirement age from 65 to 67 and raise the number of years from 15 to 25 for calculating state pensions. Nevertheless, an ageing population, low birth rates and high unemployment strained the social security system. The plan to privatise 30 per cent of Loterías y Apuestas del Estado—the body that ran the El Gordo (literally "the fat one") Christmas draw, the world's largest lottery (measured by payout)—and sell the management of the country's two largest airports (Madrid and

Barcelona) had to be scrapped after it became clear that the Socialist government would not raise anywhere near the expected €13 billion.

The only bright spots in the economy, which grew by 0.6 per cent, were tourism and exports. Thanks to the "Arab Spring", tourists cancelled holidays in countries such as Egypt and Tunisia and switched to Spain, which received close to 57 million visitors. Export growth was also impressive, as companies were forced to sell abroad in order to compensate for the depressed home market. Inflation was 2.4 per cent, the current account deficit was less than 4 per cent of GDP and the Ibex-35, the benchmark index of the Madrid stock market, dropped 13.1 per cent.

Rajoy continued the austere tone by freezing the minimum wage for 2012 for the first time since it was created in 1980. Income tax rates were also raised and further spending cuts made.

The banking sector, parts of which were still reeling under the impact of bad loans stemming from the bursting of the property bubble, continued to be restructured. Five small Spanish banks failed the revised stress test administered by the European Banking Authority (EBA) in July, the largest number of any country, but the two biggest banks, Santander, the eurozone's largest by market capitalisation, and BBVA, were among the strongest. The pass mark was a core Tier 1 capital ratio of 5 per cent. Santander and BBVA had 8.4 per cent and 9.2 per cent, respectively. The Bank of Spain, the central bank, could have presented just the four largest banks for the test as they represented more than 50 per cent of the financial system, the EBA's requirement. It presented 25 banks, however, as it wanted the maximum transparency in order to try to convince the markets that Spain was not in the same category as the three rescued eurozone countries (Ireland, Portugal and Greece). The Fund for Orderly Bank Restructuring (FROB) took over four unlisted savings banks—Caja de Ahorros del Mediterráneo (CAM), NovaCaixa-Galicia, Catalunyacaixa and Unin—the combined assets of which accounted for around 11 per cent of the banking system's total. This brought the number of savings banks that had been subject to FROB intervention since 2009 to six. The other two savings banks—Caja Sur and Caja Castilla-La Mancha—had helped to finance the aptly named Don Quixote airport at Ciudad Real, 200km from Madrid, which stopped receiving commercial flights in October after the only airline using it pulled out. The privately owned airport, built at a cost of €1.1 billion to handle 10 million passengers, filed for bankruptcy with debts of €290 million. The non-performing loans of the whole banking system represented close to 8 per cent of total credit, the highest level in 17 years.

The country's multinationals, which had mostly escaped the crisis relatively unscathed thanks to their geographic and business diversification, continued to expand abroad. Among the acquisitions was the purchase by Iberdrola, the main power utility, of Brazil's Elektro, which made it one of the main operators in the electricity sector, and the completion by Santander of its purchase of Bank Zachodni WBK, Poland's third largest bank. The fashion retailer Zara, the flagship of Inditex, added Taiwan and South Africa to the countries where it was present, bringing the total number to 80. Repsol made a big discovery of shale oil and gas in Argentina. A dozen companies formed a consortium that won a €6.7 billion contract to build and operate a high-speed railway on the Muslim pilgrim route between Mecca and Medina in Saudi Arabia.

On the social front, a tougher anti-tobacco law came into effect banning smoking in enclosed public areas and near school playgrounds and hospitals and on television broadcasts. It replaced the law in force since 2006, which the government recognised as woefully inadequate as it allowed bars and restaurants under 100 square metres (the majority) to choose whether to allow smoking or not. Unsurprisingly, almost all had opted to continue to permit smoking.

The economic crisis began to have an impact on demographics. In a striking turnaround, after a decade of growth, the National Statistics Office forecast a fall in Spain's population over the next 10 years because of the arrival of fewer immigrants, greater emigration by Spaniards and the continuing low fertility rate.

In foreign policy, the government airlifted 37 more Cuban political prisoners and 209 members of their families to Madrid, concluding the agreement reached in the summer of 2010 with the island's communist government and the Roman Catholic Church. This brought the total number freed and flown to Spain to 115 prisoners and 647 family members. The deal was part of the Spanish government's unsuccessful attempt—whilst it had held the EU presidency in the first half of 2010—to effect a softening in the EU's stance towards Cuba.

Having begun his first term in office in 2004 by withdrawing Spain's peace-keeping troops from Iraq—much to the fury of the US administration—Zapatero ended his second term by deepening the security relationship with the USA. It was agreed that four US anti-missile warships would be based at Rota, the US naval station on Spain's Mediterranean coast, as part of the NATO-wide defence system in Europe.

The year ended on an acutely embarrassing note for King Juan Carlos as his son-in-law, Iñaki Urdangarín Liebaert, the husband of Princess Cristina, was charged with misuse of public funds in a corruption case. Urdangarín was suspended from official duties amid allegations that he had abused his role as head of the Noos Institute (a non-profit organisation) by diverting public money to foreign tax havens.

William Chislett

GIBRALTAR

CAPITAL: Gibraltar   AREA: 6.5 sq km   POULATION: 31,000 ('10)
OFFICIAL LANGUAGE: English
HEAD OF STATE: Queen Elizabeth II
GOVERNOR-GENERAL: Sir Adrian Johns (since Oct '09)
RULING PARTY: Socialist Labour Party (GSLP)
HEAD OF GOVERNMENT: Chief Minister Fabian Picardo (since Dec '11)
CURRENCY: Gibraltar Pound (Dec '11 £1.00=GIP 1.00, US$1.00=GIP 0.64)
GDP PER CAPITA: £19,552 ('04-'05)

THE leader of the Socialist Labour Party (GSLP), Fabian Picardo, became the chief minister of Gibraltar in December after his party won the general election. The

GSLP obtained 48.9 per cent of the vote compared with the 46.8 per cent won by the Gibraltar Social Democrats led by Peter Caruana, the chief minister for 15 years.

Picardo's policy toward Spain, which claimed sovereignty over the UK overseas territory, was not expected to change and would continue to be channelled through the Forum for Dialogue, a body established in 2004 to air longstanding grievances between the governments of the UK, Spain and Gibraltar. However, the new Spanish government of the Popular Party (PP), which also took office in December, was less enthusiastic about the forum (which had been set up by the previous Socialist government). Some within the PP hankered for a return to the Brussels Process of "two flags, three voices", which would reduce Gibraltar's influence by emphasising bilateral discussions between Spain and the UK.

William Chislett

PORTUGAL

CAPITAL: Lisbon   AREA: 92,120 sq km   POULATION: 10,642,841 ('10)
OFFICIAL LANGUAGE: Portuguese
HEAD OF STATE AND GOVERNMENT: President Aníbal Cavaco Silva (PSD) (since March '06)
RULING PARTY: Social Democratic Party (PSD)-led coalition
HEAD OF GOVERNMENT: Prime Minister Pedro Passos Coelho (PSD) (since June '11)
DEMOCRACY INDEX: 8.02; 26th of 167   CORRUPTION INDEX: 6.1; 32nd of 183
CURRENCY: Euro (Dec '11 £1.00=EUR 1.16, US$1.00=EUR 0.74)
GNI PER CAPITA: US$21,850, Intl$24,710 at PPP ('10)

SOCIOECONOMIC woes centred upon international financial bailout, political regime change, sovereign debt crisis and unpopular austerity measures were the defining features of Portugal in 2011. The year began with President Aníbal Cavaco Silva's re-election for a second five-year term of office on 23 January. He gained 53 per cent of the votes cast and scored a convincing victory over his five rivals. On 23 March Prime Minister José Sócrates resigned after the Assembly of the Republic (legislature) rejected his fourth programme of spending cuts and tax rises in 12 months. These fiscal measures were designed to avoid having to request an international bailout to help the country meet its debt repayment obligations. However, the collapse of government led to soaring borrowing costs and triggered a downgrade in Portugal's credit rating, as Fitch cut its evaluation to A- from A+. A sense of crisis surrounded the nation and on 6 April Portugal became the third country, after Greece and Ireland, to request financial assistance from the European Union. In May Sócrates's caretaker administration negotiated a €78 billion bailout from the "troika" of the European Central Bank, the EU and the IMF. The rescue package included a string of council tax and VAT rises, changes to labour legislation to facilitate the sacking of workers, reforms to the health service and judiciary, and confirmation that several state-owned institutions (such as the electricity companies EDP and REN, and the national airline TAP) would be privatised.

A snap election was held on 5 June and Portugal's centre-right Social Democratic Party (PSD) led by Pedro Passos Coelho claimed 39 per cent of the vote. It was a crushing defeat for the outgoing Socialist Party (PS) as the PSD won 105 seats and its ally, the conservative Popular Party (CDS-PP), obtained 24 seats. A majority centre-right coalition government was formed and Portugal's smallest-ever cabinet of 11 ministers sworn in. The key finance and foreign affairs portfolios went to independent economist Vítor Gaspar and CDS-PP leader Paulo Portas, respectively. The enormity of the challenge faced by the incoming government was acknowledged by Prime Minister Passos Coelho, not least in being committed to cutting the budget deficit to 5.9 per cent of GDP by the end of the year. (In 2010, the deficit had risen to 9.1 per cent of GDP.) He warned the Portuguese population that they faced two "terrible years" of deep recession and record unemployment before the country could return to growth and regain the confidence of international investors. On 5 July the credit rating agency Moody's downgraded Portugal's sovereign debt to junk status.

In the wake of these structural reforms civil dissent was rife, with strikes a common occurrence. Civil servants, transport workers, teachers, trade unions and grass-roots demonstrators (calling themselves "indignados" as elsewhere in Europe) all staged peaceful protests. The introduction of toll charges on many of the nation's motorways was a particular source of friction. In the Algarve, tollgates on the A22/Via do Infante motorway were vandalised repeatedly, with gun shots fired at employees sent to fix the damage. Opposition to the government's austerity measures culminated in a nationwide general strike on 24 November. Portugal's two largest trade unions, the UGT and CGTP, called out their 1.2 million workers as a response to proposals to eliminate Christmas and holiday subsidies for state employees as well as reduce the number of public holidays. These measures were approved on 1 December in the 2012 state budget, which Finance Minister Gaspar described as "the most demanding budget in the history of democratic Portugal". Newly installed leader of the PS, António José Seguro, led his party to abstain in the final vote before saying that "the country needed a budget that supported growth". The criticism was not without substance, as it was estimated that 400 fuel stations, 600 car repair shops and around 3,000 catering establishments had closed down. In September, unemployment had risen to 12.5 per cent with nearly 308,000 people out of work. By December the OECD reported that the income divide between rich and poor in Portugal was the biggest in Europe and amongst the worst in the developed world.

One of the few bright spots was the performance of Portugal's tourism industry. Helped by the third hottest autumn since records began in 1931 and double-digit growth in several source markets, the sector defied the widespread effects of the economic crisis. While increasing numbers of domestic holidaymakers opted to spend their vacations at home, it was a surge in Brazilian and British tourists that helped create a record breaking summer. In November tourism authorities announced that their previously optimistic target of 40 million booked hotel nights had been surpassed. More importantly, a windfall of €8 billion had accrued to the country's beleaguered economy. On 30 December Gaspar announced that the budget deficit was about 4 per cent of GDP. It was an encouraging sign and suggested that the sacrifices of millions of Portuguese taxpayers had not been entirely in vain.

Martin Eaton

MALTA

CAPITAL: Valletta   AREA: 320 sq km   POULATION: 412,961 ('10)
OFFICIAL LANGUAGES: Maltese & English
HEAD OF STATE: President George Abela (since April '09)
RULING PARTY: Nationalist Party (PN)
HEAD OF GOVERNMENT: Prime Minister Lawrence Gonzi (since March '04)
DEMOCRACY INDEX: 8.28; 15th of 167   CORRUPTION INDEX: 5.6; 39th of 183
CURRENCY: Euro (Dec '11 £1.00=EUR 1.16, US$1.00=EUR 0.74)
GNI PER CAPITA: US$18,430, Intl$23,160 at PPP ('09)

POLITICAL turbulence from the previous year spilled into 2011, pounding Lawrence Gonzi's Nationalist (PN) government unremittingly. The controversy over ministers' salaries—found to have been quietly doubled in 2008 by simple cabinet decision—peaked in June, when Labour (PL) opposition leader Joseph Muscat tabled a motion of censure. The motion was defeated, narrowly, as the issue was grist to the mill for some PN backbenchers who had become habitually scornful of ministerial imperiousness and felt empowered by the tenuity of the government's one-seat majority. The prime minister mollified them by apologising for procedural "mistakes".

Government backbench individualism found its best expression in the volatile Jeffrey Pullicino Orlando and his private member's bill on divorce, in anticipation of which a consultative referendum was called for May. At the risk of splitting its support base along confessional lines, the PN declared itself against divorce. The PL adopted no official position but was generally in favour. The ensuing campaign mobilised society and drew the Roman Catholic Church into the fray, revealing its reduced influence in public life when an unexpected 53 per cent voted in favour of legalising divorce. During the debate on the bill that followed in Parliament, the majority expressed themselves in favour, while the prime minister, declaring himself satisfied that the arithmetic reflected the people's verdict, was one of a PN minority that voted against. The bill was passed by 52 votes to 11, with five abstentions and one absentee, and went into effect on 1 October.

The next reef was the bungled multimillion-euro public-transport reform, which disappointed expectations of an efficient service to relieve traffic congestion and pollution. In July the new *Arriva* fleet of buses took to the streets in a mayhem of bad planning and inadequate resourcing that necessitated improvised responses to mounting public criticism. An opposition motion against the minister responsible cued another PN backbencher, Franco Debono, to abstain, leaving the government dependent on the speaker's casting vote. A promoter of judicial reform, Debono had been promised that home affairs and justice, currently under one ministry, would be decoupled before the year's end. A crisis loomed when he threatened to stop supporting his government unless the pledge was honoured. It was not.

Downplaying these issues as minor, even subversive, distractions from the truly serious ones, the government pointed to the economy's buoyancy despite the euro crisis. Showing economic growth of about 2.5 per cent, with unemployment at 6 per cent and a deficit slightly below 3 per cent of GDP, the country performed above the eurozone average, although this was offset by a costly public debt that surpassed the limits imposed by the Maastricht Treaty and by European Commission alerts that the deficit could be gearing upwards, despite appearances.

Malta found itself on Europe's front line when the Arab uprising spread to Libya in February. The government rose to the occasion soberly, striking a balance between loyalty to Malta's position of neutrality and humanitarian imperatives. Whilst the island was unavailable to NATO, there were many instances where Alliance aircraft engaged over Libya made emergency landings and took off again. More usefully, Malta became a major staging post for the evacuation of foreign nationals and refugees and a supply base for humanitarian aid.

Dominic Fenech

GREECE

CAPITAL: Athens   AREA: 131,960 sq km   POPULATION: 11,319,048 ('10)
OFFICIAL LANGUAGE: Greek
HEAD OF STATE: President Karolos Papoulias (since March '05)
RULING PARTY: Panhellenic Socialist Movement (PASOK), New Democracy (ND), Popular
   Orthodox Rally (LAOS)
HEAD OF GOVERNMENT: Prime Minister Lucas Papademos (ind) (since Nov '11)
DEMOCRACY INDEX: 7.92; 28th of 167   CORRUPTION INDEX: 3.4; 80th of 183
CURRENCY: Euro (Dec '11 £1.00=EUR 1.16, US$1.00=EUR 0.74)
GNI PER CAPITA: US$27,260, Intl$27,380 at PPP ('10)

IT was a year of continual crisis, with the ever present danger of a debt default that would bring disaster to Greece, the eurozone and the global economy. The decline in the Greek economy was dramatic, as strict austerity led to a rapid deepening of recession. The government was totally dependent on EU-IMF aid, with the withholding of a loan instalment bringing the prospect of a suspension of government payments within weeks. Eighteen months after the first EU-IMF bailout, the elected government collapsed, its majority eroded after repeatedly passing austerity packages in the face of strong popular opposition. Despite two eurozone agreements on debt restructuring, Greece ended the year with no debt relief.

The May 2010 bailout programme had addressed the Greek case as a problem of short term liquidity, providing a three-year aid package while economic restructuring took place and assuming that Greece would return to the market for loans in 2012. These assumptions were overturned in 2011, as it became clear Greece would need long-term support. In February, the EU and IMF decided that Greece should reduce its debt by raising €50 billion through privatisation by 2015, an ambitious figure compared to the €20 billion raised by Greek privatisations over the previous 20 years. In March, an emergency eurozone summit agreed to reduce the interest on the EU share of the Greek bailout to just over 4 per cent. But in the same month, the European Commission forecast the Greek debt-to-GDP ratio would reach 158 per cent in 2011. The climate became even more negative in April with the publication of the final Eurostat deficit assessment for 2010. In cutting the deficit by 5 per cent of GDP, the government had set an OECD record but had missed its target by 1.1 per cent of GDP. The final deficit of 10.5 per cent not only increased the debt, but also made it harder to meet the 2011 targets. This was aggravated by falling tax revenue, a situation unlikely to improve without tax reform and a systematic attempt to combat tax evasion.

With the debt burden clearly unsustainable, observers were soon predicting imminent default. Throughout the spring, Greece was subject to repeated downgrades of its sovereign credit rating and in June became the lowest rated sovereign entity in the world. Fears that the country would leave the eurozone resulted in extensive bank deposit withdrawals and capital flight abroad throughout the year. With the EU and IMF making new measures a condition for disbursement of the fifth loan instalment, in April the government announced a €28 billion austerity package. The Medium-Term Programme included the reduction of individual tax allowances and the introduction of new taxes on the salaried and self-employed, likely to aggravate a recession which had already doubled the 2008 unemployment rate to 15 per cent. Popular rage at the new austerity measures was intensified by the fiasco of the parliamentary committees investigating government corruption scandals. Only one former minister was referred for judicial investigation while in all other cases, politicians' responsibilities were written off under the statute of limitations.

Protest was running high from the start of the year, with a series of one-day general strikes, extensive industrial action by professional groups protesting at liberalisation and a "Can't Pay, Won't Pay" movement mainly directed at public transport and road tolls. Demonstrations, usually violent, took place outside Parliament whenever new measures were debated. Attacks on governing party legislators, often by throwing yoghurt, became a regular occurrence. In May, an autonomous movement, without connection to parties or trade unions, was mobilised through social media on the model of the "Arab Spring" and the Spanish "indignados". Until the end of June, the "Indignant Citizens'" protest camp in the central square of Athens became the scene of nightly rallies with serried ranks of demonstrators making a traditional gesture of insult towards Parliament.

In this incendiary environment, there seemed a strong possibility that the Medium-Term Programme could be voted down. All the opposition parties opposed it, despite the pressure exercised on the centre-right New Democracy (ND) by fellow members of the European People's Party. Increasing numbers of legislators from the ruling Panhellenic Socialist Movement (PASOK) declared that they could not vote for more austerity. On 15 June Prime Minister George Papandreou proposed the formation of a grand coalition of the two major parties to steer the bill through Parliament. After the proposal foundered, Papandreou rallied his parliamentary group by reshuffling his cabinet for the second time since the October 2009 elections and appointing his 2007 leadership rival, Evangelos Venizelos, as finance minister and deputy prime minister. On 22 June the new government won a vote of confidence and on 29 June the Medium-Term Programme was voted through Parliament, supported only by the governing party and one ND legislator. One member of PASOK who did not support the party line was expelled, reducing the government's majority to four.

Following the passage of the Medium-Term Programme, in July a eurozone summit agreed in principle to a second bailout for Greece. The €109 billion package was to be partly financed by Greek privatisation funds, now to be used for liquidity rather than debt reduction. While including €34 billion of new loans to Greece, the deal centred on debt restructuring through a "voluntary" swap of Greek bonds by private sector investors. The agreement, initially challenged by eurozone members demanding that Greece provide collateral in exchange for their participation, was ultimately not implemented because the 21 per cent debt reduction was clearly insufficient.

On 1 September, following a Greek government attempt to renegotiate its commitments on structural reform and deficit reduction, the troika (the European Commission, IMF, and European Central Bank) suspended talks on the sixth loan instalment. The government responded by agreeing to more new measures, adding a special property tax to electricity bills and lowering the threshold at which individuals would pay income tax to 417 euros a month, a level below the official poverty line. On 20 October a new law made further cuts to pensions, introduced a unified civil service pay scale entailing drastic salary cuts, and established a labour reserve as a way of firing civil servants. The passage of the law reduced the government's majority still further, with another socialist legislator expelled for voting against the party line, while a number of her colleagues declared this was the last time that they would support new austerity measures.

By this point, Greece's economic position was increasingly precarious. In its autumn forecast, the European Commission revised its spring prediction of a 3.5 per cent fall in GDP growth in 2011 to -5.5 per cent, while the debt-to-GDP ratio was now projected to reach 198 per cent in 2012. In the early hours of 27 October another eurozone summit approved a package of measures to save the common currency. These included a further €130 billion in bailout funding to support the negotiation of an agreement between Greece and its private sector creditors for a 50 per cent "voluntary" debt write-down. The declared aim was to reduce Greek debt to 120 per cent of GDP by 2020, a level still widely regarded as unsustainable.

The following day, the 28 October national holiday parades all over Greece were marked by anti-government demonstrations. With analysts questioning the country's democratic stability, on 31 October the prime minister unexpectedly declared he would put the new debt deal to a referendum rather than attempting to pass it through Parliament. The decision, apparently taken without consultation with the cabinet or the country's EU partners, caused international turmoil with a potential "no" vote threatening the stability of the eurozone. With another legislator declaring herself independent and others threatening to do so, the government appeared finally about to lose its majority and a parliamentary vote of confidence was called. Summoned by a furious German chancellor and French president, Papandreou was told on 2 November that his actions had endangered payment of the delayed sixth tranche of the 2010 bailout. In doing so Angela Merkel and Nicolas Sarkozy made clear to Papandreou that the choice facing Greece was whether or not to remain within the eurozone. At an emergency cabinet meeting the following day, a chastened Papandreou withdrew the referendum proposal. He demanded—and won—a vote of confidence as a mandate to negotiate a government of national unity, but made clear that he would not seek to lead it.

Following difficult negotiations, on 11 November a three-party government was formed, including the radical right LAOS, a first-time government participant, alongside PASOK and ND. The new prime minister, Lucas Papademos, was a non-elected technocrat—a former governor of the Bank of Greece and vice-president of the European Central Bank. After comfortably winning a vote of confidence in the legislature on 16 November, the new government drew up an ambitious budget for fiscal 2012 that envisaged a sharp reduction in the deficit. On 29 November eurozone finance ministers, having received a written pledge of the government's adherence to the second bailout agreement, approved the disbursement of the delayed sixth tranche of funding.

In foreign policy, the year saw two successes of the pre-2009 ND government brought into question. The International Court of Justice deemed Greece's 2008 veto on the NATO entry of the Former Yugoslav Republic of Macedonia to be a violation of the 1995 Interim Agreement. The Burgas-Alexandroupolis oil pipeline project, already essentially frozen from 2010, was cancelled by Bulgaria. However, the discovery of oil off Cyprus revived Greece's hopes of becoming a regional energy hub. Claims by Turkey's former prime minister, Mesut Yilmaz, that the Turkish secret services had been behind some of Greece's major forest fires in the 1990s apparently confirmed suspicions long held by Greek intelligence.

Susannah Verney

CYPRUS

CAPITAL: Nicosia   AREA: 9,250 sq km   POULATION: Greek Cypriots 803,200 (end-'09, Cyprus Statistical Service Demographic Report); Turkish Cypriots and Turks 274,436 (Dec '10, US State Department estimate)
HEAD OF STATE AND GOVERNMENT: President Demetris Christofias (AKEL) (since Feb '08); in the TRNC President Dervis Eroglu (since April '10)
RULING PARTIES: Progressive Party of Working People (AKEL); in the TRNC National Unity Party (UBP) supported by the Democratic Party (DP)
DEMOCRACY INDEX: 7.29; 39th of 167   CORRUPTION INDEX: 6.3; 30th of 183
CURRENCY: Euro (Dec '11 £1.00=EUR 1.16, US$1.00=EUR 0.74); in the TRNC Turkish New Lira (Dec '11 £1.00=TRY 2.87, US$1.00=TRY 1.83)
GNI PER CAPITA: US$30,480, Intl$30,180 at PPP ('09); in the TRNC US$13,354

THE third year of the 2008 round of inter-communal negotiations concluded with no progress, despite intensified efforts by UN Secretary General Ban Ki Moon to secure a settlement before Cyprus assumed the presidency of the EU during the second half of 2012. The secretary general convened three high-level meetings between the Greek and Turkish Cypriot leaders, Demetris Christofias and

Derviş Eroglu, on 26 January and 7 July in Geneva and on 30-31 October at the Greentree Foundation estate on Long Island, USA. He scheduled a fourth for January 2012, saying that he expected the two sides by then to have resolved domestic aspects of a settlement so that a multilateral conference could be convened to deal with international issues. But, while the two sides reached some measure of agreement on the shape of the federal executive, the economy and foreign representation, there was no substantive progress on the key issues of territory, property rights, security and international guarantees. There was also an issue over citizenship with the Greek Cypriots calling for a demographic census which would determine who was a native Turkish-Cypriot (including all persons born on the island) and who a mainland immigrant. The Greek Cypriots allowed that some 50,000 immigrants could stay, but nearly three-fifths of the 275,000 inhabitants of the Turkish Republic of Northern Cyprus (TRNC) had arrived on the island since the Turkish invasion of 1974.

The settlement effort was again frustrated by the electoral cycle with elections for the House of Representatives in the Republic of Cyprus (ROC) on 22 May and for the General Assembly in Turkey on 12 June. The result of the latter was a foregone conclusion—the Justice and Development Party (AKP) of Prime Minister Recep Tayyip Erdogan won emphatically—nevertheless, it meant that the Turkish camp could make no concessions regarding Cyprus during the campaign. The Greek Cypriot election saw the conservative Democratic Rally (DISY) and the communist Progressive Party of the Working People (AKEL) gain seats, to 20 and 19 respectively in the 56-seat legislature, at the expense of the centrist Democratic Party (DIKO), which saw its representation reduced to nine. The Movement for Social Democracy (EDEK) took five, the European Party (EVROKO) two, and the Ecological and Environmental Movement (KOP) one. On 2 June, the House elected EDEK leader Yiannakis Omirou as speaker, replacing DIKO leader Marios Garoyian. When elected in 2008, Christofias had the support of AKEL, EDEK and DIKO; but EDEK quit his government in 2010 and DIKO, suffering from its double electoral blow, withdrew on 3 August, 2011, leaving Christofias a lame duck president having to negotiate with five parties to get legislation through the House, a particularly difficult task for much-needed economic reforms.

On 11 July, a brush fire detonated 98 shipping containers of gunpowder stored at the naval base at Zygi on the south coast of the island, causing a massive explosion that killed 13 and injured at least 60. The blast caused an estimated €1 billion in damage to the nearby Vassiliko thermal electricity generating plant, which supplied some 60 per cent of the southern territory's electricity. The TRNC authorities offered to export power to the south, which the Greek Cypriots accepted, but at an estimated cost of €18 million during the first quarter of transfers. Repairs could take years. The disaster prompted the ministers of defence and foreign affairs to resign and led to violent demonstrations against the Christofias government but, though opinion polls indicated that 85 per cent of the electorate felt that Christofias should resign, he continued as president, shuffling his 11-member cabinet on 5 August to bring in six new ministers, all from AKEL.

In the TRNC, the National Unity Party (UBP) government was shuffled on 6 April with party leader Irsen Kucuk retaining the office of prime minister but with the government's absolute majority of 26 in the 50 seat legislature reduced to 24 through the defections of deputies who henceforth sat as independents. The government was supported by the Democratic Party (DP), which had seen its parliamentary representation decline from five to two, also because of defections. The TRNC was in social turmoil for much of the year as Turkey, which provided approximately 40 per cent of budget funding, cut back its aid forcing the administration to introduce severe austerity measures. There were repeated mass demonstrations which also assumed an anti-Turkish character as Turkish Cypriots began to feel overwhelmed by mainland immigrants.

The economy of the ROC was hit hard by the global economic crisis with growth estimated at zero and the general government budget deficit forecast to reach 7 per cent of GDP. The three major international ratings agencies downgraded the state and commercial banks to near "junk", citing their exposure to Greek sovereign debt. Concerns that the country could require an EU bailout were alleviated, however, after a €2.5 billion loan facility was concluded with Russia on 27 December.

Cyprus's economic situation stood poised to change dramatically following the announcement on 28 December by the US company, Noble Energy, that it had discovered natural gas to the south-east of the island in Block 12 of the Cyprus EEZ (exclusive economic zone) adjacent to major finds in contiguous Israeli waters. The find required further appraisal drilling before development, but preliminary results put the probable resource at between 142 billion and 227 billion cubic metres. The Turkish government argued that the Cypriot government had no right to develop the find until such time as there was a settlement on the island, and in September concluded an agreement with the TRNC to delineate the continental shelf between it and the Turkish mainland, a move that the ROC deemed illegal.

Robert McDonald

TURKEY

CAPITAL: Ankara   AREA: 783,560 sq km   POULATION: 72,752,325 ('10)
OFFICIAL LANGUAGE: Turkish
HEAD OF STATE AND GOVERNMENT: President Abdullah Gül (AKP) (since Aug '07)
RULING PARTY: Justice and Development Party (AKP)
HEAD OF GOVERNMENT: Prime Minister Recep Tayyip Erdogan (since March '03)
DEMOCRACY INDEX: 5.73; 89th of 167   CORRUPTION INDEX: 4.2; 61st of 183
CURRENCY: New Lira (Dec '11 £1.00=TRY 2.87, US$1.00=TRY 1.83)
GNI PER CAPITA: US$9,890, Intl$15,180 at PPP ('10)

THE leader of the conservative Justice and Development Party (AKP), Recep Tayyip Erdogan, won a third consecutive mandate in general elections on 12 June. Buoyed by his victory and relying on the growing strength of the Turkish economy, he raised Turkey's international profile, asserting its standing as a major regional power. Ties with the USA were strengthened, but in Europe, as prospects of Turkey's membership of the EU receded, there was criticism of shortcomings in Turkey's democratic record. The AKP based its electoral campaign on the government's economic performance, stressing the targets that had already been met and setting new ones for the centenary of the Turkish republic in 2023. Coupled with the promise of a new, more liberal constitution, this fed speculation that Erdogan intended to succeed Abdullah Gül as president of the republic with enhanced powers in 2014, when Gül's seven-year mandate expired, and then serve two five-year terms as president under the provisions of the constitutional amendments approved in 2010.

The AKP received 50 per cent of the total vote, winning 327 seats in the 550-member newly-elected National Assembly, Turkey's single-chamber legislature. The new leader of the Republican People's Party (CHP), the main opposition party, Kemal Kilicdaroglu, an anti-corruption campaigner of Kurdish Alevi background (the Alevis were a heterodox community numbering up to one fifth of the population), failed to make a major impression, raising his party's share of the poll only marginally from 23 to 26 per cent and winning 135 seats. The far-right Nationalist Action Party (MHP), which appealed to ethnic Turkish nationalists, won 53 seats with 13 per cent of the total vote. Kurdish nationalists, who stood as independents to circumvent the electoral law, under which a party must receive at least 10 per cent of the total vote to gain representation in parliament, improved their position. Candidates sponsored by the Kurdish nationalist Peace and Democracy Party (BDP) received nearly 3 million votes and won 35 seats, retaining control of Diyarbakir, the unofficial capital of Turkey's Kurdish-majority south-eastern provinces.

The opposition parties had fielded a number of candidates detained on charges of sedition, and when the courts did not release successful candidates, CHP and BDP members refused to take the oath. Instead of attending parliament in Ankara, BDP deputies met in an unofficial parliament in Diyarbakir. However, faced with the threat that deputies who did not take the oath would forfeit their seats, both parties ended their boycott on 1 October in exchange for a vague promise of liberal reforms, and named representatives to a committee set up to secure consensus on a new constitution. No consensus emerged and the reforms stalled. However, at the end of the year there were signs that the government intended to liberalise anti-terrorist legislation.

In the meantime political trials continued at snail's pace, and increasing numbers of opponents of the government were detained, accused of belonging to or supporting terrorist organisations aiming to overthrow the regime. They included two prize-winning investigative journalists and a provincial police chief who had published a book claiming that the judiciary had been infiltrated by members of a fraternity formed by the Muslim preacher Fethullah Gülen, who lived in self-imposed exile in the USA. (The Gülenists ran hundreds of schools and several universities in Turkey and elsewhere, and controlled mass-circulation newspapers and TV channels.) While the arrest of government opponents continued, government supporters accused of the misuse of funds collected from Turkish workers in Germany, were released pending trial. In all, 96 journalists were held in prison.

However, the main purpose of the trials was to eliminate the danger of military intervention in politics. Thirty out of a total of some 300 generals and admirals in the Turkish armed forces were detained on charges of plotting to overthrow the government. On 29 July, the chief of the general staff, General Isik Kosaner, together with the commanders of the three armed services, resigned in protest at the detention of their colleagues. Kosaner was replaced by the gendarmerie commander, General Necdet Ozel, and the supremacy of the civil authority was demonstrated subsequently when Prime Minister Erdogan chaired the army council which determined promotions and retirements.

The main sedition trials were held in Silivri, near Istanbul in Turkish Thrace, which opposition leader Kemal Kilicdaroglu described as a "concentration camp". A total of 152 Kurdish nationalists were put on trial in Diyarbakir on charges of belonging to an organisation called KCK, the acronym of the Turkish Council of Kurdish communities. This was alleged to be the urban branch of the armed militants of the PKK (Kurdistan Workers Party), which was listed as a terrorist organisation in the USA and EU. Many more Kurdish nationalists, including mayors and other members of BDP constituency organisations, were detained pending trial.

The PKK derived most of its funds from Kurdish workers in Germany, and had its forward military base in the Qandil mountains on the frontier between Iraqi Kurdistan and Iran, from which it launched forays into Turkey. On 2 October, Prime Minister Erdogan accused German foundations of abetting terrorism by channelling aid funds to BDP-controlled local governments. As a result, Turkish-German relations, strained already by the murder of Turkish workers in Germany by neo-Nazis, were further soured.

PKK attacks on Turkish security forces continued throughout the year, claiming several hundred victims. In the worst incident, on 19 October, 26 Turkish soldiers were shot dead. The Turkish military retaliated by intensifying their sweeps of the mountainous terrain inside Turkey, where PKK militants had their hide-outs, and launching air strikes against PKK bases in Iraqi Kurdistan. In October, the parliament in Ankara authorised Turkish armed forces to operate outside the country's frontiers for a further year. On 28 December, 34 Kurdish villagers who were smuggling goods across the Iraqi frontier, were mistaken for terrorist infiltrators and killed in an air strike. The Turkish government continued its efforts to persuade the Kurdish Regional Government (KRG) in Northern Iraq to deny facilities to the PKK. Relations between Turkey and KRG improved with the opening of a Turkish consulate in Erbil, the Iraqi Kurdish capital, and the exchange of visits at ministerial level. Turkey became by far the main supplier of goods and services in Iraqi Kurdistan and gained oil exploration rights in the area.

The upheaval of the "Arab Spring" caused difficulties in Turkey's foreign policy. In September, Erdogan visited Egypt, where Turkey had been quick to press for the departure of President Hosni Mubarak, and also Tunisia and Libya, where Turkey had originally opposed NATO military involvement before switching support to the National Transitional Council in its struggle against the dictatorship of Moamar Kadhafi. After repeatedly pressing Syrian President Bashar Assad to conciliate his opponents, Turkey decided to host Syrian opposition activists and to open its frontier to Syrian refugees. Turkey's break with Assad, with whom it had originally struck up a close relationship, further alienated Iran, which had earlier criticised the Turkish decision to allow the installation of NATO radar facilities as part of an anti-missile shield. Although the supply of Iranian natural gas to Turkey was not affected, Turkey concentrated on other suppliers, signing an agreement with Azerbaijan on 26 December for the construction of a Trans-Anatolian gas pipeline (TAP), and allowing Russia on 28 December to construct the South Stream underwater pipeline in Turkey's exclusive economic zone (EEZ) in the Black Sea. Russia was awarded the contract for building Turkey's first two nuclear power stations. In October Turkey challenged the right of the Cyprus government to prospect for off-shore gas, and on 2 November it signed an agreement with the government of the Turkish Republic of Northern Cyprus (TRNC, recognised by Turkey alone) granting the Turkish oil company TPAO the right to prospect for gas in the disputed area.

Relations with France, which were already strained by President Nicolas Sarkozy's emergence as the main opponent of Turkey's membership of the EU, deteriorated further when the French National Assembly passed a bill making it a criminal offence to deny that the Armenians had been victims of a genocide in Turkey in 1915, during World War I, when the Ottoman government had decreed that they should be deported from their historic homeland. On 22 December, Erdogan retaliated by announcing a number of measures including the cancellation of courtesy visits, of automatic permits for military overflights and docking facilities, and threatening more sanctions in two stages, if the bill was ratified by the Senate, and signed into law by Sarkozy.

Trade relations were not affected by Turkey's stalled negotiations for membership of the EU—which accounted for 46 per cent the country's exports and 39 per cent of imports in the first 11 months of 2011—with Germany maintaining its position as the main trading partner. While total exports increased by a fifth to $122 billion, imports rose by a third to $220 billion, with Russia in the first place as the main supplier of fuel. Tourism and revenue from the foreign operations of Turkish enterprises helped reduce the deficit to $65 billion to end-October, as the central bank tried to discourage imports by a managed devaluation of the Turkish Lira over the year from a rate of TRY1.5 to TRY1.9 against the US dollar. At the same time, the index of the Istanbul Stock Exchange dipped from 66,124 to 51,341. However, a greater effect on public opinion was exerted by the fact that the economy grew by 9.5 per cent to end-September, and that unemployment fell from 11 to 9 per cent. The consumer price index rose by 10 per cent over the year to end-November. A public opinion survey conducted in December showed that the government's standing in the polls had risen from 50 to 54 per cent.

On October 23 a major earthquake devastated the Van district in eastern Turkey. The death toll from the earthquake and its aftershocks was estimated at 600.

A.J.A. Mango

III CENTRAL AND EASTERN EUROPE

POLAND—BALTIC STATES—CZECH REPUBLIC—SLOVAKIA—HUNGARY—
ROMANIA—BULGARIA

POLAND

CAPITAL: Warsaw   AREA: 312,690 sq km   POPULATION: 38,187,488 ('10)
OFFICIAL LANGUAGE: Polish
HEAD OF STATE: President Bronislaw Komorowski (since Aug '10)
RULING PARTIES: Civic Platform (PO)-led coalition
HEAD OF GOVERNMENT: Prime Minister Donald Tusk (PO) (since Nov '07)
DEMOCRACY INDEX: 7.05; 48th of 167   CORRUPTION INDEX: 5.5; 41st of 183
CURRENCY: Zloty (Dec '11 £1.00=PLN 5.24, US$1.00=PLN 3.34)
GNI PER CAPITA: US$12,410, Intl$19,010 at PPP ('10)

POLAND stood out in 2011 as a beacon of political stability and economic dynamism. The Civic Platform (PO) won an unprecedented second consecutive election in October, which allowed the continuation of Donald Tusk's coalition government with the Polish Peasant Party (PSL). On the international stage, Poland assumed the EU presidency in July and played a prominent role in the European financial crisis negotiations during the second half of 2011. Estimated GDP increased by 3.8 per cent and industrial production by 8.7 per cent during 2011, while inflation hovered around 3.9 per cent and unemployment remained stuck at 12.1 per cent.

Much of the first half of 2011 was dominated by a national inquest into the Smolensk air crash of 2010, in which Poland's president and a raft of elite figures had been killed (see AR 2011, pp. 75-77). From the outset, the general conclusion of pilot error in the final accident report of the Russian Interstate Aviation Committee (MAK), published on 12 January, met with strong Polish objections, especially from the opposition Law & Justice party (PiS). The mature Polish conclusions were set out in a long and detailed report, published on 29 July, by Poland's Committee for the Investigation of Air Accidents (KBWLLP), chaired by Jerzy Miller, the minister of the interior and administration. The report identified the crucial importance of a faulty altimeter setting in explaining why the Polish pilots had come in too fast and too low and why they had left it too late to pull up and make a second approach. But it also blamed Smolensk air control for poor communication, especially regarding the fog warnings, and for incorrectly confirming that the Tu-154 was on a correct glide path, as well as for defective lighting and dangerous obstacles on the approach path. The report, however, accepted that the Polish air crew were insufficiently trained and tutored for such a flight, and that the military on both sides had made inadequate contacts and preparations. The 36th Special Aviation Regiment, which provided transport for state officials, was subsequently disbanded and a number of military personnel dismissed. It was decided that military control of such official flights (a hangover from the communist era) would be replaced by civilian air crew provided by the national carrier, LOT, while the Regiment's Tu-154s were sold off and replaced by two Brazilian Embraer 170s. Finally, Defence Minister Bogdan Klich accepted responsibility and resigned. Issues such as whether Air Force Commander Andrzej Blasik's presence in the cockpit had been distracting and whether the pilots had been put under pressure to land at all costs remained open, while Polish-Russian polemics on the subject continued.

A contrasting coda to this tale of tragedy, incompetence and, arguably, bad luck came at the end of the year. A LOT airline Boeing 767, on a flight from Newark (USA), made an emergency landing, when its landing gear failed to open, at Warsaw's Chopin (previously Okecie) airport on 1 November. The pilot, Captain Tadeusz Wrona, received much deserved praise for his skill in making such a difficult belly landing safely, without endangering the lives of the 220 passengers and 11 crew on board.

Public opinion polls showed that both Tusk and his government enjoyed high levels of support in the weeks before the October parliamentary elections to both the Sejm (lower house) and the Senate. Tusk may not have been a particularly dynamic reformer, but his capable consensual style and step-by-step political management maintained the unity of his party and coalition. He was thus able to weather the gambling scandal of 2009-10 (a case of political lobbying over taxes on the casino industry) as well as the Smolensk air crash debate quite easily. The opposition, led by the temperamentally abrasive PiS leader, Jaroslaw Kaczynski, became increasingly desperate after his defeat by the PO candidate, Bronislaw Komorowski, in the 2010 presidential election. The late President Lech Kaczynski (Jaroslaw's twin brother, killed in the Smolensk crash) had been a significant constitutional and political obstacle, so the PO was now in a far easier position as it controlled the major institutions of power. Strident PiS efforts to provoke scandals, to find fault with Poland's generally positive development, and to play up inconsistencies in explanations of the Smolensk tragedy proved counterproductive.

The PO was thus in a very strong position at the outset of the electoral campaign although there was a question mark over whether the PSL, its junior partner, would achieve the 5 per cent threshold required to gain Sejm representation. Party boundaries, always fluid in democratic Poland, meant that defections such as that of Bartosz Arlukowski from the Alliance of the Democratic Left (SLD) to the PO were quite common. Joanna Kluzik Rostkowska, who had left PiS somewhat earlier to form the "Poland is Most Important" (PJN) grouping, now completed her personal move to the moderate centre by joining the PO. On the left, Grzegorz Napieralski's good showing as the SLD's presidential candidate in 2010 provided grounds for optimism that the party would continue to broaden its electoral base. On the other hand, only the most perceptive observers thought that the Palikot Movement (RP) would be successful. Janusz Palikot (born 1964), the millionaire owner of the Polmos vodka concern in Lublin, had been a colourful and controversial PO Sejm deputy. He gained notoriety through his chairmanship of the anti-bureaucratic "Friendly Poland" Sejm committee.

Outsiders often underestimated the extent to which the massive socio-economic transformation in Poland since 1989 had caused a deep pool of "losers", only partially drained by the safety valve of enormous labour emigration away from decaying small towns and the countryside, particularly in parts of eastern and northern Poland, to Western Europe, especially the UK. As in Fourth Republic France, this electoral "swamp" (or *marais*) provided support for anti-establishment populists such as Andrzej Lepper and his Samoobrona (Self-Defence) farmers' movement. In 2011 this sector responded to Palikot's vigorous populism and inflammatory attacks on a smug political and religious establishment. His anti-clerical (making abortion available, reducing the financial privileges of the Roman Catholic Church) and libertarian (decriminalising soft drugs) messages as well as his flaying of restrictive socio-cultural taboos cemented his appeal to secular progressives.

The PO gained a resounding victory in the Sejm election with 39.18 per cent of the vote and 207 seats. As the PSL gained 28 seats for its 8.36 per cent vote the coalition was assured a majority with 235 out of the 460 Sejm seats. PiS was a clear losing second with 157 seats for its 29.89 per cent share of the vote. Turnout was a touch lower than in 2007, but higher than had been expected, at 48.92 per cent. The real surprise was that the SLD was punished for failing to produce a convincing alternative programme or to run a dynamic and united campaign. With only 8.24 per cent of the vote and 27 seats (about half its 2007 representation) it not only ran behind the more dynamic RP, which took third position with 10.02 per cent of the vote and 40 seats, but also behind the PSL. In the Senate election the PO gained a huge majority winning 63 of the 100 seats to 31 for PiS, two for the PSL and four independents, who included the prominent left-wing former prime minister and presidential candidate Wlodzimierz Cimoszewicz.

Poland took contrasting steps towards modernity with the nomination of Ewa Kopacz, the previous health minister, as the country's first female Sejm Marshal (chairman), as well as the election of an openly gay individual and a transsexual, Anna Grodzka (RP), to the Sejm. Tusk promised that structural reforms would now be implemented as well as a raft of fiscal measures designed to reassure financial markets that growing budget and trade deficits would be tackled. He also pledged that Polish farmers would be incorporated within the national pension and taxation schemes. The proposal to reform the heavily subsidised farmers' social security system (KRUS) had previously been vetoed by the PSL, so there were now suggestions that Tusk might have to solicit RP and SLD votes to pass the measure against PSL opposition.

Despite Kaczynski's attacks on Germany's Chancellor Angela Merkel in a book published in October, foreign affairs did not feature prominently in the election campaign. Poland generally supported the German line over the eurozone financial crisis during its tenure of the EU presidency. After the election, Foreign Minister Radoslaw Sikorski provoked bitter PiS charges that he was undermining Poland's sovereignty by calling, in Berlin, for Germany to move towards greater European federalism and financial integration.

A large number of prominent Poles died during the year. These included the Roman Catholic cardinals Kazimierz Swiatek (born 1914) and Andrzej Maria Deskur (born 1924), film director Janusz Morgenstern (born 1922), actor and theatre director Adam Hanuszkiewicz (born 1924), mathematician and physicist Roman Ingarden (born 1920), and the trade unionist politician Jan Kulakowski (born 1930). Most poignantly, Andrzej Lepper (born 1954), the populist tribune of rural discontent, committed suicide in August.

George Sanford

ESTONIA—LATVIA—LITHUANIA

Estonia

CAPITAL: Tallinn   AREA: 45,230 sq km   POPULATION: 1,339,646 ('10)
OFFICIAL LANGUAGE: Estonian
HEAD OF STATE: President Toomas Hendrik Ilves (since Sept '06)
RULING PARTIES: Reform Party (ER)-led coalition
HEAD OF GOVERNMENT: Prime Minister Andrus Ansip (ER) (since April '05)
DEMOCRACY INDEX: 7.68; 33rd of 167   CORRUPTION INDEX: 6.4; 29th of 183
CURRENCY: Euro (Dec '11 £1.00=EUR 1.16, US$1.00=EUR 0.74)
GNI PER CAPITA: US$14,370, Intl$19,510 at PPP ('10)

Latvia

CAPITAL: Riga   AREA: 64,590 sq km   POPULATION: 2,242,916 ('10)
OFFICIAL LANGUAGE: Latvian
HEAD OF STATE: President Andris Berzins (since July '11)
RULING PARTIES: Unity (V)-led coalition
HEAD OF GOVERNMENT: Prime Minister Valdis Dombrovskis (V) (since March '09)
DEMOCRACY INDEX: 7.05; 48th of 167   CORRUPTION INDEX: 4.2; 61st of 183
CURRENCY: Lats (Dec '11 £1.00=LVL 0.81, US$1.00=LVL 0.52)
GNI PER CAPITA: US$11,620, Intl$16,350 at PPP ('10)

Lithuania

CAPITAL: Vilnius   AREA: 65,300 sq km   POPULATION: 3,320,656 ('10)
OFFICIAL LANGUAGE: Lithuanian
HEAD OF STATE: President Dalia Grybauskaite (since July '09)
RULING PARTIES: Homeland Union-Lithuanian Christian Democrats (TS-LKD)-led coalition
HEAD OF GOVERNMENT: Prime Minister Andrius Kubilius (TS-LKD) (since Oct '08)
DEMOCRACY INDEX: 7.24; 41st of 167   CORRUPTION INDEX: 4.8; 50th of 183
CURRENCY: Litas (Dec '11 £1.00=LTL 4.02, US$1.00=LTL 2.56)
GNI PER CAPITA: US$11,390, Intl$17,870 at PPP ('10)

THE three countries saw the highest economic growth in the EU as they continued to recover from the recession that had hit them hard in 2009. Unemployment declined but remained above the EU average. Despite recent austerity programs, the prime ministers were returned to power following parliamentary elections in Estonia and Latvia.

Following the adoption of the euro in January, the economy of **Estonia** was the fastest growing in the EU, GDP growth peaking at 9.5 per cent year-on-year in the first quarter. Exports increased by 42 per cent in the first nine months of the year compared with the same period in 2010. However, inflation surged to 5 per cent and unemployment continued to be higher than the EU average, even after dropping to 11.3 per cent in the third quarter.

The Riigikogu (Estonian legislature) elections in March saw the number of parties represented decrease from six to four. The Reform Party (ER) of Prime Minister Andrus Ansip remained the largest, winning 29 per cent of the vote. The Centre Party (K) remained the second largest with 23 per cent of the vote, despite a slight loss of support, partly because of a scandal in 2010 when its leader, Edgar Savisaar, was accused by the Estonian security police of being Russia's "agent of influence" and of soliciting money for the party from Russian Railways. The Union of Pro Patria and Res Publica (IRL) and the Social Democrats (SDE) both increased their vote shares (to 21 and 17 per cent respectively). The rise in the popularity of SDE was particularly notable, as its youthful new leader Sven Mikser managed to increase support by more than 6 percentage points. The Greens and the People's Union, which had suffered respectively from internal conflicts and corruption scandals, were left out of the Riigikogu. With an increased seat share and comfortable majority, the coalition of ER and IRL continued under the leadership of Ansip.

As three parliamentary parties declared their support for the re-election bid of Toomas Hendrik Ilves, the presidential election in August was an uneventful affair. K nominated Indrek Tarand—a maverick independent member of the European Parliament previously unsympathetic to the party—as an alternative candidate, triggering at least candidate debates in the media. However, the result was a foregone conclusion with Ilves beating Tarand by a comfortable margin (73 votes to 25).

In **Latvia** economic growth resumed in 2011, reaching 6.6 per cent year-on-year in the third quarter. Exports increased by nearly 30 per cent in the first 11 months compared with the same period in 2010. The budget deficit was 3.1 per cent of GDP—considerably down from 2010 and marginally above the Maastricht criterion for membership in the eurozone, which Latvia hoped to achieve in 2014. Following deflation in 2010, inflation crept up to 4 per cent. Although unemployment decreased to 14.8 per cent in the third quarter (from 20.1 per cent in 2009), it remained well above the EU average (9.7 per cent).

Allegations of high-level political corruption and the activities of KNAB (the Corruption Prevention and Combating Bureau) dominated Latvian politics in 2011. In May, the Saeima (Latvian legislature) turned down KNAB's request to lift parliamentary immunity from and search the home of Ainars Slesers, one of the country's leading tycoons, leader of Latvia's First Party/Latvia's Way (LPP/LC) and a former cabinet minister. In response to what he saw as contempt for the rule of law, President Valdis Zatlers called a referendum on the dissolution of the Saeima. But open confrontation with tycoons did not help Zatlers's chances of re-election. In June, Andris Berzins—a wealthy former banker—defeated Zatlers in the Saeima (53 to 44 votes), undisturbed by 10,000 "anti-oligarchs" demonstrators outside. He took office in July.

Later in July, the dissolution of the Saeima was overwhelmingly supported in the referendum by 95 per cent of voters (on a meagre turnout of 45 per cent). On the day of the referendum, Zatlers established a centrist anti-corruption Zatlers's Reform Party (ZRP), which was predicted to do well. Two significant mergers took place before the election, based on 2010 electoral coalitions: For Fatherland and Freedom/LNNK and "All for Latvia!" merged into "National Alliance" (NA) while New Era, the Civic Union and the Society for Different Politics joined forces in "Unity" (V).

In September's Saeima elections turnout declined slightly (59 per cent, down from 62 per cent in October 2010). With a slightly increased vote share (28 per cent), the centre-left Harmony Centre (SC) led by Nils Usakovs, the mayor of Riga, became the biggest party—the first time for a party mostly supported by Russian-speakers. ZRP won 21 per cent of the vote and became the second largest party, a position soon lost (because of defections), to "Unity", which was supported by 19 per cent of voters. NA almost doubled its vote share to 14 per cent. Meanwhile, the Union of Greens and Farmers (ZZS), the party of President Berzins, lost considerable support, coming fifth with 12 per cent of the vote. LPP/LC failed to enter the Saeima and was dissolved in December. The People's Party of Andris Skele, another tycoon and a former prime minister, had disbanded already in July. All three latter parties clearly suffered from popular anti-oligarch sentiment intensified by the presidential elections and the referendum. The success of SC increased the chances of a predominantly Russian party entering the government for the first time in independent Latvia, helped by attempts to reinvent itself as a cross-ethnic social democratic party. Eventually, SC failed to join the coalition because of differences in economic policies, interpretation of Soviet occupation and SC's connections to Vladimir Putin's United Russia. The government was formed by V, ZRP and NA, also leaving out ZZS, the only remaining party linked to an "oligarch" (Aivars Lembergs, an oil transit tycoon and the long-time mayor of Ventspils).

Political tensions over ethnic relations intensified in November as signatures were collected to call a referendum on granting Russian the status of the second state language. Over 180,000 signatures were collected, enough to bring about the referendum in 2012. Political parties were strongly divided on the issue along ethnic lines, SC being in favour of the referendum and ethnic Latvian parties dismissive of the proposed constitutional changes.

Together with Estonia and Latvia, **Lithuania** was amongst the three fastest-growing economies in the EU, seeing its GDP increase by 6.7 per cent in the third quarter year-on-year, following meagre growth in 2010. Exports grew by more than one-third in the first nine months of 2011 compared with the same period in 2010. Although it had fallen, unemployment in the third quarter (15.3 per cent) was the highest in the EU after Spain and Greece. Inflation was high but stalled at the end of the year, ending at around 3.5 per cent on an annual basis. The budget deficit declined, remaining somewhat above 3 per cent, and the government planned to lower it further in 2012.

In November, Lithuania faced a banking crisis as Snoras, the fifth largest bank in the country, with about 10 per cent market share, was nationalised following an investigation that revealed large sums (amounting to €1 billion) missing from the bank's assets. A European arrest warrant was issued for two of the bank's principal shareholders, Vladimir Antonov and Raimondas Baranauskas, who were accused of embezzlement and forgery.

Lithuania continued to push for a regional consortium (consisting of the Baltic states and Poland) to build a nuclear power plant in Visaginas to replace Ignalina, which was closed at the end of 2009 (see AR 2010, p. 80). Following the nuclear accident at Fukushima in Japan, it became easier to find contractors as the worldwide attractiveness of nuclear energy decreased. Hitachi Ltd was chosen as a new strategic investor and signed a preliminary agreement with the government. However, the project faced challenges: two planned Russian-backed nuclear plants across the Lithuanian border in Kaliningrad (Russia) and Belarus might lead to excess capacity; in December, Poland pulled out of the consortium, planning to build a nuclear power station of its own.

Relations between Lithuania and Poland deteriorated. A dispute over the spelling of Polish names in Lithuanian passports continued, Lithuania scoring a small victory as the European Court of Justice decided that the new rules did not violate EU law. In March, Lithuania passed a law that stipulated the teaching in Lithuanian of history, geography and civic education in publicly funded Polish and Russian schools, provoking a strong reaction from the Polish government. The row escalated further when the Lithuanian ambassador was summoned to the Polish foreign ministry to discuss increasing instances of hostility towards the Polish minority in Lithuania.

The Baltic states disagreed over plans to build liquid natural gas terminals (to decrease dependence on Russia's Gazprom). Latvia proposed an EU-co-funded terminal in Latvia for all three Baltic states; Lithuania and Estonia had plans of their own, calling into question the regional nature of the project and the prospect of EU funding. However, the governments were united when Lithuania quarrelled with Austria over the release of Mikhail Golovatov, the leader of a Soviet elite unit that had killed 14 civilians in Vilnius in 1991, who had been arrested in Vienna in July on a European arrest warrant and immediately released. Lithuania recalled its ambassador and co-signed a complaint with Latvia and Estonia to other EU member states and the EU justice commissioner.

Allan Sikk

CZECH REPUBLIC—SLOVAKIA

Czech Republic

CAPITAL: Prague   AREA: 78,870 sq km   POPULATION: 10,525,090 ('10)
OFFICIAL LANGUAGE: Czech
HEAD OF STATE: President Václav Klaus (ODS) (since Feb '03)
RULING PARTIES: Civic Democratic Party (ODS)-led coalition
HEAD OF GOVERNMENT: Prime Minister Petr Necas (ODS) (since June '10)
DEMOCRACY INDEX: 8.19; 16th of 167   CORRUPTION INDEX: 4.4; 57th of 183
CURRENCY: Czech Koruna (Dec '11 £1.00=CZK 29.58, US$1.00=CZK 18.86)
GNI PER CAPITA: US$17,890, Intl$23,640 at PPP ('10)

Slovakia

CAPITAL: Bratislava   AREA: 49,030 sq km   POPULATION: 5,433,456 ('10)
OFFICIAL LANGUAGE: Slovak
HEAD OF STATE: President Ivan Gasparovic (since June '04)
RULING PARTIES: Slovak Democratic and Christian Union (SDKU)-led coalition
HEAD OF GOVERNMENT: Prime Minister Iveta Radicova (SDKU) (since July '10)
DEMOCRACY INDEX: 7.35; 38th of 167   CORRUPTION INDEX: 4.0; 66th of 183
CURRENCY: Euro (Dec '11 £1.00=EUR 1.16, US$1.00=EUR 0.74)
GNI PER CAPITA: US$16,210, Intl$23,120 at PPP ('10)

WHILE the cabinet of the **Czech Republic** remained intact throughout 2011, the centre-right ruling coalition underwent several crises that harmed its credibility amongst voters. The three-party government's popularity was further damaged by the approval of long-awaited fiscal reforms, which attracted large-scale protests from trade unions as well as criticism from the political opposition. Amidst the deepening eurozone debt crisis, the deteriorating economy also dampened the mood of Czech citizens.

The first political crisis of 2011 started in March, when a series of corruption-related scandals and ministerial resignations threatened to bring down the cabinet. Most of those scandals were linked to the Public Affairs (VV) party. Prime Minister and Civic Democratic Party (ODS) leader Petr Necas was in a tough position, as the VV threatened to leave the cabinet, a step that would have led to the government's collapse. Still, Necas had pledged zero tolerance for corruption when campaigning in the May 2010 election that had brought him to power, while the third coalition partner—Tradition Responsibility Prosperity 09 (TOP09)—also favoured a strong stance against corruption. At the same time, Czech President Vaclav Klaus supported the beleaguered ministers.

After some initial personnel changes, the leaders of the three coalition parties reached a tentative agreement in mid-May. However, the government was thrown into another wave of uncertainty the following month after newly-re-elected VV leader Radek John said that he would withdraw his party from the ruling coalition unless it gained additional ministerial posts. Later in June, the VV was given a new deputy prime minister position, and the dispute was resolved.

Following the spring crisis, conflicts continued to surface as Necas struggled to retain control of both the government and his own party, the ODS. In August, TOP09 started boycotting cabinet sessions with the aim of removing an education ministry clerk who was accused of neo-Nazi affiliations. The clerk was moved to another position; however, another dispute soon emerged over the government's appointment of a co-ordinator for EU affairs, a step that TOP09 leader and Foreign Minister Karel Schwarzenberg viewed as impinging on his own position. In October, an internal conflict was exposed within the ODS after Necas dismissed his party's own agriculture minister, citing dissatisfaction with his performance. Furthermore, two additional cabinet members were removed from office over allegations of corruption: the ministers of culture and of industry and trade.

While Czechs grew increasingly disenchanted with the quality of political leadership, the death of former President Vaclav Havel just before Christmas marked the end of an era. Havel, who had led the 1989 "Velvet revolution" that brought down communism in Czechoslovakia, was widely seen as the region's most successful former dissident turned politician. He had served as president of Czechoslovakia and later of the independent Czech Republic from 1990-2003 (see Obituary).

In the policy arena, fiscal reforms ranked among the Czech Republic's top challenges in 2011, in light of the cabinet's aim of reducing the budget deficit to 3 per cent of GDP by 2013. Despite the ruling coalition's strong majority in the legislature, moving forward with those changes was more complicated than had been imagined due to squabbling among the governing parties. Nonetheless, the Necas government did manage to push through significant legislative changes. In September, the Chamber of Deputies (the lower house) backed the government's pension reform legislation as well as preliminary changes to the healthcare system. Although the opposition's majority in the upper house, the Senate, slowed the approval process, that chamber's veto was overruled in November.

The 2011 reforms attracted criticism from both ends of the political spectrum. The new pension plan, which was widely viewed as timid and poorly prepared, maintained the pay-as-you-go system, while allowing workers to divert 3 per cent from their social tax payment to private pension funds on the condition that they added 2 per cent from their salaries. The cabinet planned to finance those changes through an increase in the lower rate of VAT from 10 per cent to 14 per cent, effective in early 2012.

Several other long-awaited laws were approved by the lower house during the final months of 2011, but they still awaited Senate backing. These included a new Civil Code, as well as a constitutional amendment allowing for direct presidential elections.

The economy slowed in 2011, despite relatively strong growth in industrial production and exports. In contrast, domestic demand was hindered by fiscal austerity measures that took effect at the start of the year. By mid-2011, even industry began to show signs of weakening, as the situation elsewhere in Europe deteriorated. Consumer price inflation reached an average of 1.9 per cent in 2011, remaining below the Czech National Bank's 2 per cent target band throughout most of the year. That allowed for continued low interest rates, which remained at 0.75 per cent in 2011, below those at the European Central Bank.

Meanwhile, the Czech koruna reached an average of 24.59 to the euro in 2011, the strongest level in the country's history. That was despite a depreciation in the last four months of the year, as the eurozone crisis raised pressure on emerging market currencies.

From a social perspective, corruption remained a major burden for the Czech Republic, tainting the judicial system and education in addition to high politics. In regard to ethnic minorities, the situation of the Roma was especially challenging amid rising xenophobia among the Czech population.

The centre-right coalition government of **Slovakia** made considerable progress during the first nine months of 2011, before collapsing in a parliamentary vote of no-confidence on 11 October amidst a controversy over the country's contribution to the enlarged European Financial Stability Facility (EFSF). On the economic front, the country's performance was hampered by the slowdown elsewhere in Europe, as the eurozone debt crisis contributed to weakening industrial output and export growth in the latter part of the year.

Prime Minister Iveta Radicova's cabinet made major contributions to legislation in the labour, corruption and fiscal arenas. The government pushed through measures to help reduce unemployment, including Labour Code amendments and incentives for attracting investment to poorer regions. Indeed, Slovakia's revamped Labour Code, which took effect on 1 September, was seen as one of the most flexible in the OECD. With the aim of fighting corruption, the coalition also took steps to improve the transparency of the judicial system and the public tender process. On the fiscal front, the full-year state budget deficit came in below target and marked a considerable improvement over the 2010 level, helping to raise international confidence in the Slovak economy.

In June, the Narodna Rada (legislature) finally elected Jozef Centes as prosecutor general, ending a long-running dispute that had threatened to unravel the government in late 2010. In mid-September, Radicova survived a confidence vote put forward by the opposition, and she was supported by all four coalition parties.

Despite that progress, there were undertones of tension throughout 2011, raising concerns about the loyalty of one of the junior coalition partners, the Freedom and Solidarity (SaS) party. While the SaS was new and untested, politicians from the other three ruling parties—Radicova's Slovak Democratic and Christian Union (SDKU), the Christian Democratic Movement (KDH), and Most (Bridge)—had worked together effectively in the past. Internal tensions also surfaced within the SDKU during 2011, pitting Radicova against party leader and Foreign Minister Mikulas Dzurinda, who had served as prime minister in 1998-2006.

As the October vote on Slovakia's contribution to the EFSF approached, SaS leader Richard Sulik repeatedly expressed his opposition, claiming that Slovakia—as the second poorest eurozone member—should not be liable for the "irresponsible" fiscal policies of Greece. In an effort to bring SaS into line, Radicova tied the EFSF to a confidence vote, but to no avail. Slovak citizens were split over whether the country should contribute to the bailout: while the payment was unduly large (at nearly 12 per cent of 2010 GDP) and the impact of the EFSF's expansion uncertain, failure to back the measure would have damaged Slovakia's credibility. The controversy brought the country into the international spotlight: Slovakia was the last eurozone member state to vote on the enlarged EFSF and the only one initially to reject the measure.

Two days after the government's collapse, the opposition Smer-Social Democracy (Smer-SD) party helped push the EFSF forward. However, Smer-SD demanded in return new legislative elections, which were set for March 2012, more than two years ahead of schedule. In the meantime, a minority government between the SDKU, KDH, and Most held power, but many key legislative initiatives were put aside due to lack of parliamentary support.

One measure that was approved after the cabinet's fall was a 0.4 per cent bank tax, which was expected to generate some €80 million in revenue annually. While there was considerable uncertainty about the prospects for the 2012 state budget bill, the law was approved in early December after some Smer-SD deputies left the chamber in order to reduce the number of votes needed. The opposition decided to allow the budget's approval since the absence of a fiscal framework would have sent a negative message to financial markets and ratings agencies.

Although the 2012 budget bill was less restrictive than originally planned, Slovak doctors were unhappy with the government's continued fiscal austerity. Complaining of low pay and poor working conditions, more than a third of the 7,000 doctors at state-run hospitals submitted their resignation notices en masse in late September, once again attracting international attention to Slovakia. Although some rebels eventually backed down, the government was forced to declare a state of emergency as approximately 1,200 doctors left their jobs in early December. The dispute was settled after the government agreed to raise salaries; however, the Doctors' Trade Unions Association (LOZ) threatened another strike in mid-December, forcing the cabinet to abandon plans to turn state-run hospitals into joint stock companies.

The Slovak economy continued to recover from the 2009 downturn in 2011, and GDP returned to its pre-crisis level in the first quarter. Industrial output and exports were the biggest drivers of growth. Although there were signs of weakening by mid-year as the European debt crisis heightened, Slovakia's reliance on Germany as a key export market helped to bring some stability. Thanks to strong exports Slovakia's trade surplus widened considerably in 2011, with positive implications for the current-account balance. In terms of domestic demand, household consumption remained weak due to fiscal consolidation measures and high inflation. Despite public sector job cuts, total employment rose quite rapidly in 2011; however, jobless rates remained well above the low point of 2008.

Sharon Fisher

HUNGARY

CAPITAL: Budapest   AREA: 93,030 sq km   POPULATION: 10,008,703 ('10)
OFFICIAL LANGUAGE: Hungarian
HEAD OF STATE: President Pal Schmitt (since Aug '10)
RULING PARTY: Fidesz-Hungarian Civic Alliance (Fidesz-MPSz)
HEAD OF GOVERNMENT: Prime Minister Viktor Orban (Fidesz-MPSz) (since May '10)
DEMOCRACY INDEX: 7.21; 43rd of 167   CORRUPTION INDEX: 4.6; 54th of 183
CURRENCY: Forint (Dec '11 £1.00=HUF 354.04, US$1.00=HUF 225.75)
GNI PER CAPITA: US$12,980, Intl$19,270 at PPP ('10)

THE year 2011 saw radical changes to Hungary's post-1989 democratic structure, which led critics worldwide to argue that the country had become a "managed" democracy and showed signs of "autocratic" government. Following a landslide victory in 2010 (see AR 2011, pp. 85-86), the Fidesz-Hungarian Civic Alliance (Fidesz-MPSz)-led government was accused of curtailing the prerogatives of independent institutions and appointing party loyalists to them. Policy decisions were increasingly made in a centralised manner by Prime Minister Viktor Orban and a small group of advisors.

Ironically, this happened as Hungary took over the six-month rotating presidency of the Council of the EU, on 1 January. The presidency's motto, "Strong Europe", was soon put to the test: the European Commission forced Hungary's government to modify parts of the controversial media law that had created an international furore at the end of 2010. (A more substantial blow was delivered, on 19 December, by Hungary's Constitutional Court, which annulled several of the law's provisions limiting the freedom of the press and impeding journalists from protecting their sources.) Orban, sometimes described as a radical opportunist or political maverick, waged a war of words against the EU over which he was, temporarily, presiding. On 15 March, celebrating the anniversary of the 1848 Revolution against the Habsburg Empire (see AR 1848, pp. 404-05), he said to a crowd, which included students paid to cheer him, that he had protected Hungary against "ignoble attacks" from the EU and compared "Brussels" to Habsburg "Vienna" and Soviet-era "Moscow". Meanwhile, tens of thousands of people protested for the freedom of the media at one of the biggest anti-government demonstrations of the year.

On 18 April the unicameral legislature, the National Assembly, passed a new constitution (renamed "Fundamental Law"), which received presidential assent symbolically on Easter Monday to celebrate "Hungary's resurrection". The government argued that the old constitution, dating from 1949 though entirely rewritten after 1989, was unfit to serve the country's renewal. Fidesz was adamant that the "overly consensual" politics that the former constitution fostered had paralysed effective decision making, and argued that a move to "majoritarian democracy" would rectify many of Hungary's failings. The constitution, which would enter into force on 1 January 2012, had been rushed through the National Assembly in a matter of weeks with limited prior consultation, according to the Venice Commission, the constitutional advisory group of the Council of Europe. The opposition Hungarian Socialist Party (MSzP) and the Green-liberal Politics Can Be Different (LMP) had refused to participate in the parliamentary debate.

The new Fundamental Law removed the right of any citizen to turn directly to the Constitutional Court, the most trusted public institution, and filled this with party-loyalist new judges. Dozens of "cardinal laws" could now only be amended with a two-thirds majority. They included the electoral law, which Fidesz unrepentantly changed to mean that, under its provisions, Fidesz would have won the last three elections, even though it had actually lost two. The Fundamental Law constrained any future government without a two-thirds majority over setting its economic policy, as constitutional provisions enshrined a flat-rate tax regime and the mandatory reduction of public debt—although the current cabinet was conveniently exempted from the latter. It recognised only 14 faiths as churches, down from around 300. It tampered with the independence of the judiciary when, on 13 December, an Orban family friend was appointed to oversee the judiciary and select judges. The European Commission threatened Hungary with legal action following the removal, at the end of 2011, of the Supreme Court's president and an ombudsman, and said that laws on tax and the central bank might breach EU treaties.

The opposition claimed that the National Assembly had been reduced to a rubber stamp legislature. On 23 December, a law was passed that allowed voting on "emergency" legislation, practically without debate. Fidesz claimed that this was "still better" than governing by decree. LMP National Assembly members chained themselves to the building in protest but the police arrested them. In the evening, the opposition demonstrated against what they called the "tyranny of the majority". Although Fidesz had lost half of its voters by December, opposition parties failed to increase their support. Nevertheless, on 30 December, Fidesz wrote into the constitution that the MSzP was guilty of all crimes committed under the Communist regime.

The scope and speed of unilateral changes set off alarm bells in Europe and the USA early in the year, but the warnings went unheard. On 30 June, in Budapest, US Secretary of State Hillary Clinton called for "real commitment" to the independence of the judiciary, a free press, and government transparency. On 18 October the US ambassador handed the unfazed Orban a diplomatic démarche to reiterate Clinton's message. Fidesz insisted that as long as procedural rules were respected, the governing majority could legislate on "anything". On 23 December, in a lengthy letter sent to Orban, Clinton restated her "deep concerns" about the preservation of individual liberties and the dismantling of institutional "checks and balances". Before the end of the year, similar warnings came from European Commission President José Manuel Barroso and President Nicolas Sarkozy of France, and others.

Unlike many of the populist autocrats to whom he was frequently compared, Orban could not boast of his economic achievements. Growth was minimal and although the budget appeared to have a surplus it was only due to the one-off effect from the nationalisation of private pension funds in 2010. State debt grew to a record 83 per cent of GDP. Hopes that China would buy government bonds remained unfounded, despite the conspicuous courting of Premier Wen Jiabao during his visit on 24-25 June. The Hungarian currency, the forint, closed the year at an all-time low against the euro, having lost 20 per cent of its value in the second half of the year. This followed the passing of a law, on 19 September, that obliged banks to exchange foreign currency mortgages at significantly lower than market exchange rates. On 17 November, Hungary was forced to return to the IMF, cap in hand, to stem increasing speculation about a looming state default. Reflecting the dark mood of investors and poor economic policies, two of the three major credit rating agencies—Moody's on 24 November and Standard & Poor's on 21 December—cut Hungary's government debt to "junk" status nonetheless.

Daniel Izsak

ROMANIA

CAPITAL: Bucharest   AREA: 238,390 sq km   POPULATION: 21,442,012 ('10)
OFFICIAL LANGUAGE: Romanian
HEAD OF STATE: President Traian Basescu (since Dec '04)
RULING PARTIES: Democratic Liberal Party (PD-L)-led coalition
HEAD OF GOVERNMENT: Prime Minister Emil Boc (PD-L) (since Dec '08)
DEMOCRACY INDEX: 6.60; 56th of 167   CORRUPTION INDEX: 3.6; 75th of 183
CURRENCY: New Leu (Dec '11 £1.00=RON 5.07, US$1.00=RON 3.23)
GNI PER CAPITA: US$7,840, Intl$14,060 at PPP ('10)

ALTHOUGH parliamentary elections were not due for another year, politicians devoted much of their time and energy in 2011 to preparing for the vote, with the opposition forming a broad-based, although at times shaky, alliance and the governing Democratic Liberal Party (PD-L) drawing up plans for extensive changes to the electoral system and constituency boundaries. Economic growth returned after the recession of 2009-10, but towards the end of the year there were signs that the modest recovery was running out of steam under the impact of the prolonged debt crisis affecting several eurozone countries.

The realignment in politics began in January with the formation of the Centre-Right Alliance (ACD) by the second-largest opposition force—the National Liberal Party (PNL)—and the much smaller Conservative Party (PC). Only a month later the newly-formed ACD established an electoral alliance with the main opposition group, the Social Democratic Party (PSD). This was to be known as the Social Liberal Union (USL). Deputies and senators representing the USL outnumbered their counterparts in the governing coalition, which consisted of the PD-L and the Hungarian Democratic Union of Romania (UDMR). However, the government was able to push through legislation—albeit at times with considerable difficulty—with the help of a group of defectors from the PSD, the National Union for the Progress of Romania (UNPR), and ethnic minority representatives. Apart from its parliamentary strength, the popularity of the USL was also reflected in public opinion polls, which consistently put its support at or above 50 per cent of respondents.

In spite of the favourable opinion polls, the marriage of convenience represented by the USL had its opponents within both sides. Critics inside the PSD argued that their party, as the larger of the two, should not have agreed to a broadly equal allocation of seats that the two allies were to contest; while those in the ACD expressed concern that the alliance with the PSD would lead to a dilution of the ACD's liberal-conservative policies. Doubt was also cast on the accuracy of the opinion polls when the USL lost a parliamentary seat in August in a by-election in Neamt county, in the north east.

Divisions within the PSD itself came into the open in November when the former leader, Mircea Geoana, was expelled from the party, before being removed from his post as speaker of the Senate. Geoana was accused by Victor Ponta, his successor as PSD leader, of failing to respect party discipline and of refusing to work with the other leaders of the opposition. Geoana's dismissal led to a serious setback for the PSD, when a prominent PD-L politician, Vasile Blaga, who had previously held several ministerial portfolios, was elected as speaker. Blaga's promotion was seen as part of a move to retain his loyalty to the prime minister, Emil Boc, who had defeated him in the contest for the PD-L leadership in May.

The PD-L presented far-reaching plans at the end of the year—inspired by President Traian Basescu, the driving force behind the government—for the restructuring of the parliamentary and electoral systems. The draft proposals envisaged replacing the 41 multi-member constituencies, from which 137 senators and 334 deputies were elected, with a hybrid system, combining 200 first-past-the-post constituencies with a further 100 seats allocated in proportion to the number of votes received by each party. The changes called for the establishment of a unicameral system in place of the Senate and the Chamber of Deputies, and the postponement of the local authority elections due in June 2012 until November, to be held simultaneously with the parliamentary ballot.

The PD-L's proposals attracted considerable criticism not only from the opposition, but also from the UDMR, whose newly-elected leader, Hunor Kelemen, argued that the reforms should be postponed until after the parliamentary elections. The UDMR had earlier achieved one of its key goals, with the entry into force in January of the new education law, which made it possible for schools to teach a number of subjects in the languages of the national minorities.

A ministry of European affairs was established in September under Leonard Orban, a former EU commissioner, in order to improve co-operation with the EU. The ministry's specific task was to increase the absorption of EU funds, in which Romania had the poorest record of all EU member states with only about 10 per cent of the €20 billion in funds allocated for 2007-13 having been disbursed by the end of 2011. The European Commission's fifth annual report on Romania's performance, under the co-operation and verification mechanism—established to measure progress in judicial reform and the fight against corruption—was more positive than previous ones. However, the report pointed to persistent shortcomings, not least because of Parliament's failure to lift the immunity from prosecution of legislators accused of financial misdemeanours.

President Basescu was received by his opposite number, Barack Obama, in Washington, DC, in September, during a visit that was dedicated to the signing of a treaty on the deployment of US ballistic missiles on Romanian territory, as part of NATO's planned missile defence system. Approval of the deployment by

Romania's Supreme Council of National Defence (CSAT) had earlier prompted strong criticism by Russian leaders, including the president, Dmitry Medvedev, who warned that it would lead to his country increasing its own nuclear capability. Basescu sought to allay these concerns, arguing that the missile system was not directed against Russia. He declared that with the treaty signed, Romania's security was at its highest level ever.

Gabriel Partos

BULGARIA

CAPITAL: Sofia   AREA: 111,000 sq km   POPULATION: 7,543,325 ('10)
OFFICIAL LANGUAGE: Bulgarian
HEAD OF STATE: President Georgi Purvanov (since Nov '01)
PRESIDENT ELECT: Rosen Plevneliev
RULING PARTY: Citizens for European Development of Bulgaria (GERB) forms minority government
HEAD OF GOVERNMENT: Prime Minister Boiko Borisov (GERB) (since July '09)
DEMOCRACY INDEX: 6.84; 51st of 167   CORRUPTION INDEX: 3.3; 86th of 183
CURRENCY: Lev (Dec '11 £1.00=BGN 2.28, US$1.00=BGN 1.45)
GNI PER CAPITA: US$6,250, Intl$13,250 at PPP ('10)

THE austerity measures enacted by the minority government of Prime Minister Boiko Borisov's Citizens for European Development of Bulgaria (GERB) faced stiff resistance from the parliamentary opposition, trade unions and, at times, its allies. The government's task was made more difficult by popular protests against rising food and fuel prices. However, it managed to survive no fewer than three no-confidence votes in the course of the year. On at least two occasions it relied on a group of independent MPs, with its Ataka and Blue Coalition allies abstaining or voting against.

The government's controversial policy of extensive wiretapping, which Borisov had defended as a necessary means of combating corruption and organised crime, caused a political storm in January. A recording was leaked of Borisov asking the head of the country's Customs Agency to reinstate a friend in his job. Although the government maintained that the tape had been manipulated, the incident cast a shadow over the image of the governing party, which had come to power on a platform of cleaning up corruption and a culture of political favours. In order to prevent a further slide in popularity, Borisov ordered the launch of a working group to address the policy of wiretapping.

In its annual report under the co-operation and verification mechanism, the European Commission recognised the Bulgarian government's efforts in fighting corruption and organised crime, whilst highlighting the need for further reform in the judiciary and police. It noted a mismatch between arrests and convictions and called for more effective investigations. It was especially critical of the lack of transparency and competitiveness in the process of appointing magistrates and the lack of accountability within the judiciary.

The government suffered a setback when the EU refused to include Bulgaria into its visa-free Schengen travel zone, citing insufficient measures against crime and corruption, despite an earlier European Parliament resolution recommending the country be admitted.

In September, a combination of factors, including the presence of racism, anger at corruption and crime, as well as dissatisfaction with stalling economic growth, contributed to what was described as the worst unrest in the country since 1997 (when the Bulgarian currency had collapsed). The violence was sparked by a road accident near the city of Plovdiv involving the car of a local Roma leader; a young man was killed. The unrest spread across the country with crowds of predominantly young men on the rampage, venting their anger and frustration at poverty, unemployment and lack of opportunity.

In October, the former GERB government minister, Rosen Plevneliev, was elected president in the second round run-off with 52.6 per cent of the vote against his opposition Socialist Party (BSP) challenger Ivaylo Kalfin, who won 47.7 per cent. Plevneliev replaced Georgi Purvanov, a former BSP leader who had served the constitutional limit of two five-year terms. The Socialists conceded, but said that the elections—both local and presidential—had taken place in a climate of "unprecedented manipulation of public opinion". They accused GERB of resorting to pressure, threats and bribes. Fears about vote selling and pressure on voters were also highlighted in separate reports by the OSCE and Transparency International. The government rejected the allegations. In the mayoral elections, the Socialists won in nearly 100 of the 264 municipalities, with GERB retaining power in Sofia and winning for the first time in Plovdiv and Varna, the country's second and third largest cities.

Plevneliev's election meant that Borisov's party controlled all the major posts in Bulgaria. It also showed that, contrary to initial assessments that GERB was "a temporary set-up" or an "ebbing tide", Borisov's party had moved into territory traditionally occupied by the centre-right parties (including Blue Coalition members: the Union of Democratic Forces—SDS—and the Democrats for a Strong Bulgaria—DSB), and asserted itself as a major political force.

In his last days in office, outgoing President Purvanov vetoed pension reforms that aimed gradually to increase the retirement age from 2012, to 63 for women and 65 for men (from 60 and 63 respectively). The proposals had sparked countrywide protests. Purvanov said that the reforms were "financially unjustified and socially inexpedient".

Due to the government's tight rein on spending and an improvement in revenue collection, the budget deficit contracted by more than 50 per cent compared with 2010. Those efforts were recognised in July, when the ratings agency, Moody's, upgraded Bulgaria's sovereign debt rating by one notch to BAA2. The agency cited the government's tight fiscal policy, low public debt and the economy's relative resilience in a volatile economic and financial environment. However, the economic recovery lost momentum after the first quarter and growth stalled with the escalation of the debt crisis in the eurozone, with which Bulgaria had strong trade and financial links.

Genc Lamani

ALBANIA—MACEDONIA—KOSOVO—SERBIA—MONTENEGRO—
BOSNIA & HERZEGOVINA—CROATIA—SLOVENIA

ALBANIA

CAPITAL: Tirana   AREA: 28,750 sq km   POPULATION: 3,204,284 (World Bank figure '10);
2,800,000 (Albanian census '11)
OFFICIAL LANGUAGE: Albanian
HEAD OF STATE: President Bamir Topi (PDSh) (since July '07)
RULING PARTIES: Democratic Party of Albania (PDSh)-led coalition
HEAD OF GOVERNMENT: Prime Minister Sali Berisha (PDSh) (since Sept '05)
DEMOCRACY INDEX: 5.86; 84th of 167   CORRUPTION INDEX: 3.1; 95th of 183
CURRENCY: Lek (Dec-'11 £1.00=ALL 161.58, US$1.00=ALL 103.03)
GNI PER CAPITA: US$3,960, Intl$8,740 at PPP ('10)

ALBANIA'S slow-motion transition hit a serious obstacle in January when seething
political tensions over allegations of corruption and vote-rigging spilled into violence. A massive anti-government protest resulted in the deaths of four protestors.
The prime minister, Sali Berisha, promptly accused the opposition leader, Edi Rama,
of staging a coup d'état, claiming protestors had been armed with guns disguised as
umbrellas and pens and blaming the killings on the crowd. But his allegations evap-
orated when a reporter's video emerged, which seemed to show that the fatal shots
had been fired from inside the prime minister's compound. At the height of the argument, Berisha called the prosecutor general "a boulevard whore" and President
Bamir Topi "a thug" and claimed they had both been involved in "the coup".

The unrest followed the publication, earlier in January, of a video showing the
deputy prime minister, Ilir Meta, trying to influence a state tender for a hydroelectric power station by offering a large bribe to the government minister in
charge of the process. Meta, whose centre-left Socialist Movement for Integration
was key to the government's thin majority in Parliament, denounced the tape as
fake but still resigned. He was taken to court on graft charges.

The already tense political situation polarised further after the municipal elections in May. Rama, leader of the Socialist Party of Albania (PSSh), who was running for a fourth term as mayor of Tirana, was defeated in controversial circumstances by the challenger from the ruling Democratic Party of Albania (PDSh),
Lulezim Basha, a close aide of Berisha. The initial count gave Rama a 10-vote
lead. But a count of the "miscast votes" overturned the result in favour of Basha.
Overall, the PSSh-led opposition took most of the main cities and towns, although
the governing coalition and its allies won more votes.

The absence of political dialogue continued into early September, when the PSSh
decided to end its boycott (which had continued periodically since the 2009 elections) and return to Parliament. The PSSh proposed a 10-point plan as a condition
for the party's co-operation in resolving the deadlock. This included electoral
reform, new rules to ensure the proper functioning of Parliament, and greater support for the prosecutor's office in investigating high-profile corruption cases.

In October, the European Commission refused for the second consecutive year
to grant Albania EU candidate status on the grounds that the country had failed to

make sufficient progress in meeting key recommendations, in particular the proper working of democratic institutions, notably Parliament. The problem worsened with the deterioration of relations between Berisha's PDSh majority in Parliament and President Topi. Such was the hostility that, contrary to political tradition, Berisha publicly "dismissed" Topi from his job almost a year before the end of his mandate in mid-2012, by declaring that his party would not support Topi's candidature for a second term. Sensing the scale of animosity, Topi, who had been praised for playing a moderating role in Albania's troubled party politics, told journalists at his end-of-year reception for the media that the event would undoubtedly be his last as president. He said he would return to active politics, hinting at the formation of a new political party.

The census in October proved controversial because of the inclusion of two optional questions on ethnicity and religious affiliation. The most vocal opponent of these additions to the 2001 census form was the Red-and-Black Alliance, a nationalist movement named after the colours of the Albanian flag. It feared that people might be tempted by the benefits to be gained from being an ethnic Greek—including pensions paid by the Greek authorities and easier access to Greece's labour market—and that this could lead to an increase in the size of Albania's ethnic Greek minority. (Some Albanian migrants in Greece had already faked their ethnic identity in order to claim the benefits.) Preliminary results of the census showed that the population had shrunk by 7.7 per cent in the previous decade, to 2.8 million. (It stood at 3.07 million in 2001.) The Albanian Institute of Statistics attributed this to "large scale emigration and a decline in fertility". The results also showed more people living in urban than in rural areas (53.7 per cent to 46.3 per cent) for the first time since Albania's first census in 1923.

Despite continued pressures from the eurozone debt crisis, Albania's economy expanded, albeit below the government's 4 per cent forecast. The budget underperformed and was subject to spending cuts in the mid-year budget review. Meanwhile, the public debt was reported just under its statutory limit of 60 per cent.

Genc Lamani

MACEDONIA

CAPITAL: Skopje   AREA: 25,710 sq km   POPULATION: 2,060,563 ('10)
OFFICIAL LANGUAGE: Macedonian
HEAD OF STATE: President Gjorgje Ivanov (VMRO-DPMNE) (since May '09)
RULING PARTIES: Internal Macedonian Revolutionary Organisation-Democratic Party for
    Macedonian National Unity (VMRO-DPMNE)-led coalition
HEAD OF GOVERNMENT: Prime Minister Nikola Gruevski, (VMRO-DPMNE) (since Aug '06)
DEMOCRACY INDEX: 6.16; 73rd of 167   CORRUPTION INDEX: 3.9; 69th of 183
CURRENCY: Denar (Dec '11 £1.00=MKD 71.57, US$1.00=MKD 45.64)
GNI PER CAPITA: US$4,520, Intl$10,830 at PPP ('10)

NIKOLA Gruevski's VMRO-DPMNE party consolidated its political ascendancy over Macedonia in early general elections on 5 June, held at the insistence of the opposition Social Democrats. The government correctly estimated that while support for the opposition was growing, it was not yet powerful enough to eject Gruevski's nationalists from office. The prime minister's gamble paid off. VMRO-DPMNE (Internal Macedonian Revolutionary Organisation-Democratic Party for Macedonian National Unity) won 56 of the 123 seats in the Assembly (the unicameral legislature), seven down on the last election in 2008, but respectable enough. The Social Democrats and their allies won 42, which was 18 up on 2008—a good score but not enough to change the government. Gruevski promptly formed a new government with his previous partners in the ethnic Albanian Democratic Union for Integration (DUI), which won 15 seats, giving the government a comfortable majority.

Fears that the new government, Gruevski's third in a row, would display the same authoritarian tendencies as the last, seemed confirmed when tax officials closed down the country most watched television station. The closure on 30 July of A1, the station owned by the tycoon Velija Ramkovski, ended 18 years of broadcasting starting in 1993. The authorities said that the station closed because Ramkovski owed millions in back taxes but a feeling was widespread that the television station had been targeted selectively by the tax officials on account of its hard-hitting attacks on Gruevski's VMRO-DPMNE party, which Ramkovski had once supported but now bitterly opposed. Earlier that month, three daily newspapers linked to Ramkovski had closed for the same tax-related reasons. The result was the almost overnight disappearance of most of the remaining critical voices in the media, a situation that prompted Reporters without Borders and other press watchdogs to voice concerns about the future of the media in Macedonia. At the end of 2011, Ramkovski remained on trial for tax avoidance.

Unabashed by criticism, Gruevski continued with his tried and trusted policy of entertaining the masses with displays of pageantry. Money continued to pour into "Skopje 2014", a government project aimed at sprinkling the capital with monuments in a faux Classical style, complete with triumphal arch, various fountains, heritage museums and statues of ancient heroes. The jewel in the crown, a giant equestrian statue of Alexander the Great perched on top of a 22 m high column, was unveiled in Skopje's central "Makedonija" square on 21 June to general applause. More pomp and circumstance followed on 8 September when Macedonia celebrated 20 years of independence with parades through the new triumphal arch and son-et-lumière displays. By the end of the year the capital was preparing for the unveiling of another giant statue, this time of Philip of Macedonia.

The erection of enormous statues to Alexander and Philip, both claimed by Greece as Hellenic heroes, was widely seen as a deliberate provocation of that country—revenge for Greece's obstruction of Macedonia's attempts to join NATO in 2008. Somewhat coyly, the government insisted on terming the statues [unnamed] "equestrian statues".

The government's attempt to play on a theme of national virility received a welcome boost from an unexpected quarter when the country's hitherto obscure basketball team did unexpectedly well in the European basketball championships, EuroBasket. The team beat six teams in a row before being trounced by Russia in Kaunas, Lithuania, on 18 September. Although Macedonia only came fourth in the end, for a country that had never excelled in international tournaments, the wins seemed nothing less than a miracle and prompted frenzied celebrations.

Unsurprisingly the government's assertive nationalism and its growing habit of blaming all criticism on foreign enemies gained few plaudits in Brussels where Macedonia's application for a start to EU membership talks remained frozen as a result of the Greek blockade linked to the ancient dispute over the country's name. In October, for the third consecutive year, the European Commission declined to set a date for a start to membership talks.

Whether this setback much bothered the government was unclear. Of more interest to officials in Skopje was the outcome of Macedonia's lawsuit against Greece in the International Court of Justice, expected early in December. Macedonia accused Greece of breaking a 1995 UN agreement that obliged Greece not to use the continuing bilateral dispute over Macedonia's name—to which Greece objected—to stop Macedonia from joining international organisations. In reference to this, it claimed that Greece had vetoed the issuing of a membership invitation to Macedonia at the 2008 NATO summit in Bucharest. Greece claimed there had been a collective decision not to invite Macedonia to join. Much to Macedonia's pleasure the ICJ ruled on 5 December in Macedonia's favour, upholding the government's claim that Greece had violated the UN accord of 1995 in 2008. Greece, however, was unimpressed and insisted it changed nothing. The rather mute reaction to the ruling from the rest of the world suggested that while Macedonia had scored a moral point, it had not markedly changed the parameters of the dispute with Greece.

Marcus Tanner

KOSOVO

CAPITAL: Pristina   AREA: 10,887 sq km   POPULATION: 1,815,000 ('10)
OFFICIAL LANGUAGES: Albanian, Serbian
HEAD OF STATE: President Atifete Jahjaga (since April '11)
RULING PARTIES: Democratic Party of Kosovo (PDK)-led coalition
HEAD OF GOVERNMENT: Prime Minister Hashim Thaci (PDK) (since Dec '07)
CORRUPTION INDEX: 2.9; 112nd of 183
CURRENCY: Euro (not formal member of the Eurozone) (Dec '11 £1.00=EUR 1.16, US$1.00=EUR 0.74); Serbian Dinar (Dec '11 £1.00=RSD 121.00, US$1.00=RSD 77.16)
GNI PER CAPITA: US$3,300 ('10)

PRIME Minister Hashim Thaci put together a new coalition government after his Democratic Party of Kosovo (PDK) came first in the 12 December 2010 general election, winning 34 of the 120 seats in the Assembly (unicameral legislature), more than any other party but far short of a majority. A new coalition finally brought together the PDK, millionaire businessman Behgjet Pacolli's Alliance for a New Kosovo (AKR), and a range of ethnic minority parties. It still had only 65 seats, however.

The first convulsion involved the country's largely symbolic presidency. After Thaci agreed to make Pacolli head of state, as part of the coalition deal, the deci-

sion was met with fury, not least from members of Thaci's own party. What outraged a large section of public opinion in Kosovo was not Pacolli's party's small
share of the vote in the general election but his close business links to Kosovo's
arch-foe, Russia. The new president was forced to deliver a maiden speech to a
half-empty chamber after almost all the opposition Assembly members walked
out. The prime minister was soon seeking a way out of this situation. Fortu-
nately, the Constitutional Court solved the problem for him by declaring that the
president's election had breached the constitution, after which Pacolli agreed to
step down. This permitted the election on 7 April of a newcomer. Atifete Jahjaga
was a politically inexperienced, somewhat obscure figure; previously she had
served as deputy head of the police force. In the event, the election of Kosovo's
first woman head of state was a surprising success and Jahjaga soon established
herself as a dignified, calming presence.

Predictions that Thaci's shaky coalition would unravel as a result of these ruc-
tions proved unfounded. Instead, as the country lurched into a new phase of confrontation with Serbia, opposition parties became leery of attacking the government lest they appear unpatriotic. The dramas began on 25 July when the government abruptly ordered a special police unit to seize control of two border
crossings with Serbia that lay inside a small Serb-held enclave in northern
Kosovo. The action was unexpected as both Kosovo and Serbia had since March
taken part in EU-led talks in Brussels on technical issues aimed at easing conflict. These talks had yielded modest agreements on free movement of goods and
mutual recognition of higher educational diplomas—though Kosovo complained that Serbia had not actually implemented its share of the agreements.

The police action, therefore, came out of the blue, and caused apoplexy in the
four Serb-run municipalities of northern Kosovo, where the writ of the Kosovo
government had never run. Locals promptly erected about 18 major roadblocks
on the roads, most of which were still up in December. By then crowds of Serbs
had repeatedly clashed with NATO peacekeepers belonging to the KFOR mission, who vainly attempted to remove some of the barricades. There had been
injuries on all sides. The tense, panicky atmosphere in the north destroyed any
hopes of a thaw in relations between Serbia and Kosovo. Thaci's government,
shrilly insisting that the country's sovereignty was at stake, refused to back down
on the police action. Economics was also a factor. About half of Kosovo's annual
budget came from customs duties, but the virtually unmanned state of the border
between Serbia and Kosovo meant that vast amounts of goods could flow unimpeded into Kosovo without payment of customs, undermining Kosovo's own
businesses as well as depriving the government of much needed revenue.

The confrontations in the north overshadowed the other major development of
the latter half of the year, the trial for war crimes of the popular former transport
minister, Fatmir Limaj. Prosecutors from the EU rule of law mission in Kosovo,
EULEX, in July charged Limaj with committing war crimes in the Kosovo conflict of 1999 and his trial began in November. By then, however, matters had taken
a strange turn as the chief witness in the trial, Agim Zogaj, had died in unclear circumstances, having reportedly committed suicide in Germany in September. As

Limaj was a close ally of Thaci, the course of the trial held implications for the prime minister who had himself been accused of war crimes in 2010 in a Council of Europe report compiled by the Swiss rapporteur, Dick Marty (see AR 2011, pp. 95; 424).

With so much other news occupying the front pages, the government faced few questions about its handling of the economy. In any case, this was relatively unaffected by the crisis in the eurozone, owing to Kosovo's poor level of integration with the economies of the rest of Europe. As before, the Kosovo government staggered along mainly on a combination of foreign donations and taxes raised through VAT and customs. Much of the population survived on remittances sent home from abroad. As Kosovo barely exported anything, the marked decline in exports from most Balkan countries to Western Europe did not alter matters much.

The government's main foreign policy goal was to secure a "roadmap" from the European Union regarding eventual admission into the visa-free Schengen zone. Citizens of several former Yugoslav countries had been allowed to travel into the Schengen area without visas from December 2009. Albania and Bosnia were admitted into the same scheme in 2010. The European Commission's October progress report contained no more than hints that this might become available to Kosovo.

Besides "roadmaps", the government was also interested in roads. The government busied itself with its main infrastructural project, completing a section of the Kosovo-Albania "Patriotic Highway". This was designed to run from the north of Kosovo to the port of Durres in Albania. Thaci opened the first 38 km stretch of the highway in Kosovo in November. Being built by a Turkish-US consortium, the project was due for completion by 2013.

Marcus Tanner

SERBIA

CAPITAL: Belgrade   AREA: 88,361 sq km   POPULATION: 7,292,574 ('10)
OFFICIAL LANGUAGE: Serbo-Croat
HEAD OF STATE: President Boris Tadic (DS) (since June '06)
RULING PARTIES: For a European Serbia, coalition led by Democratic Party (DS)
HEAD OF GOVERNMENT: Prime Minister Mirko Cvetkovic (DS) (since July '08)
DEMOCRACY INDEX: 6.33; 65th of 167   CORRUPTION INDEX: 3.3; 86th of 183
CURRENCY: Serbian Dinar (Dec '11 £1.00=RSD 121.01, US$1.00=RSD 77.16)
GNI PER CAPITA: US$5,810, Intl$11,230 at PPP ('10)

KOSOVO and the quest for EU candidate country status dominated Serbian politics to the exclusion of almost all else in 2011, posing a political dilemma for the centre-right, Democratic Party-led government of Mirko Cvetkovic and President Boris Tadic.

With elections looming in spring 2012, the economy in the doldrums, and polls giving a lead to the opposition nationalist Serbian Progressive Party (SNS), the government was keen to obtain EU candidate country status for Serbia by the end of 2011, giving them at least one solid achievement to present to voters in 2012.

But growing violence in the Serb-run sliver of northern Kosovo undermined this ambition. While EU leaders grew louder in their insistence that Serbia distance itself from the militants in northern Kosovo, the Serbian government was loathe to be accused of "betraying" embattled Serbs in a land that many Serbs still viewed as "the cradle of Serbia", and whose declaration of independence in 2008 Serbia refused to recognise.

Initially, hopes were high that the EU could help Serbia and Kosovo relieve their ancient dispute of some its poison. In spring the two sides joined EU-mediated talks in Brussels, dedicated to resolving purely technical, day-to-day issues, such as the free movement of goods and people, mutual recognition of university degrees, and Kosovo's right to attend regional forums without Serbia vetoing its presence or walking out if Kosovo attended. A number of agreements were duly signed. But in July the brief thaw in relations came to an end. Tiring of the flow of duty-free goods into Kosovo via the Serb-run enclave in the north, the Kosovo government of Hashim Thaci suddenly dispatched special police units to seize the two border crossings between northern Kosovo and Serbia in an operation that appeared to enjoy the sanction of the NATO-led peacekeeping force in Kosovo, KFOR, and the EU rule of law mission there, EULEX.

The result was uproar as local Serbs threw up barricades on roads in the four municipalities of Kosovo that they controlled, as a result of which KFOR was unable to move vehicles round the area. In November, when KFOR finally undertook a few actions to dismantle barricades, a number of German KFOR soldiers were hurt in confrontations with local Serbs, angering the German government. The German chancellor, Angela Merkel, had told President Tadic in person on 23 August in Belgrade to stop encouraging troublemakers in northern Kosovo. The danger now grew that Germany would either veto or delay Serbia's application for candidacy at the EU Council of Ministers meeting on 9 December.

What was unfortunate about this development was that Serbia had worked hard to meet the other membership criteria. On 31 January, well ahead of schedule, Serbia returned a vast EU questionnaire comprising 37 volumes to the enlargement commissioner. Serbia also acted to remove the other great obstacle to its candidacy, its failure to arrest war crimes suspect former General Ratko Mladic, wanted by the International Criminal Tribunal for the Former Yugoslavia, the ICTY, over the infamous massacre of Bosniaks (Bosnian Muslims) in Srebrenica, Bosnia, in 1995. This was dealt with on 26 May, when Serbian police arrested Mladic in a village north of Belgrade and extradited him to stand trial for genocide and other grave crimes in The Hague. Serbian police arrested the country's last war crimes suspect sought by the ICTY, the former Croatian Serb leader Goran Hadzic, on 20 July.

On 11 October, the European Commission duly rewarded Serbia for its co-operative action by issuing a positive opinion, or *avis*, concerning Serbia's candidacy. But in autumn the worsening Kosovo crisis threatened to trump all those earlier achievements. On 1 December Chancellor Merkel made it clear that Germany was still not satisfied with the situation in Kosovo, warning that as matters stood Serbia did not meet the membership criteria—one of which was good relations with neighbouring countries.

In the end, Serbia paid a price for the violence in Kosovo, though not as high a price as some had predicted. On 9 December, as EU leaders met in Brussels to discuss the eurozone crisis, Serbia's application for candidate status was put on hold rather than being dismissed. There was some consolation for the government in that the EU said it would review the situation in February and possibly grant Serbia candidate status as early as March.

As was so often the case with Serbia, everything depended on unpredictable Kosovo. The problem for the government was that its room for manoeuvre remained limited. The opposition Progressives, under Tomislav Nikolic, were on the alert for any signs of backsliding over Kosovo, so recognition of Kosovo's independence was highly unlikely. The question was whether Serbia could build up a sufficiently cordial relationship with the Kosovo government without actually recognising it—and if so, how this could be done without "betraying" the Kosovo Serbs, thousands of whom had already embarrassed the authorities in Belgrade by signing a collective petition begging Russia's government to grant them Russian citizenship.

Marcus Tanner

MONTENEGRO

CAPITAL: Podgorica   AREA: 14,026 sq km   POPULATION: 631,490 ('10)
OFFICIAL LANGUAGE: Montenegrin
HEAD OF STATE: President Filip Vujanovic (since May '03 in union with Serbia)
RULING PARTIES: Democratic Party of Socialists (DPS)-led coalition
HEAD OF GOVERNMENT: Prime Minister Igor Luksic (DPS) (since Dec '10)
DEMOCRACY INDEX: 6.27; 68th of 167   CORRUPTION INDEX: 4.0; 66th of 183
CURRENCY: Euro [not formal member of eurozone] (Dec '11 £1.00=EUR 1.16, US$1.00=EUR 0.74)
GNI PER CAPITA: US$6,620, Intl$12,590 at PPP ('10)

AFTER the European Council granted Montenegro candidate country status in December 2010, the country's pro-Serbian opposition parties and the pro-independence ruling coalition largely put aside their once ferocious feuds to concentrate on expediting the EU accession process.

As Serbia itself was desperate to join the EU, membership of the European club (unlike the question of diplomatic recognition of neighbouring Kosovo, which pro-Serbian parties bitterly opposed), was an issue on which all sides could unite. In May a National Council for European Integration held a conference defining priority areas on which to work, mainly those identified in earlier European Commission reports. Key issues were defining the criteria for employment in the public service, confirming the independence and accountability of the judiciary, and strengthening the fight against corruption, including the establishment of an anticorruption taskforce. Results were mixed. In October, the European Commission's Progress Report on Montenegro commended the flurry of corruption-fighting activity on the part of the government, but said that the number of convictions for high-level graft was still far too low.

What also took much of the heat out of Montenegro's domestic politics was Milo Djukanovic's decision to step down as prime minister—though not as chief of the ruling Democratic Party of Socialists—on 21 December, 2010, and hand over to Igor Luksic. Though a member of the same party, Luksic was a far less contentious figure than Djukanovic, who remained a hate figure to the pro-Serbian parties for having taken Montenegro out of its loose "state union" with Serbia in 2006. Luksic's new government officially took office on 31 December, 2010.

Another calming factor was the country's relative success in weathering the global economic crisis. Unemployment remained stubbornly high at around 20 per cent of the working-age population, but as it had been high before the crisis the difference was not marked. Meanwhile, tourist revenues, a mainstay of the economy, remained buoyant.

In an otherwise placid year, one of the few dramas was a series of mysterious arson attacks in July on vehicles belonging to the independent newspaper *Vijesti*. The newspaper's editor blamed dark forces in the government and the judiciary both for the attacks and the failure to apprehend the perpetrators. "There is always a suspicion that such attacks are organised and ordered by some government structures and criminal circles close to them, to intimidate us and thus influence our editorial policy," Mihajlo Jovovic claimed.

On 9 December at the meeting of the European Council Montenegro received a reward for what Europe saw as its generally positive approach towards reforms. The Council did not live up to the giddy expectations of some in Podgorica, who expected a start date for accession talks, but there was plenty to celebrate from the meeting otherwise dominated by the crisis in the eurozone. The Council said that, after six months more monitoring, especially on judicial reform, it was minded to open accession talks in mid-2012. Montenegro's foreign minister, Milan Rocen, hailed the news, announcing that his country had now seized the baton from Croatia in the European integration process in the region (Croatia's membership in 2013 was approved at the same meeting). This was no exaggeration, as Montenegro had clearly leapt ahead of the next two contenders for membership, Serbia and Macedonia, and did seem likely to become the next former Yugoslav republic to join the EU, after Slovenia and Croatia.

Marcus Tanner

BOSNIA & HERZEGOVINA

CONSTITUENT REPUBLICS: Federation of Bosnia & Herzegovina (FBiH, Muslim-Croat Federation); and Republika Srpska (RS, Serb Rebublic)
CAPITAL: Sarajevo   AREA: 51,210 sq km   POPULATION: 3,760,149 ('10)
OFFICIAL LANGUAGES: Bosnian, Croatian, Serbian
HEAD OF STATE: State Presidency: Zeljko Komsic (SDP) Croat, chairman; Nebojsa Radmanovic (SNSD), Serb; Bakir Izetbegovic (SDA), Bosniak (since Nov '10)
PRESIDENTS OF REPUBLICS: FBiH: Zivko Budimir (HSP) (since March '11); RS: Milorad Dodik (SNSD) (since Nov '10)
HEAD OF GOVERNMENT: Prime Minister Nikola Spiric (SNSD) (since Jan '07), Prime Minister elect Vjekoslav Bevanda (HDZ) (since Dec '11); FBiH: Nermin Niksic (SDP) (since March '11); RS: Aleksandar Dzombic (SNSD) (since Dec '10)
HIGH REPRESENTATIVE: Valentin Inzko (Austria) (since March '09)
DEMOCRACY INDEX: 5.32; 94th of 167   CORRUPTION INDEX: 3.2; 91st of 183
CURRENCY: Marka (Dec '11 £1.00=BAM 2.28, US$1.00=BAM 1.45)
GNI PER CAPITA: US$4,790, Intl$8,970 at PPP ('10)

BOSNIA & Herzegovina approached the end of the year as it had started it, without a government. Only at the very end of December did signs emerge that, 14 months since the last general election on 3 October 2010, the political and ethnic deadlock might be broken. The country seemed increasingly forgotten by Europe, which had lost patience with the feuding Bosniak (Muslim), Serb and Croat politicians.

Predictably, the general election had returned Serbs to power in the smaller of the two autonomous entities, the Serb-dominated Republika Srpska (RS), whilst various Bosniak parties had triumphed in the mainly Bosniak and Croat Federation of Bosnia & Herzegovina (FBiH) (see AR 2011, p. 100).

In the Republika Srpska, the Alliance of Independent Social Democrats (SNSD), led by Milorad Dodik, president of the entity, quickly formed a government. In the Federation matters were more complicated. The Social Democrats, a nominally non-ethnic party but in practice a party of secular Muslims, had done best in the election in the Federation and their right to lead formation of the entity's government was not disputed. But the Social Democrats (SDP), led by Zlatko Lagumdzija, had campaigned in the election alongside two minor Bosnian Croat parties and Lagumdzija's decision to form a coalition government in the Federation in mid-March with them, not with either of the two largest Bosnian Croat parties, caused a rumpus. His move was neither illegal nor unconstitutional but the Social Democrats had manifestly broken a longstanding convention, which held that the largest Bosniak and the largest Croat parties had the right to enter any government in the Federation entity.

Dodik's Serbs profited most from this wearying dispute and his party quickly took the side of the offended Croat parties, the Croatian Democratic Union of Bosnia and Herzegovina (HDZ) and its sister party, usually known by its acronym, HDZ 1990. Claiming that the Social Democrats had undermined the 1995 Dayton peace settlement by excluding the Croats' legitimate representatives from office, Dodik refused to agree to form a state-level council of ministers, as the state government was called. The Social Democrats had handed Dodik an ace. It helped his separatist agenda if no state government could be formed, while the Social Democrats' actions appeared to reinforce his frequent assertion that Bosniaks wanted to dominate the country and were not interested in genuine power sharing.

Many observers predicted throughout the spring and summer of 2011 that Dodik would crack, have to agree to form a Council of Ministers eventually, and that "Europe" would force his hand. As the year wore on, it became clear that Dodik did not "have" to do anything, and that Europe had more or less given up on Bosnia for the time being. Only at the very end of 2011, on 28 December, did the parties reach agreement on a council of ministers, with the prime minister's post filled by a nominee of the HDZ.

Without a new council of ministers, the central government limped along, the old council of ministers continuing to operate under a so-called "technical mandate" and working under emergency budgets authorised by the international community's high representative, Valentin Inzko. But they could not undertake new initiatives, as a result of which negotiations with the European Union on Bosnia's eventual accession stalled. There was also no progress on holding a census, which the EU had urged Bosnia to undertake in 2011. Unsurprisingly, the European Commission's October Progress Report was fairly damning, many chapters opening with the phrase "No progress was made..."

Among the many complaints listed was Bosnia's failure to act on the European Court of Human Rights judgment of December 2009 in the so-called Sejdic-Finci case. This concerned the lawsuit of Jakob Finci and Avdo Sejdic, a Jew and a Roma respectively, who claimed that Bosnia's 1995 constitution violated the European Convention on Human Rights, to which Bosnia was a signatory, by limiting eligibility to the country's top posts to members of the three so-called constituent nations: Bosniaks, Croats and Serbs. As with so many other issues, Bosnia had pledged to amend the constitution to meet the judgment but had not actually done anything.

The one exception in the European Commission's doleful report on Bosnia concerned processing war crimes cases and locating missing persons. Indeed, Bosnia's relationship with the International Criminal Tribunal for the former Yugoslavia, ICTY, was deemed "satisfactory", not a word used often in the report.

One war crimes case of particular interest to everyone in Bosnia followed the capture in Serbia on 26 May of Ratko Mladic, the Bosnian Serb general indicted by the ICTY for genocide at Srebrenica in eastern Bosnia in 1995, among other crimes. The Bosnian authorities played no actual role in this affair; Mladic was caught by the Serbian police north of Belgrade and speedily dispatched from Serbia to The Hague. There was no question of such a sensitive trial being devolved to the courts in Sarajevo, either. But, as Bosnia had been the scene of his alleged crimes, the news was followed more closely in Bosnia than anywhere else.

While Bosnian Serbs felt pushed onto the defensive over the capture of Mladic, who was still a hero in the eyes of many Serbs, it was the turn of the Bosniaks to feel embarrassed on 28 October when a lone Muslim extremist staged a bizarre and ineffectual attack on the US embassy in Sarajevo, taking pot shots at the building before being disabled by a police sniper. Bosnian Serbs quickly claimed that the attack provided further proof—not that any was needed—that the Federation was a hotbed of Islamic fundamentalists. In the end, it turned out that Mevlid Jasarevic, aged 23, was not from Bosnia but the mainly Bosniak region of Sandzak in Serbia, although he had been living previously in Gornja Maoca, a hardline Muslim village in Bosnia and the centre of the small Wahhabi sect in the country.

Marcus Tanner

CROATIA

CAPITAL: Zagreb   AREA: 56,540 sq km   POPULATION: 4,424,161 ('10)
OFFICIAL LANGUAGE: Croatian
HEAD OF STATE: President Ivo Josipovic (SPH) (since Feb '10)
RULING PARTIES: Social Democratic Party (SDP)-led coalition
HEAD OF GOVERNMENT: Prime Minister Zoran Milanovic (SDP) (since Dec '11)
DEMOCRACY INDEX: 6.81; 53rd of 167   CORRUPTION INDEX: 4.0; 66th of 183
CURRENCY: Kuna (Dec '11 £1.00=HRK 8.74, US$1.00=HRK 5.57)
GNI PER CAPITA: US$13,780, Intl$18,730 at PPP ('10)

A SERIES of corruption allegations, probes and trials into leading officials of the ruling centre-right Croatian Democratic Union (HDZ) sapped the energy of Prime Minister Jadranka Kosor's government in 2011, overshadowing a significant achievement—the completion of tortuous negotiations on European Union membership.

After lengthy talks on the last four chapters of the accession process, especially on the efficiency and independence of the judiciary, the president of the European Commission, José Manuel Barroso, on 10 June announced that Croatia had crossed the finishing line and was on course to join the EU as the 28th member in 2013. If the 27 EU member states duly ratified the Commission's proposal, Croatia would be the second former Yugoslav state to join the European club after neighbouring Slovenia, which had joined in 2004 (see AR 2004, pp. 101-02).

Croatia had applied for membership in 2003 and talks started in 2005 but the process took another six years. The EU had become convinced that it had allowed Romania and Bulgaria to join prematurely in 2007 without having subjected either state to appropriate checks on its readiness. Croatia had to pay the price for this perceived error, undergoing much more scrupulous monitoring.

For Prime Minister Kosor the announcement from Brussels ought to have been a moment to savour, instead of which the good news was buried under a slew of new, damaging allegations of bribery and corruption among senior officials in her party. The HDZ in consequences failed to register any lift in the polls, which continued to suggest that the party would lose the next general election on 4 December to an opposition left-of-centre coalition, "Kukuriku". This comprised the Social Democrats (SDP), the Croatian People's Party-Liberal Democrats (HNS-LD), the Pensioners Party (HSU), and a regional party, the Istrian Democratic Assembly (IDS).

By far the most important case hanging over the government was the forthcoming trial of Kosor's predecessor as HDZ leader and prime minister, Ivo Sanader.

Arrested in Austria on a Croatian warrant in December 2010, Sanader was extradited to Croatia in July. After numerous delays his trial opened in November only to halt immediately when Sanader's lawyers voiced concerns about their client's health. The former prime minister faced several charges but the gravest concerned his alleged receipt of a €500,000 bribe in 1995 from Austria's Hypo Alpe Adria bank in return for facilitating the bank's entry into the Croatian banking market (see AR 2011, pp. 101-02). Sanader had been deputy foreign minister at the time. He denied all charges.

Adding to the government's woes, the police's special anti-corruption taskforce, USKOK, announced in November that it was extending its probes into 17 current or former HDZ officials to the whole party, which was now suspected of drawing money out of state enterprises over a period of several years into a party "slush" fund.

Kosor fought back against the dire newspaper headlines, pointing out that ever since she had taken over from Sanader in July 2009 she had consistently backed police investigations into corruption. Trying to decontaminate the issue by appropriating it, she made her strong stand against corruption one of her main pre-election slogans. The tactic did not work, however. The public was plainly bored with the HDZ and tired of its reputation for sleaze and was hungry for change. The opposition Kukuriku coalition had little more to do than promise not to be like the HDZ. Polls consistently put the centre-left coalition at between 38 and 40 per cent of the vote, more than double the rating of the HDZ.

Elections on 4 December confirmed months of pundits' predictions. The HDZ, just as expected, took a beating, dropping from 65 to 47 seats in the 151-seat legislature, the Sabor. The Social Democrats, led by Zoran Milanovic, and their partners, swept into power with 81 seats, an absolute majority. Kosor's political future at the helm of the HDZ was now in doubt, having led the party to its worst ever election result, although whether this was her fault was debatable. She received one consolation prize. On 9 December, on the fringes of the EU Council of Ministers meeting, Croatia signed its accession treaty with the European Union. As Milanovic had not yet been appointed Croatia's new prime minister, Kosor went to Brussels and signed on Croatia's behalf, thereby earning a place in Croatia's history books.

What concerned many economists, meanwhile, was the failure of the winning coalition to spell out more clearly what they intended to do in government. Croatia faced serious economic problems that had worsened as a result of the crisis in the eurozone; its banks were heavily exposed to banks in Italy, for example. It was also clear that the country needed to make large cuts to its overstaffed public sector and generous pension schemes. Many experts said the Kukuriku coalition's failure to address these challenges directly could leave it politically exposed when, as seemed likely, it had to introduce sharp cuts without having alerted the public in advance to their necessity.

Marcus Tanner

SLOVENIA

CAPITAL: Ljubljana   AREA: 20,270 sq km   POPULATION: 2,052,821 ('10)
OFFICIAL LANGUAGE: Slovene
HEAD OF STATE: President Danilo Turk (since Dec '07)
RULING PARTIES: Social Democrats (SD)-led coalition
HEAD OF GOVERNMENT: Prime Minister Borut Pahor (SD) (since Nov '08)
DEMOCRACY INDEX: 7.69; 32nd of 167   CORRUPTION INDEX: 5.9; 35th of 183
CURRENCY: Euro (Dec '11 £1.00=EUR 1.16, US$1.00=EUR 0.74)
GNI PER CAPITA: US$24,000, Intl$27,140 at PPP ('10)

BATTERED by an unexpectedly severe downturn in the export-driven economy, rising unemployment and spiralling foreign debt levels, Borut Pahor's Social Democrat-led coalition government struggled to remain afloat in 2011 as its partners defected one by one. After winning the most recent general election in 2008, Pahor had formed a coalition with the centrist Zares party, Liberal Democracy, and the Pensioners' Party. But by July the coalition was in disarray and the Pensioners' Party and Zares had both walked out. The prime minister was then left running a minority government.

In June the government lost an important referendum on the issue of raising the retirement age to 65. The vote was a disaster for the government, shattering much of its remaining credibility as more than 70 per cent of those who bothered to vote—only about 40 per cent of the electorate—said "no". After that debacle, Pahor was living on borrowed time until losing a no-confidence vote in September, after which President Danilo Turk called new elections on 4 December.

The ballot revealed the extremely febrile state of the electorate. Established parties were consigned to oblivion and none of the predictions about likely winners was confirmed. Received opinion in the months leading up to the vote had been that power would revert to Janez Jansa's right-wing, nationalist Slovene Democratic Party (SDS), which campaigned on a tough austerity programme and on demands for sharp cuts in spending. (Jansa had been prime minister from 2004 to 2008.) The result was a shock. Jansa's SDS actually lost support, falling from 28 to 26 seats in the 90-seat National Assembly, well short of a majority. That was no comfort to Pahor's Social Democrats, whose tally was slashed much more dramatically from 29 seats to 10. Zares was annihilated, falling from nine seats to none.

The real upset was the triumph of a total beginner, Positive Slovenia, a feel-good, vaguely centre-left party led by the mayor of Llubljana, Zoran Jankovic, whose party came from nowhere to win 28 seats, thereby becoming the largest party in the Assembly. Jankovic had only formed his party in October, but his claim that Slovenia needed a new kind of politics, free of the old left-right discourse, had clearly resonated. Another surprise winner was Civil List, which also came from nowhere to take eight seats. The election revealed, or rather confirmed, an urban-rural, east-west, split in Slovenia, with secular, leftist and non-nationalist parties triumphing in the capital and the west, and Catholics and conservatives retaining their grip on the rural east.

By the end of the year the likelihood was that the next administration would be led by Positive Slovenia, governing in coalition with the Pensioners' Party (which had won six seats), Civil List and possibly the humbled Social Democrats.

Jankovic had already ruled out working with Jansa, who promptly voiced doubts that the new government would last its four-year mandate.

Whoever formed the next government faced a hard task. Slovenia had been badly hit by economic downturn in 2009 and had not recovered much in 2010. The third quarter of 2011 saw a slight contraction in the economy, of 0.5 per cent. Unemployment at 12 per cent was low by regional standards but high by the standards of independent Slovenia. Spending cuts thus looked inevitable, but it was questionable whether any future master of an untidy coalition government, unavoidably composed of very different elements, would be able to steer them through.

Marcus Tanner

RUSSIA, WESTERN CIS, AND THE CAUCASUS

RUSSIA

CAPITAL: Moscow   AREA: 17,098,240 sq km   POPULATION: 141,750,000 (World Bank figure '10)
(142,914,000 census Oct '10)
OFFICIAL LANGUAGE: Russian
HEAD OF STATE: President Dmitry Medvedev (ER) (since May '08)
RULING PARTY: United Russia (ER) party
HEAD OF GOVERNMENT: Prime Minister Vladimir Putin (ER) (since May '08)
DEMOCRACY INDEX: 4.26; 107th of 167   CORRUPTION INDEX: 2.4; 143rd of 183
CURRENCY: Rouble (Dec '11 £1.00=RUB 48.22, US$1.00=RUB 30.75)
GNI PER CAPITA: US$9,910, Intl$19,190 at PPP ('10)

IN December large protests in Moscow challenged the stage-managed electoral process that had served to keep Russia's rulers in power since the late 1990s. On 10 December, up to 60,000 people joined a protest rally in the capital; the numbers were even larger at a second rally on 24 December. The demonstrations marked the overt rejection by Russia's urban middle-class of the hollow politial process in which they had been asked to acquiesce since the late 1990s, most recently in elections to the State Duma (the lower house of Russia's bicameral federal legislature) on 4 December. Like the other uprisings of 2011—the "Arab Spring", the Occupy movement, and Europe's "indignados", and to an extent inspired by them—the December protests in Russia expressed people's rejection of political and economic systems that no longer responded to their needs. In Russia's case, educated, technologically competent, and relatively prosperous young urban professionals were demanding a genuine voice in the political process. As in the other protest movements of 2011, social media websites and mobile phones with cameras were instrumental in spreading information and generating support. But, as elsewhere, it was the people's presence, their physical occupation of squares and open spaces in cities, that forced change.

The official results from the Duma elections showed that the ruling United Russia (ER) party had won 49.32 per cent, and 238 of the Duma's 450 seats.

This was already a significant decline in support since the 2007 elections when ER had won 64.3 per cent and 315 seats (see AR 2008, p. 107). However, even this reduced vote share was widely believed to have been exaggerated. There were thousands of complaints about the conduct of the election, both from the opposition parties and from independent observers. The vote rigging took various forms, including ballot stuffing and multiple voting, the latter being achieved through a process known as "the carousel", whereby people with temporary residence cards and absentee ballots were bussed from one polling station to another to cast their votes. Golos, Russia's independent election monitoring group, reported more than 2,000 complaints on election day. In many cases, abuses had been filmed by volunteer election observers on their mobile phones and posted online. In addition, before the election Golos had received 5,300 complaints on its website alleging violations of electoral law, frequently in the form of pressure from employers or superiors to vote for ER. This was given substance when opposition Duma member Gennady Gudkov released a video in October of a speech by the governor of Moscow Region, who had been filmed telling local officials to "use every opportunity to hinder our opponents' campaign staff" to ensure an ER victory.

It had long been tacitly accepted in Russia that the voting process was manipulated in various ways and that this was done with the connivance of the Central Electoral Commission (CEC) and its chairman, Vladimir Churov, whom President Medvedev described as "almost a magician". Why, then, in 2011, did this sham democracy finally provoke a reaction? Partly, it was the greater availability of online media. In 2011, 43 per cent of the Russian population, or almost 60 million citizens, had access to the Internet; in large cities this figure was as high as 70 per cent. The freedom of information and discussion online contrasted sharply with the tightly controlled main broadcast media, particularly the television news. A general weariness with the "party of crooks and thieves", as United Russia had become known, also contributed. Support for ER was declining steadily: in elections for regional legislatures in March, the party won more than 50 per cent of the vote in only three of the 12 participating regions (and less than 40 per cent in two regions), and this on a turnout of under half of the 24 million eligible voters.

The main development in 2011 that sparked sufficient anger to bring 100,000 people out to protest on 24 December was not, however, the falsification of election results but the announcement that Vladimir Putin expected two more terms as Russia's president. At the United Russia congress in September, it was announced that Prime Minister Putin, who had been president for two terms from December 1999, and President Dmitry Medvedev, elected to succeed him in 2008, had arranged to exchange roles. Putin would stand as the ER candidate for the presidential elections scheduled for March 2012, which meant that if—when—he won, he would be eligible for two further consecutive presidential terms (recently extended from four to six years), at the end of which he would be 71 years old. The reason for Putin's rumoured Botox treatment now became clear.

Prior to the announcement, speculation over whether Medvedev would choose to stand for a second presidential term, or whether his mentor would return to the presidency, had occupied political commentators for much of the year. When it was announced that Putin was to stand again, and when both he and Medvedev appeared to confirm that they had agreed on this several years ago, the implied disdain for voters and for the democratic system incensed public opinion. The cracks in the facade of sham democracy began to appear. At a martial arts event, held in Moscow in November, spectators booed Putin as he congratulated the winner; a recording of the event was swiftly posted online. A system that had been designed to restore "stability" to politics, by fostering the passive acceptance of government and curtailing expressions of dissent, had begun to break down. Even in the elite, consensus began to fracture. After the ER congress, the finance minister, Aleksei Kudrin, said that he would not serve in a Medvedev government, and was forced to resign by an irate still-President Medvedev.

The December demonstrations began with a protest the day after the elections, organised by veteran opposition groups such as The Other Russia and Solidarity. But this demonstration drew more support than usual—8,000 rather than the expected 300—from people angered by what they knew to be falsified results for United Russia. There were numerous arrests and prison sentences were imposed on some protesters, among them Aleksei Navalny, a popular blogger and anti-corruption campaigner, who had coined the phrase "party of crooks and thieves" and who became a symbol and a voice of the protests. Momentum accelerated with thousands of people committing themselves, via social media websites, to turn out for demonstrations in cities throughout Russia on 10 December, the first Saturday after the election. As the movement grew, opposition leaders in Moscow negotiated with the city authorities to find a suitable venue, eventually fixing on Bolotnaya square. This demonstration attracted up to 60,000, and a less heavy response from the police. The main breakthrough was that the Bolotnaya protest was reported by state-controlled television channels in a fairly neutral manner (until then, the television news had ignored the protests). The coverage helped to swell numbers for the next scheduled protests, on 24 December. Over 50,000 people had indicated via social media websites that they planned to attend this demonstration in Moscow. On the day itself, up to 100,000 people went to Sakharov Prospect where the protest took place in a carnival atmosphere, ending with Grandfather Frost (Russia's Father Christmas) wishing everyone a Happy New Year. As a symbol of their motivation—honesty—the protesters took to wearing white ribbons on their coats. Attitudes had changed. As Navalny said, after his release on 15 December, "I went in [to jail] from one country and came out into another." Initially inchoate, the protests coalesced around a set of demands, which were clarified by representatives of the movement on 24 December. These included fresh elections, the dismissal of Churov from the CEC, legislative changes to allow all parties to compete in elections, and that no vote be cast for Putin in the March 2012 elections.

There were some attempts at concessions from the authorities: Medvedev posted a message online, calling for an investigation into the allegations of voting fraud; the Russian Orthodox Church—normally unquestioningly supportive of the authorities—also intervened, urging them to "answer" the questions posed by protesters. The speaker of the Duma since 2003, Boris Gryzlov, stepped down. In his speech to the first session of the new Duma on 22 December, Medvedev called for "a comprehensive reform of our political system", including the reinstatement of direct elections (abolished in 2005) for Russia's powerful regional governors; simplified procedures for registering political parties (regulations often served to disqualify opposition groups from elections); and a citizen-controlled television station.

None of this was held worthy of serious consideration by the protest leaders—a mixed group of liberals, nationalists, and apolitical celebrities—who were deeply suspicious of the government. Until December's mass protests, the extra-parliamentary opposition had struggled for attention, bravely persisting in its "Strategy-31" demonstrations (see AR 2011, p. 106), but attracting little support to protests that often ended in rough treatment by the police and arrest. Opposition parties such as Yabloko or Parnas had found themselves either unable to register for elections, or with such poor figures that they did not reach the 7 per cent threshold for representation. Political parties that did achieve seats in the Duma (the Communists, the Liberal Democratic Party, and A Just Russia), had largely failed to challenge the dominance of United Russia, choosing instead to enjoy the privileges that came with providing a loyal opposition. Periodically, other nominal opposition parties were allowed to emerge to "stabilise" the system by drawing off dissent. In June, for example, the Right Cause party—a right-of-centre outfit that had been formed in 2008 from a merger of smaller groups—received a new leader in billionaire Mikhail Prokhorov, who had apparently been persuaded to head the party to infuse some life into it before the elections. However, when he began to show too much independence he found himself voted out at the party's congress in September. After the 10 December demonstration, Prokhorov announced that he was going to stand in the presidential elections, but most commentators believed that this was another attempt by the authorities to create a tame opposition.

The man who was believed to be the architect of the "stabilisation" strategy was Vladislav Surkov, the deputy head of the presidential administration (nicknamed the "grey cardinal" by some commentators). Prokhorov blamed him for the Right Cause debacle, calling him "a puppet master...who long ago privatised the political system". In December, Surkov called for the creation of a new liberal party to satisfy "disgruntled urban communities". But Surkov's strategy had apparently failed, and he was dismissed in late December, saying of his departure, "stabilisation devours its own children".

What Navalny and other opposition leaders had finally realised was that the only way to defeat sham democracy was to participate in it—to show the hollowness of ER's alleged legitimacy by casting a vote for any party on the ballot other than United Russia. This posed a threat to Putin at the presidential elections not because there was a genuine opposition leader capable of winning (even were one allowed to stand), but because votes cast for anyone other than Putin would reveal his lack of popular legitimacy.

There were some characteristics of the opposition movement at this early stage that would shape its future. First, it was co-ordinated by very diverse leaders, united only in their opposition to the establishment; second, there was no mechanism for negotiation between the authorities and the protesters. It was a dialogue conducted through the media, which produced a kind of street theatre. Putin, in a television interview, mocked the participants in the 10 December demonstration for wearing white ribbons, saying he thought they had pinned contraceptives to their coats as some sort of anti-AIDS protest. In response, banners at the 24 December event depicted the prime minister wearing a condom as a scarf.

A basic complaint voiced by the December protests was the endemic corruption of modern Russia. Much of Navalny's moral authority stemmed from his work as an anti-corruption campaigner. A lawyer by training, he had bought shares in state-owned enterprises, a move that allowed him to pressure their management into releasing accounting information. Through his website he also collated whistle-blowers' reports of corruption.

Yet despite the prevailing levels of corruption, Russia's macroeconomic figures looked generally positive. Inflation, which was running at 6.1 per cent in 2011, was at its lowest since 1991, according to the state statistical service Rosstat. This compared favourably with the hangover from the 2008 financial crisis that had produced 8.8 per cent inflation in 2009 and 2010, and 13.3 per cent in 2008. The OECD predicted growth of a respectable 4 per cent in 2011 and 2012. Yet this rosy outlook remained based on oil exports. The global oil price in 2011 was bolstered by instability in the Middle East and North Africa and by strong demand from the developing world. Russia thus had little difficulty in meeting its budget commitments and could even afford to increase spending. The breakeven price—the average price of oil that the Russian government required in order to balance its budget—therefore reached $110 per barrel in 2011. This was significantly higher than it had been in 2009 and, were the global oil price to plummet, Russia's budget would be in difficulties. Meanwhile, the much heralded "modernisation" that had been a theme of President Medvedev's tenure remained largely illusory, confined to the showcase plans for a business park at Skolkovo outside Moscow that would marry technological innovation with business development. Elsewhere, excessive bureaucratic regulation, which went hand-in-hand with corruption, was a brake on "modernisation".

In March, Medvedev announced that the link between government and business was to be broken, with ministers forced to resign from the boards of directors of state-owned companies. Had this strategy been carried through, it would have halted the appointment of government officials to the boards of strategically important companies—a policy instigated by Putin to curb the powers of the "oligarchs" but which had given the political elite access to state wealth. "During his rule," commented *Moscow News*, "every one of Putin's fellow Ozero dacha [an exclusive suburb] community members has become a billionaire." Furthermore, corruption inflated the cost of any enterprise, contributing to the failure to renew Russia's antiquated infrastructure. *Moscow News* again: "Under Putin's rule, while the country earned more than $1,500 billion from oil exports, it did not build a single modern highway."

Several major accidents in 2011 highlighted the urgent need to modernise Russia's infrastructure and to increase transparency in managing it. They included, in July, the capsizing and sinking of a passenger cruise ship, the Soviet-era *Bulgaria*, on the River Volga with the loss of 122 lives, including around 50 children; a further 79 people were rescued from the vessel, which had been built to carry a maximum of 120 passengers. Then, on 7 September, all but two members of one of Russia's most popular ice-hockey teams, Lokomotiv Yaroslavl, were killed when their Yak-42 aircraft crashed on take-off.

Beyond this physical dilapidation there was another, more corrosive form of decay at work. The dissatisfaction of an educated, urban middle-class with its life chances in such a stagnant system meant that many of the most educated and talented were tempted to emigrate abroad. It also meant that they tended to become concentrated in the largest cities (principally Moscow), leaving much of Russia in danger of long-term underdevelopment. Moreover, the population was declining. The first data from the census of October 2010 was released in March. This showed a decline since the previous census (in October 2002) from 145.2 million to 142.9 million, a 1.6 per cent fall.

Many of these problems were magnified in the North Caucasus region, contributing to the strengthening of Islamist extremism there. On 24 January there was another major terrorist incident in Moscow. A suicide bombing in the baggage reclaim hall of international arrivals at Domodedovo airport (Russia's largest) killed 37 people and seriously injured over 100. The attack joined the November 2009 derailment of the Moscow-St Petersburg express train, and the March 2010 suicide bombing on the Moscow metro as a reminder to Russians that the North Caucasus Islamist movement retained the ability to reach Russia's heartland. In March the Russian prosecutor general charged, as the mastermind of the attack, Doku Umarov, the Chechen-born leader of the "Caucasus Emirate", a group dedicated to establishing an Islamic state in the North Caucasus. Umarov had also claimed responsibility for the 2009 and 2010 attacks. There were skirmishes throughout the year between security forces and Islamist rebels, mainly in Ingushetia and Dagestan, which had become the centre of the Islamist rebellion. (The men arrested on suspicion of having carried out the Domodedovo bombing came from Ingushetia.)

The government's only positive policy for the region seemed to be the planned expansion of six ski resorts in the North Caucasus in time for the 2014 Sochi Winter Olympics. But in February, five Russian tourists from Moscow were attacked by gunmen on their way to a ski resort in the Mount Elbrus region of Kabardino-Balkaria and three of them were killed. The same day, a number of bombs were discovered in the region and one exploded, bringing down a ski-lift support pole and a number of cabins.

Chechnya, meanwhile, was largely pacified through a combination of flooding it with money and tacitly sanctioning the violent policies of its thuggish ruler, Ramzan Kadyrov. On 5 October, which happened to be his 35th birthday, Kadyrov celebrated the opening of a redeveloped zone of skyscrapers in Grozny, the Chechen capital, with a lavish concert featuring several Western film and music stars. But repercussions continued from the Chechen war of the 1990s. In June, Yury Budanov, a former Russian army colonel, was shot dead, around noon, in Moscow, near a children's playground. His alleged attacker, a Chechen, was arrested in August. Budanov was notorious for having been convicted of the murder of a teenaged Chechen girl, whom he had kidnapped and tortured after a drinking session in 2000 (a rape charge was dropped). He had been released from prison in 2009 after serving six years of a 10 year sentence. To many in Russia he was a hero, and his conviction a travesty; he was buried with full military honours.

The impact of a likely new Putin presidency began to be evident in Russia's foreign relations. The "reset" in US-Russian relations offered by the US administration of Barack Obama in 2009 and warmly accepted by the Medvedev presidency was looking less secure by the end of 2011.

In March, Russia had not used its veto at the UN Security Council against UN Resolution 1973, which authorised measures to protect civilians in Libya and established a no-fly zone. Putin had criticised the resolution, comparing international military action against Libya to "a medieval call to crusade", and in a rare example of public disagreement between them, Medvedev had called such language "unacceptable". But Russia stood firmly against UN resolutions on the Syrian regime, Syria being a close ally and a major market for Russian armaments. Towards the end of the year attitudes hardened, with much of the Russian foreign policy establishment appearing to believe that the "Arab Spring" was a Western-designed policy to reshape the region, and Putin alleging that the Russian protests of December were funded by the USA. In November, Putin presented a programme for a "Eurasian Union", a regional bloc, led by Russia, which would be "capable of becoming a pole of the modern world". The customs union between Russia, Belarus, and Kazakhstan was a start to this, although Ukraine's refusal to join made it fairly pointless. Russia did finally complete negotiations to join the WTO, however, after Georgia's objections were overcome.

A level of co-operation with NATO continued through the NATO-Russia Council, specifically involving joint military exercises, anti-piracy measures off the Horn of Africa, and in Afghanistan, where Russia continued to render logistical support to the US-led coalition war effort. But Russia remained leery of the USA's plans for a missile defence system, or shield, supported by NATO. The previous scheme (devised by the George W. Bush administration), to which Russia had objected fiercely and which involved installations in Poland and the Czech Republic, had been scrapped, but the 2010 NATO Lisbon summit had announced plans for a new missile defence system, designed as defence against a potential missile attack from Iran and covering all NATO countries. For Russia, the scheme remained a threat to its national security with the potential to disrupt Russia's ability to defend itself against a nuclear strike. NATO offered Russia "co-operation" on the system, but consistently refused to give "legal guarantees", as Russia demanded, that the system would not be aimed at Russian territory. The issue was heavily politicised in Russia: shortly before the December elections, President Medvedev threatened that Russia might deploy missiles in Kaliningrad and, more seriously, that it could withdraw from the New START nuclear arms reduction treaty of 2010 (see AR 2011, pp. 554-61).

The year saw the deaths of Elena Bonner—human rights campaigner and the widow of Andrei Sakharov—and of Svetlana Alliluyeva, writer and the daughter of Josef Stalin (see Obituary). Another member of that generation, which had come of age in Stalin's Soviet Union, was the last Soviet president, Mikhail Gorbachev, who celebrated his 80th birthday on 2 March. Over the course of 2011 Gorbachev became more outspokenly critical, denouncing the political monopoly enjoyed by United Russia as "reminding me of the worst copy of the Communist Party" and saying that the "rich debauchery" of the Russian elite made him ashamed for the country.

Wholeheartedly supporting December's protesters, Gorbachev pointed out that it was the reforms he had instigated in the late 1980s in an attempt to revitalise civil society (perestroika and glasnost) that had enabled the freedoms currently enjoyed by Russia's citizens. "We created what people make use of now," he said, "Going to church, obtaining visas, surfing the net, or buying newspapers." Twenty years, almost to the day, since his own decision to resign as Soviet president, Gorbachev called on Putin to step down. "Circles and clans", he said, had formed around the prime minister after 12 years in power. Putin's resignation seemed highly unlikely, however, and most observers expected him to win the presidential elections—although possibly not outright. Nevertheless, with the return of popular engagement in Russian politics in 2011, change was possible at last.

Wendy Slater

UKRAINE—BELARUS—MOLDOVA

Ukraine

CAPITAL: Kyiv (Kiev)   AREA: 603,550 sq km   POPULATION: 45,870,700 ('10)
OFFICIAL LANGUAGE: Ukrainian
HEAD OF STATE: President Viktor Yanukovych (since Feb '10)
RULING PARTIES: Party of Regions (PRU)-led coalition
HEAD OF GOVERNMENT: Prime Minister Mykola Azarov (PRU) (since March '10)
DEMOCRACY INDEX: 6.30; 67th of 167   CORRUPTION INDEX: 2.3; 152nd of 183
CURRENCY: Hryvna (Dec '11 £1.00=UAH 12.56, US$1.00=UAH 8.01)
GNI PER CAPITA: US$3,010, Intl$6,560 at PPP ('10)

Belarus

CAPITAL: Minsk   AREA: 207,600 sq km   POPULATION: 9,490,500 ('10)
OFFICIAL LANGUAGES: Belarusian & Russian
HEAD OF STATE: President Alyaksandr Lukashenka (since July '94)
RULING PARTY: Non-party supporters of President Lukashenka
HEAD OF GOVERNMENT: Prime Minister Mikhail Myasnikovich (since Dec '10)
DEMOCRACY INDEX: 3.34; 130th of 167   CORRUPTION INDEX: 2.4; 143rd of 183
CURRENCY: Belarusian Rouble (Dec '11 £1.00=BYR 13,526, US$1.00=BYR 8,625)
GNI PER CAPITA: US$6,130, Intl$14,250 at PPP ('10)

Moldova

CAPITAL: Chisinau (Kishinev)   AREA: 33,840 sq km   POPULATION: 3,562,062 ('10)
OFFICIAL LANGUAGE: Moldovan
HEAD OF STATE: acting President Marian Lupu (PD) (since Dec '10)
RULING PARTIES: Alliance for European Integration (AIE) coalition
HEAD OF GOVERNMENT: Prime Minister Vladimir Filat (PLDM) (since Sept '09)
DEMOCRACY INDEX: 6.33; 65th of 167   CORRUPTION INDEX: 2.9; 112nd of 183
CURRENCY: Leu (Dec '11 £1.00=MDL 18.50, US$1.00=MDL 11.80)
GNI PER CAPITA: US$1,810, Intl$3,340 ('10)

IN **Ukraine**, the main story of 2011 was the trial and imprisonment of former prime minister and leader of the opposition, Yuliya Tymoshenko. The case against her involved charges of abuse of office relating to the 2009 gas contract she had negotiated with Russia as prime minister. In court, Tymoshenko remained defiant, denouncing the trial as a political case, motivated by her rival President Viktor Yanukovych. Her famous blond plaited hairstyle intact, she communicated with her supporters from the courtroom via social media as a nervous judge conducted proceedings. Her behaviour eventually resulted in her being sent to prison for contempt of court so that by the time of her closing statement on 29 September, she had spent 57 days in Kiev's notorious Lukyanivksa detention centre, prompting concerns for her health.

Tymoshenko was convicted of abuse of office on 11 October and sentenced to seven years in prison, a ban on political activity for three further years, and a fine of 1.5 billion hryvna (around $180 million)—the alleged cost to Ukraine's budget of the gas contract. The length of the prison term was symbolic: one year for every year that had passed since the "Orange Revolution" of 2004, when Tymoshenko had led the protests against the flawed election of Yanukovych, which ultimately denied him the presidency (see AR 2004, pp. 113-15). That Yanukovych was now back in power and ready to destroy Tymoshenko, however, was in large part a consequence of the infighting and mismanagement by the "Orange" forces, which had led to their electoral defeat in 2010.

The trial of Tymoshenko highlighted Ukraine's uneasy position between Europe and Russia. The negotiation of an association agreement between the EU and Ukraine continued all year, but to demonstrate their disapproval of the "selective prosecution of political opponents" EU leaders cancelled talks with Yanukovych scheduled for 20 October. They later made clear that they would delay ratification of the association agreement—which had finally been concluded in December—because of "the risks of politically motivated justice in Ukraine".

Whilst the Tymoshenko trial jeopardised closer ties with the EU, it also met with disapproval in Russia, because a guilty verdict called into question the gas deal that lay at the heart of the case. The Yanukovych government was seeking to reduce significantly the price that Ukraine was paying for Russian gas, without having to make further painful concessions, such as the sale of Ukraine's state energy company, Naftohaz Ukrainy, to Russian investors. (Ukraine had already achieved a rebate in the cost of its gas, in 2010, in exchange for extending the lease on Sevastopol for Russia's Black Sea Fleet.) Russia wanted closer ties with Ukraine. The prime minister, Vladimir Putin, was championing the idea of a "Eurasian Union"—a body that would make little sense without Ukraine—and Russia repeatedly tried to entice Ukraine, with the promise of lower gas prices, into joining the customs union that it had established with Belarus and Kazakhstan. Although Yanukovych tried to get into bed with both the EU and Russia, suggesting in April that Ukraine could sign an association agreement with the EU before the end of 2011 and also enter a special relationship with the Russia-led customs union "under the formula 3+1", he ended the year no closer to either partner.

In February Ukraine's Verkhovna Rada (unicameral legislature) endorsed a constitutional amendment that extended the legislative term from four to five years. This meant that the general election scheduled for March 2011 was postponed until July 2012 and would take place after the Euro 2012 football championship, which was to be hosted by Ukraine. With opposition leaders behind bars and a football-induced euphoria flooding the nation, Yanukovych's Party of Regions of Ukraine (PRU) expected to do well. Another charismatic opposition leader, the former interior minister, Yury Lutsenko, was also out of the running, remaining in detention throughout the year. Arrested in December 2010, he went on trial in May 2011 on charges of abuse of office that hinged upon relatively trivial incidents, such as arranging for the award of a pension to his driver. Like Tymoshenko, Lutsenko claimed that a motive of revenge lay behind his detention: as interior minister he had initiated prosecutions against various powerful members of Yanukovych's circle.

Nevertheless, there were signs towards the end of 2011 that the president's tactics might backfire. Opposition parties, including Tymoshenko's Fatherland and Lutsenko's People's Self-Defence, announced plans to merge forces and, although Tymoshenko's popularity ratings had not improved much as a result of her trial, an opinion poll in late 2011 suggested that she had seen a 3 per cent rise in voting intention (to around 16 per cent), whilst voting intention for Yanukovych had fallen back to around 13 per cent. Even in the heartland of his support in the east, there were signs that Yanukovych was losing ground. In Donetsk, veterans of the 1986 Chernobyl nuclear cleanup operation staged a hunger strike, in the open, as a protest against cuts in their pensions. Their action inspired similar solidarity protests elsewhere in Ukraine, particularly after one man, a pensioner with heart problems, died at the Donetsk camp on 27 November as police cleared the protest.

The Chernobyl veterans' protest took place as another nuclear disaster was evolving at the Fukushima plant in Japan, and as Ukraine marked the 25th anniversary of the Chernobyl accident, still the world's worst to date. In April, at an international donors' conference in Kiev, governments pledged $785 million to complete the construction of a "new shelter", made of steel, that was designed to contain the radioactive remains of reactor number 4 at Chernobyl for another century. The current concrete "sarcophagus" around the reactor was showing signs of decay. But the amount pledged was short of the $1.07 billion thought necessary to complete the new shelter.

As Yanukovych admitted at a cabinet meeting in November, very little progress was made during 2011 in the government's 2010-14 programme of economic reforms. Only half of the measures envisaged had been met, he said. Analysts tended to agree. So far, the tax reform had squeezed small businesses out of the market, pension reform had led to significant protests, and the administrative reform had largely failed to make the overblown bureaucracy more efficient. Corruption and tax evasion were corrosive. Appointing a new interior minister, Vitaly Zakharchenko, in November, Yanukovych hailed his previous experience as head of the tax service. The new minister would ensure, said the president, "that every criminal, who is robbing the country and the people of Ukraine, knows that this money will have to be paid back and big penalties will apply". Endemic public corruption was occasionally highlighted by the media. In February, for example, a scandal erupted over the interruption of food supplies to army conscripts, who had complained of having to subsist on dry rations. Television news showed the conscripts' mothers bringing food to their sons on army bases. It was believed that the defence ministry had been involved in kickbacks between catering companies and the army, which had come unstuck leaving conscripts short of rations.

A gloomy outlook then, for Ukraine, encapsulated by broadcaster Lyudmila Savchenko, in May during her regular live weather report. Savchenko, a well-known voice on Ukrainian radio, described the arrival of spring and current spell of good weather as "compensation for the disorder, lawlessness and injustice taking place in our country. It is incomprehensible," she said, "that anyone can dislike this paradise on Earth, this country, the Ukrainian people, so much that they treat it so badly." Tymoshenko hailed her as a heroine: Savchenko was taken off the air.

Some of those who had led the protests in **Belarus** of December 2010 against flawed presidential elections spent 2011 in prison. The victor in those elections, Alyaksandr Lukashenka, spent the year trying to secure a loan to prop up the country's failing economy.

Of around 700 arrests in connection with the protests, more than 40 people were charged and 28 of these were sentenced to prison terms. Seven of the rival candidates to Lukashenka in the elections were among those arrested. By the end of 2011, two of them—Andrei Sannikov, a former foreign minister, and Mikalai Statkevich—were serving prison sentences of five and six years respectively; Vladimir Neklyayev and Vital Rymashevski were serving suspended sentences; Dmitry Uss was imprisoned but received a presidential pardon in October; Ryhor Kastyusov was not, eventually, charged; and Ales Mikhalevich obtained political asylum in the Czech republic after his release in February from a Belarusian prison, where he claimed to have been tortured. There were other opposition leaders imprisoned for their political activities. They included the leader of the Young Front group, Dmitry Dashkevich, and a member of Sannikov's campaign team, Dmitry Bandarenka. Another activist, human rights campaigner Ales Byalyatski, was sent to prison for four-and-a-half years in the autumn on tax evasion charges. To the embarrassment of Poland, which had led efforts to support Belarusian civic groups, Byalyatski was jailed on the basis of financial evidence provided by Polish officials.

Belarus did obtain a $3 billion loan, spread over 10 years, from the Russia-led Eurasian Economic Community (EurAsEC) in June, but at the cost of privatising (in effect, selling to Russian businesses) some of the country's prime assets. The IMF in May, meanwhile, turned down requests for a $8 billion loan, saying that Belarus needed to focus on privatisation and reducing inflation. There was no sign of this: instead, the macroeconomic figures were dire, with the Belarusian rouble weakening significantly in the first half of the year and inflation rising rapidly, by around 34 per cent in the first half of the year, according to government figures issued on 29 June. The National Bank of Belarus (central bank) in October held a sale of office supplies and household goods—ranging from tapestries to a Soviet-era television set—which seemed to capture the desperate plight of the country's economy, although bank officials insisted that the sale was simply a means of offloading unwanted goods, to raise $16,000.

Rising inflation prompted some protests, over which the government backed down, freezing prices of staple foodstuffs for a month in the summer and reversing petrol price rises after motorists blocked streets in Minsk in June. Political protest, on the other hand, was met with harsh repression. Nevertheless, the tiny active opposition continued to look for ways around this, summoning people, via social media, to participate in "silent protests" where hand-clapping or co-ordinated ringing of mobile phones took the place of slogans and signs. These drew a disproportionate response from the security forces. The police presence at the Independence Day ceremony in Minsk on 3 July was so heavy—to pre-empt disruptive hand-clapping by the opposition—that even Lukashenka's supporters were afraid to applaud, and his speech was met with silence. Seeking to reduce the opportunity for legal protest, a surreal piece of law submitted in July sought to criminalise "the joint mass presence of people ... for a particular action or inaction".

In April a large explosion on the Minsk metro killed 15 people—12 at the scene and three later in hospital from their injuries. The bomb was a relatively sophisticated device, detonated by remote control as a train drew into the station and opened its doors. Yet the two men convicted of the bombing in November were young mechanics, whose convictions were based largely on their apparently forced confessions. This heightened suspicions that the bombing was an attempt by the security services to justify further repression and distract attention from a worsening economic situation. The two men were sentenced to death in November; Belarus was the only country in Europe still to carry out the death penalty.

In **Moldova**, the three-party Alliance for European Integration (AIE) coalition remained in government, with a cabinet reshuffle taking place in January; but it was still unable to get its candidate elected president. The AIE, with 59 seats, was just two votes short of the three-fifths majority in Parliament that was required, under the constitution, to elect a president. Moldova thus remained under the acting presidency of parliamentary speaker Marian Lupu (see AR 2011, p. 115).

With the defection in November of three prominent members of the opposition Communist Party of Moldova (PCM)—the largest single faction in Parliament—there was briefly hope that the deadlock could be broken. However, the defectors were not prepared to support the candidacy of Lupu and the AIE was unable to agree on a compromise candidate with the PCM. Thus, at the vote on 16 December, Lupu—the sole candidate—once again narrowly failed to muster the 61 votes necessary to secure election. The PCM retained a level of support in the country, winning a significant number of mayoral and local councillor posts in June's local elections, but not that of mayor of Chisinau, which was held by incumbent Dorin Chirtoaca of the Liberal Party (PL, a member of the AIE), who narrowly defeated the PCM challenger, Igor Dodon.

Under the energetic leadership of Iurie Lenaca, the deputy prime minister and minister of foreign affairs and European integration, Moldova pursued a vigorous campaign to improve its image and forge closer ties with the West. A brief visit by US Vice President Joe Biden on 11 March was hailed as a sign of US support, and in December the EU agreed to begin negotiations on a "deep and comprehensive free trade area" with Moldova. The economy grew by 6.7 per cent in the first three quarters of 2011, year-on-year, thanks to rising domestic consumption and increased exports.

There was some movement on the Transdniester issue, the disputed independence of the self-proclaimed "Transdniester Republic", a narrow strip of Moldovan territory lying between the Dniester river and the Ukrainian border, which survived largely on financial assistance from Russia. In June there was a meeting of the "five plus two" negotiators (Moldova and Transdniester; plus Russia and Ukraine as guarantors, the OSCE as mediator, and the EU and USA as observers). The key to resolution lay with Russia. A senior Russian diplomat, quoted by *Kommersant* newspaper in June, said that a solution should include both Moldova's neutrality (i.e. it could not join NATO), and its territorial integrity within the borders of the Soviet Moldovan republic (i.e. no independence for Transdniester).

Presidential elections in Transdniester at the end of the year brought a change of leadership and with it the faint possibility of a resolution. Russia had abandoned its support for the veteran president, Igor Smirnov, who had led the region to break away from Moldova in December 1991 and whose intransigence was the major impediment to reaching a settlement. Smirnov was eliminated from the contest in the first round on 11 December. The second round, on 26 December, was won by a young businessman and politician, Yevgeny Shevchuk, who had campaigned on a platform of fighting corruption and making links with Moldova easier for Transdniester's 500,000 inhabitants.

Wendy Slater

ARMENIA—GEORGIA—AZERBAIJAN

Armenia

CAPITAL: Yerevan   AREA: 29,800 sq km   POPULATION: 3,092,072 ('10)
OFFICIAL LANGUAGE: Armenian
HEAD OF STATE: President Serzh Sarkisian (HHK) (since April '08)
RULING PARTY: Republican Party of Armenia (HHK)-led coalition
HEAD OF GOVERNMENT: Prime Minister Tigran Sarkisian (HHK) (since April '08)
DEMOCRACY INDEX: 4.09; 109th of 167   CORRUPTION INDEX: 2.6; 129th of 183
CURRENCY: Armenian Dram (Dec '11 £1.00=AMD 595.93, US$1.00=AMD 380.00)
GNI PER CAPITA: US$3,090, Intl$5,450 at PPP ('10)

Georgia

CAPITAL: Tbilisi   AREA: 69,700 sq km   POPULATION: 4,452,800 ('10)
OFFICIAL LANGUAGE: Georgian
HEAD OF STATE: President Mikheil Saakashvili (ENM) (since Jan '04)
RULING PARTY: United National Movement (ENM)
HEAD OF GOVERNMENT: Prime Minister Nika Gilauri (ind) (since Feb '09)
DEMOCRACY INDEX: 4.59; 103rd of 167   CORRUPTION INDEX: 4.1; 64th of 183
CURRENCY: Lari (Dec '11 £1.00=GEL 2.60, US$1.00=GEL 1.66)
GNI PER CAPITA: US$2,690, Intl$4,960 at PPP ('10)

Azerbaijan

CAPITAL: Baku   AREA: 86,600 sq km   POPULATION: 9,047,932 ('10)
OFFICIAL LANGUAGE: Azeri
HEAD OF STATE: President Ilham Aliev (YAP) (since Oct '03)
RULING PARTY: New Azerbaijan Party (YAP)
HEAD OF GOVERNMENT: Prime Minister Artur Rasizade (YAP) (since July '96)
DEMOCRACY INDEX: 3.15; 135th of 167   CORRUPTION INDEX: 2.4; 143rd of 183
CURRENCY: New Manat (Dec '11 £1=AZN 1.23, US$1=AZN 0.78)
GNI PER CAPITA: US$5,080, Intl$9,050 at PPP ('10)

THE prospect of legislative elections in Armenia and Georgia in 2012 set in motion intensive political manoeuvring in both countries.

Inspired by the revolutions in Tunisia and Egypt, the opposition **Armenian National Congress (HAK)**, a group of some two dozen extra-parliamentary parties headed by former President Levon Ter-Petrossian, launched in late February a series of mass protests to demand early elections and the release of jailed opposition supporters, including journalist Nikol Pashinian. President Serzh Sarkisian agreed to the latter demand. Selected officials embarked in July on a dialogue with the HAK that the latter broke off in late August in protest at the detention for hooliganism of one of its youth activists. Ter-Petrossian convened further protests in September and October to call for Sarkisian's resignation.

Then, on 25 November, Ter-Petrossian raised the possibility of co-operation with the Prosperous Armenia Party (BH) if it quit the ruling three-party coalition in which it was a junior partner. BH, together with Orinats Yerkir (Law-Based State) and Sarkisian's Republican Party of Armenia (HHK), had signed a memorandum on 17 February pledging not to compete against each other in the May 2012 legislative elections and to back Sarkisian for a second term in the presidential elections the following year. But in early October BH chairman Gagik Tsarukian declined to reaffirm his support for a second Sarkisian term and hinted that BH might participate independently in the legislative ballot.

Sarkisian repeatedly pledged that the May 2012 elections to the National Assembly (legislature) would be free and fair, but rejected in late December a proposal by the HAK and the opposition Zharangutiun (Heritage) party and the Armenian Revolutionary Federation-Dashnaktsutiun for fundamental changes in the election law.

The dismissals of the mayor of Yerevan, Karen Karapetian, in late October and of the president of the National Assembly, Hovik Abrahamian, in mid-November were widely construed as a bid by Sarkisian to sideline allies of his predecessor as president, Robert Kocharian, who had hinted in September that he would again run for president in 2013.

Economic recovery speeded up. GDP growth in 2011 was estimated at 4.6 per cent, compared with 2.4 per cent in 2010. Exports rose by 31 per cent, but the country's foreign debt grew by 6.6 per cent to $3.5 billion.

Azerbaijan's Civic Movement for Democracy-Public Chamber (GDDOP), established in December 2010 by prominent opposition politicians, drafted and unveiled in late May for public discussion a "road map" for gradual transition to democracy. But the authorities rejected as irrelevant and unnecessary both that draft and a similar document prepared by the Forum of the Intelligentsia. The Public Chamber also organised four protest demonstrations in March-May to demand democratic reforms. On every occasion, police intervened to disperse and arrest participants; 13 people were sent to prison in September and October for their role in the 2 April protest.

In early January, the leader of the unregistered Islamic Party of Azerbaijan (IPA), Movsum Samedov, and six other IPA members were arrested after Samedov publicly called for the overthrow of the country's leadership. They were sentenced in October to between 10 and 12 years' imprisonment on charges of planning a terrorist act and plotting a coup.

Two singers from Azerbaijan won the 2011 Eurovision Song Contest in mid-May, securing for Azerbaijan the right to host the contest in 2012. Later that month, President Ilham Aliyev included imprisoned journalist Eynulla Fatullayev in a list of persons pardoned and released in an amnesty to mark the 1918 declaration of the Azerbaijan Democratic Republic. Djabbar Savalan, a young blogger sentenced on 4 May on apparently fabricated drugs charges, was pardoned and released from jail on 26 December. Pressure on the media continued, however; Avaz Zeynalov, editor of the independent newspaper *Khural*, was arrested on 27 October and charged with extortion and accepting a huge bribe.

Exiled former President Ayaz Mutalibov, the first leader of independent Azerbaijan (1991-92), was allowed to visit Baku in September to attend his son's funeral.

Azerbaijan's economy stagnated, with GDP growth at 0.2 per cent. The country signed agreements with Turkey on 26 October and 26 December on the export to Europe via a Trans-Anatolia pipeline of natural gas from Azerbaijan's Shah Deniz field, beginning in 2017.

In **Georgia**, eight moderate opposition parties continued talks with the authorities but failed to reach consensus on a new election law that would create a level playing field for all participating parties. Two of those parties agreed in late June to minor changes proposed by the authorities. Ignoring key recommendations by the OSCE's Office for Democratic Institutions and Human Rights (ODIHR) and the Council of Europe, the Parliament in late December adopted a new election code that did not guarantee equality of suffrage.

Seven, more radical opposition parties, aligned in the People's Representative Assembly headed by former Parliament speaker Nino Burjanadze, launched a protest demonstration in central Tbilisi on 21 May, which police and security personnel dispersed by force early on 26 May. Four people died. The authorities claimed that two of them were hit by a car driven by Burjanadze's husband Badri Bitsadze, who was sentenced in absentia to five-and-a-half years' imprisonment.

In mid-October, billionaire philanthropist Bidzina Ivanishvili announced his intention of entering politics and winning the parliamentary election due in October 2012. Three moderate political groups aligned themselves with Ivanishvili and established a new movement, to be named Georgian Dream. The Georgian authorities retaliated to the perceived threat that the movement posed by revoking Ivanishvili's Georgian citizenship, pressuring his Cartu Bank, and passing, on 28 December, legislation barring legal entities from funding political parties.

Georgia registered 6.5 per cent GDP growth, but its gross foreign debt mushroomed to $10.8 billion.

REGIONAL AND INTERNATIONAL RELATIONS. Following talks in Sochi on 5 March hosted by Russia's President Dmitry Medvedev, hopes were raised that Presidents Aliyev and Sarkisian would finally sign, at a meeting in Kazan (Russia) on 24 June, the Basic Principles for resolving the Nagorno-Karabakh conflict drafted by the OSCE's Minsk Group, but they did not. Each side blamed the other for the failure to come to an agreement.

Four rounds of talks in Geneva co-chaired by the USA , the UN, the EU and the OSCE failed to resolve security and human rights problems created by the 2008 Georgian-Russian war, and the subsequent recognition by Russia as independent states of Georgia's separatist regions of Abkhazia and South Ossetia (see AR 2009, pp. 136-38).

Both those regions experienced changes in leadership in 2011. De facto Abkhaz President Sergei Bagapsh died suddenly on 29 May following lung surgery. The former vice president, Aleksandr Ankvab, was elected on 26 August to succeed him.

Seventeen candidates registered for the 13 November presidential election in South Ossetia, of whom six withdrew before the first round of voting, which proved inconclusive. Initial returns indicated that the opposition candidate and former education minister, Alla Djioyeva, had defeated Russia's preferred candidate, the emergency situations minister, Anatoly Bibilov, in the 27 November run-off, with 57 per cent of the vote. But the republic's Supreme Court annulled the results, adducing alleged violations by Djioyeva's campaign staff, and scheduled a repeat vote for 25 March, 2012. Mass protests by Djioyeva's supporters ended after she and outgoing President Eduard Kokoity signed an agreement on 10 December, under which Kokoity stepped down, Vadim Brovtsev took over as acting president, and the rerun elections would go ahead in March.

The EU formally agreed in December to begin talks on a visa-facilitation agreement with Armenia, and on a comprehensive free trade agreement with Georgia. Also in December, Armenia and Azerbaijan signed further Individual Partnership Actions Plans (IPAP) with NATO.

Turkey's Grand National Assembly (legislature) put back on its agenda in September ratification of the 2009 protocols on establishing formal relations with Armenia, but rapprochement was unlikely following the 22 December vote by the lower chamber of the French Parliament that designated a crime denial of the 1915 genocide of Armenians in the Ottoman Empire.

Azerbaijan stepped up defence co-operation with Turkey, but also embarked in August on talks with Russia on terms for renewing the latter's long-term lease of the Gabala radar station. In May, Azerbaijan acceded to the Non-Aligned Movement, and was elected a non-permanent member of the UN Security Council on 28 October.

Georgia's foreign policy remained focused on inflicting the maximum embarrassment on Russia. In May, the Georgian Parliament voted to designate as genocide the killing by Tsarist Russian forces in 1864 of tens of thousands of Circassians. (The Russian State Duma, the lower chamber of the legislature, had rejected in January 2006 a request by a public organisation in Russia's Republic of Adygeia to condemn the killings as genocide.) On 7 July, three Georgian photojournalists and the wife of one of them were arrested in Tbilisi and charged with spying for Russia. Two of them had circulated pictures of the 26 May police crackdown on the opposition protest. All four were released two weeks later following a plea-bargaining agreement.

In early November, Georgia ended its long-standing veto on Russia's accession to the WTO and accepted a Swiss-mediated proposal that met its demands for customs control over the flow of goods to and from its separatist territories of Abkhazia and South Ossetia.

Liz Fuller

IV THE AMERICAS AND THE CARIBBEAN

UNITED STATES OF AMERICA

CAPITAL: Washington, DC AREA: 9,632,030 sq km POPULATION: 309,050,816 ('10)
OFFICIAL LANGUAGES: English (de facto); Spanish widely used
HEAD OF STATE AND GOVERNMENT: Barack Obama (Democrat) (since Jan '09)
RULING PARTIES: Democrats control presidency and Senate; Republicans control House of
    Representatives
DEMOCRACY INDEX: 8.18; 17th of 167 CORRUPTION INDEX: 7.1; 24th of 183
CURRENCY: US Dollar (Dec '11 £1.00=USD 1.57)
GNI PER CAPITA: US$47,240, Intl$47,120 at PPP ('10)

IN 2011, the USA's slow recovery from the great recession of 2008 dominated domestic affairs, with much of the nation's political life revolving around questions of what governments should and should not to do assist the process. The contest to find the Republican Party candidate who would challenge President Barack Obama in the 2012 presidential election got under way. Abroad, the USA finally eliminated Osama bin Laden (see Obituary) and completed the withdrawal of its armed forces from Iraq, while the phenomenon called the "Arab Spring" offered the USA further lessons in the possibilities and limits of projecting US power into the lives of other nations and peoples. Near year's end a seemingly undaunted President Obama announced in Australia that the Asia-Pacific region could expect increased care and attention from the United States now that its current wars were winding down.

The year in politics got off to a shocking start in early January, when a young man called Jared Loughner shot 19 people outside a Safeway supermarket in Tucson, Arizona, killing six. The dead included John Rolls, a federal judge and Christina Taylor Green, aged nine. Both had come by to see Congresswoman Gabrielle Giffords, who was holding a "Congress on your Corner" event. Giffords was among the injured, critically wounded by a shot to the head from close range as she chatted with constituents from Arizona's eighth congressional district. Loughner was eventually disarmed by bystanders as he attempted to load another 33-round ammunition clip into his Glock 19 handgun. Their brave actions almost certainly saved further bloodshed. Giffords's gradual partial recovery from her severe brain injury would be one of the year's happier stories. Loughner was diagnosed as a schizophrenic, declared unfit to stand trial, and remanded to a federal medical facility for prisoners in Springfield, Missouri. Following the shooting, sales of the $500 Glock 19 doubled at Tucson's two Glockmeister stores and increased 5 per cent nationwide.

Another predictable response to the massacre was a heated but short-lived debate on gun control laws. The points made were familiar enough. Advocates for stricter laws noted that the same gun and clip had been among the weapons used by Seung-Hui Cho when he killed 32 people at Virginia Tech in April 2007. Attention was drawn to the high-capacity clip that had once been illegal under a federal law banning assault weapons which had been allowed to expire in 2004. What, gun control advocates asked, could justify allowing a member of the public to possess such a lethal tool? Responses to this argument were equally familiar, with gun rights advocates claiming, among other things, that gun control only prevented the law-abiding and not the criminals from possessing weapons. This left unanswered the matter of those who, like Loughner, only became criminals by using them.

Layered on top of this familiar back-and-forth exchange was the question of whether the violent rhetoric and imagery of contemporary political discourse might also have influenced events. Giffords was one of several Democratic politicians whose constituency offices had been vandalised in 2010 after they voted to support health insurance reform. Sarah Palin—a star of the right-wing of the Republican Party and a vehement advocate of gun ownership—was criticised for her Facebook posting of a map of the Democratic-held districts that Republicans should target in elections. Each district, including that of Giffords, was illustrated with the crosshairs of a gun sight. Palin responded by offering her own condemnation of the gunman and of those "journalists and pundits" who she claimed were using this "shocking tragedy" to "manufacture a blood libel" against her. (Her use of the latter term, the historical significance of which seemed unknown to her, was a cause for further criticism.) Nevertheless, Loughner's madness made it hard to draw connections between his actions and the environment of simplistic and impolite invective that passed for so much political discussion. Indeed, the simplistic linking of these two worrying social phenomena—gun violence and the nasty and vacuous nature of US political discourse—itself proved to be little more than an example of the nasty and vacuous nature of political discourse.

After the initial shock of the Tucson attack had passed, calls for greater civility in politics soon gave way to the familiar sounds of partisan conflict. A peculiar corollary seemed to be at work: the more serious the issue the more simplistic the debate. While economics and politics could never be disentangled, it seemed that in 2011 economic matters had become politicised to an unusual degree. Emblematic of this was the conflict over raising the federal debt-ceiling. In April, the 2011 federal budget was passed by both the House (260-167 votes) and the Senate (81-19 votes), and signed into law by Obama. The budget projected a deficit for the year of over $1.5 trillion. This meant that the current debt ceiling would be reached during this fiscal year, probably in August. This required, in turn, that the ceiling be raised so that the federal government could borrow enough money to meet such obligations as funding programmes, paying government workers, and servicing the nation's debts. Such increases had been approved an average of once per year since 1980, including 17 times during the administration of President Ronald Reagan. When Reagan had taken office in 1981 the national debt was less than $1 trillion. It tripled under his stewardship and had continued to grow since. It almost doubled during George W. Bush's administration to nearly $11.5 trillion. Increases did not go through without some politicking, usually by opposition politicians looking to make a point about the majority's fiscal profligacy. Senator Barack Obama had voted against an increase in 2006. But they usually passed in a routine and uncontroversial fashion—the bipartisan assumption being that it was irresponsible to risk "the good faith and credit of the United States" by causing the federal government to default on its debts or fail to meet its other obligations.

Under Obama the debt limit had already been raised three times, most recently being in February 2010 when it had increased by $1.9 trillion to $14.3 trillion. When this new ceiling was reached in May, Secretary of the Treasury Timothy Geithner took "extraordinary measures" to extend the effective deadline to early August. The administration's request for a $2.4 trillion increase was rejected by the Republicans, now in the majority in the House of Representatives. They refused to approve the increase needed to pay for a budget (that many of them had already voted for) unless it was tied to equivalent cuts in future expenditures. Thus began several months of bitter negotiations.

In April, the Republican-controlled House passed a federal budget bill for 2012, which proposed reducing spending by about $6 trillion over the next decade. A controversial element of this bill—sometimes called the Ryan Plan, after Paul Ryan, the Wisconsin congressman who had a lead role in writing it— was its impact on Medicare, the government healthcare programme for retired people. Ryan and his colleagues argued that radical change was necessary to make Medicare solvent in the longer term. Critics insisted that enacting the proposals would effectively eliminate Medicare—under which medical costs were paid directly by the government—by replacing it with a system in which the government would subsidise seniors' purchase of private health insurance. The bill had no chance of success in the Democratic-controlled Senate, no doubt something taken into account by many House Republicans when they cast affirmative votes for the dismantling of a widely popular programme. Democrats expressed surprise that so many Republicans would have even put themselves on the record in favour of "ending Medicare as we know it." Republicans in turn chided their Democratic opponents for "frightening seniors" and ignoring the government's dire fiscal circumstances.

Various sets of negotiations were conducted, none of which came to anything. The negotiations between President Obama and John Boehner, the speaker of the House, received most attention, with talk of a "grand bargain" which would raise the debt limit while also approving spending cuts and revenue increases that would save at least $4 trillion over the next decade. Rumoured elements included cuts to Medicaid, Medicare, and Social Security and approximately $1 trillion in tax increases. Details that emerged suggested that about three quarters of the reduction would be achieved through cuts and about one quarter through increased revenues. Reports that Obama was prepared to consider cuts to the social safety net greatly troubled many in his own party. On the Republican side, it became clear that, even if Boehner was prepared to compromise on a plan that included tax increases, many in his party were not. Scepticism intensified that the "grand bargain" was simply not achievable, with suspicions on both sides high that the other either could not deliver or was merely seeking a public relations advantage.

After all the talk and bluster, accusation and counter-accusation, a last-minute and far from "grand" deal was announced on 31 July by Obama and Boehner, at separate events. The following day the House passed the bill with a cross-party vote of 269 to 161 and on 2 August, the day the limit was to be reached, the Senate approved it 74 to 26 and President Obama signed it into law. Putting a positive spin on the outcome, the president insisted that it was an "important first step to ensuring that as a nation we live within our means." The markets appeared not to agree. On 5 August the mysteriously influential and far from infallible Standard & Poor's credit-rating company lowered the USA's rating from AAA to AA+.

The deal delayed a more serious and longer-lasting decision. The legislation created a cross-party "super committee" charged with formulating a plan to reduce spending. To concentrate the committee's mind, the legislation also called for across-the-board cuts, including to defence spending, to be implemented should it fail to reach agreement on targeted cuts. Any plan proposed by the committee was to be given a straight vote in the House and Senate, with no amendments allowed. Many were unhappy with this arrangement, seeing it as a dereliction of duty and perhaps even unconstitutional. The committee's work would prove less than super, its members replicating in miniature the impasses evident in Congress as a whole. After announcing that they would not be able to reach agreement its members moved on to the nearest television camera to begin blaming each other for the failure.

A final episode of brinksmanship ended the year with disagreements on whether a temporary reduction in the payroll tax should be extended for another year. This tax, intended to fund Social Security, was paid by all people in employment and so an estimated 160 million workers would benefit from the extension. Unusually for them, many Republicans opposed extending this particular tax break because, they claimed, this was a dedicated tax and to extend the cut would be to undermine Social Security. They insisted that it should be paid for by an equivalent amount in spending cuts. Critics were not slow to point out that the Republicans had not opposed any other tax cuts and indeed had opposed even the closing of some tax loopholes as a way to increase revenue. Nor, the Democrats insisted, had they expressed any desire in the past to pay for tax cuts with equivalent cuts. Eventually a two-month extension passed, but only after much opposition from House Republicans, meaning that the issue would have to be revisited when Congress reconvened in 2012. By year's end, polls showed a mere 11 per cent of respondents holding a favourable view of Congress.

Differences seemingly beyond negotiation were also much in evidence in the states, which saw some of the year's most fundamental and controversial political and economic conflicts. After the 2010 elections, Republicans occupied 29 of 50 governorships and had also made strong gains in state House and Senate races, including in so-called "battleground" or swing states such as Michigan, Wisconsin and Ohio. Many Republican victors quickly got down to implementing policies that seemed to have little to do with the biggest issue on which they ran: job creation. Instead, they introduced a range of laws that critics contended had another connecting theme: limiting the political rights and influence of various groups in society which traditionally inclined towards the Democratic Party at election time.

Wisconsin and Ohio introduced legislation that seriously curtailed the collective-bargaining rights of public sector unions. In Wisconsin, Governor Scott Walker and the Republican-controlled House and Senate passed legislation they claimed was essential to addressing a budget shortfall of almost $140 million for the year. Critics dismissed the legislation as blatant union-busting, especially since public sector unions had already agreed to proposed cuts in benefits and pensions. That the Republicans had also passed tax incentives for businesses— projected to add about $120 million to the deficit in future years—also aroused suspicions that the anti-bargaining measures were not about fiscal stability. The legislation prompted a dramatic series of events. In Wisconsin, mass protests, sometimes in the tens of thousands, were held against the legislation. At one point all the Democratic state senators not only refused to attend the legislature, thus denying it a quorum, but left the state altogether in case a way could be found to compel them to attend. Eventually the Republican majority pushed through the legislation. A lower court upheld a challenge to its legality due to the way in which it had been passed, but was eventually over-ruled by the Wisconsin supreme court. The protests did not end with the passage of the legislation. A movement began to recall Governor Walker and several of the state senators who had supported it. The recall process specified that a particular number of signatures be gathered in support of an election's result being "recalled". The official recalled would then be required to run again in a special election. Of the six Republican senators whose elections were recalled, two lost at the new elections and four retained their seats. By year's end, recall supporters had gathered over half a million signatures, with a total of 540,000 required by the 17 January deadline, for the recall of Walker.

Similar legislation was passed in Ohio, under newly elected Governor John Kasich. The law was not implemented pending a public referendum triggered after a sufficient number of voters had petitioned for it. In the referendum, Ohioans voted 69 per cent to 31 per cent to reject the legislation, a striking victory for the union movement and a severe defeat for Kasich. These state-level battles offered microcosms of nationwide conflicts. In Wisconsin, for example, the national labour movement offered strong financial and logistical support to opponents of the legislation. For their part, Governor Walker and his fellow Republicans received millions of dollars in support, through pro-legislation advertising for example, from leading right-wing individuals and groups such as the Koch Foundation of businessmen David and Charles Koch.

Another focus in Republican-controlled states was the voting system. By year's end, 22 states had passed or proposed legislation to "reform" voting practices. The stated reason was to reduce voter fraud, although proponents of the laws struggled to offer evidence that this was actually a problem, especially when balanced against the cost of reform and the potential for making electoral participation more difficult for large numbers of citizens. Critics countered that what it was really intended to do was reduce the threat of Democratic election victories. The common thread in the various reform efforts was that they would make it disproportionately more difficult for certain groups both to register to vote and to cast a vote, groups that tended to favour the Democrats. The two most common proposals would place greater restrictions on how citizens could be registered as voters and on how voters could prove their identity at polling stations. In Florida, for example, new laws significantly increased the reporting requirements associated with voter registration, adding legal penalties for registration volunteers failing to meet them. Historically, many groups—from black churches to the Boy Scouts, trade unions to the League of Women Voters—had conducted voter registration drives. The Florida Branch of The League of Women Voters found the new restrictions so onerous that they suspended their voter registration programme pending court challenges to the new laws. It was estimated that, in Florida, twice the number of people from minority groups as from the white population registered to vote through such drives.

Several states introduced more restrictive laws defining what constituted acceptable forms of voter identification. Texas and South Carolina, for example, proposed making a government-issued form of picture identification compulsory. In Texas, for example, whereas a government-issued concealed weapons permit would be acceptable, a student ID card, even from a public college or university, would not. While little evidence existed to suggest that voter impersonation was at all common, it was estimated that new rules would adversely affect as much as 11 per cent of eligible voters. Those who did not have such identification would effectively be disenfranchised unless they paid to purchase a government ID card. The people most likely not to have the most common form of government ID, a state driving licence, were the poor, particularly elderly poor people, and those groups within which the poor were disproportionately represented, most notably African Americans and Latinos. Young people too were less likely to have an acceptable form of identification, and within that group, poor and minority young people were as much as twice as likely not to have a driver's licence as were white college-age citizens. In turn, these groups were often less likely to have the kinds of identification, such as birth certificates, required to get appropriate government photo identification. Given the egregious histories of these states in matters of voting rights and minority groups, the laws in Texas and Florida, as well as similar legislation in South Carolina, had to be approved by the justice department in Washington, DC, as having neither discriminatory purposes nor effects. In December the justice department rejected the South Carolina law, noting that the state's own data showed "that non-white voters are both significantly burdened" by the law and "disproportionately unlikely to possess the most common types of photo identification." South Carolina announced its intention to fight the decision.

As established political processes seemed ever more stagnant and political leaders at state and federal level were perceived to be either deaf to public opinion or intent on limiting its expression, the year saw a rise in people seeking alternative means to make their voices heard and to achieve the kinds of political action they wanted. The protests in Wisconsin and Ohio were examples of this. Nationwide, the most prominent series of protests came in the form of the Occupy movement, itself inspired in part by the mass protests taking place in the Middle East. The Occupy movement began in September as the Occupy Wall Street movement, a deliberately diffuse and eclectic movement which set itself up in Manhattan's Zuccotti Park, close to the financial district. Its broad aim was to protest against the greed and corruption of big banks and corporations and of the nation's wealthiest people. A further source of discontent was the government's failure to bring any of these entities or individuals to legal account for their role in the financial collapse of 2008 or to sufficiently reform the financial system. For this, and other reasons, many of the protestors were at best sceptical of the Obama administration and almost all appeared determined to resist Democratic efforts to co-opt their movement in the way the Republican Party and wealthy and influential conservatives had done with much of the right-wing Tea Party movement. The Occupy movement spread to cities such as Boston, Oakland and San Francisco, and to many of the country's higher education campuses. In various cities, the authorities eventually cleared the protesters' encampments, sometimes using unnecessarily violent and destructive methods, sometimes with a reasonable degree of cooperation between protesters, police, and politicians.

An overarching concern of this eclectic movement was the extreme and growing income inequality that characterised US society; an issue eventually picked up on by the nation's media, albeit with all the tentative wonder of a child only just discovering that unicorns might actually exist. The USA, according to World Bank data, had higher income inequality than most other developed countries. The inequalities were also growing more rapidly in the USA as globalisation squeezed the middle class, as it was doing elsewhere, but without the fall-back of a more developed social structure—such as universal health care and public sector services—that helped to insulate people from such changes in most other wealthy economies. There was certainly much to question. In 1980, the average CEO compensation had been approximately 40 times that of the average worker's salary. Now that figure was well over 1,000 times greater. Dissatisfaction with such disparities in wealth and power gave rise to the protest slogan "We are the 99 per cent." The slogan reflected the striking statistic that 40 per cent of the nation's wealth was concentrated in the hands of 1 per cent of its families. Further, it spoke to the many kinds of inequities and imbalances of power and influence that followed from such concentrations of wealth.

While it could charitably be viewed as an attempt at solidarity and inclusion, albeit at the expense of the country's plutocrats, the slogan (and the thinking behind it) obscured more than it illuminated. In the early days of the twenty-first century it was also the case that the top 10 per cent owned over 70 per cent of the nation's wealth compared to less than 5 per cent for the bottom 10 per cent. Could the more than 20 per cent of the nation's children growing up in poverty really be so easily accommodated under the 99 per cent umbrella alongside the students leaving elite universities with large debts but also a prestigious diploma? Were their respective problems really susceptible to the same kinds of solutions? After all, millions of poor people had been with the USA for over a century. Masses of irate university graduates yearning to be employed at higher salaries than the ones currently on offer were a relatively new phenomenon. As winter hardened and the year drew to a close it remained an open question just how long the movement would last and how long-lasting would be its impact on the conduct of the nation's economy and politics.

Given that the roots of the recession had been so entangled in the housing market, and so much of its direct impact felt by the hundreds of thousands of individuals and families who lost their homes as a result of it, government efforts to address this core issue were not as strong or as wide-ranging as might have been expected. Perhaps, the very depth and complexity of the problem explained this neglect. Whatever the case, neither Congress nor President Obama seemed inclined to make it a priority. Data suggested that, unlike the first great waves of foreclosures, which disproportionately affected people who were over-mortgaged relative to their resources, those losing their homes in 2011 were much more likely to be homeowners who had taken on reasonable obligations given their income but who had since been made unemployed.

By the end of the year there was some brighter news on unemployment. The official unemployment rate began the year at 9 per cent and after briefly dropping below that mark spent the rest of it just above nine. It fell in November and again in December, reaching 8.5 per cent, the lowest rate since November 2009. Understanding the meaning of these numbers was made more complicated by the fact that any decline was a consequence both of people finding jobs and people giving up looking for one. By some estimates, taking into account all people without a job who wanted one as well as those in part-time work only because they could not find full-time work, the "real" rate was over 15 per cent. Nevertheless, the December figure, combined with an unexpectedly high number of newly created jobs—200,000—was generally greeted as an encouraging indicator of further economic recovery.

While there had been a strong consensus that the economic recession of 2008 was the deepest since the Great Depression, there appeared to be little patience for the idea that it might take correspondingly longer to climb out of it. "Where are the jobs?" was a handy slogan for Republicans to aim at the White House, or for the Democrats to aim at the Republicans since the latter had regained the House in 2010. For those individuals and communities who asked that question for real, its use as just one more device in the rhetorical game was one more reason to be struck, and infuriated, by the gulf between discourse in Washington DC and the facts on the ground elsewhere in the country. The pervasive public disillusionment with the nation's political leaders was entwined with widespread worries about the country's economy. A global context of uncertain revolution in much of the Middle East and of chronic financial crises in much of Europe only deepened fears, not only that the USA was in trouble but also that its ability to recover was increasingly not within its own power to control.

No doubt many of those worried about these matters looked to the ongoing campaign for the 2012 Republican presidential nomination for reassuring signs of the coming restoration of the greatness that the USA was supposedly losing. On 4 April President Obama declared his intention to run for a second term, and pretty much started doing so immediately. There were some murmurings on the Left about running a candidate against him in the primaries, such was the feeling among many self-described "progressives" that Obama's emphasis on bringing transformational change to the nation's Capitol had long given way to a compromising approach which meekly surrendered too much ground to the Republicans and was far too timid in confronting the continuing power of big business and the banks. These came to nothing, however, and attention focused on the fight on the Right.

There were several features of the Republican campaign which, taken together, distinguished it somewhat from past races. One factor was the widespread dissatisfaction with the putative front-runner, Willard Mitt Romney. The former governor of Massachusetts and self-proclaimed successful businessman had come second to Senator John McCain of Arizona in the 2008 nomination contest and had pretty much been campaigning ever since. Many of his supporters seemed unenthusiastic, however, and his opponents were outspoken as to his deficiencies. Fiscal conservatives, especially in the "Tea Party" faction, and social conservatives were particularly suspicious of Romney, convinced that he was not a genuine conservative. In "liberal" Massachusetts he had distanced himself from the economic policies of the Reagan years and had held moderate positions, at least by Republican standards, on core issues such as abortion and gay rights. Although Romney's views on these issues now reflected his party's orthodoxy, many conservatives refused to accept that he had undergone a genuine change of heart. Romney's record on healthcare also hurt him. As governor of Massachusetts he had overseen healthcare reform that had included provision for an individual mandate; that is for legally compelling those who could afford it to purchase health insurance. It was this very element of the Affordable Health Care for Americans Act—"Obamacare" to its critics—to which conservatives had taken such strong exception. With "electability" at a general election his strong suit and with a solid but uninspired support behind him, Romney's national poll numbers among Republicans remained remarkably consistent throughout the year, rarely moving in either direction beyond the 22-25 per cent range.

Following from this dissatisfaction with the frontrunner was a second major theme. Who would emerge as the "anyone-but-Romney" candidate? Could the race produce a consistent and resolute conservative capable of taking the fight to Obama in an energetic and inspiring fashion? A succession of pretenders stepped forward, each enjoying the proverbial 15 minutes in the spotlight before "getting the hook".

A third, not inconsequential, factor was that none of these challengers to Romney was electable in a general election. Even most Republicans seemed to think so. Indeed, several of the candidates themselves seemed to think so, even about themselves. For example, only Romney and Congressman Ron Paul of Texas had well-organised campaigns at the state level, with only those two gathering the required number of supporting signatures needed to even be on the ballot in Virginia.

A final factor was that an unprecedented number of nationally televised debates—a dozen or so—were conducted between May and December. By introducing a foible-laden field to a national audience, the debates played an unusually significant role in influencing voters' choices.

The importance of television and the Internet in shaping the campaign was also reflected in the amount of early attention lavished on two people who were not even running. One of them was Sarah Palin, who had become a prominent public celebrity since John McCain's extraordinary decision to make her his vice-presidential running mate in 2008. Those who speculated that Palin would not give up the lucrative business of being Sarah Palin for the serious work of running for office proved, eventually, to be correct. In any event, Palin's efforts seemed the mere posturing of an ingénue when compared to the veteran performance of Donald Trump, real estate developer and reality television show host. Trump, a man with an ironclad ego and, by general consent, one of the nation's most mysterious hairstyles, had made a quadrennial habit of declaring that he was giving serious consideration to running for the presidency. This time he supplemented the shameless touting of his business acumen and love of country with derogatory attacks on President Obama. Most notably, and with the assistance of a disdainful yet eager mainstream media, he breathed new life into the conspiratorial claims of the "birther movement": that Barack Obama had not been born in the USA. If this were true, Trump claimed, Obama's presidency would be the "greatest scam in the history of our country." A Gallup poll towards the end of April showed that one quarter of respondents believed that Obama was probably or definitely foreign-born. In April the president released the "long-form" version of his birth certificate, saying it was time to put an end to the "silliness". Trump declared himself "proud" of his efforts in having forced this revelation and hoped that the document was "real".

Trump's triumph was short-lived. At the Washington Correspondents' dinner soon afterwards, the president gave a speech worthy of a good stand-up comedian, ridiculing Trump's obsession with the birth certificate. With devastating humour Obama mocked Trump's pretentions to leadership, laughing at the kind of judgements that Trump was required to make on his reality TV show *The Apprentice*, each episode of which ended with Trump telling another contestant who had proved insufficiently entrepreneurial, "You're fired!" These were the kinds of decisions that would keep him up at night, joked Obama as a grumpy-looking Trump sat uncomfortably in the audience. When it emerged that the same weekend that Obama was taking out Trump he was up at night following the operation to take out Osama bin Laden, the contrast between a real politician and someone who just played one on television could not have been starker. Trump eventually declared in May that he would not be running for president. The new season of *The Apprentice* was announced the same day. While the speculation persisted, however, Trump showed strongly in the polls, ahead of most of the declared candidates. His popularity spoke to the powerful Republican desire for a candidate who would attack the president with no holds barred.

Trump's "boomlet" was the first of several enjoyed by a series of figures who raised brief expectations among the faithful that they might be "the one". Congresswoman Michelle Bachman of Minnesota, a social conservative and strong Tea Party supporter, was on the rise in August when she won the Iowa straw poll. Although the poll had no official standing it had taken on a certain importance over the years as a bellwether of voter intentions in the state which held the first caucus. Bachman hailed her victory as "the very first step toward taking back the White House." Yet what Bachman hailed as the light at the end of the dark tunnel of the Obama Years turned out instead to be the lights of an oncoming train called Governor Rick Perry of Texas. Perry entered the race the weekend of the straw poll. He was among several figures, including another sitting governor, the bullish and bullying governor of New Jersey, Chris Christie, who had been encouraged to get into the race by those who thought the field too lacklustre on the conservative side. As she was quickly replaced in the hearts of evangelicals and conservatives by the latest unsmooth talker from Texas, Bachman's chances melted as quickly as a honey-dipped, and deep-fried butter stick on a hot day at the Iowa state fair.

Enthusiasm for Perry proved almost as short-lived. Perry was a largely unknown quantity to most people beyond Texas. Even many of those who welcomed him to the race seemed to know little more about him than his reportedly strong job-creation record in Texas and his down-the-line correctness on issues of concern to social conservatives. In short he seemed to offer the blend of economic know-how, Christian conservative conviction, and electability for which voters on the right yearned. In his first debate appearance at the Reagan Presidential Library on 7 September, Perry won strong applause for his controversial claims that Social Security was both a fraudulent "Ponzi scheme" and a "monstrous lie to our kids", as well as for his record on capital punishment in Texas. Under Perry, 234 executions or, as he put it, acts of "ultimate justice", had been carried out. Those would prove to be the high points of his debate performances.

Even as polls and pundits established Perry as Romney's new challenger, a series of errors on and off the debate stage raised doubts about his preparedness. In one debate Perry stumbled through an attempted assault on Romney's "flip-flopping". The attack had clearly been rehearsed, just not well. Romney, in one of his better moments, responded simply "Nice try." In another debate he could not remember the third of the federal government departments that he had proudly announced he would make a priority of eliminating. Perry's "oops moment", as it came to be known, was viewed and re-viewed by millions on television and the Internet. Most damaging was that these and other "gaffes" came to be seen not as aberrant but as representative of a candidate and campaign that lacked energy, focus and seriousness. Perry fell as quickly as he had risen.

Two more frontrunners then, in turn, emerged. Both were from Georgia and both aroused strong suspicions at times that their campaigns were really an extended promotional event and book tour. That was where the similarities ended. First up was businessman Herman Cain. From early in his campaign conservative voters warmed to the former Pillsbury and Godfather's Pizza executive. They liked his "folksiness" and his claims to be a Washington outsider (despite his having spent several years as a Washington lobbyist as CEO of the National Restaurant Association—NRA). Part of Cain's attraction was the simplicity of his "problem-solver" approach and his insistence that the federal government should be run along business lines if it were to carry out efficiently the few tasks that Cain seemed inclined to leave to it. Especially appealing was his "9—9—9 plan", which called for a flat 9 per cent tax on personal and business incomes and the introduction of a national sales tax with a rate of, yes, 9 per cent. The fact that it was unworkable did not seem to deter the growing number of passengers hurrying to board what the candidate liked to call "The Cain Train". Cain showed himself to be spectacularly unversed in the recent politics and foreign policy of the nation he hoped to lead. He declared himself unfamiliar with the term neo-conservative; he appeared to be under the impression that China was still trying to acquire nuclear weapons; he insisted that abortions should be illegal *and* that it was ultimately a woman's choice whether or not to have one. The nadir was reached in an interview with the editorial board of the *Milwaukee Journal Sentinel* in which, in a response to a question on President Obama's Libya policy, Cain took five minutes to make it painfully clear that he knew little about the USA's involvement in overthrowing Kadhafi.

As long as Cain was merely impersonating a man who had not read a newspaper in quite some time, his astonishing ignorance did not seem to damage him much in the eyes of conservative voters. As Cain himself noted, the country needed "a leader not a reader". As Perry continued to plummet, Cain continued to rise, winning several non-binding straw polls, including one in Florida. By October he gained frontrunner status in the not-Romney stakes, and towards the end of that month he was even coming out ahead of the former Massachusetts governor in some polling. When substantiated reports emerged that two female employees had received cash settlements and left the NRA during his tenure, after bringing sexual harassment complaints against him, polls suggested that a fan base that despised the media even more than it liked him was sticking with Cain. Two other women came forward in November with tales of sexual harassment and although Cain adamantly denied their allegations, maintaining his claim that he was the victim of a "witch hunt", his support began to decline significantly. Later in the month another woman, Ginger White, emerged to claim a 13 year-long consensual affair with Cain. It proved to be the final blow and he withdrew from the race. He "suspended" his campaign on 3 December, vowing to continue the fight for the "solutions revolution" by opening a website instead.

From the carnage of the Cain Train's derailment stumbled Newt Gingrich, blinking into the sunlight of frontrunnership with almost as much surprise, but significantly more delight, as that felt by the many pundits and political enemies who had long ago written off his campaign. Gingrich had been a congressman from Georgia and had served as speaker of the House of Representatives from 1995 to 1999. In the 1994 elections he had led in accomplishing something the Republicans had not done in 40 years: win a majority in the House. Gingrich had later been forced to resign over ethics violations, and by the end of his time in leadership even most Republicans had wearied of his style and methods, a fact suggested by how few of them now supported his presidential run. In subsequent years Gingrich had focused his energies on book-writing and film-making, often of a supposedly historical nature, and on his Washington consulting and lobbying firm.

With little in the way of an organised campaign structure, Gingrich nevertheless came to the front of the anti-Romney pack towards the end of the year. His success was attributed to his sharp-tongued debate performances. Gingrich avoided criticising his fellow presidential contestants, instead focusing his disdain on the incumbent—"the best food stamps president the country has ever had"—and, at times, on the debate moderators and what he saw, not entirely without reason, as the vacuity of their questioning. Here were two targets guaranteed to please the Right. Barely pausing to reflect on how they had so recently got it all wrong about Gingrich the media now chalked up his success to voters' belief that here at last was someone with the intellect and belligerence, even nastiness, to beat up President Obama in the debates. Gingrich agreed, repeatedly insisting that he would challenge the president to seven three-hour "Lincoln-Douglas style" debates. It was difficult to tell where Gingrich's optimism was most misplaced: his hope that the president would ever accept such an offer or his assumption that there were many people left in the USA who knew what the Lincoln-Douglas debates were.

For those in the Republican establishment who cared about picking someone who could win the election rather than just the debates, Gingrich's rise, coming so close to the first votes, created something close to panic. Republican grandees took to the airwaves to dismiss his chances, telling tales of his erratic and confrontational ways. In this respect, Gingrich's rise may have helped Romney by pushing many previously prevaricating leaders more decisively into his camp and by pushing Romney to adopt a more open and aggressive campaign style. A Romney-supporting political action committee (PAC) called Restore Our Future flooded the airwaves of Iowa with over $3 million worth of advertisements attacking Gingrich (a huge sum for that lightly populated state). Restore Our Future was a new kind of PAC made possible by the Supreme Court's decision in the case of Citizens United v. the Federal Elections Commission. The decision held that the government could not limit groups, such as corporations and unions, or individuals from spending as much money as they liked in election campaigns. This decision paved the way for "Super PACS", or "independent-expenditure only committees", to participate in elections with none of the financial constraints such as limits on personal donations that regulated candidates' fund-raising efforts. While these Super PACs were legally forbidden from coordinating in any way with campaigns, this separation was seen widely as something of a fiction. Several leading figures in Restore Our Future, for example, were former staffers of Romney. Most candidates had such a Super PAC working in their support. Gingrich himself was supported by one that had received a multi-million dollar donation from a Las Vegas casino owner. In advertising, however, the distance was sufficient to allow advertising to be aired in the interests of a particular candidate but without any announced tie to that candidate. Each campaign-paid advertisement had to feature the candidates saying that they endorsed its message. Restore Our Future's intervention in Iowa was one of the first major forays of this kind into presidential politics. No one believed it was not a sign of things to come.

The intervention proved highly successful, and Gingrich quickly fell in the polls. Part of the problem for him was that while the advertising might have been unfair, since Romney could pretend it had nothing to do with him, for the most part it was not untrue. Gingrich had indeed done many of the conservative-displeasing things (admitting the existence of human-made climate change, for example) that the advertisements said he did. Few missed the irony of Gingrich being undone by the latest innovation in "the politics of destruction" that he had done so much to encourage when in leadership in the 1990s.

There was time yet for one more challenger to move to the front of the anti-Romney portion of the Republican field. Rick Santorum, former senator from Pennsylvania, was the only person in the field who had been running a traditional Iowa campaign, travelling the state, visiting each of its 99 counties, and meeting small groups of citizens in coffee-shops and living rooms. One of the claims made on behalf of small states like Iowa and New Hampshire going first in the process was that it allowed for this kind of "retail" politics to be conducted by candidates with little fame or money. In a year in which a surfeit of televised debates and Super PAC advertising seemed to call these claims into question, it was somewhat ironic that the traditionalist approach had brought Santorum to the fore just at the right time; that is at a time when it was too late for his opponents to tear him down before polling day. In other respects, it was not so surprising that a very conservative Christian candidate like Santorum would attract a reasonable amount of support in a very conservative Christian state like Iowa. On election eve, then, Santorum seemed best poised to be first among the group of Romney challengers from the right.

One other challenger to Romney had a wing of the party all to himself. Ron Paul was the self-proclaimed campaigner for the cause of "Liberty". Dubbed a libertarian, Paul actually had standard social conservative views on matters such as abortion. Nevertheless, his radical views on limiting the power of government in many ways—ranging from abolishing the Federal Reserve to ending the "war on drugs" to ending what he saw as the country's warmongering and adventurism overseas—struck a chord, especially with younger voters and on college campuses. With views far from the Republican mainstream, never mind the main mainstream, Paul was deemed to have no chance of winning the nomination. Not appearing to care very much what others thought of his chances, the Congressman ran a well-organised and well-funded grass roots campaign that augured well for his success in a state like Iowa. Paul joined Romney and Santorum as the candidates most likely to emerge from Iowa able to claim success. Late December polls in Iowa had leader Romney in the 23 to 25 per cent range, Paul second with 21 per cent and Santorum third and rising with 15 per cent.

The ups and downs of the campaign, the eclectic nature of the field, and the almost constant errors coming from one or another of the candidates, meant that it was difficult at times not to see the nominating process as a sideshow; the kind of mass distraction, simultaneously attracting and repelling, that was so common to the nation's television screens in this time. At one point, even the president jokingly referred to the race as resembling an episode of *Survivor*, a reality TV show in which one contestant was voted off the show each week. Others were less polite, with the phrase "clown show" frequently emanating from pundits on the Left while those on the Right found it ever more difficult to explain how this was all the Republicans could come up with to challenge a seriously vulnerable president. It remained to be seen whether the process would grow more serious as the involvement of actual voters began. For most of the year, however, it had occupied an odd, even surreal, place in the national life, between the grave challenges of a suffering economy at home and the daunting uncertainties of a wider world throwing out new challenges to the USA and its leaders. Much of the time it had indeed seemed to bear the relationship of a reality television show to, well, reality.

There was major news from the three wars that had done so much to contribute to the nation's current indebtedness: in Iraq and Afghanistan and the "war on terror." The Bush administration's name for that conflict had been jettisoned by its successors, along with some of the means of fighting it such as torture and secret prisons. Other methods continued to be employed with even greater enthusiasm and destructiveness. Numerous "enemy combatants" were attacked and killed, many of them in non-combatant countries. The high point came on Sunday 1 May. President Obama "report[ed] to the American people and to the world that the United States has conducted an operation that killed Osama bin Laden". The leader of al-Qaida had been tracked to his home in the Pakistani city of Abbottabad and was shot dead in the early hours of 2 May (local time) in his bedroom during a raid conducted by US Navy Seals and CIA operatives. His body was removed and, after formal identification, buried at sea (see Obituary).

Bin Laden joined a number of al-Qaida leaders who had met their end during the Obama presidency, during which a significant portion of its command structure had been wiped out. He at least was killed by a soldier standing before him rather than by an operative in a room somewhere in New Mexico or Nevada. It was from bases in those states that most of the Obama administration's anti-terrorist weapon of choice—the drone-delivered Hellfire missile—were operated, the drones themselves taking off from friendly countries such as Turkey. Under President Obama the number of drone attacks had increased dramatically. Over 100 were carried out in 2011 as part of the administration's secret and officially unacknowledged drone war on its enemies—what one leading newspaper described as an "emerging global apparatus" for spying upon and killing alleged enemies of the USA. Most of the attacks were in Pakistan, but there were some also in Somalia and Yemen. Among those killed in the latter was Anwar al-Awlaki, a US-born cleric considered to be an influential figure in al-Qaida in the Arabian Peninsula, who was killed on 30 September (see Obituary). The US had accused him of being connected to several attacks, including the 2009 mass shooting at the Fort Hood military base in Texas. Two weeks later, in October, another drone attack in Yemen, killed senior al-Qaida leader Ibrahim al-Banna as well as al-Awlaki's son and nephew. Bin Laden's killing and the dozens of drone raids caused great tensions with Pakistan, especially as there were persistent reports that many civilians were dying alongside acknowledged insurgents. That bin Laden was living, and may have been for years, in a Pakistani garrison town, a few hundred yards from a major military academy, was a source of embarrassment for the Pakistanis. So too was the US decision not to inform them of the raid in advance, far less involve their forces in it. US-Pakistani relations sank even lower following a US-led NATO air strike on two border checkpoints on 26 November. It seemed that miscommunications on the NATO side had led them to mistake the checkpoints for insurgent targets. Twenty-four Pakistani soldiers died.

The war in Afghanistan had begun as an attempt to get bin Laden and punish the Taliban government. Bin Laden was gone, the USA was still there, and the Taliban was very definitely back. As part of its spring offensive, it launched a series of coordinated attacks on government buildings, police stations, and schools in Kandahar. The Battle of Kandahar proved an embarrassment for the Afghan government and its allies. US forces experienced their single deadliest day yet in the Afghan conflict on 6 August when 30 troops died when the Chinook helicopter they were travelling in was shot down. The dead included 22 men from the same Navy Seal team that had participated in the killing of bin Laden (although none involved in that raid were killed in the crash). There was much discussion of withdrawal, with President Obama announcing in June that 10,000 troops would leave by the end of 2011, with more than 20,000 to follow in 2012.

In Iraq, the war was drawing to a close, at least for US forces. Under a bilateral status-of-forces agreement signed in 2008 by President George W. Bush and Iraqi Prime Minister Nouri al Maliki US troops were to leave Iraq no later than 31 December, 2011. Later negotiations between Obama and Maliki on extending some US military presence beyond 2011 proved unproductive, and on 21 October President Obama announced that full withdrawal would go ahead as agreed. Obama welcomed the troops home on a visit to Fort Bragg, North Carolina, on 14 December. He thanked them for their service and sacrifice and hailed the "sovereign, stable and self-reliant" Iraq that he claimed had emerged from the war which he had once dubbed "stupid". On 18 December the final 500 US troops left Iraq for Kuwait, under cover of darkness.

On 19 December Prime Minister Maliki ordered the arrest on terrorism charges of Vice President Tariq al Hashemi, the highest-ranking Sunni in the government. Al Hashemi, denying all charges, hurriedly left for the Kurdish territories. The move further inflamed sectarian tensions. Days later, a coordinated series of bomb blasts, for which al Qaida in Iraq claimed responsibility, killed more than 70 and wounded more than 200 in mostly Shiite neighbourhoods in Baghdad. The future for Iraq remained uncertain and deep pessimism pervaded the nation's Sunnis as they looked west to see their co-religionists being slaughtered by a Syrian leadership backed by the Iraqi and Iranian governments, and east to Iran itself, the power of which grew daily in post-Saddam and post-US occupation Iraq.

Indeed, most observers agreed that one certain outcome of the Iraq war was that Shiite-majority Iraq would fall even further under the influence of Iran. This was not only a matter of great concern for Sunnis in Iraq but also for other countries in the region such as Saudi Arabia and Israel. Iran's continuing development of a nuclear programme only added to these concerns and remained a central issue in US foreign policy. A major consideration was that if Iran ever developed nuclear weapons they would pose a mortal threat to Israel, the national security and interests of which seemed to be, for large sections of the political class, almost as important as those of the USA itself. Unsurprisingly, this attention to Israeli concerns was on display at its most intense during the Republican debates as all candidates except the anti-imperialist Ron Paul chastised Obama for "appeasing" the Iranians and neglecting the interests of a treasured ally. Candidates quick to condemn Obama for any perceived kowtowing to foreign nations, themselves boasted of how long they had known Israeli Prime Minister Benjamin "Bibi" Netanyahu and how much they would listen to Israeli advice in formulating US policy for the Middle East.

In December, a defence appropriations bill which included more sanctions on Iran passed the House and the Senate. These would punish banks which dealt with Iran's central bank. The administration did not like sanctions that might anger allies such as Japan, whose financial institutions would in effect be forced to choose between doing business in the USA or with Iran, upon whose oil the Japanese depended. With the bill passing both chambers with veto-proof majorities, and also including a pay rise for the armed services, it was clear that President Obama would sign it into law. European states were also considering more stringent sanctions. Iran reacted by threatening to close the Straits of Hormuz to sea traffic. The US military quickly responded that it would not allow this to happen. With the US Fifth Fleet by far the dominant naval force in the region there was little doubt that they could do so if the threat proved more than a signal of Iran's unhappiness with the economic conflict being waged against it.

Even these major, and familiar, concerns were overshadowed by a series of events across the Middle East that came to be known as the "Arab Spring". On 4 January Tunisian street vendor Mohammed Bouazizi died from severe burns suffered when he set himself on fire on 17 December, 2010. Bouazizi's powerful protest against persistent harassment by police and government officials inspired Tunisians to take to the streets in protest against decades of oppression. In the face of intensifying protests across Tunisian society, President Zine El Abidine Ben Ali and his family fled the country for Saudi Arabia. Ben Ali would be the first of several Arab leaders to fall in 2011 as revolutionary fervour spread. From Egypt to Syria, Bahrain to Yemen, governments faced mass protests with varying degrees of violence and varying degrees of success when it came to preserving power.

The Arab Spring raised complex diplomatic and strategic questions for the Obama administration. There were no ready answers. How should the USA respond to popular uprisings that threatened undoubtedly repressive regimes, like those of Egypt and Bahrain, which were also allies? How much should protesters against an enemy like President Bashar al Assad of Syria be encouraged when military support for them was out of the question? More generally, there were concerns that the fall of these authoritarian regimes, whether friend or foe, might bring not so much a flowering of freedom as alternative authoritarianisms no less repressive and perhaps less friendly to the USA. The administration offered for the most part cautious and measured responses to the various crises. To its supporters this was an appropriately careful approach. To some critics it was too timid in its support of freedom. To other critics it was too disloyal in its unwillingness to give stronger support to allies such as Hosni Mubarak of Egypt.

In one case the administration's measured support for the mass uprisings gave way to military action to assist in overthrowing a government. In March, NATO instituted a no-fly zone over Libya in support of a UN resolution that "all necessary measures" be taken "to protect civilians and civilian populated areas under threat of attack" from the forces of Colonel Moamar Kadhafi. The USA, France, and the UK provided most of the air and fire power. The immediate concern was that Kadhafi forces were about to launch a major attack on Benghazi, which had effectively become the rebel capital. However the NATO allies interpreted their remit with a considerable degree of flexibility, and themselves did much of the flying in the skies of Libya. Numerous targets were hit in the coming months, including Kadhafi residences, communication centres in Tripoli and Libyan government forces and materiel on the ground. It soon became clear that the NATO air war was to play a major part not only in defending civilians but in overthrowing the Kadhafi government. The leaders of the three powers admitted as much when they met in mid-April. After months of fighting, an increasingly well-armed and organised opposition—now constituted as the National Transitional Council—claimed victory in September. That same month, near his home town of Sirte, Kadhafi was captured and killed. The dictator who had successfully sought rapprochement with the West after seeing what happened to Saddam Hussein, who surrendered his weapons of mass destruction and assisted the USA in its war against al-Qaida, had met a similar fate to Saddam, albeit without the formality of a trial and a noose. Brutal dictators of the early twenty-first century had learned an important lesson. Mess with the USA and you could end up dead. Play ball with the USA and you could end up dead.

President Obama's overseas trips included visits to Brazil, Chile and El Salvador in March and to Ireland, the UK and France in May. In the latter, he attended the G-8 summit in Deauville, before rounding off his European tour with a visit to Poland. In November, it was back to France for the G-20 summit at Cannes. Later that month, in perhaps the most significant of his visits, the president attended the annual ASEAN meeting in Bali, Indonesia. Prior to that he spent two days in Australia, where he announced the coming deployment of 2500 US Marines on the northern shores of that country. The troops, it seemed, were to be a down payment on a more forceful US presence in the Asia-Pacific region. In a speech in Australia Obama said some striking things about his vision for his country's future. His visit signalled "a broader shift" in US priorities. Near the end of "two wars that cost us dearly, in blood and treasure", the USA was now "turning our attention to the vast potential of the Asia Pacific region". This "new focus" recognised the "fundamental truth" that "the United States has been, and always will be, a Pacific nation." "Here," the president continued, "we see the future." Here was a region that was "home to more than half the global economy" as well as "most of the world's nuclear powers and some half of humanity". "As president, I've therefore made a deliberate and strategic decision: as a Pacific nation, the United States will play a larger and long-term role in shaping this region and its future, by upholding core principles and in close partnership with allies and friends." "Enduring interests," the president explained, called for "our enduring presence. The United States is a Pacific power, and we are here to stay."

Clearly intended in part for the ears of the leaders of China, Obama's message would have sounded sweetly to the most ardent nineteenth-century promoter of Manifest Destiny, never mind the keenest neo-conservative of more recent times. Neither could have enunciated more precisely and robustly this enduring sense of an expansive nation ever prepared to merge the interests of the US with the interests of all, always prepared to harness its unparalleled power to the pursuit of peace for the world, just so long as it retained its inalienable right to define what those universal interests were and what that global peace would look like.

At year's end, out there in Iowa, those who would lead the empire awaited the people's first sign.

James Miller

CANADA

CAPITAL: Ottawa   AREA: 9,984,670 sq km   POPULATION: 34,108,752 ('10)
OFFICIAL LANGUAGES: English & French
HEAD OF STATE: Queen Elizabeth II (since Feb '52)
GOVERNOR-GENERAL: David Johnston (since Oct '10)
RULING PARTY: Conservative Party of Canada (CPC) (since Jan '06)
HEAD OF GOVERNMENT: Prime Minister Stephen Harper (CPC) (since Feb '06)
DEMOCRACY INDEX: 9.08; 9th of 167   CORRUPTION INDEX: 8.7; 10th of 183
CURRENCY: Canadian Dollar (Dec '11 £1.00=CAD 1.59, US$1.00=CAD 1.02)
GNI PER CAPITA: US$41,950, Intl $37,280 at PPP ('09)

ON 2 May, Prime Minister Stephen Harper's governing Conservative Party was returned to office with a comfortable majority. The election—the fourth in seven years—brought an end to a succession of Liberal and Conservative minority governments and marked the first time since 1993 that a right-of-centre party had held majorities in both the elected House of Commons and the appointed Senate. The results also substantially altered the country's political landscape as two long-dominant parties suffered steep losses while another party achieved a dramatic breakthrough.

Harper asked Governor General David Johnston to dissolve Parliament and call an election when his government lost a vote of no confidence on 25 March. The opposition had combined to pass a motion (by 156 votes to 145) which rebuked the government for failing to produce information necessary to review proposed legislation. It was the first time in history that a Commonwealth government had been found to be in contempt of Parliament. Although polls conducted during the first half of the campaign suggested that voters would re-elect a Parliament similar to the outgoing one, a strong performance by New Democratic Party (NDP) leader Jack Layton in both the English and French-language televised debates prompted his party to gain support at the expense of the centrist Liberals and the separatist Bloc Quebecois.

Although the Conservatives only marginally improved their share of the popular vote, the party benefitted from vote splitting among the opposition parties and thus carried 166 of 308 federal ridings. The Liberals, who had previously held the second largest number of seats and had therefore constituted the Official Opposition, won only 34 seats. Falling to third place and garnering less than 20 per cent of the vote, it was the worst result in the party's history. Conversely, the left-of-centre New Democrats posted their best result ever, taking 31 per cent of the popular vote and 103 seats, including 59 in the 75 seats in the province of Quebec. In its 50-year existence the NDP had only ever elected two MPs in Quebec prior to the 2011 election. The surge of the NDP in the province crushed the Bloc Quebecois; the party's representation fell from 47 seats to four, thereby losing official party status in the House of Commons. The Green Party also won its first seat with the election in British Columbia of its leader, Elizabeth May. Voter turnout increased from an historic low of 58.8 per cent in 2008 to 61.1 per cent and an unprecedented 76 women were elected to the House of Commons.

Immediately following the election Liberal leader Michael Ignatieff and Bloc Quebecois leader Gilles Duceppe both tendered their resignations. Shortly thereafter, NDP leader Jack Layton announced that he would be taking a leave of absence to seek treatment of an undisclosed type of cancer. Although he expected his leave of absence would be temporary, his condition worsened and he died on 22 August. Layton's death prompted an outpouring of grief across the country and left the opposition in Parliament in disarray. An election to choose his successor as NDP leader was scheduled for March 2012.

Prime Minister Harper's Conservative government unveiled a new agenda which included legislation to reform the Senate, eliminate public subsidies for political parties, abolish the national gun registry and end the Canadian Wheat Board's monopoly on Prairie wheat and barley sales. The government also tabled an omnibus crime bill which would mandate the imposition of compulsory minimum sentences for a range of sexual offences involving someone under the age of 16 and for some drug crimes, and eliminate pardons and certain types of conditional sentencing.

Incumbent governments were returned to office in six out of seven provincial or territorial elections held in 2011. Prince Edward Island's Liberal government, Manitoba's New Democratic Party, Newfoundland and Labrador's Progressive Conservative government, Saskatchewan's Saskatchewan Party, and Yukon Territory's Yukon Party all maintained the majorities they had held prior to the elections. In Ontario the Liberals were reduced to a minority government, falling one seat short of an outright majority. In the Northwest Territories' non-partisan system of government incumbents were re-elected in 13 of 19 ridings.

Governing parties in two other provinces selected new leaders in 2011. The British Columbia Liberal Party chose Christy Clark as its new leader on 26 February, and on 7 October Alison Redford became Alberta's first female premier after winning the leadership of the Progressives Conservatives, a party which had been in office with majority governments continuously since 1971.

Canada's GDP declined for the first time since 2009 during the second quarter of 2011. Federal Finance Minister Jim Flaherty tried to assuage fears of the onset of another recession by suggesting a 2.1 per cent decline in exports, a 3.6 per cent drop in oil and gas production, and a 0.9 per cent decline in manufacturing, would be offset by steady business investment and consumer confidence in the economy. However, the worsening economic situation did prompt the federal government to push back the date that it expected to return to a balanced budget. In November the government projected that it would eliminate its deficit by the 2015-16 fiscal year—one year later than had been announced in the June budget.

The Supreme Court of Canada issued a unanimous decision on 30 September which permitted Vancouver's Insite clinic to continue providing medically supervised injections of illegal drugs. Located in one of the country's poorest urban neighbourhoods, the clinic had begun as a pilot project in 2003 designed to reduce accidental overdoses among intravenous drug users. Although it was originally supported by all three levels of government, the federal government had subsequently withdrawn its support and stopped granting it exemptions under the Controlled Drugs and Substances Act. The court ruled that while the federal government was within its constitutional jurisdiction to control drug use, its rationale for interfering with the clinic's operations was "grossly disproportionate" to the clinic's benefit to society. Federal Health Minister Leona Aglukkaq said that the government would comply with the court's ruling, which would permit other supervised drug injection clinics to open across the country, while it reviewed its options.

William Stos

MEXICO AND CENTRAL AMERICA

MEXICO—GUATEMALA—EL SALVADOR—HONDURAS—NICARAGUA—COSTA RICA—PANAMA

MEXICO

CAPITAL: Mexico City   AREA: 1,964,380 sq km   POPULATION: 113,423,047 (10)
OFFICIAL LANGUAGE: Spanish
HEAD OF STATE AND GOVERNMENT: President Felipe Calderon (PAN) (since Dec '06)
RULING PARTY: National Action Party (PAN)
DEMOCRACY INDEX: 6.93; 50th of 167   CORRUPTION INDEX: 3.0; 100th of 183
CURRENCY: Mexican Peso (Dec '11 £1.00=MXN 21.29, US$1.00=MXN 13.58)
GNI PER CAPITA: US$8,930, Intl$14,360 at PPP ('10)

IT was a difficult year for President Felipe Calderón. There were advances in infrastructure, universal healthcare coverage and economic growth, creating 850,000 new jobs, but Mexico continued to be plagued by the drug war, a large-scale civil-military offensive against the drug cartels operating in the country. In its fifth year, and with no end in sight, it dominated the public perception of Mexico at home and abroad.

The presidential campaign season for 2012 started in December. The main contenders were the former governor of the state of Mexico, Enrique Peña Nieto, for the centre-left Party of the Institutionalised Revolution (PRI), and the former chief of government of the Federal District, Andrés Manuel López Obrador, for the leftist Party for the Democratic Revolution (PRD), while the incumbent centre-right National Action Party (PAN) had not yet decided on a single candidate at the end of the year. On 4 July, the PRI held onto the governorship of the state of Mexico, the country's most populous and second-biggest economy, with over 60 per cent of the vote; an important indicator for the upcoming presidential elections. With it, the PRI controlled 20 of the 32 Mexican states, but questions remained whether the PRI had really left behind its more authoritarian self to become a reformed and democratic party.

Despite important successes and a series of high-profile arrests, the security situation in Mexico continued to worsen. The drug war caused 13,000 deaths in 2011 alone, an increase of 11 per cent over 2010. This brought the total number of deaths to 47,500 since 2006, plus the displacement of some 230,000, and the disappearance of thousands more. Even though most of the violence remained confined to the northern states on the US border, 2011 saw a considerable increase in confrontations and attacks in areas that used to be relatively untouched by the drug-related violence, such as the cities of Veracruz and Acapulco, and to a lesser extent Guadalajara and Oaxaca.

Developments in Mexico's drug war in 2011 included, on 25 August, an attack by the Zetas drug cartel on the "Casino Royale" in Monterrey that left 53 people dead, most of them innocent civilians. State elections in Michoacán on 13 November were marred by acts of violence and threats by the drug cartels. In Tamaulipas, one of the states worst hit by extreme drug violence, mass graves were discovered in San Fernando in April, containing more than 140 bodies. The state of Veracruz became a new focal point of the drug war, after organised crime from Tamaulipas was displaced south by the government offensive there; 70 bodies were found in Boca del Río in September and October. The Familia Michoacana drug cartel was dismantled in 2011, yet splinter groups created a (smaller) successor cartel called the Knights Templar. The government focused its law enforcement and the military efforts on the Zetas, the most violent drug cartel in the country, pushing part of its operation into Guatemala.

The internationalisation of the fight against the drug cartels continued, both to the north and to the south. The USA explicitly took co-responsibility for the drug war when President Barack Obama offered help during President Calderón's state visit to Washington, DC on 3 March. The US authorities clamped down on illegal arms sales at home, increased their material support to the Mexican authorities under the Mérida Initiative, and employed unmanned drones for surveillance missions over Mexican territory. There was also increased cooperation between Mexico and Guatemala and Honduras to fight transnational crime, especially drug and human trafficking, including the violence against illegal immigrants from Central America that continued unabated.

Finally, 2011 saw the rise of civil society as a new and powerful actor in the drug war. Civil discontent with both organised crime and the way the drug war was conducted by the state reached new highs. April, May and June saw tens of thousands of Mexicans throughout the country march for peace and a demilitarisation of the drug war. Poet and father of a boy killed by cartel hitmen in March, Javier Sicilia, became the face of the popular opposition to the drug war. In an unprecedented move, President Calderón agreed to publicly meet with relatives of the victims of the drug war on 24 June to engage in a televised dialogue with them, to mourn and to apologise for not being able to protect the lives of their loved ones.

Two reports criticised the government's security strategy and gave impetus to the debate about the decriminalisation of drug use in Mexico. In March, the Global Commission on Drug Policy, an international NGO, published a report that advocated ending the repressive policies against the drug trade and instead dealing with it as a public health issue. It was written by a group of public intellectuals and eminent statesmen, mostly from Latin America. Human Rights Watch published a report on 9 November called "Neither Security nor Human Rights", denouncing extensive human rights abuses in the drug war. It stated that Mexico's public security strategy had failed; instead of improving security the all-out war against the drug cartels exacerbated a climate of violence, chaos and fear in many parts of the country.

Still, the economy grew at an estimated annualised rate of 4 per cent, with inflation at 3.8 per cent. Oil production continued to decline and stood at 2.5 million barrels per day in 2011. For the first time in 40 years private companies were allowed to participate in the exploration and extraction of crude oil. In April the national oil company Pemex stated that reserves would only last for another 10 years. The tourism industry, after a strong contraction in 2010, grew by 3.3 per cent in the first half of the year. Nevertheless, soaring private security costs and the general feeling of insecurity were a major burden for the local economy in the worst-hit areas, which included Monterrey, Veracruz and Acapulco, three of the country's main economic hubs. More important for the national economy, however, was the economic crisis in the USA—the giant neighbour that absorbed 80 per cent of Mexico's exports—negatively affecting trade, remittances and US foreign direct investment.

Christian E. Rieck

CENTRAL AMERICA

Guatemala

CAPITAL: Guatemala City AREA: 108,890 sq km POPULATION: 14,388,929 ('10)
OFFICIAL LANGUAGE: Spanish
HEAD OF STATE AND GOVERNMENT: President Alvaro Colom Caballeros (UNE) (since Jan '08)
PRESIDENT ELECT: Otto Pérez Molina
RULING PARTY: National Unity of Hope (UNE)
DEMOCRACY INDEX: 6.05; 75th of 167 CORRUPTION INDEX: 2.7; 120th of 183
CURRENCY: Quetzal (Dec '11 £1.00=GTQ 12.33, US$1.00=GTQ 7.86)
GNI PER CAPITA: US$2,730, Intl$4,600 at PPP ('10)

El Salvador

CAPITAL: San Salvador AREA: 21,040 sq km POPULATION: 6,192,993 ('10)
OFFICIAL LANGUAGE: Spanish
HEAD OF STATE AND GOVERNMENT: President Mauricio Funes (FMLN) (since June '09)
RULING PARTY: Farabundo Martí National Liberation Front (FMLN)
DEMOCRACY INDEX: 6.47; 61st of 167 CORRUPTION INDEX: 3.4; 80th of 183
CURRENCY: El Salvador Colon (Dec '11 £1.00=SVC 13.72, US$1.00=SVC 8.74)
GNI PER CAPITA: US$3,360, Intl$6,390 at PPP ('10)

Honduras

CAPITAL: Tegucigalpa AREA: 112,090 sq km POPULATION: 7,600,524 ('10)
OFFICIAL LANGUAGE: Spanish
HEAD OF STATE AND GOVERNMENT: President Porfirio "Pepe" Lobo Sosa (PNH) (since Jan '10)
RULING PARTY: National Party of Honduras (PNH) (since Jan '10)
DEMOCRACY INDEX: 5.76; 88th of 167 CORRUPTION INDEX: 2.6; 129th of 183
CURRENCY: Lempira (Dec '11 £1.00=HNL 29.67, US$1.00=HNL 18.92)
GNI PER CAPITA: US$1,880, Intl$3,740 at PPP ('10)

Nicaragua

CAPITAL: Managua AREA: 130,000 sq km POPULATION: 5,788,163 ('10)
OFFICIAL LANGUAGE: Spanish
HEAD OF STATE AND GOVERNMENT: President Daniel Ortega Saavedra (FSLN) (since Jan '07)
RULING PARTY: Sandinista National Liberation Front (FSLN)
DEMOCRACY INDEX: 5.73; 89th of 167 CORRUPTION INDEX: 2.5; 134th of 183
CURRENCY: Gold Cordoba (Dec '11 £1.00=NIO 35.89, US$1.00=NIO 22.88)
GNI PER CAPITA: US$1,090, Intl$2,630 at PPP ('10)

Costa Rica

CAPITAL: San José AREA: 51,100 sq km POPULATION: 4,658,887 ('10)
OFFICIAL LANGUAGE: Spanish
HEAD OF STATE AND GOVERNMENT: President Laura Chinchilla (since May '10)
RULING PARTY: National Liberation Party (PLN)
DEMOCRACY INDEX: 8.04; 24th of 167 CORRUPTION INDEX: 4.8; 50th of 183
CURRENCY: Costa Rican Colon (Dec '11 £1.00=CRC 789.72, US$1.00=CRC 503.57)
GNI PER CAPITA: US$6,550, Intl$10,840 at PPP ('10)

Panama

CAPITAL: Panama City AREA: 75,520 sq km POPULATION: 3,516,820 ('10)
OFFICIAL LANGUAGE: Spanish
HEAD OF STATE AND GOVERNMENT: President Ricardo Martinelli Berrocal (APC) (since May '09)
RULING PARTY: Alliance for Change (APC) coalition
DEMOCRACY INDEX: 7.15; 46th of 167 CORRUPTION INDEX: 3.3; 86th of 183
CURRENCY: Balboa (Dec '11 £1.00=PAB 1.57, US$1.00=PAB 1.00)
GNI PER CAPITA: US$6,980, Intl$12,910 at PPP ('10)

FORMER army general and ex-director of military intelligence Otto Pérez Molina won the second round of the presidential election in **Guatemala** on 6 November with 54 per cent of the vote. He and his right-wing Patriotic Party had campaigned on a law and order ticket. General Pérez Molina had retired from the army in 2000 and unsuccessfully ran for president in 2004. Some accused him of human rights abuses during the civil war (1960-96), while others saw his victory as indicative of the failure of the civilian politicians to provide security and development. An early social-democratic favourite, Sandra Torres, the wife of outgoing President Álvaro Colom, divorced her husband to run for office (close relatives of the president were not permitted to stand) but was barred from doing so by the Constitutional Court on 9 August.

The crime rate was rising steadily, from 30 (2002) to 41 (2010) homicides per 100,000 population (according to UN Office on Drugs and Crime figures), mainly because Mexico's counter-narcotics initiatives were pushing the violence into its southern neighbours; lynchings and politically motivated attacks also rose (as did spending on defence and security to combat them). The notorious Zetas drugs cartel massacred 27 peasants in La Libertad on 15 May, after having being routed from Alta Verapaz in the north of the country by national police and armed forces after a two-month siege. Argentine singer Facundo Cabral was shot dead in Guatemala City on 9 July, although the bullets were meant for a wealthy businessman in whose car Cabral was travelling. The most wanted drug kingpin, Juan Ortiz López, alias "Chamalé", was captured on 31 March.

History was ever present in Guatemala. On 15 December, President Colom apologised for a 1982 massacre in Dos Erres, carried out by government soldiers during Guatemala's 36-year civil war. On 20 October, he apologised to the family of former President Jacobo Árbenz Guzmán, who was overthrown by a US-backed coup in 1954. In September, the US Presidential Commission for the Study of Bioethical Issues delivered the results of its investigation into the conduct of human trials on Guatemalans by US medical researchers in the 1940s. The commission concluded that these experiments represented a conscious violation of ethical standards. Over 1,300 people had been deliberately infected with syphilis and other sexually transmitted diseases to test penicillin. At least 83 of the subjects died.

US President Barack Obama visited **El Salvador** on 22 March as part of his tour of Latin America. He visited the tomb of the murdered Archbishop Oscar Romero, a symbol of the fight for human rights (see AR 2011, pp. 147; 606-07), and painted El Salvador as a regional model for reconciliation and peaceful democratic change. In the 1980s, President Mauricio Funes's leftist Farabundo Martí National Liberation Front (FMLN) had fought against the Salvadorean government that was at the time backed by the USA. President Obama announced a $200 million fund, called the "Alliance for Citizen Security", to strengthen Central American institutions, such as the court system.

The crime rate was stuck at a staggering 66 homicides per 100,000 population, a situation that led to the dismissal of the interior minister on 8 November. Due to the increased influence of the Mexican cartels, El Salvador was added to the US list of important drug trafficking and drug producing countries in September.

El Salvador was the Central American country worst affected by eight days of record rainfall in October; Guatemala and Nicaragua also suffered. In El Salvador 34 people died, 56,000 lost their homes, 300,000 were affected. The UN launched an international appeal on 25 October for reconstruction funds for El Salvador, where 69 per cent of the territory had been affected.

Honduras was welcomed back into the Organisation of American States (OAS) on 1 June, after almost two years of semi-isolation from the hemispheric community. Former President Manuel Zelaya's return to the country on 28 May, from exile in the Dominican Republic, facilitated the reincorporation. Zelaya was greeted by thousands of supporters and in June announced the creation of a new political party, the Broad Front of Popular Resistance, to contest the presidential elections in 2013. On 8 July the Truth and Reconciliation Commission, set up to investigate the crisis of 2009, pronounced that there had indeed been a coup d'état (and 20 deaths in protests afterwards) and hoped to close that chapter by placing blame on both sides (see AR 2010, pp. 148-49).

Honduras, together with Guatemala and El Salvador, formed the so-called "Northern Triangle", a focal point for the international drug economy. This led to an explosion in the crime rate from 35 (2005) to 82 (2010) homicides per 100,000 population—the highest in the world—a fact that contributed to the US Peace Corps's decision to withdraw all its 158 volunteers from the country in December. Honduran and US authorities intercepted a narco-submarine on 13 July, which was carrying as much as 2.5 tons of cocaine. On 5 October President Porfirio Lobo asked the USA for help in creating a national bureau of investigation to help fight organised crime. Meanwhile, the armed forces were back on the streets in December to combat a wave of violence.

In **Nicaragua**, President Daniel Ortega of the Sandinista National Liberation Front (FSNL) was elected on 6 November for a second consecutive term. He won by a landslide, with more than 60 per cent of the vote. The main opposition candidate, Fabio Gadea, called the results fraudulent, the first such accusation in 20 years of electoral history. The EU observer mission said that the elections lacked transparency and neutrality. The election itself passed relatively peacefully, but at least four people were killed in post-election violence. The campaign was highly controversial, with its constitutionality in question, and there were several violent clashes between sympathisers and opponents of the president during the year. President Ortega's radical left-wing policies (redistribution at home; alignment with Venezuela's Bolivarian Alliance for the Peoples of Our America (ALBA) initiative abroad) now had to prove that they could sustain the moderate economic growth of recent years, of around 4 per cent per annum.

Natural disasters and the drugs trade continued to strain Nicaraguan services. President Ortega declared a state of emergency on 17 October after heavy rainfall. The rains left 16 people dead and affected 134,000. Police destroyed a regional crime network on 5 December, confiscating 700 kg of cocaine that had been smuggled onto a public bus, while on 13 November the navy seized 1.5 tons of cocaine from a speedboat in the Caribbean, killing four in the raid.

The maritime border dispute between Nicaragua and Costa Rica over an island in the mouth of the San Juan River continued in 2011. A first ruling on 8 March by the International Court of Justice (ICJ) in The Hague, in a case filed by Costa Rica, ordered both countries not to station troops in the disputed area, but allowed Costa Rica to send civilian teams to monitor the environmental impact of the dredging of the San Juan River being carried out by Nicaragua. On 8 April, Nicaragua complained that surveillance aircraft were overflying the zone, while Costa Rica went back to the ICJ on 25 June because of the presence of unauthorised civilians on the disputed Isla Calero.

Nicaragua's military occupation of Isla Calero along the San Juan river led to the installation by **Costa Rica** of surveillance cameras there and the reactivation of its border police by President Laura Chinchilla, dismantled by her predecessor in 2008. Each country continued to accuse the other of interpreting the ICJ's ruling to their own advantage.

Left-of-centre President Chinchilla bolstered her crime-fighting credentials. On 27 April, former President Miguel Ángel Rodríguez (1998-2002) was sentenced to five years in prison on corruption charges. This marked the second time that a former Costa Rican president had been successfully prosecuted for corruption, after the sentencing to prison in 2009 of Rafael Ángel Calderón (1990-94).

A mutiny in the high-security La Reforma prison was put down on 12 May, with two inmates and one policeman killed. The crime rate rose from eight (2006) to 11 (2010) homicides per 100,000 population, mainly due to the increased drugs trade and associated violence, but it was still far below that of some of Costa Rica's neighbours. The economy grew by 4.2 per cent in 2010 and continued to grow strongly in 2011, continuing Costa Rica's success story.

The **Panama** Canal was being expanded, transportation and logistics services were booming, tourism revenues were up and, in Panama City, US building tycoon Donald Trump opened the tallest building in Latin America. Between 2005 and 2010, Panama's economy grew at an average annual rate of 8 per cent, the highest in the region. After years of bilateral negotiations and heated discussions in the US Congress, the free trade agreement (FTA) between Panama and its biggest trading partner was signed into effect by US President Barack Obama on 21 October. Despite representing only a low trade volume of trade for the USA, Panama's FTA had been mired in the US Congress since being ratified by Panama in 2007.

In this context of political controversy in the USA, Panama's President Ricardo Martinelli travelled to Washington, DC on 28 April for his first meeting with his US counterpart. They discussed the stalled FTA negotiations as well as the proposed "Alliance for Citizen Security" (see above).

Despite increased regional efforts to curb the drugs trade and continuing successes in interdiction, drug trafficking remained a serious problem. The confiscation of 600 kg of heroin on 1 August was a grim reminder. Cocaine seizures in Panama, Nicaragua and Costa Rica were higher than in Mexico. The crime rate in Panama reached 21 homicides per 100,000 population, up from 11 in 2005.

On 11 December former leader, General Manuel Noriega, returned to Panama after spending a total of 22 years in US and French prisons. He was supposed to serve a further 20-year prison sentence in Panama for embezzlement, corruption and homicides carried out during his dictatorship (1983-1989), although some of his opponents feared that the ailing 77-year old might be allowed to live out the rest of his days under house arrest. The uneasiness about possible mobilisations on the day of Noriega's return, however, proved unfounded.

Christian E. Rieck

THE CARIBBEAN

CUBA—JAMAICA—DOMINICAN REPUBLIC—HAITI—WINDWARD & LEEWARD
ISLANDS—BARBADOS—TRINIDAD & TOBAGO—THE BAHAMAS—GUYANA—
BELIZE—SURINAME—UK DEPENDENCIES—DUTCH TERRITORIES—
THE US CARIBBEAN

CUBA, JAMAICA, DOMINICAN REPUBLIC AND HAITI

Cuba

CAPITAL: Havana   AREA: 110,860 sq km   POPULATION: 11,257,979 ('10)
OFFICIAL LANGUAGE: Spanish
HEAD OF STATE AND GOVERNMENT: President Raul Castro Ruz (since Feb '08)
RULING PARTY: Cuban Communist Party (PCC)
DEMOCRACY INDEX: 3.52; 121nd of 167   CORRUPTION INDEX: 4.2; 61st of 183
CURRENCY: Cuban Peso (Dec '11 £1.00=CUP 1.57, US$1.00=CUP 1.00)
GNI PER CAPITA: US$5,520 ('08)

Jamaica

CAPITAL: Kingston   AREA: 10,990 sq km   POPULATION: 2,702,300 ('10)
OFFICIAL LANGUAGE: English
HEAD OF STATE: Queen Elizabeth II
GOVERNOR-GENERAL: Patrick Allen (since Feb '09)
RULING PARTY: Jamaica Labour Party (JLP)
HEAD OF GOVERNMENT: Prime Minister Andrew Holness (JLP) (since Oct '11)
DEMOCRACY INDEX: 7.21; 43rd of 167   CORRUPTION INDEX: 3.3; 86th of 183
CURRENCY: Jamaican Dollar (Dec '11 £1.00=JMD 135.14, US$1.00=JMD 86.17)
GNI PER CAPITA: US$4,770, Intl$7,450 at PPP ('10)

Dominican Republic

CAPITAL: Santo Domingo   AREA: 48,730 sq km   POPULATION: 9,927,320 ('10)
OFFICIAL LANGUAGE: Spanish
HEAD OF STATE AND GOVERNMENT: President Leonel Fernández Reyna (PLD) (since Aug '04)
RULING PARTY: Dominican Liberation Party (PLD)
DEMOCRACY INDEX: 6.20; 70th of 167   CORRUPTION INDEX: 2.6; 129th of 183
CURRENCY: Dominican Peso (Dec '11 £1.00=DOP 60.42, US$1.00=DOP 38.52)
GNI PER CAPITA: US$5,000, Intl$8,960 at PPP ('10)

Haiti

CAPITAL: Port-au-Prince   AREA: 27,750 sq km   POPULATION: 9,993,247 ('10)
OFFICIAL LANGUAGE: French
HEAD OF STATE: President Michel Martelly (since May '11)
HEAD OF GOVERNMENT: Prime Minister Garry Conille (ind) (since Oct '11)
DEMOCRACY INDEX: 4.00; 111th of 167   CORRUPTION INDEX: 1.8; 175th of 183
CURRENCY: Gourde (Dec '11 £1.00=HTG 63.28, US$1.00=HTG 40.35)
GNI PER CAPITA: US$650, Intl$1,110 at PPP ('10)

CUBA witnessed a year of gradual change. In January, US President Barack Obama announced that restrictions would be eased on US citizens travelling and sending money to the island. The changes inter alia allowed religious organisations to sponsor religious travel to **Cuba**; permitted US citizens to send remittances (up to US$500 per quarter) to non-family members to support private economic activity; and enabled US airports to provide services to licensed charter flights. Obama said that the changes were aimed at developing "people-to-people" contacts through more academic, cultural and religious exchanges. Then, in February, Cuba saw the arrival of an undersea fibre-optic cable linking it to Venezuela, financed by the Bolivarian Alliance for the Peoples of Our America (ALBA). The cable transformed communications in Cuba, which had one of the slowest Internet speeds in the world. The new connection made download speeds 3,000 times faster—although Internet access remained tightly controlled. In December, the government announced the release of 2,900 prisoners, including several political detainees, as a "goodwill gesture".

The economy of Cuba continued to be reformed (see AR 2010, p. 153). In February the government announced the liberalisation of the sale of sugar. The state newspaper *Juventud Rebelde* said sugar would "gradually" be freed from state control and sold in shops and supermarkets where prices were much higher. Further, it was announced that the price of imported rice—another basic staple—was to go up by more than 40 per cent. In March, Cuba devalued its hard-currency convertible peso, used mostly by tourists and foreign firms, while in April, a Communist Party Congress (the first since 1997) agreed several important reforms and these were then ratified by the National Assembly in August. The changes included the right to buy and sell private homes, and the lifting of a long-standing ban on the sale of cars registered after the 1959 revolution. Then in November it was announced that farmers would be able to sell their goods directly to hotels and restaurants.

In further developments at the Party Congress, President Raúl Castro Ruz said that top political positions should be limited to two five-year terms, and promised "systematic rejuvenation" of the government. Former president Fidel Castro Ruz endorsed the changes. In an editorial published in Cuban state media, he wrote that a new generation was needed to correct the errors of the past in order to ensure that the communist system survived once the current generation of leaders had gone. This need was highlighted in September with the death at 75 of Julio Casas Regueiro, Cuban Defence Minister and veteran of the revolution.

In a general election held in **Jamaica** on 29 December, the opposition People's National Party (PNP) led by Portia Simpson Miller defeated the governing

Jamaica Labour Party (JLP) led by its new leader, Prime Minister Andrew Holness. Despite forecasts of a close race, results showed that the PNP won 42 seats (with 53.3 per cent of the vote) and the JLP 21 seats (with 46.6 per cent). The election (not constitutionally due until December 2012) was called by Holness who succeeded Bruce Golding as JLP leader in October. The departure of Golding was a surprise, but he had been damaged by the controversy surrounding the extradition to the USA of Christopher "Dudus" Coke on drug and gun-running charges (see AR 2010, p. 153). Coke pleaded guilty in a US court in August, and faced a maximum of 23 years in prison. One outcome of the Coke affair was a reduction in the murder rate as the authorities made a concerted attempt to tackle the criminal gangs operating on the island.

In the **Dominican Republic** President Leonel Fernández Reyna announced several measures on 17 March to reduce government spending in response to rising fuel prices and a large fiscal deficit. The US rating agency Standard & Poor's raised the country's credit rating, highlighting improvements in its debt structure and growth prospects. S&P said that real GDP growth had reached 7.8 per cent in 2010, and was predicted to be 4-5 per cent in 2011.

In other developments, the influx of Haitians into the Dominican Republic after the 2010 earthquake became an increasingly controversial issue. Amid rising popular anger, the government stepped up efforts to deport Haitians who had entered the country. However, the UN High Commissioner for Refugees criticised the move, arguing that Haiti "cannot yet ensure adequate protection or care especially for some vulnerable groups in case of return". But the Dominican Republic's Immigration Director, Jose Ricardo Taveras, criticised the UN's position. He claimed that "nobody can resist an invasion of that nature". Haitians born in the Dominican Republic—up to 200,000 of them—also found life more difficult. In December the country's Supreme Court endorsed a constitutional change which denied citizenship to those born in the country of parents who were illegal migrants. The Inter-American Commission on Human Rights criticised the move for leaving such people stateless.

In **Haiti**, after the disputed first round of the presidential election in November 2010 (see AR 2010, pp. 152-53), the country's electoral commission announced in early February that the run-off would be contested by Mirlande Manigat and Michel Martelly. The government-backed candidate, Jude Celestin, was excluded despite initially having come second in the first round of voting. The uncertainty surrounding the election was heightened with the return of two former presidents: Jean-Claude Duvalier in January and Jean-Bertrand Aristide in March. When the second round finally took place in April, Martelly won a clear victory with 67 per cent of the vote, and he took office on 14 May. However, without a majority in the legislature it was not until October that a prime minister was appointed and a new government was formed.

The political stalemate that characterised much of the year hindered the already poor reconstruction efforts in response to the January 2010 earthquake (see AR 2010, pp. 151-52). In October, more than 600,000 people were still homeless. In

June the BBC reported that an unpublished survey commissioned by the US Agency for International Development (USAID) said that significantly fewer people had died in the earthquake than claimed by the country's leaders. The report put the death toll between 46,000 and 85,000, while Haiti's government gave a figure of 316,000. Deaths from the cholera epidemic continued to grow, with approximately 7,000 fatalities by the end of the year; 500,000 had been infected. This meant that Haiti had the highest rate of cholera in the world.

Peter Clegg

WINDWARD AND LEEWARD ISLANDS

Antigua & Barbuda

CAPITAL: St John's   AREA: 440 sq km   POPULATION: 88,710 ('10)
OFFICIAL LANGUAGE: English
HEAD OF STATE: Queen Elizabeth II (since Feb '52)
GOVERNOR-GENERAL: Louise Lake-Tack (since July '07)
RULING PARTY: United Progressive Party (UPP)
HEAD OF GOVERNMENT: Prime Minister Baldwin Spencer (UPP) (since March '04)
CURRENCY: East Caribbean Dollar (Dec '11 £1.00=XCD 4.23, US$1.00=XCD 2.70)
GNI PER CAPITA: US$10,590, Intl$15,350 at PPP ('10)

Dominica

CAPITAL: Roseau   AREA: 750 sq km   POPULATION: 67,757 ('10)
OFFICIAL LANGUAGE: English
HEAD OF STATE: President Nicholas Liverpool (since Oct '03)
RULING PARTY: Dominica Labour Party (DLP)
HEAD OF GOVERNMENT: Prime Minister Roosevelt Skerrit (since Jan '04)
CORRUPTION INDEX: 5.2; 44th of 183
CURRENCY: East Caribbean Dollar (see above)
GNI PER CAPITA: US$5,410, Intl$9,370 at PPP ('10)

St Christopher (Kitts) & Nevis

CAPITAL: Basseterre   AREA: 260 sq km   POPULATION: 52,402 ('10)
OFFICIAL LANGUAGE: English
HEAD OF STATE AND GOVERNMENT: Queen Elizabeth II (since Feb '52)
GOVERNOR-GENERAL: Sir Cuthbert Sebastian (since Jan '96)
RULING PARTY: St Kitts-Nevis Labour Party (SKNLP)
HEAD OF GOVERNMENT: Prime Minister Denzil Douglas (SKNLP) (since July '95)
CURRENCY: East Caribbean Dollar (see above)
GNI PER CAPITA: US$9,520, Intl$12,560 at PPP ('10)

St Lucia

CAPITAL: Castries   AREA: 620 sq km   POPULATION: 174,000 ('10)
OFFICIAL LANGUAGE: English
HEAD OF STATE: Queen Elizabeth II (since Feb '52)
GOVERNOR-GENERAL: Pearlette Louisy (since Sept '97)
RULING PARTY: St Lucia Labour Party (SLP)
HEAD OF GOVERNMENT: Prime Minister Kenny Anthony (SLLP) (since Nov '11)
CORRUPTION INDEX: 7.0; 25th of 183
CURRENCY: East Caribbean Dollar (see above)
GNI PER CAPITA: US$4,970, Intl$8,520 at PPP ('10)

St Vincent & the Grenadines
CAPITAL: Kingstown   AREA: 390 sq km   POPULATION: 109,333 ('10)
OFFICIAL LANGUAGE: English
HEAD OF STATE: Queen Elizabeth II (since Feb '52)
GOVERNOR-GENERAL: Freddy Ballantyne (since Sept '02)
RULING PARTY: Unity Labour Party (ULP)
HEAD OF GOVERNMENT: Prime Minister Ralph Gonsalves (ULP) (since April '01)
CORRUPTION INDEX: 5.8; 36th of 183
CURRENCY: East Caribbean Dollar (see above)
GNI PER CAPITA: US$4,850, Intl$8,260 at PPP ('10)

Grenada
CAPITAL: St George's   AREA: 340 sq km   POPULATION: 104,487 ('10)
OFFICIAL LANGUAGE: English
HEAD OF STATE: Queen Elizabeth II (since Feb '52)
GOVERNOR-GENERAL: Sir Carlyle Glean (since Nov '08)
RULING PARTY: National Democratic Congress (NDC)
HEAD OF GOVERNMENT: Prime Minister Tillman Thomas (NDC) (since July '08)
CURRENCY: East Caribbean Dollar (see above)
GNI PER CAPITA: US$5,550, Intl$7,550 at PPP ('10)

Two elections were held during the year. In **St Lucia** the governing United Workers' Party (UWP) was defeated by the St Lucia Labour Party (SLP) in a general
election held on 28 November. The SLP won 10 seats, and the remaining seven
went to the UWP. The UWP had been weakened by two MPs resigning from the
party earlier in the year. In Nevis (of **St Kitts & Nevis**) the Nevis Reformation
Party (NRP) was voted back into office on 11 July after defeating the Concerned
Citizens' Movement (CCM). The NRP won three of the five seats with the CCM
picking up two seats. In **Dominica**, meanwhile, the opposition United Workers'
Party continued to protest about alleged voter irregularities in the December 2009
election. The party announced on 28 June that it would not be present when Prime
Minister Roosevelt Skerrit presented the 2011-12 budget to Parliament on 29 June.
Amongst the opposition's other demands was for an updated voter register and the
introduction of voter identification cards. Dominica was one of the few remaining
countries in the Caribbean without such cards.

   In economic matters **Antigua & Barbuda's** National Security Minister, Errol
Cort, was served with a $1 million lawsuit in February by investors in the Antigua-
based Stanford International Bank which was at the heart of an alleged $7 billion
fraud by Allen Stanford (see AR 2009, p. 155). The lawsuit related to the time
when Cort headed the finance ministry and had direct oversight of the country's
offshore regulatory body. In June Finance Minister Harold Lovell asked the country's Financial Services Regulatory Commission to carry out an investigation into
claims by *Euromoney* magazine that Antigua was the riskiest Caribbean country in
which to bank money. **Grenada**, in the first part of the year, saw a dramatic jump
in nutmeg production. Farmers produced 203,000 kg of nutmeg in March—five
times the amount anticipated—and one of the biggest production months since
Hurricane Ivan in 2004. The increase came after the Grenada Cooperative Nutmeg
Association increased the price per kg, and the government implemented a stimulus programme to cultivate abandoned fields.

In other developments, St Lucia launched a new television station sponsored by Taiwan. The educational channel IETV offered programmes on the subjects of English, maths, science, and health education. In April, flash flooding in **St Vincent & the Grenadines** caused millions of dollars of damage.

Peter Clegg

BARBADOS, TRINIDAD & TOBAGO, THE BAHAMAS

Barbados

CAPITAL: Bridgetown   AREA: 430 sq km   POPULATION: 273,331 ('10)
OFFICIAL LANGUAGE: English
HEAD OF STATE: Queen Elizabeth II (since Feb '52)
GOVERNOR-GENERAL: Elliot Belgrave (since Nov '11)
RULING PARTY: Democratic Labour Party (DLP)
HEAD OF GOVERNMENT: Prime Minister Freundel Stuart (DLP) (since Oct '10)
CORRUPTION INDEX: 7.8; 16th of 183
CURRENCY: Barbados Dollar (Dec '11 £1.00=BBD 3.14, US$1.00=BBD 2.00)
GNI PER CAPITA: US$12,660, Intl$18,830 at PPP ('09)

Trinidad & Tobago

CAPITAL: Port of Spain   AREA: 5,130 sq km   POPULATION: 1,341,465 ('10)
OFFICIAL LANGUAGE: English
HEAD OF STATE: President George Maxwell Richards (since Feb '03)
RULING PARTY: People's Partnership Coalition (PPC)
HEAD OF GOVERNMENT: Prime Minister Kamla Persad Bissessar (since May '10)
DEMOCRACY INDEX: 7.16; 45th of 167   CORRUPTION INDEX: 3.2; 91st of 183
CURRENCY: Trinidad & Tobago Dollar (Dec '11 £1.00=TTD 10.04, US$1.00=TTD 6.40)
GNI PER CAPITA: US$15,400, Intl$24,040 at PPP ('10)

The Bahamas

CAPITAL: Nassau   AREA: 13,880 sq km   POPULATION: 342,877 ('10)
OFFICIAL LANGUAGE: English
HEAD OF STATE: Queen Elizabeth II (since Feb '52)
GOVERNOR-GENERAL: Sir Arthur Foulkes (since April '10)
RULING PARTY: Free National Movement (FNM)
HEAD OF GOVERNMENT: Prime Minister Hubert Ingraham (FNM) (since May '07)
CORRUPTION INDEX: 7.3; 21st of 183
CURRENCY: Bahamian Dollar (Dec '11 £1.00=BSD 1.57, US$1.00=BSD 1.00)
GNI PER CAPITA: US$20,610, Intl$24,580 at PPP ('09)

THE Central Bank of **Barbados** warned in October that "prospects of a full recovery from the economic recession have become more distant" because of the weakened growth prospects for the USA and Europe. Economic growth in 2011 was projected to be "not much better than 1 per cent". Economic confidence took a further hit with criticisms from the OECD's Global Forum on Transparency and Exchange of Information for Tax Purposes that Barbados did not meet international standards. In December pressure built on Prime Minister Freundel Stuart after a letter from DLP MPs expressing dissatisfaction over his leadership was leaked to the *Barbados Sunday Sun* newspaper. Finally, Historic

Bridgetown and its Garrison were included in the UNESCO World Heritage Site list. They were considered to be "outstanding examples of British colonial architecture", offering a story "which testifies to the spread of Great Britain's Atlantic colonial empire".

Concerns over violent crime took centre stage in **Trinidad & Tobago** and the **Bahamas**. The Prime Minister of Trinidad & Tobago, Kamla Persad-Bissessar, revealed in November that police had thwarted a plot to assassinate her and members of her cabinet. The prime minister blamed the alleged plot on "criminal elements" acting in "reprisal" for a state of emergency that she declared on 21 August. During the police operation 17 people were arrested, including members of the army and police force. However, all were later released without charge. The state of emergency was introduced to tackle rising violent crime, but the opposition denounced it as a "panic response". The state of emergency expired on 5 December. In a separate development, a government proposal to amend the constitution to make it easier for the hanging of convicted murderers was defeated. Under a ruling by the London-based Privy Council, any execution carried out five years after the original death sentence had been imposed constituted torture, which was illegal under the country's constitution. The last execution in Trinidad & Tobago had taken place in 1999. In the Bahamas, a series of measures to deal with an upsurge in crime were announced by Prime Minister Hubert Ingraham on 3 October. These included the establishment of two new courts to deal specifically with crimes relating to drugs and the illegal possession of weapons, and new harsher sentencing guidelines for those convicted of unlawful possession of a firearm or ammunition.

In other news, the sale of 51 per cent of the Bahamas Telecommunications Company (BTC) to UK telecoms giant Cable & Wireless Communications (CWC) was finalised on 6 April. CWC paid $210 million for the majority share. Meanwhile in September, the Bahamas and Cuba agreed a maritime border after 15 years of negotiations, ending uncertainty over the ownership of an area that was considered rich in oil and natural gas.

Peter Clegg

GUYANA, BELIZE, AND SURINAME

Guyana

CAPITAL: Georgetown   AREA: 214,970 sq km   POPULATION: 754,493 ('10)
OFFICIAL LANGUAGE: English
HEAD OF STATE: President Donald Ramotar (since Dec '11)
RULING PARTY: People's Progressive Party-Civic (PPP-C)
HEAD OF GOVERNMENT: Prime Minister Samuel Hinds (since Dec '97)
DEMOCRACY INDEX: 6.05; 75th of 167   CORRUPTION INDEX: 2.5; 134th of 183
CURRENCY: Guyana Dollar (Dec '11 £1.00=GYD 315.53, US$1.00=GYD 201.20)
GNI PER CAPITA: US$3,300, Intl$3,560 at PPP ('10)

Belize

CAPITAL: Belmopan   AREA: 22,970 sq km   POPULATION: 344,700 ('10)
OFFICIAL LANGUAGE: English
HEAD OF STATE AND GOVERNMENT: Queen Elizabeth II (since Feb '52)
GOVERNOR-GENERAL: Sir Colville Young (since Nov '93)
RULING PARTY: United Democratic Party (UDP)
HEAD OF GOVERNMENT: Prime Minister Dean Barrow (since Feb '08)
CURRENCY: Belize Dollar (Dec '11 £1.00=BZD 3.11, US$1=BZD 1.98)
GNI PER CAPITA: US$3,740, Intl$5,970 at PPP ('10)

Suriname

CAPITAL: Paramaribo   AREA: 163,270 sq km   POPULATION: 524,636 ('10)
OFFICIAL LANGUAGE: Dutch
HEAD OF STATE AND GOVERNMENT: President Desiré "Desi" Bouterse (NDP) (since Aug '10)
RULING PARTIES: Mega Combinatie (MC) coalition, led by National Democratic Party (NDP)
DEMOCRACY INDEX: 6.65; 54th of 167   CORRUPTION INDEX: 3.0; 100th of 183
CURRENCY: Surinam Dollar (Dec '11 £1.00=SRD 5.17, US$1.00=SRD 3.30)
GNI PER CAPITA: US$5,920, Intl$7,610 at PPP ('09)

Guyana entered uncharted political territory after the governing People's Progressive Party/Civic (PPP/C) failed to win a majority in the 65-seat National Assembly in the 28 November general election. The PPP/C won 32 seats with 48.6 per cent of the vote; the main opposition coalition party, A Partnership for National Unity (APNU), won 26 seats with 40.8 per cent of the vote; and the Alliance for Change (AFC) secured seven seats with 10.3 per cent of the vote. Turnout was 73 per cent. Despite failing to win a parliamentary majority the PPP/C's Donald Ramotar won the presidency and replaced Bharrat Jagdeo, who was constitutionally barred from seeking a third successive term. The new president was sworn in on 3 December. In recognition of the PPP/C's failure to retain control of the National Assembly, Ramotar at his inauguration stated that "Pettiness must be put aside. It is time for all of us to cast off our partisan cloaks and put on our national garb." The AFC claimed that the "national political landscape has forever been changed for the better" and that the results "should engender broader participation of the representatives of the people in Parliament".

Criminal cross-border activity involving Guyana, **Suriname** and **Belize** was evident during the year. The criminal links between Guyana and Suriname were highlighted in US diplomatic cables released by WikiLeaks. According to the cables Suriname's President Desi Bouterse had helped protect the Guyanese drug lord

Shaheed "Roger" Khan who was jailed in the US in 2009 (see AR 2009, p. 158). Dutch media reported that the cables indicated that Bouterse had "social and operational links" with Khan and travelled illegally to Guyana to arrange gun running and drug smuggling operations. Further, Bouterse was alleged to have introduced Khan to "Suriname's criminal elements and structures". Cables also alleged that the two men were involved in "murders and planned murders". In Belize meanwhile, the ministry of foreign affairs and foreign trade expressed concern about the "increasing trend of illegal activities by Guatemalan nationals within Belizean territory" on 25 August after a shooting incident three days earlier involving a Belize defence force patrol and Guatemalan civilians.

In other developments the House of Representatives in Belize approved Prime Minister Dean Barrow's Ninth Amendment to the constitution on 21 October. The purpose of the amendment was to ensure that the nationalisations of Belize Telemedia Ltd (BTL) and Belize Electricity Ltd remained legally binding. The amendment was put forward in response to an appeal court ruling that the nationalisation of BTL in 2009 had been unconstitutional (see AR 2009, p. 159).

Peter Clegg

UK OVERSEAS TERRITORIES

Anguilla

CAPITAL: The Valley   AREA: 96 sq km   POPULATION: 15,962 ('09 est, FCO)
OFFICIAL LANGUAGE: English
GOVERNOR-GENERAL: William Harrison (since April '09)
RULING PARTY: Anguilla United Movement (AUM)
HEAD OF GOVERNMENT: Chief Minister Hubert Hughes (AUM) (since Feb '10)
CURRENCY: East Caribbean Dollar (Dec '11 £1.00=XCD 4.23, US$1.00=XCD 2.70)
GNI PER CAPITA: GDP per capita US$9,711 ('06)

Bermuda

CAPITAL: Hamilton   AREA: 50 sq km   POPULATION: 64,600 ('10)
OFFICIAL LANGUAGE: English
HEAD OF STATE: Queen Elizabeth II (since Feb '52)
GOVERNOR-GENERAL: Sir Richard Gozney (since Dec '07)
RULING PARTY: Progressive Labour Party (PLP)
HEAD OF GOVERNMENT: Premier Paula Cox (PLP) (since Oct '10)
CURRENCY: Bermudian Dollar (Dec '11 £1.00=BMD 1.57, US$1.00=BMD 1.00)
GNI PER CAPITA: GDP per capita US$76,400 ('06)

British Virgin Islands

CAPITAL: Road Town   AREA: 153 sq km   POPULATION: 28,000 ('08 est, FCO)
OFFICIAL LANGUAGE: English
HEAD OF STATE: Queen Elizabeth II (since Feb '52)
GOVERNOR-GENERAL: William Boyd McCleary
RULING PARTY: Virgin Islands Party (VIP)
HEAD OF GOVERNMENT: Premier Orlando Smith (since Nov '11)
CURRENCY: US Dollar (Dec '11 £1.00=US$1.57)
GNI PER CAPITA: GDP per capita US$41,700 ('06 est.)

Cayman Islands

CAPITAL: George Town, Grand Cayman   AREA: 260 sq km   POPULATION: 56,230 ('10)
OFFICIAL LANGUAGE: English
HEAD OF STATE: Queen Elizabeth II (since Feb '52)
GOVERNOR-GENERAL: Duncan Taylor (since Jan '10)
RULING PARTY: United Democratic Party (UDP)
HEAD OF GOVERNMENT: Premier McKeeva Bush (since Nov '09)
CURRENCY: Cayman Island Dollar (Dec '11 £1.00=KYD 1.29, US$1.00=KYD 0.82)
GNI PER CAPITA: GDP per capita US$46,500 ('06 est.)

Montserrat

CAPITAL: Plymouth   AREA: 102 sq km   POPULATION: 4,875 (UN est. mid-'08)
OFFICIAL LANGUAGE: English
HEAD OF STATE: Queen Elizabeth II (since Feb '52)
GOVERNOR-GENERAL: Adrian Davis (since April '11)
RULING PARTY: Movement for Change and Prosperity (MCAP)
HEAD OF GOVERNMENT: Chief Minister Reuben Meade (since Sept '09)
CURRENCY: East Caribbean Dollar (see above)
GNI PER CAPITA: GDP per capita EC$22,803 ('06)

Turks & Caicos Islands

CAPITAL: Cockburn Town   AREA: 430 sq km   POPULATION: 38,354 ('10)
OFFICIAL LANGUAGE: English
HEAD OF STATE: Queen Elizabeth II (since Feb '52)
GOVERNOR-GENERAL: Damian Roderic Todd (since Sept '11)
HEAD OF GOVERNMENT: office suspended
CURRENCY: US Dollar (Dec '11 £1.00=USD 1.57)

RELATIONS between the UK and some of its Overseas Territories remained strained—most significantly the **Turks & Caicos**, where direct rule from the UK was maintained. Elections were expected in late 2012. New constitutional and electoral arrangements were finalised (although not implemented) in an attempt to address many of the problems that had been identified by the 2009 Commission of Inquiry (see AR 2010, p. 161). They included strengthening the governor's reserved powers; introducing an enforceable commitment to good governance principles, including in relation to Crown land; establishing term limits for premiers; and improving the effectiveness of the House of Assembly. Furthermore, measures were implemented to restructure the Turks & Caicos economy and to reduce the high levels of debt bequeathed by the last Progressive National Party (PNP) government. However, the process of economic reform proved difficult, with decisions such as reducing the cost of the public service by 25 per cent, reducing public sector pay, improving tax collection and enforcement, and improving financial management and reporting, fuelling discontent. Finally, a Special Investigation and Prosecution Team (SIPT) continued to investigate and prosecute allegations of corruption highlighted in, and related to, the 2009 Commission of Inquiry report. By the end of the year, 10 people had been charged with corruption, including four former government ministers, although no charges had yet been brought against former Premier Michael Misick. In reaction against continued UK involvement the PNP announced in October that it would seek a referendum on independence if it won the next general election.

Similar sentiments were seen in **Anguilla** after clashes between the UK-appointed governor and Chief Minister Hubert Hughes. In January Hughes called on Anguillans to "throw off the yoke of oppression" and consider independence.

Peter Clegg

THE DUTCH TERRITORIES

Curaçao

CAPITAL: Willemstad   AREA: 444 sq km   POPULATION: 142,668 ('10)
OFFICIAL LANGUAGE: Dutch
HEAD OF STATE: Queen Beatrix
GOVERNOR-GENERAL: Frits Goedgedrag (since Oct '10)
RULING PARTIES: Movement for the Future of Curaçao (MFK)-led coalition
HEAD OF GOVERNMENT: Gerrit Schotte (MFK) (since Oct '10)
CURRENCY: US dollar (Dec '11 £1.00=USD 1.57)

Sint Maarten

CAPITAL: Philipsburg   AREA: 34 sq km   POPULATION: 37,850 ('10)
OFFICIAL LANGUAGE: Dutch
HEAD OF STATE: Queen Beatrix
GOVERNOR-GENERAL: Eugene Holiday (since Oct '10)
RULING PARTIES: coalition of United People's party and Democratic Party
HEAD OF GOVERNMENT: Sarah Wescot-Williams (DP) (since Oct '10)
CURRENCY: US Dollar (Dec '11 £1.00=USD 1.57)

Aruba

CAPITAL: Oranjestad   AREA: 180 sq km   POPULATION: 107,488 ('10)
OFFICIAL LANGUAGE: Dutch
HEAD OF STATE: Queen Beatrix
GOVERNOR-GENERAL: Fredis Refunjol (since May '04)
RULING PARTY: Aruban People's Party (AVP)
HEAD OF GOVERNMENT: Mike Eman (AVP) (since Sept '09)
CURRENCY: Florin (Dec '11 £1.00=AWG 2.81, US$1.00=AWG 1.79)
GNI PER CAPITA: high income: US$11,906 or more ('08 est.)

THE new coalition government in **Curaçao** suffered its first major crisis in May and June after the second largest party in the coalition, Independent People (PS), strongly criticised the actions of Prime Minister Gerrit Schotte in response to a dispute between the prime minister and Emsley Tromp, president of the Central Bank of Curaçao and Sint Maarten. Each had accused the other of corruption. In response Schotte asked the Dutch government to assist in an investigation of both the central bank and his own government. The decision of Schotte created a nationalist backlash in Curaçao, including from the PS. In response Schotte back-tracked and said that the investigation would now not involve the Dutch and would only focus on the central bank. The investigation later cleared both men, but the incident weakened the coalition government, and also support for the central bank. In early June, the parliament voted in favour of Curaçao establishing its own central bank, a potentially serious development in undermining one of the key institutions established after the dissolution of the Netherlands Antilles in 2010 (see AR 2010, p. 163). Schotte faced more trouble in October when a report commissioned by the Kingdom of the Netherlands into standards of governance in Curaçao claimed that he and two cabinet colleagues were unfit to hold public office.

Sint Maarten also had to adjust to its new relationship with the Netherlands. In the first part of the year, a draft budget that had been approved by the local legislature was rejected by the Dutch financial supervision council. The Dutch authorities demanded cuts which the local government resisted for a time. However, a new budget was then agreed after the Dutch threatened in late March that if Sint Maarten did not produce a balanced budget by mid-April, they would step in and supervise the country's economy more closely. In response, both Sint Maarten and Curaçao agitated for the termination of the Kingdom law on financial supervision.

Peter Clegg

THE US CARIBBEAN

Puerto Rico

CAPITAL: San Juan   AREA: 8,950 sq km   POPULATION: 3,978,702 ('10)
OFFICIAL LANGUAGES: Spanish & English
HEAD OF STATE: US President Barack Obama
RULING PARTY: New Progressive Party (PNP)
HEAD OF GOVERNMENT: Governor Luis Fortuño (PNP) (since Jan '09)
CORRUPTION INDEX: 5.6; 39th of 183
CURRENCY: US Dollar (Dec '11 £1.00=USD 1.57)
GNI PER CAPITA: high income: US$11,906 or more ('08 est.)

US Virgin Islands

CAPITAL: Charlotte Amalie   AREA: 350 sq km   POPULATION: 109,775 ('10)
OFFICIAL LANGUAGE: English
HEAD OF STATE AND GOVERNMENT: President Barack Obama
RULING PARTY: Democrats
HEAD OF GOVERNMENT: Governor John deJongh (Democratic Party) (since Jan '07)
CURRENCY: US Dollar (Dec '11 £1.00=USD 1.57)
GNI PER CAPITA: high income: US$11,906 or more ('08 est.)

BOTH **Puerto Rico** and the **US Virgin Islands** faced difficult economic conditions in 2011, although the news was slightly better for the former. The Fitch Rating agency reported in December that the economy of Puerto Rico was finally beginning to stabilise. The economy had begun shrinking in 2007 and had lost over 100,000 jobs in total. Fitch noted several positive signs of improvement, including a slowing of employment losses and increasing retail sales, and predicted a return to growth in 2012 of 0.5 per cent. However, debts remained "very high". In the US Virgin Islands Governor John deJongh warned on 24 January that the economy was at a "tipping point" and said that updated revenue projections showed a significant and worsening budget shortfall for 2011 and 2012. He continued that "tax increases, layoffs, salary freezes, budget cuts and unpaid holidays were unavoidable".

In other news Barack Obama became the first sitting US president since John F. Kennedy in 1961 to make an official visit to Puerto Rico. In September the Puerto Rico police department was accused by the US justice department of a "profound" and "longstanding" pattern of civil rights violations and other illegal practices that have left it "broken in a number of critical and fundamental respects". The report identified problems of violence, corruption and incompetence within the service.

Peter Clegg

SOUTH AMERICA

BRAZIL—ARGENTINA—PARAGUAY—URUGUAY—CHILE—PERU—BOLIVIA— ECUADOR—COLOMBIA—VENEZUELA

BRAZIL

CAPITAL: Brasília   AREA: 8,514,880 sq km   POPULATION: 194,946,470 ('10)
OFFICIAL LANGUAGE: Portuguese
HEAD OF STATE AND GOVERNMENT: President Dilma Rousseff (PT) (since Jan '11)
RULING PARTIES: Workers' Party (PT)-led coalition
DEMOCRACY INDEX: 7.12; 47th of 167   CORRUPTION INDEX: 3.8; 73rd of 183
CURRENCY: Real (Dec '11 £1.00=BRL 2.81, US$1.00=BRL 1.79)
GNI PER CAPITA: US$9,390, Intl$10,920 at PPP ('10)

THE year opened with the historic inauguration of Dilma Rousseff, 63, as Brazil's 36th president. Rousseff's inauguration, held in Congress (the bicameral federal legislature) in Brasilia on 1 January, was historic because it marked the first occasion that a female had held the presidency, an accomplishment that she achieved by winning the election of October 2010 as the candidate of the ruling Workers' Party (PT). During her inauguration speech, Rousseff confirmed most analysts' predictions that her administration intended to "consolidate the transforming work" of her predecessor, former President Luiz Inácio "Lula" da Silva (2000-10). Rousseff also pledged that her administration's "most determined fight" would be "to eradicate extreme poverty and create opportunities for all", adding that she would "not rest while there are Brazilians who have no food on their tables, while there are desperate families on the streets, while there are poor children abandoned to their own devices".

Rousseff had contested the presidential election under the slogan "For Brazil to keep on changing". However, the first year of her four-year term in office was blighted by corruption, an all too familiar blot on Brazil's political landscape. Allegations of corruption and other unethical practices forced six members of her nascent administration to resign from their posts in the second half of the year, and another cabinet member, Defence Minister Nelson Jobim, was forced to step down in August after making derogatory remarks about some of his colleagues. The resignations most notably included António Palocci, who resigned from the post of presidency minister (chief of staff) on 7 June, after the *Folha de São Paulo* newspaper published a report questioning why the minister's personal wealth had increased twentyfold in the past four years. The other five corruption resignations involved Transport Minister Alfredo Nascimento (7 July); Agriculture Minister Wagner Rossi (17 August); Tourism Minister Pedro Novais Lima (14 September); Sports Minister Orlando Silva de Jesus Júnior (26 October); and Labour Minister Carlos Lupi (3 December). Whilst the sense of hope which pervaded Rousseff's inauguration speech was eroded by these scandals, opinion polls showed that the president enjoyed a record level public approval as the year ended, suggesting that the resignations were perceived as evidence that the president acting on her campaign pledge to stamp out corruption. Rousseff was also named by *Forbes* magazine as the world's third most powerful woman, after Germany's Chancellor Angela Merkel and US Secretary of State Hillary Clinton.

The emergence of the scandals again raised the ugly possibility that corruption in Brazil was an intractable problem and highlighted a major defect in the character of the country's often-cited status as an "emerging power". The electorate's exasperation was clearly expressed in a series of nationwide protests against corruption in the first week of September. Tens of thousands of citizens marched in several cities to demonstrate their frustrations, with officials from the College of Lawyers, the Brazilian Press Association, and the National Bishops' Conference, describing corruption in Brazil as "a pandemic" threat to "the credibility of institutions and the entire democratic system".

Any possibility of the scandals causing vicarious damage to the popular image of da Silva, who had strongly supported Rousseff's presidential candidacy, paled in significance on 31 October, when the former president was diagnosed with a malignant throat tumour. Oncologist Artur Katz announced in December that the medical team treating da Silva's cancer, based at the Hospital Sírio-Libanés in São Paulo, Brazil's largest city, was "impressed" with the former president's ongoing recovery, revealing that three rounds of chemotherapy had yielded an "an extraordinary reduction" (of 75 per cent) in the size of the tumour. Doctors also indicated that da Silva, 66, could resume his political activities—he remained an influential member of the PT and was regarded as a close advisor to many within Rousseff's administration, including the president herself—in March 2012, after undergoing radiation treatments scheduled for January and February. Some observers speculated that if Rousseff did not seek a second consecutive term in office, then an eventual recovery from cancer by da Silva could prompt him to seek a return to office as early as 2014, a theory which was powered by a "messianic" image of the former president in the eyes of many Brazilian voters.

Just days before Palocci's resignation, on 2 June Rousseff launched her flagship social policy, Brazil Sem Miseria (BSM—Brazil Without Poverty), an ambitious social initiative aimed at helping to lift 16.2 million Brazilians out of extreme poverty by 2014. BSM effectively expanded social welfare policies implemented by the da Silva administrations, such as the Família Bolsa programme, which involved cash transfer programmes and increased access to education, health, welfare, sanitation, and electricity. Rousseff's first year in office also entailed the enactment of legislation on 18 November creating a National Truth Commission, which was given the task of investigating human rights abuses committed in Brazil between 1946 and 1988, including those committed during the country's military dictatorship era (1964-85). The bill granted a two-year mandate to a seven-strong panel, which was empowered to summon witnesses under oath and access state documents, including those from the military dictatorship era, during which at least 400 citizens were killed or "disappeared". Rousseff said that the commission was a "process of building truth and memory", declaring that "the truth about our past is fundamental, so those facts that stain our history will never happen again". Rousseff also enacted the Law of Access to Public Information, new legislation authorising public access to some previously-secret state documents.

The effects of the scheduled hosting in Brazil of two of the largest (and most lucrative) global sporting events—the Olympic Games in 2016 and the FIFA World Cup in 2014—were felt strongly in 2011. It was widely acknowledged that Brazil's preparations for both major events were behind schedule and over budget, whilst fears continued to be expressed about the reliability and capacity of Brazil's public infrastructure and the risks of violent crime, especially in major cities such as São Paulo and Rio de Janeiro. Officials from the sports ministry on 6 July made clear the economic importance of the events, revealing that Brazil's hosting of the World Cup was expected to boost GDP by at least $70 billion, including investments in private and public infrastructure, heightened consumption, increased activity in the services sector, and increased tax receipts. Government officials also estimated in 2011 that Brazil's hosting of the Olympic Games would boost the economy by some $51 billion by 2027.

In a desire to maximise these potential economic opportunities (and recognising that crime could damage those prospects), the government in 2011 intensified its attempts to "control" and "pacify" the favelas (slums) in Rio de Janiero and other major cities. Police officials announced on 11 November that areas of Rocinha, a favela in Rio de Janiero, had been "cleared" of drug gangs in an operation led by police officers and navy commandos, supported by armoured military vehicles and helicopters. A report (entitled *Mega-Events and Human Rights Abuses in Brazil*) published on 12 December by the Comites Populares da Copa, a national network of academics, community organisations, social movements and charities, alleged that a series of human rights were being violated amid Brazil's preparations for the "mega-events". The report alleged that citizens' rights were being abused in cases involving housing, information, and employment, as entire communities were demolished to make way for new developments relating to the hosting of the events. The report estimated that between 150,000 and 170,000 people had suffered "forced removal, en masse" from their homes in order to "clear the ground" "for big, money-making real estate projects".

Brazil's economy continued to develop in 2011, despite the government's announcement, on 18 November, that it had revised downwards its 2011 economic growth estimate to 3.8 per cent from 4.5 per cent, a move that it blamed on the worsening debt crisis in Europe and a sluggish US economy. In a league table published on 28 December, the UK-based think-tank, the Centre for Economics and Business Research, said that, based on data published by the IMF, Brazil was expected to replace the UK as the world's sixth largest economy in 2011.

In foreign relations, Rousseff welcomed US President Barack Obama to Brasilia on 19 March, when the two leaders signed a series of trade and energy sector agreements designed to boost bilateral ties. After the meeting, Obama praised Brazil's "extraordinary rise" on the world stage, saying that the country's economic and social developments had "captured the attention of the world". Notably, however, Obama failed to support explicitly Brazil's protracted attempts to secure a permanent seat on the UN Security Council, instead expressing an "appreciation for Brazil's aspiration".

Kurt Perry

ARGENTINA

CAPITAL: Buenos Aires AREA: 2,780,400 sq km POPULATION: 40,412,376 ('10)
OFFICIAL LANGUAGE: Spanish
HEAD OF STATE AND GOVERNMENT: President Cristina Fernandez de Kirchner (PJ) (since Dec '07)
RULING PARTY: Front for Victory—Justicialist Party (PJ)
DEMOCRACY INDEX: 6.84; 51st of 167 CORRUPTION INDEX: 3.0; 100th of 183
CURRENCY: Argentine Peso (Dec '11 £1.00=ARS 6.72, US$1.00=ARS 4.28)
GNI PER CAPITA: US$8,500, Intl$15,250 at PPP ('10)

PRESIDENT Cristina Fernández de Kirchner won her re-election bid in the first round of elections on 23 October, achieving an outright victory with 54 per cent of the vote, compared with just under 17 per cent polled by her closest rival, the Socialist governor of Santa Fé province, Hermes Binner. Her political party, the left-wing Victory Front (FPV), also took control of both houses of the national congress and won eight out of nine gubernatorial elections held on the same day. Her commanding lead in the polls since the first-ever primaries on 14 August made it even more difficult for the disjointed opposition to define a clear alternative political project and field strong candidates. Right-wing frontrunner Mauricio Macri decided early on not to run against Kirchner and was re-elected mayor of Buenos Aires on 31 July with 63 per cent of the vote. Despite a first term full of confrontations with the national executive, he defeated Kirchner ally Daniel Filmus who had hoped to benefit from the pro-Kirchner mood in the country.

Spectacular economic growth continued in 2011 at an estimated rate of 9.3 per cent. Inflation, although officially running at 9.5 per cent, in reality still hovered at around 20 per cent, some effects of which were neutralised by an activist government policy of encouraging the social partners to keep increasing wages. Agriculture boomed, generating an estimated 30 billion US dollars in exports, a new record. Tourism also grew strongly, with over 5 million visitors in 2011. In April, the Kirchner administration chose a more hands-on approach to the strategic management of the 40 companies or so that it owned shares in since the 2008 nationalisation of the pension system: positioning government representatives with real voting power in the boards of directors.

Ironically, through the national pension system (Anses) the state owned some 30 per cent of Grupo Clarín, the biggest and most influential opposition media company. Clarín continued to be at odds with Kirchner and suffered increased attacks from the state at the end of the year. Amongst these were a police operation at Cablevisión in December, Clarín's highly successful cable television provider, and the state intervention at Papel Prensa, the paper supplier for the biggest newspapers in the country, 49 per cent of which were owned by Clarín (and another 27.5 per cent by the state). The case of Papel Prensa caused particular controversy because opponents of the president saw it as state meddling and a danger to the freedom of the press, while the government claimed that it wanted to become not a regulator but the guarantor of free speech. Some feared that the government could now use its voting power on the board of directors to neutralise Clarín. For others there was concern that the Kirchner administration's efforts to create a government-controlled digital media platform through the adjudication process for a flurry of new digital TV licenses, that began in June, could be skewed towards media moguls sympathetic to the president. Coincidentally, the National University of La Plata awarded a prestigious journalism award to Venezuelan president Hugo Chávez, whose own relations with the media were rocky at best.

Judicial activism made a mark in two important areas in 2011. One was the ongoing prosecution of former members of the military government (1976-83) for crimes against humanity, by now a hallmark of both Kirchner administrations. In 2011 alone, the Argentinian judiciary convicted 83 people of such crimes committed during the dictatorship, bringing the total number of convictions to 269. Among those convicted in 2011—the 35th anniversary of the military coup that had ushered in the dictatorship—were former general Reynaldo Bignone, the last president during the period of military rule, and former Commander Alfredo Astiz, known as "the blond angel of death" for his role in the incarceration, torture and "disappearance" of political detainees at the country's largest secret prison, the navy's mechanical school, ESMA. The other area was the fight against corruption, with a series of high-profile indictments of union leaders, long considered to be untouchable. Charges of financial irregularities—in one case even murder—were brought against the leaders of the railway, banking and rural workers' unions. Even Hugo Moyano, a longtime Kirchner ally and leader of the all-powerful General Confederation of Workers (CGT), was prosecuted in three different cases. The reasons for this judicial sea change lay less in the cooling relationships between union leaders and the government, but rather in the higher degrees of autonomy enjoyed by the justice system—and in the new mood of a public tired of the corrupt and violently confrontational union politics that had regularly taken the capital hostage through roadblocks and mass demonstrations.

Regarding foreign policy, the debate about the sovereignty over the Falklands/Malvinas Islands took another turn at the end of the year, when the members of Mercosur sided with Argentina in December to start denying entry to all ships sailing under the Falklands flag. This largely symbolic measure came after the UK had allowed exploration vessels to look for oil in the continental shelf, under what it regarded as the exclusive economic zone around the disputed archipelago. Some oil had already been found and there were signs that oil production could be viable. This fuelled economic interest on both sides and further complicated the long-running sovereignty issue.

In other news, the Mothers of the Plaza de Mayo, the most important civil society organisation pushing for prosecution of crimes committed under the dictatorship and a close ally of the president, came under fire in June when charges of money laundering and embezzlement of public funds involving a housing scheme were brought against the group and its leader, Hebe de Bonafini. This represented a significant loss of credibility for the Mothers. On 13 September, former president Carlos Menem (1989-99) was acquitted of charges of illegal arms sales during his presidency to Ecuador and Croatia. This 16-year investigation was the first time that a democratically elected president had been brought before a court of law on corruption charges.

Finally, the fabled Club Atlético River Plate, once Argentina's finest football team, was relegated from the premier division in June, thereby descending into the second division for the first time in its 110-year history. In a country where football was a matter of the heart, the fans did not take it lightly, burning cars, trashing the stadium, and injuring 60 in an outpouring of anger and grief.

Christian E. Rieck

PARAGUAY—URUGUAY

Paraguay

CAPITAL: Asunción   AREA: 406,750 sq km   POPULATION: 6,454,548 ('10)
OFFICIAL LANGUAGE: Spanish
HEAD OF STATE AND GOVERNMENT: President Fernando Lugo (APC) (since Aug '08)
RULING PARTY: Patriotic Alliance for Change (APC)
DEMOCRACY INDEX: 6.40; 62nd of 167   CORRUPTION INDEX: 2.2; 154th of 183
CURRENCY: Guarani (Dec '11 £1.00=PYG 6,986, US$1.00=PYG 4,455)
GNI PER CAPITA: US$2,940, Intl$5,440 at PPP ('10)

Uruguay

CAPITAL: Montevideo   AREA: 176,220 sq km   POPULATION: 3,356,584 ('10)
OFFICIAL LANGUAGE: Spanish
HEAD OF STATE AND GOVERNMENT: President José Mujica (FA), since March '10
RULING PARTY: Broad Front (FA)
DEMOCRACY INDEX: 8.10; 21st of 167   CORRUPTION INDEX: 7.0; 25th of 183
CURRENCY: Peso Uruguay (Dec '11 £1.00=UYU 30.89, US$1.00=UYU 19.70)
GNI PER CAPITA: US$10,590, Intl$13,890 at PPP ('10)

AFTER a sharp rebound of 15 per cent in 2010, economic growth in **Paraguay** normalised at 4.5 per cent. According to the IMF, this reflected the return of agricultural growth to more normal levels, as well as the impact of cement shortfalls, and problems with accessing key beef export markets. The inflation rate was 5.5 per cent, a level achieved by lower commodity prices and the appreciation of the national currency. On 26 February Argentina and Paraguay inaugurated a joint hydroelectric power plant, "Yacyretá", on the Paraná river, close the city of Ayolas, a controversial project because of its significant environmental impact and excessive cost ($11 billion). The installed capacity of 3,100 MW, with an annual output of 20,000 GWh, was less than a quarter of that of the famed Itaipú dam situated further upriver. Nevertheless, it increased the availability of electricity an important export commodity.

July saw a short-lived controversy over whether President Fernando Lugo would be able to run for re-election in 2013, should he and his supporters so wish. On 27 June, Lugo sympathisers delivered a petition to Congress in favour of changing the 1992 constitution by referendum to allow the president to run. It contained 100,000 signatures. On 14 July the Senate dismissed this possibility, thereby closing the door on any prospect of Lugo's re-election. On 9 October, however, a constitutional amendment, supported by Lugo, was approved by referendum. This permitted Paraguayans living abroad to vote in national elections. The measure was significant in that an estimated 550,000 Paraguayans were living in neighbouring Argentina, and another 140,000 in Spain, and their remittances constituted an important source of national income.

The Army of the Paraguayan People (EPP), a small left-wing guerrilla organisation, continued to haunt the departments of Concepción and San Pedro. The Paraguayan army mounted the latest in a series of operations designed to root it out after a 21 September shootout in Capitán Giménez that left two policemen dead. Apart from such small-scale terrorist acts, however, the EPP did not have the capacity to seriously threaten the stability of the state. By contrast, drug-related criminal networks were better funded and more ruthless. From September to November, four members of the Pai Tavytera indigenous community were killed by drug traffickers in the department of Amambay simply because they had seen airplanes land in the jungle. The tribe was threatened with massacre if it did not pay a ransom of $2 million. Cartel leader Tomás Rojas Cañete was apprehended in a luxury home in Ciudad del Este on 4 September.

In the year of Paraguay's bicentenary, the country dared to look back at its more recent past. On 28 July, a permanent website, a "virtual museum", was inaugurated as a platform to disseminate the testimonials about, and information on, Latin America's longest-running dictatorship under General Alfredo Stroessner (1954-89), gathered by the Truth and Justice Commission (CVJ) from 2003 to 2008. The online museum, "Memory and Truth about Stronism" (Meves), was based on the findings of the CVJ's final report and described the characteristics of the Stroessner regime, the places of torture, as well as the long-term effects of the dictatorship on perpetrators, victims and society as a whole. As such it was part of a proud new Latin American tradition of national remembrance museums (museos de la memoria), such as the ones in Chile or Argentina, that set out to preserve the memory of the victims of the right-wing military dictatorships and return to them their dignity after being branded for too long as enemies of the state.

President José Mujica apologised on 7 September to his Haitian counterpart, Michel Martelly, for the rape of a 18-year old boy by four Uruguayan servicemen of the UN Stabilisation Mission in Haiti (MINUSTAH). The scandal broke just as representatives from MINUSTAH's troop contributing nations were meeting in Montevideo to propose a reduction by a third in the size of the deployed 12,000-strong police and military force to a level comparable to that deployed prior to the devastating 2010 earthquake. **Uruguay** had been an important contributor to MINUSTAH from the start and the rape case constituted a heavy blow to its national self-esteem and international credibility as a provider of professional military services to UN stabilisation missions.

The Uruguayan economy continued to grow, at an annualised rate of 6.5 per cent, although at 8.2 per cent inflation was higher than in 2010. Unemployment hit historic lows (around 6 per cent), while revenues from tourism overtook those from beef exports and became the main source of national income. The country also continued to attract important foreign direct investment. In January the Swedish-Finnish multinational Stora Enso, together with the Chilean firm Arauco, committed to the establishment of a large paper mill, an investment of $1.9 billion. But it was the huge mining project by Minera Aratirí, the local subsidiary of the Anglo-Swiss group Zamin Ferrous, that would, at over $2 billion, represent the largest private investment in Uruguay's history. It would include an open-air mine in the Cuchilla Grande area, close to the city of Valentines, as well as the construction of a new deep-water port in La Angostura, in the department of Rocha, for exclusive use by the mine to export its iron ore. If approved, the Aratirí project would represent a major transformation of the Uruguayan economy, creating jobs but also unknown levels of pollution.

To help decide this case, President Mujica in June asked Congress to pass a law that would regulate (non-binding) referendums, arguing that the scope, opportunities and pitfalls of the Aratirí project, and other such proposals of national importance, warranted a more direct participation of the electorate. However, this idea was not well received and inspired doubts about how consistently the government would respect the will of the people. After all, for much of the past five years the FA government had tried to overturn or hollow out the amnesty law for crimes committed during Uruguay's last dictatorship (1973-85)—a law that had been ratified by popular vote in 1989 and renewed by referendum in 2009. This amnesty law (Ley de Caducidad) was upheld by Congress on 20 May, after diverging votes in its upper and lower chambers. But on 24 March the Inter-American Court of Human Rights (IACHR) had declared that the amnesty law must not be an obstacle to the investigation of crimes against humanity committed during the dictatorship, thereby throwing its constitutionality into doubt. In the midst of this uncertainty, convicted former president and coup leader Juan María Bordaberry died under house arrest on 17 July at the age of 83.

In other news, on 28 December the Uruguayan Senate legalised abortion during the first 12 weeks of a pregnancy. The OECD removed Uruguay from its grey list of tax havens on 15 December. Former president Tabaré Vázquez (2005-10) was forced to retire from politics on 13 October after it came to light that he had analysed the possibility of war with Argentina during the Botnia paper mill conflict and had even asked the US government for support.

Uruguay won the Copa América in July, South America's most important football championship, beating Paraguay in the final. The country's premier club, Peñarol, came second at South America's international club tournament, the Copa Libertadores, after losing to Brazil's Santos in the June final.

Christian E. Rieck

CHILE—PERU—BOLIVIA—ECUADOR—COLOMBIA—VENEZUELA

Chile

CAPITAL: Santiago   AREA: 756,630 sq km   POPULATION: 17,113,688 ('10)
OFFICIAL LANGUAGE: Spanish
HEAD OF STATE AND GOVERNMENT: President Sebastian Piñera (since March '10)
RULING PARTY: Coalition for Change
DEMOCRACY INDEX: 7.67; 34th of 167   CORRUPTION INDEX: 7.2; 22nd of 183
CURRENCY: Chilean Peso (Dec '11 £1.00=CLP 808.20, US$1.00=CLP 515.35)
GNI PER CAPITA: US$9,950, Intl$13,900 at PPP ('10)

Peru

CAPITAL: Lima   AREA: 1,285,220 sq km   POPULATION: 29,076,512 ('10)
OFFICIAL LANGUAGES: Spanish, Quechua, Aymará
HEAD OF STATE AND GOVERNMENT: President Ollanta Humala (GP) (since July '11)
RULING PARTY/IES: Peru Wins (GP) alliance
PRIME MINISTER: Salomón Lerner Ghitis (since July '11)
DEMOCRACY INDEX: 6.40; 62nd of 167   CORRUPTION INDEX: 3.4; 80th of 183
CURRENCY: New Sol (Dec '11 £1.00=PEN 4.23, US$1.00=PEN 2.70)
GNI PER CAPITA: US$4,780, Intl$9,070 at PPP ('10)

Bolivia

CAPITAL: La Paz and Sucre   AREA: 1,098,580 sq km   POPULATION: 9,929,849 ('10)
OFFICIAL LANGUAGES: Spanish, Quechua, Aymará
HEAD OF STATE AND GOVERNMENT: President Evo Morales (MAS) (since Jan '06)
RULING PARTY: Movement Towards Socialism (MAS) (since Dec '05)
DEMOCRACY INDEX: 5.92; 80th of 167   CORRUPTION INDEX: 2.8; 118th of 183
CURRENCY: Boliviano (Dec '11 £1.00=BOB 10.84, US$1.00=BOB 6.91)
GNI PER CAPITA: US$1,810, Intl$4,610 at PPP ('10)

Ecuador

CAPITAL: Quito   AREA: 283,560 sq km   POPULATION: 14,464,739 ('10)
OFFICIAL LANGUAGE: Spanish
HEAD OF STATE AND GOVERNMENT: President Rafael Correa Delgado (PAIS Alliance) (since Jan '07)
RULING PARTY: PAIS Alliance
DEMOCRACY INDEX: 5.77; 87th of 167   CORRUPTION INDEX: 2.7; 120th of 183
CURRENCY: US Dollar (Dec '11 £1.00=USD 1.57)
GNI PER CAPITA: US$4,290, Intl$8,830 at PPP ('10)

Colombia

CAPITAL: Santa Fe de Bogotá   AREA: 1,141,750 sq km   POPULATION: 46,294,841 ('10)
OFFICIAL LANGUAGE: Spanish
HEAD OF STATE AND GOVERNMENT: President Juan Manuel Santos (UP) (since Aug '10)
RULING PARTY: Party of the "U" (UP)
DEMOCRACY INDEX: 6.55; 57th of 167   CORRUPTION INDEX: 3.4; 80th of 183
CURRENCY: Colombian Peso (Dec '11 £1.00=COP 3,059.58, US$1.00=COP 1,950.95)
GNI PER CAPITA: US$5,510, Intl$9,000 at PPP ('10)

Venezuela

CAPITAL: Caracas   AREA: 912,050 sq km   POPULATION: 28,834,000 ('10)
OFFICIAL LANGUAGE: Spanish
HEAD OF STATE AND GOVERNMENT: President Hugo Chávez Frías (PSUV) (since Feb '99)
RULING PARTY: United Socialist Party of Venezuela (PSUV)
DEMOCRACY INDEX: 5.18; 96th of 167   CORRUPTION INDEX: 1.9; 172nd of 183
CURRENCY: Bolívar Fuerte (Dec '11 £1.00=VEF 6.73, US$1.00=VEF 4.29)
GNI PER CAPITA: US$11,590, Intl$11,950 at PPP ('10)

THE year gave rise to a surge of popular discontent in many of the region's countries, most notably in Chile, Peru, and Bolivia, where simmering public frustrations with a variety of government initiatives spilled over into mass demonstrations of public anger and triggered frequent violent clashes with security forces. In many cases, the protests appeared successful, forcing governments to make meaningful concessions or, in some cases, to accept outright defeat.

President Sebastian Piñera faced months of protests against **Chile's** education system, which was heavily reliant on private funding, as well as widespread opposition to plans approved on 9 May for the construction of five hydroelectric dams (the HidroAysén project) in the Patagonia region. The protests by student and teacher movements, which were demanding greater state investment and control in the education sector, began in Santiago in May but were repeated intermittently in several cities throughout the remainder of the year (but most forcefully in June-September). The protesters' anger stemmed from statistics such as those showing that only 15 per cent of spending on higher education in Chile originated from public funds and nearly 40 per cent of total spending on schools and higher education came directly from households, whilst one third of secondary schools and most universities were privately owned and profit-making enterprises. Many of the protests resulted in violent clashes between a minority of protesters and the security forces, with more than 1,800 arrests being made between May and October. A two-day general strike on 25-26 August was also marred by violence, with riot police officers in Santiago and other cities using tear gas and water cannon to disperse crowds of angry youths. The strike was led by the umbrella trade union Central Unitaria de Trabajadores (CUT), which was demanding improvements to state pensions, healthcare, and education, and strongly supported by the student and teacher movements.

Piñera met with protest leaders for a series of talks in September but the meetings failed to resolve the impasse, prompting his presidential approval ratings to plunge as low as 27 per cent, regarded as the lowest suffered by a Chilean president since the restoration of democracy in 1990. The breakdown of further talks between government officials and the protesters on 5 October, as well as the negative reaction of the student protest movement, led by the undergraduate student Camila Vallejo, to Piñera's appointment on 30 December of a new education minister, Harald Bayer, suggested that the protracted dispute was likely to feature prominently in 2012. Opposition to the HidroAysén project also erupted in May, with some 40,000 opponents of the plan participating in a protest in Santiago against the government's plans to build the five controversial dams. The HidroAysén project was expected to generate more than 18,000 gigawatt hours of electricity per year, thereby meeting around one third of Chile's consumption requirements, but would also flood some 5,900 hectares of land in areas of the country's wild Patagonia region. A court ordered work on the controversial $3.6 billion development project to be suspended on 20 June but the suspension was lifted on appeal on 6 October.

Massive protests by students against government attempts to reform the education system also struck **Colombia** in 2011. A series of protests in October and November, which began in Bogota on 12 October, followed the approval of a government-sponsored bill in Congress on 3 October to restructure Colombia's higher education system. The bill proposed investing some $3.5 billion in higher education over 10 years and boosting enrolment figures by around 600,000 but also expanded the system of private, for-profit universities. Students and academics claimed that the reforms amounted to the privatisation of the university system and would reduce the quality of education and universities' independence, as well as increase costs. In response to the bill's approval, more than 500,000 students boycotted universities in October, whilst an estimated 200,000 protesters marched in Bogota on 10 November to demonstrate their opposition. In the wake of the protests legislators on 16 November rescinded the bill's approval, thereby marking the end of the protests.

In **Peru**, public anger was mainly aimed at controversial mining developments. When a protest in early April against the proposed opening of the Tia Maria open cast copper mine, near the city of Arequipa, erupted in violent clashes between protesters and police officers, one person was killed and several others were injured. The government responded to the unrest on 4 April by announcing the cancellation of the controversial project, which was being developed by Southern Copper, the world's second-largest copper mining company. The following month, however, President Alan García Pérez, who was nearing the end of his second term in office, faced fresh opposition. An estimated 10,000 people, mainly indigenous Aymara Indians, on 26 May blocked roads in the highland city of Puno in protest against the Santa Ana mining project, a proposed silver mining operation being developed by Canadian multinational mining company Bear Creek Mining Corporation. The protesters, some of whom participated in sporadic looting and other forms of unrest, were angered by claims that the development would contaminate local water supplies.

García's successor, Ollanta Humala Tasso, who won the presidency in a second round run-off vote on 5 June (see below), also faced opposition to a mining project. On 4 December, following 11 days of protests against the proposed Conga gold mine, in Cajamarca region, Humala declared a state of emergency to help control the violent clashes between the protesters and the security forces. The protests, regarded as the first major public test of Humala's nascent (and thus far moderate) administration, also forced the Newmont Mining company, the US-based multinational mining company which was developing the mine, on 30 November to announce a suspension of construction work on the $4.8 billion project. The protesters, led by Cajamarca's governor, Gregorio Santos, claimed that the mine would pollute and negatively alter sources of irrigation water by transforming natural lakes into artificial reservoirs. Earlier in the year, on 6 September, Humala had signed into law a measure granting indigenous citizens the rights of consultation prior to the development of future mining, timber or petroleum projects on their ancestral territory. Announcing the new legislation, which came into effect on 1 January 2012, Humala said that his administration wanted "the voice" of indigenous people to "be heard, and have them treated like citizens, not little children who are not consulted about anything".

Resolving the many social tensions stirred by the environmental impact of mining projects in Peru was regarded by some observers as one of the key challenges faced by Humala's administration, especially because of its need to continue attracting foreign investment, including an estimated $40 billion in mining revenues, to implement policies the president pledged during the election campaign, such as expanding social benefits for the country's poorest citizens through increased pay and pensions and cash transfer initiatives.

In **Bolivia**, President Evo Morales was forced to ask for "forgiveness" from his indigenous supporters on 28 September after riot police stormed a protest camp and fired tear gas at citizens protesting against the construction of a new 300 km road through the Isiboro Sécure (Tipnis) national park, in Bolivia's Amazon rainforest. The public anger aroused by the violent nature of the police operation also prompted Morales to order an immediate suspension of construction work on the proposed road and triggered the resignations of Defence Minister Maria Cecilia Chacon and Interior Minister Sacha Llorenti Solís. In the immediate aftermath of the incident, Maria Rene Quiroga, the head of Bolivia's migration agency, stepped down from her post, describing the violence as "unforgivable". The following month, Morales announced that the proposed road, which would have linked land-locked Bolivia to the Pacific Ocean in Chile and Peru, and the Atlantic Ocean in Brazil, was being scrapped—a clear reminder of the ability of Bolivia's traditionally powerful social movements to limit executive power.

Earlier in the year, in April, the Morales administration also faced discontent amongst members of Bolivia's largest trade union, the Central Obrera Boliviana (COB), traditionally an ally of the country's leftist president. Under an agreement reached on 18 April, the COB secured for public sector workers a pay rise of 11 per cent, more than the 10 per cent increase proposed by the government but less than the 15 per cent increase which COB had initially demanded. The settlement ended almost two weeks of nationwide protests and strike action.

The force of popular opinion was also felt by the authorities in **Venezuela** in the first month of 2011, when legislators in the National Assembly on 11 January rescinded an education reform bill following violent protests against the measure. Meanwhile, in **Ecuador**, discontent was notable in President Rafael Correa's annual state of the nation address, which he delivered to the National Assembly on 10 August. Correa's speech featured sharp criticism of Ecuador's newspapers, which he said were "corrupt and mediocre". Correa's rebuke of the media followed his victory in July in a libel case against the editor and three officials from the *El Universo* newspaper. The legal action followed the newspaper's publication of an editorial in which the president was described as a "dictator". On 21 July Correa revealed that he would not keep "one cent" of the some $40 million that he had been awarded in the libel case, confirming that the money would instead be donated to Ecuador's Yasuni National Park's Ishpingo-Tiputini-Tambococha (ITT) oil fields project, an environmental initiative designed to secure international financial donations in exchange for the government's commitment to prevent oil exploration projects in the country's northern Amazonian region.

The year was also marked by continued signs of cooperation between Colombia, on the one hand, and its neighbours Ecuador and Venezuela, on the other. In response to an upsurge of attacks by the Revolutionary Armed Forces of Colombia (FARC), Colombia's largest leftist guerrilla organisation, near Colombia and Ecuador's shared border, the two governments on 10 June signed a bilateral agreement on the exchange of military and intelligence information. Colombia's President Juan Manuel Santos made his first official visit to Ecuador on 19 December, meeting Correa in Quito for talks on improving bilateral cooperation in trade, infrastructure, and security projects. During their talks, some four years after Colombian security forces had launched a controversial military attack against a FARC camp on Ecuadorian territory in March 2008 (when Santos was Colombia's defence minister), Correa pledged his support for cross-border security, warning that "any criminal group that comes to Ecuador from Colombia will be sent back".

Earlier in the year, on 23 April, the authorities in Venezuela invoked an international arrest warrant to detain Joaquín Pérez Becerra (also known as Alberto Martinez), the editor of the New Colombia News Agency (ANNCOL), a Sweden-based independent news service frequently associated with the FARC, before extraditing him to Colombia. The extradition followed the signing on 26 January of an agreement pledging Venezuelan-Colombian bilateral co-operation in the fight against illegal drug trafficking. The recent warming in diplomatic relations between Venezuela and Colombia, following several years of diplomatic tensions, was regarded as detrimental to the FARC, whose interests were better served by Colombia being isolated from its regional neighbours. In what some analysts regarded as a warning to Venezuela's President Hugo Chávez Frías, less than one week ahead of a scheduled meeting with his Colombian counterpart, Juan Manuel Santos, FARC rebels in the Colombian department of La Guajira on 26 March used explosives to attack the Antonio Ricauarte oil pipeline, which was owned by Venezuela's state oil company PDVSA.

Santos on 24 May revealed his administration's "Integral Policy on Security and Defence for Prosperity" (PISDP), which ambitiously aimed to dismantle the principal armed groups operating in Colombia and restore peace in the country by the end of 2014, when his first term in office ended. The following month, on 10 June, Santos enacted legislation providing compensation to an estimated 4 million victims (and their relatives) of the civil conflict, which the president described as payment of "a long overdue moral debt". Santos also appointed a close ally, Juan Carlos Pinzon, as a replacement for Defence Minister Rodrigo Rivera Salazar, who resigned from his post amid criticism of the security forces and an escalation of FARC attacks, and named Alejandro Navas as the new commander of Colombia's armed forces on 8 September.

The gradual unveiling of the Santos administration's domestic security policies was met throughout the year with persistent rebel attacks and subjected to an upsurge in violence ahead of nationwide regional and municipal elections held on 30 October. At least 41 electoral candidates and more than 20 troops were killed in guerrilla attacks launched during the election campaign. Notably, the elections resulted in leftist candidates securing at least five mayoral posts, including the influential mayoral post in Bogota, which was won by former M-19 rebel group member Gustavo Petro. The Santos administration also secured some notable victories against the FARC in 2011, including the killing by Colombian troops on 13 March of Oliver Solarte, an alias of the leader of the rebels' 48th front, in the southern department of Putumayo. The security forces also captured Herminsul Arellán Barajas, a FARC guerrilla who was sentenced in absentia to 40 years in prison for his involvement in a bomb attack against a nightclub in Bogota in 2003, in which 36 people were killed and 167 others were injured.

The government's most notable victory, however, was the killing of the FARC's leader Alfonso Cano, who was shot and killed by the security forces on 4 November (see Obituary). Santos described the rebel leader's death, which followed two air strikes on a rebel camp near a jungle area of the south-western Cauca province and marked the first occasion in the FARC's 47-year history that its incumbent leader had been killed, as "the most resounding blow against the organisation in its entire history". Santos also warned other guerrillas to "demobilise" or "end up in a prison or a tomb". The FARC responded the following day by announcing the election of Rodrigo Londono (also known as Timochenko), as the new rebel leader, claiming that he would "guarantee the strategic plan for the take-over of power by the people". Saenz, regarded as an ardent Marxist, said in 2001 that the FARC's "struggle" was "to do away with the state as now it exists in Colombia... preferably by political means, but if they don't let us, then we have to carry on shooting".

Meanwhile, voters in Peru elected Ollanta Humala Tasso, 48, the candidate of Gana Perú, as the country's new president, in a second round run-off vote held on 5 June. The leftist Humala defeated his only second round rival, Keiko Fujimori, the candidate of Fuerza 2011 and the daughter of former President Alberto Keinya Fujimori (1990-2000). The second round of voting was constitutionally required as no single candidate had won a majority of the vote in the first round on 10 April. In elections to Peru's 120-strong Congress, also held on 10 April, Humala's Gana Perú secured 46 seats, whilst Fujimori's Fuerza 2011 won 38 seats, and Perú Posible, led by former President Alejandro Toledo, garnered 21 seats.

Shortly after his victory President-elect Humala visited officials in Brazil, Paraguay, Uruguay, Argentina, and Chile, notably avoiding similar trips to Venezuela, Bolivia, and Ecuador, where the region's most radical leftist leaders held power, in what many observers regarded as evidence of a strategy aimed at signalling his moderate policy intentions. During his inauguration ceremony on 28 July the new president announced that his government aimed to eradicate social exclusion and implied that he might impose a windfall tax on mining companies to help raise government funds for social spending. Humala's prime minister and cabinet leader, Salomón Lerner Ghitis, on 25 August revealed that the government aimed to avoid the violent unrest and protests against development projects that had blighted Garcia's outgoing administration. Whilst presenting the government's five-year plan to Congress, Lerner Ghitis said that Humala's administration would respect the rights of communities affected by development projects and accord greater priority to their environmental impact. The plan was presented two days after legislators unanimously approved a new law (the "Ley De Consulta Previa") granting indigenous communities the rights to consultation on proposed development projects in their vicinity and a greater say in their approval or rejection.

Lerner resigned from his post on 11 December, prompting Humala to carry out a major cabinet reshuffle, thereby making Humala's first cabinet the shortest-lived in recent Peruvian history. Ten ministers were replaced in changes that included the appointment of Interior Minister Óscar Valdés as the new prime minister. Other notable government changes included the appointment of engineer Jorge Humberto Merino as the mines and energy minister, environmental lawyer Manuel Pulgar-Vidal Otalora as the environment minister, and former deputy economic minister Luis Alberto Otárola as the new defence minister. Eight ministers retained their posts, including Finance Minister Miguel Castilla, Trade Minister José Luis Silva, Foreign Affairs Minister Rafael Roncagliolo, and Development and Social Inclusion Minister Carolina Trivelli.

A major cabinet reshuffle was also announced in Ecuador, with Correa unveiling 15 cabinet-level changes on 10 November, which he said were intended to "radicalise" his government's "citizens' revolution". The reshuffle followed Correa's request for all cabinet ministers to offer their resignation, an appeal precipitated by the approval by the US authorities on 21 October of the credentials of Nathalie Cely Suarez, the co-ordinating minister for production, employment, and competitiveness, whom the president had nominated as Ecuador's new ambassador to the USA. The appointment of a new ambassador had been required after Luis Gallegos was expelled from the post during a diplomatic spat in April, in which Correa alleged that US embassy officials in Quito were spying on Ecuador's police and military forces. The dispute erupted on 7 April, when Correa expelled the US ambassador to Ecuador, Heather Hodges, three days after a Spanish newspaper had published US diplomatic cables from July 2009 and made public by the whistleblowing website WikiLeaks. Amongst embarrassing revelations, the cables alleged that Ecuador's police commander in 2008-09, Jaime Hurtado Vaca, had used his post to "to extort cash and property, misappropriate public funds, facilitate human trafficking, and obstruct the investigation and prosecution of corrupt colleagues".

In another development affecting the USA's relationship with countries in the region, Bolivian and US officials struck a conciliatory tone on 7 November, when it was announced that the two countries had reached a bilateral agreement on a framework for restoring relations at ambassadorial level. The tone was strained on 21 November, however, when officials from the Morales administration made clear that officials from the US Drug Enforcement Administration (DEA) were not authorised to return to Bolivia "because of the effect they've had" and "for the role they've played" in the country. The remarks appeared to refer to previous Bolivian allegations, similar to those made against US officials by Ecuador, that DEA agents had engaged in spying in Bolivia and fomenting the violent unrest witnessed in the country in September 2009. Diplomatic relations within the region were also strained on 23 March, when Bolivia's Morales threatened to pursue international legal action against Chile in order to help recover Bolivian access to the Pacific Ocean, which the country lost in the War of the Pacific (1879-84).

The US Congress on 12 October approved the USA-Colombia Trade Promotion Agreement (CTPA), a free trade agreement which officials from the USA and Colombia first signed in November 2006. Approval of the CTPA, which had been delayed over concerns by US legislators about Colombia's human rights record and labour laws, was expected to boost Colombian exports to the USA by more than $30 billion a year within five years.

The region's ugly history of human rights abuses inevitably lingered in 2011, most notably in Chile and Bolivia. On 11 September, the anniversary of the military coup that removed former Chilean President Salvador Allende from power in 1973 was marked in customary fashion, with more than 10,000 citizens marching on the streets of Santiago. The demonstration was initially peaceful but erupted into violent clashes with the security forces after protesters blocked roads, threw missiles, and set fires. Earlier, on 19 July, a detailed report into Allende's death concluded that the former president had committed suicide during the military coup, which ushered in the Pinochet dictatorship and Chile's "dirty war" era (1973-90), by firing two bullets from an automatic rifle into his head. The report was part of an investigation, ordered by Judge Sergio Munoz on 27 January, designed to establish conclusively whether Allende had been killed or had committed suicide. The investigation also involved the former president's remains being exhumed on 23 May, after the Allende's family request for disinterment. As the year was drawing to a close, officials from Chile's Communist Party requested the exhumation of the remains of the Nobel prize-winning poet Pablo Neruda (born as Ricardo Eliezer Naftali Reyes y Basoalto), who died 12 days after the military coup of 1973. The request was part of an investigation, announced on 1 June, into allegations that Neruda was poisoned by Pinochet agents.

The Supreme Court in Bolivia on 30 August sentenced five senior military officers to between 10 and 15 years in prison, after convicting them for their roles in what prosecutors described as "genocide". The case, commonly referred to as "Black October" in Bolivia, related to the deaths of more than 60 citizens during the violent suppression by the security forces of anti-government protests in the city of El Alto in October 2003. Two ministers from the administration of former

President Gonzálo Sánchez de Lozada (Erik Reyes Villa and Adalberto Kua-
jarawere) were also handed prison sentences of three years for their roles in the
massacre. The convictions were the first in a civilian court for human rights violations committed by Bolivian military officials, a landmark hailed by human rights
advocates and families of the victims.

Chavez's "Bolivarian" brand of "socialism in Venezuela resulted in the nationalisation of the country's gold industry on 17 August and the nationalisation of
Agroflora, a Venezuelan subsidiary of Vestey Group, a UK-owned multinational
agricultural company, on 1 November. Chavez also ordered the repatriation of
Venezuela's foreign gold reserves, the first shipment of which arrived in the country on 25 November. According to some estimates, Venezuela held total international reserves of some $29.1 billion, including estimated foreign gold reserves of
$11 billion and domestic gold reserves of around $7 billion. The nationalisation of
Agroflora was ordered under Venezuela's Food Security and Sovereignty Law,
which allowed the state to assume control over the company's 290,000 hectares of
farmland on the grounds that it was "social property" that "cannot be converted,
as they have done, into property for just a few people, so they can enrich themselves whilst polluting waterways and rivers".

Venezuela's electoral authority, the National Electoral Council (CNE), on 13
September announced that presidential elections would be held on 7 October,
2012. The scheduling of a fresh presidential election triggered a flurry of reporting on the prospect of the opposition mounting a cohesive and serious challenge
to Chávez, whose support base was especially strong amongst Venezuela's poorest citizens. Much of the reporting claimed that popular support for Chávez was
waning, focused on increasingly alarming crime statistics, suggested that the president would boost public spending by record levels to maintain his historical electoral support, and speculated on the candidate most likely to contest the election
for the opposition. Chávez himself claimed in December that the impending election was a contest between himself "and the Yankees", adding that Venezuela must
be "attentive" to attempts by the US government to manufacture "an excuse to
attack us", which most media reports interpreted as the president indulging in
"populist" rhetoric. Despite a ban on holding public office in Venezuela, prominent opposition leader Leopoldo López announced in October that he intended to
contest the primary elections of the opposition Coalition for Democratic Unity
(MUD), which were scheduled to be held in February 2012. A ruling by the Inter
American Commission on Human Rights (IACHR) on 1 September, stating that
the Venezuelan authorities were obliged to allow López to seek public office, was
dismissed by Chávez as politically biased. The governor of Miranda state, Hen-
rique Capriles Radonski, and the governor of Zulia state, Pablo Perez, were also
acknowledged as leading contenders in the MUD's primary elections.

Chavez's response to the rising tide of violent crime included an announcement on 18 November that he was authorising the deployment of 3,650 new
troops onto the streets of Venezuela's major cities. Earlier in the year, on 25
April, Chávez announced that minimum wage was being increased by 15 per
cent on 1 May and by a further 10 per cent on 1 September, raising the monthly

rate to around $360. The increase was set against costs of living which were rising faster in Venezuela, where the rate of inflation reached an estimated 18.5 per cent in March, than any other country in Latin America. In contrast, the temporary introduction of electricity rationing in May, following intermittent power blackouts in large areas of Venezuela, was an unwelcome reminder of the "national electricity emergency" that was declared in February 2010 and which compounded the social and economic challenges which Venezuela faced in 2011. On a personal level, Chávez was struck by a health crisis as on 30 June he revealed that he had recently been diagnosed with an unspecified cancer. Detailed information about the precise nature and gravity of the president's illness was scarce but on 20 October Chávez claimed that he was "free from cancer", following four rounds of chemotherapy in Cuba.

In Colombia, President Santos announced on 31 October that the Administrative Department of Security (DAS—the intelligence service) would be dissolved on 31 December, following which it would be replaced by a new intelligence agency, the Agencia Nacional de Inteligencia (ANI). The dissolution of the DAS followed the emergence of several scandals involving the agency and its operatives, most notably the "chuzadas" scandal involving allegations of illegal intelligence-gathering. There were several developments in connection with the scandal in 2011, including the conviction of two prominent former agents and the charging of another, as well as the charging of a minister from the administration of former President Alvaro Uribe Velez (2002-10), who on 18 August gave testimony in connection with the case before a legislative investigative committee. On 5 August Gustavo Sierra, the agency's former deputy director of intelligence analysis, received a prison sentence of eight years and three months, after accepting charges of aggravated conspiracy; aggravated illicit interception of communications; prevarication; and abuse of power. The following month the former head of the DAS, Jorge Noguera, was handed a prison sentence of 24 years for his involvement in three murders committed by paramilitaries from the now-defunct, right-wing paramilitary group, the United Self Defence Forces of Colombia (AUC). Bernardo Moreno, a secretary of the presidency during Uribe's rule, and Maria del Pilar Hurtado, the agency's head in 2005-10, were charged in connection with their alleged roles in the scandal, including charges of aggravated conspiracy to commit a crime, illicit violation of communications, and abusing the position of a public servant. Hurtado was also charged with embezzlement by appropriation and the ideological forgery of a public document. However, Hurtado was living in Panama, where she had fled and was granted "territorial" asylum in November 2010. During his testimony, Uribe continued to deny that he had ordered the illegal intelligence-gathering activities. He also rejected allegations, published in the *Washington Post* on 21 August, claiming that US-government funds (from its Plan Colombia counter-insurgency initiative) had been used to pay for such activities during his time in office.

In other developments, a national referendum in Ecuador on 7 May resulted in a majority of voters approving 10 questions, including those relating to controversial judicial reforms. Correa's critics claimed that the judicial reforms were part of an attempt by the government to secure greater executive power over the judiciary.

The reforms involved replacing for 18 months an independent committee responsible for the appointment of judges with a three-person committee including a government representative, a transitional arrangement scheduled to be superseded by the creation of a five-person judicial council, including members from all three branches of the government. On 5 September Correa decreed a 60-day state of emergency to implement the controversial reform, allowing the president to reassign judges and make budget appropriations without legislative approval. The decree was enacted after the Transitional Judicial Council requested additional funding of some US$400 million to enact the reforms.

The following month, the majority of votes cast in a historic judicial election in Bolivia on 16 October were spoiled or blank. The vote, held to determine 56 judges at the Supreme Tribunal of Justice, the Plurinational Constitutional Tribunal, and the Agro-Environmental Tribunal, as well as members of the Council of the Judiciary, was historic because it marked the first occasion anywhere in the world where candidates for such posts were elected by direct popular vote. Morales claimed that the holding of the elections would make judges more accountable but many government opponents implored voters to abstain from voting or leave their papers blank, claiming that the election could "erode the independence of the judiciary".

Peru's President Humala on 9 October announced sweeping changes in the hierarchy of the national police force, replacing 30 senior officials. The changes were part of Humala's election campaign pledge to stamp-out corruption by state officials. The new director general of the force, General Raul Salazar, said that he was determined to "banish the corruption" that was "tarnishing the reputation of the police. From the least to the most significant act, it doesn't matter, it is an offence if you steal one sol or more".

The torrential rainfall which had intermittently battered Colombia during the previous two years continued to afflict the country in 2011, damaging or destroying houses and roads, causing mudslides, and leaving millions homeless. Figures released by the Red Cross showed that 114 people died as a result of the extreme weather, whilst 21 others remained missing, in the three months to 2 December.

As the year ended, large swathes of the Torres del Paine national park, a popular tourist destination in the Patagonia region of southern Chile, which attracted more than 100,000 visitors a year, was being ravaged by fire. The blaze began on 27 December, near Lake Grey, in the park's north-west area and some 3,000 km south of Santiago (the capital of Chile), but spread quickly, fanned by high winds and fuelled by dry vegetation. Within days, the fire had destroyed some 110 sq km of the park's 2,422 sq km, with Interior Minister Rodrigo Hinzpeter warning that the blaze remained "dangerous, violent and difficult to control", not least because weather conditions in the area were expected to deteriorate. An Israeli tourist, Rotem Singer, 23, whom the authorities accused of negligently starting the wildfires by failing to properly extinguish toilet tissue he was burning, was arrested in connection with the disaster on 31 December.

Kurt Perry

V MIDDLE EAST AND NORTH AFRICA

ISRAEL

CAPITAL: Jerusalem   AREA: 22,070 sq km   POPULATION: 7,624,600 ('10)
OFFICIAL LANGUAGE: Hebrew
HEAD OF STATE: President Shimon Peres (since July '07)
RULING PARTIES: Likud-led coalition
HEAD OF GOVERNMENT: Prime Minister Binyamin Netanyahu (Likud) (since March '09)
DEMOCRACY INDEX: 7.48; 37th of 167   CORRUPTION INDEX: 5.8; 36th of 183
CURRENCY: Shekel (Dec '11 £1.00=ILS 5.87, US$1.00=ILS 3.74)
GNI PER CAPITA: US$27,170, Intl$27,630 at PPP ('10)

THE astonishing developments in the Middle East and North Africa during 2011 were not embraced by the authorities in Israel, who were forced to deal with a range of new problems which added to some more familiar ones. For decades, the conflict between the Israelis and the Palestinians had dominated the region. In 2011, however, the main event was elsewhere, with the "Arab Spring"revolutions in Tunisia and Egypt, a civil war in Libya, and civil uprisings in Bahrain, Syria, and Yemen. The old Middle East order had suited the Israelis, but in 2011 it appeared to be collapsing. The fall of President Mohammed Hosni Mubarak of Egypt in February was of particular concern. Defence Minister Ehud Barak warned that the Egyptian military had lost control of the Sinai, making it an attractive place for jihadists and Palestinian militants. Barak's warning appeared prescient in mid-August when eight Israelis were killed and a further 25 injured when a squad of suspected Palestinian militants infiltrated southern Israel near the Egyptian border and carried out a series of attacks on buses and cars.

Israel's relationship with Turkey, the emerging powerhouse in the Middle East, continued on a downward trend during the year. Relations had been ruptured in May 2010 when Israeli commandos attacked a Gaza-bound flotilla of aid ships, killing nine Turkish activists in the process (see AR 2011, pp. 189-90). A UN inquiry into the raid, published in early September (see Documents), found that Israel's interception of the vessels was "excessive and unreasonable" and the use of force by Israeli commandos was "unacceptable". Israel took note of the findings but refused to issue an apology to Turkey, which was riding a wave of support in the Arab world because of its increasingly pro-Palestinian stance. Turkey responded by immediately suspending all military agreements with Israel and drastically downgraded its diplomatic representation in the country.

The sharp deterioration in Israel's relations with Turkey, hitherto one of its key non-Arab allies, heightened the Jewish state's sense of international isolation at a time when it perceived a rising existential threat from a nuclear-armed Iran. In early November, Israel test-launched a new long-range ballistic missile amid a fresh public debate triggered by reports that Prime Minister Binyamin Netanyahu was seeking support for a pre-emptive strike on Iran's nuclear facilities. A month later the Israeli Defence Forces (IDF) announced the formation of a new military command to carry out "depth" missions in distant locations. It was reported that the new so-called "Iran command" would focus on the Islamic Republic's nuclear facilities, but would also prevent arms from reaching Iran's factional proxies in Lebanon and Gaza (Hezbullah and Hamas, respectively).

The "Arab Spring" upheavals and the separation from Turkey increased speculation that Israel was actively on the lookout for new allies, including Turkey's eastern Mediterranean rivals (Greece, Cyprus, Romania and Bulgaria); predominantly Christian African countries concerned at the rise of militant Islam (Kenya, Uganda, Ethiopia, Tanzania, Nigeria and the infant state of South Sudan); and, most sensitively, Persian Gulf Arab states who shared a common concern about Iran (Saudi Arabia, the United Arab Emirates and others).

In mid-July young Israelis, inspired by the Arab Spring protests underway in neighbouring countries, pitched their tents in the centre of Tel Aviv's swanky Rothschild Boulevard and launched their own protest movement, calling for social justice, affordable housing, cheaper basic food and better social services. Some commentators tried to label the protests the "Israeli Spring", but in truth the movement had neither name nor structure, although it had obvious similarities to the Spanish "indignados" movement and to the Occupy protests. It was, as *The Economist* of 8 September noted, "a well-behaved revolution, mainly of the young, educated middle class: couples with qualifications and jobs who still find it hard to make ends meet". The movement held its final Saturday protest on 3 September when some 300,000 people congregated in Tel Aviv, with smaller gatherings in Haifa and Jerusalem.

Despite its numbers, the movement presented no immediate threat to Netanyahu's government. (The Orthodox, West Bank settlers, and Russian immigrants, all key constituencies in the ruling coalition, played no part in the protests.) Nonetheless, the prime minister could not afford to ignore the protests—especially after Tzipi Livni, leader of the opposition Kadima, effectively endorsed the protesters' demands—and in early August Netanyahu appointed a cabinet-level panel, headed by Manuel Trajtenberg, a respected professor of economics, to address the protesters' claims. In early October, a month after the final rally, the cabinet approved the recommendations of Trajtenberg's panel, which included proposals for a long-term increase in housing supply and the creation of new top tax bracket of 48 per cent.

In mid-January, Labour Party leader Ehud Barak announced the formation of a breakaway party, Atzmaut (Independence), which enabled him to retain his loyal Labour faction in the Knesset (the unicameral legislature) within Prime Minister Netanyahu's government, and prevented the departure of Labour as a whole from the 22-month-old coalition government. Barak, who retained the post of deputy prime minister and defence minister, had the support of four out of 13 Labour members of the Knesset, thereby reducing the coalition's majority in the 120-member legislature from 74 to a still-workable 66. The new Atzmaut Party was officially launched in mid-May, with Barak as chairman.

There were a number of important appointments within the military and the security services in 2011. In mid-February Lieutenant-General Benny Gantz was appointed as the new IDF chief of staff, replacing Lieutenant-General Gaby Ashkenazi, who had served in the post since 2007 (see AR 2008, p. 181). Major-

General Yoav Galant had been earmarked for the top military post, but was undone by a financial scandal. In March, Major-General Ya'akov Amidror, a noted hawk, was appointed as the new chairman of the National Security Council. Yuval Diskin was replaced as head of the Shin Bet, the domestic security service, by Yoram Cohen in mid-May.

The courts delivered a number of noteworthy verdicts and sentences during the year. In March, a district court in Tel Aviv sentenced former President Moshe Katsav to seven years' imprisonment for rape and other sexual offences. Katsav had been found guilty of the charges in December 2010 (see AR 2011, p. 186). In late October, another court in Tel Aviv sentenced Anat Kam, a journalist and former soldier, to four-and-a-half years in prison for the possession and distribution of classified documents. Kam had been found guilty of stealing more than 2,000 military documents during her compulsory army service from 2005 to 2007 and passing them on to Uri Blau, a reporter with *Ha'aretz*, one of Israel's leading liberal newspapers.

Darren Sagar

PALESTINE—EGYPT—JORDAN—SYRIA—LEBANON—IRAQ

PALESTINE

CAPITAL: Ramallah / East Jerusalem   AREA: 6,020 sq km (West Bank & Gaza)
POPULATION: 4,152,102 ('10)
OFFICIAL LANGUAGE: Arabic
HEAD OF STATE: President Mahmoud Abbas (since Jan '05)
RULING PARTIES: Hamas (in Gaza); Fatah (in West Bank)
HEAD OF GOVERNMENT: Prime Minister Salam Khalid Abdallah Fayyad (since May '09)
DEMOCRACY INDEX: 5.44; 93rd of 167
CURRENCY: Jordanian Dinar (Dec '11 £1.00=JOD 1.11, US$1.00=JOD 0.71) and Israeli Shekel
(Dec '11 £1.00=ILS 5.87, US$1.00=ILS 3.74)

DURING a day of high drama, Mahmoud Abbas, president of the Palestine National Authority (PNA), delivered a speech to the 66th session of the UN General Assembly in New York on 23 September in which he announced that he had submitted to UN Secretary-General Ban Ki Moon an application for the admission of Palestine—on the basis of the 4 June, 1967, borders, with Jerusalem as its capital—as a full member of the UN (see Documents). Palestinian officials said that Abbas had asked Ban to transmit the request to the UN Security Council and also to the General Assembly. However, US President Barack Obama had vowed that the USA would veto the Palestinian membership bid if it was ever poised to pass the Council. The USA had no veto authority in the General Assembly, but that body could not grant full membership to a country.

President Abbas—leader of the Western-backed Fatah faction which was based in the West Bank—pressed the Palestinian case for statehood in his speech and a short time later Israeli Prime Minister Binyamin Netanyahu delivered a rebuttal. Abbas contended that the Palestinians had entered into negotiations with Israel with sincere intentions, but blamed the continued construction of illegal Jewish settlements in the occupied West Bank and Jerusalem for their failure. He directly linked the Palestinians' quest for statehood with the democracy movement in the Middle East and North Africa, declaring: "At a time when Arab people are affirming their quest for democracy in what is called now the Arab Spring, the time has come now also for the Palestinian spring—the time for independence."

In his address to the General Assembly, Netanyahu struck a conciliatory note even as he blamed Palestinians for the impasse in talks and depicted their statehood bid at the UN as fruitless. He publicly called on Abbas to return to negotiations, which the Palestinians had abandoned in October 2010 after the Israelis refused to extend a 10-month moratorium on settlement building (see AR 2011, p. 189). "Now, we're in the same city. We're in the same building. So let's meet here today, in the United Nations. Who's there to stop us? What is there to stop us, if we genuinely want peace, from meeting today to begin peace negotiations?" the Israeli prime minister said.

Hours after Netanyahu's speech, the Middle East Quartet (the USA, the EU, the UN, and Russia) proposed a framework for restarting dormant peace talks between the Palestinians and Israelis. The proposal set a timeline which aimed at concluding a peace agreement no later than the end of 2012 and calling for "comprehensive proposals within three months on territory and security". The Quartet also urged both sides to avoid "provocative actions". Any slim chance of progress was quickly scuppered, however, by the Israeli interior ministry, which on 27 September approved a plan for the construction of 1,100 new housing units in the Gilo settlement in East Jerusalem. Saeb Erakat, the veteran Palestinian negotiator, described the ministry's announcement as a "slap in the face to all international efforts to protect the fading prospects of peace in the region". (Erakat himself had been under intense pressure to resign when in January the Qatar-based satellite television channel Al Jazeera had leaked a mass of confidential documents (the so-called "Palestine Papers") which appeared to show that in private meetings with Israeli negotiators, he and other Palestinian negotiators had offered far-reaching concessions and compromises on a range of issues—including the status of Jerusalem, Jewish settlements, and the right of return for Palestinian refugees—in their desperation to achieve progress on statehood.)

The threat of the US veto on the UN Security Council meant that the Palestinian bid for full UN membership was always going to be largely symbolic and by the end of the year little concrete progress had been made towards it. In mid-November the Council's admissions committee confirmed that it was unable to make a unanimous recommendation because no more than eight of the 15 members of the Council were ready to back the Palestinian bid. This left the Palestinians one short of the required majority, thus sparing the USA the need to use its veto to prevent the application being approved.

The Palestinians did achieve some success in their campaign for international recognition when, on 31 October, the UN Educational, Scientific, and Cultural

Organisation (UNESCO) became the first UN organisation to admit Palestine as a full member state. The vote was carried at the organisation's general conference in Paris by 107 votes in favour of admission and 14 votes against, with 52 abstentions (see Documents). Membership of UNESCO was largely symbolic, although it would allow the PNA to seek world heritage status for historical sites, such as the Church of the Nativity in Bethlehem. The USA, which contributed 22 per cent of UNESCO's budget, immediately suspended its dues to the organisation, claiming that the vote had triggered a long-standing congressional restriction on funding to UN bodies that recognised Palestine as a state before an Israeli-Palestinian peace deal was reached. Israel responded to the vote by announcing that it intended to accelerate the construction of new homes in Jewish settlements in the West Bank and East Jerusalem and freeze the transfer of tax and customs revenues to the PNA, although the latter measure was not fully implemented.

The Palestinian diplomatic hand had been strengthened enormously on 4 May when the two main rival factions, Fatah and Hamas, signed a reconciliation agreement in Cairo (see Documents). The two factions had been at loggerheads since Hamas won legislative elections in early 2006 (see AR 2007, p. 186), with the rift deepening a year later when Hamas forces expelled Fatah fighters from Gaza (see AR 2008, pp. 184-88). Since then Hamas had ruled Gaza whilst Fatah had controlled the PNA in the West Bank. The rivalries and divisions had weakened both factions and had been exploited by their enemies. Under the terms of the reconciliation agreement—signed by Abbas and the Syrian-based Hamas leader Khaled Meshal—the two parties promised to establish a new consensus government, and to hold presidential and parliamentary elections within a year. Attempts to implement the agreement immediately ran into difficulties when Abbas nominated current PNA Prime Minister Salam Khalid Abdallah Fayyad to head the new unity government, a move rejected by Hamas. Abbas and Meshal met again in Cairo in late November. They confirmed that legislative and presidential elections would go ahead in May 2012 as planned, but there was no progress on the formation of a new government.

After its reconciliation agreement with Fatah, Hamas was further emboldened in October when Israel agreed to release 1,027 Palestinian prisoners in exchange for one captured Israeli soldier. The exchange agreement had been brokered by German and Egyptian mediators. In the first part of the exchange, Sgt First Class Gilad Shalit, an Israeli soldier seized in June 2006 by Palestinian militants from the Gaza Strip (see AR 2007, p. 189), was returned to Israel. In return, Israel released 477 Palestinian prisoners, a number of whom were prominent militants serving life sentences for killing or injuring Israelis. A subdued Israeli homecoming ceremony for the pale and emaciated Shalit stood in stark contrast to the mood in the Gaza Strip, where buses carrying the first of the prisoners to be freed as part of the exchange were escorted through cheering crowds by heavily armed Hamas fighters. As busloads of freed Palestinians arrived in the West Bank, residents waved Hamas flags, a rare sight in the Fatah-controlled enclave. The exchange appeared to have undermined the standing of President Abbas, while raising the profile of Hamas. The exchange deal was concluded in mid-

December when Israel released another 450 Palestinians, described as "light security prisoners" who were not members of Hamas or Islamic Jihad.

Palestinian participation in, and association with, the "Arab Spring" uprisings and revolutions taking place across the region manifested itself most markedly on 15 May, the 63rd anniversary of the Nakba ("catastrophe") wherein some 750,000 Palestinians had been displaced from their homes by the creation of the state of Israel. Palestinians used social networking websites to call for co-ordinated marches to the occupied Palestinian territories to demand the right of return for all Palestinian refugees. Accordingly, thousands of Palestinians marched from Egypt, Jordan, Syria, Lebanon, the Gaza Strip, and the West Bank to confront Israeli troops stationed in sensitive areas of the occupied Palestinian territories. In Lebanon, large numbers of Palestinian refugees gathered in Maroun al-Ras, which overlooked the border with Israel. At least 11 protesters were killed, but it was not clear whether they had been shot by Israeli or Lebanese soldiers. In Syria, thousands of Palestinian refugees marched towards the border village of Majdal Shams in the Golan Heights, which Israel had captured from Syria in 1967. Israeli troops opened fire on the protesters, killing four and injuring dozens more.

The "Arab Spring" and the West's response to it featured prominently in a key note speech delivered by US President Obama four days after the Nakba protests. The speech on US policy towards the Middle East invoked the regional uprisings as a potential inspiration for an Israeli-Palestinian peace settlement. Obama offered detail—saying that negotiations should result in two states, with permanent Palestinian borders with Israel, Jordan, and Egypt, and permanent Israeli borders with Palestine. Furthermore, the borders of Israel and Palestine should be "based on the 1967 lines with mutually agreed swaps, so that secure and recognised borders are established for both states". The approach was immediately rejected by Israeli Prime Minister Netanyahu, who called the 1967 lines "indefensible". Netanyahu said that such a withdrawal would endanger Israel's security and leave major Jewish West Bank settlements within Palestinian territory.

The Israeli Defence Forces (IDF) and the main militant factions in Gaza (Hamas and Islamic Jihad) continued low-level hostilities throughout the year, but they managed to avoid the sort of full-scale conflict last seen in early 2009 after Israel had launched a massive military attack on the Strip (see AR 2010, pp. 189-93). There was a major flare-up in late March when militants fired mortars and rockets into Israel and the IDF responded with artillery and airstrikes on Gaza. Militants upped the ante in early April, firing a Kornet anti-tank missile into southern Israel which hit a school bus and critically wounded a teenage boy. It was the first time that Palestinian militants had used an advanced and accurate anti-tank missile and it prompted Israel to deploy its "Iron Dome" anti-missile system, which successfully intercepted a longer-range, Katyusha-type rocket aimed at Ashkelon. There was another upsurge in violence in Gaza triggered by a co-ordinated attack on southern Israel in mid-August in which eight Israelis were killed. Israel insisted that the assailants originally hailed from the Gaza Strip and air strikes were launched on the territory, prompting more rocket attacks into southern Israel.

Vittorio Arrigoni, a 36-year-old Italian pro-Palestinian activist, was kidnapped and killed in Gaza in mid-April. He was the first foreigner to be killed in the territory since Hamas seized control in 2007. Confusion surrounded the identity of those responsible for Arrigoni's death, although a number of reports blamed the brutal killing on militants linked to al-Qaida.

There were a few outbreaks of violence outside the Gaza Strip. Israelis were deeply shocked in early March when five members of a Jewish settler family, including two children and a baby, had their throats slit whilst they slept in their home in the isolated settlement of Itamar, deep in the West Bank. The Fatah-affiliated al-Aqsa Martyrs' Brigade reportedly claimed responsibility for the killings. Later that same month, a bomb exploded in central Jerusalem, killing a British woman—55-year-old Mary Gardner—and wounding more than 35 other people. It was the first bomb attack in Jerusalem since 2004. Whilst no faction claimed responsibility for the incident, Hamas and Islamic Jihad issued statements supporting it.

Darren Sagar

EGYPT

CAPITAL: Cairo   AREA: 1,001,450 sq km   POPULATION: 81,121,077 ('10)
OFFICIAL LANGUAGE: Arabic
HEAD OF STATE AND GOVERNMENT: Mohammed Hussein Tantawi (chairman of Supreme Council of
    the Armed Forces (since Feb '11)
RULING PARTY: none
PRIME MINISTER: Kamal Ganzouri (since Dec '11)
DEMOCRACY INDEX: 3.07; 138th of 167   CORRUPTION INDEX: 2.9; 112nd of 183
CURRENCY: Egyptian Pound (Dec '11 £1.00=EGP 9.42, US$1.00=EGP 6.00)
GNI PER CAPITA: US$2,440, Intl$6,160 at PPP ('10)

THE dramatic overthrow of the regime of President Hosni Mubarak in a mass popular uprising that started on 25 January was a highlight of the "Arab Spring" and marked 2011 as one of the most important years in Egypt's modern history. The course of the Egyptian revolution after Mubarak stepped down was far from smooth, however, as bitter conflicts erupted over the role of the army high command, the scope of constitutional reforms and the length of the period of transition to a supposedly democratic political system. Amid the turmoil, Islamist organisations seized their opportunity to consolidate their political position, and two Islamist blocs, one led by the Muslim Brotherhood, the other by the more radical Salafi tendency, won a large majority of the seats contested in a multistage parliamentary election at the end of the year. Parties and individuals representing the revolutionary movement that claimed credit for toppling Mubarak were left with only about 15 per cent of the seats. The revolution had a severe impact on the Egyptian economy, as tourism slumped and foreign investment in both projects and government securities dried up. Real GDP contracted, and the central bank's foreign exchange reserves fell by about $15 billion to a level sufficient to cover only four months of imports by the end of the year. Managing economic policy effectively was complicated by the frequent changes of government, as Egypt had four different prime ministers and four finance ministers over the turbulent 12 months.

The catalyst for the Egyptian revolution was the uprising in Tunisia, which started in December 2010 with the self-immolation of a fruit and vegetable vendor and culminated on 14 January 2011 in the enforced departure of President Zine el-Abidine Ben Ali. Political tensions were already running high in Egypt owing to the gross manipulation of the December 2010 parliamentary election by Mubarak's National Democratic Party (NDP) and the increasingly blatant promotion of the president's second son, Gamal Mubarak, as his likely successor upon the expiry of his fifth six-year term in October 2011. Activists who had come together to oppose Mubarak's re-election in 2005 (kifaya), to support labour protests in 2008 (the 6 April movement), and to protest against police brutality following the beating to death of a young man, Khaled Said, in Alexandria in June 2010, were inspired by the Tunisian events to try to mobilise a similar movement in Egypt. For their initial show of force they chose 25 January, an official holiday honouring the Egyptian police for their stand against British occupation forces in the Suez Canal zone in 1952. The intention was to contrast the image of the police in the past as patriotic heroes with the reality of the modern police force as a brutal agent of the state. Demonstrators flocked to Tahrir Square in central Cairo, as well as to public squares in several other cities, including Suez and Ismailiya. The scale of the response encouraged the activists to turn the Tahrir protests into a permanent show of opposition.

Forces under the command of the interior ministry tried to disperse the growing demonstrations, but to no avail. Mobile phone and Internet services were closed down for about 48 hours, and on 28 January the security forces went on the offensive, using live ammunition against protesters in Cairo and several other cities. It was estimated that about 800 people were killed during this violent phase of the revolution. On 30 January the army deployed a number of tanks and other armoured vehicles around Tahrir Square, but it quickly became clear to the protesters that the troops were under strict orders to hold their fire. Mubarak appeared on television on 1 February for the first time since the crisis started, and announced that he had decided to replace the government of Ahmed Nazif and appoint a vice-president for the first time since he had assumed power in 1981. Ahmed Shafiq, a former air force commander, was the new prime minister, and Omar Suleiman, the head of the intelligence services, was sworn in as vice-president. These events convinced many of the protesters that pressure was mounting on Mubarak from the military core of his regime for him to step aside. However, the president still insisted that he wished to remain in office to oversee the transition until the end of his term in September. Suleiman began to assume a more prominent role, and offered to meet representatives of the opposition. At this early point in the revolution the protesters lacked any clear leadership structure. One of the only recognised figures at the helm of the movement was Mohammed ElBaradei, the former head of the International Atomic Energy Agency, who had returned to Egypt in February 2010 to launch a campaign of constitutional reform.

Following Mubarak's speech there was a hiatus as the various interested parties, including the US government, took stock of the situation. On 6 February banks opened for business for the first time in 10 days. The Central Bank of Egypt took steps to ensure that there was sufficient liquidity in the system to avoid any panic reactions from depositors. On 10 February the Supreme Council of the Armed Forces (SCAF) made its first political intervention in the crisis through issuing Communiqué No. 1. This stated that the council was in permanent session under the chairmanship of the defence minister, Field Marshal Mohammed Hussein Tantawi, to consider the best means to safeguard the people's interests, and that it fully supported the "legitimate demands of the Egyptian people". Following the army statement Mubarak appeared on television, but he once more dashed the hopes of protesters that he had finally decided to stand down. He merely said that he would delegate the prerogatives of his office to Suleiman. The coup de grace followed swiftly, however, as on 11 February the SCAF issued a second communiqué making clear that the army council was intent on taking charge of Egypt's political future. At the end of the day Suleiman made a short statement saying that Mubarak had decided to give up the office of president and hand power to the SCAF. Mubarak left Cairo later that night and took up residence in a villa in the Sinai resort of Sharm el-Sheikh.

The main issue of debate over the next few weeks was over the sequence of constitutional reform. The Tahrir Square protest movement was supported by a number of prominent figures, including ElBaradei and Amr Moussa. (The latter, a former head of the Arab League, had presented himself as a possible presidential candidate.) These made clear that they believed the priority should be the replacement of the current constitution, and that the election of a new legislature and president should take place later. The SCAF indicated that it was in favour of proceeding quickly with legislative and presidential elections, on the basis of amendments to the existing constitution, and that the drafting of a new constitution should come at the end of the process. The SCAF entrusted the task of amending the constitution to a judicial committee, and announced that it would put these changes to a referendum. If the public voted for the amendments then this would be taken as approval for the early election option.

It was at this point that the Islamist political movement made its influence felt for the first time in the revolution. The Muslim Brotherhood, which had built up a strong nationwide network of political and social activity during the Mubarak era despite being formally banned, had provided generally low-key support to the Tahrir Square protesters. During the referendum campaign, the Brotherhood and more radical Islamists from the Salafi tendency (a puritanical version of Islam advocated by a number of popular preachers in Egypt and Saudi Arabia), mobilised support of a "yes" vote. They argued that the sooner a new parliament was in place, the sooner the government would be able to return life to normal. The revolutionary activists claimed that the Islamists merely wanted to bring forward the elections as they were in a much better position to win because of their well established political organisation. The referendum went ahead on 19 March, relatively peacefully, and with a turnout of more than 60 per cent. Of the 18.5 million Egyptians who voted, 77.3 per cent indicated that they approved of the constitutional amendments. The "yes" margin was particularly strong in rural areas; in Cairo almost 40 per cent voted "no". The result was a powerful indicator of the political strength of the Islamist movement, and of the limits to the ability of the revolutionary activists to set the political agenda. The SCAF said that the elections to the lower and upper houses of parliament would start in September, and that the presidential election would be held shortly afterwards.

Over the subsequent months the revolutionary activists grew increasingly disenchanted with the SCAF. They accused the generals of trying to minimise the changes to the government structure and of persisting in the same oppressive measures against dissent as had been practised under Mubarak, in particular through military prisons and military tribunals. The SCAF made regular tactical concessions, for example bowing to popular pressure at the start of March and appointing a new government, led by Essam Sharaf, but these failed to mollify the protesters. On 8 July Tahrir Square witnessed the largest demonstration since Mubarak's overthrow. The core demand was for the government to show more urgency in bringing to justice those responsible for having killed protesters during the revolution. Sharaf responded the following day with an assurance that the government would deal with these issues, but this did little to reassure the activists. This demonstration also witnessed the first signs of open criticism of the role of the SCAF. On 17 July Sharaf reshuffled the cabinet, replacing 14 ministers, and in the process virtually purging the government of those who had served under Mubarak. At the end of July the government and the SCAF gave an important indication of their intent to prosecute former regime officials when they started the process of bringing charges against Mubarak himself, as well as his two sons, Alaa Mubarak and Gamal Mubarak. The opening session of the trial was held on 3 August. Also in the dock was the former interior minister, Habib Adly, and six officials in his ministry. The principal charge against all of the defendants was that they bore responsibility for the deaths of more than 800 people during the revolution. The prosecution concluded its case in January 2012 by demanding the death penalty for the former president.

At the end of July the government and the SCAF were confronted for the first time by a show of political force by the Islamist movement, which objected strongly to the suggestion that a set of supra-constitutional principles, including commitment to a civil state, be drawn up prior to the drafting of a new constitution. The Islamists staged a large demonstration on 29 July to make their objections clear. Disputes also surfaced about the new election law and about the timetable for the various elections. Having originally indicated that the legislative election would be held in September, the SCAF now said that this date referred only to the start of the process. It added that it would be premature to set a date for the presidential election and for the transfer of sovereign power to a civilian authority. At the end of September, the arrangements for the elections to the lower house of parliament were finally announced. They would take place over three rounds, each with a run-off one week later, stretching from 28 November to 10 January. There would be 498 seats, of which two-thirds would be decided on the basis of party lists, proportionately in each district, and the remainder by individual candidate.

The run-up to the election was marked by a series of violent confrontations between the security forces and protesters. The first occurred in Cairo on 9 October when troops in armoured personnel carriers charged at a march supporting

Coptic Christians in their demand for action against those responsible for an attack on a church in Aswan. Twenty-four demonstrators were killed in the incident. The SCAF initially sought to blame the violence on armed infiltrators, a claim that only served to increase the resentment of the revolutionary activists. Trouble flared again in mid-November when activists converged on Tahrir Square to demand that the SCAF set a firm date for when it would relinquish power. More than 40 people were killed as security forces shot at demonstrators who had occupied a space in front of the interior ministry. On the eve of the parliamentary elections the SCAF made some fresh concessions, bringing forward the proposed date for the presidential election to June 2012, and implementing yet another change of government. The protesters had held out hope that there could be a devolution of power to a constitutional committee including a number of prospective presidential candidates. However, the SCAF decided to bring back a Mubarak-era figure, Kamal Ganzoury to serve as prime minister. Ganzoury had garnered some popular credibility as he had fallen out with Mubarak in 1999, when he was summarily dismissed as prime minister and then subjected to virtual house arrest, but was derided by the activists as being too old and out of touch.

Despite the turmoil in Cairo, the elections went ahead as scheduled. The first round was marked by a high turnout (over 60 per cent) and a resounding victory for Islamist parties. The Muslim Brotherhood had formed a new party, the Freedom and Justice Party (FJP), to head the Democratic Alliance. This bloc was widely expected to win the largest share of the vote, and it duly garnered about 45 per cent of the first round seats. It had also become clear in the aftermath of the revolution that the Salafi tendency commanded considerable support, but its performance was stronger than many had expected, and it came a close second to the FJP. The hopes of the revolutionary activists were vested mainly in a bloc of secular parties, known as the Koutla. However, this bloc and other revolutionary parties and individuals managed to win only about 15 per cent of the vote, and their tally declined in subsequent rounds. At the end of the three rounds, the FJP-led bloc held almost 45 per cent of the seats, the Salafis 25 per cent, with the remainder shared between the centrist Wafd party, the Koutla and other small parties and independents. The FJP made clear that it would seek to find common ground with the secular parties, and it ruled out forming a grand Islamist coalition with the Salafis.

The Egyptian economy suffered as a result of the revolutionary turmoil. Real GDP contracted by 4.4 per cent year-on-year in the first three months of 2011, and the economy barely registered any growth in the subsequent three quarters. The loss of tourism income and the flight of capital resulted in a large balance of payments deficit, reflected in the fall of foreign exchange reserves from $36 billion at the start of the year to $19 billion in December. The finance ministry drew up an estimate in May for the scale of short-term financial assistance that Egypt would require, and received a positive response from the International Monetary Fund (IMF), the World Bank and Arab and European donors. However, the SCAF vetoed recourse to the IMF, and little of the other promised aid materialised.

David Butter

JORDAN

CAPITAL: Amman   AREA: 88,780 sq km   POPULATION: 6,047,000 ('10)
OFFICIAL LANGUAGE: Arabic
HEAD OF STATE: King Abdullah ibn al-Husain (since Feb '99)
RULING PARTY: none
HEAD OF GOVERNMENT: Prime Minister Awn Shawkat al-Khasawneh (since Oct '11)
DEMOCRACY INDEX: 3.74; 117th of 167   CORRUPTION INDEX: 4.5; 56th of 183
CURRENCY: Jordanian Dinar (Dec '11 £1.00=JOD 1.11, US$1.00=JOD 0.71)
GNI PER CAPITA: US$4,390, Intl$5,810 at PPP ('10)

KING Abdullah II came under sustained political pressure in 2011, as the popular protest movements associated with the "Arab Spring" resonated with opposition groups within Jordan. The king sought to appease the protesters with modest political reforms and with two changes of government during the year. This paid off to some extent, as the protests in Jordan never attained the size and intensity of movements elsewhere in the region. The success of Islamist parties in elections held in Tunisia, Morocco and Egypt provided a source of inspiration for Jordan's Islamic Action Front (IAF), a branch of the Muslim Brotherhood, but the party's chances of taking political advantage were impaired by its decision to boycott Jordan's previous general election, which took place in November 2009.

Protest demonstrations broke out in Jordan in January in emulation of events in Tunisia and Egypt. The IAF played a prominent role in the demonstrations— in contrast to Tunisia and Egypt, where Islamist parties kept a low profile during the initial unrest—together with professional associations, left-wing groups and social media activists. The crowds focused its anger on the government rather than on the monarchy, thus allowing the king some room for manoeuvre. He responded quickly, acceding on 1 February to the protesters' demand for the removal of the prime minister, Samir Rifai, a businessman who had been closely involved in Jordan's privatisation programme, a policy that was regarded with suspicion by many Jordanians. Rifai, who was of Palestinian origin, had only recently been reappointed to the position after the November election. His replacement was Marouf Bakhit, a former head of national security who had previously been prime minister between 2005 and 2007. Bakhit promised that he would introduce far-reaching political reforms, but his appointment was criticised by the IAF, which made clear that it had little confidence in this promise. One of the main reasons advanced for the choice of Bakhit was that he came from the staunchly loyal East Bank tribes that formed the backbone of the king's security forces.

Despite the protesters' lack of enthusiasm for Bakhit, the change of government brought a lull in opposition activity and the king set up a National Dialogue Committee (NDC) to discuss political reforms. The attention of Jordanian political activists was also drawn to the increasingly violent events in Syria, where protests had erupted in Deraa, close to the Jordanian border, in mid-March. The Syrian experience may have had a sobering effect on Jordan. The trouble in Syria and the wider regional unrest depressed growth in Jordan, as trade and tourism both suffered. However, Jordan did benefit from a sense of solidarity among Arab monarchies, and Saudi Arabia provided a $1 billion grant in July, as well as proposing to bring Jordan (and Morocco) into the Gulf Co-operation Council (GCC).

The NDC came forward with proposals for limited changes to the electoral system, retaining the bias towards loyalist rural and tribal constituencies. In August the Royal Commission on Constitutional Review (RCCR) recommended some more far-reaching reforms through 42 amendments to the constitution. These included a number of substantial measures, for example abolishing military trials (other than for espionage or terrorism), outlawing torture, providing for greater parliamentary scrutiny of ministers, extending media freedoms and lowering the minimum age for legislators to 25 from 30. However, they stopped short of imposing any significant limits on the powers of the king, beyond curtailing his right to postpone elections and limiting the period that he may rule by decree between elections to four months from two years. The opposition was unimpressed by the reforms, and staged protest demonstrations outside parliament, but there were still few signs of direct criticism of the king.

The tenure of Bakhit as prime minister lasted only eight months. He provoked strong opposition from MPs following his summary dismissal of the central bank governor, Faris Sharaf, and the king intervened in mid-October and replaced Bakhit with Awn Khasawneh, a judge, who had been serving on the International Court of Justice. Khasawneh was considered to have good relations with the IAF, but the Islamist party turned down his offer of inclusion in the new cabinet. The government nevertheless had 16 ministers without previous experience, which sent a signal of intent about setting Jordan on a path of reform. The IAF indicated that it would boycott municipal elections that were scheduled to take place on 20 December, but Khasawneh left the way open for the group to revise its position as he decided to postpone these elections until early 2012.

David Butter

SYRIA

CAPITAL: Damascus   AREA: 185,180 sq km   POPULATION: 20,446,609 ('10)
OFFICIAL LANGUAGE: Arabic
HEAD OF STATE AND GOVERNMENT: President Bashar al-Assad (since July '00)
RULING PARTY: Ba'ath Party
PRIME MINISTER: Abel Safar (since April '11)
DEMOCRACY INDEX: 2.31; 152nd of 167   CORRUPTION INDEX: 2.6; 129th of 183
CURRENCY: Syrian Pound (Dec '11 £1.00=SYP 78.41, US$1.00=SYP 50.00)
GNI PER CAPITA: US$2,790, Intl$5,150 at PPP ('10)

THE wave of unrest unleashed at the start of 2011 by the "Arab Spring" appeared at first to have passed Syria by. However, a small act of defiance by schoolchildren in the southern town of Deraa in early March, emulating the uprisings in Tunisia and Egypt, led to a spiralling of protests across the country. The resort to force by the regime of President Bashar Assad, in an attempt to quell the protests, merely inflamed the situation, resulting in a state of rebellion in many parts of the country lasting throughout the year. Assad managed to cling on to power, but faced mounting international pressure, and as the year ended the survival of his regime continued to hang in the balance.

Assad's initial reaction to the Arab uprisings was broadly positive. The popular anger in Tunisia, Egypt, Bahrain and, to a lesser extent, in Jordan was directed at leaders regarded as allies of the West, whereas Assad had positioned Syria at the heart of a so-called front of resistance against Western and Israeli attempts to dominate the Middle East region. In toppling President Hosni Mubarak, the Egyptian people had also removed one of the harshest critics of Assad among Arab leaders. The Syrian president's confidence had been further enhanced at the start of the year by the change in government in neighbouring Lebanon, marking the ascendancy of pro-Syrian factions over a coalition supported by Saudi Arabia, France and the USA. In an interview published in the *Wall Street Journal* at the end of January, Assad acknowledged that Syria did share some of the characteristics of Egypt and Tunisia, but he argued that his regime was more secure because its policies on issues such as Palestine and the US invasion of Iraq were more closely aligned with popular sentiment. One week later, an effort by opposition activists to inspire protest demonstrations through social media networks fell flat, in an apparent validation of Assad's analysis.

The trouble in Deraa started in mid-March when reports filtered out of the town that there had been protest demonstrations over the arrest of 15 schoolchildren after graffiti had appeared echoing the slogans of revolutionaries in Egypt and Tunisia and turning them against the Syrian regime. Activists posted videos on Facebook and Twitter showing security forces shooting at the crowds in Deraa and outlying villages, and these were replayed on Arab satellite television channels, ensuring that most of the population could see them. The unrest quickly spread to several other towns, including Banias and Latakia, on the Mediterranean, where some of the clashes took on a sectarian tinge, pitting members of Assad's Alawi minority against Sunni Muslims, the majority sect in Syria. Assad's first public reaction to the unrest came on 24 March when he issued a number of decrees providing financial benefits to the public, including higher public-sector wages, better pension entitlements, an increase in the personal tax threshold and a measure relating to the use of state-owned land. The latter appeared to be Deraa-specific, as there had been much resentment in the area at the appropriation of land by Rami Makhlouf, Assad's first cousin, for a large duty-free shopping centre. The decrees were issued on a Thursday, marking a pattern for the next few months, whereby the regime attempted to pre-empt protests starting after Friday prayers. Official spokespeople and state media commentators blamed externally backed Islamist extremists and the foreign and Arab media for stirring up the unrest, a theme picked up by Assad on 30 March in a speech in parliament, his first public utterance since the crisis started. At the end of March, the Jordanian bureau-chief of Reuters news agency was expelled from Syria, and one of his colleagues, also of Jordanian nationality, was detained for several days, before also being told to leave. The two main Arab satellite television channels, Al Jazeera and Al Arabiya, were also barred from continuing to broadcast from Syria.

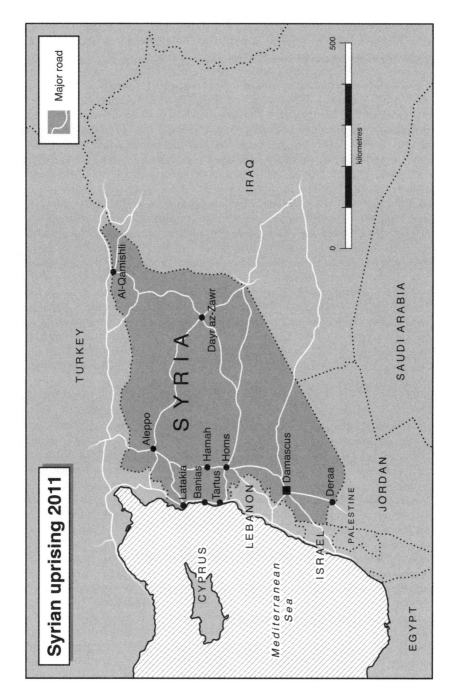

Over the following weeks, Assad offered more political and economic concessions, while his security forces intensified their suppression of the continuing demonstrations. The main military strike force was the Fourth Army, a division commanded by the president's younger brother, Maher Assad, backed up by units of the various state intelligence services and militiamen referred to as Shabiha, an Alawi force known for its involvement in smuggling. On 4 April Assad dismissed the government headed by Naji Otari, who had first been appointed prime minister in 2003. The new prime minister was Adel Safar, who had been agriculture minister in the outgoing cabinet. One of the most notable casualties of the reshuffle was Abdullah Dardari, who had been deputy prime minister for economic affairs since 2005, and who had been at the forefront of Syria's market-oriented economic reforms for most of Assad's rule. Dardari's efforts to cut subsidies and court foreign investment had made him unpopular with vested interests bent on preserving the old state-dominated model, and he was regularly attacked in sections of the state and Baath party media. He was thus a convenient scapegoat for Assad as the president sought to placate the protesters with populist economic measures. Assad made a televised address to the cabinet on 16 April, in the course of which he announced plans to lift the emergency laws, which had been in force since 1963 (when the Baath party seized power), pass a new political parties law, enhance the powers of local government and give more freedoms to the media, all in the cause of making Syria a model for democratic reform. Most of the these measures were rushed through parliament before it was suspended at the end of May, having completed its allotted four-year term without fresh elections being held. The parliament reconvened three months later, in line with the constitutional provisions covering the legislature.

As the civilian death toll rose over 1,000, the Syrian uprising started to attract increased international attention, and in mid-May US President Barack Obama made his first comments, calling on Assad to "lead the transition" to a democratic system or "get out of the way". The EU meanwhile issued a second round of sanctions, designating a large number of Syrian officials as people that Europeans should have no business with, and suspending its economic aid programme. Syria's relations with Turkey also took a sharp turn for the worse. Over the previous few years, relations had improved markedly, with the signing of a free-trade agreement and frequent meetings between Assad and the Turkish prime minister, Recep Tayyip Erdogan. Turkey made some efforts to resolve the escalating crisis in Syria diplomatically, but concluded that the Syrian government was not acting in good faith. After an incident in Jisr al-Shughour, a town near the Turkish border, at the start of June, when more than 100 policemen were killed in what the regime described as an attack by extremists, the Syrian army attacked several villages in the area, prompting thousands of Syrians to seek refuge in Turkey.

The USA became more directly involved in early July when its ambassador, Robert Ford, together with his French colleague, Eric Chevalier, visited the central Syrian city of Hama, renowned for the massacre that took place there in 1982 when Syrian troops confronted an Islamist uprising. Ford said that he wished to witness the protests at first hand. His action was strongly criticised by the authorities as he had not sought prior permission, and on his return to Damascus, the US embassy was attacked by a mob. The visit to Hama came after the city had come close to turning itself into a no-go area for the regime, setting a potentially dangerous precedent. At the end of June Assad took steps to reassert control, removing the governor, who had taken a liberal approach to demonstrations. On 4 July Ibrahim Qashoush, a singer from Hama who had gained a huge following on YouTube for a song calling for Assad's departure, was found dead, with his throat cut and his vocal chords ripped out. The regime gradually reasserted control over Hama, but the focus of the revolt then shifted to Homs, 50km to the south of Hama, and the third-largest city in Syria.

The opposition movement took some time to develop any sort of coherent political structure. Protest activity within Syria was organised by a network of local co-ordinating committees (LCCs), which disseminated information via groups using the Internet outside the country. A number of political figures within Syria who had opposed the regime over the past few decades and had been in and out of jail set up a National Co-ordinating Body for Democratic Change, which was able to hold a few public meetings within the country. The most substantial effort to create a unified opposition front came from the Syrian National Council (SNC), a coalition of liberal intellectuals in exile, members of the banned Muslim Brotherhood, Kurdish groups and representatives of the LCCs. The SNC formally announced itself at a conference in Istanbul on 15 September as the main address for the Syrian opposition. It called for Assad to step down immediately and for a democratic consultation to take place about how to replace his regime with a freely elected government. The SNC ruled out negotiation with the current government, but it stopped short of advocating armed opposition or foreign intervention. Bourhan Ghalioun, a Paris-based professor originally from Homs, became its first chairman.

Foreign pressure on the regime increased in the latter part of the year, but was mitigated by the refusal of Russia and China to endorse UN sanctions. The EU decided on 2 September to impose a ban on importing Syrian oil, a severe measure owing to the fact that virtually all of Syria's oil exports (about 150,000 barrels per day) was purchased by European buyers. By the end of the year most foreign oil companies had stopped production in Syria, and oil exports had virtually ceased. The Arab League finally became engaged in the Syrian crisis in mid-October after Russia and China had vetoed a UN Security Council resolution on 4 October on the grounds that it was unbalanced. The Arab League served notice on 16 October that it would suspend Syria's membership if the regime did not stop its violent suppression of the protests—by this time the death toll was estimated to have risen over 3,000. The Arab League voted on 2 November to go ahead with the suspension, and proposed to send observers to Syria to monitor the situation. After several weeks of discussion, Syria and the Arab League agreed on a protocol covering the deployment of the observers, and the first batch arrived on 26 December, led by Mohammed al-Dabi, a former head of military intelligence in Sudan.

As the Arab League diplomacy ground slowly forward, the levels of violence had increased markedly, partly as a result of the emergence of the Free Syrian Army, a group made up of defectors from the regime's forces. Large numbers of civilians were still being killed, mainly in Homs and in the area around Idleb, in the north-west, but casualties among the security forces were also rising. The UN Commission on Human Rights estimated in mid-December that more than 5,000 Syrian civilians had been killed since the uprising began in March. In parts of the country, notably Homs, the conflict had taken on an overtly sectarian guise, pitting Sunnis against Alawis, but the opposition claimed that much of this stemmed from regime incitement. The opposition made similar claims after an apparent suicide bomb attack in Damascus on 23 December killed about 40 people. The government said the attack had been carried out by Islamist extremists linked to al-Qaida.

As the year ended it was clear that Syria faced a prolonged period of violent internal conflict. The Assad regime had managed to avoid any major defection from within its ranks, and retained the important external support of Russia, Iran, Lebanon's Hezbullah and, with some reservations, Iraq. Assad had mixed repression with a process of political reform that, while it lacked credibility, gave the regime's active and passive supporters a notion that the crisis could be resolved without traumatic change. However, the opposition movement had shown great resilience in the face of the regime's brutal crackdown, and there was a powerful consensus among large swathes of the Syrian public, the majority of Arab governments and most Western powers that there could be no accommodation with Assad after the actions that his regime had taken.

David Butter

LEBANON

CAPITAL: Beirut   AREA: 10,400 sq km   POPULATION: 4,227,597 ('10)
OFFICIAL LANGUAGE: Arabic
HEAD OF STATE: Gen. Michel Suleiman (since May '08)
RULING PARTY: 8 March Alliance, led by Hezbullah
HEAD OF GOVERNMENT: Prime Minister Najib Mikati (since June '11)
DEMOCRACY INDEX: 5.82; 86th of 167   CORRUPTION INDEX: 2.5; 134th of 183
CURRENCY: Lebanese Pound (Dec '11 £1.00=LBP 2,361, US$1.00=LBP 1,505)
GNI PER CAPITA: US$9,080, Intl$14,260 at PPP ('10)

AT the start of 2011 Lebanon was in the throes of a political crisis involving a trial of strength between the respective external sponsors of the two principal political groupings in the country. The conflict was typical of the function that Lebanon had performed for decades as the arena for settling wider political scores. However, the tumultuous events elsewhere in the Middle East marked an historic shift in the region's political dynamics, and although Lebanon had a relatively tranquil year it could not entirely avoid some impact from the "Arab Spring", as the Syrian uprising spilled over the border and the Lebanese economy suffered from a decline in trade, investment and tourism.

The Lebanese government had been paralysed for much of 2010 by the political battle between its two main constituent blocs over how to deal with the Special Tribunal for Lebanon (STL), set up under UN auspices to investigate the assassination of Rafiq Hariri in 2005 and bring the perpetrators to justice. In January the national unity government led by Saad Hariri, the late statesman's son, collapsed following a shift of allegiance of the Druze leader, Walid Junblatt, from Hariri's 14 March bloc, which had a slender majority in the parliament elected in 2009, to the 8 March bloc, comprising the two Shia movements, Hezbullah and Amal, and the mainly Christian Free Patriotic Movement (FPM), led by Michel Aoun, a former commander of the army. Hariri resigned on 12 January after the failure of diplomatic efforts by his main external sponsor, Saudi Arabia, to persuade Syria and the 8 March bloc to withdraw their demand for the government formally to end co-operation with the STL. The timing of the crisis was influenced by the strong indications that the STL was coming close to issuing its first indictments and speculation that Hezbullah members would be among the accused.

After a tense fortnight the Lebanese parliament convened on 25 January to vote on which candidate to recommend to the president, Michel Suleiman, for the post of prime minister. Thanks to Junblatt's support, the 8 March candidate, Najib Mikati—a businessman from the northern city of Tripoli who had previously served as a caretaker prime minister for a few months in 2005 after Hariri's assassination and who had been minister of public works in the late 1990s—was duly appointed. However, it then took almost five months of wrangling among the members of the 8 March coalition before he was finally able to form a cabinet. The main obstacle had been the demand of Aoun for a large share of ministerial portfolios. The breakthrough came after the Syrian president, Bashar Assad, intervened in early June by making clear that he did not consider that the state of political limbo in Lebanon was in Syria's interest. Assad was increasingly preoccupied with the popular uprising against his own regime, but retained a strong interest in being able to demonstrate that Syria had no intention of giving up its traditional role of supreme arbiter of Lebanese political affairs. The Aoun problem was resolved through reducing the number of ministers selected by President Suleiman to two from the five specified in the Doha agreement that had resolved a previous political crisis in May 2008. The new government finally took office on 13 June.

Another factor in the formation of the government was the timing of the publication of the STL indictments. On 29 June the government issued its policy programme, including a section stating that Lebanon would continue to co-operate with the tribunal as long as this did not threaten to undermine national cohesion and stability. On 30 June the STL passed the indictments to the Lebanese prosecutor, Said Mirza. The Lebanese media immediately published the names of the four men named in the indictments, all described as being members of Hezbullah. The leader of the alleged assassination squad was named as Mustafa Badreddin, a relative and close associate of Imad Mughniyeh, Hezbullah's military commander, who had been killed by a bomb placed in his car in Damascus in February 2008. The indictments largely confirmed media reports over the preceding two to three years which had indicated that the STL had amassed evidence from patterns of mobile phone use that implicated Hezbullah operatives.

Hezbullah's leader, Hassan Nasrallah had already rejected this hypothesis in a presentation in 2010 in which he claimed that the mobile phone evidence had been fabricated by Israel.

The STL stated that if the four men did not come forward or were not arrested by Lebanon's police, there was provision for them to be tried *in absentia*. A dispute over whether the Lebanese government should pay its share of the STL's costs, as specified in the UN Security Council resolution establishing the tribunal, rumbled on for the remainder of 2011, and was finally resolved in early 2012 by the expedient of the Association of Lebanese Banks offering the necessary funds.

The Mikati government remained comfortably in power for the remainder of 2011, and made progress in some areas of economic policy. These included making preparations for an international bid round for oil and gas exploration licences off the Lebanese coast. The recent discovery of large reserves of gas in Israeli and Cypriot waters provided a strong incentive for Lebanon to determine whether it too might have the potential to become a significant energy producer. The new government sought to get the UN involved in resolving a dispute about maritime border demarcations between Lebanon and Israel. According to Lebanon, the Israeli government had in effect annexed 1,500 sq km of Lebanese territory in its version of the border, based on an unratified 2007 maritime border agreement between Lebanon and Cyprus. Lebanon and Israel had had no direct negotiations about the border.

The worsening security situation in Syria was a major preoccupation for Lebanon for most of 2011. Hundreds of Syrian refugees fleeing the Assad regime's violence streamed over the border, particularly in the Wadi Khaled area in north-east Lebanon. The Syrian government accused Lebanese Sunni Muslim groups of providing arms and weapons to the regime's opponents, and there were persistent reports of Syrian military incursions over the Lebanese border in pursuit of rebels or army deserters. Syrian opposition groups accused the Lebanese security services of collaborating with their Syrian counterparts and arresting refugees and sending them back to Damascus. The Syrian crisis had a damaging impact on Lebanon's services oriented economy, particularly affecting trade, tourism and property investment, with the result that economic growth slumped to about 1.5 per cent after averaging 8 per cent in the previous four years. Events in Syria also looked as though they could undermine the Lebanese government's stability, as Junblatt, who wielded considerable influence over the Druze minority in Syria, took an increasingly critical stance towards the Assad regime, suggesting that he could move back into the 14 March camp.

David Butter

IRAQ

CAPITAL: Baghdad   AREA: 438,320 sq km   POPULATION: 32,030,823 ('10)
OFFICIAL LANGUAGES: Arabic and Kurdish
HEAD OF STATE: President Jalal Talabani (since April '05)
RULING PARTY: United Iraq Alliance (UIA)
HEAD OF GOVERNMENT: Prime Minister Nouri al-Maliki (UIA, Da'wa Party), (since April '06)
DEMOCRACY INDEX: 4.00; 111th of 167   CORRUPTION INDEX: 1.8; 175th of 183
CURRENCY: New Iraqi Dinar (Dec '11 £1.00=IQD 1,830, US$1.00=IQD 1,167)
GNI PER CAPITA: US$2,340, Intl$3,350 at PPP ('10)

ON 18 December the last US forces withdrew from Iraq, travelling south across the desert by much the same route that US and other coalition forces had attacked the country in 2003 (see AR 2003, pp. 229-48). The withdrawal concluded the USA's most ambitious and bloodiest military campaign since the Vietnam War, and the departing troops left behind a country that was not exactly at war and not exactly at peace. At a ceremony in Fort Bragg, North Carolina, on 14 December, US President Barack Obama marked an end to the war he had once described as "dumb" by declaring the conflict in Iraq a success. Obama avoided displaying the hubris of his predecessor, George W. Bush, who, only two months after the invasion of Iraq, had declared that major combat operations had ended, just as the worst of the carnage in the country was about to begin (see AR 2003, p. 551). Obama, who entered office promising to end the war, told the soldiers at Fort Bragg, "It's harder to end a war than begin one. Indeed, everything that American troops have done in Iraq—all the fighting and all the dying, the bleeding and the building, and the training and the partnering—all of it has led to this moment of success."

Figures recorded by the independent, US-based iCasualties.org showed that 4,484 US servicemen had been killed in Iraq between March 2003 and December 2011. When the UK's military operation in Iraq officially ended on 21 May, a total of 179 British troops had died in the conflict. Other member countries of the US-led coalition had suffered 139 military fatalities in total, notably Italy (33), Poland (23), Ukraine (18) Bulgaria (13), and Spain (11).

More than 100,000 Iraqi civilians were killed in the war and its aftermath. However, violence had decreased significantly since the US "troop surge" of 2007 (see AR 2008, pp. 198-203). Nonetheless, by any standards, in 2011 Iraq remained one of the most dangerous and violent countries in the world. According to the US military, there were between 500 and 750 attacks a month during the year, including suicide bombings, rocket attacks and assassinations carried out by Sunni and Shia insurgent groups and militias, including the local branch of al-Qaida.

Whilst the violence had declined in relative terms, deep sectarian rifts had certainly not healed and the spectre of fresh bloodletting hung over the country as the year drew to a close. On 22 December—only a few days after the final US military withdrawal—around a dozen car bombs exploded within a space of two hours in Baghdad, killing at least 72 people and injuring over 200 others. The co-ordinated attacks led to one of the highest death tolls of the year, matched only by a similar spate of bombings on 15 August in which as many as 89 people had died. Shia areas of Baghdad took the brunt of both attacks, although some Sunni areas of the capital were hit in the December bombings. There was no immediate claim of responsibility, but the attacks appeared similar to others conducted by the Iraqi branch of al-Qaida.

The December wave of violence followed hard upon a clash between Nouri al-Maliki, the Shia prime minister, and one of the country's most prominent Sunni politicians. Maliki had been gradually consolidating his position and that of Iraq's new, Shia-led establishment since he became prime minister in 2006. On 19 December he declared that a warrant had been issued for the arrest of Vice President Tariq al-Hashemi, one of the country's most prominent Sunni leaders, on charges of terrorism. State television broadcast the confessions of three men said to be Hashemi's bodyguards, who claimed that they had been paid to carry out attacks on civil servants and traffic police. Hashemi fled north, to Iraq's semi-autonomous Kurdish area, from where he insisted that the charges against him had been fabricated by the prime minister. Maliki told the Kurdish authorities to send Hashemi back to Baghdad, which they refused to do. The standoff, involving as it did the Shias, the Sunnis and the Kurds, set alarm bells ringing in the USA, where many commentators expressed serious concern that the fragile political accommodation, which had followed the formation of a broad coalition government in late 2010 (see AR 2011, p. 201), was unravelling and could hasten attempts by the three main Sunni-dominated provinces—Salahuddin, Anbar and Diyala—to seek Kurdish-style autonomy. Four predominantly Shia provinces—Basra, Missan, Dhiqar and Muthanna—were reported to have discussed plans to make themselves autonomous regions, and some Shias had advocated the construction of a larger federal region that would include all nine southern and central provinces, which were predominately Shia.

Iran, which like Iraq was majority Shia, continued to exert great influence over its neighbour during the year, much to the consternation of the Sunni monarchs in the Gulf region. In January, Muqtada al-Sadr returned to Iraq after three years of voluntary exile in Iran and by the end of the year the mercurial and enigmatic cleric was flexing his political muscle anew. Sadr had insisted, against Maliki's initial wishes, that all US troops had to depart before 2012 or face a new insurgency from his Iranian-backed militia, the "Mahdi Army". Iran's ability to affect Iraq's powerful Shia religious establishment, led by the revered Grand Ayatollah Ali Sistani in Najaf, had always been limited. However, it was reported in mid-December that Iran, with the backing of Maliki, was close to installing a high-ranking cleric in Najaf. The cleric, Ayatollah Mahmoud Hashemi Shahroudi, was a former head of the Iranian judiciary and was regarded as close to Iran's supreme leader, Ayatollah Ali Khamenei.

During its occupation of Iraq, the USA had tried but failed to resolve the delicate problem of how to divide the country's vast oil wealth. Some analysts, citing recent geological surveys and seismic data, believed that oil reserves in Iraq would soon be shown to be the largest in the world. Furthermore, after years of stagnant production during the US occupation, oil output starting to increase during the latter half of 2011. Oil production had hovered at around 2 million barrels-per-day (bpd) for much of the post-US invasion period, but during 2011 production increased to around 2.6 million bpd, according to the US Energy Information Administration. Foreign companies were again operating in the oil-rich south, but they had been wary of making deals in the Kurdish north, since the government in Baghdad and the Kurds' regional authority (the Kurdistan Regional Government, KRG) had failed to agree on how to divide the income, despite years of acrimonious negotiations. Eventually, in mid-October, the US multinational ExxonMobil signed a landmark deal with the KRG to explore for oil and gas in north-eastern Iraq. The Maliki government responded furiously, threatening to penalise any company that dealt with the Kurds without its agreement. Royal Dutch Shell took heed of the threat and, in mid-November, pulled out of oil development talks with the KRG in an effort to protect lucrative operations in southern Iraq, including a large natural gas deal.

The "Arab Spring" uprisings and revolutions of 2011 largely passed Iraq by. There were a number of protest marches in Baghdad and other cities in February and March, with outbreaks of violence, but the protesters were not concerned with toppling the government, but rather with ending electricity blackouts and reducing the level of corruption.

Darren Sagar

SAUDI ARABIA—YEMEN—ARAB STATES OF THE GULF

SAUDI ARABIA

CAPITAL: Riyadh   AREA: 2,000,000 sq km   POPULATION: 27,448,086 ('10)
OFFICIAL LANGUAGE: Arabic
HEAD OF STATE AND GOVERNMENT: King Abdullah ibn Abdul Aziz (since Aug '05), also prime minister
HEIR APPARENT: Crown Prince and Deputy Prime Minister Mayef bin Abdul Aziz al-Saud
   (since Oct '11)
DEMOCRACY INDEX: 1.84; 160th of 167   CORRUPTION INDEX: 4.4; 57th of 183
CURRENCY: Saudi Riyal (Dec '11 £1.00=SAR 5.88, US$1.00=SAR 3.75)
GNI PER CAPITA: US$16,190, Intl$22,540 at PPP ('09)

SECURITY and internal stability continued to be priorities for the kingdom. In 2011 concerns went beyond threats from al-Qaida affiliates and incursions by Zaydi (Houthi) rebels on the southern flank, as Saudi Arabia found itself engulfed by the events unfolding in Tunisia and later in Egypt, Yemen and Bahrain. By March it was evident that the kingdom was in the forefront of efforts to slow the unprecedented uprisings that came to be known as the "Arab Spring". As protests reached its eastern front, Saudi Arabia had more than one reason for a further cooling of relations with Iran. The ruling family exerted all its diplomatic and military efforts along its borders and as far away as Libya in order to stave off any threats to internal stability.

Domestic policy focused on the economy and continuing uncertainty over the line of succession. The budget for 2011 proposed an increase of just under 8 per cent in state expenditure, emphasising infrastructure and social spending. Analysts estimated that this increase amounted to around $155 billion (SAR 580 billion), but in March King Abdullah ibn Abdul Aziz announced an economic stimulus package that raised expenditure to nearly SAR 1,000 billion. The package included the creation of 60,000 jobs and the construction of 500,000 residential units. The announcement was made as unrest surfaced in the eastern province of Qatif after a botched "day of rage" for 11 March, which had been organised online by activists such as Faisal Ahmed Abdul-Ahadwas (who was believed to have been shot dead by the security forces on 2 March).

The economic stimulus helped the country's booming economy. At the Saudi-US business forum held in Atlanta, Georgia in December Abdullah Zainal Alireza, the commerce and industry minister, announced that GDP was expected to grow by 6.5 per cent in 2011. The kingdom was ranked as the 12th most business-friendly country out of 183 economies and considered a "high growth market" by the British government. Members of the ruling family, such as Prince Alwaleed bin Talal, the head of Kingdom Holding Company (KHC), expanded their operations into satellite television, with the new Alarab channel, and into social media. Alwaleed and KHC invested $300 million in the microblogging site Twitter, obtaining around 3 per cent of shares in the company.

Many outside observers remained focused on the potential for instability arising from uncertainty over the line of succession, a concern magnified as a number of the elder Sudeiri princes had suffered from poor health since late 2009. On 22 October Crown Prince Sultan ibn Abdul Aziz succumbed to colon cancer, dying in New York at the age of 80. However, the swift, uncontested transition to Prince Nayef ibn Abdul Aziz, the interior minister, as the new crown prince served to allay many of the concerns over the succession.

The resignation of Tunisia's President Zine El Abidine Ben Ali on 14 January, and his welcome to exile in Jeddah, placed Saudi Arabia at the centre of the "Arab Spring". Saudi Arabia's image was eroded further as its rulers moved to support Egypt's President Hosni Mubarak after US President Barack Obama on 4 February called on Mubarak to "make the right decision" to meet the demands of youth protesters camping at Tahrir square in Cairo.

Concerns increased when the "Arab Spring" reached Bahrain and Yemen, states vital for stability in the Arabian peninsula. The Saudi ruling family was condemned by many for its heavy-handed approach in support of Bahrain's Sheikh Hamad bin Isa al-Khalifa since the first protests in February, and for its unyielding backing of Yemen's President Ali Abdullah Saleh. Saudi troops were despatched to Bahrain as part of a GCC force at the request of Sheikh Hamad, and Saleh received medical treatment in Riyadh after being wounded in a bomb attack in June. Yet whilst the kingdom exerted all its diplomatic and military efforts to end the protests in Bahrain and Yemen, Saudi Arabia, along with Qatar, was instrumental in NATO's support for the rebels in Libya against Colonel Moamar Kadhafi. Within the Arab League, Saudi Arabia also became a very outspoken opponent of Syria's President Bashar al-Assad. Saudi support for the Syrian opposition and the suspension of Syria's membership in the Arab League eventually led to an attack on Saudi Arabia's embassy in Damascus on 12 November by pro-Assad crowds.

This dual track approach to popular uprisings in North Africa and the Middle East was a very delicate balancing act by the ruling family as it faced its own domestic challenges, in part inspired by the "Arab Spring". Calls for demonstrations against the government focused first on domestic issues such as unlawful detentions, economic conditions, and high unemployment. Protests then developed among the minority Shia population over grievances relating to lack of equality. This led to confrontation between the Saudi rulers and Iran, over claims that the Islamic Republic was providing support to Saudi Shia protesters. Relations deteriorated further with the news, in October, that US law enforcement agencies had disrupted a plot by Iranian-Americans Manssor Arbabsiar and Gholam Shakuri to assassinate Saudi Arabia's ambassador to Washington, DC, and bomb the embassies of Saudi Arabia and Israel in the USA. Iran rejected the allegations.

Fernando Carvajal

YEMEN

CAPITAL: Sana'a   AREA: 527,970 sq km   POPULATION: 24,052,514 ('10)
OFFICIAL LANGUAGE: Arabic
HEAD OF STATE: President Ali Abdullah Saleh (GPC) (since May '90)
RULING PARTY: General People's Congress (GPC)
HEAD OF GOVERNMENT: Mohammed Salim Basundwa (from Dec '11)
DEMOCRACY INDEX: 2.64; 146th of 167   CORRUPTION INDEX: 2.1; 164th of 183
CURRENCY: Yemeni Riyal (Dec '11 £1.00=YER 343.05, US$1.00=YER 218.75)
GNI PER CAPITA: US$1,070, Intl$2,350 at PPP ('09)

POLITICAL instability continued as result of protests against President Ali Abdullah Saleh, led by the journalist and activist Tawakkol Karman—Nobel Peace Prize laureate in 2011—and the Joint Meeting Party (JMP). Early in January, Karman and the JMP continued to organise protests against Saleh's restructuring of the Supreme Electoral Commission and his proposed amendments to the constitution that would, in effect, make him president for life and ensure succession by his son Ahmed Ali Abdullah Saleh (see AR 2011, p. 206). Prior to the overthrow of President Zine el-Abidine Ben Ali of Tunisia in January, Karman led a march from the main gate of Sana'a University along a one-way street towards the office of the president's son, and then continued to the Tunisian embassy in support of the overthrow of Ben Ali. The protest movement in Yemen that would become part of the "Arab Spring" uprising did, in fact, have its own spark, beyond the inspiration provided by the self-immolation of Tunisian street vendor, Mohammed Bouazizi.

Two weeks after Ben Ali's resignation and exile to Jeddah in Saudi Arabia, Yemen's organised opposition, the JMP, called for a "day of rage" on 3 February. In an attempt to pre-empt the emulation of Tunisian- or Egyptian-style mass protests, President Saleh appeared before the Assembly of Representatives (the legislature) on 2 February and promised to withdraw the proposed constitutional amendments and work with the opposition on a new schedule for legislative elections, previously set for 27 April. As President Saleh addressed the Assembly, a number of tents and a stage were erected by the authorities a block away within Tahrir (Freedom) Square. This was symbolic, since it deprived the JMP of a location similar (and identically named) to that occupied by the protesters in Cairo. The JMP had requested a permit to hold a demonstration at Tahrir square in

Sana'a, but this had been denied on the grounds of the venue's proximity to the Assembly, the Republican Palace, and the presidential offices.

The "day of rage" organised by the JMP included speeches by young activists and leaders from opposition parties within the JMP, such as the Islamist al-Islah party, the Yemeni Socialist Party, and the Zaydi (al-Haq) party. Notably absent from this demonstration, which convened in front of the main gate of Sana'a University, were Sheikh Hamid al-Ahmar and Tawakkol Karman. The former had become President Saleh's most outspoken critic since 2009, and the latter would become a major figure recognised by Western media as a leader of the "youth revolution". This demonstration, along with the parallel pro-government rally at Tahrir square, ended at mid-day as planned but, to the surprise of opposition and government alike, a small group of independent youth took it upon themselves to clean the streets around Sana'a University and later set up a small tent at the spot occupied by the main stage during the JMP rally. By Saturday morning the young university students had been dispersed by soldiers guarding the university gate. The students gathered more support and continued to demonstrate near the university until the JMP announced the first Friday prayer protest in Sana'a—similar to those being held in Cairo—for 11 February. These Friday rallies became the official launch of a permanent protest movement in Sana'a and the city of Taiz, where Karman gave a fiery speech against the regime and propelled the protest motto "asShab yurid isqa't al-nitham" ("the people want to overthrow the regime"). Tents began to appear along streets radiating from Sana'a University and near Taiz city centre. Although the political climate was tense, the protests remained peaceful and without major incidents except in the port city of Aden, where at the end of February protests were dispersed with tear gas and live ammunition.

Tension was managed through mediation between the JMP, as the presumed leader of the protests, and President Saleh by the council of clerics headed by Sheikh Abd al-Majid al-Zindani. For two weeks Zindani shuttled between the presidential palace and meetings with JMP leaders to draft an agreement that would end the protests. After reaching a tentative deal, on 2 March Zindani made an impromptu appearance at the protest area outside Sana'a University, now renamed "Change square". The sheikh, who was on the US state department's list of terrorists, began his speech by mentioning the coming of the Islamic caliphate that would spread from Yemen to the rest of the world, then congratulated the youth for an unprecedented movement and promised their demands would be met. While Zindani's presence at Change square failed to convince people to abandon the protests, it did succeed in bringing more Islah party followers to the protest area and solidified the role of Islah in supplying the majority of protesters and dominating the main stage. This marked the beginning of a protracted conflict between independent university students and Islah members at Change square in Sana'a; a similar conflict in Taiz would develop after the summer.

The political dispute escalated to armed conflict following the 18 March massacre of unarmed protesters in Sana'a by government troops. About 52 young protesters, marching after prayers, were killed, sparking defections to the opposition by dozens of government officials and military officers, most of whom were associated with General Ali Muhsin al-Ahmar, the head of the 1st Armoured Division al-Firqa. The list of defectors included diplomats stationed in the Arab world and western Europe, military officers of the Eastern Command (Hadhramawt), and all brothers of Sheikh Hamid al-Ahmar who held government positions, such as the deputy speaker of the Assembly, Himyar al-Ahmar. The defections served to sharpen the conflict within the regime that had been brewing since 2009 when General Ali Muhsin and President Saleh had clashed over the strategy against Houthi rebels in the north and the role of Ahmed Ali Saleh during the war. As the diplomatic cables published by WikiLeaks had revealed, Sheikh Hamid al-Ahmar had warned that he could organise mass protests against Saleh and be able to gain the support of General Ali Muhsin. By 21 March, Firqa armed personnel were manning the security line around Change square's perimeter where they set up cement blocks and sand bags. This divided the city of Sana'a into Firqa dominated areas in the north and east, and government controlled areas in the south and west of the capital.

Defections from the regime also brought about an expansion of protests beyond Aden, Sana'a and Taiz. By the start of April, protest camps were being organised in tribal areas like Mareb and al-Jawf, port cities like Hodeida and Mukalla, and Friday demonstrations were seen nationwide. But these were countered by pro-government demonstrations in Sana'a and other areas. Both the opposition and the government supported the protests financially, which led to accusations against regional powers, who provided food, water and tents for protesters on both sides, for directly funding the protest leaders.

After nearly two months of further negotiations led by the Gulf Co-operation Council (GCC) and repeatedly broken promises by President Saleh to sign an agreement, he was targeted by a bomb on 3 June as he prayed with many cabinet members inside the presidential palace. He then spent four months convalescing in the Saudi capital, Riyadh, yet no deal was reached between the regime and the opposition. Even as proxy wars flared in Arhab (near Sana'a airport), Hadhramawt, Mareb, and Taiz, the regular army did not engage in direct conflict. Battles also ignited in al-Jawf, near the Saudi border, between Houthi loyalist tribesmen and Islah tribesmen. Two ceasefires failed to end the clashes. In addition, the power vacuum created by the withdrawal of government troops in southern areas led to a takeover of Abyan province by Ansar al-Sharia, an affiliate of al-Qaida in the Arabian Peninsula (AQAP). (Many analysts claimed that Ansar al-Sharia was a creature of the regime.) Also, the increased focus on AQAP led to the killing of US-born cleric Anwar Awlaki on 30 September (see Obituary), and his teenage son, Abd al-Rahman Awlaki, on 14 October, in both instances by US unmanned aerial vehicles.

President Saleh finally signed the GCC transition agreement, as amended and mediated by UN special envoy Jamal Ben Omar, on 23 November in Riyadh. This agreement delegated some of the president's authority to Vice President Abdo Rabo Mansour al-Hadi, called for a military commission to oversee demilitarisation of the capital, established a coalition government led by Prime Minister Mohammed Salim Basundwa, and set presidential elections for 90 days after the signing of the agreement, on 21 February 2012.

Fernando Carvajal

ARAB STATES OF THE GULF

Bahrain

CAPITAL: Manama   AREA: 710 sq km   POPULATION: 1,261,835 ('10)
OFFICIAL LANGUAGE: Arabic
HEAD OF STATE: Sheikh Hamad bin Isa al-Khalifa (since March '99)
HEAD OF GOVERNMENT: Sheikh Khalifa bin Sulman al-Khalifa, Prime Minister (since Jan '70)
DEMOCRACY INDEX: 3.49; 122nd of 167   CORRUPTION INDEX: 5.1; 46th of 183
CURRENCY: Bahraini Dinar (Dec '11 £1.00=BHD 0.59, US$1.00=BHD 0.38)
GNI PER CAPITA: US$18,730, Intl$24,710 at PPP ('08)

Kuwait

CAPITAL: Kuwait   AREA: 17,820 sq km   POPULATION: 2,736,732 ('10)
OFFICIAL LANGUAGE: Arabic
HEAD OF STATE AND GOVERNMENT: Sheikh Sabah al-Ahmad al-Jaber al-Sabah (since Jan '06)
 PRIME MINISTER: Sheikh Nasser al-Mohammad al-Ahmad al-Sabah (since Feb '06)
DEMOCRACY INDEX: 3.88; 114th of 167   CORRUPTION INDEX: 4.6; 54th of 183
CURRENCY: Kuwaiti Dinar (Dec '11 £1.00=KWD 0.43, US$1.00=KWD 0.28)
GNI PER CAPITA: US$47,790, Intl$58,350 at PPP ('07)

Oman

CAPITAL: Muscat   AREA: 309,500 sq km   POPULATION: 2,782,435 ('10)
OFFICIAL LANGUAGE: Arabic
HEAD OF STATE AND GOVERNMENT: Shaikh Qaboos bin Said al-Said (since July '70)
DEMOCRACY INDEX: 2.86; 143rd of 167   CORRUPTION INDEX: 4.8; 50th of 183
CURRENCY: Rial Omani (Dec '11 £1.00=OMR 0.60, US$1.00=OMR 0.38)
GNI PER CAPITA: US$18,260, Intl$24,960 at PPP ('09)

Qatar

CAPITAL: Doha   AREA: 11,000 sq km   POPULATION: 1,758,793 ('10)
OFFICIAL LANGUAGE: Arabic
HEAD OF STATE: Sheikh Hamad bin Khalifa al-Thani (since June '95)
HEIR APPARENT: Crown Prince Shaikh Tamin Bin Hamad al-Thani (since Aug '03)
PRIME MINISTER: Sheikh Hamad Bin Jassem Bin Jabr al-Thani (since April '07)
DEMOCRACY INDEX: 3.09; 137th of 167   CORRUPTION INDEX: 7.2; 22nd of 183
CURRENCY: Qatar Riyal (Dec '11 £1.00=QAR 5.71, US$1.00=QAR 3.64)
GNI PER CAPITA: GDP per capita US$29,400 ('06)

United Arab Emirates (UAE)

CONSTITUENT REPUBLICS: Abu Dhabi, Dubai, Sharjah, Ras al-Khaimah, Fujairah, Umm al-Qaiwin,
    Ajman
CAPITAL: Abu Dhabi   AREA: 83,600 sq km   POPULATION: 7,511,690 ('10)
OFFICIAL LANGUAGE: Arabic
HEAD OF STATE: Shaikh Khalifa Bin Zayed al-Nahyan (Ruler of Abu Dhabi), President of UAE
    (since Nov '04)
HEAD OF GOVERNMENT: Gen. Shaikh Mohammed bin Rashid al-Maktoum (ruler of Dubai), Vice-
    President and Prime Minister of UAE (since Jan '06)
DEMOCRACY INDEX: 2.52; 148th of 167   CORRUPTION INDEX: 6.8; 28th of 183
CURRENCY: UAE Dirham (Dec '11 £1.00=AED 5.76, US$1.00=AED 3.67)
GNI PER CAPITA: high income: US$11,906 or more ('08 est.)

IN **Bahrain**, the ruling family, led by Sheikh Hamad bin Isa al-Khalifa, faced
renewed challenges to the established pace of reform. Bahrain's political environment deteriorated as popular consent weakened in the light of the movement of

dissent sweeping across North Africa and the Middle East. This affected the communal politics of Bahrain, which existed in a tense and fragile balance between the Sunnis (to which the ruling family belonged) and the majority Shia (nearly 70 per cent of the population).

Soon after the "Arab Awakening" had sent shockwaves through Tunisia and Egypt, it reached the Arabian peninsula in February through Yemen and Bahrain. As the country had already experienced five months under a state of emergency, the events in North Africa became a visual inspiration for voicing political grievance, and young Bahrainis called for their own "day of rage" on 14 February. Social turmoil was also fuelled by delays in the trial of 225 Shia Bahrainis, charged in 2010 with attempts to overthrow the regime. Defence lawyers and human rights observers claimed that torture and other violations of civil liberties were being used against the Shia, as the regime utilised military courts to try the demonstrators. A project reclaiming 65 sq km of land for government use and distributed among the ruling family also exacerbated relations with the population, which was demanding increased transparency and accountability.

When the protest camp centred on the Pearl Roundabout in Manama was raided by police on the night of 17 February, calls were heard for the overthrow of Sheikh Hamad. A month of demonstrations was ended in March when Saudi Arabia and the UAE sent troops and police officers to Bahrain as part of the Gulf Co-operation Council's Peninsula Shield Force, whose deployment had been requested by Sheikh Hamad. Among the nearly 3,000 people arrested in the crackdown were a number of doctors and medical personnel, whose sentencing by a military court in September to prison terms for "incitement to overthrow the government" drew international condemnation. Their retrial in a civilian court was ordered in October.

Even as Crown Prince Salman bin Hamad bin Isa al-Khalifa promoted political freedoms as a priority, and the state of Kuwait offered on 17 March to mediate between the government and the opposition, dialogue was accepted by the Shia opposition al-Wefaq party but obstructed by the government and rejected by the al-Haq Movement for Civil Liberties and Democracy. Following further protests in June, which led to the cancellation of the Bahrain Grand Prix Formula One race, dialogue eventually began on 2 July with five delegates from al-Wefaq and ended nearly 15 days later.

In June, Sheikh Hamad established the Bahrain Independent Commission of Inquiry to examine the events of February and March. The commission's report, released in November, confirmed the use of torture on detainees (see Documents).

Economic woes also presented challenges for the ruling family, as the sheikh aimed at stabilising the internal family relationships that were threatened by the modernisation of government structures. While the IMF predicted 5 per cent growth for 2011, unemployment was reported stable at just under 4 per cent. The government also moved ahead with a $1.25 billion sovereign bond, attracting investors from Asia, Europe, and the USA, and lobbied Saudi Arabia's Prince Alwaleed bin Talal to establish his new satellite television channel, Alarab, in Manama.

A brief cosmetic reshuffling of government early in the year served to strengthen the hand of Sheikh Sabah al-Ahmed al-Jaber al-Sabah, ruler of **Kuwait**, and his prime minister, Sheikh Nasser Mohammed al-Ahmed al-Sabah, who was reappointed on 5 March. The government also acted to stave off any potential social disturbances caused by the torture and death in police custody in January of a Kuwaiti man, Mohammed Ghazzai al-Mutairi, by accepting the resignation of Interior Minister Jaber Khaled al-Sabah; he was replaced by Sheikh Ahmed Homoud al-Sabah. Protests against the government were partly organised by a youth group named Fifth Fence.

Even as the Kuwaiti government extended its good offices to mediate between Bahrain's government and the opposition in March, it hoped to deter any further protests in its own territory. This changed on 16 November when around 100 protesters, led by a member of the National Assembly, Musallam al-Barrak, stormed the legislature building on what was called "Black Wednesday". The protests had more to do with long standing corruption accusations against members of the Assembly and Sheikh Sabah's reluctance to intervene than with the "Arab Spring". Observers suggested that this incident served to weaken the opposition but also exacerbated family rivalries between the al-Salem and al-Jaber branches of the ruling family.

Soon after the capture of the tanker *Irene SL* off the coast of Oman by Somali pirates on 9 February, with 2 million barrels of Kuwaiti oil en route to the USA, Kuwait joined forces with the UAE to engage in security projects in Puntland in northern Somalia.

The sultanate of **Oman** was often sidelined in regional politics and international relations, but new realities presented fresh challenges and opportunities. Early in the year Oman found itself the target of a spy ring with direct links to the ruling family of the UAE. The UAE's state security service was publicly identified by media outlets, which speculated that the Duqm industrial maritime project was the target. Relations remained heated until the Gulf Co-operation Council (GCC) closed ranks to confront the "Arab Spring" torrent that was sweeping through North Africa and creeping into the Arabian Peninsula through Bahrain and Yemen.

Sultan Qaboos bin Said al-Said quickly responded to potential threats from the Arab Spring by meeting one of the existing demands in Oman and issuing a decree on 20 February to raise the minimum wage from the equivalent of $364 to $520. But on 26 February demonstrations erupted in the northern port city of Sohar to protest against unemployment, low wages and corruption. Protests later expanded to the capital, Muscat, where demands centred on limiting terms in office to four years and asking the government to reduce the number of foreign workers. As in the case of Bahrain, the GCC came to the sultanate's aid and provided $10 billion to supplement the government's budget and prevent further disturbances.

The country also held elections for the Majlis al-Shura (consultative council) in October. One woman was elected to the advisory body for the first time, and by royal decree members were able to elect the chairman of the Majlis directly.

The small emirate of **Qatar** expanded its sphere of influence. The Al Jazeera satellite television station became its soft-power tool, and its wealth provided financial support for the rebels in Libya and the other protests movements extending from the "Arab Spring". The emir, Sheikh Hamad bin Khalifa al-Thani, also made economic development a priority, although the policy neglected the lower echelons of society. Elderly nationals continued to receive a monthly stipend of only QAR 3,000. The government's budget expenditure was estimated at around $38.4 billion, while revenue was estimated at $44.5 billion.

In April Qatar shifted the full power of its purse in support of the Benghazi-based rebel government fighting the forces of Colonel Moamar Kadhafi in Libya. It signalled a first move in what was perceived to be a foreign policy independent from the GCC. Qatar supported the NATO-imposed no-fly zone over Libyan airspace and recognised the interim National Transitional Council (NTC), the rebel Libyan government. This policy position led to heated relations with a former ally, Algeria, which opposed Qatar's activist foreign policy and support for revolutions in Egypt, Libya and Syria. Algeria's President Abdelaziz Bouteflika, who visited Doha in November, also feared that Qatar would assist Abbassi Madani, the 80-year old founder of the Islamic Salvation Front (FIS) who was living in exile in Doha, to return to Algeria.

Commercial interests were often identified as driving Qatar's new approach to relations in the region. Early in the year, Qatar Petroleum reached an agreement with the UK's Centrica, owner of British Gas, on a liquid natural gas project, which was expanded in November to include oil and gas exploration. Moves to support Libya's rebel government also brought criticism upon Qatar for its work to secure oil fields in the eastern provinces. This included funding the Libyan rebel militia, the 17 February Martyrs' Brigade, to secure oil pipelines for Libya's National Oil Corporation. The militia was led by Ismael al-Salabi, brother of cleric Ali al-Salabi, who was living in exile in Doha.

Qatar also expended its competitive edge in international sports. Although Qatari football administrator Mohammed bin Hamam was dropped from the executive committee of FIFA in July over claims of corruption, Qatar continued attracting international sporting events, which already included the 2022 FIFA World Cup.

Dubai, having survived the global financial crisis, managed to stay out of the spotlight in 2011. Of more concern to observers was the manner in which the ruler of Abu Dhabi and president of the **UAE**, Sheikh Khalifa bin Zayed al-Nahyan, and the crown prince, Sheikh Mohammed bin Zayed al-Nahyan, managed their approach to deterring social unrest inspired by the "Arab Spring".

The succession within the UAE became an issue of concern to observers, as Crown Prince Sheikh Mohammed became more involved in matters concerning the northern emirates. As the government began to recognise the social and economic conditions of the less successful emirates, questions were raised about the crown prince's more active approach to the federation. Expanding his engagement with the population beyond Abu Dhabi was thought to signal a move to strengthen federal authority over the other emirates.

Fernando Carvajal

SUDAN—SOUTH SUDAN—LIBYA—TUNISIA—ALGERIA—MOROCCO—
WESTERN SAHARA

SUDAN AND SOUTH SUDAN

Sudan

CAPITAL: Khartoum   AREA: 1,886,068 sq km   POPULATION: 43,551,941 ('10, including South Sudan)
OFFICIAL LANGUAGES: Arabic, English
HEAD OF STATE AND GOVERNMENT: President (Gen.) Omar Hasan Ahmed al-Bashir (since Oct '93),
   previously Chairman of Revolutionary Command Council (since June '89)
RULING PARTY: National Congress Party (NCP)-led coalition
DEMOCRACY INDEX: 2.42; 151st of 167   CORRUPTION INDEX: 1.6; 177th of 183
CURRENCY: Sudanese Pound (Dec '11 £1.00=SDG 4.20, US$1.00=SDG 2.68)
GNI PER CAPITA: US$1,270, Intl$2,020 at PPP ('10)

South Sudan

CAPITAL: Juba   AREA: 619,745 sq km   POPULATION: 8,079,000 ('10)
OFFICIAL LANGUAGE: English
HEAD OF STATE AND GOVERNMENT: President Salva Kiir Mayardit (since July '11)
RULING PARTY: Sudan People's Liberation Movement (SPLM)
CURRENCY: South Sudanese Pound
GNI PER CAPITA: US$984 ('10 South Sudan National Bureau of Statistics)

THE defining event of the year for Sudan was the secession of South Sudan on 9
July, marking the creation of the independent Republic of South Sudan, and a
redrawing of the boundaries of Sudan. The secession of South Sudan followed a
referendum on self-determination conducted in January, in accordance with the
2005 Comprehensive Peace Agreement which had ended the civil war begun in
1983 (see AR 2005, pp. 201-03). Decisively, the referendum produced a 98.8 per
cent vote in favour of independence for South Sudan (3,792,518 for; 44,888
against), from a turnout of 97 per cent of registered voters.

When the final results were announced in February, the government of Sudan
reiterated its position that it would accept and honour a vote for secession. What
remained to be done by July (when the 2005 Comprehensive Peace Agreement
was due to end) was for the two governments to negotiate post-secession arrangements, especially for the export of South Sudanese oil, the border between the two
countries, Sudan's external debt stock, and citizenship. However, as had often been
the case before, this proved too much for the parties to negotiate in the time available. Instead, by June they had agreed little more than the principle that the border
between the two countries should be a "soft" border, allowing people and goods
to move freely across it.

In the meantime, both governments faced uncomfortable pressures. Encouraged
by the example of the protests and popular uprisings of the "Arab Spring" in North
Africa, from late January protests began to occur in northern Sudan, with protestors voicing discontent primarily about the difficult economic conditions. The
protests were not confined to Khartoum but were forcefully stifled by the security
forces and did not gain the momentum of the protests in North Africa. In South

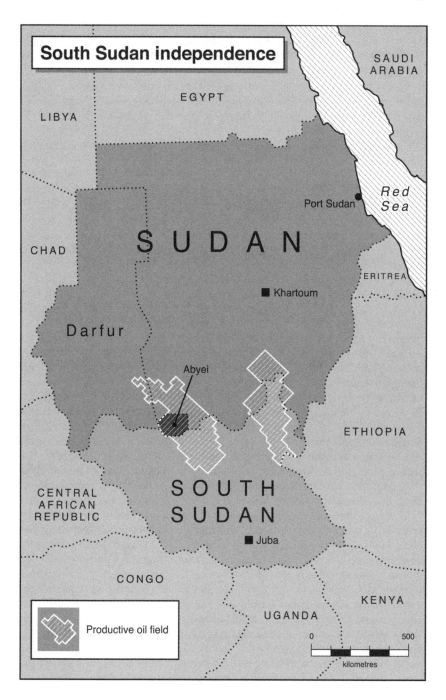

South Sudan independence

SAUDI ARABIA

LIBYA

EGYPT

CHAD

Red Sea

Port Sudan

S U D A N

ERITREA

Khartoum

Darfur

Abyei

ETHIOPIA

CENTRAL AFRICAN REPUBLIC

S O U T H
S U D A N

Juba

CONGO

KENYA

UGANDA

Productive oil field

0   500
kilometres

Sudan, fighting between the army and rebel militias escalated, with one bout of fighting in northern Jonglei State in early February reportedly causing 197 deaths, and another bout in late February causing another 92 fatalities. Rebel militias also clashed with the army and attacked civilians in Unity and Upper Nile states, close to the border with Sudan. Tensions also escalated between the Lou Nuer and the Murle tribes in Jonglei State, leading to unusually large attacks and counter-attacks, exemplified by clashes in June and August in which around 200 and 600 civilians were reportedly killed.

Under the Comprehensive Peace Agreement, a referendum to determine the future status of the disputed border area of Abyei was meant to happen in January and "popular consultations" were meant to be held in Blue Nile and South Kordofan states, concerning their future governance. The Abyei referendum did not happen, and how far the consultations occurred was disputed. However, in late May the national army seized control of the disputed border area of Abyei, expelling forces from the Sudan People's Liberation Army (SPLA), the South Sudan military. A larger pre-emptive campaign followed in South Kordofan in June, with the army trying to swiftly defeat local SPLA forces. For its part, the SPLA in northern Sudan refused to be disarmed or disbanded, and the opposition SPLM-North disputed the results of elections held in South Kordofan in May, in which the ruling National Congress Party (NCP) increased its control of the state at the expense of the SPLM-N. In the ensuing fighting, civilians once more bore the brunt of the violence, and the government restricted access for local and foreign journalists.

Despite these troubles, in July the secession of South Sudan itself passed off smoothly and peacefully. After hurrying to spruce up the capital, Juba, the South Sudan government received a host of foreign dignitaries, including the president of Sudan, Omar al-Bashir, and the secretary-general of the United Nations, Ban Ki-Moon. At the independence ceremony a statue of John Garang, the leader of the South Sudan rebel movement, the SPLM/A, was unveiled and the flag of Sudan was taken down and in its place the South Sudan national flag was hoisted on a 32-metre high flagpole. Poignantly, the president of South Sudan, Salva Kiir, said that South Sudan would keep the flag of Sudan that had been lowered, rather than return it to Khartoum, saying that it would be kept in the new country's archives in recognition of the "common history" which the two countries shared.

In August President Kiir appointed a new cabinet and soon afterwards a new national legislature was convened, comprising an enlarged 332-seat Parliament and a newly appointed 50-seat second chamber, the Council of States. Meanwhile among the people of South Sudan, expectations were high that independence would allow them to make a better future for their country. What remained unchanged, however, was that South Sudan was very poor and under-developed, even if it was nominally better off than some of its neighbours, thanks to oil revenues. It also continued to face internal insecurity, with renewed fighting between the Lou-Nuer and Murle in December causing many deaths.

The impact on Sudan of the loss of South Sudan was muted. Few in Sudan were surprised that southerners had voted for secession, but many outside government were inclined to blame the NCP for failing to make unity more attractive and instead presiding over the break-up of the country. President Bashir talked of launching a "second republic", but with a few exceptions the NCP resisted the temptation to invoke a renewed Islamist ideology to shield itself from criticism. A more pressing need for the NCP was to find a new partner in government, to replace the SPLM. Eventually it succeeded, persuading members of the opposition Democratic Unionist Party to join a new cabinet announced in December.

Meanwhile, the government sought to secure its control of what remained of Sudan. In September the army launched a campaign against the SPLM in Blue Nile State. Although the army suffered some setbacks, by October it had secured control of the main towns in Blue Nile. On the back foot, in November the SPLM-Northern Sector announced that it was forming an alliance with the main Darfur rebel groups, to be known as the Sudan Revolutionary Front. Nevertheless, as with other such alliances, the front struggled to present a unified challenge to the NCP.

With each government facing internal armed opposition, each accused the other of supporting its respective rebel forces, and Sudanese air force planes repeatedly bombed targets within adjoining areas of South Sudan, either denying the incidents or claiming that they were chasing rebels. Nonetheless, overall relations were maintained, and in November President Kiir visited Khartoum and was received by President Bashir as a foreign head of state.

Throughout the year, economic conditions were difficult and levels of foreign and domestic investment remained depressed. In July South Sudan launched its own currency, the South Sudanese pound, and Sudan issued a new series of bank notes, replacing the old shared currency. From July through to September, authorities in Sudan imposed a partial economic blockade on the south, preventing the export of fuel, food and other goods, and causing severe shortages in South Sudan. In November a dispute escalated about terms for the export of South Sudanese oil through the export pipeline and terminals in Sudan. This culminated in Sudan saying that it would confiscate some South Sudanese oil because South Sudan had not paid any transit fees. All the same, despite threats and accusations, neither country (nor the foreign oil companies involved) wanted to jeopardise production.

Richard Barltrop

LIBYA

CAPITAL: Tripoli   AREA: 1,759,540 sq km   POPULATION: 6,355,112 ('10)
OFFICIAL LANGUAGE: Arabic
HEAD OF STATE: Chairman of NTC, Mustafa Adbul Jalil (since March '11)
HEAD OF GOVERNMENT: acting prime minister Abdurrahim El-Keib (since Nov '11)
DEMOCRACY INDEX: 1.94; 158th of 167   CORRUPTION INDEX: 2.0; 168th of 183
CURRENCY: Libyan Dinar (Dec '11 £1.00=LYD 1.93, US$1.00=LYD 1.23)
GNI PER CAPITA: US$12,320, Intl$16,740 at PPP ('10)

As for much of the region, 2011 was a year of monumental upheaval and historic change for Libya. The country's contribution to the "Arab Spring", like those of neighbouring Tunisia and Egypt, began with popular protests against an authoritarian leader. Following the government killing of protesters it quickly escalated into the most violent revolution of 2011. The Libyan uprising plunged the country into an eight-month civil-war between forces loyal to Colonel Moamar Kadhafi and those seeking to oust his government. The rebellion ended with the total victory of the NATO-backed National Transitional Council (NTC) on 20 October. Kadhafi's capture and sordid execution by rebel forces ended 42 years of rule and marked the beginning of a new but uncertain political future for Libya.

Libya was infected by the contagion of the Arab Spring. Immediately after the Tunisian uprising, leading Libyan activists began calling for similar protests, although they enjoyed little initial success and were quickly suppressed by the government. Despite the regime's efforts, however, four days after the fall of Egyptian President Hosni Mubarak, Libyan protests began in earnest. The arrest of human rights lawyer Fathi Terbil on unknown charges on 15 February sparked mass protests in the city of Benghazi. Terbil was the official spokesman for over 1,000 of the families of victims who had been killed in the Abu Slim prison massacre in June 1996. In response to his arrest, approximately 200 relatives of the dead prisoners gathered in front of the police headquarters in Benghazi, chanting slogans against "the corrupt rulers of the country". The residents of Benghazi had suffered heavily under the Kadhafi regime and often been subject to severe repression as much of the membership of Libya's banned political groups, such as the Libyan Islamic Fighting Group, were from the city. By the early hours of 16 February the number of protesters had swelled to over 500, some armed with rocks and petrol bombs. Police dispersed the crowds using tear gas, rubber bullets and water cannon, and arrested 20. The unrest quickly spread to other cities. In Zentan (120 km south of Tripoli) hundreds of protesters marched through the streets on 16 February setting fire to a police station and pitching tents in the city centre. In Al-Beida, east of Benghazi, hundreds of protesters burned police outposts and chanted slogans demanding a change of government.

A "Day of Rage" was organised for 17 February—the anniversary of anti-government demonstrations in Benghazi five years earlier—by the National Conference for the Libyan Opposition, an organisation formed in London in 2005 and composed primarily of activists living outside Libya. The demonstrations were co-ordinated through social networking sites such as Facebook, and saw mass turnouts in a number of places, including Benghazi, Ajdabiya and Al-Beida. Libyan security forces fired live ammunition into the demonstrations and protesters burned government buildings and police stations in the three cities. Protests also began in Tripoli, where state controlled television and public radio stations were sacked, and protesters set fire to governing Revolutionary Committee offices, the interior ministry building, and the People's Hall building of the national legislature. The protests initially overwhelmed security forces and on 18 February police and army units withdrew from Benghazi with some army personnel even defecting to the protesters. It was also reported in Al-Beida that members of the local police force and riot-control units had joined the protesters following the withdrawal of the army from the city.

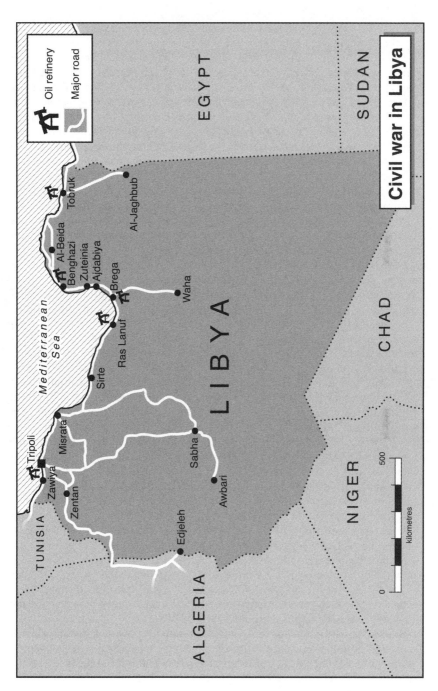

Civil war in Libya

On 19 February reports began to emerge of the use of helicopters by the security forces, firing live ammunition into crowds of unarmed anti-government protesters in an attempt to disperse them. The unleashing of such violence against the protesters coincided with public speeches in which Kadhafi denounced the demonstrators as "rats" and "cockroaches". His terminology echoed that used by the perpetrators of the 1994 Rwandan genocide and caused growing unease in the international community. Kadhafi also threatened to hunt down the protesters, cleansing the country "house by house" and executing all opponents, stating that "Those who don't love me do not deserve to live." With his usual eccentricity, the Libyan leader also claimed that the protesters were acting under the influence of hallucinogenic drugs ingested through drugged milk, coffee and Nescafé that had been disseminated by Osama bin Laden and the al-Qaida organisation. In addition to this crude attempt to curry Western favour by portraying himself as assailed by Islamist terrorism, Kadhafi simultaneously claimed that the protests against his rule were a "neo-colonialist plot" by foreign countries that were seeking to control the region's oil and "enslave" the Libyan people.

Despite the government violence, the protests continued to grow, spreading to other cities, including Tobruk, Misrata, and Zawiya. Indications that support for the government was crumbling came with the resignation of a number of senior government officials, including ministers, diplomats and military officers, many of whom pledged their support to the protesters. Isolated internationally, it seemed that Kadhafi was about to suffer a fate similar to that of his counterparts in Tunisia and Egypt, for by late February the regime had lost control of vast swathes of the country and numerous major cities, including Benghazi. On 25 February the Al Jazeera television station reported that talks were taking place between "personalities from eastern and western Libya" to form an interim government for the post-Kadhafi era, and on the following day former Justice Minister Mustafa Abdul Jalil announced the formation of an interim body to be based in Benghazi. Immediate support came from the Libyan ambassador to the USA, Ali Suleiman Aujali, and the Libyan deputy ambassador to the UN, Ibrahim Omar al-Dabashi, assisting in establishing its international legitimacy. Thus, the National Transitional Council (NTC) was formally established on 27 February with the purpose of acting as the "political face of the revolution" both domestically and internationally, and to co-ordinate resistance efforts between the different towns under rebel control. On 5 March, the NTC issued a statement in which it declared itself to be the "only legitimate body representing the people of Libya and the Libyan state". Politically it was careful to outline a pro-democracy agenda based on the principles of the 1952 constitution and promised an eventual transition to multi-party democracy. France, on 10 March, became the first country to recognise the rebel council as the legitimate government of Libya.

But Kadhafi did not intend to release his grip on Libya without a fight. Having recovered from the shock of the uprising, the regime launched a fierce counter-offensive on 6 March designed to re-establish its authority in areas lost to the rebels. Loyalist forces soon recaptured Ras Lanuf and Brega, and began pushing further east along the coast road towards Ajdabiya and the ultimate prize, Benghazi. Government units also struck west, attempting to retake Misrata by sending infantry and armour into the city. These were beaten back by determined rebel resistance and thereafter the city was the site of months of bitter fighting with Kadhafi destroying large areas of it but failing to capture or subdue it. A similar government attack on the western city of Zawiya led to heavy fighting and widespread destruction. But although the rebels controlled eastern Libya as well as important towns such as Misrata in the west, loyalist pro-Kadhafi forces held onto the centre, including Tripoli, Sirte (Kadhafi's hometown), and Sabha (640 km south of the capital). Furthermore, the balance of forces favoured the regime as the rebels were forced to use courage and determination to overcome their evident lack of heavy weapons, training, discipline, co-ordination, unified command structure and tactical acumen. By contrast, Kadhafi had heavy weapons—including armour and air power—and could call upon some well trained and well equipped military units. As the uprising evolved into a military struggle, these advantages became ever more evident and loyalist forces began a seemingly inexorable advance eastwards towards the rebel capital in Benghazi. By mid-March Kadhafi's men had taken Ajdabiya after subjecting it to days of aerial bombing and artillery fire and had overcome resistance in Zuteinia, the last major town before Benghazi. Anticipating victory, the government spoke with relish of the vengeance that it would enact once its forces had penetrated the heart of the rebellion.

Faced with a rapidly deteriorating military situation the NTC appealed for intervention by the international community to establish a no-fly zone to negate Kadhafi's air force. Under the shadow of what threatened to be a genocidal catastrophe in the city, on 17 March, the UN Security Council passed Resolution 1973 authorising member states to take all necessary measures to protect civilians under threat of attack in Benghazi and elsewhere, while specifically excluding a foreign occupation force in any part of Libyan territory (see Documents). In response to the UN resolution, on 18 March the Kadhafi government declared an immediate ceasefire, although this proved no more than a ruse designed to buy time enough for its forces to reach Benghazi and secure the decisive victory that seemed within reach. The city was shelled by artillery on 19 March as loyalist armoured units forced their way into its outskirts. With the notional ceasefire in ruins, enforcement of Resolution 1973 by NATO forces began on the same day with French aircraft attacking Kadhafi armour in the vicinity of the threatened city. US and British warships also contributed, firing cruise missiles at Libyan air defence systems. Having rapidly established air superiority NATO aircraft operated against government targets with impunity and NATO enforced a naval blockade.

The NATO aerial campaign had a dramatic impact as it systematically destroyed Kadhafi's armoured and mechanised forces, and disrupted his vulnerable supply lines along the main coastal road. With the government advance halted in its tracks, the rebels began an offensive on 20 March, rapidly advancing west from Benghazi. They retook Zuteinia and, after fierce fighting in which they were supported by NATO airstrikes, they regained control over Ajdabiya and then retook Brega and Ras Lanuf. Thoughts that the regime might collapse were once again proved to be premature as a government counter-offensive on 29 March regained lost ground, driving the rebels out of Ras Lanuf and Brega. There followed a stalemate which involved a fluid frontline in the area between Brega and Ajdabiya, with neither side strong enough to force a breakthrough. In the west there was deadlock too, as the shattered city of Misrata remained defiant in the face of all that Kadhafi threw against it.

Amid stalemate on the ground, NATO intensified its aerial operation, sparing no aspects of the regime's military infrastructure from its attritional attentions. Although NATO denied that it was attempting to target Kadhafi himself, his compound in Tripoli was subjected to repeated air strikes. On 30 April a NATO airstrike hit the home of Saif al-Arab Kadhafi, the leader's youngest son, killing him and three of Kadhafi's grandchildren. Following the attack, angry mobs of Kadhafi loyalists ransacked and set fire to the British embassy and several UN buildings. In May UK and French forces also stepped up the pressure on Kadhafi by deploying ground attack helicopter gunships to provide rebel forces with close air support. The attack helicopters were used against communication and control facilities, and were able to target government troops in populated areas while minimising the risks of civilian casualties.

The rebels were also assisted by advisers, trainers and special forces from NATO countries. The aim was to help fashion a force capable of launching a sustained and co-ordinated attack that could take advantage of the opportunities provided by the air campaign and defeat the regime's depleted and increasingly demoralised forces. The difficulties of this task were illustrated on 28 July when the head of the rebel army, Major General Abdul Fatah Younis, was recalled from the frontline near Brega to be placed under arrest. The move apparently followed suspicions over the loyalties of Younis, who had been a right-hand man of Kadhafi for 40 years as minister of defence and head of special forces before defecting. Despite orders for his arrest, however, at a press conference on 29 July, the NTC announced that Younis had been assassinated, stating that rebel fighters dispatched to bring him to Benghazi had instead, acting upon their own initiative, killed him.

Younis was replaced as head of the National Liberation Army by his deputy, Suleiman Mahmoud, and the war continued, with signs at the end of July that the rebels were making slow but steady progress. On 31 July, assisted by intensive NATO bombing, rebel units finally broke through the frontline in several places west of Misrata, and advanced upon Tripoli. Further progress was made in the ensuing weeks, particularly with the capture in mid-August of the coastal oil city of Zawiya to the west of Tripoli, a move that deprived the regime of its largest remaining source of refined petroleum. By mid-August the capital was effectively under siege. Then, on 21 August, rebel Berber units (who were reportedly armed by Qatar and assisted by British special forces), advanced from the Nafusa mountains and broke through the outer defences of Tripoli. Rebel pressure from the outside was assisted by a co-ordinated anti-Kadhafi uprising, supported by NATO air strikes, which took place in the city on the evening of 20 August. After several days of fighting the city fell. By the evening of 23 August the rebels had seized Kadhafi's heavily fortified compound in the city and by 26 August the final pockets of loyalist resistance had been liquidated. During the fighting a number of Kadhafi's family fled to Algeria but the leader himself chose to make a final stand in Sirte, his birthplace.

As Libyans celebrated their victory and the NTC began constructing a post-Kadhafi regime, the rebel army closed inexorably upon the former leader's final redoubt. As the city fell, Kadhafi met a bloody and public end. On 20 October he was in a convoy of vehicles that tried to break out of the falling city but which was attacked by NATO aircraft. Wounded, he was found hiding in a storm drain by rebel militia. Mobile phone videos captured his brutal end, showing him covered in blood and being abused by rebel fighters: beaten, half stripped, and sodomised with a bayonet. Shortly afterwards he was shot dead. His body, together with those of Defence Minister Abu-Bakr Yunis Jabr and his son and national security adviser Mutassim Kadhafi—both of whom were captured alive but, like their master, ended up dead—were put on public display for four days in a industrial refrigeration unit in Misrata, the city that Kadhafi had battered but failed to break. After being viewed by a steady stream of sightseers, the body of the former dictator, now showing signs of physical decay, was buried at an undisclosed desert location on 25 October.

The NTC on 23 October declared that the war was over and that Libya had been liberated. However, the formidable task of rebuilding a country within which constitutional politics, civil institutions and the rule of law had been systematically eradicated over several decades still lay ahead. Furthermore, with the dictator dead and the war over, the amalgam that had united the rebels was significantly weakened. This had been illustrated a day earlier when Mahmoud Jibril had stood down as chairman of the NTC executive committee, a post equivalent to that of prime minister, amid factional infighting between the representatives of various Libyan cities. He was succeeded by Abdurrahim El-Keib, a professor of electrical engineering who had returned to Libya after 35 years of exile. On 22 November this interim prime minister announced an interim government that sought to reconcile the country's dangerous regional rivalries and which was notable chiefly for its absence of Islamists. In line with the NTC declaration of 3 August, the interim government was committed to create an framework whereby a constituent assembly would be elected within eight months and a new constitution submitted to a referendum within a further year, thereby opening the way for legislative and presidential elections. It promised to be a long and arduous road—more so than that which linked Tripoli and Benghazi and which had witnessed the ebb and flow of this most bitterly contested war.

D.S. Lewis and Josh Bird

TUNISIA

CAPITAL: Tunis   AREA: 163,610 sq km   POPULATION: 10,549,100 ('10)
OFFICIAL LANGUAGE: Arabic
HEAD OF STATE: President Moncef Marzouki (CPR) (since Dec '11)
HEAD OF GOVERNMENT: Prime Minister Hamadi Jebali (Ennahda) (since Dec '11)
DEMOCRACY INDEX: 2.79; 144th of 167   CORRUPTION INDEX: 3.8; 73rd of 183
CURRENCY: Tunisian Dinar (Dec '11 £1.00=TND 2.30, US$1.00=TND 1.47)
GNI PER CAPITA: US$4,060, Intl$8,130 at PPP ('10)

THE illusion of permanent dictatorship in the Arab world, created by the longevity of incumbents' terms and reinforced by the apparent grooming of family successors, was shattered on 14 January when nationwide protests in Tunisia that had begun in late 2010 finally ousted President Zine el-Abidine Ben Ali, forcing his departure to Saudi Arabia (see AR 2011, pp. 214-16). Twenty-eight days of uninterrupted protests brought to an end 23 years of uninterrupted power. The proven fragility of the North African dictatorship under sustained popular pressure had a profound influence on the rest of the Arab world, and the resulting "Arab Awakening" saw societies across the region mount their own bids for change, in what became known as the 2011 "Arab Spring".

Having refused to follow orders from Ben Ali to open fire on unarmed demonstrators, the military leadership withdrew their support from the president, forcing him to step down. Army Commander Rashid Ammar pledged to "protect the revolution", and on 14 January Ben Ali dissolved his government and declared a state of emergency. Public gatherings of three or more people were made illegal in an attempt to prevent continued demonstrations, although, according to officials, the declaration was enacted to protect Tunisians and their property from further rioting. On the same day Ben Ali fled the country, eventually arriving in Jeddah, Saudi Arabia, after being refused entry into France, and Prime Minister Mohamed Ghannouchi took over as acting president.

On the morning of 15 January, Tunisian state television announced that Ben Ali had officially resigned his position and that, under pressure from Tunisia's judiciary, Ghannouchi had handed power to Fouad Mebazaa, the president of the Chamber of Deputies (the lower chamber of Parliament). Fethi Abdennadher, the head of Tunisia's Constitutional Court, declared that Ben Ali would not be permitted to return, that Ghannouchi had no legitimate right to power, and that Mebazaa would only be given 60 days in which to organise new elections. Mebazaa accepted the role of interim president under the terms stipulated, and stated that it was in the country's best interest to form a national unity government. Interpol's National Central Bureau in Tunis also issued an international arrest warrant for Ben Ali, charging him with money laundering and drug trafficking. On 20 June he and his wife were sentenced in absentia to 35 years in prison.

Protests against the presence of members of the former ruling Constitutional Democratic Rally (RCD) in the new government began immediately after the announcement of its composition on 17 January, and continued daily. Following rallies attended by thousands of anti-RCD protesters, cabinet members from the Tunisian General Labour Union (UGTT) resigned on 18 January to signal their disapproval of the inclusion of RCD members in the cabinet. The interim president and prime minister resigned from the RCD, with Ghannouchi claiming that all members of the national unity government had "clean hands". However, mass demonstrations against the RCD spread across the country, with protestors in Tunis, Sfax, Gabes, Bizerta, Sousse and Monastir demanding that no "former allies" of Ben Ali remain in government and that the RCD be disbanded. On 20 January hundreds of people began demonstrating outside the RCD headquarters in Tunis, which finally forced the resignation of all remaining RCD members from the cabinet and the disbanding of the RCD central committee.

Although Ghannouchi promised on 21 January that he would resign after the elections, which were to be organised within the next six months, this was not enough to satisfy the protestors, and hundreds of people set up camp outside the prime minister's office to demand his resignation. On 27 January Ghannouchi carried out a major reshuffle that removed all former RCD members, other than himself, from government. This sparked a new wave of protests, in response to which Ghannouchi resigned as prime minister to be replaced by Beji Caid el Sebsi.

Following this purge of RCD members from the interim government, the initial instability of the immediate post-revolutionary period subsided. In the following months political activity centred around the practicalities of arranging free and fair, transparent elections for the Constituent Assembly that was to approve a government and draft a new constitution for a post-Ben Ali Tunisia.

The key debates centred over which political parties would be permitted to stand for election to the Constituent Assembly and how to prepare for the elections by addressing technical difficulties, such as providing and distributing nearly 400,000 voter cards to those with outdated identification documents. Although it had been announced on 20 January that all banned political parties would be legalised and all political prisoners be freed—meaning that the long-isolated, moderate Islamist Ennahda party was immediately granted a permit—limitations remained on more extreme politics. A ban on the more radical Islamist Hizb ut-Tahrir was due to be lifted on 12 March after review, but the party was again banned. Meanwhile, on 9 March a court in Tunis officially announced the dissolution of the RCD and the liquidation of all party assets and funds, a decision the party said it would challenge. Over 70 political parties were eventually permitted to stand in the assembly elections.

Furthermore, although the interim government announced on 25 February that elections would be held by mid-July "at the latest", there were calls from the opposition to delay. The head of the Higher Political Reform Commission and prominent lawyer, Yadh Ben Achour, warned that Tunisia risked anarchy if the transitional period was not handled with care, as the state institutions were either in disarray or still tainted by links to the Ben Ali regime. Prime Minister Sebsi also agreed on the need to move slowly: "The most important thing is the transparency of the elections. There are parties who disagreed with this...but our mission is to hold elections that are free and transparent. We must protect the good name of the revolution."

The election of the Constituent Assembly was therefore postponed until 23 October. The assembly was elected on a strictly proportional system, with parties required to present equal numbers of male and female candidates, and the polling was monitored by 10,000 domestic and 500 international observers, including delegations from the OSCE, the EU and the Carter Center.

In their campaigning, the main parties presented different constitutional models for the new system. Ennahda advocated a parliamentary system with a strong prime minister; the Progressive Democratic Party (PDP) and the Congress for the Republic (CPR) argued for a semi-presidential system, similar to that of France. The principal discussion during the campaign, however, centred on the extent of secularism and the role of Islam in public life. Historically, Islamism had been repressed under the French-style, strictly secular republic of Tunisia's first president, Habib Bourguiba (1957-87), a policy continued under the regime of Ben Ali (1987-2011). As Tunisia's largest and best organised party, the moderate Islamist Ennahda led calls for Islam to have a greater presence in public life and outlined its vision of an Islamic democracy, with guarantees for civil freedoms and equality. The PDP and CPR, however, claimed that such a system would endanger civil rights and would permit the election to government of illiberal political parties.

Ennahda proved most successful in the election, gaining 37 per cent of votes cast and winning 89 of the 217 seats in the Constituent Assembly. Second placed was the CPR, which gained only 8.7 per cent of the vote (29 seats), followed by Popular Petition with 6.7 per cent (26 seats), Democratic Forum for Labour and Liberties (Ettakatol) with 7 per cent (20 seats), and the PDP with 3.9 per cent (16 seats). Ennahda's leader, Rachid Ghannouchi, did not stand for election, saying that he had no ambitions to be in government. Instead, the party proposed Hamadi Jebali, Ennahda's secretary-general, as the new prime minister. The post of interim president was taken by veteran dissident Moncef Marzouki of the CPR, whose secularist credentials balanced Ennahda's Islamist stance. On 10 December, after heated debate and with the assent of 141 delegates (with 37 voting against and 39 abstaining), the assembly adopted provisional measures on state institutions, pending the drafting of a new constitution. Just before the turn of the year, the assembly approved Jebali's new 41-member cabinet, in which Ennahda took key posts with Ettakatol, the CPR, and independents also represented.

Josh Bird and Wendy Slater

ALGERIA

CAPITAL: Algiers   AREA: 2,381,740 sq km   POPULATION: 35,468.208 ('10)
OFFICIAL LANGUAGE: Arabic
HEAD OF STATE AND GOVERNMENT: President Abdelaziz Bouteflika (FLN) (since April '99)
RULING PARTIES: Coalition including National Liberation Front (FLN) and National Democratic Rally (RND)
PRIME MINISTER: Ahmed Ouyahia (RND) (since June '08)
DEMOCRACY INDEX: 3.44; 125th of 167   CORRUPTION INDEX: 2.9; 112nd of 183
CURRENCY: Algerian Dinar (Dec-'11 £1.00=DZD 116.43, US$1.00=DZD 74.24)
GNI PER CAPITA: US$4,450, Intl$8,120 at PPP ('10)

BETWEEN 3 and 10 January, riots and protests broke out in towns across Algeria, triggered by large increases in the prices of basic foods including oil, sugar and flour. Whilst localised riots had been a frequent occurrence in Algeria (especially in the Kabylie region) since the end of the civil crisis in 2005, the rioting of 2011 was markedly different in that it quickly spread across the country rather than being confined to a particular area. Inspired by the "Arab Spring", the protests became politicised, but a combination of government concessions and heavy policing prevented them from gaining the kind of momentum that led to government change in Tunisia and Egypt.

Protests began in the Ras El Ain quarter of the major port city of Oran, as well as in Fouka and Staoueli near Algiers, and by 4 January they had spread to other areas near the capital, including Tipaza and Kolea. The following day, major riots erupted simultaneously in the working-class district of Bab El Oued in Algiers, in Oran, and in other towns including Djelfa, Boumerdes, Annaba and Tipaza. The rioters blocked roads and ransacked government buildings in protest at the sudden increase in the cost of living and widespread unemployment. Bab El Oued suffered the most criminal damage, with several shops and car showrooms being set ablaze. The former deputy leader of the banned Islamic Salvation Front (FIS), Ali Belhadj, joined the Bab El Oued demonstrations, allegedly to encourage the protestors, addressing a crowd and pledging, "We will defend the concerns of young people if God allows, and this whatever the cost." Belhadj was arrested and charged with "harming state security and inciting an armed rebellion".

Within days the riots had spread to over 20 of Algeria's 48 provinces—almost the whole of the northern part of the country, including the Kabylie region—and to some towns in the Sahara, including Ouargla and Bechar. On 8 January, the government responded with a temporary tax cut and reduction in the duties on sugar and cooking oil. It also restricted access to social media websites in some areas. By 11 January the unrest had largely subsided, although attempted demonstrations that day in Algiers were harshly repressed by the police. In total, the rioting resulted in the deaths of three demonstrators, over 800 wounded, and approximately 1,100 arrested, the majority of whom were minors.

The demonstrators appeared to have no overt political affiliations, but a number of left-wing opposition parties and trade unions, as well as the Algerian League for the Defence of Human Rights (LADDH), met on 20 January to discuss how to respond to the situation. They announced the creation of an umbrella group, the National Co-ordination for Change and Democracy (CNCD), which demanded fundamental change and called on people to join nationwide marches. On 3 February, President Abdelaziz Bouteflika signalled that the government was prepared to make some concessions, including a promise to lift the state of emergency that had been in force since 1992. He also instructed ministers to draw up a job creation programme and declared that radio and television should give airtime to all political parties. This was too little for the protest leaders, who were given new vigour by the success of Egypt's revolutionaries in forcing the resignation of President Hosni Mubarak. On 12 February, the day after Mubarak stepped down, the CNDC organised what they hoped would be the largest protest yet in Algiers, despite the continued ban on marches in the city.

Ahead of the planned protest, police blocked roads and erected a security cordon consisting of 28,000 police officers around the 1 May square in central Algiers. Despite this, a few thousand protesters managed to force their way onto the square where their slogans included "système dégage" ("government out") and "yesterday Egypt, today Algeria". The police responded with tear gas and hundreds of arrests, and most protesters left the square that night. The demonstration was not followed by any similarly organised or well-attended protests in Algiers, although low-level protests continued to occur sporadically across the country throughout the rest of February and March.

On 23 February the state of emergency was officially lifted, satisfying one of the main demands of the protesters. This legalised protests held outside Algiers, although they remained banned within the capital. The LADDH dismissed the move as a "ruse aimed at fooling international opinion at a time when Arab regimes are under pressure". Despite the ban, the CNCD attempted to organise further anti-government demonstrations in Algiers on 5 March, but these were again blocked by police and countered by pro-government demonstrations.

On 15 April President Bouteflika made a television statement in which he sought to pre-empt opposition demands. He said that he would introduce constitutional amendments to "reinforce representative democracy". He also proposed changes to the legislation governing elections, the media and political parties. A committee charged with drafting reforms presented its report in July, but did not publish the document. In September, media reforms ended the state monopoly of broadcasting that had existed since 1962 and other concessions were made that were designed to take the heat out of the protest movement, including an increase in state sector wages and subsidies on food staples.

Algeria suffered no further substantial unrest in 2011, the regime apparently having successfully weathered the "Arab Spring". But it did not remain untouched by events in neighbouring Libya. On 27 August the Egyptian news agency, Mena, reported that five armoured cars, possibly carrying senior figures from the Kadhafi regime, had crossed the south-western border into Algeria. At the time, the Algerian authorities denied it but on 29 August they announced that the widow of Colonel Moamar Kadhafi, Safia Farkash, together with their daughter Ayesha and sons Muhammad and Hannibal, accompanied by their spouses and children, had crossed into Algeria earlier that day.

Josh Bird and Wendy Slater

MOROCCO

CAPITAL: Rabat   AREA: 446,550 sq km   POPULATION: 31,951,412 ('10)
OFFICIAL LANGUAGES: Arabic; Tamazight and Hassani
HEAD OF STATE: King Mohammed VI (since July '99)
RULING PARTY: Justice and Development Party (PJD)-led coalition
HEAD OF GOVERNMENT: Prime Minister Abdelilah Benkirane (PJD) (since Nov '11)
DEMOCRACY INDEX: 3.79; 116th of 167   CORRUPTION INDEX: 3.4; 80th of 183
CURRENCY: Dirham (Dec '11 £1.00=MAD 13.04, US$1.00=MAD 8.32)
GNI PER CAPITA: US$2,900, Intl$4,620 at PPP ('10)

On 20 February protests began in Morocco's main cities of Rabat, Casablanca, and Marrakesh, with unrest also reported in Tangier, Larache, Fez and Tétouan. The protests had been organised by the February 20 Youth Movement, a group consisting mainly of students from the three main cities who, inspired by events in Egypt, had called for demonstrations on 20 February. The "Day of Dignity" revolved around several broad complaints, including the infringement of civil liberties, the high illiteracy rate, inequality of incomes, corruption, the failure of the healthcare system, and the absence of free and fair democratic elections. The group relied heavily on social media websites like Facebook and Twitter to coordinate their protests and created a YouTube channel with videos to spread their message. Their success was helped by the high Internet penetration in Morocco— the highest in North Africa—where 41.3 per cent of the population was online in 2011, according to Internet World Stats. (For comparison, figures for Egypt and Tunisia were 24.5 per cent and 33.9 per cent, respectively.)

According to the interior ministry, 37,000 people joined the protests, though organisers put the figure higher. In Rabat thousands took to the streets demanding a new constitution redefining the role of the monarchy, a change to the Makhzen (political elite)-dominated government of palace cronies, and an end to political corruption. During the march towards the Parliament building on Hassan II Avenue, demonstrators shouted slogans demanding that King Mohammed VI give up some of his powers, but not calling for his abdication.

In response, on 9 March the king went on television to announce that a special commission was to draft a revised constitution containing "comprehensive" reforms. The commission, chaired by academic lawyer Abdellatif Menouni, would present its proposals to the king for consideration by June. The draft would then be put to a national referendum. However, the February 20 Movement turned down an invitation to participate in the commission's work, and there were further protests, including fairly large-scale demonstrations in a number of cities on 20 March and again on 24 April, organised in an attempt to maintain pressure on the reform process. Yet, although the protests continued into May and June, they did not enjoy a level of participation close to the high tide of 20 February, the opposition movement having failed to capitalise on its momentum and the king's concessions seeming to have satisfied the majority of protestors.

There were further concessions to protestors on 14 April when King Mohammed pardoned or reduced the sentences of 190 political prisoners, including Islamist militants and Sahrawi independence activists. However, the same month Morocco suffered its worst terrorist attack since the 2003 Casablanca bombings when 16 people, mainly tourists, were killed by a remotely controlled bomb at a cafe in central Marrakech.

In a televised speech on 17 June, the king unveiled the new draft constitution and asked voters to endorse it in the forthcoming referendum. The proposed reforms gave the prime minister and Parliament more executive authority, empowering the prime minister to appoint ministers and other government officials and to dissolve Parliament—powers hitherto held exclusively by the king. However, the new constitution maintained the king as commander-in-chief of the military and chair of the council of ministers and the Supreme Security Council (the primary bodies responsible for security policy), and reaffirmed his role as the highest religious authority in the land. The new constitution also named the Berber Tamazight and Saharawi Hassani languages as official languages (together with Arabic), a long-standing demand of the two ethnic groups.

The leaders of both the secularist February 20 Youth Movement and the banned Islamist Justice and Spirituality movement rejected the proposals as insufficient and called for a boycott of the referendum. Despite their efforts, turnout on 1 July reached 73 per cent (according to official statistics) and the new constitution was accepted with a 98 per cent "yes" vote. Hailing the result in a televised speech on 30 July, the king said that the changes should be implemented swiftly, since "any delay may jeopardise this dynamic of trust and squander opportunities offered by the new reform".

Early parliamentary elections were duly called, almost a year ahead of the scheduled date of September 2012. They were initially postponed due to Eid al-Adha, but campaigning began on 12 November and the vote took place on 25 November. Fears that the typically low turnout for Moroccan elections would be exacerbated by further calls for a boycott proved unfounded, with the interior ministry announcing that turnout was 45 per cent, 8 per cent higher than the previous elections in 2007.

The results of the election to an expanded House of Representatives (the lower chamber of Parliament) produced victory for the moderate Islamist Justice and Development Party (PJD), which secured 107 of the 395 seats, followed by the Istiqlal party with 60, the National Rally of Independents (RNI) with 52 seats, the Authenticity and Modernity Party (PAM) with 47 seats, the Socialist Union of Popular Forces (USFP) with 39, and Popular Movement (MP) with 32 seats. A further 12 parties were also represented. The result meant that the PJD had overtaken the conservative monarchist Istiqlal as the largest party in the house, and on 29 November the PJD leader, Abdelillah Benkirane, was duly nominated as the new prime minister by the king. Benkirane said that the PJD would still "need alliances", and in December signed an agreement to form a coalition government with Istiqlal, Popular Movement, and the Party for Progress and Socialism (PPS). Together, the four parties controlled 217 seats in the house. As one of his first priorities in government, Benkirane pledged to tackle the rural poverty and urban shanty towns that blighted areas of Morocco.

Josh Bird and Wendy Slater

WESTERN SAHARA

CAPITAL: Al Aaiún   AREA: 284,000 sq km   POPULATION: 497,000 (UN est. '08)
HEAD OF STATE AND GOVERNMENT: President Mohamed Abdelaziz (since Aug '76)
RULING PARTY: Polisario
PRIME MINISTER: Prime Minister Abdelkader Taleb Omar (since Oct '03)
CURRENCY: Moroccan Dirham [de facto] (Dec '11 £1.00=MAD 13.04, US$1.00=MAD 8.32)

WESTERN Sahara also witnessed rioting and political protests in early 2011. However, the unrest was not linked to the revolutions of the "Arab Spring" but rather to continued cultural tension. On 25 February a concert organised in the coastal city of Dakhla as part of the Sea and Desert festival—a popular Sahrawi cultural event—was interrupted by Moroccan youths. According to Sahrawi sources, they attacked the gathering and went on to loot properties of Sahrawi families in Dakhla. The next day, Sahrawis gathered in the city centre to protest against police inaction and the failure to protect Sahrawis and their property. The festival was suspended. There had long been tension in Dakhla between the indigenous Sahrawi population and the Moroccans who had settled there in large numbers since 1976.

On 2 March, a group of about 500 people took part in a sit-down protest in front of the mining and energy ministry in Al Aaiún, demanding the release of all Sahrawi political prisoners. Moroccan security forces dispersed the demonstration, injuring up to 68 people according to reports from Polisario. A further peaceful protest to draw attention to the alleged maltreatment of Sahrawi detainees was held on 8 April by families of Sahrawi political prisoners. Then, on 20 April an "indefinite" sit-in was organised by unemployed university graduates outside the ministry of labour building in Al Aaiún. The students planned to continue their peaceful protest three times a week until their demands were met.

The worst violence of the year however occurred on 25 September during football riots in Dakhla. Seven people were killed after a football match in which Mohammedia Club Chebab, from just north of Casablanca, beat the local Mouloudia team 3-0. Local officials claimed that "criminals" had taken advantage of the fighting between rival fans to attack people with knives and clubs. However, the Al Jazeera satellite television station said that Morocco had "totally besieged" the city with security forces, and Polisario condemned the "wave of repression" in Dakhla.

An eighth round of informal talks in the UN-sponsored negotiation process on the future of Western Sahara took place in the USA in June, attended by representatives of Polisario and Morocco, together with Algeria and Mauritania, and mediated by UN envoy Christopher Ross. As widely expected, they produced no progress.

Josh Bird and Wendy Slater

VI EQUATORIAL AFRICA

HORN OF AFRICA—KENYA—TANZANIA—UGANDA

ETHIOPIA—ERITREA—SOMALIA—DJIBOUTI

Ethiopia
CAPITAL: Addis Ababa   AREA: 1,104,300 sq km   POPULATION: 82,949,541 ('10)
OFFICIAL LANGUAGE: Amharic
HEAD OF STATE: President Girma Woldegiorgis (since Oct '01)
RULING PARTY: Ethiopian People's Revolutionary Democratic Front (EPRDF)
HEAD OF GOVERNMENT: Prime Minister Meles Zenawi (EPRDF), (since Aug '95)
DEMOCRACY INDEX: 3.68; 118th of 167   CORRUPTION INDEX: 2.7; 120th of 183
CURRENCY: Ethiopian Birr (Dec '11 £1.00=ETB 27.07, US$1.00=ETB 17.26)
GNI PER CAPITA: US$390, Intl$1,030 at PPP ('10)

Eritrea
CAPITAL: Asmara   AREA: 117,600 sq km   POPULATION: 5,253,676 ('10)
OFFICIAL LANGUAGES: Arabic & Tigrinyam
HEAD OF STATE AND GOVERNMENT: President Isayas Afewerki (since May '93)
RULING PARTY: People's Front for Democracy and Justice (PFDJ)
DEMOCRACY INDEX: 2.31; 152nd of 167   CORRUPTION INDEX: 2.5; 134th of 183
CURRENCY: Nakfa (Dec '11 £1.00=ERN 23.52, US$1.00=ERN 15.00)
GNI PER CAPITA: US$340, Intl$540 at PPP ('10)

Somalia
CAPITAL: Mogadishu   AREA: 637,660 sq km   POPULATION: 9,330,872 ('10)
OFFICIAL LANGUAGES: Somali & Arabic
HEAD OF STATE: President Sheikh Sharif Ahmed (since Jan '09)
HEAD OF GOVERNMENT: Prime Minister Abdiweli Mohamed Ali (since June '11)
CORRUPTION INDEX: 1.0; 182nd of 183
CURRENCY: Somali Shilling (Dec '11 £1.00=SOS 2,470, US$1.00=SOS 1,575)
GNI PER CAPITA: low income: US$975 or less ('08 est.)

Djibouti
CAPITAL: Djibouti   AREA: 23,200 sq km   POPULATION: 888,716 ('10)
OFFICIAL LANGUAGES: Arabic & French
HEAD OF STATE AND GOVERNMENT: President Ismail Omar Guelleh (since April '99)
RULING PARTY: Union for a Presidential Majority (UMP) coalition
PRIME MINISTER: Dilleita Mohamed Dilleita (since March '01)
DEMOCRACY INDEX: 2.20; 154th of 167   CORRUPTION INDEX: 3.0; 100th of 183
CURRENCY: Djibouti Franc (Dec '11 £1.00=DJF 273.67, US$1.00=DJF 174.50)
GNI PER CAPITA: US$1,270, Intl$2,440 at PPP ('09)

DESPITE significant economic growth during the year, the political scene in **Ethiopia** continued to be characterised by authoritarian rule. An "Arab Spring"-style "day of rage" organised by democracy activists in May to protest against high levels of unemployment, rising prices and the government's poor human rights and media freedom record, failed to shake Prime Minister Meles Zenawi's two-decade-old grip on power. Ethiopian journalists Woubshet Taye Abebe and Reeyot

Alemu Gobebo remained in detention, and in December two Swedish freelancers, Johan Persson and Martin Schibbye, were each sentenced to 11 years for entering the Ogaden region illegally with the Ogaden National Liberation Front (ONLF), officially designated a terrorist group by the government. The Committee to Protect Journalists (CPJ) rated Ethiopia the second worst country in Africa for jailing media workers, and claimed that at least 79 reporters had been forced into exile over the last 10 years.

With its neighbours, the country was hard hit by the regional drought, with over 3 million people needing emergency aid by mid-year. Flooding was also forecast for the rainy season between June and September, with the Lake Tana region, Gambella and the Awash basin especially under threat. In August the BBC reported that the government was using food aid to punish opposition supporters and human rights activists by denying access to micro-finance, seeds and fertiliser. However, the claim was rejected by Tadesse Bekele, a senior official in the food security programme, who insisted that food and cash were available to all Ethiopians in exchange for working on public construction projects, adding that "nobody has died because of a lack of food".

In June Ethiopia deployed a detachment of 4,200 soldiers to take part in the peace-keeping mission in the contested Abyei border region between Sudan and South Sudan.

The economy continued to boom, despite an inflation rate of nearly 30 per cent in April, with growth for 2011 anticipated in June at between 7 and 11 per cent. At mid-year, the Council of Ministers tabled a record budget of $7 billion for FY 2011-2012, of which $3.6 billion was to be sourced from local revenue. Ethiopia, with a growing middle class, remained one of Africa's fastest growing economies, pursuing business-friendly policies to attract foreign investment and taking advantage of strong global demand for mineral and other resources.

In May Ethiopia hosted the second Africa-India Forum, attended by Indian Prime Minister Manmohan Singh, who met with several heads of state from African countries. India was ranked second only to China as a trading partner in Africa, with the China-Africa Development Fund especially active in Ethiopia in areas such as leather, cement and glass manufacturing.

The government continued to implement a controversial large-scale land-leasing policy that allowed foreign agri-businesses from over 30 different countries including India, China, Pakistan and Saudi Arabia long-term access to around three million hectares of arable farmland. Part of the national five-year Growth and Transformation Plan, the scheme was officially intended to boost commercial farming to supplement the country's mainly smallholder agricultural sector, employing around 80 per cent of the population. Critics complained of forced relocation of local populations, poor working conditions, negative environmental impact and a failure to deliver promised infrastructural improvements.

Controversy also continued to dog the Gibe III dam on the Omo river, with critics from Survival International and other groups claiming that the project, the largest ever undertaken in Ethiopia, would destroy the traditional way of life of hundreds of thousands of people in eight tribal groups in the South Omo region and around Lake Turkana in neighbouring Kenya. Prime Minister Meles rejected the criticisms, however, claiming that the foreign organisations "don't want to see developed Africa; they want us to serve their tourists as a museum".

The veteran British Ethiopianist Edward Ullendorff (1920-2011), former intimate of Emperor Haile Sellassie and the author of many books and articles on the country, died in May at the age of 91.

Despite cautious attempts to rebuild links with its neighbours, **Eritrea** remained isolated under UN sanctions throughout the year, mainly as a result of independently-unverified accusations that it was providing arms for the Somali fundamentalist group al-Shabaab. In November the foreign ministry issued a statement rejecting such claims as "pure fabrications and outright lies". Nevertheless, in December the UN Security Council voted 13-0 with two abstentions to renew sanctions and impose tough controls on foreign mining companies operating in the country.

The UN issued a report in July stating that Eritrea had planned a car bomb attack on an African Union meeting in Addis Ababa in January, as well as other acts that would have resulted in civilian casualties, but were not carried out. The report claimed that Eritrean security operatives were active in Kenya, Somalia, newly-independent South Sudan, and Uganda.

Despite these disputes, in August Eritrea attempted to rejoin the regional Inter-Governmental Authority on Development (IGAD), which it had left in 2007 after the Ethiopian intervention in Somalia. At the same time President Isaias Afewerki visited Uganda to discuss the allegations that his country was supporting al-Shabaab with President Yoweri Museveni.

In September Amnesty International appealed for the release of 11 political prisoners, who in 2001 had published an open letter calling for democratic reforms and who had been detained ever since. The group included senior political figures at ministerial and vice-presidential level, as well as one woman, Aster Fissehatsion, a veteran of the independence struggle.

Officially, the government stated that the country had escaped the major effects of the regional drought, claiming a bumper harvest early in the year. However, according to independent reports and satellite imaging surveys, the northern parts of the country in fact suffered from significant food shortages, and US sources claimed that there was a "clear-cut denial of access by the government of Eritrea of food and other humanitarian support" for the people.

On 13 June, the Nabro volcano, located in the Danakil Depression and previously believed to have been dormant, erupted with an ash-plume of around 15 km, after an earthquake of magnitude 5.7. The event disrupted air traffic in the region, forcing US Secretary of State Hillary Clinton to shorten a planned three-nation tour of East Africa. It also killed livestock and some people, and contaminated water supplies in both Eritrea and neighbouring Ethiopia, affecting nearly 170,000 pastoralists.

The twentieth anniversary of the fall in 1991 of **Somalia's** last effective government passed with instability spilling over into neighbouring Kenya, a drought and famine that threatened thousands of lives, further fracturing of the country into local fiefdoms, ongoing and massive population displacement, and sporadic violent attacks by the fundamentalist al-Shabaab militia in the capital, Mogadishu.

In September and October suspected al-Shabaab fighters raided northern Kenyan coastal resorts, killing and kidnapping British and French tourists, as well as taking two Spanish aid workers from a refugee camp near the border. The negative impact on Kenyan tourism was felt immediately, and Kenya reacted in October—the middle of the difficult rainy season—by sending troops into southern Somalia, pushing forward according to some reports with logistical and other support from the USA and France. It remained unclear whether Kenya would establish a buffer zone (possibly to be called "Jubaland", or Azania) along the border, and the invading force stopped short of taking the southern port city of Kismaayo. Later, a war of words erupted with the Somali fighters warning that they would bring the "flames of war" to Nairobi, destroying skyscrapers and tourism.

In August al-Shabaab fighters abruptly abandoned the capital "for tactical reasons", raising hopes that the weak Transitional Federal Government (TFG) under President Sheikh Sharif Ahmed might be able to facilitate aid for up to 100,000 city residents facing food shortages and public health problems. But in October a suicide bomb attack killed around 70 civilians, many of them students, when a truck loaded with explosives drove into a government compound in the Harkaha area of Mogadishu. The death toll later rose to over 100. A protest rally was organized by the TFG in a local stadium, and was attended by several thousand city residents, who condemned the militants as "cowards" and "fugitive criminals". Troops from the African Union mission, together with TFG soldiers, subsequently assaulted al-Shabaab mortar positions near the city.

Somalis continued to flee unrest in large numbers, some attempting to cross into Yemen in overcrowded boats, while others risked arrest or deportation while trying to reach Mozambique or South Africa, which began to turn asylum-seekers back.

The drought and famine that affected an estimated 12 million people across the Horn of Africa—described by aid workers as the worst in 60 years—was exacerbated in southern Somalia (where over two million people were affected) by the ongoing violence, as well as by a delayed response to the crisis by the international community and a lack of reliable information about the situation. In July, al-Shabaab allowed some relief agencies access to areas under its control, but later in November banned 16 groups, including United Nations organisations, accusing them of "illicit activities and misconduct".

Increasingly violent pirate activity by groups based in Puntland continued to threaten sea-lanes in the Gulf of Aden and the western Indian Ocean throughout the year, with gangs targeting fishing boats, large freight vessels and private yachts. Ships attacked included Bulgarian, Greek, Iranian, Maltese, and Thai flagged vessels. In an incident in February four US citizens were killed aboard a sailing ship, and a Virginia court subsequently sentenced three captured pirates to life imprisonment. In January the South Korean navy seized a chemical carrier from pirates; the Indian navy also conducted rescue operations and some captures were made.

Low-level violence continued in the semi-independent region of Puntland, with improvised roadside bombs planted by Islamist insurgents targeting inhabitants of the central city of Gaalkacyo. In an interview in January, President Ahmed Mohamed Silanyo of the "Republic of Somaliland" expressed optimism that the independence of South Sudan would have a positive impact on his state's search for international recognition. In September Somaliland sent a humanitarian mission to Mogadishu, distributing food and medicine to around 9,000 drought-displaced families in the capital. Both Puntland and Somaliland introduced schemes to control the influx of displaced persons from Somalia and Ethiopia during the year.

President Ismael Omar Guellah of **Djibouti** won a third term in elections in April, with 80 per cent of the vote against independent candidate Mohamed Warsama Ragueh. The main opposition parties boycotted the polls, claiming that conditions for free elections did not exist. In February, in the run-up to the elections, two days of violent demonstrations saw thousands of protesters clashing with security forces in an unprecedented outburst of popular anger. Three leading opposition politicians were arrested, and two deaths were reported as military police patrolled the streets of the capital.

Together with neighbouring countries, Djibouti was hard hit by drought and high food prices early in the year, with an estimated 120,000 people from a total population of over 800,000, many of them pastoralists, affected by food insecurity. In an interview in February, President Guellah identified drought and famine as the "main challenge" facing the country, and criticised his own government's failure to plan for weather shocks.

Economic growth was estimated at over 5 per cent, fuelled by a construction boom. In November, the Djibouti Ports and Free Zones Authority announced plans to build a large ship maintenance yard at a cost of $400 million, as well as to add general cargo facilities, an oil terminal, and a livestock port at points along the Djibouti coast, located strategically on the main shipping route from Europe to the Far East.

In May, the International Criminal Court (ICC) in the Hague appealed to the UN Security Council to take action against Djibouti after President Omar Hassan al-Bashir of Sudan, who was wanted under an ICC war crimes indictment, visited the country but was not arrested.

US Defence Secretary Leon Panetta visited Djibouti in December for talks with President Guellah about joint counter-terrorism efforts. At the same time a contingent of 200 Djibouti troops joined the African Union peace-keeping forces in Somalia.

Colin Darch

KENYA

CAPITAL: Nairobi   AREA: 580,370 sq km   POPULATION: 40,512,682 ('10)
OFFICIAL LANGUAGES: Kiswahili & English
HEAD OF STATE AND GOVERNMENT: President Mwai Kibaki (PNU) (since Dec '02)
RULING PARTIES: Party of National Unity (PNU) and Orange Democratic Movement (ODM)
PRIME MINISTER: Raila Odinga (ODM) (since April '08)
DEMOCRACY INDEX: 4.71; 101st of 167   CORRUPTION INDEX: 2.2; 154th of 183
CURRENCY: Kenyan Shilling (Dec '11 £1.00=KES 140.20, US$1.00=KES 89.40)
GNI PER CAPITA: US$790, Intl$1,630 at PPP ('10)

NATIONAL politics was dominated by efforts to recover from the post-election crisis of 2007-08, and by preparations for the next general election, despite uncertainty over the eligibility of presidential candidates, the political alignment of key figures, and the election date. Slow progress was made in the implementation of the 2010 constitution, but significant changes were evident, such as in the public vetting that followed President Mwai Kibaki's attempt to unilaterally select judicial officials and subsequent appointment of Willy Mutunga—a prominent human rights activist—as Chief Justice. Popular support for the new constitution was coloured by ongoing fears that the spirit and letter of the document would be manipulated and undermined by vested interests.

The government failed in its efforts to stop legal proceedings at the International Criminal Court (ICC) against six prominent Kenyans for their alleged involvement in post-election violence. In March the ICC issued summonses against the six, who included Deputy Prime Minister Uhuru Kenyatta, politicians William Ruto and Henry Kosgey, radio broadcaster Joshua arap Sang, former Police Commissioner Mohammed Hussein Ali, and head of the civil service Francis Muthaura. Their appearance in April was surrounded by fanfare and mass "prayer meetings", but a cautionary ruling encouraged defendants and their supporters to become much more muted, and calm prevailed during the confirmation of charges hearings that ran from September to October. The Truth, Justice, and Reconciliation Commission, which began in 2009, continued taking statements and held public hearings across the country. These gained little public attention but the Commission was given an extension, pushing the deadline for a final report to 3 May 2012.

The fight against corruption had a disappointing year. In August, the outspoken head of the Kenyan Anti-Corruption Commission (KACC), Patrick Lumumba, was removed from office following revelations that he had received money from an assistant minister's husband—whose business interests were under investigation by the KACC—and the year ended with political deadlock over nominations to the new Ethics and Anti-Corruption Commission (EACC). During the year, protesters staged an unsuccessful sit-in at the education ministry to demand the minister's resignation following the loss of millions of shillings from the country's primary education budget, while William Ruto was acquitted of defrauding a state corporation of KSh 97 million in 2001, and Moses Wetangula was reappointed minister of foreign affairs despite controversy surrounding the purchase of diplomatic properties in Japan. However, the director of public prosecutions did agree to the extradition of a former head of Kenya Power and Lighting and former energy minister to face charges of fraud and money laundering in the UK.

Extra-judicial killings continued and gained particular attention in January when commuters photographed what was allegedly a plain-clothes police officer shooting two prostrate men on a busy Nairobi street. Police also failed to solve the death of Mercy Keino, a student widely believed to have been recruited as a "drug mule" by a prominent politician, or the shooting of Joseph Cheptarus, a Kenya Revenue Authority official investigating a large gold smuggling operation.

In September, a British man was killed and his wife abducted from a resort near the Kenya-Somali border, and soon afterwards a French woman was abducted further down the coast. Kenya accused al-Shabaab of the attacks and, after two Spanish aid workers were abducted from the Dadaab refugee camp near the Somali border, it confirmed in October that it had launched a military incursion into Somalia. The government denied reports of civilian targets including an alleged aerial bombardment of a refugee camp in southern Somalia. Regional neighbours, together with the USA, the UK and Israel announced their support for Kenya, but there were concerns that the country would be drawn into a prolonged conflict and suffer further terrorist attacks. In October, grenades killed one and wounded 29 in Nairobi, and bomb attacks in northern and eastern Kenya in November and December killed several others. Kenya's strategy remained unclear. One idea was the possible creation of a buffer zone state called "Azania" (Jubaland): a nascent state which enjoyed a flag and a president-in-waiting, elected during a meeting at a Kenyan hotel.

The year also witnessed a regional famine which threatened approximately 4 million Kenyans, while hundreds of thousands of refugees fled from conflict-ridden Somalia into overcrowded camps in the north. Media attention prompted a successful "Kenyans for Kenya" campaign, which raised over KSh 677 million to feed the country's starving and fund future food security initiatives.

Famine, together with a rise in food prices, global financial crisis, regional economic problems, a drop in tourism, a dramatic fall in the Kenyan shilling, and an inflation rate of almost 20 per cent by November, meant many faced severe economic difficulties. However, as the year ended, inflation began to fall and the Kenyan shilling began to recover.

Gabrielle Lynch

TANZANIA

CAPITAL: Dodoma   AREA: 947,300 sq km   POPULATION: 44,841,226 ('10)
OFFICIAL LANGUAGES: Kiswahili & English
HEAD OF STATE AND GOVERNMENT: President Jakaya Kikwete (CCM) (since Dec '05)
RULING PARTY: Chama Cha Mapinduzi (CCM)
 PRIME MINISTER: Mizengo Pinda (since Feb '08)
DEMOCRACY INDEX: 5.64; 92nd of 167   CORRUPTION INDEX: 3.0; 100th of 183
CURRENCY: Tanzanian Shilling (Dec '11 £1.00=TZS 2,639, US$1.00=TZS 1,683)
GNI PER CAPITA: US$530, Intl$1,420 at PPP ('10)

THE year marked the 50th anniversary of independence from British colonial rule, and celebrations culminated in a mass rally at Dar es Salaam's Uhuru Stadium in December attended by over 40 heads of state. The celebratory mood was offset, however, by new levels of political opposition and protest. Early in the year there was uncharacteristic political violence as a dispute over Arusha's mayoral elections led to the detention of Freeman Mbowe, chairman of the main opposition party (the Party for Democracy and Progress—CHADEMA), and confrontations between protesters and police in which three people died. Furthermore, in the aftermath of the October 2010 general election—which saw opposition parties gain 51 new seats—debate in the National Assembly became more heated and adversarial. The government sought to revive the ruling party, Chama Cha Mapinduzi (CCM), through the appointment of a new secretariat in April, and "clarified" legislative rules, including designating the official opposition as all opposition parties rather than just the party with the second-largest number of parliamentary seats.

The need for constitutional reform dominated political debate. In March, a draft constitutional review bill was unveiled but met with popular demands for greater consultation and more extensive reform. In response, public hearings were held in Zanzibar, Dar es Salaam and Dodoma in April, but meetings ended early because of local protests. Proposals for a new constitutional review body were subsequently presented to parliament, but when an amended bill was returned in November, opposition legislators staged a walk-out to protest against the absence of earlier parliamentary recommendations. Nevertheless, the bill was passed and President Jakaya Kikwete reaffirmed his commitment to have a new constitution in place by 2014.

Another talking point was the all-purpose "miracle cure" dispensed by a pastor in a northern village. Thousands flocked to buy it, including a number of public figures, and some politicians arranged transport for constituents. Unfortunately, the year was also marked by several avoidable disasters. These included explosions at a military base in Dar es Salaam in February where 23 people were killed, and the deaths of around 200 people (and perhaps many more) when an overloaded ferry sank between Unguja and Pemba islands in September.

Like other countries in the region, Tanzania faced a difficult economic situation. The shilling fell in value, the price of food rose by 22 per cent and fuel by more than 37 per cent, and there was electricity rationing. However, a number of oil and gas exploration agreements were signed during the year, while China agreed to support the development of the Mchuchuma coal and Liganga iron ore projects.

Gabrielle Lynch

UGANDA

CAPITAL: Kampala   AREA: 241,040 sq km   POPULATION: 33,424,683 ('10)
OFFICIAL LANGUAGE: English
HEAD OF STATE AND GOVERNMENT: President Yoweri Museveni (since Jan '86)
RULING PARTY: National Resistance Movement (NRM)
PRIME MINISTER: Patrick Amama Mbabazi (since May '11)
DEMOCRACY INDEX: 5.05; 98th of 167   CORRUPTION INDEX: 2.4; 143rd of 183
CURRENCY: Uganda Shilling (Dec '11 £1.00=UGX 3,975, US$1.00=UGX 2,535)
GNI PER CAPITA: US$500, Intl$1,240 at PPP ('10)

Amidst heightened security, President Yoweri Museveni was re-elected in February with 68 per cent of the vote, while the ruling party, the National Resistance Movement (NRM), secured 263 of 375 parliamentary seats in a general election that —according to African Union and EU election observers—was characterised by "several shortcomings" and "avoidable administrative and logistical failures". However, in contrast to previous elections—when the leading opposition candidate, Kizza Besigye of the Forum for Democratic Change (FDC), had been charged with terrorism and rape—the campaign and voting proved relatively uneventful. Museveni and the NRM spent heavily and emphasised the importance of security and development, while Besigye (who came second with 26 per cent of the vote) focused on corruption, poverty and the likelihood of vote rigging.

Problems began after the election as Besigye led a "walk to work" campaign to protest against the rising cost of living. Museveni denounced these protests and Besigye was arrested four times, while nine people were killed in confrontations with security forces, and the government cracked down on journalists and social media sites. However, the government's strong-armed response reinvigorated opposition support, and Museveni's inauguration was marked by pro-Besigye demonstrations, some of which were violent.

Little progress was made in the fight against corruption. Charges against former Vice-President Gilbert Bukenya for abuse of office and fraud—linked to the supply of luxury cars to Commonwealth Summit delegates in 2007—were dropped, while claims that government ministers had accepted bribes from oil companies prompted parliament to suspend all new deals until a new law could be introduced.

Uganda also gained unwanted international attention on the issue of gay rights, which recaptured the headlines after the murder of a local gay rights activist, David Kato, in January.

In September, two Ugandans were jailed for the 2010 bomb attack that killed 76 people, planned by the Somali Islamist group al-Shabaab in retaliation for Uganda's military support for the Somali government. Concern over the possibility of further attacks remained throughout the year, as did worries over the activities of the rebel Lord's Resistance Army (LRA), which continued to operate outside the country's borders. In July, the first LRA commander to face charges at the special war crimes court was granted an amnesty, a decision that raised questions regarding the court's future role.

Ugandans faced a difficult year economically as the shilling dropped to a record low against the US dollar in August, and inflation reached 29 per cent with a 45 per cent increase in food prices. However, by the year's end inflation had begun to fall and the shilling had recovered some lost ground. The development of oil projects continued, although a dispute between Heritage Oil and the Ugandan government meant that the first oil was not expected to flow until 2012.

Gabrielle Lynch

NIGERIA—GHANA—SIERRA LEONE—THE GAMBIA—LIBERIA

NIGERIA

CAPITAL: Abuja   AREA: 923,770 sq km   POPULATION: 158,423,182 ('10)
OFFICIAL LANGUAGE: English
HEAD OF STATE AND GOVERNMENT: President Goodluck Jonathan (since May '10)
RULING PARTY: People's Democratic Party (PDP)
DEMOCRACY INDEX: 3.47; 123rd of 167   CORRUPTION INDEX: 2.4; 143rd of 183
CURRENCY: Naira (Dec '11 £1.00=NGN 252.89, US$1=NGN 161.25)
GNI PER CAPITA: US$1,180, Intl$2,160 at PPP ('10)

IT was a tumultuous year in Africa's most populous country, with national elections that deepened political divisions between north and south, and violence in parts of the north. The year began inauspiciously, when a market outside an army barracks near the federal capital of Abuja was bombed on New Year's Eve, killing at least 11 people. Until 2010 bombings were rare in Nigeria, but since then bomb attacks had become more frequent, as a method of political violence and in religious conflicts. Some of the insecurity in 2011 was connected to the elections, but by the end of the year the violence being perpetrated under the rubric of Boko Haram, an Islamist militant group, had become a major focus of domestic and international attention.

The first half of the year was dominated by the elections, which were held in April. The party campaigns and buying of patronage consumed vast amounts of money and political attention across the country. On 14 January, President Goodluck Jonathan won the nomination of the ruling People's Democratic Party (PDP) with a 77 per cent majority. This was controversial because according to an informal principle within the PDP—which had been in power since the transition from military to civilian rule in 1999—the presidency was meant to rotate between north and south every two terms. The president in the first two terms (1999-2007) had been Olusegun Obasanjo, a Christian southerner from Ogun state, but his successor, Umaru Musa Yar'Adua, a Muslim from Katsina state in the north, had died in office in May 2010. Goodluck Jonathan, a Christian southerner from Bayelsa state in the Niger Delta, was vice president in the Yar'Adua administration, and thus succeeded him. This led to much political wrangling within the PDP over who should stand for the presidency in 2011, with northern politicians arguing that they had not completed their two terms. The problem was compounded because the PDP stalwarts from the north were not unified behind their candidate, Atiku Abubakar, who had been vice president under Obasanjo. The powers of incumbency gave the Jonathan camp a crucial advantage, as it used state resources and patronage to gain support. In the PDP primaries, the southern delegates were united behind him, but many northern politicians also supported Jonathan instead of Abubakar.

The opposition was divided between multiple parties, the most prominent of which were the Congress for Progressive Change (CPC), the Action Congress of Nigeria (ACN), the All Nigeria People's Party (ANPP), and the Labour Party (LP). The most significant opposition candidate for the presidency was Major General Muhammadu Buhari, a respected figure in the north and to a lesser extent elsewhere who was still remembered for his "War Against Indiscipline" and clampdown on corruption when he was military ruler of Nigeria (1983-85). Buhari, a Muslim from Katsina, was especially popular at the grassroots in northern Nigeria, but was opposed by much of the northern political establishment. This disconnect between elite and popular politics in the north became a source of instability and violence after the elections.

Attahiru Jega, an academic and democracy activist, was chairman of the Independent National Election Commission (INEC) during the 2011 elections. His predecessor, Maurice Iwu, was widely condemned as corrupt and complicit in the rigging of the 2007 elections. The previous electoral register was so flawed that voter registration had to be done from scratch and a new one created. Logistical problems at INEC meant that some of the voting materials did not reach their destinations in time, leading to a last minute announcement that the Senate and State House of Assembly elections were to be delayed in some constituencies. In the event, in most areas the National Assembly elections were held on 9 April, the presidential vote on 16 April, and gubernatorial elections on 26 April, along with elections to the Senate and state assemblies in constituencies that had been affected by the delays. The timing of the governorship elections after the presidential vote was a tactic used by the PDP to pressurise its governors—especially in the north—into supporting Jonathan's candidacy.

The ruling PDP emerged from the electoral process as the dominant party, but with a substantial erosion in support, especially in the north and south-west. The ACN won 17 out of the 18 senatorial seats in the south-west and controlled all six governors in this predominantly Yoruba region. In the presidential election, however, support in the south-west went to Jonathan rather than to ACN candidate Nuhu Ribadu, the former anti-corruption chief, who was from Adamawa in the north. In the Niger Delta (the south-south) and in the south-east the PDP received an increased share of the vote, and Jonathan received overwhelming support in the presidential contest. In central Nigeria support was divided between the PDP and CPC, with more for the former.

Goodluck Jonathan was declared outright winner of the presidential election, with 22.5 million votes to Buhari's 12.2 million. Buhari and the CPC failed to make any impact in the south, but Jonathan gained some votes in the north. This was essential for the PDP because in order to avoid a run-off the constitution stipulated that a presidential candidate must win a majority of the popular vote and at least 25 per cent of votes in at least two-thirds of the states (i.e. 24 of the 36 states in the federation). This was one of the points on which the opposition CPC and Buhari's supporters protested, claiming that the ruling PDP had used its control of the electoral machinery and its vastly superior financial resources to rig up to the 25 per cent threshold in northern states where it had little popular support. The official figures from the south-south—Jonathan's home region—were also questioned, as they showed unusually high turnout and more than 98 per cent support for the president in several states. However, the international observers, from the EU, USA, and UN, while noting some irregularities, declared the elections to have been broadly "free and fair" and a marked improvement on the widely condemned 2007 contests.

When the presidential results were announced pro-Buhari riots broke out across northern Nigeria. Buhari had won 12 states, all of them in the north, but in eight of these the PDP also made sizeable inroads, winning 25 per cent or more of the vote. It emerged that most of the traditional rulers—the emirs—and some state governors in the north had backed Jonathan and the PDP rather than Buhari. The rioters directed their considerable anger at northern politicians and traditional rulers who were deemed to have supported the PDP. There followed a spree of killing and looting that was particularly bad in Kaduna state where hundreds died. The unrest included communal violence between Muslims and Christians (the latter had tended to support Jonathan) which reinforced religious and regional divisions that had already surfaced in the run-up to the election.

The amnesty for Niger Delta militants continued in 2011 and reduced the level of militancy there, even though doubts remained over whether the policy could offer a durable solution to the problems of Nigeria's oil-producing region. Militants were being paid off, but oil bunkering continued, kidnapping was still occurring, and piracy was a growing a menace for shipping along the coast. But the biggest security concern was at the opposite end of the country, in the north-east, especially in Borno and Yobe states. This was the stronghold of Boko Haram, an Islamist movement that the government had attempted to crush in 2009. Having regrouped, during 2011 the movement stepped up its attacks against the Nigerian state and, increasingly, upon Christians. Boko Haram claimed responsibility for the attempted bombing of the national police headquarters on 16 June, and for the destruction of the UN building in Abuja on 26 August in an apparent suicide bombing, in which 27 people were killed.

Meanwhile, there was serious inter-group violence in parts of Plateau state, central Nigeria, at different points of the year. Rioting and low-level violence between Muslims and Christians occurred in Jos during the first three months of the year. Some degree of calm was then restored, but renewed violence occurred when Christian youths attacked Muslims from the reformist group Izala (JIBWIS) during Eid el Fitr (sallah) celebrations at the end of August when the Muslim worshippers were at their prayer ground, which was located in what had become a mainly Christian area of the city. By the end of September an uneasy calm had returned to metropolitan Jos, but violence continued in some rural areas.

By the end of the year the security situation in the north was very precarious. Boko Haram launched some audacious attacks in November and December in Yobe state, and claimed responsibility for a string of attacks on churches in the north on Christmas Day. The bombing of St Theresa Catholic Church in Madalla, near Abuja, killed 37 people. On 31 December President Jonathan declared a state of emergency in 15 local government areas of Borno, Yobe, Plateau, and Niger states. The practical effects of such a move were limited, because the security forces were already heavily engaged in those states, but it suggested that the government would continue to pursue a military solution. This was also reflected in the 2012 budget, announced in December, which allocated more than 20 per cent of expenditure to the security forces. Much of the rest was recurrent expenditure: Nigerian politicians were among the highest paid in the world, with allowances that dwarfed their already high salaries. At the same time, the federal government was pushing to remove a fuel subsidy, partly to plug the hole in government finances created by extravagant spending during the election.

Adam Higazi

GHANA—SIERRA LEONE—THE GAMBIA—LIBERIA

Ghana

CAPITAL: Accra   AREA: 238,540 sq km   POPULATION: 24,391,823 ('10)
OFFICIAL LANGUAGE: English
HEAD OF STATE AND GOVERNMENT: President John Atta Mills (NDC) (since Jan '09)
RULING PARTY: National Democratic Congress (NDC)
DEMOCRACY INDEX: 6.02; 77th of 167   CORRUPTION INDEX: 3.9; 69th of 183
CURRENCY: Cedi (Dec '11 £1.00=GHS 2.58, US$1.00=GHS 1.65)
GNI PER CAPITA: US$1,230, Intl$1,600 at PPP ('10)

Sierra Leone

CAPITAL: Freetown   AREA: 71,740 sq km   POPULATION: 5,867,536 ('10)
OFFICIAL LANGUAGE: English
HEAD OF STATE AND GOVERNMENT: President Ernest Bai Koroma (APC) (since Sept '07)
RULING PARTY: All People's Congress (APC)
DEMOCRACY INDEX: 4.51; 105th of 167   CORRUPTION INDEX: 2.5; 134th of 183
CURRENCY: Leone (Dec '11 £1.00=SLL 6,914, US$1.00=SLL 4,409)
GNI PER CAPITA: US$340, Intl$820 at PPP ('10)

The Gambia

CAPITAL: Banjul   AREA: 11,300 sq km   POPULATION: 1,728,394 ('10)
OFFICIAL LANGUAGE: English
HEAD OF STATE AND GOVERNMENT: President Yahya Jammeh (APRC) (since Sept '96)
RULING PARTY: Alliance for Patriotic Reorientation and Construction (APRC)
DEMOCRACY INDEX: 3.38; 128th of 167   CORRUPTION INDEX: 3.5; 77th of 183
CURRENCY: Dalasi (Dec '11 £1.00=GMD 45.53, US$1.00=GMD 29.03)
GNI PER CAPITA: US$450, Intl$1,290 at PPP ('10)

Liberia

CAPITAL: Monrovia   AREA: 111,370 sq km   POPULATION: 3,994,122 ('10)
OFFICIAL LANGUAGE: English
HEAD OF STATE AND GOVERNMENT: President Ellen Johnson-Sirleaf (since Jan '06)
RULING PARTY: Unity Party
DEMOCRACY INDEX: 5.07; 97th of 167   CORRUPTION INDEX: 3.2; 91st of 183
CURRENCY: Liberian Dollar (Dec '11 £1.00=LRD 110, US$1=LRD 70)
GNI PER CAPITA: US$200, Intl$340 at PPP ('10)

IN the first quarter of the year, **Ghana** received refugees from the conflict in Côte d'Ivoire; at the end of 2011 some 16,000 remained in the country. The conflict affected diplomacy between the two countries as well. President John Atta Mills was slow to recognise Alassane Ouattara as the winner in the Ivorian election, and Côte d'Ivoire subsequently challenged Ghana's claim to parts of the Jubilee oil field, a challenge perceived by many observers to have been political retaliation.

Increasing prospects for oil revenues brought Ghana into the international financial news. Ghana was listed as one of the fastest growing economies in the world in 2011, at 13.6 per cent growth, mostly due to expanded oil and gas exploration and production in the offshore Jubilee field. The Jubilee field, operated by Tullow Oil, a UK company, began producing in December 2010. Cocoa and gold also remained important exports, although a shipping dispute in December lowered the cocoa export projections for the year. Throughout the economy, growth had yet to translate into more jobs or increased capacity, however, two results which relied on the political process.

Campaigning intensified in 2011 as the political parties solidified their bases and chose their candidates for the December 2012 presidential election. President Mills was challenged in the National Democratic Congress (NDC) party's selection process by Nana Konadu Agyeman-Rawlings, wife of the former president, Jerry Rawlings. In the end, Mills won the nomination on 8 July with 96.9 per cent of his party's votes. Nana Akufo-Addo, who had lost to Mills in the runoff of the 2008 election, won the opposition New Patriotic Party (NPP) nomination.

Despite an impending election year, in December Ghana's National Petroleum Authority (NPA), the country's regulatory body, set about cutting oil subsidies in response to rising fuel prices and the decreasing value of the currency. The action was part of continuing austerity measures, adopted to reduce the deficit inherited from the previous administration. The NPA was likely responding to pressure from the IMF, from which it was hoping to receive approval of a Chinese loan to build a gas pipeline and gas processing facility that would enable exploitation of the natural gas reserves also located in the Jubilee field. Some international financial authorities nevertheless expressed concern that the campaign year could cause an increase in borrowing as the government attempted to spend its way to re-election.

The year 2011 marked the 50th anniversary of **Sierra Leone's** independence from the UK. President Ernest Bai Koroma announced a "year of national unity" in honour of the occasion. Celebrations took place around the week of 27 April, and included national parades, a thanksgiving service, cultural displays, a sports competition and the women of excellence awards.

These awards were part of a broader policy to highlight women's issues in the country. Women's health initiatives remained high on the agenda, with the experiment in free maternal and infant care continuing. The opposition Sierra Leone People's Party (SLPP) announced in November that it would nominate a woman, Dr Kadi Sesay, as its vice presidential candidate. However, despite the positive turn for women, other issues of human rights remained controversial. An anti-gay rights protest took place on 30 December in reaction to US Secretary of State Hillary Clinton's new aid initiative, which tied foreign aid to human rights, including gay rights.

The government promoted a new tourism initiative to coincide with the 50th anniversary celebrations, and 2011 also marked a new beginning for Sierra Leone's extractive industries. Both African Minerals and London Mining exported their first shipments of iron ore in 2011, and African Petroleum announced in November that it would begin offshore drilling in 2012. The government, in response to initial criticisms of the deal with London Mining, considered adjusting the tax rate on the company's profits in Sierra Leone from 6 to 25 per cent, bringing it closer to the National Mines and Minerals Code's suggested 37.5 per cent rate.

This economic news may have been heartening for incumbent president and ruling All People's Congress (APC) candidate Koroma. Elections were scheduled for August 2012, and the contest had already begun in the press. Mohamed Bangura was selected as the United Democratic Movement (UDM) candidate, while Julius Maada Bio won as candidate for the SLPP over Usman Boie Kamara. Bio, who had led a coup in 1996, was formerly head of state under the National Provisional Ruling Council (NPRC) military government from January to March 1996. In 2011, he focused on corruption and the economy as the cornerstone issues of his campaign, particularly noting the continuing problems of drug trafficking and alleged instances of police and government collusion.

A police ban on political meetings and rallies, imposed on 29 September as a result of violence in the Bo and Kono districts, was lifted in December as it became clear that political parties were finding ways around the rules.

The Gambia's three-term president, Yahya Jammeh, won a further five-year term on 24 November, with 71 per cent of the vote. He had already served for 17 years. Ousainou Darboe, representing the opposition United Democratic Party (UDP), won 17 per cent of the vote, after campaigning on a promise to balance the economy of one of the most highly-indebted poor countries. Hamat Bah, of the United Front, won 11 per cent. The Economic Community of West African States (ECOWAS) did not monitor the elections, after determining that the conditions in which they were being held were not free, fair or transparent. The UDP rejected the election results. President Jammeh countered international criticism with the statement that he would rule the country for one billion years "if Allah said so". He also rejected comparisons with toppled Libyan leader and Gambian ally, Moamar Kadhafi, or deposed Egyptian President Hosni Mubarak.

A more positive impression of The Gambia was given by the election, unanimously, of Fatou Bom Besouda as the next prosecutor of the International Criminal Court (ICC), to replace Argentine Luis Moreno-Ocampo. She was the first Gambian to hold a high-level international position. She promised to make the prosecution of sexual and gender-based war crimes a priority.

Eight foreign drug traffickers, arrested in June 2010, were sentenced to 50 years in prison in October as part of the attempt to stem the flow of drugs through the country. The Gambia's approach to tackling drug trafficking was praised in a US embassy cable released by WikiLeaks earlier in the year, although the US diplomats also criticised the government for its approach to gay rights, AIDS prevention, and press freedom.

The international community continued to have a presence in **Liberia**, eight years after the end of the country's 23-year long conflict. The mandate of the UN Mission in Liberia (UNMIL) was renewed until September 2012; the IMF also agreed to continue Liberia's extended credit facility until March 2012.

The year began with an influx of refugees from neighbouring Côte d'Ivoire. Villages in eastern Liberia, in particular those in Grand Gedeh and Nimba counties, were affected. The UN High Commissioner for Refugees (UNHCR) estimated that more than 125,000 Ivorian refugees had entered Liberia between December 2010 and April 2011, with over 80,000 arriving between February and the end of hostilities in Côte d'Ivoire in April.

With presidential elections due at the end of the year, a referendum on constitutional amendments held in August proved controversial. The referendum, organised by the National Elections Commission, proposed increasing the retirement age for judges from 70 to 75; postponing the presidential elections from October until November; shortening the residency requirement for presidential and vice-presidential candidates from 10 years to five; and changing the requirement for election from an absolute majority to a simple majority, for all candidates other than the president. The opposition parties claimed that the timing of the referendum would confuse voters and benefit the ruling Unity Party. None of the four issues passed with a two-thirds majority of registered voters, however, although the Supreme Court later ruled that the simple majority rule had, in fact, passed.

Another source of controversy before the elections was the award, just days before the first round, of the Nobel Peace Prize to President Ellen Johnson Sirleaf and peace activist Leymah Gbowee for their role as women's rights leaders. (The third laureate was Yemeni activist, Tawakkol Karman). Gbowee had been integral to the establishment of peace in Liberia in 2003, and had continued to play a role in politics, particularly advocating for women's issues.

President Sirleaf, the ruling Unity Party candidate, won the first round on 11 October with 44 per cent of the vote. The Congress for Democratic Change (CDC) had nominated Winston Tubman, while Charles Brumskine stood for the Liberty Party. Controversially, Prince Johnson—the former rebel leader and warlord—also stood for election. Tubman won 32.7 per cent of the vote in the first round, but called for voters to boycott the second round, leading some supporters to violence in the period before the election in November. President Sirleaf won 90 per cent of the vote in the run-off, although turnout was recorded as only 37 per cent of eligible voters. ECOWAS, the African Union, and the Carter Center all declared the elections legitimate.

Bronwen Everill

WEST AFRICAN FRANCOPHONE STATES—CENTRAL AFRICAN FRANC ZONE

SENEGAL—MAURITANIA—MALI—GUINEA—CÔTE D'IVOIRE— BURKINA FASO—TOGO—BENIN—NIGER

Senegal

CAPITAL: Dakar   AREA: 196,720 sq km   POPULATION: 12,433,728 ('10)
OFFICIAL LANGUAGE: French
HEAD OF STATE AND GOVERNMENT: President Abdoulaye Wade (since April '00)
RULING PARTIES: Sopi Coalition, led by Senegalese Democratic Party (PDS)
PRIME MINISTER: Souleymane Ndéné Ndiaye (PDS) (since April '09)
DEMOCRACY INDEX: 5.27; 95th of 167   CORRUPTION INDEX: 2.9; 112nd of 183
CURRENCY: West African CFA Franc BCEAO (Dec '11 £1=XOF 763, US$1.00=XOF 487)
GNI PER CAPITA: US$1,090, Intl$1,910 at PPP ('10)

Mauritania

CAPITAL: Nouakchott   AREA: 1,030,700 sq km   POPULATION: 3,459,773 ('10)
OFFICIAL LANGUAGES: French & Arabic
HEAD OF STATE AND GOVERNMENT: President General Mohamed Ould Abdelaziz (since Aug '09)
PRIME MINISTER: Moulaye Ould Mohamed Laghdhaf (since Aug '08)
DEMOCRACY INDEX: 3.86; 115th of 167   CORRUPTION INDEX: 2.4; 143rd of 183
CURRENCY: Ouguiya (Dec '11 £1.00=MRO 450.99, US$1.00=MRO 287.57)
GNI PER CAPITA: US$1,030, Intl$1,950 at PPP ('10)

Mali

CAPITAL: Bamako   AREA: 1,240,190 sq km   POPULATION: 15,369,809 ('10)
OFFICIAL LANGUAGE: French
HEAD OF STATE AND GOVERNMENT: President Amadou Toumani Touré (since June '02)
PRIME MINISTER: Prime Minister Cissé Mariam Kaïdama Sidibé (since April '11)
DEMOCRACY INDEX: 6.01; 79th of 167   CORRUPTION INDEX: 2.8; 118th of 183
CURRENCY: West African CFA Franc (see above)
GNI PER CAPITA: US$600, Intl$1,020 at PPP ('10)

Guinea

CAPITAL: Conakry   AREA: 245,860 sq km   POPULATION: 9,981,590 ('10)
OFFICIAL LANGUAGE: French
HEAD OF STATE AND GOVERNMENT: Alpha Condé (RPG) (since Dec '10)
RULING PARTY: Rally of the Guinean People (RPG)
PRIME MINISTER: Mohamed Said Fofana (since Dec '10)
DEMOCRACY INDEX: 2.79; 144th of 167   CORRUPTION INDEX: 2.1; 164th of 183
CURRENCY: Guinean Franc (Dec '11 £1.00=GNF 10,805.30, US$1=GNF 6,890.00)
GNI PER CAPITA: US$400, Intl$1,020 at PPP ('10)

Côte d'Ivoire

CAPITAL: Yamoussoukro (official) Abidjan (de facto)   AREA: 322,460 sq km   POPULATION: 19,737,800 ('10)
OFFICIAL LANGUAGE: French
HEAD OF STATE AND GOVERNMENT: President Alassane Ouattara (RDR) (since Dec '10)
RULING PARTY: Rally of the Republicans (RDR)
PRIME MINISTER: Guillaume Kigbafori Soro (Forces Nouvelles) (since March '07)
DEMOCRACY INDEX: 3.02; 139th of 167   CORRUPTION INDEX: 2.2; 154th of 183
CURRENCY: West African CFA Franc (see above)
GNI PER CAPITA: US$1,160, Intl$1,800 at PPP ('10)

Burkina Faso

CAPITAL: Ouagadougou AREA: 274,000 sq km POPULATION: 16,468,714 ('10)
OFFICIAL LANGUAGE: French
HEAD OF STATE AND GOVERNMENT: President (Capt.) Blaise Compaoré (CDP) (since Dec '91); previously chairman of Popular Front (from Oct '87)
RULING PARTY: Congress for Democracy and Progress (CDP)
PRIME MINISTER: Luc Adolphe Tiao (since April '11)
DEMOCRACY INDEX: 3.59; 120th of 167 CORRUPTION INDEX: 3.0; 100th of 183
CURRENCY: West African CFA Franc (see above)
GNI PER CAPITA: US$550, Intl$1,250 at PPP ('10)

Togo

CAPITAL: Lomé AREA: 56,790 sq km POPULATION: 6,027,798 ('10)
OFFICIAL LANGUAGES: French, Kabiye & Ewem
HEAD OF STATE AND GOVERNMENT: President Faure Gnassingbé (RPT) (since May '05)
RULING PARTY: Rally of the Togolese People (RPT)
PRIME MINISTER: Gilbert Fossoun Houngbo (since Sept '08)
DEMOCRACY INDEX: 3.45; 124th of 167
CURRENCY: West African CFA Franc (see above)
GNI PER CAPITA: US$490, Intl$890 at PPP ('10)

Benin

CAPITAL: Porto Novo AREA: 112,620 sq km POPULATION: 8,849,892 ('10)
OFFICIAL LANGUAGE: French
HEAD OF STATE AND GOVERNMENT: President Yayi Boni (since April '06)
RULING PARTY: Cauri Forces for an Emerging Benin (FCBE)
PRIME MINISTER: Pascal Irénée Koupaki (since May '11)
DEMOCRACY INDEX: 6.17; 72nd of 167 CORRUPTION INDEX: 3.0; 100th of 183
CURRENCY: West African CFA franc (see above)
GNI PER CAPITA: US$780, Intl$1,580 at PPP ('10)

Niger

CAPITAL: Niamey AREA: 1,267,000 sq km POPULATION: 15,511,953 ('10)
OFFICIAL LANGUAGE: French
HEAD OF STATE AND GOVERNMENT: President Mahamadou Issoufou (PNDS) (since April '11)
RULING PARTY: Niger Party for Democracy and Socialism (PNDS)
PRIME MINISTER: Brigi Raffini (since April '11)
DEMOCRACY INDEX: 3.38; 128th of 167 CORRUPTION INDEX: 2.5; 134th of 183
CURRENCY: West African CFA Franc (see above)
GNI PER CAPITA: US$370, Intl$720 at PPP ('10)

THERE were signs of mounting political crisis in **Senegal**, as discontent with the rule of octogenarian President Abdoulaye Wade increased. The focal point was the coming election in February 2012, and although there were several potential candidates, they came together in a massive day of protest on 23 June. The cause was the plan by the president to amend the constitution to reduce the proportion of votes needed to win the presidential election from more than 50 per cent to 25 per cent. He also proposed the creation of the post of vice president. Both of these measures were allegedly designed to facilitate the succession of Wade's son, Karim Wade, already a "super-minister" holding several portfolios.

The demonstration was organised by a coalition of most of the main opposition parties, named Benno Siggil Senegaal (United to Boost Senegal). This had originally been formed for the municipal elections in 2009, when it had achieved important successes. Its main leaders were Moustapha Niasse (leader of the Alliance of the Forces of Progress, AFP) and Ousmane Tanor Dieng, leader of the Socialist Party, both potential rivals for the presidency. It was supported by a massive crowd and saw scenes of violence, with several policemen among over 100 injured. One report said that Karim Wade had even called on France's President Nicolas Sarkozy to request intervention by French troops. This was denied, especially as Wade had requested the closure of French bases in Dakar.

The impact of 23 June was immediate. The president decided to withdraw his constitutional amendment, and also reaffirmed his own intention to run in the forthcoming elections, and although the appointment of a vice president was not abandoned, no attempt was made to fill the post. Karim told an interviewer in July that he considered power should be "merited, not inherited," and several reports suggest that the president, although now nearly 90, was still lively, and bristling with ideas and "far from geriatric". Ironically, as Wade's own power seemed increasingly threatened, the Senegalese economy was performing better than it had done for many years.

In February a car bomb attack in **Mauritania's** capital, Nouakchott, reportedly organised by al-Qaida in the Islamic Maghreb (AQIM), was foiled by the military. Its target had been the French embassy and the neighbouring ministry of defence. This was followed by a massive operation to hunt down AQIM accomplices, described by Mauritanian security sources as being "as important as the AQIM fighters themselves". Because of the cross-border nature of AQIM, Mauritanian troops had often attacked rebels over the long border with Mali, at the same time as developing closer ties with affected countries within the Sahel counter-terrorism initiative, backed by the USA and France (see AR 2011, pp. 217; 241).

In October, just as several AQIM supporters were jailed in Nouakchott, the Mauritanian army announced that it had killed an AQIM leader, Tiyib Ould Sidi Ali, in an air raid in northern Mali.

Meanwhile, politics showed increased restiveness, under the influence of the "Arab Spring". On 25 April a "day of danger" was organised in the capital, in which hundreds of youths protesting against government "corruption" tried to march on a square in central Nouakchott. Teargas was used and a number of arrests were made. Legislative elections that had been scheduled first for April and then for October were postponed indefinitely. The government said that the delay was in order to introduce biometric voting.

In September, President Mohamed Ould Abdelaziz convened a 10-day "national dialogue" to discuss governance, national unity and the rule of law, but this was boycotted by the Co-ordination of the Democratic Opposition (COD), which grouped most opposition parties. It was followed by a new outbreak of discontent focused on proposals for a national census. A movement called "Don't Touch My Nationality" complained that the exercise was biased against Negro-Mauritanians who lived in the south of the country, generally believed to be one-third of the population. Demonstrations at the end of September were followed by the arrest of 31 people said to be "foreigners".

The impact on **Mali** of the activities of AQIM was one of the running stories of the year. In March a team from the African Union spent several days in the country advising on anti-terrorism measures, in the face of an increased spate of hostage-taking. In May there was a summit of Sahel nations (Mali, Algeria, Niger, Mauritania) in Bamako to discuss security matters.

There were serious repercussions from the civil war in Libya that eventually led to the overthrow and killing of Libyan leader, Moamar Kadhafi. A further crisis meeting was held in the southern Algerian town of Tamanrasset in September, at which concern was expressed at the increased circulation of arms, including heavy mortars, in the Sahel region, as well as the influx of participants in the war. There was particular concern that over 1,000 Touareg combatants (who had originally been in Kadhafi's Islamic Legion and had returned to fight for him in his last campaign against the NATO-supported rebels) had moved to the mountains of northern Mali.

Repercussions from Libya somewhat eclipsed preparations for the next presidential elections, also a leap into the unknown. The eight-year rule of President Amadou Toumani Touré was due to come to an end, and because of his prestige as the army leader who had handed power to civilians in 1991, he had been able to offer the country a useful period of stability. This had to some extent been illusory, as he was often criticised for the weakness of the way in which he handled the continuing Touareg rebellions, but there was no clear candidate emerging for 2012, although forces were becoming mobilised.

This was year of difficult consolidation for Alpha Condé, the veteran 73-year old opposition leader in **Guinea**, who had won convincingly the democratic elections in November 2010 (see AR 2011, p. 242). His election had followed a tense and crisis-bound period of military rule, under first the erratic would-be dictator Captain Dadis Camara, followed by General Sékouba Konaté, who had been keen to withdraw the army from power as soon as possible. Hostility to the military was one of the issues that continued to confront Condé. There were anti-army demonstrations in March, and in May three soldiers were jailed for taking part in an "illegal demonstration" in support of Cellou Dalein Diallo, the defeated candidate in the previous year's elections. Diallo left for overseas in May because he said he felt increasingly insecure in the violent atmosphere which had continued since the elections, which he had alleged were fraudulent.

Tensions in the country were worsened by an attempt to assassinate President Condé in a rocket attack on his residence in Conakry on the night of 18 July. It was followed by a three-hour battle in which three people was killed. The president linked the attack to discontented army officers who had been dismissed early in the year, and hinted that there was complicity by neighbouring countries, which remained to be proven. The situation was not helped by the ruthless suppression of a human rights demonstration on 28 September. Although it had been designated a "day of national reconciliation", the bloody clashes with the police brought to mind similar violence two years previously. The stadium massacre on that date in 2009, in which 157 people died, had precipitated the chain of events which led to the fall of the Dadis Camara military regime (see AR 2010, p. 244).

Condé's troubles were rendered more difficult by ethnic tensions, as Diallo had massive support from the Peulh, the largest ethnic group in the country, now feeling increasingly marginalised and isolated. Many Guineans who had had their hopes raised by Condé's election, warned that escalating violence threatened the democratic process. In early December, legislative elections that had been scheduled for 29 December were postponed by the electoral commission, claiming pressure from opposition parties for a role in the electoral process. Disappointment was greater in that it had been hoped that the new dispensation might finally unlock Guinea's huge economic potential, especially in the mining sector.

The arrest on 13 April of President Laurent Gbagbo of **Côte d'Ivoire** in the presidential palace in the Abidjan suburb of Cocody marked a turning point in the long Ivorian political crisis. This had lasted since the coup d'état of December 1999 and had seen a de facto partition of the country and several periods of low intensity fighting. There were many international dimensions to the conflict, including a French military intervention, which came under a UN peacekeeping force (UNOCI).

The year had begun with one of the country's worst crises after the refusal of President Gbagbo to accept the result of the presidential election of November 2010 (see AR 2011, pp. 242-44). This had given a convincing victory to Gbagbo's main rival, Alassane Ouattara, and was endorsed by the UN and almost all the international community, including African states. Angola and South Africa, however, continued to endorse Gbagbo, claiming that Ouattara's wide backing had been engineered by the French. African intellectuals also protested along the same lines, supporting Gbagbo's claim that the results had been rigged in parts of the north. The UN and the EU implemented an increased sanctions regime against the Gbagbo administration.

While Gbagbo occupied the main institutions of government, Ouattara held out in Abidjan's Golf Hotel, protected by UN troops against attempts by militia to take it. Anti-Gbagbo demonstrations were put down violently, and diplomatic attempts to produce a settlement, such as a unity government or an arranged exile for Gbagbo, proved fruitless. By March the country looked as if it was drifting towards civil war. As Gbagbo's own arguments became more extreme, there was increasing evidence of divisions within the armed forces. Notably, the head of the armed forces, General Philippe Mangou, distanced himself from the regime (though he later returned to the Gbagbo camp).

In the end, it was the former rebel forces (linked to the political movement of the northern "Forces Nouvelles") that ended the crisis. The FRCI (Republican Forces of Côte d'Ivoire), set up by President Ouattara in March in an effort to bring together different warlord-led militias, was ready by the end of that month to make its move rapidly southwards from its headquarters in Bouaké to end the stalemate. The FRCI entered Abidjan on 31 March, and although it met fierce resistance from a hard core of pro-Gbagbo forces, the discreet presence of French troops gave critical backing. This was the rump of Operation Epervier that had been brought in to police the buffer zone in October 2002, and was operating under the umbrella of the 9,000 UN troops.

A crack unit of the FRCI was able to enter the Cocody Palace through a secret passage from the French embassy. This was originally an escape route during the presidency of Félix Houphouët-Boigny and had been used by President Konan Bedié to seek asylum during the coup of 1999. President Gbagbo and his influential wife, Simone, were arrested with members of their inner circle and sent to different points of detention in northern Côte d'Ivoire. Other members of the Gbagbo government sought asylum in Ghana. On 29 November, after a case for prosecution for human rights offences was presented by the International Criminal Court (ICC), Gbagbo was transferred to the Hague to await trial. He and his wife would also face trial in Côte d'Ivoire on charges of looting the treasury, it was stated.

It was expected that there would be other trials after completion of the proceedings of the 11-member Truth and Reconciliation Commission, chaired by a former prime minister, Charles Konan Banny. Members included religious leaders and the star footballer, Chelsea player Didier Drogba, who came from Gbagbo's home area. The commission was one aspect of Ouattara's wider policy of reconciliation and reconstruction set out on 21 May when he was formally sworn in as democratically elected president in the presence of UN Secretary General Ban Ki-Moon, President Sarkozy of France, and a number of African leaders. He called for unity and peace and said, "The new Côte d'Ivoire will be built only on the basis of our core values."

The process of reconciliation proved difficult for the new president when it came to meeting charges of atrocities committed by his supporters, especially in the western part of the country, and bringing some of the pro-Ouattara militias under control. There was also concern that the supporters of Gbagbo's Ivoirian Popular Front (FPI), most of whom were in the southern part of the country, would find it hard to come to terms with defeat. This was seen in the legislative elections of 11 December, which the FPI boycotted, saying they had been intimidated by members of the ruling Rally of the Republicans (RDR) and their newspaper, *Notre Voie*, had been banned. The RDR won 127 seats and its ally, the Cote d'Ivoire Democratic Party (PDCI) of Konan Bedié, won 77 seats. Guillaume Soro, leader of the Forces Nouvelles during the rebellion, was reappointed prime minister, but there was speculation that it might not be possible to have another northerner in the second top job for too long.

As a landlocked Sahelian state, **Burkina Faso** had often survived by playing off a number of countries that were seeking regional influence. Although in the past its southern neighbour, Ghana, had played an important role, the two powers of which most account had to be taken were Libya and Côte d'Ivoire. Both of these went through grave crises of power in 2011. Because of the close ties between Burkina's President Blaise Compaoré and the northern rebels in Côte d'Ivoire, the triumph of Alassane Ouattara in that country was also in a sense a victory for the Burkinabé leader, who in the previous few years had been able to recover his standing with France by acting as peacemaker. Compaoré, despite his earlier closeness to Libya's Moamar Kadhafi, was also able expertly to disengage from the "brother leader" and align himself with the West African states, such as Nigeria, that were strong supporters of the new regime in Tripoli.

The "Arab Spring" was also not without influence in Burkina, as the regime, in power for 24 years, went through a rough patch in public opinion, facing a series of demonstrations. Wisely, the government decided to postpone for one year legislative elections due in May 2012, to permit the introduction of biometric voting.

In May, the Truth and Reconciliation Commission of **Togo** submitted a report on the violence that had occurred in the election of April 2005, the first for President Faure Gnassingbé after coming to power that year. This was not exactly the promised inquiry into the abuses of the dictatorship of Faure's father, Gnassingbé Eyadema, but it played a part in the present government's pursuit of reconciliation with the opposition, still only partly implemented. Troubles in May at the university in Lomé indicated that although the 2010 presidential election had been a much more placid affair this was still a regime with problems, despite a measure of economic recovery.

The key political event of the year was the trial of the president's half-brother, Kpatcha Gnassingbé, a former minister of defence, who was charged with attempting to overthrow the government in 2009. He was jailed for 20 years, along with Ahmed Tijane, a former army chief. Another half-brother, Esizinma Gnassingbé, was acquitted. The trial and sentence helped reinforce the president's position, as it had been felt that he could not always stand up to the stronger personality of Kpatcha, who had important backers in the ethno-military cabal that still governed Togo.

After two short delays because of complaints of people left off electoral lists, presidential elections took place in **Benin** on 13 March in a highly charged atmosphere. The delays had been linked to a computerisation of the electoral list, and days before the vote many voter cards had not been distributed. President Yayi Boni, whose popularity had reportedly declined since his first election five years before, ordered that the vote should go ahead in spite of calls from the opposition for a third postponement. The result gave the president a first round victory with 53.24 per cent, against 35.65 per cent for his main opponent Adrien Houngbedji, who subsequently proclaimed himself president, claiming that more than a million potential voters were missing from the electoral roll. The only other among 14 candidates to secure over 5 per cent was Abdoulaye Bio Tchane, who took 6.14 per cent. The post-election situation was so fraught that the UN secretary general intervened with an appeal to respect the final results.

Elections to the National Assembly (the unicameral legislature), delayed for two weeks to the end of April, helped reinforce the president's position as there was lower turnout due to organisational problems and growing voter apathy. The ruling party, the Cauri Forces for an Emerging Benin (FCBE), obtained 41 seats and Houngbedji's party, Union Makes the Nation (UN), 30 seats. The remaining 12 seats were divided between minority parties.

After the shock treatment of the military takeover of 2010 in **Niger** (see AR 2011, p. 245), the military were able to leave power in February with their heads held high. The elections they organised on 31 January (a year after taking power, as had been promised) were a smoothly democratic exercise that gave 36 per cent to Mahamadou Issoufou, the candidate of the Niger Party for Democracy and Socialism (PNDS), with his nearest rivals Seini Oumarou and Amadou Hama securing about 23 and 19 per cent respectively. In a second round on 12 March, Issoufou secured first place through some skilful alliance-making with some of the smaller parties. Issoufou's party had already obtained 39 seats out of 113 in the National Assembly elections, which were held parallel to the first round of the presidential poll, but the party had a number of allies which would help with an overall majority.

President Issoufou was sworn in on 7 April, and the outgoing military head of the Supreme Council for the Restoration of Democracy, General Salou Djibo, received a tribute from his successor for the transparency and honesty with which the elections had been organised. The renewal of institutions was completed with the swearing in of Amadou Hama as president of the National Assembly.

The new government was faced with serious challenges. Notably Niger had to face the annual problem of food shortages arising from persistent drought and desertification, which in 2011 triggered a number of famine alerts from relief organisations. There was also a growing threat from AQIM, which had targeted Niger, making it one of the countries most vulnerable to the taking of hostages from among Westerners working there, especially in the increasingly valuable uranium mines in the north. Niger also had to cope with the side effects of the civil war in Libya, including increased circulation of arms in the Sahel region and the aggravation of Touareg dissidence in both Niger and Mali.

Speaking in London in December, Foreign Minister Mamadou Bazoum said that Niger had considered attacking Touareg rebels within Mali who had been fighting for Libya's leader Moamar Kadhafi, but that talks with Mali had led to a stepping up of counter-terrorist co-operation. One of Kadhafi's less politically-minded sons, Saadi, had been given temporary asylum in Niger in September, but there was a strong disinclination to accommodate more controversial figures. Bazoum said that, on top of drought problems, his country was also having to cope with the return of 250,000 Nigeriens who had been working in Libya.

Kaye Whiteman

CAMEROON—CHAD—GABON—CONGO—CENTRAL AFRICAN REPUBLIC—EQUATORIAL GUINEA

Cameroon

CAPITAL: Yaoundé   AREA: 475,440 sq km   POPULATION: 19,598,889 ('10)
OFFICIAL LANGUAGES: French & English
HEAD OF STATE AND GOVERNMENT: President Paul Biya (since Nov '82)
RULING PARTY: Cameroon People's Democratic Movement (RDPC)
PRIME MINISTER: Yang Philemon (since July '09)
DEMOCRACY INDEX: 3.41; 126th of 167   CORRUPTION INDEX: 2.5; 134th of 183
CURRENCY: Central African CFA Franc (Dec '11 £1.00=XAF 763, US$1.00=XAF 487)
GNI PER CAPITA: US$1,180, Intl$2,230 at PPP ('10)

Chad

CAPITAL: Ndjaména   AREA: 1,284,000 sq km   POPULATION: 11,227,208 ('10)
OFFICIAL LANGUAGES: French & Arabic
HEAD OF STATE AND GOVERNMENT: President (Col.) Idriss Déby (MPS) (since Dec '90)
RULING PARTIES: Patriotic Salvation Movement (MPS)
PRIME MINISTER: Emmanuel Nadingar (MPS) (since March '10)
DEMOCRACY INDEX: 1.52; 166th of 167   CORRUPTION INDEX: 2.0; 168th of 183
CURRENCY: Central African CFA Franc (see above)
GNI PER CAPITA: US$620, Intl$1,210 at PPP ('10)

Gabon

CAPITAL: Libreville   AREA: 267,670 sq km   POPULATION: 1,505,463 ('10)
OFFICIAL LANGUAGE: French
HEAD OF STATE AND GOVERNMENT: President Ali-Ben Bongo Ondimba (since Oct '09)
RULING PARTY: Gabonese Democratic Party (PDG)
PRIME MINISTER: Paul Biyoghe Mba (since July '09)
DEMOCRACY INDEX: 3.29; 133rd of 167   CORRUPTION INDEX: 3.0; 100th of 183
CURRENCY: Central African CFA Franc (see above)
GNI PER CAPITA: US$7,740, Intl$13,150 at PPP ('10)

Congo

CAPITAL: Brazzaville   AREA: 342,000 sq km   POPULATION: 4,042,899 ('10)
OFFICIAL LANGUAGE: French
HEAD OF STATE AND GOVERNMENT: President Denis Sassou Nguesso (PCT) (since Oct '97)
RULING PARTY: Congolese Labour Party (PCT)
DEMOCRACY INDEX: 2.89; 142nd of 167   CORRUPTION INDEX: 2.2; 154th of 183
CURRENCY: Central African CFA Franc (see above)
GNI PER CAPITA: US$2,150, Intl$3,050 at PPP ('10)

Central African Republic

CAPITAL: Bangui   AREA: 623,000 sq km   POPULATION: 4,401,051 ('10)
OFFICIAL LANGUAGE: French
HEAD OF STATE AND GOVERNMENT: President Gen. François Bozizé (since March '03)
RULING PARTY: National Convergence "Kwa Na Kwa" (KNK) coalition
PRIME MINISTER: Faustin-Archange Touadera (since Jan '08)
DEMOCRACY INDEX: 1.82; 162nd of 167   CORRUPTION INDEX: 2.2; 154th of 183
CURRENCY: Central African CFA Franc (see above)
GNI PER CAPITA: US$470, Intl$780 at PPP ('10)

Equatorial Guinea

CAPITAL: Malabo   AREA: 28,050 sq km   POPULATION: 700,401 ('10)
OFFICIAL LANGUAGES: Spanish & French
HEAD OF STATE AND GOVERNMENT: President (Brig.-Gen.) Teodoro Obiang Nguema Mbasogo (since
    Aug '79)
RULING PARTY: Equatorial Guinea Democratic Party (PDGE)
PRIME MINISTER: Ignacio Milam Tang (since July '08)
DEMOCRACY INDEX: 1.84; 60th of 167   CORRUPTION INDEX: 1.9; 172nd of 183
CURRENCY: Central African CFA Franc (see above)
GNI PER CAPITA: US$14,540, Intl$23,570 at PPP ('10)

IN hotly contested elections on 9 October, 78-year old Paul Biya won with nearly 78 per cent of the vote, the largest tally he had ever received in his 29 years leading **Cameroon**. According to the Supreme Court, his nearest rival was John Fru Ndi with 10.71 per cent of the vote. Fru Ndi had stood against Biya in all four elections since multi-party democracy was introduced in 1990. None of the 21 other candidates took more than just over 3 per cent. The results were rejected by Biya's opponents, who alleged fraud, an accusation raised at each previous election.

There was considerable disorganisation and some violence reported during the vote, but in most parts of the country it took place peacefully. Both the International Organisation of Francophonie (OIF) and the Commonwealth observer teams found no obvious violations. There was, however, disbelief among many Cameroonians at the result, which charitably could only be explained by an increasing desire for stability, at the cost of an ossified system and economic stagnation. Since presidential terms had been extended to seven years, and in 2018 Biya would be 85, many felt that by then (assuming he lived that long) the system would have to be shaken up. The message from the elections of 2011, however, was "not now".

Presidential elections in **Chad** in April saw incumbent President Idriss Déby Itno returned to power with a first-round majority of 83.59 per cent. He was only opposed by leaders of two minor parties: Albert Pahimi Padacké, who won 8.6 per cent, and Nadji Madou (7.81 per cent). The main opposition leaders, such as Abdelkader Kamougué, Ngarlejy Yorongar and Saleh Kebzabo, had all withdrawn from the poll after they charged that Déby's Patriotic Salvation Movement (MPS) had won legislative elections in February by fraudulent means, including the hasty issuing of new voters' cards. The MPS had obtained 113 of the 188 National Assembly seats. The remainder were divided between a large number of political parties. Chad had more than 100 fragmented and under-funded parties; moreover, it was the first time legislative elections had been contested for over 10 years.

Relations with Chad's eastern neighbour, Sudan, once a persistent source of conflict, showed further signs of improvement during the year. A joint Chad-Sudan military force stepped up its activities policing the border, and in May there was a tripartite summit in Ndjaména with Sudan and Central African Republic (CAR), which joined the joint military operation. The summit discussed border security, in view of continued conflict in Sudan's Darfur province still adding to the numbers in refugee camps in both Chad and CAR. The small UN force MIN-

URCAT (UN Mission in CAR and Chad), which monitored the refugee camps, had been wound up at the end of 2010, and there was concern in humanitarian circles that the new friendship between the leaders of Chad and Sudan might make the monitoring exercise more difficult.

Chad also felt the effect of the Libyan war, although the departure of Colonel Kadhafi was something of a relief for Libya's immediate southern neighbour. In an interview in December, President Déby said that as many as 150,000 Chadians, mainly from the Toubou ethnic group which spanned the border, had returned home from Libya

In **Gabon** frictions from the presidential elections of 2009 spilled over into an argument on how soon legislative elections were to be held. It had originally been decided that elections due in December 2011 should not be held until December 2012, because of the need to implement satisfactorily biometric polling. It was later decided that the polls should go ahead in 2011, without biometric voting, although the opposition parties and civil society opponents in a grouping called "ça suffit comme ça" (that's enough of that) maintained support for the delay.

Frontier problems with both Cameroon and Equatorial Guinea led to talks with both countries, but left the problems apparently unresolved. The matter was contentious because Gabon's offshore waters still contained large deposits of unexploited oil.

It was a quiet political year for **Republic of Congo**, with only indirect Senate (upper house) elections in October, in which the ruling Congolese Labour Party (PCT) of President Denis Sassou Nguesso consolidated its position.

In the same month the National Commission against Fraud, Corruption and Embezzlement said that corruption had cost the country over $100 million between 2003 and 2007. The commission's secretary, Laurence Tengo, said that it was getting worse but it was also no longer taboo to talk about it. President Sassou Nguesso was also under international pressure from allegations made by Transparency International and a French group, CCFD-Terre Solidaire, that he possessed 16 properties in Paris, worth millions of euro. The charges (which also cited the presidents of Gabon and Equatorial Guinea) were contained in a dossier presented to French prosecutors.

On 2 February, President François Bozizé was declared winner of the 23 January presidential elections in **Central African Republic** with a majority of over 66 per cent. His main opponent was Ange-Félix Patassé, who received just over 20 per cent. The third main candidate was Martin Ziguélé, who obtained 6.46 per cent of the votes. It was Bozizé's second election, having stood in 2005 following his seizure of power from Patassé two years before. Patassé himself stood for the last time in 2011, as he died in March from diabetes.

According to the UN Office for the Co-ordination of Humanitarian Affairs (OCHSA), a series of political crises, coups and rebellions, and deficient governance had left the country with its health services in tatters and a large percentage of the population vulnerable to disease. Rebellion in the north-east and insecurity on the borders with both Chad and Sudan had driven nearly 200,000 displaced persons—many from the troubled Darfur region—into refugee camps.

The tenor of the year for **Equatorial Guinea** was set at the summit of the African Union in Addis Ababa, Ethiopia, in January, at which it was decided that the country should hold the chair for the next one year, and host the summit in its capital, Malabo, in June. Although the AU (like the Organisation of African Unity before it) had had some fairly awkward customers in its chair before—notably Uganda's Idi Amin and, on two occasions, Libya's Moamar Kadhafi—this was the first time that Equatorial Guinea had deemed itself fit for such a role.

Some argued that to have this kind of international responsibility would help bring a regime with a notorious human rights record in from the cold, but there were still some raised eyebrows. Fears were confirmed with the intensive security clampdown prior to the June summit. According to Amnesty International, political opponents and over 100 students had been arrested in the period prior to the summit and been badly treated in prison. There was also an increased number of roadblocks in Malabo, and more arbitrary stop-and-search operations. Police raids on foreign neighbourhoods in the port city of Bata intensified just before the summit, and "undocumented foreign nationals" were arrested. There was also a news blackout on state-owned television of all reports on the "Arab Spring", especially the fighting in Libya. News of events in Côte d'Ivoire was also suppressed.

Security was at its highest around the new city of Sipopo, several miles outside Malabo, with 52 villas for heads of state, a conference centre, a heliport, shopping and medical centres, a 200-room Sofitel hotel, an 18-hole golf course and an artificial beach. The cost was reported to have been more $500 million and it was intended for subsequent use as a tourist resort. It also attempted to give a new image to one of Africa's most deeply unattractive regimes.

This, it seemed, might become an uphill struggle as the president, Teodoro Obiang Nguema Mbasogo, in power since 1979, was increasingly subject to publicity over his ill-gotten wealth. Transparency International put reports to French prosecutors that indicated he owned a number of expensive properties in Paris, including a six-storey block on the Avenue Foch worth $15 million. Stories of corruption involving the president's playboy son, Teodorin, included his attempts early in 2011 to buy a $300 million super yacht, and reports that he had spent, in one year, more than twice the national education budget on luxury goods. In October the US department of justice unsealed an asset forfeiture claim against a $30 million house in Malibu, a Gulfstream jet, and other assets belonging to Teodorin. The USA, where oil companies such as Mobil were prominent in exploiting Equatorial Guinea's petroleum resources, was openly expressing alarm that the ageing president (who would turn 70 in 2012) was still planning for Teodorin to succeed him. But in such an autocracy, ruled by a family clique, anything was possible.

Kaye Whiteman

CAPE VERDE—GUINEA-BISSAU—SÃO TOMÉ & PRÍNCIPE

Cape Verde

CAPITAL: Praia   AREA: 4,030 sq km   POPULATION: 495,999 ('10)
OFFICIAL LANGUAGE: Portuguese
HEAD OF STATE: President Jorge Carlos Fonseca (MpD) (since Sept '11)
RULING PARTY: African Party for the Independence of Cape Verde (PAICV)
HEAD OF GOVERNMENT: Prime Minister José Maria Pereira Neves (PAICV) (since Feb '01)
DEMOCRACY INDEX: 7.94; 27th of 167   CORRUPTION INDEX: 5.5; 41st of 183
CURRENCY: CV Escudo (Dec '11 £1.00=CVE 124.58, US$1.00=CVE 79.44)
GNI PER CAPITA: US$3,270, Intl$3,790 at PPP ('10)

Guinea-Bissau

CAPITAL: Bissau   AREA: 36,120 sq km   POPULATION: 1,515,224 ('10)
OFFICIAL LANGUAGE: Portuguese
HEAD OF STATE AND GOVERNMENT: President Malam Bacai Sanha (PAIGC) (since Sept '09)
RULING PARTY: African Party for the Independence of Guinea Bissau and Cape Verde (PAIGC)
PRIME MINISTER: Carlos Gomes Junior (PAIGC) (since Jan '09)
DEMOCRACY INDEX: 1.99; 157th of 167   CORRUPTION INDEX: 2.2; 154th of 183
CURRENCY: West African CFA Franc (Dec '11 £1.00=XOF 763, US$1=XOF 487)
GNI PER CAPITA: US$590, Intl$1,180 at PPP ('10)

São Tomé e Príncipe

CAPITAL: São Tomé   AREA: 960 sq km   POPULATION: 165,397 ('10)
OFFICIAL LANGUAGE: Portuguese
HEAD OF STATE AND GOVERNMENT: President Manuel Pinto da Costa (ind.) (since Sept '11)
RULING PARTIES: Independent Democratic Alliance (ADI)-led coalition
PRIME MINISTER: Patrice Emery Trovoada (ADI) (since Aug '10)
CORRUPTION INDEX: 3.0; 100th of 183
CURRENCY: Dobra (Dec '11 £1.00=STD 28,487, US$1.00=STD 18,165)
GNI PER CAPITA: US$1,200, Intl$1,910 ('10)

THE reputation of **Cape Verde** as one of Africa's most stable democracies was enhanced in 2011, a year in which both legislative and presidential elections were held peacefully. In the legislative election, in February, the ruling African Party for the Independence of Cape Verde (PAICV) gained a majority in the National Assembly by winning 38 seats to the 32 won by the Movement for Democracy (MpD). Having been president for two consecutive terms, Pedro Pires of the PAICV was not eligible to stand in the country's fifth presidential election. In the first round, none of the four candidates achieved enough votes for outright victory. Jorge Carlos Fonseca of the MpD and Manuel Inocencio Sousa of the PAICV campaigned against each other in the second round. In the decisive election on 21 August, Fonseca polled 54.2 per cent of the vote. Sousa, who won 45.8 per cent, immediately conceded defeat. Fonseca, who then had to govern with a PAICV prime minister, promised measures to attract foreign investment and boost tourism, both sorely needed, given the island state's lack of resources and fragile ecology.

Towards the end of the year Pires, the former president, was awarded the $5 million Mo Ibrahim Foundation African Leadership Prize, given to African leaders who voluntarily left office after demonstrating a commitment to good governance.

On Pires's watch, Cape Verde had experienced sound economic growth and become recognised as a middle-income country.

In December Cesária Évora, known as the "barefoot diva", who had made the music of her country popular around the world and became Cape Verde's leading unofficial ambassador, died in her home town of Mindelo, on the island of São Vicente, at the age of 70.

Though **Guinea-Bissau** remained one of the poorest countries in the world—placed by the UN 175th out of 177 countries in its Human Development Index—it saw relative political stability until the last week of the year. However, there were tensions between President Malam Bacai Sanhá and Prime Minister Carlos Gomes Júnior. In July thousands demonstrated against Gomes for hindering a probe into the 2009 assassinations of the former president, João Vieira, and others (see AR 2010, p. 253). Sanhá, who left the country on several occasions during the year for medical treatment, nevertheless retained Gomes in his post when he reshuffled the cabinet in August.

The Community of Portuguese-Speaking Countries (CPLP) and the Economic Community of West African States (ECOWAS) helped to prepare a road map for reform of the security sector in Guinea-Bissau, and Angola provided support for the restructuring of the armed forces. Guinea-Bissau's international debt was cut by 87 per cent and production of the country's main crop, cashew nuts, increased significantly. This positive news was tempered by the fact that drug trafficking continued, with Guinea-Bissau a transit point for drugs shipped from Latin America to Europe, as did food shortages. Gomes's announcement in September that Guinea-Bissau would give refuge to Colonel Moamar Kadhafi, Libya's ousted leader, did not enhance the country's reputation.

Then, in the last week of December, Rear-Admiral Bubo Na Tchuto, who had been accused of drug trafficking by the EU and the USA, attempted a military coup. Rebel soldiers stormed the headquarters of the armed forces in the capital, Bissau, and Gomes had to flee to the Angolan embassy for safety. The coup attempt failed, however, and Tchuto was arrested. President Sanhá remained abroad undergoing medical treatment, with his country near the bottom of most economic and health indices. Life-expectancy was only 46 years, most people lived without electricity or clean water, and there were few job opportunities for young people. On 9 January, 2012, Sanhá died in a Paris hospital.

The key political event of 2011 for **São Tomé and Príncipe** was the presidential election. Having served two consecutive five-year terms as president, Fradique de Menezes was not eligible for a third term. In the first round there was no clear winner, but in the run-off, which took place peacefully in August, Manuel Pinto da Costa won 53 per cent of the vote to the 47 per cent cast for his main rival, Evaristo Carvalho of the ruling Independent Democratic Alliance (ADI).

Da Costa, who had ruled the archipelago from its independence in 1975 until the first multi-party elections in 1991, now promised to tackle the island state's endemic poverty. Half the population of 170,000 continued to live below the poverty line and the economy remained highly dependent on foreign aid and agriculture, although vast oil fields had been discovered off-shore. The challenge for the new president would be to tap into the potential oil bonanza without destabilising the country, while at the same time diversifying the economy.

Christopher Saunders

VII CENTRAL AND SOUTHERN AFRICA

DEMOCRATIC REPUBLIC OF CONGO—BURUNDI AND RWANDA—
MOZAMBIQUE—ANGOLA

DEMOCRATIC REPUBLIC OF CONGO

CAPITAL: Kinshasa   AREA: 2,344,860 sq km   POPULATION: 65,965,795 ('10)
OFFICIAL LANGUAGE: French
HEAD OF STATE AND GOVERNMENT: President Joseph Kabila (APM) (since Jan '01)
RULING PARTY: Alliance for the Presidential Majority (APM) coalition
PRIME MINISTER: Aldophe Muzito (since Oct '08)
DEMOCRACY INDEX: 2.15; 155th of 167   CORRUPTION INDEX: 2.0; 168th of 183
CURRENCY: Congo Franc (Dec '11 £1.00=CDF 1,375.77, US$1.00=CDF 877.26)
GNI PER CAPITA: US$180, Intl$320 at PPP ('10)

THE second presidential elections in the DRC since the end of fighting in 2002 were held on 28 November. After a lengthy delay, the National Independent Electoral Commission (CENI) announced on 9 December that incumbent President Joseph Kabila had won a second mandate with 49 per cent of the vote, defeating the runner-up, 79-year-old Étienne Tshisekedi wa Mulumba, with 32 per cent. The announcement was followed by violent protests and some looting in the capital, Kinshasa, an opposition stronghold. The Atlanta-based Carter Center stated that the voting was "too flawed to be credible" and European Union observers pointed to "serious deficiencies". France, the USA and the local Catholic Church (which deployed 30,000 monitors), were also highly critical, although stopping short of calling for a re-run. On 23 December Tshisekedi attempted to have himself declared president by holding a "swearing in" ceremony at a football stadium, but was prevented by police who used tear gas to disperse his supporters.

The 30-day campaign period before the elections was marred by fatalities and arbitrary arrests, with the government closing some opposition radio stations and banning public meetings in some areas. On the eve of the campaign, a coalition of 41 organisations issued a statement calling for increased security to prevent violence, but CENI refused to consider opposition calls for a postponement. Just before the announcement of the results, several thousand Kinshasa residents fled by ferry to Brazzaville in the neighbouring Republic of Congo to escape anticipated violence.

The security situation in eastern Congo, described as a "quagmire", remained serious, especially in Ituri and both North and South Kivu provinces, as approximately eight different local militias and splinter groups continued to battle with units of the Congolese army, the Armed Forces of the Democratic Republic of Congo (FARDC). Some of the groups numbered fewer than 100 armed men. Sexual violence remained a prominent feature of the conflict, with one study, later disputed, estimating that 400,000 women had been raped in an earlier 12-month period. Reports also emerged for the first time of sexual violence and rape being used as a weapon of war against men in the Kivus.

In October the United States agreed to send 100 military advisors to the DRC border with South Sudan and Uganda to assist in operations against the Lord's

Resistance Army (LRA), a fanatically religious rebel group responsible for the killing of several thousand villagers and the enforced conscription of even more. Ugandan-led military operations against the group had been largely ineffective.

Cholera and measles threatened to run out of control in several parts of the country throughout the year. A cholera outbreak in the town of Kisangani in the eastern DRC was aggravated by heavy rains that slowed a chlorination project, and vaccination programmes against measles were hampered by population movements as people fled from local militias. In July the World Health Organisation reported over 115,000 cases of measles in seven provinces, with 1,100 deaths, despite the vaccination of nearly 6 million children in previous months. In October, confirmed cases of cholera, spread by poor hygienic conditions and dirty water, had climbed to nearly 7,000, with just under 300 deaths.

In April, the Dodd-Frank Act came into force in the United States. Among other provisions, this required US manufacturers to report the sources of supply of key "conflict minerals" such as coltan, wolframite and cassiterite. The minerals, essential components of mobile phones and other portable electronic devices, were mined mainly in the eastern DRC and constituted a major source of revenue for local militias. According to some estimates, up to 80 per cent of production was being smuggled out of the country, mainly through Rwanda. Some former rebels claimed in December, however, that the regulations would only push the trade deeper into criminal control, and export figures at year's end indicated a sharp drop of up to 90 per cent in production as major companies such as Apple backed off Congolese supplies. The government introduced a code of conduct in March in an attempt to control artisanal mining. The regulations banned barter trade in minerals and prohibited the use of child labour.

The trials for war crimes and human rights abuses of Thomas Lubanga Dyilo, former Congolese vice-president Jean-Pierre Bemba, and militiamen Mathieu Ngudjolo and Germain Katanga at the International Criminal Court (ICC) in the Hague continued to make slow progress throughout the year, with a judgment expected only in the Lubanga case. Commentators disagreed on the effectiveness of the ICC as a deterrent, but after the DRC elections in December Luis Moreno-Ocampo, chief prosecutor at the ICC, warned Congolese politicians that "electoral violence is no longer a ticket to power, I assure you. It is a ticket to The Hague."

In February an IMF representative expressed cautious optimism about economic growth, praising an "improved business climate". Inflation had slowed, the exchange rate had settled down and the 2010 debt reduction, of $12 billion, had had a positive effect. The IMF official dismissed fears that fiscal discipline might suffer in an election year.

Before the elections, the UN Security Council extended the mandate of MONUSCO, the stabilisation mission in the DRC, until 30 June 2012, and also renewed the arms embargo and related sanctions until the end of November 2012. In April, 32 UN employees died when their aircraft crashed in heavy rain while attempting to land at Kinshasa airport. There was one survivor.

Colin Darch

BURUNDI AND RWANDA

Burundi

CAPITAL: Bujumbura   AREA: 27,830 sq km   POPULATION: 8,382,849 ('10)
OFFICIAL LANGUAGES: French & Kirundi
HEAD OF STATE AND GOVERNMENT: President Pierre Nkurunziza (CNDD-FDD) (since Aug '05)
RULING PARTY: National Council for the Defence of Democracy-Forces for the Defence of
   Democracy (CNDD-FDD)
DEMOCRACY INDEX: 4.01; 110 of 167   CORRUPTION INDEX: 1.9; 172nd of 183
CURRENCY: Burundi Franc (Dec '11 £1.00=BIF 2,088, US$1.00=BIF 1,332)
GNI PER CAPITA: US$170, Intl$400 at PPP ('10)

Rwanda

CAPITAL: Kigali   AREA: 26,340 sq km   POPULATION: 10,624,005 ('10)
OFFICIAL LANGUAGES: French, Kinyarwanda & English
HEAD OF STATE AND GOVERNMENT: President Paul Kagame (RPF) (since April '00)
RULING PARTIES: Rwandan Patriotic Front (FPR)-led coalition
PRIME MINISTER: Pierre Habumuremyi (since Oct '11)
DEMOCRACY INDEX: 3.25; 134th of 167   CORRUPTION INDEX: 5.0; 49th of 183
CURRENCY: Rwanda Franc (Dec '11 £1.00=RWF 945.39, US$1.00=RWF 602.83)
GNI PER CAPITA: US$520, Intl$1,150 at PPP ('10)

IN a deadly attack in September, unidentified men in military uniform machine-gunned a crowded bar in Gatumba, near **Burundi's** capital Bujumbura, killing over 40 people and wounding another 15. The attack was the worst in a period marred by sporadic assassinations in the aftermath of disputed elections in mid-2010.

Despite initial suggestions that the shooting was the work of the rebel National Liberation Forces (FNL), led by exiled Agathon Rwasa, no evidence emerged to support this, and in a subsequent trial in December one of the 20 defendants implicated three senior police officers, although judges declined to summon them. In November, former policeman Pierre-Claver Kabirigi announced the formation of a new rebel group, the Abanyagihugu Front for the Restoration of Democracy (FRD-Abanyagihugu).

In December, in a resolution sponsored by France and passed unanimously, the UN Security Council noted its "grave concern" over the role of the Burundi security forces in extra-judicial killings, totalling 57 deaths up to November. The UN called on President Pierre Nkurunziza to bring those responsible to justice. The Security Council also extended the mandate of the United Nations Integrated Office in Burundi (BINUB) until mid-February 2013, demanding the "thorough, credible, impartial and transparent investigation of serious crimes".

In a separate incident in July, a farm belonging to the president was attacked with grenades and fires were set, causing some damage.

Food insecurity, including high prices, and public health problems continued to trouble the country. In March heavy rains and hailstorms destroyed cassava, banana and other crops in Ruyigi province, with 40,000 people needing food aid. In August and September a cholera outbreak in the south spread rapidly to other areas, with an estimated 600 infections reported.

Burundi climbed several places in the World Bank's "Doing Business" ranking, to 169th out of 183 countries. Simplified bureaucratic procedures led to an increase in foreign direct investment in 2011, with 4 per cent growth to $104 million. Most of the investments were in tourism and agro-business. Coffee remained the top foreign-exchange-earning crop, although aging bushes, planted in colonial times, produced a yield of only 13,000 tonnes in the 2010-11 season. Around 48 per cent of the national budget was funded by foreign donors.

Some 4,000 troops from Burundi continued to serve with the African Union peace-keeping mission in Somalia, AMISOM; in February it was reported that the soldiers were complaining that salaries were being paid five months in arrears.

President Paul Kagame of **Rwanda** struck an upbeat note in his end of year message to the nation for 2011, claiming an 8.8 per cent growth rate and inflation under 7.4 per cent for the year, despite turmoil in the global economy. The governor of the National Bank of Rwanda, Claver Gatete, announced in December that he was planning to issue seven-to-ten-year bonds in the near future. The government also announced plans to provide programmes for the basic health care and educational needs of "each and every Rwandan". Systematic reform of business regulations with World Bank support began in 2001, and the bank's latest "Doing Business" report identified the country as the world's best performer, jumping 76 places to 67th out of a total of 183 nations.

In September, President Kagame began to mend broken links with France, after having broken off diplomatic relations in 2006 amidst accusations that France had "played an active part" in preparing the 1994 genocide. Meeting with President Nicolas Sarkozy in Paris, the Anglophone Kagame spoke cautiously of "a new relationship"; the French president had earlier admitted to "errors of judgement" during a visit to Kigali in 2010.

Ignace Murwanashyaka, a former leader of the Democratic Forces for the Liberation of Rwanda (FDLR), and his deputy Straton Musoni went on trial in May in Germany on a total of 65 charges of crimes against humanity and war crimes. The trial was the first under a new German law covering crimes committed on foreign soil. In December, Callixte Mbarushimana, also a former leader of the FDLR, was acquitted at the International Criminal Court in The Hague of charges of murder, torture and rape in the Democratic Republic of Congo, and released. He returned to France, where he was detained subject to strict parole conditions while further charges were investigated.

At year's end the UN High Commissioner for Refugees (UNHCR) invoked a "cessation clause", allowing host countries to revoke the refugee status of Rwandans by mid-2012. But both former militia members and civilian refugees—hosted mainly in the Congo, the DRC, Kenya, Malawi, South Africa, Uganda and Zambia—remained reluctant, citing a lack of guarantees of safety.

In December it was reported that mountain gorillas, which constituted the country's major attraction for tourism, were showing signs of increasing their numbers, registering a three-fold growth to nearly 800 individuals, including infants. Visitors typically paid up to $500 for a permit to observe gorilla families in the wild.

Colin Darch

MOZAMBIQUE

CAPITAL: Maputo   AREA: 799,380 sq km   POPULATION: 23,390,765 ('10)
OFFICIAL LANGUAGE: Portuguese
HEAD OF STATE: President Armando Emilio Guebuza (Frelimo) (since Feb '05)
RULING PARTY: Front for the Liberation of Mozambique (Frelimo)
HEAD OF GOVERNMENT: Prime Minister Aires Bonifacio Aly (since Jan '10)
DEMOCRACY INDEX: 4.90; 99th of 167   CORRUPTION INDEX: 2.7; 120th of 183
CURRENCY: Metical (Dec '11 £1.00=MZN 41.74, US$1.00=MZN 26.61)
GNI PER CAPITA: US$440, Intl$920 at PPP ('10)

DESPITE its low world ranking in terms of overall poverty and inequality, the country maintained the rapid economic growth that it had sustained over the previous 15 years, in the range of 7 to 8 per cent per year. President Armando Guebuza continued to focus on the struggle against poverty and inequality as the country's main challenge, stating in May that "the right not to be poor is our right and it's a human right".

In October economic prospects received a boost when the Italian energy company, Eni, announced that it had discovered a very large field of natural gas in the Indian Ocean about 2,000 km north of the capital, Maputo. The field was believed to contain as much as 425 billion cubic metres of gas. In May the Brazilian mining company, Vale S.A., began to operate its large open-cast coal mine in Moatize, exporting a first shipment of 35,000 tonnes along the Sena railway to Beira port. The mine, which employed around 8,000 workers, most of them Mozambicans, was described as "one of the last great unexploited coal basins in the world". In November, Prime Minister Aires Aly announced that total exports in the first six months of 2011 were valued at $1.3 billion, just over half of the targeted total for the whole year.

The Mozambican policy of reliance on "mega-projects", such as the Mozal aluminium smelter, the Sasol natural gas project in Inhambane, and the Kenmare heavy mineral sands project in Nampula, came in for criticism from local economists in January for allowing excessive tax breaks to foreign interests and for inadequate investment in infrastructure.

The government continued to take action against corruption, and in March a former minister of the interior, Almerino Manhenje, and two of his deputies, Rosário Fidelis and Álvaro de Carvalho, were sentenced to prison terms on counts of ignoring budget regulations, abuse of power and making unauthorised payments. More serious charges had been dropped for lack of evidence.

In February heavy rains caused flooding in the central province of Manica, but by the end of the month the government had downgraded a "red alert" to orange for southern and central rivers—the Incomati, the Limpopo, the Save, the Pungoe, the Buzi and the Licungo. Food security remained a preoccupation, but nonetheless the government announced in May that it would be phasing out the subsidies for such staples as maize, flour, rice, fish, beans, groundnuts, vegetable oil and bread by the end of June. A similar attempt to remove subsidies had provoked serious rioting in September 2010 (see AR 2010, p. 257).

President Guebuza visited Portugal in November and met Prime Minister Pedro Passos Coelho, but the two sides failed for "technical and financial motives" to reach final agreement over the outstanding issue of Portugal's continuing 15 per cent stake in the Cahora Bassa dam. Co-operation agreements were signed on the issues of gender and diplomatic archives, with a stated intention to extend bilateral co-operation into other spheres.

Three mayoral elections were held in northern cities in December, with Manuel de Araújo of the Mozambique Democratic Movement (MDM) winning power in Quelimane, while Frelimo candidates held on in Pemba and Cuamba. Voter turnout was low, topping 25 per cent only in Quelimane.

Tensions rose along the northern border with Tanzania in the first part of the year as large numbers of Somali and Ethiopian refugees crossed the Rovuma river into the country. The refugees had been brought by boat down the coast and dropped off in Mtwara, south-eastern Tanzania, to trek the last distance on foot but reportedly were beaten and robbed by locals, who forced them back into Tanzania. In May the government had introduced strict controls on the movement of asylum seekers, confining them to camps in the northern provinces.

On 19 October, at a ceremony to mark the 25th anniversary of the death of former President Samora Machel in the air disaster at Mbuzini (see AR 1986, p. 249), President Guebuza repeated accusations that Machel had been murdered by South Africa's then minority apartheid regime. Following "repeated public threats" against the president by senior South African officials, stated Guebuza, Machel's plane "was diverted from its flight path" by a false navigational beacon.

Beginning on 3 September, the Maputo suburb of Zimpeto hosted the 10th edition of the All-Africa Games, which were opened by President Guebuza in a colourful ceremony that concluded with a 10-minute firework display. The games ended two weeks later with Mozambique having won four silver medals and eight bronze in nine sporting disciplines including athletics, boxing and basketball.

The Mozambican artist Malangatana Valente Ngwenha (1936-2011) died in Portugal at the age of 74. Widely known simply as Malangatana, he had been active in the liberation struggle with Frelimo and was imprisoned by the Portuguese colonial secret police in the 1960s. He was given a state funeral.

Colin Darch

ANGOLA

CAPITAL: Luanda   AREA: 1,246,700 sq km   POPULATION: 19,081,912 ('10)
OFFICIAL LANGUAGE: Portuguese
HEAD OF STATE AND GOVERNMENT: President José Eduardo dos Santos (MPLA) (since Sept '79)
RULING PARTIES: Popular Movement for the Liberation of Angola-Workers' Party (MPLA) heads
    nominal coalition
DEMOCRACY INDEX: 3.32; 131st of 167   CORRUPTION INDEX: 2.0; 168th of 183
CURRENCY: Readj. Kwanza (Dec-'11 £1.00=AOA 148.91, US$1.00=AOA 94.95)
GNI PER CAPITA: US$3,940, Intl$5,400 at PPP ('10)

IN 2011 influential members of the ruling Popular Movement for the Liberation of Angola (MPLA), which held its fourth extraordinary congress in Luanda in April, started talking about plans for the succession to its leader, the 69-year-old José

Eduardo dos Santos, who had been president of the country for 32 years. The decision would now be an entirely party one, as the constitution of 2010 provided that presidents would be chosen by majority party in the National Assembly (the unicameral legislature), in which the MPLA had 82 per cent of the seats (see AR 2011, p. 259).

The impact of the "Arab Spring" began to be felt in Angola from late February, first with an online protest movement calling for change. Beginning in March small groups of protestors took to the streets of Luanda. That month President dos Santos was widely criticised for his support of Laurent Gbagbo, then trying to cling on to power in Côte d'Ivoire. In September the Angolan government violently suppressed a rally in which mostly young protestors openly called for an end to dos Santos's rule and rejected the proposed amendments to the electoral law. Though the MPLA blamed the main opposition party—the National Union for the Total Independence of Angola (UNITA)—for the protests, the demonstrators appeared not to be politically affiliated. The state-controlled media strongly condemned the protests, but in October the Supreme Court ordered those arrested after the September protest to be freed because of lack of evidence. In his state of the nation address to the National Assembly that month, dos Santos denied that Angola was ruled by a dictatorial regime and confirmed that there would be a legislative election at the end of 2012. While he did not say whether he would lead his party into the election, he said that he would accept any mission his party asked him to undertake. In December the various political parties finally agreed, after much haggling, on a new electoral law, with UNITA failing to achieve an independent electoral commission. In an end-of-year speech, dos Santos promised that a well-organised, transparent and fair election to the National Assembly would be held in late 2012.

With the vice president, Fernando Dias dos Santos, in poor health, the name most often mentioned as a successor, one who would be likely to maintain the status quo and keep oil investors happy, was that of Manuel Vicente, a close friend of the president. Vicente said he would step down as chief executive of the state oil company, Sonangol, at the end of 2011. Angola remained sub-Saharan Africa's second-largest exporter of crude oil, making its economy the third largest after those of South Africa and Nigeria. With oil exports continuing to bring in vast sums, the country's reserves reached record highs. Angola remained a very closed society, but it was common knowledge that state funds were looted by party and state officials, and Angola remained one of the 20 most corrupt countries in the world on Transparency International's Corruption Perceptions Index. Angola also remained near the bottom of the countries on the UN Human Development Index, with more than half of its population continuing to live below the international poverty line. In December, as a new huge offshore oil find in the Kwanza Basin was announced, the New York-based Human Rights Watch claimed that the IMF had found that $32 billion in revenues had not gone into state coffers but had "disappeared" between 2007 and 2010.

Angola continued with vast infrastructural schemes, including upgrading and modernising the port of Lobito. Rebuilding the Benguela railway was further delayed, however, preventing the export of copper from the Democratic Republic of Congo (DRC) and Zambia via Angola. Though Angola had made substantial investments in the energy sector, and planned even larger investments, electricity supply continued to be unreliable and only an estimated 30 per cent of the country's population had access to power. Recognising this as a problem, President dos Santos sacked the energy minister at the beginning of December and replaced him with a technocrat.

Angola continued to enjoy close ties with China and Brazil, and there was talk of Angola helping to bail Portugal out of its economic mess. President Joseph Kabila of the DRC visited in August to talk about a dispute over offshore oil fields and the expulsion of illegal immigrants. That month Angola became chair of the Southern African Development Community (SADC). Angola also kept close ties with the other Portuguese-speaking countries in Africa, and played an active role in trying to stabilise Guinea Bissau.

Christopher Saunders

ZAMBIA—MALAWI—ZIMBABWE—BLNS STATES

ZAMBIA

CAPITAL: Lusaka   AREA: 752,610 sq km   POPULATION: 12,926,409 ('10)
OFFICIAL LANGUAGE: English
HEAD OF STATE AND GOVERNMENT: President Michael Sata (PF) (since Sept '11)
RULING PARTY: Patriotic Front (PF)
DEMOCRACY INDEX: 5.68; 91st of 167   CORRUPTION INDEX: 3.2; 91st of 183
CURRENCY: Zambian Kwacha (Dec '11 £1.00=ZMK 7,967, US$1.00=ZMK 5,080)
GNI PER CAPITA: US$1,070, Intl$1,370 at PPP ('10)

ECONOMICALLY, Zambia did well in the first half of 2011. The largest maize harvest in its history was recorded, while the price of copper, which accounted for 75 per cent of the country's export earnings, recovered from its collapse in 2008 to reach record highs. In January the government launched a sixth national development plan, which looked forward to the diversification of the economy and to Zambia becoming a prosperous middle-income country by 2030. In the second half of the year, however, the copper price fell. Well over half of Zambia's population remained poor, with an estimated 37 per cent living in extreme poverty.

The key event of 2011 was the hotly contested campaign leading to the legislative and presidential elections held in September, in which the incumbent president, Rupiah Banda, and his party—the Movement for Multiparty Democracy (MMD), which had been in power for 20 years—were defeated. Banda's election campaign was weakened when his sons insisted he dismiss his long-time campaign manager, Vernon Mwaanga. The 74-year-old leader of the Patriotic Front (PF), Michael Chilufya Sata, ran for president for the fourth time. When he was investigated for alleged money laundering early in the year, he accused Banda of trying to exclude him from the contest. Known as "King Cobra" because of his venomous attacks, Sata accused Banda of corruption, cronyism and incompetence. Long critical of China's role in Zambia, Sata demanded that Chinese employers treat Zambian workers properly. He promised, if elected, that he would act rapidly to restore Zambia's dignity and tackle poverty and unemployment.

Sata beat the nine other candidates to win with 43 per cent of the vote, while Banda received only 36 per cent. The PF became the largest party in the National Assembly (the unicameral legislature) with 60 seats, MMD won 55 seats, and the next largest party 28. Before the final result was announced both main parties grew anxious at the slow count, but when it was announced Banda was quick to accept it and Sata was sworn in as the country's fifth president.

He chose as his vice president Dr Guy Scott, an economist and former minister of agriculture, the first white person to occupy so senior a post since Zambia's independence. Sata acted quickly on some of his populist campaign promises, rapidly firing numerous leading officials in the military, the police, the Anti-Corruption Commission and the state-owned media, along with diplomats and the central bank governor. He demanded information on copper exports, claiming there had been much misreporting and corruption involved, and announced that all export payments must now be routed via the central bank. While Zambia was Africa's largest copper exporter, the mining industry contributed only about 10 per cent of the country's tax revenue, and Banda had said in March that audits showed that the Zambian mining sector owed up to $200 million in unpaid taxes. Sata's new finance minister doubled royalties on the base metal, and said that the increased revenue would help pay for increases in social spending and farming subsidies.

Sata cancelled the sale of Finance Bank Zambia to a South African bank, and ordered an investigation into the Libyan purchase of a controlling stake in Zambia Telecommunications, which a commission found to have been illegal. Sata's election, and his rapid post-election actions, unsettled investors, who wondered what the government would do were the copper price to drop dramatically again.

Meanwhile, at the Southern African Development Community summit in August, President Banda had joined four others in signing a treaty that created the Kavango-Zambezi Transfrontier Conservation Area (Kaza), the world's largest conservation area, a large portion of which lay in Zambia.

Christopher Saunders

MALAWI

CAPITAL: Lilongwe   AREA: 118,480 sq km   POPULATION: 14,900,841 ('10)
OFFICIAL LANGUAGE: English
HEAD OF STATE AND GOVERNMENT: President Bingu wa Mutharika (DPP) (since May '04)
RULING PARTY: Democratic Progressive Party (DPP)
DEMOCRACY INDEX: 5.84; 85th of 167   CORRUPTION INDEX: 3.0; 100th of 183
CURRENCY: Kwacha (Dec '11 £1.00=MWK 259.70, US$1.00=MWK 165.60)
GNI PER CAPITA: US$330, Intl$850 at PPP ('10)

IN 2011 Malawi's reputation as an African success story, which had lasted at least until President Bingu wa Mutharika's re-election in 2009, was further tarnished. When a lecturer at the country's main university spoke of the popular uprisings in North Africa in February he was interrogated by the police, after which the president spoke of "academic anarchy". When it was revealed by the WikiLeaks website that the British high commissioner in Malawi had referred to Mutharika in a diplomatic cable as "autocratic and intolerant of criticism", the high commissioner was expelled. In response, the UK expelled Malawi's acting high commissioner.

The donor community, which provided 40 per cent of Malawi's development budget, was by this time uneasy about trends in the country. In 2010, Mutharika had remarried in an extraordinarily lavish ceremony and built an ornate mausoleum for his first wife. The US Millennium Challenge Corporation, an aid agency, had delayed approving a $350 million grant for Malawi's collapsing electricity network because of the government's opposition to gay marriages and threats to media freedom. That grant was approved in April, but after the expulsion of its high commissioner, the UK, Malawi's single largest bilateral donor, announced in May that it was freezing new aid to Malawi pending a review of its ties with the country. After the British international development secretary expressed concerns about corruption and government accountability, Malawi's finance minister said that the country would not back down, but take tough decisions.

The already postponed local government elections were again postponed until 2014. In mid-December 2010 Joyce Banda, the country's first female vice president, had been expelled from Mutharika's ruling Democratic Progressive Party (DPP) after she refused to endorse Mutharika's brother Peter, then minister of education, science and technology, as the party's 2014 presidential nominee. Some suspected she wished to run for president herself. Mutharika found himself unable constitutionally to dismiss Banda as the country's vice president and she remained popular. Her new People's Party began to explore ties with other opposition parties ahead of the 2014 election.

Perhaps triggered by the "Arab Spring" and by the spat with the UK leading to the withdrawal of British donor aid, some 80 civil society organisations came together to arrange a peaceful protest in July, which the government tried but failed to prevent. The police, ordered to be tough, killed at least 18 protestors. Mutharika blamed civil society for refusing to enter into dialogue to solve problems peacefully and said that he would "smoke out" opposition to his rule. The UN sent a team to mediate between him and civil society, one of the demands of which was that he reduce the size of his cabinet. In August he dismissed his entire cabinet.

When he appointed a new, smaller one, in September, it included not only his brother Peter (his heir apparent) as the new minister of foreign affairs, but also his wife, Callista Mutharika.

Though further civil society protests were postponed and the UN-led mediation effort was abandoned, political tensions remained high as the year ended, with many, especially in urban areas, complaining of chronic fuel shortages, interruptions to power and water supply, and increases in the cost of living. There were demands that the government repair relations with donors and development finance institutions, for the president's actions had sorely damaged Malawi's international standing.

Christopher Saunders

ZIMBABWE

CAPITAL: Harare   AREA: 390,760 sq km   POPULATION: 12,571,454 ('10)
OFFICIAL LANGUAGE: English
HEAD OF STATE: President Robert Mugabe (since Dec '87); previously Prime Minister (from April '80)
RULING PARTIES: Zimbabwe African National Union-Patriotic Front (ZANU-PF) and Movement for
    Democratic Change (MDC) coalition
HEAD OF GOVERNMENT: Prime Minister Morgan Tsvangirai (MDC) (since Feb '09)
DEMOCRACY INDEX: 2.64; 146th of 167   CORRUPTION INDEX: 2.2; 154th of 183
CURRENCY: Zimbabwe Dollar (Dec '11 £1.00=ZWL 592.95 US$1.00=ZWL 378.10)
GNI PER CAPITA: US$460 ('10)

THE year was dominated by the shifting prospect of national elections, the first since the violently contested—and disputed—poll of 2008 and the formation in February 2009 of the Global Political Agreement (GPA) that resulted from it. The GPA had created a tense coalition of President Robert Mugabe's Zimbabwe African National Union-Patriotic Front (ZANU-PF) and the opposition Movement for Democratic Change (MDC), led by Morgan Tsvangirai. By the start of 2011 the coalition was bitterly divided with the president, in office for 31 years, having deftly marginalised the MDC, disempowered its ministers and appropriated full control over the army, police, the courts and the media.

Mugabe, who was impatient to escape from the GPA and restore autonomous power to his party, declared his intention to call national and presidential elections before the end of the year. But an all-party constitutional commission—charged with addressing key issues such as the flawed electoral roll, the probability of voter intimidation and proper access for independent monitors—had still to table its recommendations. The commission's progress, however, was painfully slow as ZANU-PF resisted every move towards reform while opposition parties filibustered on the grounds of cost and transparency. The pace was forced in March by a Southern African Development Community (SADC) summit in Livingstone, Zambia, when leaders of neighbouring countries pressured ZANU-PF into backing a co-operative political environment.

In particular the South African president, Jacob Zuma, argued that without meaningful reform an election would simply repeat the stalemate of 2008, with the same consequences. A South African team of facilitators was posted to Harare during the early months of the year to sustain the momentum for change. Initiatives included a code of conduct in public affairs aimed at reducing violence, and the establishment of a national peace and reconciliation council to help resolve political disputes. Yet an election plan agreed in July broke down over the issue of the role of security forces and the staffing of the Zimbabwe Electoral Commission. The plan remained unimplemented at the end of the year.

Meanwhile, an ominous increase in political violence brought strong reminders of 2008: the harassment of opposition meetings and intimidation of MDC officials, including a direct challenge to the MDC-controlled Harare city council. Alongside this were state-sponsored rallies in the rural areas from which ZANU-PF traditionally drew its support, and the coercion or "re-education" of local voters— priming the electorate to deliver the desired outcome.

Polls during the year highlighted a sharp fall in ZANU-PF's popularity, the result of the continued regression of the country's economy, its agricultural base and job opportunities for the poor. Economic growth of almost 9 per cent, aided by a rise in world commodity prices, was undermined by inflation of 5.6 per cent, a shortage of currency and an inability to service the country's external debt of $7 billion. A government proposal to promote economic indigenisation and empowerment through the nationalisation of foreign-owned companies was repeatedly vaunted, thereby damaging international confidence and investment.

A key factor in the country's ability to withstand financial pressure was the growth in revenue from the Marange diamond field on Zimbabwe's eastern border (see AR 2010 p. 264). Though the diamond industry watchdog, the Kimberley Process, had previously ruled against the sale of rough diamonds from the Chiadzwa mine, it repealed the ban in November, opening international markets to Zimbabwean gems. Described by Tendai Biti, the MDC finance minister, as "the biggest find of alluvial diamonds in the history of mankind", the Marange field promised to be massively lucrative, delivering a reputed $100 million a month. The question was who would benefit?

Despite the diamond windfall, ZANU-PF showed increasing signs of paranoia, particularly given the events of the "Arab Spring". In mid-February the fall from office of Egyptian President Hosni Mubarak brought the uncomfortable parallel of a nation tipped over the edge after 30 years of abusive rule by an ageing autocrat. A group of Zimbabwean students and political activists caught watching news reports of demonstrations in Egypt and Tunisia was arrested on suspicion of "plotting to oust" Mugabe and charged with treason. Reports indicated that several hundred Zimbabwean soldiers had been sent to Libya to support Mugabe's long-term ally, Colonel Moamar Kadhafi, and indeed the country was mentioned as a possible refuge for a vanquished Kadhafi.

In November the whistle-blowing website WikiLeaks released further interesting revelations. Evidence that senior ZANU-PF leaders had covertly met US embassy officials to discuss Mugabe's overthrow, and that a faction associated with the vice-president, Joice Mujuru, had proposed links with the MDC, exposed rivalry within the ruling party itself. Rumours of political jostling between the

Mujuru camp and a faction supporting Mugabe's allegedly "anointed" successor, Defence Minister Emmerson Mnangagwa, were brought to a head by the circumstances of the death of Solomon Mujuru, husband of the vice-president and one of the heroes of Zimbabwe's liberation struggle. The 62-year-old retired general was found burnt beyond recognition following an unexplained fire at his Beatrice farmhouse, 54 km south of Harare. As the only member of the ZANU-PF politbureau with the standing to restrain Mugabe, and a man with influence across the political spectrum, Mujuru's death—or perhaps assassination—had far reaching political implications. Zimbabwe had lost its kingmaker. Nevertheless, in December the ZANU-PF annual party congress, meeting in Bulawayo, once again nominated Mugabe to fight the next presidential election. This would probably occur in 2013, by which time he would be aged 89.

By the close of the year there appeared to be two Zimbabwes. On one hand was an impoverished state with almost no social provision, in which a third of the children were malnourished. The country's antiquated water system was close to collapse, and its power supply at risk of being severed by Mozambique after years of defaulted payments. Half the workforce was unemployed, with poorly paid teachers, civil servants and nurses threatening to strike. On the other hand was an assertive and stylish urban elite—straddling both parties—with disposable cash, luxurious vehicles, up-to-date telecommunications and a taste for international travel. Two decades of cultural isolation, fiscal mismanagement and political stasis had enriched a privileged few but devastated the country as a whole.

Robert Baldock

BOTSWANA—LESOTHO—NAMIBIA—SWAZILAND

Botswana

CAPITAL: Gaborone   AREA: 581,730 sq km   POPULATION: 2,006,945 ('10)
OFFICIAL LANGUAGES: English and Setswana
HEAD OF STATE AND GOVERNMENT: President Lt-Gen. Seretse Khama Ian Khama (since April '08)
RULING PARTY: Botswana Democratic Party (BDP)
DEMOCRACY INDEX: 7.63; 35th of 167   CORRUPTION INDEX: 6.1; 32nd of 183
CURRENCY: Pula (Dec '11 £1.00=BWP 11.65, US$1.00=BWP 7.43)
GNI PER CAPITA: US$6,790, Intl$13,710 at PPP ('10)

Lesotho

CAPITAL: Maseru   AREA: 30,350 sq km   POPULATION: 2,171,318 ('10)
OFFICIAL LANGUAGES: English & Sesotho
HEAD OF STATE: King Letsie III (since Jan '96)
RULING PARTY: Lesotho Congress for Democracy (LCD)
HEAD OF GOVERNMENT: Prime Minister Bethuel Pakalitha Mosisili (since June '98)
DEMOCRACY INDEX: 6.02; 77th of 167   CORRUPTION INDEX: 3.5; 77th of 183
CURRENCY: Maloti (Dec '11 £1.00=LSL 12.69, US$1.00=LSL 8.09); South African Rand (Dec '11 £1.00=ZAR 12.69, US$1.00=ZAR 8.09)
GNI PER CAPITA: US$1,040, Intl$1,840 at PPP ('10)

Namibia

CAPITAL: Windhoek   AREA: 824,290 sq km   POPULATION: 2,283,289 ('10)
OFFICIAL LANGUAGES: Afrikaans & English
HEAD OF STATE: President Hifikepunye Pohamba (SWAPO) (since March '05)
RULING PARTY: South West Africa People's Organisation (SWAPO)
HEAD OF GOVERNMENT: Prime Minister Nahas Angula (since March '05)
DEMOCRACY INDEX: 6.23; 69th of 167   CORRUPTION INDEX: 4.4; 57th of 183
CURRENCY: Namibia Dollar (Dec '11 £1.00=NAD 12.69, US$1.00=NAD 8.09), South African
    Rand (Dec '11 £1.00=ZAR 12.69, US$1.00=ZAR 8.09)
GNI PER CAPITA: US$4,500, Intl$6,380 at PPP ('10)

Swaziland

CAPITAL: Mbabane   AREA: 17,360 sq km   POPULATION: 1,186,056 ('10)
OFFICIAL LANGUAGES: English & Siswati
HEAD OF STATE: King Mswati III (since '86)
RULING PARTY: none
HEAD OF GOVERNMENT: Prime Minister Sibusiso Barnabas Dlamini (since Oct '08)
DEMOCRACY INDEX: 2.90; 141st of 167   CORRUPTION INDEX: 3.1; 95th of 183
CURRENCY: Lilangeni (Dec '11 £1.00=SZL 12.69, US$1.00=SZL 8.09)
GNI PER CAPITA: US$2,630, Intl$4,950 at PPP ('10)

BOTSWANA, Lesotho, Namibia and Swaziland were integrated with each other and linked to South Africa through the Southern African Customs Union (SACU). Concerns about SACU's future persisted as disputes over an economic partnership agreement (EPA) with the European Union remained unresolved (see AR 2010, p. 269). A study prepared for the South African government suggested restructuring the way in which customs revenues were distributed, raising the proportion retained by South Africa. Given that SACU contributed considerable resources to the other states, this was viewed with concern.

Botswana's short-term economic prospects looked poor, as its diamond exports depended on the economic health of Europe and North America. The Botswana government and the De Beers company concluded an agreement that would see sorting and marketing activities transferred to Gabarone from London and give Botswana the right to sell 10 per cent of diamond production.

The Botswana Democratic Party (BDP), which had dominated the country's politics since independence, and the incumbent president, Ian Khama, remained under criticism for their stewardship of the country and its political direction, not least over allegations of growing authoritarianism. Such allegations also emerged from within the BDP. The BDP's secretary general Kentse Rammidi expressed this view when he resigned from the party in August.

In April and May Botswana suffered a major public sector strike, with the government refusing to concede 16 per cent pay rises following several years of salary freezes. The opposition came out in support of the unions—a significant development, as it had not previously seen the unions as part of its constituency—and suggested that the strike could precipitate a North African-style uprising along the lines of the "Arab Spring". The strike was resolved with a combination of dismissals and modest pay rises. Several services were also deemed essential, meaning that workers in those sectors were not permitted to strike.

In June, four opposition parties announced an agreement to co-operate in the 2014 elections and to field a single presidential candidate. In the elections of 2009 the BDP had lost support, although it emerged as the winner. However, negotiations proved difficult and late in the year the country's Federation of Trade Unions warned that it would not co-operate with the parties unless they resolved their differences.

The position of the San (Bushman) minority, whose alleged mistreatment had attracted international attention, continued to be an issue. Reversing a High Court decision, the Court of Appeals in January ruled that a San group could access water from a borehole in the central Kalahari game reserve (see AR 2011, p. 266). This gave the relevant community the means to remain on the territory from which the government had controversially attempted to evict them.

Lesotho, entirely landlocked by South Africa and heavily dependent on the latter's economy, continued to suffer from the international economic situation, notably in the decline of SACU revenues. The finance minister, Timothy Thahane, warned early in the year that the unfavourable environment demanded that the country make "hard choices".

Strategically, the government noted that Lesotho needed to develop its own sources of revenue as it was too dependent on SACU revenues. It was also overly reliant on its textile industry, which was significantly dented by economic troubles in the USA. However, given Lesotho's extensive unemployment and the social welfare impact of the loss of wages earned by the 33,000 textile workers, the government committed itself to spending some $12.7 million to support the industry, pending improvements in the global economy.

Controversy continued around new land legislation, which was intended to formalise tenure and act as a spur for modernisation and investment. It would also, hopefully, resolve conflicts arising from the informal nature of landholding and would assist in addressing the poor use of farm land—a major concern for a country with a large subsistence agriculture sector and constant food deficits. However, pastoralists feared that it would take away their livelihood, through, for example, depriving them of traditional communal grazing lands.

A simmering dispute over the 2007 parliamentary election reached a conclusion (see AR 2008, p. 272). In April, the participating parties reached agreement that the relevant issues had been dealt with, and that peaceful elections were possible in 2012. Among the concrete outcomes of the process were a new Electoral Act and a constitutional amendment.

Local government elections took place in October. Reports of divisions within the ruling Lesotho Congress for Democracy (LCD) prompted speculation that the opposition might make significant gains, but the LCD secured control of 69 of the country's 77 councils. However, there was concern over the low turnout, which in some districts did not exceed 15 per cent.

In **Namibia**, dissatisfaction on the part of opposition groups with the outcome of the 2009 parliamentary elections remained unresolved (see AR 2010, p. 271). In February, the country's High Court ruled that there was no evidence of electoral fraud, but criticised the conduct of the country's Electoral Commission. By the end of the year, the Supreme Court had not ruled on an appeal.

The succession to President Hifikepunye Pohamba after the end of his term as head of state in 2015 emerged as an important political issue. The ruling South West African People's Organisation (SWAPO) was unlikely to face a serious electoral threat, so the key contestation would likely take place within the party. SWAPO officials expressed fears that this could lead to divisions within the party, possibly even fracturing it.

In a move heavy with symbolism for a multicultural society attempting to come to terms with its deeply divided history, the Namibian government repatriated from Germany the skulls of several Nama and Herero people killed by German forces in the genocide of the early 20th century. The Namibian delegation complained of humiliating treatment in Germany, and a government minister, Kazenambo Kazenambo, responded with a furious outburst to criticism by a journalist of the cost of the trip. He accused white people of failing to respond to conciliatory overtures and said that the country's constitution should be ignored if it hampered efforts to redistribute land.

Along with unstable communal relations, poverty continued to dog Namibia. Although technically a middle-income country, extreme levels of inequality meant that acute poverty was widespread, a problem that was brought into sharp focus with revelations in August about people scavenging in Windhoek rubbish tips for food.

Swaziland, Africa's last absolute monarchy, was in parlous straits. Its economy had taken a severe battering from the decline in SACU revenues over recent years, and it was estimated that over 10 per cent of the population depended on food aid.

The country's fiscal position was the focus of particular concern. In January, a report by the IMF called for reforms, including cutting the size of the public sector, which it viewed as excessive for the country's needs. The Swazi government refused. Instead, it attempted to deal with the crisis by cutting social services, including suspending pension payments. Failure by the government to pay the school fees of orphaned and vulnerable children—a constitutional requirement—led to some schools not opening in September. These problems were compounded by corruption. According to the finance minister, Majozi Sithole, Swaziland lost some $128 million annually to corruption, a figure amounting to twice the social services budget.

Having failed to secure IMF support, it was announced in August that Swaziland had obtained a $350 million loan from South Africa. The news was received with anger by activist groups, who argued that the country's economic problems stemmed in significant measure from its political arrangements, in particular, the extensive power wielded by the monarch, King Mswati III, and his profligate lifestyle. The loan's memorandum included calls for "confidence-building" measures but these were seen as tokenism. However, by September it appeared that Swaziland was unwilling to commit to the terms and the memorandum remained unsigned. Economists familiar with Swaziland indicated that the economy was likely to grind to a halt within six months.

Terence Corrigan and Elizabeth Sidiropoulos

SOUTH AFRICA

CAPITAL: Pretoria   AREA: 1,219,090 sq km   POPULATION: 49,991,300 ('10)
OFFICIAL LANGUAGES: Afrikaans, English & nine African languages
HEAD OF STATE AND GOVERNMENT: President Jacob Zuma (ANC) (since May '09)
RULING PARTY: African National Congress (ANC)
DEMOCRACY INDEX: 7.79; 30th of 167   CORRUPTION INDEX: 4.1; 64th of 183
CURRENCY: Rand (Dec '11 £1.00=ZAR 12.69, US$1.00=ZAR 8.09)
GNI PER CAPITA: US$6,090, Intl$10,280 at PPP ('10)

SOUTH Africa's political life was dominated by municipal elections held in May. Taking place in circumstances unpropitious for the ruling African National Congress (ANC)—including a failure to deal with extensive socio-economic problems and divisions within the ANC and its allied formations—the elections were viewed as an important barometer of the country's mood and likely direction. The performance of the Democratic Alliance (DA)—the largest opposition party nationally and the governing party in the Western Cape province and several municipalities—was closely watched. The DA sought to position itself as a performance-oriented alternative to the ANC, drawing notably on its record in office in Cape Town, South Africa's legislative capital, and to project an image of racial inclusivity.

In the election the ANC garnered some 62 per cent of the vote (excluding votes for District Councils—a third ballot available to rural voters). The DA won 24 per cent, the Inkatha Freedom Party 4 per cent, the National Freedom Party 2 per cent, and the Congress of the People 2 per cent. Thus, the ANC managed to maintain support but was unable to regain ground lost to the DA, despite considerable effort in areas such as Cape Town and Midvaal (Gauteng). The DA, meanwhile, breached the psychologically important 20 per cent mark, consolidating its support among the minority communities and making some headway among African voters. Estimates put the DA's share of the African vote at around 5 per cent. While this represented considerable progress, it remained far from a serious challenge to the ANC, however.

The campaign took place against widespread failings in municipal governance. Complaints were unremitting about the inability of many municipal governments to manage finances and ensure the maintenance of infrastructure and provision of services. Frustration regularly expressed itself in violent protests. The heavy-handed response from law enforcement agencies generated controversy, notably the beating and shooting by police—captured on camera—of a protester named Andries Tatane in Ficksburg in April; he died of his injuries.

During the election campaign, senior ANC members regularly invoked racial and class solidarity, sometimes in a tenor that called into question their supposed commitment to non-racism. Debate was brought into sharp relief by the broadcast in February of video footage of the government's chief spokesman, Jimmy Manyi, saying that there were too many coloured (mixed-race) people in the Western Cape, and that people of Indian extraction had "bargained" a more prominent position for themselves than their numbers warranted. The ANC Youth League (ANCYL) and its leadership were notable exponents of this tendency. During 2011, ANCYL leader Julius Malema became embroiled in a legal dispute with the advocacy group AfriForum over the singing of a song calling for "Boers"—a pejorative term meaning, variously, farmers, Afrikaners, white people and apartheid-era security forces—to be shot. The ANC supported Malema, arguing that it was a "struggle" song and part of the country's heritage. It was, conversely, noted that the ANC had previously distanced itself from such calls and that there appeared to be no record of this song having actually been sung during the ANC's struggle. The Equality Court deemed the song to be hate speech and the ANC indicated that it would appeal against the ruling.

The internal politics of the ANC attracted much attention. President Jacob Zuma had ascended to power on an unstable coalition of interests, motivated largely by animosity towards former President Thabo Mbeki. Zuma's failure to commit fully to any particular faction's agenda produced widespread dissension, and some prominent party members were known to be working towards his removal as party leader in 2012, probably to be replaced by his deputy, Kgalema Motlanthe. The ANCYL and Malema emerged as key elements of this strategy, with Malema making frequent oblique critiques of Zuma. Towards the end of the year, Malema and several senior ANCYL members were subjected to party disciplinary charges and suspended from their positions. It was widely suspected that the move was intended to remove a source of dissent threatening the incumbent leadership. However, some of the offences—in particular a publicly mooted proposal by Malema to form a team to co-ordinate the removal of Botswana's President Ian Khama for being in league with "imperialists"—were severely embarrassing to the government.

South Africa's social and economic impasse remained a dominant concern. Real GDP had grown by some 2.9 per cent in 2010, and was projected to grow by something over 3 per cent in 2011. This remained inadequate to address the country's unemployment crisis. The unemployment rate stood at 25 per cent and some analysts calculated that around half of young people of African extraction would likely never find work. Instability in North Africa (the "Arab Spring") and rioting in the UK in the summer were invoked as warnings of the consequences should South Africa fail to address this issue. Although President Zuma declared 2011 "the year of job creation", little progress was made. The country's National Planning Commission—a body given the task of mapping a long term vision for the country—produced a set of reports, which made proposals for large scale development and job creation. These recognised the central role of the private sector, in contrast to the state-centric thinking of the *New Growth Path* report (see AR 2011, p. 269). The commission noted forthrightly that many of the country's institutions were weak and compromised. While it was well received by business and many commentators, it was viewed with scepticism by the ANC's leftist factions. It was further noted that, given President Zuma's desire to remain in office and his fear of alienating possible supporters, he was unlikely to exercise decisive leadership on the matter.

Officially, economic policy remained stable, but the extent of the social problems and the lack of inspiring leadership allowed populist demands to take prominence. This was the case with regard to the ANCYL's calls for mines (and possibly other parts of the economy) to be nationalised and for land owned by white people to be seized without compensation. During the year, a number of formations with the ANC's alliance also came out in favour of nationalising the mines. An economist linked to the Congress of South African Trade Unions (COSATU) told a business audience in August that nationalisation was a certainty and that business would need to accept it. However, some voices in cabinet, such as the planning minister, Trevor Manuel, opposed it publicly, arguing that the state had neither the expertise nor the resources to run industries effectively. A drive for greater government intervention was, however, evident in an ongoing attempt by a group of cabinet ministers to prevent investment by the US discount retailer, Walmart, in South Africa. They argued that Walmart's global supply chains would harm local industry and employment.

Observers and opposition parties charged the ANC with undermining the constitution. An especially bitter contest developed over legislation designed to protect state information. Critics charged that it would create a culture of secrecy and that the extensive prison terms mandated for possession of particular types of information could be used to intimidate journalists. Pleas for a "public interest" defence to be included were rejected. An extensive civil society mobilisation, the Right2Know campaign, continued to press for changes but the bill was passed by the National Assembly (one of Parliament's two chambers) in November. Unusually, all opposition parties voted against, with only the ANC supporting it. It remained to be processed by the National Council of Provinces, amid concerns about its constitutionality.

The appointment in September of Mr Justice Mogoeng Mogoeng as the country's chief justice was widely condemned: his judicial record was undistinguished and he had made controversial rulings which appeared to trivialise gender violence. In December, the Supreme Court of Appeal set aside the appointment of the national director of public prosecutions, Menzi Simelane, ruling him unfit for the position. Simelane's appointment in 2009 had been controversial as he was widely viewed as primarily loyal to the ANC and had shown a lack of understanding of the constitution.

Interpretations of this trend differed. Some felt that the ANC had drifted from its roots, was struggling with the prudent exercise of power, and was poorly led. Other saw in purported attacks on the constitution the hand of the ANC's commitment to its "national democratic revolution" (NDR), an ill-defined ideological programme for the remaking of society and the building of ANC hegemony. That the ANC frequently criticised the judiciary—less on the substance of judgments than by casting aspersions on the motives for particular decisions—lent credence to the view that its position was informed by political and ideological concerns. A newspaper column in September by Ngoako Ramathlodi, a deputy minister, drew much attention for arguing that the country's constitutional settlement was a "fatal compromise", and, by implication, that the ANC needed to reformulate it in its own interests.

In one area, there was significant consensus that the ANC's pursuit of the NDR had damaged governance. This was the ANC's programme of "cadre deployment", in which activists were "deployed" to state positions. That many lacked the necessary skills and were focused on advancing the party's agenda, rather than the interests of the bodies in which they worked, was increasingly recognised. Although the ANC at times conceded the problem, it indicated that cadre deployment would continue.

Corruption and maladministration also remained prominent concerns. High profile cases, notably revelations that leases on buildings for the police had been concluded corruptly, underlined this. The official response to a report in July by Public Protector Thuli Madonsela calling for action on the leases was seen as a test of the government's commitment to combating corruption. After some delay, a minister was demoted and Police Commissioner Bheki Cele was suspended. Zuma was commended for having acted decisively, but a scandal around the police commissioner, following the conviction of his predecessor for corruption in 2010 (see AR 2011, p. 270), was a demoralising indication of the deficiencies of the country's crime-fighting apparatus.

South Africa achieved international visibility during 2011. Accession to the BRIC group of emerging economies—which thus became the BRICS (Brazil, Russia, India, China, South Africa)—was seen as endorsement of the country's global importance, although the role of this body remained unclear. South Africa once again assumed a seat on the UN Security Council, where it supported in March the imposition of a no-fly zone over Libya. However, it subsequently argued that the NATO air campaign had exceeded its mandate and argued for an "African" solution, which would have left Libya's leader Moamar Kadhafi with a significant role in the country's affairs. Initially South Africa opposed recognition of Libya's National Transitional Council, but it later relented and acknowledged the new government.

Terence Corrigan and Elizabeth Sidiropoulos

VIII SOUTH ASIA AND INDIAN OCEAN

IRAN—AFGHANISTAN—CENTRAL ASIAN STATES

IRAN

CAPITAL: Tehran   AREA: 1,745,150 sq km   POPULATION: 73,973,630 ('10)
OFFICIAL LANGUAGE: Farsi (Persian)
SPIRITUAL GUIDE: Ayatollah Seyed Ali Khamenei (since June '89)
HEAD OF STATE AND GOVERNMENT: President Mahmoud Ahmadinejad (since Aug '05)
DEMOCRACY INDEX: 1.94; 158th of 167   CORRUPTION INDEX: 2.7; 120th of 183
CURRENCY: Iranian Rial (Dec '11 £1.00=IRR 17,059, US$1.00=IRR 10,877)
GNI PER CAPITA: US$4,520, Intl$11,380 at PPP ('09)

ALTHOUGH President Mahmoud Ahmadinejad had announced price increases on 18 December 2010, the full implementation of legislation—entitled the Targeted Subsidies Reform Act—designed to remove subsidies for goods and services, estimated to be between $70 and $100 billion, began in January 2011. Prices for fuel, utilities, flour, bread, and transportation were raised by between 20 and 500 per cent in an orderly fashion and without undue popular reaction. To counter these increasing costs for the population, cash subsidies of 45,000 rials per month per person were deposited directly in the bank accounts of heads of households who signed up based on the number of people in the family. These cash transfers continued throughout 2011 and, according to the government, led to higher real incomes in rural households which, based on Iran's Statistical Centre's latest census data in 2011, constituted 29 per cent of the population. In the cities, however, high inflation, increased unemployment, and sluggish economic growth hit the middle and working classes hard. Reliable figures regarding both inflation and unemployment were difficult to arrive at as various government ministries offered competing data. But close observers of Iran's economy estimated that the unemployment rate (including discouraged workers) increased to 15.2 per cent and inflation to close to 30 per cent in 2011.

The government nevertheless remained steady in the implementation of subsidy reform despite increasing external economic pressure imposed by the USA and the EU. But sanctions, on Iran's financial sector in particular, did stress the Iranian currency—the rial—eventually forcing devaluation of more than 40 per cent by the end of the year. Many critics, however, blamed government mismanagement of the economy more than sanctions. In particular, the 2007 forced lowering of interest rates, from 17 to 12 per cent, well below the inflation rate, was blamed for the increased demand for foreign currency and gold as a hedge against inflation and a reason for the Central Bank of Iran's inability to stabilize the currency market.

On the political front, a major conflict brewed over the control of the intelligence ministry. The resignation of Intelligence Minister Heydar Moslehi in April was accepted by Ahmadinejad but was immediately overturned by the order of the Leader Ayatollah Ali Khamenei. This confrontation led to Ahmadinejad's refusal to go to work for 11 days. But his threat to resign unless the intelligence minister was removed remained unfulfilled. Ahmadinejad returned to work and faced severe criticism from an array of politicians and clerics in his own conservative camp who saw his refusal to work as a challenge to Khamenei's guardianship of the Islamic state. The tensions increased to the point of calls for Ahmadinejad's impeachment by the Iranian parliament. However, the parliament's leadership let it be known that Khamenei remained in favour of Ahmadinejad serving out his full presidential term until 2013.

Leader Khamenei's treatment of other challengers was more severe. After street protests in February, called by former presidential candidates Mir Hossein Mousavi and Mehdi Karrubi in solidarity with the "Arab Spring" popular protests which were sweeping the region, these leaders and their spouses were placed under house arrest. With the exception of Karrubi's wife, they remained incarcerated throughout the year despite the fact that no legal proceedings were initiated against them.

Pro-Khamenei forces also called for the removal of former president Akbar Hashemi Rafsanjani from his position as the chair of the Assembly of Experts, an elected body with the authority to appoint and dismiss the country's supreme leader. Hashemi Rafsanjani was criticised for his advocacy of political pluralism—including the release of political prisoners and the free operation of political parties and press—and was accused of aligning with those "forces of sedition" which challenged the legitimacy of President Ahmadinejad's re-election in 2009. Eventually Mohammadreza Kani, an 81-year old cleric who had served as acting prime minister in 1980, ran unopposed and became the chair of the Assembly.

Charges of sedition and acting against national security were also used against several other reformist political figures, as well as against a number of well-known student leaders, women's rights activists, journalists, filmmakers, and human rights lawyers who either remained in detention without trial or were handed harsh prison sentences. The UN Human Rights Council in August appointed Special Rapporteur Ahmed Shaheed to investigate human rights violations in Iran. But despite Shaheed's repeated requests, the government of Iran did not allow him to visit the country. In October he nevertheless presented his report to the UN General Assembly's third committee, which dealt with social, humanitarian and cultural affairs, voicing concern over alleged violations in the country's judicial system, citing practices such as torture, cruel or degrading treatment of detainees, and the imposition of the death penalty without proper safeguards. He also identified denial of access to legal counsel and medical treatment, and widespread use of secret and public executions, as other issues of concern.

In the area of foreign policy, the issue of the country's nuclear programme remained a significant cause of international concern. Iran continued to insist that its nuclear ambitions were solely for civilian purposes. As such it refused to suspend its ongoing efforts at uranium enrichment, the process which lay at the heart of civil nuclear power and the creation of nuclear weapons.

In January an Iranian delegation met representatives of the five permanent members of the UN Security Council plus Germany, a group known as the P5+1, for talks in Istanbul. After the meeting failed to achieve any results, the USA and European officials attempted to institute new UN sanctions against Iran but were blocked by Russia and China. As a result, the USA and EU began to take their own actions to increase pressure on Iran. Their coordinated action to impose sanctions and restrictions on individuals, companies and Iran's banking system was boosted by a November report by the International Atomic Energy Agency (IAEA), which suggested that Iran might have carried out studies relevant to the development of a nuclear explosive device. The IAEA report also indicated that prior to the end of 2003, these activities had taken place under a structured programme and that some activities could still be ongoing.

New US sanctions were announced in November which targeted Iran's petrochemical sector for the first time, prohibiting the provision of goods, services, and technology to this sector and authorising penalties against any person or entity that engaged in such activity. These new sanctions also targeted for the first time the entire Iranian banking sector—including the Central Bank of Iran (CBI)—governments or financial institutions that did business with Iranian banks. The USA was joined in this action by the UK and Canada, which also acted to cut off Iran from their financial systems. Iran reacted to the sanctions by allowing demonstrators to storm the British embassy and a diplomatic residence in Tehran on 29 November. The embassy attack came a day after Iran's parliament had approved a measure to expel the British ambassador and downgrade diplomatic relations between the two countries, in retaliation for the new economic sanctions. In response, the British government closed its vandalised embassy in Tehran and expelled all Iranian diplomats from the UK.

The year ended with Tehran threatening to close the Strait of Hormuz, the world's most important oil transit point, if Western powers attempted to impose an embargo on Iranian petroleum exports. There were also growing fears that Israel, which was suspected of pursuing a campaign of sabotage and assassination in an effort to impede Iran's nuclear programme, might go further and seek to preserve its monopoly of nuclear weapons in the Middle East by launching a direct military strike against Iranian nuclear facilities.

Farideh Farhi

AFGHANISTAN

CAPITAL: Kabul   AREA: 652,090 sq km   POPULATION: 34,385,068 ('10)
OFFICIAL LANGUAGES: Pushtu, Dari (Persian)
HEAD OF STATE AND GOVERNMENT: President Hamid Karzai (since Dec '04)
DEMOCRACY INDEX: 2.48; 150th of 167   CORRUPTION INDEX: 1.5; 180th of 183
CURRENCY: Afgani (Dec '11 £1.00=AFN 67.40, US$1.00=AFN 42.98)
GNI PER CAPITA: US$290, Intl$860 at PPP ('08)

> ...looks like freedom but it feels like death
> it's something in between, I guess
> it's Closing Time... (Leonard Cohen)

THIS was the year that marked the beginning of the end for the US-led coalition war effort in Afghanistan. The troop surge that had characterised 2010 was over and had not produced the decisive military breakthrough that had been promised by its advocates. Instead it seemed as if the surge had stiffened the will of the Taliban to wait out the foreign armies as they began their preparations for departure. Militarily the war remained in a state of stalemate but as 2011 moved towards its conclusion, and the first US troops were withdrawn, time seemed unmistakeably on the side of the insurgents. Western politicians no longer talked of victory but instead all eyes were becoming fixed upon what would happen after 2014 when the last of the coalition troops were scheduled to have completed their withdrawal.

This then was the beginning of the fourth and final phase of the Afghan war. The first had been the Era of Illusions (2001-04) when the Taliban seemed to have been beaten and Afghanistan was to be recast in the mould of a liberal democracy. The second, the Period of Neglect (2005-09), had seen the war effort starved of resources and relegated to a sideshow by the US concentration on the conflict in Iraq. The third phase (2009-10) had been the Surge and the fourth, Closing Time, was characterised by drawdown and transition. For the aim was no longer to win the war. Instead, even for the most belligerent of hawks, "victory" had been redefined as an orderly withdrawal from Afghanistan, leaving behind a viable state. The self-sufficiency and longevity of that state would be the memorial to the enormous human and material cost of the conflict, and would provide an important measure against which the legitimacy of the war would be judged historically.

But although the redefined objective was clear, the inefficiency and corruption of the regime presided over by Afghan President Hamid Karzai made it an elusive goal. Afghanistan's constitutional fragility was illustrated during the year by a protracted dispute over the composition of the 249-member Wolesi Jirga (House of the People), the lower chamber of the National Assembly that had been elected in September 2010 amid a tide of fraud and malpractice. The Assembly was due to convene in January, but Karzai intervened to delay it, ostensibly on the grounds of allowing a special court on electoral fraud—that he had established over the objections to the constitutionally designated adjudicating bodies, the Independent Election Commission (IEC) and Electoral Complaints Commission (ECC)—to have more time to rule on hundreds of cases of alleged fraud arising from the poll. To many, however, the president (himself the notorious beneficiary of electoral fraud on an industrial scale) was motivated by a desire to keep the legislature suspended, thereby leaving him free to rule by degree.

Amid threats by elected legislators to go ahead and convene without the president's consent, and protests from defeated candidates claiming that they had been fraudulently denied their rightful seats, the National Assembly did eventually open on 26 January. Karzai rose to the occasion with a speech that set the tone for the year by acknowledging that "it is not possible to achieve peace through a military option alone". As such he promised "talks and reconciliation" with Taliban insurgents and political opponents alike in order to "put an end to the present misery through any possible means". The mercurial president also made one of his characteristically bizarre forays against his Western backers, lamenting the "abuse and foreign interventions" which he claimed had marred the legislative elections, and calling for "an end to foreign intervention and ambiguity in our democracy, elections and affairs". Thereafter, the lower house descended into a protracted squabble over the election of a speaker, which went on until the end of February, and an even more lengthy dispute over ruling on individual cases of electoral malpractice which went on until the latter half of the year. Karzai's special court, the legality of which was itself challenged in the courts, provoked fury amongst legislators who deemed it nothing more than an instrument for manipulating the composition of the National Assembly into a more compliant shape. This ill feeling between executive and legislature was also fuelled by a continuing dispute arising from Karzai's refusal to submit his cabinet for approval by the legislature. His defiance of this constitutional obligation appeared a gesture of contempt for the status of the legislature and the concept of the rule of law, and helped to cement the image of a capricious government presiding over a dysfunctional state.

This impression was heightened by the president's persistent reluctance to act against the endemic corruption which characterised Afghanistan. This was symbolised by the ongoing scandal at the Kabul Bank which was revealed in January to have run up losses even greater than had been initially estimated. It transpired that Afghan politicians and businessmen had plundered up to $900 million from the institution with much of the money being taken abroad and significant amounts invested (and lost) in the Dubai property bubble. Amongst the beneficiaries of this financial bonanza were many of the bank's shareholders, men who enjoyed powerful political and family connection with Karzai and his government. Their connections gave them protection. The head of the Afghan central bank, Abdul Qadir Fitrat, fled to the USA in June, claiming that his investigation into conduct at the Kabul Bank had been obstructed and that his life had been threatened after he had pointed the finger at some of those who had benefitted from the corruption.

The Kabul Bank scandal was emblematic of the cancerous corruption that riddled Afghanistan at all levels. It swallowed aid money from foreign countries and non-governmental organisations alike, and its corrosive effects undermined Western ambitions to construct a state capable of defending itself after the 2014 troop withdrawal. A detailed report commissioned by the US Senate, released in June, estimated that US aid to Afghanistan over the previous decade had amounted to $18.8 billion, a sum that excluded the cost of the war itself, estimated to be running at around $2 billion per week. Much of this money had been wasted on expensive short-term stabilisation projects that had had a limited or negative long-term impact. The report noted that foreign aid, which constituted some 97 per cent of the Afghan economy, had fuelled corruption, inflated the cost of labour and goods, undermined the authority of the central government, and created a "culture of dependency". It warned that the impact of the troop withdrawal could trigger a severe economic depression. A World Bank assessment compiled in November made a similar prediction, suggesting that Afghanistan would suffer a recession from 2014, trigged by the departure of Western troops and a reduction in the aid upon which it was almost wholly dependent. This was the most optimistic scenario. Were the security situation to worsen, the report warned, the economy could face total collapse.

Against this gloomy backdrop of viability, the move towards Western disengage-
ment continued with a firming up of planned troops withdrawals. The US commander of coalition forces in Afghanistan, General David Petraeus, in March
attempted to put a brave face on the retreat, claiming that since 2005 rebel gains
had been halted or even reversed. He confirmed that the withdrawal of troops,
which would begin during the year, would be slow enough not to jeopardise these
military gains. This point was underlined by US Defence Secretary Robert Gates
when chiding his NATO colleagues for being too keen to rush towards the exit.
Nevertheless, the ebbing tide of the coalition war effort was clear to see. In a televised address to the US public on 22 June President Barack Obama promised that
10,000 US troops would be withdrawn in 2011 and that the rest of the "surge"
would have been removed by September 2012. Thereafter there would be withdrawal at "a steady pace" to be completed in 2014. Significantly Obama presented
the US goal in Afghanistan not as trying to make the country "a perfect place" but
rather to ensure that it was "no safe haven" from which terrorists could attack the
USA or its allies. He specifically ruled out long-term responsibility for
Afghanistan's security, but talked instead of a vague but ongoing "partnership with
the Afghan people". He also publicly expressed his support for "a political settlement" to the conflict, which could include any party that renounced violence and
accepted the terms of the Afghan constitution.

This framework for US withdrawal was mirrored by those allies that were
fighting alongside it, particularly the UK, France and Germany, all of which had
significant contingents of troops in Afghanistan. It was accompanied also by a
piecemeal formal handover of authority by coalition troops to the expanding (but
still largely inadequate) Afghan armed forces and police force. This transfer
began with a low-key ceremony on 17 July in Bamiyan, a province chosen
because it was one of the most peaceful areas of the country. Nevertheless, concerns over security meant that the ceremony was not announced in advance nor
carried live on television.

But clandestine ceremonies of withdrawal were easier to manage than the realities of taking responsibility for security on the ground. By the end of the year the
combined strength of the Afghan police and army totalled around 308,000 and was
due to reach a peak of 352,000 by the end of 2012. Yet there remained grave
doubts over the quality of this rapidly expanded and largely ill-trained force. There
were also fears over its reliability and loyalty, particularly in the light of the continuing phenomenon of rogue attacks, wherein individual Afghan soldiers turned
their weapons on Western troops in sudden and deadly point-blank killing sprees.
There were also concerns over the ethics of the security appartus of the Afghan
state. A detailed report by the UN Assistance Mission in Afghanistan (UNAMA),
released in October, catalogued abuses in prisons administered by the Afghan
National Police and the National Directorate of Security (NDS—the intelligence
agency). It found "compelling evidence" of the use of torture to extract confessions or information from suspects, included beatings, genital abuse, the ripping
out of toenails, suspension, the use of electric shocks, stress positions, and sexual
assault. In response to these findings General John Allen, who in July had suc-

ceeded Petraeus as the commander in Afghanistan, ordered a halt in the transfer of detainees from coalition custody to a number of Afghan prisons. It was a necessary gesture of disapproval but only a gesture. A month before the UNAMA report, Human Rights Watch had issued a study which showed the degree to which the Western military effort had had a detrimental effect on human rights. It exposed a process whereby the Karzai government and the US military had financed and armed thousands of men in village-level paramilitary groups, known collectively as the Afghan Local Police (ALP). Distinct from the Afghan National Police, the ALP was the latest of several attempts to build a militia that could offer protection for communities against insurgent attack. The report showed that in practice these paramilitary groups frequently terrorised local civilians, often engaging with impunity in a range of criminal activities that included murder, rape, torture, extortion, smuggling and the seizure of land.

The imminence of the Western military withdrawal raised two other significant political issues that had a crucial bearing on the viability of the Afghan regime which was to be left behind. These were the nature of a long-term US presence in the country after 2014 and the necessity of negotiating a peace agreement with the Taliban insurgents. Both matters were shrouded in secret negotiations.

It was widely accepted that after the Western troops had withdrawn, a significant US military presence would remain in the form of "advisers". Karzai also suggested that the USA was demanding permanent military bases in his country as part of a long-term "strategic partnership" agreement. He recognised that this was a prospect not attractive to many of his compatriots. In mid-November he convened a Loya Jirga (grand assembly), consisting of 2,000 hand-picked delegates— elders, local and regional leaders, and government officials—which debated the issue and, unsurprisingly, endorsed Karzai's objective of negotiating a strategic agreement to maintain a long-term US military presence after 2014. In his address to the jirga Karzai welcomed the fact that the "foreigners are leaving Afghanistan" and shared his somewhat improbable vision of a strong and independent Afghanistan commanding respect upon the international stage. Warming to his theme he insisted that any future relationship with the USA would have to be based on mutual respect. "Yes, America is rich, strong... but we are lions. A lion is a lion even if even it gets old... America should treat us as a lion. We are ready to sign a strategic treaty between a lion and America." A more conventionally phrased assessment of future relations came from the US ambassador in Afghanistan, Ryan Cocker, who expressed optimism that the 2014 withdrawal timetable would be achieved but stressed that this was "not the date when the United States and the international community just walk away from Afghanistan... We don't want to repeat the mistakes of 1990—we got out when the Soviets left and that was the road to 9/11." Instead he envisaged a bilateral security agreement between the USA and Afghanistan that "would lay out the framework for strategic partnership well beyond 2014 in a wide range of areas—the economy, education... as well as security".

The Loya Jirga also inconclusively discussed the issue of peace talks with the Taliban. Throughout the year there had been rumours of unofficial talks and "back channel" contacts. Defence Secretary Gates had confirmed in June that the USA was engaged in direct talks with Taliban representatives but qualified this by emphasising that these were "very preliminary" contacts. The UN Security Council had also amended its sanctions regime in a move designed to make it easier to draw the Taliban into the negotiating framework. There remained, however, no clear or reliable conduit for meaningful negotiations. In theory Karzai's High Peace Council, created in 2010, continued to pursue peace but neither its efforts, nor those of the coalition, made any tangible progress towards a negotiated ceasefire. For the stark truth remained that the Taliban had no pressing incentive to negotiate. With the troop surge having failed and the 2014 deadline for withdrawal fast approaching, the insurgents could afford to play a patient endgame.

Thus the war continued along its well-worn attritional path. The steady trickle of coalition casualties continued, with each death helping to further undermine public and political resolve in the troop-contributing countries to which the bodies of dead husbands and sons were repatriated. Occasionally there were spectacular Taliban successes, most notably the shooting down of a US helicopter in the Tangi valley, in Wardak province, in August, killing all 38 people on board. (In additional to Afghan troops, the dead included 25 US special operations personnel and five members of the US National Guard, thus making it the deadliest single US loss of the 10-year war.) In general, however, the guerrillas preferred to avoid direct clashes in which the superior training and weaponry of the coalition invariably prevailed. Instead they continued to perfect their use of the much feared "improvised explosive devices" (IEDs), which became ever more sophisticated and powerful, capable of killing the occupants of even the most heavily armoured of vehicles.

Suicide bombings also remained a routine feature of daily life. Individuals detonating explosive vests or at the wheel of a vehicle packed with explosives regularly struck targets such as government offices, police recruitment centres, and military convoys. Although the Taliban professed a commitment to targeting the "foreign invaders" and representatives of the "puppet" Afghan government, in practice they also hit the softest of non-military targets, such as hospitals and crowded marketplaces, and were responsible for the majority of civilian deaths. In addition to the threat of bombs, the insurgents continued to administer their own brand of justice in many areas of the country, with a sharp rise in the summary execution of those accused of being collaborators or informants. Some of the death squads accused of these killings were associated with the Haqqani network, an insurgent-clan structure operating in the Afghanistan-Pakistan border region, that had fought the Soviets in the 1980s (with US support) but had more recently been associated with al-Qaida. Regardless of authorship of the increased rate of murder, the result of such tactics was widespread fear. According to the assessment of the outgoing UN deputy special representative, Robert Watkins, in late February, security in Afghanistan was at its worst since 2001 with 40 per cent of the country virtually "off limits" to UN personnel because it was simply too dangerous.

In a world inured to decades of violence in Afghanistan only the most spectacular insurgent attacks made an impact in the international media. To this end, the

Taliban enlivened its routine diet of bombing and killing with attacks on high-profile targets deliberately chosen for their propaganda value. The greatest prize was central Kabul, which offered proof that the rebels could penetrate the city's inner security cordon and strike at the heart of the Karzai government. The city suffered a number of attacks during the year. In January a suicide bomber killed nine in a supermarket much patronised by Westerners in one of the wealthiest and most heavily guarded areas of the city centre. In June three suicide bombers attacked a central police station killing at least nine people. Later that month, 21 were killed when a nine-member suicide squad struck inside the prestigious Inter-Continental hotel in central Kabul, leading to a five-hour gun battle before Afghan and NATO forces were able to overcome them. On 19 August insurgents overran the British Council building in Kabul, leading to another prolonged gun battle. Less than a month later, on 13 September, insurgents launched multiple attacks upon the capital in which at least 27 people died. The targets included the US embassy and NATO's headquarters. Parts of the city were paralysed for 20 hours as government troops fought to regain control of buildings that had been occupied and fortified by the attackers. Several of these assaults were blamed upon the Haqqani network.

In addition to Kabul there were other attacks during the year with high propaganda value. These included police stations and government offices, particularly in centres of provincial government, which at times were overrun by insurgents, particularly in remote areas. The major southern city of Kandahar was also a repeated target, although here the greatest propaganda coup of the year was a mass escape by Taliban prisoners from the city's main Sarposa prison in the early hours of 25 April. It was later discovered that Taliban members on the outside had spent five months digging a 320-metre tunnel into the prison. When it was completed, a total of 541 Taliban inmates (including more than 100 "commanders"), assisted by some prison staff, escaped in an orderly fashion. Their guards, who apparently routinely alleviated the boredom of their duties with the assistance of marijuana and heroin, slept soundly through the night and did not discover the escape until the next morning. In addition to having the practical value of supplementing the Taliban's force pool and command structure, the embarrassing prison debacle was a perfect metaphor that encapsulated the methodical patience of the insurgency and the dissolute corruption of the regime with which it was at war.

The insurgents also stepped up their assassination of significant political figures. Those targeted tended to be former Mujahedeen commanders, tribal leaders, and advisers to President Karzai. Chief amongst these was the president's powerful half-brother, Ahmed Wali Karzai, the key power-broker in southern Afghanistan, who was shot dead at his home on 12 July by a trusted member of his security staff (see Obituary). In the same month insurgents assassinated Jan Muhammad Khan, a powerful warlord and close confidant of Karzai, and Ghulam Haider Hamidi, the mayor of Kandahar, who had been a childhood friend of the president. The latter was killed by a suicide bomber who had hidden explosives in his turban. This new method of concealment was used increasingly during the year and accounted for another high-profile victim with the death on 20 September of Burhanuddin Rabbani, a former president of Afghanistan and the chief peace envoy of Karzai (see Obituary). Rabbani was killed at his home in Kabul by a man—posing as a Taliban commander come to discuss peace terms—who detonated a bomb concealed within his turban as he leaned forward to greet his host in an embrace.

By such means the insurgents harassed, intimidated and demoralised their enemies as they waited for the 2014 withdrawal to alter decisively the balance of forces on the ground. For the coalition armies which opposed them there was also a move away from the grand but ultimately unsuccessful offensive operations of 2010. Instead there was a campaign of increasing intensity designed to disrupt and decapitate the insurgency by assassinating Taliban senior and middle-ranking commanders. The mechanism for this was a combination of night raids by special forces—averaging around 10 per night but sometimes reaching as many as 40 per night—and airstrikes. The latter were often conducted by unmanned drone aircraft, which increasingly patrolled the skies of Afghanistan. The tactic was effective in achieving kills and there was some evidence that the Taliban was struggling to replace the loss of seasoned commanders. It was also cheap in terms of Western casualties as the drones were operated remotely from the USA and night raids tended not to result in high coalition casualties (with the notable exception of the Tangi valley helicopter disaster.)

The problem with this strategy was that air attacks and night raids on civilian compounds thought to harbour insurgents inevitably produced civilian casualties. (Some research suggested that for every rebel leader killed in night raids, eight other people also died.) The result was deep resentment at all levels of Afghan society over tactics that seemed designed to minimise coalition military casualties by inflicting death on innocent Afghan civilians. Underlying such a policy, of course, was the implicit assumption that Western lives were worth more than those of ordinary Afghans. As always, it was the worst of the atrocities that made the news. More than 60 civilians (half of whom were children) were killed during a night operation, including air strikes, in Kunar province in February. The Afghan sense of outrage over the massacre was inflamed by US military suggestions that some of the injuries sustained by the children could have been inflicted by their parents in order "to create a civilian casualty claim". Within days of the incident a coalition helicopter killed nine children who were collecting firewood, although at least on this occasion there were prompt and profuse apologies, from Obama downwards. Yet in May an air strike in Helmand province killed 14 people, 11 of whom were children under the age of seven, whilst in November an air strike killed seven civilians, including six children.

Such acts were repeatedly denounced by an exasperated Karzai and other public figures, and led to public demonstrations in which Afghans screamed "Death to America". They were also acts that undermined the moral basis of the Western military intervention in Afghanistan and whipped up anti-US feeling. This was also fuelled by other incidents during the year, including the ongoing prosecution in the USA of a group of soldiers who had killed Afghan civilians for sport, photographing their crimes and retaining body parts as souvenirs. Popular fury was also provoked by the burning in Florida in March of a copy of the

Koran by an otherwise insignificant US pastor who possessed a small congregation but a supersize ego. In the rioting which followed this act of senseless bigotry the compound of UNAMA in Mazar-i-Sharif was overrun, and seven UN personnel butchered by an enraged mob.

Air attacks on, and over, the border with Pakistan also had a significant impact on the West's relationship with Afghanistan's powerful neighbour. This was most evident with the hostility generated by an air strike on 26 November on an outpost in Pakistan that killed 24 Pakistani troops. The incident provoked a furious diplomatic response from Pakistan which included the closure of its supply lines to Western troops operating in Afghanistan. It was a costly act of carelessness as Pakistan would be a key player in determining the stability of any future Afghan regime. Karzai himself had acknowledged this, even whilst launching a new strategic partnership with India in early October. He insisted that better relations with India would not compromise his country's bond with Pakistan, which he referred to as "a twin brother". Yet the suspicion remained that this twin was co-ordinating insurgent activity in Afghanistan, particularly via the Haqqani network. Speaking on Pakistani television in October, Karzai claimed that the Taliban "would not be able to move a finger" without Pakistani support. But with characteristic unpredictability the Afghan president went on to promise that Afghanistan would support its twin if it were involved in a military conflict with any other power, including the USA or India.

Resentment over the US air strike in November meant that Pakistan did not participate in the second Bonn conference, an international gathering of more than 100 countries and international organisations held in early December to discuss Afghanistan's future. The conference marked the anniversary of a similar gathering that had been held in the German city almost exactly 10 years earlier, during happier times. After a decade of war the mood of the second conference was sombre, particularly as its opening coincided with a leaked German intelligence report which suggested that Karzai was intent upon retaining power even after the expiry of his current (second) term of office as president in 2014. When the conference got under way the president contributed to the downbeat mood by suggesting that his government would require up to $10 billion per year in support after the Western military withdrawal. In response, the conference did no more than offer a vague commitment to continued support in the post-2014 era and appeal to Karzai to strengthen democracy and anti-corruption efforts. As the conference ended Karzai was forced to rush back to Kabul to confront the aftermath of co-ordinated suicide bombings on 6 December that killed around 60 people. The worst of the bombs was at the Abul Fazal mosque in Kabul where at least 55 were killed and 130 wounded. The attacks displayed a murderous sectarianism rarely seen in Afghanistan in that they had specifically targeted the minority Shia community, which constituted 20 per cent of the population and was tribally distinct from the (Sunni) Taliban who were predominantly Pashtun.

These two events of December were ominous notes upon which to end the year. One highlighted the problems posed by the need for a huge future commitment to Afghanistan by Western economies already facing economic austerity. The other carried the fear that even if long-term financial support were forthcoming, the future of Afghanistan would be bloody and bleak. Upon these discordant notes hung an echo of the old adage that it was easier to get into a war than to get out, and a realisation that 2014 would not mark the end of this unhappy conflict.

D.S. Lewis

KAZAKHSTAN—KYRGYZSTAN—UZBEKISTAN—TAJIKISTAN— TURKMENISTAN

Kazakhstan

CAPITAL: Astana   AREA: 2,724,900 sq km   POPULATION: 16,316,050 ('10)
OFFICIAL LANGUAGES: Kazakh & Russian
HEAD OF STATE AND GOVERNMENT: President Nursultan Nazarbayev (since Feb '90)
RULING PARTY: Nur-Otan People's Democratic Party
PRIME MINISTER: Karim Masimov (since Jan '07)
DEMOCRACY INDEX: 3.30; 132nd of 167   CORRUPTION INDEX: 2.7; 120th of 183
CURRENCY: Tenge (Dec '11 £1.00=KZT 231.47, US$1=KZT 147.6)
GNI PER CAPITA: US$7,440, Intl$10,610 at PPP ('10)

Kyrgyzstan

CAPITAL: Bishkek   AREA: 199,900 sq km   POPULATION: 5,365,167 ('10)
OFFICIAL LANGUAGES: Kyrgyz & Russian
HEAD OF STATE AND GOVERNMENT: President Almazbek Atambayev (SDP) (since Dec '11)
RULING PARTIES: Social Democratic Party (SDP)-led coalition
PRIME MINISTER: Bakyt Beshimov (since Dec '11)
DEMOCRACY INDEX: 4.31; 106th of 167   CORRUPTION INDEX: 2.1; 164th of 183
CURRENCY: Som (Dec '11 £1.00=KGS 73.25, US$1.00=KGS 46.71)
GNI PER CAPITA: US$880, Intl$2,180 at PPP ('10)

Uzbekistan

CAPITAL: Tashkent   AREA: 447,400 sq km   POPULATION: 28,160,361 ('10)
OFFICIAL LANGUAGE: Uzbek
HEAD OF STATE AND GOVERNMENT: President Islam Karimov (since March '90)
RULING PARTY: People's Democratic Party (PDP)
PRIME MINISTER: Shavkat Mirziyoev (since Dec '03)
DEMOCRACY INDEX: 1.74; 164th of 167   CORRUPTION INDEX: 1.6; 177th of 183
CURRENCY: Sum (Dec '11 £1.00=UZS 2,792, US$1.00=UZS 1,780)
GNI PER CAPITA: US$1,280, Intl$3,090 at PPP ('10)

Tajikistan

CAPITAL: Dushanbe   AREA: 142,550 sq km   POPULATION: 6,878,637 ('10)
OFFICIAL LANGUAGE: Tajik
HEAD OF STATE AND GOVERNMENT: President Imamoli Rahmon (formerly Rahmonov) (since Nov '92)
RULING PARTY: People's Democratic Party of Tajikistan
PRIME MINISTER: Akil Akilov (since Dec '99)
DEMOCRACY INDEX: 2.51; 149th of 167   CORRUPTION INDEX: 2.3; 152nd of 183
CURRENCY: Somoni (Dec '11 £1.00=TJS 7.46, US$1.00=TJS 4.76)
GNI PER CAPITA: US$800, Intl$2,120 at PPP ('10)

Turkmenistan
CAPITAL: Ashgabat   AREA: 488,100 sq km   POPULATION: 5,041,995 ('10)
OFFICIAL LANGUAGE: Turkmen
HEAD OF STATE AND GOVERNMENT: President and Prime Minister Gurbanguly Berdymukhamedov
   (since Feb '07)
RULING PARTY: Democratic Party of Turkmentistan (DPT)
DEMOCRACY INDEX: 1.72 165th of 167   CORRUPTION INDEX: 1.6; 177th of 183
CURRENCY: New Manat (Dec '11 £1.00=TMT 4.45, US$1.00=TMT 2.84)
GNI PER CAPITA: US$3,800, Intl$7,350 at PPP ('10)

IN December 2010, Nur Otan, **Kazakhstan's** largest political party, proposed
holding a referendum to extend President Nursultan Nazarbayev's tenure until
2020 without elections. By January 2011 over 5 million citizens had signed up to
it. However, at home and abroad there was widespread condemnation of this idea.
Consequently, it was abandoned in favour of a snap election on 3 April. Unsurprisingly, Nazarbayev won a landslide victory, gaining 95.5 per cent of the vote
and securing another five-year term of office. There were allegations of misconduct and media bias in his favour, but there was general acknowledgement that the
result largely reflected the mood of the electorate. A few months later, political
parties began to position themselves for the next bout of parliamentary elections,
scheduled for August 2012. However, in December it was suddenly announced
that these would be brought forward to January 2012. The aim was to create a
more representative parliamentary-presidential system, but it was anticipated that
Nur Otan, the president's own party, would win an overwhelming majority.

In January Kazakhstan hosted the Asian Winter Games, a prestigious event
attended by over 1,000 athletes, from 27 countries. Yet domestically there were
signs of instability. In April, copper workers in Zhezqazgan began demanding
better wages and the right to form independent trade unions. Thousands of oil
workers soon followed their lead, some going on hunger strike, others setting up
roadblocks. The company owners (mostly foreign corporations) and the government tried to crush the "illegal" protests by sending in the police, but opposition
parties and NGOs, both foreign and domestic, supported the workers. The
British singer Sting cancelled his scheduled performance at President
Nazarbayev's 71st birthday celebrations in July as a mark of solidarity with the
protesters. In December, there were further disturbances, leading to the deaths
of at least 16 people in Zhanaozen.

Another worrying trend was the rise in Islamist-inspired terrorist attacks, including in May the first instance of a suicide bombing in Kazakhstan. An estimated
total of 30 people were killed in these various incidents. In an attempt to curb this
extremist element, a tough new law on religion was enacted in October, but many
believed that this would further exacerbate the situation. The independent media
also experienced severe restrictions. Meanwhile, the former British prime minister, Tony Blair, accepted (allegedly for a fee of £8 million) a one-year post as consultant to President Nazarbayev; he opened an office in Astana in October.

Kyrgyzstan, following the violent clashes of 2010 (see AR 2011, pp. 288-90),
had a relatively calm year. However, the coalition government that had been

formed in December 2010 was crippled by internal divisions and was unable to implement a coherent programme of reforms; consequently, little was done to address the country's massive socio-economic problems. Moreover, the political scene was dominated by preparations for the presidential election, scheduled for 30 October. The long and varied list of presidential hopefuls (83 candidates sought registration, including farmers, businessmen, teachers and unemployed people) was reduced to 16 by polling day. As expected, the winner was 56-year-old Almazbek Atambayev, leader of the Social Democrats and former prime minster (he had resigned in September, in order to stand for president). He gained some 63 per cent of the vote and, despite allegations of electoral fraud, was generally recognised as the popular choice. Interim President Roza Otunbayeva stepped down as promised, in the country's first peaceful transfer of power. Yet the political situation remained fragile. Two days after the inauguration ceremony the government resigned over proposed reforms. Shortly after this, the speaker also resigned "in order to maintain stability"; more probably, his departure was linked to serious allegations of criminal ties. In mid-December, the Social Democrats, supported by three of the largest parties, Respublika, Ata-Meken (Fatherland), and Ar-Namys (Dignity), formed a new, somewhat fragile, coalition. The Ata-Zhurt (Homeland) faction formed the parliamentary opposition.

President Atambayev signalled his intention to build good relations with neighbouring states, likewise with the "big powers"—Russia, China and the USA. Nevertheless, he insisted that the US transit centre at Manas airport would have to be closed by 2014. This facility had long been a source of contention and there had been previous attempts to close it (see AR 2010, p. 293). One reason for closing the Manas base was the risk of attracting retaliatory attacks from militant Islamist groups. As in Kazakhstan, such attacks were already occurring. Yet, given the vital role played by the Manas base in transporting NATO-ISAF operations in Afghanistan (it handled some 15,000 servicemen and 500 tons of cargo per month) it was probable that negotiations to reach a mutually acceptable arrangement would soon take place.

Uzbek President Islam Karimov's visit to Brussels in January marked a warming of the relationship between **Uzbekistan** and the West, which had been derailed by the violent clashes in the Uzbek city of Andijan in 2005 (see AR 2005, pp. 267-68). He had meetings with European Commission President José Manuel Barroso and NATO Secretary General Anders Fogh Rasmussen. A memorandum of co-operation on energy was signed. Substantive discussions on co-operation between NATO and Uzbekistan were also held. Subsequently, the Uzbek government hosted several US generals and senior diplomats, who described Uzbekistan as a key partner, not only for the "movement of critical supplies into Afghanistan", but because of "co-operation on countering terrorism and narcotics smuggling". A railway connecting Uzbekistan with Afghanistan became operational in December; this was expected to be a key link in NATO-ISAF's supply chain (the "Northern Distribution Network").

Uzbekistan's role in assisting operations in Afghanistan was heightened by the deterioration in US-Pakistan relations. However, human rights organisations were outraged by the West's growing ties with the Uzbek government and published numerous reports of torture and other abuses taking place in the country, claims that were firmly denied by the Uzbek authorities. Moreover, international organisations, such as Save the Children and the OSCE, highlighted positive trends in the country. In December, Uzbekistan's parliament cut the presidential mandate from seven to five years (it had been extended from five to seven years by referendum in 2002) as part of a wider programme to devolve power and to strengthen civil society. The new law would not affect the incumbent's current term of office, which would run until 2014.

Addressing the 66th Session of the UN General Assembly in September, the Tajik foreign minister stressed the dangerous effects of climate change, particularly on Central Asia's hydrology. Some 60 per cent of the region's water resources originated in **Tajikistan**, but in the previous 30 years more than 35 per cent of the glaciers had melted. He called for the establishment of an international fund to save glaciers in the region.

Water issues were also on the agenda during the visit of Iran's President Mahmoud Ahmadinejad to Dushanbe earlier that month. Iran was involved in the financing and construction of several large projects in Tajikistan, including the Sangtuda-2 hydroelectric power plant and dam (HPP). When completed, this would not only help to alleviate the chronic energy shortage in Tajikistan, but would allow for energy to be exported to Afghanistan. Other HPPs were also under construction. However, there were still problems surrounding the monumental Roghun HPP project, planned for the Vakhsh Cascade in southern Tajikistan. Most of the funding was provided by the state budget, supplemented by semi-compulsory contributions from Tajik citizens. Uzbekistan strongly objected to the project, insisting that it would adversely affect water flows to downstream states. In August, following detailed assessment studies, World Bank experts reported that it was inadvisable to start the project immediately, owing to environmental and social impact concerns. The Uzbek side claimed that the Tajiks were ignoring these warnings and covertly proceeding with construction work.

Tajikistan maintained a carefully balanced foreign policy. In October, US Secretary of State Hillary Clinton made her first visit to Tajikistan. She focused on the need for economic development, also religious and other fundamental freedoms. Tajik officials responded by calling for a "political dialogue" with the USA; they also sought US investment in developing their natural resources, and support in the fight against terrorism, drug trafficking and transnational crime. A few weeks earlier Russia's President Dmitry Medvedev, too, had visited Dushanbe. A significant outcome of his visit was the agreement to extend the lease on the Russian military base in Tajikistan by 49 years (under the original agreement, it would have expired in 2013). The base housed around 6,000 servicemen, the largest deployment of Russian ground troops beyond its borders.

Turkmenistan's hydrocarbon reserves continued to attract attention. The discovery of major new gas fields resulted in a substantial upgrade of its estimated reserves, placing it second only to Iran. There were also discoveries of new oil deposits in Turkmenistan's sector of the Caspian Sea, now estimated at 12 billion tons. International interest in securing energy supplies from Turkmenistan thus intensified. In November, China concluded a deal to purchase 65 billion cubic metres (bcm) of natural gas annually, 25 bcm more than had been originally agreed when the 7,000 km pipeline from Turkmenistan to China was inaugurated in 2009 (see AR 2010, p. 295). The transaction was part of a larger package of agreements that included Chinese soft loans of more than $8 billion. Russia, another major consumer of Turkmen gas, had experienced strains in its relationship with Turkmenistan. Notably, in 2009 the Russian company Gazprom suddenly cut the volume of its imports of Turkmen gas, causing financial loss as well as infrastructural damage in Turkmenistan (see AR 2010, p. 296). This matter was resolved in 2010, but there were other areas of tension, including Russia's objections (shared with Iran) to the laying of a subsea trans-Caspian pipeline from Turkmenistan to Azerbaijan, to carry Turkmen gas to European markets. Yet despite these problems, bilateral relations between the two countries were largely amicable and Russia remained Turkmenistan's second-largest trading partner.

Turkmenistan's largest trading partner was neighbouring Iran. Ties between the two countries were underpinned by co-operation in a number of fields, including energy. In January 2010 Turkmenistan inaugurated the first stage of a new pipeline to Iran to transport natural gas from Dovletabat (eastern Turkmenistan), a field previously reserved for deliveries to Russia. In November 2011, Iranian President Ahmadinejad and his Turkmen counterpart inaugurated the last section of this 1,024 km pipeline.

The EU was also eager to receive energy supplies from Turkmenistan. In January, European Commission President Barroso made his first official visit to Turkmenistan, primarily to secure agreement to contribute Turkmen gas to the planned Nabucco pipeline (a project backed by the EU and the USA to transport natural gas from Turkey to Europe, bypassing Russia). Yet despite encouraging statements, Turkmenistan was not as yet prepared to make a firm commitment.

A project that did have its full backing was the 1,680 km-long TAPI (Turkmenistan-Afghanistan-Pakistan-India) pipeline. Russia and the USA also supported the project. However, reaching consensus amongst all the participants was difficult. Pakistan and Turkmenistan inked the gas sale purchase agreement in November, but negotiations over financial details continued into 2012.

Shirin Akiner

INDIA—PAKISTAN—BANGLADESH—SRI LANKA—NEPAL—BHUTAN

India

CAPITAL: New Delhi   AREA: 3,287,260 sq km   POPULATION: 1,170,938,000 ('10)
OFFICIAL LANGUAGES: Hindi & English
HEAD OF STATE: President Pratibha Patil (since July '07)
RULING PARTIES: Indian National Congress (INC)-led United Progressive Alliance (UPA)
HEAD OF GOVERNMENT: Prime Minister Manmohan Singh (INC) (since May '04)
DEMOCRACY INDEX: 7.28; 40th of 167   CORRUPTION INDEX: 3.1; 95th of 183
CURRENCY: Indian Rupee (Dec '11 £1.00=INR 80.71, US$1.00=INR 51.46)
GNI PER CAPITA: US$1,340, Intl$3,560 at PPP ('10)

Pakistan

CAPITAL: Islamabad   AREA: 796,100 sq km   POPULATION: 173,593,383 ('10)
OFFICIAL LANGUAGE: Urdu
HEAD OF STATE AND GOVERNMENT: President Asif Ali Zardari (PPP) (since Sept '08)
RULING PARTY: Pakistan People's Party (PPP)
PRIME MINISTER: Yusuf Raza Gillani (PPP) (since March '08)
DEMOCRACY INDEX: 4.55; 104th of 167   CORRUPTION INDEX: 2.5; 134th of 183
CURRENCY: Pakistan Rupee (Dec '11 £1.00=PKR 134.23, US$1.00=PKR 88.78)
GNI PER CAPITA: US$1,050, Intl$2,780 at PPP ('10)

Bangladesh

CAPITAL: Dhaka   AREA: 144,000 sq km   POPULATION: 148,692,131 ('10)
OFFICIAL LANGUAGE: Bengali
HEAD OF STATE: President Mohammad Zillur Rahman (AL) (since Feb '09)
RULING PARTIES: Awami League (AL)-led coalition
HEAD OF GOVERNMENT: Prime Minister Sheikh Hasina Wajed (AL) (since Jan '09)
DEMOCRACY INDEX: 5.87; 83rd of 167   CORRUPTION INDEX: 2.7; 120 of 183
CURRENCY: Taka (Dec '11 £1.00=BDT 120.65, US$1=BDT 76.93)
GNI PER CAPITA: US$700, Intl$1,800 at PPP ('10)

Sri Lanka

CAPITAL: Sri Jayawardenapura (Kotte)   AREA: 65,610 sq km   POPULATION: 20,859,949 ('10)
OFFICIAL LANGUAGES: Sinhala, Tamil, English
HEAD OF STATE AND GOVERNMENT: President Mahinda Rajapakse (SLFP) (since Nov '05)
RULING PARTIES: United People's Freedom Alliance (UPFA) coalition, led by Sri Lanka Freedom
   Party (SLFP)
PRIME MINISTER: Disanayaka Mudiyanselage Jayaratne (since April '10)
DEMOCRACY INDEX: 6.64; 55th of 167   CORRUPTION INDEX: 3.3; 86th of 183
CURRENCY: Sri Lankan Rupee (Dec '11 £1.00=LKR 178.58, US$1.00=LKR 113.87)
GNI PER CAPITA: US$2,240, Intl$4,980 at PPP ('10)

Nepal

CAPITAL: Kathmandu   AREA: 147,180 sq km   POPULATION: 29,959,364 ('10)
OFFICIAL LANGUAGE: Nepali
HEAD OF STATE: President Ram Baran Yadav (since July '08)
RULING PARTY: coalition led by Unified Communist Party of Nepal (Maoist) (UCPN-M)
HEAD OF GOVERNMENT: Prime Minister Baburam Bhattarai (since Aug '11)
DEMOCRACY INDEX: 4.24; 108th of 167   CORRUPTION INDEX: 2.2; 154th of 183
CURRENCY: Nepalese Rupee (Dec '11 £1.00=NPR 129.14, US$1=NPR 82.34)
GNI PER CAPITA: US$480, Intl$1,200 at PPP ('10)

Bhutan

CAPITAL: Thimphu   AREA: 47,000 sq km   POPULATION: 725,940 ('10)
OFFICIAL LANGUAGE: Dzongkha
HEAD OF STATE: Dragon King Jigme Khesar Namgyel Wangchuk (since Dec '06)
RULING PARTY: Bhutan Harmony Party (DPT)
HEAD OF GOVERNMENT: Prime Minister Jigme Yoser Thinley (since April '08)
DEMOCRACY INDEX: 4.68; 102nd of 167   CORRUPTION INDEX: 5.7; 38th of 183
CURRENCY: Ngultrum (Dec '11 £1.00=BTN 80.71, US$1.00=BTN 51.46)
GNI PER CAPITA: US$1,880, Intl$4,950 at PPP ('10)

WHILE 2011 witnessed a change of leadership in only one of the six states in South
Asia (Nepal), the year was one in which the governments of India and Pakistan
struggled in the face of powerful challenges to their authority, while those of Sri
Lanka and Bangladesh were accused by their opponents of creeping authoritarianism. Tiny Bhutan held its first ever local government elections. Growth slowed
in the subcontinent's major economies as the impact of the global recession, as
well as local factors, began to bite. The year ended on a note of uncertainty, especially in Pakistan where apprehensions grew that the country might yet again be
on the verge of an extra-parliamentary removal of the government.

As in 2010, the issue of corruption dominated politics in **India**, with the Indian
National Congress-led United Progressive Alliance (UPA) government of Prime
Minister Manmohan Singh facing relentless pressure from a new mass movement
launched by Anna Hazare, a hitherto obscure 74-year-old veteran social activist
and anti-corruption campaigner from the western state of Maharashtra who held
repeated public fasts to force the government to introduce stringent anti-corruption
legislation. His campaign recalled the methods of non-violent civil protest pio-
neered by Gandhi in India's independence struggle. Despite being criticised for
allegedly reactionary attitudes by some commentators, Hazare's campaign won
the attention of the media and attracted widespread support, especially among
middle class urban Indians disillusioned by the corruption apparently pervasive
among politicians, bureaucrats and businessmen.

  While there was a plethora of corruption scandals (see AR 2011, pp. 293-296),
the four most controversial involved the possible loss to the public exchequer of
up to $40 billion in the government's sale of lucrative electro-magnetic spectrum
licences in 2008, the mismanagement of the 2010 Commonwealth Games in
Delhi, the alleged bribery that enabled the UPA government win a parliamentary
confidence vote in 2008, and land and mining deals that forced the resignation of
the Bharatiya Janata Party (BJP) chief minister of the southern state of Karnataka.
The first was the source of greatest difficulty for the government. Former communications minister Andimuthu Raja was arrested in February and soon afterwards
Prime Minister Singh gave in to opposition demands for a joint parliamentary
committee inquiry into the telecom scam. In April Raja was charged with conspiracy, forgery and fraud. In further blows to the Dravida Munnetra Kazhagam
(DMK), the UPA component to which he belonged, in May M.K. Kanimozhi—a
DMK member of parliament and the daughter of the party's longtime leader, M.
Karunanidhi—was also arrested and in July DMK Textile Minister Dayanidhi

Maran had to resign after allegations of involvement in the scandal. In November Kanimozhi, Raja and 12 others, including former civil servants, top company executives and businessmen, were put on trial on charges including criminal conspiracy, forgery, accepting bribes and misuse of office. The Congress Party, too, continued to be caught up in the scandal—the year ended with the opposition BJP-led National Democratic Alliance (NDA) demanding the resignation of Home Minister P. Chidambaram for failing to prevent the scam while serving as finance minister. In October a new draft telecom policy, reforming how mobile licences were sold and boosting consumer rights, was unveiled.

Congress was directly in the line of fire in connection with two of the other major corruption scandals. In April Suresh Kalmadi, the ex-chairman of the Commonwealth Games organising committee and former secretary of the Congress parliamentary party, was arrested on charges of conspiracy in the awarding of contracts. A report by the comptroller and auditor general of India subsequently concluded that there had been serious irregularities with bidding and contracts. In March the WikiLeaks website published a US diplomatic cable suggesting that Congress had bribed opposition MPs to win a parliamentary vote of confidence in 2008. Although this was dismissed by Prime Minister Singh, in August Amar Singh, the former general secretary of the Samajwadi Party, formerly allied to Congress, was charged, along with three BJP members of parliament, for his role in the alleged cash-for-votes affair. The prime minister's reputation for probity suffered another blow in March when he had to admit an "error of judgement" after the Supreme Court quashed his appointment of P.J. Thomas as chief vigilance commissioner, the head of the country's anti-corruption body, on the grounds that Thomas faced fraud allegations dating back to when he had been a senior civil servant in the southern state of Kerala.

It was against this backdrop that in April Anna Hazare began an indefinite fast at Jantar Mantar, the historic Delhi observatory, demanding that the government accept a joint committee—including civil society representatives from the new India Against Corruption movement—in drafting a rigorous anti-corruption Jan Lokpal (Citizens' Ombudsman) bill. After four days, during which support for the demand was expressed in demonstrations across India, the government agreed to the formation of a joint committee. However, differences over the scope of the Lokpal soon emerged and the authorities' harsh suppression in June of a BJP-backed anti-corruption fast by the Hindu yoga guru Baba Ramdev at the Ram Lilla Maidan in Delhi, venue of historic popular demonstrations since the 1930s, further soured the atmosphere. When the draft bill was tabled in parliament in early August its ambit excluded the prime minister and senior judges and Hazare proclaimed his intention to go ahead with a new fast against it, describing the struggle as the "second war of independence". His detention in Delhi, along with hundreds of supporters, on the eve of the fast on 16 August provoked nationwide protests and a storm of criticism, forcing the police to release him after three days to undertake the remainder of his 15-day fast at the Ram Lilla Maidan. Hazare ended this fast on 28 August after MPs expressed willingness to make changes to the bill.

The redrafted bill still excluded the judiciary, the lower level bureaucracy and the conduct of MPs in parliament, as well as the country's main investigative agency, the Central Bureau of Investigation (the Lokpal would not have its own investigative agency). Although Hazare undertook further fasts and threatened a protest campaign of civil disobedience, the bill was passed by the Lok Sabha (the lower house of parliament), with debate in the Rajya Sabha (the upper house) adjourned at the end of December amidst heated scenes and uncertainty about whether the ruling UPA could muster enough votes to secure its approval.

The opposition BJP called on the prime minister to resign following the impasse in the Rajya Sabha, thus ending the year scenting a more realistic prospect of the NDA returning to office than for some time. However, this was due more to the UPA's discomfiture than its own achievements. In November the party's 84-year-old leader L.K. Advani completed a 38-day nationwide anti-corruption Jan Chetna Yatra (public awareness tour). Yet only four months earlier the party had to instruct B.S. Yeddyurappa, the chief minister of the southern state of Karnataka, to resign after an anti-corruption panel named him as a suspect in an illegal iron ore mining scam that allegedly cost the state $3 billion between 2006 and 2010. In September G. Janardhan Reddy, a former BJP minister and one of the richest politicians in Karnataka, was arrested in connection with the case. Yeddyurappa was arrested in October in another case which had brought him into confrontation with the state governor after the latter had sanctioned his prosecution for illegally allotting valuable real estate to family members and other associates.

The BJP's Hindu chauvinist reputation also continued to haunt it. In a confession in January (later retracted) Swami Aseemanand, a former activist of the Rashtriya Swayam Sevak Sangh, the parent organisation of the BJP, admitted that he and other Hindu militants had been behind several terrorist attacks in 2006-07 including one on a Muslim graveyard previously attributed to seven Muslims. In May the Supreme Court, hearing rival appeals against it, suspended the Uttar Pradesh High Court ruling (see AR 2011, p. 296) partitioning the controversial site of the Babri Masjid (Babar's mosque) in Ayodhya razed by Hindu militants allied to the BJP in 1992. In August the BJP state government in the western state of Gujarat charged two senior police officers with misconduct after they gave evidence suggesting the complicity of chief minister Narendra Modi and his officials in the mass killing of Muslims in 2002 (see AR 2011, p. 296). In November a special court sentenced 31 people to life imprisonment for killing 33 Muslims in an arson attack during the 2002 riots; in March 11 Muslims had been sentenced to death for the arson attack on a train carrying Hindu pilgrims that had set off the rioting.

If the BJP's better position at the year's end was largely not the product of its own efforts, Congress was more the author of its own misfortune. The mishandling of the backlash against corruption weakened the prime minister. Despite the removal of five ministers, cabinet reshuffles in January and July (described by Manmohan Singh as the last before the general election due in 2014) did little to mitigate this impression. The most noteworthy change was the shift of Environment Minister Jairam Ramesh, who had won credit for enforcing long-neglected environmental norms, to the ministry of rural development. The absence abroad of Congress party president Sonia Gandhi for five weeks in August-September, reportedly for surgery at the Memorial Sloan-Kettering Cancer Centre in New York, coincided with the government's clumsy handling of Anna Hazare's second fast, further undermining Singh's credibility as prime minister.

There were elections to four state assemblies in April-May. These included a crushing defeat for the Communist Party of India (Marxist) (CPM)-led Left Front in its stronghold of West Bengal at the hands of the UPA, spearheaded by Congress's regional ally, the Trinamool Congress, led by the mercurial Mamata Banerjee, who gave up her position as central railway minister to become the state's first woman chief minister. The longest serving democratically elected Communist government lost power after 34 years, having alienated many of its erstwhile supporters by its complacent arrogance. (This had been symbolised by the controversial 2007 Nandigram police firing on peasants protesting against the expropriation of land for a foreign company to build a chemical facility.) The CPM-led Left Democratic Front also narrowly lost power in Kerala to the Congress-led United Democratic Front, but in neighbouring Tamil Nadu, Congress's DMK ally lost office to the rival All India Anna DMK, led by the controversial J. Jayalalitha, who became chief minister for the fourth time despite facing a court case over alleged illegitimate assets worth $13 million. Congress returned to power in a landslide victory in the eastern state of Assam.

The year ended with parties jockeying for advantage ahead of state assembly elections in India's largest state, Uttar Pradesh (UP). The Bahujan Samaj Party chief minister, Mayawati, played to sub-regional sentiments by proposing the division of UP into four smaller states, while Congress appeared to court the support of UP's sizeable Muslim electorate through a central government order that 4.5 per cent of government jobs and places in educational centres be reserved for religious minorities.

Longstanding regional tensions continued to simmer through the year. The equivocal report by the Srikrishna Committee (see AR 2011, p. 298) on the proposed grant of statehood to the Telengana region of the southern state of Andhra Pradesh resolved nothing. In July a mass resignation of state assembly members from Telengana in support of the statehood demand was rejected by the assembly speaker and in October an indefinite strike by government employees in Telengana ended after 42 days without a result. In Jammu and Kashmir after the civil unrest in 2010 (see AR 2011, p. 297), the government announced in January that it intended to cut the security forces stationed in populated areas by a quarter over the next 12 months. In the north east, while several low intensity separatist and ethnic conflicts continued, in July the Gorkha Janamukti Morcha, which in 2008 had resumed its agitation for a separate state for Nepali-speaking Gorkhas, in the Darjeeling region, signed an agreement with the new government of West Bengal and the central government on the creation of an elected Gorkhaland Territorial Administration.

One conflict that continued was that involving Maoist rebels across a swathe of isolated tribal districts in central and eastern India. However, it was less intense than in 2010 with the death toll nearly halved to around 600, the lowest in a decade. In July the Supreme Court instructed the government of Chhattisgarh, the worst affected state, to disband anti-Maoist civilian militias accused of human rights abuses. In other judgments the court also granted bail to Binayak Sen, a doctor and human rights activist whose imprisonment in Chhattisgarh had attracted international protests, and ordered an inquiry into the controversial killing of Maoist leader Cherukuri Rajkumar, alias Azad (see AR 2011, p. 297). In November Maoists ended a month-long ceasefire in West Bengal reached with mediators appointed by Chief Minister Mamata Banerjee, who had advocated conciliation while in opposition, on the grounds that the government had resumed operations. Days later Koteshwar "Kishenji" Rao, one of the most senior Maoist leaders, was killed by security forces in West Bengal.

Terrorism by suspected Muslim extremists continued to concern the Indian government. However, in contrast to previous suggestions of Pakistani involvement in attacks, Home Minister P. Chidambaram indicated that Indian groups might have been responsible for coordinated bomb blasts in central Mumbai in July that claimed 26 lives, as well as a bomb blast outside the high court in Delhi in September that killed 13.

By the end of the year the outlook for the Indian economy had become markedly less buoyant. After years of high growth, GDP growth slowed to 7 per cent with inflation still around 9 per cent, a central bank interest rate of 8.5 per cent (the highest in any major economy aside from Brazil), the Mumbai stock market falling to a two-year low, and the Reserve Bank forced to sell US dollars after in November the rupee hit a new low of 52.50 to the dollar. It was also apparent that high growth was far from resolving the issue of mass poverty. An OECD report showed income inequality having doubled in two decades, with two-fifths of Indians still living on less than $40 a month. Another report, this time by the World Bank, found that despite over 2 per cent of GDP being devoted to anti-poverty programmes, the effectiveness of these was impaired by corruption, poor administrative capacity and under-payments. In the wake of the microfinance crisis (see AR 2011, p. 308), the Reserve Bank recommended a cap on interest and tighter guidelines on lending to the poor.

There was more evidence during the year of a backlash against the demands of rapid development with a wave of violent protest against the acquisition of land for infrastructural and industrial projects, most notably by farmers in the Noida area of UP adjoining Delhi. In attempts to assuage the farmers the UP state government announced a new policy on the sale of rural land and the central government introduced a Land Acquisition Relief and Rehabilitation bill containing a proposal to pay farmers up to six times more than the market rate for land.

In May environmental clearance was finally given to the largest foreign investment project, a steel plant in Orissa to be constructed by the South Korean firm Posco (see AR 2011, p. 308). In July Prime Minister Singh announced that in future an independent National Environment Appraisal and Monitoring Authority would be responsible for a streamlined system of granting clearances and ensuring industrial compliance with "green norms".

In November the government approved long-awaited proposals to open India's huge retail sector to global supermarket chains by agreeing to 51 per cent foreign ownership of multi-brand retail stores. The decision was vehemently opposed in parliament by virtually all opposition parties as well as two regional parties allied to the government, the Trinamool Congress and the DMK. Although the Federation of Indian Chambers of Commerce and Industry backed the move, apprehensive local retailers reacted furiously calling a one-day strike. After two weeks of parliamentary paralysis, the government backed down and suspended its plans pending a consensus on the issue.

The Indian space programme rebounded from its setbacks in 2010 (see AR 2011, p. 308) with four successful satellite launches.

In May the country's most famous, albeit controversial, spiritual guru, Sri Satya Sai Baba, revered by many foreigners as well as wealthy and influential Indians, died at the age of 84.

The 2011 census revealed that the country's population had grown by 181 million (or 17.6 per cent) to 1.21 billion over the last decade—a 4.9 per cent drop in the growth rate compared to the 1991-2001 period. A cause for concern was the sex ratio of only 914 female births for every 1,000 males.

The year was marked by the repercussions of the active presence of militant Islamist groups, both within **Pakistan** and in Afghanistan, which led to a severe worsening of relations with Pakistan's most important ally, the USA, especially following the US killing of the al-Qaida leader Osama bin Laden in May. This also contributed to a developing confrontation between the government and the country's powerful military establishment. Economic growth remained sluggish at below 3 per cent and in December the World Bank committed $5.5 billion to Pakistan to support growth and poverty reduction.

The intensity of militant Islamic sentiment in sectors of Pakistani society was underlined by two assassinations: that of Salman Taseer, the governor of the country's largest province, Punjab, by one of his bodyguards in January; and of the Christian minister for minorities, Shahbaz Bhatti, in March (see Obituary). Both men, senior members of the ruling Pakistan People's Party (PPP), had called for reform of the country's draconian blasphemy law and had defended a Christian woman sentenced to death under its provisions (see AR 2011, p. 298). Taseer's assassin, Mumtaz Qadri, hailed as a hero by hardline Muslims, declared that he was acting to punish a blasphemer and a month after Taseer's murder, PPP MP Sherry Rahman was forced by her party leadership to drop a controversial attempt to amend the blasphemy law. After Qadri was sentenced to death in October, the trial judge fled the country with his family in fear of his own life, Salman Taseer's son Shahbaz having been abducted in August.

While the estimated death toll in militant attacks and sectarian violence marginally fell to just over 6,000 (from a peak of close to 12,000 in 2009), this brought the total since March 2008—when the PPP-led government came to office—to nearly 31,000, almost a tenfold increase compared to the preceding last four years of former military ruler Pervez Musharraf's administration. The worst violence was once again in the Federally Administered Tribal Areas and the province of Khyber Pakhtunkhwa along the north-western border with Afghanistan, although hundreds also died in Balochistan and Punjab. As in previous years Sunni militants particularly targeted those regarded as heterodox such as the Shia minority and worshippers at Sufi shrines, as well as the security forces. Over 600 people were killed in suicide attacks with 90 dying in a single incident in May when two suicide bombers blew themselves up at a paramilitary forces training centre in Khyber Pakhtunkhwa. In an especially daring attack in the same month, six militants attacked the Mehran naval aviation base in the country's largest city, Karachi, killing 10 soldiers. At the end of the year Maulvi Faqir Mohammad, the deputy commander of the Tehrik-e-Taliban Pakistan, said that peace talks were taking place with the government, though, in an indication of differences among the militants, this was denied by a Taliban spokesman.

Apart from the violence connected to Muslim militant groups, the conflict between security forces and separatist insurgents in the south-western border province of Baluchistan and the ethnic and criminal gang related strife in Karachi, exacerbated by the recent influx of hundreds of thousands of Pashtuns and Balochis fleeing counterinsurgency operations in their home provinces, also claimed many lives. In October an inquiry by the Supreme Court into the violence in Karachi blamed political parties, particularly the Muttahida Qaumi Movement (MQM) supported by many Muhajirs (Urdu-speaking migrants from India) (see AR 2011, p. 299), for many of the over 800 killings in the city during the first nine months of 2011. In January the MQM had temporarily withdrawn its support from the PPP-led government of Prime Minister Yusuf Raza Gillani forcing it to rescind a 9 per cent fuel price increase, a decision criticised by the USA and the IMF. A 9.9 per cent price rise in March had to be halved following a second ultimatum from the MQM.

An aspect of the violence in the country that evoked particularly strong feelings across Pakistani society were the frequent bombing raids by pilotless US drone aircraft against al-Qaida, Afghan and Pakistani Taliban targets. A tactic favoured by the Obama administration (see AR 2011, p. 299), nearly 60 such attacks were carried out during 2011, perhaps claiming over 500 lives. In March army chief General Afshaq Kayani joined in strongly condemning a raid in North Waziristan in FATA in which 40 people, said to be mostly civilians, died. Nevertheless, the raids continued with Ilyas Kashmiri, a senior al-Qaida figure and military leader of the banned Harkat-ul Jihad al-Islami, among those killed in South Waziristan in June, al-Qaida operations chief Atiyah Abd al-Rahman dying two months later, and two British nationals with militant links reported killed in November. In an increasingly rare instance of cooperation between US and Pakistani intelligence a senior al-Qaida leader, global operations chief Younis al Mauritani was captured in Quetta, the capital of Balochistan, in September.

Disquiet over drone attacks was only one symptom of a deteriorating relationship with the USA that had a direct bearing on politics in Pakistan. The year began badly with Raymond Davis, a US national who the USA claimed had diplomatic status, detained by Pakistani police after shooting dead two men he said were attempting to hijack his car in the city of Lahore. It later emerged that Davis was a private security contract worker for the US Central Intelligence Agency (CIA). In mid-February US Senator John Kerry visited Pakistan on behalf of the US government expressing regret for the incident and promising a criminal inquiry if Davis was released. Despite intense public outrage in Pakistan over the affair, a month later he was released when relatives of the men he had killed pardoned him after accepting "blood money" in conformity with the country's Islamic Sharia law. This followed the first visit by the new US special envoy to Pakistan and Afghanistan, veteran diplomat Marc Grossman, but hardly marked a positive turning point in the bilateral relationship. In early April the *New York Times* reported that a delegation to Washington DC, headed by the chief of Pakistan's Inter-Services Intelligence (ISI), had asked for the withdrawal of hundreds of US agents and the limitation of drone attacks. Shortly afterwards, Admiral Mike Mullen, the outgoing chairman of the US joint chiefs of staff, on a visit to Pakistan, accused the ISI of having long supported a terrorist network run by the Afghan insurgent Jalaluddin Haqqani that was killing US and other troops combating the Afghan Taliban. (Testifying before the US Senate Foreign Relations Committee in September, Mullen termed the Haqqani network a "veritable arm" of the ISI.)

The biggest shock to US-Pakistani relations followed when on 2 May US special forces raided Osama bin Laden's hideout, located close to the Pakistan Military Academy in Abbottabad, in Khyber Pakhtunkhwa, killing the Saudi founder and leader of al-Qaida (see Obituary) and three of his associates. The raid was a huge embarrassment to the Pakistani government and military—apparently ignorant of the whereabouts of the world's most wanted terrorist and not being trusted by the US government with advance knowledge of the operation to eliminate him. Prime Minister Gillani described the action as a violation of Pakistani sovereignty, denied any official knowledge of bin Laden's whereabouts and announced an investigation into how the al-Qaida leader had escaped detection. The National Assembly subsequently unanimously condemned the raid, also urging an end to NATO supply convoys to Afghanistan via Pakistan unless drone attacks were halted.

Visits by Senator Kerry, US Secretary of State Hilary Clinton and CIA Director Leon Panetta to Pakistan in the weeks immediately following the raid did little to repair the damage done to bilateral relations and at the end of May the USA announced the withdrawal of some of its military training personnel in response to a Pakistani request. In mid-June five Pakistani CIA informants were detained on suspicion of having aided the Abbottabad raid. A month later two Muslim US citizens of South Asian origin were charged with operating an illegal front for the Pakistani government, one of them later pleading guilty to secretly receiving millions of dollars from the ISI. Adding to the strain in relations, in July the US administration decided to suspend $800 million in military aid, about a third of its annual military assistance to Pakistan, and in December a US Congressional panel froze $700 million of aid pending Pakistani assurances that it was tackling the problem of the improvised explosive devices (IEDs) allegedly being made by militants based in Pakistan for use against US and NATO troops in Afghanistan.

US-Pakistani relations suffered a further serious blow at the end of the year. In late November 24 Pakistani soldiers were killed in a strike by US helicopters on two border posts in the Mohmand Agency of FATA. Pakistan responded by suspending the movement of NATO supply convoys, ordering a review of all cooperation with the USA and NATO, and boycotting the international conference on the future of Afghanistan in Bonn, Germany, in early December. Although the US government expressed its condolences, Pakistan rejected a US report blaming mistakes, poor coordination and a lack of trust for the incident.

On the domestic political front, the Pakistani government's future was imperilled by a revelation in an article by Mansoor Ijaz, a Pakistani-American businessman and lobbyist, in the *Financial Times* of London in October. This alleged that in a memo, which US Joint Chiefs of Staff Chairman Mullen confirmed having received, President Asif Ali Zardari expressed fears that the army might stage a coup if the civilian government tried to set up an independent inquiry to determine who had been protecting bin Laden, and also offered, in return for US help, to replace his country's military leadership and cut all ties with militant groups. Despite denying drafting or conveying the memo, Pakistan's ambassador in Washington Husain Haqqani, was forced to resign and replaced by the PPP MP Sherry Rahman. The year ended with Prime Minister Gillani alleging conspiracies to overthrow the government but both army chief Kayani and Iftikar Chaudhry, the Chief Justice of the Supreme Court, dismissing the prospect.

As well as the tensions with the military, the government's relationship with the judiciary also continued to be fractious (see AR 2011, p. 300). In March the Supreme Court quashed Zardari's appointment of Deedar Hussain Shah as head of the National Accountability Bureau, the country's top anti-corruption body, and in May the Lahore High Court ruled that the president, the joint leader of the PPP, could not take part in political activities. In December the Supreme Court also intervened in the controversy over the memo to the USA by establishing its own inquiry.

President Zardari, for his part, accused the Supreme Court of failing to investigate the assassination in 2007 of his wife, former prime minister Benazir Bhutto. In November an anti-terrorism court charged two senior police officers, arrested nearly a year before (see AR 2011, p. 298), with security breaches and a failure to protect her; five alleged Taliban militants were charged with criminal conspiracy over her death. In February the court had issued a warrant for the arrest of former military ruler Pervez Musharraf, living in self-imposed exile in London, in connection with the case.

Although the main opposition party, the Pakistan Muslim League (Nawaz) of former prime minister Nawaz Sharif was not able to take advantage of the government's difficulties, one Pakistani politician appeared to strike a popular chord. This was the charismatic former cricketer Imran Khan, the founder-leader of the Tehreek-e-Insaf (Movement for Justice), who attracted crowds of over 100,000 at rallies in Lahore in October and Karachi in December. Though hitherto lacking a strong political base, Khan's nationalist stance, strongly critical of US policy and of the corruption of the country's political establishment, attracted support among young and urban Pakistanis. Favouring a peaceful resolution of the conflict with the Pakistani Taliban, he also won a degree of acceptance from Muslim parties. It was noteworthy that Khan forbore from criticising the military and, in addressing the rally in Lahore, first named Husain Haqqani in the US memo affair. Among prominent figures who defected to the Tehreek-e-Insaf in late 2011 were senior PPP leader Shah Mahmood Qureshi, foreign minister in the Gillani government until February, and Javed Hashmi, who had been a minister under Nawaz Sharif.

The political rise of Imran Khan, who had led Pakistan to victory in the 1992 cricket World Cup, came at a time when many Pakistanis felt angered and let down by the conviction in Britain of three Pakistani Test cricketers, former captain Salman Butt and bowlers Mohammad Asif and Mohammad Amir, on charges of cheating and conspiracy to accept corrupt payments for fixing passages of play in matches. The charges, arising from incidents during the 2010 Pakistan tour of England, resulted in the trio receiving custodial sentences of between six and 30 months.

In January the trial opened of 800 soldiers and 20 civilians charged with some of the most serious offences—including murder and arson—in connection with the bloody mutiny by the paramilitary **Bangladesh** Rifles in 2009 (see AR 2010, p. 302; AR 2011, p. 301). The mass trial in a civilian court was the largest in the country's history. In a separate mass trial in a military court for lesser offences, in June a total of 657 mutineers were sentenced to prison terms of up to seven years with nine men being acquitted. In July Human Rights Watch (HRW), the international human rights organisation, expressed concerns about the fairness of the procedures and called for a halt to the mass trials. Both HRW and Amnesty International also issued reports on alleged unlawful killings of hundreds of people by the elite Rapid Action Battalion. In December an inquiry was announced into a spate of unexplained killings and disappearances.

Within Bangladesh the Awami League government of Sheikh Hasina Wajed came under fire for making liberal and secular changes to the law. In February Muslim religious parties called a national one-day strike in protest at changes that gave female children an equal share in inherited property instead of the half share under customary Islamic Sharia law. In May the Supreme Court relaxed a decade-long ban on Muslim religious leaders pronouncing fatwas (edicts), introduced after it had resulted in a number of cases in which brutal punishments had been imposed on women. However, the court held that while fatwas might be pronounced they could not be legally enforced. In July Islamic parties called another general strike to protest against a constitutional amendment dropping the phrase "absolute faith and trust in Allah" from the preamble to the country's constitution.

The trial began in November of Delawar Hossain Sayedee, a leader of the Jamaat-e-Islami, on charges of genocide, rape, and religious persecution arising from the 1971 liberation struggle in what was then East Pakistan. He was the first of seven men, including four other Jamaat members and two members of the main opposition Bangladesh Nationalist Party (BNP), facing war crimes trial by an International Crimes Tribunal established in 2010.

In November the National Assembly passed legislation enabling people belonging to the country's shrinking Hindu minority (less than a tenth of the population) to reclaim property taken from them under an order first introduced at the time of the 1965 Indo-Pakistan War. This fulfilled an election promise made by the Awami

League. In December a judicial commission of inquiry held thousands of supporters of the BNP responsible for attacks on Hindus and political opponents following the victory of the BNP-Jamaat-e-Islami alliance in the 2001 elections.

The most controversial change introduced by the government was the National Assembly's resolution to end the 15-year-old requirement that general elections be overseen by non-partisan caretaker administrations, introduced to address the violence and fraud that marred elections. The vote in June followed a Supreme Court ruling that such interim administrations were unconstitutional but was boycotted by the BNP which held strikes and demonstrations in protest.

BNP leaders continued to be pursued in the courts. In June a special court sentenced Arafat Rahman Koko, the younger son of party leader Khaleda Zia, to six years' imprisonment in a money laundering case. Koko was said to be in Malaysia while his elder brother Tarique Rahman, for whom an arrest warrant was issued in July in connection with a grenade attack on an Awami League rally in 2004, also lived in exile. In August the country's Anti-Corruption Commission filed cases against Rahman (again for money laundering) and Khaleda Zia for acquiring wealth exceeding her known income.

In March the country's central bank removed Muhammad Yunus, the Nobel Peace Prize-winning founder of the pioneering microcredit institution Grameen Bank, from his position as the bank's managing director on the grounds that at 70 he was past the retirement age for private bank executives. The move attracted international criticism and speculation that the decision was prompted by Prime Minister Sheikh Hasina's unhappiness with Yunus' attempt to set up a rival political party in 2007.

The Dhaka stock exchange, which had enjoyed a spectacular rise in 2010 on the back of annual GDP growth of 5.8 per cent, lost 40 per cent of its value in volatile trading early in the year provoking the suspension of trading and violent protests by angry investors. The government then moved to set up a $700 million investment fund to stabilise the market.

Meeting the country's growing demand for power was also a major concern with an offshore gas exploration deal with the US company ConocoPhillips and a 19 per cent fuel price hike provoking strikes. In November a deal was signed with Russia to build two new nuclear power plants.

Following its victory in presidential and parliamentary elections in 2010, the United People's Freedom Alliance (UFPA) led by President Mahinda Rajapaksa's **Sri Lanka** Freedom Party, further consolidated its position in elections to local councils held during the year. It won 56 per cent of the popular vote and 270 of the 322 authorities, compared with 32 per cent and nine authorities for the opposition United National Party; the Tamil National Alliance, a coalition of parties supporting self determination for the country's Tamil minority, took 32 authorities in the north and east of the island, and the Sri Lanka Muslim Congress secured five authorities. The polls were marred by incidents of violence and allegations of corrupt practice and the misuse of state resources and media by the ruling coalition. In one of the worse instances a presidential adviser, Bharatha Lakshman Premachandra, was among four killed in a clash within the UFPA in a suburb of the capital, Colombo, in October. A warrant was later issued for the arrest of Duminda Silva, an MP leading a rival UFPA faction and aide to Defence Secretary Gotabaya Rajapaksa, the president's brother. Silva had been seriously injured in the incident.

Although longstanding emergency laws were allowed to lapse in September, more than two years after the defeat of separatist Tamil Tigers (LTTE), Human Right Watch pointed out that anti-terrorism and other laws permitting detention without trial for up to 18 months remained in force. Moves also continued to be made to reinforce the position of the military and police. A new scheme came into force in May requiring all university entrants to undergo three weeks of military training. The military steadily expanded its commercial activity, opening a tourist resort, engaging in marketing agricultural produce, and taking over the running of the country's main cricket grounds.

The government continued to face criticism for its intolerance of opposition. In January the Paris-based Reporters Without Borders urged a boycott of the Galle international literary festival in protest at the restrictions on press freedom. An arson attack on the offices of Lankaenews.com, a website critical of the government, served to highlight the issue. The editor of Lankaenews was later briefly detained and the operation temporarily suspended by a court order. The government subsequently sought to block access to it and several other websites hostile to President Rakjapaksa and in November warned that any site dealing with Sri Lankan affairs that failed to register with the ministry of mass media and information would face prosecution. In November Sarath Fonseka, Rajpaksa's defeated opponent in the 2010 presidential contest, already serving a 30-month sentence for corruption (see AR 2011, p. 302), was sentenced by the High Court in Colombo to an additional three-year prison term for "spreading disaffection" through having given a newspaper interview in which he apparently backed allegations that Defence Secretary Gotabaya Rajapaksa had ordered that surrendering Tamil Tiger leaders be shot in May 2009.

The government continued to have to deal with the troublesome legacy of the civil war. It sought to highlight signs of progress such as the induction of several hundred Tamil recruits into the hitherto majority Sinhala dominated police in January, the lifting of restrictions on the entry of journalists and foreigners to the Tamil north of the island, and the closure in October of the notorious Menik Farm camp with the relocation of the last of the 300,000 Tamils displaced at the end of the war. Yet actions such as the building of a new military headquarters in the north on the site of a Tamil Tiger cemetery and a huge military festival commemorating the second anniversary of the war's end smacked of triumphalism. In August the police acted to repress a wave of public hysteria and vigilante violence in Tamil and Muslim areas of northern and central Sri Lanka prompted by widespread fear of mysterious nocturnal prowlers termed "grease devils" who assaulted women and were suspected by local people of being fostered by the security forces.

In April a UN panel appointed to investigate alleged human rights abuses during the final stages of the war (see AR 2011, p. 303) reported that, while the Tigers had used civilians as human shields, most of the tens of thousands killed had died as a result of the army shelling targets including hospitals and UN centres. It found credible "allegations, which if proven, indicate that a wide range of serious violations of international humanitarian law and international rights law was committed both by the government of Sri Lanka and the LTTE, some of which would amount to war crimes and crimes against humanity". The Sri Lankan government rejected the findings of the panel, which had not been permitted to visit the island, as biased. Though UN Secretary General Ban Ki Moon submitted the panel report to the UN Human Rights Council in September, the Council did not act on its recommendation for an international investigation.

In December the Sri Lankan government's own Lessons Learned and Reconciliation Commission submitted its report to parliament. A report by the human rights organisation Amnesty International described the Commission's inquiry as "flawed at every level". While calling for action on missing people, it absolved the military of the charge of targeting civilians, finding that "the protection of the civilian population was given the highest priority".

The country's post-war economic boom continued with the IMF praising its macroeconomic performance. However, there was concern that the replacement of free visas on arrival for foreign visitors by a fee paid visa to be obtained in advance might undermine the lucrative tourist industry.

In mid-January the UN mission established in 2007 to monitor the peace process in **Nepal** following the end of the Maoist rebellion ceased operating. The Nepali political parties having decided not to renew its mandate, a multi-party committee agreed to take over its monitoring duties.

In February, after seven months of stalemate and at the 17th attempt, the Constituent Assembly elected Jhalanath Khanal, the leader of the Communist Party of Nepal (Unified Marxist-Leninist), the third largest party in the assembly, to succeed his party colleague, Madhav Kumar Nepal, as prime minister. Having come to power as a result of a pact with Prachanda, the leader of the largest party, the Unified Communist Party of Nepal (Maoist) (UCPN(M)), Khanal resigned after six months, unable to achieve consensus on either completing the peace process or on a new constitution. He was succeeded by Baburam Bhattarai, the vice chair of the UCPN (M), who defeated Ram Chandra Poudel of the Nepali Congress Party, the main rivals of the Maoists.

Bhattarai's coalition government succeeded in getting the rebels to finally hand over their weapons to the multi-party committee overseeing the peace process. In November the political parties reached agreement on the future of 19,000 rebel fighters; a third of them were to be integrated into the armed forces and the rest given cash incentives and training. However, the year ended in renewed discord over a demand that twice as many rebels be absorbed into the military.

The first ever elections in **Bhutan** for three tiers of local government, originally slated for 2008, were held in the course of the year with over 1,100 representatives (including 76 women) being elected from among the nearly 2,200 candidates, who had to be born of Bhutanese parents and not possess any political party affiliation.

In July the UN General Assembly adopted a non-binding resolution, based on

Bhutan's model of Gross National Happiness (GNH) to make happiness a "development indicator".

In October 31-year-old King Jigme Khesar Namgyel Wangchuck married 21-year-old Jetsun Pema, the daughter of an airline pilot.

REGIONAL RELATIONS WITHIN SOUTH ASIA. After the nadir of the 2008 Mumbai attacks attributed to Pakistani militants and in spite of Indian dissatisfaction with Pakistan's action against anti-Indian terrorist groups, relations between the two countries continued to thaw with meetings between their respective foreign, home and defence secretaries. Prime Minister Gillani attended the cricket World Cup semi-final match between the two countries in Mohali, in March at the invitation of Prime Minister Singh, and Hina Rabbani Khar, newly appointed Pakistan's first female foreign minister, visited Delhi in July. In September Makhdoom Amin Faheem became the first Pakistani commerce minister to lead a business delegation to India for 35 years and agreed to aim to double bilateral trade to $6 billion within three years. Despite having previously linked trade liberalisation to a resolution of the dispute over Kashmir, Pakistan reciprocated India's extension of "most favoured nation" status and at the regional SAARC summit in the Maldives, in November, the prime ministers of both countries spoke of a new chapter in bilateral relations.

Despite an exchange of visits by Prime Minister Gillani and President Hamid Karzai of Afghanistan, mutual suspicions were worsened by the assassination in September of former Afghan president Burhanuddin Rabbani, head of the effort to negotiate peace with the Taliban (see pp. 285-86). The Afghan interior minister accused the Pakistani ISI of involvement. Pakistan for its part regarded with unease Karzai, on a visit to Delhi in October, reaching a strategic partnership with India. Prime Minister Singh pledged that India, having already committed $2 billion in aid, would "stand by Afghanistan" when foreign forces withdrew in 2014.

India's relations with Bangladesh remained close but problematic. Manmohan Singh, making the first visit to Dhaka by an Indian prime minister in 12 years, was unable to conclude planned treaties on sharing river water and transit across Bangladesh to India's isolated north-east because of the last-minute refusal of his UPA ally, and West Bengal chief minister, Mamata Banerjee to go along with the Teesta river deal. However, the two countries did reach a protocol on exchanging border enclaves and India agreed to lift tariffs on the import of Bangladeshi readymade textiles.

In February, after a strong protest from India, Sri Lanka released 136 Indian fishermen held for allegedly fishing in Sri Lankan waters. As well as sensitivity over the treatment of the Tamil minority on the island, as in the case of Bangladesh, India's relations with Sri Lanka increasingly reflected concern over growing Chinese economic and political influence. (China was the largest trading partner of Bangladesh and Pakistan, and second only to India for Sri Lanka.)

SOUTH ASIA AND THE GLOBAL ORDER. After the flurry of visits to India by the leaders of the other major powers in 2010 (see AR 2011, p. 305), 2011 was a quieter year in Delhi. A visit by Indonesia's President Susilo Bambang Yudhoyono as the guest of honour at the Republic Day celebrations in January saw trade deals worth $16.8

billion being signed. India reached a free trade deal with Japan in an effort to boost flagging bilateral trade, also agreeing a $15 billion currency swap agreement in December in an effort to boost the Indian rupee and ease liquidity problems for both countries in an unstable global economic environment.

In May Prime Minister Singh offered African countries $5 billion in development credit at the 2nd India-Africa Forum summit in the Ethiopian capital Addis Ababa. Singh also attended summits of the BRICS (Brazil-Russia-India-China-South Africa) states in China, and the IBSA (India-Brazil-South Africa) Dialogue Forum in South Africa, as well as the G-20 summit in France and an East Asia Summit in Indonesia. He chose to miss the Commonwealth summit in Australia where India joined Sri Lanka and other states in successfully deferring a recommendation from an Eminent Persons Group on human rights to create a Commonwealth commissioner for democracy, the rule of law and human rights.

There were no major developments in India's relations with the other major powers. As a non-permanent member of the UN Security Council, India, like its BRICS and IBSA counterparts, adopted a cautious attitude towards European and US backed initiatives to intervene in the internal conflicts arising from the "Arab Spring", abstaining in votes on taking action against the governments of Libya and Syria. Pakistan was elected to join the Security Council in 2012.

A study by the Stockholm International Peace Research Institute reported that India had overtaken China as the world's largest arms importer. In April India shortlisted the pan-European Eurofighter and the French Rafale, in preference to US, Swedish and Russian aircraft, for a $11 billion contract for 126 fighter jets. A link was drawn by some with the resignation immediately afterwards of Timothy Roemer, the US ambassador to India. On a visit by Prime Minister Singh to Russia in December India signed a deal for the licensed production of another 42 of the jointly developed Sukhoi Su-30MKI, currently the Indian air force's primary fighter jet.

South Korea became the ninth country to sign a civil nuclear deal with India in July and in December Australia's ruling Labour Party backed Prime Minister Julia Gillard in voting to overturn the long-standing ban by the country, which held an estimated 40 per cent of the world's uranium, on exporting uranium to India.

In March the UK outlined major changes to its overseas aid policy, freezing aid to India, still the biggest recipient. Bangladesh and Pakistan, currently the third and fourth biggest recipients, were two countries slated to receive large increases, although the Pakistani opposition politician Imran Khan called for aid to be cut, arguing that it only fuelled corruption. In April UK Prime Minister David Cameron made his first visit to Pakistan since taking office. Having provoked anger with his criticism of Pakistan when visiting India (see AR 2011, p. 305), he called for a fresh start in bilateral relations and pledged £650 million of additional aid over the next four years for Pakistan's run down school system. However, with Pakistani relations with the Western powers severely strained in the wake of the killing of Osama bin Laden, Prime Minister Gillani, on the eve of a visit to the country in May, described China as "our best and most trusted friend".

James Chiriyankandath

INDIAN OCEAN STATES

The Comoros

CONSTITUENT REPUBLICS: Anjouan, Grande Comore, Mohéli
CAPITAL: Moroni   AREA: 1,861 sq km   POPULATION: 734,750 ('10)
OFFICIAL LANGUAGES: Arabic & French
HEAD OF STATE AND GOVERNMENT: Ikililou Dhoinine, Union President (since May '11)
DEMOCRACY INDEX: 3.41; 126th of 167   CORRUPTION INDEX: 2.4; 143rd of 183
CURRENCY: Comoro Franc (Dec '11 £1.00=KMF 572.77, US$1.00=KMF 365.23)
GNI PER CAPITA: US$750, Intl$1,080 at PPP ('10)

Madagascar

CAPITAL: Antananarivo   AREA: 587,040 sq km   POPULATION: 20,713,819 ('10)
OFFICIAL LANGUAGES: Malagasy, French & English
HEAD OF STATE AND GOVERNMENT: President Andry Rajoelina (since March '09, de facto)
PRIME MINISTER: Omer Beriziky (since Nov '11)
DEMOCRACY INDEX: 3.94; 113rd of 167   CORRUPTION INDEX: 3.0; 100th of 183
CURRENCY: Malagasy Ariary (Dec '11 £1.00=MGA 3,296, US$1.00=MGA 2,102)
GNI PER CAPITA: US$430, Intl$950 at PPP ('10)

Maldives

CAPITAL: Malé   AREA: 300 sq km   POPULATION: 315,885 ('10)
OFFICIAL LANGUAGE: Divehi
HEAD OF STATE AND GOVERNMENT: President Mohammed Nasheed (Anni) (MDP) (since Nov '08)
RULING PARTY: Democratic Party (MDP)-led coalition
CORRUPTION INDEX: 2.5; 134th of 183
CURRENCY: Rufiyaa (Dec '11 £1.00=MVR 24.12, US$1.00=MVR 15.38)
GNI PER CAPITA: US$4,240, Intl$5,450 at PPP ('10)

Mauritius

CAPITAL: Port Louis   AREA: 2,040 sq km   POPULATION: 1,281,214 ('10)
OFFICIAL LANGUAGE: English
HEAD OF STATE: President Sir Anerood Jugnauth (since Oct '03)
RULING PARTIES: Alliance of the Future coalition, including Mauritian Labour Party
HEAD OF GOVERNMENT: Prime Minister Navin Ramgoolam (MLP) (since July '05)
DEMOCRACY INDEX: 8.04; 24th of 167   CORRUPTION INDEX: 5.1; 46th of 183
CURRENCY: Mauritius Rupee (Dec '11 £1.00=MUR 45.79, US$1.00=MUR 29.20)
GNI PER CAPITA: US$7,750, Intl$13,670 at PPP ('10)

Seychelles

CAPITAL: Victoria   AREA: 460 sq km   POPULATION: 86,525 ('10)
OFFICIAL LANGUAGES: Seychellois, English & French
HEAD OF STATE AND GOVERNMENT: President James Michel (since April '04)
RULING PARTY: People's Party (PP)
CORRUPTION INDEX: 4.8; 50th of 183
CURRENCY: Seychelles Rupee (Dec '11 £1.00=SCR 20.59, US$1.00=SCR 13.13)
GNI PER CAPITA: US$9,760, Intl$21,050 at PPP ('10)

IN the **Comoros** on 13 January the constitutional court confirmed the results of the presidential elections held in December 2010. The new president, Ikililou Dhoinine, was declared to have secured 61 per cent of the vote with a 52.8 per cent turnout. Dhoinine had been supported by the outgoing president, Ahmed Abdallah Sambi and his "Baobab" coalition. Dhoinine was the first president to come from Mohéli, in accordance with the provision in the 2001 constitution that the presidency would be filled by each of the three islands in turn.

Dhoinine's election promised continuity with the rule of President Sambi and the possibility of an end to the political instability that had plagued the islands. The new president announced his cabinet on 30 May. Although only two of Sambi's ministers were retained in the new administration, many of his supporters continued to occupy key posts. One of Dhoinine's first acts was to implement the anti-corruption legislation that had been passed in 2008 and which required politicians and civil servants to declare their assets.

New island governors were also elected: Mauigni Baraka Said Soilihi for Grande Comore; Anissi Chamisidie for Anjouan; and Mohamed Ali Said for Mohéli. The assumption by Mayotte, the fourth island of the archipelago, of the status of a French department led to tensions with France which focused on the issue of illegal migrants entering Mayotte from the other islands. In July the AU reaffirmed that Mayotte "belongs to the Union of the Comores" but Dhoinine, speaking at the UN in September, suggested that the Mayotte issue should be resolved by negotiation.

The economy of the islands remained fragile and in September a 10 per cent rise in fuel prices led to hostile demonstrations.

Political deadlock continued throughout the year in **Madagascar**. The Haute Autorité de la Transition (HAT), led by self-styled president, Andry Rajoelina, remained in power with the support of the army but was not recognised by the Southern African Development Community (SADC), the wider international community or the competing political factions within Madagascar.

In January the SADC negotiator, Leonardo Simão, produced a "road map" pointing the way to a political settlement but the HAT continued to block any attempt by former president Marc Ravalomanana to return to Madagascar. Throughout the year this remained the principal obstacle to any political settlement with the army strongly objecting to the former president's return. On 10 March Camille Vital resigned as prime minister in accordance with the road map proposals and was reappointed a week later. On 26 March a new government, including some members of TIM (Ravalomanana's party), was sworn in. On 11 September all political factions, except the supporters of Didier Ratsiraka, at last signed up to the SADC road map. A government of national unity was formed and on 17 October Prime Minister Camille Vital resigned once again. Rajoelina then appointed Jean Omer Beriziky as prime minister but this appointment was objected to by Ravalomanana on the grounds that Beriziky was too close a political associate of the president.

Elections, originally promised for 2011, were not held as the main parties demanded that there first be an amnesty for Ravalomanana. Elections were rescheduled for 2012. A proposal was agreed to reform the upper and lower chambers of parliament by adding nominees of the rival parties and only then would a proposal for an amnesty for Ravalomanana be considered.

The unresolved political standoff prevented any revival in Madagascar's economy. Nickel mining receipts rose and tourism showed a 16 per cent increase, endangered however by the Eurozone financial crisis. Rice production, however, declined, and a report indicated that 77 per cent of households were living in poverty. The government's austerity programme led to a cut in all capital expenditure but the World Bank approved a $52 million loan to assist environmental protection in the national parks where illegal logging was endangering the natural environment.

The **Maldives** continued to experience political paralysis in 2011 with President Mohammed Nasheed at loggerheads with the Dhivehi Rayyithunge Party (DRP), the party of his predecessor, Maumoon Abdul Gayoom, which controlled the Majlis (the Maldives parliament). Although following his electoral defeat in 2008, Gayoom had stated in 2010 that he would retire from politics, it became clear that he had set his sights on contesting the next presidential election, due in 2013.

On 1 May street protests began, ostensibly over rising food prices, which had resulted from the government's decision to allow the rufiya (the Maldivian currency) to float. The protests were organised by the DRP and there were counter-demonstrations by Nasheed's supporters in the Maldivian Democratic Party (MDP). The demonstrations, often accompanied by violence, continued until banned by the police on 6 May. The president claimed that the unrest was an attempt to create a revolution similar to that which had emerged from the Tahrir Square protests in Egypt.

In December there were further mass demonstrations calling on the people to "protect Islam". This followed a speech made on 24 November in the Majlis by the visiting UN High Commissioner for Human Rights Navi Pillay condemning the flogging of women. The Adhaalath party, an Islamic opposition party, called for the closure of all spas and beauty salons in tourist areas claiming they were fronts for brothels. The Maldives Association of Tourism objected and the ban was later overturned. Gayoom denied that his party had supported the ban. Nasheed, meanwhile, called on Maldivians to support a "tolerant form of Islam"

The pressures on the fragile Maldives environment reached crisis point in December when Thilafushi, the island set aside as the Maldives rubbish disposal site, had to be closed because of waste being tipped illegally into the lagoon.

In **Mauritius**, in January the Union Nationale, led by Ashok Jugnauth, which had failed to win any seats in the previous year's general election, suffered a mortal blow when 11 of its members defected to the Militant Socialist Movement (MSM), led by Pravind Jugnauth, a member of the Alliance de l'Avenir, a coalition that also contained the Labour Party. However, the MSM came under increasing scrutiny when the Independent Committee against Corruption investigated the sale of the Med-Point clinic owned by Jugnauth's brother-in-law. On 22 July the health minister, Maya Hanoomanjee, was arrested in connection with the investigation. This prompted Pravind Jugnauth to resign his ministerial post and on 7 August to take the MSM out of the coalition. Jugnauth began co-operation with Paul Berenger's MMM, but the Labour Party continued to rule with the support of the small PMSD (Parti Mauricien Social Democrate) which was led by Xavier-Luc Duval who took over Jugnauth's portfolio of finance and economic development. The new coalition had a parliamentary majority of five.

The political crisis deepened when Pravind Jugnauth was arrested on 22 September for his role in the Med-Point affair. He asserted that he had declared an interest in cabinet and demanded that the cabinet minutes be released. This was resisted by the prime minister.

Constitutional changes to bring an end to the "Best Loser System"—whereby legislative seats were given to eight "best losers" representing ethnic minorities in a measure designed to ensure their representation in parliament—was moved to the top of the political agenda when the Privy Council in London agreed to hear an appeal brought by the small party Rezistans ek Alternativ party over the continued use of the system in parliamentary elections. Although it remained a sensitive issue, Labour and the MMM were in broad agreement that the constitution should be amended to allow for proportional representation. The prime minister appointed former finance minister Rama Sithanen to report on the options available.

The Mauritian economy weathered the global economic storm well, registering 4.6 per cent growth in the first 6 months and 3.9 per cent in the second. Tourism proved the weakest sector of the economy, not helped by the murder in January of Michaela McAreavey, daughter of a well known Irish football manager, while on her honeymoon.

Presidential elections in the **Seychelles** were held in May and were won by the incumbent, James Michel with 55 per cent of the vote. His main rival, as in previous elections, was Wavel Ramakalawan who received 41 per cent of the vote (down from the 45.7 per cent that he had achieved in 2006). Although the polls were given a clean bill of health by Commonwealth observers, Ramakalawan alleged that votes had been "bought"' by his rival and refused to attend the official poll declaration. He then withdrew himself and his Seychelles National Party (SNP) from parliament, thereby precipitating a general election. As the SNP boycotted the election, a new party of opposition, the Popular Democratic Party (PDP), led by David Pierre, was quickly formed hoping to attract disillusioned SNP voters. The withdrawal of the SNP was widely seen as marking the end of Ramakalawan's political career.

The general election held in October resulted in a sweeping victory for Michel's Parti LEPEP which won 88.56 per cent of the vote and all 25 seats that were contested. The new PDP secured only 10.89 per cent of the vote.

Malyn Newitt

IX SOUTH-EAST AND EAST ASIA

SOUTH-EAST ASIAN STATES

BURMA—THAILAND—MALAYSIA—BRUNEI—SINGAPORE— VIETNAM—CAMBODIA—LAOS

Burma

CAPITAL: Naypyidaw (Pyinmana)   AREA: 676,580 sq km   POPULATION: 47,963,012 ('10)
OFFICIAL LANGUAGE: Burmese
HEAD OF STATE AND GOVERNMENT: Thein Sein (since March '11)
DEMOCRACY INDEX: 1.77; 163rd of 167   CORRUPTION INDEX: 1.5; 180th of 183
CURRENCY: Kyat (Dec '11 £1.00=MMK 10.05, US$1.00=MMK 6.41)

Thailand

CAPITAL: Bangkok   AREA: 513,120 sq km   POPULATION: 69,122,234 ('10)
OFFICIAL LANGUAGE: Thai
HEAD OF STATE: King Bhumibol Adulyadej (Rama IX), since June '46
RULING PARTY: Pheu Thai Party (PTP)-led coalition
HEAD OF GOVERNMENT: Prime Minister Yingluck Shinawatra (PTP) (since Aug '11)
DEMOCRACY INDEX: 6.55; 57th of 167   CORRUPTION INDEX: 3.4; 80th of 183
CURRENCY: Baht (Dec '11 £1.00=THB 48.46, US$1.00=THB 30.90)
GNI PER CAPITA: US$4,150, Intl$8,120 at PPP ('10)

Malaysia

CAPITAL: Kuala Lumpur   AREA: 329,740 sq km   POPULATION: 28,401,017 ('10)
OFFICIAL LANGUAGE: Bahasa Malaysia
HEAD OF STATE: King Mizan Zainal Abidin Sultan of Terengganu (since Nov '06)
RULING PARTY: National Front (BN) coalition
HEAD OF GOVERNMENT: Prime Minister Najib Razak (since April '09)
DEMOCRACY INDEX: 6.19; 71st of 167   CORRUPTION INDEX: 4.3; 60th of 183
CURRENCY: Ringgit (Dec '11 £1.00=MYR 4.92, US$1.00=MYR 3.14)
GNI PER CAPITA: US$7,760, Intl$14,110 at PPP ('10)

Brunei

CAPITAL: Bandar Seri Bagawan   AREA: 5,770 sq km   POPULATION: 398,920 ('10)
OFFICIAL LANGUAGES: Malay & English
HEAD OF STATE AND GOVERNMENT: Sultan Sir Hassanal Bolkiah (since Oct '67)
CORRUPTION INDEX: 5.2; 44th of 183
CURRENCY: Brunei Dollar (Dec '11 £1.00=BND 2.01, US$1.00=BND 1.28)
GNI PER CAPITA: US$31,800, Intl$49,730 at PPP ('09)

Singapore

CAPITAL: Singapore   AREA: 699 sq km   POPULATION: 5,076,700 ('10)
OFFICIAL LANGUAGES: Malay, Chinese, Tamil & English
HEAD OF STATE: President Tony Tan Keng Yam (since Sept '11)
RULING PARTY: People's Action Party (PAP)
HEAD OF GOVERNMENT: Prime Minister Lee Hsien Loong (since August '04)
DEMOCRACY INDEX: 5.89; 82nd of 167   CORRUPTION INDEX: 9.2; 5th of 183
CURRENCY: Singapore Dollar (Dec '11 £1.00=SGD 2.01, US$1.00=SGD 1.28)
GNI PER CAPITA: US$41,430, Intl$55,380 at PPP ('10)

Vietnam

CAPITAL: Hanoi   AREA: 329,310 sq km   POPULATION: 86,936,464 ('10)
OFFICIAL LANGUAGE: Vietnamese
HEAD OF STATE: President Truong Tan Sang (since July '11)
RULING PARTY: Communist Party of Vietnam (CPV)
HEAD OF GOVERNMENT: Prime Minister Nguyen Tan Dung (since June '06)
DEMOCRACY INDEX: 2.94; 140th of 167   CORRUPTION INDEX: 2.9; 112nd of 183
CURRENCY: Dong (Dec '11 £1.00=VND 32,950, US$1.00=VND 21,010)
GNI PER CAPITA: US$1,110, Intl$2,960 at PPP ('10)

Cambodia

CAPITAL: Phnom Penh   AREA: 181,040 sq km   POPULATION: 14,138,255 ('10)
OFFICIAL LANGUAGE: Khmer
HEAD OF STATE: King Norodom Sihamoni (elected Oct '04)
RULING PARTY: Cambodian People's Party (CPP)
HEAD OF GOVERNMENT: Prime Minister Hun Sen (since July '97)
DEMOCRACY INDEX: 4.87; 100th of 167   CORRUPTION INDEX: 2.1; 164th of 183
CURRENCY: Riel (Dec '11 £1.00=KHR 6,299, US$1.00=KHR 4,017)
GNI PER CAPITA: US$760, Intl$2,040 at PPP ('10)

Laos

CAPITAL: Vientiane   AREA: 236,800 sq km   POPULATION: 6,200,894 ('10)
OFFICIAL LANGUAGE: Laotian
HEAD OF STATE: President Choummaly Sayasone (since June '06)
RULING PARTY: Lao People's Revolutionary Party (LPRP)
HEAD OF GOVERNMENT: Prime Minister Thongsing Thammavong (since Dec '10)
DEMOCRACY INDEX: 2.10; 156th of 167   CORRUPTION INDEX: 2.2; 154th of 183
CURRENCY: New Kip (Dec '11 £1.00=LAK 12,510, US$1.00=LAK 7,977)
GNI PER CAPITA: US$1,040, Intl$2,390 at PPP ('10)

THE government in Burma (Myanmar) took several steps towards reform, winning support from the South-East Asian region and beyond. Thailand's elections brought to power the country's first-ever woman prime minister, with her government almost immediately challenged by massive flooding that threatened the capital, Bangkok.

Following elections in November 2010 to the new National Assembly (see AR 2011, pp. 314-16), **Burma's** first parliamentary session for 22 years was convened on 31 January, meeting in a capital city, Naypyidaw, that did not even exist the last time a parliamentary meeting had taken place in the country. On 4 February, an electoral college drawn from the National Assembly named Thein Sein, a member of the out-going military junta and the military regime's last prime minister, to be the country's new president, choosing him from a pool of three vice-presidents selected the previous day. A week later the National Assembly unanimously approved all of the president's cabinet nominees, most of them former military officers. Subsequently state media announced that the junta—the State Peace and Development Council—had been officially dissolved with the installation of the new cabinet. Initial signs were that little had changed, however. In February the junta's chief, Senior-General Than Shwe, stated that he would lead the "State Supreme Council", a body not even mentioned in the 2008 constitution that had introduced the reforms.

As early as January the regional organisation, ASEAN, called for an end to sanctions imposed on Burma, highlighting the elections and the release from house arrest, in November 2010, of opposition leader, Aung San Suu Kyi. In April, however, the US government stated that it was premature to lift sanctions and that it would be unwilling to work with ASEAN if Burma were permitted to be its chairman, given the country's poor record on human rights and democracy. However, the USA nominated a special envoy to Burma, a move welcomed by Suu Kyi's National League for Democracy (NLD). The NLD also described President Thein Sein's first public speech as positive and stated that it was looking forward to dialogue and face-to-face discussion.

The new government's stance towards Suu Kyi was more lenient than that of its predecessor. In June she was able to celebrate her 66th birthday with her supporters and with her son, Kim Aris, who returned to Burma for the second time since his mother's release. On 28 June and 5 July, the BBC broadcast two lectures by Suu Kyi—one on freedom, the other on dissent—as part of its prestigious Reith Lectures. On 1 July Suu Kyi gave a video address to the Community of Democracies, meeting in Lithuania, thanking democratic countries for their support and saying that she expected Burma to achieve democracy and go on to become a member of the organisation.

In July Suu Kyi was able to take her first trip outside Rangoon since 2003, travelling to the city of Pagan. In August she attended commemorations of the failed 1988 uprising, which had marked her emergence, aged 44, as leader of Burma's pro-democracy movement (see AR 1988, pp. 328-29). On 19 August Suu Kyi had her first meeting with the president, Burmese media showing the two of them beneath a picture of Suu Kyi's father, General Aung San, Burma's martyred independence hero. Suu Kyi said that she was "happy and satisfied" and looked forward to further meetings. On 22 August, at the opening of the second parliamentary session, the president described his government as willing to make efforts to "work with everyone".

Subsequently the government took a number of steps towards liberalisation. Trade unions were legalised in September and bans were lifted on the websites of several international news organisations, including some running articles frequently critical of the government. Access to the YouTube website, previously blocked, was reestablished. The following month the director of Burma's Press Scrutiny and Registration Department—its censorship body—called for an end to censorship, describing it as "not in harmony with democratic practices". In September Burma's National Human Rights Commission was established. Its chairman subsequently wrote an open letter to the president, urging him "to grant amnesty" to prisoners who did not pose to a threat to the stability of the state or to public tranquillity—a letter notable for openly acknowledging the existence of political prisoners. In October one of Burma's senior parliamentarians likewise admitted that the NLD had indeed won the 1990 election—a concession never before made. In October, Burmese exiles were invited to return, the president indicating that a law would be enacted offering amnesty. The same month, a partial prisoner release took place, though with only a few hundred political prisoners among the several thousand freed.

On 4 November the president signed a revised law on political parties, repealing provisions that would have barred the NLD, or Suu Kyi, from taking part in elections. Two weeks later the party decided to re-register and to compete in forthcoming by-elections, with Suu Kyi herself standing as a candidate. On 23 December the NLD was formally registered and Suu Kyi stated that she hoped that joining the National Assembly would speed up the process of dialogue and national reconciliation. In December the president also approved a new law allowing citizens to request permission to stage peaceful protests; previously all demonstrations had been banned.

Domestic reform initiatives were complemented by other developments. In September the government cancelled construction of the Myitsone dam, citing popular disapproval of the scheme. The $3.6 billion hydroelectric project had been agreed in 2006 and was to be a joint venture between China and Burma, with most of the electricity generated by the project to be exported to China. The US special envoy to Burma, Derek Mitchell, made three trips to the country, meeting with government officials and with Suu Kyi. In mid-November, with Suu Kyi describing Burma's president as "very genuine in his desire for change", US President Barack Obama announced that Hillary Clinton would make the first visit to Burma by a US secretary of state since 1955. President Obama had spoken by telephone with Suu Kyi on 17 November, confirming her support for the visit. In announcing the decision, Obama said that there had been "flickers of progress", citing the opening of dialogue between the government and Suu Kyi, the release of some political prisoners, and the relaxation of media restrictions. The ASEAN summit, showing regional approval, accepted Burma's proposal to chair the organisation in 2014.

During Clinton's three day visit, from 30 November to 2 December, she told President Thein Sein that the USA had been "encouraged by the steps" taken to date. Clinton and Suu Kyi met in Rangoon on 1 December—the first meeting between two of the world's most prominent female politicians—with Clinton saying that Americans "admired" Suu Kyi and that they had been "inspired by her fearlessness in the face of intimidation" and by "her devotion to her country and to the freedom and dignity of her fellow citizens". On 30 November, French film-maker Luc Besson's film about the life of Suu Kyi, *The Lady*, was released in France. Suu Kyi, contacted by Besson, thanked him, saying "it sheds light on my country".

Clinton made some modest concessions while urging further reforms. She announced that the USA would no longer block cooperation between Burma and the IMF, that it would support intensified UN health and other programmes in Burma, and that it would allow the country to participate in the US-initiated "Friends of the Lower Mekong", a group of countries which held their first meeting (without Burma) in July to promote sustainable development in the Mekong region. Clinton also stipulated the USA's preconditions for lifting economic sanctions: these included the release of all political prisoners, the peaceful resolution of ethnic conflicts in the country, and an end to illicit military, nuclear and ballistic missile cooperation with North Korea. Clinton's visit was followed by one from Japan's foreign minister in an attempt to continue the momentum towards democratisation and national reconciliation.

There were other developments ushering in Burma's return from isolation. On 14 October India announced the extension of a $500 million credit line to Burma to help it develop its infrastructure, agreeing to expand cooperation in oil and gas exploration. On 19 October a delegation from the IMF arrived in Naypyidaw for consultations with government officials on reforming the country's exchange rate system. On 5 December the main border route for trade between Burma and Thailand, the Mae Sot-Myawaddy Friendship Bridge, was reopened after being closed by Burmese authorities in 2010 for reasons of border security.

However, despite calls for the government to achieve reconciliation with the country's ethnic minorities, attempts at ceasefire agreements with groups long at odds with the state produced results both uneven and fragile. While government negotiators met with various ethnic group representatives, comprehensive and durable peace agreements proved elusive. Clashes between the Burmese military and ethnic groups continued, contributing to casualties among both soldiers and civilians as well as the displacement of thousands of villagers.

In **Thailand**, parliamentary elections on 3 July led to Yingluck Shinawatra, the sister of deposed former prime minister Thaksin Shinawatra, becoming the country's new prime minister. Aged 44, she was Thailand's youngest prime minister and the first woman to hold the office. Her Pheu Thai party, which she had been chosen to lead only six weeks prior to the election, won 265 seats, ousting the Democrat Party's incumbent prime minister, Abhisit Vejjajiva, who had been in office for 32 often turbulent months. Abhisit had called the elections six months early and resigned as opposition leader following his defeat. The new prime minister brought together a six-party coalition holding 300 seats (in a 500-member lower house), giving the government a commanding lead over the Democrat Party, which won only 159 seats. Following the election the country's outgoing defence minister said that the military would accept the result.

The inexperienced new prime minister immediately came under pressure as Thailand faced a national emergency from massive flooding caused by heavy rains, with rivers overflowing their banks. About one-fifth of the population was affected by the crisis, which began in July. Flood-related deaths rose to more than 600 people (as well several hundred in Burma, Cambodia, Vietnam and Laos). Large numbers of people were made homeless and unemployed as the flooding damaged homes and businesses and destroyed rice fields and other food crops. The disaster extended over several months, with some areas still under water in December, and affected millions of people across most of the country.

The flooding came after Yingluck had been in office for just over two months and led at least initially to a decline in public confidence in her leadership. The government was criticised for failing to predict the magnitude of the threat to the capital, with the prime minister and experts having given different assessments of the flooding situation, many of which turned out to be overly optimistic. Assurances that certain areas would be safe from flooding proved unfounded. The government resisted calls to invoke a state of emergency, which would have involved its sharing power with the military. (The military had staged a coup in 2006 to oust Yingluck's brother Thaksin, then prime minister.) At one point, Bangkok's governor urged people in the capital to ignore the national government's statements and listen only to him.

The prime minister's call for "cooperation from all sides" was reflected in her willingness to be seen listening to suggestions from former prime minister Abhisit. Yingluck was also photographed receiving advice from Thailand's hugely respected but increasingly frail king, at Siriraj hospital in Bangkok. In November, the king was reported to have lost consciousness temporarily, and his daughter, Princess Chulabhorn, linked the event to stress over the country's crisis. On 5 December, in remarks on his 84th birthday, the king called for national unity in response to the floods.

The prime minister's association with her brother remained an issue. The family connection had been stressed during her campaign, as Yingluck asked voters, "If you love my brother, will you give his younger sister a chance?" Her party's slogan, linked directly to the former prime minister, was "Thaksin thinks, Pheu Thai acts". Yingluck's election campaign, like those of her brother, emphasised populist welfare policies, including an increase in the minimum wage and the distribution of computers to schoolchildren. Her brother, living in Dubai, stated that he had no desire to be prime minister again, but plans for a possible pardon, which would enable him to return to Thailand, attracted criticism. In November, the Thai cabinet approved a draft Royal Decree for the 2011 royal pardon, incorporating legal changes that would have the effect of allowing Thaksin to return to Thailand without having to serve a two-year jail sentence handed down in 2008 for a conflict-of-interest conviction. The prime minister stated that she knew nothing of the cabinet's decision, reportedly made while she was out of the capital visiting flood victims. In December, the annual pardon was granted to thousands of people, but it did not include the former prime minister. Controversy also surrounded reports in December that the government had issued Thaksin with a new Thai passport, his previous one having been rescinded in 2009 by the former government.

Controversy also focused on whether Thaksin might be exerting undue influence over government actions and policies. On 15 December Thaksin travelled to Burma, meeting with President Thein Sein and former junta leader Than Shwe. Four days later, Yingluck arrived in Burma's capital to attend the Greater Mekong sub-region summit and met with opposition leader Aung San Suu Kyi the following day. The prime minister's talks with government officials, accompanied by Thailand's energy minister, included discussions on energy cooperation. The two visits together aroused concerns that Thai investment in Burma's energy sector would serve Thaksin's business interests, reviving questions about his government's alleged corruption. Subsequently Thailand's state-run oil and gas company received permission to purchase an extensive quantity of natural gas from Burma.

During the year there were further cases of foreigners being convicted of insulting the country's monarch, with US and EU citizens receiving prison sentences. In December, a court sentenced a US citizen to two-and-a-half years in prison for posting excerpts online of a locally banned biography of the king. He had done so while living in the USA, but was convicted and sentenced while on a visit to Thailand. Other high profile cases involved Thai nationals, including academics and journalists, leading to concerns about restrictions on freedom of expression. In October, a UN official called for Thailand to amend its law to conform with the country's international human rights obligations.

Intermittent public protest continued, the pro-Democrat "yellow shirts" demanding strong action against Cambodia in the border dispute between the two countries, and the "red shirts" continuing to express anger at the crackdown in Bangkok and elsewhere in 2010 (see AR 2011, pp. 317-19). The low-level insurgency in the south of Thailand continued as well, with the government extending the state of emergency in the three southernmost provinces for a further three months—the 22nd such extension since the law was introduced in mid-2005. Ambushes and random attacks on both civilians and defence personnel caused further loss of life and injuries.

In **Malaysia**, the prime minister, seeking to promote change under his "1Malaysia" concept, promised a series of initiatives, including reform of the country's system of press censorship, a review of the electoral system, and repeal of controversial internal security laws, including the Internal Security Act 1960, which allowed for indefinite detention without trial. In late November, however, the lower house of Malaysia's legislature approved a bill which would increase restrictions on public assembly. Opposition lawmakers boycotted the vote, but the ruling coalition defended the measure as intended to strike a balance between public order and the right to peaceful assembly.

Several months earlier, in July, more than 20,000 people had gathered in Kuala Lumpur calling for free and fair elections. More than 1600 people were detained and later released, as police met the demonstration with tear gas and water cannon. Opposition parties and international human rights groups denounced the government's response to the rally, but the prime minister defended police intervention as necessary, claiming that the rally was not going to be peaceful and accusing opposition leader Anwar Ibrahim of being behind it.

After nearly two years of conflicting testimony, Anwar's trial (on sodomy charges) ended in December, with a verdict expected in January 2012. Anwar accused the prime minister (and his wife) and government officials of framing him, with the connivance of the high court judge who was presiding over the trial. The prime minister and his wife were subpoenaed to testify but were excused, the court ruling that their testimony was not "material"—a decision criticised by Anwar.

Opposition parties had other problems as well. In October, the Democratic Action Party (DAP)—one of three parties forming the People's Alliance in opposition to the governing coalition—reprimanded one of its members who had posted on his Facebook page that he would be distributing party flags on the country's national holiday instead of the national flag, described as representing the government and in need of redesign because of its similarity to the US flag. Two of the People's Alliance parties clashed over proposals from the Pan-Malaysian Islamic Party (PAS) to implement Islamic punishments, with the DAP stating that these would require constitutional amendments to which it would "never agree". Reflecting the sensitivity of religious issues, in March the government reversed a decision to stamp Malay-language Bibles with serial numbers and government seals in a dispute over the use of the word "Allah" as a translation for the deity.

Customs authorities released the 35,000 Bibles, held since 2009, with the words "For Christianity" stamped on them.

In February the acting chairman of the **Brunei** Economic Development Board was removed and the board was merged with the Brunei Economic Planning and Development Department. The administrative step moved the board from the auspices of the foreign ministry, where the sultan's younger brother, Prince Mohamed Bolkiah, served as minister of foreign affairs and trade, to an entity more directly under the sultan's control. This was seen as further ensuring that economic development projects under the country's 9th National Development Plan (2007-12) would not be undertaken without the sultan's knowledge and consent.

Parliamentary elections in **Singapore** on 7 May returned the governing People's Action Party (PAP) to power, but with a reduced popular vote. The prime minister conceded the need for change, while the head of the opposition Workers' Party virtually claimed victory, stating that voters had "made history". The PAP's popular vote fell from 66.6 per cent in 2006 to around 60.1 per cent. Nevertheless the PAP—which had governed Singapore throughout its history— retained its large majority in Parliament, giving it the power to legislate and to amend the constitution. The PAP won all but six seats—81 out of 87—although its share of the vote was its lowest since the country split from Malaysia in 1965. The Workers' Party had its best showing, taking 13 per cent of the vote (and six seats), and another opposition group, the National Solidarity Party, won 12 per cent of the vote.

Prime Minister Lee Hsien Loong, describing the parliamentary elections as a vote for change, a "watershed election", said that the government would change its "style and approach". Subsequently his two predecessors (the country's only previous prime ministers) left the cabinet: one of them Lee's father, Lee Kuan Yew, prime minister from independence until 1990, and the other, Goh Chok Tong, in office until 2004. The two former leaders remained members of Parliament, however, although they also resigned from other important positions: Lee as chairman of one of the country's two sovereign wealth funds, Government of Singapore Investment Corp., and Goh as the country's central bank chairman.

The election reflected public anger over rising living costs and high government salaries, as well as concerns about immigration. Subsequently the prime minister pledged better access to university education, healthcare and housing, while defending his government's economic policies, stating that Singapore's economy had rebounded strongly, experiencing substantial growth despite internationally difficult circumstances.

There was also a more competitive election for Singapore's largely ceremonial presidency, which experienced its first contested poll since 1993 (the only previous time that an actual election needed to take place). The PAP's preferred candidate, former deputy prime minister Tony Tan, defeated three other candidates on 27 August, his slim margin of victory a further setback for Prime Minister Lee, who had backed him in the election campaign. Tan, who became the country's seventh head of state, won only 35 per cent of about 2.1 million votes, beating the second-highest polling candidate by 7269 votes.

Singapore's political and legal system continued to attract criticism. In May a British author, Alan Shadrake, lost an appeal against his conviction for contempt of court, refusing to apologise for his book, *Once a Jolly Hangman: Singapore Justice in the Dock*, which was critical of the use of the death penalty for crimes such as drug trafficking. The author was given a jail sentence of several weeks, released in July and deported to the UK.

Vietnam held the 11th national congress of the ruling Communist Party in January. Nguyen Phu Trong, chairman of the National Assembly, was named general secretary of the Communist Party, replacing Nong Duc Manh, who had held the position since April 2001. The party congress also agreed to the choice of the country's president and prime minister, giving the latter, Nguyen Tan Dung, a second term and selecting Truong Tan Sang as the country's new president. These choices were confirmed by the National Assembly at its meeting in July.

Conflicting territorial and resource claims in the South China Sea, involving China and several South-East Asian nations, led to concerns about possible military confrontation. In June, China sent a patrol ship through the South China Sea to "monitor security" after Vietnam held live fire naval exercises there. Relations between Vietnam and China hit a low point at mid-year when Vietnam accused China of interfering with its oil exploration activities. Vietnam also protested about incidents in which Chinese naval ships threatened Vietnamese fishermen. Public demonstrations took place in Hanoi during June and July, with official permission, as young Vietnamese, prompted in part by calls on Facebook and other social media websites, marched through the capital to protest against China's actions. In August, however, police broke up an anti-China rally, arresting dozens of protesters after loudspeakers warned residents to stay away from the demonstrations. In October, China and Vietnam signed an agreement on the principles to be followed in relation to maritime issues between the two countries. At the same time, India and Vietnam agreed to cooperate on oil exploration in the region. In December, ASEAN and China agreed to begin negotiations in January 2012 on a code of conduct to govern activities in the area.

On 1 August the Vietnamese and US militaries signed their first formal agreement since the Vietnam War, providing for cooperation on health and medical issues. However, Vietnam's human rights policies continued to attract criticism. In June the US government condemned the conviction of seven Vietnamese, including a church pastor, during a one-day closed trial at which the defendants, who had been lobbying for land rights, were convicted of attempting to overthrow the government and sentenced to between two and eight years in prison. Later that month Vietnam released a dissident writer, Tran Khai Thanh Thuy, a pro-democracy activist, and deported her to the USA on humanitarian grounds, following requests by the US state department for her release. There were arrests and trials of other pro-democracy and human rights campaigners, which attracted protests both within and outside the country.

National Assembly elections (held every five years) took place on 30 April in **Laos**, followed by the convening of the National Assembly on 15 June. Members re-elected the general secretary of the ruling Lao People's Revolutionary Party, Choummaly Sayasone, as president, and party Politburo member Thongsing Thammavong as prime minister.

A proposed dam in Laos across the Mekong River attracted controversy. The \$3.5 billion Xayaburi project, intended to provide revenue from hydroelectric power (mostly to be sold to Thailand), was opposed by Vietnam, environmental groups and by villagers along the river. Vietnam urged at least a 10-year moratorium on all mainstream dams on the Mekong because of concerns about the consequences for the country's fish and rice production. Following agreement at a meeting in December of the intergovernmental Mekong River Commission, the Lao government agreed to suspend construction of the dam pending the results of a study of the project's potential impact.

In **Cambodia** the trial of four surviving Khmer Rouge leaders by a special tribunal, meeting in Phnom Penh, began in November (following pre-trial hearings in June). The defendants, charged with crimes against humanity, genocide, religious persecution, homicide and torture, included Ieng Sary, foreign minister in the 1975-79 Khmer Rouge regime; Nuon Chea, second-in-command to Khmer Rouge leader Pol Pot and the regime's chief ideologist; Khieu Samphan, the regime's head of state; and Ieng Thirith, social affairs minister and the wife of Ieng Sary and sister-in-law of Pol Pot. All declared their innocence and claimed that the tribunal had no authority over them. The trial was the second to be held by the Extraordinary Chambers in the Courts of Cambodia, following the conviction of Kaing Guek Eav ("Duch") in 2010 (see AR 2011, pp. 322-23). It aimed to contribute to a better understanding among Cambodians, particularly young people, of what had occurred, and to provide some consolation for Cambodians with family members among the estimated 1.7 million people who had died under the Khmer Rouge. In December the tribunal ordered that Ieng Thirith, earlier ruled unfit to stand trial, remain in detention to see if her mental condition improved.

The tribunal came under criticism after two judges, one German and one Cambodian, ruled out initiating further cases. This sparked concerns about political interference, as the Cambodian government had earlier indicated that it opposed allowing further cases to be investigated or additional indictments to be issued. There were calls for the two judges to resign and for the UN to re-evaluate its relations with the Cambodian government. In response, the UN secretary-general affirmed his support for the panel and expressed confidence in its impartiality.

Cambodia's conflict with Thailand over the tenth-century Preah Vihear temple and surrounding lands (see AR 2011, pp. 319-20) led to further exchanges of both gunfire and rhetoric. In May, talks in Indonesia at the ASEAN summit failed to resolve the border dispute. Subsequently a ceasefire was arranged with the 2011 ASEAN chair, Indonesia, acting as mediator, and military observers were sent to the area to monitor it. In July, following a request from Cambodia for an interpretation by the International Court of Justice (ICJ) of its 1962 ruling that the temple was situated in Cambodian territory, the court called for an immediate withdrawal of Thai and Cambodian troops from the area, a request with which neither side complied.

In June, Thailand announced its withdrawal from UNESCO's World Heritage Convention in Paris, after UNESCO's World Heritage Committee agreed to consider Cambodia's management plan for the contested temple. Two days later there were reports of military reinforcements at the border. In November, Thailand's legal team submitted a report to the ICJ seeking to document Thailand's claim to ownership of the area adjacent to the temple. In December, the Thai and Cambodian defence ministers announced that they had agreed to withdraw their forces "completely and simultaneously" in the presence of Indonesian observers.

Stephen Levine

INDONESIA—PHILIPPINES—TIMOR-LESTE

Indonesia

CAPITAL: Jakarta   AREA: 1,904,570 sq km   POPULATION: 239,870,937 ('10)
OFFICIAL LANGUAGE: Bahasa Indonesia
HEAD OF STATE AND GOVERNMENT: President Susilo Bambang Yudhoyono (DP) (since Oct '04)
RULING PARTY: Democratic Party (DP)
DEMOCRACY INDEX: 6.53; 60th of 167   CORRUPTION INDEX: 3.0; 100th of 183
CURRENCY: Rupiah (Dec '11 £1.00=IDR 14,106, US$1.00=IDR 8,995)
GNI PER CAPITA: US$2,500, Intl$4,170 at PPP ('10)

Philippines

CAPITAL: Manila   AREA: 300,000 sq km   POPULATION: 93,260,798 ('10)
OFFICIAL LANGUAGE: Filipino
HEAD OF STATE AND GOVERNMENT: President Benigno "Noynoy" Aquino III (since June '10)
RULING PARTY: Liberal Party (LP)
DEMOCRACY INDEX: 6.10; 74th of 167   CORRUPTION INDEX: 2.6; 129th of 183
CURRENCY: Philippine Peso (Dec '11 £1.00=PHP 67.88, US$1.00=PHP 43.28)
GNI PER CAPITA: US$2,060, Intl$3,950 at PPP ('10)

Timor-Leste

CAPITAL: Dili   AREA: 14,870 sq km   POPULATION: 1,124,355 ('10)
OFFICIAL LANGUAGES: Portuguese, Tetum and Bahasa Indonesian
HEAD OF STATE: President José Ramos Horta (since May '07)
RULING PARTIES: National Congress for Timorese Reconstruction (CNRT)-led coalition
HEAD OF GOVERNMENT: Prime Minister Kay Rala Xanana Gusmao (CNRT) (since Aug '07)
DEMOCRACY INDEX: 7.22; 42nd of 167   CORRUPTION INDEX: 2.4; 143rd of 183
CURRENCY: US Dollar (Dec '11 £1.00=USD 1.57)
GNI PER CAPITA: US$2,220, Intl$3,570 at PPP ('10)

THE year 2011 was relatively free of unexpected drama in **Indonesia**, but a number of long-standing issues which had dogged the country over recent years—the terrorist threat, separatism, corruption—continued to make their presence felt.

Indonesia's violent Islamists appeared to be selecting more focused targets in their somewhat desultory campaign of terror during the year. This was at least in part a response to the counterproductive revulsion provoked by earlier undirected attacks (such as those of 2009 on hotels and other public buildings), which had killed and maimed local people (see AR 2010, p. 330). In March explosive devices were sent to a number of prominent "liberal" Muslims and in mid-April a suicide bomber attacked a Java mosque used predominantly by police personnel. This appeared to be part of a campaign aimed at supposedly moderate Muslims complicit in the state's anti-Islamist stance. Later in the month, suspects led police to unexploded bombs planted in the vicinity of a Catholic church near Jakarta.

Whatever their change in tactics, the standing and credibility of the militants' ideology was damaged in June with the public execution of an Indonesian maid, Ruyati binti Satubi, in Saudi Arabia for killing her allegedly abusive employer. The incident not only highlighted the general plight of Indonesia's mass of migrant workers in the Middle East oil states but also generated huge public hostility to the Saudi-inspired Wahhabist Islamism to which the local Islamists adhered.

In June the four month-long trial of the 72-year old Abu Bakar Bashir, widely regarded as the founder of Jemaah Islamiya, the region-wide affiliate of al-Qaida, concluded with a 15-year prison sentence. The charges related specifically to his support for jihad training camps in the deeply conservative Muslim region of Aceh in Sumatra, but Bashir was widely regarded as one of the key planners of earlier attacks, most notably those in Bali in 2002 (see AR 2002, p. 340). The government's approach to the pursuit and punishment of terrorists was nothing if not pragmatic and cautious, however. In August it was reported that Indonesia was reluctant to accept the extradition of another of the alleged prime movers in the Bali attacks, Umar Patek, who had been detained in Pakistan. Fearful of garnering public sympathy for the fugitive, the government in Jakarta evidently favoured his extradition to Australia (whose citizens had formed the majority of the victims in 2002).

Aceh, now an area of concern to the national government in respect of militant Islam, had been one of the "successes" in Indonesia's attempts to manage the multi-fronted challenge of regional separatism in the late 1990s and early 2000s. In other parts of the national archipelago, however, difficulties persisted. In particular, violent confrontation continued in the province of Papua (formed by the western half of the island of New Guinea), which had been more or less continuously restive since its absorption by Indonesia in 1963. In August thousands of indigenous Papuans demonstrated against Indonesian rule in the provincial capital, Jayapura. The demonstration itself passed off reasonably peacefully, but it was accompanied by killings away from the main events and the authorities were accused of having deliberately engendered an atmosphere of violence. In August the government faced criticism internationally for initiating an Interpol "red notice" for the apprehension of a leading figure in the separatist Free Papua Movement, Benny Wenda, who was living in exile in Oxford. The government's claim that Wenda should be arrested as a terrorist suspect brought accusations of abuse of process and caused considerable embarrassment to Interpol.

The problem of corruption, a venerable and deeply rooted aspect of public life at all levels in Indonesia, continued to attract attention during 2011. While President Susilo Bambang Yudhoyono himself was widely credited as being genuinely committed to tackling the problem, many of those around and below him continued to be viewed with suspicion. Indonesia scored three out of 10 in Transparency International's annual Corruption Perception Index for 2011 (higher numbers indicating relative "cleanness"). Against this background the president continued to support the national Anti-Corruption Commission in its campaign against *"Korupsi, Kolusi and Nepotisme"* ("corruption, collusion and nepotism"). In August the former treasurer of the president's own Democratic Party, Muhammad Nazaruddin, was arrested in Colombia and returned to Indonesia, where he was immediately taken into custody in relation to kickbacks of some $3 million from a company contracted to construct the athletes' village for the 2011 South-East Asian Games. On his return Nazaruddin announced his intention to implicate other corrupt holders of high office. The process and outcome of the proceedings against him were likely to shape perceptions of the true extent of the government's commitment to the anti-corruption crusade.

Indonesia's relations with Australia during 2011 followed a long-familiar pattern of managed mutual suspicion. This was evident in August when Australia suddenly suspended livestock exports to Indonesia after a television documentary was aired showing gross mistreatment of cattle in Indonesian slaughter-houses. While the Australian public was genuinely shocked by the footage and forced its government's hand, there was a feeling in Indonesia that the affair was merely another example of Australia's "colonial" attitude to the country.

Relations with Indonesia's actual former colonial master, meanwhile, enjoyed an unexpected boost when the Dutch government issued a formal public apology and announced compensation for the massacre in 1945 of some 430 Javanese villagers at the beginning of Indonesia's four-year war of independence. As some commentators rather unhelpfully pointed out, however, the principle of compensation for past atrocities might well work the other way if the government of Timor Leste chose to make an issue of the hundreds of thousands who died there during Indonesia's occupation between 1975 and 1999.

Indonesia's foreign policy was also affected during 2011 by its leading position in the larger South-East Asian region and by its identity as the world's most populous Muslim state. International actors from beyond the region saw it as a potential diplomatic bridgehead and source of influence. The moderate Islamic government of Turkey considered Indonesia as the obvious starting point for the development of its relationship with the Association of Southeast Asian Nations (ASEAN). To this end the Turkish head of state, President Abdullah Gül, made a much heralded state visit in April. Indonesia was also regarded as a key ally by those seeking formal recognition of Palestinian statehood at the United Nations.

During 2011 the political vicissitudes of public life in the **Philippines** maintained their customary high colour. More gravely, however, political violence, whether actual, past or threatened, remained ever-present. Moreover, following a recent pattern, 2011 saw the Philippines suffer disproportionately from natural disaster.

A long-running and unedifying wrangle over the remains of the dictator Ferdinand Marcos, who died in 1989, took a new turn during the year. Marcos's
widow, the formidable Imelda, had resolutely refused to allow his body to be
disposed of in the quiet way favoured by successive governments, demanding
instead a state funeral and maintaining his body in a Perspex coffin in the
interim. By 2011 the issue had passed to another generation with Marcos's
politician son, Ferdinand junior, taking over the campaign and facing, in President Benigno Aquino III, the son of his own father's most famous victim,
Benigno senior, assassinated on his return from exile in 1983. With some dignity
President Aquino passed the decision, with its potentially serious implications
for political stability and public order, to his deputy. But there appeared to be
little prospect of an early resolution.

In June a more recent act of political violence was revisited when 70-year old
Andal Amputuan, patriarch of the powerful clan responsible for the massacre of
at least 57 political opponents in 2009, finally got underway (see AR 2010, p.
331). His son, accused of leading the actual killings, was already on trial but the
older man was widely seen as the mastermind behind the crime. The Amputuans
had been supporters of the former president, Gloria Macapagal Arroyo, and typical of the breed of local political fixers who were able to operate with impunity
as virtual warlords in their own districts. This was a particularly dark aspect of
Filipino political culture that President Aquino committed himself to root out.

Former President Arroyo herself came back into the public eye in November
when she was stopped at Manila airport when attempting to leave for Singapore. Although Arroyo pleaded a need for urgent specialist treatment for a bone
disorder, the Benigno government suspected that she and her husband were
aiming to flee to a non-extraditable jurisdiction in the face of an inquiry into
alleged corruption during her period in office between 2001 and 2010. Despite
arming themselves with a Supreme Court order preventing the government
from blocking their departure, the couple still faced airport police acting for the
ministry of justice who refused to allow them to board their flight. Whilst in
many countries such a conflict between judiciary and executive might have
been expected to provoke a constitutional crisis, in the Philippines it was not
regarded as exceptional.

Carefully organised kidnappings, whose motivation lay in the misty border-
lands between political militancy, Islamic terrorism and plain criminality, continued to afflict the country in 2011. In April, 16 people, mostly teachers, were
abducted from a college graduation ceremony in a remote part of the generally
lawless south. The kidnappers' demands related to a previous mass abduction:
fellow tribesmen had been jailed for their part in an even larger incident in 2009
and their release was now the objective of the later crime. Following the disastrous events of 2010 in Manila, when several foreign tourists were killed in a
botched attempt to release them from a hostage-taker who was holding them on
a minibus, the authorities had adopted a new caution in such situations (see AR
2011, pp. 326-27). Later, in July, a carefully planned assault on a resort centre
near Zamboanga, also in the insurgency-prone south, saw two US citizens and

their Filipino relative captured and taken away by speedboat. This was a more ominous incident as it bore the hallmarks of the al-Qaida-inspired kidnappings by the Islamist Abu Sayyaf group, which had afflicted the region earlier in the decade. In the event, the apparent professionalism of the initial abduction was belied by subsequent developments. The Filipino hostage escaped, one of the US hostages was released, and her 14-year old son was later rescued by villagers following a two-day jungle trek after slipping away from his captors.

The evident impact of global climate change continued to afflict the Philippines in 2011. In June tropical storms and catastrophic flooding created chaos in the north and in Manila. The capital was left reeling again in September when Typhoon Nesat struck, killing more than 50. The extreme experiences of recent years meant that the authorities were better prepared than in the past, however, and the loss of life was much less than it might have been. The forces of malign nature had, however, kept their worst in store for the end of the year when perhaps 1000 people lost their lives and about 10,000 homes were destroyed in flash floods following a huge tropical storm—Typhoon Washi—across 13 southern provinces.

Timor Leste continued to enjoy a reasonable level of stability and calm in 2011 after the difficulties of recent years. In part, this was due to the continued presence of a substantial United Nations security force but, more positively, the regionalist tensions which had driven much of the post-independence violence in the country appeared to have been substantially eased. This was an important element in the relative optimism with which the new country looked forward to its second sequence of national elections in 2012.

In 2011 President José Ramos-Horta was particularly active internationally. During a visit to Palestine in February he offered an echo of his revolutionary past when he proclaimed that "the Palestinian and East Timorese peoples [had] the same experience of occupation and struggle for self-determination." Despite such resonances of previous conflict, relations with the former occupying power, Indonesia, remained good. Indonesia, for example, undertook to sponsor securing Timor Leste's admission to ASEAN when the country presented its formal application to that organisation in March. The general feeling in the region, however, was that Timor Leste would not be admitted during 2011.

Relations with another previous occupier were also developed during the year. In September it was announced that Timor Leste military personnel would be incorporated in Portugal's contingent to the UN force in Lebanon, UNIFIL. This was in part a natural extension of the relationship developed as a result of the extensive Portuguese military presence in international forces in Timor Leste itself. But it also reflected Portugal's long-held ambition to develop a Lusophone "commonwealth" from its former colonial territories, as well as Timor Leste's anxiety to maximise the range of its international relations.

Norman MacQueen

EAST ASIAN STATES

PEOPLE'S REPUBLIC OF CHINA—HONG KONG—TAIWAN

People's Republic of China

CAPITAL: Beijing   AREA: 9,598,088 sq km   POPULATION: 1,338,299,512 ('10)
OFFICIAL LANGUAGE: Mandarin Chinese
HEAD OF STATE: President Hu Jintao (since March '03)
RULING PARTY: Chinese Communist Party (CCP)
PARTY LEADER: Hu Jintao
CCP POLITICAL STANDING COMMITTEE MEMBERS: Hu Jintao, Wu Bangguo, Wen Jiabao, Jia Qinglin, Li
    Changchun, Xi Jinping, Li Keqiang, He Guoqiang, Zhou Yongkang
CCP CENTRAL COMMITTEE SECRETARIAT: Xi Jinping, Liu Yunshan, Li Yuanchao, He Yong, Ling Jihua,
    Wang Huning
HEAD OF GOVERNMENT: Premier Wen Jiabao (since March '03)
CHAIRMAN OF CENTRAL MILITARY COMMISSION: Hu Jintao (since March '04)
DEMOCRACY INDEX: 3.14; 136th of 167   CORRUPTION INDEX: 3.6; 75th of 183
CURRENCY: Renminbi, denominated in Yuan (Dec '11 £1.00=CNY 9.98, US$1.00=CNY 6.36)
GNI PER CAPITA: US$4,260, Intl$7,570 at PPP ('10)

Hong Kong SAR

CAPITAL: Victoria   AREA: 1,092 sq km   POPULATION: 7,067,800 ('10)
CHIEF EXECUTIVE: Donald Tsang Yam-Kuen (since June '05)
ADMINISTRATIVE SECRETARY: Rafael Hui (since June '05)
DEMOCRACY INDEX: 5.92; 80th of 167   CORRUPTION INDEX: 8.4; 12th of 183
CURRENCY: Hong Kong Dollar (Dec '11 £1.00=HKD 12.19, US$1.00=HKD 7.77)
GNI PER CAPITA: US$32,780, Intl$47,130 at PPP ('10)

Taiwan

CAPITAL: Taipei   AREA: 35,980 sq km   POPULATION: 23,146,090 (Sept '10, Taiwan gvt)
OFFICIAL LANGUAGE: Chinese
HEAD OF STATE AND GOVERNMENT: President Ma Ying-jeou (KMT) (since May '08)
RULING PARTY: Kuomintang (KMT)
PRIME MINISTER: Wu Den-yi (KMT) (since Sept '09)
DEMOCRACY INDEX: 7.52; 36th of 167   CORRUPTION INDEX: 6.1; 32nd of 183
CURRENCY: New Taiwan Dollar (Dec '11 £1.00=TWD 47.25, US$1.00=TWD 30.13)
GNI PER CAPITA: GNP per capita US$16,471 ('06, FCO figure)

THE Chinese economy in 2011, in terms of raw growth statistics, remained a bright spot on an otherwise gloomy looking global landscape. Its growth rate came in at 9.2 per cent, 1.1 per cent lower than the year before, but back to the same level as 2009, and consistent with China's growth over the past two decades. Two long-standing problems remained: the rate of inflation, which hovered around the 5 to 6 per cent mark, and caused particular problems in the food sector; and property, where despite numerous government policies at central and local level to calm the market, prices continued to be highly volatile, and there were persistent rumours of an imminent collapse in the market. The final issue was the value of the Chinese currency, the Renminbi, which the USA and others continued to state was overvalued. Even so, China's exports weakened as the year proceeded, partially due to the weakening of demand in its main markets in the USA and EU, but also because of some competition from neighbouring countries, such as Vietnam and India, as manufacturing bases.

The key milestone for 2011 was the 12th Five Year Plan, which set the blueprint for economic development from 2011 to 2015, and was formally approved at the annual session of the National People's Congress (NPC), China's legislature, held in Beijing on 4-14 March. Premier Wen Jiabao made the key presentation, setting out the overall context of the new five-year programme. In the period 2006 to 2011, China had seen growth of 11.2 per cent, the creation of 57.71 million new urban jobs, and increases of per capita income in rural and urban areas of 9.7 and 8.9 per cent respectively. Major investments had occurred in infrastructure, in education and in building social infrastructure. But according to his statement, there was a need for greater concentration by central and local government in the areas of reinforcing market mechanisms in society, co-ordinating China's economic relations with the outside world, and implementing reforms that helped to build social harmony and stability. All of this was simply code for addressing once more the issue of big imbalances, between the cities and the countryside, between the rich and the poor, and between different social classes in Chinese society. Wen stated that the growth rate target from 2011 to 2015 would be 7 per cent per year, with major investments made in improving energy efficiency, creating a greener economy, and building social welfare in order to address social imbalances. The word "innovation" was used throughout the final text of the plan, with a clear intent to use it as the basis to create, by 2020, a middle income country, increasingly orientated towards production for domestic consumption, making goods further up the value-added chain, with greater indigenous input.

2011 was also a year in which China's relations with its closest neighbours, and the wider world, became more vexed. This was partly due to the poor state of the global economy, and unrealistic expectations that, as one of the few countries with strong growth, China would be able to involve itself in activities such as the purchasing of European debt or acquisition of troubled US companies at a greater level than was desired by the Chinese government. Vice Premier Li Keqiang's visit to Europe from 4 to 12 January, and US Secretary of Defence Robert Gates's visit to China from 9 to 12 January, were precursors to the larger visit of President Hu Jintao to the USA and raised some of the general issues that were to recur throughout the year. For Li, the expectation while he was in Spain, the UK and Germany was that the Chinese would become more heavily involved in assisting with the euro crisis through buying European debt. For Gates, his meeting with Hu was overshadowed by news that China had tested its first stealth fighter, the J-20, a major technological advance in its defensive and offensive capacities. When Hu went to the USA, from 18 to 21 January, he had the uneasy memory of President Barack Obama's controversial November 2009 trip, where China had stood accused of belittling the USA. Perhaps as a concession, Hu agreed to one of his rare press conferences while at the White House, taking a question on human rights, and giving one of his most candid responses. "China recognises and respects the universality of human rights," he said, going on to suggest that China's size and complexity meant there would inevitably be problems in realising this principle.

This did not detract from the increasing feeling given by Chinese leaders that the USA was now firmly back in the Asian region, something confirmed at the end of the year by the agreement between the US and Australia that there would be marines based in Darwin, Australia. It was also confirmed by the effective diplomatic work at the Asia Pacific Forum in November, where Premier Wen Jiabao was forced to sit in a meeting while he heard other members of the forum—from Indonesia to Vietnam to the USA—express their concerns over China's increasing assertiveness in regard to maritime borders in the South and East China Sea. The visit by Secretary of State Hillary Clinton to Burma in November too, after the government there had cancelled Chinese involvement in a dam construction project earlier in the year, compounded this. China was facing a USA where the big distractions of wars in Iraq and Afghanistan were coming to an end, and Asia was to become, once again, the key area of influence and concern for the world's sole remaining superpower. In this respect it was significant that the contenders for the Republican nomination for the 2012 US presidential election frequently highlighted ongoing issues with China, such as the overvalued currency, lack of market access, and, perhaps most emotive of all, the claims that China was waging cyber warfare and online espionage for political and economic advantage.

China took its seat at the world stage, attending the G-20 meeting at presidential level in Cannes on 3-4 November. (This followed the cancelling of an EU-China summit, scheduled for Beijing in October, because of the euro crisis.) Hu Jintao repeated the reassuring remarks made by a spokesperson for the ministry of foreign affairs a month earlier at the end of Cannes, saying that he "believed in the wisdom of the European leaders to resolve their economic issues". Fu Ying, the Chinese vice foreign minister, reinforced this, stating that the failure of the euro and the impact of economic problems in the EU, as China's largest trading partner, would be a disaster. Premier Wen, however, suggested that the crisis presented an opportunity for the EU to confront and resolve some of its long-term issues of financial governance, thus echoing language usually used by the EU about China. Excited rumours in late October that the Chinese government might even be a major stakeholder on the European Financial Stability Facility (EFSF) were quashed, however, when the head of the facility visited Beijing on 25 October and made it clear that, at least for this moment, China would not be a direct contributor, particularly in view of the fact that per capita levels of income in poorest areas of the EU were still 5 to 6 times higher than in China.

The raft of revolutions and toppled leaders resulting from the "Arab Spring" continued to pose huge challenges for China's traditional foreign policy of non-interference in the affairs of other countries. China voted in favour of UN Security Council Resolution 1970 on 26 February, which expressed concern over the deteriorating situation in Libya, and imposed sanctions on the Kadhafi regime. Thousands of Chinese personnel, mostly working in the construction sector, were evacuated from the country. Even so, when the vote to use "all necessary measures" to protect civilians came before the Security Council on 17 March (Resolution 1973), China, together with Russia, abstained. It watched the NATO military intervention with misgivings, and was the last major country to recognise the transitional authority in Libya after the overthrown of Kadhafi. This caused caustic criticisms within the Chinese blogosphere, with many on Weibo—China's microblogging network—questioning their government's Middle East policy as slow to respond, passive, and heavy handed. China's official reaction to the fall of the governments in Tunisia and in Egypt was equally low key.

This wave of unexpected popular uprisings led to fears within the Chinese leadership and a sharper response to domestic dissent. Zhou Yongkang, member of the Politburo's standing committee with responsibility for security, addressed an internal meeting on 25 February calling for "measures to sustain public order and stability by enhancing social management and firmly preventing accidents and incidents which might harm social order". Dozens of people who were calling for China's own version of the Jasmine Revolution throughout February were detained, with one demonstration planned for 20 February quickly dispersed, and those posting information on it investigated and, in some cases, arrested. Wen Jiabao, in his annual press conference after the close of the NPC session in March, acknowledged that events in the Middle East were disturbing, but said that while China's leaders were responding to people's aspirations and concerns, those in the Middle East had failed to do this.

The other two events of 2011 which had a major impact in China were the Fukushima nuclear disaster in Japan in March, and the death of the North Korean leader, Kim Jong Il on 17 December. In the case of Fukushima, initial fears that nuclear fallout might spread to the Chinese mainland proved unfounded. However, the accident had an impact on China's own ambitious plans to build over 20 nuclear plants in the coming decade, adding to the dozen or so that were already in operation. Nuclear power plant production was put on hold as the Fukushima crisis unfolded, with a review of the safety procedures in place for the production of each site. As for Kim Jong Il, his visit to China in May was interpreted, by the Chinese and international press, as a desire to examine Chinese economic reforms that might be applied to the moribund economy of North Korea and to cement the position of his third son and chosen successor, Kim Jung Un. In fact it provided evidence that Kim Jong Il's health was even worse than had been expected. Upon Kim's death, Politburo member Zhang Dejiang (who had studied in Pyongyang) was the only foreign dignitary at the funeral, a sign of the continuing closeness of the two neighbouring states. The impact of Kim's death, leaving a nuclear power in the hands of a young and wholly untested successor, created yet more uncertainty at a time when China was already stretched and preoccupied.

President Hu and Premier Wen, in pursuing their shared vision of "putting people first", and addressing some of the issues in creating social harmony that had been prefigured in the discussions of the 12th Five Year Plan, had to face two areas of critical concern. The first of these was the proper implementation of the intra-party democracy measures, which had been pursued since the mid 2000s. For these, the continuing fight against corruption was key, with the former minister of railways, Liu Zhijun, representing a seminal case. Prior to his dismissal from his position at the 19th meeting of the NPC's Standing Committee in November, Liu had been in charge of one of the most ambitious, fast-paced expansions of a high speed rail network ever undertaken. But he had also been accused of misappropriating billions of dollars and taking massive kickbacks. Tragically underlining the nature of the risks that had been taken, on 23 July two high speed trains crashed into each other in the suburbs of Wenzhou, Zhejiang province, killing 40 and injuring at least 192. That there were issues with the safety regime, construction and operation of the trains was clear, but all of this was compounded by the inept response of local leaders and national rail officials who attempted a news cover-up, ignored requests for information from family members of the victims, and even buried one of the damaged carriages in a bid to hide evidence pertaining to the disaster. Public outrage over such behaviour meant that national leaders had to step in to pacify angry and alarmed citizens. The humiliating accident also meant that the high speed rail network in China—a high-profile prestige project—was placed under review and seemed likely to be dramatically scaled back.

The second area of concern was how to deal with deepening unrest and dissent. Wen visited the state bureau for letters and calls on 25 January, during the Spring Festival, the first premier to have done so since 1949. Petitions to the central government had increased markedly since 2002, with a reported 9 million in 2009, although, according to one estimate by Professor Yu Jianrong of the Chinese Academic of Social Science (CASS), only 0.2 per cent of these received a satisfactory resolution. Meanwhile, the ruling Chinese Communist Party (CCP) was approaching the celebration of its 90th anniversary, and had just issued for the first time ever (in January) a history from the official archives spanning the period 1949 to 1978, an era of party-led social upheavals. "The CCP has proven itself to be a great, glorious and correct Marxist political party," stated the official Xinhua news agency on 5 May, "Only the CCP can save China. Only the CCP can develop China. Only the CCP can make China prosperous." A movie, *Beginnings of the Great Revival*, celebrating the founding of the party was issued in June, and the high profile party secretary of Chongqing (and future Politburo contender) Bo Xilai continued his campaign of nostalgic Red Guard songs.

All of this clashed with increased problems of managing dissent and social unrest in an era of rapid economic change and the rise of social media websites as tools of political expression. Some 400 million users were registered by the end of the year on Weibo. On 30 May, reflecting language in the 12th Five Year Plan, Wen had chaired a Politburo meeting to discuss social management. But only four days earlier, 2,000 people had gone on to the streets in Lichuan, Hubei, to protest at the death in suspicious circumstances of a local official, Ren Jianxin. Harrowing pictures of his body, posted online, showed what appeared to be the ugly marks of beating and torture. On 10 June there were major clashes in Xintang, Sichuan, when a pregnant migrant labourer was allegedly mishandled by village security personnel. But the most striking protest was the rebellion in November-December by villagers in Wukan, Fujian, who rose up against corrupt land seizures by local officials. The protest was aggravated by the detention of some of its leaders, one of whom died in custody, allegedly as a result of ill treatment. Amid increasing interest by local and international media the villagers fortified their community and, in effect, became a self-governing enclave. Provincial Party Secretary Wang Yang, whose bid to become a member of the Standing Committee during the leadership succession scheduled for 2012 was being threatened by the protest, intervened and brokered a compromise. The protest ended peacefully, with improved democracy promised for the community and a change of local officials, but the intensity of the action and the publicity that it generated illustrated how much anger there was over corrupt officials and land seizures.

As a background to this, the ongoing detainment of rights lawyers, those who dealt with some of the most contentious issues in contemporary China, continued throughout 2011. The most high profile of these were Jiang Tianyong, released on 19 April after two months in detention; Liu Xiaoyuan, and Li Zhuang, the latter a defence lawyer from Chongqing. Wu Bangguo, the chairman of the NPC Standing Committee, had stated on 26 January at a seminar on law, that "No organisation or individual is above the constitution and the nation's laws. All acts that violate the constitution and the laws must be punished." Yet despite this lip service to the rule of law, throughout 2011 activists were detained without trial (such as Gao Zhisheng); released from prison but then subject to "soft detention" (such as AIDS activist Hu Jia); or, as in the case of international artist Ai Weiwei, prosecuted for ill-defined tax reasons after extended periods in detention. Attempts to clarify the law of soft detention and produce new criminal procedures were issued on 30 August, tightening the ability of police and security personnel to detain suspects. Writers Chen Xi and Chen Wei were awarded prison sentences of nine and 10 years respectively in late December 2011, showing that the clampdown on activists, writers challenging the CCP, and other "subversive" forces was set to continue into 2012.

The leadership in Beijing was aware that the impact of unrest was particularly problematic in China's huge border areas, and that these had been sites of particular discontent since the Tibet uprising in March 2008. In 2011, the last major border area with a significant ethnic minority population, the Inner Mongolian Autonomous Region, erupted in student protests after the death of a Mongolian herdsman at the hands of two Han truck drivers on 10 May. (The two accused were put on trial and sentenced, respectively, to death and life imprisonment.) However anger in the region boiled over, with marches in the provincial capital of Hohhot on the seat of local government. Vice Premier Wang Qishan toured the area on 17 June, stating that economic development and environmental protection would be accelerated. For Tibet, the issue was the election of Lobsang Sangay as prime minister of the Tibetan government-in-exile on 26 April 2011, a move initiated by Tibet's exiled spiritual leader, the Dalai Lama, but condemned by the Chinese government which continued to demonise the Dalai Lama and his representatives. Meanwhile anger over Chinese rule expressed itself in more than a dozen cases of self-immolation by Tibetan monks.

HONG KONG. In 2011, the economy of the Hong Kong Special Administrative Region grew by 5.4 per cent, a slight fall from the previous year. It had an inflation level of 5.8 per cent, and unemployment of 3.6 per cent. For a territory that was overwhelmingly reliant on financial services (99 per cent of its economic activity lay in this sphere) the impact of the continuing global financial crisis was offset by the fact that the Hong Kong stock exchange was able to attract more fresh capital over the course of 2011 than any other international bourse.

On 2 January the veteran local politician and campaigner for democracy, Szeto Wah, died. It was a symbolic moment, as the controversy over constitutional changes—for direct elections for the chief executive and changes in the numbers making up the electoral college from 800 to 1,200 representatives—which had been proposed in 2009 and finally passed in 2010 (with their implementation from 2012), continued to have an impact. Donald Tsang, the current chief executive, was assaulted by demonstrators while visiting the Hong Kong Museum of History on 1 March. His official spokesperson said that the incident had caused grave concern, and the perpetrators needed to be punished. But Tsang's case had not been helped at the start of the year by the refusal of the Hong Kong immigration authorities to issue entry permits to well known Chinese dissidents Wang Dan and Wuer Kaixi, both of whom had intended to attend Szeto Wah's funeral.

The situation deteriorated further when Chinese executive Vice Premier—and one of the main contenders for promotion in the Chinese leadership changes due in 2012—Li Keqiang, visited Hong Kong in August. The ostensible reason for his visit was to promote the 12th Five Year Plan recently passed in Beijing, and to look at financial co-operation between Hong Kong and mainland entities. As part of the celebrations of Hong Kong university's centenary, Li attended an event hosted by the chancellor of the university on 18 August, during which it was claimed the Hong Kong police mishandled demonstrating students, and imposed a lockdown on the area around the campus. The fallout from this saw teachers and students demonstrate later in the month.

For most of the latter part of 2011, Hong Kong was preoccupied with the continuing political manoeuvring over who might replace Donald Tsang as chief executive in the elections scheduled for 25 March 2012. The key candidates were Henry Tang, former chief secretary in Tsang's administration, who resigned from his post in September in order to run for the position, and Leung Chun-ying, formerly convener of the Executive Council. Both were regarded as pro-Beijing candidates. The main pro-democracy candidate was Albert Ho, who announced his candidature in October. Others who were also talked of as being interested in standing were Rita Fan, Regina Ip, and Alan Leong.

TAIWAN. Taiwan's economy grew by 4.4 per cent in 2011, with the key issue being the signing into law on 1 January of the Economic Framework Cooperation Agreement (ECFA) with the People's Republic of China, a comprehensive free-trade agreement which had been reached in June 2010. ECFA had lifted tariffs on 539 types of goods on the Taiwanese side, and 267 on the Chinese side. Expectations that it would dramatically increase cross-Strait trade, however, had to be managed carefully, with the first conference between both sides to monitor the progress of the accord's implementation being held in Taoyuan on 24 February. The ECFA agreement had been heralded as creating a new era of stability in the region, and with showing that politicians were focused on the economic links rather than military ones. Yet the detention of four Chinese fishermen by Taiwanese coastguards when caught fishing illegally in Lesser Kinmen on 13 January—although they were subsequently released—was the first of a series of rows around the status of the island and the limits of its self-determination. Taiwan's protests against the decision by the Philippines to send 14 Taiwanese fraud suspects back to China rather than to Taiwan only underlined the island's feeling of isolation as China continued to grow more economically important and more politically assertive. Claiming that the Philippine action was a violation of its jurisdiction and political integrity, police officers from Taipei visited Beijing on 24 February to discuss the case.

President Ma Ying-jeou complained in May of the description by the World Health Assembly (WHA), of which Taiwan had been granted observer status in 2009, of its health minister being described in internal WHO memos as representing "Taiwan province of China." On the positive side, at meetings on 8 June between the Taiwanese Straits Exchange Foundation and the Chinese Association for Relations Across the Taiwan Straits, in Taipei, a decision was taken to lift the ban on private Chinese tourists visiting Taiwan.

For 2011, the key domestic issue was the preparation for elections for president and for the Legislative Yuan (Taiwan's legislature) due in January 2012. For the Democratic Progressive Party (DPP), the presidential candidate was Tsai Ing-wen, who had won a close victory over her main competitor, Su Tseng-chang, in April. Tsai had run a spirited campaign in opposition to the signing of ECFA in 2010, and was the first ever female leader of a Taiwanese political party. For the newly established People's First Party, the candidate was the politically maverick James Soong Chu-yu, who announced his bid on 20 September. For the incumbent party, the Kuomintang (KMT), President Ma Ying-jeou was standing for his second four-year term, after his landslide victory over the DPP in 2008. The greatest difference between the KMT and DPP remained attitudes towards the mainland, with Tsai stating during the campaign that she did not stand by the 1992 consensus position, in which it was stated that there was only one China, but that this needed to be ratified by democratic process. There was also controversy over reports in the USA during Tsai's visit there in September that officials in the Obama administration had expressed concern over her possible victory (something that was subsequently denied) because of her attitude to China, and over press reports very late in the campaign that the Taiwanese National Intelligence Council and the Intelligence Bureau had monitored Tsai and other opposition candidates, and delivered reports on their movements and activities to President Ma.

Kerry Brown

JAPAN

CAPITAL: Tokyo   AREA: 377,910 sq km   POPULATION: 127,450,459 ('10)
OFFICIAL LANGUAGE: Japanese
HEAD OF STATE: Emperor Tsugu no Miya Akihito (since Jan '89)
RULING PARTIES: Democratic Party of Japan-led coalition
HEAD OF GOVERNMENT: Prime Minister Yoshihiko Noda (DPJ) (since Sept '11)
DEMOCRACY INDEX: 8.08; 22nd of 167   CORRUPTION INDEX: 8.0; 14th of 183
CURRENCY: Yen (Dec '11 £1.00=JPY 121.87, US$1.00=JPY 77.71)
GNI PER CAPITA: US$42,130, Intl$34,780 at PPP ('10)

It was a year defined by triple catastrophe. A sequence of cataclysmic events began in the early afternoon of 11 March when a huge undersea earthquake occurred off the north-east coast of Honshu. What became known as the Great East Japan Earthquake was one of the largest ever recorded and the biggest ever to have hit Japan. In addition to the damage that it wrought, it unleashed a vast tsunami that devastated the coastal region, wiping out whole communities and leaving around 20,000 people dead or missing. The disaster also severely damaged the Fukushima nuclear power plant, triggering the world's gravest nuclear crisis since Chernobyl, depositing radioactive contamination across a swathe of Japanese territory and polluting the neighbouring ocean. The disaster had an impact on almost all areas of life, highlighting the strengths and weaknesses of Japanese society. Thus, 2011 proved to be a year with a powerful but unquantifiable half-life, whose legacy would affect Japan for decades to come.

Prior to the earthquake it had been an unremarkable year. It began with Prime Minister Naoto Kan reshuffling his cabinet as he struggled to remain at the helm of his Democratic Party of Japan (DPJ)-led government. Kan had entered office in 2010 as a reformer and he continued to make a convincing case for more open politics, a liberalisation of trade, a reduction in subsidies for the agricultural sector and changes to the country's social security and taxation structure. He stressed the necessity of such reforms for tackling the country's chronic level of public debt and for addressing the social security burden attendant upon Japan's aging population. But, as ever, he experienced the difficulties of effecting fundamental change in the face of the inertia of a deeply orthodox society, whose post-war political structure had been built around a comfortable (and often corrupt) consensus between a single conservative ruling party—the Liberal Democratic Party (LDP), whose half-a-century in office had been ended in 2009—and a powerful and entrenched bureaucracy.

Kan's efforts at reform were also impeded by the gridlock in a divided Diet (the bicameral legislature). Although the DPJ commanded a majority in the House of Representatives (the lower house), the House of Councillors (the upper chamber) was controlled by the LDP-led opposition. This former party of government spurned Kan's calls for bipartisan co-operation in pursuit of fiscal reform, choosing instead to obstruct the legislative process in a bid to force an early general election. There followed a bitter impasse with the prime minister unable to secure approval for the financial reforms which he had defined as the "historical mission" of his government, or even to enact a budget. This standoff severely eroded Kan's authority. By February the opinion polls showed that support for his administration had fallen to below 20 per cent and there were increasing calls for the prime minister's resignation.

Kan's difficulties with the opposition were compounded by problems within his own party where he faced continuing hostility from the supporters of Ichiro Ozawa, a hugely influential former party leader who had been indicted in January in connection with a long-running scandal over undeclared political donations. Relations between Kan and Ozawa, which had long been strained, had worsened following an unsuccessful attempt by the latter in late 2010 to oust Kan and thereby regain the DPJ leadership. For Ozawa's many supporters within the DPJ, Kan was encouraging the prosecution of the "Shadow Shogun" in order to neutralise a leadership rival and to curry favour with the electorate and the opposition (amongst whom Ozawa was deeply unpopular). For Kan, Ozawa embodied the tradition of patronage and "money politics" that bedevilled Japan's political culture and impeded much needed reform. This dichotomy remained at the heart of the DPJ although by the end of the year both Kan and Ozawa had been marginalised, the former ejected from office and the latter, whose criminal trial opened amid a media frenzy in October, suspended from the party and terminally discredited in the eyes of the public.

At the beginning of March Kan used the constitutional primacy of the House of Representatives to force through a budget for the fiscal year beginning in April, but the opposition continued to block supplementary financial legislation. A group of 16 DPJ legislators expressed their loyalty to Ozawa and their hostility to Kan by abstaining on the budget vote. The government was also shaken on 6 March by the resignation of Foreign Minister Seiji Maehara in a political funding scandal. Kan's position seemed untenable and there was intense speculation about the likelihood of his resignation. Then, in the early afternoon of 11 March everything changed—the political perspective altering fundamentally with a shift in the Earth's tectonic plates.

The magnitude 9 earthquake occurred at 2.46pm local time, 72 km off the eastern Oshika peninsula of the Tohoku region, on the main Japanese island of Honshu. Its epicentre, at a depth of 32 km, was a point on the ocean's floor where the Pacific tectonic plate was forcing its way beneath the Honshu landmass. During its six-minute duration the earthquake released energy equivalent to 600 million times that of the atomic bomb dropped on Hiroshima. It recast the landscape of the ocean floor and shifted parts of northern Japan by up to 2.4 metres. It even moved the Earth's axis by 10-25 cm, making a small alteration to the speed of the planet's rotation and the length of its day. Throughout the remainder of the year there were frequent aftershocks, some of them reaching magnitude 7, with some geophysicists suggesting that these would continue for a decade or more.

Although the earthquake caused extensive damage, Japan's infrastructure—built to withstand earthquakes—fared remarkably well and helped to keep casualties to a minimum. Of the 20,000 or so people killed in the disaster, most were drowned

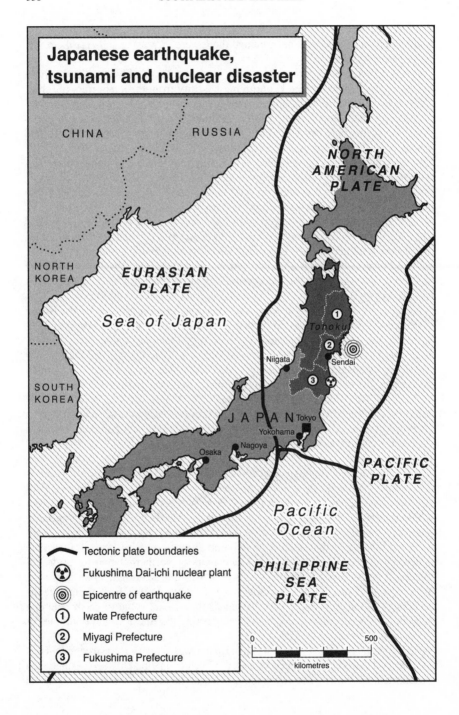

Japanese earthquake, tsunami and nuclear disaster

CHINA

RUSSIA

NORTH AMERICAN PLATE

NORTH KOREA

EURASIAN PLATE

Sea of Japan

Tohoku

①

②

◎

Niigata

Sendai

③

SOUTH KOREA

J A P A N Tokyo

Yokohama

Osaka Nagoya

PACIFIC PLATE

Pacific Ocean

PHILIPPINE SEA PLATE

Tectonic plate boundaries
Fukushima Dai-ichi nuclear plant
Epicentre of earthquake
① Iwate Prefecture
② Miyagi Prefecture
③ Fukushima Prefecture

0   500
kilometres

as the earthquake unleashed a tsunami that devastated parts of Japan's north-east coast. The wave was more than 10 metres high in many areas and attained a height of almost 40 metres in parts of Iwate prefecture. It even reached the west coast of the USA and the Pacific coast of South America, with 2 metre-high waves being recorded in Chile, some 17,000 km from the site of the earthquake. In north-eastern Japan the tsunami overwhelmed coastal defences and inundated an area of around 500 sq km. The city of Sendai was badly hit and a number of smaller towns along the coast, including Ofunato, Kuji, and Rikuzentakata, were largely obliterated. The disaster also ravaged the region's infrastructure, leaving millions without access to water or electricity. Road, rail and air links with the north east were disrupted by the disaster, as were telephone lines. Some 350,000 people were displaced and the misery of the region's inhabitants was exacerbated by the onset of freezing temperatures and heavy snow in the immediate aftermath of the disaster.

Despite their ordeal the survivors behaved with a stoicism and dignity that elicited praise from the watching world. Stories of great individual heroism and self-sacrifice emerged from the mud and the wreckage. There were few reports of looting or violence as inhabitants returned to their stricken communities. Indeed, an astonishingly large amount of recovered cash and valuables was handed in to the authorities in the hope that it could be returned to its rightful owners. Quietly co-operating and displaying little ostentatious emotion, the survivors began patiently and systematically to clear the debris and begin reconstructing their shattered lives. They were assisted by more than 100,000 troops from Japan's Self Defence Forces who brought temporary shelters and emergency supplies to the region and who searched for survivors and began burying the dead, often in mass graves. The troops were joined by aid teams from numerous other countries and non-governmental organisations. The rescue effort and cleanup operation was overseen by Prime Minister Kan who made frequent television appearances—having exchanged his suit and tie for a set of overalls—in which he reported on progress and appealed for calm. On 17 March Emperor Akihito also made a rare television appearance, praising the conduct of his people and encouraging them to retain hope in the face of the disaster (see Documents).

The nature of the catastrophe was captured to an unprecedented extent on the cameras and mobile phones of those who witnessed it. This meant that it was shared like never before. Within hours of the event the world was watching images of a disaster unfolding in real time. Even in an age inured to spectacle, these endlessly replayed recordings captured the sheer power of the tsunami as it swept away houses, boats, cars and infrastructure—a dirty brown, debris-strewn wave advancing relentlessly inland and consuming all that lay before it. No sooner had the wave subsided than the international news media swarmed to the scene to report on the misery. Invariably they reported on the courageous forbearance of the victims and the systematic industry of the relief effort. These characteristic qualities of Japanese culture remained present as the relief and rescue operation evolved into a giant cleanup and reconstruction effort that by the end of the year had achieved remarkable results. But whereas the response to the tsunami encapsulated many of the strengths of Japan, the reaction by the authorities to the nuclear crisis at the Fukushima nuclear power plant epitomised the weaknesses of a society that too often elevated deference and obfuscation to a cultural art form.

As the events of 11 March unfolded it quickly became apparent that there was an emergency at the large Fukushima power plant, which contained six light-water nuclear reactors which were used by Tokyo Electric Power Company (Tepco) to generate electricity. At the time of the disaster, reactors 4, 5 and 6 were already closed for maintenance. Reactors 1, 2 and 3, each housed in a separate building, were automatically shut down when the earthquake struck. Within minutes of the earthquake the Fukushima installation was hit by a 14 metre tsunami which overwhelmed its 5.7 metre-high sea-wall and knocked out the plant's main and back-up electricity supplies, causing the failure of its cooling systems. With the reactors facing the threat of overheating, the government ordered an evacuation of those living within a 3 km radius of the plant.

The situation worsened dramatically on 12 March when a hydrogen explosion destroyed the building housing reactor number 1 after hydrogen and steam had been vented from the overheating reactor. Although the containment vessel of the reactor was reported to be intact, the explosion raised fears that there could be a meltdown of fuel rods in the reactor's core. Tepco began using seawater for emergency cooling, and the government extended the evacuation zone to 20 km, a move that encompassed some 200,000 people. The Japan Atomic Energy Agency (JAEA) assessed the situation as a level 4 nuclear emergency—constituting an "accident with local consequences". As efforts continued to cool the reactors with seawater and boric acid (a compound capable of slowing the rate of nuclear fission), the building housing reactor number 3 exploded on 14 March. Although Tepco insisted that the reactor's containment vessel remained intact and that there was no release of radioactive material above that which was already being vented, the second explosion complicated the situation by impeding efforts already under-way to cool reactor number 2. On 15 March there were explosions at reactors 2 and 3 and a fire at the pool containing the spent fuel rods of reactor number 4. This increased fears that exposed rods could become "critical" and trigger an uncontrolled chain reaction. In the following days there were successful efforts to douse the fuel rods in the pools of reactors 3 and 4 by dropping water from helicopters and spraying from fire engines.

As the authorities struggled to contain the situation, engineers worked to reconnect electrical supplies. By 22 March this had been largely achieved, a breakthrough which greatly assisted cooling efforts. Nevertheless, the extent of the damage to the reactors remained unclear and with it the seriousness of the accident. The JAEA raised its official assessment to level 5—defined as an "accident with wider consequences". This placed it on a par with the Three Mile Island incident in 1979, though less serious than the level 7 accorded to the 1986 Chernobyl disaster. Many foreign experts disputed the JAEA's assessment, however, suggesting that Fukushima warranted a rating of level 6 or more. Increasingly it was suggested that the true extent of the disaster was being concealed by Japan's tradition of close and secretive ties between government officials, civil servants and corporate interests. These fears undermined the confidence of a public already unnerved by reports of traces of radioactive contamination being detected in tap water in Tokyo, 240 km south of Fukushima, and in foodstuffs from other prefectures. Many foreign journalists fled the country and governments withdrew diplomatic staff from their embassies. Although there was no panic within Japan, there was a steady exodus of people heading south and an increasingly vociferous public debate over the desirability of nuclear energy which played such a major role in meeting Japan's energy demands.

On 12 April the accident rating was raised to level 7. This maximum rating was reserved for nuclear disasters with serious global ramifications and had hitherto only ever been applied to Chernobyl. The decision followed estimates by both the Nuclear and Industrial Safety Agency and the Nuclear Safety Commission (both Japanese bodies) over the quantity of radioactive material that had been released into the environment from the Fukushima plant. It also followed the acknowledgment that efforts to cool the reactors had left vast pools of highly contaminated water inside the turbine buildings and the underground service tunnels of the plant. Some of this had leaked into the ocean and some had been discharged into the sea from storage tanks in order to make room for more heavily contaminated water. For even as engineers attempted to drain and capture contaminated water, huge quantities of fresh water was also still being used to cool the reactors and fuel rods which remained dangerously hot.

On 17 April Tepco unveiled a plan for making the plant safe. It envisaged taking three months to lower the temperature of the reactors and spent fuel ponds, and to reduce radiation levels in the surrounding area, and then six months to remove the contaminated water and clear the wreckage of damaged buildings. With this done a "cold shutdown" could be achieved and thereafter the damaged reactor buildings could be shrouded—initially with fabric but later with concrete—in order to prevent further atmospheric radiation releases. The company promised to monitor radiation levels systematically but neither Tepco nor the government would give any indication as to when evacuees, living in temporary accommodation, would be able to return to their homes.

The first heavily protected workers were able to enter the damaged housing of reactor number 1 on 5 May. A week later it was confirmed that a meltdown had occurred. By the end of the month it was admitted that the reactor had undergone meltdown within 16 hours of the accident, its molten mass having burned through the pressure vessel and damaged the concrete floor of the reactor's containment vessel. When workers entered rectors 2 and 3 it was confirmed that they, too, had undergone meltdown within days of the accident. The admissions fuelled anger over what was seen as a pattern of persistent underestimation of the gravity of the accident by Tepco, and increased fears over the extent of the radiation that had been released.

Amid this growing public hostility, Tepco announced losses of ¥1,250 billion, the largest ever recorded by a Japanese company outside the financial sector. On 20 May the company's president, Masataka Shimizu, apologised to the country and announced his resignation "to take managerial responsibility for undermining confidence in nuclear power and causing trouble for society".

Prime Minister Kan was also under pressure both within the Diet and the country at large. Although he managed to enact legislation to help finance reconstruction in the aftermath of the 11 March disaster, he was widely criticised for having shown insufficient leadership during the crisis. In early May he acknowledged that the government's response had been "inadequate". On 10 May he went further and admitted that his government bore "a major responsibility for having promoted nuclear energy as national policy" and apologised for "failing to prevent the nuclear accident". He promised an independent investigation into its causes, improved safety standards, and a revised energy policy that would focus on conservation and on renewable sources of power. Kan later clarified his position by stating that the country would continue to use nuclear energy but that its significance within the overall matrix of power generation would be reduced. In the meantime around two-thirds of Japan's 54 nuclear reactors remained inactive as the nuclear industry was subjected to a rigorous safety inspection. This resulted in power shortages and rolling electricity cuts which affected industry and domestic consumers alike.

Facing a no-confidence motion against him in early June, the prime minister said that he would step down but only after further progress had been made in the reconstruction effort. Eventually he agreed to go in August in return for opposition co-operation in enacting the legislative framework for long-term reconstruction in the disaster-stricken north-eastern region. This included a government agency presided over by a cabinet minister, funding (which included an additional budget), and the creation of special zones with tax incentives and preferential business regulations within the region. With his legislative objectives achieved, Kan announced his resignation on 26 August. A lightning DPJ leadership election was won by Yoshihiko Noda, who on 30 August became Japan's sixth premier in five years. A former finance minister with a low public profile, Noda selected a cabinet which tried to balance the DPJ's competing factions, an approach which differentiated him from Kan and reinforced his perception as a conciliator within the fractious party.

In outlining the priorities of his new government, Noda acknowledged the fragility of the country's economy and its huge level of public debt by stressing the need to "strike a balance between economic growth and fiscal discipline". He also identified "speeding up the recovery and reconstruction process" in the aftermath of the March disaster as "our biggest mission" and warned that tax rises and the sale of some state-owned assets would be required to fund this in ways that would not worsen the already parlous state of public finances. He vowed to maintain the post-tsunami move towards phasing out Japan's reliance on nuclear energy, stating that it was "unrealistic" to build any new nuclear reactors in the aftermath of the Fukushima disaster, or to prolong the use of reactors that were reaching the end of their lives. In the short-term, however, he promised to restart the country's nuclear power plants as soon as the ongoing round of safety checks had been completed.

Although the effort to shut down the crippled Fukushima plant continued to make progress, the credibility of the nuclear industry was deeply compromised not just by the accident itself but also by the constant drip of bad news concerning its severity. In early June the Nuclear and Industrial Safety Agency doubled its assessment of how much radiation had escaped from the damaged plant to 770,000 terabecquerels, around 20 per cent of the total released at Chernobyl. In the same month plutonium was detected in soil outside the Fukushima complex and radioactive elements were discovered in the urine samples of local children. In August cattle and rice in Fukushima prefecture were found to be contaminated as were fish caught near the nuclear plant. Although the government announced structural reforms to increase the regulation of the nuclear industry, the extent to which it had become discredited was shown by a rare protest rally in Tokyo in September with up to 60,000 people demanding a clear timetable for the phasing out of nuclear power.

The continued discovery of "hot spots" of radioactive contamination, some of which were found hundreds of kilometres away from the site of the accident, fuelled public disquiet. These areas were often discovered in tests conducted by groups of private citizens concerned that the authorities had not been sufficiently open or energetic in assessing the risks to public health. There was also public mistrust of government declarations over what were acceptable levels of exposure to radiation both for people and the foods which they ingested. As a result, fearful Japanese consumers shunned some agricultural produce, especially rice and fruit originating from the Fukushima area, despite efforts by some politicians to restore confidence by publicly eating produce from the prefecture. The paucity of clear and reliable information fuelled the belief that both Tepco and the government had misled the public by downplaying the seriousness of the accident. This belief was encouraged by the revelation that in the immediate aftermath of the Fukushima disaster bureaucrats had withheld information—derived from sophisticated predictive computer systems—about the spread of contamination.

Reports issued in late October gave further credence to the argument that the severity of the Fukushima disaster had been systematically underestimated. According to a study in the *Atmospheric Chemistry and Physics* journal the damaged plant had possibly emitted 35,800 terabecquerels of caesium-137 into the atmosphere. This amounted to more than 40 per cent of that released at Chernobyl and more than twice the 15,000 terabecquerels estimated by the Japanese authorities. Although caesium-137 was a harmful long-term pollutant, the report suggested that the consequences would be less serious than at Chernobyl as 79 per cent of the radioactive isotope had fallen into the ocean, with only 19 per cent landing in Japan and 2 per cent in other countries. A second report, this one by the Institute for Radiological Protection and Nuclear Safety, a French monitoring agency, estimated that more than 27,000 terabecquerels of caesium-137 had entered the ocean in the vicinity of the Fukushima plant between March and mid-July, up to 20 times more than Tepco's estimate.

At the end of October Tepco completed the fitting of an airtight polyester outer shell around reactor number 1. Rejoicing was tempered, however, by the assessment that it would take at least 30 years to safely decommission the Fukushima plant. Nevertheless, at a televised press conference on 16 December Prime Minister Noda announced that a "cold shutdown" had been achieved at the plant. He promised to press ahead with "off-site issues", including cleaning contaminated areas and ensuring that compensation payments were received by those affected by the disaster.

However, the month also saw the release of the interim report of the independent body established by the government to investigate the nuclear disaster. Compiled after interviewing more than 400 workers and officials, the 507-page document was scathing in its assessment of the response to the crisis by both Tepco and the government. The report found that the authorities had underestimated the risks posed by a magnitude 9 earthquake, assuming that the highest tsunami wave would be only 5 metres. It had also been incorrectly assumed that the Fukushima plant's emergency cooling system would continue to work after a tsunami. The report suggested that workers were untrained to handle emergencies such as that which occurred on March 11 and had made mistakes that worsened the situation. It also criticised officials for delays in making decisions to staunch radiation leaks as the situation worsened in the immediate aftermath of the disaster. The confusion was compounded by poor communication and delays in releasing data relating to the seriousness of the situation (see Documents).

The impact of the 11 March disaster tipped the Japanese economy back into recession. There was some recovery during the course of the year as, assisted by a 6.2 per rise in exports and a 1 per cent increase in private domestic consumption, GDP grew by 1.5 per cent in the third quarter—its first expansion in four quarters—to achieve an annualised growth rate of 6 per cent. However, throughout the year Japanese exporters struggled with the soaring value of the yen. In March G-7 finance ministers made a rare, co-ordinated intervention in the global currency markets after the yen had reached its highest level against the US dollar in the post-war period. The finance ministers expressed "our solidarity with the Japanese people in these difficult times, our readiness to provide any needed co-operation and our confidence in the resilience of the Japanese economy and financial sector". Although the yen had been on an upward trajectory for some time, its value had spiked in the aftermath of the earthquake, thereby hampering Japan's reconstruction effort. Ostensibly the cause of this spike was "repatriation"—the process whereby some of the large funds held by Japanese savers and businesses in overseas bank accounts was being converted to yen and returned to Japan in order to pay for reconstruction work. Analysts agreed, however, that it was also a function of huge speculation by currency dealers. Fumihiko Igarashi, Japan's deputy finance minister, welcomed the G-7 action against the speculators whom he denounced for putting the global economic recovery at risk and for behaving "like sneaky thieves at the scene of a fire". The palliative effect proved short-lived, however, and the Bank of Japan (BoJ) made further interventions during the course of the year as it promised to maintain decisive action against speculators.

In December the BoJ downgraded its forecast of the county's economic prospects from "moderate recovery" to zero growth. Data for the year as a whole showed that Japan had recorded a trade deficit of ¥2,490 billion in 2011, its first annual trade deficit for 31 years. Despite the third quarter rebound, overall exports fell by 2.7 per cent to total ¥65,500 billion. They were hampered by the strong value of the yen, the disruption caused by the 11 March disaster, and sluggish global demand. By contrast, imports rose by 12 per cent to reach ¥68,000 billion, a significant share of which resulted from higher demand for imported fossil fuels because of the shutdown of much of the nuclear power industry.

Of greater long-term concern, however was the country's level of sovereign debt which, even before the events of 11 March, was estimated by the OECD as likely to rise to almost 220 per cent of GDP in 2012, the largest debt-to-GDP ratio in the world. Faced with such debt, and an apparent absence of political will to address it, Japan's credit rating was downgraded during the course of the year. By the year's end it faced the prospect of revenue from bond issuance exceeding that from taxes for the fourth consecutive year and total debt of an eye watering ¥937,000 billion. Noda was criticised as being too ready to concede to ministerial spending requests and too apt to rely on accountancy sleights of hand to give an impression of controlling spending. Furthermore, despite a tax take that had fallen as a proportion of GDP from 21 per cent in 1991 to 17 per cent in 2008, there was no indication of imminent tax rises.

That Japan was not facing an economic crisis similar to that of Greece was because it continued to be able to borrow at nominal interest rates as a result of its debt being held by domestic investors. This thrift was an established feature of Japanese culture, like social deference and public trust in ruling elites. They were qualities that were simultaneously admirable and dangerous, contributing to political and economic stability but also to passivity and complacency. Public trust was also a delicate creature. Bespattered by radioactive fallout, it remained to be seen whether in the long-term its fragility would survive the corrosive effect of the official mendacity which had been such an intrinsic part of the Fukushima experience.

D.S. Lewis

SOUTH AND NORTH KOREA

South Korea

CAPITAL: Seoul   AREA: 99,260 sq km   POPULATION: 48,875,000 ('10)
OFFICIAL LANGUAGE: Korean
HEAD OF STATE AND GOVERNMENT: President Lee Myung Bak (GNP) (since Feb '08)
RULING PARTY: Grand National Party (GNP)
PRIME MINISTER: Kim Hwang Sik (GNP) (since Oct '10)
DEMOCRACY INDEX: 8.11; 20th of 167   CORRUPTION INDEX: 5.4; 43rd of 183
CURRENCY: Won (Dec '11 £1.00=KRW 1,766, US$1.00=KRW 1,126)
GNI PER CAPITA: US$19,890, Intl$29,010 at PPP ('10)

North Korea

CAPITAL: Pyongyang   AREA: 120,540 sq km   POPULATION: 24,346,229 ('10)
OFFICIAL LANGUAGE: Korean
HEAD OF STATE: Kim Il Sung [died 1994], Eternal President (ceremonial); Kim Jung Un (since Dec '11)
RULING PARTY: Korean Workers' Party (KWP)
PRIME MINISTER: Choe Yong Rim (since June '10)
DEMOCRACY INDEX: 1.08; 167 of 167   CORRUPTION INDEX: 1.0; 182nd of 183
CURRENCY: North Korean Won (April '12 €1.00=KPW 132.2, US$1.00=KPW 100)

AFTER the excitement of 2010, the Korean peninsula attracted less international attention for most of 2011. In the Republic of Korea (ROK—South Korea), the 2013 presidential election began to cast a shadow. In the Democratic People's Republic Of Korea's (DPRK—North Korea) the induction of a successor to Kim Jong Il, a process begun at the Korean Workers' Party (KWP) conference in September 2010, seemed to proceed smoothly. Then on 19 December, the DPRK media announced that Kim Jong Il had died of a heart attack two days earlier. An international media feeding frenzy got underway, fuelled by a general lack of information about Kim Jung Un, the dead leader's third son and chosen successor, and by pictures of apparently grief-stricken mourners from all walks of life. An announcement at the end of the year that "foolish politicians" should not expect any changes in the DPRK's policies failed to end speculation.

SOUTH KOREA. Following the sinking of the corvette *Cheonan* in March and the shelling of Yeonpyeong Island in November 2010 (see AR 2011, pp. 346-347), the ROK expected more challenges from the DPRK. However, despite continued verbal hostility, there were no further "provocations". Rather than confrontation, the DPRK went into conciliatory mode at the beginning of the year, with an early proposal for a variety of talks. ROK President Lee Myung Bak said in his New Year address that he was open to contacts. Later, he even said that he was willing to hold a summit meeting. But the ROK rejected the proposed talks, arguing that without an apology for the events of 2010, the DPRK was not sincere. The only meeting, held between colonels from the two sides on 8-9 February to examine the events of 2010, broke up without agreement. There were moments of tension and irritations. Groups in the ROK persisted in sending balloons carrying anti-DPRK materials into the DPRK (see AR 2009, p. 357). The

DPRK threatened to shoot-up the south side of the Demilitarised Zone (DMZ) if the balloons did not stop but did not do so.

Both the USA and the ROK alleged that the DPRK was engaged in cyber warfare and that it had jammed GPS equipment during US-ROK military exercises. A ROK newspaper, the *Chosun Ilbo*, said in March that should the DPRK collapse, the ROK military had teams ready to destroy the symbols of the regime, and in June it emerged that ROK army units had been using pictures of the two Kims for target practice. Ignoring ROK protests, the DPRK took over ROK assets at the Mount Kumgang resort in August, giving the remaining ROK caretakers 72 hours to leave. The project, run by the Hyundai group, had been suspended following the shooting of a South Korean woman in 2008 and the DPRK's refusal to allow an ROK enquiry. Hyundai wanted to reopen it but the government would not agree. In December, the DPRK threatened to fire on Christmas trees that the ROK proposed to establish along the DMZ. The ROK abandoned the idea after Kim Jong Il's death. The ROK also arrested several people for alleged spying.

Yet despite these signs of tension, there were also indications that that both sides wished to move away from confrontation. The DPRK Red Cross reopened its office at Panmunjom and re-established the telephone link across the DMZ. Fears that the Kumgang takeover might lead to pressure on the Kaesong Industrial Zone, as in the past, proved unfounded. Kaesong not only continued to function but the ROK quietly resumed construction work. The ROK allowed some non-governmental contacts with the DPRK and it also offered aid after summer floods. The offer was not taken up. In June, the DPRK revealed that there had been North-South contacts in April and May, aimed at an eventual summit between leaders. Embarrassed ROK officials argued that they were seeking an apology from the DPRK. The DPRK said that the approach was to find a formula that looked like an apology but the real aim was for the DPRK leader to attend a summit.

No summit materialised but a shift was discernible in the ROK's position. At the ASEAN Regional Forum meeting in Bali in July the two sides' nuclear negotiators held "constructive" talks, and the foreign ministers also met briefly. At the end of August, Lee replaced his hard-line unification minister, Hyun In Taek, with Yu Woo Ick, a former chief of staff to Lee and later ambassador to China. The DPRK dismissed the change, but in the ROK it was seen as a move away from the tough line followed since 2008. In September Lee was positive about the prospects for a Russian gas pipeline via the DPRK to the ROK (see below), a position he maintained during his visit to Russia in November. Hong Joon Pyo, appointed chairman of the ruling Grand National Party in July, regularly stressed the need for a new approach, and in September visited the Kaesong Zone.

Behind these developments was the April 2012 general election, and even more, the 2012 presidential election. Although Lee was not eligible to stand again, he wished to retain influence in the selection of a successor. A deal with the North would have been a major coup. The DPRK, while willing to string out the contacts to see what it could gain, probably saw little advantage in boosting Lee's position, and Kim Jong Il's death put everything on hold.

In June, the *Economist* noted that while Lee was seen abroad as successful, at home he was viewed more sceptically. His support hovered around 28 per cent—it had been 75 per cent in the heady days of 2008—and there was criticism of various grandiose schemes. Although the ROK had not suffered too much from the 2008 global recession, there were problem areas. Economic growth in 2011 was 3.9 per cent, but there were signs of a slowing over the year. The Japanese tsunami had negative effects, since ROK companies were very dependent on Japanese components. It also raised issues about the ROK's nuclear energy programme. The European economic crisis affected sales of automobiles and electronic goods. Foot and mouth disease reached a peak in the spring. As food prices, especially for imported vegetables, rose steadily, the government cut duties in June. Surveying the year in December, the *JoongAng Ilbo* said that it been bad for most. Inflation had increased. Real wages had grown by 3.8 per cent in 2010 but by minus 3.5 per cent in the first nine months of 2011. Youth unemployment was high. Forecasts for 2012 saw growth slackening, while the government announced in September that planned spending in 2012 would increase by 5.5 per cent compared with 2011, to $275 billion.

Developments in Seoul showed that the conservatives were generally unpopular. The incumbent mayor, Oh Se Hoon, re-elected by a slender majority in 2010, tried to restrict free school meals to those on welfare benefits, a measure that required a referendum. The opposition saw its chance and called for a boycott, and the referendum failed. Oh resigned and in the ensuing election, an independent, Park Won Soon, won against the GNP candidate, with support from Ahn Chul Soo, a businessman and a professor at Seoul National University, whom many tipped as a likely opposition candidate in the presidential election. For the conservatives, the most likely candidate was Park Geun Hye, daughter of the late President Park Chung Hee, who lost out to Lee Myung Bak in 2007 (see AR 2008, p. 344). She made no open break with Lee but indicated that she would follow a different line on several issues, including relations with the DPRK. Vocal opposition to a proposed naval base on Cheju Island and to the ratification of the ROK-US Free Trade Agreement (FTA—passed by the ruling party by sheer weight of numbers after fighting in the National Assembly) indicated that election year politics would be rough.

Relations with the USA were good. For Lee the passing of the FTA was both a trade and a foreign policy triumph, even if a belated one. Originally signed in 2007 (see AR 2008, p. 345), it had been strongly contested in both countries right to the end. Its US ratification in October cleared the way for a triumphant Lee visit to the USA, a trip which included an address to both Houses of Congress. Other foreign relations were generally good, although old issues emerged with Japan from time to time. Clashes between the ROK coastguard and Chinese fishing boats left one coastguard dead.

NORTH KOREA. Until December, 2011 was a quiet year by recent standards. Kim Jong Il seemed to have made a good recovery from his 2008 stroke and carried out many tours of inspection, as well as two visits to China and one to Russia. Kim

Jung Un, who had publicly appeared for the first time at the 2010 Party Congress (see AR 2011, p. 351), frequently accompanied him. He was never formally identified as Kim Jong Il's son, although officials made no secret of the fact. Kim Jong Il's visits were, as in recent years, heavily geared towards the military, but some commentators thought that the Korean Workers' Party was making a comeback, and was backing the younger Kim.

The nuclear issue made no progress. Kim Jong Il told various visitors that the DPRK was ready to return to the six-party talks but there seemed no question of a unilateral DPRK denuclearisation. The DPRK was prepared to talk about managing its programme, not abandoning it. This struck no chord with the ROK, the USA or Japan. Russian and Chinese officials indicated that they thought some form of acceptance of the DPRK as a nuclear weapons' state might be required. There were moments of hope. In July, the US allowed DPRK Vice Foreign Minister Kim Kye Gwan to visit. He met with the US chief negotiator, Stephen Bosworth, and said that the talks had been "very constructive and businesslike". Meetings at the ASEAN Regional Forum were described in similar fashion. But nothing happened. Rumours that the DPRK might conduct another nuclear test proved unfounded.

The major debate was over food aid. In 2010, the DPRK had appealed for food aid, citing a series of natural disasters as the major reason for the shortfall. These claims aroused scepticism. Some argued that the DPRK was attempting to stockpile food so that it could make special allowances in 2012, the 100th anniversary of Kim Il Sung's birth, and the year in which it was to become a "strong and prosperous country". In March, the UN organised a "Rapid Assessment Mission", which visited 40 counties in nine of the 11 provinces, including 20 where there was no international assistance. Their report supported the DPRK claims. Heavy rain in August and September 2010 and a cold and prolonged winter had damaged crops. As in the ROK, foot and mouth disease began in the autumn. This had a wider effect than the meat supply because diseased cattle were unable to plough. They noted that the Public Distribution System was in theory functioning, but that at best it delivered only part of the allocated supplies and often dried up altogether. People were then thrown back on private plots, markets, or private barter trade. In more remote provinces, they found serious food shortfalls, leading to stunting, wasting and malnutrition. In general, people suffered from chronic undernourishment. Recent appeals had produced much less than was required and the report concluded that some 297,000 metric tonnes of food aid was needed for the most vulnerable.

Although the report noted no stockpiling of food, the accusations continued. Some claimed that the report exaggerated North Korea's needs and that much food aid was diverted to the military. During the following months, others also investigated the situation. A delegation from The Elders, led by former US President Jimmy Carter, accompanied by other senior political figures, toured in March. Despite the eminence of the group, its members were not seen by Kim Jong Il in Pyongyang or by Lee Myung Bak in Seoul, and there were claims that they had been deceived by the North Koreans. The US "Special Envoy for North Korean

Human Rights", Robert R. King, led a food assessment team in May, the first time the DPRK had accepted a visit from King or his predecessor. This concluded that while there was no overall food shortage, certain areas were in difficulties; any food aid should not be of a quality that would lead to diversion. King also secured the release of another US citizen arrested for illegally entering the DPRK.

There was aid, although it fell short of what the UN team thought was needed. The ROK, which had argued that there should be no food aid until the DPRK apologised for the 2010 incidents, changed its position after flooding in June and July and offered assistance. The offer was not taken up and the ROK eventually withdrew it. The USA apparently gave $950,000 worth of aid in August, which led to an offer to resume the missing in action programme, suspended by the US authorities in May 2005. Talks began in October.

The DPRK's main international partner remained the People's Republic of China. This was particularly marked in trade. Figures from ROK sources showed that the Chinese share of DPRK trade was some 87 per cent of $4.2 billion, up from 48.5 per cent in 2004. Coal and steel were the main DPRK exports, while the country imported fuel and machinery. The increasing Chinese involvement in the DPRK economy was evident. Chinese goods flooded the shops and the markets. Chinese tour groups flocked to visit a country they said reminded them of their own past. The Chinese were also major suppliers of aid. This led to much hand wringing in the ROK as well as speculation that China was ready to turn the DPRK into a Chinese province. There was no evidence that this was China's intention. Kim Jong Il made two "unofficial" visits to China, in May and August; the latter while returning from Russia. He met with senior Chinese leaders, including President Hu Jintao and there were the usual pledges of mutual friendship. It was widely believed that the chief purpose of the visits was to obtain China's endorsement of the succession arrangements. In early August, two Chinese naval vessels from the Chinese Northern Fleet visited Wonsan to mark the 50th anniversary of the 1961 Sino-DPRK Treaty of Friendship.

Relations with Russia were more active. Deputy Foreign Minister Aleksei Borodavkin was in the DPRK in March, discussing economic co-operation in a number of fields, including railways, a gas pipeline and power transmission. Kim Jong Il went to eastern Russia in August and met President Dmitry Medvedev at Ulan-Ude. On both occasions, the DPRK said that it was willing to return to the nuclear talks. The most substantive discussions, however, seem to have been on the gas pipeline issue. Preliminary agreements were signed with Gazprom, the Russian gas exporting company, and the two Koreas in September.

Although not carried by the DPRK media, events in the Middle East were clearly known to senior officials and those who had dealings with foreigners. DPRK workers in Libya were apparently told not to come home. As they had done when Saddam Hussein fell, officials greeted the news of the death of Moamar Kadhafi by noting that it was a mistake for a regime to give up the nuclear weapons' option.

Kim Jong Il's death in December overshadowed all other events in the DPRK. Following the 19 December announcement, the country entered a 100-day period of mourning, although the most extreme manifestations were confined to the days between the announcement and the funeral ceremonies on 28 and 29 December. The announcement was a surprise as Kim seemed to have made a good recovery from his 2008 stroke. The succession apparatus swung into action. There was no doubt that Kim Jung Un, for the first time identified as his father's son, was his designated successor. He was the chief mourner at the ceremonies and by the end of the year had been given a variety of titles to signify his role. But it remained unclear where real power lay. The day of the funeral, the younger Kim was seen as leading the mourners beside the hearse, with party dignitaries on one side and military figures on the other. Immediately behind Kim was his uncle by marriage, Jang Song Taek. That, and the fact that a few days previously, Jang had appeared wearing the uniform of a four-star general for the first time, indicated that he was the man to watch. Thus, the DPRK entered the year of Kim Il Sung's centenary facing many uncertainties.

J.E. Hoare

MONGOLIA

CAPITAL: Ulan Bator   AREA: 1,566,500 sq km   POPULATION: 2,756,001 ('10)
OFFICIAL LANGUAGE: Halh (Khalkha) Mongolia
HEAD OF STATE: President Tsakhiagiyn Elbegdorj (MDP) (since June '09)
RULING PARTY: Mongolian People's Party (MAN)
HEAD OF GOVERNMENT: Prime Minister Suhbaataryn Batbold (MAN) (since Oct '09)
DEMOCRACY INDEX: 6.36; 64th of 167   CORRUPTION INDEX: 2.7; 120th of 183
CURRENCY: Tugrik (Dec '11 £1.00=MNT 2,108, US$1.00=MNT 1,344)
GNI PER CAPITA: US$1,850, Intl$3,630 at PPP ('10)

THE economy of Mongolia grew rapidly in 2011 as foreign investment rose three-fold from the previous year to a record $5.3 billion. Economic growth rose by 17.3 per cent over 2010. The main forces driving this spectacular boom were the mining project underway at Oyu Tolgoi (Turquoise Hill), a copper and gold mine in the Gobi Desert, and the planned development of Tavan Tolgoi (Five Hills), the world's largest untapped coal deposit, also in the Gobi, with an estimated 6 billion tonnes of coal.

According to the IMF, Mongolia could expect average annual economic growth of 14 per cent between 2012 and 2016, peaking at almost 23 per cent in 2013 when production was due to begin at Oyu Tolgoi. However, government spending was also growing fast—by 56 per cent in 2011 according to the World Bank—stimulating inflation, which reached 11 per cent in December. There were fears that the elections to the Great Hural (unicameral legislature), due in June 2012, could tempt the government to raise spending even further.

In September, the government tried, and failed, to increase its stake in the joint venture concluded in 2009 with Ivanhoe Mines of Canada to develop Oyu Tolgoi. The existing contract gave the Mongolian government a 34 per cent stake in OT with the remaining 66 per cent owned by Ivanhoe, itself 49 per cent owned by Rio Tinto, the mining giant that would invest most of the $10 billion needed to develop

Oyu Tolgoi. Under pressure from the opposition Mongolian Democratic Party (MDP), the government sought to increase its stake to 50 per cent, but the foreign mining companies refused to renegotiate the contract, which allowed for a revision of terms only after 30 years. Opposition politicians failed to force the resignation of Prime Minister Suhbaataryn Batbold over the issue.

The economic boom engendered a movement to protect Mongolia's traditional way of life and vast wilderness. US Vice President Joe Biden visited in August amidst controversy over reports that Mongolia had reached an informal agreement with Japan and the USA to host a regional nuclear waste storage facility. However, the signing of the agreement had been delayed following the disaster at Japan's Fukushima nuclear power station in March. Biden said, after holding meetings with the president and prime minister, that the USA was interested in investing in Mongolia's renewable energy sector.

A lengthy case involving Bat Khurts, the head of Mongolia's National Security Council (intelligence agency), ended in October. Khurts had arrived in the UK in August 2010, expecting to hold talks on security co-operation (although British officials claimed that no formal invitation had been issued to him). But on arrival, Khurts had been detained on a European arrest warrant for his alleged part in the abduction of a Mongolian dissident in France in 2003. Khurts fought extradition to Germany through the British courts but was finally deported in August 2011. The affair ended with Khurts's release in early October, after Germany dropped charges shortly before a planned visit to Mongolia by Chancellor Angela Merkel, on 12-13 October, accompanied by a large business delegation.

Wendy Slater

(11 February) Opposition supporters attend Friday prayers in Tahrir Square, Cairo, on the day that popular protests succeeded in ousting President Mubarak from office. (REUTERS/Suhaib Salem)

(19 January) A woman poses with a soldier in front of a tank in Tunis during celebrations following the overthrow of President Ben Ali. (REUTERS/Finbarr O'Reilly)

(4 March) An Egyptian girl films with her mobile phone during a pro-democracy rally in Tahrir Square, Cairo. (REUTERS/Peter Andrews)

(9 March) Anti-Kadhafi rebel forces advance on the road between Ras Lanuf and Bin Jawad, Libya. (REUTERS/Asmaa Waguih)

(16 December) a young girl gestures to demonstrators marching through the streets after Friday prayers in Idlib, Syria, in protest against President Assad. (REUTERS/Handout)

(5 October) A father and his daughter participate in a protest by the Occupy movement in Foley Square, New York city. (REUTERS/Mike Segar)

(8 July) Space shuttle Atlantis is launched from NASA's Kennedy Space Centre in Cape Canaveral, Florida, its 12-day mission to the International Space Station marking the final flight of the space shuttle programme. (NASA/Bill Ingall)

(1 May) US President Barack Obama and members of his national security team crowd into the Situation Room in the White House to monitor the progress of the mission by US special forces that killed Osama bin Laden. (REUTERS/White House/Pete Souza/Handout)

(2 May) Crowds in Times Square, New York city, celebrate news of the killing of Osama bin Laden by US special forces in Pakistan. (REUTERS/Eric Thayer)

(6 July) Christine Lagarde, the first woman to be appointed head of the International Monetary Fund, holds a news briefing at the IMF's headquarters in Washington, DC. (REUTERS/Kevin Lamarque)

(16 May) Outgoing International Monetary Fund (IMF) chief Dominique Strauss-Kahn appears in Manhattan Criminal Court during his arraignment on charges (later dropped) of having sexually assaulted a hotel maid. (REUTERS/Shannon Stapleton)

(28 March) Japanese police officers wearing protective suits search for victims of the 11 March earthquake and tsunami in an area 30km north of the critically damaged Fukushima nuclear power station. (REUTERS/Yomiuri Shimbun)

X AUSTRALASIA AND THE PACIFIC

AUSTRALIA—PAPUA NEW GUINEA

AUSTRALIA

CAPITAL: Canberra   AREA: 7,741,220 sq km   POPULATION: 22,328,800 ('10)
OFFICIAL LANGUAGE: English
HEAD OF STATE: Queen Elizabeth II (since Feb '52)
GOVERNOR-GENERAL: Quentin Bryce (since Sept '08)
RULING PARTY: Australian Labor Party (ALP) forms minority government
HEAD OF GOVERNMENT: Prime Minister Julia Gillard (Labor) (since June '10)
DEMOCRACY INDEX: 9.22; 6th of 167   CORRUPTION INDEX: 8.8; 8th of 183
CURRENCY: Australian Dollar (Dec '11 £1.00=AUD 1.53, US$1.00=AUD 0.98)
GNI PER CAPITA: US$43,590, Intl$38,380 at PPP ('09)

For the first full year in more than half a century, Australia was governed by a hung parliament. By tradition, and by dint of majoritarian electoral rules, Australians were accustomed to a two-party system. Yet electoral volatility, generated by the decline in the core support of the major parties, was rendering minority governments less of a novelty. For in addition to the national government, parliaments in four of the eight states and territories were also hung in 2011.

Despite lacking a majority, Prime Minister Julia Gillard and her Australian Labor Party (ALP) cabinet could feel superficially pleased with a year in which Australia was ranked second only to Norway on the 2011 United Nations Human Development Index. Despite predictions of parliamentary gridlock and global economic crisis, over 170 bills were enacted and the economy remained robust. These measures included landmark legislation to help address global warming by pricing carbon. An initial "carbon tax'" on 500 major industrial emitters was to be followed by an emissions trading scheme intended to dovetail with similar international endeavours. Another initiative was a "mineral resource rent tax". Levied on the booming coal and iron ore sectors, this profits tax supplemented corporate tax and sidelined traditional state royalties. Social measures included plain packaging for all tobacco products and a requirement that gamblers nominate a limit on their betting on electronic gaming machines, a measure that generated much debate.

Far from winning public approval, however, Gillard's success as a legislative negotiator only reinforced an image of weakness. Various currents mingled to produce this perceived lack of authority. Some believed that Australia's first female prime minister lacked gravitas, whether personally or because of her gender. The public also seemed dubious about a minority government that was dependent on three independents and a Green MP. (In November the government's slender majority improved by one, when it wooed a renegade opposition MP to assume the speakership—the first independent to hold this office since 1909.) By the second-half of the year, the press was consumed with speculation about Gillard's survival, although she was barely a year into her post as ALP leader. The shadow of her predecessor, Kevin Rudd, whom she had deposed in 2010, lingered like Banquo's ghost. Serving as foreign minister in Gillard's administration, Rudd spent the year—when he was not undergoing heart surgery—pursuing Australia's case for a temporary seat on the UN Security Council. He remained as popular with the public as he was unpopular with his colleagues.

But leadership woes could not fully explain the ALP's predicament. Just three years earlier it had been in power at all levels. Yet in March it was swept from office in the country's most populous state, New South Wales, attracting just 24 per cent of the vote. By year's end, its ratings nationally and in another large state, Queensland, hovered around 30 per cent. A spectre seemed to hang over Australia's oldest party and it was unclear whether 2011 was merely a temporary nadir or a portent of permanent decline.

The steady emergence of the Australian Greens as a political (and social) force was cemented in 2011. From 1 July the party's nine senators assumed the balance of power in the Australian upper chamber. Also cemented was the position of Tony Abbott, the conservative Liberal-National opposition leader. Abbott's pugilistic image was reinforced by his penchant for being photographed in swimming briefs, on dawn cycling excursions, and in hard-hats bemoaning the decline of manufacturing industries. His "blokey" reputation helped open a distinct gender gap in public opinion. Under Abbott's leadership, the opposition pledged to repeal carbon pricing and the minerals tax. The opposition cloaked its scepticism on climate change with a taxpayer-funded "direct action" proposal to encourage carbon reductions. Abbott's negativity proved a double-edged sword, however, and by year's end his disapproval rating, nearly 60 per cent, matched that of Gillard.

In the one area where government and opposition agreed—the utility of offshore processing for asylum seekers arriving by sea—there was a standoff. After the High Court ruled that such processing could only occur in countries with humanitarian guarantees, the government insisted on Malaysia as a destination and the opposition on Nauru, despite problems with both proposals.

The year also saw an intensification of the recent phenomenon of large-scale, third-party issue campaigning. Miners, carbon intensive industries, and pubs and clubs opposed to gaming reforms, launched multimillion dollar campaigns, taking advantage of the climate of political disgruntlement. The policy ramifications of a shift from party-centric to vested interest politics could take years to unfold. Whilst two states passed laws restricting election donations and expenditure (though not political campaigns generally) the national parliament continued to dither on regulating political finance.

Internationally, the two most influential Australians remained Rupert Murdoch, the head of News Corporation, and Julian Assange, the founder of Wiki-Leaks. These polar political opposites of the media world each weathered ongoing legal battles in the UK: phone tapping scandals brought down Murdoch's *News of the World* (see pp. 9-11) whilst Assange fought extradition from the UK to Sweden to face charges of sexual assault. In response to Murdoch's difficulties, the Australian government established an inquiry into the accountability of the online and print media.

Turbidity dominated financial markets worldwide, and the fiscal positions of most Western governments declined. Yet Australia remained a relative economic oasis. Unemployment crept above 5 per cent, and inflation subsided. For engineering the Keynesian stimulus that helped keep Australia out of recession during the global financial crisis, Treasurer Wayne Swan was named "2011 Finance Minister of the Year" by an international journal. Others thought the achievement belonged to China, whose demand for commodities drove Australia's terms of trade to a 140-year high. The mining boom spread beyond coal and iron ore exports, into the burgeoning liquid natural gas and coal seam gas industries. But relative prosperity was tempered with the challenge of a "two-speed" economy, courtesy of the boom. Some expressed glee at four new mining ventures involving A$80 billion of capital expenditure. Others leapt at opportunities to earn up to A$300,000 on offshore rigs. But despite its profitability, mining employed barely 2 per cent of the workforce. Its insatiable demands distorted labour and capital markets, and its success drove the Australian dollar to record levels, exceeding US$1.10. The tourism, education and manufacturing sectors winced in response. Tourism was also buffeted when the management of Qantas, the national airline, took industrial action, stranding 70,000 passengers worldwide.

Although the mineral legacy of the world's oldest continent provided a continuing export cornucopia, Nature, or at least the La Niña cycle of the southern oceans, remained fickle. The first decade of the twenty-first century had been overshadowed by a deep, eight-year drought. As if to confirm the stereotype of Australia as a land of extremes, 2011 dawned with a series of record breaking floods. Large areas of Victoria were inundated, and over 75 per cent of Queensland, including the central business district of its capital, Brisbane, was declared a disaster zone. Tropical cyclones also devastated parts of far north Queensland. Reconstruction work and insurance claims remained pending as the year ended.

On lighter matters, Australians continued to make their mark on popular culture, winning five Academy Awards for motion pictures. With victory in the US Open, Samantha Stosur became the first Australian woman to win a Grand Slam tennis tournament for over 30 years. Stosur's upset win mollified some of the pride leached by the national cricket team. In January, the English cricketers completed a convincing Ashes series victory for the first time in 25 Australian summers. By midyear the Australian team had slid from first to fourth in the world rankings. It has often been said, albeit wryly, that the highest Australian office was not that of prime minister, but national cricket captain. With politics marooned in a state of grumpiness, and cricket fortunes in decline, for once neither office had reason to be jealous of the other.

Graeme Orr

PAPUA NEW GUINEA

CAPITAL: Port Moresby   AREA: 462,840 sq km   POPULATION: 6,858,266 ('10)
OFFICIAL LANGUAGES: Pidgin, Motu & English
HEAD OF STATE: Queen Elizabeth II (since Feb '52)
GOVERNOR-GENERAL: Sir Michael Ogio (since Feb '11)
RULING PARTIES: National Alliance Party (NAP)-led coalition
HEAD OF GOVERNMENT: Parliament-elected Prime Minister Peter O'Neill (since Aug '11)
DEMOCRACY INDEX: 6.54; 59th of 167   CORRUPTION INDEX: 2.2; 154th of 183
CURRENCY: Kina (Dec '11 £1.00=PGK 3.37, US$1.00=PGK 2.15)
GNI PER CAPITA: US$1,300, Intl$2,400 at PPP ('10)

IT was a year of considerable trial for Papua New Guinea across the political, economic and social fronts. A failing state, with an economy perpetually teetering on
the verge of collapse and with social tensions past breaking point, represented a
kind of normality for Papua New Guinea by 2011 and, as in the past, the country
muddled on with characteristic insouciance.

The year ended with two parallel and mutually hostile "governments" claiming legitimacy. The saga began with the position of 76-year old veteran Prime
Minister Michael Somare undermined by his referral to the country's Leadership
Tribunal over his financial affairs. The tribunal, which consisted of three overseas judges (from Australia, New Zealand and the UK), found him guilty of misconduct in public office. There followed a period of confusion over whether or
not he was suspended from office. Further uncertainty was added when Somare
flew to Singapore in April for treatment for evidently quite serious heart problems. No one, it seemed, was very clear about the country's constitutional position or whether it actually had a head of government, though Somare had unilaterally appointed his deputy, Sam Abal, as acting prime minister.

In August Abal was ousted in a parliamentary coup and replaced by opposition leader Peter O'Neill, an experienced political operator of mixed Australian
and Papua New Guinean descent. When Somare returned to the country at the
end of the year, however, he sought to resume his position as prime minister on
the grounds that O'Neill's appointment by the National Parliament had been
unconstitutional. Initially Somare had some success, with the older political
establishment, who owed their advancement to him during his accumulated
years in power, rallying to his support. This group included, crucially, the governor-general, Michael Ogio (elected in January after his predecessor's reap-
pointment was declared unlawful). Parliament was not to be overruled, however,
and the Somare faction was physically excluded. Henceforward O'Neill performed the functions of head of government, with the provisional title of "Parliament-elected prime minister". At year's end Somare gave no sign that he
would accept the situation, however.

In the meantime the country was confronted by long-standing economic and
social problems. The year began with another bout of violence around the Hides 4
liquid natural gas (LNG) workings in the Southern Highlands. Competing and
shifting "landowner" claims had long been the bane of large scale resource
exploitation and development in Papua New Guinea, with the intensity of the con-

flict directly correlated with the size of the potential rewards. As the LNG programme had come to form the central plank of the country's economic future, the stakes were particularly high. In January ExxonMobil, the principal operators of the project, responded to yet another violent invasion of the site by disgruntled claimants. Personnel were evacuated, production shut down, and the company suggested to the government that its patience was close to exhaustion. There could be little optimism that any Port Moresby administration would have sufficient will or authority to impose order, however.

Throughout the year leading aid donors sounded warnings about the drift in central authority. In March the US ambassador articulated a long-standing concern that the country's weak central authority and porous borders could make it a regional hub of transnational crime. The problem for the government was that robust action ran considerable political risks. At the beginning of the year, for example, a major joint operation with Indonesian security forces on the common border brought accusations that the government was doing Indonesia's dirty work in suppressing separatist activity in its restive Papua province (formed by the western half of the island of New Guinea). In March the Australian high commissioner warned of the threat posed by fraud and corruption to his country's crucial aid programme in Papua New Guinea. Reflecting deep concern in both countries, he insisted that Australia would henceforward adopt a zero-tolerance policy. At the same time, Papua New Guinea continued during the year to foster its economic relations with major Asian powers, in particular China and Japan.

Norman MacQueen

NEW ZEALAND—PACIFIC ISLAND STATES

NEW ZEALAND

CAPITAL: Wellington   AREA: 267,710 sq km   POPULATION: 4,367,800 ('10)
OFFICIAL LANGUAGE: English
HEAD OF STATE: Queen Elizabeth II (since Feb '52)
GOVERNOR-GENERAL: Sir Jeremiah Mateparae (since Aug '11)
RULING PARTY: National Party (NP)-led coalition
HEAD OF GOVERNMENT: Prime Minister John Key (NP) (since Nov '08)
DEMOCRACY INDEX: 9.26; 5th of 167   CORRUPTION INDEX: 9.5; 1st of 183
CURRENCY: New Zealand Dollar (Dec '11 £1.00=NZD 2.02, US$1.00=NZD 1.29)
GNI PER CAPITA: US$29,050, Intl$28,050 at PPP ('09)

PARLIAMENTARY elections on 26 November gave the National Party's leader, Prime Minister John Key, a second consecutive term. Opinion polls over the previous three years had consistently shown Key with an overwhelming advantage over Labour's Phil Goff, who was replaced as party leader after the election. The National Party's 47.3 per cent share of the vote was an increase in support from 2008, when it had won 44.9 per cent.

The elections were accompanied by a referendum on New Zealand's voting system, known as "mixed member proportional" (MMP). The system, approved by voters in referendums held in 1992 and 1993, had first been used in parliamentary elections in 1996 and made it difficult for either of the two largest parties—National and Labour—to govern on their own. While the prime minister indicated his personal preference for a less proportional alternative, known as "supplementary member", neither he nor his ministers campaigned for or against MMP or any of the four alternatives on the ballot. The result was a substantial 57.8 per cent of the votes in favour of retaining MMP.

The MMP system complicated National's post-election governance arrangements. National won 59 parliamentary seats, an increase of one from 2008. However, its coalition partners polled poorly: ACT and United Future won only one seat apiece, and the Maori Party won three seats, losing one to Labour and another to a rival Maori political party, the Mana Party.

National's principal opponent, the Labour Party, suffered a significant defeat, gaining only 27.5 per cent of the vote—its lowest proportion since 1928—and winning only 34 seats (a loss of nine). The opposition Green Party achieved its best-ever result, winning more than 10 per cent support for the first time, allowing it to win 14 seats (a gain of five). Another party, New Zealand First, which had lost its parliamentary representation at the 2008 election, returned to Parliament, opposed to Prime Minister Key, winning 6.6 per cent of the vote and eight seats.

The overall result for National, in spite of its substantial triumph over Labour, was a narrow victory, giving it the lead role in a four-party coalition of 64 seats in a 121-seat Parliament. National's loss of its mid-campaign lead in opinion polls, which had suggested that it might gain more than 50 per cent of the vote and win enough seats to be able to govern alone, reflected public unease with plans to sell state-owned assets such as electric power companies, as well as tactical campaign errors.

National failed to win convincingly despite the boost to national feeling provided in the autumn by the Rugby World Cup, which was hosted by New Zealand for the first time since 1987 and won by the New Zealand team, the All Blacks. The international rugby competition dominated public and media attention for nearly two months and aroused national feeling, with New Zealand flags and All Blacks banners displayed from public buildings, private houses and vehicles. On 23 October the undefeated All Blacks narrowly beat France in the final, by 8 points to 7, winning the Rugby World Cup for only the second time since the inaugural event in 1987. Within a week the team was given three victory parades—in Auckland, Christchurch and Wellington—and the All Blacks' captain, Richie McCaw, ended the year with an offer of a knighthood from the prime minister, which he declined.

The All Blacks' victory in New Zealand's national sport lifted a public mood dampened by the country's dim economic performance—its credit rating was downgraded by three international ratings agencies—and by a devastating earthquake in the South Island city of Christchurch on 22 February. The city had experienced an earthquake in November 2010 but with no loss of life (see AR 2011, p. 358). The February earthquake, magnitude 6.3, destroyed much of the central business district and there were 181 fatalities.

The government declared a national state of emergency. Exactly one week later, on 1 March, at 12.51 pm, New Zealanders stood in silence for two minutes as a mark of respect for those who had died. Subsequently, amidst ongoing aftershocks, the government announced a commitment to rebuild Christchurch, but at great expense and with portions of the city excluded from the rebuilding programme. Thousands of homes were expected to be demolished and some areas of the city were to be abandoned. In April Parliament passed a bill assigning sweeping powers to the new Canterbury Earthquake Recovery Authority, and a cabinet minister was given special responsibility for overseeing Christchurch reconstruction. The earthquake also set back government hopes of a return to surplus, with the rebuilding programme increasing borrowing requirements.

A March visit to Christchurch from Prince William, grandson of New Zealand's head of state, Queen Elizabeth II, lifted morale and the prince also visited Pike River, paying respects to those killed in the November 2010 coal mine disaster (see AR 2011, p. 358). The prince's visit, shortly before his marriage to Kate Middleton in April, strengthened public support for the monarchy.

In September the Pacific Islands Forum (PIF)—the islands' principal regional organisation—met in Auckland, marking the 40th anniversary of the founding meeting in Wellington in 1971. The prime minister enjoyed other international successes. In June he addressed the Australian Parliament—the first time that a New Zealand leader had done so—and in July he met with US President Barack Obama in Washington, DC.

New Zealand's involvement in the war in Afghanistan saw several major developments. On 1 February, Key announced an extension of the deployment of New Zealand's Special Air Services (SAS) for a further year but with a 50 per cent reduction in the size of the 70-person contingent. Two SAS members were killed within several weeks of each other, in August and September, the unit's first fatalities in the conflict. In December the prime minister announced that the SAS deployment would not be extended beyond March 2012.

New Zealand's marine and coastal environment attracted attention from lawmakers, protesters and, until year's end, a salvage crew. In March the controversial Marine and Coastal Area Act was passed, repealing and replacing the contentious 2004 Foreshore and Seabed Act (see AR 2004, p. 345), which had led to the formation of the Maori Party. The new act sought to secure public access to New Zealand's marine and coastal areas while allowing Maori tribal groups opportunities to gain recognition of claims to ownership.

In October a container ship, the *Rena*, hit a reef, discharging hundreds of tons of oil, endangering North Island fisheries, seabirds and beaches. The oil spill led to difficult and lengthy salvage operations, intended to remove oil from the ship amid fears that it would break apart, but oil continued to wash ashore at popular holiday beaches in late December. Concerns about the exposure of New

Zealand's environment to damage from oil spills had been displayed in April when protesters disrupted oil and gas survey work off the North Island coast.

The country's film industry continued to flourish, with director Peter Jackson beginning filming of *The Hobbit*, following on from his success with the *Lord of the Rings* trilogy, based on the work of J.R.R. Tolkien. Another Jackson film, *The Adventures of Tintin*, made in association with Steven Spielberg, opened in December.

Stephen Levine

PACIFIC ISLAND STATES

Fiji

CAPITAL: Suva   AREA: 18,270 sq km   POPULATION: 860,623 ('10)
OFFICIAL LANGUAGES: Fijian, Hindi & English
HEAD OF STATE: President Ratu Epeli Nailatikau (since July '09)
PRIME MINISTER: acting Prime Minister Commodore Voreqe "Frank" Bainimarama (since Jan '07)
DEMOCRACY INDEX: 3.62; 119th of 167
CURRENCY: Fiji Dollar (Dec '11 £1.00=FJD 2.87, US$1.00=FJD 1.83)
GNI PER CAPITA: US$3,580, Intl$4,450 at PPP ('10)

Kiribati

CAPITAL: Tarawa   AREA: 810 sq km   POPULATION: 99,546 ('10)
OFFICIAL LANGUAGES: English & Kiribati
HEAD OF STATE AND GOVERNMENT: President Anote Tong (since July '03)
RULING PARTY: Pillars of Truth
CORRUPTION INDEX: 3.1; 95th of 183
CURRENCY: Australian Dollar (Dec '11 £1.00=AUD 1.53, US$1.00=AUD 0.98)
GNI PER CAPITA: US$2,010, Intl$3,510 at PPP ('10)

Marshall Islands

CAPITAL: Dalap-Uliga-Darrit   AREA: 180 sq km   POPULATION: 54,038 ('10)
OFFICIAL LANGUAGES: English & Marshallese
HEAD OF STATE AND GOVERNMENT: President Jurelang Zedkaia (since Oct '09)
CURRENCY: US Dollar (Dec '11 £1.00=USD 1.57)
GNI PER CAPITA: US$3,450 ('10)

Federated States of Micronesia

CAPITAL: Palikir (Pohnpei)   AREA: 700 sq km   POPULATION: 111,064 ('10)
OFFICIAL LANGUAGE: English
HEAD OF STATE AND GOVERNMENT: President Emanuel "Manny" Mori (since May '07)
CURRENCY: US Dollar (see above)
GNI PER CAPITA: US$2,700, Intl$3,420 at PPP ('10)

Nauru

CAPITAL: Domaneab   AREA: 21.4 sq km   POPULATION: 13,770 ('08 estimate, FCO)
OFFICIAL LANGUAGES: Nauruan & English
HEAD OF STATE AND GOVERNMENT: President Marcus Stephen (since Dec '07)
CURRENCY: Australian Dollar (see above)
GNI PER CAPITA: GDP per capita US$6,133 ('04)

Palau (Belau)

CAPITAL: Koror   AREA: 460 sq km   POPULATION: 20,472 ('10)
OFFICIAL LANGUAGE: English
HEAD OF STATE AND GOVERNMENT: President Johnson Toribiong (since Jan '09)
CURRENCY: US Dollar (see above)
GNI PER CAPITA: US$6,470, Intl$10,780 at PPP ('10)

Samoa

CAPITAL: Apia   AREA: 2,840 sq km   POPULATION: 183,081 ('10)
OFFICIAL LANGUAGES: English & Samoan
HEAD OF STATE: Tupua Tamasese Tupuola Tufuga Efi (since June '07)
RULING PARTY: Human Rights Protection Party (HRPP)
HEAD OF GOVERNMENT: Prime Minister Tuilaepa Aiono Sailele Malielegaoi (since Nov '98)
CORRUPTION INDEX: 3.9; 69th of 183
CURRENCY: Tala (Dec '11 £1.00=WST 3.66, US$1.00=WST 2.33)
GNI PER CAPITA: US$2,860, Intl$4,200 at PPP ('10)

Solomon Islands

CAPITAL: Honiara   AREA: 28,900 sq km   POPULATION: 538,148 ('10)
OFFICIAL LANGUAGE: English
HEAD OF STATE: Queen Elizabeth II (since Feb '52)
GOVERNOR-GENERAL: Frank Ofagioro Kabui (since July '09)
RULING PARTY: National Coalition for Reform and Advancement (NCRA)
HEAD OF GOVERNMENT: Prime Minister Gordon Darcy Lilo (NCRA) (since Nov '11)
CORRUPTION INDEX: 2.7; 120th of 183
CURRENCY: Solomon Islands Dollar (Dec '11 £1.00=SBD 11.38, US$1.00=SBD 7.25)
GNI PER CAPITA: US$1,030, Intl$2,200 at PPP ('10)

Tonga

CAPITAL: Nuku'alofa   AREA: 750 sq km   POPULATION: 104,058 ('10)
OFFICIAL LANGUAGES: Tongan & English
HEAD OF STATE: King Siaosi (George) Tupou V (since Sept '06)
RULING PARTY: Friendly Islands Democracy Party
HEAD OF GOVERNMENT: Prime Minister Lord Tuivakano (since Dec '10)
CORRUPTION INDEX: 3.1; 95th of 183
CURRENCY: Pa'anga (Dec '11 £1.00=TOP 2.69, US$1.00=TOP 1.71)
GNI PER CAPITA: US$3,390, Intl$4,640 at PPP ('10)

Tuvalu

CAPITAL: Fongafale   AREA: 26 sq km   POPULATION: 9,827 ('10)
OFFICIAL LANGUAGE: English
HEAD OF STATE: Queen Elizabeth II (since Feb '52)
GOVERNOR-GENERAL: Sir Iakoba Taeia Italeli (since April '10)
HEAD OF GOVERNMENT: Prime Minister Willy Telavi (since Dec '10)
CURRENCY: Australian Dollar (see above)
GNI PER CAPITA: US$3,700 ('10)

Vanuatu

CAPITAL: Port Vila   AREA: 12,190 sq km   POPULATION: 239,651 ('10)
OFFICIAL LANGUAGES: English, French & Bislama
HEAD OF STATE: President Iolu Abil (VP) (since Sept '09)
RULING PARTY: Vanua'aku Pati (VP)-led coalition
HEAD OF GOVERNMENT: Prime Minister Sato Kilman (People's Progress Party) (since Dec '10)
CORRUPTION INDEX: 3.5; 77th of 183
CURRENCY: Vatu (Dec '11 £1.00=VUV 147.96, US$1.00=VUV 94.35)
GNI PER CAPITA: US$2,760, Intl$4,450 at PPP ('10)

THE "interim" government in **Fiji**—a military regime in power since 2006—took
further steps to consolidate control while continuing to promise that parliamentary
elections would be held in 2014 under a new constitution and electoral system.
The regime extended public emergency regulations—which gave it the authority
to ban public meetings and censor the news media—and issued a new decree that
further restricted trade union activity, requiring unions in industries designated as
"essential" to re-register and to renegotiate collective agreements. Conflict continued with the country's largest church, with the military first approving, then cancelling, the Methodist church's annual conference, and banning church leaders
from travelling abroad. China's support for Fiji's government helped the regime
resist Western criticism. In October, Fiji's chief censor flew to China to attend
workshops for officials involved in information dissemination. In November, the
Fiji government opened the country's first bauxite mine, in the presence of Chinese officials, and stated that the first exports to China would be made in early
2012. Fiji continued with other moves to diversify its foreign policy, opening
embassies in Indonesia, South Africa and Brazil. In May, Fiji was admitted to the
Non-Aligned Movement, and in August it hosted an international "Engaging with
the Pacific" conference, with development partners from Asia and Africa attending the meeting along with Pacific island states.

In May, two senior military figures, former Land Force Commander Brigadier-
General Pita Driti and former Commander of the Third Fiji Infantry Regiment
Lieutenant-Colonel Ratu Tevita Mara, were arrested for allegedly inciting mutiny
and sedition. Relations with **Tonga** deteriorated when, released on bail, Mara, the
son of Fiji's founding prime minister and former president (Ratu Sir Kamisese
Mara) and related to the Tongan royal family, was picked up in Fijian waters by a
Tongan patrol boat. Subsequently Tonga refused a Fiji request for Mara's extradition, describing its rescue of him as a humanitarian act, and granting Mara Tongan
citizenship. In the aftermath of the incident Tonga and Fiji also clashed over their
rival claims to Minerva Reefs (also known as the Teleki Reefs), with Tonga claiming that Fiji had destroyed a navigation beacon that it had erected there.

Elections and parliamentary votes of no-confidence—impossibilities in Fiji in
the absence of either elections or a parliament—were responsible for changes of
leadership elsewhere in the Pacific.

Nauru experienced three heads of government in a month, beginning with the
resignation of its president, Marcus Stephen, on 10 November, prior to a scheduled vote of no-confidence over corruption allegations. His successor, Freddie
Pitcher, elected by Parliament, held office for only six days before losing a no-confidence vote on 15 November when a former cabinet minister, Sprent Dabwido,
defected to the opposition. Parliament then elected Dabwido as president (by nine
votes to eight).

Vanuatu likewise went through several changes of leadership as the result of
cabinet defections and court rulings. On 24 April Prime Minister Sato Kilman
(who had assumed office in December 2010—see AR 2010, p. 362) was defeated
on a no-confidence vote, 26-25, and was replaced by a former prime minister,
Serge Vohor. Nineteen days later the Court of Appeal ruled that Kilman be rein-

stated, along with his ministers, as the country's constitution required an "absolute majority"' of MPs (i.e. at least 27 of the 52 members) for a no-confidence motion to be approved. Subsequently Kilman narrowly survived a new motion of no-confidence, but on 15 June his December 2010 election was ruled invalid as it had not been conducted by secret ballot as required by the constitution. Vanuatu's chief justice appointed the then prime minister, Edward Natapei, as interim prime minister, until on 25 June Kilman once again took office when he defeated Vohor by 29-23 votes.

The prime minister of the **Solomon Islands**, Danny Philip, resigned on 11 November ahead of a vote of no-confidence, proposed following allegations that he had diverted a multi-million dollar Taiwanese development grant to businesses owned by members of his family. Four days later, former finance minister Gordon Darcy Lilo was elected as prime minister. Extra police, both local and from overseas, were deployed in the capital as a precaution against a repeat of the April 2006 riots which had followed a previous prime ministerial election.

Each of France's major Pacific territories also experienced changes of government, amid French impatience. In **French Polynesia**, Gaston Tong Sang was replaced as president by Oscar Temaru on 1 April following the territorial assembly's approval of a motion of no-confidence against his 15-month old government. In July France altered the territory's electoral system ahead of scheduled 2013 elections in an attempt to increase political stability. As a result, no-confidence motions were required to win the support of at least 60 per cent of assembly members (rather than a simple majority) in order to succeed. France's other major Pacific territory, **New Caledonia**, experienced its own distinctive instability. In February, one of the coalition partners of the multi-party government, the Union Calédonienne, left the territory's executive, bringing about the coalition's collapse. The move reflected disagreement over a decision that the territory have a double flag: the French national flag and the Kanak flag (i.e., the banner of the pro-independence FLNKS party), each flying alongside each other. Subsequent re-elections of a new executive failed to resolve the issue until, in June, at the fourth attempt, a new government was elected. Later that month the French Parliament approved a proposal to give the territorial government an 18-month grace period, replacing arrangements under which the government collapsed if a single minister resigned.

Elsewhere in the Pacific, stability rather than change was the outcome as elections confirmed incumbents in office. Toke Talagi was re-elected premier by **Niue**'s Legislative Assembly in May following legislative elections. In March, the **Federated States of Micronesia** (FSM) held congressional elections, with the FSM Congress re-electing Emanuel ("Manny") Mori as president for a second successive four-year term. In October the FSM Congress approved the appointment of the FSM's first woman ambassador, Jane Jimmy Chigiyal, who became the country's permanent representative to the UN.

The president of **Kiribati** retained his seat in parliamentary elections in October, subsequently becoming a candidate for a third successive four-year term. National elections for president, scheduled for 30 December, were postponed until January 2012. Parliamentary elections were also held in the **Marshall Islands**, on

21 November, with the presidential election scheduled for January 2012 following the seating of the new parliament. The chiefs of Kwajalein atoll, in the Marshalls, signed an agreement in May granting the USA use of a key missile testing range for a further 50 years, thereby ending an eight-year impasse with landowners over lease rental payments.

Elections in **Samoa** in March led to the re-election of the governing Human Rights Protection Party, in power since 1982, and its leader and prime minister since 1998, Tuilaepa Lupesoliai Sailele Malielegaoi. On 29 December Samoa switched time zones, moving west of the international dateline in order to be on the same day as New Zealand, Australia, and the country's Asian trading partners—but a day ahead of neighbouring American Samoa. New Zealand's territory of **Tokelau**, which shared close ties with Samoa, followed suit.

Following **Tonga**'s November 2010 elections under a new electoral system (see AR 2010, p. 362), the new prime minister, Lord Tuivakano, named a government, which included opposition leader Akilisi Pohiva, who criticised the appointment process. Eight days after taking office Pohiva resigned from the cabinet, opposing the appointment of two ministers from outside the legislature as well as a letter of agreement that he had asked to sign. In February the new government officially ended Tonga's state of emergency—which had lasted more than four years—lifting regulations adopted following the November 2006 riots. In April all four men—the captain, his first mate, the former director of Tonga's ministry of transportation, and the former chief executive officer of the government-owned Shipping Corporation of Polynesia (SCP)—charged in the sinking of a ferry in 2009 in which 74 people had died, were found guilty (as was the SCP).

Pacific states also confronted regional challenges of various kinds. Serious shortages of fresh water in several island states and territories, brought on by drought, led to rationing and emergency shipments of bottled water and desalination units. Environmental issues encouraged donors to provide, and island governments to accept, renewable energy sources such as solar-powered lighting equipment. Opposition to trade in dolphins brought acceptance by the Solomon Islands of a ban on dolphin exports in return for external assistance.

Applications by **Vanuatu** and **Samoa** for World Trade Organisation (WTO) membership were approved. In December Vanuatu's Parliament ratified membership, with Samoa's accession expected to become valid following legislative approval in 2012.

Violence recurred in two non-self-governing territories, **Rapa Nui/Easter Island** and **Papua**. In February, a group of Rapa Nui protesters, seeking a return of ancestral lands and a greater share in profits from tourism, were evicted from the grounds of a hotel. Following their removal the Organization of American States' Inter-American Commission for Human Rights asked for a report from Chile about Rapa Nui land claims and demanded the cessation of violence against Rapa Nui protesters. In Papua—territory annexed by Indonesia but the site of a long-running pro-independence rebellion—violence and alleged human rights violations occurred alongside a protracted industrial dispute around the Grasberg copper mine, owned by the US mining company Freeport-McMoRan. There were also clashes and arrests elsewhere in the territory, with hundreds of delegates to a meeting of the Papuan People's Congress being detained and concerns over the killing, beating and abduction of journalists in the territory. In September, UN Secretary-General Ban Ki Moon called for the West Papua issue to be discussed by the UN General Assembly's Decolonization Committee.

The 14th Pacific Games, a sporting event held every four years since 1963, was hosted by Nouméa, New Caledonia, and included 22 participating countries and approximately 5,000 athletes and officials. The event was opened on 27 August by French President Nicolas Sarkozy during his first presidential visit to the Pacific, and closed on 10 September with New Caledonia having won the most gold and silver medals (and twice as many medals overall—288—as any other competing country).

Stephen Levine

XI INTERNATIONAL ORGANISATIONS

UNITED NATIONS AND ITS AGENCIES

DATE OF FOUNDATION: 1945   HEADQUARTERS: New York, USA
OBJECTIVES: To promote international peace, security and co-operation on the basis of the equality
    of member-states, the right of self-determination of peoples and respect for human rights
MEMBERSHIP (END-'11): 193 sovereign states
SECRETARY GENERAL: Ban Ki Moon (South Korea) (since Jan '07)

IT was yet another demanding year for the United Nations. Thirty-five UN personnel were killed—25 civilians, nine peacekeepers and a military officer—an increase of 20 compared with 2010. Four contracted security guards working for the UN were also killed. The dead included 23 killed in terrorist attacks upon UN premises in Mazar-i-Sharif and Kandahar in Afghanistan, and in the Nigerian capital of Abuja. The secretary general took a prominent stand in defending principles he believed were at stake when the UN mission in Côte d'Ivoire had to resort to force to protect civilians, peacekeepers and the mission headquarters from heavy weapon attacks in the dispute over the presidential elections in that country (see pp. 246-47). He was equally vocal in relation to the "Arab Spring", stating that it was a once-in-a-generation opportunity to advance freedom and democracy and that the UN would support those efforts to the maximum.

THE ARAB SPRING. A tragedy set off the Arab Spring. In Tunisia an unemployed graduate, Mohammed Bouazizi, forced to earn a living as an unlicensed fruit and vegetable seller, committed suicide in December 2010 by setting himself alight when his produce was seized by the authorities. The protests that followed in Tunisia and which quickly resonated across states in North Africa and the Middle East via satellite television, the Internet, and social media were stimulated by simmering resentment at varying combinations of low economic growth, high unemployment, endemic corruption, tainted judiciaries, social inequalities, and governments without political legitimacy. These governments responded with varying levels of force against peaceful demonstrators, who were advocating democratic change, often using arbitrary arrests and detention, torture, and show trials without due process.

The Secretariat was active from the outset of the Arab Spring. The secretary general took a stand of principle in relation to each crisis. He talked to government leaders and, where they could be identified, opposition figures, insisting that there must be respect for the rights of peaceful protest and assembly, for freedom of the press and for access to information. Equally, he warned that those responsible for violence against civilians would be held to account. He urged government leaders to listen to their people and respond to their legitimate aspirations with bold reforms before it was too late. When criticised by some of those leaders, he replied that he was not interfering in domestic politics but was determined to speak out when fundamental human rights were at stake, particularly when governments were perpetrating violence against their own citizens. After the revolutions in

Tunisia and Egypt, he sent senior staff to assist the transitional governments with their immediate humanitarian needs and offered a wide range of constitutional, economic and social help, visiting both countries to assess conditions on the ground. He also met the sheikh and the foreign minister of Bahrain, sent envoys to Libya and Yemen, and appointed a special representative for post-conflict planning in Libya.

Like the Secretariat, the Security Council found that each state affected by the Arab Spring presented a different problem. The Council responded in a variety of ways. In three cases—those of Tunisia, Egypt and Bahrain—the Security Council did not formally become involved, although there were occasional secretariat briefings and informal consultations In the case of Tunisia, this was partly because of the difficulties of assessing the speedy and unpredictable events. When it came to Egypt and Bahrain, there were other reasons for standing back. First, because the USA discouraged Council involvement in the difficulties of close allies with whom it had important military ties, particularly Bahrain where the 5th Fleet was stationed. Secondly, because China and Russia viewed the uprisings, and the forceful response to them, as internal matters and not threats to international peace, and did not believe that the UN should offer political advice on such sensitive issues as changes to governments. And thirdly because a regional organisation which appeared to have a disproportionate influence upon the Security Council— the Gulf Co-operation Council (GCC)—had provided a political and military mantle for Bahrain when two of its members—Saudi Arabia and the United Arab Emirates—had supplied troops to help the Bahraini government (see p. 205). The GCC believed that if the majority Shia protests in Bahrain were to succeed, Iran would expand its influence and cause further unrest.

In the other three cases of the Arab Spring—Libya, Yemen and Syria—the degree to which the United Nations could intervene differed extensively.

LIBYA. In responding to Colonel Kadhafi's use of force by land and air against his own citizens, the Security Council passed two very important resolutions. The first—Resolution 1970 of 26 February, which was adopted unanimously— attempted to deter further coercive action by reminding the Libyan authorities that they had a responsibility to protect their population. The resolution condemned the use of violence; imposed an arms embargo on Libya; subjected the Kadhafi family and named government officials to a travel ban and a freeze on assets; and made referrals to the International Criminal Court for possible prosecution for crimes against humanity. When this resolution was ignored by the authorities in Libya, the Council adopted Resolution 1973 by 10 votes with five abstentions (Brazil, China, Germany, India and Russia) on 17 March (see Documents). This second resolution imposed a no-fly zone over Libya and tighter sanctions on the Kadhafi regime. It called for an immediate ceasefire and authorised "all necessary measures" to enforce the arms embargo and to protect civilians and civilian-populated areas under the threat of attack (while excluding a foreign occupation force). The expanded sanctions imposed by the resolution included measures to stem the flow of mercenaries, further travel bans, and the application of a broader asset freeze to affect the central bank, the national oil company, and the Libyan sovereign wealth fund.

The passage of Resolution 1973 resulted from a unique set of circumstances. First, there was the importance attached to the rhetoric used by Kadhafi and the belief that he had the means and intent to massacre the citizens of Benghazi, the centre of the revolt, unless international action was taken urgently (see pp. 214-15). Secondly, there was the appeal for help from the National Transitional Council (NTC, the rebel government) in Benghazi and from the Libyan ambassador to the UN and his deputy in New York, who had defected from the regime. Thirdly, there was active secretariat pressure for intervention. The secretary general and his senior staff had consulted widely with key states in the Security Council, in the wider United Nations, and with the regional organisations about the need for resolute action. The secretary general's advisers on the prevention of genocide and on the responsibility to protect had already warned about the systematic attacks upon the civilian population, and the UN high commissioner for human rights had called for an international investigation into Libyan violence and justice for the victims. Fourthly, Kadhafi was friendless among his fellow Arabs and within the Security Council. Fifthly, the regional organisations—the Arab League, the Organisation of the Islamic Conference and the GCC—had sought a no-fly zone to prevent any further aerial attacks upon protestors. This effectively neutralised the potential vetoes of China and Russia and allowed the USA to participate in the military action without attracting Arab odium. And finally, three national governments initially and then NATO had the resources and were willing to undertake the necessary aerial and naval action to enforce the terms of the resolution.

THE RESPONSIBILITY TO PROTECT. It was perhaps inevitable that the NATO mission—"Operation Unified Protector", which ran from 23 March (the arms embargo), 25 March (the no-fly zone) and 31 March (the protection of civilians) until 31 October, and which at its peak deployed 260 air and 21 naval assets—should attract criticism from the outset. Resolution 1973 had been passed quickly and lacked unanimity and varying interpretations of it quickly emerged. The "mandate to protect" was imprecise, no political outcome had been established, and it was impossible for the Security Council to micro-manage the NATO operation.

The first criticism was that the NATO air campaign was disproportionate to the threat. In response, NATO argued that to enforce a no-fly zone required the destruction of aircraft, airfields, air defence systems and other weapons that could attack NATO planes. To protect civilians necessitated the elimination of military command and control centres. It also meant destroying weapon and logistics stores, and attacking tanks, armoured personnel carriers, and those troops and mercenaries who were preparing to attack cities and ground held by the rebels, in order to prevent these falling back into the control of the Libyan authorities. NATO attempted, by very careful targeting, strict rules of engagement and the use of precision weapons, to keep civilian casualties to an absolute minimum.

The second criticism was that the responsibility to protect was regime change by stealth. Even if the intention was not to help the rebels achieve their objective of overthrowing Colonel Kadhafi, critics claimed that the military practice seemed to indicate otherwise. This perception gained further support when NATO planes attacked presidential palaces, when NATO bombing coincided with rebel attacks, and when states within the NATO alliance (or partner states taking part in the campaign) on a national basis assisted the National Transitional Council. Such assistance included sending diplomatic agents to work with the NTC, offering an outlet for oil sales, and supplying arms and communication equipment, military intelligence, training and strategic direction to turn what had been predominately ill disciplined civilian groups into more cohesive units. These were then able to undertake a campaign (after the military stalemate had been broken) that culminated in the fall of Tripoli on 23 August (see pp. 216-17).

During the hostilities the Secretariat briefed the Council monthly on conditions in Libya and circulated the reports that it had received from NATO. The Security Council was informed that the International Criminal Court had issued arrest warrants for Colonel Kadhafi, his son Saif al-Islam Kadhafi, and his intelligence chief Abdullah al-Senussi on charges of crimes against humanity. The secretary general's special envoy, Abdulilah Khatib (the former foreign minister of Jordan), made repeated visits to Libya to assess conditions, establish links with the parties, and attempt to persuade them to agree to a ceasefire and negotiate a settlement. His task was bedevilled by each side's insistence on conditions that were unacceptable to the other. Efforts were also made to provide humanitarian assistance to refugees and migrant workers who had fled the country, as well as to the internally displaced and those workers in Libya from sub-Saharan Africa, who were often subject to brutal treatment because they were viewed as mercenaries. The secretary general maintained links with the groupings that had emerged to consider the future of Libya, particularly the Contact Group that arose from the London Conference of 29 March. Finally, it was decided that the UN should begin planning for post-conflict Libya in a way that would ensure that the multilateral, regional and international efforts complemented each other and were responsive to Libyan wishes.

On 16 September in Resolution 2009 the Council unanimously established the United Nations Support Mission in Libya (UNSMIL), initially for three months but extended in December for a further three months, to assist the Libyan interim authorities in restoring security and promoting the rule of law and political dialogue. The Council modified some of the sanctions imposed in earlier resolutions in order to foster economic recovery. Following the formal declaration of liberation on 23 October, the Council unanimously (in Resolution 2016 of 27 October) terminated the provisions of Resolution 1973. The Council remained concerned about the proliferation of weapons from Libya to the wider region, especially the possibility of portable surface-to-air missiles coming into terrorist hands. It asked the sanctions committee to prepare a report on how this threat might be countered and asked UNSMIL to assist Libyan non-proliferation efforts.

YEMEN. Although the Security Council discussion of Libya and Syria overshadowed that of Yemen, from April the Council started to receive briefings from the Secretariat and the secretary general's special envoy, who visited Sana'a on many occasions. The Council was briefed on the evolving developments in this strategically important state, where the uprising that began in January, and its brutal repression, overlaid existing problems (see pp. 201-03). The government led by President Ali Abdullah Saleh faced an intermittent civil war in the north, potential secession in the south, active agents belonging to al-Qaida in the Arabian Peninsula (AQAP), and acute economic problems. The Council encouraged the regional organisation, the Gulf Co-operation Council, which had the resources, cultural affinities and contacts with different political elements in Yemen, to seek to mediate. It was hoped that a settlement that led to the formation of a national unity government and presidential elections would help to preserve the independence and territorial integrity of the state. The wider implications of such a settlement could be to ensure the security of the shipping lanes, contain AQAP, and enhance the internal stability of Yemen's neighbours.

The Council approved three press statements (24 June, 9 August and 24 September) in which it expressed concern at the deteriorating security situation and called upon all parties to show maximum restraint. The Council welcomed the mission to Yemen of the UN high commissioner for human rights, the mediation efforts of the Gulf Co-operation Council, and the continuing engagement of the secretary general and his special adviser Jamal Ben Omar (whose role had gradually enlarged to become that of a mediator, facilitator and provider of good offices in the political negotiations underway in Yemen). In Resolution 2014 of 21 October, which condemned the government for continued human rights violations and called for humanitarian assistance for the country, the Council sent a signal to President Saleh that he was expected to sign the GCC agreement on peaceful political transition, which the Security Council had endorsed, and fulfil a promise that he had failed to honour on three previous occasions. On 28 November the Council was finally able to welcome the signing of the GCC agreement by the president on 23 November. On 21 December it welcomed the formation of a government of national unity and called for the implementation of the remaining parts of the GCC initiative in a timely fashion.

SYRIA. The Security Council had great difficulty in reaching any consensus on how to handle the Syrian government's use of snipers, tanks and heavy weapons in urban areas, as peaceful demonstrations demanding the removal of President Bashar al-Assad spread across the country (see pp. 189-94). Those members—particularly the UK, France, Germany and Portugal—who believed that the Council should send a warning to President Assad that his government's reprehensible behaviour towards its own citizens had to cease, and that sanctions would have to be considered if it did not, faced a number of difficulties.

First, the Russian government was strongly opposed to any Council intervention. It stated initially that the matter was internal; when Syrians started to flee the country and became refugees in adjoining states, which internationalised the issue, it argued for talks between the government and the opposition; and when reforms were introduced, it claimed that time should be allowed for them to become effective. Russia was fearful that if President Assad was forced to stand down, Russia's own interests would be jeopardised. These included longstanding political ties; the strategic naval base at the Syrian port of Tartus, which gave Russia access to the Mediterranean; its string of vital listening posts; its weapon sales; and its considerable investment in Syria, including infrastructure and the gas and oil industries. Moreover, if civil war broke out in this important regional state, the country could split along religious and ethnic lines and states like Iran and Israel might be drawn in. (This concern was shared at times by the United States.)

A second difficulty was that there was support from China and the non-permanent members India, Brazil and South Africa for the Russian view that the Council must not provide NATO with the mandate to intervene in Syria, because it had already abused that mandate in Libya where it had sought regime change by stealth. Thirdly, Lebanon, with its umbilical link to Syria, would not support any measures against the Assad government. Fourthly, there were concerns that were a proposed Security Council resolution to provoke the use of the veto, this might embolden and encourage the Syrian government. Finally, the leadership in Syria was to a large degree impervious to outside demands, although it made some cosmetic changes in response to widespread criticism. The president still commanded considerable domestic political support, the armed forces and the internal security agencies remained loyal, there were no important defectors, and the opposition lacked political cohesion.

Although the Council received regular Secretariat briefings, had extensive informal consultations, and held four formal meetings which allowed critics to place their views on the public record, it was only able to find sufficient consensus to issue a presidential statement (rather than a resolution) on 3 August. This expressed regret over the many hundreds of deaths in Syria, condemned the authorities' widespread violation of human rights, called for an immediate end to the violence, and urged all sides to act with the utmost restraint. In a tense Security Council meeting on 4 October, the draft resolution that had been considered in various forms and subject to long and hard negotiations since May was vetoed by Russia and China, and four non-permanent members abstained. The draft had called on the Syrian government to cease its repression, to allow freedom of expression, to undertake a Syrian-led political transition, and stated that if these terms were not met within 30 days the Council would consider other options but explicitly excluding any military action. The US delegation led by Ambassador Susan Rice left the chamber during the speech of the Syrian permanent representative.

While the Security Council remained supine, the Arab League in November reached an agreement with Syria to end the violence, and when the Syrian government failed to comply the League suspended Syria and imposed economic sanctions. After further arduous negotiations the Syrian government agreed on 19 December to allow Arab League monitors to establish whether Syria had met its pledges to end the violence against peaceful demonstrators, and to open unhindered access to all parts of Syria for Arab and international media. The UN Secretariat provided training and other assistance for the Arab League monitors, but later estimated that a further 400 people had been killed since the arrival of the monitors on 26 December, adding to the 5,000 civilian deaths established since March.

PEACEKEEPING, SANCTIONS, MILITARY FORCES. With the emergence of the new Republic of **South Sudan** following the successful conduct of the referendum (see pp. 208-11), the Security Council—with some members' misgivings—withdrew the United Nations Mission in Sudan (UNMIS) at the request of the host state, Sudan, on 11 July. It established UNISFA, the United Nations Interim Security Force for Abyei—an area whose status was still to be determined—initially for six months. UNISFA had a monitoring, verification, security, training, and demining mandate with the authority to use force if necessary to protect UN personnel and facilities, and civilians in the Abyei area under imminent threat of physical danger. It also created the United Nations Mission in the Republic of South Sudan (UNMISS), with an initial one-year mandate to consolidate peace and security, establish conditions for development, strengthen the capacity of the government of South Sudan to govern effectively and democratically, and help it to establish good relations with its neighbours.

One new sanctions regime was established, one regime was divided into two parts, and two were expanded. The Council by Resolutions 1970 and 1973 imposed an arms embargo, travel ban, and assets freeze against **Libya**, and a ban on flights by Libyan aircraft and by any other aircraft that might be violating the sanctions. It established a sanctions committee to monitor these and an expert panel to assist. These sanctions were later modified by Resolution 2009 (see above).

In an attempt to divide the **Taliban** from **al-Qaida** following the death of Osama bin Laden, and to encourage reconciliation in Afghanistan, the Security Council (in Resolutions 1988 and 1989) divided into two the consolidated list of individuals and entities deemed to be associated with al-Qaida, bin Laden or the Taliban, and assigned each list to a different sanctions committee. The new Taliban committee would consider petitions for removal from the list every six months. The request would need to include a recommendation from the Afghan government's High Peace Council. It was hoped that delisting petitioners who had met the criteria of renouncing violence, severing links to international terrorist organisations and recognising the Afghan constitution would contribute to political reconciliation in Afghanistan by inducing the Taliban into meaningful negotiations about ending violence.

The Council also extended for 18 months and enhanced the mandate of the ombudsperson for the al-Qaida sanctions regime, in order to make the process of seeking removal from that list more equable.

In **Côte d'Ivoire** the Security Council decided in Resolution 1975 to impose a travel ban and financial sanctions against the defeated presidential candidate, Laurent Gbagbo, who had refused to leave office, and against his wife and two associates. The sanctions were imposed because of their obstruction of peace and reconciliation in the country, their impeding the work of UNOCI, the United Nations Mission in Côte d'Ivoire, and other international actors, and their serious violations of human rights.

The Council also expanded the sanctions regime relating to **Somalia** and **Eritrea**. In Resolution 2002 the Council decided to expand the criteria for targeted sanctions to include those individuals who engaged in non-local commerce via ports controlled by the al-Shabaab militia, which was deemed to be a threat to the peace, security and stability of Somalia. Sanctions were also to be imposed upon political and military leaders who recruited children for armed conflict, and those who targeted civilians including children and women.

In Resolution 2023 (on which Russia and China abstained) the Council decided that Eritrea should cease using threats of violence and extortion to collect a diaspora tax from people of Eritrean descent living abroad. Funds raised in this manner were being used to finance violations of existing sanctions and illicit acts in neighbouring states, which threatened peace and stability in the Horn of Africa.

The Council extended the mandates for a further year of the African Union Mission in **Somalia** (AMISOM) on 30 September; of the International Security Assistance Force (ISAF) in **Afghanistan** on 12 October; of the European Union Force in **Bosnia & Herzegovina** (EUFOR ALTHEA) on 16 November; and on 22 November of those entities co-operating with the Transitional Federal Government of **Somalia** "to use all necessary means" to combat piracy in the Gulf of Guinea.

ELECTIONS. On 21 June the General Assembly, acting upon a recommendation of the Security Council, formally appointed Ban Ki Moon to the office of secretary general for a second term (to run from 1 January 2012 to 31 December 2016). Nasser Abdulaziz al Nasser of Qatar was elected president of the 66th Session of the General Assembly on 22 June.

On 14 July, acting upon a recommendation of the Security Council, the General Assembly admitted the Republic of South Sudan as the 193rd member of the United Nations.

On 21 October the General Assembly selected Guatemala, Morocco, Pakistan and Togo, and on 24 October Azerbaijan (following Slovenia's withdrawal after 16 rounds of voting) to serve as non-permanent members of the Security Council for two-year terms starting on 1 January 2012. These states replaced Bosnia & Herzegovina, Brazil, Gabon, Lebanon and Nigeria. The terms of Colombia, Germany, India, Portugal and South Africa would be completed on 31 December 2012.

The Security Council and the General Assembly independently but concurrently elected to the International Court of Justice on 10 November Giorgio Gaja (Italy), Hisashi Owada (Japan), Peter Tomka (Slovakia), Xue Hanqin (China) and on 14 December Julia Sebutinde (Uganda), to serve terms of nine years starting on 6 February 2012.

THE GENERAL ASSEMBLY. One hundred and ninety-six speakers, including the president of South Sudan and the foreign minister of the National Transitional Council of Libya, discussed "the role of mediation in the settlement of disputes by peaceful means"—the theme of the General Debate of the 66th Session of the General Assembly (21-24 and 26-27 September).

In his address to the Assembly on 23 September, the president of the **Palestinian Authority**, Mahmoud Abbas, announced that he had that day transmitted to the secretary general Palestine's application for full membership of the United Nations, on the basis of the 4 June 1967 borders (see pp. 179-81; Documents). The president referred the application to the Security Council's committee on the admission of new members. But the committee was unable to make a unanimous recommendation to the Council, unsurprisingly, since US President Barack Obama had threatened to veto the application.

The Assembly held a high-level meeting on nuclear safety and security to discuss the UN system-wide study, commissioned by the secretary general in May, exploring the implications of the accident at the **Fukushima** Daichi nuclear power station in Japan (see pp. 337-44).

On 16 September the Assembly approved the credentials of the delegation representing the National Transitional Council as the legal representatives of **Libya**. On 18 November, the Assembly reinstated Libya as a member of the UN Human Rights Council (UNHRC), from which it had been suspended in March over human rights violations. On 19 December the General Assembly passed a resolution which condemned the continued grave and systematic human rights violations by the authorities in **Syria** and called for the implementation of the Arab League's plan in its entirety.

THE SECURITY COUNCIL. The Council held 213 public meetings in 2011; adopted 66 resolutions, 57 of which were unanimous; and issued 22 presidential statements. One draft resolution on Israeli settlements on the West Bank was vetoed by the USA, and another draft on Syria was vetoed by China and the Russian Federation (see above). The Council issued press statements condemning terrorists attacks in Russia, Morocco, Norway, Iraq, India, Somalia, Afghanistan, Syria and Nigeria; attacks upon United Nations peacekeeping forces in Lebanon and Darfur; and attacks upon diplomatic premises in Syria and Iran.

On 6 June members were briefed about the Council's mission to Ethiopia, Sudan and Kenya between 19 and 26 May.

Despite its heavier work load, the Council continued to improve its working methods by making its debates and consultations more interactive, continuing the use of videoconferencing to provide updates from the field, and by enhancing the quality of the monthly briefings on current and emerging conflicts produced by the department of political affairs.

FINANCE. On 11 October the under-secretary general for management, Angela Kane, provided her assessment of the financial health of the United Nations. She stated that, despite the global financial climate, she anticipated a positive cash balance at the end of the year: regular budget $244 million, peacekeeping $3.08 billion, international tribunals $129 million, and the capital master plan $861 million, and a reduction in debt to member states, even though unpaid assessments for all these categories had increased slightly. The final outcome would crucially depend upon contributions from member states in the final quarter.

Assessments and payments for the regular budget were higher in 2011 than in 2010 by $249 million and $184 million respectively. By October 133 states had paid their assessments in full, which was 14 more than the previous year; unpaid assessments were $867 million, which was $81 million higher than in 2010. The outstanding sum was highly concentrated with the USA owing $758 million (87.4 per cent); three states—Mexico ($40 million), Spain ($19 million) and Venezuela ($11 million)—8.1 per cent; and 55 members 4.5 per cent.

United Nations peacekeeping operations had outstanding assessments of $3.3 billion in October, which was $113 million higher than in 2010. This had a similarly concentrated spread. The sum, however, included assessments for UNIFIL (Lebanon) of about $474 million, which had only been issued on 16 September. The cash balance of about $4.3 billion was divided between active missions ($3.8 billion), the peacekeeping reserve fund ($143 million) and closed missions ($314 million). But there were restrictions on using these funds to assist active missions with inadequate cash flows: no peacekeeping operation could be financed by borrowing from other active missions; the peacekeeping reserve fund was restricted to supporting new operations and the expansion of existing missions; only some of the cash available in the closed accounts was available for cross borrowing, and in 2010 the General Assembly had authorised the return of $180 million from closed mission accounts.

It was calculated that there would be $3.2 billion in cash in all peacekeeping accounts at the end of 2011, comprising $2.8 billion in active missions, $140 million in the peacekeeping reserve fund, and $316 million in the accounts of closed missions. But $263 million in the closed accounts would have to be paid to member states for troops, equipment and outstanding credits, leaving $53 million for possible cross-borrowing by active missions. In 2011 $130 million had been borrowed for MINURSO (Western Sahara), UNFICYP (Cyprus), UNMIT (Timor-Leste), UNMIK (Kosovo), MONUSCO (DRC), and UNOCI (Côte d'Ivoire). This compared with $33 million borrowed in 2010 for three missions—MINURSO, UNFICYP and UNMIT.

The United Nations' debt to member states providing troops and equipment was expected to be $448 million at 31 December 2011, compared with $539 million in 2010. The organisation owed Pakistan $63 million, India $52 million, Bangladesh $52 million and the USA $34 million. Obligations had increased in 2011 mainly because of a unique single supplementary payment to troop-contributing states authorised by the General Assembly and the deployment of a contingent to the new mission, UNISFA (Abyei). These were partly mitigated by reductions of military personnel in UNMIL (Liberia) and of police in UNMIT. Payment for contingent-owned equipment (June 2011) and troops and formed police units (August 2011) was being broadly met for 10 active missions, but not in MINURSO, UNFICYP and UNMIL where there were insufficient funds in their special accounts.

The financial position of the International Criminal Tribunal for Rwanda and the International Tribunal for the Former Yugoslavia had improved slightly, with 93 states compared with 88 in the previous year paying their assessments in full. But unpaid assessments were higher by $6 million. This debt again was highly concentrated, with one state—the USA owing 64 per cent of the total ($36 million), four other states owing 18 per cent, and the remaining 94 states a further 18 per cent. It was expected that the tribunals would have a positive balance at the end of the year but the final outcome would depend upon the action taken by the debtor states.

The capital master plan for the refurbishment of UN headquarters had a total budget of $1.88 billion. Twelve states had paid their total assessment in a single payment; 180 members paid yearly. By October 124 states had paid their assessments. The remaining members owed $88 million. Cash balances at the end of the year were expected to be positive.

On 24 December, after tough negotiations, the General Assembly approved a budget of $5.5 billion for 2012-13. This was lower than that proposed by the secretary general and smaller than the previous biennium—a reflection of global financial austerity.

David Travers

UNITED NATIONS PEACEKEEPING MISSIONS 2011

MISSION	Established	Present Strength	Renewal Date
UNTSO: United Nations Truce Supervision Organisation	May 1948	152 military observers; 101 international civilians; 131 local civilians. Total personnel: 384. Fatalities: 50. Budget: $60,704,800 (2010-11)	
UNMOGIP: United Nations Military Observer Group in India and Pakistan	January 1949	39 military observers; 25 international civilians; 51 local civilians. Total personnel: 115. Fatalities: 11. Budget: $16,146,000 (2010-11)	
UNFICYP: United Nations Peacekeeping Force in Cyprus	March 1964	856 military; 69 civilian police; 39 international civilians; 112 local civilians. Total personnel: 1,076. Fatalities: 181. Budget: $58,204,247, including voluntary contributions of one-third from Cyprus and $6.5 million from Greece	19 July 2012
UNDOF: United Nations Disengagement Observer Force	June 1974	1,047 military; 41 international civilians; 103 local civilians. Total personnel: 1,191. Fatalities: 43. Budget: $50,526,100	30 June 2012
UNIFIL: United Nations Interim Force in Lebanon	March 1978	11,959 military; 355 international civilians; 666 local civilians. Total personnel: 12,980. Fatalities: 293. Budget: $545,470,600	31 August 2012
MINURSO: United Nations Mission for the Referendum in Western Sahara	April 1991	25 military; 198 military observers; 7 civilian police; 101 international civilians; 162 local civilians; 18 UN volunteers. Total personnel: 511. Fatalities: 15. Budget: $63,219,300	30 April 2012
UNMIK: United Nations Interim Administration Mission in Kosovo	June 1999	9 military observers; 7 civilian police; 146 international civilians; 215 local civilians; 27 UN Volunteers. Total personnel: 404. Fatalities: 54. Budget: $44,914,800	Established for an initial period of 12 months; to continue unless the Security Council decides otherwise

UNITED NATIONS PEACEKEEPING MISSIONS 2011 *continued*

MISSION	Established	Present Strength	Renewal Date
UNMIL: United Nations Mission in Liberia	September 2003	7,769 military; 131 military observers; 1283 civilian police; 481 international civilians; 993 local civilians; 252 UN volunteers. Total personnel: 10,909. Fatalities: 163. Budget: $525,612,730	30 September 2012
UNOCI: United Nations Operation in Côte d'Ivoire	April 2004	9,417 military; 194 military observers; 1,367 civilian police; 392 international civilians; 741 local civilians; 277 UN volunteers. Total personnel: 12,388. Fatalities: 86. Budget: $486,726,400	31 July 2012
MINUSTAH: United Nations Stabilisation Mission in Haiti	June 2004	8,856 military; 3,582 civilian police; 573 international civilians; 1,351 local civilians; 240 UN volunteers. Total personnel: 14,602. Fatalities: 167. Budget: $793,517,100	15 October 2012
UNMIS: United Nations Mission in Sudan	March 2005	119 international civilians; 579 local civilians; 12 UN volunteers. Total personnel: 710	Officially closed on 9 July 2011, but civilian personnel were still employed
UNMIT: United Nations Integrated Mission in Timor-Leste	August 2006	33 military observers; 1,202 civilian police; 396 international civilians; 887 local civilians; 207 UN volunteers. Total personnel: 2,725. Fatalities: 12. Budget: $196,077,500	26th February 2012
UNAMID African Union-United Nations Hybrid Operation in Darfur	July 2007	17,626 military; 247 military observers; 4,977 civilian police; 1,131 international civilians; 2,916 local civilians; 482 UN volunteers. Total personnel: 27,379. Fatalities: 104. Budget: $1,689,305,500	31 July 2012

UNITED NATIONS PEACEKEEPING MISSIONS 2011 *continued*

MISSION	Established	Present Strength	Renewal Date
MONUSCO United Nations Organisation Stabilisation Mission in the Democratic Republic of Congo	July 2010	16,813 military; 714 military observers; 1,362 civilian police; 983 international civilians; 2,820 local civilians; 599 UN volunteers.Total personnel: 23,291. Fatalities: 33. Budget: $1,419,890,400	30 June 2012
UNISFA: United Nations Interim Security Force for Abyei	June 2011	2,779 military; 74 military observers; 7 international civilians; Total personnel: 2,860. Fatalities: 5	31 May 2012
UNMISS: United Nations Mission in the Republic of South Sudan	July 2011	4,914 military; 168 military observers; 446 civilian police; 706 international civilians; 1,056 local civilians; 223 UN volunteers. Total personnel: 7,513. Fatalities: 1	9 July 2012

NOTES.

Different Categories of personnel serving in the 15 peacekeeping missions as of 30 November 2011:

Military troops, observers and civilian police: 98,322 (82,061 troops, 14,302 civilian police and 1,959 military observers)

Countries contributing uniformed personnel: 115

International civilians (as of 30 September 2011): 5,596

Local civilians (as of 30 September 2011): 12,795

United Nations volunteers: 2,337

Total number of personnel serving in the 15 peacekeeping operations: 119,038

Total number of personnel serving in the 16 Department of Peacekeeping-led peace operations: 121,272

Total number of fatalities from all categories in all peace operations between 1948 and 30 November 2011: 2,960

Finance:

Approved budgets for the period 1 July 2011 to 30 June 2012: about $7.06 billion.

Estimated total cost of operations from 1948 to 30 June 2010: about $69 billion.

Outstanding contributions to peacekeeping: about $3.81 billion.

(UNTSO and UNMOGIP are funded from the United Nations regular biennial budget. The costs to the United Nations of the 13 other current peacekeeping operations are financed from their own separate accounts on the basis of legally binding assessments on all Member States. For these missions budget figures are for one year July 2011 to June 2012, unless otherwise specified.)

Number of peacekeeping operation since 1948: 66.

(Sources: United Nations Background note 30 November 2011, United Nations current peacekeeping operations website, and United Nations press releases.)

UNITED NATIONS POLITICAL AND PEACEBUILDING MISSIONS 2011

Mission	Established	Present Strength	Current Authorisation
UNPOS: United Nations Political Office for Somalia	15 April 1995	Special Representative of the Secretary General: Augustine Mahiga (Tanzania); 53 international civilians; 28 local civilians; 3 military advisers and 3 civilian police	
UNSCO: Office of the United Nations Special Co-ordinator for the Middle East	1 October 1999	Special Co-ordinator for the Middle East Peace Process and Personal Representative of the Secretary General to the Palestine Liberation Organisation and the Palestinian Authority: Robert H. Serry (Netherlands); 32 international civilians; 29 local civilians	
UNOWA: Office of the Special Representative of the Secretary General for West Africa	29 November 2001	Special Representative of the Secretary General: Said Djinnit (Algeria); 19 international civilians; 16 local civilians; 3 military advisers	31 December 2013
UNAMA: United Nations Assistance Mission in Afghanistan	28 March 2002	Special Representative of the Secretary General: Staffan de Mistura (Sweden); 427 international civilians; 1,713 local civilians; 13 military advisers; 4 civilian police; 77 UN volunteers	23 March 2012
UNAMI: United Nations Assistance Mission for Iraq	14 August 2003	Special Representative of the Secretary General for Iraq: Martin Kobler (Germany). (Staff are based in Iraq, Jordan and Kuwait.) 394 international civilians; 503 local civilians; 294 military; 13 military advisers; 4 civilian police	28 July 2012
UNSCOL: Office of the United Nations Special Co-ordinator for Lebanon	16 February 2007	Special Co-ordinator for Lebanon (acting): Robert Watkins (Canada); 19 international civilians; 59 local civilians	

UNITED NATIONS POLITICAL AND PEACEBUILDING MISSIONS 2011 *continued*

Mission	Established	Present Strength	Current Authorisation
UNRCCA: United Nations Regional Centre for Preventive Diplomacy for Central Asia	10 December 2007	Miroslav Jenca (Slovakia); 8 international civilians; 20 local civilians	
UNIPSIL: United Nations Integrated Peacebuilding Office in Sierra Leone	1 October 2008	Executive Representative of the Secretary General: Michael von der Schulenburg (Germany); 36 international civilians; 28 local civilians; 6 civilian police; 8 UN volunteers	15 September 2012
BINUA: United Nations Integrated Peacebuilding Office in the Central African Republic	1 January 2010	Special Representative of the Secretary General: Margaret Vogt (Nigeria); 66 international civilians; 75 local civilians; 2 military advisers; 2 civilian police; 5 UN volunteers	31 January 2013
UNIOGBIS: United Nations Integrated Peacebuilding Office in Guinea-Bissau	1 January 2010	Special Representative of the Secretary General: Joseph Mutaboba (Rwanda); 55 international civilians; 49 local civilians; 2 military advisers; 15 civilian police; 6 UN volunteers	28 February 2013
BINUB: United Nations Office in Burundi	1 January 2011	Special Representative of the Secretary General: Karin Landgren (Sweden); 43 international civilians; 65 local civilians; 1 military adviser; 1 civilian police; 6 UN volunteers	13 February 2013

UNITED NATIONS POLITICAL AND PEACEBUILDING MISSIONS 2011 *continued*

Mission	Established	Present Strength	Current Authorisation
UNOCA: United Nations Regional Office for Central Africa	1 January 2011	Special Representative of the Secretary General: Abou Moussa (Chad); 11 international civilians; 5 local civilians	1 January 2013
UNSMIL: United Nations Support Mission in Libya	16 September 2011	Special Representative of the Secretary General: Ian Martin (UK); 16 international civilians	16 March 2012

NOTES:

Mission ended in 2011: **UNMIN**: United Nations Mission in Nepal: 23 January 2007—15 January 2011.

Current number of Missions: 13.

Personnel:

    Uniformed personnel: 366

    International civilian personnel (as of 30 September 2011): 1,179

    Local civilian personnel (as of 30 September 2011): 2,590

    United Nations volunteers: 102

Total number of personnel serving in political and peacebuilding missions: 4,237

(UNAMA in Afghanistan is directed and supported by the Department of Peacekeeping Operations; all other political and peacebuilding missions are directed by the Department of Political Affairs.)

(Sources: United Nations Political and Peacebuilding Missions Fact Sheet 30 November 2011; United Nations resolutions, press releases and websites of individual departments and missions.)

UNITED NATIONS SANCTIONS REGIMES 2011

Regime	Current sanctions	Sanctions committee	Panel/Group of Experts/ Monitoring Group	Criteria for lifting santions	Current authorisation
Somalia since 1992; and **Eritrea** since 2009	(a) arms embargos which are territorial and a targeted ban on arms transfers to identified individuals and entities for both Somalia and Eritrea Cargoes to both states may be inspected; (b) travel ban and assets freeze on listed individuals deemed a threat to peace and the national reconciliation process or obstructing delivery or access to humanitarian assistance in Somalia; individuals and entities engaged in non-local commerce via al-Shabaab controlled ports that constitutes financial support for a designated entity; political and military support or using children in armed conflict; and individuals and entities violating applicable international law involving the targeting of civilians including women and children in situations of armed conflict. And in relation to Eritrea the political and military leadership and other individuals and entities violating the arms embargo; providing support to armed opposition groups destabilising the region; obstructing the resolution concerning Djibouti; supporting or inciting individuals or groups to perpetuate violence or terrorists acts against other states or their citizens in the region. And obstructing the investigation or the work of the monitoring group;	Yes: appointed in 1992	Yes: appointed in 1992; since 2009 also monitored sanctions against Eritrea	Considered when Eritrea is no longer undermining peace and reconciliation in Somalia and the sub-region. And when there is peace and stability in Somalia and the sub-region	Monitoring Group 29 July 2012. Sanctions presently do not require a 12 month renewal

UNITED NATIONS SANCTIONS REGIMES 2011 *continued*

Regime	Current sanctions	Sanctions committee	Panel/Group of Experts/ Monitoring Group	Criteria for lifting santions	Current authorisation
Somalia since 1992; and **Eritrea** since 2009 *continued*	(c) Eritrea to cease using extortion, threats of violence, fraud and illicit means to collect taxes outside of Eritrea from its nationals or individuals of Eritrean descent; (d) states to undertake appropriate measures to hold accountable, consistent with international law, those individuals on their territory who are acting, officially or unofficially, on behalf of the Eritrean government or the PFDJ to collect taxes; (e) states to prevent funds, derived from the mining sector of Eritrea, contributing to the violations of any aspect of the sanctions regime, by undertaking appropriate measures to promote the exercise of vigilance by their nationals, persons subject to their jurisdiction and firms incorporated in their territory or subject to their jurisdiction that are undertaking business in that sector in Eritrea including through the issuance of due diligence guidelines.				

UNITED NATIONS SANCTIONS REGIMES 2011 *continued*

Regime	Current sanctions	Sanctions committee	Panel/Group of Experts/ Monitoring Group	Criteria for lifting santions	Current authorisation
Al Qaida, and associated individuals and entities since 1999 and 2011	The sanctions apply to individuals and entities designated to be associated with al-Qaida, or any cell, affiliate, splinter group or derivative WHEREVER LOCATED. The sanctions are: (a) arms embargo: states are required to prevent direct or indirect supply, sale and transfer from their territories or by their nationals outside their territories using their flag vessels, or aircraft of arms, and related material of all types, spare parts, and technical advice, assistance or training, related to military activities to designated individuals and entities; (b) Asset freeze including funds used for internet hosting, derived from property and from the illicit cultivation, production, and trafficking of narcotic drugs and their precursors, and payments of ransoms to individuals, Groups, undertakings or entities; and travel ban on designated individuals and entities who participate in the financing, planning, facilitating, preparing or perpetuating of acts or activities by, in conjunction with, under the name of, on behalf of, or in support of; supplying, selling, or transferring arms and related material to; and recruiting for, or otherwise supporting the acts or activities of the above named group.	Yes: appointed in 1999	Yes: appointed in 2004		Sanctions and the mandate of the Monitoring Group to be reviewed on 17 December 2013

UNITED NATIONS SANCTIONS REGIMES 2011 *continued*

Regime	Current sanctions	Sanctions committee	Panel/Group of Experts/ Monitoring Group	Criteria for lifting santions	Current authorisation
Iraq since 2003	(a) arms ban on the supply. sale or transfer to Iraq of arms or related material (excludes arms and related material required by the Government of Iraq); (b) ban on dealings with illegally removed Iraqi cultural property; (c) funds, other financial assets and economic resources both within and without Iraq of individuals and entities (identified by the sanctions committee) associated with the regime of the former President Saddam Hussein should be frozen and transferred to the Development Fund for Iraq	Yes: appointed in 2003	No: consequently there is no monitoring of the arms ban in particular	To be considered when there is security and stability in Iraq	Sanctions and Panel of Experts 14 December 2012
Liberia since 2003	(a) embargo on arms and related material against non governmental entities and individuals operating in Liberia; states have to notify the sanctions committee in advance of any shipment of arms and related materials to, and any assistance, advice or training related to military activities for, the Government of Liberia; (b) freezing of funds and economic resources and a travel ban on persons and entities associated with the former President Taylor.	Yes: appointed in 2003	Yes: appointed in 2003	Considered when sufficient progress had been achieved in stabilisation throughout the country and parliamentary and presidential elections had been held	

UNITED NATIONS SANCTIONS REGIMES 2011 *continued*

Regime	Current sanctions	Sanctions committee	Panel/Group of Experts/ Monitoring Group	Criteria for lifting sanctions	Current authorisation
Democratic Republic of the Congo since 2003	(a) arms and related material embargo against non-governmental entities and individuals operating in the DR Congo; (b) freezing of funds and economic resources and a travel ban on individuals and entities violating the arms embargo; leaders of foreign armed groups and leaders of Congolese militias receiving support from abroad who impede disarmament, demobilisation repatriation, resettlement and reintegration processes; leaders recruiting or using children in armed conflict; individuals committing serious violations of international law involving the targeting of children and women in situations of armed conflict including killing, maiming, sexual violence, abduction and forced displacement; and obstructing provision of humanitarian assistance in the eastern parts of the DR Congo and individuals and entities supporting illegal armed groups through illicit trade of natural resources	Yes: appointed in 2004	Yes: appointed in 2004	Considered in the light of the security situation in the DRC, in particular progress in security sector reform including the integration of the armed forces and the reform of the national police and in the disarming, demobilising, repatriating, resettling and reintegrating, as appropriate, of Congolese and foreign armed groups	Sanctions and Group of Experts: 30 November 2012

UNITED NATIONS SANCTIONS REGIMES 2011 *continued*

Regime	Current sanctions	Sanctions committee	Panel/Group of Experts/ Monitoring Group	Criteria for lifting santions	Current authorisation
Côte d'Ivoire	(a) embargo on the supply, sale or transfer of arms or related material to Côte d'Ivoire; (b) embargo on assistance, advice or training related to military activities; (c) ban on the import of rough diamonds; (d) the freezing of the assets and economic resources and a travel ban on those individuals deemed to be a threat to the peace and reconciliation process, violating the arms embargo, seriously violating human rights and international humanitarian law, inciting publicly hatred and violence and attacking or obstructing the action or the freedom of movement of UNOCIL.	Yes: appointed in 2004	Yes: appointed in 2005	Considered when there was stabilisation throughout the country, parliamentary elections had been held, key processes of the peace process had been implemented and human rights record has been improved	Sanctions and Group of Experts 30 April 2012

UNITED NATIONS SANCTIONS REGIMES 2011 *continued*

Regime	Current sanctions	Sanctions committee	Panel/Group of Experts/ Monitoring Group	Criteria for lifting sanctions	Current authorisation
Sudan since 2004. These sanctions do NOT apply to the Republic of South Sudan	(a) arms embargo on the supply of arms and related material of all types and on technical training and assistance related to the provision, maintenance or use of arms to the following operating in the States of North Darfur, South Darfur and West Darfur: all non-governmental entities and individuals including the Janjaweed; all parties to the N'djamena Ceasefire Agreement and any other belligerents; (b) the government of Sudan is required to obtain advanced approval from the sanctions committee for the movement of equipment and supplies into the Darfur Region. And any state that sells or transfers arms to Sudan that are not proscribed has to ensure that these are conditional on the necessary end user documentation that ensures that the sale is consistent with the provisions of Security Council resolutions on Sudan; (c) assets freeze and travel ban on any individual or entity that impedes the peace process, constitutes a threat to the stability in Darfur and the region; commits violations of the arms embargo, international humanitarian law and human rights or other atrocities and is responsible for offensive military overflights.	Yes: appointed in 2005	Yes: appointed in 2005	Considered when significant progress has been made in establishing and maintaining stability in Sudan and the sub-region	Panel of Experts: 19 February 2012

UNITED NATIONS SANCTIONS REGIMES 2011 *continued*

Regime	Current sanctions	Sanctions committee	Panel/Group of Experts/ Monitoring Group	Criteria for lifting santions	Current authorisation
Lebanon since 2005	(a) arms embargo on the supply, sale or transfer of arms to Lebanon but does not apply to arms, related material and training authorised by the government of Lebanon or UNIFIL; (b) assets freeze and travel ban on individuals suspected of involvement in the planning, sponsoring, organising, or perpetration of the murder of the former Prime Minister of Lebanon Rafiq Hariri and 22 others on 14 February 2005	Yes: appointed in 2005. The committee, however, has not listed any individuals	No	The arms embargo will be terminated when the government of Lebanon believes that its writ extends throughout its territory. The assets freeze and the travel ban will terminate when Sanctions Committee reports to the Security Council that all investigative and judicial proceedings relating to the attack on 14 February 2005 have been completed unless the Security Council decides otherwise.	

UNITED NATIONS SANCTIONS REGIMES 2011 *continued*

Regime	Current sanctions	Sanctions committee	Panel/Group of Experts/ Monitoring Group	Criteria for lifting santions	Current authorisation
DPR Korea (North Korea) since 2006	(a) arms embargo on the supply, sale or transfer to and from the DPRK of all conventional arms and related material and nuclear, ballistic and other Weapons of Mass Destruction and related items; (b) the prevention of any transfers of technical training, advice, services or assistance related to the provision, manufacture, maintenance or use of nuclear, ballistic missile and WMD related programmes; (c) a freeze of funds, financial assets and economic resources of any person or entities engaged in DPRK nuclear related programme; (d) a travel ban against designated persons contributing to DPRK's various prohibited programmes and their families; (f) and where there are export of luxury goods; (f) and where there are reasonable grounds for believing that cargos to and from North Korea contain prohibited items states could inspect, seize and dispose of those items; and states should deny bunkering and other facilities to ships from DPRK if it is believed they are carrying prohibited items; (g) prevent the provision of financial	Yes: appointed in 2006	Yes: appointed in 2009	Considered (a) when North Korea abandons all nuclear weapons and existing nuclear programmes in a complete and verifiable and irreversible manner and returns to the non-proliferation treaty; (b) abandons all other Weapons of Mass Destruction and ballistic missile programmes in a similar fashion and refrains from conducting further nuclear and ballistic missile tests	Panel of Experts 12 June 2012

UNITED NATIONS SANCTIONS REGIMES 2011 *continued*

Regime	Current sanctions	Sanctions committee	Panel/Group of Experts/ Monitoring Group	Criteria for lifting santions	Current authorisation
DPR Korea (North Korea) since 2006 *continued*	services or transfer of any financial or other assets or resources that could contribute to DPRK's Weapons of Mass Destruction Programmes; (h) prevent any new commitments for grants, financial assistance or concessional loans to DPRK except for humanitarian and development or denuclearisation purposes and reduce current commitments; (i) no public support to be provided for trade with DPRK that could contribute to its WMD programmes; and (j) states should prevent specialised teaching or training of DPRK nationals in their territories of disciplines which could contribute to DPRK proliferation sensitive nuclear activities and the development of nuclear weapon delivery systems.				

UNITED NATIONS SANCTIONS REGIMES 2011 *continued*

Regime	Current sanctions	Sanctions committee	Panel/Group of Experts/ Monitoring Group	Criteria for lifting santions	Current authorisation
Iran since 2006	(a) a ban on the export of any goods and technology that might contribute to the development of nuclear weapons and of ballistic missiles in Iran including those contained in the Nuclear Suppliers Group and the Missile Technology Control Regime lists; (b) states must prevent Iran acquiring an interest in any commercial activity in another state involving uranium mining, the production or use of nuclear materials and technology particularly relating to ballistic missiles capable of delivering nuclear weapons; (c) a ban on the export of seven categories of conventional weapons to Iran and a ban on the import of any arms from Iran; (d) a freeze on the assets and economic resources of and a travel ban on any individual or entity involved in the nuclear programme or helping in the evasion of sanctions; (e) states are required to inspect cargoes to and from Iran if there are reasonable grounds for believing that the cargo contains banned items; similarly with the consent of the flag state vessels on the high seas may be inspected. Any banned item	Yes: appointed in 2006	Yes: appointed in 2010	Will be considered when Iran has complied with Security Council resolutions and when the IAEA verifies that Iran has stopped its uranium enrichment activities and that its nuclear programme is for exclusively peaceful purposes	Panel of Experts 9 June 2012

UNITED NATIONS SANCTIONS REGIMES 2011 *continued*

Regime	Current sanctions	Sanctions committee	Panel/Group of Experts/ Monitoring Group	Criteria for lifting santions	Current authorisation
Iran since 2006 *continued*	should be seized and disposed of. And states are also required to withdraw bunkering and other services to Iranian vessels if it is believed that they are carrying banned items. (f) states are requested to supply information to the sanctions committee on how Iran state transport systems might be evading sanctions by transferring activity to other states and by renaming or re-registering vessels, ships and aircraft; and (g) states must prevent their nationals or financial institutions providing financial services to or within Iran and prevent Iran from entering into any form of banking relationship within their territory if they have easonable grounds for believing that such activities could contribute to Iran's nuclear proliferation activities or the development of nuclear weapon delivery systems.				

UNITED NATIONS SANCTIONS REGIMES 2011 *continued*

Regime	Current sanctions	Sanctions committee	Panel/Group of Experts/ Monitoring Group	Criteria for lifting santions	Current authorisation
Libya since 2011	Arms embargo: (a) states to prevent the direct or indirect supply, sale, or transfer to Libya, from or through their territories or by their nationals, or using their flag, vessels or aircraft, of arms and related material of all types, including weapons and ammunition, military vehicles, and equipment, paramilitary equipment and spare parts for the forementioned and technical assistance, training, financial or other assistance, related to military activities, or the provision, maintenance or use of any arms and related material, including the provision of armed mercenary personnel whether or not originating in their territories; (b) that Libya cease the export of all arms and related material and that all member states should prohibit the procurement of such items from Libya by their nationals or using their flagged vessels or aircraft whether or not originating in the territory of Libya; (c) Enforcement of the Arms Embargo: states were called upon to inspect in their territories including seaports and airports and on the high seas vessels and aircraft bound to or from Libya if they had information that provided reasonable grounds to believe that the cargo contained prohibited items including armed mercenary personnel and called upon flag states of such vessels and aircraft to co-operate with such inspections;	Yes: appointed in 2011	Yes: appointed in 2011		Panel of Experts 17 March 2012

UNITED NATIONS SANCTIONS REGIMES 2011 *continued*

Regime	Current sanctions	Sanctions committee	Panel/Group of Experts/ Monitoring Group	Criteria for lifting sanctions	Current authorisation
Libya since 2011 *continued*	and authorised states to use all measures commensurate with the specific circumstances to carry out such inspections; (d) Ban on Flights: all states were required to deny permission to any aircraft registered in Libya or owned or operated by Libyan nationals or companies, or any aircraft that they had reasonable grounds to believe contained prohibited items including armed mercenary personnel to take off from, land in or overfly their territory except in the case of an emergency landing; (e) Travel Ban. All states were required to deny entry or transit through their territory of persons listed by the Security Council or the Sanctions Committee; (f) Financial Freeze: all member states should freeze without delay all funds, other financial assets and economic resources which were on their territories, which were controlled, directly or indirectly, by the Libyan authorities, individuals or entities listed, or by individuals or entities acting on their behalf or at their direction, or by entities owned or controlled by them; and ensure that they prevented their nationals making any assets available to or for the benefit of those listed; and their nationals should exercise vigilance when conducting business with Libyan entities if states had information that provided reasonable grounds for believing that such business could contribute to violence				

UNITED NATIONS SANCTIONS REGIMES 2011 *continued*

Regime	Current sanctions	Sanctions committee	Panel/Group of Experts/ Monitoring Group	Criteria for lifting santions	Current authorisation
Libya since 2011 *continued*	and the use of force against civilians. (g) the travel ban and the assets freeze would apply to those Libyan authorities, entities and individuals involved in or complicit in ordering, controlling, or otherwise directing the commission of serious human rights abuses against people in Libya, including by being involved in or complicit in planning, commanding, ordering or conducting attacks in violation of international law, including aerial bombardment on civilian populations and facilities. And those who violated the provisions of Resolution 1970 (2011) particularly the arms embargo or assisted others in so doing. Resolution 2009 (2011) modified some of these measures by making exemptions to the arms embargo and the asset freeze and allowed commercial flights by Libyan aircraft.				

UNITED NATIONS SANCTIONS REGIMES 2011 *continued*

Regime	Current sanctions	Sanctions committee	Panel/Group of Experts/ Monitoring Group	Criteria for lifting santions	Current authorisation
the Taliban since 2011	The following measures were to be taken against any individuals, groups, undertakings and entities associated with the Taliban in constituting a threat to the peace, stability and security of Afghanistan. (a) arms embargo: states must prevent the direct or indirect supply, sale and transfer from their territory or by their nationals outside their territories, or using their flag vessels or aircraft, of arms and related materials of all types, spare parts, and technical advice, assistance or training related to military activities to designated individuals and entities; (b) assets freeze: freeze without delay the funds and financial assets or economic resources of designated individuals and entities; (c) travel ban: prevent the entry into or transit through their territories by designated individuals.	Yes: appointed in 2011	1267 Monitoring Team would support the committee for 18 months		Monitoring Team 17 December 2012

NOTES:

Each regime normally has a sanctions committee composed of the 15 members of the Security Council normally chaired by a non-permanent member and assisted by the Secretariat. The committee works by consensus. The committee has a range of functions including but not limited to: monitoring the implementation of the sanctions; examining and taking action on information alleging violations of these measures; designating additional individuals and entities to be subject to sanctions; deciding upon exemptions to sanctions; regularly briefing the Council on its work and making recommendations on how the effectiveness of sanctions might be strengthened.

Most regimes have a monitoring group or expert panel which is established by the Security Council to report to and assist the sanctions committee. The members who have specialised technical knowledge in the areas of the sanctions are appointed by the secretary general after consultation with the sanctions committees, and serve in their individual capacity. Their principal functions are to investigate the implementation and violation of sanctions: in particular to explore who are the violators, how these generate revenue for their activities, and what transport routes and facilities they use to undermine sanctions; and to suggest how states' capacities, especially those in the region adjacent to the target, might be improved to help in the implementation of sanctions and to make recommendations on enhancing compliance with sanctions.

(Sources: the sanctions websites of the UN, the EU, the UK Foreign and Commonwealth Office, the Treasury and the Australian Department of Foreign Affairs and Trade.)

DEFENCE AND ECONOMIC ORGANISATIONS

NORTH ATLANTIC TREATY ORGANISATION (NATO)

DATE OF FOUNDATION: 1949   HEADQUARTERS: Brussels, Belgium
OBJECTIVES: To ensure the collective security of member states
MEMBERSHIP (END-'11): Albania, Belgium, Bulgaria, Canada, Croatia, Czech Republic, Denmark,
    Estonia, France, Germany, Greece, Hungary, Iceland, Italy, Latvia, Lithuania, Luxembourg,
    Netherlands, Norway, Poland, Portugal, Romania, Slovakia, Slovenia, Spain, Turkey, UK, USA
    (total 28)
SECRETARY GENERAL: Anders Fogh Rasmussen (Denmark) (since Aug '09)

WHERE the organisations of European security and defence were concerned, it was NATO that was the focus of attention during 2011—politically, strategically and operationally. Politically, the alliance projected itself as a cohesive inter-governmental organisation, involving alliance members and partners, with the aspiration and the capability to act in both a regional and an international context. Strategically, NATO continued to transform its organisation and its outlook in order more effectively to meet emerging international security challenges and threats. These political and strategic goals meant that the alliance was especially concerned to implement decisions made during the previous year, particularly the New Strategic Concept endorsed by the NATO leadership in November 2010. Operationally, NATO found itself with demanding military commitments in the course of 2011. Afghanistan continued to absorb the larger part of the alliance's military effort, but from March to October NATO played a decisive role in a much smaller, but no less significant, operation: the international intervention in Libya.

Aspiration and experience combined in 2011 to generate mounting interest in NATO's forthcoming 25th summit meeting, due to take place in Chicago in May 2012. The Chicago summit was seen increasingly as an opportunity to present NATO as an alliance which had rebalanced itself politically between the USA and its European allies; as an alliance which had transformed itself strategically, principally as the result of an initiative known as "smart defence"; and as an alliance which had learned from, and capitalised upon, the operational experience gained during 2011.

NATO AND LISBON. NATO's summit meeting in Lisbon in November 2010 was described by the secretary general, Anders Fogh Rasmussen, as "the most important summit in NATO's history". There were several good reasons for describing the alliance's 24th summit in this way. In 2010 NATO remained embroiled in a particularly complex conflict in Afghanistan; alliance governments were experiencing ever tighter fiscal constraints, with predictable effects on defence spending; and it had become clear that a range of new threats and security challenges had matured to the point that NATO would have to respond in one way or another. But without doubt the principal achievement of the summit was the launch of NATO's New Strategic Concept, entitled *Active Engagement, Modern Defence* (see AR 2011, pp. 397-98; for text see AR 2011, pp. 573-80).

The New Strategic Concept (NSC) was intended by member governments to "guide the next phase in NATO's evolution, so that it continues to be effective in a changing world, against new threats, with new capabilities and partners". The NSC described a distinctly outward-looking alliance, with an explicit mission "to help promote common security with our partners around the globe". In perhaps the most expansive and ambitious passage of the document, it was accepted that "crises and conflicts beyond NATO's borders can pose a direct threat to the security of Alliance territory and populations". In such circumstances, NATO would "engage, where possible and when necessary, to prevent crises, manage crises, stabilise post-conflict situations and support reconstruction". More ambitiously still, and with an eye to a global role for the alliance, the NSC also committed NATO member governments to deepening "political dialogue and practical co-operation with the United Nations", including through "enhanced practical co-operation in managing crises where both organisations were engaged". Within months, these ringing declarations of intent were found to have been rather prophetic, and NATO was to discover that it had positioned itself for a decisive role in the "Arab Spring".

The NSC's interest in "new threats" and "emerging security challenges" had been anticipated some months earlier by the establishment within the International Staff at NATO headquarters of a seventh staff division: the ponderously entitled Emerging Security Challenges Division (ESCD). In reality, the ESCD was more of a reorganisation of existing capabilities within NATO headquarters than a wholly new departure. Beginning work in August 2010, the ESCD aimed to address a disparate collection of threats and challenges, including terrorism, the proliferation of weapons of mass destruction, cyber-security and defence, and energy security.

For at least two decades NATO had acknowledged the need to transform itself in order to meet the challenges of the post-Cold War world. In 2011 the ESCD emerged as the latest symbol of NATO's efforts to do so. With an eye to the 2012 Chicago summit, the ESCD claimed a number of significant "evolutionary" achievements in 2011. The 2010 New Strategic Concept had emphasised NATO's growing interest in conflict prevention: "The best way to manage conflicts is to prevent them from happening. NATO will continually monitor and analyse the international environment to anticipate crises and, where appropriate, take active steps to prevent them from becoming larger conflicts." With this objective in mind, a Strategic Analysis Capability (SAC) had been created within the ESCD with the task of monitoring and assessing international developments that could affect NATO's security. In the course of its work in 2011 the SAC was credited with nudging the alliance away from its traditionally reactive approach to crises and towards a more anticipatory and "forward-leaning" stance, in the spirit of NATO as an organisation with a special competence in the field of conflict prevention. The ESCD was also closely involved in the production, in June 2011, of a revised NATO policy on cyber defence, which promised a "co-ordinated approach to cyber defence across the Alliance with a focus on preventing cyber threats and building resilience".

In 2011 the ESCD thus began to assume the role of NATO's "operations cell" for non-traditional and largely (although not exclusively) non-military security threats and challenges. As one component of the broader project of transforming NATO into a political-military alliance with a wide range of capabilities and a particular interest in conflict prevention, the ESCD was best understood as work-in-progress that would doubtless be closely examined at the May 2012 Chicago summit. For the transformation of NATO, there were a number of areas that required further development: identifying the key capabilities (civil as well as military) that NATO would need if it was to undertake ESCD missions; and liaising with allies, partners and other organisations (including the European Union).

NATO AND LIBYA. In the more than two decades since the end of the Cold War, NATO had sought to consolidate its reputation as an operationally effective political-military alliance. In 2011 NATO remained closely involved in Afghanistan. This almost decade-long commitment remained politically contentious, strategically uncertain, operationally frustrating and militarily demanding. By the end of 2011 the International Security Assistance Force (ISAF), led by NATO since 2003, commanded some 130,000 troops from as many as 50 troop-contributing countries (NATO member nations and partners). ISAF's mission continued to be to support the government of Afghanistan in the pursuit of a "secure and stable environment", to conduct counter-insurgency operations and to assist in the training and development of the Afghan National Security Forces (ANSF, comprising military and police). With the decision having been made to withdraw ISAF by the end of 2014 (when the USA was to end its combat mission in Afghanistan), a successful transition to an effective ANSF became steadily more imperative—though seemingly less achievable—as 2011 progressed (see pp. 282-86).

While NATO's involvement in Afghanistan continued to be the focus of the Alliance's work in 2011, it was a much smaller operation that occupied the attention of the international media. On 31 March 2011 NATO assumed control of all military operations concerning Libya, mandated by United Nations Security Council Resolutions 1970 and 1973. Under the code name "Operation Unified Protector", NATO's involvement lasted until 21 October when the North Atlantic Council (NATO's political leadership) took the decision to wind down the operation by the end of that month. Led by Lieutenant General Charles Bouchard of the Canadian Air Force based in NATO's Allied Joint Force Command headquarters in Naples, the alliance's operational commitment lasted 204 days and at its peak involved over 40 warships and submarines from NATO and partner countries together with over 250 aircraft of all types (i.e. combat, surveillance, refuelling, transport and helicopters). By 31 October 2011 NATO aircraft had flown as many as 26,500 sorties in accordance with Security Council resolutions. Although by the end of 2011 there was widespread doubt as to the stability of Libya and its longer-term future, NATO was confident that it had performed as expected and was able to indulge in a certain amount of self-congratulation. In a statement released shortly before the conclusion of Operation Unified Protector, Secretary General Rasmussen insisted that NATO had "fully complied with the historic mandate of the United Nations" and described the operation as "one of the most successful in NATO history".

The United Nations mandate certainly was historic. UN Security Council Resolution 1973 of 17 March 2011 (UNSCR 1973), known in international law as a Chapter VII enforcement measure (referring to the relevant chapter of the UN Charter), authorised UN member states "acting nationally or through regional organisations or arrangements ... to take all necessary measures" to protect civilians, to enforce a no-fly zone over Libya and to enforce an arms embargo on Libya (see Documents). The resolution was very carefully worded. The 1949 North Atlantic Treaty—NATO's founding document—had deliberately not described the alliance as a "regional agency" under Chapter VIII of the UN Charter, because to have done so would have been to subject aspects of NATO decision-making—and most importantly the decision to resort to armed force—to United Nations deliberations, thereby exposing NATO decision-making to the Security Council vetoes of China and the Soviet Union. Yet in March 2011 NATO took control of military operations over and around Libya and showed that the alliance could act as a regional agency under a specific UN Security Council mandate.

As well as cementing a closer relationship between the United Nations (as the international authority for the use of armed force in such circumstances) and NATO (as a political-military alliance with the capacity to act internationally), the significance of UNSCR 1973 was that it was concerned primarily with the need to protect civilians. In this respect, the resolution and the mandate it gave for action by NATO's member states and partners reopened a long-running debate about the international community's response to situations of the sort seen in Libya, and particularly about the evolution of a doctrine known as the "responsibility to protect".

"Responsibility to protect" (often abbreviated to R2P) was first formulated in the December 2001 report of the International Commission on Intervention and State Sovereignty (ICISS), an ad-hoc body consisting of UN Security Council members and co-chaired by Gareth Evans, former foreign minister of Australia. The essence of R2P was summarised in an early sentence of the report: "Where a population is suffering serious harm, as a result of internal war, insurgency, repression or state failure, and the state in question is unwilling or unable to halt or avert it, the principle of non-intervention yields to the international responsibility to protect."

Although generally considered to be a norm of international society, rather than an instrument of international law strictly defined, R2P steadily acquired respect and moral authority as the first decade of the 21st century progressed. But it then appeared to lose energy, to the point in 2008 when Gareth Evans wondered whether, as far as the consolidation of the R2P idea was concerned, 2005 had been "the high-water mark from which the tides recede". Libya seemed to act as an antidote to such pessimism, however, with Evans prompted to declare in October 2011: "Libya has shown that the responsibility to protect has come of age."

With the shooting dead of Colonel Moamar Kadhafi on 20 October 2011 (see p. 217), the last remnants of his regime collapsed and the Libyan intervention was concluded. But almost immediately doubts began to be raised about the conduct of the operation and, in particular, about the nature of the relationship between the United Nations and NATO. Rather than provide a mandate for NATO to act in the spirit (at least) of a Chapter VIII regional organisation, had the UN effectively devolved responsibility and decision-making upon NATO? As a result, did the mission "creep" from the relatively restrained aim of protecting civilians to the much more ambitious goal, both politically and practically, of regime change? In April 2011, shortly after Operation Unified Protector began, Russia's Foreign Minister Sergei Lavrov had been explicit in warning against the use of UNSCR 1973 to bring about regime change. Yet in the view of both China and Russia, regime change was precisely what took place in Libya under the guise of a UN Security Council resolution. This was not what either country had intended when they had abstained in the vote for UNSCR 1973 earlier in the year. The outcome was that both countries, wracked by what some described as "buyer's remorse" on a grand scale, used their veto in the UN Security Council in early October 2011 to prevent the passage of a resolution which would have threatened sanctions against the regime of Syria's President Bashar al-Assad.

There were also doubts that the Libyan intervention had been the unqualified success for NATO that some (including the alliance's secretary general) had claimed it to be. Although Operation Unified Protector was explicitly not a US-led NATO operation and although the spirit of the enterprise was that European members of the alliance should take the lead in the provision and deployment of military capability, as much as 70-80 per cent of air power tasks (including intelligence, surveillance, reconnaissance, air-to-air refuelling and suppression of Libyan air defence systems) were provided by manned and remotely piloted aircraft from the USA. With this level of dependence on US equipment, the Libyan intervention—rather than demonstrate NATO's strength—may have shown the alliance to be something of a paper tiger. It was the perception of a major capability imbalance at the heart of NATO that generated renewed interest in "smart defence" and the approach to NATO's Chicago summit in May 2012.

NATO AND CHICAGO. It became increasingly clear during 2011 that NATO's 25th summit meeting in May 2012 would be an important, even a vital, moment in the alliance's post-Cold War history. Libya had shown that there was a good deal more work to be done across NATO to ensure efficient and effective collaboration in key areas of military capability. In many ways, therefore, Libya was but the latest phase in a very lengthy, yet so far inconclusive, debate between the United States and its European allies concerning the means by which the costs and commitments of the NATO defence and security project would be shared across the alliance. The USA would not necessarily object to finding itself in the position of "enabling" NATO operations, as it had done in Libya, but the US administration became more insistent during 2011 that it expected its allies in Europe to take a more equitable share of the burden and to find more imaginative and better co-ordinated ways in which to make the best use of limited resources in times of financial austerity. The US administration also argued, as it had in the past, that the gap between US and European defence spending must be closed and that European members of NATO should therefore maintain (or, in the majority of cases, restore) a level of defence spending equivalent to 2 per cent of GDP. Without such a commitment, European governments could reasonably be described as "free riders" on US defence spending—a position that could no longer be tolerated in the United States, particularly as the global recession persisted.

The latest round of the US-European burden-sharing debate came to be symbolised in 2011 by the term "smart defence". According to NATO, the purpose of the initiative was to encourage allies "to co-operate in developing, acquiring and maintaining military capabilities to meet current security problems in accordance with the new NATO strategic concept. That means pooling and sharing capabilities, setting priorities and co-ordinating efforts better." As agreed at the Lisbon summit in 2010, the core capabilities to be addressed included ballistic missile defence, ISR (intelligence, surveillance and reconnaissance), and force protection. But smart defence also came to be seen as a timely opportunity to capitalise upon the more positive aspects of Operation Unified Protector. Whatever the implications of the operation for the credibility of the emergent doctrine of "responsibility to protect" (particularly where the situation in Syria was concerned), for the relationship between the United Nations and NATO, and for the longer term situation in Libya, in the end the consolidated view of NATO and its member governments was that the alliance had succeeded in its mission. In conjunction with NATO's operational experience in 2011, the smart defence initiative therefore represented a chance to confirm a positive trend in the transformation of the alliance.

Some commentators and officials took to describing NATO's development metaphorically in terms of the release of ever-improving versions of computer software. Thus, if "NATO 1.0'" could be considered the alliance of the Cold War, then "NATO 2.0" might be described as the alliance of post-Cold War enlargement. The latest and much improved version of the software—"NATO 3.0"— would be revealed with a flourish at the Chicago summit. By this view, Chicago would project NATO as a united, responsible and credible political-military alliance, strengthened internally by an equitable burden-sharing arrangement and known externally for its operational effectiveness. Much of the language of unity, burden-sharing and transformation had of course been heard before over the several decades of NATO's existence. At the end of 2011 it remained open to question whether the 2012 Chicago summit would see the consolidation of initiatives pursued and experience gained in 2011, or whether the summit would be more concerned with organising an orderly exit for the International Security Assistance Force from Afghanistan in 2014.

Paul Cornish

ECONOMIC ORGANISATIONS

International Monetary Fund (IMF)

DATE OF FOUNDATION: 1945   HEADQUARTERS: Washington DC, USA
OBJECTIVES: To promote international monetary co-operation and to assist member states in
    establishing sound budgetary and trading policies
MEMBERSHIP (END-'11): 187 members
MANAGING DIRECTOR: Christine Lagarde (France) (since July '11)

*World Bank (International Bank for Reconstruction and Development (IBRD) and
International Development Association (IDA))*

DATE OF FOUNDATION: 1944   HEADQUARTERS: Washington DC, USA
OBJECTIVES: To make loans on reasonable terms to developing countries with the aim of increasing
    their productive capacity
MEMBERSHIP (END-'11): 187 members
PRESIDENT, WORLD BANK GROUP: Robert Zoellick (USA) (since July '07)

World Trade Organisation (WTO)

DATE OF FOUNDATION: 1995 (successor to General Agreement on Tariffs and Trade, GATT)
    HEADQUARTERS: Geneva, Switzerland
OBJECTIVES: To eliminate tariffs and other barriers to international trade and to facilitate
    international financial settlements
MEMBERSHIP (END-'11): 153 members
DIRECTOR GENERAL: Pascal Lamy (France) (since Sep '05)

Organisation for Economic Co-operation and Development (OECD)

DATE OF FOUNDATION: 1961   HEADQUARTERS: Paris, France
OBJECTIVES: To promote economic growth in member states and the sound development of the
    world economy
MEMBERSHIP (END-'11): Australia, Austria, Belgium, Canada, Chile, Czech Republic, Denmark,
    Estonia, Finland, France, Germany, Greece, Hungary, Iceland, Ireland, Israel, Italy, Japan,
    South Korea, Luxembourg, Mexico, The Netherlands, New Zealand, Norway, Poland, Portugal,
    Slovakia, Slovenia, Spain, Sweden, Switzerland, Turkey, UK, USA (total 34)
SECRETARY GENERAL: Angel Gurria (Mexico) (since June '06)

INTERNATIONAL MONETARY FUND (IMF). Early in 2011 there was widespread speculation that the managing director, Dominique Strauss-Kahn, would soon announce
his resignation in order to seek nomination as the socialist party candidate in the
French presidential election in 2012. The names of possible successors to replace
him at the head of the IMF were already being bandied about in April. On 14 May
Strauss-Kahn was arrested in New York on criminal charges of sexual assault,
charges that were eventually withdrawn in August. On 18 May he resigned with
immediate effect, the third successive managing director of the IMF to leave the
post before completing the standard five-year term.

The appointment of Strauss-Kahn in September 2007 had been controversial
(AR 2008, pp. 389-390) because it continued the long-standing, informal arrangement whereby the head of the IMF was always a European and that of the World
Bank was from the USA. The developing country members of both institutions
objected strongly to these monopolies and to the way in which the selection
process was conducted. Their protests had increased as their voting strength in the

IMF, despite recent reforms (AR 2011, p. 403), continued to lag behind their share of global output (the principal criterion determining quotas and voting power) while the developed economy members, especially the Europeans, retained a disproportionate influence over IMF governance.

The European members had appeared to accept the force of these arguments. In May 2011 a joint statement by the BRICS (Brazil, Russia, India, China and South Africa) pointedly recalled the words of Jean-Claude Juncker, president of the Euro-group, in 2007, that "the next managing director will certainly not be a European". Yet, even before Strauss-Kahn had formally resigned, the president of the European Commission, José Manuel Barroso, said that a European candidate would be proposed and a number of eurozone leaders, including the German Chancellor Angela Merkel, argued that the role of the IMF in dealing with the eurozone's sovereign debt problems spoke strongly in favour of a European as managing director, an argument that failed to impress Latin American and Asian members who had survived their own financial crises in the 1980s and 1990s, respectively, without one of their own at the head of the IMF.

European governments quickly united behind Christine Lagarde, finance minister of France, as their preferred candidate and when nominations closed on 10 June the only other contender was Augustin Carstens, governor of the central bank of Mexico. Despite their objections to another European at the head of the IMF, the developing countries failed to unite behind a single candidate. On 28 June the executive board chose Lagarde to become the first woman to be managing director and her five-year term started on 5 July.

Behind the familiar objections to another European becoming managing director, there were genuine concerns, and not a little resentment, at the way and on the scale that the IMF had become involved with the problems of the eurozone. Strauss-Kahn, a man with clear political ambitions in Europe, was seen as an important influence in getting the IMF to provide a third of the very large rescue loans for Greece, Ireland and Portugal and effectively to accept the demand of rich eurozone countries that the IMF's *imprimatur* be a condition for their own lending to the European periphery. This contingency essentially provided eurozone members with an escape from their own rules. Critics within and outside the Fund, many of whom regarded the bailouts as poorly conceived and insufficiently financed, feared that its minority role risked compromising both the Fund's independence and its balance sheet. They also contended that the Fund had bowed to political pressures defending the interests of German and French banks. There was also concern at the possible damage to the IMF's credibility and indeed its legitimacy as a global institution. The prospect of the poorer members of the IMF bailing out a group of the richest countries in the world—and one that collectively was in current account surplus—was not regarded as helpful for its reputation or, indeed, as morally acceptable.

Lagarde, as a former minister involved in the eurozone bailouts and sensitive to the difficult situation in which she was taking over as managing director, rejected any suggestion of a conflict between her past and present roles and insisted she was not at the IMF to represent any region but the entire membership. She promised to push for continued reform of the Fund's system of governance, aware that if reforms were blocked by the richer countries the emerging market economies might seek regional alternatives and thus undermine the global body that a highly interconnected world economy needed. Whatever the strength of the various criticisms, it was clear that the eurozone debt crisis had exacerbated tensions within the Fund, as in the global economy at large.

Strauss-Kahn had started to move away from the neo-liberal orthodoxy usually associated with the Fund, speaking out early in support of fiscal stimuli in 2008 and emphasising issues such as unemployment and inequality. Many commentators expected Lagarde to adopt a more conservative approach but instead she repeated her predecessor's view that rapid and severe deficit cutting risked tipping the global economy into recession which, in turn, would worsen the problems of deficits and debt. She also continued to stress employment and social issues which had been "peripheral components of the traditional economics".

IMF lending to its members had grown considerably since the onset of the financial crisis. At the end of 2011, its outstanding net loans were SDR92.6 billion, more than nine-fold above their level at the end of 2007 and more than 50 per cent up on 2010. The flow of net lending in 2011 was some SDR32 billion against SDR18.2 billion at the end of 2010. (These data refer to the main General Resources Account and the Poverty Reduction and Growth Trust.)

Allowing for various adjustments, the Fund's resources available for new lending—what it called its forward commitment capacity—at the end of 2011 were SDR251.4 billion, considerably more than in December 2010 (SDR132.1 billion). It was clear, however, that these would still be inadequate to meet any marked increase in the demand for loans following a further deterioration in Europe. A 10-fold increase in the Fund's standing credit lines—the New and General Agreements to Borrow—went into effect in March, raising the total to SDR387 billion, but, for prudential reasons, not all of this could be lent. By end year the managing director was asking member countries for another $500 billion to prepare for a possible escalation in the demand for loans. Not all members were keen to contribute: the USA appeared to be unwilling, there was opposition in the UK to providing €30 billion of the EU's pledge of €200 billion, and some of the emerging market economies, while not opposed, wanted the eurozone to finance its own members in difficulty.

Against this uncertain outlook, the Fund continued to develop its various financial instruments to make them more effective in times of heightened tension and in particular to try to limit the damage to "bystanders" from specific crises. In November the Executive Board approved a more flexible Precautionary and Liquidity Line to provide countries that had "sound policies and fundamentals" with some insurance against contagion from exogenous shocks, and a new Rapid Financing Instrument replaced two previous arrangements for emergency help to countries coping with the balance of payments effects of national disasters and a range of external shocks.

An important work programme concerned international capital flows and the controversial issue of unfettered capital account liberalisation, one of the central pillars of globalisation. The view of the Board was that such flows generally facilitated more efficient resource allocation and economic growth but that episodes of high volatility could be very disruptive of macro-economic stability. The work was still in progress but it was accepted that "capital flow management measures" did belong in the policy toolbox. Some Board members thought there should be a coherent framework for such measures—"rules of the road" as existed for international trade in goods—that could be included in the Fund's Articles of Agreement, but there was no consensus and further analysis was promised for 2012.

WORLD BANK (WB). The World Bank had generally been seen as a financial institution providing funds for infrastructure investment and other concrete projects in developing countries. Although such lending remained a core activity, the institution increasingly saw itself as a "think tank" supplying the public good of useful knowledge on development issues. In September, the Bank released the first comprehensive review of the large sums ($600 million in 2010) spent on research, macroeconomic analysis, and on technical assistance and training (*The State of World Bank Knowledge Services: Knowledge for Development*). The WB's President, Robert Zoellick, argued that in "this new world economy, good data and information will be at least as important as financial assistance". This "knowledge report" was henceforth to be an annual publication.

The 2011 edition of the Bank's flagship publication, the *World Development Report*, focused on the impact of violent conflict in undermining development prospects and noted that no low-income, conflict-affected state had yet achieved a single Millennium Development Goal. It drew lessons from a range of countries and, while suggesting a basket of policy options, warned against a single solution to all such problems. Fragile, post-conflict states often lacked external support for restoring domestic peace and creating jobs, in the absence of which violent crime tended to flourish. Delivering aid in such circumstances was highly problematic.

Discrimination against women was another brake on development in many low and medium income countries and in 2011 the Bank launched a three-year (2011-13) Road Map for Gender Mainstreaming to improve the opportunities for women. Gender equality and development was included as a special theme for IDA assistance (see below) and was the focus of the *2012 World Development Report* (released in September 2011).

Agriculture and food security remained a priority and the Bank's *Global Food Crisis Response Program* was extended in 2011 as food prices again approached the levels of 2008 when it was created. Apart from emergency assistance, investment in agriculture directly accounted for some 5 per cent of all IBRD lending in 2011 while much of the infrastructure programmes for transport, water supply and flood control also supported agricultural development. The Bank was also working within the G-20 policy process to strengthen food security.

Although earlier attempts to deal with allegations of fraud and corruption in WB programmes were controversial (AR 2007, p. 387), efforts to improve matters followed a report by an independent panel, led by Paul Volker, former Chairman of the US Federal Reserve (AR 2008, p. 393). In 2011 a report from the Independent

Evaluation Group, however, considered that the Bank's anti-corruption strategy had yet to show significant results, although it conceded that the task was difficult since it involved institutional change in borrowing countries. In June, the Bank's department of institutional integrity published its first global report on the vulnerability of the road-building sector to fraud and corruption. Based on the experience of both developed and developing countries, it made a number of suggestions on how to reduce such risks.

As with the IMF, the global financial and economic crisis led to a rapid expansion in WB lending in 2009 and 2010, but in 2011 there was a marked slowdown. At the end of the fiscal year (to June) total lending commitments by the IBRD and the IDA were $43 billion, down from $58.7 billion in 2010 but still well above the pre-crisis levels of some $24 billion a year in 2006-08. (For the component members of the World Bank Group see AR 2009, p. 411.) Loans and credits outstanding, however, were some 10 per cent up on 2010 and about 25 per cent above pre-crisis levels. The fall in new lending was all on the IBRD account: IDA concessional lending to the poorest countries, some 38 per cent of the total, rose by 12 per cent.

Just under one-quarter of all IBRD-IDA lending in 2011 went to South Asia, with another 22 per cent going to Latin America, 19 per cent to East Asia and the Pacific and 14 per cent to central and south-east Europe and the CIS. Africa's share of 14 per cent was almost entirely due to funds from IDA and, indeed, accounted for over two-fifths of all IDA lending. Nearly one half of all loans in 2011 were made to just three sectors: transport; water, sanitation and flood control; and energy and mining. Another 22 per cent went to strengthening institutional structures (public administration, law and justice etc.) and some 16 per cent to health and social services.

Although distributed across all regions of the globe, lending was nevertheless relatively concentrated on a handful of countries. Eight of them—China, Turkey, Mexico, India, Brazil, Indonesia, Colombia and Poland, in descending order of the WB's exposure—accounted for 62 per cent of the WB's outstanding loans in 2011, the individual positions ranging from some $13 billion in China and Turkey to $5.6 billion in Poland.

In April 2010 it was agreed that, given the financial crisis and the uncertain outlook, the lending capacity of the Bank should be strengthened (see AR 2011, p. 404). In March 2011, the Board of Governors approved an increase of $86.2 billion in the Bank's authorised capital, taking the total to $278.4 billion. (Not all of this would be available for lending to member countries: nearly two-thirds of it remained as "callable", i.e. available only if needed to meet the Bank's obligations on borrowed funds or guaranteed loans. There had never yet been a call on the Bank's callable capital.)

An important feature of the general capital increase was a selective component aimed at raising the capital subscriptions and, hence, the votes of the developing and transition countries. As a result, their voting strength increased from 44.06 per cent of the total to 47.19 per cent. (This was phase two of the voice reforms agreed in 2010.)

The IDA was financed by contributions from donor governments and transfers from the IBRD and the IFC. Every three years its funding was reviewed and 2011 marked the end of the 15th Replenishment which provided $43.7 billion for 2009-11. Funding for the 2010-14 triennium was agreed at SDR32.8 billion ($49.3 billion) which included contributions from 52 countries, as well as some debt forgiveness, credit reflows, and transfers from within the WB Group. The policy emphasis for the 16th IDA included gender issues and development, climate change, and the problems facing post-conflict countries.

WORLD TRADE ORGANISATION (WTO). The now traditional end-of-year promise by trade ministers and officials to bring the Doha Round of trade negotiations (DR) to a speedy and successful conclusion resembled a scene from the 1960s satirical show, *Beyond the Fringe*. Peter Cook invites his companions to a mountain top to witness the end of the world. They sit through the countdown to the predicted hour—nothing happens and Cook says: "Same time again next year chaps?"

In November 2010 the G-20 governments instructed the trade negotiators to conclude the Round in 2011 and the WTO's director-general, Pascal Lamy, promised an intensive effort for revised negotiating texts to be ready by the end of March 2011, so enabling the necessary trade-offs to be made in the following months. At the end of March, however, the differences between the member countries on a wide range of issues remained as large as ever and when the Trade Negotiations Committee met at the end of April to consider a 600 page report on the state of play it was clear there would be no conclusion in 2011.

Acknowledging the "unbridgeable gaps" between the developing countries and the advanced economies, Lamy nevertheless proposed concentrating on a subset of issues, mainly dealing with support for the trade of the least developed countries (LDCs), on which agreement might be reached in time to be presented to the 8th Ministerial Conference of the WTO in Geneva in December. But even this suggestion was effectively vetoed by the USA which insisted, as a matter of principle, that improving market access for LDC exports or eliminating cotton subsidies had to be accompanied by major contributions from all major players—i.e., that the major developing countries (China, Brazil, India and South Africa) should provide more market access for goods and services from the developed economies. The attempt to save a small part of the negotiations failed for much the same reasons that the Round as a whole was paralysed: namely, a fundamental clash of entrenched interests between North and South.

When the biennial ministerial conference met in December, the session devoted to the DR was very low key: not all the ministers bothered to attend and the outcome was little more than expressions of regret at the lack of progress and the ritual pledge to continue working towards a successful conclusion. A former US Trade Representative, Susan Schwab, declared (in *Foreign Affairs*, May/June 2011) that the Round was doomed and that world leaders should liberate themselves from its stranglehold. No government, however, was prepared to declare that the Round had failed for fear of being blamed for its failure. But neither was there a sense from the Conference of how to move forward, no "road map" that some negotiators had asked for, and no longer a promise to conclude "next year".

A number of explanations have been suggested for this stalemate. In 2007, Charlene Barshevsky, US Trade Representative 1997-2001, argued that the Round was launched as a hasty gesture of solidarity with the USA in the aftermath of the September 11 terrorist attacks, that no-one had been pressing for it and its description as a "development round" was largely window dressing. Indeed, a major complaint of the developing countries in 2011 was that the development dimension had largely disappeared from the negotiations. A number of critics argued that the agenda was ill-prepared, was far too large and that the mixture of proposals for regulation and for market opening made trade-offs more difficult. Some saw the single undertaking—"nothing is agreed until everything is agreed"—as a handicap, although developing countries were against abandoning it.

The deterioration in the global economy since 2008 had increased the domestic constraints on negotiators seeking more trade liberalisation at a time of high and rising unemployment in many countries. Changes in the structure of the world economy also increased the influence of the "emerging" market economies (EMEs) which, despite their own differences, frequently acted as an informal coalition in the negotiations and were no longer passive participants as had often been the case in previous trade rounds. The advanced economies, especially the USA, insisted that the big emerging economies were now sufficiently developed to accept parity of reciprocity in trade negotiations: the EMEs responded that in terms of income per head and other indicators they were still "developing" and that adopting a "level playing field" with the rich countries would be premature.

Another factor was that the benefits of the DR had been oversold from the start. Most of the quantitative estimates used to gather support for the Round had been shown to be fragile, resting on disputable initial assumptions, dubious models, and often on very uncertain or, in the case of services, missing data. The benefits in any case were small in relation to global trade and output and accrued mainly to the advanced economies.

The lack of consensus on how to revive the DR negotiations was amplified during the year by the developed countries proposing to add to the agenda what they called "21st century issues", such as competition policy, investment rules, energy security and climate change, while developing countries complained that little had been done on 20th century issues such as agricultural protectionism in the USA and the EU. The developed economies also wanted more "plurilateral" agreements, with the USA proposing one for services. Plurilaterals were essentially "coalitions of the willing" focused on single issues and which did not automatically extend market opening to non-joiners. They ran counter to the principles of multilateralism and "most favoured nation" treatment and, as such, were strongly opposed by most developing countries.

Whenever the DR negotiations had previously faltered or were suspended there had been immediate cries from G-7 governments and various pressure groups that the entire global trading system was at risk. This rhetoric began to give way in 2011 as the same voices emphasised that the WTO was bigger than the DR and stressed the importance of its work in areas such as dispute settlement, the monitoring of trade policies, and the creation of trade capacities in developing countries.

Despite the problems facing the WTO, countries still wanted to be inside rather than outside the organisation. In December, the ministerial council approved Russia's membership, after an 18-year process, as well as those of Samoa and Montenegro. Vanuatu's accession was approved by the WTO general council in October and, when ratified by its parliament, would raise the WTO's membership to 154.

ORGANISATION FOR ECONOMIC CO-OPERATION AND DEVELOPMENT (OECD). In 2011 the OECD celebrated its 50th anniversary. Having evolved from the Organisation for European Economic Co-operation (OEEC), which had been created in 1948 to administer the Marshall Plan for the post-war reconstruction of Europe, the OECD had begun life at the end of September 1961. Its aims were much the same as those of the OEEC: to promote "policies designed to achieve the highest sustainable economic growth and employment and a rising standard of living in member countries, while maintaining financial stability". A key principle inherited from OEEC was that these objectives would be best achieved by co-operation among countries in contrast to the destructive economic nationalism of the inter-war years.

Initially regarded as a body of more-or-less like-minded Europeans and their allies, the institution became more diverse in the 1990s. Following governance reforms in 2006—including qualified majority voting and changes in the basis for calculating membership dues—extending the membership was judged a priority in a world where the distribution of economic power was shifting away from Europe and North America towards the developing world. After a three-year negotiation process, Chile, Estonia, Israel and Slovenia joined in 2010. (Russia's candidature was still under discussion in 2011.) Alongside the start of those negotiations, the OECD also launched in 2007 its Enhanced Engagement Process, starting with five major "emerging economies"—Brazil, China, India, Indonesia and South Africa (EE5). The aim was to draw them into an ever closer relationship with OECD activities and philosophy, with a view to eventual membership.

Thus, 50 years on, the OECD was in the midst of a major effort to transform itself from a "rich-country club" into a more inclusive global organisation. But for the OECD to attract a significantly more global membership it would have to face the same demands for changes in governance as those addressed to the IMF and the World Bank, namely, an equal voice for emerging and developing countries. It would also need to show a greater understanding and acceptance of alternative approaches to supporting economic growth and macro-economic management. Until the 1970s OECD was generally associated with Keynesian ideas on economic policy, but from the early 1980s it became an important vector for propagating a neo-liberal, one-size-fits-all approach, downplaying the role of the state and promoting labour market "flexibility", privatisation, and public-private partnerships in infrastructure. In his report to ministers Secretary-General Angel

Gurria acknowledged the need to "challenge the conventional wisdom, including our own, and to revise our analytical frameworks" but he still spoke of "*the* economic growth model we should champion" (emphasis supplied), albeit taking into account "the impact on the environment, its redistributive capacity, and the international linkages".

In practice, much of OECD's work has focused on market failures, such as environmental degradation, inadequate investment in education and health, and labour market problems. In December it published an important report on growing inequality in OECD countries (*Divided We Stand: Why Inequality Keeps Rising*) which the secretary general said dispelled the claims of neo-liberal, "trickle down" theories that economic growth would automatically benefit the disadvantaged and that "without a comprehensive strategy for inclusive growth, inequality will continue to rise". Nevertheless, a perceptive analysis of OECD reforms—Judith Clifton and Daniel Diaz-Fuentes in *Global Policy* (October 2011)—concluded that without substantial reform and a more decisive shift from the habits of "unidirectional policy advice" it would face a decisive challenge: "the organisation needs the emerging economies, but do they need the OECD?"

Paul Rayment

OTHER WORLD ORGANISATIONS

THE COMMONWEALTH

DATE OF FOUNDATION: 1949 (London Declaration)   HEADQUARTERS: London, UK
OBJECTIVES: To maintain political, cultural and social links between (mainly English-speaking)
    countries of the former British Empire and others subscribing to Commonwealth democratic
    principles and aims
MEMBERSHIP (END-'11): Antigua & Barbuda, Australia, The Bahamas, Bangladesh, Barbados, Belize,
    Botswana, Brunei, Cameroon, Canada, Cyprus, Dominica, Fiji (suspended), the Gambia,
    Ghana, Grenada, Guyana, India, Jamaica, Kenya, Kiribati, Lesotho, Malawi, Malaysia,
    Maldives, Malta, Mauritius, Mozambique, Namibia, Nauru, New Zealand, Nigeria, Pakistan,
    Papua New Guinea, Rwanda, St Kitts & Nevis, St Lucia, St Vincent & the Grenadines, Samoa,
    Seychelles, Sierra Leone, Singapore, Solomon Islands, South Africa, Sri Lanka, Swaziland,
    Tanzania, Tonga, Trinidad & Tobago, Tuvalu, Uganda, UK, Vanuatu, Zambia (total 54)
SECRETARY GENERAL: Kamalesh Sharma (India) (since April '08)

A GENERAL feeling that the organisation was beginning to lose its relevance and sense of direction pervaded the Commonwealth as 2011 began, but by the end of the year, after the biennial Commonwealth Heads of Government Meeting (CHOGM) had been held in Perth, Australia (28-30 October), the mood had changed for the better. Nonetheless, the meeting itself, which was chaired by Australia's Prime Minister Julia Gillard, was a difficult one.

Controversy centred on the report of the 11-member Commonwealth Eminent Persons Group (EPG), which had been set up in 2009 with Tun Abdullah Ahmad Badawi, former prime minister of Malaysia, as chair. The Group had agreed that the report should be published several weeks before CHOGM to allow public debate on the proposals. Some heads of government wanted it published only as CHOGM met. Importantly, these included Kamla Persad-Bissessar, the prime minister of Trinidad, who was at that point still chairperson-in-office of the Commonwealth. Publication was delayed (although in the weeks between, it was widely leaked), with the result that many delegation officials at the table had still not read the report.

Mishandling internationally of the Commonwealth's public affairs (of which this was an example) was one of the matters highlighted in the EPG report. It said, "the Commonwealth needed a higher international profile together with greater credibility."

The report, published under the title *A Commonwealth of the People: Time for Urgent Reform*, was widely regarded as pointing the way ahead for the organisation but because of the earlier confusion only 30 of its 106 recommendations were adopted without reservation and 12 more if judged financially possible, while 43 others were referred to foreign ministers and 11 were rejected. One agreed recommendation was that a "Charter of the Commonwealth" should be drawn up. A draft for such a charter was published as an annex to the EPG report.

Most controversy centred round the EPG recommendation for the establishment of a commissioner for democracy, the rule of law and human rights. It was decided that the secretary general and the long-standing Commonwealth Ministerial Action Group (CMAG) of foreign ministers should evaluate the options for a commissioner. Governments had always been slow to take stronger action on human rights and no real advances had been made since CMAG had been set up at the Auckland CHOGM meeting in 1995, which had created a rules-based Commonwealth (see AR 1995, pp. 381-82). For some years CMAG had been considered too weak, and the so-called "good offices role" of the secretary-general—since 2008, Kamalesh Sharma of India—was slow in producing better discipline that would render member countries like the Gambia more democratic. The EPG said that the secretary general should speak out more. "Silence," its report said, "should not be an option." This failure of the Commonwealth to speak out when its values were violated, the report added, "is seen as a decay that has set into the body of the organisation and one that will occasion the association's irrelevance—if not its actual demise—unless it is promptly addressed." CMAG had been asked to recommend ways in which the organisation could be strengthened "to deal with the full range of serious or persistent violations of Commonwealth values". It duly reported to CHOGM and the Perth communiqué said that the leaders had agreed to its recommendations, but these were not published before 2011 ended.

Another controversy in Perth concerned Sri Lanka. As the meeting neared, the prospect of the 2013 CHOGM being held in Sri Lanka, as planned, worried some countries. Disturbing UN reports about atrocities at the end of the civil war there in 2009 (see pp. 305-06) led Canada's Prime Minister Stephen Harper to threaten not to attend in 2013, but it was decided that the plans should stand. Mauritius had already been lined up to host the 2015 summit.

In Perth, heads of government re-elected Kamalesh Sharma for a second four-year term as Commonwealth secretary general. He was unopposed, although the

EPG report had suggested that he should be more outspoken publicly. The report was also critical of the structures and operations of the secretariat which needed "a higher international profile with greater credibility". It also needed to recruit higher calibre staff, but the report did not say how this was to be done on its current tiny budget, one-quarter that of the charity, Oxfam. In 1995 the secretariat staff had numbered 420; by 2011 this had fallen below 300.

Derek Ingram

INTERNATIONAL ORGANISATION OF FRANCOPHONIE

DATE OF FOUNDATION: 1997   HEADQUARTERS: Paris, France
OBJECTIVES: To promote co-operation and exchange between countries wholly or partly French-speaking and to defend usage of the French language
MEMBERSHIP (END-'11): Albania, Andorra, Armenia, Belgium, Benin, Bulgaria, Burkina Faso, Burundi, Cambodia, Cameroon, Canada, New Brunswick (Canada), Québec (Canada), Cape Verde, Central African Republic, Chad, Comoros, Congo, Côte d'Ivoire, Croatia, Cyprus, Dominican Republic, DRC, Egypt, Equatorial Guinea, France, French-speaking community of Belgium, Gabon, Georgia, Greece, Guinea, Guinea-Bissau, Haiti, Laos, Lebanon, Luxembourg, Madagascar, Mali, Mauritania, Mauritius, Moldova, Monaco, Morocco, Niger, Romania, Rwanda, St Lucia, São Tomé & Príncipe, Senegal, Seychelles, Switzerland, Togo, Tunisia, UAE, Vanuatu, Vietnam (total 56)
OBSERVER MEMBERS: Austria, Bosnia & Herzegovina, Czech Republic, Djibouti, Dominica, Estonia, Ghana, Hungary, Latvia, Lithuania, Macedonia, Monetenegro, Mozambique, Poland, Serbia, Slovakia, Slovenia, Thailand, Ukraine (total 19)
SECRETARY GENERAL: Abdou Diouf (Senegal) (since Jan '03)

IN years like 2011 when there was no summit (every second year), the Organisation International de la Francophonie (OIF) seldom received much global attention. It continued, however, to engage in routine activities that formed an essential part of the life of the organisation. Apart from the ritual celebration of its International Day on 20 March, in 2011 there was substance in the annual meetings of the two principal institutions.

December saw the 19th meeting of francophone ministers, attended by representatives of a record 75 countries (56 full members and nineteen observers). They reviewed implementation of decisions taken at the last summit, at Montreux, Switzerland, in 2010, including an impending reduction of resources by an expected 20 per cent due to the global financial crisis. These had already been reduced from €89 million to €81 million, from 2009 to 2010. Pressing political and economic issues, notably in the Arab world and Africa, were also discussed.

July had seen the OIF's Permanent Council meeting in Paris in its 81st session, at which representatives of francophone heads of government discussed major issues. This meeting examined at length the "Arab spring", especially as two of the most influential member states in North Africa, Tunisia and Egypt, had experienced dramatic changes of leadership.

Another prominent Arab OIF member, Morocco, had hosted a regional parliamentary meeting in Rabat in May, at which the issue was also discussed. The Association of Francophone Parliamentarians, set up before La Francophonie itself in 1967, worked closely with the OIF, holding an assembly once a year, as well as regional assemblies. The 2011 assembly, in July, was held in Kinshasa in the Democratic Republic of Congo. This was, on paper, one of the largest of the countries described as French-speaking, but the number of actual French-speakers in the DRC was far smaller. The parliamentarians' session was seen as a prelude to the next OIF summit, due to take place in Kinshasa in 2013.

Abdou Diouf, the secretary general, his prestige reinforced with a third four-year mandate, which had been agreed at the 2010 Montreux summit (see AR 2011, p. 411), could be seen taking up more decisive political positions. At the July meeting of the Permanent Council he noted particularly that, "strong in its experience of assisting transition processes, Francophonie has been engaged in Tunisia, in reinforcing the capacity of electoral structures; in the training of forces in charge of electoral security, and of the media and national observers; and in the administration and treatment of electoral disputes." He was also very supportive of the political change in Côte d'Ivoire, which had brought to power President Alassane Ouattara (see pp. 246-47). The OIF had supported consolidation of the rule of law there, as well as national reconciliation.

Aware of the need to play a role in the global economic crisis, the OIF convened a meeting of francophone bankers in Paris early in the year, and in October France's President Nicolas Sarkozy invited both Abdou Diouf and Commonwealth Secretary General Kamalesh Sharma for a discussion in Paris prior to the G-20 summit in Cannes (which Sarkozy chaired). They told the French president of the problems that weighed on poor and vulnerable countries, saying that apart from traditional financial support, the rich countries should also provide resources for adapting to climate change, ensuring food security, and improving infrastructure, health and education. They observed that 90 per cent of the world's GDP was represented at the G-20 table, but 90 per cent of the world's population was not invited.

Kaye Whiteman

NON-ALIGNED MOVEMENT AND DEVELOPING COUNTRIES

Non-Aligned Movement (NAM)

DATE OF FOUNDATION: 1961   HEADQUARTERS: rotating with chair
OBJECTIVES: Originally to promote decolonisation and to avoid domination by either the Western
industrialised world or the Communist bloc; since the early 1970s to provide a authoritative
forum to set the political and economic priorities of developing countries; in addition, since the
end of the Cold War, to resist domination of the UN system by the USA
MEMBERSHIP (END-'11): Afghanistan, Algeria, Angola, Antigua & Barbuda, Azerbaijan, Bahamas,
Bahrain, Bangladesh, Barbados, Belarus, Belize, Benin, Bhutan, Bolivia, Botswana, Brunei,
Burkina Faso, Burma (Myanmar), Burundi, Cambodia, Cameroon, Cape Verde, Central African
Republic, Chad, Chile, Colombia, Comoros, Congo, Côte d'Ivoire, Cuba, Democratic Republic
of Congo, Djibouti, Dominica, Dominican Republic, East Timor, Ecuador, Egypt, Equatorial
Guinea, Eritrea, Ethiopia, Fiji, Gabon, the Gambia, Ghana, Grenada, Guatemala, Guinea,
Guinea-Bissau, Guyana, Haiti, Honduras, India, Indonesia, Iran, Iraq, Jamaica, Jordan, Kenya,
Kuwait, Laos, Lebanon, Lesotho, Liberia, Libya, Madagascar, Malawi, Malaysia, Maldives,
Mali, Mauritania, Mauritius, Mongolia, Morocco, Mozambique, Namibia, Nepal, Nicaragua,
Niger, Nigeria, North Korea, Oman, Pakistan, Palestine, Panama, Papua New Guinea, Peru,
Philippines, Qatar, Rwanda, St Kitts & Nevis, St Lucia, St Vincent & the Grenadines, São
Tomé and Príncipe, Saudi Arabia, Senegal, Seychelles, Sierra Leone, Singapore, Somalia,
South Africa, Sri Lanka, Sudan, Suriname, Swaziland, Syria, Tanzania, Thailand, Togo,
Trinidad & Tobago, Tunisia, Turkmenistan, Uganda, United Arab Emirates, Uzbekistan,
Vanuatu, Venezuela, Vietnam, Yemen, Zambia, Zimbabwe (total 120)
CHAIRMAN: acting President of Egypt Mohamed Hussein Tantawi (since Feb '11)

Group of 77 (G-77)

DATE OF FOUNDATION: 1964   HEADQUARTERS: UN centres
OBJECTIVES: To act as an international lobbying group for the concerns of developing countries
MEMBERSHIP (END-'11): Afghanistan, Algeria, Angola, Antigua & Barbuda, Argentina, Bahamas,
Bahrain, Bangladesh, Barbados, Belize, Benin, Bhutan, Bolivia, Bosnia & Herzegovina,
Botswana, Brazil, Brunei, Burkina Faso, Burma (Myanmar), Burundi, Cambodia, Cameroon,
Cape Verde, Central African Republic, Chad, Chile, Colombia, Comoros, Congo, Costa Rica,
Côte d'Ivoire, Cuba, Democratic Republic of Congo, Djibouti, Dominica, Dominican
Republic, Ecuador, East Timor, Egypt, El Salvador, Equatorial Guinea, Eritrea, Ethiopia,
Federated States of Micronesia, Fiji, Gabon, the Gambia, Ghana, Grenada, Guatemala, Guinea,
Guinea-Bissau, Guyana, Haiti, Honduras, India, Indonesia, Iran, Iraq, Jamaica, Jordan, Kenya,
Kuwait, Laos, Lebanon, Lesotho, Liberia, Libya, Madagascar, Malawi, Malaysia, Maldives,
Mali, Marshall Islands, Mauritania, Mauritius, Mongolia, Morocco, Mozambique, Namibia,
Nauru, Nepal, Nicaragua, Niger, Nigeria, North Korea, Oman, Pakistan, Palestine, Panama,
Papua New Guinea, Paraguay, Peru, Philippines, Qatar, Rwanda, St Kitts & Nevis, St Lucia,
St Vincent & the Grenadines, Samoa, São Tomé and Príncipe, Saudi Arabia, Senegal,
Seychelles, Sierra Leone, Singapore, Solomon Islands, Somalia, South Africa, Sri Lanka,
Sudan, Suriname, Swaziland, Syria, Tajikistan, Tanzania, Thailand, Togo, Tonga, Trinidad &
Tobago, Tunisia, Turkmenistan, Uganda, United Arab Emirates, Uruguay, Vanuatu, Venezuela,
Vietnam, Yemen, Zambia, Zimbabwe (total 131)
CHAIRMAN: Argentina (2011); Algeria (2012)

THE regular triennial conference of foreign ministers of the Non-Aligned Movement took place in Bali, Indonesia, on 23-27 May 2011. Events were held during
the year in Bali, Belgrade and New York to commemorate the 50th anniversary of
the first NAM summit in September 1961 (see AR 1961, pp. 136-37). The Group
of 77 held their 35th annual ministerial meeting at the UN on 23 September 2011.
   In general, the NAM were silent on the "Arab Spring". However, at the Bali conference they did take the unusual step of making negative comments about the
internal politics of a member country. They expressed "deep concern" about the

situation in Libya, calling for "a complete end to violence and all attacks against, and abuses of, civilians".

The Palestinians were in a much stronger political position than in previous years. They had recently re-established unity with the signing by all Palestinian political factions of a reconciliation agreement in Cairo on 4 May (see p. 181; and Documents). In addition, due to a campaign launched in August 2009, there had been an expansion of the number of countries recognising the Palestinian Authority as a state. At Bali, in a special "Declaration on Palestine", the Non-Aligned endorsed the goal of the admission of Palestine as a member of the United Nations "as soon as possible". Nevertheless, on 31 October, when UNESCO decided to admit Palestine, only 81 of the 119 NAM members voted in favour (see Documents).

Anti-colonialism continued as a current issue on the agenda of the Non-Aligned, albeit for small territories. The Bali conference objected to the British decision to suspend the constitution of the Turks & Caicos Islands and to postpone elections there (see p. 155). In addition, after Mayotte had changed its status on 31 March to that of a French Overseas Department (see p. 310), the NAM ministers insisted the island remained under the sovereignty of Comoros. Argentina was able to exploit its position as chair of the G-77 to gain their endorsement of a call for the UK to "resume negotiations ... to find ... a peaceful solution to the sovereignty dispute" relating to the "Malvinas [Falkland] Islands".

The developing countries were pleased that the theme chosen for the UN General Assembly's 65th Session was reinstating the Assembly "at the centre of global governance". While larger developing countries had been incorporated into the G-20 global economic policy forum, smaller countries felt excluded. Both the NAM and the G-77 ministerial meetings affirmed the role of the UN in global economic governance, because it was the "only global body with universal membership and unquestioned legitimacy". The Non-Aligned also had a range of more specific proposals. They pressed for better staffing and more office space to strengthen the role of the President of the Assembly. They argued for the Assembly to have greater authority over the UN Secretariat, especially on budgetary questions, on "the development of concepts, policies and strategies" for peacekeeping operations, and on the election of the secretary general. On the review of the first five years' work of the UN Human Rights Council, the approach was very different. The NAM did not want a strengthened Council. They defended the weak processes for considering each country's human rights record under the Universal Periodic Review and objected to the Assembly adopting its own country-specific resolutions. They rejected discussion of "issues related to the reform of the Council such as its composition, geographical distribution of its membership, and membership criteria".

The Group of 77 in New York focused on denying the prevailing optimism in the media that the worst of the global financial crisis was over. While growth had been resilient in some developing countries, the majority still faced "numerous shared and common problems". They were worried that the continuing crisis, in its "second wave", would result in past commitments on development and climate change not being met. Indeed, in order to "bridge the gap between policy-making and implementation of commitments", the G-77 proposed the establishment within the UN of a Financing for Development Commission. Similarly, both the NAM and the G-77 rejected moves to reduce payments from developed countries to the UN's budget by increasing developing country contributions.

In 2011, the G-77 showed significantly greater concern than previously about the multiple threats presented to developing countries by climate change. Even some of the major oil producers were disturbed by the increased impact of sand storms in the Middle East. There was more concern for loss of marine biodiversity and the G-77 called for the creation of a legal regime to cover conservation and sustainable use of biodiversity in the high seas, beyond national jurisdictions.

In September 2010, an offer by Libya to host a third South Summit had been accepted, but in mid-2011 the summit was officially postponed. Problems over the third summit and domestic political upheavals in Egypt, the NAM chair, reduced the number of South-South initiatives in 2010-11. Nevertheless, the Consortium on Science, Technology and Innovation for the South (COSTIS) was launched by the G-77, in order to pool expertise on science-based economic development. A meeting of the NAM ministers of health did go ahead in May on the margins of the World Health Assembly and a South-South Development Expo focusing on food security was held in Rome in December. However, a Ministerial Meeting on the Advancement of Women, due to be held in Qatar in November, was postponed until February 2012.

The number of countries in the NAM increased in 2011 from 118 to 120 (including Palestine) when Azerbaijan and Fiji (see AR 2011, p. 414) were admitted as full members in Bali. At the September annual meeting of the Group of 77, Nauru joined the Group, increasing its size to 131 members, excluding China. At the end of 2011, Argentina handed the chairmanship of the G-77 to Algeria for 2012.

Peter Willetts

EUROPEAN ORGANISATIONS

THE EUROPEAN UNION

DATE OF FOUNDATION: 1952   HEADQUARTERS: Brussels, Belgium
OBJECTIVES: To promote peace, its values and the well-being of its peoples
MEMBERSHIP (END-'11): Austria, Belgium, Bulgaria, Cyprus, Czech Republic, Denmark, Estonia,
    Finland, France, Germany, Greece, Hungary, Ireland, Italy, Latvia, Lithuania, Luxembourg,
    Malta, Netherlands, Poland, Portugal, Romania, Slovakia, Slovenia, Spain, Sweden, United
    Kingdom (total 27)
PRESIDENT OF EUROPEAN COMMISSION: José Manuel Durao Barroso (Portugal) (since Nov '04)

THE year was dominated by the EU's attempts to shore up the euro and prevent the economic and financial crisis from spreading and fatally undermining the single currency. EU leaders met on a record number of occasions to tackle the economic challenges. There were five formal European Council meetings, one extraordinary and one informal summit and four meetings of the heads of state or government of the eurozone. Each reaffirmed the Union's unwavering commitment to the euro and took measures to try to reassure financial markets of the currency's long-term health and viability. Invariably, the lull lasted just a few days before market pressure again began to batter countries such as Greece, Portugal, Spain and Italy perceived as weak links in the single currency chain, raising their cost of borrowing and prompting credit rating agencies to talk of potential downgrades.

However, by the end of the year the EU appeared to be turning a corner. The prospects for the euro appeared brighter as a second rescue package was being assembled for Greece, technocratic governments took office in Greece and Italy, and agreement was reached on a new fiscal treaty with the prospect of sanctions for governments which broke single currency rules. While emphasis was on budgetary consolidation and debt reduction to restore public finances and confidence in financial markets, with Greece in the forefront, there was also growing emphasis as the year progressed on policies to promote economic growth.

The EU responded to the "Arab Spring" and the seismic events in North Africa by overhauling its southern Mediterranean policy. It also prepared for major changes in its internal policies and tabled proposals to cover all EU expenditure between 2014 and 2020. There were also changes of government in seven countries: Ireland, Finland, Portugal, Denmark, Greece, Italy and Belgium.

ECONOMIC GOVERNANCE. The EU spent all year trying to bolster credibility in the euro. The first attempt came on 24 March with the formal adoption of the Euro+ Pact, whose contents had been agreed some two weeks earlier as a way to strengthen the economic pillar of monetary union. This committed the 17 euro members and six other member states (Bulgaria, Denmark, Latvia, Lithuania, Poland and Romania) to closer economic co-ordination. By endorsing the pact, the signatories committed themselves to take all necessary measures to foster competitiveness and employment, contribute further to the sustainability of public finances and to reinforce financial stability. Each country promised to agree a package of concrete actions that it would implement in the following 12 months to meet those objectives. The heads of state or government of the participating countries were to monitor the progress made towards these objectives.

The EU used two other main vehicles to improve economic governance: a package of six pieces of new legislation, dubbed "the six pack" and, at the end of the year, under pressure from Germany, a new intergovernmental treaty, known as the Fiscal Compact. The former had been proposed by the Commission in 2010. It aimed to strengthen the Stability and Growth Pact underpinning the single currency and budgetary frameworks generally, and to prevent and correct macroeconomic imbalances. It was eventually adopted by EU governments and the European Parliament in November and came into force on 13 December. The package included stricter surveillance of national budgets, greater attention to debt reduction, minimum requirements for national budgetary frameworks, a scoreboard of indicators to identify imbalances earlier and the possibility of financial sanctions on governments which failed to honour the commitments they had made. The package made it easier than under the Stability and Growth Pact arrangements for fines to be imposed on a country breaking the new rules, since a Commission proposal to this effect would be adopted unless a qualified majority of member states opposed it. This reverse qualified majority procedure represented a victory for the European Parliament, which won the trial of strength with EU governments that had initially opposed it since they felt it gave the Commission, which had the right to propose sanctions, too much power.

On 23 November the Commission tabled two further proposals to strengthen surveillance in the euro area and enhance the coordination and surveillance of budgetary processes for all member states using the single currency. The first would require the countries to present their draft budgets at the same time each year to the Commission, which would be able to ask for the draft to be revised if it was considered to be in contravention of the Stability and Growth Pact. The second would give the Commission the power to decide whether enhanced surveillance should be applied to a member state experiencing severe difficulties.

To emphasise publicly the importance which economic governance and defence of the euro occupied on the EU agenda, the Economic Affairs Commissioner Olli Rehn was promoted to the post of a Commission vice-president in October with specific responsibility for the euro and given a wider role in coordinating, monitoring and enforcing economic governance in the euro area.

Shortly before Christmas, on 9 December, the European Council, under pressure from Germany, agreed to strengthen further economic union through a fiscal compact among euro area member states which enshrined fiscal rules and an automatic correction mechanism within their national legal systems. The groundwork had been prepared by European Council President Herman Van Rompuy, Commission President José Manuel Barroso and Eurogroup President Jean-Claude Juncker—all three of whom had been given a mandate by EU leaders in October to come up with ideas to strengthen economic governance. The initiative led to a major rift between the UK and its EU partners. British Prime Minister David Cameron refused to sign up to the compact since he feared that it would have a detrimental impact on financial services and the City of London in particular. His opposition prompted "Britain isolated" headlines as most other non-eurozone countries signalled their readiness to participate, subject to approval by their national parliaments. (In the end, when the fiscal compact, by now rechristened the Treaty on Stability, Coordination and Governance in the Economic and Monetary Union, was formally signed on 2 March 2012, the only countries not to endorse it were the UK and the Czech Republic.)

To many observers the fiscal compact was unnecessary since most of what it set out to achieve could have been managed through the "six pack" and the EU's existing treaties. However, it was important for the German government to demonstrate that other member states now had a firm commitment to put their finances in order. The whole incident also confirmed the EU's ability to compromise. Despite the clear tensions at the December summit meeting, the UK was invited to participate as an observer in the drafting of the short treaty. In addition, the treaty, while legally an intergovernmental text outside the EU's ambit (since only 25 of the 27 member states signed up to it), was to be brought into the EU institutional framework within five years and the European Commission, as the official guardian of the EU's spirit and mores, was to have a central role in its application from the very outset.

The year also saw the launch of the first European semester—a new six month cycle beginning in January to coordinate member states' macroeconomic, budgetary and structural policies. This was designed to ensure that all policies were analysed and assessed together and that areas—such as macroeconomic imbalances and the financial sector—which were previously not covered by economic surveillance were included, in order to strengthen the EU dimension of national budgetary and economic policy by requiring national capitals to submit their policy plans in these areas for assessment by the European Commission. The exercise ended in June when EU governments adopted a series of specific recommendations for each country, which their governments were expected to implement in their national policies and budgets. These focused on macroeconomic stability, structural reforms and labour markets, and ranged from moves to reduce over-indebtedness of private households to facilitating access to finance and increasing the retirement age. The Commission started preparations for the 2012 semester exercise even earlier by issuing its 2012 annual growth survey in November 2011, setting out the budgetary policies and structural reforms it considered as priorities.

On 23 November the European Commission published a Green Paper on stability bonds—an idea which, had first been aired almost 20 years earlier, in the form of euro bonds, but which had resurfaced as the EU tackled the challenges of joint issuance of debt in the euro area. Supporters saw such bonds as a long-term response to the sovereign debt crisis, while critics feared that they could reduce pressure for fiscal discipline and might encourage moral hazard.

By the end of the year the various moves to strengthen economic governance were beginning to calm the financial markets and restore confidence in the euro. These had also been helped by the arrival of technocratic-led governments in Greece and Italy with new reform programmes. But, arguably, more important in the immediate term was the decision by the new European Central Bank president,

Mario Draghi, who took office in November, to allow longer-term refinancing operations (LTRO) the following month. The first involved €489 billion and was a turning point for the eurozone as it provided 523 banks with cheap, unlimited three-year loans. Not only did this increase liquidity, but many used the finance to buy government bonds, thereby helping to reduce the cost of government borrowing in countries such as Italy and Spain.

Ironically, the unprecedented pressure on the euro throughout 2011 came just as the single currency was preparing to celebrate—on 1 January 2012—the 10th anniversary of the introduction of euro notes and coins. These were now used by over 330 million people. On 1 January 2011 Estonia had replaced its national currency (the kroon) with the euro, making it the 17th EU member of the euro area. An agreement between the EU and Andorra in the middle of the year confirmed the principality's right to use the euro as its official currency and issue its own euro coins.

CREATING FIREWALLS AND TACKLING SOVEREIGN DEBT. Efforts were made during the year to strengthen the two temporary bailout funds established in 2010: the European Financial Stability Facility (EFSF) with €440 billion in guarantees from the euro countries; and the European Financial Stabilisation Mechanism (EFSM), which was based on guarantees from the EU budget of up to €60 billion. The funds were designed to strengthen the overall credibility of the euro and to help individual single currency countries that were in financial difficulty and under severe market pressure.

In July, EU leaders agreed to increase the EFSF's flexibility by lowering lending rates in an effort to better address the debt sustainability of countries receiving loans from the fund and by increasing maturities. Further powers came in October. These allowed the Fund to enter into precautionary programmes, provide loans to recapitalise financial institutions and intervene in primary and secondary markets. The EFSF and EFSM were to be replaced on 1 July 2012—a year earlier than originally intended—by a permanent financial crisis resolution fund, the European Stability Mechanism, which was to carry out the same tasks. This was to have an effective lending capacity of €500 billion, a total subscribed capital of €700 billion, of which €80 billion would be in the form of paid-in capital and €620 billion in committed callable capital from the euro member countries. Before access to financial assistance from the ESM was granted, the Commission, IMF and European Central Bank would conduct a thorough analysis of a country's public debt sustainability. The green light to create the permanent mechanism came on 15 January when the European Commission gave a favourable opinion to change the relevant article (Art 136) in the Lisbon Treaty. The new ESM Treaty was signed by the 17 euro finance ministers on 11 July.

Various calls were made on the crisis resolution mechanisms during the year. After receiving a €110 billion assistance programme in 2010 from EU member states and the IMF, Greece returned to Brussels for a second loan. In October, EU leaders agreed on a new EU-IMF financial assistance programme of up to €100 billion. This included a higher voluntary private sector contribution, compared with an arrangement which they had agreed earlier on 21 July. Under the new terms, private investors would contribute through a voluntary bond exchange with a nominal discount of 50 per cent on their holdings of Greek debt. Eurozone member states would contribute up to €30 billion for the debt rescheduling. It was made clear that this was an exceptional, one-off measure and would not apply to private bond holders in other situations. The overall aim was to lower Greece's debt ratio from around 160 per cent of GDP in 2011 to 120 per cent by 2020.

However, no sooner had the terms been laboriously agreed than the Greek prime minister, George Papandreou, surprised his EU colleagues by announcing that he intended to put the terms of the loan—which had attracted strong opposition in Greece—to a referendum. With hindsight, this was probably more of a political ploy to emphasise the gravity of the country's situation to its bickering politicians. If so, it worked, as Lucas Papademos, a former vice-president at the European Central Bank, succeeded Papandreou as head of a cross-party government charged with implementing the structural reforms and austerity measures attached to the second loan (see pp. 64-65). However, by the end of the year the final terms of the package still had to be agreed as EU member states, especially Germany, placed pressure on Greece to give binding commitments to deliver its side of the bargain and negotiations with private bond holders continued.

In September, the Commission created a task force of senior EU officials to provide Greece with technical assistance to deliver the EU/IMF adjustment package and to help it make better use of EU funding. It provided quarterly reports to the Greek government and the European Commission.

Ireland, which had negotiated an EU and IMF assistance package of €85 billion over three years in November 2010, received €12.6 billion during 2011 from the two temporary bailout funds. In May, Portugal agreed its own economic adjustment programme with the Commission and the IMF for €78 billion over three years with €33.23 disbursed in 2011. The EFSM and the EFSF would each provide up to €26 billion, while the IMF was to provide the remaining €26 billion (see p. 59).

FINANCIAL REGULATION AND TAXATION. The EU continued to put in place new regulations to reduce the risk of a repetition of the financial crisis, to improve consumer protection and restore confidence in the industry. On 1 January, shortly after the European Systemic Risk Board came into being to monitor the entire financial security system and provide early warning of systemic-wide risks, three new European supervisory authorities began operating: the European Banking Authority, European Securities and Markets Authority and European Insurance and Occupational Pensions Authority. They were considered the cornerstone of the EU's financial reforms and worked together with national supervisors to develop harmonised rules and ensure their strict and coherent implementation. In emergencies, such as turbulent market conditions, they had extensive powers.

Importance was also paid to the recapitalisation of banks. In July, the first stress tests on 90 banks in 21 EU countries were carried out by the European Banking Authority. After crisis-related losses by European banks between 2007 and 2010 that were estimated as totalling €1,000 billion—equivalent to 8 per cent of the EU's GDP—the Commission tabled proposals in the same month to raise the capital requirements of the 8,000 banks that operated within the Union. This would require them to hold more and better quality capital and liquid assets and to avoid excessive lending. It was estimated that the banks would have to find extra capital of up to some €460 billion.

Legislation was approved on alternative investment fund managers and short selling and credit default swaps. Overall, the European Commission tabled 25 legislative proposals during 2011 on financial services regulation. These included measures to make financial markets more transparent; to tackle market abuse with criminal sanctions for insider dealing and market manipulation; to tighten controls on credit rating agencies; and to revise statutory audit requirements in order to introduce more competition in a market dominated by four multinational auditors.

In September, the Commission presented a proposal for a financial transaction tax—a controversial move favoured by France and Germany, but strongly opposed by the UK and many other countries. The tax would be levied on all transactions between financial institutions when at least one party was based in the EU. The Commission estimated the tax would raise €57 billion a year. The rationale behind the initiative was that the financial sector, which was at least partly responsible for the crisis, should make a contribution to resolving it. Ten member states already had some form of financial transaction tax.

The Commission proposed legislation to create a common set of rules to calculate the corporate tax base for companies operating in the EU's single market. Currently, 27 separate systems applied. This would be optional, but was designed to make life easier for companies since they would only need to file a single consolidated return to one tax administration for all their EU activities. Given national sensitivities towards tax and the fact that any EU legislation had to be agreed unanimously, it was far from clear that the proposals would be approved in their original form by all 27 member states. However, it was possible that a smaller group of countries might go ahead with either or both initiatives under the EU's enhanced cooperation arrangements.

ECONOMIC AGENDA. The EU continued to develop its economic agenda for the rest of the decade, known as the Europe 2020 strategy. This contained five main targets: 75 per cent of the population between 20 and 64 should be employed; 3 per cent of the EU's GDP should be invested in research and development; the EU should reduce its greenhouse emissions by at least 20 per cent compared with 1990 levels; the share of early school leavers should be under 10 per cent with at least 40 per cent of the younger generation having a higher education degree or diploma; and 20 million fewer people should be at risk of poverty or social exclusion. The Europe 2020 strategy contained seven flagship initiatives: youth on the move, agenda for new skills and jobs, platform against poverty and social exclusion, innovation union, digital agenda, industrial policy for the globalisation era and resource efficiency. During the year, more detailed proposals were tabled to achieve these objectives.

On 13 April the Commission presented the Single Market Act to breathe new life into a policy considered to bring benefits to businesses, employees and the general public. This identified a dozen measures to be approved by the end of 2012. They covered revision of existing legislation on energy taxation, European standards, public procurement, mutual recognition of professional qualifications, electronic signatures, and on employees posted from one member state to another. It also included legislation on a single EU patent, energy infrastructure, alternative dispute resolution and access to venture capital across Europe. The remaining initiatives covered measures to support entrepreneurship, stimulate funding for social businesses and simplification of accounting standards rules.

On 29 June 2011, the European Commission presented its forward looking expenditure proposals for all EU policies until the end of the decade, known as the multiannual financial framework (MFF) for 2014-20. The overall amount for the seven-year period was €1,025 billion—a €49 billion increase on the current MFF which ran from 2007 to the end of 2013. The priorities included boosting jobs and growth, investing in Europe's regions, talents and skills, making Europe safer for citizens and increasing Europe's influence in the world. The Commission argued that the proposals respected the general need to reduce public expenditure, represented only 1.05 per cent of the Union's gross national income, and were calibrated to add value to specific policy areas. Many member states immediately criticised them, however, and they were likely to be pared back by EU governments during negotiations throughout 2012.

In November, the Commission's economic forecasts demonstrated the challenges ahead in reviving the economy. They painted a picture of GDP growth in 2012 of just 0.5 per cent and 1.5 per cent in 2013. Unemployment was predicted to remain at around 9.5 per cent, while inflation would return to below 2 per cent.

ENLARGEMENT. Accession negotiations with Croatia were closed on 30 June 2011, just under six years after they began in October 2005. The European Commission gave its positive opinion in October, the European Parliament its assent on 1 December and the treaty was signed on 9 December (see p. 100). Providing this was ratified in all 27 EU member states, Croatia was set to become the 28th EU member on 1 July 2013, 10 years after the country applied to join. In the interim, Croatia was to participate in the proceedings of the European Parliament, the Council and its preparatory bodies as an active observer. The Commission was to monitor developments in the country to ensure that it met all its membership commitments and could comply with its EU responsibilities from the first day of accession.

Iceland was the next in line to join the EU. By the end of the year 11 of the 35 negotiating chapters had been opened and eight provisionally closed. Although Iceland already applied much EU legislation—being a member of the European Economic Area—sensitive negotiations remained in many areas, notably fisheries, the environment, financial services, taxation and financial controls.

Turkey's hopes of joining the EU remained stalled. No new negotiating chapters were opened during the year and EU foreign ministers in December noted that

Turkey had still not made progress towards the necessary normalisation of its relations with the Republic of Cyprus. The deadlock was unlikely to be broken, particularly as Cyprus would hold the rotating six-month EU presidency in the second half of 2012 and Turkey had indicated it would freeze its relations with the EU presidency during that period.

By contrast, it was likely that Montenegro would be able to open accession negotiations in June 2012 after the EU agreed that it was in a position to take on its membership obligations in most policy areas in the medium-term. So, too, it was decided by the European Council in December, should the former Yugoslav Republic of Macedonia. Albania, however, still had some way to go before it could receive candidate status—a necessary step on the road to opening membership negotiations. Bosnia & Herzegovina was required to make even more progress, including amending its constitution to conform to the European Convention on Human Rights. In October, the European Commission recommended granting candidate status to Serbia, but while certain member states—including France—favoured this, Germany insisted that Serbia first had to normalise its relationship with Kosovo (see pp. 94-95). In December, the European Council agreed that, subject to certain conditions being met, this status could be granted in March 2012. Kosovo also progressed on its journey towards a closer relationship with the EU, particularly with the prospect of a trade agreement.

RELATIONS WITH THE WIDER WORLD. On 1 January, the EU's European External Action Service (EEAS), the new diplomatic service created by the Lisbon Treaty, formally came into being. This involved integrating EU officials from the European Commission and the Council of Ministers and recruiting national diplomats from the 27 EU member states. Getting the service up and running under one roof was a considerable logistical challenge and some EU officials were unhappy when senior posts went to national diplomats. By the end of 2011 the new service had just over 3,600 employees, of whom 1,550 worked in Brussels and the remaining 2,060 in 140 EU delegations around the world. The two most recent delegations to be opened were in South Sudan and Libya. The annual EEAS budget of €464 million was divided between €184 million on its Brussels headquarters and €280 million for its delegations.

The biggest challenge to the fledgling service was the "Arab Spring", which forced the EU to reassess its relations with its southern partners. In early March, the EEAS issued a communication—"A Partnership for Democracy and Shared Prosperity with the Southern Mediterranean"—following popular uprisings and the transition to democracy in several countries in North Africa and the Middle East. This set out three priority areas: governance, employment and youth, and pledged EU support of a further €1 billion between 2011 and 2013 in addition to the €3.5 million already allocated to the southern Mediterranean countries. It was followed in May by a second communication—"A new response to a changing Neighbourhood"—which overhauled EU strategy towards the 16 countries on its southern and eastern borders. This emphasised the importance of human rights, democracy and the rule of law and confirmed that the EU would differentiate its relations with neighbouring countries according to their aspirations, needs and capacities. Those that wished to, and were able to do so, would enjoy closer economic integration and political cooperation with the EU, possibly leading to their involvement in the EU's single market. The EU also allocated €22 million (2011-13) to helping the development of civil society; €66 million (2011-15) to encourage student and academic exchanges; and €350 million (2011-12) to assist the countries with their transition to democracy.

As the "Arab Spring" unfolded and some member states participated in NATO military action, the EU provided humanitarian and civil protection help to the area with €60 million allocated to Libya and neighbouring countries, €10 million to help Chadian migrants return home, and some €10.5 million to civil protection. The EU also gave its support for elections in Tunisia, Morocco and Egypt, condemned violence against peaceful demonstrations in Bahrain, Yemen and Syria, and applied economic sanctions against Syria and the Kadhafi regime in Libya. These included trade embargos, asset freezes and visa bans. An international task force, representing the EU, third countries and international financial institutions, was created to ensure the coherence of the support from different sources to countries in transition in the Southern Mediterranean. The EU opened a representative office in Tripoli, Libya, in September and upgraded this to full delegation status on 12 November. In December, it approved a €10 million support package to develop public sector capacity building, education and support for civil society.

During the year the Union gave special attention to strengthening alliances with strategic partners such as the USA, Russia, China and India. The bilateral EU-US summit in Washington, DC, on 28 November agreed to establish a joint high-level working group on jobs and growth to develop further the transatlantic economic relationship and report back by June 2012.

The EU was also active providing humanitarian aid after natural or man-made disasters. It continued its support for the reconstruction effort in Haiti after the 2010 earthquake and provided financial and practical assistance to Japan after the 11 March earthquake, tsunami and nuclear accident. Apart from its involvement in North Africa, it also sent resources to specific crisis zones such as the Horn of Africa, Sudan, the Middle East and Sahel.

Since early 2010, the EU had sought to consolidate its relations with the UN, following the entry into force of the Lisbon Treaty. On 3 May, the UN General Assembly adopted Resolution 65/276 on the participation of the EU's representatives (the president of the European Council, the Foreign Policy High Representative, the European Commission and EU delegations) in the General Assembly, its committees, working groups and international UN meetings and conferences. On 22 September, for the first time, the president of the European Council, Herman Van Rompuy, addressed the UN General Assembly.

TRADE. The EU-South Korea free trade agreement (FTA)—the biggest EU trade arrangement with an Asian country—came into force on 1 July 2011. The Commission estimated that it would create some €19 billion of new export opportunities for EU companies and could double bilateral trade in the medium- to long-term.

During the year, against the backdrop of the stalled multilateral WTO Doha Round trade talks, the EU continued negotiations on bilateral trade agreements with India, Canada, MERCOSUR, Singapore and Malaysia. Progress was made on the EU-India FTA with the latter agreeing to improve market access for EU firms in the banking, consulting and legal sectors. After postponing several times the original spring 2011 target date for concluding negotiations, however, that objective was moved into 2012. In October the EU and Russia resolved the final bilateral issues, notably on car production and agricultural, foodstuffs and wood exports, that had been standing in the way of Russia's joining the WTO.

In December EU foreign ministers gave the Commission approval to open trade negotiations with Egypt, Jordan, Morocco and Tunisia on deep and comprehensive free trade areas (DCFTAs). These went further than simply removing tariffs, for they encompassed all regulatory issues relevant to trade such as investment protection, public procurement, technical barriers and competition policy. In the same month, the EU decided to launch DCFTAs with Georgia and Moldova. At the end of December the EU and Ukraine completed the technical negotiations of the DCFTA that would form part of the future association agreement. In the same month the EU and its member states agreed to sign the anti-counterfeiting trade agreement negotiated a month earlier by the EU, USA, Japan and several developed countries to strengthen enforcement of intellectual property rights.

During the year, the Commission also proposed changes to its preferential trading system with developing countries to help their integration into the global trading system. The reform focused on countries most in need and encouraged respect for human and labour rights and environmental and good governance standards.

CITIZENS' INITIATIVE. Early in 2011, legislation establishing a Citizens' Initiative was adopted to give the public the possibility of direct participation in the EU policy-making process for the first time. Introduced by the Lisbon Treaty, the innovation stated that from April 2012, if citizens and other groups could muster at least one million signatures and satisfy other conditions, they could call on the European Commission to propose specific legislation on issues where the EU had responsibility.

Rory Watson

OSCE AND COUNCIL OF EUROPE

Organisation for Security and Co-operation in Europe (OSCE)
DATE OF FOUNDATION: 1975   HEADQUARTERS: Vienna, Austria
OBJECTIVES: To promote security and co-operation among member states, particularly in respect of
the resolution of internal and external conflicts
MEMBERSHIP (END-'11): Albania, Andorra, Armenia, Austria, Azerbaijan, Belarus, Belgium, Bosnia &
Herzegovina, Bulgaria, Canada, Croatia, Cyprus, Czech Republic, Denmark, Estonia, Finland,
France, Georgia, Germany, Greece, Holy See (Vatican), Hungary, Iceland, Ireland, Italy,
Kazakhstan, Kyrgyzstan, Latvia, Liechtenstein, Lithuania, Luxembourg, Macedonia, Malta,
Moldova, Monaco, Montenegro, Netherlands, Norway, Poland, Portugal, Romania, Russia, San
Marino, Serbia, Slovakia, Slovenia, Spain, Sweden, Switzerland, Tajikistan, Turkey,
Turkmenistan, Ukraine, UK, USA, Uzbekistan (total 56)
SECRETARY GENERAL: Lamberto Zannier (Italy) (since July '11)

Council of Europe
DATE OF FOUNDATION: 1949   HEADQUARTERS: Strasbourg, France
OBJECTIVES: To strengthen pluralist democracy, the rule of law and the maintenance of human rights
in Europe and to further political, social and cultural co-operation between member states
MEMBERSHIP (END-'11): Albania, Andorra, Armenia, Austria, Azerbaijan, Belgium, Bosnia &
Herzegovina, Bulgaria, Croatia, Cyprus, Czech Republic, Denmark, Estonia, Finland, France,
Georgia, Germany, Greece, Hungary, Iceland, Ireland, Italy, Latvia, Liechtenstein, Lithuania,
Luxembourg, Macedonia, Malta, Moldova, Monaco, Montenegro, Netherlands, Norway,
Poland, Portugal, Romania, Russia, San Marino, Serbia, Slovakia, Slovenia, Spain, Sweden,
Switzerland, Turkey, Ukraine, UK (total 47)
SECRETARY GENERAL: Thorbjørn Jagland (Norway) (since Oct '09)

AT the turn of the year the presidency of the **Organisation for Security and
Co-operation in Europe (OSCE)** passed from Kazakhstan, a serial violator of
OSCE values, to Lithuania, which proved a safer pair of hands. Much of the
OSCE's work was necessarily conducted away from the public gaze, notably
the Minsk Group's work towards a peaceful settlement of the Nagorno-
Karabakh dispute, talks on the Transdniester issue in Moldova, and the promoting of reconciliation in southern Kyrgyzstan. The need for privacy was
much less evident at the annual Ministerial Council, held in Vilnius in December. This endorsed uncontentious declarations on human trafficking, equal
opportunities in the economy, conflict prevention, and illegal circulation of
small arms, light weapons and ammunition. However, the meeting failed to
reach consensus on a wide range of issues, including the protection of journalists and freedom in the digital age, sponsored by a group of Western countries.
The OSCE Parliamentary Assembly's human rights committee pressed for
Council meetings to be held in public so that it would be clear which countries
were blocking change.
   The OSCE Office for Democratic Institutions and Human Rights (ODIHR)
observed 17 national elections. While invariably giving credit where it was due, its
reports invariably also found some scope for improvement. Sometimes, as with
Finland and Cyprus, it raised only mild suggestions. Other reports raised more
substantial issues within a generally satisfactory assessment, as with Latvia and
Estonia, where minorities were unable to exercise full democratic rights; or Albania, which had created a thorough technical foundation for democratic elections

but still needed improvements to the quality of the process. Some countries raised much graver concerns. In Azerbaijan, "certain conditions necessary for a meaningful competitive election were lacking"—notably an effective registration process, freedom of assembly and expression. The report also found media coverage to be unbalanced, a disparity in access to resources and misuse of administrative resources. In Kazakhstan, so recently presiding over the OSCE, the absence of opposition candidates and of "a vibrant political discourse" resulted in a "noncompetitive environment" in which "democratic elections have still to materialise". In Kyrgyzstan observers found ballot stuffing and vote buying.

Belarus had ordered closure of the OSCE's Minsk office after a critical report on its presidential election in December 2010. In January, the OSCE imposed a travel ban on the Belarus president and 160 officials over the harassing of reporters. The director of ODIHR issued a highly critical report on the lack of due process in the trial of people, including five presidential candidates, allegedly involved in demonstrations following the announcement of the election result. Belarus complained of hypocrisy and double standards, while Russia called the OSCE action "counterproductive". That country would shortly be receiving an adverse report on its own legislative election.

As always, the **Council of Europe** addressed an eclectic range of issues including online child abuse, microwave radiation from mobile devices, alleged organ trafficking in Kosovo, the plight of rural women, media freedom in Turkey, denial of service attacks on the Internet, pressure on Internet sites used by human rights activists and whistleblowers, "black sites" used by the CIA for rendition, and alleged violations of the human rights of Roma by France, Romania and Bulgaria. It also voiced concern at political trials in Ukraine. Such concerns were even greater over Belarus, with its unashamed retention of the death penalty, electoral malpractices, harassing and imprisonment of journalists and political opponents. The political affairs committee of the Parliamentary Assembly of the Council of Europe (PACE) found that the authorities in Belarus were "deliberately turning their backs on Europe".

There was a heightened awareness of the need for the Council and its associated bodies to change. The speed with which matters passed between the Assembly and the Council was a relic of more leisurely times. The limit for the Council to respond to initiatives from the Assembly was cut from nine months to six. The Council would now have biennial programmes and budgets; staffing would be reduced and resources redeployed to priority areas of human rights. The UK, assuming the presidency in November, declared reform of the European Court of Human Rights to be its first priority, including tackling the Court's immense backlog of cases and improving the recruitment and training of judges, notoriously of worryingly variable calibre. There was also a need to tighten up execution of the Court's judgments.

Martin Harrison

AMERICAN, ARAB, AFRICAN, EURASIAN, AND ASIA-PACIFIC ORGANISATIONS

AMERICAN AND CARIBBEAN ORGANISATIONS

Organisation of American States (OAS)

DATE OF FOUNDATION: 1951   HEADQUARTERS: Washington DC, USA
OBJECTIVES: To facilitate political, economic and other co-operation between member states and to defend their territorial integrity and independence
MEMBERSHIP (END-'11): Antigua & Barbuda, Argentina, Bahamas, Barbados, Belize, Bolivia, Brazil, Canada, Chile, Colombia, Costa Rica, Cuba, Dominica, Dominican Republic, Ecuador, El Salvador, Grenada, Guatemala, Guyana, Haiti, Honduras, Jamaica, Mexico, Nicaragua, Panama, Paraguay, Peru, St Kitts & Nevis, St Lucia, St Vincent & the Grenadines, Suriname, Trinidad & Tobago, USA, Uruguay, Venezuela (total 35)
SECRETARY GENERAL: José Miguel Insulza (Chile) (since May '05)

Union of South American Nations (UNASUR)

DATE OF FOUNDATION: 2008   HEADQUARTERS: Quito, Ecuador
OBJECTIVES: To improve political and economic integration in the region, and defence co-operation
MEMBERSHIP (END-'11): Argentina, Bolivia, Brazil, Chile, Colombia, Ecuador, Guyana, Paraguay, Peru, Suriname, Uruguay, Venezuela (total 12)
OBSERVER MEMBERS: Mexico, Panama
SECRETARY GENERAL: Maria Emma Mejia Velez (Colombia) (since May '11)

Southern Cone Common Market (MERCOSUR)

DATE OF FOUNDATION: 1991   HEADQUARTERS: Montevideo, Uruguay
OBJECTIVES: To build a genuine common market between member states
MEMBERSHIP (END-'11): Argentina, Brazil, Paraguay, Uruguay (total 4; Venezuela's membership is awaiting formal ratification)
ASSOCIATE MEMBERS: Bolivia, Chile, Colombia, Ecuador, Peru
PRESIDENCY: Argentina

Organisation of Eastern Caribbean States (OECS)

DATE OF FOUNDATION: 1981   HEADQUARTERS: Castries, St Lucia
OBJECTIVES: To co-ordinate the external, defence, trade and monetary policies of member states
MEMBERSHIP (END-'11): Anguilla (associate), Antigua & Barbuda, British Virgin Islands (associate), Dominica, Grenada, Montserrat, St Lucia, St Kitts & Nevis, St Vincent & the Grenadines (total 9)
DIRECTOR GENERAL: Len Ishmael (St Lucia) (since May '03)

Caribbean Community (CARICOM)

DATE OF FOUNDATION: 1973   HEADQUARTERS: Georgetown, Guyana
OBJECTIVES: To facilitate economic, political and other co-operation between member states and to operate certain regional services
MEMBERSHIP (END-'11): Antigua & Barbuda, Bahamas, Barbados, Belize, Dominica, Grenada, Guyana, Haiti, Jamaica, Montserrat, St Kitts & Nevis, St Lucia, St Vincent & the Grenadines, Suriname, Trinidad & Tobago (total 15)
ASSOCIATE MEMBERS: Anguilla, Bermuda, British Virgin Islands, Cayman Islands, Turk & Caicos Islands
DIRECTOR GENERAL: Irwin LaRocque (Dominica) (since Aug '11)

IN early December a new regional organisation, the **Community of Latin American and Caribbean States (CELAC)**, held its first summit meeting. Its host,

Venezuelan President Hugo Chávez Frías, claimed that CELAC would fulfil Simon Bolivar's dream of regional integration, weaken US influence, and replace the **Organisation of American States (OAS)** as the key body for the hemisphere. Chávez said, "the OAS is old, a space that was manipulated, dominated by the US, while CELAC is born with a new spirit of political, economic and social integration". He described CELAC as a "historic and transcendental agreement". However, the rhetoric appeared to surpass the reality. CELAC included all 33 countries of Latin America and the Caribbean, but key members—Brazil, Mexico, Argentina, Chile and Colombia—indicated they were not eager for the new grouping to replace the OAS. Furthermore, CELAC was created without a permanent institutional structure, agreed budget, or headquarters. Rather, it had a nominal leadership committee composed of a pro tempore chairman, and the hosts of the previous summit and the subsequent one. Venezuela also tried to persuade the other members to accept majority voting on CELAC resolutions, but this was resisted so all resolutions were non-binding. It was felt by some countries that the **Union of South American Nations** (UNASUR), established in 2008, would, with its more defined structure and set of responsibilities, be more important than CELAC in the long run.

A long running trade dispute within the **North American Free Trade Agreement** (NAFTA) was resolved in July. The US government signed a deal with Mexico that allowed Mexican trucks and their drivers to deliver goods across the USA. The US had originally agreed to liberalise the trucking market in 1995, but US trade unions fearful of the competition lobbied Congress and the move was blocked. This was a significant restriction because 70 per cent of the $400 billion trade between the two countries was delivered by lorry. In response to the US decision, the Mexican government removed its retaliatory tariffs that amounted to $2.3 billion a year. The Mexican government said that the agreement would reduce Mexican exporters' transport costs by 15 per cent.

While trade tensions reduced in NAFTA, they increased in the **Southern Cone Common Market** (MERCOSUR). In February Argentina placed quotas on a dozen imported goods, including automobiles, consumer electronics and textiles. This was necessary, according to Industry Minister Debora Giorgi, to protect local industry "from unfair competition from South-East Asia and China". However, Argentina's MERCOSUR partners were also affected by the quotas, and the new restrictions came after a period of increasing trade protectionism by Argentina. Indeed, a study by an Argentine consultancy, Acebeb, found that 23.9 per cent of Brazilian goods entering Argentina were subject to import barriers, a far higher amount than the 2010 figure of 13.5 per cent. In response Brazil imposed non-tariff barriers on imports of cars, car parts and tyres. Although the measure was applicable to all countries it was seen as a retaliatory measure against Argentina, which sent over 80 per cent of its car exports to Brazil. Giorgi criticised the Brazilian decision as "tempestuous" and complained that it would affect 50 per cent of bilateral trade. But Rubens Barbosa, president of the foreign trade council at São Paulo's Confederation of Industries, stated "Brazil took a measure already adopted by Argentina years ago. Mercosur no longer exists from a commercial point of view." Underlying these tensions was the fact that Brazil had a large trade surplus with Argentina: $4.09 billion in 2010, up from $1.5 billion in 2009.

In the Caribbean the **Organisation of Eastern Caribbean States** (OECS) introduced full freedom of movement for its citizens from 1 August. This allowed OECS citizens to enter any of the six independent countries of the organisation and stay for an indefinite period. The development followed an agreement on Economic Union which came into force in January. The progress towards substantive regional integration in the OECS compared very favourably to the still halting pace of integration in the **Caribbean Community** (CARICOM). The "implementation deficit" was not helped by a leadership vacuum in CARICOM. Former Secretary General Edwin Carrington retired in December 2010 and it was not until late July that his successor was appointed: Irwin LaRocque from Dominica.

In September, Trinidad & Tobago hosted the third China-Caribbean Economic and Trade Co-operation Forum. At the meeting the Chinese pledged $2 billion in financial assistance, along with the conclusion of several bilateral agreements. The level of co-operation between the two parties was significant. In 2010 the value of trade amounted to $7.2 billion, while Chinese investments totalled $400 million in sectors such as bauxite, agriculture, and infrastructure. However, there was concern on the part of CARICOM over the significant imbalance in trade relations, with 95 per cent of trade flows being imports from China.

Peter Clegg

ARAB ORGANISATIONS

League of Arab States (Arab League)

DATE OF FOUNDATION: 1945   HEADQUARTERS: Cairo, Egypt
OBJECTIVES: To co-ordinate political, economic, social and cultural co-operation between member states and to mediate in disputes between them
MEMBERSHIP (END-'11): Algeria, Bahrain, Comoros, Djibouti, Egypt, Iraq, Jordan, Kuwait, Lebanon, Libya, Mauritania, Morocco, Oman, Palestine, Qatar, Saudi Arabia, Somalia, Sudan, Syria (suspended), Tunisia, United Arab Emirates, Yemen (total 22)
SECRETARY GENERAL: Nabil al-Araby (Egypt) (since May '11)

Gulf Co-operation Council (GCC)

DATE OF FOUNDATION: 1981   HEADQUARTERS: Riyadh, Saudi Arabia
OBJECTIVES: To promote co-operation between member states in all fields with a view to achieving unity
MEMBERSHIP (END-'11): Bahrain, Kuwait, Oman, Qatar, Saudi Arabia, United Arab Emirates (total 6)
SECRETARY GENERAL: Abdullatif bin Rashid al-Zayani (Bahrain) (since April '11)

FOR decades the **Arab League** was regarded as a self-serving club of Arab autocrats and dictators, but the "Arab Spring" of 2011 redrew the diplomatic map of the Middle East and forced the organisation to adopt a new vibrant and dynamic role in the region. The League's secretary general, Amr Mohammed Moussa, told an Arab economic summit in Egypt in mid-January that the recent toppling of President Zine el-Abidine Ben Ali of Tunisia (see p. 218) was linked to deteriorating economic conditions throughout the Arab world, warning that the people's anger had reached unprecedented heights. "The Tunisian revolution is not far from us," Moussa warned. "The Arab citizen has entered an unprecedented state of anger and frustration."

In late February the League suspended Libya from its proceedings after hundreds of people had been killed at the start of an uprising against Colonel Moamar Kadhafi. The League gave its full support for the anti-Kadhafi rebellion on 12 March when it voted, with only Algeria and Syria dissenting, for the establishment of a no-fly zone over Libya and also recognised the opposition National Transitional Council (NTC). The move led directly, five days later, to the adoption by the UN Security Council of Resolution 1973 (see Documents) which provided for NATO intervention in Libya, with active military participation by Arab League members Qatar and the United Arab Emirates (UAE). Without the Arab League vote, the NATO intervention would not have been possible and Kadhafi might not have met his ignominious end at the hands of rebel forces in October (see p. 217).

In an almost equally dramatic step, in mid-November the League suspended Syria's membership in response to the government's brutal response to months of street protests demanding the dismantling of the regime of President Bashar al-Assad. The move meant that one of the standard-bearers of Arab nationalism, the Syrian Arab Republic, was excluded from the organisation created in 1945 to "draw closer the relations between member states and co-ordinate their political activities with the aim of realising a close collaboration between them". The League's bold decision to challenge Assad was not driven by the traditional Arab leader, Egypt, but by tiny Qatar, with the support of neighbouring Saudi Arabia.

In late August the League had issued its first condemnation of Syrian government repression of nationwide uprisings, calling for an immediate end to the violence. Shaikh Hamad Bin Jassem Bin Jabr al-Thani, the prime minister and foreign minister of Qatar, drew up an Arab League peace plan aimed at launching a dialogue between Assad and the opposition. Assad accepted the plan in early November, but he was wary of Thani's insistence that the League be allowed to send monitors into Syria. The League repeatedly extended deadlines for Syria to formally abide by the terms of the plan, but it eventually suspended Syria's membership on 16 November (see Documents) and on 27 November imposed wide-ranging and unprecedented sanctions. Qatar's hard-line approach forced Assad to reassess and in late December Arab League monitors were allowed into Syria, which by this stage appeared to be on the verge of full-scale civil war (see p. 193).

The turmoil sweeping the Middle East meant that the Arab League failed to meet in formal session during the year. In early May it was announced that the League's 23rd regular summit meeting scheduled to be held in Baghdad, the Iraqi capital, had been postponed until 2012 at the request of the Iraqi government. The League's 22nd regular summit meeting had been held in the Libyan city of Sirte— Kadhafi's place of birth and death—in March 2010 (see AR 2011, p. 429). Also in May, Egyptian Nabil al-Araby was unanimously elected as the League's new secretary general, replacing another Egyptian, Moussa, who had held the post since 2001 (see AR 2001, p. 453).

The 32nd summit of the **Gulf Co-operation Council** (GCC) took place in Riyadh, the Saudi capital, on 19-20 December. The summit was attended by new GCC secretary general Abdullatif bin Rashid al-Zayani (Bahrain), who had taken office on 1 April in succession to Abdulrahman al-Attiyah (Qatar). The summit approved an initiative put forward by King Abdullah ibn Abdul Aziz of Saudi Arabia for the Council to "move beyond the stage of co-operation to the stage of union so that the GCC countries form a single entity to achieve good and repel evil".

The summit was attended by the king of Bahrain, Sheikh Hamad bin Isa al-Khalifa, who in March had responded to street protests by the majority Shia Muslim population by requesting the deployment of detachments of the GCC's Peninsula Shield Force to guard key facilities in his kingdom. Accordingly, some 1,500 troops and police officers from Saudi Arabia and the UAE were deployed in Bahrain—home of the USA's Fifth Fleet—for a three-month period to protect strategic facilities (see pp. 204-05).

Darren Sagar

AFRICAN ORGANISATIONS AND MEETINGS

African Union (AU)

DATE OF FOUNDATION: 2002 HEADQUARTERS: Addis Ababa, Ethiopia
OBJECTIVES: To promote the unity, solidarity and co-operation of African states, to defend their sovereignty, to promote democratic principles, human rights and sustainable development and to accelerate the political and socio-economic integration of the continent
MEMBERSHIP (END-'11): Algeria, Angola, Benin, Botswana, Burkina Faso, Burundi, Cameroon, Cape Verde, Central African Republic, Chad, Comoros, Congo, Côte d'Ivoire, Democratic Republic of Congo, Djibouti, Egypt, Equatorial Guinea, Eritrea, Ethiopia, Gabon, the Gambia, Ghana, Guinea, Guinea-Bissau, Kenya, Lesotho, Liberia, Libya, Madagascar (suspended), Malawi, Mali, Mauritania, Mauritius, Mozambique, Namibia, Niger, Nigeria, Rwanda, São Tomé and Príncipe, Senegal, Seychelles, Sierra Leone, Somalia, South Africa, South Sudan, Sudan, Swaziland, Tanzania, Togo, Tunisia, Uganda, Western Sahara, Zambia, Zimbabwe (total 54)
CHAIR OF AU COMISSION: Jean Ping (Gabon) (since Feb '08)

Southern African Development Community (SADC)

DATE OF FOUNDATION: 1992 HEADQUARTERS: Gaborone, Botswana
OBJECTIVES: To work towards the creation of a regional common market
MEMBERSHIP (END-'11): Angola, Botswana, Democratic Republic of Congo, Lesotho, Madagascar, Malawi, Mauritius, Mozambique, Namibia, Seychelles, South Africa, Swaziland, Tanzania, Zambia, Zimbabwe (total 15)
EXECUTIVE SECRETARY: Tomaz Augusto Salomão (Mozambique) (since Sept '05)

Economic Community of West African States (ECOWAS)

DATE OF FOUNDATION: 1975 HEADQUARTERS: Abuja, Nigeria
OBJECTIVES: To seek the creation of an economic union of member states
MEMBERSHIP (END-'11): Benin, Burkina Faso, Cape Verde, Côte d'Ivoire, the Gambia, Ghana, Guinea, Guinea-Bissau, Liberia, Mali, Niger, Nigeria, Senegal, Sierra Leone, Togo (total 15)
PRESIDENT OF THE COMMISSION: James Gbeho (Ghana) (since March '10); Kadré Désiré Ouedraogo (Burkina Faso) (from March '12)

East African Community (EAC)

DATE OF FOUNDATION: 2000   HEADQUARTERS: Arusha, Tanzania
OBJECTIVES: To widen and deepen economic, political, social and culture integration in order to
   improve the quality of life of the people of East Africa through increased competitiveness,
   value added production, trade and investments
MEMBERSHIP (END-'11): Burundi, Kenya, Rwanda, Tanzania, Uganda (total 5)
SECRETARY GENERAL:: Richard Sezibera (Rwanda) (since April '11)

Common Market for Eastern and Southern Africa (COMESA)

DATE OF FOUNDATION: 1994   HEADQUARTERS: Lusaka, Zambia
OBJECTIVES: To co-operate in developing its members' natural and human resources for the good of
   all their people
MEMBERSHIP (END-'11): Burundi, Comoros, Democratic Republic of Congo, Djibouti, Egypt, Eritrea,
   Ethiopia, Kenya, Libya, Madagascar, Malawi, Mauritius, Rwanda, Seychelles, Sudan,
   Swaziland, Uganda, Zambia, Zimbabwe (total 19)
SECRETARY GENERAL:: Sindiso Ndema Ngwenya (Zimbabwe) (since May '08)

THE annual **African Union** (AU) heads of state meeting in Addis Ababa, Ethiopia, in January confirmed as the new AU president the president of Equatorial Guinea, Teodoro Obiang Nguema Mbasogo, despite his poor human rights record. He had a luxurious new venue built, allegedly at a cost of $830 million, for the 17th AU summit that was held outside Malabo, the capital of Equatorial Guinea, in late June (see p. 253). The theme of the Malabo summit was "Accelerating Youth Empowerment for Sustainable Development"; however, the "hot" issue was Libya. Though the three African countries serving as non-permanent members of the UN Security Council (Nigeria, South Africa and Gabon) had voted in favour of Security Council Resolution 1973 in March, there was much unhappiness in the AU with the way in which NATO had ignored the AU's Libyan roadmap and sought to remove Colonel Moamar Kadhafi from power. The AU's proposed standby force was nowhere near ready for action, however; there were divisions within the AU; and the organisation failed to communicate effectively what it wished to happen in Libya. At Malabo the AU leaders proposed that ceasefire talks be held in Addis Ababa between the Libyan government and Libyan rebels, but nothing came of this, and once again the AU was marginalised.

The fall of Kadhafi increased concerns, long expressed in the AU, about its funding, for many countries failed to pay their annual dues and Kadhafi had helped bankroll the organisation. The **Southern African Development Community** (SADC) put forward Nkosanana Dlamini-Zuma of South Africa as its candidate for the post of chair of the AU Commission, and she stood against the incumbent, Jean Ping of Gabon. The South African government argued that her election would help rejuvenate the AU, but neither candidate emerged a clear winner at the 18th summit in January 2012. As it prepared to assume the presidency of the UN Security Council in January 2012, South Africa also focused attention on the issue of the relationship between the UN and the AU. This was the subject of an AU report recommending better co-ordination and clearer modalities on how the two could work together.

In the first months of the year the **Economic Community of West African States** (ECOWAS) failed in its efforts to resolve the crisis in Côte d'Ivoire. Some in the AU blamed the UN mission there for supporting the French military involvement that eventually ended Laurent Gbagbo's attempt to cling on to power (see pp. 246-47). By the end of November he was at the International Criminal Court (ICC) at the Hague.

Many Africans continued to claim that the ICC was biased against Africa, and President Omar al-Bashir of Sudan brushed aside the warrant for his arrest issued by the ICC in 2009 and travelled to a number of African countries. The joint AU-UN hybrid mission in Darfur (UNAMID) continued to try to keep the peace there, and its life was extended. Though the AU's high level implementation Panel on Sudan, led by former President Thabo Mbeki of South Africa, helped to pave the way for the independence of South Sudan in early July (see pp. 208-10), many issues arising out of the 2005 Comprehensive Peace Agreement continued to threaten peace between Sudan and South Sudan and the Panel continued its engagement with the two countries on these.

The AU enhanced its work in Somalia, where its peacekeeping mission (AMISOM) and the forces of the Transitional Federal Government forced the withdrawal of al-Shabaab from Mogadishu (see p. 229). Among other issues before the AU's Peace and Security Council during the year were piracy in both the Indian Ocean and the Gulf of Guinea, and the terrorism that spread in the Sahel region, leading to increased activity in that area by the United States Africa Command (AFRICOM).

Though the Pan African Parliament met again in Midrand in South Africa, no progress was made in defining its future role, and plans to build a permanent building for it were put on hold.

At a tripartite summit held in South Africa in June, SADC, the **East African Community** (EAC) and the **Common Market for Eastern and Southern Africa** (COMESA) agreed to negotiate a free trade agreement that would embrace the three sub-regional organisations, constituting half the African continent. SADC summits held in Livingstone, Zambia, in March, in Sandton, South Africa, in June, and in Luanda, Angola, in August discussed the crises in Zimbabwe and Madagascar, but made no real progress on either. ECOWAS held a number of summits in Abuja, Nigeria, but at its October meeting the heads of state were unable to reach agreement on who should take over as the new president of the ECOWAS Commission.

In short, 2011 was not a good year either for the AU or for its sub-regional organisations, though at the end of the year it seemed that the efforts being made to revive the five-nation **Arab Maghreb Union** (comprising Algeria, Libya, Mauritania, Morocco and Tunisia), in the aftermath of the so-called "Arab Spring" in North Africa, might bear fruit in 2012.

Christopher Saunders

EURASIAN ORGANISATIONS

Shanghai Co-operation Organisation (SCO)

DATE OF FOUNDATION: 2001   HEADQUARTERS: Beijing, China
OBJECTIVES: To strengthen mutual trust and good-neighbourly relations among member states
MEMBERSHIP (END-'11): China, Kazakhstan, Kyrgyzstan, Russia, Tajikistan, Uzbekistan (total 6)
OBSERVER MEMBERS: India, Iran, Pakistan, Mongolia
SECRETARY GENERAL: Muratbek Imanaliyev (Kyrgyzstan) (since Jan '10)

Eurasian Economic Community (EurAsEC)

DATE OF FOUNDATION: 2000   HEADQUARTERS: Moscow, Russia
OBJECTIVES: To form a customs union and common market in the former Soviet space
MEMBERSHIP (END-'11): Belarus, Kazakhstan, Kyrgyzstan, Russia, Tajikistan, Uzbekistan (total 6)
SECRETARY GENERAL: Tair Mansurov (Kazakhstan) (since Oct '07)

Commonwealth of Independent States (CIS)

DATE OF FOUNDATION: 1991   HEADQUARTERS: Minsk, Belarus
OBJECTIVES: To facilitate economic and humanitarian integration between member states
MEMBERSHIP (END-'11): Armenia, Azerbaijan, Belarus, Kazakhstan, Kyrgyzstan, Moldova, Russia, Tajikistan, Turkmenistan, Uzbekistan, Ukraine (total 11)
EXECUTIVE SECRETARY: Sergei Lebedev (Russia) (since Oct '07)

Collective Security Treaty Organisation (CSTO)

DATE OF FOUNDATION: 2002   HEADQUARTERS: Moscow, Russia
OBJECTIVES: To further co-operation and develop joint structures in security, defence and intelligence
MEMBERSHIP (END-'11): Armenia, Belarus, Kazakhstan, Kyrgyzstan, Russia, Tajikistan, Uzbekistan (total 7)
SECRETARY GENERAL: Gen. Nikolai Bordyuzha (Russia) (since April '03)

THE **Shanghai Co-operation Organisation** (SCO) held its 10th anniversary summit in Astana, Kazakhstan on 15 June. In addition to heads of state of the six full members, the meeting was attended by high-ranking delegations from observer states and affiliated organisations such as the Eurasian Economic Community (EurAsEC). The guest of honour was Afghan President Hamid Karzai. Reports at the conference covered SCO activities in such fields as culture, environmental protection, science, technology, innovation, healthcare, tourism and sport. A key concern was the need to strengthen economic integration, thereby minimising the negative effects of the global crisis on SCO banking and financial sectors. Improving security co-operation to fight terrorism, drug trafficking, cyber-crime and other threats was also high on the agenda. Procedures for accepting new members were formally approved; this was welcomed by Iran and Pakistan, both of which hoped to acquire full membership. One result of the SCO's activities was the growth in trade turnover between China and other SCO members, from $12 billion in 2001 to $84 billion in 2011. In September heads of energy agencies in SCO member states discussed ways in which to speed up the creation of an SCO energy club. The SCO Regional Anti-Terrorist Structure (RATS) implemented its programme of co-operation 2010-12, which was aimed at combating terrorism, separatism and extremism.

The **Eurasian Economic Community** (EurAsEC) became a two-tier organisation when the customs union (CU) was launched in 2010 (see AR 2011, p. 435), encompassing Belarus, Kazakhstan and Russia, but postponing the accession of Tajikistan and Kyrgyzstan (and possibly others) to an unspecified later date. The division became sharper on 1 July 2011, when Kazakhstan, Russia, and Belarus abolished their internal customs borders. All customs procedures were now shifted to the common outer border of the CU, except for control over migration. On 18 November, the leaders of Kazakhstan, Russia, and Belarus signed an agreement to establish the Eurasian Economic Commission, a supranational body to manage integration into a new EU-style Eurasian Economic Union, to be established by 2015. The idea of such a union was first raised by Kazakh President Nursultan Nazarbayev in 1994 and consistently advocated by Kazakhstan thereafter. Some experts saw these developments as positive and predicted substantial GDP growth within the CU, but others were more sceptical, regarding it as an obstacle to growth. There were also concerns as to how moves towards integration would affect trade with the SCO bloc.

The 20th anniversary jubilee summit of the **Commonwealth of Independent States** (CIS) was held in Dushanbe, Tajikistan, in September. One of the aims of the meeting was to formulate a comprehensive development strategy for the next decade. However, members failed to agree a draft accord on the creation of a CIS free trade zone, preferring bilateral arrangements. An informal meeting of CIS heads of state was held in Moscow on 20 December, to mark the actual date of the founding of the CIS (see AR 1991, pp. 183-84). The general conclusion of the participants was that the organisation had much to offer and should be developed further. Turkmenistan, previously a dormant member, now showed new enthusiasm for the CIS and agreed to chair it in 2012.

Leaders of the members of the **Collective Security Treaty Organisation** (CSTO)—Armenia, Belarus, Kazakhstan, Kyrgyzstan, Russia, Tajikistan and Uzbekistan—held a working summit in Moscow in December. The main issue was to improve the organisation's efficacy, especially with regard to the challenges and threats from Afghanistan. Another priority was to develop systems-based approaches to the countering of cyber-terrorism and other non-traditional security threats. During the year, drills and manoeuvres of varying scale and purpose were held in member states. These included the Shygys-2011 (East-2011) exercises in eastern Kazakhstan in June, which involved more than 3,000 Kazakh and Russian troops; the manoeuvres focused for the first time on repelling a Cruise missile attack. Kazakhstan also hosted Centre-2011, CSTO's large-scale joint strategic training operations, in September.

The **Co-operation Council of Turkic-speaking States** (CCTS), launched in Istanbul in 2010 (see AR 2011, p. 435), held its inaugural summit meeting in Kazakhstan on 20-21 October. It was attended by the presidents of Kazakhstan, Azerbaijan, Kyrgyzstan and the prime minister of Turkey; the leaders of Uzbekistan and Turkmenistan, despite repeated invitations, did not participate. The Business Council of Turkic-speaking states was established, aimed at deepening economic ties between member states and facilitating trade.

In November, the UN Special Programme for Central Asia (SPECA), comprising Afghanistan, Azerbaijan, Kazakhstan, Kyrgyzstan, Tajikistan, Turkmenistan and Uzbekistan, convened a major international conference on ways to strengthen regional economic ties with Afghanistan. The event was hosted by Turkmenistan, incumbent chairman of SPECA (elected in October 2010). One of the most viable proposals was the plan to establish a unified legal framework dealing with rail-freight, which in turn would provide a basis for a free-trade agreement between Afghanistan and the Central Asian states.

Shirin Akiner

ASIA-PACIFIC ORGANISATIONS

Association of South-East Asian Nations (ASEAN)

DATE OF FOUNDATION: 1967 HEADQUARTERS: Jakarta, Indonesia
OBJECTIVES: To accelerate economic growth, social progress and cultural development in the region
MEMBERSHIP (END-'11): Brunei, Burma (Myanmar), Cambodia, Indonesia, Laos, Malaysia, Philippines, Singapore, Thailand, Vietnam (total 10)
SECRETARY GENERAL: Surin Pitsuwan (Thailand) (since Jan '08)

Asia-Pacific Economic Co-operation (APEC)

DATE OF FOUNDATION: 1989 HEADQUARTERS: Singapore
OBJECTIVES: To promote market-oriented economic development and co-operation in the Pacific Rim countries
MEMBERSHIP (END-'11): Australia, Brunei, Canada, Chile, China, Hong Kong, Indonesia, Japan, South Korea, Malaysia, Mexico, New Zealand, Papua New Guinea, Peru, Philippines, Russia, Singapore, Taiwan, Thailand, USA, Vietnam (total 21)
EXECUTIVE DIRECTOR: Muhamad Noor Yacob (Malaysia) (since Jan '10)

Asian Development Bank (ADB)

DATE OF FOUNDATION: 1966 HEADQUARTERS: Manila, Philippines
OBJECTIVES: To improve the welfare of the people in Asia and the Pacific, particularly the 1.9 billion who live on less than $2 a day
MEMBERSHIP (END-'11): REGIONAL MEMBERS: Afghanistan, Armenia, Australia, Azerbaijan, Bangladesh, Bhutan, Brunei, Burma (Myanmar), Cambodia, China, Cook Islands, East Timor, Fiji, Georgia, Hong Kong, India, Indonesia, Japan, Kazakhstan, Kiribati, Kyrgyzstan, Laos, Malaysia, Maldives, Marshall Islands, Federated States of Micronesia, Mongolia, Nauru, Nepal, New Zealand, Pakistan, Palau, Papua New Guinea, Philippines, Samoa, Singapore, Solomon Islands, South Korea, Sri Lanka, Taiwan, Tajikistan, Thailand, Tonga, Turkmenistan, Tuvalu, Uzbekistan, Vanuatu, Vietnam (total 48); NON REGIONAL MEMBERS: Austria, Belgium, Canada, Denmark, Finland, France, Germany, Ireland, Italy, Luxembourg, the Netherlands, Norway, Portugal, Spain, Sweden, Switzerland, Turkey, UK, USA (total 19)
PRESIDENT: Haruhiko Kuroda (Japan) (since Nov '04)

South Asian Association for Regional Co-operation (SAARC)

DATE OF FOUNDATION: 1985 HEADQUARTERS: Kathmandu, Nepal
OBJECTIVES: To promote collaboration and mutual assistance in the economic, social, cultural and technical fields
MEMBERSHIP (END-'11): Afghanistan, Bangladesh, Bhutan, India, Maldives, Nepal, Pakistan, Sri Lanka (total 8)
OBSERVER MEMBERS: Australia, Burma (Myanmar), China, EU, Iran, Japan, Mauritius, South Korea, USA (total 9)
SECRETARY GENERAL: Fathimath Dhiyana Saeed (Maldives) (since March '11); Ahmed Saleem (Maldives) (since March '12)

Pacific Islands Forum (PIF)
DATE OF FOUNDATION: 1971 (as South Pacific Forum)   HEADQUARTERS: Suva, Fiji
OBJECTIVES: To enhance the economic and social well-being of the people of the Pacific, in support
   of the efforts of the members' governments
MEMBERSHIP (END-'11): Australia, Cook Islands, Fiji (suspended), Kiribati, Marshall Islands,
   Federated States of Micronesia, Nauru, New Zealand, Niue, Palau, Papua New Guinea, Samoa,
   Solomon Islands, Tonga, Tuvalu, Vanuatu (total 16)
SECRETARY GENERAL: Tuiloma Neroni Slade (Samoa) (since Aug '08)

THE **Association of South-East Asian Nations** (ASEAN) held summits in Indonesia in May and November. Member states welcomed positive developments in Burma during 2011 and agreed to its becoming the ASEAN chair in 2014, hosting that year's summits (see p. 316). The November ASEAN meeting was followed by the sixth **East Asia Summit** (EAS), including participation by new members Russia and the USA, with US President Barack Obama in attendance. The summit emphasised the value of the EAS in contributing to peace, stability and prosperity in the region, with some countries criticising China's assertiveness in a dispute over competing territorial and resource claims in the South China Sea.

The **Asia-Pacific Economic Co-operation** (APEC) annual conference was held in Hawaii, USA, in November. APEC ministers committed themselves to further economic integration, trade expansion, and the development of a future free trade area of the Asia-Pacific. Representatives from 11 Pacific island nations met with US President Obama in parallel with the APEC leaders' meeting. Ten countries attending the APEC meeting—Australia, Brunei, Chile, Japan, Malaysia, New Zealand, Peru, Singapore, the USA and Vietnam— approved the framework for a free trade agreement based on the Trans-Pacific Partnership.

The **Asian Development Bank** (ADB) held its 44th annual meeting in May, in Hanoi, Vietnam, attended by finance ministers, policy-makers, business leaders, civil society representatives, journalists and academics. The ADB warned that climate change threatened to increase hunger and malnutrition among the Pacific region's poorest people, as a result of flood, drought, storms, and damage to coastal areas. Governments in Asia and the Pacific were warned of the need to prepare for a significant increase in climate-induced migration in the future. The ADB was funding renewable energy programmes in the Pacific in an attempt to reduce reliance on fuel imports and mitigate the effects of these on local economies and the environment.

The **South Asian Association For Regional Co-operation** (SAARC) held its 17th summit in November, in Addu City, the Maldives. The organisation emphasised that its principal goal was the alleviation of poverty, with members urged to implement the SAARC Plan of Action on Poverty Alleviation (endorsed at the 2004 summit) as part of the SAARC Decade of Poverty Alleviation (2006-15). Four agreements were signed at the summit, including a measure to facilitate rapid joint action in response to natural disasters. The organisation re-emphasised its concerns about terrorism and piracy, as well as the dangers of climate change, to which some member states were especially vulnerable.

The **Pacific Islands Forum** (PIF) held its annual heads of government meeting in September in New Zealand, marking the 40th anniversary of the Forum's founding meeting in New Zealand in 1971 (see AR 1971, p. 319). Leaders agreed to invite Fiji to participate in regional trade talks—an offer subsequently rejected by Fiji—but the country remained suspended from the PIF. The organisation declined to endorse the bid by the president of French Polynesia to win PIF support for his effort to have the territory reinscribed on the UN's decolonisation list (from which it had been removed in 1947). With US state department approval, representatives from American Samoa, Guam and the Northern Mariana Islands were able to participate for the first time as observers. The summit focused on regional efforts to boost productivity, and leaders reaffirmed the dangers of climate change, which they described as "'the single greatest threat to the livelihoods, security and well-being of the peoples of the Pacific". The summit's Waiheke Declaration on Sustainable Economic Development committed Pacific leaders to the goal of "ensuring a sustainable economic environment" for Pacific communities.

Pacific island states took part in the UN climate change conference in December in Durban, South Africa, partnering with AOSIS (the Alliance of Small Island States) to work for a binding agreement to limit global warming. Recognition of the growing importance at the UN of Pacific Island states—and their voting power—came in late August when the Asian Group changed its name to the Asia-Pacific Group, with island states making up more than one-fifth of the group's members.

Indonesia and East Timor were each granted observer status in March by the **Melanesian Spearhead Group** (MSG), with acceptance of Indonesia criticised by representatives of the Papuan independence movement. In November the MSG agreed to give West Papua the opportunity to apply for observer status, but only as part of the group representing Indonesia. With Fiji's prime minister, Frank Bainimarama serving as MSG chairman, the group's March summit held in Fiji endorsed his plans for a return to democracy in 2014. In September MSG leaders signed a Treaty on Traditional Knowledge, intended to promote respect for Melanesian cultures, traditions and values, and safeguard the legal rights of traditional knowledge holders.

In November, leaders from eight Polynesian island states and territories, meeting in Samoa, reached agreement on the establishment of a new sub-regional organisation, the **Polynesian Leaders Group**. The founding members were five PIF members—Cook Islands, Niue, Samoa, Tonga and Tuvalu—and three non-independent territories: American Samoa, French Polynesia and Tokelau.

Stephen Levine

XII THE INTERNATIONAL ECONOMY IN 2011

"Society may subsist, though not in the most comfortable state,
without beneficence; but the prevalence of injustice must utterly destroy it...
Justice, on the contrary, is the main pillar that upholds the whole edifice."
(Adam Smith, *The Theory of Moral Sentiments,* 6th ed., 1790)

"None of the cruelties exercised by wealth and power upon indigence and dependence,
is more mischievous in its consequences, or more frequently practised with wanton
negligence, than the encouragement of expectations which are never to be gratified, and the
elation and depression of the heart by needless vicissitudes of hope and disappointment."
(Samuel Johnson, *The Rambler,* No. 163, 1751)

"To convert the business man into the profiteer is to strike a blow at capitalism, because
it destroys the psychological equilibrium which permits the perpetuance of unequal
rewards. The economic doctrine of normal profits, vaguely apprehended by everyone,
is a necessary condition for the justification of capitalism. The business man is only
tolerable so long as his gains can be held to bear some relation to what, roughly and in
some sense, his activities have contributed to society."
(John Maynard Keynes, *A Tract On Monetary Reform,* 1923)

"Some have suggested that footballers' salaries and fees are as offensive as bankers'
pay deals. This newspaper disagrees. Footballers contribute more than bankers to the
sum of human happiness and entertainment...clubs are at least the product of a free—
if rarefied—market in which entities are able to fail."
(*The Financial Times,* editorial, 5 February 2011)

THE world economy appeared to start the year well but it all ended badly. It began with the prospect of a continuing recovery from the Great Recession of 2008-09 but from late spring the outlook deteriorated rapidly. By December there were widespread fears of renewed recession; the sovereign debt crisis in Europe was threatening renewed turbulence throughout the global economy; and the managing director of the IMF was raising the spectre of a return to the 1930s.

In April the IMF concluded that the recovery had "solidified" and was continuing "broadly as anticipated", that is, towards a rise in global output of about 4.5 per cent in both 2011 and 2012. At the end of May the OECD similarly judged the global recovery to be "firmly under way" and it, too, was expecting similar growth rates of global GDP. With business confidence rising, governments were urged to stabilise and reduce high levels of public debt as soon as possible. By January 2012, however, the estimate for growth in 2011 was 3.8 per cent, falling to 3.3 per cent in 2012.

The deterioration in the global outlook was largely due to the developed economies. In the spring the IMF was expecting these to grow by an average of 2.4 and 2.6 per cent in 2011 and 2012, respectively, but by the end of the year these forecasts were revised to 1.6 and 1.2 per cent. Specific factors, such as higher commodity prices, aggravated the situation and matters were made worse from midsummer by increasing scepticism as to the ability of eurozone leaders to contain the eurozone sovereign debt crisis. Matters deteriorated further in September when revised data for the US revealed that the slowdown in the early months of the year had been underestimated and that GDP had decelerated sharply in the second quarter in Europe, Canada and Japan, the last reflecting the consequences of the March earthquake and tsunami. But the underlying weakness basically reflected the aftershocks of the financial crisis. A key insight from the work of a number of writers—Gottfried Haberler (1941), Christopher Dow (1998), Carmen M. Reinhart and Kenneth S. Rogoff (2009)—was that recessions triggered by banking crises were not only extremely costly in terms of lost output and jobs, but that recovery from them tended to be slow and more protracted than from the more familiar cyclical downturn. This reflected the attempts of households, companies and banks to restore their balance sheets, which in turn reduced spending by consumers and the corporate sector and restricted the supply of credit.

The emerging and developing economies were less directly affected by the financial crisis and with reduced, but still rapid, rates of economic growth were able to wind down the fiscal stimuli of 2009 more easily than the developed countries. The IMF originally expected average growth of 6.5 per cent in both 2011 and 2012 and although these rates were lowered to 6.2 and 5.4 per cent by end year, the revisions were smaller than those for the developed economies. The principle challenge for the developing economies was to check rising inflation, which they did for the most part by raising interest rates, tightening fiscal policy and, in a number of cases, deploying controls to restrain a sharp increase in capital flows from the low-yield markets of the north. The emerging economies also relied more on domestic rather than external demand which had weakened as a result of the slowdown in the developed economies.

After four-and-a-half years of economic crisis, rising discontent across much of the global economy gave birth to a variety of slogans and key words that may eventually be seen as emblematic of 2011. In addition to the "Arab Spring", Stéphane Hessel's famous pamphlet of October 2010, *Indignez-vous!*, translated into several languages, was echoed in Europe and Latin America by los indignados, les indignés, and indignant Anglo-Saxons. These and the "squeezed middle" and the banner of the Occupy Movement—"We are the 99 per cent"—all focused on the growth of inequality and a general sense of unfairness at the costs of the crisis falling most heavily on those who had profited least, or not at all, from the preceding boom (see below). The popular focus on the large bonuses of top bankers even led to the revival of the 1930s pejorative of "banksters", while the claims of several developed governments that their fiscal consolidation efforts were really an "expansionary contraction" were best regarded as an ironic oxymoron with little analytical foundation.

Growth in the USA decelerated in the first half of 2011 and although it improved in the second, GDP for the year as a whole rose just 1.7 per cent against 3 per cent in 2010. At the end of the year most of the forecasts suggested continued weak growth in 2012 with a gradual improvement through 2013. Several factors were behind this sluggishness: a high rate of unemployment—falling slowly but running at around 9 per cent for most of the year—and minimal growth in household income; debt reduction by households, badly hit by the collapse in the housing market; and a shift to a more restrictive fiscal policy. The housing market remained a drag on the economy: sales of new homes were still falling at end year and about a third of homeowners were in negative equity. A more general problem was the constant paralysis in the decision-making process.

Although the fiscal stimulus of 2009 was widely criticised as inadequate by many economists, the fiscal tightening in 2011 was less severe than in Europe but, with continuing worries about a return to recession, the Federal Reserve announced in September a variant of its quantitative easing (QE) policy in which $400 billion of Treasury securities maturing within three years were to be exchanged by the end of June 2012 for securities of much longer maturities (six years and more), the aim being to lower (already very low) long-term interest rates. Despite signs of improvement at the end of 2011, the US economy did not appear to be much stronger than a year earlier. Federal Reserve chairman Ben Bernanke observed that Congress could still "throw a spanner in the works of recovery".

The developed economies in Asia and the Pacific were all hit by natural disasters in 2011. In Japan the massive earthquake in March was followed by a fall in national output in the first half of the year but there was a strong recovery in the third quarter and, although there was a setback in the fourth, the fall in GDP for the year as a whole was provisionally estimated at just under 1 per cent, against 4 per cent growth in 2010. In Australia, recovery from the extensive flooding of the eastern states was slow and growth for the year was reduced from 2.5 per cent in 2010 to about 0.5 per cent. Considerable damage was caused in New Zealand by the February earthquake centred on Christchurch, but the economy as a whole avoided recession, GDP rising by about 1.5 per cent. In all three economies reconstruction programmes were set to continue through 2012 but their financing presented problems for governments attempting to stick to tight budget targets.

In Western Europe the recovery was relatively strong in the first quarter of 2011 (with GDP up 0.8 per cent). A sharp deceleration in the second quarter (0.2 per cent) was at first attributed to interruptions in manufacturing supply chains due to the Japanese earthquake in March, the closure of nuclear power plants in Germany and the large increase in oil prices. But there was little improvement in the third quarter and in the fourth output in the EU fell by 0.3 per cent. The fall was widespread—France and Sweden being the principle exceptions among the 15 "old" members of the EU. In several countries (Belgium, Italy, and the Netherlands), output had also fallen in the third quarter and so they were technically in recession, while in Greece and Portugal output fell throughout the year. There were large differences within the region. Among the "old" members of the EU relatively high annual growth rates in Finland, Germany, Austria and Sweden (2.7 to 4.3 per cent) contrasted with large falls in GDP in Greece (-8 per cent) and Portugal (-1.5 per cent) while elsewhere growth rates were stuck at or below 1 per cent. The characterisation of Europe as divided into a dynamic North and a depressed South was not without substance but there was a large grey area in between.

Among the central and south-east European members of the EU there were relatively high rates of growth in the Baltic states (5.3 to 7.5 per cent) and Poland (4.3 per cent) but much weaker out-turns elsewhere. Relatively stronger growth in these countries partly reflected a bounce-back from very deep recession in 2008-09, but in most of them there was a loss of momentum in the second half of 2011 as their principal export markets in the EU weakened. The outstanding exception continued to be Poland: the least export dependent of all the new EU members, its growth was largely driven by domestic demand and especially by infrastructure investment, stimulated in part by the prospect of hosting the Euro 2012 football championship. Household spending in the region was limited by efforts to reduce indebtedness, which was especially difficult in several countries given the large share of private borrowing denominated in Swiss francs—more than half of all outstanding mortgages in Hungary and Poland, for example. The appreciation of the Swiss franc in 2011 put considerable pressure on households and companies with foreign currency debts.

For Europe as a whole GDP growth in 2011 averaged 1.5 per cent, pretty much in line with forecasts at the start of the year except that the recovery was expected to strengthen rather than weaken through the year. Consequently, expectations for 2012 were considerably reduced and by the end of 2011 the IMF and other institutions were forecasting a fall in eurozone GDP of around 0.5 per cent.

The underlying reasons for the deterioration in the European economies were debt reduction in the private sector and the cutbacks in government deficits. The purpose of fiscal consolidation was to stem the rise in government debt with the aim of creating confidence in the sustainability of the debt burden and restoring stability to the financial markets. But there was increasing doubt in 2011 as to whether consolidation might be counter-productive insofar as it appeared to be undermining the prospects for economic growth and hence of debt sustainability. There were at least two dimensions to this issue. The first was that fiscal tightening was taking place simultaneously in a group of economies that were deeply inter-connected by trade and finance, so the negative impact of each country's consolidation included a spillover to its neighbours and vice versa. The overall impact of consolidation was therefore likely to be larger than anticipated when considering each country's programme in isolation. The second concerned the timing of consolidation in relation to the progress of debt reduction in the rest of the economy.

In the long credit boom that ended in 2007-08 the private sector became heavily indebted and was enabled to do so by an extraordinary expansion of bank lending. Following the crash, and especially the collapse of property bubbles in the USA and several European countries, a process of deleveraging began, i.e. the reduction of debts in the face of collapsing asset prices in order to avoid insolvency. Thus, households cut their expenditure, companies cut back on investment and reduced their labour and other costs, and the banks reduced their lending and tried to dispose of non-performing assets. Reducing the burden of debt created a deflationary environment that threatened a collapse of output. With the corporate and household sectors moving into surplus, the government sector, in the absence of a sufficiently large current account surplus, must automatically have moved into deficit. Had governments resisted the increase in their deficits in 2008-09 the result, in the judgement of leading policy makers at the time, would have been a slump on a scale to match that of the 1930s (AR 2009, p. 455).

It was therefore highly misleading to argue, as several European governments have done in the past two years, that government overspending ("profligacy") was responsible for the crisis. Deficits increased dramatically but mainly because of the impact of the crisis on government revenues and increased expenditure on unemployment and other social security benefits. The fiscal stimuli of 2009 contributed only a small amount, some 10-20 per cent, of the overall increase in debt. Effectively, private sector debts were shifted to the general government sector and, with the exception of Greece, this was also true of the countries of the so-called periphery of the EU.

The shift from fiscal stimulus to austerity, which started in 2010 (AR 2011, p. 439), helped to undermine the recovery in Europe in 2011 and would continue to do so in 2012. The recommendation of institutions such as the IMF and the OECD, was for governments to draw up coherent and transparent adjustment plans for the medium term but to judge carefully the pace of implementation: not so fast as to kill economic growth but not so slow as to lose credibility in the financial markets. The difficulty with this Goldilocks approach to fiscal policy was that it was not easy to calibrate the trade-off and, in practice, European governments made little or no effort to do so. Either because they felt they already had little choice or for political or ideological reasons, most of them launched front-loaded programmes of deficit cuts. In terms of the sectoral balances, however, the IMF/OECD advice implied that it would have been more appropriate to first try to accelerate deleveraging in the household sector, for example with programmes for mortgage relief as introduced in the USA, and to encourage the corporate sector to start converting part of its record cash surplus into fixed investment. The corporate sector's reluctance to invest largely reflected uncertainty about future demand but also worries about whether the banks would be able or willing to supply it with capital when needed. There were increasing calls during the year from independent research institutes and academics for some front-end loosening of fiscal policy within existing medium-term plans, preferably with an emphasis on infrastructure investment. Governments, however, generally held to the line of fiscal austerity, combined with loose monetary policy and structural reforms to tackle rising unemployment and lay the basis for improved growth. Debt reduction and structural reforms were recognised as important medium and long-term objectives but the neglect of growth in the short run risked undermining both.

As the economic outlook deteriorated in the summer amid uncertainty surrounding the sovereign debt crisis in the eurozone, government leaders, central banks and the international economic institutions all agreed that a comprehensive and co-ordinated plan to defuse the threat to global stability was urgently required. Yet 18 months after the first bail-out was agreed for Greece (AR 2011, pp. 442-

443) there was still no convincing strategy that combined measures to contain the debt crisis and stabilise financial markets with a credible prospect of stronger economic growth. At the European summit in December, the eighth meeting of EU leaders in 2011, the centrepiece of the discussion was the proposal for a new "fiscal pact" that would insist on legally binding fiscal rules with automatic penalties for breaking them and central oversight of national budgets by the European Commission. This was seen by many analysts as addressing the wrong problem: apart from Greece, the vulnerable countries were not in difficulty because of mismanagement of their budgets—Spain and Ireland were in balance or surplus before the crisis, Italy had one of the smallest deficits in the eurozone and was in primary surplus. Instead, their problems arose from the failure to deal with the current account imbalances within the eurozone, the result of 13 years of diverging competitiveness.

By the end of the year a measure of calm had been restored to the financial markets by the ECB. In August, as the debt crisis began to spread to Italy and Spain, it resumed its programme of buying bonds in an effort to stabilise the markets and of supporting the banks with offers of unlimited loans for up to one year. But the more substantial boost to confidence followed the ECB's introduction in December of its offer to eurozone banks of three-year loans at its policy rate of 1 per cent. This action—the Long-Term Refinancing Operation (LTRO), to be repeated at the end of February 2012—by addressing the liquidity problem of European banks, avoided another major cut-back in credit and, essentially, bought time for governments and banks to deal with the more fundamental problem of solvency. It was highly favourable to the banks, but the impact on the real economy was minimal as the banks used the money (€489 billion) to repair their balance sheets and to invest in the bonds of their own governments yielding much more than the cost of their borrowing. At the end of the year, the pressing issue was whether agreement would be reached on a new bail-out for Greece in time to remove the risk of a default on a large repayment of its bonds in March.

Among the transition economies, those in south-eastern Europe continued to recover from recession in 2011 but at relatively modest rates (from 0.8 per cent in Croatia to 3 per cent in Albania) and well below the pace of expansion before the financial crisis. On average the region's GDP grew less than 2 per cent, an improvement on 2010 (0.6 per cent) but still insufficient to offset the fall of output in 2009 (-3.7 per cent). The weaker EU performance led to decelerating growth in the latter half of the year but domestic demand was also subdued by marginal gains in real income, tight credit and declining inflows of foreign direct investment (except into Albania). Household spending in a number of countries (Albania, Croatia and Serbia) was also weakened by the appreciation of the Swiss franc which led to an increase in non-performing loans and in the burden of debt servicing. (In Croatia, some 40 per cent of mortgages were in Swiss francs as were a still larger proportion of loans for car purchase.) This part of Europe remained highly vulnerable to spillovers from the eurozone debt crisis: Greek banks had a significant presence in the region and Italy was a key export market and source of remittances.

In the Commonwealth of Independent States (CIS), higher commodity prices and export volumes helped to maintain an average growth of GDP at just over 4 per cent, albeit considerably lower than the annual average (just under 8 per cent) before 2008. Improved terms of trade and falling unemployment, particularly in Russia, boosted domestic demand, and there was a significant rise in agricultural output following the drought of 2010. Growth was fairly robust across the region, with GDP ranging from 4 to over 9 per cent among the net energy exporters—the exception was Azerbaijan (0.9 per cent) where oil production was interrupted by major oil-rig repairs—and 4.3 to 6 per cent among the net energy importers.

The global economy continued to get strong support from the developing countries in 2011. Their average growth rate of some 6 per cent, while below the 7.5 per cent average of 2004-07, was over four times higher than that of the developed economies. With a similar growth differential likely to be maintained in 2012 and 2013, the shift in the global balance of economic strength towards developing countries looked set to continue at a fairly rapid pace, at least within the time-frame of current forecasts. Their superior performance reflected in part their relative insulation from the financial shocks centred in North America and Europe, their policy support for domestic demand until recovery was firmly established, and increasing trade with one another. Growth, however, began to slow from the second quarter, partly because of efforts to control rising inflation and asset price bubbles and, from mid-year, weaker demand in the developed economies. Macro-economic policy was also complicated for many countries in Latin America and East Asia by the volatility of foreign capital which moved from large inflows in the first half of the year, to outflows in the second, and to renewed inflows towards the end of the year. By the end of 2011 the outlook for most developing countries was for a further deceleration of growth in 2012 but this was not universal: an improvement was expected in North Africa, subject to political uncertainties, and in many of the poorer countries that are influenced more by commodity than financial markets.

Despite numerous shocks, economic growth in most of Africa remained relatively strong in 2011. The average rise in GDP was about 2.7 per cent, down from just under 4 per cent in 2010, but this largely reflected a fall in North Africa (of about 0.5 per cent); for Sub-Saharan Africa output rose on average by just over 4.5 per cent, down from 4.8 in 2010. The dramatic political changes in North Africa led to sharp falls in domestic spending and a collapse in fixed investment in the early months of the year in Egypt, Tunisia and Morocco, but after the initial dislocation the rate of decline seemed to have stabilised. The World Bank estimated the fall in GDP for the first three quarters of the year at no more than 1.2 per cent. For the year as a whole, output in Tunisia may have fallen by 0.5 per cent and in Egypt it may have risen slightly. The Libyan economy was estimated to have contracted by more than 20 per cent. The countries affected by the political upheaval of the "Arab Spring" suffered large falls (30 to 50 per cent) in the number of tourist arrivals, but migrant remittances from Europe, surprisingly, appeared to have been largely maintained as were those from the Middle East.

Preliminary estimates put growth in Sub-Saharan Africa at much the same rate (4.8 per cent) as in 2010. Excluding South Africa, the increase was closer to 6 per cent, with Nigeria, the region's second largest economy, accelerating from under 3 per cent in 2010 to more than 6 per cent. Rising domestic demand was the principal source of growth with private consumption continuing to rise and with strong public investment in infrastructure. Despite the troubles in the global economy, the region's exports grew more than 30 per cent in value in the first half of the year due to the rise in commodity prices. Foreign direct investment (FDI) increased by some 25 per cent, most of it going into the oil and minerals sectors. But not all of Africa was doing better in 2011. Large areas in the Horn of Africa—Eritrea, Ethiopia, Djibouti, and Somalia—were suffering the worst drought in 60 years leading to famine and to humanitarian and economic disasters.

In East Asia, economic growth slowed in 2011 as a result of several factors: weaker demand in the developed economies and financial turmoil in Europe; disruption of international supply chains for manufacturing production following the earthquake and tsunami in Japan in March and the flooding of much of Thailand from July to November; the tightening of monetary policy from 2010 to counter inflationary pressures—in China, for example, policy interest rates were raised five times in the 12 months to July 201—and the return to more balanced fiscal policies in some countries after the considerable loosening in 2008-09. The average rise in GDP was just over 7 per cent against over 9 per cent in 2010. Inflationary pressures eased in the first half of the year and, from the summer, monetary policy began to ease or stabilise, the emphasis of policy shifting towards supporting growth. In China, GDP rose some 9.3 per cent in 2011 (10.5 per cent in 2010) and forecasts for 2012 were around 8-8.5 per cent although the government's target was set at 7.5 per cent. At the same time the shift in the structure of the Chinese economy, with private consumption and fixed investment providing most of the rise in GDP, was set to continue.

Growth in South Asia slowed in 2011, to around 6.5 per cent from 7 per cent in 2010. A mixture of domestic and external factors was at play: domestically, macroeconomic policy was tightened to deal with persistently high inflation (averaging over 10 per cent) and large fiscal deficits in most of the region. The region's exports grew strongly in the first half of the year and although there was a deceleration in the second half, especially from October, for the year as a whole export earnings were around 20 per cent higher than in 2010. This reflected in part a gain in market share for textiles and clothing at the expense of China, where costs had risen sharply, and North Africa where production was disrupted by the political turmoil of the "Arab Spring". The slowdown in regional growth largely reflected developments in India which accounted for about 80 per cent of the region's GDP.

In West Asia, GDP rose on average by just over 6.5 per cent. The oil-exporting countries benefited from higher oil prices and from increased public spending and private consumption, their average growth rate rising to some 7.3 per cent from just under 5 per cent in 2010. Large increases in social spending by several Arab governments were a reaction to the widespread popular protests that followed the revolts in North Africa. In Syria and Yemen, GDP certainly fell but the orders of magnitude were uncertain. Although Iran faced international sanctions, rising oil prices and improved agricultural output helped to raise GDP by around 2.5 per cent, albeit somewhat less than the estimate of just over 3 per cent in 2010. In the energy-importing countries of the region GDP growth fell below 6 per cent in 2011, down from just under 8 per cent in 2010. Political and social unrest, rising oil prices and import bills, and falling revenues from tourism were among the negative factors. Unemployment, particularly among young men, remained one of the most serious problems in the region.

In Latin-America and the Caribbean, growth slowed to some 4.3 per cent from 6 per cent in 2010. There were large differences among countries, with growth rates ranging from 7.6 per cent in Argentina to 3 per cent in Venezuela. Growth was particularly strong in South America in the first half of 2011, the result of increased domestic demand, in turn supported by rising employment and higher commodity prices which boosted export earnings and, via taxes and royalties, government revenues. With signs of overheating in several economies, fiscal and monetary policies were tightened in the second quarter. The consequent weakening of demand, however, coincided with the softening of external demand and commodity prices, prompting moves towards a new round of expansionary measures. In general, however, there was little scope for stimuli on the scale of those introduced in 2008-09. Growth in the economies of Mexico and Central America (3.5 to 3.8 per cent), was more subdued than in the south, partly because exports and workers' remittances were reduced by the slowdown of the US economy. As in East Asia, the monetary authorities in a number of countries—Argentina, Brazil, Colombia, Mexico, and Uruguay, for example—intervened in the foreign exchange markets to control currency appreciation. At the end of the year there were concerns that possible sovereign defaults in the eurozone might lead to the liquidation or repatriation of assets by Spanish banks which had a large presence in Latin America.

World trade continued to recover in 2011 but by much less than in 2010 when it bounced back by some 14 per cent from the collapse of 2009. Provisional estimates put the increase in volume at between 6 and 6.5 per cent. The recovery was led, as in 2010, by the developing country exporters of manufactures, especially those in Asia; its relative weakness was almost entirely due to the depressed state of import demand in the developed economies. The volatility of commodity prices continued to be a feature of world trade: food prices peaked in the first quarter and oil prices fell in the third, but the average price level for the year was still some 20-30 per cent higher than in 2010. Despite—or because of—continual warnings, fears of an upsurge of protectionism proved unfounded. WTO-OECD-UNCTAD reports showed that new import restrictions concerned just 0.6 per cent of G-20 imports in 2011, less than in 2008-09. Nevertheless, with slowing growth and high unemployment, the political pressures for import protection remained strong.

The long-running problem of large current account imbalances remained a concern of the G-20 finance ministers. Relative to GDP, the principal imbalances were roughly half their pre-crisis levels—the US deficit in 2011 was about 3 per cent of

GDP while the counterpart surpluses were under 4 per cent of GDP in China, 2.5 per cent in Japan, and 5 per cent in Germany. It was uncertain whether the narrowing of the imbalances was cyclical or structural or a mixture of both. Policy commitments to the necessary structural adjustments were made by the G-20 in their Cannes Action Plan for Growth, adopted in November, but given the weakness of the global economy, the problem was not an immediate priority. But the accumulation of large stocks of liabilities by deficit countries and of assets by those in surplus remained potential risks to exchange rate stability in the event of doubts about the direction and credibility of economic policies. Such doubts concerning the US and the eurozone triggered large fluctuations of international capital flows and exchange rates in 2011.

Although accounts of the global economy—including this one—frequently referred to "recovery" in 2010 and 2011, this was not a term that would be recognised by the millions who lost their jobs in the recession of 2008-09 or the young people who had been increasingly unable to find work upon leaving school or university. Despite much talk by G-20 finance ministers of "growth for jobs" and "growth friendly structural adjustment", the reality was that the priority given to rapid fiscal consolidation meant that growth was too feeble to have a significant impact on job creation. This was especially the case in the developed economies where the failure of labour markets to lower unemployment and absorb new entrants to the labour force was due essentially to a lack of effective demand rather than a sudden intensification of structural problems. This was less true of the developing countries where official unemployment rates fell or stabilised in 2010 and 2011, with the exception of the Middle East and North Africa.

Globally, the ILO estimated the number of unemployed in 2011 at 197 million, an unemployment rate of 6 per cent, with both figures set to rise in 2012. The average rates varied from around 4 per cent in the Asian and Pacific region through just over 7 per cent in Latin America, around 8.5 per cent in the developed economies, and to more than 10 per cent in the Middle East and North Africa—and there were much larger differences within each region. Among the developed economies, for example, the unemployment rate in 2011 averaged 9.1 and 9.6 per cent in the USA and the EU respectively, while in the eurozone the rates in Portugal, Italy, Greece and Spain ranged between 13 and 21 per cent and were rising throughout the year.

There were also rising numbers of the long-term unemployed, those without a job for more than a year: in the USA they increased from 10 per cent of total unemployment in 2007 to nearly 30 per cent in 2011 and the ILO put the proportion at 35 per cent of all jobseekers in the EU. In the developing economies, although open unemployment rates in urban areas were much higher than the country averages, a large proportion of employed people were in fact unpaid family helpers or own-account workers, poorly paid and without access to any social security. The ILO estimated that for the global economy, vulnerable employment was nearly half of total employment in 2011 with the proportion ranging from 10 per cent in the developed economies to 32 per cent in Latin America and 78 per cent in South Asia.

One of the most disconcerting aspects of the labour market was the high rate of unemployment among young people aged 15-24: globally, this rose from under 12 per cent in 2003 to just under 13 per cent in 2009 where it has remained. Young people in the developed countries were particularly hard hit, their average unemployment rate rising from 12.5 per cent in 2007 to 18 per cent in 2011, considerably higher than for adults. In the EU, rates were rising throughout 2011, ending the year at an average of just over 22 per cent. Youth unemployment was especially high in the countries at the centre of the sovereign debt crisis: 35 per cent in Portugal, 48 per cent in Greece and nearly 50 per cent in Spain; not far behind were Ireland and Italy at over 30 per cent. But the problem was widespread: in the UK, young people aged 16-24 without work and not in education or training reached one million in the last quarter of 2011, an unemployment rate of 22 per cent; in the "new" EU members from central and south east Europe, youth unemployment was 27 per cent in Bulgaria, Hungary and Poland, and 34 per cent in Lithuania. Young women and young men were more or less equally affected.

The jobs crisis that continued unabated in 2011 was one of the largest costs of the financial crisis, and the increase in social unrest around the world was hardly surprising. High rates of unemployment among the young, as is well researched, tend to have long-term effects on their acquisition of skills and lifetime earnings as well as on the economy's long-run prospects for growth and increased prosperity. It could also lead to widespread disillusionment with the economic and political system. Large numbers of young people faced the prospect of joining what Professor Guy Standing described in 2011 as the "precariat", a significant and rising part of the labour force subject to multiple sources of employment, income and social insecurity. With diminished expectations of secure employment, of reduced opportunities to acquire and maintain skills and of "upward mobility in terms of status and income", the precariat was under pressure to focus on the present without a sense of development through work "as there is no future in what they are doing". This economic and social waste of the young, unemployed or in part time or temporary work, was perhaps the most signal failure of the present configuration of the market economy.

These same groups were at the forefront of most of the popular protests that erupted across the world in 2011. In North Africa, where youth unemployment rates had been at 25 per cent or more for many years, the frustrated young—educated and not so educated—led the revolts that brought down autocratic regimes in Tunisia and Egypt, with effects that were still reverberating throughout the Middle East at the end of the year. From Spain to Chile there were demonstrations against cuts in education budgets and the lack of educational reforms. Protests occurred throughout Europe, especially in Spain, Greece and Italy. In the UK, student protests were followed by violent riots by the more underprivileged youth in August. The start of the Occupy Wall Street movement in September was followed by similar occupations in London and many other cities across the world.

Dismissed at first by political and financial leaders as incoherent groups of anti-capitalists, these various movements actually resonated with large sections of their respective populations by highlighting the degree of inequality in most market economies and the failings of political and financial elites. The slogan of Occupy Wall Street—"We are the 99 per cent"—found a sympathetic audience in the American middle class—"the squeezed middle"—which had suffered a prolonged stagnation of real incomes while the rewards of several decades of productivity growth were captured almost entirely by the top 1 per cent. At the start of 2011, 15.1 per cent of the US population were below the poverty line and one estimate put the assets held by the richest 400 people in the USA as equal to those of the poorest 140 million.

What disarmed many of the protesters' early critics, however, was that they called not for the end of capitalism but for a better regulated capitalism that would actually meet the promise of prosperity for all, a promise—as the Secretary General of the OECD noted—that the neo-liberal approach to economic growth had failed to deliver. Their protests, which for the most part were outside the traditional frameworks of political action, reflected a widespread distrust of governments and established political parties, a distrust that often focused on the close relations between high finance and state institutions, as well as the increased role of powerful vested interests in financing political parties. There was a general sense that democratic governments, instead of defending the broader national interest, had too often failed to resist the capture of government policies and regulatory systems by private power. In this, the protesters not only struck a chord with much of the population, including a number of commentators and even members of the financial sector, but they also echoed Keynes' conclusion in 1926 that "capitalism, wisely governed, can probably be made more efficient for attaining economic ends than any alternative yet in sight".

As these arguments found a wider audience in 2011, political leaders began to speak of the need for "responsible capitalism", of the importance of "morality in the markets", and to argue for "productive" instead of "predatory" activities. The model of the last three decades had failed but the key problem for governments and policy makers remained: how to govern capitalism more wisely?

For many analysts and commentators, not just the protest movements, a key test for restoring trust in the market economy and credibility in its surrounding institutions, was whether governments were prepared to admit that there was no automatic identity between the interests of the financial sector and those of the population as a whole and, therefore, whether they were prepared to insist on comprehensive and effective reforms to reduce systemic risk and create a more stable global environment for the real economy. A scatter of micro and macro reforms were at various stages of negotiation and implementation in 2011, but financial interests were resisting strongly: seeking exemptions from the application of agreed legislation, such as the Volcker rule in the USA (which aimed at restricting proprietary trading by universal banks), or attempting to modify or postpone the introduction of other regulations such as higher capital ratios. Despite the public protests over bankers' bonuses, the incentive structures encouraging excessive risk-taking (and large bonuses) remained largely unexamined and intact. The fundamental issue of institutions "too big to fail", many of which were bigger in 2011 than before 2008, had still to be convincingly resolved despite the provisions of the Dodd-Frank legislation in the USA and the proposals of the Independent Commission on Banking in the UK (published in September).

At the same time, reform of the international monetary system received less attention as governments pursued their own, national, solutions to the crisis and with the EU preoccupied with its debt crisis. IMF participation in solving the latter led to increased tensions between members of the Fund while, in the WTO, the Doha Round of trade negotiations was deadlocked (see Economic Organisations). International cooperation on economic policy and financial reform was much weaker than had been promised in early 2009. Whether 2011 would eventually prove to be a tipping point towards a wiser, better managed capitalism or just a pause before restoring "business as usual", with the prospect of another financial crisis in the not-too-distant future, was far from clear at the end of the year.

Paul Rayment

XIII THE SCIENCES

SCIENTIFIC, INDUSTRIAL AND MEDICAL RESEARCH

MEDICAL AND BIOLOGICAL SCIENCES. The results of a final stage trial of the first working vaccine against malaria, which involved 6,000 children in seven African countries, showed that vaccination reduced the risk of developing malaria over the course of a year by 56 per cent, and the risk of severe malaria by 47 per cent. Currently, malaria infected 225 million people each year and killed almost 800,000. The results of vaccinating babies aged 6-12 weeks would be available in 2012 and if they showed a similarly positive picture the vaccine would be inserted into existing vaccination programmes for African children. The World Health Organisation (WHO) also reported remarkable progress in tackling malaria by conventional means, such as the use of insecticide-treated bed nets. The number of deaths worldwide from the disease had fallen from 985,000 in 2000 to 781,000 in 2009.

The prospect of the conception of babies with three biological parents moved nearer to acceptance by the UK Human Fertilisation and Embryology Authority (HFEA). A new IVF technique, developed by a team led by Professor Doug Turnbull of Newcastle University, was designed to replace faulty mitochondria inherited from the mother. Mitochondria provide the energy needed by human cells to function. One in 200 children was born each year with a genetic mutation in mitochondria but in 1 in 6,500 cases the mutations could cause fatal liver, neurological and heart conditions. The new IVF technique involved removing the nucleus from the donor egg, leaving the rest of the egg contents including the healthy mitochondria, and replacing it with the nucleus from the mother's egg. The process could be carried out either before or after the mother's egg was fertilised with the father's sperm. Mitochondria contain minute quantities of DNA, believed not to influence appearance or personality. The embryo would thus inherit 99.8 per cent of DNA from the mother and father. Whilst scientists believed that this technique would help to eradicate certain incurable genetic diseases, others were concerned with its ethics. Currently, in the UK, it was illegal to place embryos created in this way into the womb but there was strong scientific support to suggest that this technique would become legal within two years.

The first deposit of stem cells that could be safely used to treat humans was made at the UK Stem Cell Bank in December. The human embryonic stem cell lines were the first to have been grown without animal products (which had the potential for introducing infections and immune reactions). The deposit of clinical-grade cells would advance efforts to develop clinical trials based on embryonic stem cells. A UK government-supported initiative to develop a centre for translating stem cell research into commercial therapies had been dealt a heavy blow by a decision of the European Court of Justice to block patents on stem cell products that involved destroying an embryo. The European Court of Justice did, however, rule that a patent could be granted where an embryo was used for therapeutic or diagnostic purposes useful to the embryo, such as to correct a malformation and improve the chances of life.

The team led by Professor Paolo Macchiarini, of the Karolinska Institute in Stockholm, which had transplanted the first trachea (windpipe)—created out of a collagen scaffold donor trachea stripped of its own cells and infiltrated with the patient's own stem cells (see AR 2011, pp. 450-51)—succeeded in dispensing with the need for a donor trachea by creating a custom-made synthetic windpipe framework, using nanotechnology. The synthetic organ, which was successfully transplanted into a cancer sufferer in July, was an exact replica of the patient's original trachea and ran no risk of rejection. Later in the year, in October, a surgical team at the University of California's Davis Centre succeeded in transplanting a whole larynx (voice-box) into a 52-year-old-woman whose own larynx had been damaged to the extent that she could neither breathe nor speak normally. This first complete laryngeal transplant, which simultaneously included the trachea and thyroid glands, enabled the patient to regain her voice for the first time in 11 years.

A nanotechnology cancer therapy which targeted tumours was given to a patient, suffering from ovarian cancer, in the first human test of this promising technique. A common cancer drug, docetaxel, packed into a nanoparticle which had been designed to escape the body's immune system, had bound to the cancer cell and spared surrounding healthy tissue. This technique delivered higher and more effective doses of drugs to tumours whilst at the same time, by limiting damage to other cells, reducing the disturbing side effects of conventional chemotherapy. The treatment, called BIND 014, had been developed by BIND Biosciences, a US company based in Cambridge, Massachusetts, and was thought by the scientists to be suitable for patients suffering from ovarian, hand and neck, breast, prostate and lung cancer.

Astra Zeneca, a leading pharmaceutical company, based in Cheshire, UK, reported closure of their dog research facility after having replaced animal experiments to evaluate drug solubility and absorption rates with a synthetic intestinal tract consisting of glass tanks, plastic tubes, filters and valves which mimicked the conditions of the human stomach and gut. Traditionally, because their gastro-intestinal physiology was similar to that of humans, dogs had been used to test the uptake of orally administered drugs into the blood stream. This change had been welcomed by Humane Society International.

A blood test for pregnant women that could detect haemophilia without putting an unborn baby at risk was developed by scientists from Hong Kong and the UK. Haemophilia, a sex-linked recessive genetic disorder, affected one in 5,000 boys and caused problems with blood clotting. The gene responsible was carried on the X chromosome and was transmitted by the female but only males suffered from haemophilia. An affected male who married a normal female would have normal sons and daughters but the daughters would be carriers of the condition. When they had children with a normal male, an average of half of the male offspring would be affected and half the female offspring would be carriers. At present women who were known to carry the mutation were advised to give birth in a hospital with a specialist haemophilia centre, as an affected baby had an increased risk of haemorrhage during labour and the mother, as a carrier, had a slightly raised risk of severe bleeding. Previous methods of prenatally determining whether the unborn child was a haemophiliac involved invasive techniques such as amniocentesis which carried a risk in one in 100 of causing miscarriage. A new test, developed by Dr. Dennis Lo, of the Chinese University of Hong Kong, detected traces of the foetus's DNA in the mother's bloodstream and thus did not put the pregnancy at risk. The test was used in a clinical trial, conducted by a team at the Royal Free Hospital, London, and was found to have a 100 per cent accuracy rate. As a result of the test only those mothers known to be carriers and to have an affected child would need to be delivered at a hospital with a specialist haemophilia centre.

A Dutch woman, who became the world's oldest person in 2004 until she died in 2005 at the age of 115, in October became the oldest person to have had her complete genetic code sequenced in a study that could further the understanding of the biology of ageing.

The Nobel Prize in Physiology or Medicine was awarded in one half equally to Professor Bruce A. Beutler and Professor Jules Hoffman for their discoveries concerning the activation of innate immunity, and the other half to Dr. Ralph M. Steinman for his discovery of the dendrite cell and its role in adaptive immunity. These Nobel Laureates had revolutionised the understanding of the immune system by discovering the key principles for its activation. Scientists had long searched for the gatekeepers of the immune system response whereby humans and other animals defended themselves against attack by bacteria and other micro-organisms. Beutler and Hoffman discovered receptor proteins that could recognise such micro-organisms and activate innate immunity, the first step in the body's immune response. Steinman, who unbeknown to the Nobel Assembly had died of pancreatic cancer prior to his receiving the award, had discovered the dendritic cells of the immune system and their unique capacity to activate and regulate adaptive immunity, the later stage of the immune response during which micro-organisms were cleared from the body. Their work opened up new avenues for the development of prevention and therapy against infections, cancer, and inflammatory diseases. The Nobel Assembly agreed that, notwithstanding its own statutes which disqualify posthumous awards, the prize would still be awarded in the name of Dr Ralph Steinman.

Neil Weir

PHYSICS AND CHEMISTRY. This was a remarkable and hugely exciting year for physics with two major and extremely tantalising discoveries that had the potential to transform particle physics.

Researchers at CERN (Conseil Européen pour la Recherche Nucléaire or European Council for Nuclear Research) announced on 13 December that they might have found the Higgs boson. This particle, postulated by Peter Higgs in 1962, was vital to the currently accepted "standard model" of physics which explained the weight of other particles as their interaction with the Higgs field. As particles moved through the field, they would leave behind small particles—

"Higgs bosons". These particles had never been found before and were the only undetected fundamental particle. Scientists analysing the debris of billions of collisions between protons believed that they may have found around a dozen Higgs bosons, each between 115 and 127 times heavier than a proton (a hydrogen atom). Tantalising hints of the particle were seen by two different experiments in this region of mass, but the results were not yet strong enough to claim a definite discovery. There was still a small chance that the result was not statistically significant and further experiments were planned to confirm the finding.

Astonishingly, another experiment at CERN appeared to show particles travelling faster than the speed of light. Neutrinos (very small, light, subatomic particles) were fired from CERN in Switzerland to a detector at Gran Sasso in Italy, a distance of 730 km, where they arrived some nanoseconds sooner than if they had travelled at the speed of light. The difference in velocity was small, but highly significant as it would violate Einstein's Law of Relativity. Those conducting the experiment, called Opera, and based at CERN, announced the finding in September. Scientists found it extremely difficult to believe, but many, many examinations of the measurements, both by the highly-respected Opera team and others, found no errors and the experiment was repeated 20 times with the same result. Most physicists believed that there must be a flaw in the experiment as Einstein's theory had proved correct in every other way. String theorists were excited as, if the finding proved to be true, the only explanation would seem to be that the neutrinos were in some way accessing hidden dimensions, as predicted in string theory, and were able to shortcut long distances.

Single particles of antimatter had been produced in particle accelerators before but as they were destroyed in contact with matter, they had never been captured for long enough to analyse. On 2 May scientists at CERN managed to capture 309 antihydrogen atoms and isolate them for over 15 minutes.

Development of nuclear energy took a step backwards during 2011 as a result of the disaster in March at the Fukushima power plant in northern Japan. Many countries delayed plans to develop new nuclear reactors, and some, notably Germany, announced that they would phase out nuclear power altogether.

Work continued on applications of graphene, the two-dimensional carbon that was the subject of the Nobel Prize for Physics in 2010 (see AR 2011 p. 454), in minute transistors and highly-sensitive gas sensors.

The 2011 Nobel Prize for Physics was awarded to Saul Perlmutter, from the University of California; Brian P. Schmidt, of the Australian National University; and Adam G. Riess, from Johns Hopkins University, for the discovery of the accelerating expansion of the universe through observations of distant supernovae. The acceleration was thought to be driven by dark energy about which almost nothing was known.

The Nobel Prize for Chemistry was awarded to Dan Shechtman, of the Technion Institute in Israel, for the discovery of quasicrystals in alloys. These showed a non-repeating crystal geometry which had been thought impossible, indeed Shechtman had been forced to leave his job in the USA when he first suggested the concept in the early 1980s. Now accepted as genuine, the definition of a crystal had to be rewritten to accommodate the new structures. Several different quasicrystals had been found in alloys and in a fragment of meteorite.

ASTRONOMY. The discovery of "exoplanets"—those outside the Earth's solar system—continued during 2011 and by the end of the year several hundred had been confirmed (see AR 2011 p. 453). The process had stimulated interest in extraterrestrial life and astronomers were increasingly trying to identify potentially habitable planets. In January the discovery of Kepler 10b was announced, the first rocky rather than gaseous planet outside the solar system. Later, on 5 December, came the identification of Kepler 22b, the first rocky planet discovered in the "Goldilocks zone", i.e. at a distance from its sun which suggested that it could be sufficiently temperate to support life.

Also in December, two giant black holes were discovered, each with a mass around 10 billion times that of the Earth's sun. Their event horizon, the region within which nothing could escape, was seven times larger than the Earth's solar system.

Analysis of moon rock samples gathered during the Apollo missions 40 years ago showed that the volcanic rock had very similar concentrations of fluorine, chlorine, sulphur and water as the Earth's crust. The analysis, published in May, supported the theory that the Moon had broken off the Earth early in the development of the solar system, as a result of a massive impact.

Further exploration of Mars continued during the year, with NASA sending a six-wheeled rover, *Curiosity*, to investigate the canyons which had first been discovered by the Mariner Mars 9 Orbiter in 1971. These were believed to be channels which had been made by running water at some stage in the history of the planet. Launched on 26 November, *Curiosity* carried 10 times as much analytical equipment as the previous Mars rovers *Spirit* and *Opportunity*.

The NASA spacecraft, *Messenger*, launched by NASA in 2004 (see AR 2004 p. 427) entered orbit around Mercury on 18 March. Over 70,000 images of the planet's heavily-cratered surface were sent back to Earth.

The building of the world's largest observatory, Atacama Large Millimeter/sub-millimeter Array (ALMA), in the Atacama desert, Chile, was completed during 2011 and began scientific observations. Currently consisting of 20 linked dishes, each 12 metres across, the first images from the linked telescopes were released on 3 October.

Six astronauts who had been held in an isolation module for 520 days emerged from their confinement on 4 November. The windowless compartment in Moscow, cut off from the outside world, was an experiment to simulate a journey to Mars. The crew worked as if on a spacecraft and were very closely monitored with daily urine and blood tests. Communication with the outside world was limited and subject to a time delay of up to 25 minutes to simulate the communications lag between Mars and Earth. The crew stayed motivated and in good spirits, with no sign of physical or psychological problems.

The 30 year NASA space shuttle programme ended on 21 July when *Atlantis* made the 135th and final US shuttle flight. *Discovery*, the spacecraft with the highest mileage, was retired on 7 March having completed 38 voyages. Russian Soyuz shuttles continued to operate. The US government announced that it expected privately-owned transporters to replace the shuttle fleet in the future.

ARCHAEOLOGY AND PALAENTOLOGY. A huge Stone Age temple complex was excavated on Orkney, Scotland. By the end of the year 14 buildings had been discovered, but archaeologists estimated that there could be more than a hundred in total at the Ness of Brodgar site. The excavation showed that Neolithic man had lived in a highly structured society and suggested that Orkney might have had even more cultural importance than Stonehenge.

A total of 17 new pyramids, 1,000 tombs and 3,000 ancient buildings were discovered in Egypt by archaeologists studying satellite images. Equipment for pressing grapes and fermentation jars for wine were found in Armenia. Thought to date from around 4,000 years BC, this was the earliest known evidence of wine-making.

Tiny microfossils, clearly preserved and dating back more than 3.4 billion years, were found in Strelley Pool, Western Australia. These would have lived at a time when there was little or no oxygen on Earth and these microbes would have metabolised sulphur instead. The creatures showed a cell-like structure and were preserved in ancient sedimentary rocks thereby making dating accurate, claimed the team from the Universities of Oxford and Western Australia, on 21 August.

Palaeontologists had always assumed that dinosaurs, being reptiles, were cold-blooded but an analysis of brachiosaurus teeth suggested otherwise. Isotopic analysis of carbonates in the teeth suggested that they had had a temperature of 38C, similar to humans. This would have enabled them to be more active, but would also have required huge quantities of food to sustain them.

Fossils were rare in Antarctica, but in December, a fossil sauropod (long-necked plant eating dinosaur) was found. Palaeontologists believed that it could have reached the site 75 million years ago by travelling along an isthmus which then linked the Antarctic continent to South America.

Lorelly Wilson

INFORMATION TECHNOLOGY

STEVE Jobs, charismatic leader of the technology company Apple, died in October at the age of 56 (see Obituary). Known for an exacting leadership style and a meticulous eye for simplicity, Jobs had been a major figure in computing and entertainment ever since his company launched the Apple II personal computer from his garage in 1977. Under his leadership, Apple repeatedly created profitable, high-end consumer markets featuring innovative technology designs. Products such as the Macintosh computer, iPod, iPhone, iTunes, and iPad introduced the general public to graphical user interfaces, desktop publishing, portable digital music devices, Internet music stores, electronic books, touchscreen phones, and tablet computers. Jobs also started the film company Pixar, which popularised computer animated films. The month before Jobs's death from cancer, Apple briefly passed ExxonMobil as the most valuable US corporation. Jobs's net worth was estimated at $7 billion.

Dennis Ritchie also passed away, at the age of 70. The UNIX operating system, which Ritchie co-developed at Bell Labs in 1969, remained in 2011 the most widely used operating system on any general computational device, including personal computers, phones, Internet servers, and interplanetary satellites. The C language, which Ritchie released in 1972, fundamentally influenced all computer programming that followed and was still widely used in 2011.

Computer scientist John McCarthy, who coined the term "artificial intelligence" and created the influential LISP programming language, died at 84. Ken Olsen, founder of Digital Equipment Corporation, which dominated the computer industry from the 1960s to the 1980s, passed away at 81. Michael Hart, who invented the electronic book in 1971, also died. The first text in Hart's pioneering digital library, Project Gutenberg, was the American Declaration of Independence, which he typed into a computer terminal by hand. By 2011, the project had become an online scanning and transcription community which shared over 38,000 e-books in 60 languages online for free.

Consumer technology continued to focus on handheld devices, as Google Android and the Apple iOS platforms became the dominant players in mobile communications and tablet computing. In March, Google launched their tablet operating system, Android Honeycomb. Chinese manufacturer Huawei released the IDEOS Android smartphone at $80 in February. By August, over 350,000 units had been sold in Kenya alone. In India, a partnership between UK-based DataWind and Indian manufacturer Quad produced a $35 Android-based tablet computer intended for rural education. In September, Amazon announced the Kindle Touch and Kindle Fire, Android-based tablet computers whose low cost was subsidised by advertising revenue. By December, Amazon was selling over a million Kindles a week. Nevertheless, Apple remained the strongest player in the 2011 tablet market, having sold 27.7 million iPads by September. Apple also released Siri, a voice-activated computer interface for handheld devices.

The entertainment company Sony experienced a data security breach of names, addresses and, possibly, credit card information from 77 million customers. On the Web, Google launched a new social network, Google+, which invited users to share media with circles of curated recipients. Computer company IBM celebrated its 100th birthday. In May, the Bitcoin decentralised digital currency system rose to prominence, renewing interest in global currencies and prompting financial speculation.

Decentralised models of production reached the mainstream in 2011, amplified by Internet media. A lighting system for favela (slum) homes, invented by Filipino designer Illac Diaz, spread to thousands of dwellings in South-East Asia and South America after appearing on the video website, YouTube. Since the "Litre of Light" solar bulb could be easily made from any plastic bottle, its adoption outpaced any centralised model of production and distribution. In Japan, after the Fukushima nuclear accident, volunteers on the Internet created Safecast, a free technology platform for Japanese citizens to report radiation levels. In the USA, the UK, and some African countries, public institutions established "hackerspaces" for local manufacturing and media education.

In education, Internet content and collaboration were increasingly seen as viable alternatives to institutions. Harvard innovation expert Clayton Christensen argued in *Disrupting Class* for the transformative power of online education. He shifted debate away from older regulatory concerns about the quality of online learning to concerns about the viability of traditional institutions. Khan Academy, a non-profit organisation which offered free online education videos in 16 languages, served 2 million learners per month. In the USA, three disgruntled students at the University of Pennsylvania created CourseKit, a learning management technology, launched in summer 2011, which was adopted by thousands of university classes in the same year. Stanford University offered a free Artificial Intelligence course to more than 160,000 students online, an unprecedented number for any university class. Approximately 23,000 students completed the course. To integrate non-institutional learning with existing bodies, a consortium of US institutions, including the MacArthur Foundation, NASA, Mozilla and the US department of education, launched the Badges for Lifelong Learning initiative. This Internet technology was expected to permit learners to be rewarded for learning outside school. Online learning innovation was expected to be most transformative in China, where university enrolment had grown five-fold since 1990 and was probably higher than 25 million, 20 per cent more than in the United States.

Media produced by non-professionals and shared on the Internet were prominent in popular political movements worldwide in 2011. Lively debate occurred all year on what role the Internet played in those movements. In January, writer Evgeny Morozov argued against the liberating potential of the Internet in his book *The Net Delusion*, even as Tunisia's President Zine el-Abidine Ben Ali fled the country in response to popular protests, coordinated partly over the Internet (see p. 218). Tunisians had taken to the streets in December 2010 in reaction to the self-immolation of Mohammed Bouazizi, which had been recorded on a mobile phone and published on the social website, Facebook. The popular revolution in Egypt, which began in January, was also partially coordinated through a Facebook page. The page denounced the murder of Khaled Said, a businessman who had posted evidence of police corruption online. Wael Ghonim, Google executive and creator of the page, used it to invite people to join a mass protest in Cairo, which eventually led to the removal of President Hosni Mubarak (see pp. 183-85). In September, the Occupy Wall Street movement recruited supporters online and motivated the creation of over a thousand "Occupy" protest camps worldwide.

Governments debated the role of communications networks in mass movements, as they considered cutting off communications during periods of unrest. In London in December 2010 student protesters developed Sukey, a mobile application to coordinate avoidance of the police tactic of "kettling". While hemmed in by police in Trafalgar Square in January 2011, they also developed SukeyDating, a mobile dating service for protesters. Mobile technologies were initially blamed for coordinating the August 2011 riots in England, which resulted in five deaths and £200 million-worth of damage (see p. 18). Although subsequent enquiries did not support this explanation, UK Prime Minister David Cameron considered blocking Internet communications during future disturbances. More generally, the decision whether to permit or suspend Internet communications during civil unrest became known as the "dictator's dilemma" and the "cute cat theory of the Internet". Theorist Ethan Zuckerman argued that the political cost of censorship was proportional to the number of "cute cat pictures" in the censored medium: if cutting off the opposition's communications led the general public to experience disrupted entertainment, a government risked fostering greater popular dissatisfaction. This applied in Egypt. When the government shut down Internet sites to limit protesters' organising capacity, formerly uninvolved citizens were politicised by frustration at the disruption of media technologies. During the Libyan uprising in February and March 2011, rebel engineers were able to restore parts of the Libyan mobile network shut down by the government, thereby enabling the popular revolution to be coordinated using mobile telephones.

In the autumn of 2011, the Occupy movement took a self-conscious approach to information technology to build a decentralised organisation and create prefigurative politics—organising in a way that reflected their vision of the society of the future. "Occupy" camps developed power generators, libraries and schools as part of their strategy to prefigure a society of consensus. The movement spread its messages through Internet memes—creative templates, which supporters could remix in respect to their own experience. Adherents published stories online which identified with the global "99 per cent" of the world's least wealthy people. As it became a decentralised global movement, Occupy broadcast hundreds of live videos to the Internet and facilitated "Inter-Occupy" discussion online. Occupy also used confrontation with police to amplify its message into the media ecosystem of online sources, television, and print. After police evicted many of the Occupy movement camps in the United States (see pp. 124-25), Occupy shifted online to coordinate directed protests and plan its actions for the spring of 2012.

The "hacktivist" group "Anonymous" (see AR 2011, p. 455) moved its actions to the physical world in 2011, showing support for Occupy. Loosely organised in public on the Internet, under the protection of anonymous communication technologies, Anonymous demonstrated unexpected power in its physical protests. Anonymous participants also continued to apply online techniques to overwhelm the websites of organisations which they opposed or considered incompetent.

The United States withdrew funding from and closed its Data.gov digital transparency technologies, even as Kenya became the first developing country to develop an open data initiative. The European Commission also launched a Europe-wide open data strategy, pledging to make data produced by the EU available on the Internet for commercial and non-commercial users.

J. Nathan Mathias

This entry of *The Annual Register 2012* was "crowdsourced" online by nine technology experts from seven countries.

THE ENVIRONMENT

Two great forces were shaping the future of the Earth in the early years of the 21st century, two forces which seemed destined to combine and present civilisation with a daunting challenge: the immense rise in human numbers, and the advent of climate change. The year 2011 saw notable landmarks in the progress of both of these phenomena, but neither prompted public anxiety on any significant scale. That was reserved for a natural disaster with world-wide social, political and environmental effects: the earthquake and subsequent tidal wave off the coast of Japan in March, which overwhelmed the Fukushima atomic power plant and brought about modern technology's long-anticipated nightmare—nuclear meltdown.

Fukushima had consequences which were immediate and grave and could have been truly catastrophic, and the alarm they engendered was entirely understandable. Yet they presented not a scrap of the systemic threat to the whole human enterprise that was posed by population growth and global warming. But although the warning signs from these latter forces were eminently visible during 2011, they were passed over largely in blithe unconcern, an oversight which may be something to which future historians will devote their attention.

It was in population that developments were more starkly obvious. On 31 October the UN declared that human numbers had passed the seven billion mark. To reach seven billion from six billion had taken a mere 12 years; it was a significant milestone on the ascent from under two billion people on Earth at the start of the 20th century, to a likely 10 billion-plus by the end of the 21st, a progression spelled out in detail when the UN published its *2010 Revision of World Population Prospects* earlier in the year.

About this historic shift there were sharply differing opinions, with governments, and churches, and liberal commentators who viewed the world from a humanist perspective generally, all taking the view that this was of no matter of urgent concern. Environmentalists, however, or let us say, those who viewed the world from the point of view of its natural systems—the ecosystems which, it was increasingly recognised, provided the services which underpinned all of human existence—took a different view entirely, seeing the pressures on the natural world remorselessly increasing with the swelling billions. It was the view voiced, for example, by Britain's leading environmentalist, Jonathon Porritt, formerly the UK government's principal Green adviser, who greeted the breaking of the seven billion barrier—under a headline referring to "Overpopulation: the global crisis that dare not speak its name"—with the comment: "The simple truth is that continuing population growth is a multiplier of every one of today's converging sustainability pressures."

Environmentalists accepted that population growth rates had fallen in many countries from a peak in the 1980s; the problem, as they saw it, was that there was a group of 55 nations, defined in *World Population Prospects* as "high-fertility countries", where growth was still soaring. Many of these were in regions of the world—39 of them were in sub-Saharan Africa—which were not only desperately poor already, but were most likely to be adversely affected by climate change (for example, with the increasing frequency and intensity of droughts threatening to make agriculture unviable).

Climate change itself, however, presented a more complex picture in 2011. According to the World Meteorological Organisation (WMO), it was the 10th hottest year in the global temperature record (which went back to 1850). Even though the 13 warmest years in the record had all occurred in the 15 years since 1997, the 2011 result might at first have been seen as a major change of direction, a significant reverse from 2010 which had been ranked by the WMO as the joint hottest-ever (together with 2005 and 1998). But 2011 was influenced by a very strong La Niña, the recurring phenomenon of a cooling of the eastern tropical Pacific which affected the whole globe—the better-known El Niño was its warming counterpart—and the WMO went on to say that 2011 was the hottest year on record with a La Niña event. (In the UK the year was the second-warmest ever, after 2006, with the warmest April and the warmest spring on record, the second warmest autumn, and the warmest-ever October day, with the mercury reaching 29.4 degrees Celsius—85.8 degrees Fahrenheit—at Gravesend in Kent on the first of the month.)

There were many other indications of a warming world in 2011. The extent of the Arctic sea ice at its summer minimum in September was the second-lowest on record, stated the WMO, and its volume was the lowest. According to data compiled by the Washington-based Earth Policy Institute, seven countries set all-time temperature records: Armenia, China, Iran, Iraq, Kuwait, the Democratic Republic of the Congo (DRC) and Zambia. Kuwait experienced the year's highest temperature, with thermometers measuring a searing 53.3 degrees Celsius (127.9 degrees Fahrenheit), the highest temperature ever recorded on Earth during the month of August. Oklahoma and Texas had the hottest summer ever experienced by a US state, breaking by a wide margin the record set in 1934 during the Dust Bowl.

The vast majority of the world's climate scientists believed that the warming of the climate system was "unequivocal" and that it was largely being caused by the emission of greenhouse gases such as carbon dioxide (CO_2) from industry, energy generation and transport, which retained the sun's heat in the atmosphere. There was an enigma, however, for the climate science community: the upward progress of the warming, in global terms, appeared over the last decade to have paused, although emissions were growing rapidly, and this was in contrast to the 1980s and 1990s when the annual upward progression of global average temperatures was startlingly obvious.

The globe, climatologists believed, should be heating up faster than it was; and 2011 was notable for two scientific studies (which were not mutually exclusive) that attempted to account for this phenomenon. One, from Robert Kaufman of Boston University and others, published in July, suggested that the true temperature rise was being "masked" by the Chinese sulphur aerosol—the huge volumes of sulphur particles emitted by Chinese coal-burning power stations—which once in the atmosphere reflected back the heat of the sun and had a cooling effect. The other, by a team from the US National Centre for Atmospheric Research, published in September, suggested that much of the "missing heat" was currently being taken up by the deep ocean.

Both theories created widespread interest, as data released during the year confirmed that atmospheric carbon was growing faster than anyone had believed possible even five years ago. Global CO_2 emissions in 2010, said the US department of energy in November 2011, had reached 33.51 billion tonnes, up from 31.63 billion tonnes in 2009—an increase of nearly 6 per cent that was believed to be the highest-ever percentage increase year-on-year. China led the way: Chinese emissions in 2010 were the world's highest by a wide margin, at 8.15 billion tonnes, up from 7.46 billion tonnes the year before, a 9.3 per cent increase in 12 months. China thus accounted for 24 per cent of global carbon emissions, whereas the USA—which had been the world's largest carbon emitter for decades until 2007—emitted a total of 5.49 billion tonnes in 2010—up from 5.27 billion tonnes in 2009, an increase of 4.1 per cent—and was responsible (in second place) for 16 per cent of the total. India, the world's third-biggest carbon polluter, was rapidly catching up. In 2010, its annual emissions passed two billion tonnes of CO_2 for the first time, totalling 2.06 billion tonnes, which represented just over 6 per cent of the global total.

When the international community met for its annual round of climate change negotiations in Durban in December, the fact that these three huge economies now accounted for 46 per cent of all greenhouse gas emissions presented a specific problem: none had agreed to any binding emissions cuts, such as those enshrined in the 1997 Kyoto Protocol governing many other advanced economies. But the meeting concluded with the "Big Three" polluters agreeing that they would be legally bound to cut carbon by a future treaty, to come into force by 2020. Depending on one's point of view, this was either a triumph—the meeting had nearly collapsed, with nothing being agreed—or a hopeless failure, as no action was scheduled for 10 years, and many observers felt the chance of controlling rising temperatures would have come and gone during that decade. But perhaps the defining characteristic of the Durban agreement, as of the issue of climate change generally in 2011, was how little it was noticed in the real world of ordinary citizens.

Contrast this with Fukushima, whose meltdown in March, the most momentous nuclear incident since the Chernobyl disaster of 1986, held the world spellbound—partly, of course, because it was a by-product of the catastrophic tsunami which struck the east coast of Japan on 11 March following an undersea earthquake of magnitude 9, one of the most powerful seismic movements ever recorded (see pp. 337-41).

Killing at least 16,000 people, causing perhaps \$35 billion-worth of damage and wiping out whole towns, the giant wave, some 14 metres high, overtopped the 5.7 metre-high sea-wall protecting Fukushima's six reactors and knocked out all power, which meant that water could no longer be pumped in to cool them. The reactors overheated and eventually melted down, with the reactor housings exploding spectacularly when hydrogen built up inside them. The principal fear, before the emergency was contained, was that large amounts of radioactive material would be released and might spread over vast areas, as had happened with Chernobyl, and a 20 km exclusion zone was set up around the plant. Current estimates suggest that Fukushima released about a tenth of the radioactivity discharged by Chernobyl. This was still being measured around the world and accurate casualty figures remained unclear. A significant policy consequence of the accident was that it damaged the "nuclear renaissance" taking place around the world—most spectacularly in Germany, which announced plans to sever its links with nuclear power altogether—although by the end of the year, adverse opinion in some countries had lessened.

In the natural world, 2011 was notable for the mounting assault on one of the great beasts, one of the "charismatic megafauna": the rhinoceros. This was prompted by the soaring price in Asian markets for rhino horn, shooting up to above $40,000 per kilo as a result of an urban myth: that the powdered horn could cure cancer. In South Africa alone, 448 rhinos were illegally shot for their horn in 2011 (up from 12 in 2007), and during the year it was announced that no fewer than three rhinoceros subspecies had been driven to extinction: the Javan rhino in Vietnam (only discovered in 1988), the western black rhino in West Africa, and the northern white rhino, last seen in the DRC. The year was marked also by the loss of a great defender of the natural world: Wangari Maathai, the Kenyan woman who founded the Green Belt movement to promote conservation and women's rights in Africa, and who received the Nobel Peace Prize in 2004, died on 25 September.

The UK faced its own, much smaller animal disappearance: the humble hedgehog was found to be tumbling in numbers, for reasons which were not entirely clear. But one piece of good news was that otters, nearly wiped out by pesticides in the 1950s and slowly recovering ever since, had returned to every county in England. Britain had its own environmental policy controversies too: a government attempt to sell off the public forest estate was scrapped in the face of overwhelmingly hostile public opinion; a somewhat similar attempt to neuter the planning system, in an effort to promote economic growth, met a similar response, and the government was mulling over its options as the year ended.

Both of these disputes caught the public imagination and excited public feeling in 2011 far more than did the truly existential threats of population growth and climate change, whose outlines were very clear. But the arguments about forests and planning concerned the here-and-now, while soaring human numbers and global warming threatened to converge somewhere in the future. And the future, as Czechoslovakia once was, is a faraway country of which we know nothing.

Michael McCarthy

XIV THE LAW

INTERNATIONAL LAW

THE killing of Osama bin Laden and other targeted killings of alleged terrorists by the USA raised controversial questions as to whether such actions could be lawful self-defence and whether they violated human rights law and international humanitarian law. Other legal questions arose with regard to the revolution in Libya. There was disagreement whether the military operations had gone beyond the UN Security Council authorisation in Resolution 1973 (2011) (see p. 215 and Documents), and on the scope of the doctrine of the "responsibility to protect" the population of Libya against crimes against humanity by the Kadhafi government. The African Commission on Human and People's Rights brought a case to the African Court on Human and People's Rights against Libya for serious and massive violations of human rights. The Court on its own initiative ordered provisional measures because the situation was one of extreme gravity and urgency and measures were necessary to avoid irreparable harm. It ordered Libya to refrain from any action that would result in loss of life or violation of physical integrity. The UN Security Council unanimously referred the situation in Libya to the International Criminal Court (ICC) which started its sixth investigation. Subsequently, on 27 June the Pre-Trial Chamber issued arrest warrants for Colonel Moamar Kadhafi, his son Saif al-Islam Kadhafi and former intelligence chief Abdullah al-Senussi for crimes against humanity committed since 15 February. However, the African Union (AU) called on its member states to disregard the arrest warrant for Colonel Kadhafi. The AU also challenged the ICC's role by calling on it to defer proceedings against President Omar al-Bashir of Sudan, who in 2009 had become the first head of state to be indicted by the Court, and in the cases arising from the 2007-08 post-election violence in Kenya (see p. 231). However, the ICC confirmed the admissibility of the Kenyan cases. It also informed the UN Security Council of the non-cooperation of Malawi and Chad, both parties to the ICC's Rome Statute, in the arrest and surrender of Bashir.

The ICC authorised a new investigation into war crimes and crimes against humanity committed in Côte d'Ivoire after the 2010 presidential elections; this was the first time the ICC had opened a case in a state not party to the Rome Statute, which had, however, accepted the jurisdiction of the Court. The ICC later issued an arrest warrant for former President Laurent Gbagbo (see p. 247). It brought an end to one of the Democratic Republic of Congo cases when it refused to confirm the charges against Rwandan rebel leader Callixte Mbarushimana and ordered his release (see p. 260).

Two new cases were submitted to the International Court of Justice (ICJ). The first was *Request for Interpretation of the Judgment of 15 June 1962 in the case concerning the Temple of Prihear Vihear* (*Cambodia v Thailand*). Cambodia claimed that the Court's earlier 1962 judgment had not merely recognised its sovereignty over the temple, but had also recognised that a legally established frontier existed between the two parties in the area in question. Thailand rejected this interpretation. The 1962 judgment had declared that Thailand was under an obligation to withdraw its forces stationed at the temple and in its vicinity on Cambodian territory. Cambodia now asked the ICJ to declare that the obligation on Thailand to withdraw its forces was a particular consequence of the general and continuing obligation to respect Cambodia's territorial integrity. It also asked for provisional measures to bring an end to Thailand's incursions into its territory in the area of the temple and along the border. The ICJ held that there appeared to be a dispute between the parties as to the meaning and scope of the 1962 judgment. It considered that the alleged rights were plausible, and that there was a risk of irreparable prejudice such that provisional measures were urgently required. It used its powers to indicate measures that were in whole or in part other than those requested, and defined a provisional demilitarised zone to prevent conflict between the parties (see pp. 322-23).

The ICJ also indicated provisional measures in *Certain Activities carried out by Nicaragua in the Border Area* (*Costa Rica v Nicaragua*). Costa Rica claimed that without its consent Nicaragua had constructed a canal across its territory, causing serious damage to a fragile eco-system. It asked the ICJ to order the withdrawal of Nicaraguan troops, the cessation of the construction of the canal and the suspension of the dredging programme. However, Nicaragua said that the operations in the canal were finished and that its troops had been withdrawn from the contested area. The Court ordered both parties to refrain from sending any personnel to the disputed territory until the dispute on the merits had been decided, except in so far as Costa Rica needed to send civilian personnel for the protection of the environment. In the second new case brought to the Court, Nicaragua instituted a related action against Costa Rica with regard to "violations of Nicaraguan sovereignty and major environmental damages to its territory" arising out of Costa Rica's major construction works along the border area (see p. 145).

The ICJ gave judgment on the merits in one case: *Application of the Interim Accord of 13 September 1995* (*the former Yugoslav Republic of Macedonia v Greece*). This case arose out of the long-standing dispute between Greece and the former Yugoslav Republic of Macedonia (FYROM) over the name "Macedonia". Greece objected to the use of this name by the former Yugoslav Republic as the term "Macedonia" covered an important part of its own territory. Accordingly, Macedonia had been admitted to the UN under the provisional name FYROM. It now claimed that Greece had blocked its accession to NATO in violation of a 1995 Interim Accord in which Greece had agreed not to object to FYROM's admission to international or regional organisations of which it was a member. Disputes concerning the interpretation or implementation of the accord should be decided by the Court, except for disputes about the definitive name of FYROM. Greece challenged the Court's jurisdiction on several grounds: first, the dispute was one about FYROM's name; second, the dispute concerned the conduct of NATO; third, any judgment would not be effective as it could not secure FYROM's admission to NATO; and, fourth, a judgment would interfere with the ongoing diplomatic negotiations. However, the Court asserted its jurisdiction and held on the merits that Greece had violated the Interim Accord in objecting to FYROM's membership of NATO (see p. 91).

The ICJ found it had no jurisdiction in another case, *Application of the International Convention on the Elimination of All Forms of Racial Discrimination (Georgia v Russia)*. Georgia claimed that Russia had repeatedly violated the 1965 *Convention on the Elimination of All Forms of Racial Discrimination* (CERD). The Court held that there was no dispute between the parties under CERD until the outbreak of conflict in South Ossetia in August 2008. After that date Georgia's claims were primarily about the use of force in that conflict, but they also expressly referred to alleged ethnic cleansing by Russian forces. However, the Court held by 10 votes to six that it had no jurisdiction as Georgia had not exhausted the procedural requirements under CERD. Thus, it took a different line from that in its earlier decision on provisional measures when it had held by eight votes to seven that there was prima facie jurisdiction on the merits. After a full hearing of the arguments the Court now held that the topic of ethnic cleansing had not been the subject of genuine negotiations or attempts at negotiations between the parties. Therefore it did not have jurisdiction to decide on the merits of the case.

Judges Hisashi Owada (Japan), Peter Tomka (Slovakia) and Xue Hanqin (China) were re-elected as members of the Court; Giorgio Gaja (Italy) and Julia Sebutinde (Uganda) were elected as new members.

The Court of Arbitration, established in 2010 under the 1960 Indus Waters Treaty to settle a dispute between Pakistan and India concerning a hydroelectric project, made an order for interim measures. This was the first time in the 50-year history of the treaty that a Court of Arbitration had been established to resolve a dispute between the parties. Pakistan claimed that India's proposed diversion of a river and depletion of the water supply would violate its obligations under the treaty. It also submitted a request for interim measures, asking the tribunal to order India to cease work on certain parts of the hydroelectric project. The tribunal was satisfied that Pakistan's claims were plausible, but the construction schedule meant that it was not necessary to order a halt of all construction to safeguard its ability to render an effective award. India could proceed with some projects at its own risk. However, the construction of a permanent dam did create a significant risk of prejudice to the final solution and the tribunal ordered that this should not proceed pending its final award.

The Seabed Disputes Chamber of the International Tribunal for the Law of the Sea (ITLOS) unanimously issued its first Advisory Opinion on the *Responsibilities and Obligations of States Sponsoring Persons and Entities with Respect to Activities in the Area*. The request for an opinion arose out of proposals by Nauru and Tonga, small island states, to sponsor commercial firms to carry out activities in the deep seabed beyond national jurisdiction. The Chamber held that the 1982 *Law of the Sea Convention* required that sponsoring states ensure that contractors carry out activities in conformity with their contracts and the Convention. The Chamber set a high standard of due diligence: states should apply the precautionary principle and follow best environmental practice. No special allowance should be made for developing states in this context. If damage occurred and the sponsoring state had failed to take all necessary and appropriate measures for securing compliance by its contractor, it would be liable.

Panama and Guinea-Bissau agreed to submit a new case to ITLOS concerning the oil tanker *Virginia G*, flying the flag of Panama. Panama claimed that the *Virginia G* was carrying out refuelling operations for fishing vessels in Guinea-Bissau's exclusive economic zone when it was arrested by Guinea-Bissau and detained for 14 months. Panama claimed reparation for the serious damage it suffered during detention. An arbitral tribunal was established under the *Law of the Sea Convention* to decide a dispute between Mauritius and the UK concerning the latter's proclamation of a Marine Protected Area around the Chagos Archipelago.

The International Labour Organisation (ILO) adopted a *Convention concerning Decent Work for Domestic Workers* in an attempt to improve the conditions of the 53 million (mainly women and girls) domestic workers around the world. A *Convention on Preventing and Combating Violence against Women and Domestic Violence* was opened for signature on 11 May. This was the first international treaty on the subject; it covered forced marriage, female genital mutilation, and physical and psychological violence. The International Law Commission finished its work on two major topics. After 17 years it adopted a "Guide to Practice on Reservations to Treaties". It also adopted draft articles on the responsibility of international organisations.

The European Court of Human Rights (ECtHR) continued to face an enormous backlog of cases. It codified for the first time in the Rules of the Court the pilot-judgment procedure that it had adopted to deal with repetitive cases. It also adopted a new Filtering Section to streamline decision-making on the admissibility of applications under Protocol 14 (which had come into force in 2010). This centralised the handling of cases from five of the highest case-count countries—Russia, Turkey, Romania, Ukraine and Poland. These states accounted for over half the cases pending before the Court. The Court also issued a Practice Direction to deal with the vastly increased number of requests for interim measures in immigration and asylum cases.

It issued two important judgments on freedom of conscience and religion. In *Bayatyan v Armenia* the ECtHR Grand Chamber for the first time held that refusal to allow conscientious objectors an alternative to military service violated Article 9 on freedom of religion. Although in the past the Court had understood that the European Convention on Human Rights (ECHR) allowed member states to choose whether to recognise conscientious objectors, there was now a virtual consensus among member states on the right of conscientious objection; this had brought about a shift in the interpretation of Article 9. Another, more controversial, case was brought by parents who objected to the display of crucifixes in Italian state schools as an interference with their freedom of conscience. In *Lautsi* the Grand Chamber reversed the earlier unanimous decision by a Chamber of the Court and held that this display of religious symbols came within the margin of appreciation of the domestic authorities. It took account of the great diversity between states in Europe with regard to their culture and history.

The Court also decided several cases on asylum and deportation. In *MSS v Belgium and Greece* the Grand Chamber found that the treatment of asylum seekers in Greece violated the prohibition of inhuman treatment in Article 3 ECHR, and that Belgium had also violated this Article in returning asylum seekers to Greece. Bulgaria had also violated Article 3 through its failure to carry out an adequate risk assessment in returning a Palestinian suspected terrorist to Lebanon; it could not invoke national security to escape this obligation. In *AA* the UK had violated the right to private life by its deportation of a Nigerian national for a serious offence committed while he was a minor, despite his subsequent exemplary conduct. In contrast, Sweden had been justified in returning a Rwandan Hutu to Rwanda where he could expect a fair trial for genocide and crimes against humanity.

Finally, the Grand Chamber decided two important cases against the UK on the territorial scope of the application of the Convention. In *Al-Skeini*, it held that because the UK had assumed the exercise of some public power in Iraq after the end of the conflict it was bound to uphold the ECHR there; its failure to carry out effective investigation into deaths caused by British soldiers in Basra amounted to a violation of Article 2 ECHR on the right to life. In *Al-Jedda* it found that the preventive detention of Iraqi nationals by British armed forces in Iraq was attributable to the UK rather than to the UN which had authorised the deployment of the troops. Security Council Resolution 1546 could not be interpreted to justify detention in violation of ECHR rights.

Five years after its creation the UN Human Rights Council completed its appraisal of the human rights situation of every member state through its Universal Periodic Review mechanism. It also carried out a review of its working methods. It held special sessions on Côte d'Ivoire, Libya and Syria. On 16 June it endorsed "Guiding Principles on Business and Human Rights".

The International Criminal Tribunal for the former Yugoslavia (ICTY) secured the arrest of the two last remaining fugitives—Ratko Mladic, the former commander of the Bosnian Serb armed forces, and Goran Hadzic, a former leader of the breakaway Serb republic in Croatia (see p. 94). They made their initial appearances before the tribunal. Mladic had been indicted in 1995 for genocide for the murder of about 8,000 men in the 1995 Srebrenica massacre. The ICTY Trial Chamber refused to sever the charges against Mladic to allow two separate trials, one to deal with the crimes in Srebrenica, and the other concerning crimes committed in Sarajevo and elsewhere in Bosnia. It held that this could prejudice the accused, make the trial less efficient and unduly burden witnesses. It did however, reduce the charges from 196 to 106 in the interests of an expeditious trial. Hadzic had been indicted in 2004 for crimes against humanity and war crimes.

The Trial Chamber completed three major trials. First, Momcilo Perisic, former chief of general staff of the Yugoslav Army, was sentenced to 27 years' imprisonment for military aid to Bosnian Serbs responsible for the Srebrenica massacre and for the siege of Sarajevo. This was the first conviction of a Yugoslav official for war crimes in Bosnia. Second, in the trial of three Croatian generals for their actions against Croatian Serb civilians in 1995 as part of a joint criminal enterprise to drive Croatian Serbs out of Croatia, Ante Gotovina and Mladen Markac were convicted and Ivan Cermak was acquitted. Third, Vlastimir Djordjevic, a former senior Serbian police officer, was convicted for crimes against humanity and war crimes against Kosovo Albanian civilians in 1999.

The International Criminal Tribunal for Rwanda (ICTR) for the first time referred a case, that of Jean Uwinkindi, a former pastor in a Pentecostal church, to the Rwandan courts, a mechanism crucial to its completion strategy. The Referral Chamber requested that the African Commission on Human and People's Rights be appointed to monitor the trial in Rwanda. The Trial Chamber decided several important cases involving multiple accused. In the *Military II* cases Augustin Bizimungu, former chief of staff of the Rwandan armed forces and one of the main architects of the genocide, and Augustin Ndindiliyimana, a former chief of the military police, were convicted of genocide and crimes against humanity; they were acquitted of conspiracy to commit genocide. Bizimungu was sentenced to 30 years' imprisonment. However, Ndindiliyimana was released for time served as his effective command had been limited and he had opposed the massacres. Two other military commanders were found guilty of lesser offences. In the *Government II* cases Justin Mugenzi and Prosper Mugiraneza, both former government ministers, were convicted for conspiracy to commit genocide and public incitement of genocide. Two other ministers were acquitted. In the *Butare* cases all six accused were convicted, including Pauline Nyiramasuhuko, former government minister and the first woman to be charged with genocide. Also Matthieu Ngirumpatse and Edouard Karemera, president and vice-president of the ruling party in Rwanda, were found guilty of genocide and crimes against humanity through their joint criminal enterprise to destroy the Tutsi population of Rwanda. They were also responsible for the widespread rape of Tutsi women which was a foreseeable consequence of their joint criminal enterprise. The Appeal Chamber decided five cases. These generally affirmed the convictions of the accused, but in some cases the Chamber reduced the sentences.

The Prosecutor of the Special Tribunal for Lebanon (STL) filed an indictment against four members of Hezbullah in connection with the attack on former Prime Minister Rafiq Hariri and others on 14 February 2005. This marked the beginning of the judicial phase of the tribunal's work. The Pre-Trial Judge subsequently confirmed the indictments and issued international arrest warrants for the four accused. In February the STL Appeals Chamber unanimously issued a landmark ruling on the applicable law. This 152-page interlocutory decision covered 15 questions. Most notably it ruled on the definition of terrorism, the first time an international tribunal had confirmed a general definition of terrorism under international law. It also ruled on the modes of criminal responsibility.

The Extraordinary Chambers in the Courts of Cambodia (ECCC) began the trial of four Khmer Rouge leaders, Nuon Chea, Ieng Sary, Ieng Thirith, Khieu Samphan in Case 002 (see p. 322). They were indicted for crimes against humanity, grave breaches of the 1949 Geneva Conventions and genocide. The Trial Chamber issued a severance order to split the case into a series of smaller trials, starting with a trial on forced movement of people and related crimes against humanity. The Trial Chamber decided in November that Ieng Thirith was mentally unfit to stand trial and ordered her release. However, this decision was reversed by the Supreme Court Chamber which found that the Trial Chamber must exhaust all available measures capable of helping the accused to stand trial.

Christine Gray

EUROPEAN UNION LAW

THE dominating theme for the European Union during 2011 was the economy and specifically the currency problems of the 17 nations of the eurozone ("the Member States which have the euro as their currency"). This led to a feeling that constitutional changes would be needed, involving alterations to the founding treaties—only 18 months after the substantial Lisbon Treaty amendments had come into effect (see AR 2010, p. 475). But treaty amendment would require unanimous approval of all 27 Member States and not just the eurozone states. This was impossible, not least because the United Kingdom was ideologically opposed to any involvement. The increasingly fraught political negotiations culminated, therefore, in two eurozone treaties in December.

The first of these, the ESM Treaty, created machinery—the European Stability Mechanism—to safeguard financial stability in the euro area. It was signed, on 11 July 2011, by the 17 members of the eurozone and applied to them only. However, before it could be signed it was necessary to amend the Treaty on the Functioning of the European Union (TFEU) to provide the requisite legal basis. This was done, by all 27 EU Member States, by a decision of the European Council on 25 March 2011, acting under the accelerated amendment procedure laid down in Article 48(6) of the Treaty on European Union (TEU). That decision added a paragraph to Article 136 of TFEU, which specifically authorised the eurozone Member States to "establish a stability mechanism".

In effect, therefore, the full EU of 27 authorised the eurozone of 17 to legislate to create the ESM. Both the March decision and, of course, the July treaty had treaty status and required ratification by the 27 or 17 Member States respectively.

Events, however, moved on quickly and the ESM Treaty was immediately altered by the leaders of the eurozone-17, on 21 July and again on 9 December. On the latter occasion it was decided to incorporate these unofficial alterations (i.e. without legal status) into a revised version of the treaty, the text of which was agreed, to be made ready for signature early in 2012. It was hoped that after ratifications the ESM Treaty would come into force and the ESM would be set up in July 2012.

Whilst this relatively focused development was pursuing its course, pressure built in the latter part of the year for a more generalised, constitutional solution to the perceived lack of fiscal discipline in some eurozone states. This came to a head in a discussion by the 17 eurozone states, in the margins of the European Council meeting on 9 December, with a decision to conclude a Fiscal Compact Treaty. This would contain more effective rules of economic governance. Owing to fierce opposition from the UK (see p. 19), this new treaty could not adopt the route taken when creating the ESM (amending Article 136 of TEFU), but had to remain wholly distinct from the EU founding Treaties. The decision of the 9 December Euro Summit therefore (a new term for a new concept: a formal meeting of the leaders of the eurozone Member States) envisaged a treaty to be ready for signature by the eurozone Member States by March 2012 but, unlike the ESM Treaty, open to accession by non-eurozone Member States and capable of being incorporated into the EU founding Treaties at some propitious time in the future.

The Fiscal Compact Treaty would, therefore, not use the Article 136 TFEU procedure (as used for the ESM Treaty), or the "enhanced cooperation" facility to legislate for only part of the EU (as was done for the Divorce Regulation of December 2010, see AR 2011, p. 474). Both these techniques were attached to EU texts and so were precluded by the UK veto. Instead, the Fiscal Compact Treaty was closely comparable to the Schengen and Prüm Treaties on a common external frontier for the movement of aliens into and within the EU. These had started with a small nucleus of Member States acting independently of the EU, and had gradually expanded until they were eventually brought into the basic EU Treaties themselves, although subject to opt-outs for some dissident Member States. A similar progression was clearly in the minds of the authors of this new treaty.

Important constitutional change was not exhausted by these events. The venerable Western European Union (WEU), which pre-dated the European Union itself and for many years had represented the European interest in cooperating for military purposes, had gradually lost its will to live—first with the arrival of NATO and latterly as the EU took over many of its remaining functions. The decision was therefore taken in 2010 to wind it up, and this was done on 30 June 2011. Its physical and financial debris was absorbed by the European Space Agency, another wholly-owned subsidiary of the EU. Perhaps as part of the same development of the EU's defence capability, the statute of the European Defence Agency (established in 2004, see AR 2005, pp. 373) was rewritten by the Council in July.

Membership of the EU was increased in December by signature of the treaty of accession of Croatia, as the 28th Member State, effective when the treaty would receive full ratification (see pp. 99-100). Turkey, the second state ever to apply for EU (at the time, European Economic Community) membership, saw its application recede ever more into the distance. On the other hand, the application from Iceland made swift progress but still had to surmount the hurdles of fisheries policy and domestic public opinion, as well as Iceland's refusal to reimburse the

British and Dutch governments for compensation to depositors in the crashed Icelandic banks (see p. 47).

Internationally, the legal status of the EU continued to harden. Since, in recent years, only two types of legal person were recognised—sovereign states and international organisations—international lawyers placed the EU in the second category, ignoring the powerful, state-like elements in its governmental system. A third category had recently been invented by the Hague Conference on Private International Law (the body harmonising conflict of laws between countries in personal or commercial situations), specifically to permit the EU to join its system alongside the sovereign states which had, until then, constituted its membership. As a result, the EU was able to sign in April and ratify the Hague Convention on Child Support, in its capacity as a "regional economic integration organisation". The content of that convention thereby became a binding part of the domestic law of the EU Member States as such. The same technique had been used by the Council of Europe to enable the EU to become a party to the European Convention on Human Rights (ECHR). Difficult technical negotiations on the EU's accession to the ECHR, however, continued throughout 2011 and culminated in the presentation to the Committee of Ministers of the Council of Europe in October of a draft treaty of accession, which formed the basis of further political negotiations lasting beyond the end of the year.

The entry into force in 2010 of Protocol 14 to the European Convention on Human Rights (see AR 2011, p. 475) did not halt the calls for reform of the Convention system, to solve the problem of the severe overload and backlog of the European Court of Human Rights. Discussions and papers, especially within the Council of Europe and the Court itself, continued throughout the year. The same occurred within the EU's Court of Justice (ECJ) which, together with its junior, the General Court, was also experiencing case load difficulties, not unconnected with the massive recent enlargement of the EU. Only the specialist Civil Service Tribunal succeeded in mastering its case list. One useful, albeit somewhat overdue, contribution to quicker justice was the adoption in September by all three EU courts of electronic methods of lodging formal documents.

In the field of legislation a number of significant developments took place. The Lisbon Treaty had introduced a new power for ordinary people to take part in creating legislation by means of a "citizens' initiative", which would allow a "petition" by EU citizens to initiate laws. The detailed procedure for operating this was laid down in a regulation in February. Also following Lisbon, the "comitology" procedure governing the European Commission's use of delegated legislative power was heavily revised and the underlying implementing powers regulation was reissued in February. Finally, the special legislative procedure of "enhanced cooperation", whereby a group of Member States smaller than the total membership might legislate for themselves alone but using, and with permission of, EU procedures, was used for a second time (the first was the Divorce Regulation in December 2010). In March the Council authorised its use to bring to fruition the long disputed EU patent regulation. The blockage by two Member States of its language provisions was thus turned. But no sooner was that problem solved than other causes for delay were found by other states, and by the year's end little further progress had been made.

More traditional was the revision and repeal of the venerable Regulation 1612/68 on the free movement of workers. This had formed one of the key elements in the EEC's fundamental freedoms since 1968, near the beginning of the EU project. In April it was replaced by Regulation 492/2011 and brought more into harmony with current EU legislation on free movement.

Neville March Hunnings

LAW IN THE UNITED KINGDOM

THE UK Supreme Court saw a changing of the guard. It was announced that Lord Saville of Newdigate and Lord Brown of Eaton-under-Heywood would on retirement be succeeded by Lords Justices Wilson and Carnwath respectively. In June, Lord Rodger of Earlsferry died in office aged 66. His untimely death made the unprecedented *ad hominem* attacks upon the Scottish judges of the Court by Alex Salmond, first minister of Scotland—when Lord Rodger was seriously ill—particularly maladroit. Lord Reed was chosen to replace Lord Rodger. Even more controversial was the announcement that Jonathan Sumption QC would replace the retiring Lord Collins of Mapesbury. This was the first appointment direct from the Bar to the ultimate tribunal since that of Lord Radcliffe in 1949; a previous attempt to elevate Mr Sumption in 2009 had foundered amid objections from disappointed judges of the Court of Appeal (see AR 2010, p. 477). Jonathan Sumption was disinclined to avoid controversial topics. In his F.A. Mann lecture at the British Institute of International and Comparative Law in November, he argued trenchantly for judicial restraint in reviewing discretionary decisions of the executive. He suggested that courts frequently substitute their own view of the better policy without admitting it. English administrative law was unprincipled and incoherent; it was time for an open debate about the constitutional merits of greatly increased judicial review.

Lord Sumption finally joined the Supreme Court in January 2012. Some cases of 2011 saw sharp public disagreements in judicial review cases, providing evidence for his thesis. In *Regina (McDonald) v. Kensington and Chelsea Royal London Borough Council* the local authority decided to provide incontinence pads instead of night nursing care for the claimant. The Supreme Court held that this had not infringed her right to private life under the European Convention on Human Rights; even if the right was engaged, the decision was a proportionate one (respecting the claimant's rights with a significant cost saving). Baroness Hale of Richmond dissented, holding the council's policy unworthy of a civilized society and deeming it irrational in the "*Wednesbury*" sense—so unreasonable that no reasonable authority could have adopted it. Lord Brown dismissed these comments as "little short of remarkable". *Regina (Quila and another) v. Home Secretary* challenged the Home Office policy that non-European spouses under the age of 21 were not allowed to enter Britain. This was intended to deter the "appalling evil" of forced marriages (Lord Brown). However, the 18-year-old Chilean applicant, refused entry to the UK, had been married by his British wife with her enthusiastic consent. The Supreme Court held that applying a blanket policy to such unsuitable cases was arbitrary and unlawful. It had not been shown that the policy itself would have any discernible deterrent effect on forced marriage. Lady Hale suggested that it might be counterproductive—leading British brides to be sent abroad to live with foreign husbands. Lord Brown this time dissented, holding that in this sensitive area it was "positively unwise for the courts yet again to frustrate government policy except in the clearest of cases". Forced marriage created enormous suffering and Lord Brown did not think the government's response to it "demonstrably wrong".

In *Regina (Lumba and Mighty) v. Home Secretary* the claimants were foreign nationals convicted of criminal offences. They had been detained pending deportation, purportedly under a policy requiring such detention only when justified. In fact, however, the Home Office was operating a secret, unpublished policy of detaining all foreigners convicted of crimes (in reaction to public disquiet on the subject). The Supreme Court held this unlawful. The government had committed the tort of false imprisonment even though, had the correct policy been applied, the claimants might still have been detained. This simply meant that they had suffered no loss from the unlawful conduct; but it was of constitutional importance to vindicate the liberty of the subject through a finding of liability. Exemplary damages were not appropriate; although there had been a deliberate decision to conceal the policy at the highest level the conduct was not "unconstitutional, oppressive or arbitrary". In *Rahmatullah v Foreign Secretary* a writ of *habeas corpus* was issued against the foreign secretary ordering him to request the release of the claimant from a US-controlled detention camp in Afghanistan. The claimant had been captured in Iraq in 2004 by British forces and handed to the US authorities. The British government had sufficient control of the claimant to be amenable to the writ because, arguably, they were entitled to demand his return to their custody under the Geneva Convention. The argument that this might damage diplomatic relations with the USA was dismissed as a "flimsy basis" for refusing *habeas corpus*.

There was a raft of constitutionally significant legislation. The Fixed-Term Parliaments Act mandated general elections be held every five years from the first Thursday in May 2015. Parliament could be dissolved earlier only if there was a vote of no-confidence in the government or two-thirds of the House of Commons approved a motion for an early election (see pp. 14-15). The House of Lords took the view that this should be a temporary measure born of the expediencies of coalition government, but the Commons resisted an expiry or "sunset" clause. The compromise was that the prime minister must hold an inquiry into the operation of the Act in 2020. The European Union Act required that future amendments to the EU treaties must be approved in a national referendum before being ratified. Constitutional scholars debated the effect, if any, of this Act. Parliament is not able to bind its successors, according to orthodoxy, so what was to stop a future Parliament ignoring or indeed repealing the 2011 Act? On the other hand, the European Communities Act 1972 had famously prevailed over the Merchant Shipping Act 1988 in the *Factortame* litigation, altering orthodoxy.

Following the government's review of anti-terror laws, the Terrorism Prevention and Investigation Measures Act repealed the 2005 law on control orders (see AR 2004, p. 451; AR 2005, pp. 16-17). However, the new "TPIM"s could be used to impose overnight residence and travel measures, exclusions of entering specified places, control over bank accounts and transfers of property, restrictions on possession or use of electronic communications devices, restrictions on work, study and associations, and a duty to report to the police. The Police Reform and Social Responsibility Act repealed the 2005 restrictions on demonstrations in the vicinity of Parliament, while making unlawful camping, sleeping or using amplified sound equipment in Parliament Square.

The Supreme Court was obliged (in *Jones v. Kernott*) to explain what the House of Lords had meant by its decision on *Stack v. Dowden* (2007) on the co-ownership of homes by non-married couples. The Court of Appeal held that a nightclub owed a duty of care to its patrons to protect them from violent behaviour by fellow guests (*Everett v. Comojo*). In *Jones v. Kaney* the Supreme Court held that expert witnesses in court cases should no longer enjoy immunity from suit should their evidence contain negligent inaccuracies. Lord Hope and Lady Hale, dissenting, thought that the courts did not have sufficient information to predict the effect of the change and so reform should be left to the Law Commission. *Sienkiewicz v. Greif* established that the exceptional approach to proving causation of mesothelioma in *Fairchild* (2002) applied when a single defendant added to the claimant's environmental exposure to asbestos. In *AXA General Insurance v. Lord Advocate* the Supreme Court rejected a challenge to the Damages (Asbestos-related Conditions) (Scotland) Act 2009. This legislation deemed asymptomatic pleural plaques to be compensable injury (reversing the House of Lords' decision in *Rothwell*, 2007). The court dismissed the insurers' argument that the statute interfered with their right to their possessions under the European Convention. It was, moreover, doubtful that an Act of the Scottish Parliament could be quashed as "irrational", save in the most exceptional circumstances. Lord Hope pointed to the democratic legitimacy that the Parliament enjoyed but judges did not.

In *Regina v. Williams* the defendant had correctly been convicted of causing death while driving without insurance, even though the victim had walked out in front of his car and his driving was impeccable. The offence did not require blameworthy conduct (other than being uninsured). This had been criticised for "perverting" principles of causation but it was what Parliament had intended when creating the offence in 2006. In *Regina v. Gnango* an innocent bystander had been killed in the cross-fire from a fight between the defendant and an untraced adversary, "Bandana Man", who had fired the fatal shot. The defendant was guilty of murder since he was engaged in a murderous joint enterprise with "Bandana Man". This curiously suggested that the defendant was party to a scheme to ensure his own death at the hands of the other gunman. In *D Borough Council v. AB* the Court of Protection found that the defendant, "seriously challenged in all aspects of his mental functionality", was incapable of understanding the nature of, or therefore consenting to, sexual activity. The authority had therefore acted lawfully in preventing sexual contact. But in this case of "legal, intellectual and moral" difficulty having such a profound effect on the liberty of the subject, Mr Justice Mostyn ordered the authority to give the defendant a course of sex education in the hope that he would come to understand such matters and be able to form consensual sexual relationships.

Jonathan Morgan

LAW IN THE USA

Four federal Circuit Courts of Appeal decided challenges to the validity of the Obama administration's signature healthcare reform legislation, the Patient Protection and Affordable Care Act. The Sixth and District of Columbia Circuits upheld the law, the Eleventh Circuit held it invalid on the grounds that Congress's power to regulate commerce did not include compelling individuals to buy health insurance, and the Fourth Circuit held that the plaintiffs did not have standing to bring such proceedings. The US Supreme Court agreed to hear the appeal of the Eleventh Circuit decision and scheduled five-and-a-half hours of argument in 2012, the most allocated to a case since the 1960s.

The number and importance of the cases questioning measures to combat terrorism declined in 2011. Federal courts divided over whether US citizens could sue officials for unlawful detention and torture. In *Doe v. Rumsfeld*, Judge James Gwin held that an action against former Defence Secretary Donald Rumsfeld for torture could proceed, though the plaintiff would have to prove Rumsfeld's personal involvement in the alleged actions. In *Padilla v. Rumsfeld*, Judge Richard Mark Gergel held that no suit for unlawful detention or torture could proceed against Rumsfeld and other officials because they enjoyed qualified immunity. The Supreme Court, in *Ashcroft v. al-Kidd*, held that Abdullah al-Kidd, who had been arrested, shackled, strip-searched and detained in a high-security cell for 16 days under a federal statute that allowed judges to order the arrest of a person whose testimony was material in a criminal proceeding and his presence would have been difficult to secure, could not challenge the warrant on the basis of the official's improper motive.

Anwar al-Awlaki, a US-born Muslim cleric—whose father had unsuccessfully challenged, in a court case in 2010 (see AR 2011, p. 479), a presidential order to assassinate him—was killed in 2011 by a missile fired by an unmanned drone aircraft directed by the CIA (see Obituary).

Federal courts were asked to decide if state laws enacted to scare out illegal immigrants usurped federal immigration powers. In *U.S. v. Arizona*, the Supreme Court upheld an Arizona law that empowered state and local officials to revoke and suspend licenses of businesses that knowingly hired illegal immigrants, because the federal law specifically allowed states to impose sanctions on such businesses through licensing and similar laws. The Ninth Circuit Court of Appeals invalidated another Arizona law that required police officers to determine the immigration status of persons stopped, penalised persons for violating federal registration laws, penalised undocumented aliens for seeking work, and authorised police officers to make warrantless arrests of persons that committed an offence that made him removable from the USA. In *U.S. v. Alabama*, federal district court Judge Sharon Lovelace Blackburn held invalid the provisions in an Alabama law that required immigrants to carry residency documents and required public schools to determine and report the immigration status of all students, but upheld provisions that required police officers to verify the status of suspected undocumented aliens, that required that police officers arrest and verify the immigration status of persons found driving without a licence, that prohibited state courts from enforcing contracts signed by illegal aliens, and that prohibited undocumented persons from entering into business transactions with state and local governments. Similar laws were passed in Georgia, Utah and South Carolina.

Efforts to diminish the influence of money in political campaigns witnessed another setback. In *Arizona Free Enterprise Club v. Bennett* and *McComish v. Bennett*, the Supreme Court held invalid an Arizona law that entitled candidates who elected to receive public funds for their campaigns to additional funds when their opponents received significant amounts from private sources. Such levelling of the "playing field" in campaign finance was held an unacceptable burden on free speech.

Novel issues concerning young persons' rights and liberties were decided by the courts during the year. The Supreme Court, in *Brown v. Entertainment Merchants Association*, held invalid a California law that prohibited the sale to persons under the age of 18 of video games that depict "killing, maiming, dismembering or sexually assaulting an image of a human being", on the basis that only pornographic material could be banned. The Supreme Court held, in *J.D.B. v. North Carolina*, that police officers should consider a juvenile's age when considering whether to give him his Miranda warnings prior to questioning him, because of a child's vulnerability. Prior to this decision, a Miranda warning was required only after a suspect was in custody. In *State v. Ninham*, the Wisconsin supreme court upheld a life sentence without parole for a 16-year old tried as an adult, who, at age 14, without any provocation, had stopped a 13-year old on an errand for his parents, accosted and thrown him to his death from a five-storey parking ramp. The case was expected to be appealed to the Supreme Court, which, in 2010, had held that a life sentence without parole for a juvenile offender who had committed a crime less than homicide was unconstitutional.

The New Jersey Supreme Court, in *State v. Henderson*, held, in a landmark decision, that because of the unreliability of eyewitness testimony a judge must conduct a full pre-trial hearing on the admissibility of such evidence where the police had been suggestive and, if such testimony was admitted, a judge must give detailed instructions that explained the factors that affect the reliability of such evidence. In two other cases, the District of Columbia Circuit Court, in *Bame v. Dillard*, and the Tenth Circuit Court, in *Archuleta v. Wagner*, held that law enforcement officers could strip-search demonstrators arrested for non-violent, non-drug related misdemeanours. An appeal to the Supreme Court in the first case was expected.

In two decisions the Supreme Court significantly curbed class actions. In *Wal-Mart v. Dukes* the court held that female employees of Wal-Mart could not bring a class action for sex discrimination, alleging such discrimination was a company-wide policy, because local managers had discretion to award promotions and raises. In *AT&T Mobility v. Concepcion*, the Court held the contractual agreement between AT&T and its customers to submit disputes to arbitration and not to join classwide proceedings was binding, notwithstanding a California law that held such agreements unenforceable where the individual claim was for a small amount and the bargaining power between the parties uneven, and such arbitration precluded a class action.

Robert J. Spjut

XV RELIGION

CHRISTIANITY. Inter-religious tensions—particularly Muslim-Christian violence—escalated in some parts of the world. Thirty minutes into the New Year 2011, a bomb in the Egyptian city of Alexandria killed 21 Coptic Christians. On 2 March Pakistan's minister for religious minorities—and the only Christian cabinet member—Shahbaz Bhatti was assassinated after expressing opposition to the country's blasphemy law (see p. 299 and Obituary). On 25 December—Christmas day—a suicide bomber in Madalla, Nigeria, detonated a bomb after Mass, killing around 40 (see p. 237). Despite such atrocities, several leaders of Christian churches, including Pope Benedict XVI, challenged the triumphalism which had greeted the killing of Osama bin Laden in May (see p. 133). In October, the pope visited Assisi in Italy for a day of reflection, dialogue and prayer for peace and justice with leaders of the world's faiths and churches.

The Roman Catholic Church, which claimed a membership of 1.18 billion adherents, continued to be torn apart by the allegations of sexual abuse of children by its clergy. This led to an official condemnation of "sexual exploitation in all its forms, especially when perpetrated against minors" and a set of guidelines issued in May. In Ireland, following the report on abuse in the diocese of Cloyne released in July, both houses of the Irish parliament as well as the Archbishop of Dublin deplored the Vatican's delay in publishing the findings of its own investigation. In November Ireland withdrew its ambassador to the Holy See. Matters were particularly tense in Austria where, in June, 361 clergy led by Helmut Schüller, former vicar-general, issued a "Call to Disobedience" in areas such as clerical marriage and the ordination of women. Cardinal Christoph Schönborn of Vienna compared this to a football team refusing to play by the rules. In April relations between the Chinese Patriotic Catholic Church and the Vatican were stretched after a number of men were ordained bishop without papal approval.

Pope Benedict, who celebrated 60 years as a priest in July, made a number of foreign visits: to Croatia in June for the first national family day; to Madrid in August for World Youth Day (a visit that provoked criticism over its cost and the closure of public spaces); and to Germany in September where, amid much opposition, he spoke to the Bundestag and met with victims of sexual abuse at Erfurt. There was disappointment following an ecumenical service at which he failed to make any concessions to Protestants. In November he was greeted more enthusiastically in Benin.

Benedict continued to promote conservative causes. In January the "Personal Ordinariate of Our Lady of Walsingham" was established for disaffected Anglicans. Three Anglican bishops were ordained priest, taking with them about 600 people. The third round of the Anglican-Roman Catholic International Commission began in May under the shadow of these events. As well as trying to revive Eucharistic adoration, Benedict also issued an Instruction, *Universae Ecclesia*, which allowed for greater use of the old Mass. A new English-language translation in a far more traditional style was introduced in September. On 1 May Pope John Paul II was declared blessed (a step on the path to sainthood). The church showed that it could deploy social media by using official Facebook and YouTube pages to promote the cause of the former pope. In November the Vatican acted against an unauthorised use of a papal image by the fashion chain, Benetton. Fashion also created a stir in Sicily in May where Bishop Domenico Mogavero sported silk vestments designed by Armani.

The patriarchs of three ancient Orthodox churches met on 1-2 September in Istanbul to discuss the situation of Christian minorities in the Middle East, as well as the possibility of a pan-Orthodox council, an event which seemed as elusive as ever. The year concluded with a brawl between Greek Orthodox and Armenian clergy armed with brooms, over the cleaning of Bethlehem's Church of the Nativity, birthplace of the "Prince of Peace".

In the Anglican Communion a number of senior bishops (primates) absented themselves from a meeting in Dublin, which aimed to solve some of the divisions over human sexuality. In Zimbabwe the official Anglican church suffered persecution at the hands of state-supported dissidents, although matters began to improve following a visit by the archbishop of Canterbury in October. In London, St Paul's Cathedral was surrounded by activists from the "Occupy" movement (see p. 13), which led to its temporary closure and the resignation of a canon and dean amid much publicity. The Church of Scotland, and the Presbyterian Church of the USA, voted to move towards the acceptance of gay and lesbian candidates for ordination. In California there was a media frenzy—and a degree of relief—as the beginning of the end of world failed to materialise on 21 May, contrary to the predictions of evangelist Harold Camping.

Mark Chapman

HINDUISM. The Hindu year began in 2011 on 4 April, coinciding with the World Economic Forum in Davos, Switzerland. The organisers invited 94 spiritual leaders, senior Hindus among them, to address issues of healing, spiritual life and happiness. In February the Hindu American Seva Charities launched the UtsavSeva initiative, another attempt to draw attention to spiritual matters. In the spirit of Gandhi's often-quoted maxim, "service to man is service to God", its aim was to raise awareness of *seva*, or selfless service, and to encourage US Hindus to engage in community service for the common good.

It was a good year for Hindu chaplains, a growing community and a product of interaction with non-Indian institutions. Oxford University acquired its first Hindu chaplain in its 900-year history, as did the younger Duke University in North Carolina. These were followed by the appointment of the first Hindu chaplain to the US defence department. In July, the Bhumi Project, named after Mother Bhumi, goddess of the earth, was launched at the White House. This represented an international Hindu response to issues of environmental change. Facilitated by the Oxford Centre for Hindu Studies, in partnership with the Alliance of Religions and Conservation, the project worked with a number of national Hindu forums to raise awareness of global responsibility from Hindu sources. In the UK, the Hindu-Christian Forum was relaunched in November, hosted by the Archbishop of Canterbury.

In March India's Supreme Court made passive euthanasia legal, ruling that life-support machines or medical treatment could be withdrawn in cases of terminal disease, under "guarded conditions". This decision inspired some debate, but Hindu tradition, opposed to active euthanasia, had always supported the concept of *prayopavesa*—allowing individuals to end their life by refusing food. In Kerala, south India, remarkable treasures were discovered in the underground chambers of the Shree Padmanabhaswamy temple. The hoard of gold, silver, precious stones and jewels, deposited as offerings to the deity of Lord Vishnu, was estimated to be worth at least $24 billion. It had its origins in generations of rulers of Travancore, the royal family who were custodians of the temple. This made Padmanabhaswamy the wealthiest Hindu temple in the world. In August a collection of a different kind of treasure, from the Indian research institute Bharat Itihas Sanshodhak Mandal in Pune, was set to be digitised by India's National Manuscripts Mission. An historical collection of about 40,000 Sanskrit manuscripts on Indian philosophy, art and the Ayurveda would be made accessible over the next two years.

The academic world was stirred by the controversial decision made by Delhi University to withdraw from its history syllabus A.K. Ramanujan's essay *Three Hundred Ramayanas: Five examples and three thoughts on translations*. The Indian division of Oxford University Press (OUP) decided not to reprint the work. The essay described the different retellings of the *Ramayana*, some of which had offended Hindu nationalist groups. OUP recanted after strong reaction from scholars around the world.

April saw the death of Sathya Sai Baba, a well-known holy man, and guru for millions of followers, including many prominent industrialists and politicians in India and the diaspora. For his followers he was a manifestation of God, a miracle worker, healer and spiritual leader. He was also a source of controversy—his acts of materialising objects had made him famous worldwide—and the subject of sexual abuse allegations, which were pursued the media but not in court.

In July the Hindu temple in Leicester in the UK registered a 551kg churma ladoo, made as an offering to the deity Ganesh, as a new Guinness World Record for the largest Indian sweet ever made. Its preparation kept three chefs and more than 20 volunteers busy for four days, and the finished product fed about 5,500 people.

Shaunaka Rishi

ISLAM. The toppling of several pro-Western governments as part of the "Arab Spring", or "Arab awakening", increased expectations in many Muslim countries for greater democracy and public accountability. In Tunisia (see p. 220) and in Egypt (see pp. 185-87), formerly persecuted Islamic opposition movements outperformed secularist rivals in generally free elections, raising hopes for a more equitable distribution of wealth, as well as the reintroduction of Sharia-based legislation. The situation was still fluid by the year's end, but it appeared that conservative clerics who had been lukewarm to the revolutionary movements had lost popularity to the Islamists. In Egypt, although some veteran leaders such as Grand Mufti Ali Goma held their positions, Shaykh Ahmad al-Tayyib, head of Islam's leading Al-Azhar University, was rumoured to have offered his resignation following the departure of President Hosni Mubarak. Al-Tayyib, a lifelong opponent of the Muslim Brotherhood and more radical Salafist tendencies, helped to draft the "Al-Azhar Document" following the deposition of Mubarak, which called on the authorities to respect Al-Azhar's independence, in the framework of a government based on an Islamic democracy. Al-Tayyib also expressed the hope that the new conditions would allow the Arab world to support the Palestinians and Hezbullah more effectively. In neighbouring Libya, the National Transitional Council replaced Kadhafi-era appointees with a new religious hierarchy, led by Mufti Assadiq Gheriani, a Salafi who had previously called for the suppression of Sufi and other traditional sites and practices across Libya.

Against the backdrop of the uprisings, 57 Muslim foreign ministers met in June in Kazakhstan to establish the Independent Permanent Human Rights Commission, based on Muslim principles. The new body was composed of 18 independent experts appointed by member states of the Organisation of the Islamic Conference (OIC). Its remit was primarily to investigate human rights violations inside member states. Observers saw this as a break with the OIC's historic policy of directing criticism outwards at the record of non-OIC states in their treatment of Muslim minorities.

In Istanbul the city's deputy mufti, Kadriye Erdemli, dispatched 30 teams to report on provisions for women in the city's 3,100 mosques. She issued instructions requiring mosque administrators to ensure ablution and worship facilities for women. The campaign was backed in an outspoken sermon by Mehmet Gomez, the official responsible for Turkey's religious establishment. This triggered a backlash from the country's most popular religious conservative columnist, Ali Bulac, who expressed fears that encouraging women to attend mosques was a first step to promoting their fuller incorporation in the workplace, thus undermining the institution of the family. A national debate ensued, with the woman theologian Ozlem Albayrak condemning Bulac's attitude as "a form of persecution against women".

The growth of far-right parties in many European countries appeared to underlie the intensifying pressure on Muslim women to dress in ways considered culturally acceptable. In August, a commission appointed by the Italian government approved legislation that banned the wearing of any form of face-covering in public places. A spokesman for Italy's Union of Islamic Organisations called the ban a "media dramatisation", which would raise prejudice and oblige conservative Muslim women to remain at home. New laws against forms of Islamic dress in several European countries were criticised in July by the Council of Europe, whose human rights commissioner, Thomas Hammarberg, claimed that there was "very little evidence" that such laws liberated women and that they were, instead, "a sad capitulation to the prejudices of xenophobes". In France, where a ban on Muslim face-veils came into force on 11 April, President Nicolas Sarkozy, in a speech in March praising "France's Christian heritage", publicly supported the ending of halal food options in schools and a possible ban on minaret construction. France's education minister stated that women in headscarves would not be allowed to accompany their children on school expeditions. A ban on praying in the streets was introduced in Paris in September, provoking complaints from Muslims who claimed that their mosques were overcrowded and permission to construct new mosques difficult to obtain.

Meanwhile, in Tunisia Muslim students staged sit-ins demanding the repeal of legislation passed by the secularist regime toppled in January, which banned the wearing of the Muslim headscarf on university campuses. But a similar ban was more strictly enforced in Tajikistan, which also, during the fasting month of Ramadan, prohibited mosque attendance by anyone under the age of 18. The ban, denounced by theologian Akbar Turajonzoda, was seen as part of a general pattern of religious restrictions in post-Soviet Central Asia.

Timothy Winter

JUDAISM. The Jewish settlements in the West Bank had long been an obstacle in negotiations between Israelis and Palestinians. In Israel opinion polls suggested that a majority of citizens were opposed to them. Diaspora Jews had similar views: a 2010 survey of British Jews suggested that 74 per cent opposed the settlement drive. Nevertheless, Israelis often elected a right-wing government to protect them in times of perceived violence, which brought with it the settlement agenda. Thus, the 2011-12 state budget allocated 900 million shekels to support Ariel College, Orot College in Elkana and Herzog College in Alon Shvut—all institutions within the occupied territories. In 2011 there were more than 300,000 Jews living in West Bank settlements and although the settlements amounted to less than 5 per cent in terms of area, the control which they exerted, according to the municipal lines drawn, covered more than 40 per cent of the West Bank. Those who lived there for religious reasons as opposed to the purely economic ones of affordable housing and a better quality of life tended to live in the remoter areas, often in places which evoked a Biblical resonance, rather than closer to the Green Line—the pre-1967 border.

Ehud Barak, the defence minister, attempted to implement a tougher approach against violence by settlers, and especially against illegal outposts erected by the "Hilltop Youth" extremists. Major-General Avi Mizrachi called for the yeshiva (religious seminary) in the settlement of Yizhar to be closed down and implied that it was a source of "Jewish terror" in instigating attacks on West Bank Palestinians. In November, the ministry of education closed down the high school which was attached to the yeshiva. This, in turn, induced a rise in attacks against Israeli Defence Force (IDF) personnel and against Palestinians. The Israeli far Right supported this campaign against the military, one member of the Knesset (legislature) labelling the outgoing military commander of the West Bank, Brigadier-General Nitzan Alon, "a post-Zionist". However, some religious settlers such as Menachem Froman, the chief rabbi of the settlement of Tekoa, had long proclaimed their willingness to live under Palestinian rule. In August he visited the president of the Palestine National Authority, Mahmoud Abbas, in Ramallah, and proclaimed his support for the Palestinian bid for recognition of statehood at the United Nations (see pp. 179-81).

The revival of Jewish life in post-Holocaust and post-Communist Eastern Europe proceeded apace. In May, the American Jewish Joint Distribution Committee published the results of a two-year investigation by leading demographers of religious observance and Jewish identity in Eastern Europe. The survey, *Identity à la Carte*, found that a majority no longer felt the need to conceal their Jewish identity, in contrast to attitudes during the overt anti-Semitism of the pre-war years or the assimilationist policies of Communist governments. Over 20 per cent admitted that they had not known, as children, that they were Jewish. Conducted amongst Jewish adults in Bulgaria, Hungary, Latvia, Poland and Romania, the survey revealed a confidence that their communities would grow in the future.

In the USA, the American Jewish Committee (AJC) joined the Council on American Islamic Relations (CAIR) to appeal against a measure that would have prevented the use of Sharia law to solve private disputes, a situation which religious Jews recognised as similar to when the Halakhah (Jewish law) was utilised to resolve legal disputes. Attacking the proponents of the bill, the AJC stated that it regarded "the recent phenomena of legislative initiatives directed at a mythical imminent take-over of our legal system by sharia law, as yet another manifestation of anti-Muslim bigotry".

A Simchat Torah (festival of the Rejoicing of the Law) service was held for Jews involved in the "Occupy London" protests outside St Paul's Cathedral in the autumn of 2011. Several liberal rabbis penned a letter of support. Many Jews questioned the morality of large bonuses paid to bankers.

In Israel, meanwhile, the gap between the rich and the poor was widening. While the Israeli government could point to growing GDP, low unemployment and low inflation, the advent of tent cities and waves of protest during the summer of 2011 pointed to a different, darker reality (see p. 178). A first tent was pitched on Tel Aviv's Rothschild Boulevard on 14 July. By August 2011, there were 90 tent cities. An estimated 300,000 protestors, religious and non-religious, came onto the streets to make their voice heard. There were also tent camps in several Arab villages. The government was disparaging at first, labelling the first Tel Aviv demonstrators as "sushi eaters", spoilt middle class youngsters. Yet all over Israel, it was clear that such social protests knew neither class nor political boundaries.

Colin Shindler

XVI THE ARTS

OPERA

WITH ongoing financial difficulties besetting opera companies worldwide—sponsorship, state grants and audience figures were all falling—there was a tendency for programmes to be curtailed or made safer. Some new operas nevertheless continued to be staged alongside the classics. At London's Royal Opera House, Mark-Anthony Turnage's *Anna Nicole* opened on 17 February. To a libretto by Richard Thomas, the composer of the West End musical *Jerry Springer: the Opera*, it told the contemporary story of the US model and TV personality Anna Nicole Smith in tragicomic mode. With a score drawing on the composer's love of jazz that some critics found less memorable than his earlier works, it received a lavish production by Richard Jones, and featured Dutch soprano Eva-Marie Westbroek excelling in the title role.

More memorable was *Kommilitonen!*, by Master of the Queen's Music Sir Peter Maxwell Davies and director/librettist David Pountney, which premiered at London's Royal Academy of Music on 18 March. The title, meaning *Fellow Students!*, referred to the background of the piece in political action undertaken by students in the US Civil Rights movement, Nazi Germany and the Chinese Cultural Revolution. Naive and nostalgic though the dramatic result might be, it was considerably livelier from a musical point of view and moved on successfully to the Juilliard School in New York in November.

Two Boys, by the prominent, media-friendly 30-year-old US composer Nico Muhly opened at English National Opera on 24 June. With its cyber-mystery plot based in bizarrely tragic events that took place in Manchester in 2003, it provided a thin and anonymous accompaniment to a compelling drama. Muhly's second new opera of the year, the chamber piece *Dark Sisters*, concerning a polygamous, renegade Mormon family, opened in New York (9 November). Other notable premieres included Marco Tutino's *Senso* in Palermo (20 January) and his *The Servant* in Plzen (11 September); Lorenzo Ferrero's *Risorgimento* in Modena (26 March); the posthumous stage premiere of Karlheinz Stockhausen's *Sonntag aus Licht* in Cologne (9-10 April); James MacMillan's *Clemency* in London (6 May); Judith Weir's *Miss Fortune* in Bregenz (21 July); Tarik O'Regan's *Heart of Darkness* in London (1 November); and Manfred Trojahn's *Orest* in Amsterdam (8 December).

Of personal losses during the year, the most shocking was that of Salvatore Licitra, who died following a scooter accident in Sicily aged 43. The Italian tenor was one of the few able to tackle the big Verdi assignments with credibility; his sudden disappearance left a gap in the plans of many major companies.

Other artists to pass on were mostly long retired. They included the distinguished Welsh soprano Margaret Price, particularly admired for her creamy tone in Mozart and Verdi, aged 69; and her older colleagues, German 20th-century specialist Helga Pilarczyk, aged 86; Canadian Pierrette Alarie, aged 89; and the Italian Alda Noni, aged 95. The Croatian-Austrian Sena Jurinac, who died aged 90, will long be remembered as an especially searching artist. The recently retired Welsh tenor Robert Tear died, at the age of 72; his still active Italian colleague Vincenzo La Scola at just 53. Lamented among international baritones were the American Cornell MacNeil, long a mainstay at the Metropolitan in New York, aged 88, and the Swede Ingvar Wixell, aged 80, a famous Scarpia who also represented his country in the Eurovision Song Contest in 1965. The American bass Giorgio Tozzi, who also appeared in Broadway musicals, and notably provided the singing voice for actor Rossano Brazzi in the 1958 film of *South Pacific*, died aged 88.

American composer Lee Hoiby (best known for his 1971 Tennessee Williams-based *Summer and Smoke*) died aged 85, and the Mexican Daniel Catán aged 62, less than six months after the successful premiere of his *Il postino* (starring Plácido Domingo) had been given in Los Angeles.

Author of the monumental study of singing on record, *The Grand Tradition*, the English critic John Steane, who died aged 82, knew as much about the subject as anyone living. The highly successful administrator George Lascelles, the 7th Earl of Harewood, who died aged 88, ran the Edinburgh Festival from 1961 to 1965, English National Opera from 1972 to 1985, and established Opera North in 1978. He also edited *Kobbé's New Opera Book*, and back in 1950 founded the respected magazine *Opera*.

News from individual companies was occasionally positive but more often reflected funding difficulties. The Bolshoi in Moscow finally reopened after an extensive and expensive rebuilding programme. Garsington Opera moved to exceptional new premises at Wormsley, in Berkshire. In Prague, it was announced that the National Theatre and the State Opera would be reorganised into one company; there was also a threat to the continued existence of a company in the Czech Republic's second city, Brno. In the Netherlands, the touring Nationale Reisopera lost 60 per cent of its funding. Barcelona's Liceu announced that it would begin its 2011-12 season one month later than usual following a 30 per cent cut from the Spanish government, and one of 15 per cent from the Catalan government. Opera Boston announced its closure on 22 December—to surprise as well as dismay, since its $750,000 deficit had looked manageable. Created out of two existing companies, the new Irish National Opera Company was wound up before it had actually performed, leaving the country more bereft of opera than ever.

Kasper Holten assumed the artistic directorship of London's Royal Opera, following a successful decade in Copenhagen. David Pountney was announced as the new leader of Welsh National Opera. Anthony Freud moved from Houston to Chicago Lyric Opera. Paul Curran resigned from the Norwegian Opera following a short tenure. Daniel Barenboim was appointed music director of La Scala. In a similar post, Glyndebourne announced that Robin Ticciati would succeed incumbent Vladimir Jurowski.

New York City Opera moved out of its Lincoln Centre home and offered a smaller, peripatetic season in various venues around the city; to outsiders it looked like yet another disastrous step by a company in serious disarray. Continued health problems and slow recovery kept James Levine from conducting at the Met, where he remained music director; it was announced that he would not return to the podium until at least 2013. Fabio Luisi cancelled European dates, took over his performances and was given the title principal conductor. The second and third instalments of the Met's ongoing *Ring* cycle, directed by Robert Lepage, however, were only moderately well received. On a more positive note, the Met's live HD transmissions rose to 11 per season, playing at 1,600 cinemas in 54 countries, adding in for the first time Israel, Russia and China.

George Hall

CLASSICAL MUSIC

THIS was a year of orchestral tumult. In 2011 strikes swept through institutions in the Americas and Europe—most notably for six months at the Detroit Symphony—as corporate and state funds dried up and ensembles were forced to restructure. One of the USA's most celebrated orchestras, the Philadelphia Orchestra, filed for bankruptcy in April. Several others (including the Baltimore Symphony and Houston Symphony) teetered on the edge of solvency, found themselves losing key principals or even, as with the Netherlands Radio Philharmonic, saw themselves facing abolition.

In response to this financial Armageddon, many began to rethink the very foundations of the art form and the whole concept of concert-going in its current 18th-century pattern. The Decca-sponsored classical club nights, Yellow Lounge, which had been such a success in Germany throughout the 2000s, made their first successful foray overseas to Amsterdam and London. The Berlin Philharmonic relayed a 3-D broadcast of Sir Simon Rattle conducting Mahler's Symphony No 3 to packed cinemas around Britain. And Ivan Fischer and the Budapest Festival Orchestra brought tombola-style audience-led programming to a late night Prom, with thrilling results. This was, no doubt, a sign of things to come.

There was still room, however, for traditional concerts in the 18th century mould, with lavish celebrations of Gustav Mahler's centenary and Franz Liszt's bicentenary buoying up audience figures. This was the year you could get your Mahler and Liszt in any shape, size or form. Riccardo Chailly delivered one of the most ambitious Mahler festivals in Leipzig with the Gewandhaus over the week of the 100th anniversary of Mahler's death, on 18 May, offering what was in essence a back-to-back symphonic cycle. The Pittsburgh Symphony Orchestra and their live-wire chief conductor, Manfred Honeck, produced a feverish recorded cycle. In Ljubljana you could have witnessed possibly the largest ever performance of Mahler's Eighth Symphony at the hands of Valery Gergiev. And at the Proms you could have caught one of the most controversial Mahler performances of the year, Sir Roger Norrington bringing his period performance practices to bear on Mahler's Ninth, to the fury of some and the delight of others.

Every pianist worth his or her salt had a Liszt programme to showcase. Of these, the most memorable recitals were given by Stephen Hough, Evgeny Kissin and Yevgeny Sudbin. Several also flung themselves at the concertos—including Daniel Barenboim, Lang Lang and a young Benjamin Grosvenor—with mixed critical success.

Cancellations accompanied the cuts. Sir Colin Davis, Mariss Jansons, Riccardo Muti and James Levine all took time out for health reasons. Levine subsequently quit his post at the Boston Symphony Orchestra. Riccardo Chailly was widely tipped to take over; however, he was forced to withdraw from a series of concerts scheduled between the orchestra and the conductor to assess the suitability of the partnership, also owing to health concerns. In June the Salzburg Easter Festival announced that Christian Thielemann and the Dresden Staatskapelle would take over from Sir Simon Rattle and the Berlin Philharmonic (respectively as musical director and resident orchestra) from 2013. With orchestras in choppy waters, it was not surprising to find conductors, on the whole, holding tight, waiting out the financial storms, and cautiously renewing contracts.

In new music, the voice of Minimalism was strong. Everyone wanted a piece of Steve Reich during his 75th birthday celebrations. His string quartet, *WTC 9/11*, received its UK premiere. Philip Glass completed his Ninth and Tenth Symphonies, Louis Andriessen a Violin Concerto, and in London the Labeque sisters presented a festival celebrating the 50th anniversary of Minimalism. There were major new works from several Neo-Romantics, including a large orchestral piece and string quartet from Thomas Adès, a rearrangement of several Brahms songs by German Detlev Glanert, and eight quirky vignettes, *Feldman's Sixpenny Editions*, from the eccentric Irishman Gerald Barry. Esa-Pekka Salonen won the prestigious Grawemeyer Award for his new Violin Concerto. One of the most fascinating batch of commissions came courtesy of Riccardo Chailly and the Leipzig Gewandhaus. Each concert in their Beethoven cycle, which toured Europe in the autumn, was accompanied by five Beethoven-inspired new works from five living composers: Colin Matthews, Steffen Schleiermacher, Bruno Mantovani, Carlo Boccadoro and Friedrich Cerha.

Though Modernism's grip on contemporary music continued to loosen, the high priests of the movement could be seen and heard in several retrospectives. Pierre Boulez toured Europe with what many considered his masterpiece, *Pli selon pli*; this was possibly the last chance one had to hear the 86-year-old titan conduct the work in public. The Barbican dedicated a day to the British standard bearer of the school of New Complexity, Brian Ferneyhough. And a 102-year-old Elliott Carter went on a wild Modernist goose chase in his new double concerto for piano and percussion, a work that was as fresh and energetic as anything he had ever written.

Like the live tradition, the classical recording industry found itself experimenting in 2011. Vinyl made a return to Deutsche Grammophon's output. Venezuelan Gustavo Dudamel's recording of Mendelssohn's Third Symphony with the Vienna

Philharmonic appeared on LP, complete with a retro-style cover. Paavo Järvi followed suit, with the announcement that his entire Beethoven cycle, with the Deutsche Kammerphilharmonie Bremen, would be released on vinyl. Deutsche Grammophon's new signings were also unconventional. Montenegrin Milo Karadaglic became the first classical guitarist to join their roster for many years, and Israeli Avi Avital became their first ever virtuoso mandolin player. Beyond these novelties, there were two new acclaimed Beethoven cycles from Chailly and the Leipzigers and La Chambre Philharmonique and Emmanuel Krivine. Finally, Chandos celebrated Percy Grainger's semi-centenary with an epic 19-CD box set.

The year saw the deaths of two musical giants. The godfather of integral Serialism—the man who did more than anyone else to entrench high Modernist principles in post-war US music departments—Milton Babbitt, died, aged 95 (see Obituary). The former principal conductor of the Leningrad Philharmonic and acclaimed interpreter of the German classics, Kurt Sanderling, died aged 98. The year also saw two tragically premature deaths. US composer Peter Lieberson, winner of the Grawemeyer Award and husband of the late mezzo-soprano Lorraine Hunt Lieberson, died of cancer aged 66, while Russian-born Yakov Kreizberg, chief conductor of the Netherlands Philharmonic Orchestra and former musical director of the Komische Oper Berlin, died in March, aged 51.

Igor Toronyi-Lalic

ROCK AND POP MUSIC

On 5 December the Official Charts Company declared Adele's album *21* to be "the biggest-selling album of the century". The century in question was only 10 years old, but the achievements of Adele Adkins, the 23-year-old singer and songwriter from Tottenham, London, were already sufficiently astounding for her to have been recognised as one of the most successful British acts in pop history. In the USA, *21* had sold more than 5.5 million copies by the end of the year, three times as many as Adele's closest rival Lady Gaga had managed with her album, *Born This Way* (1.9 million).

It was difficult to comprehend the magnitude of Adele's success, let alone to overstate it. Global sales of *21* were put at 17 million copies, and it topped the charts in more than 26 countries. She bulldozed through barriers of genre and geography, defying the rules of radio formatting and marketing demographics with a sound that appealed to all age groups. Her trick was simply to write profoundly emotional music and sing it brilliantly. No hype. No hysteria. Her game-changing single *Someone Like You* was a volcanic outpouring of lovelorn emotion, which would surely live on as a pop favourite for as long as such songs are sung.

With poignant timing, the album which *21* overtook to become the "biggest-selling album of the century" was Amy Winehouse's *Back to Black* (released in 2006). Winehouse, whose personal and professional life had long been blighted by drugs and relationship issues, died of alcohol poisoning on 23 July (see Obituary). She was just 27, her death a salutary reminder of the perils of playing the fame game too hard. A posthumous album, *Lioness: Hidden Treasures*, topped the UK chart in December, a hollow success if ever there was one.

PJ Harvey became the only act to win the Mercury Music Prize for a second time, when *Let England Shake* was declared the Album of the Year on 6 September. Harvey's bittersweet rumination on her relationship with the country of her birth and its history of wars married pop music to an intellectual tradition stretching from the poems of Tennyson and Kipling to the novels of Sebastian Faulks. "The West's asleep. Let England shake/Weighted down with silent dead," she sang with a brittle intensity that left a nation bewitched.

The UK's military tradition found popular expression of a rather different nature thanks to the extraordinary success of a recording by a choir comprising the wives and girlfriends of personnel deployed in Afghanistan. *Wherever You Are*, by the Military Wives, under the direction of Gareth Malone, a spin-off single from a reality TV series, sold more than 500,000 copies in the week of its release to become the UK Christmas number one. It was hardly the most exciting of songs, but the proceeds went to charity and its success did loosen the grip of *The X-Factor* on the singles chart, if not on the popular imagination.

There were bullish reports of an accelerated increase in digital sales of music, suggesting that the commonly-held belief that nobody paid for recorded music any more was perhaps becoming out of date. In the USA, *Billboard* magazine reported a full-year increase in revenue of $314 million from digital sales of music, compared to a gain of about $100 million calculated at the same point in 2010. And in the UK, sales of albums in the digital format increased by as much as 25 per cent in the year from 2010. But this was still not nearly enough to offset the continuing steep decline in physical (CD) sales, which was such that overall sales of digital, CD and vinyl albums once again dropped by more than 10 per cent in the UK. Although the recording industry was slowly getting to grips with the digital revolution, its revenues were still a long way from bottoming out.

The age of austerity did not impinge on U2. The Irish group's monumental *360°* world tour, which had begun in 2009, ended in Canada on 31 July. This was a spectacle on a scale that was unlikely to be repeated in a hurry. The steel "claw" stage structure under which the band played was the biggest set for a touring music production ever to have been erected, let alone carted across five continents. With declared takings of $736 million and 7.2 million tickets sold, it was the highest-grossing and best-attended concert tour ever.

In June, U2 headlined the Friday night at Glastonbury. But even they were upstaged by Beyoncé who closed the festival on Sunday night with a stunning performance which underlined why she had risen to become the biggest R&B star in the world. Her forthright expressions of personal empowerment, as summed up in her song *Run the World (Girls)*, was a message which resonated throughout the year in popular music during which acts such as Jessie J, Rumer, Florence and the Machine, Rihanna and Katy Perry could all be found calling the shots with increasing style and confidence.

While a handful of boy bands, including JLS, One Direction and the Wanted, scampered across TV screens and the big stages, along with talent-show stars such as Olly Murs, it was all so much froth compared with the return of the heavy hitters Coldplay. Their mysteriously titled album, *Mylo Xyloto*, released in October, topped the charts in 30 countries, becoming the London group's third album to reach number one in the US and their fifth to do so in the UK.

In February, Tinie Tempah, the 22-year-old rap star from Plumstead, was one of the big winners at the BRIT Awards. By the end of the year, his debut album, *Disco-very*, had been certified double-platinum (for sales of 600,000 copies) making him the most successful British hip hop act, by some distance. Like Adele, he wove the story of an ordinary London life into songs of inspirational power. "I don't ever want to hear another siren/Them high rises can block your horizons," he declared in his appropriately-named song, *Simply Unstoppable*.

David Sinclair

BALLET AND DANCE

COMMISSIONED scores—including those by Joby Talbot for The Royal Ballet's *Alice's Adventures in Wonderland*, by the Pet Shop Boys (*The Most Incredible Thing*), and by Sir Paul McCartney for New York City Ballet's reportedly rather muddled *Ocean's Kingdom*—were a feature of dance productions in 2011. *The Most Incredible Thing* at Sadler's Wells, a fable concerning the arts in times of hardship, was rich in quotations from dance works and choreographers that Javier De Frutos, the ballet's choreographer, admired. Thus audiences saw *Apollo*, *Les Noces*, *The Green Table* and extracts from Broadway musicals flash before their eyes in a narrative inspired by a story from Hans Christian Andersen. The work needed editing but proved popular, its Soviet-style socialist realist designs reflecting a shared interest between composers and choreographer indicative of the partners' close collaboration.

It was a year of narrative creations and The Royal Ballet's season was dominated by Christopher Wheeldon's *Alice* with effective designs by Bob Crowley, albeit dominated by projections. A prologue was set in Dean Liddell's Oxford garden and the "real" world found parallels in Alice's adventures. Lauren Cuthbertson made an effective heroine, although she was given too many similar linking solos, and there were impressive dances for Sergei Polunin as the gardener's boy/Knave of Hearts, Steven McRae as the tap-dancing Mad Hatter and Zenaida Yanowsky as the Queen of Hearts performing a spoof "Rose Adagio". The actor Simon Russell Beale was wasted as the Duchess.

Overall, however, this critic preferred the more imaginative *Alice* choreographed by Ashley Page, designed by Antony McDonald and with a new score by Robert Moran for Scottish Ballet. Visually this included references to Charles Dodgson's photographs and began with Lewis Carroll (Erik Cavallari) and Alice Liddell (the delightful Sophie Martin) embarking on a journey through a camera lens rather than down a rabbit hole. Characters were neatly delineated; Page seized his opportunities to create dances in his neo-classical style and the set included appropriately Monty Pythonesque film by Annemarie Woods. Nevertheless, the more productions there are of *Alice* the less appropriate the source appears for dance. Riddles and puns do not work in movement and however attractive river bank, croquet and floral scenes may be, there are others—such as the trial—that simply do not translate into dance.

The Royal Ballet also presented *Ballo della regina*, one of George Balanchine's tributes to the world of 19th-century opera-ballet, in which dancers both skimmed across the stage and paraded with dignity. Polunin's dancing was impressive and both Cuthbertson and Marianela Nuñes tackled the speedy choreography fluently. However, in another production at The Royal, Wayne McGregor's *Live Fire Exercise*, the slow-motion projection of an explosion of an army truck distracted from the six dancers

From Russia came the disappointments. In April the Kremlin Ballet presented a week-long *Les Saisons Russes XXI* with three programmes. Six works from the Diaghilev repertoire were a mish-mash of research and conjecture. Some audience members enjoyed seeing designs by Léon Bakst "come to life" but others felt frustrated knowing the wealth of sources that the company had failed to consult. *The Blue God* and *Thamar* had new choreography by Wayne Eagling and Jurijus Smoriginas respectively, and the season strayed far from Diaghilev's policy of presenting stimulating new ballets to excite audiences.

The Mariinsky Ballet on their visit to London in July also presented their homage to Diaghilev—or rather to his first choreographer Mikhail Fokine. Interpretations of *Firebird* and *Schéhérazade* both dating from 1910 were muddled but the company understood the romantic heart of *Les Sylphides*. Their other disappointment was Alexei Ratmansky's production of *Anna Karenina*. Told in two hours, the narrative focused exclusively on Anna, losing the depth of Tolstoy's novel. In fairness it must be acknowledged that this was one of Ratmansky's early creations and could be regarded as an effective vehicle for a dramatic ballerina like Diana Vishneva. *La Bayadère* and the mixed bill of ballets by Balanchine and Jerome Robbins revealed that this great company could still be impressive.

English National Ballet subjected their company to close scrutiny in the three-part television series, *Agony and Ecstasy*, but emerged from the ordeal with a new following. One of the dancers who came across most sympathetically was the mature ballerina Daria Klimentova, whose career in partnership with youthful Vladimir Muntagirov shone even more brightly in 2011 than before. Although some ENB productions, such as *Strictly Gershwin*, were presented with an eye on box office appeal, the company did venture into the more risky area of mixed programmes. Performances of Serge Lifar's *Suite en blanc* revealed the strength of the dancers and the triple bill of ballets by Roland Petit was the highlight of 2011. Intended as a tribute to a now somewhat undervalued choreographer, it became a memorial as Petit died two weeks before the opening night. Surely he would have been proud of performances by Esteban Berlanga as the tortured young man who deserts his Bride in *L'Arlésienne*, a mature work full of subtle choreographic references. Similarly Petit would have been thrilled by performances by Yonah Acosta as the youthful existentialist in *Le Jeune homme et la mort*. Ivan Vasiliev, then at the Bolshoi, also flew in at the last minute to take on the role of the Young Man and stun audiences—his personal tribute to a great master.

Vasiliev's other performances in London in 2011 were less satisfying. For all his virtuosity, Frederick Ashton's style seemed to elude him. He danced Romeo to Natalia Osipova's moving but over-sophisticated Juliet in the Peter Schaufuss production, which convinced the audience that the plague was rife in Verona it was such an under-populated city. While chamber versions had their place when touring regionally, it was absurd that this same production was brought to one of London's largest stages. Nevertheless, the opportunity to see the nimble Royal Danish Ballet rising star, Alban Lendorf, as Mercutio justified the evening in the theatre. To the astonishment of Russia's dance world, Vasiliev and Osipova left the Bolshoi in November, shortly after its theatre in Moscow re-opened following extensive repairs, to be based with the Mikhailovsky Company in St Petersburg. Meanwhile, US danseur David Hallberg signed a contract to join the Bolshoi.

Other companies visiting London included Dutch National Ballet in a well-danced if slightly dated celebration of ballets by Hans van Manen, and the Royal New Zealand Ballet in a dull programme of works by Jorma Elo, Andrew Simmons (a former company member) and De Frutos. The end of 2011 saw the final farewell of the Merce Cunningham Dance Company in New York. Throughout the year the company took a repertoire of major works that had changed the face of dance to the cities world-wide where Cunningham's dancers had been appreciated.

On the home front, Richard Alston Dance Company continued to fascinate. *Caravaggio: Exile and Death* by choreographer and film-maker Darshan Singh Buller had an integrity in its combination of film and dance that was missing in many productions. His use of digital images was beautifully realised for a small-scale production and enhanced the production rather than detracting from the dancers.

In response to the earthquake in Japan, Sylvie Guillem invited her favourite choreographers, William Forsythe and Mats Ek, to create new works for her, for *6000 miles away*. Forsythe's post-modern pas de deux, *Rearray*, for Guillem and Paris Opéra star Nicolas Le Riche combined balletic and modern dance to create a revealing portrait of two artists with a shared heritage. Akram Khan's *Desh* (Bengali for "homeland") was an outstanding full-evening contemporary dance solo to celebrate the 40th anniversary of the independence of Bangladesh from Pakistan. With sets and costumes from Tim Yip, lighting by the ever-brilliant Michael Hulls and a score from Jocelyn Pook, it was a mesmerising evening.

Elsewhere the Royal Swedish Ballet presented a *Coppélia* inspired by the magician of film, Georges Méliès. This was a brilliant idea and the opening and closing scenes, set in his film studio, were effective. However, the creators lost confidence in the idea, leaving the other scenes in too traditional a form. Jan-Erik Wikstrom brought a lively virtuosity to the role of Franz. Another dancer it was good to see was Chase Finlay in New York City Ballet's *Apollo*. Here was a committed dancer taking on a masterpiece of a role, so that one really believed he was the young god assuming his responsibilities. The novelty from the Paris Opéra in 2011 was a new production of *La source* that continued the company's tradition of looking back at its long, rich heritage. Re-using the music by Delibes and Minkus gave it some semblance of original narrative but programme notes were needed to make sense of the action. The confusion was not helped by the generalised theatre setting rather than the specific locations of the original.

The growth in transmissions of ballets to theatres worldwide provided an opportunity for wider audiences to share productions. Both The Royal Ballet and Birmingham Royal Ballet reached out to new audiences with arena performances at London's O2. Rather than rethinking productions for a popcorn-eating audience, they "enhanced" their stage productions with video screens as at a pop concert. In respect of dance on screen the most significant dance film release in 2011 was the 3-D *Pina*, in which extracts from four of Bausch's creations truly sprang from the screen

Jane Pritchard

NEW YORK AND LONDON THEATRE

THIS would be remembered as the theatre year in which comedy was king. That was not so unusual a scenario on Broadway, a commercial thoroughfare that used to emblazon upon empty playhouses the exhortation, "See a Broadway show for the fun of it"—thereby rather begging the question, what if the show concerned happened not to be, well, fun? London, however, had long been characterised by a different ecology, whereby dark, even tragic fare could co-exist alongside happier offerings, and where the heyday of such farceurs as Brian Rix, Ray Cooney, and even Alan Ayckbourn (though many of his plays left farce well behind) had long been forgotten in favour of a climate given over season after season to the likes of Henrik Ibsen, Eugene O'Neill, and Tennessee Williams, to name just three playwrights who were not exactly a laugh-a-minute.

So it was with surprise that one saw throughout 2011 various London offerings vying to outdo one another on the mirthometer, the stakes set very high by the opening at the Royal National Theatre in May of *One Man, Two Guvnors*, Richard Bean's adaptation of the Venetian dramatist Carlo Goldoni's 1743 repertoire mainstay, *A Servant of Two Masters*. The action relocated to the gangland underworld of 1960s Brighton, Bean's play quickly emerged as the breakout hit of the year, transferring from the National's midsized Lyttelton auditorium to the West End's capacious Adelphi Theatre, at which point it became the first non-musical in over 25 years to play one of London's largest venues. The self-evident attraction was the appearance in the principal role of the servant with two "guvnors" (for which, read "bosses" or "masters") of TV personality and erstwhile British bad boy James Corden, here reunited with the director of the play, *The History Boys*, that had first brought him to public attention before small-screen sitcoms like *Gavin & Stacey* cemented his fame. (Well, that and also appearing on TV in 2010 in an awards-night slanging match with none other than Patrick Stewart, a contretemps that did neither gentleman any favours.)

But deft and physically limber though Corden undeniably was in a play that amounted to its own eight-times-a-week aerobic workout, director Nicholas Hytner's entire cast did sterling comic service, abetted throughout by an array of physical business from associate director Cal McCrystal. Repeated viewings at different theatres (once as part of NT Live, in which specific National Theatre stagings were shown in cinemas throughout the UK and worldwide) only proved the agility and acumen of such co-stars as Oliver Chris, playing a handsome if dim-witted toff with a habit of hurling random exclamations like "Country life!", and newcomer Tom Edden, a 35-year-old cast as a doddering 87-year-old waiter with a precarious hold on both soup tureens and, it would appear, life.

Suddenly, on the back of Bean's pretty much wholesale rewrite of his Italian source, everyone was in on the comic act. The play with which *One Man, Two Guvnors* was most frequently compared, Michael Frayn's now-classic 1982 award-winner *Noises Off*, reappeared for its second major London revival, opening just prior to Christmas at the Old Vic Theatre, where it quickly sold out, necessitating a transfer of its own for a longer commercial run in March 2012. Director Lindsay Posner's cast was highlighted by a comically savage turn from Robert Glenister as the director in charge of a disastrous touring production of a cheesy sex farce called *Nothing On* and by his colleague Jamie Glover's ability to jump up a set of steps with his shoelaces tied together: something, presumably, that one does not learn at drama school.

Elsewhere, the laughs kept coming, or at least that was the hope. The National Theatre gave over pride of place in its largest auditorium, the Olivier, to a fitfully entertaining production of Shakespeare's *The Comedy of Errors*, transposed to the modern day and featuring the celebrated comedian Lenny Henry in the co-starring role of Antipholus of Syracuse—this robust actor's sophomore appearance in the Bard following acclaim in the title role of *Othello* two years earlier. Shaftesbury Avenue, the heart of the commercial West End, had an unexpected hit with *The Ladykillers*, directed by Sean Foley and based on the venerable Ealing Studios film comedy from 1955 but with Clive Rowe, Marcia Warren, and the inimitable Peter Capaldi instead of such screen notables of a bygone era as Alec Guinness and Peter Sellers. Staying with Shakespeare, there were not one but two productions of his beloved comedy, *Much Ado About Nothing*, the first at the Globe far and away trumping its starrier West End successor, the al fresco pairing of Charles Edwards and Eve Best finding a mixture of melancholy and joy that eluded the better-known David Tennant and Catherine Tate across town.

In fact, one often saw double (in Shakespearean terms) across the year, the Old Vic opening their barnstorming *Richard III*, directed by Sam Mendes and with Kevin Spacey camping it up mightily in the title role, within seeming minutes of a scarier, lower-profile staging of the same play from the director Edward Hall, with Richard Clothier as a silver-haired, saturnine Richard possessed of a blood-lust that was not easily slaked. The Anglo-Irish director Declan Donnellan returned to *The Tempest*, a play he had previously staged in English many years before, this time with a Russian-language staging of the late-Shakespearean Romance that featured multiple Ariels and among the few sensible (i.e. non-twee) stagings of that play's climactic masque that most spectators had ever seen. Indeed, that same masque proved just one of several stumbling blocks when the director Trevor Nunn tackled the same play as part of a patchy season of four shows that began with a bang and fizzled out with each successive opening. Nunn's Prospero—*The Tempest*'s magus-like central character—was none other than a bearded, resonantly spoken Ralph Fiennes, who seemed to belong to an altogether different play from most of his fellow performers, a young newcomer called Elisabeth Hopper, playing Prospero's daughter Miranda, the notable exception.

Far more potent across the board was Nunn's reclamation of the World War II Terence Rattigan drama *Flare Path*, a potentially grievous tale that against expectation turned out to have a happy ending but not before the ever-popular actress Sheridan Smith reduced audiences to audible sobs with a second-act scene involving the reading of a letter that scooped Smith every award going. The previous season's Elle Woods in the London transfer of the Broadway musical *Legally Blonde* turned out to possess formidable chops in the straight play arena, not just the world of song and dance. The Nunn quartet of productions ended with a superfluous revival of the historical drama from James Goldman, *The Lion in Winter*, a play long-associated with its 1968 Oscar-winning screen version which had paired Katharine Hepburn and Peter O'Toole as Eleanor of Aquitaine and Henry II of England. In the event, English TV name Joanna Lumley simply was not up to the mercurial demands of the distaff lead, though TV and theatre draw Robert Lindsay suggested an embryonic *King Lear* in his shaggy-maned occupancy of a royal husband who keeps his spouse under what in effect was house arrest.

Activity was busy, as ever, across the capital's not-for-profit sector and the fringe, the latter arena dominated against the odds by a 50-seat pub theatre in southwest London, Earl's Court, called The Finborough which found success after success in a room not much bigger than many a front parlour. Their productions ranged from an atmospheric staging of Caryl Churchill's haunting and haunted 1983 play *Fen* to a major discovery in the form of an all-but-unknown Emlyn Williams play from 1950 called *Accolade*, the latter title delivered up in a production from the fast-rising young director Blanche McIntyre that brought her precisely the kudos promised by her play's title. Aden Gillett brought a quiet pathos to the tricky role of a much-lauded novelist who leads a double life—devoted family man by day, frequenter of orgies by night—of which his wife, unusually, is fully apprised. A longer-established venue, north London's Almeida Theatre, effected a comparable resuscitation on a more frequently seen play, *A Delicate Balance*, from the American dramatist Edward Albee. On this occasion, Gillett lookalike Tim Pigott-Smith found commendable reserves of fury in the part of Tobias, the well-heeled husband of the gallopingly neurotic Agnes (played with a reined-in regality by Penelope Wilton).

The small but mighty Donmar Warehouse in Covent Garden saw out the last year of artistic director Michael Grandage's near-decade in that job with a magnificent rendering of *Richard II*, Shakespeare's manboy of a monarch played with near-definitive passion and precision by Eddie Redmayne, the Eton-educated actor whose previous Donmar entry, the John Logan play *Red,* had brought him both 2010 Olivier and Tony Awards for Best Supporting Actor. Watching Redmayne tear into some of the most luxuriant passages in all of Shakespeare within the intimate confines of the Donmar (251 seats) was to bear witness to a quick learn from an actor—in only his second-ever Bardic assignment—in complete hold over his own craft and the audience's emotions.

Broadway, as ever, could not compete quantitatively with London and only occasionally, alas, did it deliver the quality goods. Whereas the London musical scene was more or less dominated by the Roald Dahl-inspired *Matilda*—the only English musical all year to get across-the-board raves—New York apportioned copious amounts of love to the deliberately rude, take-no-prisoners *The Book of Mormon*, which swept the June 2011 Tony Awards, but also to such classy revivals as the director Eric Schaeffer's superlative take on *Follies*, the Stephen Sondheim musical from 1971 that occupies a particularly privileged position in many playgoers' hearts. That may be due in part to the fact that the show always loses money, as it did again this time out, notwithstanding the putative box office appeal of Sondheim veteran Bernadette Peters, in a tearful and tear-inducing star turn as the hapless Arizona housewife, Sally Durant Plummer. *Mormon*, by contrast, quickly became the city's must-see ticket, asking (and getting) close to $500 a seat in a fiercely competitive town where theatre tickets, like so much else, were a sign of cachet and status.

"Tuners" (as the trade newspaper *Variety* was wont to call the genre of the musical) aside, straight plays were there to be found on Broadway, some better than others. *Seminar* proved a rickety vehicle for the definably languid insouciance of its English leading man, Alan Rickman, just as Terrence McNally's *Master Class* was showing its age, however formidable the presence of erstwhile Tony winner Tyne Daly as Maria Callas, who is seen in the play giving a version of her actual master classes in 1971 at The Juilliard School, the notable New York dance, drama, and music conservatoire. A revival of the 1946 Garson Kanin play *Born Yesterday* got raves for Nina Arianda in the role associated perhaps forever with the late Judy Holliday, but that production proved a quick casualty of New York's merciless commercial climate. So, for that matter, did the director David Leveaux's New York reappraisal of the magisterial Tom Stoppard play *Arcadia*. That was despite a Tony nomination for its (over-the-top) male lead, film name Billy Crudup, and a wonderfully warm central performance from English actress Lia Williams as the keen-minded literary sleuth and historian, Hannah Jarvis, who sows erotic discontent in her wake.

In context, one could only lament the now-you-see-it, now-you-don't mentality of a Broadway industry where deserving shows were sent packing almost as brusquely as non-deserving ones. It was hard to shed a tear over the fast fade achieved by the crooner Harry Connick Jr's dour occupancy of the central role in

On A Clear Day You Can See Forever, a 1965 musical (later filmed with Barbra Streisand) set amidst the world of psychiatry, that made little sense to contemporary audiences more than four decades on, even with some controversial gender-bending in the director Michael Mayer's conception of the piece this time out. (The actor David Turner, fresh from a small role in that ill-fated *Arcadia*, took on a role traditionally filled by a woman.) On the other hand, that always galvanising, classically trained performer Norbert Leo Butz was so thrilling as one half of the star pairing in the stage premiere of the 2002 Steven Spielberg film *Catch Me If You Can* that one could have watched his bespectacled FBI investigator, Carl Hanratty, gyrate across the stage of the Neil Simon Theatre forever. Butz won his second Tony Award for the performance, giving an emotional acceptance speech that referenced the murder of his sister Teresa in Seattle two years before. Yet, the lively and engaging musical, co-starring Aaron Tveit in the role of the real-life fraudster Frank Abagnale Jr played by Leonardo DiCaprio on screen, closed after 170 performances at a huge financial loss: another casualty in a town that insisted upon fun for theatre patrons but where a show's premature demise was serious business, indeed.

Matt Wolf

CINEMA

IF anyone had predicted a year earlier that a silent film from France would win several 2012 Oscars, including that for Best Picture, they would have been considered out of their minds. But it happened. Michel Hazanavicius's *The Artist*, rather more than just a pastiche of a film made shortly before sound ruined so many reputations in the 1920s, carried all before it, and most people would say rightly so. Strangely, despite all the attendant publicity, some would-be customers were still heard leaving the cinemas complaining that they had had no idea there was no sound except for the musical accompaniment.

When you come to think about it, it was odd, too, that an American star playing Mrs Thatcher in a British film won the Best Actress award. But Meryl Streep was as hot a favourite for her performance in *The Iron Lady* as was *The Artist* before the event. Clearly the American Academy, whose members had been criticised for being largely white and distinctly middle-aged, wanted to show some spunk this year. The other award that was as merited as either of these was that of Best Foreign Film for Iran's Berlin Festival winner, Asghar Farhadi's *A Separation*. This was, in the opinion of many, the best film of the year from any source—an extraordinary portrait of a failing marriage in contemporary Iran, which was largely non-political but still gave us an intimate view of what it must be like to live in that country as an ordinary middle-class family. Tiny incidents, such as when the family's home help had to ring the local religious authorities to find out whether she could change the underclothes of grandfather, suffering from dementia, because he was a man and she a woman, were particularly memorable. It was rather strange, though, that it was dubbed the best foreign film when *The Artist* won the main award.

Another clutch of Oscars for the films of 2011 went to Martin Scorsese's *Hugo*, a fine, special effects-laden tribute to Georges Méliès and the beginnings of cinema. Scorsese, having been denied much from the Academy for most of his career, now could not help picking up awards as one of the world's leading auteurs.

The end of a long and sometimes tedious awards season, taking in the British Film and Television Academy, the Golden Globes, the American and British critics and more besides, seemed to tell us that the cinema—fighting off recession, the partial collapse of the DVD market and the fact that practically any movie could now be downloaded from the Internet shortly after its release, and sometimes before—was still in fairly good health. But it was certainly true that Hollywood, upon which receipts depended in well over half of the world, hardly distinguished itself over 2011. Its big budget films were often either dreary if expensive sequels or special effects-infested giants with little in the way of screenplay or characterisation to commend them. If they made money at the box office it was because they had spent so much on hype that your average young film-goer (who still represented 75 per cent of the worldwide audience) could hardly have avoided them. But there were a few exceptions, like *The Descendents* or *Young Adult*, which proved that you did not have to spend millions to make films of some distinction that made their money back.

There was also, of course, a new film from Terrence Malick called *The Tree of Life*, which took painful years to make and edit and won the Cannes Festival and much praise from many of his diehard fans. Others, however, found it both portentous and long-winded in its telling of the trials and tribulations of an American suburban family at the time of the Vietnam War. Animation prospered and so did documentary, though the renewal of 3-D did not prove more than occasionally merited and the fact that customers paid more for tickets to wear the glasses provided was surely more than a little exploitative. Half of the time, they made precious little difference.

It was not a particularly great year for European film, though Denmark's Lars von Trier made *Melancholia* about a group of people facing the end of the world, which won Best European Film of the Year from the European Film Academy, and Germany provided *Pina*, a 3-D tribute to dancer Pina Bausch from Wim Wenders that proved his most successful film for over a decade and used 3-D intelligently for once. Turkey produced Nuri Bilge Ceylan's impressive *Once Upon A Time In Anatolia*, and the always reliable Jean-Pierre and Luc Dardenne brothers from Belgium made the delightful *The Kid With A Bike*. From Finland came Aki Kaurismaki's sympathetic *Le Havre*, made in France but Finnish to a tee, and from Poland there was Jerzy Skolimowski's stylish thriller *Essential Killing* (premiered in 2010). Hungary's auteur of auteurs, Béla Tarr, made the difficult if memorable *The Turin Horse*, which justly won Best Director at Berlin. There was nothing much from Russia until Aleksandr Sokurov's version of Goethe's *Faust* won the Venice Festival. But the British cinema, very much part of Europe because, if nothing else, it raised so much money there, seemed on the brink of revival with at least half a dozen films of considerable artistic and commercial success.

If *The Iron Lady* relied almost entirely on Meryl Streep, and was so short on political and cultural detail that it had Mrs Thatcher wearing a hat at Question Time in the House of Commons, there were other performances which matched that of Streep. For example Michael Fassbender as a sex addict in Steve McQueen's audacious *Shame*, Tilda Swinton in Lynne Ramsay's fine adaptation of *We Need To Talk About Kevin*, Rachel Weisz in the second film version of Terence Rattigan's *The Deep Blue Sea* directed by Terence Davies, and Gary Oldman reprising Alec Guinness's famous role as Smiley in *Tinker Tailor Soldier Spy*. All of these were films of considerable merit, and there were others—like *Weekend*, one of the most intelligent of gay films—that made Hollywood look distinctly unoriginal and lacking in audacity. The disappearance of the British Film Council did not appear to have affected things adversely, since the British Film Institute was given a large part of the seed money instead. It was noticeable that most of the better British films had been helped by the BFC during the last few months of its existence.

This was an era when it was no surprise that almost every country in the world produced films, and when the East and Latin America (particularly Argentina and Mexico) were as likely to come to the fore internationally as Europe. India, a sanctuary against Hollywood since Bollywood still held sway, continued to sell its commercial wares to the Indian diaspora all over the world and appeared to be at least attempting to freshen up the old clichés, musical and otherwise, for contemporary audiences at home and abroad who were clearly growing more sophisticated. But Bollywood, just like Hollywood, still produced many more flops than successes. Censorship prevented China from producing more than a very few films worth international release and several of its premier directors seemed to have given up, producing huge, battle-strewn historical epics of little merit apart from their spectacle.

Among those who died during the year were actors Elizabeth Taylor, a superstar for some 40 years; Dev Anand, an Indian superstar for even longer; Jane Russell, famed Hollywood sex symbol, especially for *The Outlaw*; Peter Falk, collaborator with John Cassavetes but best known for television's *Columbo*; Jackie Cooper, child star of *The Champ*; Farley Granger, used effectively by Hitchcock; Annie Girardot, celebrated French star; Shammi Kapoor, rebellious Bollywood star; Anna Massey, leading actress in the controversial *Peeping Tom*; Maria Schneider, Brando's lover in *Last Tango in Paris*; Cliff Robertson, Hollywood star of *Charly* and *Obsession*; and Pete Postlethwaite, British star of *Distant Voices, Still Lives* and *Brassed Off*. (For Taylor, Russell, Massey, Schneider and Postlethwaite, see Obituary.)

The directors who died include Theo Angelopoulos, the Greek maker of at least one masterpiece in *The Travelling Players*; Michael Cacoyannis, who immortalised Anthony Quinn in *Zorba the Greek*; John Mackenzie, British director of the classic *The Long Good Friday*; Sidney Lumet, New York maker of *12 Angry Men* and many others; Ken Russell, who transformed television with a series of *Moni-*

tor films about classical composers and then made controversial films like *Women In Love* and *The Devils*; Tareque Masud, the premier Bangladeshi film-maker; Raúl Ruiz, prolific Chilean director who worked in France; Peter Yates, British director of *Bullitt* and *Breaking Away*; and Richard Leacock, pioneering documentary maker. (For Lumet and Russell, see Obituary.)

Derek Malcolm

TELEVISION AND RADIO

IF there was a single image that conveyed the sense of excitement and immediacy provided by television coverage of what became known as the "Arab Spring" it came from Sky News on Sunday 21 August. Sky correspondent Alex Crawford was travelling with anti-Kadhafi forces a couple of hours away from the Libyan capital, Tripoli. Crawford risked heavy gunfire to travel all the way to the heart of Kadhafi's capital, broadcasting live to the world as she went using simple satellite equipment plugged into the truck's cigarette lighter. Later, one newspaper headlined the feat with a touch of hyperbole: "Sky scoops the world with cigarette lighter." Crawford who seemed certain to scoop many journalist awards for her work also broadcast the storming of Kadhafi's inner compound two days later. "I could sense the excitement in Sky presenter Steve's voice and soon afterwards realised everyone was watching our pictures as incredulity spread around the world ...first reaction from the US State Department, Downing Street, the UN ...it went on. We realised our pictures were having an impact but never anticipated the scale of it," Crawford wrote later.

Despite the power and ubiquity of television, the medium had to share the limelight with social media networks such as Facebook and Twitter as never before in North Africa. It was Facebook users, taking advantage of camera phones, who had sent out the pictures of the riots following the death of a Tunisian vegetable seller who poured petrol on himself in the provincial town of Sidi Bouzid. The events, and the fact that pictures went out to a wider world, forced Tunisian president Zine el-Abidine Ben Ali to step down after 23 years in power (see p. 218) and, more importantly, provided the catalyst for revolutions across the region. It was also Twitter that on 2 May transmitted the first public reports of the US operation in Pakistan that killed al-Qaida leader Osama bin Laden.

While pictures on Facebook and breaking news on Twitter were an internal part of dramatic change in the Arab world, in Egypt it was live satellite television, and the Arab broadcaster Al Jazeera in particular, which played the key role. The then director-general Wadah Khanfar, delivering the James Cameron Memorial lecture in London in October, told how the then Egyptian government had taken Al Jazeera Live off the air. "We feared we were broadcasting only to ourselves," admitted Khanfar. The channel was being broadcast again across the Middle East within two hours as other regional broadcasters changed their own schedules and put the channel, with its live coverage of demonstrations and repression in Cairo, on no fewer than 14 satellites. The results were devastating for the regime of Egyptian President Hosni Mubarak. Yet despite the powerful influence of Al Jazeera on a reputational high, Khanfar was replaced as director-general by Sheikh Ahmed bin Jassim bin Mohammed Al Thani, a prince of the Qatari ruling family which ultimately funded Al Jazeera. Al Khanfar insisted that he left voluntarily and that it had simply been time to go. A number of Middle East specialists, however, believe the royal family wanted to exercise greater control over Al Jazeera given the sensitivity of coverage of the affairs of two of Qatar's closest allies, Saudi Arabia, and Bahrain where demonstrations were suppressed violently.

Another sign of the growing importance of the Middle East to Western broadcasters came when Sky announced it would launch an Arabic language channel, Sky News Arabia, in 2012 in a joint venture with billionaire Sheikh Mansour bin Zayed al-Nahyan.

The immediacy of television and its ability to cover human tragedy was once more in evidence in a news year that stretched the budgets of television news organisations round the world when the massive earthquake and resulting tsunami hit the north-east coast of Japan on 11 March (see pp. 337-39). Pictures of the effect of the tremors in the Japanese capital, Tokyo, were almost immediately posted on YouTube and a camera crew from the Japanese national broadcaster NHK, on their way to a routine story by helicopter, filmed live the devastating tsunami coming ashore.

It may not have involved matters of life and death but the biggest broadcasting story of the year in the UK was the gradual unwinding of Rupert Murdoch's attempts to pull off the biggest deal of his life—the £9-10 billion acquisition of the 61 per cent of satellite broadcaster BSkyB that his parent company, The News Corporation, did not already own. Opponents argued vociferously that such a move would put too great a concentration of power in one pair of hands. In particular the opponents said that a Sky News channel completely controlled by Murdoch would enable him to create a British version of his controversial right-wing US channel Fox News. Culture Secretary Jeremy Hunt insisted he had a legal duty to seek potential remedies before referring the deal to the Competition Commission. Hunt had been given the task of deciding on the matter after Business Secretary Vince Cable, whose job it would have been, told undercover *Daily Telegraph* reporters that he had "declared war on Murdoch and I think we are going to win". Cable was allowed to keep his job but Prime Minister David Cameron made it clear he thought the remarks "totally unacceptable and inappropriate".

An acceptable remedy was found for the Sky issue involving the spinning off of Sky News as a separate, independent organisation to be quoted on the Stock Exchange complete with independent chairman and board. As a result, Hunt said on 30 June that he was "minded to allow the takeover", although there would still have been tense negotiations with BSkyB's minority shareholders to agree a price. Less than two weeks later, however, everything span out of control for Murdoch, who turned 80 in March, as the phone-hacking scandal at his *News of the World* intensified with the revelation by *The Guardian* that the mobile phone of murdered schoolgirl Milly Dowler had been hacked. In the light of such behaviour by a Murdoch-owned newspaper Hunt came under intense political pressure to refer the proposed deal to the Competition Commission. Amid growing public revulsion over the revelations, particularly in the case of Milly Dowler, Murdoch closed down the *News of the World*, a paper launched in 1843 and selling 2.7 million copies a week, with its last edition appearing on Sunday 10 July. The next day, in what was seen as an attempt to buy time, Murdoch withdrew his undertakings on Sky News. Half an hour later the inevitable happened and Hunt announced the formal referral. Soon afterwards News Corporation withdrew its bid to take over all of BSkyB with few observers believing that it was likely to return to the battle anytime soon (see pp. 9-11).

Although the satellite broadcaster had no involvement in the phone-hacking scandal, the creation of the committee chaired by Lord Justice Leveson to investigate press ethics and standards could yet have an effect on BSkyB. James Murdoch, the chairman of BSkyB, was also executive chairman of News International, which published the *News of the World* and which continued to publish *The Sun*. Critics argue that regulators should look at whether the alleged scale of the illegalities at the Murdoch national newspapers called into question whether News Corporation was a fit and proper organisation to hold broadcasting licences in the UK.

Amidst the outcry BSkyB continued to prosper in commercial terms. A new high profile channel, Sky Atlantic, specialising in American mini-series was launched, and in the year to June 2011 revenue reached £6.6 billion and underlying profits £1.4 billion, while subscriber numbers rose to 10.3 million. There had been another blow, however, in February when a Portsmouth pub landlady, Karen Murphy, went to the European Court of Justice seeking the right to by-pass Sky and show Premier League football games in her pub using a much cheaper Greek decoder. She won and although it would be some time for the full legal implications to emerge, the decision could ultimately undermine Sky's control over the essential main packages of live Premier League football rights.

For the BBC it was a year of working through the implications of 2010's agreement with the government which saw no increase in the licence fee for six years while taking on extra financial responsibilities for the World Service and the Welsh Fourth Channel. Mark Thompson, the BBC director-general, who was expected to leave the corporation after the 2012 London Olympics, embarked on a Delivering Quality First (DQF) programme designed to protect the BBC's mainstream broadcasting services while cutting 20 per cent from the budget over six years. In October plans were unveiled that would mean savings of £670 million a year by 2016-17 and the loss of 2,000 jobs. The BBC director-general warned that the cost-cutting meant that in his opinion, "this is the last time the BBC will be able to make this level of savings without a substantial loss of services or quality or both." Lord Patten, the former Conservative politician who took over the BBC chairmanship from Sir Michael Lyons in May, said that the BBC, while far from perfect, was "a great institution and at its best a great broadcaster". Earlier in the year Patten had made it clear that he intended to tackle what he regarded as a "toxic" public relations problem by cutting the pay of some of the BBC's most senior executives.

The proposals, which were subject to public consultation and final ratification by the BBC Trust, did not involve the closure of BBC services. There would be more repeats, particularly on BBC 2 during daytime, and BBC Three would follow services such as children's programmes and BBC Breakfast to the BBC's new northern headquarters in Salford. BBC staff foreign correspondents criticised plans to save money by hiring locally recruited reporters in some countries. Radio 5 Live was to eliminate the second commentator's role for football matches, and controversy also continued over the cuts proposed for BBC local radio with many arguing they were too severe. During the year the BBC also lost a significant employment tribunal case when it was found to have discriminated on grounds of age, but not sex, against the 53-year-old presenter Miriam O'Reilly who was dropped as a presenter from the *Countryfile* programme. Afterwards Thompson conceded there were too few "older women" on British television and promised remedial action.

In the commercial sector ITV had a strong year despite the recession and in the year to March announced a tripling of pre-tax profits to £312 million thanks to a 16 per cent surge in advertising revenue. The rise in advertising was not sustained although ITV channels still outperformed the UK advertising market and the broadcaster was ahead of schedule in the second year of its five year "transformational programme", mainly designed to reduce dependence on advertising revenue. Overall earnings rose by 13 per cent during the year. Communications regulator Ofcom permitted product placement in commercial television for the first time but the liberalisation appeared to have made only a limited initial impact.

The second series of ITV's hit show *Downton Abbey* was the highest rated drama of the year but the *X Factor* fell to a three-year ratings low and the BBC's *Strictly Come Dancing* even managed to take a slender lead over its ITV entertainment rival on occasions. The overall ratings winner was the royal wedding of Prince William and Kate Middleton in April, which attracted one of the biggest audiences in UK television history—a total of 26 million viewers across all channels and outlets.

Culture Secretary Hunt pushed ahead with plans for local television stations across the UK and in December announced that London, Manchester, Edinburgh and Cardiff would be among the first 20 cities and towns to get local stations. He also promised a new Communications Bill to be put in place by 2015 and suggested that he was prepared to rethink radically the way everything is done. "This is not about tweaking the current system, but redesigning it—from scratch if necessary—to make it fit for purpose," Hunt told a conference in Oxford in January.

Commercial radio had a surprisingly good year despite a sharp drop in revenue in the first quarter caused largely because of the government's closure of the Central Office of Information, one of the UK's largest radio advertisers. The recovery was swift, partly because radio remained good value in a recession and growth rates of nearly 10 per cent were achieved heading towards expected revenue of £518 million for the year. Research also showed that the medium, which had more than 34 million listeners in the UK, was also good at driving Internet traffic. The claim was that allocating 10 per cent of a media budget to radio boosted brand browsing by more than 50 per cent.

In the USA major structural change continued in the broadcasting market with final approval by the Federal Communications Commission of the creation of "a media powerhouse" through the acquisition by cable group Comcast of NBC Universal, the studio and network television group. Extensive conditions were imposed to ensure that Comcast played fair with rival programmers, cable providers and broadband Internet operators.

Two events in October marked the old and the new of broadcasting during the year. The BBC announced that its Radio 4 longwave broadcasts, the traditional home of *Test Match Special*, depended on the last two specially crafted glass valves which are no longer manufactured. Its demise, therefore, would only be a matter of time. Later in the month, Google-owned YouTube unveiled its latest challenge to the TV industry with the launch of 100 channels of online original programming from a range of partners that included the *Wall Street Journal*, Madonna and the online magazine *Slate*.

Raymond Snoddy

VISUAL ARTS—ARCHITECTURE

VISUAL ARTS

At the Venice Biennale, with more countries present than ever before, the Egyptian pavilion commemorated Ahmed Basiony, the artist killed by a sniper in the Tahrir Square protest of 28 January. Apart from the pathos of the death itself, it was striking that the organisers felt free to be so radically political. The "Arab Spring" seemed to be omnipresent also at the Sharjah Biennial, full of videos and conceptual works expressing political frustration and the search for civic freedom, yet put together, before the revolts started, by curators who were exceptionally sensitive to the changing mood. The only work to run into trouble there was an installation by Mustapha Benfodil, with inscriptions in Arabic about the violent, sexual misappropriation of Islam during the recent Algerian civil war. This work was seen two weeks after the opening by families visiting the old town for the Sharjah Heritage Days. Unexplained, it was inevitably misunderstood; protests were tweeted and the ruler of the relatively conservative emirate sacked the director of the Sharjah Art Foundation, Jack Persekian, who admitted he had not noticed the work.

In Damascus, a major international cultural meeting under the patronage of the president's wife, Asma Assad, due to take place in April, was cancelled when the police first started firing into the crowds of Syrian protesters. There was also some looting of the Egyptian Museum, a treasure of Roman and Greek gold artefacts was stolen from a bank in Benghazi, and works of art in the British Embassy in Tripoli were burned during the Libyan revolution, but generally the Arab Spring was respectful of the heritage.

What was almost certainly the largest work of art to be made during the year, Anish Kapoor's *Leviathan*, was dedicated to the Chinese artist, Ai Weiwei, who on 3 April was arrested by the Chinese authorities. Although eventually charged with tax evasion, Ai was actually paying the price for having denounced public corruption and political oppression too loudly at home and abroad. *Leviathan* filled the 13,500 sq metre Grand Palais (by comparison the Tate Modern's Turbine Hall is a mere 3,400 sq metres), a red, womb-like form through whose walls filtered light from the cast iron and glass roof. The Tate, the Guggenheim and Museum of Modern Art in New York, the Guangju Biennial in South Korea, and the Musée nationale d'Art Moderne in Paris signed a petition to the Chinese government for Ai's liberation. In Germany, the directors of three major museums who, with the support of the German government, had sent an exhibition about the art of the Enlightenment to China were widely criticised for collaborating with its regime. China continued, however, to show signs of wanting to engage with the world outside. Thirty Chinese delegates attended the annual meeting of the Association of American Museums to learn about good museum practice (the meeting was sponsored by the Saudi King Abdulaziz Centre for World Culture, due to open in 2013). Furthermore, in a remarkable sign of détente, the Zhejiang Provincial Museum in China lent its half of a 14th-century scroll painting so that it could be temporarily reunited with its other half which was held in the Taipei National Palace Museum, in Taiwan. The Chinese premier, Wen Jiabao, himself gave permission for the move.

Excited by data that seemed to prove that the Chinese art auction market had overtaken that of the UK and was second only to that of the USA, Western dealers rushed to set up shop in the region, usually in Hong Kong. The powerful US dealer Gagosian opened with a show of Damien Hirst, which included a small version of his diamond-studded skull. The Art Basel fair bought a 60 per cent share of the Hong Kong fair, ArtHK, and Sotheby's increased its consultancy expenditure in the second quarter of 2011 to $7.9 million (24 per cent) as part of developing its China strategy, while cutting back on operations in continental Europe.

A national market upheld essentially by a single buyer, Sheikha Al Mayassa Al-Thani, daughter of the Emir of Qatar, was revealed by US and UK trade statistics, which showed that the small Gulf State was the biggest importer of modern and contemporary Western art in the world, by value at least. The works included, among others, Rothkos, Warhols, a Hirst and a Serra.

Japan, in the economic doldrums for two decades, suffered the additional hit of the 11 March earthquake, which led to five major exhibitions and many smaller ones from abroad being cancelled or postponed, including "300 Years of French Paintings" from the Pushkin Museum in Moscow. In the West, the best attended exhibition of the year was "A Savage Beauty", at the Metropolitan Museum, New York, about the British dress designer, Alexander McQueen, who died in 2010. This was seen by 661,000 people over the four summer months. In London,

"Leonardo da Vinci: Painter at the Court of Milan" at the National Gallery, opened in November and remained sold out for its entire run. It united 10 of the Renaissance master's 15 surviving works to make a once-in-a-lifetime event, and presented the newly rediscovered *Salvator Mundi*, painted in 1498-1506.

Just before his retrospective at the Guggenheim in New York, the joking Italian conceptual artist, Maurizio Cattelan, author of the famous sculpture of Pope John Paul II floored by a meteorite, announced his retirement, aged 51. He said: "Now my peers are continuously opening new studio spaces and producing art at an almost industrial level; I can't compete." He was not joking. The continuing boom in the market for contemporary art had led to galleries putting more and more pressure on their successful artists to produce, and for these top galleries, the profits were so large as to allow them to put on museum-style, ostensibly uncommercial shows, such as "Picasso and Marie-Thérèse: *l'Amour Fou*", at Gagosian New York, with the famous Picasso biographer, John Richardson as co-curator.

"Pacific Standard Time" was a six-month, 60-venue event, largely financed by the Getty Foundation, to unite the museums, big and small, of southern California in a focus on the art produced there between 1945 and 1980. It started as a project to record as much about the period as could be found about those years and ended up generating 125 exhibitions. Many critics agreed that it helped put the amorphous art scenes of the West Coast on the map to an unprecedented extent.

Renewed confidence in the future of the economy could perhaps be deduced from the fact that donations to US museums were $1 billion higher in the first half of 2011 than the equivalent period in 2010. In Europe, however, where public funding for culture was more important, the situation was less happy. In the UK, for example, national museums (the National Gallery, the British Museum, the Victoria and Albert Museum etc) had a 15 per cent cut in their aid grants from fiscal years 2011-12 to 2014-15, which they said they would face by cutting the number of exhibitions and leaving vacant posts unfilled. The Dutch government was even more drastic and announced that the culture budget would be slashed by 25 per cent from 2013 against overall spending cuts of 16 per cent. This led to major public protests by institutions and individuals. On the grounds that the private ownership of art and private backing for the arts were of benefit to the nation, Nicholas Sarkozy, the French president, successfully led opposition to the sixth attempt since 1997 in the National Assembly to impose a tax on the ownership of art.

A four-year "cold war" between Russia and the UK, in which the Russian government expressed its displeasure by closing down two British Council offices and accusing it of being a nest of spies, ended in July with the unveiling of a monument to the Soviet cosmonaut, Yuri Gagarin, in front of the British Council's London office, with important exhibitions from the UK to Russia following.

Turku, in Finland, and Tallinn, capital of Estonia, shared the title of European Capital of Culture.

Amongst those connected to the art world who died in 2011 were US Abstractionist Cy Twombly and British figurative painter Lucian Freud, in July, and British Pop artist Richard Hamilton in September (for each of whom see Obituary). Others who died included Sir Denis Mahon, a British collector, scholar and benefactor (24 April, aged 101); Leonora Carrington, a British Surrealist (25 May, aged 94); Maqbool Fida Husain, an Indian painter (9 June, aged 95); and John Hoyland, a British Abstractionist (31 July, aged 76).

Finally, in a development that suggested that the fraudsters were more popular than bankers, a trial was held in Cologne of a group of art forgers who had earned an estimated €16 million over the previous decade through faking works by artists such as Max Ernst, André Derain and Fernand Léger, which had been unwittingly sold by reputable auction houses and galleries. The trial was marked by widespread public sympathy for the accused. "Compared with crooked bankers, Wolfgang Beltracchi [the ringleader of the forgers] and his co-conspirators haven't swindled common people out of their savings, but only people who may have wanted to be deceived," commented the weekly *Der Spiegel*. Nevertheless, on 27 October Beltracchi was convicted and sentenced to six years in prison.

Anna Somers Cocks

ARCHITECTURE

PERHAPS the slowest of all the arts, architecture runs many years behind the economy, a fact never more keenly demonstrated than in the buildings of 2011. Just as analysts warned of the arrival of a triple-dip recession, vast numbers of cultural buildings were completed, glittering baubles of the boom years, unveiled in a bust.

Nowhere was the contrast more jarring than in Spain, where the €400 million City of Culture of Galicia in Santiago de Compostela was opened in January. Designed by US architect Peter Eisenman, this sprawling campus of libraries, theatres and exhibition halls ruptured from the ground in huge stone arcs across 70 hectares of hillside. Locally denounced as a political vanity project, it had already cost four times the original budget when it opened, still only half-complete.

A little way to the east, in the coastal town of Avilés, Brazilian architect Oscar Niemeyer opened his €44 million Niemeyer Cultural Centre, a characteristic concoction of curvaceous white dome and spiralling watch-tower. With all hopes vested in it bringing the "Bilbao effect" to the area, the building was instead closed down by the municipality nine months after its inauguration, following irregularities with the accounts, shortly before the architect's 104th birthday.

In England, David Chipperfield finished two major galleries in quick succession, after receiving the RIBA (Royal Institute of British Architects) Gold Medal in February. Both buildings were articulated as composite clusters of rooms, top-lit containers of art huddled together. The £17 million Turner Contemporary opened in Margate in April, a collection of six monopitched warehouse-like volumes perched on the seafront, dressed in a sharp skin of milky white glass, a stark arrival to the ailing seaside town. Further north, Chipperfield's £35 million Hepworth Gallery, which opened in Wakefield the following month, was a fittingly robust affair.

Entailing chiselled volumes of exposed concrete that rose from the churning waters of the weir, it appeared to grow out of its rugged industrial setting.

A rather less contextual monument landed on Liverpool's Pier Head in August, the long-awaited £72 million city museum, designed by Danish practice 3XN and executed by British firm AEW. A twisted cliff face of limestone, stretched open at each end to frame big, tinted windows, the Museum of Liverpool looked like a brash cruise liner run aground in front of the Three Graces—the compromised product of seven years of cost-cutting, legal battles and replacement architects.

The result of a similarly confused ambition, the £28 million firstsite gallery by Uruguayan-born and US-based architect Rafael Viñoly, opened in Colchester in September. Nicknamed "the golden banana", its lustrous façade brought a touch of Essex bling to the town centre but, at twice the original budget, it seemed like another expensive trophy, its tilted walls strangely at odds with displaying the art-work it was intended to house.

The shimmering metallic carapace proved a popular dressing for these super-sized containers of art and culture, the signature language for their role as gleam-ing beacons of regeneration. In Mexico City, Fernando Romero built a strikingly torqued tower, draped with a chainmail skin of aluminium hexagons, for the $34 million Soumaya Museum, which was to house the 6,200 piece art collection of Carlos Slim, the richest man in the world—and also the architect's father-in-law.

In Glasgow, Zaha Hadid wrapped the £60 million zigzag Riverside Museum of transport in an a curvaceous envelope of brooding grey zinc, like the snaking hull of some enormous upturned ship. An object building with little care for its sur-roundings, it joined a slew of similar structures along the riverside, bulky orna-ments severed from the city by a motorway.

On Abu Dhabi's Saadiyat Island—an invented cultural playground—Jean Nouvel was to craft a vast steel lattice dome for a satellite Louvre museum, while Frank Gehry was to bring his billowing flanks of titanium for a Guggenheim twice the size of the one in Bilbao. Conceived in an artificial bubble, thought to be immune from the troubles of the global economy, both projects were finally halted in 2011. One flamboyant gesture that did get built here was Zaha Hadid's $300 million Sheikh Zayed Bridge, a sinuous ripple of concrete, writhing up and down to support a 842 metre-long four-lane road deck.

Back in London, her adopted home city, Hadid picked up the RIBA Stirling Prize for the £36 million Evelyn Grace Academy, a strident, muscular structure for a deprived part of Brixton. Sponsored by hedge fund playboy Arpad Busson, it looked more like part of his power yacht fleet than an inner-city comprehen-sive school, providing an apt metaphor for the increasing encroachment of the private sector on state education.

It was a prolific year for Hadid, who also completed the spectacular $200 mil-lion Guangzhou Opera House in China, a pair of gigantic boulders from which the auditoria were carved out like sculpted grottoes. Time would tell whether the build quality would stand up to the ambition of the design; by the end of the year, cladding panels were already falling off.

A more modest, but equally powerful, theatrical space was unveiled in Belfast, Ireland, in the form of the £18 million Lyric Theatre by Dublin-based architects

O'Donnell and Tuomey. A sensitive response to the neighbouring grain of redbrick terraces, the building took advantage of its sloping site to form a series of sheer-faced geological brick volumes, housing a carefully crafted interior sequence, cleverly composed to make the most of the tight budget.

Continuing the tradition started by the Empire State Building of completing sky-scrapers in the depths of recession, Frank Gehry unveiled his 76-storey Spruce Street tower, clad in rippling sheets of stainless steel; and Kohn Pedersen Fox Associates (KPF) finished their 46-storey Heron Tower in London, the tallest building in the City. Work also began on KPF's Pinnacle tower, Rafael Viñoly's "walkie-talkie" and Richard Rogers's "cheese grater" towers, while Renzo Piano's Shard continued to race towards the clouds, becoming the tallest building in London while still under construction.

China's unstoppable tower boom continued apace, with estimates that the country contained 53 per cent of skyscrapers being built in the world. Terry Far-rell's 100-storey KK100 tower in Shenzhen became the tallest structure ever designed by a British architect, a slender glassy blade soaring over the sprawl-ing city at 442 metres.

An altogether stealthier office block appeared in London in the form of OMA's Rothschild Bank headquarters, a disaggregated series of volumes climbing up to peek over the walls of the Bank of England—which the company once bailed out. The Dutch practice also completed their Maggie's Cancer Caring Centre in Glas-gow, a similarly sleek collection of glassy blocks arranged in a doughnut around a courtyard; and they enjoyed a rambling retrospective at the Barbican gallery, curated by Belgian group Rotor. Rem Koolhaas also published his long-awaited seven-year investigation into the Japanese Metabolist movement of the 1960s, undertaken with Hans Ulrich Obrist, which celebrated a time when the state believed in the visionary powers of utopian architectural plans (*Project Japan: Metabolism Talks*).

A project on a similar scale of state sponsorship finally took shape in east London, as much of the Olympic park was revealed. Originally conceived as the austerity Games, with a budget of £3 billion and a host of temporary structures, the venture had since mushroomed to £9 billion. Zaha Hadid's Aquatics Centre was the iconic centrepiece, a lithe, slippery fin that swelled with sinuous energy along its length—although it was then clamped between two hulking temporary seating stands for the Games. Michael Hopkins's Velodrome demonstrated that it was possible to build something of equal elegance and similar span, with one-30th of the amount of steel, in the form of a stripped down cable-net roof that spanned across a taut timber bowl. The main Olympic Stadium itself was an essay in lean structural design by Populous, although it looked likely to become a white elephant with an uncertain future, designed for a "legacy" brief that had rapidly changed by its completion.

Towering above the stadium like its lunatic red twin, Anish Kapoor and Cecil Balmond's ArcelorMittal Orbit topped out in November, a writhing tangle of steel christened the "mutant trombone" by London's mayor Boris Johnson. Dreamed up in 2008, as Johnson feared the Olympics needed "something extra...

to arouse the curiosity and wonder" of visitors, the 115 metre sculpture/structure proved to be the perfect symbol for a year that saw the excesses of the iconic tendency writ large.

The trend for the primacy of image over content, the blurring of building and sculpture, was the focus of art critic Hal Foster's book, *The Art-Architecture Complex*. With sinister echoes of Eisenhower's warnings about the military-industrial complex in its title, as well as intimations of a psychological complex, the book examined how the co-mingling of the two disciplines had created "a primary site of image-making and space-shaping in our cultural economy". Foster dismissed the a-contextual "global style" of Norman Foster, Richard Rogers and Renzo Piano as "banal cosmopolitanism", and warned that our "experience economy" was leading to a "stunned subjectivity and arrested sociality supported by spectacle". Any pretence that the cultural was separate from the economic, said Foster, was finished. At the end of a year characterised by bloated cultural projects from aging "starchitects", predicated on selling cities to global investors, this was perhaps exactly the wake-up call we needed.

Oliver Wainwright

LITERATURE

THE year 2011 saw a new record set in instantaneous publication. Andrew Morton, whose best-selling biography of the late Princess Diana in 1992 exposed the British royal family to more intimate scrutiny than it had perhaps ever experienced, wrote and saw published *William & Catherine: Their Lives, Their Wedding* within three days of the royal nuptials on 29 April 2011. It was an indication of the upheaval that had shaken publishing globally since the digital revolution. Book buyers increasingly demanded the immediacy which online ordering—and particularly the downloading of e-books—had brought about. This was the year in which sales of many popular titles through Amazon and other Internet outlets overtook bookshop sales. It was, therefore, not surprising that the supply-on-demand which the majority of book buying customers could now find was beginning to be matched by an expectation that certain kinds of publication should also appear within moments of the events they recorded. It was too early to know if this would affect scholarly publication, with a consequent loss of thoroughness in research, but it was part of a trend that many observers felt would eventually spell the death of the traditional publishing industry.

It was a mixed year for publishing. The rapid expansion of digital media obliged all publishers to review their working practices and to take note of changing customer habits. It was a boom year for sales of the Kindle and iPad electronic reading devices, with a consequent shift for many readers in how they received the written word. For some firms this was a challenge to be welcomed, not least because this dependency on technology allowed the more dexterous of them to reduce staffing, and hence costs, in the name of streamlined modernisation. The less adaptable presses simply went to the wall.

The failure to survive of Borders, the bookstore chain which even at its demise accounted for over 10 per cent of US trade book sales, was the most high profile and emblematic collapse of the year. It forced every publisher to take stock of its distribution network. It made the more alert of them aware that the powerful agents of the new technology were closing in on their markets—Amazon, for example, commanded over 50 per cent of e-book sales. They also had to recognise that these interlopers would not be content just to sell books. They were rapidly turning their attention to publishing them, too. In 2011 e-books accounted for 7 per cent of both the US and the British adult trade market, with signs of continuing growth.

Even with this turmoil swirling around them, some publishers did well. There were over 280,000 new titles published by traditional methods in the USA and well over 200,000 in the UK. China and India reported steady expansion of their publishing industries, though these were almost entirely focused on indigenous markets, with as yet no aspirations to make an international impact. Every publisher was looking for the new J.K. Rowling, or for an identifiable trend in popular taste, which might lead to the replenishment of their dwindling coffers, but overall the economic difficulties of the world at large made life very tough for them, and hence for writers, booksellers and literary agents. Publishers' advances to authors were at their lowest for many years. "Change is everywhere", pronounced the chief executive of Penguin, UK. "The one constant factor is that authors must remain at the very heart of our business."

Authors did not disappoint. This was a notably good year for fiction, biography and social history. The choice of Julian Barnes as the winner of the Man Booker Prize for his novel *The Sense of an Ending* was generally welcomed, though with some relief that an otherwise eccentric short-list had not delivered a surprise result. The choice of Stella Rimington, former head of the secret service in Britain, as the chair of the judges was extremely controversial, not least because she herself had since retirement from that post produced some rather poor spy novels. Earlier in the year Julian Barnes was also named as the winner of the prestigious David Cohen prize for a lifetime's achievement, the youngest recipient to date.

The Nobel Prize for Literature, awarded annually in Sweden, stayed close to home in the person of the Swedish poet Tomas Tranströmer. His poetry, tinged with mysticism and imbued with a deep love of nature, had long been at the forefront of Scandinavian literature, with a worldwide reach through the quality of many excellent translations. It was a popular choice, made more poignant by the recipient's inability through stoke damage to make his acceptance speech in person, though from his wheelchair he warmly acknowledged the applause which greeted him at the ceremony.

If not the richest year for poetry, there was a splendid new collection from the poet laureate of England and Wales, Carol Ann Duffy. *The Bees* was thought to be among her best collections. She travelled widely to promote it and in the meantime extended the traditional role of the laureate by commissioning other poets to write on social themes and international affairs, refusing to see her post as merely about honouring royalty. Another poetry collection which made a mark was Michael Longley's *A Hundred Doors*, the Northern Irish poet writing as well in old age as he had ever done. However, perhaps the most remarkable book of poems of 2011 was *Black Cat Bone* by the Scottish writer John Burnside. It won both the major poetry awards in the UK, the T.S. Eliot Prize and the Forward Prize, and made many people feel that they might have among them a new Robert Burns. Meanwhile Scotland's greatest Gaelic poet, Sorley MacLean, who died in 1996, was the subject of a posthumous collection, *White Leaping Flame/Caoir Gheal Leumraich*, which brought together all his poems, accompanied by English translations. There was another notable collection, published after its author's death: Mick Imlah's *Selected Poems*, recalling a poet who died far too young in 2009.

It was a distinguished year for fiction. It was good to see a revaluation of Margaret Drabble, who for many years seemed to have been unfairly treated as passée. Her collection of short stories, *A Day in the Life of a Smiling Woman*, was outstanding. Her sister A.S. Byatt's re-telling of a Norse myth, *Ragnarok: The End of the Gods*, was also deemed a huge success. Veteran novelists Anita Desai, Michel Houellebecq, Siri Hustvedt, David Lodge, Edna O'Brien and Barry Unsworth were all on good form with their new books, whilst P.D. James, at over 90 years of age, produced one of the big popular hits of the year with *Death Comes to Pemberley*, a clever tale of crime embracing the characters of *Pride and Prejudice*. The experienced but not quite leading writers, Andrew Miller and Edward St. Aubyn, wrote two of the most highly praised novels of the year, *Pure* and *At Last*. Alan Hollinghurst with *The Stranger's Child* was considered by some to have written his best book to date, but it missed out on all the major awards.

American fiction flourished. Jeffrey Eugenides excited much interest with *The Marriage Plot*. Partly a campus novel, it tracked three destinies in an intricate tale, which en route paid homage to the narrative techniques of Jane Austen and George Eliot. Among newer talents, the final novel of David Foster Wallace, who committed suicide in 2008 at the age of 46, was regarded as one of his bleakest, though it confirmed that with his death modern American literature had lost a massive talent. *The Pale King* was a study of boredom as a human condition; it was not hard here to see the link with the recurring depression that had destroyed the author whilst feeding his fiction. An outstanding new talent in American fiction was introduced in 2011: Amy Waldman. Her novel *The Submission* joined a growing corpus of "post-9/11" writing, which took the historic turning point of the destruction of the Twin Towers in New York on 11 September 2001 as a template for exploring the USA's contemporary identity and its likely path in the decades to come.

In the field of biography, Claire Tomalin's *Charles Dickens: A Life* was published ahead of the Dickens bicentenary in 2012. It was praised by generalist critics but less enthusiastically received by some Dickens scholars. There was a remarkable autobiography from the novelist Jeanette Winterson, *Why Be Happy When You Could Be Normal?* The title quoted something her rather grim adoptive mother had said to her, when the author was trying as a very young woman to assert her own personality. One of the best accounts of adoption in modern writing, this book had the immediate makings of a classic. There was also an impressive memoir by the award-winning Kenyan writer Binyavanga Wainana, *One Day I Will Write About This Place*, a penetrating and at times caustically ironic view of life in East Africa over the last three generations.

The year 2011 saw the 400th anniversary of the publication of the King James Authorised Version of The Bible. In a supposedly secularist age the attention this received was huge, with celebratory readings, broadcasts and symposia held all over the Christianised world. Many publications assessed the influence of the Bible as a work of literature as well as a spiritual guide. The year also saw the 150th anniversary of the birth of the polymath poet Rabindranath Tagore, an event widely honoured in India, and the same anniversary of Elizabeth Barrett Browning's death. William Golding's centenary was notable for the publication of his daughter Judy Golding's memoir of her father. Terence Rattigan's centenary was widely acknowledged through many productions of his plays.

A number of prominent writers died in 2011. Perhaps the most internationally noted was Václav Havel, the Czech playwright and the first president of the Czech Republic (see Obituary). Best known in the theatre for the plays featuring Vanek, an alter ego of the author himself, Havel awaited final judgement in terms of his importance as a writer, but as a spokesman for free speech in the late 20th century he was a major historical figure. The deaths in Britain of two notable playwrights, Dennis Cannan and N.F. Simpson, did not carry the same political resonance.

Ernesto Sabato, often described as Argentina's "last classic writer", died in April aged almost 100. He had been invited by his government to chair an enquiry into the *desaparecidos*, the "disappeared", the findings of which were published in 1984 as *Nunca Más (Never Again)*. Another loss was the Icelandic poet and novelist Thor Vilhjálmsson. Finland's most prominent poet and author Bo Carpelan also died, in the same year as the outstanding translator into English of Finnish writing, Herbert Lomas, himself a fine poet. Ewald Osers, another remarkable translator, mainly of Slavonic languages, died, as did Ulli Beier, one of the pioneer commentators on modern African writing. US authors who died in 2011 included the poets Edwin Honig and Paul Violi, and the playwright Lanford Wilson. The Canadian novelist Robert Kroetsch and the Jamaican playwright Barry Reckord were both lamented; and in Germany there were major assessments of Christa Wolf, whom many considered one of the giant figures of the post-war period.

In Britain Stan Barstow died. Part of the generation that included John Braine and Alan Sillitoe, Barstow brought a new undefensive working class energy into modern English fiction, strongly regional and wholly lacking in moral censoriousness, especially in his first novel, *A Kind of Loving*. This novel became the basis of one of the defining films of the early 1960s. Two doyen poets died, Peter Reading and Christopher Logue; as did well-loved children's authors, Diana Wynne Jones and Dick King-Smith; the feminist playwright Pam Gems; and the creator of Inspector Ghote, mainstay of a series of "thrillers" set in India, H.R.F. Keating. Patrick Leigh Fermor, perhaps the foremost travel writer of his generation, died aged 96 (see Obituary).

Alastair Niven

Among the books published in 2011, the following were of particular note:

FICTION: Aravind Adiga, *Last Man in Tower* (Atlantic); Chris Adrian, *The Great Night* (Granta); Jamil Ahmad, *The Wandering Falcon* (Hamish Hamilton); Tahmima Anam, *The Good Muslim* (Canongate); Paul Bailey, *Chapman's Odyssey* (Bloomsbury); Beryl Bainbridge, *The Girl in the Polka Dot Dress* (Little, Brown); Julian Barnes, *Pulse* (Cape); Julian Barnes, *The Sense of an Ending* (Cape); Rahul Bhattacharya, *The Sly Company of People Who Care* (Picador); Stefan Merrill Block, *The Storm at the Door* (Faber); John Burnside, *A Summer of Drowning* (Cape); A.S. Byatt, *Ragnarok: The End of the Gods* (Canongate); Lucy Caldwell, *The Meeting Point* (Faber); Justin Cartwright, *Other People's Money* (Bloomsbury); Teju Cole, *Open City* (Faber); Anita Desai, *The Artist of Disappearance* (Chatto and Windus); Roddy Doyle, *Bullfighting* (Cape); Margaret Drabble, *A Day in the Life of a Smiling Woman: The Collected Stories* (Penguin Classics); Anne Enright, *The Forgotten Waltz* (Cape); Jeffrey Eugenides, *The Marriage Plot* (Fourth Estate); Amitav Ghosh, *River of Smoke* (John Murray); Juan Goytisolo, trans. Peter Bush, *Exiled from Almost Everywhere (The Posthumous Life of the Monster of Le Sentier)* (Dalkey Archive); Abdulrazak Gurnah, *The Last Gift* (Bloomsbury); David Guterson, *Ed King* (Bloomsbury); Dermot Healy, *Long Time, No See* (Faber); Philip Hensher, *King of the Badgers* (Fourth Estate); Susan Hill, *A Kind Man* (Chatto and Windus); Edward Hogan, *The Hunger Trace* (Simon and Schuster); Alan Hollinghurst, *The Stranger's Child* (Picador); Christopher Hope, *Shooting Angels* (Atlantic); Michel Houellebecq, trans. Gavin Bowd, *The Map and the Territory* (Heinemann); Siri Hustvedt, *The Summer Without Men* (Sceptre); P.D. James, *Death Comes to Pemberley* (Faber); Manju Kapur, *Custody* (Faber); Shehan Karunatilaka, *Chinaman: The Legend of Pradeep Mathew* (Cape); A.L. Kennedy, *The Blue Book* (Cape); Nicole Krauss, *Great House* (Viking); Hari Kunzru, *Gods Without Men* (Hamish Hamilton); David Lodge, *A Man of Parts* (Harvill Secker); Earl Lovelace, *Is Just a Movie* (Faber); Adam Mars-Jones, *Cedilla* (Faber); China Miéville, *Embassytown* (Macmillan); Andrew Miller, *Pure* (Sceptre); William Nicholson, *The Golden Hour* (Quercus); Téa Obreht, *The Tiger's Wife* (Weidenfeld and Nicolson); Edna O'Brien, *Saints and Sinners* (Faber); Andrew O'Hagan, *The Life and Opinions of Maf the Dog, and of his Friend Marilyn Monroe* (Faber); Michael Ondaatje, *The Cat's Table* (Cape); Helen Oyeyemi, *Mr. Fox* (Picador); Edward St. Aubyn, *At Last* (Picador); José Saramago, trans. Margaret Jull Costa, *Cain* (Harvill Secker); Ali Smith, *There but for the* (Hamish Hamilton); Graham Swift, *Wish You Were Here* (Picador); Barry Unsworth, *The Quality of Mercy* (Hutchinson); Mirza Waheed, *The Collaborator* (Viking); Amy Waldman, *The Submission* (Heinemann); David Foster Wallace, *The Pale King* (Hamish Hamilton); Alan Warner, *The Stars in the Bright Sky* (Vintage).

POETRY: Neil Astley (ed.), *Being Human* (Bloodaxe); John Burnside, *Black Cat Bone* (Cape); Wendy Cope, *Family Values* (Faber); Carol Ann Duffy, *The Bees* (Picador); Jane Duran, *Graceline* (Enitharmon); Annie Freud, *The Mirabelles* (Picador); Lavinia Greenlaw, *The Casual Perfect* (Faber); Geoffrey Hill, *Clavics* (Enitharmon); Mick Imlah, *Selected Poems* (Faber); Jenny Joseph, *Nothing Like Love* (Enitharmon); Michael Longley, *A Hundred Doors* (Cape); Glyn Maxwell, *One Thousand Nights and Counting: Selected Poems* (Picador); Sorley MacLean, *White Leaping Flame/Caoir Gheal Leumraich: Collected Poems in Gaelic with English Translations* (Polygon/Birlinn); Les Murray, *Taller When Prone* (Carcanet); Daljit Nagra, *Tippoo Sultan's Incredible White-Man-Eating Tiger Toy-Machine !!!* (Faber); Sean O'Brien, *November* (Picador); Bernard O'Donoghue, *Farmers Cross* (Faber); Alice Oswald, *Memorial* (Faber); Craig Raine, *How Snow Falls*

(Atlantic); Peter Reading, *Vendange Tardive* (Bloodaxe); Gertrude Schnackenberg, *Heavenly Questions* (Bloodaxe); Penelope Shuttle, *Sandgrain and Hourglass* (Bloodaxe); Anthony Thwaite, *Late Poems* (Enitharmon).

AUTOBIOGRAPHY AND BIOGRAPHY: Paul Allen, *Idea Man: A Memoir by the Co-Founder of Microsoft* (Portfolio); Julian Assange, *The Unauthorised Biography* (Canongate); John Baxter, *The Inner Man: The Life of J.G. Ballard* (Weidenfeld); Tracy Borman, *Matilda: Queen of the Conqueror* (Cape); Gordon Bowker, *James Joyce: A Biography* (Weidenfeld); Frank Brady, *Endgame: The Spectacular Rise and Fall of Bobby Fischer* (Constable); Anthony Brandt, *The Man Who Ate His Boots: Sir John Franklin and the Tragic History of the Northwest Passage* (Cape); Jane Brown, *The Omnipotent Magician: Lancelot 'Capability' Brown, 1716-1783* (Chatto and Windus); Deborah Bull, *The Everyday Dancer* (Faber); Carolyn Burke, *No Regrets: The Life of Edith Piaf* (Bloomsbury); Rachel Campbell-Johnston, *Mysterious Wisdom: The Life and Work of Samuel Palmer* (Bloomsbury); Alistair Darling, *Back from the Brink* (Atlantic); Philip Eade, *Young Prince Philip* (Harper Press); Daniel Mark Epstein, *The Ballad of Bob Dylan: A Portrait* (Souvenir); Roger Garfitt, *The Horseman's Word* (Cape); Martin Gayford, *A Bigger Message: Conversations with David Hockney* (Thames and Hudson); Judy Golding, *The Children of Lovers: A Memoir of William Golding by His Daughter* (Faber); Richard Greene, *Edith Sitwell: Avant Garde Poet, English Genius* (Virago); Susie Harries, *Nikolaus Pevsner: The Life* (Chatto and Windus); Stefan Kanfer, *Tough Without a Gun: The Extraordinary Life of Humphrey Bogart* (Faber); Ian Ker, *G.K. Chesterton: A Biography* (OUP); Jennifer Kloester, *Georgette Heyer: Biography of a Bestseller* (Heinemann); Peter Longerich, *Heinrich Himmler* (OUP); Fiona MacCarthy, *The Last Pre-Raphaelite: Edward Burne-Jones and the Victorian Imagination* (Faber); Oliver Matuschek, trans. Allan Blunden, *Three Lives: a Biography of Stefan Zweig* (Pushkin Press); Franny Moyle, *Constance: The Tragic and Scandalous Life of Mrs Oscar Wilde* (John Murray); Stephen Naifeh and Gregory White Smith, *Van Gogh: The Life* (Profile); John Julius Norwich, *The Popes: A History* (Chatto and Windus); William Rees-Mogg, *Memoirs* (Harper Press); Margaret Rhodes, *The Final Curtsey* (Umbria Press); Donald Rumsfeld, *Known and Unknown: A Memoir* (Sentinel); Michael Scheuer, *Osama bin Laden* (OUP); John T. Spike, *Young Michelangelo: The Path to the Sistine* (Duckworth); Jonathan Steinberg, *Bismarck: A Life* (OUP); Claire Tomalin, *Charles Dickens: A Life* (Viking); Giles Tremlett, *Catherine of Aragon: Henry's Spanish Queen* (Faber); Hugo Vickers, *Behind Closed Doors: The Tragic, Untold Story of the Duchess of Windsor* (Hutchinson); Binyavanga Wainana, *One Day I Will Write About This Place* (Granta); David Waller, *The Perfect Man: the Muscular Life and Times of Eugen Sandow, Victorian Strongman* (Victorian Secrets); Jeanette Winterson, *Why Be Happy When You Could Be Normal?* (Cape).

OTHER: Margaret Atwood, *In Other Worlds: Science Fiction and the Human Imagination* (Virago); Melissa Benn, *School Wars: The Battle for Britain's Education* (Verso); Peter L. Bergen, *The Longest War: The Enduring Conflict Between America and Al-Qaeda* (Simon and Schuster); Vernon Bogdanor, *The Coalition and the Constitution* (Hart); Melvyn Bragg, *The Book of Books: The Radical Impact of the King James Bible 1611-2011* (Hodder); Rodric Braithwaite, *Afgantsy: The Russians in Afghanistan 1979-1989* (Profile); Jason Burke, *The 9/11 Wars* (Allen Lane); John Casey, *After Lives: A Guide to Heaven, Hell and Purgatory* (OUP); Michael Dobson, *Shakespeare and Amateur Performance: A Cultural History* (CUP); Dave Eggers, *Zeitoun* (Penguin); Peter Englund, *The Beauty and the Sorrow: An Intimate History of the First World War* (Profile); Patrick French, *India: A*

Portrait (Allen Lane); Francis Fukuyama, *The Origins of Political Order: From Prehuman Times to the French Revolution* (Profile); Misha Glenny, *Dark Market: CyberThieves, CyberCops and You* (Bodley Head); Peter Godwin, *The Fear: The Last Days of Robert Mugabe* (Picador); Hannibal Hamlin and Norman W. Jones, *The King James Bible after 400 Years: Literary, Linguistic and Cultural Influences* (CUP); Eric Hobsbawm, *How to Change the World: Tales of Marx and Marxism 1840-2011* (Little, Brown); Adam Hochschild, *To End All Wars: How the First World War Divided Britain* (Macmillan); David Hoffman, *The Dead Hand: Reagan, Gorbachev and the Untold Story of the Cold War Arms Race* (Icon); Robert Hughes, *Rome* (Weidenfeld); Henry Kissinger, *On China* (Allen Lane); Hanif Kureishi, *Collected Essays* (Faber); David Lammy, *Out of the Ashes: Britain After the Riots* (Guardian Books); Jeremy Paxman, *Empire: What Ruling the World Did to the British* (Viking); Ross Perlin, *Intern Nation: How to Earn Nothing and Learn Little in the Brave New Economy* (Verso); Jonathan Sacks, *The Great Partnership: God, Science and the Search for Meaning* (Hodder and Stoughton); John Stubbs, *Reprobates: The Cavaliers of the English Civil War* (Viking); Frederick Taylor, *Exorcising Hitler: The Occupation and Denazification of Germany* (Bloomsbury); Colin Thubron, *To a Mountain in Tibet* (Chatto and Windus); Marina Warner, *Stranger Magic: Charmed States and the Arabian Nights* (Chatto and Windus).

XVII SPORT

ASSOCIATION FOOTBALL. The international year was dominated by qualification for the 2012 European Championship in Poland and Ukraine. The major nations all made it to the finals, while the Republic of Ireland, Portugal, Croatia and the Czech Republic secured their places via the play-offs. England qualified by topping their group, but had Wayne Rooney sent off in a 2-2 draw against Montenegro in their final match. The Manchester United striker was initially banned for three matches, which would have seen him ruled out of the whole group phase in 2012, but his suspension was reduced on appeal to two matches. The Republic of Ireland beat Estonia 5-1 on aggregate in the play-offs, while Scotland kept alive their hopes of qualifying until a 3-1 defeat to Spain in their last match allowed the Czech Republic to take second place in the group. Northern Ireland and Wales also failed to qualify. Nigel Worthington stepped down as Northern Ireland's manager at the end of the qualifying tournament and was replaced by the former manager of Shamrock Rovers, Michael O'Neill. Wales, meanwhile, were shocked by the death of their manager, Gary Speed, who was found hanged at his family home in late November (see p. 25 and Obituary). Uruguay won the Copa America after beating Paraguay 3-0 in the final in Buenos Aires.

FIFA, the sport's international governing body, became embroiled in major corruption scandals. A report by the organisation's ethics committee said that Mohamed Bin Hammam, an executive committee member who had challenged Sepp Blatter for the presidency, had attempted to bribe officials. He was banned from all international and national football activity for life. His later appeal was rejected. Meanwhile Jack Warner, a FIFA vice-president and the longest-serving member of its executive committee, resigned from all his positions after the ethics committee's report said he was "an accessory to corruption". Blatter, who was re-elected unopposed as FIFA president for a fourth term, caused a storm of controversy later in the year when he suggested that racist abuse between players could be resolved with a handshake at the end of matches. He later apologised for his comments. Racism returned to football's agenda after two incidents in Premier League matches in England. The Crown Prosecution Service authorised criminal charges to be brought against John Terry, the Chelsea and England captain, over alleged racist comments towards a Queens Park Rangers player, Anton Ferdinand. Meanwhile Luis Suarez, the Liverpool striker, was banned for eight matches by the Football Association for allegedly racially abusing Manchester United defender Patrice Evra. Both Terry and Suarez denied the allegations.

Barcelona, for whom Lionel Messi scored 53 goals in all competitions, won the Champions League for the third time in six years, beating Manchester United 3-1 in the final at Wembley, having earlier disposed of Arsenal, Shakhtar Donetsk and Real Madrid. United had put out Olympique Marseille, Chelsea and Schalke. Tottenham Hotspur went out to Real Madrid in the quarter-finals, having beaten Milan in the second round. Porto beat Braga 1-0 in an all-Portuguese final of the

Europa League. Arsenal and Chelsea both qualified for the knock-out stage of the 2011-12 Champions League, but Manchester United and Manchester City both went into the Europa League.

Manchester United won the Premier League by nine points from Chelsea. United's record 19th title took them one clear of their old rivals, Liverpool. Manchester City, who finished third in the league, beat Stoke City 1-0 in the FA Cup final to win their first major honour for 35 years. Birmingham City were surprise winners of the League Cup, beating Arsenal 2-1 in the final to win their first major piece of silverware since 1963. Fernando Torres completed a record transfer between two British clubs when he moved from Liverpool to Chelsea for £50 million in the January transfer window. On the same day Liverpool signed Andy Carroll for £35 million from Newcastle United and completed the £23 million purchase of Suarez from Ajax. Earlier in the month Kenny Dalglish had been appointed as Liverpool manager for a second time following the departure of Roy Hodgson, who had joined them the previous summer. Manchester City continued their big spending. Their recruits included Edin Dzeko, signed from Wolfsburg for a reported £27 million, and Atletico Madrid's Sergio Aguero for a reported £38 million. Kolo Touré, the City defender, was suspended for six months after failing a drugs test. Rangers won the Scottish Premier League for the third year in a row, clinching the title from Celtic on the final day to give their retiring manager, Walter Smith, the perfect send-off. Smith was replaced by his assistant, Ally McCoist. Rangers also beat Celtic in the Scottish League Cup final, winning 2-1 after extra time. Celtic beat Motherwell 3-0 in the Scottish Cup final.

Japan won the women's World Cup in Germany, beating the USA 3-1 on penalties after the final had ended 2-2 after extra time. England were knocked out at the quarter-final stage after a penalty shoot-out defeat to France. Sunderland won the FA Women's Premier League, while Arsenal beat Bristol Academy 2-0 to win the Women's FA Cup.

RUGBY. After a series of disappointments, New Zealand's rugby union team finally came good to win the World Cup on home soil. Graham Henry's men, led by their exemplary captain, Richie McCaw, were deserved winners of the tournament. It was 24 years since the All Blacks had last won the event and the fact that 200,000 people turned out for the team's victory parade in Auckland showed what it meant to the country. Henry, who had been coach for eight years, had rebuilt the team to such an extent that only three of the side who had lost to France in Cardiff in 2007 were in the starting line-up. The All Blacks even recovered from the blow of losing Dan Carter, their inspirational fly half, in the pool stages because of a groin injury. Piri Weepu, the scrum half, assumed Carter's mantle as the team's inspiration and also took over his goalkicking duties. New Zealand won all of their pool matches with something to spare and beat Argentina to earn a semi-final against Australia, their greatest rivals, who had won the Tri-Nations title earlier in the year. Henry's men won 20-6 to set up a final against France, who had been a disappointment for much of the tournament, having lost to both Tonga (19-14) and the All Blacks (37-17) in the pool stage. However, Marc Lièvremont's team came desperately close to winning the trophy and dashing New Zealand hopes, as they had in 1999 and 2007. The final was tight from start to finish. Both teams scored a try and it was a second-half penalty by Stephen Donald, the hosts' fourth-choice fly half, that proved the difference in the All Blacks' 8-7 victory. Ireland had pulled off one of the best wins of the tournament by beating Australia 15-6 in the group phase, but then lost 22-10 to Wales in the quarter-finals. Wales, who received widespread praise for playing attractive and attacking ruby, deserved to beat France in the semi-finals but went down 9-8 despite scoring the game's only try. Their inspirational captain, Sam Warburton, was controversially sent off after 18 minutes for a tackle which the referee deemed dangerous. Australia subsequently beat Wales 21-18 in the third-place play-off match.

It was a poor tournament for England. Martin Johnson's team were not helped by injuries to Danny Care, who did not even make the trip, and Andrew Sheridan, but revelations of late-night drinking escapades by players were equally damaging. Even after England went out of the tournament they continued to be dogged by controversy as Manu Tuilagi was fined £3,000 by the Rugby Football Union after he was warned by Auckland police for jumping off a ferry. England had qualified for the quarter-finals when a late try by Chris Ashton secured a 16-12 victory over Scotland, but they then lost 19-12 to France. Johnson stood down after the tournament, while leaked extracts from an internal report later exposed rifts within the England camp. Stuart Lancaster, coach of the England Saxons team, was installed as interim coach in place of Johnson. It was a year of turmoil at the Rugby Football Union, where John Steele left his post as chief executive and Martyn Thomas stood down as chairman. At the end of the year it was announced that Steele would be replaced in 2012 by Ian Ritchie, chief executive of the All England Club at Wimbledon. Rob Andrew, the RFU's elite rugby director, resisted calls to resign and was appointed as the English governing body's professional rugby director.

Earlier in the year England had ended a run of eight years without a title by winning the Six Nations Championship. Ashton had a fine tournament, scoring six tries, including four at Twickenham in a 59-13 victory over Italy. However, Johnson's team were denied the Grand Slam when they were beaten 24-8 by Ireland on the final weekend, when Welsh hopes of winning the championship were dashed by their defeat in Paris against France, who finished as runners-up. Italy took the wooden spoon, despite recording their first championship victory over France, winning 22-21 in Rome. Shane Williams scored his 58th and last try for Wales in the closing minutes of his 87th and final appearance for his country as Warren Gatland's team were beaten 24-18 by Australia in a one-off international in Cardiff in December.

Leinster won the Heineken Cup, beating Northampton 33-22 in the final at the Millennium Stadium, while Harlequins won the Amlin Challenge Cup thanks to a dramatic 19-18 win over Stade Français. Saracens beat Leicester 22-18 to win their first Premiership title and Gloucester beat Newcastle 34-7 to win the Anglo-Welsh Cup. Munster won the Magners League for a third time.

Leeds came from behind to beat St Helens in rugby league's Grand Final and claim their fourth Super League title in five years. Wigan won the Challenge Cup final by beating Leeds 28-18 at Wembley but lost 21-15 to St George Illawarra in the World Club Challenge. Australia beat England 30-8 in the Four Nations Series final at Elland Road.

CRICKET. The World Cup was a triumph for India, one of the host countries. Millions of supporters took to the streets across the country after their team beat Sri Lanka by six wickets to win the title for a second time. The tournament ended in appropriate fashion with the captain, Mahendra Singh Dhoni, hitting a match-winning six. The all-rounder Yuvraj Singh was named player of the tournament, which also provided the veteran batsman Sachin Tendulkar with one of the rare honours to have eluded him. India had secured their place in the final by beating Pakistan, their historic rivals, by 29 runs. Led by Shahid Afridi, Pakistan put their recent troubles behind them to enjoy a fine run in the tournament. Sri Lanka had reached the final by beating New Zealand by five wickets, having beaten England by 10 wickets in the quarter-finals. Australia, who had been attempting to win the tournament for the fourth time in a row, were beaten in the quarter-finals by India, which prompted Ricky Ponting's resignation as Test and one-day captain. He was replaced by Michael Clarke. England had a poor World Cup. Kevin Pietersen and Stuart Broad were both injured, but that could not excuse some below-par performances. England were beaten by both Ireland, for whom Kevin O'Brien hit a 50-ball century, the fastest in World Cup history, and Bangladesh.

England had begun the year by completing a 3-1 Ashes series victory when they beat Australia by an innings and 83 runs in the final Test in Sydney, during which Paul Collingwood announced his retirement from Test cricket. England went on to claim a world record eighth successive Twenty20 victory, but Australia won the second match and went on to win the one-day series 6-1. In May Alastair Cook was named as England's new one-day captain, with Broad appointed to lead the Twenty20 side. Andrew Strauss, the Test captain, confirmed his retirement from the one-day game. England began their home summer by beating Sri Lanka 1-0 in a three-Test series. Their only victory came in the First Test in Cardiff, where Strauss' team won by an innings after bowling out Sri Lanka for 82 in their second innings. Sri Lanka won a Twenty20 international in Bristol, but England won the one-day series 3-2.

England replaced India at the top of the world rankings thanks to a stunning 4-0 win in the main Test series of the summer. The home team never looked back after Pietersen hit an unbeaten double century—his first Test century in England for three years—at Lord's in a 196-run victory. At Trent Bridge England won by 319 runs and at Edgbaston they triumphed by an innings and 242 runs after declaring on 710 for seven, with Cook hitting a career-best 294 in an innings that lasted more than 12 hours. India's humiliation was completed at the Oval, where Pietersen and Ian Bell shared a stand of 350 in another innings victory. England went on to win a Twenty20 international and the one-day series before drawing a two-match Twenty20 series at home to the West Indies. In October India gained a measure of revenge over England by winning a home one-day series 5-0. Two Indian batsmen broke significant records during the year. Tendulkar became the first player to score 15,000 Test runs, while Virender Sehwag scored 219 against the West Indies, a record for a one-day international. Australia, meanwhile, were bowled out for just 47 by South Africa in Cape Town and lost a Test on home soil to New Zealand for the first time in 26 years.

A good year for Pakistan on the pitch was overshadowed by a "spot-fixing" scandal that ended with three international players being given prison sentences. The former captain, Salman Butt, and a bowler, Mohammad Asif, were found guilty by a court in London of conspiracy to cheat and conspiracy to accept corrupt payments. This followed a plot to bowl no-balls at specific times during a Test match against England in 2010. Another bowler, Mohammad Amir, had already pleaded guilty to the same charges. Butt was jailed for 30 months, Asif for one year and Amir for six months. The three players had earlier been handed lengthy suspensions by the International Cricket Council. The cricket agent Mazhar Majeed was jailed for two years and eight months.

Lancashire won their first outright county championship title since 1934, Surrey won the Clydesdale Bank 40 final by beating Somerset at Lord's and Leicestershire took the Friends Life Twenty20 title after beating Somerset in the final at Edgbaston.

TENNIS. There could be no doubting the player of the year as Novak Djokovic enjoyed one of the most remarkable seasons in the history of the sport. The Serb won 10 titles, including three of the four Grand Slam tournaments, and went unbeaten for 41 matches at the start of the season, falling just one victory short of John McEnroe's Open era record. His only defeat in Grand Slam play came at the French Open, where he lost to Roger Federer in the semi-finals. Rafael Nadal went on to beat Federer in the final in Paris, but the Spaniard lost to Djokovic in all six finals they played during the year.

The game's top four players, Djokovic, Nadal, Federer and Andy Murray, would have formed the semi-final line-ups at all four Grand Slam tournaments but for David Ferrer's victory over an injured Nadal in the Australian Open quarter-finals and Federer's remarkable defeat by Jo-Wilfried Tsonga at the same stage at Wimbledon, when the Swiss lost after winning the first two sets for the first time in his Grand Slam career. Djokovic began the year by beating Murray in the Australian Open final. His subsequent winning run was such that he replaced Nadal as world No 1 by beating him in the Wimbledon final. The Serb went on to beat Nadal again in the final of the US Open, but only after saving two match points against Federer in the semi-finals. Djokovic saved the first with a thumping forehand return of serve that summed up the confidence and self-belief that was evident throughout the year. Nadal won only three titles but led Spain to victory over Argentina in the Davis Cup final. Federer and Murray also enjoyed good finishes to the year. Federer won his last 17 matches and claimed a record sixth title in the year-end championships, while Murray won three titles in a row in Asia.

Petra Kvitova was the outstanding female performer during a year in which four different players took the Grand Slam singles titles. Kim Clijsters won in Melbourne, Li Na became Asia's first major singles champion when she triumphed in Paris, Kvitova held off a resurgent Maria Sharapova at Wimbledon, and Samantha

Stosur beat Serena Williams in New York. The achievement of Williams in reaching the US Open final was remarkable considering that she had only returned to the court in June after an absence of almost a year following injury and health problems, including life-threatening blood clots on her lungs. Venus Williams, her sister, played in only four tournaments and revealed that she was suffering from Sjogren's syndrome, a condition that affected the immune system. Caroline Wozniacki again finished the season on top of the world rankings, but Kvitova, who won the season-ending WTA Championships and led the Czech Republic to the Fed Cup title, was named player of the year.

GOLF. As Tiger Woods had another season to forget, golfers from the British Isles provided the most memorable moments of the year. If Luke Donald was the most consistent performer, finishing the year as world No. 1 after winning four titles, two men from Northern Ireland were the greatest headline-makers. At 22 years of age Rory McIlroy became the second youngest player to win a major since 1934 when he claimed the US Open at Congressional, while Darren Clarke rolled back the years at the Open at Royal St George's, Sandwich, to win his first major at the age of 42. All four majors went to players who had never previously won one of the game's great prizes. South Africa's Charl Schwartzel won the Masters, finishing two shots ahead of the Australians Adam Scott and Jason Day, but only after McIlroy had squandered his four-shot lead going into the last day with a final round of 80. Given McIlroy's meltdown at Augusta, his response at the US Open was all the more commendable as he won the title by eight strokes, with Day again runner-up. Clarke won the Open by three strokes, using all his experience to master the wet and windy conditions and keep at bay the Americans Phil Mickelson and Dustin Johnson. The US rookie Keegan Bradley won the USPGA Championship at the Atlanta Athletic Club after a play-off against his fellow countryman, Jason Dufner.

Woods's year was disrupted by injuries, a fine for spitting on the green during the Dubai Desert Classic and a controversial parting of the ways with his long-time caddie, Steve Williams. However, the American enjoyed his first tournament victory for more than two years when he won the Chevron World Challenge in December and also hit the winning putt as the USA retained the Presidents Cup with a 19-15 victory over the International team at Royal Melbourne. Europe's women regained the Solheim Cup, beating the USA 15-13 at Killeen Castle in Ireland. The Americans also lost the Walker Cup as Great Britain and Ireland won 14-12 at Royal Aberdeen to secure their first victory in the event since 2003.

ATHLETICS. The most remarkable story from the world championships in Daegu, South Korea, was Usain Bolt's disqualification for a false start in the final of the 100m. Bolt, the outstanding sprinter of his generation, had been the clear favourite to take the gold medal, which subsequently went to his fellow countryman, Yohan Blake. Bolt nevertheless went on to win the 200m gold in a time of 19.40 seconds and teamed up with Blake, Nesta Carter and Michael Frater as Jamaica won the sprint relay in 37.04 seconds, which was the only world record set at the championships. The USA topped the medals table with 25 in total, including 12 golds.

Britain won seven medals, including two golds, to record their best performance at the event since 1993. Dai Greene won a gold medal in the men's 400m hurdles, but the outstanding British performer was Mo Farah, who won gold in the 10,000m and silver in the 5,000m. Having been caught 20m from the line by Ethiopia's Ibrahim Jeilan in the longer event, Farah bounced back to win the 5,000m, holding off the challenges of Bernard Lagat and Imane Merga. Farah had gone to the championships in the form of his life, having broken the British and European 10,000m records in June and his own 5,000m British record the following month. Jessica Ennis and Hannah England won silver medals in Daegu in the heptathlon and 1500m respectively, while Phillips Idowu was runner-up in the triple jump behind the USA's Christian Taylor.

Earlier in the year Russia led the medals table at the European indoor championships in Paris. The highlight of the competition came in the final event, when the French triple jumper, Teddy Tamgho, won gold with a world record leap of 17.92m. Britain's two golds both came in the 3,000m events. Farah won the men's competition, while Helen Clitheroe won her first international title at the age of 37. Emmanuel Mutai of Kenya won the men's London Marathon in a course record time of 2 hours 4 minutes and 38sec. Mary Keitany, also of Kenya, won the women's race.

MOTOR SPORT. Sebastian Vettel, who celebrated his 24th birthday in the middle of the season, became the youngest driver to win back-to-back Formula One world titles. The Red Bull driver did it in style, securing the championship at the Japanese Grand Prix at Suzuka with four races to spare. By the end of the year he had won 11 of the season's 19 races and claimed a record 15 pole positions. Mark Webber, Vettel's teammate, had run the German close in 2010, but struggled this time. McLaren's Jenson Button, who won three races, was runner-up, with Ferrari's Fernando Alonso third and Webber fourth. Red Bull won the constructors' title from McLaren and Ferrari, for whom Alonso's victory in the British Grand Prix at Silverstone was a rare high point.

Formula One continued to expand its horizons by staging a grand prix in India, but the race in Bahrain was called off because of political unrest. Sebastian Loeb held off Mikko Hirvonen to win the world rally championship for the eighth year in a row, while Yvan Muller won the world touring car championship for a third time. Dan Wheldon, a British driver, was killed in a crash at the Las Vegas Indy 300. Australia's Casey Stoner won his second MotoGP world championship, securing the title with victory in his home race. The Italian rider Marco Simoncelli was killed in a crash at the Malaysian MotoGP. Spain's Carlos Checa, riding a Ducati, won the world superbikes championship for the first time at the age of 38.

BOXING. The most eagerly anticipated fight of the year ended in disappointment for David Haye, Britain's world heavyweight champion. Haye put his World Boxing Association (WBA) title on the line in a unification bout against Wladimir Klitschko, who held the International Boxing Federation (IBF) and World Boxing Organisation (WBO) belts. Some 10,000 British supporters were in a 45,000 crowd in Hamburg, but their man was outboxed and outmuscled by the Ukrainian, who won a unanimous points decision. Haye was one of nine British boxers who lost world title fights abroad during the year. Amir Khan, who lost his WBA and IBF light-welterweight titles to Lamont Peterson, was one of only two British fighters to win a world title bout overseas, having earlier beaten Zab Judah in Las Vegas. In his first fight of the year Khan had retained his WBA title with a points win over Paul McCloskey in Manchester. Carl Froch successfully defended his World Boxing Council (WBC) title against Glen Johnson, but went on to lose a unification bout against Andre Ward. The other British losers overseas were Matthew Hatton (to Saul Alvarez), Brian McGee (to Lucian Bute), Matthew Macklin (to Felix Sturm), Ryan Rhodes (also to Alvarez), Darren Barker (to Sergio Martinez) and John Murray (to Brandon Rios).

HORSE RACING. Frankel was the undisputed horse of the year, taking his record to nine wins from nine starts. His victory in the 2,000 Guineas at Newmarket, in which he had established a 15-length lead by the halfway mark, was hailed as one of the great Classic performances of all time. Sir Henry Cecil's three-year-old, ridden by Tom Queally, also won the Greenham Stakes at Newbury, the St James's Palace Stakes at Royal Ascot, the Sussex Stakes at Goodwood and the Queen Elizabeth II Stakes at Ascot. Carlton House, owned by the Queen, would have been a popular winner of the Derby, but could finish only third behind Pour Moi, ridden by Mickael Barzalona. André Fabre's Pour Moi was the first French-trained winner of the race since 1976. Dancing Rain, trained by William Haggas and ridden by Johnny Murtagh, won the Oaks 24 hours earlier. John Gosden and William Buick won a second consecutive St Leger with Masked Marvel and Godolphin's Blue Bunting, ridden by Frankie Dettori, was an impressive winner of the 1,000 Guineas. The German filly Danedream sprang a surprise to take the Prix de l'Arc de Triomphe. Paul Hanagan was champion jockey for the second year in a row, while Joseph O'Brien, the 18-year-old son of the Coolmore trainer Aidan O'Brien, rode St Nicholas Abbey to victory at the Breeders' Cup Turf at Churchill Downs.

Tony McCoy rode 218 winners—his best return for eight years—to win the National Hunt jockeys' title in a year bookended by contrasting fortunes for one of the sport's great equine stars. Kauto Star began by failing in his quest to win a fifth King George VI Chase at Kempton, which had been delayed until January because of bad weather. Victory went instead to Nicky Henderson's Long Run, who went on to win the Cheltenham Gold Cup in one of the greatest races the Festival had ever seen as the amateur rider Sam Waley-Cohen overhauled both Kauto Star and Paul Nicholls's other classy stayer, Denman. After Kauto Star ran poorly at Punchestown, there were calls for the horse to be retired. However, he went on to beat Long Run at Haydock and ended the year in a blaze of glory, winning his record fifth King George VI Chase on Boxing Day to huge acclaim from the Kempton crowd. Denman's career ended when he was retired after suffering a tendon injury, but another inmate of the Nicholls stable, Big Buck's, extended his unbeaten run to 14 wins over hurdles, just two short of the record set by Sir Ken in the 1950s. Hurricane Fly, trained by Willie Mullins, won the Champion Hurdle at Cheltenham, while Aintree witnessed yet another Grand National triumph for the McCain family. Donald McCain, son of the legendary trainer Ginger McCain, enjoyed the biggest triumph of his career when Ballabriggs, ridden by Jason Maguire, won a race in which only 19 of the 40 starters finished.

Four jockeys as well as two owners and five of their associates were banned for a total of 66 years by the British Horseracing Authority as the largest race-fixing ring in British history was exposed. The jockeys Paul Doe and Greg Fairley were banned for 12 years for deliberately riding horses to lose, while the owners Maurice Sines and James Crickmore were banned for 14 years for betting on their own horses to lose and conspiring with others to corrupt races.

MISCELLANEOUS. Cadel Evans became the first Australian winner of the Tour de France, holding off the challenge of Andy Schleck, while Mark Cavendish became the first British cyclist to win the sprinters' green jersey. Cavendish went on to become Britain's first world road-race champion for 46 years and was the runaway winner of the BBC's Sports Personality of the Year award. At the end of the year he completed his much-anticipated move to Team Sky. Alberto Contador, who was cleared by the Spanish cycling federation after winning his appeal against a provisional one-year doping ban, finished only fifth in the Tour de France but won the Giro d'Italia, in which a Belgian rider, Wouter Weylandt, died in a crash on the third stage. Britain dominated the European Track Championships in Apeldoorn in the Netherlands, winning seven gold medals.

The USA and China, with 17 and 15 golds respectively, headed the medals table at the world swimming championships in Shanghai. Three Britons won gold. Keri-Anne Payne became the first British athlete to qualify for the 2012 London Olympics by winning the 10km open water race, Rebecca Adlington won the 800m freestyle and Liam Tancock took the 50m backstroke. Britons won three Olympic-class gold medals at the world rowing championships in Slovenia with victories in the men's lightweight double sculls (Mark Hunter and Zac Purchase), the men's four (Matt Langridge, Ric Egington, Tom James and Alex Gregory) and women's double sculls (Katherine Grainger and Anna Watkins). Oxford beat Cambridge, the favourites, by four lengths in the Boat Race.

New Zealand's Mark Todd, riding NZB Land Vision, won Badminton for the fourth time. Great Britain's dressage team, consisting of Carl Hester, Laura Bechtolsheimer, Charlotte Dujardin and Emile Faurie, were crowned European team champions for the first time in Rotterdam, seeing off competition from Germany and the Netherlands. Adrian Lewis won the PDC World Darts Championship. His 7-5 victory over Gary Anderson in the final included a nine-dart finish. John Higgins won the world snooker championship for the fourth time, beating Judd Trump 18-15.

St Louis Cardinals beat the Texas Rangers 4-3 in baseball's World Series, while the Green Bay Packers won the Super Bowl with a 31-25 victory over the Pittsburgh Steelers. The Dallas Mavericks were National Basketball Association champions after beating Miami Heat 4-2. The Boston Bruins won ice hockey's Stanley Cup thanks to a 4-3 victory over the Vancouver Canucks.

Paul Newman

XVIII OBITUARY

Awlaki, Anwar al- (b. 1971), radical Islamist cleric and propagandist for jihadism. Born in New Mexico, to a Yemeni father who was studying in the USA, Awlaki held dual US-Yemeni nationality. He spent his early childhood in the USA, completed his secondary education in Sana'a, and then attended college in the USA where he gained a degree in civil engineering and a Master's in education. Subsequently, he served as imam at mosques in Colorado, California and Virginia, in which capacity he was known to have had contact with several of the perpetrators of the 11 September 2001 terrorist attacks. As vice chairman of an Islamic charity he was also alleged to have assisted in the channelling of terrorist funds. In 2002 he moved to the UK where he built up a following amongst alienated young British Muslims. He returned to Yemen in 2004 and spent time preaching and lecturing at al-Iman university, a Sunni religious school in Sana'a. Arrested in 2006 on kidnapping and terrorism charges, he was released in December 2007, without facing trial, following lobbying by senior members of his tribe. Thereafter he moved to his family's home in the rugged and remote Shabwa mountains where he expressed a more open support of violent jihad. His fluency in English and his skill with online communications made him the most prominent of Islamist propagandists in the West. In addition to posting blogs and online sermons in which he urged Muslims to attack the USA, he also edited an Islamist magazine, *Inspire*. He was accused of enjoying a close relationship with the al-Qaida organisation and was known to have mentored a number of individuals who later committed acts of terrorism in the USA and UK. In April 2010 President Obama approved his elimination. He was killed in Yemen by missiles fired from an unmanned drone aircraft. Died 30 September.

Babbitt, Milton (b. 1916), avant-garde US composer and academic known for his advocacy of serial and electronic music. Born in Philadelphia, Pennsylvania, but raised in Jackson, Mississippi, Babbitt showed early promise as both a mathematician and musician. He enrolled at the University of Pennsylvania to study the former in 1931 but soon left to study music at New York University. After graduating in 1935 he completed a Master's degree at Princeton University, an institution with which he was to have a lifelong affiliation, teaching in its music and mathematics faculties. As a composer, Babbitt applied mathematical set theory to the creation of music and from the 1950s began using a synthesiser as he increasingly experimented with electronic music. Self-consciously esoteric and elitist in his approach, Babbitt composed works that were often difficult for musicians to perform and audiences to endure. He made no concessions to convention, however, and was often equally dismissive of performers and consumers. As late as 1994 he derided "permissive, diluted and vocation-oriented" music education, and performers who were "less concerned about the future of music than their own careers". Although never popular with the public, Babbitt was influential within the world of music theory. He lectured widely within the USA and Europe with a number of his students achieving musical prominence in their own right, most notably Stephen Sondheim. He also received numerous awards and honorary degrees including, in 1982, a Pulitzer Prize special citation for "his life work as a distinguished and seminal American composer". Died 29 January.

Bailey, Trevor, (b. 1923), tenacious English Test cricketer renowned for his defensive play. Born in Westcliff-on-Sea, Bailey was educated at Dulwich College and served in the Marines during World War II. Thereafter he attended St John's College, Cambridge where he also earned a Blue in both cricket and football. He played cricket for Essex, representing the county on 482 occasions between 1946 and 1967, and captaining the side in 1961-66. A talented all-rounder, he also represented England in 61 Test matches between 1949 and 1959, taking 132 wickets, holding 32 catches (a feat made all the more remarkable by his unusually small hands), and scoring 2,290 runs (at an average of 29.74). As a batsman (sometimes playing as an opener but more often in the middle order) he became notorious for his stubborn occupancy of the crease, prodding defensively for hours on end whilst scoring few runs. Such obduracy was instrumental in frustrating opponents and saved his side from defeat on numerous occasions. It earned him a variety of nicknames, the least offensive of which was "Barnacle Bailey". For it was a style of play that was not easy on the eye and many spectators came to dread the sight of Bailey emerging from the pavilion to begin another glacial innings. Following his retirement from cricket he combined a career in business with sports journalism and broadcasting, providing an authoritative analytical voice on BBC Radio's *Test Match Special* for 26 years. He also wrote a well-received autobiography and was awarded a CBE in 1994. He died as a result of a fire at his retirement home in Westcliff-on-Sea which he shared with his wife, Greta, to whom he had been married for more than 60 years. Died 10 February.

Ballesteros Sota, Severiano, (b. 1957), Spanish golfer widely regarded as the greatest European player of all time. Born in humble circumstances in Pedreña, a small fishing village on the Bay of Santander, "Seve" Ballesteros was the youngest of four brothers, all of whom became professional golfers. Despite learning the game with only an improvised golf club, he proved to be a child prodigy and turned professional at the age of 17. He gained international recognition in 1976 when he finished second in the British Open and went on to win five major championships (including the British Open three times) between 1979 and 1988. Eschewing safety, he opted for high-risk brilliance, often trying for breathtaking shots— not all of which were successful—and emitting a degree of sporting charisma that was widely credited with galvanising the world of European golf and leading to hugely increased prize money and sponsorship deals. He was also the mainstay of a European team that won the Ryder Cup on five occasions, the last of which, held in Spain in 1997, saw Ballesteros captain (in a non-playing

capacity) the victorious side. By this time, however, his game was in decline, with his last significant victory as a player being achieved in the Spanish Open in 1995. Plagued by back problems and increasingly inclined towards altercations with the golfing authorities, he retired from competitive golf in July 2007 and was thereafter reported to have suffered from bouts of severe depression. After collapsing at Madrid airport in October 2008 he was diagnosed with a brain tumour and underwent surgery and chemotherapy. Died 7 May.

Bhatti, Shahbaz (b. 1968), Pakistani government minister assassinated because of his adherence to Christianity and his advocacy of religious tolerance. Born into a Roman Catholic family in Lahore, Bhatti grew up in Faisalabad and gained a Master's degree in public administration from the University of Punjab. During this period he also fully embraced his Christian heritage and in 1985 helped to found the Christian Liberation Front (CLF), an organisation that advocated religious pluralism in a society where blasphemy against the majority Islamic faith was, in theory at least, a capital offence. The CLF also sought to defend other minorities, as did the All Pakistan Minorities Alliance (APMA) which Bhatti helped to found in 2002 and which he served as chairman. In the same year he joined the Pakistan People's Party and was elected in 2008 to the National Assembly. Shortly thereafter he was appointed to the federal cabinet as minister for minorities affairs. It was the first time that a Christian—a faith followed by only 2 per cent of the county's population—had held such a post. He stated that he was joining the government to assist the "oppressed, down-trodden and marginalised and to send a message of hope to the people living a life of disappointment, disillusionment and despair". As such, he fearlessly defended Christians and other minorities, denounced the country's blasphemy laws, and promoted religious tolerance and interfaith understanding. He received repeated death threats from Islamic extremists, particularly after he spoke out in support of Aasia Noreen, a Christian peasant woman who was convicted of blasphemy and sentenced to death in 2010 for allegedly insulting the Prophet Muhammad. Bhatti was subsequently shot dead by unknown gunmen who ambushed his car near his home in Islamabad. Died 2 March.

Bonner, Elena (b. 1923), Soviet dissident and human rights activist who was married to Andrei Sakharov. Born in Merv, Turkmenistan (then part of the Soviet Union), to prominent Bolshevik parents, Bonner witnessed the disgrace and arrest of her Armenian father and Jewish mother in the late 1930s (the former being executed). Thereafter she was raised in Leningrad by her grandmother and served as a nurse in the Great Patriotic War, during which she was wounded. She qualified as a paediatrician, married, had two children, and was later divorced. In the 1960s she also became gradually more disillusioned with the Communist Party and increasingly involved in the dissident movement, particularly in support of "refuseniks"—Soviet Jews who were being denied visas to emigrate. In 1970 she met (and in 1972 married) physicist Andrei Sakharov, by then a prominent dissident, and together they became central to the Helsinki Group of human rights activists. In 1975 she travelled to Oslo to collect Sakarov's Nobel Peace Prize, and in 1984 was sentenced to join him in internal exile in Gorky. The couple were freed by Gorbachev in 1986 and returned to Moscow where they resumed their political activities. Sakharov died there in 1989, whereupon Bonner founded the Andrei Sakharov Foundation to preserve his memory. An implacable critic of Russian presidents Yeltsin and Putin, and an unflinching opponent of the country's military intervention in Chechnya, Bonner remained an outspoken commentator on Russian politics despite spending much of her later years living in the USA. Died 15 February.

bin Laden, Osama (b. 1957), global jihadist and founder of the al-Qaida movement which was responsible for the 11 September 2001 terrorist attacks against the USA. Born in Saudi Arabia as the 17th of 52 children of a father who had amassed a fortune in the construction industry, Osama bin Laden grew up as a shy and courteous child in the Wahhabi Islamic tradition. Keen on writing, poetry and football, where his height made him a natural centre forward, he was exposed to radical Islamist teachings whilst at university and became an advocate of the creation of a new Islamic Caliphate through the pursuit of violent jihad. He graduated in civil engineering at the King Abdulaziz University in Jeddah in 1979 and worked briefly in the family business before going to Afghanistan in 1981 to assist in the struggle by Islamist rebels against the Soviet-supported, communist Afghan government. Drawing upon his family's resources, he assisted with logistics—apparently receiving support from the CIA—and the recruitment of Arab fighters for the guerrilla war. His work in Afghanistan led directly to the creation of the al-Qaida organisation, an avowedly internationalist Sunni Islamist group created in 1988 or 1989 and dedicated to the pursuit of global jihad. Following the withdrawal of the Soviet Union from Afghanistan in 1989, bin Laden returned to Saudi Arabia in 1990. He was bitterly opposed to the Saudi government, however, particularly over the latter's close relationship with the USA during the 1991 war against Iraq, and he went into exile in Sudan in 1992. With al-Qaida being held responsible for a number of terrorist attacks, bin Laden was stripped of his Saudi nationality, disowned by his family, and expelled from Sudan in 1996. Thereafter he found refuge in Afghanistan where al-Qaida established extensive training facilities. Having declared war on the USA, the organisation launched a number of spectacular attacks including the June 1996 bombing of a US barracks in Dhahran, Saudi Arabia; the August 1998 suicide bombings of US embassies in Nairobi and Dar es Salaam; and the October 2000 attack on the *USS Cole*. In 2001 al-Qaida launched the 11 September attacks upon Washington DC and New York city, using hijacked airliners to damage the Pentagon and to destroy the World Trade Centre, thereby killing almost 3,000 people. Although bin Laden did not acknowledge authorship of these attacks—which traumatised the USA and shocked much of the world—until 2004, they were widely seen as his work. In response, the USA led an attack upon Afghanistan that overthrew the Taliban government but failed to kill or capture bin Laden who slipped away from his remote stronghold and seemingly vanished. There were no confirmed reports of his whereabouts and many speculated that, given his poor health, he had probably died. Although over the years he released a number of video and audio statements, their authenticity was never entirely proven. It later transpired that he had been living anonymously with his family in a secluded house in the Pakistani garrison town of Abbottabad. Although he was still nominally the head of al-Qaida, the movement—which had always been decentralised—had by this time evolved into a loose ideology rather than a formally constituted terrorist organisation. When this hiding place was eventually uncovered by US intelligence, a team of US Navy Seals covertly flew to Pakistan from Afghanistan and attacked the compound, killing bin Laden and his bodyguards. His corpse was removed by the raiders and, after formal identification, was later "buried at sea" in the Persian Gulf. Died 2 May.

Buckles, Frank (b. 1901), the last surviving US soldier to have participated in the Great War. Born in Missouri, Buckles joined the army at 16 years of age (by lying about his date of birth) and was shipped to France in late 1917 where he served as an ambulance driver behind the front line. He left the army in 1919 and, after a succession of jobs in the interwar period, was in Manila in December 1942 when the USA entered World War II. He was subsequently imprisoned in a Japanese internment camp for three years where he suffered great privations. Buckles spent the remainder of his life as a cattle farmer in West Virginia, continuing to drive his tractor until he was 104 years of age. In his later years he was fêted, giving interviews and being received at the White House, the Pentagon and Capitol Hill, having in 2008 become the country's only surviving veteran of World War I. He ascribed his longevity to a healthy diet, exercise, an optimistic disposition, and the will to survive, explaining that "when you start to die... don't". Although Buckles did not meet the criteria for entitlement to a burial in Arlington National Cemetery—having never served in combat—an exception was made and he was interred there with full military honours on 15 March. Died 27 February.

Cano, Alfonso (b. 1948), Marxist intellectual who became leader of FARC, Colombia's largest guerrilla army. Born into a professional family in Bogotá, Guillermo León Sáenz Vargas entered the National University of Colombia in 1968 to study anthropology. It was here that he became radicalised, becoming a student leader and joining the youth wing of the Colombia Communist party (PCC). He spent several years in the Soviet Union before returning to his homeland and joining the Revolutionary Armed Forces of Colombia (*Fuerzas Armadas Revolucionarias de Colombia*, FARC), an agrarian, Marxist, revolutionary organisation loosely affiliated to the PCC. He rose rapidly within its ranks and after a spell in prison in 1981-83 became a full-time guerrilla, adopting the *nom de guerre* Alfonso Cano. Operating from FARC's headquarters in the mountains, he played a key role in formulating ideology, building bridges with other guerrilla organisations and conducting peace negotiations with the government. In 1990 Cano joined FARC's seven-member leadership body, the Secretariat. An enthusiastic proponent of guerrilla struggle, he justified kidnapping (taking of "prisoners of war") and other controversial military tactics and weapons, arguing that in an "asymmetrical" struggle the underdog was not bound by conventional rules. At the time of his death more than 200 arrest warrants had been issued against him on charges including terrorism, murder and abduction. The US government also offered a $5 million reward for his capture on charges related to cocaine trafficking, although Cano consistently denied FARC's involvement in the drugs trade, despite abundant evidence to the contrary. In 2008 he became leader of FARC after the death of Manuel Marulanda Vélez, the movement's founder. Although the organisation had declined in numbers since its peak in 2000, it remained well-funded and well-armed. Under Cano's leadership it intensified its class war against the rich, and signed a strategic pact in 2009 with its smaller rival, the National Liberation Army (ELN). However, using intelligence from government infiltrators, the army closed in on Cano, forcing him to abandon his mountain stronghold in the west-central department of Tolima and move to less familiar terrain in the south-western province of Cauca.

It was here that he was eventually killed in a raid by elite army units. Died 4 November.

Christopher, Warren (b. 1925), lawyer, diplomat and US Secretary of State with a reputation for lacking ruthlessness. Born in Scranton, North Dakota, Christopher was brought up in reduced circumstances in California after the bankruptcy and death of his father. He won a scholarship to the University of Southern California and, after graduating from Stanford Law School in 1949, he successfully practised law, interrupted only by a period as deputy attorney general in 1967-69. In February 1977 he was appointed deputy secretary of state by Jimmy Carter, a president infamous for pursuing inconsistent foreign policy goals. A cautious figure, Christopher seemed uncomfortable in the limelight and was renowned for his rigorous attention to detail and his willingness to search for compromise rather than pursue bold policy gestures or confrontation. During these years his principal task was to negotiate the release of the 52 US diplomats taken hostage in Tehran in November 1979 by Iran's new Islamist regime. The talks dragged on for more than a year and the hostages were not released until January 1981 when Ronald Reagan became president. Though Christopher, by then out of office, was sent to greet the liberated hostages in Algiers (and was awarded the Medal of Freedom for his unsuccessful efforts to secure their release), his inability to end a crisis that had humiliated his country was seen as indicative of his lack of steel. He returned once again to public life to serve as President Clinton's secretary of state from 1993 to 1997, where he presided over the signing of the Oslo Peace Accords, the expansion of NATO, the normalisation of relations with Vietnam, and the Dayton Agreement of 1995 which ended the war in Bosnia. However, critics were quick to point out that tough negotiations in all of these areas were done by other parties. Furthermore, Christopher was lambasted for feebleness in failing to respond to—or even acknowledge—the genocide in Rwanda in 1994. After his retirement, he returned briefly to the public stage when he supervised the vote recount in Florida on behalf of Al Gore in the disputed presidential election of 2000. Died 18 March.

Cooper, Henry (b. 1934), British heavyweight boxing champion known for modesty, humour and a ferocious left hook. Cooper was born in Southwark, south-east London, in humble circumstances. His twin brother, George, also became a boxer, fighting under the name Jim, although he achieved less success. A gifted amateur boxer, Cooper won 73 of 84 contests, including the Amateur Boxing Association (ABA) light-heavyweight championship in 1952 and, in the same year, participated in the Helsinki Olympic Games. After completing his national service he turned professional. Although comparatively light for a heavyweight boxer, Cooper, a natural left-hander, had a formidable left hook which was affectionately known as "'Enry's 'Ammer". His greatest limitation was a prominent bone structure and delicate skin, especially around the eyes, which made him vulnerable to sustaining cuts. Nevertheless, in a career lasting from 1954 until 1971 he won 40 of his 55 professional fights (27 by knockout) and drew one. He was the only British boxer to win three Lonsdale Belts outright, and held the British, Commonwealth and European heavyweight titles. Perhaps his greatest moment in the ring came at Wembley stadium, on 18 June 1963, when he caught Muhammad Ali (at the time still known as Cassius Clay) with a hook that knocked the young American challenger to the canvas. The punch came in the final seconds of the fourth round and Ali was literally saved by the bell. He went on to win the contest after the fight was stopped because of a cut to Cooper's eye. (Reflecting on the punch, Ali later said that he had been hit so hard that the blow had been felt by his ancestors in Africa.) The two men fought again in May 1966, with the contest ending in a similar fashion, and thereafter retained the greatest respect for each other throughout the rest of their lives. After his retirement at the age of 37 Cooper served as a boxing commentator, after-dinner speaker, and sports personality. His natural humour and modesty, together with his fundraising for charity, meant that in his later years he became something of a national treasure, affectionately known as "Our 'Enry". In 2000 he was knighted (having received an OBE in 1969). Died 1 May.

Delaney, Shelagh (b. 1939), English playwright and screenwriter renowned for her ground-breaking debut work, *A Taste of Honey*. Born into a working class background in Salford, Delaney left school at 16 and worked in a range of menial jobs. At the age of 18 she wrote *A Taste of Honey*, which proved to be one of the defining plays of the 1950s in its willingness to defy the conventions of the era. Rooted in her own humble background, the play vibrantly portrayed a group of dysfunctional characters, at the centre of which was a feisty young girl who becomes pregnant after a one night stand with a black sailor and is thereafter befriended by a gay man. The play opened in May 1958 in London and, although controversial, proved a critical and commercial success. It transferred to Broadway in 1960 and was made into an award-winning film, released in 1961. Although Delaney wrote further plays during her career, none captured the same unself-conscious spontaneity of her initial work. She also wrote a collection of short stories, *Sweetly Sings the Donkey* (1963), and created scripts for radio, television and film. Amongst her best known screenplays were *Charlie Bubbles* (1967), starring Albert Finney, and *Dance With a Stranger* (1985), based on the life of Ruth Ellis, the last woman to be hanged in the UK. Died 20 November.

D'Oliveira, Basil (b. c1931), genial England cricketer who became a symbol of the struggle against the apartheid regime in South Africa. "Dolly", as he was known affectionately throughout his career, was born in Cape Town, South Africa, probably in 1928 although he reduced his official age by revising his official birth date to 1931. Under the apartheid laws of the country he was categorised as "coloured", a status which meant that despite his outstanding talent—he dominated non-white cricket in South Africa—he was prohibited from playing at first class level. In 1960 he emigrated to the UK where he played minor league cricket before making his debut for Worcestershire in 1964, becoming the first non-white South African to play county cricket. A right-handed middle-order batsman with powerful arms, he could hit the ball formidably hard. He was also an expert slip fielder and could bowl medium pace seam as well as off-spin. Having qualified by residence, he was selected for England in 1966 and established himself in the national side. When the team to tour South Africa in 1968-69 was named, however, he was controversially omitted from the squad. Although the MCC insisted that D'Oliveira's exclusion was purely the result of cricketing considerations, it was widely perceived as a cowardly and unjust concession to official South African pressure not to select him. In the face of widespread public outrage the MCC back-tracked. When one of the squad dropped out through injury it was announced that D'Oliveira would take his place. The South African government responded by stating that he would not be permitted to play, whereupon the tour was cancelled. The decision marked a watershed in establishing South Africa's international sporting isolation, a boycott that was to last until the collapse of the apartheid system. D'Oliveira continued to represent England until 1972, playing in a total of 44 Tests, and scoring 2,484 runs (including five centuries) at an average of 40.06, taking 47 wickets (at 39.55 runs apiece), and holding 29 catches. He played county cricket until 1980, retiring after 367 first class matches having scored 19,490 runs (at an average of 40.26), taken 551 wickets (at 27.45 apiece), and held 215 catches. In 2004 the trophy for Test series between South Africa and England was named in his honour and in 2005 he was awarded a CBE (having received the OBE in 1969). Died 19 November.

Erbakan, Necmettin (b. 1926), engineer, academic, and first Islamist prime minister of Turkey. Born in Sinop, on the Black Sea coast, Erbakan graduated in 1948 with a degree in mechanical engineering from Istanbul Technical University (UTI) before completing a PhD at the Rhenish-Westphalian Technical University of Aachen, Germany. After working in the German motor industry he returned to Turkey where he taught at UTI from 1953, becoming a professor in 1965. His political career began in 1969 with his election to the legislature and his founding of the first of a series of Islamist political parties. As chairman of the National Salvation Party he twice served as deputy prime minister in the 1970s. The party was closed down after the 1980 military coup, however, and Erbakan was excluded from politics. He returned to politics as leader of the Welfare Party, founded in 1983, and in 1995 led it to a surprise election victory. As prime minister in a coalition government Erbakan was seen by Turkey's urban middle class as threatening the secular, pro-Western foundations of the modern state. In 1997 the military forced his resignation and in the following year the Welfare Party was banned for violating the constitutional principle of secularism. Although once again barred from active politics, Erbakan played a key role as the mentor of a younger generation of more inclusive Islamists. They founded the Virtue Party in 1997 and, when this was declared illegal in 2001, the Justice and Development Party (AKP) which swept Recep Tayyip Erdogan, a former follower of Erbakan, to power at the election of 2002. Offering a brand of Islamism that combined religious belief with liberal democracy, capitalism and existing Western alliances, Erdogan's AKP had the effect of marginalising Erbakan, who had by then returned to political activity as leader of the Felicity Party. In his final years Erbakan was found guilty of corruption charges over cash that went missing when the Welfare Party was closed down. He was pardoned on health grounds by President Abdullah Gül, a former political colleague. Died 27 February.

Feiwel, Penny (b. 1909), the last surviving British woman to have served with the International Brigades in the Spanish Civil War. Born Ada Louise "Penny" Phelps to a working class family in north London, Feiwel left school at 13 and, after unhappy spells as a domestic servant and factory worker, trained as a nurse. In her mid-20s she attended Hillcroft College in Surrey, which specialised in teaching working women from poor backgrounds, and as a result began moving in a more politically aware, left-wing, milieu. In January 1937 she travelled to Spain to work as a nurse for the International Brigades, a cosmopolitan organisation of left-wing volunteers who were helping to defend the Spanish Republic against the right-wing Nationalist

forces of General Franco. Although she had never before been abroad, and spoke no Spanish, Feiwel (who at the time was known by her maiden name of Phelps) distinguished herself in the difficult wartime conditions and rapidly secured promotion. In 1938, however, she was severely wounded during a bombing attack whilst working near Valencia and was evacuated back to Britain to convalesce. Here she met and married Michael Feiwel, a surgeon at Saint James's hospital, Balham, and thereafter worked with him in his Harley Street practice. Although she regretted that her wounds meant that she could never bear children, she had no reservations concerning her decision to volunteer for the war. She later wrote that she regarded it as a seminal struggle against fascism: "Spain was a warning of what would happen to all of us. If we let Spain go, then it would be our fate, too, to go to war." She published a memoir, *English Penny*, in 1992, and in 2009 was honoured with the award of a Spanish passport in recognition of her wartime service. Died 6 January.

Ferraro, Geraldine (b. 1935), lawyer and politician who became the first woman to be chosen by a major US political party as its vice-presidential candidate. Born in Newburgh, New York state, of Italian immigrant parents, Ferraro was raised in relative poverty by her widowed mother in New York city. Academically gifted, she won a university scholarship to Marymount College and later worked as a school teacher to finance taking evening classes at law school. In 1960 she married a Manhattan property developer, John Zaccaro and, after being admitted to the bar in 1961, practised as a part-time lawyer in her husband's real estate company whilst bringing up three children. In 1974 she was appointed (by her cousin) as an assistant district attorney for Queens County, specialising in cases of rape and family violence. Determined to tackle some of the causes of the crimes that she was prosecuting, she entered politics in 1978, winning a New York seat in the House of Representatives for the Democratic Party, assisted by cash (later deemed illegal) from her husband. As a legislator she was particularly active in areas regarding women's equality and established a growing national reputation. In 1984 Democratic presidential candidate Walter Mondale chose her as his vice-presidential running mate. Although an effective campaigner, her suitability for the post was widely questioned on the grounds of her gender. There was also public consternation over her husband's refusal to release tax records, a stance that she made light of, telling reporters, "You people who are married to Italian men, you know what it's like." The matter became a major campaign issue which eventually forced the release of financial information, which damagingly showed the couple to be multimillionaires and revealed that Ferraro owed more than $50,000 in back taxes. At the subsequent election she and Mondale suffered one of the most crushing electoral defeats in US history at the hands of the incumbent Republican president, Ronald Reagan. Thereafter Ferraro held various appointed posts, made two fruitless runs for the Senate, and pursued a successful career as a lobbyist and political commentator. In 2001 she revealed that she was being treated for cancer that had been diagnosed in 1998. Died 26 March.

Ford, Betty (b. 1918), former US First Lady and founder of well-known addiction treatment centre which bears her name. Born Elizabeth Bloomer in Chicago and brought up in Grand Rapids, Michigan, Ford gave up an early career as a dancer and model because of her mother's disapproval. After a failed first marriage she married Gerald Ford, an aspiring politician, in 1948. Despite leading an ostensibly ordinary life as a political wife and mother, Betty Ford became secretly addicted to powerful analgesics prescribed to help her cope with the pain of arthritis. In 1973 her life changed when her husband was chosen by President Nixon to replace his disgraced vice president, Spiro Agnew. In August 1974 Nixon himself was forced to resign in the face of the Watergate scandal and the Fords entered the White House. As First Lady Ford was remarkably forthright, supporting a range of woman's causes, including the right to abortion, and being willing to discuss openly the possibility of her daughter engaging in pre-marital sex or smoking marijuana. She also admitted to having been diagnosed with a lump in her breast and

allowed publication of the details of her subsequent mastectomy and recuperation with a frankness that was credited with having saved lives by encouraging breast screening. After her husband's defeat in the presidential election of 1976, Ford acknowledged her addiction to painkillers and alcohol and successfully sought treatment. With her recovery complete, in 1982 she founded the not-for-profit Betty Ford Centre, near her home at Palm Springs, which rapidly became one of the most well-regarded clinics for the treatment of addiction, and which was frequented by numerous celebrity clients. Died 8 July.

Frazier, Joe (b. 1944), former heavyweight boxing champion known for his relentless aggression and fearsome left hook. Born in poverty in California, Frazier dropped out of school at the age of 13 and became a successful amateur boxer. After winning a heavyweight gold medal at the 1964 Olympic Games, he turned professional and by 1970 had become world heavyweight champion. That same year Muhammad Ali—the former champion who had been stripped of his title for refusing to fight in Vietnam—returned to the ring, thereby setting up the series of three lucrative and epic encounters with which Frazier would be forever associated. The two boxers were starkly contrasting in almost every respect: the light skinned, dancing Ali was tall, handsome, witty and outspokenly political; "Smokin' Joe" was dark, squat and taciturn, relying on fitness, unyielding aggression and raw courage. There was also deep antagonism between the two, with Frazier being the long-suffering butt of Ali's taunts that he was "ignorant", a "gorilla" and an "Uncle Tom". The two met first at Madison Square Garden in March 1971 in a contest billed "the Fight of the Century" and watched by a global audience of 300 million. The dogged Frazier wore down the former champion, knocking him to the canvas in the 15th round and going on to win the fight on points. At the height of his success, Frazier bought a 150-hectare plantation near his boyhood home and became the first black man since the Reconstruction era to address the legislature of South Carolina. In January 1974—with Frazier having already lost his title after being savagely knocked out the previous year by George Fore-man—Ali secured some measure of revenge by beating him in a non-title fight. Their final encounter was in Manila on 30 September 1975—a contest dubbed the "Thrilla in Manila" and often cited as the greatest heavyweight fight of all time. Ali, who had by then regained the world title from Foreman, prevailed in a brutal spectacle that was stopped by Frazier's trainer before the final round when damage to the boxer's eyes meant that he was fighting almost blind. An exhausted Ali said of his defeated opponent, "He is the greatest fighter of all times, next to me." Frazier retired in 1976 having lost once more to Foreman. During the course of his professional career he won 32 fights (27 by knockouts), drew one and lost only four. Died 7 November.

Freud, Lucian (b. 1922), widely regarded as the greatest figurative artist of the late 20th century. Freud was born into a prosperous family in Berlin—his father was the youngest son of Sigmund Freud—but the family fled to London in 1933 following the rise of Nazism. There, Freud underwent a privileged but chequered education before studying at the Central School of Arts and Crafts and later at the East Anglian School of Painting and Drawing. Thereafter, assisted by a number of wealthy and influential patrons, Freud built a reputation based upon capturing the essence of his subject through penetrating observation. Whilst this sometimes involved inanimate objects, he was best known for portraits and nudes wherein he seemed able to strip the protective layers from an individual and reveal a corporeal and astonishingly vulnerable level of nakedness. He worked exclusively from life but eschewed the use of professional models, preferring to paint friends, neighbours, lovers and his children. (Of these, he fathered at least 13, by a number of wives and lovers, but was rumoured to have had many more amid a personal life notorious for promiscuity and an addiction to gambling.) He frequently employed an impasto technique but used canvases which varied in size from tiny to vast and sought always to avoid being formulaic in his approach to a subject. An individual picture could take thousands of hours

to complete and Freud demanded that a model be present throughout its execution, a commitment leavened by the artist's reputation as a lively conversationalist and amusing mimic. The revival of interest in figurative art in the early 1980s rapidly augmented Freud's growing reputation. International exhibitions and honours followed and the monetary value of his works soared as they were sought after by wealthy American collectors and newly rich Russian oligarchs. In May 2008 his *Benefits Supervisor Sleeping* (1995) was sold in New York for $33.6 million, a record auction price for a living artist. Died 20 July.

Granado, Alberto (b. 1922), Argentinian doctor who accompanied his friend and compatriot Ernesto "Che" Guevara on an idealistic motorcycle journey through South America in 1952. Born in Hernando, Granado studied at the University of Cordoba and in 1943 spent a year in prison for protesting against Argentina's Peronist government. At this time he became close friends with Che Guevara, the two men sharing similar political views and literary tastes, together with a mutual idealism and intellectual curiosity. After working as a biochemist for a number of years, Granado accompanied Guevara on their iconic motorcycle tour between December 1951 and July 1952, with both men recording the experiences in diaries. Both were deeply affected by the level of poverty and deprivation that they encountered and sought to use their medical skills to ameliorate it. Following the Cuban revolution, Che—who was by then a senior figure in the new government—invited Granado to Cuba where he lived from 1961 until the end of his life. In 1963-64 he assisted Che in organising an unsuccessful guerrilla campaign in northern Argentina. He made a more lasting impact, however, by playing a significant role in developing Cuba's impressive medical and research facilities, becoming in the process an international authority in the field of genetics. A lifelong Marxist, in 1978 he published an account of his motorcycle odyssey, *Con el Che por Sudamerica*. The book finally appeared in English in 2003, coinciding with *The Motorcycle Diaries*, a highly acclaimed film by Walter Salles, based on the diaries of the two participants. Despite his advanced years Granado served as an on-set advisor for the film, retracing the journey that he had made 50 years earlier and expressing shock and dismay that so much of the poverty that he and Che had encountered remained unchanged. He was invited to attend the film's world premier at the Sundance film festival in 2004, but was denied a visa by the US authorities. Died 5 March.

Hamilton, Richard (b. 1924), influential British artist widely considered to be the "father of Pop Art". Born in London, the son of a lorry driver, Hamilton left school at 14 to work at an engineering firm, later taking evening classes in painting and enrolling as a student at the Royal Academy Schools. He was experimental in style, a characteristic that he attributed to his love of James Joyce's *Ulysses*, which he first read whilst doing National Service. He was also heavily influenced by the Dadaist and Surrealist work of Marcel Duchamp, an artist whom he knew and admired greatly. In 1956 Hamilton produced the work with which he was forever associated. Titled *Just What is it that Makes Today's Homes So Different, So Appealing?*, it was a collage composed largely of cuttings from US consumer magazines. It was the first Pop Art image to achieve iconic status and would later be cited as emblematic of the emergence of a major artistic movement. In addition to capturing images of the London pop music scene in the 1960s, Hamilton also consistently produced political works, notably a series of paintings in the early 1980s concerning the conflict in Northern Ireland (which included the portrayal of hunger striker Bobby Sands as Jesus), and opposition to Britain's involvement in the Iraq war. In addition to painting and printmaking, he also experimented with new technologies, being quick to recognised their impact on the process of producing art in a digital age. He received a number of awards from the 1960s onwards and was the subject of regular international exhibitions, his work being much sought after by collectors and galleries alike. Died 13 September.

Havel, Václav (b. 1936), dissident playwright who became the first president of the Czech Republic. Born into a wealthy Prague family that suffered discrimination at the hands of Czechoslovakia's communist government, Havel worked as a laboratory assistant and then performed military service (1957-59). Thereafter he found work as a theatre stagehand and pursued a drama correspondence course. In 1963 his first full length play, *The Garden Party*, was publically performed to critical acclaim and numerous others followed in the ensuing years. His growing international reputation as a dissident voice was boosted by his radio broadcasts during the 1968 Soviet invasion which crushed the "Prague Spring". Thereafter Havel was banned from the theatre and his works were suppressed. He continued to write, however, and also became more actively involved in the politics of the underground Czech dissident movement. In 1977 he was a founder of the Charter 77 civil rights group and thereafter suffered persistent official harassment and spent periods in prison. Nevertheless, he remained an influential artistic and political force, producing several significant works of non-fiction in the latter half of the 1980s. As the leader of Civic Forum, a loose alliance of anticommunist political forces, Havel was the natural choice to become president of Czechoslovakia in December 1989 after the overthrow of the communist regime by the Velvet Revolution. He was confirmed in the post in the country's first free election in 1990 and served until July 1992 when he stood down in order to avoid presiding over the breakup of the country into its Czech and Slovak constituent elements. In January 1993 he was elected president of the new Czech Republic, a post that he held until February 2003 (having been re-elected in 1998). His years as head of state were characterised by an informal style, a respect for human rights and democracy, and a willingness to forgive the transgressions of the past. Having completed his second term as president Havel returned to writing, and his first play in almost two decades, *Leaving*, was published in 2007. Despite ill health—a heavy smoker, he had been diagnosed with lung cancer in 1996, and later underwent a colostomy after rupturing his colon—he remained politically active in the cause of international human rights, and from 2004 was a supporter of the Czech Green Party. Died 18 December.

Hitchens, Christopher (b. 1949) polemical British journalist. Born in Portsmouth, Hitchens was educated at Leys School in Cambridge, before gaining a third class degree in philosophy, politics and economics at Balliol College, Oxford. His university years were notable for his adherence to leftwing politics—he was a member of International Socialists, a Trotskyist group, from 1966 to 1976—whilst also pursuing an active social life that included sexual relationships with men as well as women. After graduating he began a career in journalism, becoming part of a literary group at the *New Statesman* that included his lifelong friend, Martin Amis. In 1981 he emigrated to the USA where he wrote for *The Nation* and in 1992 became a contributing editor of *Vanity Fair*. He also travelled widely, reporting from a range of countries. A fiercely combative and often brilliant writer, Hitchens used his incendiary prose and oratory to lambast a wide range of targets that included US foreign policy, international human rights abuses, capitalist exploitation and the Israeli occupation of Palestinian territory. He wrote passionately about figures that he admired, with books on Thomas Jefferson, George Orwell and Tom Paine, but was scathing about a host of others—including Ronald Reagan, the Dalai Lama, Bill Clinton, Mother Teresa, Jerry Falwell, Mel Gibson, Michael Moore and Jesse Helms—who were often the subject of biting personal attack. His years in Washington saw a shift in his politics as he moved in increasingly exalted social circles and seemed to enjoy his growing celebrity. Although continuing to claim that he was a Marxist, Hitchens eschewed socialism and found common cause with US neoconservatives. He declared himself a Jew (having learnt that his mother was of Jewish descent) and became an implacable opponent of Islamism, which he described as "fascism with an Islamic face". This became more marked after the 2001 terrorist attacks upon the USA, with Hitchens deploying his rhetorical skills in defence of the US-led invasion of Iraq. Denounced by many of his former comrades on the Left, he appeared to relish engaging them in public debate wherein he frequently displayed his trademark combination of vitriolic erudition and intellectual thuggery. In April 2007 he became a US citizen at a ceremony presided over by Michael Chertoff, the head of the Homeland Security department in the Bush administration. A notoriously heavy drinker and smoker, Hitchens was also an assertive atheist, a view to which he adhered with increased strength after his 2010 diagnosis with oesophageal cancer. Died 15 December.

Jobs, Steve (b. 1955), innovative technology entrepreneur and co-founder of Apple Inc. Born in California to an unmarried young mother and a Syrian father, Jobs was put up for adoption immediately after his birth. Fascinated by technology from an early age, he completed high school in 1972 and attended Reed College, Oregon, but dropped out after only a few months. In 1974 he spent several months travelling in India, experimenting with eastern religion and psychedelic drugs. In 1976 he founded Apple together with fellow electronics buff Steve Wozniak, whom he had known since his teenage years. The Apple computers that they produced were distinguished by a sense of aesthetic style which raised them from utilitarian gadgets to personalised lifestyle accessories and design statements. Apple grew rapidly but the dictatorial style of Jobs was not always appreciated by those with whom he worked. In 1985, with the company's development having stalled, Jobs was ousted from Apple in a boardroom coup. After the shock had subsided his loss unleashed a period of renewed creativity. He founded NeXT, a company which manufactured innovative computers and software and which was eventually bought in 1996 by Apple. He also developed the computer graphics company Pixar into a hugely successful concern, collaborating with Disney on a range of popular and lucrative children's films. Having returned to Apple he was instrumental in developing its almost unrivalled reputation for innovative and attractive designs, although the company continued to command only a relatively small share of a personal computer market that remained dominated by Microsoft's Windows operating system. Under the guidance of Jobs, Apple branched out into the massively successful iPod digital music player in 2001, which transformed the way in which music collections were stored and played.

In 2007 Apple unveiled the iPhone, which combined the functions of mobile phone, media player and personal organiser in one stylish unit. In January 2010 the company launched the iPad, a successful touch-sensitive tablet computer. Diagnosed with pancreatic cancer in 2004, Jobs battled ill health in his later years, undergoing a liver transplant in 2009, before eventually succumbing to the disease. Died 5 October.

Kadhafi, Moamar (b. 1942), eccentric and narcissistic Libyan dictator. Born in a Bedouin tent near Sirte, as a teenager Kadhafi was much influenced by Colonel Nasser and the concepts of pan-Arabism and renaissance that the Egyptian leader personified. He graduated from the Royal Libyan Military Academy in 1966 and around this time also studied in Europe. Driven by a mystical sense of personal destiny, the young officer led a bloodless coup in 1969 which deposed the monarchy and established him as Libya's preeminent leader, a position that he retained until his overthrow in 2011. After Nasser's death in 1970 Kadhafi inherited his mantle, championing the creation of a Federation of Arab Republics which unsuccessfully united Libya, Egypt and Syria between 1972 and 1977. Internally, he advocated a form of socialism with Islamic characteristics, espousing modernisation together with an implacable opposition to Zionism and Western imperialism. He forced Western oil companies to cede a greater share of their profits, using the vast revenues to construct roads, school and hospitals which resulted in striking levels of increased literacy and life expectancy. In 1977 he proclaimed the Socialist People's Libyan Arab Jamahiriya (Jamahiriya being his Arabic term for "state of the masses"), where power was theoretically exercised by the people through local councils. In practice, Kadhafi continued as a dictator, eliminating—often with extreme violence—all possible sources of opposition and creating a country without conventional political, civil or military institutions. His ideology was contained in his *Green Book* in which he advanced a "third universal theory" as an alternative to capitalism and socialism. Disillusioned with Arab unity, Kadhafi increasingly identified Libya as an African country, intervening widely in regional affairs, including involvement in a number of conflicts and support for some notorious dictators. Meanwhile, in the West his government was denounced for its support of terrorist organisations and its attempts to acquire weapons of mass destruction. In 1986 Kadhafi survived a US airstrike against him but Libya's isolation was intensified after the 1988 Lockerbie bombing when he refused to surrender the alleged perpetrators of the crime. The regime finally emerged from isolation in the early 21st century when sanctions were lifted after Kadhafi compensated the victims of Lockerbie, scrapped his weapons of mass destruction, and co-operated with the West in its conflict with al-Qaida. Although rehabilitated internationally, however, the regime was reviled by many Libyans as corrupt and inefficient—faults personified by the leader's sons who combined their official positions with capricious power and a shamelessly extravagant lifestyle. Amid such conspicuous consumption Kadhafi—whose many titles included "the leader of the revolution", "the brother leader", "the guide to the era of the masses" and the "king of kings of Africa"—seemed an increasingly distant figure. The once handsome and charismatic leader appeared eccentric, narcissistic and detached, sporting a vast wardrobe of African robes, a glamorous troop of female bodyguards, and the face of an aging rock star who had undergone cut-price cosmetic surgery. When the Libyan people rose up against the regime in early 2011, inspired by popular revolutions in Tunisia and Egypt, Kadhafi fought a prolonged and vicious civil war, the balance of which was eventually tipped against him by the deployment of Western air power. Despite the fall of Tripoli Kadhafi refused to flee the country, choosing instead to make a final stand in an enclave in Sirte. Wounded by a Western airstrike he was captured by rebel forces and publicly beaten and humiliated before being summarily executed and his body put on display. Died 20 October.

Karzai, Ahmed Wali (b. 1961), influential power-broker in Afghanistan and half-brother of the country's president. Karzai was born in the small southern town of Karz, the son of a senior leader of the Popalzai Pashtun tribe

(Afghanistan's main ethnic group) who was killed by the Taliban in 1999. As a teenager he fled Afghanistan to escape the civil war that followed the 1979 Soviet military intervention in support of the country's communist government. Thereafter he lived in Chicago where he worked in the family-owned Afghan restaurant. He returned to his native country following the US-led overthrow of the Taliban regime in 2001 and profited from the West's choice of Hamid Karzai, his paternal half-brother, as the county's new president. As the new regime struggled to establish itself in Kabul, Ahmed Wali Karzai rapidly became a major power-broker in the family's native south-east. Much of his authority was exercised informally, backed by his private militia, although he was elected to the Kandahar provincial council in 2005 and was the council's chairman at the time of his death. His informal power was such that he presided over a parallel government structure through a network of patronage involving local tribes, political clans and drug barons. He was widely accused of having amassed a huge private fortunate through corruption and involvement in the county's narcotics industry, although he consistently denied all criminal allegations. He was also deeply implicated in both financing and fraudulently manipulating his half-brother's re-election as president, particularly in 2009 when electoral malpractice on an almost industrial scale stripped the Afghan government of any vestige of legitimacy. Despite repeated calls by Western officials that he be held to account, Karzai was well protected by the president and also by his alleged connections with the CIA. He was believed to have been on the agency's payroll for more than a decade, providing information on the insurgency and using his militia against Taliban targets. He survived several assassination attempts before finally being gunned down at point blank range in his house in Kandahar by Mohammed Sadar, a trusted associate and his long-time head of security. Died 12 July.

Kevorkian, Jack (b. 1928), US pathologist whose participation in assisted suicides led to the nickname "Dr Death". Born in Pontiac, Michigan, Jacob Kevorkian gained a medical degree from the University of Michigan in 1952. He served as an army doctor, first during the Korean War and then in Colorado, before returning to Pontiac to work as a hospital pathologist. He was also an inventor, writer, musician and composer, as well as an accomplished artist—his chosen medium was usually oils but sometimes he painted in his own blood. An avowed advocate of the right-to-die, Kevorkian achieved national fame for assisting Janet Adkins, an Alzheimer's sufferer, to kill herself in 1990. Operating from the back of his Volkswagen van, Kevorkian hooked Adkins up to a machine he called "the Thanatron", a homemade device that, when the patient pressed a button, dispensed sodium pentathol to render them unconscious and then potassium chloride to kill them. The state of Michigan subsequently pressed murder charges against him but later dropped them as it became clear that, technically, Adkins had killed herself. Over the next eight years Kevorkian assisted in some 130 suicides, in the process becoming a hugely controversial figure and stimulating an impassioned national debate over the ethics of suicide. He commanded widespread public support from those who saw him as an angel of mercy enabling the terminally ill to end their agony. For others, he was a serial killer deriving a ghoulish pleasure from his role in facilitating death. He was prosecuted four times between 1994 and 1997, being acquitted on three occasions and the fourth ending in a mistrial. Although stripped of his medical licences, Kevorkian appeared to thrive on his celebrity status. He replaced the Thanatron with the "Mercitron", a lethal machine that administered carbon monoxide, a method of death that he said he preferred as it left the corpse with a more life-like pallor. In 1998 Kevorkian actually administered the fatal injection (at the patient's own request) to a terminally ill man, Thomas Youk, and later allowed videotape of the procedure to be broadcast on television. The authorities took up his apparent challenge and this time secured a conviction for second-degree murder. In 1999 he was sentenced to 10-25 years in prison. Terminally ill, he was eventually paroled in 2007 on condition that he did not return to his former activities. Died 3 June.

Kim Jong Il (b. c.1942), reclusive and autocratic leader of North Korea. Kim was the son of Kim Il Sung, the founder of North Korea and the object of a huge personality cult. According to legend the younger Kim was born in 1942 at Mount Baekdu, one of the country's most revered sites, an event heralded by twin rainbows and the emergence of a brilliant new star. From Soviet records, however, it seems more likely that he was born (possibly in 1941) in Siberia, where his father was serving as a military officer. After graduating from university in Pyongyang in 1964, Kim held a number of posts within the ruling Workers' Party as it presided over the country's rapid industrialisation with the assistance of the Soviet Union and China. Kim Il Sung espoused an ideology know as "juche"—a mixture of nationalism, autarky and state communism—that saw the development of a grotesque personality cult which elevated both Kims to an almost divine level. In 1974 Kim Jong Il was designated his father's successor and in 1980 he joined the politburo and was given the title "Dear Leader", as opposed to the "Great Leader" designation enjoyed by his father. Historians are divided as to the degree of influence wielded by Kim at this stage of his career, although there is no such disagreement over the profligacy of his playboy lifestyle, which included an insatiable fondness for vintage cognac and wine, tobacco, luxury food and the services of multiple prostitutes. He was also believed to have been deeply implicated in planning acts of state terrorism, including the 1983 assassination of 17 South Korean officials in Burma, the 1987 bombing of a South Korean airliner, and the systematic abduction of more than a dozen Japanese citizens in the 1970s and 1980s. Kim became leader of North Korea in 1994 following the sudden death of his father, although it was not until 1997 that he officially became general secretary of the ruling party. By this time the country's economy was in sharp decline and a series of famines in the latter half of the 1990s claimed up to a million lives. Nevertheless, North Korea continued to develop nuclear weapons, the presence of which gave Kim a degree of international significance that was disproportionate to the stature of his impov-

erished and isolated country. Meanwhile, at the centre of one of the most oppressive regimes in the world, Kim's personality cult reached ever more absurd levels. Behind this facade, however, the Dear Leader's excessive lifestyle exacted its price in terms that were all too human. His health declined and in 2008 he suffered a serious stroke, after which he nominated his youngest son, Kim Jung Un, as his heir. Died 17 December.

Leigh Fermor, Patrick (b. 1915), English autodidact whose many facets included heroic soldier, intrepid traveller and much admired writer. Born in London, Leigh Fermor later described himself as a "wild-natured boy" unsuited to "the faintest shadow of constraint". He chose not to attend university but instead, in December 1933—at the age of 18 and with little money and few possessions—set out to walk the length of Europe. Assisted by his natural charm and an astonishing ability with foreign languages, he interacted with a wide range of characters before arriving in Constantinople (as he insisted on calling Istanbul) in January 1935. He later wrote about his adventures in *A Time of Gifts* (1977) and *Between the Woods and the Water* (1986), although the final part of the planned trilogy remained unpublished at the time of his death. In Athens he fell in love with Balasha Cantacuzene, a Romanian princess 12 years his senior, and lived with her on her family's "Tolstoyan" estate in Moldavia. After the outbreak of World War II he joined the British army and utilised his local knowledge and linguistic skills in the Balkans and Greece. He joined the Special Operations Executive in 1941 and helped to co-ordinate the resistance in German-occupied Crete. This included leading the audacious mission in 1944 that kidnapped the German commander on the island, General Heinrich Kreipe, and spirited him away to captivity in Alexandria. In the 1950s Leigh Fermor led a nomadic existence, producing a series of admired books, beginning with *Travellers' Tree* (1950) and including *A Time to Keep Silence* (1957) and his much acclaimed *Mani - Travels in the Southern Peloponnese* (1958). He also wrote his only novel, *The Violins of Saint-Jacques* (1953); a screenplay, *The Roots of Heaven* (1958); and worked on a number of translations. In 1964 he settled in the Mani with his long-time companion, Joan Eyres-Monsell (whom he married in 1968) and produced a further volume on Greece, *Roumeli* (1966). Although less prolific in his later years, he continued to write and to travel. He also remained physically robust, swimming daily until the last year of his life and even swimming the Hellespont at the age of 70. He was knighted in 2004, having been awarded the OBE (military) in 1943 and the DSO in 1944. Died 10 June.

Litvinoff, Emanuel (b. 1915), poet and writer who chronicled his Jewish upbringing in East London. Born in poverty in Whitechapel to immigrant parents from Russia, Litvinoff worked in a series of menial jobs in the interwar period and suffered periods of destitution. In 1939 he joined the Pioneer Corps, serving in Africa and the Middle East and emerging with the rank of Major. He was later to describe World War II as his "salvation" and it was during this period that his first poems were published. Although he claimed that after the sinking in 1942 of a Jewish refugee ship, the *Struma*, which had been denied entry to Palestine, he would never again regard himself as an Englishman, he returned to London after the war where he struggled to make a living from writing. He was supported financially by his wife, Irene Pearson, who pursued a successful modelling career under the name Cherry Marshall. Litvinoff worked for a number of Jewish publications and in the mid-1950s began publicising the plight of Jews within the Soviet Union. Assisted by information supplied by Israel's intelligence service, Mossad, he spearheaded an effective international campaign that prepared the way for eventual large-scale Jewish emigration. He achieved literary success in 1960 with his first novel, *The Lost Europeans*, and thereafter produced a number of television plays and novels dealing with aspects of Jewish history and anti-Semitism. The last of these, *Falls the Shadow* (1983), was a thriller in which an Israeli is revealed to be a former Nazi concentration camp guard. As a writer, however, he was best known for *Journey Through a Small Planet* (1972), which vividly chronicled his experience of growing up in London's East End. Died 24 September.

Lofthouse, Nat (b. 1925), talismanic English footballer whose work ethic and sheer physicality exemplified the simple virtues of the post-war game. Born into a working class family in Bolton, Lofthouse joined Bolton Wanderers as an amateur in 1939 before turning professional in 1941. Although only 5 feet 9 inches tall, he was heavily built and possessed a strength that had been honed by his earlier work in a tannery and then as a miner. Thus, although never blessed by abundant skills, his physical presence and hard work made him an effective centre forward. He played for Bolton throughout his career, appearing in the senior squad in 452 league games and scoring 255 goals between 1946 and his retirement in 1960. He represented England on 33 occasions between 1950 and 1958, his 30 international goals representing one of the best goals-to-games ratios of any English player. In a brutal match against Austria in May 1952 he scored twice to secure a 3-2 English victory—a performance that earned him the title of "Lion of Vienna". In 1953 he won the accolade of English Footballer of the Year, but was on the losing side in the FA Cup final. Five years later, as captain of Bolton, Lofthouse won the Cup against a Manchester United side depleted by the Munich air disaster. Lofthouse scored both goals in the game, although he later acknowledged that the second—which had involved him in a characteristically robust aerial challenge that had bundled both goalkeeper and ball into the opponents' goal—had been illegitimate. After retiring from the game he ran a pub and remained closely involved with his beloved Bolton Wanderers, including several brief but unsuccessful stints as manager before becoming club president in 1986. In 1994 he was appointed OBE. Died 15 January.

Lumet, Sidney (b. 1924), prolific US film director renowned for films of social conscience and moral complexity. Lumet was born in Philadelphia in 1924, the son of distinguished Yiddish theatre actors. A child performer, he continued acting after attending Columbia University and completing wartime military service in the army signal corps. Lumet began directing television dramas in 1950 and his flair for fast shooting and fluid camerawork brought him immediate acclaim. His first feature film, *12 Angry Men* (1957), was a critical success and later became acknowledged as a classic work of cinema. Together with cinematographer Boris Kaufman, Lumet used a range of camera angles and varying focal lengths to heighten the claustrophobia of the jury room in which almost the entire film is set. The movie also characterised Lumet's style in its exploration of a range of complex moral issues with its hero, Henry Fonda, courageously defying the pressure of conformity in a bid to do what is right. The film was the first of four to earn Lumet an Oscar nomination for best director, the others being *Dog Day Afternoon* (1975), *Network* (1976) and *The Verdict* (1982). For most of his career Lumet averaged a film per year—not all of which were critically or commercially successful—with many being adapted from stage plays and shot not in Hollywood but in and around New York. It was a productivity rate which was widely seen as having undermined his chances of receiving an Oscar, although he did receive an Academy Award for lifetime achievement in 2005. In presenting the award Al Pacino summed up the high esteem in which Lumet was held by actors: "If you prayed to inhabit a character, Sidney was the priest who listened to your prayers—helped them come true." Died 9 April.

Massey, Anna (b. 1937), English actress of stage, film and television who was renowned for her intelligent portrayal of repressed women. Born in Thakeham, West Sussex, to parents who were actors, Massey had a privileged but lonely upbringing. Although never trained as an actress, she made a confident stage debut at the age of 17 at the Theatre Royal, Brighton, in William Douglas Home's play *The Reluctant Debutante* (1955). The play later went to London and Broadway and led to further roles for Massey with the result that for the next quarter of a century she was a regular on the West End stage. Keys roles included Penelope Shawn in *Dear Delinquent* (1957), Lady Teazle in *School for Scandal* (1962), Laura Wingfield in *The Glass Menagerie* (1965), the eponymous schoolteacher in *The Prime of Miss Jean Brodie* (1966) and Driver in *Donkey's Years* (1977). She made her film debut in 1958 and later secured a lead role in Michael Powell's notorious *Peeping Tom* (1960). Although she appeared in numerous subsequent films, her somewhat pinched features gave her an unconventional look that did not conform to the stereotypes demanded for females leads in the mainstream film industry. As such, she was more successful on television, with notable roles in *David Copperfield* (1969), *The Mayor of Casterbridge* (1978), *Rebecca* (1979)—where she embodied an authentically creepy and threatening Mrs Danvers—*Mansfield Park* (1983) and *Hotel du Lac* (1986), where her portrayal of the lonely Edith Hope won her Best Actress awards from both BAFTA and the Royal Television Society. In 2005 she was appointed CBE for services to drama. The following year she acknowledged that she had worn less and less makeup as she had aged, arguing that "the unadorned face is far more interesting, if less flattering, but it requires courage". Died 3 July.

Mitterrand, Danielle (b. 1924), mould-breaking former first lady of France and human rights campaigner. Danielle Gouze was born in Verdun, the daughter of left-wing schoolteachers. During the Nazi occupation that followed France's defeat in 1940 her parents assisted the French Resistance. At the age of 17 Danielle joined the movement and fell in love with a comrade, François Mitterrand, whom she married in 1944. When Mitterrand was elected in 1981 for the first of his two seven-year terms as French president, Danielle became an unconventional première dame. Always more radical than her socialist husband—Mitterrand called her "my left-wing conscience"—Danielle gave militant support to a range of causes, sometimes to the embarrassment of the French government. These included Fidel Castro's revolutionary regime in Cuba, the struggle for Tibet's liberation, the Marxist guerrilla movement in El Salvador, the struggle for autonomy by Kurds in Iraq and Turkey, and by the Polisario Front in Western Sahara, and the rights of indigenous peoples of South America. She was a fierce opponent of the death penalty and championed humanitarian and ecological causes in developing countries through the non-profit human rights foundation, France-Libertés, which she created in 1986. In July 1992 she narrowly survived a huge car bomb whilst travelling through Iraq to inspect the town of Halabja, where 5,000 Kurds had died in a chemical attack by Saddam Hussein. Although she and her husband enjoyed a close relationship, he was an inveterate adulterer and it later transpired that she had allowed him to pursue this appetite in return for his recognition of her intellectual freedom to speak her mind. In 1974 Mitterrand fathered a daughter, Mazarine, with his long-time mistress, Anne Pingeot, although this did not become public knowledge until 1994. Danielle later described it as "neither a discovery, nor a drama". When her husband died in 1996 she was widely praised for the generosity that she showed in permitting Mazarine to stand beside her own sons at Mitterrand's state funeral. Died 22 November.

Peters, Lana (b. 1926), restless daughter of Josef Stalin who spent a lifetime trying to escape from her father's tyrannical shadow. Peters was born in Moscow as Svetlana Stalina, the youngest child and only daughter of Stalin and his second wife, Nadezhda Alliluyeva, who committed suicide in 1932. Although reputedly her father's favourite child, Svetlana's upbringing was harshly defined by the distant but domineering presence of the Soviet dictator. When she was 16 he sent her first love to a labour camp. Two brief, failed marriages followed and after Stalin's death in 1953 Svetlana—living under the name Svetlana Iosifovna Alliluyeva—worked as a lecturer and translator, exploiting her fluency in four languages, to support her two children. In 1963 she fell in love with Brajesh Singh, an Indian communist visiting Moscow, and although she was prevented from marrying him she was permitted, following his early death, to escort his ashes back to India in 1966. She stayed there for several months and in March 1967 defected via the US embassy in New Delhi. Arriving in the USA in April, she vehemently denounced the Soviet regime and her father's monstrous legacy. She lived in her adopted country for more than a decade, producing two memoirs—*Twenty Letters to a Friend* and *Only One Year*—and in 1970 marrying for a third time but divorcing in 1973. Although by now a US citizen, using the name

Lana Peters, she moved to the UK in 1982, before returning to Moscow—with her US-born daughter, Olga—in 1984. She publicly denounced her 17 years in the West, saying that she had not enjoyed a "single day of freedom" and that she had been a "pet" of the CIA, comments which she later claimed had been mistranslated. After living in Tbilisi she returned to the USA in 1986 and she spent the remainder of her life in a peripatetic existence, ending her days living in anonymous austerity in Wisconsin. Prior to her death she acknowledged that "wherever I go... I always will be a political prisoner of my father's name." Died 22 November.

Postlethwaite, Pete (b. 1946), Oscar-nominated English character actor who played a wide range of leading roles on stage, film and television. Born into a working class, Roman Catholic family in Warrington, Cheshire, Postlethwaite qualified as a teacher prior to training as an actor at the Bristol Old Vic Theatre School. Thereafter he pursued an acting career, appearing in numerous roles at the Liverpool Everyman theatre, the Royal Shakespeare Company, the Bristol Old Vic and many other prestigious venues. From the mid-1970s he supplemented his stage appearances with television and film roles. His first major cinematic success came in the film *Distant Voices, Still Lives* (1988) in which he powerfully portrayed a drunken and abusive husband. He received an Oscar nomination for his performance in *In the Name of the Father* (1993), a moving depiction of the agony endured by those who had been wrongly convicted of the IRA's 1974 Guildford pub bombings. His distinctive face and wide acting range gave him an ability to shine in comic as well as tragic roles. Thus he won wide acclaim for his performances in the darkly disturbing *The Usual Suspects* (1995) as well as the popular comedy *Brassed Off* (1996), and was once described by the director Steven Spielberg as "probably the best actor in the world today". He received an OBE in 2004. A committed socialist, Postlethwaite was also a keen supporter of environmentalism and lived in an "eco-house" that he constructed in Shropshire. Despite battling cancer, Postlethwaite made a final appearance in Nick Hamm's film *Killing Bono*

(2011). Unable to play the part in which he had been originally cast, he appeared in another role which was written specifically for him. Died 2 January.

Rabbani, Burhanuddin (b. 1940), religious scholar, political leader and former president of Afghanistan. An ethnic Tajik, Rabbani was born in Faizabad, in Badakhshan province. He attended the Abu Hanifa religious high school in Kabul and then studied Islamic law and theology at Kabul University. After graduating in 1963 he taught there, becoming well known as an Islamist speaker and theoretician. He then spent two years in Cairo (1966-68) where he developed close ties with the Muslim Brotherhood whilst acquiring a Master's degree in Islamic Philosophy from Al-Azhar University. Upon returning to Afghanistan he became closely associated with the Jamiat-i-Islami, an established Islamist movement, becoming its leader in 1972. In 1974 he fled to Pakistan to escape arrest but returned after the 1979 Soviet military intervention in Afghanistan. The Jamiat-i-Islami became a key element in the Mujahedeen—the common front of Islamic fighters who engaged in a guerrilla war against the Soviets and their Afghan government allies. Rabbani's forces were the first to enter Kabul after the fall of the Soviet-backed government in 1992 and shortly thereafter he became president. Despite an agreement that the office should rotate amongst the Mujahedeen's leaders, Rabbani retained the presidency (together with military control of Kabul) until 1996. As president he imposed strict Islamic codes, banning alcohol, closing cinemas, conducting public executions and forcing women to wear the hijab. The period was also marked by vicious fighting between the erstwhile Mujahedeen allies, and Rabbani's forces were involved in widespread human rights abuses. He was eventually driven out of the capital by the rise of the Taliban, a younger generation of more extreme Pashtun Islamists. Thereafter Rabbani was the political head of the main source of anti-Taliban military resistance, the Northern Alliance. He served briefly as temporary president in 2001, after the US-led invasion and overthrow of the Taliban regime. In 2010 he became head of the High Peace Council, created by President Hamid Karzai with the aim of finding a political solution to the Afghan war, including peace negotiations with the Taliban. He was killed at his home in Kabul by a man posing as a Taliban commander intent upon discussing peace terms. The assassin detonated an explosive device hidden in his turban as he leaned forward to greet Rabbani with an embrace. Died 20 September.

Rojas Pizarro, Gonzalo (b. 1917), leading Chilean poet who was exiled by the Pinochet dictatorship. The seventh of eight children born to a coal miner in the small town of Lebu, Rojas was educated at a school run by German Jesuits in the city of Concepción, an experience which inculcated within him a lifetime's love of German Romantic poetry and the German language. Influenced by Surrealism, he published his first volume of verse in 1948 and taught Spanish literature at the universities of Concepción and Valparaiso. He was a close friend of the country's democratically elected Marxist president, Salvador Allende, and was appointed by him as ambassador to China and then to Cuba. Whilst Rojas was in Havana, Allende's government was overthrown in 1973 by a military coup led by General Augusto Pinochet whose military regime subsequently stripped him of his nationality. After spending years in exile, including time in East Germany, he eventually returned to Chile in 1979, but lived subsequently in the USA (1980-94). Although never a prolific poet, Rojas continued to publish works of great intensity and sensuality, and was translated into numerous languages. In 1992 he was awarded the Chilean National Prize for Literature and in 2003 received the prestigious Miguel de Cervantes Prize, awarded annually to honour the lifetime achievement of an outstanding writer in Spanish. Died 25 April.

Russell, Jane (b. 1921), American actress and sex symbol of the 1940s and 1950s. Ernestine Jane Geraldine Russell was born in Bemidji, Minnesota, to a mother who was an actress (and later became a lay preacher) and a father who was an office manager. She grew up in California and in 1940, whilst working as a model, she was spotted by the eccentric millionaire and film mogul

Howard Hughes and cast in a leading role in *The Outlaw*. The film emphasised Russell's statuesque physique—Hughes even designed a special bra for her—and publicity stills for the movie which dwelt upon her ample cleavage became popular pinups. The film was considered so risqué at the time that it caused a furore and, although completed in 1941, did not secure a general certificate of release until 1946. Russell went on to star in more than 20 films although only *The Paleface* (1948), a comedy with Bob Hope, and *Gentlemen Prefer Blondes* (1953), a musical co-starring Marilyn Monroe, were of any lasting significance. Increasingly at odds with the values of Hollywood, roles for her dried up in the 1960s and she struggled with alcoholism. Ironically, despite having become an overnight sex symbol at the outset of her film career, she was throughout her life a devout Christian. She married three times and adopted three children as she was unable to have children of her own because of the backstreet abortion that she had endured in her youth. Having finally overcome her alcohol addiction in old age, she described herself in 2003 as "a teetotal, mean-spirited, right-wing, narrow-minded, conservative Christian bigot, but not a racist". Died 28 February.

Russell, Ken (b. 1927), flamboyant, provocative and controversial British film director. Born in Southampton, Russell was educated at Pangbourne naval college and studied photography at Walthamstow School of Art. After serving in the Merchant Navy (1945) and the RAF (1946-49), he worked as a ballet dancer and as a freelance photographer before finding success at the BBC. He made a number of critically acclaimed arts documentaries for the corporation between 1959 and 1970, including *Elgar* (1962), *The Debussy Film* (1965), *Isadora Duncan, the Biggest Dancer in the World* (1967), *Song of Summer* (about Delius) (1968) and *Dance of the Seven Veils* (1970), a film about Richard Strauss. Russell's work was marked by an increasing flamboyance and controversy that resulted in the outraged Strauss family withholding the music rights in order to prevent his film about the composer from being aired. His willingness to shock his audiences was also evident in his feature films. In 1969 he made *Women in Love*, an adaptation of the D.H. Lawrence novel, which included a nude wrestling scene between Oliver Reed and Alan Bates that breached the prohibition on showing male genitalia in mainstream films. Further controversy and explicit sexuality was evident in *The Music Lovers* (1970), which dealt with the life of Tchaikovsky; and *The Devils* (1971), based on a novel by Aldous Huxley, a film that was considered so obscene and blasphemous that it was widely banned. Their combination of moments of cinematic brilliance within a context of consistent excess, garnished lavishly with religious and sexual imagery, became a trademark which the director seemed to savour. Other, if less controversial, successes were *The Boy Friend* (1971), *Savage Messiah* (1972), *Mahler* (1974), and *Tommy* (1975), the latter, an extravagant rock opera featuring the Who, proving to be his last major triumph. Later films, including *Lisztomania* (1975), *Valentino* (1977), *Altered States* (1980) and *Crime of Passion* (1984), received neither consistent critical acclaim nor significant box office success and Russell found himself increasingly shunned by the Hollywood establishment. Although he continued to make independently financed films, and received praise for an adaptation of Lawrence's *The Rainbow* (1989), his output dwindled. His last film of note, *Whore* (1991), an unflinching examination of the life of a prostitute, sparked typical controversy. Died 27 November.

Savile, Jimmy (b. 1926), colourful British broadcaster and charity worker. James Wilson Vincent Savile, the youngest of seven children, was born in humble circumstances in Leeds. After leaving school at the age of 14 he was called up as a "Bevin boy" in 1942 and worked for six years as a miner before his underground career was ended when he received serious spinal injuries in a pit explosion. By this time he was already developing an alternative career as a disc jockey in local dance halls, being an early exponent of using two turntables, side by side, to enable the playing of continuous music. He also worked as a nightclub manager, hospital porter and professional wrestler. From the late 1950s he began broadcasting, first for Radio Luxembourg and then for the "pirate" Radio Caroline, and in 1964 he introduced the BBC's first *Top of the Pops* programme (he also hosted the last programme in the series in July 2006). He joined Radio 1 as a disc jockey in 1968, shortly after its launch, and found even greater fame as the host of *Jim'll Fix It* (1975-94), a popular television programme that gave viewers (particularly children) the opportunity to realise particular ambitions. Nevertheless, he was perceived as having an odd attitude towards children, remaining unmarried throughout his life and admitting that "I actually don't care for children". He maintained a very close but physically undemonstrative relationship with his mother—Agnes, whom he called "The Duchess"—until her death in 1973, and thereafter maintained her clothes and personal effects in pristine order. A shrewd promoter of his own image, Savile was known for his ubiquitous large cigar, peroxide blond hair, garish clothing and ostentatious jewellery. However, he also exploited his fame in the cause of good works, raising an estimated £30 million for charity, including some £12 million for Stoke Mandeville's National Spinal Injuries Centre. His philanthropy led to admiration from a broad spectrum—including royalty, politicians and celebrities—and resulted in a series of awards including an OBE (1971) and a knighthood (1990). Died 29 October.

Schneider, Maria (b. 1952), French actress whose career was defined but damaged by her lead role in *Last Tango in Paris*. Born (as Marie Christine Gelin) in Paris, the illegitimate daughter of a Romanian teenage model and a married French actor who refused to acknowledge her, Schneider was brought up near the German border by her mother (whose surname she later adopted). As a teenager she moved back to Paris where she found work as a film extra and model. Although an unknown, she auditioned for and secured the female lead in *Last Tango in Paris* (1972), a Bernardo Bertolucci film that provoked global controversy because of its explicit sexual content. Detailing the anonymous and often brutal relationship between a young French woman and her older American lover (played by Marlon Brando), the film included a notorious scene in which Schneider is shown being sodomised with the assistance of a handful of butter. Although the film was an enormous commercial and critical success, Schneider later accused Brando and Bertolucci of exploiting her youth and inexperience. She likened the experience to having been "raped" and claimed that the film had taught her, "Never take your clothes off for a middle-aged man who claims that it's art." In 1974 she confirmed her bisexuality. Although she appeared in a number of later films—most notably Michelangelo Antonioni's *The Passenger* (1975) with Jack Nicholson—she complained that "I was treated like a sex symbol and I wanted to be recognised as an actress." Her subsequent career was also adversely affected by her long struggle with drug addiction and mental health issues. Died 3 February.

Shalikashvili, John (b. 1936), army general and the first foreign-born soldier to serve as chairman of the US joint chiefs of staff. Shalikashvili was born in Warsaw to a father who, as a Georgian prince, had fled the Russian Revolution and would go on to fight for the Waffen-SS during World War II. The family emigrated to the USA in 1952 where Shalikashvili learned English and in 1958 became a US citizen. In the same year he graduated in mechanical engineering from Bradley University in Peoria, and later received a Master's degree in international affairs from George Washington University. He joined the army as a private in 1958 but soon earned promotion. After serving in Vietnam (where he was decorated for bravery) he returned to the USA where he held further military appointments, attended the US Army War College, and in 1987 became commander of the 9th Infantry Division. He achieved distinction as the head of the peacekeeping and humanitarian "Operation Provide Comfort", which protected the Kurdish community of northern Iraq in the aftermath of the 1990-91 Gulf War, a role that involved difficult and complex negotiations with both the Turkish government and the Iraqi military. He then served as supreme allied commander in Europe in 1992-93, assisting in the reshaping of NATO from an anti-Soviet pact into a more flexible security institution. In 1993 he became chairman of the joint chiefs of staff, a position that he held until his retirement from the military in 1997. Thereafter he served as a visiting professor at the Centre for International Security and Cooperation at Stanford University, held a number of directorships in defence-related commercial companies, and was an adviser to John Kerry's unsuccessful 2004 presidential campaign. Died 23 July.

Shriver, Robert Sargent (b. 1915), US politician, public official and diplomat who improved countless lives through government programmes and charitable works. Born in Westminster, Maryland, Shriver graduated from Yale in 1938 and from Yale Law School in 1941 before serving with distinction in the Navy in the Pacific (despite having initially opposed US entry into World War II.) After a seven-year courtship he finally succeeded in marrying Eunice Kennedy in 1953, and was given a job in her father's business empire. He worked on behalf of the successful campaign for the presidency in 1960 of his brother-in-law, John F. Kennedy, and was the driving force behind the creation of the Peace Corps, serving as its first director from 1961 to 1966. After Kennedy's assassination Shriver served as Special Assistant to President Lyndon Johnson. As such he was the architect of the "War on Poverty" and was instrumental in founding numerous social programmes and organisations, including giving assistance to underprivileged children ("Head Start") and providing health, legal and employment services to the poor. His commitment to philanthropy and civil rights sprang not from an ideological belief in big government but from his profound Christian faith, although his devout Catholicism also made him a staunch opponent of abortion. Having served as ambassador to France in 1968-70, Shriver ran as the Democratic vice-presidential candidate in the election of 1972, which the party lost resoundingly. Thereafter he devoted himself to his legal practice apart from one brief foray into elective politics when he unsuccessfully contested the Democratic presidential nomination in 1976. For two decades he also served as president, then chairman, of the Special Olympics, an organisation developed by his wife to offer sports training and competition to those with learning

difficulties. In 1994 his long record of public service was recognised with the award of a Presidential Medal of Freedom. Died 18 January.

Speed, Gary (b. 1969), Welsh footballer and manager widely respected for his integrity and inspirational leadership. Born in Mancot, Flintshire, as a boy Speed excelled at both football and cricket. He joined Leeds United in 1988 and helped the team to win promotion to the First Division in the 1989-90 season. An athletic and attacking player, Speed was the youngest element of a balanced and creative Leeds midfield that saw the team win the title in 1992, the year before the Premier League was formed. In total, he played 312 games for the club, scoring 57 goals and serving as team captain, before moving to Everton in 1996. During his long career he also enjoyed successful spells at Newcastle (1998-2004) and Bolton Wanderers (2004-08), becoming in 2006 the first player ever to make 500 Premier League appearances. Speed placed great emphasis on fitness and nutrition, characteristics that—together with the honest sportsmanship with which he played the game—meant that his career was rarely interrupted by injury or suspension. His final years were spent at Sheffield United (2008-10) and by the time he retired he had played 535 Premier League games, an achievement surpassed by only two other players. Speed also enjoyed a successful international career, making his debut for Wales in May 1990 and winning a total of 85 caps—a record for a Welsh outfield player—over the course of 14 years. As at club level, his professionalism, tactical acumen and popularity with his fellow players made him a natural choice for captain. Speed briefly managed Sheffield United in 2010 before becoming manager of the Welsh national side in December of that year. He galvanised the lacklustre Welsh team, blending youth with experience and providing inspired leadership and a renewed sense of self-belief. Of his 10 games in charge he won four of the last five and established a reputation as one of the most promising young mangers in the world. His early death—apparently as a result of having hanged himself at his home—was greeted by widespread grief and bewilderment. Died 27 November.

Styrene, Poly (b. 1957), British punk rock singer and songwriter whose flamboyant originality made her a modern feminist icon. Born in Bromley and raised in Brixton, Marianne Elliott-Said was the daughter of a legal secretary mother and an (absent) dispossessed Somali aristocrat father. She ran away from home at the age of 15 and, inspired by the punk rock group the Sex Pistols, formed her own punk band, X-Ray Spex, in 1975. Although at times shambolic, the band was energised by Styrene's unorthodox appearance and her powerful if discordant vocal style. X-Ray Spex received critical acclaim for their first single "Oh Bondage, Up Yours!", the anti-consumerist thrust of which was further developed with the release of their 1978 album *Germ Free Adolescents*, subsequently regarded as amongst the greatest punk albums ever recorded. Numerous concerts followed and the band participated in many key events of the punk rock era. Exhausted by touring, Styrene left the band in 1979 but as a solo artist failed to replicate her earlier success. She joined the Hare Krishna movement, an experience that she later said meant that "you end up as a complete space cadet". X-Ray Spex reformed for a concert in 1991 and again in 1995, although on the latter occasion its activities were curtailed after Styrene was injured by being knocked down by a fire engine in central London. The band's final performance was in September 2008 when it played to a packed audience of 3,000 at the Roundhouse in London. Died 25 April.

Taseer, Salman (b. 1944), Pakistani businessman and politician who advocated religious tolerance and the rights of minorities. Born in Simla, Taseer grew up in a left-wing family in Lahore. After the death of his father, a poet, Taseer and his two sisters were raised by their English mother in relative poverty. After completing school he lived in London where he supported himself with casual work whilst studying accountancy. During this period Taseer pursued left-wing causes and associated with radicals such as his childhood friend Tariq Ali. Impressed by Ali Bhutto's charisma and nationalism, Taseer joined the Pakistan People's Party (PPP) in the late 1960s. Upon his return to Pakistan his opposition to the "brutal and medieval dictatorship" of General Zia-ul-Haq (who had overthrown Bhutto's government in 1977) led to frequent periods of arrest, imprisonment and ill treatment. Zia's death in 1988 opened up a new democratic era for Pakistan and in that year Taseer was elected to the Punjab legislature. Electoral defeat in the 1990s, however, led him to concentrate upon building a successful business empire, although his youthful idealism remained in the form of his commitment to the cause of minority rights. Following a further military coup and a subsequent restoration of democracy, Taseer served in the federal government in 2007 as minister for industry and production. In 2008 he was appointed governor of Punjab and, in accordance with his vision of a "liberal and tolerant Pakistan", distinguished himself through his commitment to the rights of religious minorities. He opposed the country's blasphemy laws and received repeated death threats from Islamic extremists after he spoke out in support of Aasia Noreen, a Christian woman sentenced to death in 2010 for allegedly insulting the Prophet Muhammad. Subsequently, Taseer was assassinated by one of his own bodyguards. Died 4 January.

Taylor, Elizabeth (b. 1932), British-US actress who became an international film star renowned for her beauty, glamour and multiple romantic involvements. Born in London to American parents, Taylor's striking beauty—with violet eyes and dark hair—contributed to her success as a child actress from the age of 10. She achieved international fame for her performance in *National Velvet* (1945), a sentimental tale of a young girl who wins the Grand National disguised as a boy. Other notable performances followed, including *A Place in the Sun* (1951), *Giant* (1956), *Cat On a Hot Tin Roof* (1958), *Suddenly, Last Summer* (1959), *Butterfield 8* (1961) and *Who's Afraid of Virginia Woolf?* (1966). For the latter two she won Academy Awards for Best Actress. The first of her eight marriages (to seven different men) came in 1950. After two divorces she converted to Judaism and married flamboyant impresario Mike Todd in 1957 but he was killed in an air crash the following year. Whilst filming *Cleopatra* (1963)—an overblown epic for which

Taylor received a fee of $1 million and thereby became at the time the highest paid actress in history—Taylor met Richard Burton (playing Mark Anthony) and each left their spouses to embark upon a highly publicised relationship. They married in 1964 and, as the world's most famous couple, made a number of films together—although few were of great merit—before their tempestuous relationship ended in divorce in 1974. They remarried briefly in the following year and divorced once more in 1976. Thereafter Taylor continued to appear on stage, television and in films, but such projects were generally characterised by their mediocrity. She also suffered a range of health problems which were exacerbated by huge fluctuations in weight and addiction to cigarettes, alcohol, sleeping pills and pain killers. She had two further husbands, including US Senator John Warner, but both marriages ended in divorce. Throughout her life she was a supporter of numerous charities, particularly those connected to HIV and AIDS, and was a staunch supporter of Jewish causes and the state of Israel. Died 23 March.

Titmus, Fred (b. 1932), English cricketer and practitioner of subtly flighted off-spin bowling. Born in London and educated at William Ellis Grammar School, Titmus—who was also a promising footballer—made his debut for a depleted Middlesex team in 1949, thereby becoming, at the age of 16, the county's youngest ever player. He went on to make a record 642 appearances for Middlesex, his last being in 1982 at the age of almost 50 when, as a spectator, he was prevailed upon to join the team in a game against Surrey on a turning pitch. (Middlesex won the match with Titmus taking three wickets.) Initially a batsman who could also bowl seam deliveries, Titmus rapidly became an accomplished off-spinner despite lacking the stature or long fingers traditionally associated with this art. During his county career he took 2,361 wickets for Middlesex and scored over 20,000 runs, achieving on eight occasions the renowned "double" feat of taking 100 wickets and scoring 1,000 runs in a season. He captained the side from 1965 to 1968. He also played in 53 Test matches for England between 1955 and 1975,

scoring 1,449 runs (at an average of 22.29) and taking 153 wickets (at an average of 32.22). His career was blighted during a Test tour to the West Indies in 1967-68 when, whilst swimming in Barbados, his left foot was mangled by a boat's propeller causing the loss of four toes. After recovering, he soon returned to cricket and was even recalled to the England side, at the age of 42, to tour Australia in 1974-75, where he courageously faced the ferocious bowling of Dennis Lillee and Jeff Thomson. After his retirement as a player he served briefly as a coach with Surrey and in the 1980s was an England selector. He was awarded an MBE in 1977. Died 23 March.

Twombly, Cy (b. 1928), innovative and influential US artist whose non-figurative, often cryptic paintings divided critics and public alike. Edwin Parker Twombly Jr. was born in Lexington, Virginia, and inherited his father's nickname "Cy", itself derived from the renowned baseball pitcher "Cyclone" Young. Having been privately tutored in art, Twombly won a scholarship to the Art Students League in New York in 1950, where he was exposed to the works of seminal modern American painters such as Mark Rothko and Jackson Pollock. Thereafter he studied at the influential and experimental Black Mountain College, in North Carolina, in 1951-52, and held his first solo exhibition in Chicago in 1951. He was drafted into the US Army in 1954, where he trained as a cryptographer and used his time to practise the Surrealist technique of drawing in the dark, a form that would later become evident in his work. In 1957 he moved to Italy where he lived for the rest of his life. From an early age Twombly developed the distinctive abstract technique of applying thin white lines to dark canvasses, a style that formed the basis of his celebrated "Blackboard Paintings". This series was characterised by continuous scrawls applied whilst the artist sat astride the shoulders of an assistant who galloped back and forth in front of the canvas. In addition to paintings characterised by lines and muted colours, during the course of his career Twombly also produced blank or monochrome canvasses, abstract paintings involving dots and smudges executed in luminous, watery tones, and sculptures derived from found materials. Although denounced by some critics as devoid of real significance, at the end of his life Twombly's work was commanding high prices at auction and he had received a range of international awards. In 2010 he was commissioned to paint a ceiling at the Louvre, the first artist to be given this honour since Georges Braque in the 1950s. Died 5 July.

Vann Nath (b. 1946), Cambodian artist who survived the Khmer Rouge regime and later documented its horrors. Born in rural poverty in the village of Phum Sophy, in north-west Cambodia, Vann Nath spent several years as a monk before, inspired by the paintings that he saw on the walls of Buddhist temples, he enrolled in painting school in 1965. His subsequent career, painting landscapes and cinema posters, was interrupted by the Khmer Rouge's seizure of power in April 1975. Extolling a bizarre form of agrarian communism, the new government emptied the country's cities and Vann Nath, like many others, found himself forced to work in the rice fields. During their murderous period in power, the Khmer Rouge killed some 2 million people—particularly targeting intellectuals and artists—through execution, starvation and overwork. In 1978 Vann Nath was imprisoned at Tuol Sleng, a notorious facility (also known as "S-21"), where some 16,000 people were tortured and killed before the Khmer Rouge were driven from power in 1979 by invading Vietnamese troops. He was one of only seven inmates to have survived the incarceration, being spared solely because his artistic skills were required to paint likenesses of Khmer Rouge leader Pol Pot. After liberation Vann Nath used those skills to record the horrors he had witnessed and his paintings were hung at the Tuol Sleng site after its conversion into a public memorial to the genocide. He also wrote a 1998 memoir, *A Cambodian Prison Portrait: One Year in the Khmer Rouge's S-21 Prison*, and participated in a prize-winning 2003 documentary, *S21, la machine de mort Khmère rouge*, which brought him face-to-face with some of his former captors. Although suffering ill health in his final years, Vann Nath was able to testify at the trial of Duch, a leading member of the Khmer Rouge, who in 2010 was sentenced to 35 years in prison for his role in administering the Tuol Sleng facility. Died 5 September.

Varas, José Miguel (b. 1928), Chilean author and broadcaster. The son of an army colonel, Varas's first novel, *Cahuín* (Binge), was published in 1946 when he was just 18 years old. During the course of his literary career he went on to write more than 20 others, as well as several collections of short stories and biographies, thereby becoming one of his country's most prolific authors. He joined the Chilean Communist party as a young man and served on its central committee for many years. From 1959-61 he worked as a journalist for the party in Prague and thereafter returned to Chile to become editor of the party's daily newspaper *El Siglo* ("The Century"). He was also a prominent radio presenter and served as the press chief at Chile's national television channel during the administration of Salvador Allende, the country's first democratically elected Marxist president. When Allende was overthrown by a right-wing military coup in 1973, Varas fled into exile in Moscow from where he broadcast a daily programme to his homeland, *Escucha Chile!* ("Listen Chile!"). In this role he became a key figure of opposition to the oppressive regime of General Augusto Pinochet and provided an important source of alternative information to those living under the military dictatorship. After the 1988 plebiscite—in which Chileans voted to dismantle the regime—Varas returned to his homeland and was once more able to dedicate the remainder of his life to his writing. Throughout his literary career he wrote about the common people, displaying a deep empathy with both worker and peasant. His enduring popularity, as well as his literary talent, led to the award in 2006 of Chile's national prize for literature. He continued to write until the end of his life and was working on his memoirs at the time of his fatal heart attack. Died 23 September.

von Habsburg, Otto (b. 1912), son of last Austro-Hungarian emperor and pretender to the defunct thrones of Austria, Hungary, Croatia and Bohemia. He was born Franz Josef Otto Robert Maria Anton Karl Max Heinrich Sixtus Xavier Felix Renatus Ludwig Gaetan Pius Ignatius von

Habsburg in Reichenau an der Rax, Lower Austria, and became crown prince in 1916 when his father, Charles, succeeded Emperor Franz Josef. Following the breakup of Austria-Hungary in the aftermath of its World War I defeat, the family went into exile but retained its private fortune. Upon the death of his father in 1922 Otto became Duke of Lorraine and the formal head of the house of Habsburg. He read politics and social science at the Catholic University of Louvain, Belgium, graduating with a doctorate in 1935. An opponent of the Anschluss, von Habsburg was sentenced to death by the Nazis and fled to the USA during World War II. After the war he spent several years in France and Spain before, in 1961, renouncing his claim to the Austrian throne. This act (which in later years he admitted had been inspired by pragmatism rather than a sincere conversion to republicanism) led to the lifting of the ban on his entering his native land but sparked political and constitutional dispute (the Habsburg "crisis"). It was only in 1966 that he finally entered Austria for the first time in 48 years. However, he lived mostly in Germany (whose citizenship he also held) and spent 20 years as an MEP for Bavaria, having been elected in 1979 as a candidate of the right-wing Christian Social Union (CSU). A firm advocate of European integration, he also served as president of the international Pan-European Union from 1973 to 2004 and was a co-creator of the 1989 Pan-European Picnic at the Austria-Hungary border, which helped to open the hitherto sealed frontier with Eastern Europe and advance the collapse of its communist regimes. Died 4 July.

Winehouse, Amy (b. 1983), English singer-songwriter renowned for her contralto voice and eclectic musical style. The daughter of a north London taxi driver who loved jazz, Winehouse showed early promise as a singer and attended a number of stage schools. She proved a rebellious teenager and by the age of 16 was performing locally, writing songs and smoking marijuana. The quality of her soulful voice was quickly recognised and she was signed up by Island records. Her debut album, the jazz-infused *Frank*, was released in 2003 to enthusiastic reviews and sold well. Her second album, *Back to Black*, released in 2006

and influenced by the all-female bands of the 1950s and 1960s, became the best-selling record in the UK in 2007. It was also a huge international success, becoming the world's seventh best-selling album of 2008 and reaping its creator a series of music industry awards. By this time, however, Winehouse was suffering the effects of alcohol abuse and drug addiction, reportedly consuming heroin and crack cocaine as well as heavy cigarette smoking. Her international celebrity status meant that her private life became a staple for the tabloid press, which monitored her tempestuous, drug-fuelled relationship with boyfriend Blake Fielder-Civil, whom she married in May 2007. She admitted to physically abusing him and the couple, constantly pursued by the paparazzi, were frequently photographed with physical injuries. Although she continued to attract large audiences to her concerts, her performances were sometimes shambolically impaired by her addictions. Her lifestyle also led to a number of arrests for drugs offences and violence, intermittent health scares, and periods spent in rehab. Although she reportedly gave up illegal drugs in 2008, and divorced Fielder-Civil in 2009 after his imprisonment for attempting to pervert the course of justice, she continued to battle alcoholism and was found dead at her home after a drinking bout. Died 23 July.

York, Susannah (b. 1939), versatile British actress of film, theatre and television. Born in London as Susannah Yolande Fletcher, she grew up in Scotland and graduated from the Royal Academy of Dramatic Art in 1958. Thereafter she enjoyed success in a number of acclaimed film roles including *Tunes of Glory* (1960), *Tom Jones* (1963), *A Man for all Seasons* (1966), and *They Shoot Horses, Don't They?* (1969), for which she received an Oscar nomination. Although often praised for possessing a delicate and quintessentially English beauty, York also appeared in a number of dark roles. One of the most memorable of these was in *The Killing of Sister George* (1968), where she played Alice "Childie" McNaught, the naïve sexual companion of a disturbed older woman. The film generated controversy with a lesbian sex scene involving York who later said of the project, "I could accept the idea of lesbianism philosophically, but playing intensely emotional scenes with another woman taxed all my resources as an actress." She won an Emmy nomination for her role as the eponymous heroine in a US television production of *Jane Eyre* (1970) and won the Best Actress award at Cannes for her starring role in Robert Altman's bewildering psychological drama, *Images* (1972). In her later years she appeared in a number of theatrical roles and television dramas. She was active in left-wing causes and a staunch supporter of CND. Appearing in a play in Tel Aviv in June 2007, she dedicated the performance to Mordechai Vanunu, the dissident who was kidnapped and imprisoned by Israel for revealing details of the country's secret nuclear weapons programme. Died 15 January.

D.S. Lewis

XIX DOCUMENTS AND REFERENCE

SPEECH BY PRESIDENT MUBARAK

Extracts from the speech by Egyptian President Hosni Mubarak, carried on Egyptian television on 10 February, in which he made limited concessions to the nationwide protests against his rule. His attempt to placate the protesters failed and he was forced to step down from office the following day, thereby ending almost three decades in power.

I am addressing the youth of Egypt today in Tahrir Square and across the country. I am addressing you all from my heart, a father's dialogue with his sons and daughters. I am proud of you, the new Egyptian generation, dreaming and calling for a better future.

First, I tell you that the blood of your martyrs and injured will not have been shed in vain. I assure you that I will not shrink from harshly punishing those responsible... I tell the families of those innocent victims that I suffered for them as much as they did. My heart was in pain because of their fate...

Heeding your voice, your message and demands, here is an irreversible commitment. I am determined to live up to my promises with all firmness and honesty and I am totally determined to implement them without hesitation or reconsideration. This commitment springs from a strong conviction that your intentions are honest and pure and so are your actions...

I am telling you that as a president I find no shame in listening to my country's youth and interacting with them. But it would be shameful and humiliating to listen to foreign demands, whatever may be the source or pretext. I have not done this and never will.

My sons, the youth of Egypt, brother citizens, I have unequivocally declared that I will not run for president in the next elections, satisfied with what I have given my country in over 60 years during war and peace. I declared my commitment to that, and my equal commitment to carrying out my responsibility in protecting the constitution and the people's interests until power and responsibility are handed over to whoever is elected next September, following free and open elections, held with guarantees of freedom and candour...

I have set a defined vision for what should come out of this crisis, to carry out what the citizens and the youth have called for in a way which will respect constitutional legitimacy and not undermine it. It will be carried out in a way that will bring stability to our society and achieve the demands of its youth, and, at the same time, propose an agreed framework for a peaceful transfer of power through responsible dialogue with all factions of society and with the utmost sincerity and transparency...

From now to next September, day after day, we will see the peaceful transition of power. This national dialogue has focused on establishing a constitutional committee that will look into the required amendments of the constitution and the needed legislative reforms...

These top-priority constitutional amendments aim to ease the conditions for presidential nominations and to fix presidential term limits to ensure the transfer of power, and to strengthen oversight of elections to guarantee their freedom and fairness...

The proposal to delete Article 179 from the constitution aims to achieve the required balance between the protection of the nation from the dangers of terrorism and safeguarding the civil rights and freedoms of the citizens. This opens the way to lifting the emergency law, following the return of calm and stability and the presence of suitable conditions to lift the state of emergency...

The current moment is not to do with myself, it is not to do with Hosni Mubarak; it is to do with Egypt, its present and the future of its children. All Egyptians are in one boat now, and it is incumbent upon us to continue the national dialogue which we have started...so that we can get Egypt past its current crisis...

I was as young as Egypt's youth today when I learned the meaning of Egyptian military honour, allegiance and sacrifice for my country. I have spent a lifetime defending its soil and sovereignty. I witnessed its wars, with its defeats and victories. I lived through the days of defeat and occupation, I also lived through the Suez crossing, victory and liberation. It was the happiest day of my life when I raised the flag of Egypt over Sinai. I faced death many times as a pilot, in Addis Ababa, and numerous other times.

I never succumbed to foreign pressure or demands. I kept the peace. I worked towards the stability and security of Egypt. I worked hard for its revival and for its people. I never sought power or fake popularity. I trust that the overwhelming majority of the people know who Hosni Mubarak is. It pains me to see how some of my countrymen are treating me today...

I saw fit to delegate presidential jurisdictions to the vice president as defined by the constitution...

I say again that I lived for the sake of this country, preserving its responsibility and trust. Egypt will remain above all and above everyone. It will remain so until I hand over this trust and post. This is the goal, the objective, the responsibility and the duty.

It is the beginning of life, its journey, and its end. It will remain a country dear to my heart. It will not part with me and I will not part with it until my passing. Egypt will remain immortal with its dignified people with their heads held high.

May God preserve the safety of Egypt and watch over its people.

May peace be upon you.

(*Source: Al-Misriyah television, Cairo, unofficial translation*)

EGYPTIAN ARMY STATEMENTS

Two Statements by the Supreme Council of the Egyptian Armed Forces, issued on 11 February, which made it clear that the army was taking power from President Mubarak.

STATEMENT No. 2

In consideration of the rapid developments that are shaping the country's destiny, and as part of the ongoing monitoring of the domestic and foreign situations, given what has been decided through delegating powers to the vice-president, and from our belief in our national duty to protect and maintain the stability of the homeland and its safety, the Council has decided to implement the following decisions:

1. Ending the state of emergency as soon as the current conditions end. Arbitrating in electoral appeals and procedures. Implementing the required legislative reforms and holding free and fair presidential elections under the agreed constitutional reforms.

2. The Armed Forces are committed to protecting legitimate popular demands and to work to achieve them by implementing these procedures at the specified times with all precision and resoluteness until a peaceful transfer of power is achieved, in order to arrive at the free democratic society to which the children of the nation are aspiring.

3. The Armed Forces confirm that honourable people, those who rejected corruption and called for reform, will not be pursued by the security forces. They warn against damaging the safety and security of the homeland and its citizens. The Council also confirms the need to resume work in state bodies and to return to normal life in order to preserve the interests and property of our great people.

May God protect the homeland and the its citizens.

(*Source: Al-Misriyah television, Cairo, unofficial translation*).

STATEMENT NO. 3

Citizens, we are all aware of the significance of this distinctive and historic moment in the history of Egypt that follows the decision by His Excellency President Muhammad Hosni Mubarak to step down as president of the republic and to entrust the High Command of the Armed Forces with managing the country's affairs.

In response to demands from our great people throughout the country to bring about radical change, the Higher Council of the Armed Forces is studying the matter, with the help of God Almighty, in order to realise these hopes. The High Command of the Armed Forces will later issue statements setting out the measures and provisions that will be taken. Meanwhile, the High Command of the Armed Forces does not represent an alternative to legitimate government sanctioned by the people.

The High Command of the Armed Forces salutes and thanks President Hosni Mubarak for his service to his country, both in peace and wartime, and for his patriotic stand in favouring the higher interest of the homeland.

In this respect, the High Command of the Armed Forces asks God to have mercy on the souls of the martyrs who sacrificed their lives for the sake of their country's freedom and security. We also salute our great people.

May God help us to succeed! May God's peace, mercy and blessings be upon you!

(Source: Al-Misriyah television, Cairo, unofficial translation).

EGYPTIAN ARMY DECLARATION OF INTENT TO RULE

The statement issued by the Supreme Council of the Egyptian Armed Forces on 13 February, announcing temporary military rule.

In the name of God, the Merciful and the Compassionate! The following is a constitutional statement:

Given the requirements of this crucial phase in the history of the homeland, and faithful to its historic and constitutional duties to protect the country and its territorial integrity and to ensure its security, the Higher Council of the Armed Forces notes that the real challenge faced by our dear homeland, Egypt, is to achieve progress by releasing the creative energies of all the sons of our great people. This will be achieved by preparing the way for freedom and by facilitating the route for democracy through amendments to the constitution and the laws which will realise the legitimate demands expressed by our people in recent days. The Higher Council of the Armed Forces will progress further, in a manner that befits the prestige of Egypt, a country whose people drew the first lines of human civilization.

The Higher Council of the Armed Forces strongly believes that popular freedom, the rule of law and the establishment of equality, multi-party democracy, social justice and eradicating corruption are legitimate foundations for any political system and will guide the country in the near future.

The Higher Council of the Armed Forces also strongly believes that the dignity of the homeland is a reflection of the dignity of every individual in the country. The free citizen, proud of his humanity, is the cornerstone in the construction of a strong homeland.

On the basis of the aforementioned, and hoping to achieve the progress of our people, the Higher Council of the Armed Forces has taken the following decisions:

1. To suspend the constitution.

2. The Higher Council of the Armed Forces will take over the management of the country's affairs temporarily for six months; or until the election of the People's Assembly, of the Consultative Council and of the president of the republic.

3. The head of the Higher Council of the Armed Forces will represent the council in the country and abroad.

4. To dissolve the People's Assembly and the Consultative Council.

5. The Higher Council of the Armed Forces will issue decrees during the transitional phase.

6. To set up a committee to amend some articles of the constitution and determine the rules for a referendum on these amendments.

7. To give Dr Ahmad Muhammad Shafiq responsibility for running the government until a new government is appointed.

8. To hold elections to the People's Assembly and the Consultative Council as well as presidential elections.

9. The state commits itself to upholding all international conventions and treaties to which it is signatory.

God is the One from whom we seek help and success.

Signed: Commander in Chief of the Armed Forces and Chairman of the Higher Council of the Armed Forces, Field Marshal Hussein Tantawi.

(Source: Al-Misriyah television, Cairo, unofficial translation)

SPEECH BY SAIF AL-ISLAM KADHAFI IN RESPONSE TO THE VIOLENT PROTESTS.

Excerpts from a speech made on Libyan state television on 20 February in which Saif al-Islam condemned protesters but also acknowledged mistakes by the army in responding to the violence and offered the prospect of political reform. The alternative, he warned, was civil war and foreign domination, and he promised that the supporters of his father's regime would fight to the bitter end.

...We all know that the region is passing through an earthquake, a hurricane or change. If this change does not come from the governments it will come from the people, we have seen this in other Arab countries. Today I will tell you only truth. We know that there are opposition figures living abroad who have support in Libya. There people try to use Facebook for a revolution to copy Egypt. These people want to bring Libya to what happened in Egypt and Tunisia. We saw this on Facebook and on emails. The country did a pre-emptive move by arresting some people before the protests, shots were fired, people died. The anger was directed at the police in Benghazi. People wanted to storm the police stations, people died, funerals occurred. This is a summary of what happened in Benghazi, now there is a major... threat to the unity of Libya. Of course there were many deaths, which angered many people in Benghazi, but why were there people killed? The army was under stress, it is not used to crowd control so they shot, but I called them. The army said that some protesters were drunk, others were on hallucinogens or drugs. The army has to defend its weapons. And the people were angry. So there were deaths, but in the end Libyans were killed.

...It is no lie that the protesters are in control of the streets now. Libya is not Tunis or Egypt. Libya is different, if there was disturbance it will split to several states. It was three states before 60 years. Libya are Tribes not like Egypt. There are no political parties, it is made of tribes. Everyone knows each other. We will have a civil war... There will be a war and no future. All the firms will leave... You can say we want democracy and rights, we can talk about it, we should have talked about it before. It's this or war. Instead of crying over 200 deaths we will cry over hundreds of thousands of deaths. You will all leave Libya, there will be nothing here. There will be no bread in Libya, it will be more expensive than gold.

Before we let weapons come between us, from tomorrow, in 48 hours, we will call for a new conference for new laws. We will call for new media laws, civil rights, lift the stupid punishments, we will have a constitution. Even the Leader Kadhafi said he wants a constitution. We can even have autonomous rule, with limited central government powers. ...We will have a new Libya, new flag, new anthem. Or else, be ready to start a civil war and chaos and forget oil and petrol...The country will be divided like North and South Korea we will see each other through a fence. You will wait in line for months for a visa. If we don't do the first scenario be ready for the second scenario...Be ready for a new colonial period from America and Britain. You think they will accept an Islamic Emirate here, 30 minutes from Crete? The West will come and occupy you. Europe and the West will not agree to chaos in Libya, to export chaos and drugs so they will occupy us.

...Kadhafi is not Mubarak or Ben Ali, a classical ruler, he is a leader of a people. Tens of thousands of Libyans are coming to defend him...The army is also there, it will play a big part whatever the cost. The army...is not the army of Tunisia or Egypt. It will support Kadhafi to the last minute. ...we will not lose one inch of this land. Sixty years ago they defended Libya from the colonialists, now they will defend it from drug addicts. ...We will flight to the last man and woman and bullet. We will not lose Libya...We will live in Libya and die in Libya.

(Source: transcribed and disseminated live on Twitter.)

SPEECH BY COLONEL KADHAFI IN RESPONSE TO LIBYAN PROTESTS

A small extract from a long, rambling and sometimes incoherent address given by Moamar Kadhafi in Tripoli on 22 February, in which he accused outsiders of inciting protests in Libya by dispensing money and drugs to Libyan youths.

...I am talking to you from the house which was bombarded by 170 planes from America and Britain. ... Moamar al Kadhafi is not occupying a position to resign from, the same way other presidents did. Kadhafi is not a president; he is a leader of a revolution. History. Resistance. Liberation. Glory. Revolution. This is an admission by the biggest power in the world that Kadhafi is not a president or an ordinary person that you can poison or lead a demonstration against. When this place was bombed, here at my home, killing my children, where were you, you rats? Where were you? You men with big beards? Where were you? You were with America. You were applauding your American masters... when Kadhafi and his family were here at this place bombed by America.

... Now, a few groups of people, groups of youths, who were given hallucinogenic pills are raiding police stations here and there like rats. ...They raided barracks and police stations and they burned their previous criminal records. But I don't blame these youths. They are young people, 16, 17 years old, they are imitating what's happening in Tunisia. ... But there is a group ...who is giving money and these hallucinogenic pills to these young people, pushing them towards this civil war. The people who were killed are members of the police and armed forces, but not those who are behind it, they are home, outside the country enjoying safety with their families and children...

(Source: unofficial translation from Al-Jazeera broadcast.)

UNITED NATIONS SECURITY COUNCIL RESOLUTION 1973 (2011) AUTHORISING INTERVENTION IN LIBYAN CIVIL WAR

Text of UN Security Council Resolution 1973 (2011), adopted on 17 March by a vote of 10 in favour, none against, and five abstentions (Brazil, China, Germany, India and Russia). The resolution demanded an immediate ceasefire, established a no-fly zone over Libya, and authorised all necessary measures short of foreign occupation to protect civilians.

The Security Council,

Recalling its resolution 1970 (2011) of 26 February 2011,

Deploring the failure of the Libyan authorities to comply with resolution 1970 (2011),

Expressing grave concern at the deteriorating situation, the escalation of violence, and the heavy civilian casualties,

Reiterating the responsibility of the Libyan authorities to protect the Libyan population and *reaffirming* that parties to armed conflicts bear the primary responsibility to take all feasible steps to ensure the protection of civilians,

Condemning the gross and systematic violation of human rights, including arbitrary detentions, enforced disappearances, torture and summary executions,

Further condemning acts of violence and intimidation committed by the Libyan authorities against journalists, media professionals and associated personnel and *urging* these authorities to comply with their obligations under international humanitarian law as outlined in resolution 1738 (2006),

Considering that the widespread and systematic attacks currently taking place in the Libyan Arab Jamahiriya against the civilian population may amount to crimes against humanity,

Recalling paragraph 26 of resolution 1970 (2011) in which the Council expressed its readiness to consider taking additional appropriate measures, as necessary, to facilitate and support the return of humanitarian agencies and make available humanitarian and related assistance in the Libyan Arab Jamahiriya,

Expressing its determination to ensure the protection of civilians and civilian populated areas and the rapid and unimpeded passage of humanitarian assistance and the safety of humanitarian personnel,

Recalling the condemnation by the League of Arab States, the African Union and the Secretary-General of the Organization of the Islamic Conference of the serious violations of human rights and international humanitarian law that have been and are being committed in the Libyan Arab Jamahiriya,

Taking note of the final communiqué of the Organization of the Islamic Conference of 8 March 2011, and the communiqué of the Peace and Security Council of the African Union of 10 March 2011 which established an ad hoc High-Level Committee on Libya,

Taking note also of the decision of the Council of the League of Arab States of 12 March 2011 to call for the imposition of a no-fly zone on Libyan military aviation, and to establish safe areas in places exposed to shelling as a precautionary measure that allows the protection of the Libyan people and foreign nationals residing in the Libyan Arab Jamahiriya,

Taking note further of the Secretary-General's call on 16 March 2011 for an immediate ceasefire,

Recalling its decision to refer the situation in the Libyan Arab Jamahiriya since 15 February 2011 to the Prosecutor of the International Criminal Court, and *stressing* that those responsible for or complicit in attacks targeting the civilian population, including aerial and naval attacks, must be held to account,

Reiterating its concern at the plight of refugees and foreign workers forced to flee the violence in the Libyan Arab Jamahiriya, *welcoming* the response of neighbouring States, in particular Tunisia and Egypt, to address the needs of those refugees and foreign workers, and *calling on* the international community to support those efforts,

Deploring the continuing use of mercenaries by the Libyan authorities,

Considering that the establishment of a ban on all flights in the airspace of the Libyan Arab Jamahiriya constitutes an important element for the protection of civilians as well as the safety of the delivery of humanitarian assistance and a decisive step for the cessation of hostilities in Libya,

Expressing concern also for the safety of foreign nationals and their rights in the Libyan Arab Jamahiriya,

Welcoming the appointment by the Secretary General of his Special Envoy to Libya, Mr. Abdul Ilah Mohamed Al-Khatib and supporting his efforts to find a sustainable and peaceful solution to the crisis in the Libyan Arab Jamahiriya,

Reaffirming its strong commitment to the sovereignty, independence, territorial integrity and national unity of the Libyan Arab Jamahiriya,

Determining that the situation in the Libyan Arab Jamahiriya continues to constitute a threat to international peace and security,

Acting under Chapter VII of the Charter of the United Nations,

1. *Demands* the immediate establishment of a ceasefire and a complete end to violence and all attacks against, and abuses of, civilians;

2. *Stresses* the need to intensify efforts to find a solution to the crisis which responds to the legitimate demands of the Libyan people and *notes* the decisions of the Secretary-General to send his Special Envoy to Libya and of the Peace and Security Council of the African Union to send its ad hoc High-Level Committee to Libya with the aim of facilitating dialogue to lead to the political reforms necessary to find a peaceful and sustainable solution;

3. *Demands* that the Libyan authorities comply with their obligations under international law, including international humanitarian law, human rights and refugee law and take all measures to protect civilians and meet their basic needs, and to ensure the rapid and unimpeded passage of humanitarian assistance;

Protection of civilians

4. *Authorizes* Member States that have notified the Secretary-General, acting nationally or through regional organizations or arrangements, and acting in cooperation with the Secretary-General, to take all necessary measures, notwithstanding paragraph 9 of resolution 1970 (2011), to protect civilians and civilian populated areas under threat of attack in the Libyan Arab Jamahiriya, including Benghazi, while excluding a foreign occupation force of any form on any part of Libyan territory, and *requests* the Member States concerned to inform the Secretary-General immediately of the measures they take pursuant to the authorization conferred by this paragraph which shall be immediately reported to the Security Council;

5. *Recognizes* the important role of the League of Arab States in matters relating to the maintenance of international peace and security in the region, and bearing in mind Chapter VIII of

the Charter of the United Nations, requests the Member States of the League of Arab States to cooperate with other Member States in the implementation of paragraph 4;

No-fly zone

6. *Decides* to establish a ban on all flights in the airspace of the Libyan Arab Jamahiriya in order to help protect civilians;

7. *Decides further* that the ban imposed by paragraph 6 shall not apply to flights whose sole purpose is humanitarian, such as delivering or facilitating the delivery of assistance, including medical supplies, food, humanitarian workers and related assistance, or evacuating foreign nationals from the Libyan Arab Jamahiriya, nor shall it apply to flights authorised by paragraphs 4 or 8, nor other flights which are deemed necessary by States acting under the authorization conferred in paragraph 8 to be for the benefit of the Libyan people, and that these flights shall be coordinated with any mechanism established under paragraph 8;

8. *Authorizes* Member States that have notified the Secretary-General and the Secretary-General of the League of Arab States, acting nationally or through regional organizations or arrangements, to take all necessary measures to enforce compliance with the ban on flights imposed by paragraph 6 above, as necessary, and *requests* the States concerned in cooperation with the League of Arab States to coordinate closely with the Secretary General on the measures they are taking to implement this ban, including by establishing an appropriate mechanism for implementing the provisions of paragraphs 6 and 7 above,

9. *Calls upon* all Member States, acting nationally or through regional organizations or arrangements, to provide assistance, including any necessary overflight approvals, for the purposes of implementing paragraphs 4, 6, 7 and 8 above;

10. *Requests* the Member States concerned to coordinate closely with each other and the Secretary-General on the measures they are taking to implement paragraphs 4, 6, 7 and 8 above, including practical measures for the monitoring and approval of authorised humanitarian or evacuation flights;

11. *Decides* that the Member States concerned shall inform the Secretary-General and the Secretary-General of the League of Arab States immediately of measures taken in exercise of the authority conferred by paragraph 8 above, including to supply a concept of operations;

12. *Requests* the Secretary-General to inform the Council immediately of any actions taken by the Member States concerned in exercise of the authority conferred by paragraph 8 above and to report to the Council within 7 days and every month thereafter on the implementation of this resolution, including information on any violations of the flight ban imposed by paragraph 6 above;

Enforcement of the arms embargo

13. *Decides that* paragraph 11 of resolution 1970 (2011) shall be replaced by the following paragraph : "Calls upon all Member States, in particular States of the region, acting nationally or through regional organisations or arrangements, in order to ensure strict implementation of the arms embargo established by paragraphs 9 and 10 of resolution 1970 (2011), to inspect in their territory, including seaports and airports, and on the high seas, vessels and aircraft bound to or from the Libyan Arab Jamahiriya, if the State concerned has information that provides reasonable grounds to believe that the cargo contains items the supply, sale, transfer or export of which is prohibited by paragraphs 9 or 10 of resolution 1970 (2011) as modified by this resolution, including the provision of armed mercenary personnel, *calls upon* all flag States of such vessels and aircraft to cooperate with such inspections and authorises Member States to use all measures commensurate to the specific circumstances to carry out such inspections";

14. *Requests* Member States which are taking action under paragraph 13 above on the high seas to coordinate closely with each other and the Secretary-General and *further requests* the States concerned to inform the Secretary-General and the Committee established pursuant to paragraph 24 of resolution 1970 (2011) ("the Committee") immediately of measures taken in the exercise of the authority conferred by paragraph 13 above;

15. *Requires* any Member State whether acting nationally or through regional organisations or arrangements, when it undertakes an inspection pursuant to paragraph 13 above, to submit promptly an initial written report to the Committee containing, in particular, explanation of the grounds for the inspection, the results of such inspection, and whether or not cooperation was provided, and, if prohibited items for transfer are found, further requires such Member States to submit to the Committee, at a later stage, a subsequent written report containing relevant details on the inspection, seizure, and disposal, and relevant details of the transfer, including a description of the items, their origin and intended destination, if this information is not in the initial report;

16. *Deplores* the continuing flows of mercenaries into the Libyan Arab Jamahiriya and *calls upon* all Member States to comply strictly with their obligations under paragraph 9 of resolution 1970 (2011) to prevent the provision of armed mercenary personnel to the Libyan Arab Jamahiriya;

Ban on flights

17. *Decides* that all States shall deny permission to any aircraft registered in the Libyan Arab Jamahiriya or owned or operated by Libyan nationals or companies to take off from, land in or overfly their territory unless the particular flight has been approved in advance by the Committee, or in the case of an emergency landing;

18. *Decides that* all States shall deny permission to any aircraft to take off from, land in or overfly their territory, if they have information that provides reasonable grounds to believe that the aircraft contains items the supply, sale, transfer, or export of which is prohibited by paragraphs 9 and 10 of resolution 1970 (2011) as modified by this resolution, including the provision of armed mercenary personnel, except in the case of an emergency landing;

Asset freeze

19. *Decides* that the asset freeze imposed by paragraph 17, 19, 20 and 21 of resolution 1970 (2011) shall apply to all funds, other financial assets and economic resources which are on their territories, which are owned or controlled, directly or indirectly, by the Libyan authorities, as designated by the Committee, or by individuals or entities acting on their behalf or at their direction, or by entities owned or controlled by them, as designated by the Committee, and *decides further* that all States shall ensure that any funds, financial assets or economic resources are prevented from being made available by their nationals or by any individuals or entities within their territories, to or for the benefit of the Libyan authorities, as designated by the Committee, or individuals or entities acting on their behalf or at their direction, or entities owned or controlled by them, as designated by the Committee, and directs the Committee to designate such Libyan authorities, individuals or entities within 30 days of the date of the adoption of this resolution and as appropriate thereafter;

20. *Affirms* its determination to ensure that assets frozen pursuant to paragraph 17 of resolution 1970 (2011) shall, at a later stage, as soon as possible be made available to and for the benefit of the people of the Libyan Arab Jamahiriya;

21. *Decides* that all States shall require their nationals, persons subject to their jurisdiction and firms incorporated in their territory or subject to their jurisdiction to exercise vigilance when doing business with entities incorporated in the Libyan Arab Jamahiriya or subject to its juris-

diction, and any individuals or entities acting on their behalf or at their direction, and entities owned or controlled by them, if the States have information that provides reasonable grounds to believe that such business could contribute to violence and use of force against civilians;

Designations

22. *Decides* that the individuals listed in Annex I shall be subject to the travel restrictions imposed in paragraphs 15 and 16 of resolution 1970 (2011), and *decides* further that the individuals and entities listed in Annex II shall be subject to the asset freeze imposed in paragraphs 17, 19, 20 and 21 of resolution 1970 (2011);

23. *Decides* that the measures specified in paragraphs 15, 16, 17, 19, 20 and 21 of resolution 1970 (2011) shall apply also to individuals and entities determined by the Council or the Committee to have violated the provisions of resolution 1970 (2011), particularly paragraphs 9 and 10 thereof, or to have assisted others in doing so;

Panel of Experts

24. *Requests* the Secretary-General to create for an initial period of one year, in consultation with the Committee, a group of up to eight experts ("Panel of Experts"), under the direction of the Committee to carry out the following tasks:

(a) Assist the Committee in carrying out its mandate as specified in paragraph 24 of resolution 1970 (2011) and this resolution;

(b) Gather, examine and analyse information from States, relevant United Nations bodies, regional organisations and other interested parties regarding the implementation of the measures decided in resolution 1970 (2011) and this resolution, in particular incidents of non-compliance;

(c) Make recommendations on actions the Council, or the Committee or State, may consider to improve implementation of the relevant measures;

(d) Provide to the Council an interim report on its work no later than 90 days after the Panel's appointment, and a final report to the Council no later than 30 days prior to the termination of its mandate with its findings and recommendations;

25. *Urges* all States, relevant United Nations bodies and other interested parties, to cooperate fully with the Committee and the Panel of Experts, in particular by supplying any information at their disposal on the implementation of the measures decided in resolution 1970 (2011) and this resolution, in particular incidents of non-compliance;

26. *Decides* that the mandate of the Committee as set out in paragraph 24 of resolution 1970 (2011) shall also apply to the measures decided in this resolution;

27. *Decides* that all States, including the Libyan Arab Jamahiriya, shall take the necessary measures to ensure that no claim shall lie at the instance of the Libyan authorities, or of any person or body in the Libyan Arab Jamahiriya, or of any person claiming through or for the benefit of any such person or body, in connection with any contract or other transaction where its performance was affected by reason of the measures taken by the Security Council in resolution 1970 (2011), this resolution and related resolutions;

28. *Reaffirms* its intention to keep the actions of the Libyan authorities under continuous review and underlines its readiness to review at any time the measures imposed by this resolution and resolution 1970 (2011), including by strengthening, suspending or lifting those measures, as appropriate, based on compliance by the Libyan authorities with this resolution and resolution 1970 (2011);

29. *Decides* to remain actively seized of the matter.

(Source: UN Security Council)

STATEMENT BY UN SECRETARY GENERAL ON LIBERATION OF LIBYA

A statement issued by UN Secretary-General Ban Ki Moon on 23 October 2011 in response to the ending of the civil war in Libya.

Today in Benghazi, the Libyan National Transitional Council (NTC) declared the full liberation of Libya, marking a historical juncture that signifies a people attaining their freedom after decades of dictatorship.

Today marks an occasion for Libyans to celebrate, to look forward to a future of liberties and opportunities, from the right to express an opinion freely to the right to elect their own government.

From this day onward, the Libyan people will be in full charge of their future—a future that their new leaders have declared will be based on justice and national reconciliation. Their commitment is to building accountable democratic institutions, guided by respect for human rights and the rule of law, and to the transparent management of Libya's resources to the benefit of all Libyans.

The end of the war is only the beginning of what Libyan fighters, youth and women have struggled for: their determination now is to build a truly new Libya, overcoming the grim legacy of human rights abuse and corruption, and now so many killed or disabled during the conflict.

My Special Representative for Libya attended the ceremonies today in Benghazi at which liberation was declared. On this momentous day, the United Nations restates it commitment, through the United Nations Support Mission in Libya, to support the Libyan people and their authorities as they work to build this brighter future.

(Source: UN)

REPORT OF THE BAHRAIN INDEPENDENT COMMISSION OF INQUIRY INTO THE EVENTS OF FEBRUARY/MARCH 2011

Extracts from the report of the commission of inquiry, established by King Hamad bin Isa Al-Khalifa on 1 July to investigate the "events occurring in Bahrain in February/March 2011", when a mainly Shia protest movement was violently suppressed by the Bahraini security forces. The 489-page report was presented to the king in Manama on 23 November 2011. The "Bassiouni commission", consisting of five independent international legal experts under the chairmanship of Mahmoud Cherif Bassiouni, found that the authorities had deployed excessive force, and torture, against protesters.

CHAPTER XII: General Observations and Recommendations.

A.   General Observations

1690. The events that were the subject of the Commission's mandate appear to have been unpredictable. The Government responded in a manner that suggests that it was not prepared for such a situation. It is not the task of the Commission to determine which side is responsible for what outcomes, but in order to understand the evolution of events it is necessary to look at the facts and their underlying causes. In that respect, there is no doubt that what occurred in February/March, and subsequently, was the result of an escalating process in which both the Government and the opposition have their share of responsibility in allowing events to unfold as they did.

1691. A series of events occurred during February/March that affected the progression of the protest movement that began in Bahrain on 14 February 2011. This is covered extensively in Chapter IV on the Narrative of Events and in the Concluding Observations in that Chapter. The forceful confrontation of demonstrators involving the use of lethal force and resort to a heavy deployment of Public Security Forces led to the death of civilians. This caused a marked increase in the number of persons participating in protests and led to a palpable escalation in their demands. As protests continued into mid-March 2011, the general state of security in Bahrain deteriorated considerably. Sectarian clashes were reported in a number of areas, attacks on expatriates took place, violent clashes occurred between students at the University of Bahrain and other educational institutions, and major thoroughfares, including the vital King Faisal Highway, were blocked by protesters. This situation led the GoB to declare a State of National Safety on 15 March 2011.

1692. With the approval of HM King Hamad, HRH the Crown Prince engaged in negotiations with various political parties, especially Al Wefaq, with a view to reaching a peaceful resolution to the unfolding situation in Bahrain. Notwithstanding the best efforts of HRH the Crown Prince, negotiations to reach a political solution were not successful. If HRH the Crown Prince's initiative and proposals, at the time, had been accepted, it could have paved the way for significant constitutional, political and socioeconomic reforms and precluded the ensuing negative consequences. This was a particularly important initiative bearing in mind that Bahrain is located in an important regional and international strategic location.

1693. The Government believed that the domestic situation reached a point that was threatening the complete breakdown of law and order, the safety of citizens and the stability of the country, all of which impacted upon the economic and social condition of the country. Therefore, on 15 March 2011, HM King Hamad issued Royal Decree No. 18 of 2011 pursuant to which a State of National Safety was declared in Bahrain. The GoB used the BDF [Bahrain Defence Force] and National Guard to assist MoI [Ministry of Interior] units in restoring public order. The NSA [National Security Agency] was also used in arresting prominent members of the political leadership of the protest movement. A substantial number of arrests were made, including of senior political and clerical leadership of opposition and Shia groups. In particular, the security forces carried out the arrests without presenting an arrest warrant or informing the arrested individual of the reasons for arrest. In many cases, the security services of the GoB resorted to the use of unnecessary and excessive force, terror-inspiring behaviour and unnecessary damage to property. The fact that a systematic pattern of behaviour existed indicates that this is how these security forces were trained and were expected to behave.

1694. Many detainees were subjected to torture and other forms of physical and psychological abuse while in custody. This again indicates certain patterns of behaviour by certain government agencies. Not all of the detainees were subjected to all of the techniques of mistreatment. Rather, there was a more discernible pattern of ill-treatment with regard to certain categories of detainees. The extent of this physical and psychological mistreatment is evidence of a deliberate practice, which in some cases was aimed at extracting confessions and statements by duress, while in other cases was intended for the purpose of retribution and punishment. The Commission notes that this systematic practice ceased after 10 June. As of that time no further mistreatment is reported to the Commission to have taken place in prisons. However, mistreatment has been reported as continuing in police stations where persons arrested for localized demonstrations and stone throwing at the police have occurred from July to date.

1695. The Commission received 559 complaints concerning the mistreatment of persons in custody. These complainants included individuals who had been released from detention and individuals who remained in custody at the time of the Commission investigations. All but nine of these complainants were Shia Muslims. Forensic medical experts appointed by the Commission examined 59 of these detainees, and Commission investigators also conducted further interviews with these individuals as well as with their family members and their lawyers. The 59 detainees who underwent a forensic medical examination were selected on the basis of one of the following criteria: (i) the severity of the alleged injuries and the existence of physical marks on the bodies of certain detainees; or (ii) the high profile nature of their case. The 59 selected detainees included the 14 political leaders as well as the SMC [Salmaniya Medical Complex] doctors who were charged with offences relating to the events of February/March 2011.

1696. The most common techniques for mistreatment used on detainees included the following: blindfolding; handcuffing; enforced standing for prolonged periods; beating; punching; hitting the detainee with rubber hoses (including on the soles of the feet), cables, whips, metal, wooden planks or other objects; electrocution; sleep-deprivation; exposure to extreme temperatures; verbal abuse; threats of rape; and insulting the detainee's religious sect (Shia). The MoI opened investigations into cases of alleged torture. However, with the exception of 10 prosecutions for torture relating to death, no prosecutions ensued.

1697. Many of the detainees who claimed to have been physically mistreated were also subjected to coercion in signing confessions or admitting to accusations of criminal conduct. Consequently, these measures fall within the meaning of torture as defined in the Convention Against Torture (CAT), to which Bahrain is a State Party. They also constitute violations of the Bahrain Criminal Code. These forced confessions have been used in criminal proceedings, either in the special courts established pursuant to the National Safety Decree or, in some cases, in the ordinary criminal courts.

1698. The Commission is of the view that the lack of accountability of officials within the security system in Bahrain has led to a culture of impunity, whereby security officials have few incentives to avoid mistreatment of prisoners or to take action to prevent mistreatment by other officials. The Commission received evidence indicating that, in some cases, judicial and prosecutorial personnel may have implicitly condoned this lack of accountability. In the light of this culture of impunity, the Commission acknowledges the immense courage that was required for the victims of torture and ill-treatment to report their experiences to the Commission....

1703. Thirty-five deaths occurred between 14 February and 15 April 2011 that have been linked to the events of February/March 2011. The deaths of 19 of these civilians have been attributed to Security Forces (MoI, NSA, BDF); the deaths of 2 civilians have been attributed to other civilians; and the deaths of 9 civilians have not been attributed to any specific perpetrator, group or government agency. Five of the thirty-five deaths were members of security forces (MoI, BDF) personnel. The deaths of 3 police officers have been attributed to demonstrators;

that of 1 police officer has been attributed to the BDF; and that of 1 BDF officer has not been attributed to specific perpetrators. Thirty-two out of thirty-five death were investigated by the GoB, but the Commission has reservations as to the effectiveness of these investigations which were limited to the personnel of each of the concerned security agencies.

1704. Between 21 March and 15 April 2011, security forces systematically raided houses in order to arrest individuals, and in so doing terrified the occupants. These arrests were performed during the night and in pre-dawn raids by hooded persons, who intentionally broke down doors, forcibly entered and sometimes ransacked the houses. This practice was often accompanied by sectarian insults and verbal abuse. Women and children and other family members frequently witnessed these events. In many of the reported cases, the women were asked to stand in their sleeping clothes, thus humiliating the women and other relatives present, and terrifying the children. The arrested persons were taken blindfolded to places of detention that at the time were unknown to the arrested persons. The pattern of these arrests indicated the existence of an operational plan which involved personnel from three government agencies, the MoI, the NSA and the BDF.

(Source: Bahrain Independent Commission of Inquiry)

UNHRC REPORT ON SYRIAN UPRISING

Summary of the UN Human Rights Council report on Syria, a three-member expert commission appointed on 12 September to investigate human rights abuses in Syria. The Report estimated that at least 3,500 civilian deaths had occurred at the hands of the security forces since the uprising began in March 2011, and described numerous instances of torture and ill treatment, including against children.

Summary

The deteriorating situation in the Syrian Arab Republic prompted the Human Rights Council to establish an independent international commission of inquiry to investigate alleged violations of human rights since March 2011. From the end of September until mid- November 2011, the commission held meetings with Member States from all regional groups, regional organizations, including the League of Arab States and the Organization of Islamic Cooperation, non-governmental organizations, human rights defenders, journalists and experts. It interviewed 223 victims and witnesses of alleged human rights violations, including civilians and defectors from the military and the security forces. In the present report, the commission documents patterns of summary execution, arbitrary arrest, enforced disappearance, torture, including sexual violence, as well as violations of children's rights.

The substantial body of evidence gathered by the commission indicates that these gross violations of human rights have been committed by Syrian military and security forces since the beginning of the protests in March 2011. The commission is gravely concerned that crimes against humanity have been committed in different locations in the Syrian Arab Republic during the period under review. It calls upon the Government of the Syrian Arab Republic to put an immediate end to the ongoing gross human rights violations, to initiate independent and impartial investigations of these violations and to bring perpetrators to justice. The commission also addresses specific recommendations to opposition groups, the Human Rights Council, regional organizations and States Members of the United Nations.

The commission deeply regrets that, despite many requests, the Government failed to engage in dialogue and to grant the commission access to the country. The Government informed the commission that it would examine the possibility of cooperating with the commission once the work of its own independent special legal commission was completed. The commission reiterates its call for immediate and unhindered access to the Syrian Arab Republic.
23 November 2011.

(Source: UN General Assembly.)

SUSPENSION OF SYRIA BY ARAB LEAGUE

Text of Arab League statement on Syria, issued on 12 November 2011, in which the organisation suspended Syrian delegations from its meetings; imposed sanctions against the government; urged the army to stop violence against civilians; and took steps towards recognising the Syrian opposition.

The Council of the Arab League, meeting at ministerial level, resuming its extraordinary session on 12 November 2011, having reviewed the Arab ministerial committee's assessment of developments in Syria, having listened to the report of the secretary-general and the speech of the head of the Syrian delegation, and having heard the deliberations of ministers and heads of delegations, and due to the Syrian government's failure completely and immediately to implement the Arab League initiative which the Council approved in its ministerial session of 2 November 2011, has decided as follows:

1. To suspend Syrian delegations activities in Arab League meetings and meetings of its affiliate bodies and organisations, as of 16 November 2011, until the Syrian government fully meets its commitments towards the Arab League initiative to resolve the Syrian crisis, which the Council endorsed on its session on 2 November 2011.
2. To provide protection for Syrian civilians through immediate contact with relevant Arab organizations. If the violence and killing do not stop, the secretary-general will contact concerned international human rights organisations, including the UN, in coordination with the Syrian opposition, to draw up a programme for measures to stop that bloodshed and will refer that programme for discussion to the Arab League ministerial meeting, due to be held on 16 November.
3. To call on the Arab Syrian army not to participate in violence against and killing of civilians.
4. To implement economic and political sanctions against the Syrian government.
5. To call on Arab countries to withdraw their ambassadors from Damascus, aware that this is a sovereign decision for each country.
6. To invite all sections of the Syrian opposition to a meeting at Arab League headquarters within three days to agree on a unified vision for the transitional period in Syria. The Council of the Arab League will study the outcome of that meeting and will take appropriate decisions regarding the recognition of the Syrian opposition.
7. To hold a meeting on the ministerial level with all parties of the Syrian opposition after they reach agreement as described in Point 6.
8. To keep the Council in open session to monitor the situation.

(Source: unofficial translation from Egyptian television)

PRESIDENTIAL STATEMENT ON DEATH OF OSAMA BIN LADEN

Text of the speech by US President Barack Obama, given from the East Room at the White House, at 11.35 pm on 1 May 2011, in which he announced the killing of Osama bin Laden by US special forces, in Pakistan.

THE PRESIDENT: Good evening. Tonight, I can report to the American people and to the world that the United States has conducted an operation that killed Osama bin Laden, the leader of al Qaeda, and a terrorist who's responsible for the murder of thousands of innocent men, women, and children.

It was nearly 10 years ago that a bright September day was darkened by the worst attack on the American people in our history. The images of 9/11 are seared into our national memory—hijacked planes cutting through a cloudless September sky; the Twin Towers collapsing to the ground; black smoke billowing up from the Pentagon; the wreckage of Flight 93 in Shanksville, Pennsylvania, where the actions of heroic citizens saved even more heartbreak and destruction.

And yet we know that the worst images are those that were unseen to the world. The empty seat at the dinner table. Children who were forced to grow up without their mother or their father. Parents who would never know the feeling of their child's embrace. Nearly 3,000 citizens taken from us, leaving a gaping hole in our hearts.

On September 11, 2001, in our time of grief, the American people came together. We offered our neighbors a hand, and we offered the wounded our blood. We reaffirmed our ties to each other, and our love of community and country. On that day, no matter where we came from, what God we prayed to, or what race or ethnicity we were, we were united as one American family.

We were also united in our resolve to protect our nation and to bring those who committed this vicious attack to justice. We quickly learned that the 9/11 attacks were carried out by al Qaeda—an organization headed by Osama bin Laden, which had openly declared war on the United States and was committed to killing innocents in our country and around the globe. And so we went to war against al Qaeda to protect our citizens, our friends, and our allies.

Over the last 10 years, thanks to the tireless and heroic work of our military and our counterterrorism professionals, we've made great strides in that effort. We've disrupted terrorist attacks and strengthened our homeland defense. In Afghanistan, we removed the Taliban government, which had given bin Laden and al Qaeda safe haven and support. And around the globe, we worked with our friends and allies to capture or kill scores of al Qaeda terrorists, including several who were a part of the 9/11 plot.

Yet Osama bin Laden avoided capture and escaped across the Afghan border into Pakistan. Meanwhile, al Qaeda continued to operate from along that border and operate through its affiliates across the world.

And so shortly after taking office, I directed Leon Panetta, the director of the CIA, to make the killing or capture of bin Laden the top priority of our war against al Qaeda, even as we continued our broader efforts to disrupt, dismantle, and defeat his network.

Then, last August, after years of painstaking work by our intelligence community, I was briefed on a possible lead to bin Laden. It was far from certain, and it took many months to run this thread to ground. I met repeatedly with my national security team as we developed more information about the possibility that we had located bin Laden hiding within a compound deep inside of Pakistan. And finally, last week, I determined that we had enough intelligence to take action, and authorized an operation to get Osama bin Laden and bring him to justice.

Today, at my direction, the United States launched a targeted operation against that compound in Abbottabad, Pakistan. A small team of Americans carried out the operation with extraordinary courage and capability. No Americans were harmed. They took care to avoid civilian casualties. After a firefight, they killed Osama bin Laden and took custody of his body.

For over two decades, bin Laden has been al Qaeda's leader and symbol, and has continued to plot attacks against our country and our friends and allies. The death of bin Laden marks the most significant achievement to date in our nation's effort to defeat al Qaeda.

Yet his death does not mark the end of our effort. There's no doubt that al Qaeda will continue to pursue attacks against us. We must—and we will—remain vigilant at home and abroad.

As we do, we must also reaffirm that the United States is not—and never will be—at war with Islam. I've made clear, just as President Bush did shortly after 9/11, that our war is not against Islam. Bin Laden was not a Muslim leader; he was a mass murderer of Muslims. Indeed, al Qaeda has slaughtered scores of Muslims in many countries, including our own. So his demise should be welcomed by all who believe in peace and human dignity.

Over the years, I've repeatedly made clear that we would take action within Pakistan if we knew where bin Laden was. That is what we've done. But it's important to note that our counterterrorism cooperation with Pakistan helped lead us to bin Laden and the compound where he was hiding. Indeed, bin Laden had declared war against Pakistan as well, and ordered attacks against the Pakistani people.

Tonight, I called President Zardari, and my team has also spoken with their Pakistani counterparts. They agree that this is a good and historic day for both of our nations. And going forward, it is essential that Pakistan continue to join us in the fight against al Qaeda and its affiliates.

The American people did not choose this fight. It came to our shores, and started with the senseless slaughter of our citizens. After nearly 10 years of service, struggle, and sacrifice, we know well the costs of war. These efforts weigh on me every time I, as Commander-in-Chief, have to sign a letter to a family that has lost a loved one, or look into the eyes of a service member who's been gravely wounded.

So Americans understand the costs of war. Yet as a country, we will never tolerate our security being threatened, nor stand idly by when our people have been killed. We will be relentless in defense of our citizens and our friends and allies. We will be true to the values that make us who we are. And on nights like this one, we can say to those families who have lost loved ones to al Qaeda's terror: Justice has been done.

Tonight, we give thanks to the countless intelligence and counterterrorism professionals who've worked tirelessly to achieve this outcome. The American people do not see their work, nor know their names. But tonight, they feel the satisfaction of their work and the result of their pursuit of justice.

We give thanks for the men who carried out this operation, for they exemplify the professionalism, patriotism, and unparalleled courage of those who serve our country. And they are part of a generation that has borne the heaviest share of the burden since that September day.

Finally, let me say to the families who lost loved ones on 9/11 that we have never forgotten your loss, nor wavered in our commitment to see that we do whatever it takes to prevent another attack on our shores.

And tonight, let us think back to the sense of unity that prevailed on 9/11. I know that it has, at times, frayed. Yet today's achievement is a testament to the greatness of our country and the determination of the American people.

The cause of securing our country is not complete. But tonight, we are once again reminded that America can do whatever we set our mind to. That is the story of our history, whether it's the pursuit of prosperity for our people, or the struggle for equality for all our citizens; our commitment to stand up for our values abroad, and our sacrifices to make the world a safer place.

Let us remember that we can do these things not just because of wealth or power, but because of who we are: one nation, under God, indivisible, with liberty and justice for all.

Thank you. May God bless you. And may God bless the United States of America.

(Source: The White House, Office of the Press Secretary)

RECONCILIATION AGREEMENT BETWEEN FATAH AND HAMAS

Text of the "Palestinian National Reconciliation Agreement", signed in Cairo on 4 May. The agreement sought to end a four-year schism between the two main Palestinian groups—the Fatah movement, based in the West Bank, and the Islamist Hamas organisation, based in the Gaza Strip. The agreement was due to run for one year, pending the holding of elections to Palestinian governing bodies.

1. Elections

A. Election Committee:
Both Fatah and Hamas agree to identify the names of the members of the Central Election Commission in agreement with the Palestinian factions. This list will then be submitted to the Palestinian President who will issue a decree of the reformation of the committee.

B. Electoral Court:
Both Fatah and Hamas agree on the nomination of no more than twelve judges to be members of the Electoral Court. This list will then be submitted to the Palestinian President in order to take the necessary legal actions to form the Electoral Court in agreement with the Palestinian factions.

C. Timing of Elections:
The Legislative, Presidential, and the Palestinian National Council elections will be conducted at the same time exactly one year after the signing of the Palestinian National Reconciliation Agreement.

2. Palestine Liberation Organization

The political parties of both Fatah and Hamas agree that the tasks and decisions of the provisional interim leadership cannot be hindered or obstructed, but in a manner that is not conflicting with the authorities of the Executive Committee of the Palestine Liberation Organization.

3. Security

It was emphasized that the Higher Security Committee, which will be formed by a decree of the Palestinian President, will consist of professional officers in consensus.

4.Government

A. Formation of the Government:
Both Fatah and Hamas agree to form a Palestinian government and to appoint the Prime Minister and Ministers in consensus between them.

B. Functions of the Government:
1. Preparation of necessary condition for the conduction of Presidential, Legislative and the Palestinian National Council elections.
2. Supervising and addressing the prevalent issues regarding the internal Palestinian reconciliation resulting from the state of division.
3. Follow-up of the reconstruction operations in the Gaza Strip and the efforts to end the siege and blockade that is imposed on it.
4. Continuation of the implementation of the provisions of the Palestinian National Accord.
5. To resolve the civil and administrative problems that resulted from the division.
6. Unification of the Palestinian National Authority institutions in the West Bank, Gaza Strip and Jerusalem.
7. To fix the status of the associations, Non-Governmental Organizations and charities.
5. Legislative Council: Both Fatah and Hamas agree to reactivate the Palestinian Legislative Council in accordance to the Basic Law.

(Source: Translated by Al Mubadara, the website of the Palestinian National Initiative (PNI) party)

PALESTINIAN APPLICATION FOR MEMBERSHIP OF THE UNITED NATIONS

The documents relating to Palestine's request for admission as a full member of the United Nations. In a speech to the UN General Assembly on 23 September, Palestinian President Mahmoud Abbas said that Palestine sought admission on the basis of the 4 June 1967 borders with East Jerusalem as its capital. The request was transmitted to the UN Security Council (the General Assembly not having the authority to grant full membership in the UN); but the USA had warned that it would veto any move by the Security Council to grant Palestine full UN membership.

Application of Palestine for admission to membership in the United Nations

Note by the Secretary-General

In accordance with rule 135 of the rules of procedure of the General Assembly and rule 59 of the provisional rules of procedure of the Security Council, the Secretary-General has the honour to circulate herewith the attached application of Palestine for admission to membership in the United Nations, contained in a letter received on 23 September 2011 from its President (see annex I). He also has the honour to circulate a further letter, dated 23 September 2011, received from him at the same time (see annex II).

Annex I
Letter received on 23 September 2011 from the President of Palestine to the Secretary-General

I have the profound honour, on behalf of the Palestinian people, to submit this application of the State of Palestine for admission to membership in the United Nations.

This application for membership is being submitted based on the Palestinian people's natural, legal and historic rights and based on United Nations General Assembly resolution 181 (II) of 29 November 1947 as well as the Declaration of Independence of the State of Palestine of 15 November 1988 and the acknowledgement by the General Assembly of this Declaration in resolution 43/177 of 15 December 1988.

In this connection, the State of Palestine affirms its commitment to the achievement of a just, lasting and comprehensive resolution of the Israeli-Palestinian conflict based on the vision of two-States living side by side in peace and security, as endorsed by the United Nations Security Council and General Assembly and the international community as a whole and based on international law and all relevant United Nations resolutions.

For the purpose of this application for admission, a declaration made pursuant to rule 58 of the provisional rules of procedure of the Security Council and rule 134 of the rules of procedure of the General Assembly is appended to this letter (see enclosure).

I should be grateful if you would transmit this letter of application and the declaration to the Presidents of the Security Council and the General Assembly as soon as possible.

(Signed) Mahmoud Abbas
President of the State of Palestine
Chairman of the Executive Committee of the
Palestine Liberation Organization

Enclosure
Declaration

In connection with the application of the State of Palestine for admission to membership in the United Nations, I have the honour, in my capacity as the President of the State of Palestine and as the Chairman of the Executive Committee of the Palestine Liberation Organization, the sole legitimate representative of the Palestinian people, to solemnly declare that the State of Palestine is a peace-loving nation and that it accepts the obligations contained in the Charter of the United Nations and solemnly undertakes to fulfil them.

(Signed) Mahmoud Abbas
President of the State of Palestine
Chairman of the Executive Committee of the
Palestine Liberation Organization

Annex II
Letter dated 23 September 2011 from the President of Palestine to the Secretary-General

After decades of displacement, dispossession and the foreign military occupation of my people and with the successful culmination of our State-building program, which has been endorsed by the international community, including the Quartet of the Middle East Peace Process, it is with great pride and honour that I have submitted to you an application for the admission of the State of Palestine to full membership in the United Nations.

On 15 November 1988, the Palestine National Council (PNC) declared the Statehood of Palestine in exercise of the Palestinian people's inalienable right to self-determination. The Declaration of Independence of the State of Palestine was acknowledged by the United Nations General Assembly in resolution 43/177 of 15 December 1988. The right of the Palestinian people to self-determination and independence and the vision of a two-State solution to the Israeli-Palestinian conflict have been firmly established by General Assembly in numerous resolutions, including, inter alia, resolutions 181 (II) (1947), 3236 (XXIX) (1974), 2649 (XXV) (1970), 2672 (XXV) (1970), 65/16 (2010) and 65/202 (2010) as well as by United Nations Security Council resolutions 242 (1967), 338 (1973) and 1397 (2002) and by the International Court of Justice Advisory Opinion of 9 July 2004 (on the Legal Consequences of the Construction of a Wall in the Occupied Palestinian Territory). Furthermore, the vast majority of the international community has stood in support of our inalienable rights as a people, including to statehood, by according bilateral recognition to the State of Palestine on the basis of the 4 June 1967 borders, with East Jerusalem as its capital, and the number of such recognitions continues to rise with each passing day.

Palestine's application for membership is made consistent with the rights of the Palestine refugees in accordance with international law and the relevant United Nations resolutions, including General Assembly resolution 194 (III) (1948), and with the status of the Palestine Liberation Organization (PLO) as the sole legitimate representative of the Palestinian people.

The Palestinian leadership reaffirms the historic commitment of the Palestine Liberation Organization of 9 September 1993. Further, the Palestinian leadership stands committed to resume negotiations on all final status issues — Jerusalem, the Palestine refugees, settlements, borders, security and water — on the basis of the internationally endorsed terms of reference, including the relevant United Nations resolutions, the Madrid principles, including the principle of land for peace, the Arab Peace Initiative and the Quartet Roadmap, which specifically requires a freeze of all Israeli settlement activities.

At this juncture, we appeal to the United Nations to recall the instructions contained in General Assembly resolution 181 (II) (1947) and that "sympathetic consideration" be given to application of the State of Palestine for admission to the United Nations.

Accordingly, I have had the honour to present to Your Excellency the application of the State of Palestine to be a full member of the United Nations as well as a declaration made pursuant to rule 58 of the provisional rules of procedure of the Security Council and rule 134 of the rules of procedure of the General Assembly. I respectfully request that this letter be conveyed to the Security Council and the General Assembly without delay.

(Signed) Mahmoud Abbas
President of the State of Palestine
Chairman of the Executive Committee of the
Palestine Liberation Organization

(Source: United Nations: General Assembly, Security Council)

ADDRESS BY UNESCO DIRECTOR GENERAL ON THE ADMISSION OF PALESTINE AS A FULL MEMBER

Text of the address by Irina Bokova, director general of UNESCO, to the plenary session of the UNESCO General Conference in Paris on 31 October 2011, which voted by 107 votes to 14, with 52 abstentions, to admit Palestine as a member. This decision made UNESCO the first UN organisation to admit Palestine as a full member state. In her speech, Bokova raised concerns that US funding for UNESCO could be withdrawn as a result of the admission of Palestine.

Madam President of the General Conference, Madam Chair of the Executive Board, Excellencies, Ladies and Gentlemen,

We are witnessing a historic event, and we all sense, at this time, the symbolic significance and the importance of this decision for the Palestinian people and for UNESCO.

It is the fruit of a people's aspiration to join fully the family of world nations, linked together by the same ambition for peace and shared values.

As the United Nations Secretary-General, Mr Ban Ki-moon, has emphasized, a two-State solution, each living in peace and security, has been long awaited in the region.

I welcome Palestine and wish to take this opportunity to recall that our cooperation dates back many years.

I think of our efforts to train teachers and to enrol students in the Gaza Strip.

I also think of the fellowships that we fund and of the training workshops held on safety for journalists.

I should like to say that UNESCO has made tremendous efforts to preserve cultural heritage and implement a sustainable management plan for the Tell Balata site in Nablus, the mosaics at the Qasr Hisham Archaeological Park, the Church of the Nativity, and the Riwaya Museum in Bethlehem.

I have heard, and more loudly than ever, the call of the Palestinian people for UNESCO to strengthen its commitment and bolster its efforts in its fields of competence.

In reply, I wish to say once more that I will continue this cooperation, motivated by the deepest conviction that a high-quality education system, a dynamic culture and pluralistic media are the solid foundations of any society.

Ladies and Gentlemen, The admission of a new Member State is a mark of respect and confidence.

This must be an opportunity to strengthen the Organization and not weaken it, a chance for all to commit once again to the values we share and not to be divided.

Let me be frank. As Director-General, it is my responsibility to say that I am concerned by the potential challenges that may arise to the universality and financial stability of the Organization.

I am worried we may confront a situation that could erode UNESCO as a universal platform for dialogue. I am worried for the stability of its budget.

It is well-known that funding from our largest contributor, the United States, may be jeopardized.

I believe it is the responsibility of all of us to make sure that UNESCO does not suffer unduly as a result.

I am thinking of those thousands of girls and women in Afghanistan, in Africa and around the world, who have learned to read and write, with the help of UNESCO.

I have in mind Khalida, a young Afghan woman from the Paktika Province, enrolled in a UNESCO training course, who said [I quote]:

"My family was hesitant at first about me joining this programme. But I have learned many new techniques and realized that, as an Afghan woman, I can work together with men and service my community."

Khalida benefits from UNESCO's work to enhance literacy in Afghanistan.

I am thinking about the illiterate policemen in Kabul, in Kandahar and other cities, who are learning to read and write to better protect their citizens, thanks to us.

I am thinking of the Iraqi education satellite channel that supports learning to Iraqi girls and boys, including refugees and internally displaced persons.

I am thinking of the hundreds of journalists around the world who are at this very moment harassed, killed or imprisoned, because they stand by the truth—UNESCO stands by them and speaks out for them.

I am thinking also about the stolen treasure of Benghazi, Libya, for which UNESCO was first to ring the alarm bell.

I am thinking of the millions of lives that may be saved by the Tsunami warning system we launched in the Indian Ocean on 12 October, in response to the 2004 natural disaster.

At this time, I know these thoughts are also on your mind.

The fabric of our societies can be easily torn and is long to mend. I am saddened by the possible loss of momentum and energy in UNESCO.

I cannot imagine we would let these women and men down.

UNESCO's work is too important to be jeopardized.

Our Organization was created sixty six years ago to ensure that education, the sciences, culture and communication bring people together and foster a culture of peace.

This is our role as a specialized agency of the United Nations.

We are committed to taking our vital mandate forward. I appeal to you all to upkeep UNESCO's ability to act.

In welcoming once again Palestine to the UNESCO family, let me state clearly that we need each and every member of this Organization to be fully engaged.

(Source: United Nations Educational, Scientific and Cultural Organization)

CONCLUSIONS OF THE TURKEL REPORT

Conclusions of The Public Commission to Examine the Maritime Incident of 31 May 2010 (The Turkel Commission), established by the Israeli government to investigate the May 2010 attack by Israeli commandos on a flotilla of aid ships, which was attempting to deliver humanitarian supplies to the Gaza Strip. The flotilla had been organised and funded by the Free Gaza Movement and a Turkish NGO, IHH Humanitarian Relief Foundation, in an attempt to break the Israeli blockade. Israeli commandos boarded the vessels, and on one of them, the Mavi Marmara, killed nine activists—eight of whom were Turkish nationals. The Commission published its report on 23 January 2011.

Chapter A: The naval blockade of the Gaza Strip

Conclusions

112. Here we shall summarize the conclusions that the Commission has reached in this part of the report:
     - The conflict between Israel and the Gaza Strip is an international armed conflict.
     - Israel's 'effective control' of the Gaza Strip ended when the disengagement was completed.
     - The purpose of the naval blockade imposed by Israel on the Gaza Strip was primarily a military-security one.
     - The naval blockade was imposed on the Gaza Strip lawfully, with Israel complying with the conditions for imposing it.
     - Israel is complying with the humanitarian obligations imposed on the blockading party, including the prohibition of starving the civilian population or preventing the supply of objects essential for the survival of the civilian population and medical supplies, and the requirement that the damage to the civilian population is not excessive in relation to the concrete and direct military advantage anticipated from the blockade.
     - The imposition and enforcement of the naval blockade on the Gaza Strip does not constitute 'collective punishment' of the population of the Gaza Strip.
     - International law does not give individuals or groups the freedom to ignore the imposition of a naval blockade that satisfies the conditions for imposing it and that is enforced accordingly, especially where a blockade satisfies obligations to *neutral parties*, merely because in the opinion of those individuals or groups it violates the duties of the party imposing the blockade vis-à-vis *the entity subject to the blockade*.

Chapter B: The actions undertaken by Israel to enforce the naval blockade on May 31, 2010

Conclusions

255. The Commission has reached the following conclusions:
     - A vessel that attempts to breach a blockade is subject to international law governing the conduct of hostilities: international humanitarian law, including the rules governing use of force.
     - The Israeli armed forces' interception and capture of the Gaza Flotilla vessels in international waters - seaward of the blockaded area - was in conformity with customary international humanitarian law.
     - The tactics chosen to intercept and capture the Flotilla vessels -including having Shayetet 13 naval commandoes board from Morena speedboats and fast-rope from helicopter onto the roof of the vessels - was consistent with established international naval practice.
     - The participants in the Flotilla were predominantly an international group of civilians whose main goal was to bring publicity to the humanitarian situation in Gaza by attempting to breach the blockade imposed by Israel.

- On board the *Mavi Marmara* and the other flotilla vessels was a group of IHH [IHH Humanitarian Relief Foundation] and affiliated activists (the "IHH activists") that violently opposed the Israeli boarding. The IHH activists who participated in that violence were civilians taking a direct part in hostilities.
- The force used against civilians on board the flotilla was governed by the principles of "necessity" and use of "proportionate force" associated with human rights based law enforcement norms. However, the IHH activists lost the protection of their civilian status for such time as they directly participated in the hostilities. The use of force against these direct participants in hostilities is governed by the applicable rules of international humanitarian law.
- The Rules of Engagement for the operation provided an authority to use force that reflected the nature of a law enforcement operation.
- The IHH activists carried out the violence on board the *Mavi Marmara* by arming themselves with a wide array of weapons, including iron bars, axes, clubs, slingshots, knives, and metal objects. These were weapons capable of causing death or serious injury. Further, the hostilities were conducted in an organized manner with IHH activists, *inter alia*, operating in groups when violently assaulting the IDF soldiers.
- The IHH activists used firearms against the IDF soldiers during the hostilities.
- The Commission has examined 133 incidents in which force was used. The majority of the uses of force involved warning or deterring fire and less-lethal weapons.
- Overall, the IDF personnel acted professionally in the face of extensive and unanticipated violence. This included continuing to switch back and forth between less-lethal and lethal weapons in order to address the nature of the violence directed at them.
- The Commission has concluded that in 127 cases, the use of force appeared to be in conformity with international law.
- In six cases, the Commission has concluded that it has insufficient information to be able to make a determination.
- Three out of those six cases involved the use of live fire and three cases involved physical force; two incidents of kicking and one strike with the butt of a gun.
- In five out of the 127 incidents that appeared to be in conformity with international law, there was insufficient evidence to conclude that the use of force was also in accordance with law enforcement norms. However, in these cases, force appeared to be used against persons taking a direct part in hostilities and, as a consequence, was in conformity with international law.
- The planning and organization of the IDF mission to enforce the blockade did not include anticipation that there would be a violent opposition to the boarding, which had a direct impact on the operational tactics, Rules of Engagement, and training before the operation. However, the focus of the planning and organization of the operation on a lower level of resistance did not lead to a breach of international law.

(Source: Turkel Commission. Report Part one)

CONCLUSIONS OF THE TURKISH NATIONAL COMMISSION OF INQUIRY

Conclusions from the Report of the Turkish National Commission of Inquiry, published in February 2011, into the Israeli operation against the Gaza aid flotilla on 31 May 2010.

III. CONCLUSIONS

In light of the foregoing, the Commission has reached the following factual and legal conclusions:

1. The international humanitarian aid convoy was a civilian initiative. Its aims were peaceful. It constituted no threat to Israel.

2. All the Turkish ports used by the convoy possessed ISPS Certificates. All participants, ships and cargo departing from Turkish ports were subjected to the entire range of border and boarding checks, in a manner consistent with international standards.

3. There were no firearms on board the ships.

4. Prior to the convoy's departure, an understanding was reached among Turkish, Israeli and American officials that the convoy would eventually steer towards the Egyptian port of Al-Arish, when faced with compelling opposition. Events demonstrated that Israel did not abide by this understanding.

5. No attempt was made by the Israeli forces to visit and search the vessels before taking any other action.

6. Israeli forces severed the ships' communication capabilities. This put the vessels, passengers and crew at risk.

7. The Israeli forces launched an attack against the convoy approximately 2 hours after the last communication with the vessels.

8. The attack took place in international waters, 72 nautical miles from the nearest shore.

9. When the Israeli forces took control of the ship, nine passengers had been killed. Israel seriously breached the fundamental right of a human being, namely the "Right to Life".

10. Five of the deceased were shot in the head at close range. Furkan Dogan received 5 gunshots wounds, three of them in the head. After he fell down receiving the first bullet in his foot, two Israeli soldiers kicked and shot him in execution style. Cevdet Kiliclar, a photographer, was killed by a single distant shot to the middle of the forehead. The nine dead passengers suffered a total of 30 bullet wounds.

11. As a result of the attack over 50 had sustained wounds of varying gravity. One wounded passenger remains in coma.

12. The attack was carried out by an overwhelming Israeli force comprising frigates, zodiacs, helicopters, submarines, and fully-equipped elite commando units.

13. Prior to their attack, the Israeli forces did not proceed with standard warning practices, i.e. firing across the bow, to indicate an imminent use of force.

14. Israeli forces initially tried to board the *Mavi Marmara* from zodiacs. At this stage, the Israeli forces fired the first shots.

15. The nature and magnitude of the Israeli attack caused panic among the passengers who, in fear for their lives, reacted in self-defence.

16. The Israeli military did not at any time pause to re-assess the situation with a view to consider the least violent options in face of the passengers' self-defence.

17. The Israeli forces opened fire with live ammunition from the zodiacs and helicopters onto the passengers on deck, resulting in the first casualties.

18. As soon as the attack started, the Captain changed the course of *Mavi Marmara* to a bearing of 270° heading West, in opposite direction of the Israeli coast. However, Israeli frigates approached from the starboard bow and closed in, forcing the convoy to turn to the direction of Israel.

19. Israeli soldiers fast-roped down to the *Mavi Marmara* from helicopters. Three were subdued by the passengers. They were taken to the lower decks where they were treated for their non-lethal injuries.

20. Israeli soldiers shot indiscriminately, killing and wounding passengers, once on the upper deck.

21. The shooting spree of the Israeli soldiers continued in spite of the white flags waved by the passengers and multilingual surrender announcements made over the ship's PA system.

22. The Israeli forces attacked the other ships as well. Violence by Israeli soldiers occurred on all the ships of the convoy.

23. The total number of wounded on the convoy exceeded 70 from a host of nationalities.

24. On no occasion did the passengers use firearms against their Israeli assailants.

25. Once the Israeli military assumed control of the entire convoy, the vessels were diverted to the Israeli port of Ashdod.

26. Throughout the hours-long journey to Ashdod, the passengers aboard the *Mavi Marmara*, including the Captain, and some on the other ships were subjected to severe physical, verbal and psychological abuses.

27. These abuses continued at Ashdod, during the transfer to prisons/hospitals, en route to the Ben Gurion Airport until the passengers boarded the airplanes for departure.

28. Throughout the ordeal, passengers from virtually all the nationalities represented in the convoy were indiscriminately and brutally victimized by Israeli forces.

29. Freedom of navigation on the high seas is a long-standing universally accepted rule of international law.

30. The high seas are governed by the laws of peace time.

31. The law of naval blockade applies only in international armed conflicts.

32. Israel does not recognize Palestine as a State. Israel has, therefore, consistently treated its conflict with Hamas as a non-international armed conflict.

33. The international community and the UN continue to regard Israel as an occupying power of the Palestinian Territory, which includes the Gaza Strip.

34. The "naval blockade" imposed by Israel off the Gaza Strip is unlawful under international law and its enforcement is therefore unlawful.

35. The "blockade" was also unlawful in its implementation and practice.

36. The "blockade"'s "open-ended" nature did not comply with mandatory notification requirements under customary international law, particularly those relating to duration and extent.

37. The "blockade" was unlawful as it was not reasonable, proportional or necessary.

38, The "blockade" was excessive in the damage it inflicted on the population of the Gaza Strip in comparison to the expected military advantage.

39. The "blockade" was unlawful as it constituted collective punishment of the entire civilian population of the Gaza Strip.

40. Israel's ultimate objective through its "blockade" has been to punish the people of the Gaza Strip for supporting Hamas. This is why Israel chose in 2007 to impose a "blockade" although there were other options, and to persistently maintain it even though it did not yield its purported military objectives.

41. The international community has condemned the Israeli "blockade" of the Gaza Strip as a form of collective punishment.

42. Under customary international law, vessels carrying humanitarian aid cannot be lawfully attacked.

43. As a consequence of its attack on 31 May 2010, Israel has violated *inter alia* the right to life, the right to liberty and security of the person, freedom from arbitrary arrest or detention, prohibition of torture and other cruel, inhuman or degrading treatment or punishment of the passengers.

44. Israel is liable for compensating the damages and losses it caused.

45. Israel's attack must be condemned as unlawful. Any other disposition would establish a danger-ous precedential derogation from the paramount right of freedom of navigation on the high seas.

(Source: Turkish ministry of foreign affairs.)

REPORT OF PALMER INQUIRY

Excerpt from the report of the UN Secretary-General's Panel of Inquiry, chaired by former New Zealand Prime Minister Sir Geoffrey Palmer and published on 2 May 2011, into the Israeli intercep-tion of the Gaza aid flotilla on 31 May 2010. After examining the analysis of both Israel and Turkey, the UN panel concluded that the Israeli blockade of the Gaza Strip was lawful but that the attack on the flotilla, which had occurred in international waters, had used excessive force. Most of the nine activists killed by the Israeli forces had been shot multiple times or at point blank range, and many of the survivors had been mistreated and robbed by Israeli military personnel.

1 Summary

On 31 May 2010 at 4.26 a.m. a flotilla of six vessels was boarded and taken over by Israeli Defense Forces 72 nautical miles from land. The vessels were carrying people and humanitarian supplies. The flotilla had been directed to change course by the Israeli forces who stated that the coast of Gaza was under a naval blockade. Nine passengers lost their lives and many others were wounded as a result of the use of force during the take-over operation by Israeli forces.

The Secretary-General established the Panel of Inquiry on the 31 May 2010 Flotilla Incident on 2 August 2010. The Panel received and reviewed reports of the detailed national investigations con-ducted by both Turkey and Israel. Turkey established a National Commission of Inquiry to examine the facts of the incident and its legal consequences, which provided an interim and final report to the Panel along with annexes and related material. Israel provided the report of the independent Public Commission that it had established to review whether the actions taken by the State of Israel had been compatible with international law.

The Panel reviewed these reports and further information and clarifications it received in written form and through direct meetings with Points of Contact appointed by each government. In light of the infor-mation so gathered, the Panel has examined and identified the facts, circumstances and context of the incident and considered and recommended ways of avoiding similar incidents in the future. In so doing it was not acting as a Court and was not asked to adjudicate on legal liability. Its findings and recom-mendations are therefore not intended to attribute any legal responsibilities. Nevertheless, the Panel hopes that its report may resolve the issues surrounding the incident and bring the matter to an end.

The Panel's Method of Work provided that the Panel was to operate by consensus, but where, despite best efforts, it was not possible to achieve consensus, the Chair and Vice-Chair could agree on any procedural issue, finding or recommendation. This report has been adopted on the agreement of the Chair and Vice-Chair under that procedure.

Facts, Circumstances and Context of the Incident

The Panel finds:

i. The events of 31 May 2010 should never have taken place as they did and strenuous efforts should be made to prevent the occurrence of such incidents in the future.

ii. The fundamental principle of the freedom of navigation on the high seas is subject to only cer-tain limited exceptions under international law. Israel faces a real threat to its security from militant groups in Gaza. The naval blockade was imposed as a legitimate security measure in order to prevent weapons from entering Gaza by sea and its implementation complied with the requirements of international law.

iii. The flotilla was a non-governmental endeavour, involving vessels and participants from a number of countries.

iv. Although people are entitled to express their political views, the flotilla acted recklessly in attempting to breach the naval blockade. The majority of the flotilla participants had no violent intentions, but there exist serious questions about the conduct, true nature and objectives of the flotilla organizers, particularly IHH. The actions of the flotilla needlessly carried the potential for escalation.

v. The incident and its outcomes were not intended by either Turkey or Israel. Both States took steps in an attempt to ensure that events did not occur in a manner that endangered individuals' lives and international peace and security. Turkish officials also approached the organizers of the flotilla with the intention of persuading them to change course if necessary and avoid an encounter with Israeli forces. But more could have been done to warn the flotilla participants of the potential risks involved and to dissuade them from their actions.

vi. Israel's decision to board the vessels with such substantial force at a great distance from the blockade zone and with no final warning immediately prior to the boarding was excessive and unreasonable:

    a. Non-violent options should have been used in the first instance. In particular, clear prior warning that the vessels were to be boarded and a demonstration of dissuading force should have been given to avoid the type of confrontation that occurred;

    b. The operation should have reassessed its options when the resistance to the initial boarding attempt became apparent.

vii. Israeli Defense Forces personnel faced significant, organized and violent resistance from a group of passengers when they boarded the Mavi Marmara requiring them to use force for their own protection. Three soldiers were captured, mistreated, and placed at risk by those passengers. Several others were wounded.

viii. The loss of life and injuries resulting from the use of force by Israeli forces during the take-over of the Mavi Marmara was unacceptable. Nine passengers were killed and many others seriously wounded by Israeli forces. No satisfactory explanation has been provided to the Panel by Israel for any of the nine deaths. Forensic evidence showing that most of the deceased were shot multiple times, including in the back, or at close range has not been adequately accounted for in the material presented by Israel.

ix. There was significant mistreatment of passengers by Israeli authorities after the take-over of the vessels had been completed through until their deportation. This included physical mistreatment, harassment and intimidation, unjustified confiscation of belongings and the denial of timely consular assistance.

How to Avoid Similar Incidents in the Future

The Panel recommends:

<u>With respect to the situation in Gaza</u>

i. All relevant States should consult directly and make every effort to avoid a repetition of the incident.

ii. Bearing in mind its consequences and the fundamental importance of the freedom of navigation on the high seas, Israel should keep the naval blockade under regular review, in order to assess whether it continues to be necessary.

iii. Israel should continue with its efforts to ease its restrictions on movement of goods and persons to and from Gaza with a view to lifting its closure and to alleviate the unsustainable humanitarian and economic situation of the civilian population. These steps should be taken in accordance with Security Council resolution 1860, all aspects of which should be implemented.

iv. All humanitarian missions wishing to assist the Gaza population should do so through established procedures and the designated land crossings in consultation with the Government of Israel and the Palestinian Authority.

General

v. All States should act with prudence and caution in relation to the imposition and enforcement of a naval blockade. The established norms of customary international law must be respected and complied with by all relevant parties. The San Remo Manual provides a useful reference in identifying those rules.

vi. The imposition of a naval blockade as an action in self-defence should be reported to the Security Council under the procedures set out under Article 51 of the Charter. This will enable the Council to monitor any implications for international peace and security.

vii. States maintaining a naval blockade must abide by their obligations with respect to the provision of humanitarian assistance. Humanitarian missions must act in accordance with the principles of neutrality, impartiality and humanity and respect any security measures in place. Humanitarian vessels should allow inspection and stop or change course when requested.

viii. Attempts to breach a lawfully imposed naval blockade place the vessel and those on board at risk. Where a State becomes aware that its citizens or flag vessels intend to breach a naval blockade, it has a responsibility to take proactive steps compatible with democratic rights and freedoms to warn them of the risks involved and to endeavour to dissuade them from doing so.

ix. States enforcing a naval blockade against non-military vessels, especially where large numbers of civilian passengers are involved, should be cautious in the use of force. Efforts should first be made to stop the vessels by nonviolent means. In particular, they should not use force except when absolutely necessary and then should only use the minimum level of force necessary to achieve the lawful objective of maintaining the blockade. They must provide clear and express warnings so that the vessels are aware if force is to be used against them.

Rapprochement

x. An appropriate statement of regret should be made by Israel in respect of the incident in light of its consequences.

xi. Israel should offer payment for the benefit of the deceased and injured victims and their families, to be administered by the two governments through a joint trust fund of a sufficient amount to be decided by them.

xii. Turkey and Israel should resume full diplomatic relations, repairing their relationship in the interests of stability in the Middle East and international peace and security. The establishment of a political roundtable as a forum for exchanging views could assist to this end.

(Source: UN.)

DOWNGRADING OF TURKISH RELATIONS WITH ISRAEL

Press statement issued on 2 September 2011 by Ahmet Davutoglu, Turkey's minister of foreign affairs, in the aftermath of the release of the Palmer report and the refusal by Israel to apologise or pay compensation to those whom it killed during the attack on the Gaza aid flotilla. Davutoglu announced a downgrading of diplomatic relations with Israel to the level of second secretary and suspended all military agreements between the two states.

Distinguished Members of the Press,

You all know very well the reason why I will deliver this statement today.

Approximately 15 months ago on the 31st of May 2010, Israel carried out an armed attack in the international waters of the Mediterranean, against an international aid convoy in which hundreds of passengers from 32 countries participated to bring humanitarian aid to Gaza.

During this attack, Israeli soldiers killed 9 civilians, 8 of whom were Turkish and 1 was a US citizen, they injured many passengers and also forcefully brought the ship and its passengers to Israel.

These people were subjected to all sorts of degrading treatment throughout their two-day captivity at the hands of Israel.

Dear Friends,

Approximately 15 months have elapsed since this unlawful attack.

However, the concrete facts remain unchanged.

I find it necessary to repeat them.

The Israeli attack took place in international waters.

Those killed by Israeli soldiers were innocent civilians.

Those, whose lives were claimed, were civilians who wished to respond to the cry for help of the Palestinian people under the plight of the blockade enforced by Israel in violation of international law and human values.

War is a harsh reality of the history of humanity.

And war, above all, is the gravest violation of the human right to life, which constitutes the most sacred value.

Indeed, all civilizations have developed the concept of a "just war" in order to regulate even war according to certain rules.

For this reason, the use of military force has been restricted by very strict conditions in the United Nations Charter.

Furthermore, it is for the conviction of the sanctity of the right to life, that even when the war is warranted, the killing of innocent civilians is accepted as a war crime.

However, Israel, not in war but in peace time, not in a military but a civilian convoy; killed civilians who participated in a peaceful event organized to bring aid to innocent people suffering under a cruel embargo. This is the picture!

Moreover, it did so, neither in its territory nor territorial waters, but in international waters, where freedom of navigation prevails as the most fundamental principle of international law.

The crime committed by Israel is not a simple offense.

It is international law that has been violated.

It is the conscience of humanity and the most fundamental human value, the right to life that have been violated.

There is an irreversible truth:

And that is, the fact that attacking civilians in a ship part of an aid convoy, firing multiple times at unarmed people at the back of their neck is a crime against humanity.

This crime cannot be covered under any guise nor justified under any circumstances.

One other thing must also be underlined.

No state is above the law.

The world is currently changing.

Those who claim the lives of civilians, or commit crimes against humanity are sooner or later brought before justice and face trial for their crimes.

Neither the Israeli Government who ordered the attack against the *Mavi Marmara* nor the ones that actually carried out the attack are above or immune from the law. They all must be held accountable.

In fact, they have already been convicted by the conscience of humanity.

Distinguished Members of the Press,

You will recall that, as Turkey, we promptly acted to ensure that this clear crime would not go unpunished and that justice would to take its course.

To this end, within hours of the Israeli attack we called for an urgent session of the UN Security Council that very same day.

In my speech before the UN Security Council, I stated that humanity had drowned in the waters of the Mediterranean with this Israeli attack which totally disregarded all norms of law, human conscience and values of humanity.

Indeed, the UN Security Council, in the first hours of 1 June 2010, adopted a Presidential Statement with the agreement of all its members—an agreement of the entire international community.

With this Statement, the Security Council called for a prompt, impartial, credible and transparent investigation conforming to international standards, into the tragedy caused as a result of Israel's use of armed force.

Furthermore, the UN Human Rights Council based in Geneva, adopted a resolution by which it established a Fact-Finding Mission comprising highly prominent and specialized lawyers and launched an investigation process into the attack.

The UN Secretary General also set up an Inquiry Panel in line with the call by the Security Council.

As Turkey, we have fully cooperated with the Panel. We provided every contribution to speed up the investigation process and submitted our national report.

Whereas Israel, despite being represented in the Panel, continuously acted with the intention to delay its work.

Again, as you all very well know, we requested the Government of Israel to issue a formal apology and pay compensation to the families of and those close to the deceased. Moreover, we continued to emphasize that the blockade enforced against Gaza, which was explicitly criticized in the UN Security Council Presidential Statement, must be lifted.

We also declared that if our conditions were not met, the Turkish-Israeli relations would not be normalized.

On the other hand, upon being informed by the Government of Israel of its readiness to meet with Turkey with a view to apologize from the Turkish public and pay compensation to the families of and those close to the deceased, we held a total of 4 rounds of meetings at different times.

During these meetings, agreement was reached a couple of times between the Turkish and Israeli delegations negotiating the texts of an agreement, which accommodated our claims for an apology and compensation.

Indeed, ad referendum agreement was reached for the first time over two separate texts as a result of the meetings held in Geneva upon the request by the Israeli Prime Minister following Turkey's contribution to the relief efforts to put out the forest fires in Israel in December 2010. This agreement was also endorsed by the Israeli Prime Minister Netanyahu. However, due to the disagreements within the Israeli Council of Ministers, this agreement could not be implemented.

Throughout this process, all the delays in the publication of the Palmer Commission's report—I am emphasizing this since we are faced with a serious press manipulation—were caused as a result of the Government of Israel's request for additional time to form its internal consensus over apology and compensation, in other words every postponement was at the request of the Government of Israel.

The last request made by Israel for a 6 month-additional period was not accepted by Turkey. Because it was understood that all these requests for delay were aimed at prolonging the process.

The leaking to the press of the report, to which neither Turkey nor Israel is a side, bearing only the signatures of its Chair Palmer and Vice-Chair Uribe, and before it was officially submitted to the UN Secretary General on 1 September, is quite thought-provoking in this sense. Yesterday I spoke in a frank manner to the UN Secretary General Mr. Ban Ki-moon on this subject. He expressed great astonishment and dismay that this report which had not yet been submitted to him and whose details he was not yet fully acquitted with would be leaked to the press as it had. Unfortunately, the Israeli side has not acted in a manner compatible with State solemnity and confidentiality in this process.

First of all it should be stated that this report reflects only the views of the people abovementioned.

The report clearly establishes and expresses the crimes committed by Israeli soldiers and other officials.

In this respect, it explicitly concludes that attacking vessels with substantial force at a great distance from the blockade zone was excessive and unreasonable.

It also states that the loss of life and injuries caused by Israeli soldiers was unacceptable, none of the nine deaths was accounted for by Israel and that the evidence showed that most of the deceased were shot multiple times, including in the back, or at close range.

The report clearly documents serious mistreatment of passengers, including physical mistreatment, harassment and intimidation, unjustified confiscation of belongings and denial of consular assistance.

The report however alleges that the inhumane blockade enforced by Israel against Gaza is lawful.

It is not possible and even out of the question to accept this approach.

The Fact Finding Mission, comprising highly competent and specialized lawyers mandated by the UN Human Rights Council have reported that the Gaza blockade is unlawful. They clearly documented this in their work following the incident last year.

This conviction was both endorsed by the UN Human Rights Council and supported by the UN General Assembly.

When this is the case, clearly then the controversial views put forward by the Chair and Vice-Chair of the Panel exceeding their mandates are based on political motives, rather than on legal grounds.

Turkey in no way accepts this approach, which jeopardizes the functioning and integrity of the panel.

Turkey totally rejects this approach, which it finds incompatible with the letter and spirit of the Presidential Statement adopted by the UN Security Council by consensus.

In this vein, we are determined to refer this issue to the competent international legal authorities.

Dear Friends,

Turkey's stance against this unlawful act of Israel from the first moment has been very clear and principled. Our demands are known.

Our relations with Israel will not be normalized until these conditions are met.

At this juncture, Israel has wasted all the opportunities it was presented with.

Now, the Government of Israel must face the consequences of its unlawful acts, which it considers above the law and are in full disregard of the conscience of humanity. The time has come for it to pay a price for its actions.

This price is, above all, deprivation of Turkey's friendship.

The only side responsible in reaching this stage, is the Government of Israel and the irresponsible act of the Government of Israel.

In this context, our Government has decided to take the following measures at this stage:

1. Diplomatic relations between Turkey and Israel will be downgraded to the Second Secretary level. All personnel starting with the Ambassador above the Second Secretary level, will return to their countries on Wednesday at the latest.

2. Military agreements between Turkey and Israel have been suspended.

3. As a littoral state which has the longest coastline in the Eastern Mediterranean, Turkey will take whatever measures it deems necessary in order to ensure the freedom of navigation in the Eastern Mediterranean.

4. Turkey does not recognize the blockade imposed on Gaza by Israel. Turkey will ensure the examination by the International Court of Justice of Israel's blockade imposed on Gaza as of 31 May 2010. To this end we are starting initiatives in order to mobilize the UN General Assembly.

5. We will extend all possible support to Turkish and foreign victims of Israel's attack in their initiatives to seek their rights before courts.

Distinguished Members of the Press,

I would like to emphasize another point.

We in Turkey, we are the representatives of an understanding that advocates peace instead of eternal conflict and wants to establish justice instead of tyranny. Our foreign policy is based on this fundamental understanding.

That is why, in the same manner that we have raised our voice against the massacres in Bosnia, in Kosovo, we have also shown our reaction following the brutal Israeli attacks on Gaza.

Today, the Government of Israel must make a choice and the time has come to make that choice.

Those who rule Israel need to see that it will only be possible to ensure real security by building a real peace.

They should also understand that the path to building real peace passes through the strengthening of friendships, not by murdering citizens of friendly countries.

However, it is also clear that the current Government of Israel is incapable of seeing this simple reality and comprehending the consequences of the huge changes taking place in the Middle East.

On this occasion, I would like to emphasize that the measures we have adopted and we will adopt are linked only to the current Government of Israel's attitude.

Our aim is not to harm or jeopardize the historic Turkish-Jewish friendship, on the contrary, we aim to encourage the Government of Israel to correct this mistake that does not befit this exceptional friendship.

Turkey has always demonstrated a sincere and constructive attitude regarding the prevention of developments that adversely affect regional and global peace and stability and has always sought to correct their negative impact.

Turkey has made known her demands and expectations in a very clear manner from the beginning and has done her part.

I would like to underline it once more.

The Government of Israel is the responsible party for the point we have reached today.

As long as the Government of Israel does not take the necessary steps, we will not be able to revert from this point.

I thank you.

(Source Turkish ministry of foreign affairs.)

ADDRESS BY JAPANESE EMPEROR

Text of televised message to the Japanese nation from Emperor Akihito, broadcast on 16 March, in the aftermath of the devastating earthquake and tsunami. The unprecedented video message conveyed the Emperor's sadness at the destruction wrought by the disaster and voiced his deep concern over the nuclear crisis at the damaged Fukushima power plant. He praised the manner in which his subjects had responded to the tsunami and called upon them to continue to co-operate with each other.

I am deeply saddened by the devastating situation in the areas hit by the Tohoku-Pacific Ocean Earthquake, an unprecedented 9.0-magnitude earthquake, which struck Japan on March 11th. The number of casualties claimed by the quake and the ensuing tsunami continues to rise by the day, and we do not yet know how many people have lost their lives. I am praying that the safety of as many people as possible will be confirmed. My other grave concern now is the serious and unpredictable condition of the affected nuclear power plant. I earnestly hope that through the all-out efforts of all those concerned, further deterioration of the situation will be averted.

Relief operations are now under way with the government mobilizing all its capabilities, but, in the bitter cold, many people who were forced to evacuate are facing extremely difficult living conditions due to shortages of food, drinking water and fuel. I can only hope that by making every effort to promptly implement relief for evacuees, their conditions will improve, even if only gradually, and that their hope for eventual reconstruction will be rekindled. I would like to let you know how deeply touched I am by the courage of those victims who have survived this catastrophe and who, by bracing themselves, are demonstrating their determination to live on.

I wish to express my appreciation to the members of the Self-Defense Forces, the police, the fire department, the Japan Coast Guard and other central and local governments and related institutions, as well as people who have come from overseas for relief operations and the members of various domestic relief organizations, for engaging in relief activity round the clock, defying the danger of recurring aftershocks. I wish to express my deepest gratitude to them.

I have been receiving, by cable, messages of sympathy from the heads of state of countries around the world, and it was mentioned in many of those messages that the thoughts of the peoples of those countries are with the victims of the disaster. These messages I would like to convey to the people in the afflicted regions.

I have been told that many overseas media are reporting that, in the midst of deep sorrow, the Japanese people are responding to the situation in a remarkably orderly manner, and helping each other without losing composure. It is my heartfelt hope that the people will continue to work hand in hand, treating each other with compassion, in order to overcome these trying times.

I believe it extremely important for us all to share with the victims as much as possible, in whatever way we can, their hardship in the coming days. It is my sincere hope that those who have been affected by the disaster will never give up hope and take good care of themselves as they live through the days ahead, and that each and every Japanese will continue to care for the afflicted areas and the people for years to come and, together with the afflicted, watch over and support their path to recovery.

(Source: The Imperial Household)

DESIGNATION OF LEVEL 7 NUCLEAR ACCIDENT

Excerpt from the press release on 12 April by the Japanese Nuclear and Industrial Safety Agency (NISA) announcing the upgrading of the Fukushima disaster to a Level 7 nuclear accident, the most severe classification. NISA was the regulatory arm of the Agency for Natural Resources and Energy, which was a part of the Ministry of Economy, Trade and Industry.

INES (the International Nuclear and Radiological Event Scale) Rating on the Events in Fukushima Daiichi Nuclear Power Station by the Tohoku District - off the Pacific Ocean Earthquake.

The Rating of the International Nuclear and Radiological Event Scale (INES) on the events in Fukushima Daiichi Nuclear Power Station (NPS), Tokyo Electric Power Co. Inc. (TEPCO), caused by the Tohoku District - off the Pacific Ocean Earthquake is temporarily assessed as Level 7, considering information obtained after March 18th.

However, the amount of discharged radioactive materials is approximately 10 percent of the Chernobyl accident which was assessed on the same level.

1. INES

INES is the rating, which International Atomic Energy Agency (IAEA) and Nuclear Energy Agency, Organization for Economic Cooperation and Development (OECD/NEA) established and proposed to the Member States in March 1992, in order to indicate the impact on safety by the individual event in a nuclear facility and so on. Japan has also utilized it since 1 August 1992.

2. Events in Fukushima Daiichi NPS, TEPCO, by the Tohoku District - off the Pacific Ocean Earthquake

On 18 March, the ratings of the events in Fukushima Dai-ichi NPS by the Tohoku District - off the Pacific Ocean Earthquake were informed to be temporarily assessed as Level 5, considering information obtained before March 18th. However, Nuclear and Industrial Safety Agency (NISA) estimated the total amount of discharged radioactive materials from the reactors of Fukushima Dai-ichi NPS to the air, making a trial calculation using the result of analysis of the situation of the reactors and so on, which was carried out by Japan Nuclear Energy Safety Organization (JNES). This estimation resulted in the value corresponding to Level 7 of INES rating...

Although Level 7 is the highest level of INES rating, it is estimated that the amount of discharged radioactive materials to the environment in the current stage is approximately 10 percent of the Chernobyl accident, which was assessed on the same level in the past.

3. Procedures to be taken

This information is about the result of the total amount of the discharge from Fukushima Dai-ichi NPS in the current stage. As radioactive materials are being released to the environment, NISA will continuously gather and evaluate information.

In addition, the official level of INES will be determined, considering the technical evaluation from specialist view points made by INES Evaluation Subcommittee (Chairman: Dr. Naoto Sekimura, Professor of University of Tokyo, Nuclear Professional School Engineering, Department of Nuclear Engineering and Management), which set up in the Nuclear and Industrial Safety Subcommittee of the Advisory Committee for Natural Resources and Energy, after the recurrence prevention measures are confirmed based on the concrete causes found.

(Source: NISA/METI.)

REPORT TO IAEA CONFFERENCE

Extracts from the report of the Japanese government to the International Atomic Energy Agency's Ministerial Conference on Nuclear Safety, which was held at the IAEA's headquarters in Vienna on 20-24 June, in order to discuss the Fukushima accident.

I. Introduction

The Tohoku District - off the Pacific Ocean Earthquake and tsunami caused by the earthquake attacked the Fukushima Dai-ichi and Fukushima Dai-ni Nuclear Power Stations (hereinafter referred to as Fukushima NPS) of Tokyo Electric Power Co. (TEPCO) at 14:46 on March 11, 2011 (JST, the same shall apply hereinafter) and a nuclear accident followed at an unprecedented scale and over a lengthy period.

For Japan, the situation has become extremely severe since countermeasures to deal with the nuclear accident have had to be carried out along with dealing with the broader disaster caused by the earthquake and tsunami.

This nuclear accident has turned to be a major challenge for Japan, and Japan is now responding to the situation, with the relevant domestic organizations working together, and with support from many countries around the world. The fact that this accident has raised concerns around the world about the safety of nuclear power generation is a matter which Japan takes with the utmost seriousness and remorse. Above all, Japan sincerely regrets causing anxiety for people all over the world about the release of radioactive materials. Currently, Japan is dealing with the issues and working towards restoration from the accident utilizing accumulated experience and knowledge. It is Japan's responsibility to share correct and precise information with the world continuously in terms of what happened at Fukushima NPS, including details about how the events progressed, and how Japan has been working to restore from the accidents. Japan also recognizes its responsibility to inform the world of the lessons it has learned from this process.

This report is prepared based on the recognition mentioned above, as the report from Japan for the International Atomic Energy Agency (IAEA) Ministerial Conference on Nuclear Safety which is convened in June 2011.

The Government-TEPCO Integrated Response Office is engaged in working toward restoration from the accidents under the supervision of Mr. Banri Kaieda, the Minister of Economy, Trade and Industry in conjunction with and joining forces with the Nuclear and Industrial Safety Agency, and TEPCO. Preparation of this report was carried out by the Government Nuclear Emergency Response Headquarters in considering the approach taken by the Government-TEPCO Integrated Response Office toward restoration and by hearing the opinions from outside experts. The work has been managed as a whole by Mr. Goshi Hosono, special advisor to the Prime Minister, who was designated by the Prime Minister in his capacity as Director-General of the Government Nuclear Emergency Response Headquarters.

This report is a preliminary accident report, and represents a summary of the evaluation of the accident and the lessons learned to date based on the facts gleaned about the situation obtained so far. In terms of the range of the summary, technical matters related to nuclear safety and nuclear emergency preparedness and responses at this moment are centered on, and issues related to compensation for nuclear damage and the wider societal effects and so on are not included.

On top of preparing this report, the Government has established "Investigation Committee on the Accident at the Fukushima Nuclear Power Stations" (hereinafter referred to as "the Investigation Committee") in order to provide an overall verification of the utility of countermeasures being taken against the accidents that have occurred at the Fukushima NPS. In the Investigation Committee, independence from Japan's existing nuclear energy administration, openness to the public and international community, and comprehensiveness in examining various issues related not only to technical elements but also to institutional aspects, are stressed. These concepts are used as the base to strictly investigate all activities undertaken so far, including activities by the Government in terms of countermeasures against accident. The contents of this report will also be investigated by the Investigation Committee, and the progress of the investigation activities will be released to the world.

Japan's basic policy is to release the information about this accident with a high degree of transparency. In terms of the preparation of this report under this policy, we have paid attention to providing as accurately as possible an exact description of the facts of the situation, together with an objective evaluation of countermeasures against the accident, providing a clear distinction between known and unknown matters. Factual descriptions are based on the things that were found by May 31, this year.

Japan intends to exert all its power to properly tackle the investigation and analysis of this accident, and to continue to provide information on its policy to both the IAEA and to the world as a whole....

XIII. Conclusion

The nuclear accident that occurred at the Fukushima Nuclear Power Station (NPS) on March 11, 2011 was caused by an extremely massive earthquake and tsunami rarely seen in history, and resulted in an unprecedented serious accident that extended over multiple reactors simultaneously. Japan is extending its utmost efforts to confront and overcome this difficult accident.

In particular, at the accident site, people engaged in the work have been making every effort under severe conditions to settle the situation. It is impossible to resolve the situation without these contributions. The Japanese Government is determined to make its utmost effort to support the people engaged in this work.

We take very seriously the fact that the accident, triggered by a natural disaster of an earthquake and tsunamis, became a severe accident due to such causes as the losses of power and cooling functions, and that consistent preparation for severe accidents was insufficient. In light of the lessons learned from the accident, Japan has recognized that a fundamental revision of its nuclear safety preparedness and response is inevitable.

As a part of this effort, Japan will promote the "Plan to Enhance the Research on Nuclear Safety Infrastructure" while watching the status of the process of settling the situation. This plan is intended to promote, among other things, research to enhance preparedness and response against severe accidents through international cooperation, and to work to lead the results achieved for the improvement of global nuclear safety.

At the same time, it is necessary for Japan to conduct national discussions on the proper course for nuclear power generation while disclosing the actual costs of nuclear power generation, including the costs involved in ensuring safety.

Japan will update information on the accident and lessons learned from it in line with the future process of restoration of stable control and also further clarification of its investigations. Moreover, it will continue to provide such information and lessons learned to the International Atomic Energy Agency as well as to countries around the world.

Moreover, we feel encouraged by the support towards restoration from the accident received from many countries around the world to which we express our deepest gratitude, and we would sincerely appreciate continued support from the IAEA and countries around the world.

We are prepared to confront much difficulty towards restoration from the accident, and also confident that we will be able to overcome this accident by uniting the wisdom and efforts of not only Japan, but also the world.

(Source: Japanese government.)

ANNOUNCEMENT OF COLD SHUTDOWN AT FUKUSHIMA

Transcript of the press conference given by Prime Minister Yoshihiko Noda in Tokyo, on 16 December, at which he announced that a state of cold shutdown had been achieved at the damaged Fukushima plant.

Today the situation relating to the accident at the nuclear power station reached a significant milestone and I would like to provide a report to the people of Japan in my opening statement.

"Without the revival of Fukushima Prefecture there can be no revival for Japan." Since my appointment as Prime Minister of Japan I have used this phrase on frequent occasions. The single largest precondition for the revival of Fukushima is that the nuclear power station accident is brought to a conclusion. Since the accident occurred on March 11, the Government of Japan has been engaged in comprehensive efforts to respond to the situation, first and foremost by seeking to stabilize the status of the nuclear reactors. In the areas affected by the accident outside the power station grounds, the impact of the accident is still being strongly felt and it is a fact that there are many challenges that remain outstanding, including full-fledged decontamination efforts, the disposal of debris and work to enable the return home of the people who have evacuated. On the other hand, after implementing a meticulous inspection operation by experts, it has been confirmed technologically that coolant water is now circulating stably and that the temperature at the base of the reactors and inside the containment vessel is now secured below 100 degrees Celsius, which means that even if trouble were to reoccur, radiation dose beyond the grounds of the power stations can be maintained at sufficiently low levels.

Given this situation, today I convened a meeting of the Nuclear Emergency Response Headquarters, over which I preside, and the members of the meeting confirmed the judgment that the nuclear reactors had thus reached a state of cold shutdown and that this element of the power station accident had thus been brought to a conclusion. I would therefore like to announce the conclusion of Step 2 of the roadmap towards the conclusion of the nuclear power station accident.

Since the accident occurred, it has caused tremendous worry and great inconvenience for the people of Fukushima, as well as all the people of Japan and indeed the people of the world. I would like to express my apologies for this. Now that the status of the reactors has been stabilized, I believe that one of the major causes for concern has been eliminated.

It has been the dedicated efforts of countless people that have led us to this milestone today. I would like to mention the efforts of those people once again today. There are the members of the fire departments, Self Defense Forces and police service, who were involved in operations to inject water into the reactors from the immediate aftermath of the accident, working under the threat of irradiation and with the awareness that their very lives may be threatened. There are also all the workers at the power station, who worked day and night in an extreme environment, where during the summer months there was the added concern of heat exhaustion. There are the people from companies and research institutions in Japan and overseas who generously provided their knowledge and technical expertise. On behalf of the people of Japan, I would like to reiterate my appreciation for all these heroic and dedicated efforts, which were undertaken to save Japan from the clutches of the nuclear accident.

In addition, within the grounds of the nuclear power station there are still countless origami paper cranes, letters of hope and banners that have been sent from all around the country. I believe that such items have provided tremendous support and encouragement to those working at the site. I would also like to express my appreciation to all the members of the public who have taken the trouble to send warm messages of encouragement to the people working diligently at the power station.

With this milestone we have reached the conclusion of Step 2, but this does not mean that the struggle to tackle the nuclear accident is over. With regard to the nuclear reactors, we will now move from the stage where we seek to stabilize the situation, to a stage where we look toward decommissioning. The Government will once again clearly lay out the roadmap from now, and will continue to make every effort until the very end of the decommissioning process for the reactors, all the while taking every precaution to ensure the safety of the power station. Outside the grounds of the power station the three future challenges are decontamination operations, health management and compensation payments. We will engage in committed actions relating to these three challenges to ensure that the residents who have been obliged to evacuate are able to return to their homes and that an environment is created as soon as possible that will allow residents to rebuild their lives as they used to be. To this end the Government plans to set out its concept for a revision of the evacuation zones.

Next, I would like to provide a brief explanation of the individual challenges and the Government's response to them.

The first challenge is decontamination. The Government will promote the resumption of public services, such as hospitals and schools, in order to enable residents to return, but it goes without saying that the most significant factor in such efforts will be the thorough decontamination of residual radiation. In order to enable decontamination operations to progress as soon as possible, the Government will provide large-scale budgetary and manpower resources. In terms of the budget, a total of 464 billion yen has been secured to date, and I am seeking to prepare a total budget allocation of over 1 trillion yen, including the budget requests for next fiscal year. If further budgetary allocation is deemed to be required, depending on the status of progress, the Government will take responsibility to secure the required budget. With regard to manpower resources, the number of personnel to advance decontamination operations will be significantly increased. By the end of January next year a total of 200 personnel will be available, which will further increase to 400 personnel in April. A training and education structure will be rapidly developed for the personnel who will actually be engaged in decontamination operations on-site and by April we aim to have secured more than 30,000 personnel.

The second challenge is thorough measures to manage the health of the residents of Fukushima. In specific terms, there are already two whole body counters in place in Fukushima Prefecture, which are capable of testing for internal exposure to radiation, and a further five such counters will be purchased to significantly expedite testing and examination. In addition, the Government will expend all possible means to gain an understanding concerning the degree of exposure to radiation and its impact on the health of children. Already from October thyroid gland examinations for all children in Fukushima Prefecture who were under 18 years of age at the time of the disaster were initiated. From mid-November these examinations were launched not only at prefectural hospitals in Fukushima, but also by five teams of doctors and diagnosticians, which were formed to engage in visits to schools and civic halls, where they are also implementing examinations. Currently approximately 10,000 people are being examined each month. Furthermore, dosimeters have been installed in all locations that have requested them, in locations within the prefecture where people tend to gather in large numbers, including schools, kindergartens, child day care centers and parks. These dosimeters are being used to monitor radiation volumes on a real-time basis. By mid-February it is anticipated that 2,700 dosimeters will have been installed. In addition, with regard to food safety, the Government will further strengthen and thoroughly implement a structure to engage in detailed examinations, in order to ensure that food showing residual radiation in excess of the regulation values is not distributed in the food chain. I have previously noted that I am enjoying delicious rice from Fukushima Prefecture at the Prime Minister's Office. I would like the people of Japan to also feel safe and secure about eating food that has been confirmed to be safe, as a means of supporting the reconstruction of Fukushima.

The third challenge is the payment of compensation for damages arising from the nuclear accident. The Government is also working to develop a support structure through which an expedited and appropriate response can be made that is based on the perspective of those people who have been affected. In specific terms, in addition to providing the funds required for compensation payments through the Nuclear Damage Liability Facilitation Fund, the Government has also decided to expand the scope of eligibility for compensation to residents in the vicinity of the power station who evacuated voluntarily. Furthermore, teams comprising lawyers and other experts are engaging in visits to provide consultation services to residents. We are steadily progressing with assistance that will help to facilitate the compensation claims of the people affected by the accident.

Finally, I would like to state that my resolve remains unwavering that "Without the revival of Fukushima Prefecture there can be no revival for Japan." This is something that I intend to keep on repeating time and again. This is a challenge for the nation and also a challenge for the whole of humanity. I believe that the day will definitely come when the word "Fukushima" evokes an image of a place where the knowledge and wisdom of Japan and the world is amassed, and where the bravery and force of will of the people have opened up a new chapter for humanity. Already in Fukushima, initiatives are being created that seek to create a new Fukushima, through projects to promote renewable energies and clusters of medical-related industries, among other matters. The Government will work with the local communities to promote and aid the realization of such initiatives. Already, under the third supplementary budget, which was recently passed by the Diet, a fund for the revival of Fukushima has been established and assistance measures in excess of 500 billion yen, including 170 billion yen to promote the relocation of businesses to Fukushima Prefecture, have been set up. Moreover, in next year's ordinary session of the Diet, the Government will be submitting a special measures bill for the reconstruction and revival of Fukushima. I intend to proceed with work to draft this legislation while listening intently to the wishes of the local communities. The Government will continue to make concerted efforts to ensure that the residents who have been forced to move away from the familiar surroundings of their home towns will be able to return to their homes and rebuild their lives as soon as possible. We will pour every effort into the revival of Fukushima. It is this unwavering resolve that I would like to emphasize in my statement today.

(Source: Japanese government)

REPORT BY FUKUSHIMA INVESTIGATION COMMITTEE

The Executive Summary of the interim report, dated 26 December, of the Investigation Committee on the Accidents at the Fukushima Nuclear Power Station of Tokyo Electric Power Company. The report, compiled after interviewing more than 400 people involved in all aspects of the accident, was scathing in its assessment of the response to the crisis by both the government and TEPCO and also found that the risks posed to the plant by an earthquake and tsunami had been grossly underestimated.

1. Introduction

The Investigation Committee on the Accident at the Fukushima Nuclear Power Stations (the Investigation Committee) of Tokyo Electric Power Company (TEPCO) was established by the Cabinet decision on May 24, 2011. Its objectives are: to conduct investigation for finding out the causes of accidents (the Accident) at the Fukushima Dai-ichi Nuclear Power Station (Fukushima Dai-ichi NPS) and Fukushima Dai-ni Nuclear Power Station (Fukushima Dai-ni NPS) of TEPCO as well as the causes of accident damage; and to make policy recommendations for limiting the expansion of damage and preventing reoccurrence of similar accidents.

The Investigation Committee has conducted its investigation and evaluation since its first meeting on June 7, 2011. Its activities included: site visits to the Fukushima Dai-ichi and Dai-ni NPSs, as well as to other facilities; hearing of heads of local governments around the Fukushima Dai-ichi NPS; and hearing of people concerned through interviews mainly arranged by the Secretariat. As of December 16, 2011, the number of interviewees reached 456.

The investigation and evaluation by the Investigation Committee are still ongoing and the Interim Report does not cover every item that the Committee aims at investigating and evaluating. Fact-finding of even some of those items discussed in the Interim Report are not yet completed.

The Investigation Committee continues to conduct its investigation and evaluation and will issue its Final Report in the summer of 2012...

2. Outline of the Accident

On March 11, 2011, the Fukushima Dai-ichi and Dai-ni NPS were hit by off the Pacific Coast of Tohoku District Earthquake ("the Earthquake") and accompanying tsunami waves ("the Tsunami"). The Earthquake was of Magnitude 9.0 and the Tsunami waves height at the Fukushima Dai-ichi NPS exceeded 15 meters above O.P. (Reference sea level at Onahama Peil).

Six nuclear power units stood at the Fukushima Dai-ichi NPS: Units 1 to 3 were in operation, and Units 4 to 6 were in maintenance modes for scheduled outage at the time of the Earthquake. It is believed that Units 1 to 3 were automatically scrammed at the Earthquake, but external power supplies and almost all in-house AC power supplies were lost due to the Earthquake and the Tsunami. Reactors and spent fuel pools at the Fukushima Dai-ichi NPS lost their cooling capabilities. Explosions occurred on Units 1, 3 and 4, which were caused presumably by the hydrogen released from the possible core damage and filled in the reactor buildings. The reactor core of Unit 2 also seems to have been damaged, although the investigation is still incomplete.

A large amount of radioactive materials were released and spread from the Fukushima Dai-ichi NPS. The zone up to 20km from the site was designated as the Access Restricted Areas and no entry is allowed unless authorized. Some areas outside 20km from the site were also designated as the Deliberate Evacuation Area. As many as more than 110,000 people have evacuated. Many people are still forced to live in evacuation, and radiation contaminations have caused serious impacts on extended areas.

3. Problems of the Responses by Government Organizations to the Accident

(1) Problems of the local nuclear emergency response headquarters
a) Loss of functionality at the Off-site Center

The Act on Special Measures Concerning Nuclear Emergency Preparedness ("Nuclear Emergency Preparedness Act") and the Nuclear Emergency Response Manual ("NER Manual") of the Government stipulate that once a nuclear accident occurs, a local nuclear emergency response headquarters ("local NERHQ") shall be established close to the accident site, as the center of the emergency response coordination. A local NERHQ is to be located at a local standing facility for emergency responses and measures ("Off-site Center").

The Off-site Center of the Fukushima Dai-ichi NPS was located about 5km from the Fukushima Dai-ichi site but it could not function as intended.

The Off-site Center had to be evacuated because of the following reasons: difficulty in collecting its personnel due to damaged transportation and heavily congested traffic caused by the Earthquake; Moreover, the staff had to evacuate finally from the Off-site Center because of loss of telecommunication infrastructures, power cut, shortages of food, water and fuel; and the elevated radiation levels in the building which was not equipped with air cleaning filters.

In other words, the Off-site Center lost its functionality because:

i. It was not assumed that nuclear disasters may strike simultaneously with outbreak of an earthquake; and

ii. Its building structure was not designed to withstand elevated radiation levels, although it was intended for use in nuclear emergencies.

The Ministry of Internal Affairs and Communications identified the latter point in its "Recommendations based on the results of administrative evaluation and inspection of nuclear disaster prevention programs (Second Issue)" in February 2009. However the Nuclear and Industrial Safety Agency (NISA) of the Ministry of Economy, Trade and Industry (METI) did not take concrete steps for installing air cleaning filters, etc.

The Government should take prompt actions to ensure that off-site centers are able to maintain their functions even during a major disaster.

b) Problems concerning delegation of authority to the local NERHQ

The Nuclear Emergency Preparedness Act stipulates that the head of the Nuclear Emergency Response Headquarters ("NERHQ") may delegate part of its authority to the head of the local NERHQ. However, in the case of the Accident, necessary notification concerning delegation of authority was not issued. In order to execute necessary actions in a timely manner, the head of the local NERHQ had to make various decisions such as implementation of evacuation and carry out those decisions assuming the formal notifications had been provided and he had been given the authority. The Investigation Committee will continue to investigate why such a situation had happened.

(2) Problems of the government nuclear emergency response headquarters
a) Responses at the NERHQ at the Prime Minister's Office

Once a nuclear disaster occurs, the Government's Nuclear Emergency Headquarters (NERHQ), headed by the prime minister, is to be established at the Prime Minister's Office and to execute the emergency responses. Also the Director-General level officials of relevant ministries and agencies are to assemble at the Crisis Management Center of the Government located on the underground floor of the Prime Minister's Office, and to serve as members of an emergency operations team. The team is expected to promptly put together the information from respective ministries and agencies, and coordinate their views with flexibility.

At the time of the Accident, decisions on emergency responses were made primarily by the NERHQ (located on the 5th Floor of the Prime Minister's Office). All relevant Ministers and the Chairman of the Nuclear Safety Commission ("NSC") of Japan assembled there. Senior executives of TEPCO were convened and also present.

The emergency operations team members (on the underground floor) could hardly get hold of the discussions that took place on the fifth floor. When all resources of the entire Government were demanded, there was poor communication between the fifth floor (NERHQ) and the emergency operations team at the underground floor.

b) Problems of collection of information

The Nuclear Emergency Response Manual stipulates that, in the event of emergency, nuclear operators must report information about the accident to the Emergency Response Center (ERC) at the Ministry of Economy, Trade and Industry (METI), and that the information is transferred to the NERHQ at the Prime Minister's Office via the ERC. At the Accident, however, such routes for collection and transfer of information did not function in a satisfactory manner. NISA staff and others at the ERC were aware of slowness in the collection and transfer of information but they did not think of setting up a terminal for the teleconference system that had been employed extensively by TEPCO. Neither did they dispatch their members to TEPCO HQ for information collection. After all they failed to make positive efforts to collect information.

The problem is serious because the collection of accurate and most up-to-date information is a prerequisite for prompt and exact decision-making., and moreover, it is important from the view point of the need to provide information to the public.

(3) Remaining issues

The Nuclear Emergency Preparedness Act was established and the Nuclear Emergency Manual (NER Manual) was prepared to enable to the prompt implementation of appropriate measures in response to nuclear disasters. However existing manuals and designated emergency organizations set-up did not function properly. Therefore, the Integrated Headquaters for the Response to the Accident had to be established outside the scope of the Manuals, etc..

- Why procedures in the Manuals did not work as intended?
- What problems existed in the crisis management operations at the Prime Minister's Office?
- Were the emergency response procedures assumed in the existing NER Manuals realistic?

The Investigation Committee will conduct further interviews with the persons concerned to be able to address these questions in the final report.

4. Problems of Responses to the Accident at the Fukushima Dai-ichi NPS

(1) Misjudgment of operational situation of IC at Unit 1

Unit 1 lost its all power supplies shortly after the arrival of the Tsunami. The isolation condensers (IC) seemed to have lost its functionality as its isolation valves were fully or almost fully closed by the fail-safe circuits. But at the initial stage of the Accident, appropriate corrective actions were not taken, nor were instructions given. This was because it was erroneously assumed that the IC had been operating normally. Later on, aided by partial restoration of the status display on the control panel, for example, shift operators on duty began to have doubts about the normal operation of IC and eventually switched off the IC. This judgment was not necessarily incorrect, but the decision was not properly reported to, or consulted with, the NPS emergency response center.

On the other hand, besides the information and consultation from the shift operators on duty, the emergency response centers at the NPS and at the TEPCO head office in Tokyo ("NPS ERC" and "TEPCO ERC", respectively) could have become aware of the loss of functionality of the IC at many opportunities. But they failed to become aware of this and continued to assume the normal operation of the IC. These incidents in sequence indicate that not only the shift operators on duty but also the staff members of the emergency response centers, both at the station and at the head office, lacked sufficient understanding about the functioning of the IC. Such situation is quite inappropriate as a nuclear operator.

As soon as the IC had become inoperable, Unit 1 required alternative water injection for core cooling as quickly as possible, and it became necessary to depressurize the reactor vessel for allowing water injection. In the view of the Investigation Committee, misjudgment of the operational situation of the IC caused unwarranted delay in alternative water injection and primary containment vessel (PCV) venting. As a result, an earlier opportunity for core cooling was missed.

(2) Poor handling of alternative water injection at Unit 3

At Unit 3, the high pressure coolant injection (HPCI) system had been running at a low rpm (revolutions per minute) below the operating ranges of the driving turbine, as specified in the operating procedures, for long duration while the reactor pressure vessel (RPV) had been in low pressures. Therefore, shift operators on duty became concerned about insufficient water injection by the HPCI and switched off the HPCI manually at 2:42 a.m. on March 13, 2011. In doing so, the shift operators underestimated the risk of battery depletion in spite of the absence of assurance concerning the successful implementation of alternative water injection means. Eventually, they failed to lower the reactor pressure to a level that would allow the implementation of alternative water injection means. These decisions were made only among shift operators and the limited number of staff of the operation team of the NPS emergency response center. They did not seek for instructions from the senior executives and moreover, a post fact report about these operating decisions was submitted only much later from the operation team of the plant's emergency response center to senior executives. Such situation is problematic in light of crisis management. It is highly regrettable that this caused the delay of alternative water injection until 9:25 a.m. on March 13.

Furthermore, due attention should have been paid to the depletion of battery that was essential for HPCI operation under the station blackout (SBO) conditions. If it had been done, the NPS emergency response center could have initiated much earlier alternative water injections by using fire engines, for example, as an alternative means for water injection. In reality, however, the NPS emergency response center did not prepare for the injection of water by alternative means using fire engines until they were informed by the shift operators at Unit 3 of their failure in implementing an alternative means of water injection after the manual switching off of the HPCI even though the NPS emergency response center had been considering and preparing for mid- to long-term programs of water injection from the Standby Liquid Control System after the restoration of power. It must be concluded that the delay to the implementation of necessary measures was caused solely due to the lack of recognition at the NPS emergency response center of the necessity and urgency of alternative water injections into Unit 3.

(3) **Possible contribution to the explosions in the Units 1 and 3 reactor buildings**
It is still too early to judge at this stage whether earlier depressurization and alternative water injection of Units 1 and 3 could have prevented the explosions of reactor buildings.

5. Problems of the Hazard Control Measures

(1) **Problems of the initial radiation monitoring**
Monitoring data of radiation levels in the environment are indispensable to the protection of people from radiation exposure and also evacuation planning.

However, as many monitoring posts were carried away by the Tsunami or became inoperable by the loss of power, monitoring activities could not be conducted in a satisfactory manner due to the consequences of the earthquakes and tsunami.

Furthermore, in the initial stage of responses to the Accident, there were confusions over utilization of monitoring data. In particular, the government lacked an attitude of making the monitoring data promptly available to the public. Even when some data were made public, they were only partial disclosure.

The Investigation Committee calls on the relevant organizations concerned to take prompt actions for improvement on the following points:

(i) To ensure that the monitoring system does not fail at critical moments, and to ensure the collection of data and other functions, the system should be designed against various possible events, including not only an earthquake but also a tsunami, etc. Measures should be taken for them to function even in a complex disaster. Furthermore, measures should be developed to facilitate the relocation of monitoring vehicles and their patrols even in a situation where an earthquake has damaged roads.

(ii) Training sessions and other learning opportunities should be enhanced to raise awareness among competent authorities and personnel of the functions and importance of the monitoring system.

(2) **Problems of the utilization of SPEEDI**
The Network System for Prediction of Environmental Emergency Dose Information (SPEEDI) is also expected to play an important role in protecting local population from radiation exposure and the planning of evacuation. However, the system was not utilized when evacuation was instructed.

The communication links were disrupted and inoperative due to the earthquakes, and the SPEEDI could not receive the basic source term information of released radioactivity. It was therefore not possible for the SPEEDI to estimate atmospheric dispersion of radioactive materials on the basis of the basic source term information.

Nevertheless, it is possible for the SPEEDI to estimate the course of dispersion of radioactive materials, making assumption of the reference release rate of 1 Bq/h. And actually those estimates were then calculated by the system. Such calculation only predicts the direction of dispersion and relative distribution of radioactivity. But, if the information had been provided timely, it could have helped local governments and population to choose more appropriate route and direction for evacuation.

Since the local NERHQ lost its functionality, the Government NERHQ or NISA should have taken the role of providing the SPEEDI results to the public. But none of them had the idea of making use of this information. The Ministry of Education, Culture, Sports, Science and Technology (MEXT), the competent ministry for SPEEDI, also did not come to realize the provision of the SPEEDI information to the public on its own or through the Government NERHQ. Furthermore, since March 16, the clear division of responsibility was kept undefined between MEXT and NSC on the utilization of the SPEEDI. This was one of the reasons for the delay of making the SPEEDI results public.

In order to prevent the spread of harm from the disaster, measures should be developed to improve SPEEDI's management system so that crucial radiation dose rate information is provided promptly in a way that the Japanese people find persuasive. Measures, including hardware and infrastructure-related measures should be developed and implemented to ensure that SPEEDI functions remain operable even during a complex disaster.

(3) Problems of the decision-making of evacuation of residents and confusion experienced by the affected communities
The government issued instructions for evacuation over several times. The decisions were made at the Government NERHQ solely on the basis of the information and views of the senior members of relevant ministries and TEPCO who assembled at the fifth floor of the Prime Minister's Office. There is no evidence that any official representing MEXT as the competent ministry of SPEEDI was present at the Government NERHQ. No knowledge of SPEEDI was utilized in the decision-making process. Since the SPEEDI had not been functional in a full form, the conclusions of evacuation zoning might have been the same as the government decisions. But it should be pointed out as problematical that the point of view of utilizing the SPEEDI was totally missing in planning the evacuation strategy.

The government instructions for evacuation did not reach promptly all the relevant local governments in the designated evacuation areas. Moreover, the instructions were not specific nor in detail. The local governments had to, without sufficient information, make decisions to evacuate, locate evacuation destination, and evacuation procedures. One of major reasons for such confusion is considered to be the background factors that the government and electric power companies had not tackled fully the problem of evacuation once a nuclear disaster occurs.

The Investigation Committee notes the following points in order to prepare for possible recurrence of such an accident.

i. Activities to raise public awareness are needed to provide residents with basic, customary knowledge of how radioactive substances are released during a major nuclear accident, how they are dispersed by wind and other agents, and how they fall back to earth, as well as knowledge of how the harm exposure to radiation can do to health.

ii. Local government bodies need to prepare evacuation readiness plans that take into account the exceptionally grave nature of a nuclear accident, periodically conduct evacuation drills realistic circumstances, and take steps to promote the earnest participation of residents in those drills.

iii. Beginning in times of normalcy, there is a need for readiness preparations, such as drafting detailed plans for ensuring modes of transportation, organizing transportation, establishing

evacuation sites in outlying areas, and ensuring water and food supplies in places of refuge, taking into consideration the situation that evacuees may number in the thousands or tens of thousands. It is especially important to develop measures that support the evacuation of the disadvantaged, such as seriously ill or disabled people in medical institutions, homes for the aged, social welfare facilities, or in their own homes.

iv. The above types of measures should not be left up to the local municipal governments, but need in addition to involve the active participation of the prefectural and national governments in drawing up and administering evacuation and disaster readiness plans, in consideration of the situation that a nuclear emergency would affect a large area.

(4) **Problems of provision of information to the nation and international society**
In the wake of the Accident, quite a few cases were observed where the manner of providing information by the government gave rise to questions and suspicion on the populations in the areas around the Fukushima Dai-ichi NPS and people in the whole nation that the government was not providing truth promptly and accurately. The manner in which the government provided information about the status of the reactor cores (core meltdowns, in particular) and the critical conditions of Unit 3, as well as the repeated announcement of an unclear statement that the radiation "will not immediately affect human bodies", aroused such suspicions.

The following tendency was observed: transmission and public announcement of information of urgent matters were delayed, press releases were withheld, and explanations were kept ambiguous. Whatever the reasons behind, such tendency was far from the ideal response as to how the public should be informed of risks in an emergency.

The Investigation Committee will continue its investigation on this subject, and will make necessary recommendations in the final report.

As regards providing information to the international society, contaminated water was discharged to the ocean immediately after the decision had been made without prior explanation to the neighboring countries. It may not violate legal obligations under the relevant international conventions, but the case may have caused mistrust of the international communities in the adequacy of Japan's response to nuclear disasters. We should take this an important lesson for the future.

(5) **Review of other hazard control measures**
The Investigation Committee is still in the process of investigating problems relating to the raising of screening levels, the criteria about the use of contaminated school grounds, and the medical institutions that provide emergency medical care to the victims of radiation exposure.

6. Inappropriate Precautionary Measures against Tsunami and Severe Accidents

(1) **Inappropriate measures against tsunami and severe accidents**
a) **Problems on tsunami assumptions**

(a) **Regulatory bodies concerned**
The Nuclear Safety Commission (NSC) of Japan started its revision process of the Regulatory Guide for Reviewing Seismic Design of Nuclear Power Reactor Facilities ("seismic design regulatory guide") in July 2001 within its Sub-committee on the seismic design regulatory guide. But no tsunami specialist was included among the Sub-committee members. This seems to demonstrate the NSC's insufficient awareness of the significance of tsunamis in nuclear safety. The revision of the seismic design regulatory guide (NSCRG L-DS-I.02) took five years of work and it was finally completed in September 2006. It is appreciable that a clause on the countermeasures against tsunami was included in

the final version of the revised seismic design regulatory guide, but it did not lead to additional implementation of specific measures against tsunami.

It is the role of the regulators to set up the methodology for tsunami evaluation and the criteria for evaluating the effectiveness of measures against tsunami. The Investigation Committee is unable to find, however, evidence of such efforts made by the regulatory organizations concerned. NISA received from TEPCO in 2002 its safety evaluation report based on the "Tsunami Assessment Method for Nuclear Power Plants in Japan" (Ref. 1). But NISA did not provide TEPCO with any particular comment or instructions in return. In August/September 2009 and in March 2011, NISA received from TEPCO reports on the results of its test calculations of the wave height of possible tsunamis, etc. but failed to respond to them positively by requesting TEPCO to take specific measures such as implementing additional construction works to enhance protection against tsunamis.

(Ref. 1) Tsunami Assessment Method for Nuclear Power Plants in Japan, the Tsunami Evaluation Subcommittee, the Nuclear Civil Engineering Committee, Japan Society of Civil Engineers, 2002.

(b) TEPCO and others

The licenses for the Fukushima Dai-ichi NPS were granted between 1966 and 1972 assuming a maximum tsunami height of 3.1m as part of design conditions. This height was set based on the maximum wave height observed at the Onahama Port (about 40km south of the Fukushima Dai-ichi NPS) when a tsunami originating from the 1960 Great Chilean Earthquake reached the port.

In February 2002, the Tsunami Evaluation Subcommittee of the Japan Society of Civil Engineers (JSCE, then an incorporated association and now a non profit foundation) compiled the "Tsunami Assessment Method for Nuclear Power Plants in Japan" (Ref.1). The methodology estimates a possible tsunami wave height, based on the historic records of tsunamis that could be judged fairly reliable from evident traces of wave heights. Prehistoric tsunamis, even if they might have occurred, were not considered in the methodology, so long as there are no records. And its limits of application or remarks for application were not mentioned in the compiled document.

Using the JSCE's tsunami assessment method, TEPCO revised the assumed maximum tsunami height for the Fukushima Dai-ichi NPS to 5.7m (later revised again to 6.1m).

In 2008, TEPCO reevaluated the tsunami risks at the Fukushima Dai-ichi NPS and got the wave heights exceeding 15m. TEPCO got another estimated wave heights of exceeding 9m on the basis of the wave source model of the Jogan Tsunami in 869 A.D. (the Satake paper, Ref. 2). However, it did not lead TEPCO to take concrete measures against tsunami at the Fukushima Dai-ichi NPS. The reasons for this attitude was that: in their view, the former value (>15m) was a virtually derived value obtained by repositioning the source wave model of the Off-Sanriku coast (about 200km north of the site) to the Off-Fukushima coast, while the latter value (>9 meters) was not sufficiently reliable, because the source model had not yet been finalized in the Satake paper.

(Ref. 2) Kenji Satake, Yuichi Namegaya, Shigeru Yamaki,, Numerical simulation of the AD 869 Jogan tsunami in Ishinomaki and Sendai plains, katsudannsou kojishinkennkyuuhoukoku, No.8, pp.71-89, 2008. (http://unit.aist.go.jp/actfault-eq/seika/h19seika/pdf/03.satake.pdf)

The Investigation Committee is of the view that specific measures against tsunami should have been implemented including measures against severe accidents for the purpose of preventing nuclear disasters, because it is considered that: i) natural phenomena entail by nature major uncertainties ii) with regards to tsunamis in particular, we must take note that we can closely examine only a limited number of tsunami disasters in the past by means of studying existing literatures, and iii) once a tsunami far exceeding the design basis hits nuclear power plants, a wide range of safety functions of nuclear facilities could be lost simultaneously by common mode failures. Nuclear power stakeholders, including the national government and industries, should seriously review the history of assessment activities conducted before the Fukushima nuclear accidents and learn lessons for the future.

Severe accident management measures

As stated, if a tsunami far exceeding the design basis hits nuclear power plants, it is very likely that a broad range of safety functions could be lost simultaneously by common mode failures, which will lead immediately to a severe accident. But in the past, risks of tsunamis were not fully considered in the context of severe accident management that deals with incidents exceeding design basis assumptions.

In July 1992 the Ministry of International Trade and Industry (MITI, later reformed into METI) published a document titled the "Roadmap of Accident Management (AM)", and initiated considerations on the Accident Management as measures against severe accidents. However, the scope of incidents was limited only to internal incidents such as mechanical failures and human factor errors. External incidents such as earthquakes and tsunamis were not included in the scope of consideration. Moreover, AM was regarded as voluntary initiatives by nuclear operators and not as part of regulatory requirements.

Measures against severe accidents should not be left to the operator's voluntary initiatives. The nuclear safety regulatory bodies should consider and determine legal requirements when they deem them necessary. This is a lesson learned from the experience with the Accident.

(2) **Problems of measures against natural disasters that had been taken by TEPCO**

TEPCO did not implement measures against tsunami as part of its AM strategy and was very poorly prepared to cope with an accident of a degree of severity that reactor cores are seriously damaged by natural disasters. Listed below are some of the specific problems that were revealed through the Accident.

(i) **Lack of preparedness against the total loss of power**

The risk of tsunami exceeding design basis assumptions had not been considered. Therefore, no preparation was made for an eventuality such as "simultaneous and multiple losses of power" and the "Station Blackout including the loss of DC power supplies". No operational manuals were in place for recovering measurement hardware, power supplies, and PCV venting, etc. in such situations. Staff education was not implemented for such eventuality. No stock of equipment and materials were available for such restoring operations.

(ii) **No preparative plan for injection of freshwater and seawater by fire engines**

Fire engines were brought in for the injection of freshwater and seawater for responding to the Accident. These steps were not placed as part of the AM. Therefore, specific procedures were not established in advance and extra time was needed for their operation.

(iii) **Breaking down of emergency telecommunication lines**

The in-house telecommunication lines in an emergency were not sufficiently in place. As a result of the SBO, all PHS (personal handy phone system) became inoperative and information sharing among the people concerned was seriously disrupted.

(iv) **Securing of materials and operators in an emergency**

There were no specific procedures arranged in advance for handling equipment and materials for an emergency or in an extraordinary situation, which caused delay in securing operators of fire engines and heavy machinery.

7. Why Were the Measures against Tsunami and Severe Accident Insufficient?

i. Limitation of voluntary safety measures

TEPCO did not incorporate measures against tsunamis exceeding their heights of design basis assumptions. This indicates the limitation of voluntary safety measures.

ii. Insufficient organizational capabilities of regulatory bodies

Relevant research and knowledge continue to advance quickly on daily basis. The regulatory bodies should focus their efforts on formulating and updating the guidelines and criteria, taking into account the latest applicable knowledge. To this end, it is essential to ensure sufficient organizational capabilities of regulatory bodies. Scholarly discussion with inconclusive nature could be left to the work of academic communities.

iii. Adverse effects of specialization and sectoral subdivisions

The successful implementation of tsunami protection measures requires knowledge and technology from different field of expertise. It is important to notice that problems should be solved by the joint effort of different groups of experts and engineers, where each has its own unique culture. It is necessary to make arrangements toward the formation of cross-sectoral organizations.

iv Difficulties in presenting risk information

It is a paradox that the effort to further improve safety is met with negative reactions by others, because such effort may be interpreted as the negation of the past practices.

It is not easy to admit an idea that an absolute safety never exists, and to learn to live with risks. But it is necessary to make effort toward building a society where risk information is shared and people are allowed to make reasonable choices.

8. Recommendations on the New Nuclear Safety Regulatory Body

The Government made a cabinet decision on August 15, 2011 to reorganize the nuclear safety regulatory bodies into a new government agency under the Ministry of Environment, by separating NISA from METI and combining its function with that of NSC. The Investigation Committee suggests the Government to take the following points into account in establishing the new agency.

i. The need for independence and transparency

The new nuclear safety regulatory organization should be granted independence and should maintain transparency. The new nuclear safety regulatory organization must be granted the authority, financial resources and personnel it needs to function autonomously, and should also be given the responsibility of explaining nuclear safety issues to the Japanese people.

ii. Organizational preparedness for swift and effective emergency response

The new nuclear safety regulatory organization should, beginning in times of normalcy, draw up disaster preparedness plans and implement drills to facilitate rapid response if a disaster occurs, should foster the specialized skills to provide expert advice and guidance that competent personnel and organizations responsible for emergency response will need, and should foster the management potential it needs to apply its resources effectively and efficiently.

In addition, the nuclear safety regulatory organization must be well aware that its role is to respond responsibly to crises. It should prepare systems that can deal with a major disaster if it occurs, and develop partnerships with relevant government ministries and agencies and with relevant local governing bodies to create mechanisms for cross-organizational response, with the role of the nuclear safety regulatory organization clearly demarcated.

iii. Recognition of its role as a provider of disaster-related information to Japan and the world

The new entity must be fully conscious that the way it provides information is a matter of great importance, and must also, beginning in times of normalcy, establish an organizational framework that ensures it will, during an emergency, be able to provide information in a timely and appropriate manner.

iv. Retention of first-rate human resources; greater specialized expertise

The new nuclear safety regulatory organization should consider establishing a personnel management and planning regime that encourages personnel to develop lifetime careers. For example, it should offer improved working conditions to attract and retain talented human resources with excellent specialized expertise, expand opportunities for personnel to undergo long-term

and practical training, and promote personnel interaction with other administrative bodies and with research institutions, including those involved in nuclear energy and radiation.

v. Efforts to collect information and acquire scientific knowledge
The new regulatory organization to be established should keep abreast of trends embraced by academic bodies and journals in the field (including those in foreign countries) and by regulatory bodies in other countries, in order to continue absorbing knowledge that will contribute to its regulatory activities. It must also understand the implications of that knowledge, share it and use it systematically, and convey it and pass it on as befits an organization of its nature.

9. Interim Conclusions
Based on the examination of various facts found up to now, the Investigation Committee is of the view that the following three factors contributed greatly to the arising of many problems related to the Accident and the responses after the Accident.

i. Lack of severe accident preparedness for tsunamis
TEPCO did not take precautionary measures in anticipation that a severe accident could be caused by a tsunami such as the one which hit at this time. Neither did the regulatory authorities.

The tsunami that caused the Accident is an example of events that are believed to have a very small probability of happening but are likely to produce enormous damage if they do happen. We must refresh our awareness of the risks of such events. We should take the necessary measures to address such risks, which should never be ignored.

ii. Lack of awareness of the ramifications of a complex disaster
A lack of foresight is identified as a great problem for the safety of both nuclear power plants and surrounding communities that nuclear accident had not been assumed to occur as complex disaster. Disaster prevention program should be formulated by assuming a complex disaster, which will be the major point in reviewing nuclear power plant safety for the future.

iii. Lack of an all-encompassing perspective
It cannot be denied that the nuclear emergency response programs in the past lacked an overall perspective. This is a great shortfall in nuclear emergency response programs. The excuse cannot be justified that it had been difficult to make sufficient preparations for such an exceptional event because the plant was struck by a tsunami beyond design basis assumptions.

The Investigation Committee is convinced of the need of a paradigm shift in the basic principles of disaster prevention programs for such a huge system, whose failure may cause enormous damage.

10. Final Remarks
Whatever to plan, design and execute, nothing can be done without setting assumptions. At the same time, however, it must be recognized that things beyond assumptions may take place. The Accident presented us crucial lessons on how we should be prepared for such incidents that we had not accounted for.

The Investigation Committee will continue its investigation, bearing in mind following points:
- Many people are still forced to spend restricted life in evacuation for a prolonged period of time;
- Many people are suffering from the consequences of radiation contamination or troubled by anxieties concerning the consequences of radiation exposure which they may face in the future; and also
- Many people continue to face anxieties concerning the contamination of air, soil and water or concerning the safety of food.

(Source: Japanese government.)

AIMS OF THE "OCCUPY" MOVEMENT

Statement from the website of the Occupy Wall Street protest seeking to explain the rise of the "Occupy" movement and to describe its aims.

OccupyWallSt.org is the unofficial *de facto* online resource for the growing occupation movement happening on Wall Street and around the world. We're an affinity group committed to doing technical support work for resistance movements. We're not a subcommittee of the NYCGA* nor affiliated with Adbusters, Anonymous or any other organization.

Occupy Wall Street is a people-powered movement that began on September 17, 2011 in Liberty Square in Manhattan's Financial District, and has spread to over 100 cities in the United States and actions in over 1,500 cities globally. Occupy Wall Street is fighting back against the corrosive power of major banks and multinational corporations over the democratic process, and the role of Wall Street in creating an economic collapse that has caused the greatest recession in generations. The movement is inspired by popular uprisings in Egypt and Tunisia, and aims to fight back against the richest 1% of people that are writing the rules of an unfair global economy that is foreclosing on our future.

The occupations around the world are being organized using a non-binding consensus based collective decision making tool known as a "people's assembly". To learn more about how to use this process to organize your local community to fight back against social injustice, please read this quick guide on group dynamics in people's assemblies.

Solidarity Forever!

*NYCGA: New York City General Assembly: "The NYC General Assembly is composed of dozens of groups working together to organize and set the vision for the Occupy Wall Street movement."

(Source: occupywallst.org)

OCTOBER 2011 EURO SUMMIT

Published below is the statement issued at the 26-27 October Euro Summit in Brussels, which was held in the context of the sovereign debt crisis affecting Greece and several other eurozone countries. Leaders of eurozone countries agreed to strengthen the governing structures of the euro area by holding twice-yearly meetings and, possibly, making changes to the EU Treaties that would formalise their hitherto ad hoc summit meetings (these changes were subsequently agreed in the form of a new Treaty, "the Fiscal Compact" in March 2012). The meeting also agreed measures to strengthen the eurozone and tackle the debt crisis, including a "voluntary" reduction in the value of Greek debt held by private creditors; the recapitalisation of Europe's banks; and a further enhancement to the capacity of the European Financial Stability Facility (a bailout fund created in 2010 and which, in July 2011, had already seen its lending capacity increased to €440 billion).

Brussels, 26 October 2011

EURO SUMMIT STATEMENT

1. Over the last three years, we have taken unprecedented steps to combat the effects of the worldwide financial crisis, both in the European Union as such and within the euro area. The strategy we have put into place encompasses determined efforts to ensure fiscal consolidation, support to countries in difficulty, and a strengthening of euro area governance leading to deeper economic integration among us and an ambitious agenda for growth. At our 21 July meeting we took a set of major decisions. The ratification by all 17 Member States of the euro area of the measures related to the EFSF significantly strengthens our capacity to react to the crisis. Agreement by all three institutions on a strong legislative package within the EU structures on better economic governance represents another major achievement. The introduction of the European Semester has fundamentally changed the way our fiscal and economic policies are co-ordinated at European level, with co-ordination at EU level now taking place before national decisions are taken. The euro continues to rest on solid fundamentals.

2. Further action is needed to restore confidence. That is why today we agree on a comprehensive set of additional measures reflecting our strong determination to do whatever is required to overcome the present difficulties and take the necessary steps for the completion of our economic and monetary union. We fully support the ECB in its action to maintain price stability in the euro area. Sustainable public finances and structural reforms for growth

Sustainable public finances and structural reforms for growth

3. The European Union must improve its growth and employment outlook, as outlined in the growth agenda agreed by the European Council on 23 October 2011. We reiterate our full commitment to implement the country specific recommendations made under the first European Semester and on focusing public spending on growth areas.

4. All Member States of the euro area are fully determined to continue their policy of fiscal consolidation and structural reforms. A particular effort will be required of those Member States who are experiencing tensions in sovereign debt markets.

5. We welcome the important steps taken by Spain to reduce its budget deficit, restructure its banking sector and reform product and labour markets, as well as the adoption of a constitutional balanced budget amendment. Strictly implementing budgetary adjustment as planned is key, includ-

ing at regional level, to fulfil the commitments of the stability and growth Pact and the strengthening of the fiscal framework by developing lower level legislation to make the constitutional amendment fully operative. Further action is needed to increase growth so as to reduce the unacceptable high level of unemployment. Actions should include enhancing labour market changes to increase flexibility at firm level and employability of the labour force and other reforms to improve competitiveness, specially extending the reforms in the service sector.

6. We welcome Italy's plans for growth enhancing structural reforms and the fiscal consolidation strategy, as set out in the letter sent to the Presidents of the European Council and the Commission and call on Italy to present as a matter of urgency an ambitious timetable for these reforms. We commend Italy's commitment to achieve a balanced budget by 2013 and a structural budget surplus in 2014, bringing about a reduction in gross government debt to 113% of GDP in 2014, as well as the foreseen introduction of a balanced budget rule in the constitution by mid 2012.

Italy will now implement the proposed structural reforms to increase competitiveness by cutting red tape, abolishing minimum tariffs in professional services and further liberalising local public services and utilities. We note Italy's commitment to reform labour legislation and in particular the dismissal rules and procedures and to review the currently fragmented unemployment benefit system by the end of 2011, taking into account the budgetary constraints. We take note of the plan to increase the retirement age to 67 years by 2026 and recommend the definition by the end of the year of the process to achieve this objective.

We support Italy's intention to review structural funds programs by reprioritising projects and focussing on education, employment, digital agenda and railways/networks with the aim of improving the conditions to enhance growth and tackle the regional divide.

We invite the Commission to provide a detailed assessment of the measures and to monitor their implementation, and the Italian authorities to provide in a timely way all the information necessary for such an assessment.

Countries under adjustment programme

7. We reiterate our determination to continue providing support to all countries under programmes until they have regained market access, provided they fully implement those programmes.

8. Concerning the programme countries, we are pleased with the progress made by Ireland in the full implementation of its adjustment programme which is delivering positive results. Portugal is also making good progress with its programme and is determined to continue undertaking measures to underpin fiscal sustainability and improve competitiveness. We invite both countries to keep up their efforts, to stick to the agreed targets and stand ready to take any additional measure required to reach those targets.

9. We welcome the decision by the Eurogroup on the disbursement of the 6th tranche of the EU-IMF support programme for Greece. We look forward to the conclusion of a sustainable and credible new EU-IMF multiannual programme by the end of the year.

10. The mechanisms for the monitoring of implementation of the Greek programme must be strengthened, as requested by the Greek government. The ownership of the programme is Greek

and its implementation is the responsibility of the Greek authorities. In the context of the new programme, the Commission, in cooperation with the other Troika partners, will establish for the duration of the programme a monitoring capacity on the ground, including with the involvement of national experts, to work in close and continuous cooperation with the Greek government and the Troika to advise and offer assistance in order to ensure the timely and full implementation of the reforms. It will assist the Troika in assessing the conformity of measures which will be taken by the Greek government within the commitments of the programme. This new role will be laid down in the Memorandum of Understanding. To facilitate the efficient use of the sizeable official loans for the recapitalization of Greek banks, the governance of the Hellenic Financial Stability Fund (HFSF) will be strengthened in agreement with the Greek government and the Troika.

11. We fully support the Task Force on technical assistance set up by the Commission.

12. The Private Sector Involvement (PSI) has a vital role in establishing the sustainability of the Greek debt. Therefore we welcome the current discussion between Greece and its private investors to find a solution for a deeper PSI. Together with an ambitious reform programme for the Greek economy, the PSI should secure the decline of the Greek debt to GDP ratio with an objective of reaching 120% by 2020. To this end we invite Greece, private investors and all parties concerned to develop a voluntary bond exchange with a nominal discount of 50% on notional Greek debt held by private investors. The Euro zone Member States would contribute to the PSI package up to 30 bn euro. On that basis, the official sector stands ready to provide additional programme financing of up to 100 bn euro until 2014, including the required recapitalisation of Greek banks. The new programme should be agreed by the end of 2011 and the exchange of bonds should be implemented at the beginning of 2012. We call on the IMF to continue to contribute to the financing of the new Greek programme.

13. Greece commits future cash flows from project Helios or other privatisation revenue in excess of those already included in the adjustment programme to further reduce indebtedness of the Hellenic Republic by up to 15 billion euros with the aim of restoring the lending capacity of the EFSF.

14. Credit enhancement will be provided to underpin the quality of collateral so as to allow its continued use for access to Eurosystem liquidity operations by Greek banks.

15. As far as our general approach to private sector involvement in the euro area is concerned, we reiterate our decision taken on 21 July 2011 that Greece requires an exceptional and unique solution.

16. All other euro area Member States solemnly reaffirm their inflexible determination to honour fully their own individual sovereign signature and all their commitments to sustainable fiscal conditions and structural reforms. The euro area Heads of State or Government fully support this determination as the credibility of all their sovereign signatures is a decisive element for ensuring financial stability in the euro area as a whole.

Stabilisation mechanisms

17. The ratification process of the revised EFSF has now been completed in all euro area Member States and the Eurogroup has agreed on the implementing guidelines on primary and secondary market interventions, precautionary arrangements and bank recapitalisation. The decisions we took concerning the EFSF on 21 July are thus fully operational. All tools available will be used in an effective way to ensure financial stability in the euro area. As stated in the implementing

guidelines, strict conditionality will apply in case of new (precautionary) programmes in line with IMF practices. The Commission will carry out enhanced surveillance of the Member States concerned and report regularly to the Eurogroup.

18. We agree that the capacity of the extended EFSF shall be used with a view to maximizing the available resources in the following framework:
    • the objective is to support market access for euro area Member States faced with market pressures and to ensure the proper functioning of the euro area sovereign debt market, while fully preserving the high credit standing of the EFSF. These measures are needed to ensure financial stability and provide sufficient ringfencing to fight contagion;
    • this will be done without extending the guarantees underpinning the facility and within the rules of the Treaty and the terms and conditions of the current framework agreement, operating in the context of the agreed instruments, and entailing appropriate conditionality and surveillance.

19. We agree on two basic options to leverage the resources of the EFSF:
    • providing credit enhancement to new debt issued by Member States, thus reducing the funding cost. Purchasing this risk insurance would be offered to private investors as an option when buying bonds in the primary market;
    • maximising the funding arrangements of the EFSF with a combination of resources from private and public financial institutions and investors, which can be arranged through Special Purpose Vehicles. This will enlarge the amount of resources available to extend loans, for bank recapitalization and for buying bonds in the primary and secondary markets.

20. The EFSF will have the flexibility to use these two options simultaneously, deploying them depending on the specific objective pursued and on market circumstances. The leverage effect of each option will vary, depending on their specific features and market conditions, but could be up to four or five.

21. We call on the Eurogroup to finalise the terms and conditions for the implementation of these modalities in November, in the form of guidelines and in line with the draft terms and conditions prepared by the EFSF.

22. In addition, further enhancement of the EFSF resources can be achieved by cooperating even more closely with the IMF. The Eurogroup, the Commission and the EFSF will work on all possible options.

Banking system

23. We welcome the agreement reached today by the members of the European Council on bank recapitalisation and funding (see Annex 2).

Economic and fiscal coordination and surveillance

24. The legislative package on economic governance strengthens economic and fiscal policy coordination and surveillance. After it enters into force in January 2012 it will be strictly implemented as part of the European Semester. We call for rigorous surveillance by the Commission and the Council, including through peer pressure, and the active use of the existing and new instruments available. We also recall our commitments made in the framework of the Euro Plus Pact.

25. Being part of a monetary union has far reaching implications and implies a much closer coordination and surveillance to ensure stability and sustainability of the whole area. The current crisis shows the need to address this much more effectively. Therefore, while strengthening our crisis tools within the euro area, we will make further progress in integrating economic and fiscal policies by reinforcing coordination, surveillance and discipline. We will develop the necessary policies to support the functioning of the single currency area.

26. More specifically, building on the legislative package just adopted, the European Semester and the Euro Plus Pact, we commit to implement the following additional measures at the national level:
    a. adoption by each euro area Member State of rules on balanced budget in structural terms translating the Stability and Growth Pact into national legislation, preferably at constitutional level or equivalent, by the end of 2012;
    b. reinforcement of national fiscal frameworks beyond the Directive on requirements for budgetary frameworks of the Member States. In particular, national budgets should be based on independent growth forecasts;
    c. invitation to national parliaments to take into account recommendations adopted at the EU level on the conduct of economic and budgetary policies;
    d. consultation of the Commission and other euro area Member States before the adoption of any major fiscal or economic policy reform plans with potential spillover effects, so as to give the possibility for an assessment of possible impact for the euro area as a whole;
    e. commitment to stick to the recommendations of the Commission and the relevant Commissioner regarding the implementation of the Stability and Growth Pact.

27. We also agree that closer monitoring and additional enforcement are warranted along the following lines:
    a. for euro area Member States in excessive deficit procedure, the Commission and the Council will be enabled to examine national draft budgets and adopt an opinion on them before their adoption by the relevant national parliaments. In addition, the Commission will monitor budget execution and, if necessary, suggest amendments in the course of the year;
    b. in the case of slippages of an adjustment programme closer monitoring and coordination of programme implementation will take place.

28. We look forward to the Commission's forthcoming proposal on closer monitoring to the Council and the European Parliament under Article 136 of the TFEU. In this context, we welcome the intention of the Commission to strengthen, in the Commission, the role of the competent Commissioner for closer monitoring and additional enforcement.

29. We will further strengthen the economic pillar of the Economic and Monetary Union and better coordinate macro- and micro-economic policies. Building on the Euro Plus Pact, we will improve competitiveness, thereby achieving further convergence of policies to promote growth and employment. Pragmatic coordination of tax policies in the euro area is a necessary element of stronger economic policy coordination to support fiscal consolidation and economic growth. Legislative work on the Commission proposals for a Common Consolidated Corporate Tax Base and for a Financial Transaction Tax is ongoing.

Governance structure of the euro area

30. To deal more effectively with the challenges at hand and ensure closer integration, the governance structure for the euro area will be strengthened, while preserving the integrity of the European Union as a whole.

31. We will thus meet regularly - at least twice a year- at our level, in Euro Summits, to provide strategic orientations on the economic and fiscal policies in the euro area. This will allow to better take into account the euro area dimension in our domestic policies.

32. The Eurogroup will, together with the Commission and the ECB, remain at the core of the daily management of the euro area. It will play a central role in the implementation by the euro area Member States of the European Semester. It will rely on a stronger preparatory structure.

33. More detailed arrangements are presented in Annex 1 to this paper.

Further integration

34. The euro is at the core of our European project. We will strengthen the economic union to make it commensurate with the monetary union.

35. We ask the President of the European Council, in close collaboration with the President of the Commission and the President of the Eurogroup, to identify possible steps to reach this end. The focus will be on further strengthening economic convergence within the euro area, improving fiscal discipline and deepening economic union, including exploring the possibility of limited Treaty changes. An interim report will be presented in December 2011 so as to agree on first orientations. It will include a roadmap on how to proceed in full respect of the prerogatives of the institutions. A report on how to implement the agreed measures will be finalised by March 2012.

Annex 1

Ten measures to improve the governance of the euro area

There is a need to strengthen economic policy coordination and surveillance within the euro area, to improve the effectiveness of decision making and to ensure more consistent communication. To this end, the following ten measures will be taken, while fully respecting the integrity of the EU as a whole:

1. There will be regular Euro Summit meetings bringing together the Heads of State or government (HoSG) of the euro area and the President of the Commission. These meetings will take place at least twice a year, at key moments of the annual economic governance circle; they will if possible take place after European Council meetings. Additional meetings can be called by the President of the Euro Summit if necessary. Euro Summits will define strategic orientations for the conduct of economic policies and for improved competitiveness and increased convergence in the euro area. The President of the Euro Summit will ensure the preparation of the Euro Summit, in close cooperation with the President of the Commission.

2. The President of the Euro Summit will be designated by the HoSG of the euro area at the same time the European Council elects its President and for the same term of office. Pending the next such election, the current President of the European Council will chair the Euro Summit meetings.

3. The President of the Euro Summit will keep the non euro area Member States closely informed of the preparation and outcome of the Summits. The President will also inform the European Parliament of the outcome of the Euro Summits.

4. As is presently the case, the Eurogroup will ensure ever closer coordination of the economic policies and promoting financial stability. Whilst respecting the powers of the EU institutions in

that respect, it promotes strengthened surveillance of Member States' economic and fiscal policies as far as the euro area is concerned. It will also prepare the Euro Summit meetings and ensure their follow up.

5. The President of the Eurogroup is elected in line with Protocol n°14 annexed to the Treaties. A decision on whether he/she should be elected among Members of the Eurogroup or be a full-time President based in Brussels will be taken at the time of the expiry of the mandate of the current incumbent. The President of the Euro Summit will be consulted on the Eurogroup work plan and may invite the President of the Eurogroup to convene a meeting of the Eurogroup, notably to prepare Euro Summits or to follow up on its orientations. Clear lines of responsibility and reporting between the Euro Summit, the Eurogroup and the preparatory bodies will be established.

6. The President of the Euro Summit, the President of the Commission and the President of the Eurogroup will meet regularly, at least once a month. The President of the ECB may be invited to participate. The Presidents of the supervisory agencies and the EFSF CEO / ESM Managing Director may be invited on an ad hoc basis.

7. Work at the preparatory level will continue to be carried out by the Eurogroup Working Group (EWG), drawing on expertise provided by the Commission. The EWG also prepares Eurogroup meetings. It should benefit from a more permanent sub-group consisting of alternates/officials representative of the Finance Ministers, meeting more frequently, working under the authority of the President of the EWG.

8. The EWG will be chaired by a full-time Brussels-based President. In principle, he/she will be elected at the same time as the chair of the Economic and Financial Committee.

9. The existing administrative structures (i.e. the Council General Secretariat and the EFC Secretariat) will be strengthened and co-operate in a well coordinated way to provide adequate support to the Euro Summit President and the President of the Eurogroup, under the guidance of the President of the EFC/EWG. External expertise will be drawn upon as appropriate, on an ad hoc basis.

10. Clear rules and mechanisms will be set up to improve communication and ensure more consistent messages. The President of the Euro Summit and the President of the Eurogroup shall have a special responsibility in this respect. The President of the Euro Summit together with the President of the Commission shall be responsible for communicating the decisions of the Euro Summit and the President of the Eurogroup together with the ECFIN Commissioner shall be responsible for communicating the decisions of the Eurogroup.

Annex 2

Consensus on banking package

1. Measures for restoring confidence in the banking sector (banking package) are urgently needed and are necessary in the context of strengthening prudential control of the EU banking sector. These measures should address:
   a. The need to ensure the medium-term funding of banks, in order to avoid a credit crunch and to safeguard the flow of credit to the real economy, and to coordinate measures to achieve this.
   b. The need to enhance the quality and quantity of capital of banks to withstand shocks and to demonstrate this enhancement in a reliable and harmonised way.

Term funding

1. Guarantees on bank liabilities would be required to provide more direct support for banks in accessing term funding (short-term funding being available at the ECB and relevant national central banks), where appropriate. This is also an essential part of the strategy to limit deleveraging actions.

2. A simple repetition of the 2008 experience with full national discretion in the setting-up of liquidity schemes may not provide a satisfactory solution under current market conditions. Therefore a truly coordinated approach at EU-level is needed regarding entry criteria, pricing and conditions. The Commission should urgently explore together with the EBA, EIB, ECB the options for achieving this objective and report to the EFC.

Capitalisation of banks

3. Capital target: There is broad agreement on requiring a significantly higher capital ratio of 9 % of the highest quality capital and after accounting for market valuation of sovereign debt exposures, both as of 30 September 2011, to create a temporary buffer, which is justified by the exceptional circumstances. This quantitative capital target will have to be attained by 30 June 2012, based on plans agreed with national supervisors and coordinated by EBA. This prudent valuation would not affect the relevant financial reporting rules. National supervisory authorities, under the auspices of the EBA, must ensure that banks' plans to strengthen capital do not lead to excessive deleveraging, including maintaining the credit flow to the real economy and taking into account current exposure levels of the group including their subsidiaries in all Member States, cognisant of the need to avoid undue pressure on credit extension in host countries or on sovereign debt markets.

4. **Financing of capital increase:** Banks should first use private sources of capital, including through restructuring and conversion of debt to equity instruments. Banks should be subject to constraints regarding the distribution of dividends and bonus payments until the target has been attained. If necessary, national governments should provide support , and if this support is not available, recapitalisation should be funded via a loan from the EFSF in the case of Eurozone countries.

State Aid

5. Any form of public support, whether at a national or EU-level, will be subject to the conditionality of the current special state aid crisis framework, which the Commission has indicated will be applied with the necessary proportionality in view of the systemic character of the crisis.

(Source: Consilium.Europa)

THE GLOBAL CLIMATE IN 2010

Extract from the UN World Meteorological Organization (WMO) report on the global climate in 2010, published in March 2011. The report—prepared annually since 2003 on the basis of three extensive temperature datatsets—said that the year 2010 was notable in that global surface temperature had "reached record values at the same level as in 1998 and 2005, consistent with the acceleration of the warming experienced over the last 50 years". In addition, "large and extended climate extremes were recorded in several parts of the world".

WMO statement on the status of the global climate in 2010

Global temperatures in 2010

Average global temperatures were estimated to be 0.53°C ± 0.09°C above the 1961-1990 annual average of 14°C. This makes 2010 tied for warmest year on record in records dating back to 1880. The 2010 nominal value of +0.53°C ranks just ahead of those of 2005 (+0.52°C) and 1998 (+0.51°C), although the differences between the three years are not statistically significant, due to uncertainties mainly associated with sampling the Earth's land and sea surface temperatures using only a finite number of observation sites, and the way estimates are interpolated between those sites. Data from the ECMWF* Interim Reanalysis (ERA) indicate that 2010 ranks as the world's second warmest year, with the difference between it and 2005 within the margin of uncertainty.

The decade 2001-2010 was also the warmest on record. Temperatures over the decade averaged 0.46°C above the 1961-1990 mean, 0.21°C warmer than the previous record decade 1991-2000. In turn, 1991-2000 was warmer than previous decades, consistent with a long-term warming trend.

*ECMWF: European Centre for Medium-Range Weather Forecasts.

(Source: World Meteorological Organization)

UNITED KINGDOM COALITION GOVERNMENT

(as at 31 December 2011)

Members of the Cabinet

Prime Minister, First Lord of the Treasury and Minister for the Civil Service	Rt Hon David Cameron MP (Con)
Deputy Prime Minister, Lord President of the Council (with special responsibility for political and constitutional reform)	Rt Hon Nick Clegg MP (LibDem)
First Secretary of State, Secretary of State for Foreign and Commonwealth Affairs	Rt Hon William Hague MP (Con)
Chancellor of the Exchequer	Rt Hon George Osborne MP (Con)
Lord Chancellor, Secretary of State for Justice	Rt Hon Kenneth Clarke QC MP (Con)
Secretary of State for the Home Department; and Minister for Women and Equalities	Rt Hon Theresa May MP (Con)
Secretary of State for Defence	Rt Hon Phillip Hammond MP (Con)
Secretary of State for Business, Innovation and Skills; and President of the Board of Trade	Rt Hon Dr Vincent Cable MP (LibDem)
Secretary of State for Work and Pensions	Rt Hon Iain Duncan Smith MP (Con)
Secretary of State for Energy and Climate Change	Rt Hon Chris Huhne MP (LibDem)
Secretary of State for Health	Rt Hon Andrew Lansley CBE MP (Con)
Secretary of State for Education	Rt Hon Michael Gove MP (Con)
Secretary of State for Communities and Local Government	Rt Hon Eric Pickles MP (Con)
Secretary of State for Transport	Rt Hon Justine Greening MP (Con)
Secretary of State for Environment, Food and Rural Affairs	Rt Hon Caroline Spelman MP (Con)
Secretary of State for International Development	Rt Hon Andrew Mitchell MP (Con)
Secretary of State for Culture, Olympics, Media and Sport	Rt Hon Jeremy Hunt MP (Con)
Secretary of State for Northern Ireland	Rt Hon Owen Paterson MP (Con)
Secretary of State for Scotland	Rt Hon Michael Moore MP (LibDem)
Secretary of State for Wales	Rt Hon Cheryl Gillan MP (Con)
Chief Secretary to the Treasury	Rt Hon Danny Alexander MP (LibDem)
Minister without Portfolio (Minister of State)	Rt Hon Baroness Warsi (Con)
Leader of the House of Lords, Chancellor of the Duchy of Lancaster	Rt Hon Lord Strathclyde (Con)

Also attending Cabinet meetings

Minister for the Cabinet Office and Paymaster General	Rt Hon Francis Maude MP (Con)
Minister of State - Cabinet Office (providing policy advice to the Prime Minister in the Cabinet Office)	Rt Hon Oliver Letwin MP (Con)
Minister of State (Universities and Science) - Department for Business, Innovation and Skills	Rt Hon David Willetts MP (Con)
Leader of the House of Commons, Lord Privy Seal	Rt Hon Sir George Young Bt MP (Con)
Parliamentary Secretary to the Treasury and Chief Whip	Rt Hon Patrick McLoughlin MP (Con)

Also invited to attend Cabinet meetings when required

Attorney-General	Rt Hon Dominic Grieve QC MP (Con)

UNITED STATES DEMOCRATIC ADMINISTRATION

(as at 31 December 2011)

President of the United States   Barack Obama

Members of the Cabinet

Vice President of the United States	Joseph R. Biden
Secretary of State	Hillary Rodham Clinton
Secretary of the Treasury	Timothy F. Geithner
Secretary of Defence	Leon E. Panetta
Attorney General and Head of Department of Justice	Eric H. Holder, Jr
Secretary of the Interior	Kenneth L. Salazar
Secretary of Agriculture	Thomas J. Vilsack
Secretary of Commerce	John E. Bryson
Secretary of Labour	Hilda L. Solis
Secretary of Health and Human Services	Kathleen Sebelius
Secretary of Housing and Urban Development	Shaun L.S. Donovan
Secretary of Transportation	Ray LaHood
Secretary of Energy	Steven Chu
Secretary of Education	Arne Duncan
Secretary of Veterans' Affairs	Eric K. Shinseki
Secretary of Homeland Security	Janet A. Napolitano

status of Cabinet-rank

White House Chief of Staff	Bill Daley
Administrator of Environmental Protection Agency	Lisa P. Jackson
Director of Office of Management and Budget	Jacob J. Lew
United States Trade Representative	Ambassador Ronald Kirk
United States Ambassador to the United Nations	Ambassador Susan Rice
Chairman of Council of Economic Advisers	Alan B. Krueger

THE EUROPEAN COMMISSION

(as at 31 December 2011)

The members of the Barroso Commission (2010-2014)

José Manuel Barroso (Portugal)	*President*
Catherine Ashton (UK)	*Vice-President; High Representative of the Union for Foreign Affairs and Security Policy*
Viviane Reding (Luxembourg)	*Vice-President; Justice, Fundamental Rights and Citizenship*
Joaquín Almunia (Spain)	*Vice-President; Competition*
Siim Kallas (Estonia)	*Vice-President; Transport*
Neelie Kroes (Netherlands)	*Vice-President; Digital Agenda*
Antonio Tajani (Italy)	*Vice-President; Industry and Entrepreneurship*
Maros Sefcovic (Slovakia)	*Vice President; Inter-Institutional Relations and Administration*
Olli Rehn (Finland)	*Vice President; Economic and Monetary Affairs and the Euro*
Janez Potocnik (Slovenia)	*Environment*
Andris Piebalgs (Latvia)	*Development*
Michel Barnier (France)	*Internal Market and Services*
Androulia Vassiliou (Cyprus)	*Education, Culture, Multilingualism and Youth*
Algirdas Semeta (Lithuania)	*Taxation and Customs Union, Audit and Anti-Fraud*
Karel De Gucht (Belgium)	*Trade*
John Dalli (Malta)	*Health and Consumer Policy*
Maire Geoghegan-Quinn (Ireland)	*Research, Innovation and Science*
Janusz Lewandowski (Poland)	*Financial Programming and Budget*
Maria Damanaki (Greece)	*Maritime Affairs and Fisheries*
Kristalina Georgieva (Bulgaria)	*International Co-operation, Humanitarian Aid and Crisis Response*
Günther Oettinger (Germany)	*Energy*
Johannes Hahn (Austria)	*Regional Policy*
Connie Hedegaard (Denmark)	*Climate Action*
Stefan Fule (Czech Republic)	*Enlargement and European Neighbourhood Policy*
Laszlo Andor (Hungary)	*Employment, Social Affairs and Inclusion*
Cecilia Malmström (Sweden)	*Home Affairs*
Dacian Ciolos (Romania)	*Agriculture and Rural Development*

NOBEL LAUREATES 2011

THE NOBEL PRIZE IN PHYSICS

Saul Perlmutter (one half of the prize), Brian P. Schmidt and Adam G. Riess
"for the discovery of the accelerating expansion of the Universe through observations of distant supernovae"

THE NOBEL PRIZE IN CHEMISTRY

Dan Shechtman
"for the discovery of quasicrystals"

THE NOBEL PRIZE IN PHYSIOLOGY OR MEDICINE

Bruce A. Beutler and Jules A. Hoffmann
"for their discoveries concerning the activation of innate immunity"
Ralph M. Steinman
"for his discovery of the dendritic cell and its role in adaptive immunity"

THE NOBEL PRIZE IN LITERATURE

Tomas Tranströmer
"because, through his condensed, translucent images, he gives us fresh access to reality"

THE NOBEL PEACE PRIZE

Ellen Johnson Sirleaf, Leymah Gbowee and Tawakkol Karman
"for their non-violent struggle for the safety of women and for women's rights to full participation in peace-building work"

THE PRIZE IN ECONOMIC SCIENCES

Thomas J. Sargent and Christopher A. Sims
"for their empirical research on cause and effect in the macroeconomy"

(*Source: Nobelprize.org.*)

INTERNATIONAL COMPARISONS: POPULATION, GDP AND GROWTH (2011)

The following table gives population, gross domestic product (GDP) and growth data for the main member states of the Organisation for Economic Co-operation and Development, plus selected other countries.

	Population		Gross Domestic Product	
	($ millions) 2010	Avg. annual % growth 2000-10	($ millions) 2010	Avg. annual % growth 2000-10
Algeria	35	1.5	159,426	3.8
Argentina	41	1.0	368,712	5.6
Australia	22	1.5	924,843	3.3
Austria	8	0.5	376,162	1.9
Bangladesh	164	1.6	100,076	5.9
Belgium	11	0.6	467,472	1.6
Brazil	195	1.1	2,087,890	3.7
Canada	34	1.0	1,574,052	2.0
Chile	17	1.1	203,443	4.0
China (excl Hong Kong)	1,338	0.6	5,878,629	10.8
Colombia	46	1.5	288,189	4.5
Denmark	6	0.4	310,405	0.9
Egypt	84	1.9	218,912	5.3
Finland	5	0.4	238,801	2.2
France	65	0.7	2,560,002	1.3
Germany	82	-0.1	3,309,669	1.0
Greece	11	0.4	304,865	2.9
Hungary	10	-0.2	130,419	1.9
India	1,171	1.4	1,729,010	8.0
Indonesia	233	1.2	706,558	5.3
Iran	74	1.4	331,015	5.4
Irish Republic	4	1.6	203,892	3.0
Italy	61	0.6	2,051,412	0.3
Japan	127	0.0	5,497,813	0.9
Kenya	41	2.6	31,409	4.3
South Korea	49	0.4	1,014,483	4.1
Malaysia	28	1.8	237,804	5.0
Mexico	109	1.0	1,039,662	2.2
Netherlands	17	0.4	783,413	1.6
New Zealand	4	1.2	126,679	2.6
Nigeria	158	2.4	193,669	6.7
Norway	5	0.8	414,462	1.8
Pakistan	173	2.3	174,799	5.1
Philippines	94	1.9	199,589	4.9
Poland	38	-0.1	468,585	4.3
Portugal	11	0.4	228,538	0.7
Russia	142	-0.3	1,479,819	5.4
South Africa	50	1.3	363,704	3.9
Spain	46	1.4	1,407,405	2.4
Sweden	9	0.6	458,004	2.2
Switzerland	8	0.8	523,772	1.9
Thailand	68	0.9	318,847	4.5
Turkey	76	1.3	735,264	4.7
United Kingdom	62	0.6	2,246,079	1.6
USA	310	0.9	14,582,400	1.9
Venezuela	29	1.7	387,852	4.5
Vietnam	88	1.3	103,572	7.5

(Source: World Bank, Washington, DC)

XX CHRONICLE OF 2011

1	**Brazil:** President Dilma Rousseff took office. **Hungary:** assumed the presidency of the EU, amidst international disquiet over the provisions of a new media law.
4	**Pakistan:** Salman Taseer, the governor of Punjab province and a prominent critic of the country's blasphemy laws, was assassinated in Islamabad by one of his own bodyguards. **Tunisia:** Mohammed Bouazizi, the street vendor, whose attempted self-immolation in December 2010 had sparked demonstrations against the government, died from his injuries, giving further impetus to the popular revolt.
5	**Algeria:** rioting began in Algiers in protest at price rises for staple foods, turning into general anti-government demonstrations across the north of the country in emulation of Tunisia's popular revolt. **Iraq:** Shia cleric Muqtada al-Sadr returned from three years of voluntary exile in Iran, after the Sadrist-dominated Iraqi National Alliance decided to support the coalition cabinet of Prime Minister Nouri al-Maliki that was formed in December 2010.
6	**Egypt:** at the start of Coptic Christmas, security was increased at the main Coptic Christian cathedral in Cairo, following the suicide bombing of a Coptic church in Alexandria in the early hours of 1 January.
8	**USA:** Democratic congresswoman Gabrielle Giffords was shot in the head at an open-air meeting near Tucson, Arizona. The assassination attempt on Giffords, in which six people died, raised concerns about the polarisation of political discourse in the USA.
9	**Sudan:** voting began in the referendum on independence for South Sudan. Preliminary results, after polls closed on 15 January, showed over 98 per cent in favour. **Thailand:** anti-government "Red Shirts" held the first demonstration in Bangkok since the state of emergency imposed in April 2010 had been lifted in December.
11	**USA:** a presidential commission delivered its report on the 2010 Gulf of Mexico oil spill, apportioning blame and calling for stricter regulation of deepwater drilling. **Brazil:** exceptionally heavy rains began in south-eastern Brazil; by the end of the month they had caused at least 800 deaths. **Tunisia:** popular protests reached the centre of Tunis as the "jasmine revolution" gathered strength.
12	**Australia:** serious flooding in the state of Queensland caused by exceptionally heavy rainfall reached Brisbane, the state capital. **China:** US defence secretary Robert Gates ended a visit to China that both demonstrated improved military contacts and underlined the growing capability of Chinese weaponry. **Lebanon:** the national unity government collapsed after Hezbullah withdrew its support.
13	**Mexico:** the government released a detailed database on drug-related murders since 2006. Of a total of almost 35,000 deaths, over 15,000 had occurred in 2010 alone. **USA:** William Daley became presidential chief of staff, replacing Rahm Emanuel, who had resigned in October 2010.
14	**Japan:** Prime Minister Naoto Kan reshuffled his cabinet to enhance his reform strategy to tackle Japan's chronic economic problems.

Tunisia: President Zine el-Abidine Ben Ali fled to Saudi Arabia, prompting popular rejoicing after weeks of protest.

Russia: oil company BP signed a share swap deal with Russia's Rosneft; the two companies would explore Rosneft's licence blocs in the Arctic Circle.

16 **France:** at a party congress, Marine Le Pen was elected to succeed her father, Jean-Marie Le Pen, as leader of the far-right National Front.

Haiti: Jean-Claude ("Baby Doc") Duvalier, Haiti's dictator from 1971 to 1986, unexpectedly returned from exile in France amidst growing tension over results of the first round of presidential elections, held on 28 November 2010, and was immediately charged with corruption and assassination.

17 **Israel:** Ehud Barak, the defence minister, announced that he was leaving Labour (a party within the ruling coalition) to form a new faction, Atzmaut ("Independence").

Oman: defying a ban on demonstrations, several hundred young men protested in the government district of the capital, Muscat, against corruption and price rises.

Somalia: the annual report of the International Maritime Bureau showed that piracy off Somalia was increasing; 49 vessels were hijacked in 2010.

Tunisia: Prime Minister Mohamed Ghannouchi formed a government of national unity, including former opposition members.

18 **Iraq:** a suicide bombing outside a police recruitment centre in Tikrit killed at least 60 people; a further attack occurred at a police headquarters in Baquba the following day.

19 **India:** a cabinet reshuffle of the United Progressive Alliance (UPA) coalition was announced to defuse criticisms of steep price rises and corruption scandals.

Vietnam: the Communist Party of Vietnam congress concluded with the election of a new general secretary. In his closing remarks, outgoing general secretary Nong Duc Manh admitted that he had "not met the expectations" of the people.

20 **Environment:** the UN World Meteorological Organisation announced that 2010 ranked as the warmest year on record (together with 2005 and 1998), and that Arctic sea ice cover in December 2010 was the lowest on record.

Sri Lanka: a senior UN official launched an appeal for flood victims after touring affected areas of eastern Sri Lanka. Exceptionally heavy rains since December had affected over 1 million people.

Yemen: demonstrations began against proposals to guarantee a further presidential term for Ali Abdullah Saleh. These developed into nationwide protests demanding his departure, organised by the Joint Meeting Parties opposition coalition.

21 **Albania:** three men were shot dead during anti-government protests by around 20,000 people in Tirana in support of fresh elections.

Algeria: as popular protests continued, leftist parties and trade unions formed the National Co-ordination for Change and Democracy.

Iran: talks in Istanbul between Iran and the P5+1 group on Iran's nuclear programme ended in stalemate.

22 **China:** President Hu Jintao ended a ceremony-laden state visit to the USA that resulted in trade and investment contracts worth US$45 billion.

23 **Belgium:** more than 30,000 demonstrators marched in Brussels calling for national unity, after negotiations to form a new government broke down again on 6 January. Belgium had been without a government since the legislative elections of June 2010.

Central African Republic: presidential elections were won by the incumbent, François Bozizé, but opposition candidates denounced the result as fraudulent.

Ireland: the governing coalition collapsed as the junior partner, the Green Party, withdrew in frustration at turmoil within the senior coalition partner, Fianna Fail.

Portugal: President Aníbal Cavaco Silva was re-elected to a second term. Meanwhile, the country faced pressure to seek an EU rescue package.

Palestine: Qatar-based satellite television station Al-Jazeera, and the UK's *Guardian* newspaper, began releasing leaked documents relating to the Israel-Palestine conflict that showed Palestinian negotiators had in 2008 offered major concessions over Israeli-occupied East Jerusalem.

24   **Russia:** a suicide bombing at Moscow's Domodedovo airport caused the deaths of 37 people; it was attributed to extremists from the North Caucasus.

25   **Egypt:** a "day of rage" called by a coalition of opposition groups on a public holiday in honour of the police developed into nationwide popular demonstrations calling for the removal of President Mohammed Hosni Mubarak.

Lebanon: Najib Mikati became prime minister, with the backing of Hezbullah, replacing Saad Hariri.

USA: President Barack Obama delivered his State of the Union speech to a Congress still shocked by the shooting of Gabrielle Giffords. In addition to the official Republican response, the Tea Party organised its own response speech, delivered by Michelle Bachman.

USA: the Congressional Budget Office forecast a budget deficit in 2011 of $1,480 billion.

26   **Afghanistan:** the National Assembly convened after several days of intense negotiations with President Hamid Karzai, who had earlier decided to postpone its inauguration, ostensibly to allow investigation of alleged electoral fraud but widely believed to be a ploy to continue ruling by decree.

Uganda: prominent gay rights activist, David Kato, was murdered in Kampala.

27   **USA:** reporting on the financial crisis of 2007-10, the Financial Crisis Inquiry Commission concluded that it had been "avoidable" and caused by "widespread failures in financial regulation".

28   **Egypt:** as anti-government protests gathered momentum, demonstrators ignored the curfew that had been announced in Cairo, Alexandria and Suez.

31   **Côte d'Ivoire:** the African Union announced a mediation panel consisting of five African presidents to resolve the crisis resulting from President Laurent Gbagbo's refusal to step down after losing the November 2010 elections to Alassane Ouattara.

Egypt: President Mubarak appointed a new cabinet as calls for his resignation continued during massive protests in Cairo and major cities.

Indonesia: pop star Nazril Irham (known as Ariel) was sentenced to three-and-a-half years in prison for violating the 2008 anti-pornography laws after a sex tapes scandal.

Niger: presidential and legislative elections were held, in the context of the 12-month transition to democracy following the February 2010 coup.

FEBRUARY

1   **Jordan:** King Abdullah II dismissed the government of Samir Rifai and appointed Marouf Bakhit as prime minister in response to month-long protests.

2   **Australia:** following January's floods, Queensland was hit by cyclone Yasi.

Egypt: protesters continued their occupation of Tahrir Square in Cairo, resisting attempts by regime supporters to drive them out in the "battle of the camels".

India: Andimuthu Raja, a former telecommunications minister, was arrested in connection with a corruption scandal involving the sale of licences for mobile networks that had potentially cost the government $38 billion.

3 **Haiti:** election officials reversed preliminary presidential election results, giving Michel Martelly and not Jude Celestin the right to contest a second round against Mirlande Manigat.

Yemen: a "day of rage" saw 20,000 protesters in Sana'a calling for the departure of President Ali Abdullah Saleh.

4 **Burma:** the outgoing prime minister, Thein Sein, became the first civilian president of Burma after nearly 50 years of military rule.

EU: Most European leaders objected to proposals from France and Germany at an EU summit in Brussels for tighter co-ordination of fiscal and social policies in return for bailing out troubled eurozone economies through the European Financial Stability Facility.

Russia: Chechen Islamist leader Doku Umarov claimed responsibility for the Domodedovo airport suicide bombing.

6 **Cape Verde:** the ruling PAICV won elections to the National Assembly.

Kuwait: the interior minister resigned over revelations about torture in prisons.

Nepal: Jhala Nath Khanal became prime minister, after a successful election was finally held in the Constituent Assembly.

Tunisia: in response to demands by protesters, the former ruling Constitutional Democratic Rally (RCD) was suspended.

7 **Japan:** in an escalation of the territorial dispute with Russia over the Northern Territories/Southern Kurile Islands, Prime Minister Naoto Kan called a recent visit to the islands by Russia's President Medvedev "an unforgivable outrage".

Sudan: official results showed that 98.83 per cent of 3.9 million registered voters in the 10 southern provinces had approved independence in January's referendum.

8 **China:** the UN Food and Agriculture Organisation issued an alert that the drought affecting China could threaten the country's wheat crop.

North and South Korea: military delegations met in Panmunjom in the DMZ, but the talks quickly collapsed.

9 **Somalia:** in a sign of the increased range of Somali piracy, the *Irene LS*, a Greek-flagged super tanker, was captured by Somali pirates more than 1,600 km from Somalia.

Sudan: a rebel general launched renewed attacks in the border region of Sudan and South Sudan, breaking a ceasefire agreement with the South's armed forces, the SPLA.

10 **Bangladesh:** a second post-mortem ordered by the High Court showed that a girl who died after a public flogging imposed by a Sharia court had perished from internal bleeding.

North Korea: officials admitted that foot and mouth disease had broken out, threatening severe food shortages.

Pakistan: a teenage suicide bomber killed 31 soldiers at a military base in Mardan, north-west Pakistan.

Portugal: as yields rose, the ECB intervened to buy Portuguese government bonds.

11 **Egypt:** President Mohammed Hosni Mubarak finally stepped down after weeks of mass protest against his rule. The military took over.

Yemen: daily protests began, inspired by the fall of the Egyptian regime, calling for the departure of President Saleh.

USA: a proposal by Republican governor of Wisconsin, Scott Walker, to curtail union rights within a proposal to address the state's budget deficit prompted mass popular protests.

12 **Algeria:** large pro-democracy demonstrations were held

Italy: the government declared a humanitarian emergency after several thousand Tunisian migrants had arrived on the island of Lampedusa.

13 **Chad:** the first National Assembly elections since April 2002 were won by the ruling Patriotic Salvation Movement (MPS) of President Idriss Déby Itno and its allies.

Mexico: drug gang members murdered the most senior intelligence official of Nuevo Leon state in Monterrey.

14 **Ecuador:** at the end of an 18-year lawsuit, a judge ruled that oil firm Chevron was responsible for contamination of the Amazon basin dating back to the 1960s and levied more than $18 billion in fines and damages.

Iran: opposition supporters marched in Tehran.

USA: President Barack Obama presented a $3,730 billion budget request for fiscal 2012 that included proposals for $1,100 billion deficit reduction over 10 years.

15 **Italy:** Prime Minister Silvio Berlusconi was indicted on charges of paying for sex with an underage girl, Karima El Mahroug (aka Ruby Rubacuori).

Libya: protests against Colonel Moamar Kadhafi began in Bengazi.

18 **Bahrain:** security forces fired on demonstrators in Manama; protests against the ruling family had begun on 14 February and continued until the end of the month.

Palestine: in the first veto exercised by the Obama administration, the USA vetoed a UN Security Council resolution that declared illegal the Israeli settlements in Palestinian territories.

Uganda: President Yoweri Museveni won re-election with an increased majority for a fourth consecutive term; legislative elections the same day were won by Museveni's National Resistance Movement.

19 **Libya:** a "day of revolt" was held as anti-Kadhafi protests spread across the east of the country and moved towards Tripoli. The regime deployed tanks and fighter jets to suppress the protests.

Zimbabwe: 46 activists were arrested after viewing a video on anti-government protests in Tunisia and Egypt and charged with treason.

20 **Afghanistan:** allegations by local officials surfaced that an ISAF operation had killed 64 civilians, including 29 children, in Kunar province.

China: an anonymous online campaign calling for popular protests mirroring the "jasmine revolution" in North Africa prompted a heavy response from police and censors.

Germany: state legislative elections in Hamburg produced a crushing defeat for the ruling CDU.

Iceland: President Olafur Ragnar Grimsson vetoed the government's revised bill to compensate the UK and Netherlands for bailing out investors in the collapsed Icesave bank.

Morocco: there were street demonstrations in Rabat, Casablanca, Tangier and other cities in support of demands for a democratic constitution, an end to corruption and the dismissal of the government.

21 **DRC:** in a landmark case, a court sentenced a militia leader, Lieutenant-Colonel Kibibi Mutware, to 20 years' imprisonment for crimes against humanity, having found him guilty of ordering mass rape by his troops.

Germany: Defence Minister Karl-Theodor zu Guttenberg relinquished the title of doctor after accusations that he had plagiarised parts of his 2006 doctoral thesis.

India: an appeals court upheld the conviction of Ajmal Kasab for his part in the 2008 attacks on Mumbai.

22   **Cambodia and Thailand:** agreed to allow ASEAN to send military observers to the disputed border area near the Preah Vihear temple where recent exchange of fire had occurred.

Kosovo: formed a new government, with Hashim Thaci approved for a second term as prime minister.

Libya: Colonel Kadhafi made a brief television appearance in Tripoli to dispel rumours that he had fled to Venezuela.

New Zealand: an earthquake devastated parts of Christchurch in what Prime Minister John Key described as the country's "darkest day".

Somalia: pirates killed four US citizens whom they had taken hostage on a private yacht, the *SV Quest,* as US forces stormed the captured vessel.

23   **Brazil:** federal prosecutors opened an investigation into former President Lula da Silva for alleged mis-spending of around $3.5 billion of public funds in 2004.

Saudi Arabia: a major spending package announced by the king was seen as an attempt to avert popular unrest.

24   **Algeria:** the state of emergency in force since 1992 was lifted, as had been promised on 3 February by President Abdelaziz Bouteflika, but large pro-democracy protests continued.

25   **China:** Railways Minister Liu Zhijun was dismissed following a corruption investigation.

Ireland: in an early general election the opposition Fine Gael, led by Enda Kenny, won an historic victory over Fianna Fáil.

Iraq: in imitation of the revolutionary movements in North Africa, Internet groups called for a "revolution of Iraqi rage" and protests were held throughout the country.

26   **Oman:** a minor cabinet reshuffle by Sultan Qaboos bin Said al-Said failed to halt demonstrations, with serious clashes occurring in Sohar, an industrial town north of Muscat.

27   **DRC:** the home of President Joseph Kabila was attacked in an apparent assassination or coup attempt.

France: Michèle Alliot-Marie lost the post of foreign and European affairs minister to Alain Juppé after criticism of her response to the Tunisian revolution and revelations that she had enjoyed holidays in Tunisia at the expense of prominent Tunisians.

Tunisia: after a large protest rally, Mohamed Ghannouchi, head of the government of national unity, announced his resignation; he was replaced by Beji Caid-el Sebsi.

28   **Belarus:** Ales Mikhalevich, an opposition leader arrested after December's protests, said that he had been tortured during his detention.

Yemen: the opposition, represented by the Joint Meeting Parties, rejected a proposal from President Ahmed Ali Abdullah Saleh to form a unity government.

MARCH

1   **Afghanistan:** NATO helicopters opened fire on group of boys, having mistaken them for Taliban, killing nine out of the 10 children and provoking outrage in Afghanistan.

Germany: Karl-Theodor zu Guttenberg resigned as defence minister and from his seat in the Bundestag over the scandal arising from allegations that he had plagiarised parts of his doctoral thesis.

India: a court in Gujarat sentenced 11 Muslim men to death and 20 to life imprisonment for the deaths of 59 Hindu activists in a fire at a train station in 2002.

Iran: protesters against the arrests in February of opposition figures Hossein Moussavi and Mehdi Karrubi were dispersed by police.

Libya: as fighting continued, and a refugee crisis caused by Libyans fleeing to Tunisia and Egypt intensified, the UN suspended Libya from its Human Rights Council (UNHRC) and the International Criminal Court (ICC) began investigating possible crimes against humanity committed by Libya's leaders.

2   **Pakistan:** the minister for minorities, Shahbaz Bhatti, was shot dead in Islamabad; like the Punjab governor assassinated in January, Bhatti had been a critic of the blasphemy laws.

USA: the US army laid a further 22 charges against Bradley Manning, the former intelligence analyst accused of supplying the archive of US military and diplomatic files to WikiLeaks.

3   **Egypt:** the prime minister, Air Marshal Ahmed Shafiq, resigned; President Mubarak had appointed him shortly before his own resignation on 11 February. Shafiq was replaced by Essam Sharaf.

India: the Supreme Court ordered the head of the anti-corruption commission (the CVC) to resign, because he faced corruption charges.

Wales: a referendum (on a turnout of 35.2 per cent) approved the granting of additional legislative powers to the Welsh Assembly.

4   **Iraq:** anti-government protests were held in Baghdad for the second consecutive Friday.

Samoa: in elections to the Fono (legislature), the ruling Human Rights Protection Party retained its majority.

Somalia: officials said that at least 50 AU peacekeepers from AMISOM had been killed during a major offensive aiming to drive the Islamist al Shabaab militia out of central and southern areas of the country.

Saudi Arabia: anti-government protests were held in Riyadh and in the eastern regions by minority Shias.

Turkey: demonstrators marched in protest at the arrests on 3 March of journalists suspected of membership of the illegal Ergenekon organisation.

6   **Estonia:** legislative elections saw gains for the ruling coalition parties, the Estonian Reform party (ER) and the Union of Pro Patria and Res Publica (IRPL).

Ireland: the Fine Gael and Labour Party leaders announced an agreement on the formation of a coalition government, with Fine Gale leader Enda Kenny as Taoiseach.

Japan: the foreign minister, Seiji Maehara, resigned after admitting having accepted campaign donations from a Korean-born resident of Japan.

Lebanon: there were protests against the sectarian political system in Lebanon, with slogans echoing those of demonstrators in Tunisia and Egypt.

Libya: Colonel Kadhafi's forces launched a counter-offensive against the rebels, pushing them back to Benghazi in a rapid advance along the coast. The UK, France and the Arab League endorsed the imposition of a no-fly zone as Kadhafi warned that his forces would show no mercy to the rebels.

7   **Egypt:** a new interim council of ministers was appointed under Essam Sharaf, who had replaced the Mubarak-appointed Air Marshal Ahmed Shafiq on 3 March.

USA: trials of inmates at the Guantanamo Bay prison camp by "military commission" were allowed to resume, having been suspended by executive order of the president in January 2009.

8   **Egypt:** sectarian violence broke out in Cairo suburbs when Coptic Christians protested against the burning down of a church by Muslims on 4 March.

Federated States of Micronesia: elections were held to the 14-seat Congress (legislature).

Iran: Akbar Hashemi Rafsanjani, the former president and a critic of current president, Mahmoud Ahmadinejad, was removed as chairman of the Assembly of Experts.

Kosovo: talks with Serbian representatives opened in Brussels.

Kuwait: in the first demonstration of its kind, around 1,000 people called for greater democracy in a protest in Kuwait city.

Pakistan: the Pakistani Taliban detonated a bomb near a police station in Faisalabad killing 25; the next day a suicide bombing killed 37 members of an anti-Taliban militia in Peshawar.

9   **Morocco:** King Mohammed VI announced constitutional reform plans in response to pro-democracy protests.

Tunisia: a court dissolved the former ruling Constitutional Democratic Rally (RCD), which had been suspended in February. The banned opposition Ennahda party, an Islamist party, had been formally legalised on 1 March.

UAE: intellectuals and human rights activists petitioned President Sheikh Khalifa bin Zayed al-Nahyan for free elections and parliamentary democracy.

10   **Afghanistan:** among a number of high profile attacks during March, the police chief of Kunduz province was killed by a Taliban suicide bomber.

Environment: a UN Environment Programme report concluded that colony collapse disorder (CCD) among honey bees was becoming a global phenomenon.

Tibet: the Dalai Lama announced his intention to resign as leader of Tibet's government-in-exile, based in Dharamsala in India, and devolve his authority to an elected politician.

Zimbabwe: bringing the governing coalition close to collapse, President Mugabe's ZANU-PF ensured that the MDC lost control of the post of speaker of the House of Assembly and a ministerial post.

11   **Azerbaijan:** student groups participating in a "great people's day" anti-government demonstration, and opposition parties protesting on 12 March, met stern repression by the police.

Côte d'Ivoire: Laurent Gbagbo refused AU demands to step down in favour of Alassane Ouattara as heavy fighting between their supporters continued.

Japan: a magnitude-9 earthquake triggered a tsunami that devastated Japan's northeast coastal region and damaged nuclear reactors at the Fukushima power complex.

Palestine: five members of a Jewish settler family in the West Bank were murdered as they slept. The Palestinian National Authority condemned the murders. Israel immediately announced the construction of new West Bank settlements.

USA: the Republican governor of Wisconsin, Scott Walker, succeeded in enacting a controversial measure to curb the bargaining rights of public sector workers.

12   **Japan:** the building housing reactor No. 1 at the Fukushima power complex was destroyed in a hydrogen explosion, raising fears that fuel rods in the reactor's core could melt down.

Niger: Mahamadou Issoufou, an opposition leader, won a run-off election (after a first round on 31 January) to become president.

13   **Benin:** the president, Yayi Boni, won a second five-year term; the results of the elections were confirmed, despite opposition claims of fraud.

Oman: responding to a wave of protests, Sultan Qaboos bin Said al Said granted legislative and audit powers to an advisory body, the council of Oman, and announced improved popular economic benefits.

Russia: The ruling United Russia party won elections to 12 regional legislatures, but by a slimmer margin than expected.

Somalia: the Indian navy recaptured the Mozambique-flagged *Vega 5* in the Arabian Sea. Since being hijacked in December 2010, the *Vega-5* had been used as a mother ship for pirate attacks between East Africa and India.

Sudan: the SPLM, the ruling party of South Sudan, suspended talks with the government over preparations for South Sudan's independence, accusing it of supporting various rebel militias that were attacking the southern government's armed forces.

14 **China:** the fourth session of the 11th National People's Congress closed. The NPC approved the draft 12th five-year plan, which sought to increase domestic demand in order to prevent overheating of the economy.

Greece: the third tranche of the emergency loan package from the EU and IMF, approved in May 2010, was disbursed to Greece; eurozone members had extended the repayment period for the loan and lowered the interest rate paid on it, at a meeting on 11 March.

Japan: the building housing reactor No. 3 at the Fukushima complex exploded. There was a further explosion the following day at the pool containing the spent fuel rods of No. 4.

15 **Afghanistan:** in testimony to the armed services committee of the UN Senate, General David Petraeus, US commander of coalition troops in Afghanistan, confirmed the start of US troop withdrawals in July but warned that progress against the Taliban was "fragile and reversible".

Algeria: responding to pro-democracy protests, President Abdelaziz Bouteflika announced plans for possible constitutional reforms.

Bahrain: the king, Sheikh Hamad al-Khalifa, declared a three-month period of martial law in response to continued anti-government protests; the announcement followed the arrival in Bahrain, on 14 March, of 1,500 troops and police from Saudi Arabia and the UAE.

Pakistan: a Christian man serving a life sentence for infringing the Islamic blasphemy law died in prison in Karachi.

16 **Japan:** Emperor Akihito made a rare television appearance to raise morale in the face of the tsunami disaster.

17 **Armenia:** an opposition rally summoned by the Armenian National Congress called for new elections.

UN: the Security Council approved Resolution 1973 (2011) authorising a no-fly zone and action to protect civilians in Libya.

Pakistan: missiles fired from two US pilotless drone aircraft killed 44 civilians in North Waziristan agency on the Afghanistan border.

18 **Haiti:** the former president, Jean-Bertrand Aristide, returned from exile in South Africa where he had been living since his removal from power in February 2004.

Japan: the central banks of G-7 countries made a rare co-ordinated intervention in currency markets to stabilise the soaring value of the Japanese yen.

Syria: in response to protest calls on online forums, serious unrest erupted after Friday prayers in Damascus, Deraa, Homs and Bnaiyas.

Yemen: during continued anti-government protests, around 50 demonstrators were killed in Sana'a.

19 **Egypt:** a referendum approved constitutional amendments that triggered early elections to be held before the end of 2011.

Libya: French warplanes launched attacks on Kadhafi's forces.

Mexico: the US ambassador to Mexico resigned over a diplomatic cable, published by WikiLeaks in December 2010, in which he had criticised the Mexican government for its failure to tackle drug cartels.

20 **USA:** Terry Jones, a fundamentalist pastor in Florida, held a "trial" of the Koran and publicly burned a copy of the Muslim holy book, leading to violent protests in a number of countries including Afghanistan and Pakistan.

23 **India:** the prime minister, Manmohan Singh, defended his government against allegations of a new corruption scandal and rejected demands from the opposition BJP that he resign.

Israel: in the first attack in Jerusalem since 2004, a bomb at a bus stop killed one person after Israeli jets had launched air raids in Gaza in retaliation for rockets and mortars fired by Palestinian militants earlier in March.

Portugal: José Sócrates resigned as prime minister after his government lost a vote on austerity measures.

Yemen: the House of Representatives granted President Ali Abdullah Saleh emergency powers for 30 days; the measure had last been used in 1994.

USA: one of five US soldiers accused of killing Afghan civilians for sport received a 24-year prison sentence after pleading guilty. Jeremy Morlock escaped life imprisonment because of a plea bargain arrangement.

24 **Jordan:** as part of continued protests demanding political reforms, a camp was set up in Amman, leading to violence in the capital.

Ukraine: a former president, Leonid Kuchma, was charged with abuse of office in relation to the murder in 2000 of investigative journalist Georgy Gongadze.

25 **Canada:** the minority Conservative government lost a vote of no-confidence in Parliament; elections were scheduled for 2 May.

Mauritania: a demonstration in Nouakchott calling for political and economic reforms, and organised through online social media, was broken up by the police.

Syria: more Friday protests occurred, particularly in Deraa where the funeral processions of those killed by security forces in earlier demonstrations turned into anti-regime protests.

26 **Australia:** the ruling ALP lost state elections in New South Wales.

Libya: assisted by NATO-led air strikes against Kadhafi's forces, the Libyan rebels launched a new offensive to the west from their Benghazi stronghold.

UK: in one of the largest demonstrations in recent British history, a march was staged in central London to protest against government policy to cut spending.

27 **France:** in the second round of cantonal elections for half of the seats in departmental general councils, the ruling UMP saw substantial losses, whilst the opposition Socialist Party made gains; the right-wing National Front obtained almost 12 per cent of the vote.

Germany: the ruling CDU lost state elections in Baden-Württemberg, which it had governed since 1953.

28 **Bosnia & Herzegovina:** the EU high representative quashed an election commission ruling relating to the election of a new presidency in the FBiH (the Bosniak-Croat component of the state).

Libya: US President Barack Obama made a speech explaining why the USA should be involved in the Libyan conflict.

29 **Iraq:** attacks on provincial council offices in Tikrit by suicide bombers killed over 50 people.

Syria: the cabinet resigned in an apparent attempt to defuse the protests, as thousands gathered in pro-government rallies.

30   **Burma:** the military government handed power to a nominally civilian president, Thein Sein, and government.

    Kosovo: Behgjet Pacolli resigned as president because of procedural violations during his election by the Assembly in February.

    Libya: Kadhafi's long-serving foreign minister, Moussa Koussa, fled to London.

    Russia: President Dmitry Medvedev proposed removing government ministers from the boards of directors of state-owned companies in an effort to break the link between businesses and government.

31   **Côte d'Ivoire:** forces loyal to Alassane Ouattara took several towns from Laurent Gbagbo's troops.

    Kuwait: the cabinet resigned over the National Assembly's demand to question three ministers about their performance.

    Ireland: stress tests of the banking sector showed that the four largest banks needed an extra €24 billion in capital.

    Libya: NATO took full command of operations to enforce a no-fly zone over Libya; other military operations remained the responsibility of the individual states involved.

    Mayotte: the Indian Ocean island became the 101st department of France (the fifth overseas department), in accordance with the March 2009 referendum on changing from territorial collectivity to departmental status.

APRIL

1   **Afghanistan:** a mob attacked the compound of the UN Assistance Mission in Afghanistan (UNAMA) in Mazar-i-Sharif and killed seven UN personnel. The violence had been inflamed by the burning of a copy of the Koran on 20 March by a fundamentalist Christian pastor in Florida. Anti-Western rioting took place in other cities.

    French Polynesia: President Gaston Tong Sang was removed in a no-confidence vote in the Legislative Assembly and replaced by pro-independence leader Oscar Temaru.

    Syria: tens of thousands marched in towns and cities after Friday prayers in protest against the government; security forces responded with violence.

2   **Northern Ireland:** a young police constable was killed by a bomb planted under his car by Republican extremists opposed to the peace process.

3   **Andorra:** elections to the General Council of the Valleys (the 28-seat legislature) were won by the opposition Democrats for Andorra (DA).

    China: artist and dissident Ai Weiwei was arrested at Beijing airport.

    Kazakhstan: Nursultan Nazarbayev was re-elected president with over 95 per cent of the vote.

    Mali: President Amadou Toumani Touré appointed the country's first female prime minister, Cissé Mariam Kaïdama Sidibé.

    Pakistan: in Punjab province, an attack by two suicide bombers near a Sufi shrine killed at least 50 people.

4   **Japan:** engineers began releasing low-level radioactive water from the damaged Fukushima nuclear plant into the Pacific Ocean in order to create space in the plant's waste disposal system for more highly contaminated water that had accumulated from efforts to cool the reactors damaged by the tsunami.

Syria: President Assad dismissed the government of Naji Otari, appointing Adel Safar as prime minister in his place.

USA: Barack Obama formally announced his intention to seek re-election as president in 2012.

6   **China:** the central bank raised interest rates by a quarter of a percentage point—the fourth rise in five months—in an attempt to tackle inflation and to slow the pace of economic growth.

Mexico: as protests against organised crime were held across the country, seven mass graves containing 59 bodies were discovered in north-eastern Tamaulipas state.

Portugal: requested financial aid from the European Commission after 10-year government bond yields rose to almost 9 per cent; it was the third eurozone country (after Greece and Ireland) to seek an international bailout.

7   **EU:** the European Central Bank raised interest rates for the eurozone to 1.25 per cent from the 1 per cent level set in May 2009. It was the first rate rise since July 2008.

Niger: the inauguration of Mahamadou Issoufou as president was followed by the appointment, on 21 April, of a new cabinet that replaced the transitional government appointed by the military junta in March 2010.

8   **Djibouti:** in presidential elections, Ismael Omar Guellah was elected for a third consecutive term with over 80 per cent of the vote. Opposition parties boycotted the poll.

USA: as the budget for 2011 remained in dispute, Republicans in Congress reached an agreement with the White House to continue funding services in return for wider spending cuts, narrowly averting a shutdown of federal government.

9   **Iceland:** a referendum rejected, for the second time, a deal to reimburse the governments of the UK and the Netherlands over the Icesave bank collapse.

11   **Belarus:** a bomb on the metro system in Minsk killed 12 people.

Côte d'Ivoire: troops loyal to Alassane Ouattara, supported by French and UN forces, detained Laurent Gbagbo, who had lost to Ouattara in the 2010 presidential election but had refused to leave office.

France: the ban on wearing the full Muslim face veil (the burqa and the niqab) in public places came into force.

12   **Japan:** the government raised the severity rating of the accident at the Fukushima nuclear plant to seven—the highest point on the International Nuclear Event Scale—reflecting the cumulative effect of the radiation leak since the tsunami in March.

13   **Egypt:** the deposed former president, Mohammed Hosni Mubarak, was arrested (together with his two sons), suffered a heart attack, and was transferred to hospital.

USA: President Barack Obama presented new proposals in response to the alternative budget for 2012 put forward by Republican Congressman Paul Ryan. Obama's proposals would reduce the deficit by $4,000 billion over 12 years through spending cuts and tax rises for the wealthy; Ryan's scheme to reduce the budget by a similar amount was based on tax reductions and radical cuts to welfare provision.

USA: a bipartisan Senate committee produced a report into events and practices on Wall Street prior to the banking collapse of 2008, with some of its heaviest criticism directed against Goldman Sachs.

14   **Greece:** yields on government bonds soared after Germany's finance minister, Wolfgang Schäuble, said that Greece might have to restructure its debt.

Syria: a new government was formed under Adel Safar, who had been appointed prime minister on 3 April.

15 **Algeria:** President Abdelaziz Bouteflika made a televised address proposing constitutional reforms; the same day, there was a major attack by 150 AQIM (al-Qaida in the Islamic Maghreb) militants on an army base outside Azazga in northern Algeria.

16 **Nigeria:** Goodluck Jonathan, the incumbent, won the presidential election with almost 60 per cent of votes cast. His People's Democratic Party also won the legislative elections held on 9 April.

Syria: in a televised address to the cabinet, President Bashar Assad promised reforms, including lifting the emergency law of 1963, in an attempt to pre-empt further protests.

17 **Finland:** in a general election, the eurosceptic True Finns (PS) party increased its representation in the 200-member legislature from five to 39 seats.

18 **Bolivia:** an 11-day general strike by trade unions came to an end after public sector wages were raised in line with inflation.

Hungary: the National Assembly passed a rewritten constitution (replacing that of 1989), which contained several controversial provisions.

19 **Cuba:** Raúl Castro replaced his brother, Fidel Castro, as central committee first secretary at the sixth congress of the ruling Cuban Communist Party; the congress approved reforms giving greater freedom to small businesses.

20 **Haiti:** musician Michel Martelly secured the presidency, defeating Mirlande Manigat in the second round of elections.

21 **Burkina Faso:** in an attempt to quell an army mutiny and spreading civil unrest, President Blaise Compaoré appointed a new government and a new head of the armed forces.

22 **Cambodia:** troops exchanged fire with Thai forces along the disputed border; by 30 April a total of 16 soldiers had been killed and 60,000 civilians displaced.

23 **Libya:** Colonel Kadhafi's forces withdrew from central Misrata where there had been intense fighting with the rebels but continued to shell the port area.

Yemen: Gulf Co-operation Council states negotiated a deal between government and opposition that involved Ali Abdullah Saleh stepping down as president; Saleh developed "reservations" about the deal on 30 April.

24 **Vanuatu:** Sato Kilman lost a no-confidence vote; he was replaced as prime minister by Serge Vohor.

25 **Afghanistan:** nearly 500 prisoners, mostly Taliban, staged a mass escape from Kandahar's main jail, with suspected official complicity.

Chad: Idriss Déby was elected to a fourth consecutive presidential term with over 88 per cent of the vote in a contest boycotted by the main opposition contenders.

Libya: NATO air strikes targeted Colonel Kadhafi's residential compound in central Tripoli.

Syria: security forces attacked the southern city of Deraa, where the popular protest movement had begun in mid-March.

26 **Afghanistan:** ISAF announced that it had killed a senior al-Qaida leader, Abdul Ghani (Abu Hafs al-Najdi), in an air strike on 13 April.

Jordan: King Abdullah II appointed a royal committee to revise the constitution, in response to recent demonstrations.

Ukraine: as the world watched the unfolding Fukushima disaster in Japan, ceremonies marked the 25th anniversary of the Chernobyl nuclear disaster.

27 **Palestine:** Fatah and Hamas announced a reconciliation agreement, brokered by Egypt, and pledged to form a unity government.

Tibet: the Tibetan community in exile selected Lobsang Sangay, a Harvard University academic lawyer, to replace the Dalai Lama as prime minister.

USA: the White House released the full version of Barack Obama's birth certificate to dismiss the rumours—amplified by Donald Trump—that the president had not been born in the USA.

USA: tornadoes and storms killed at least 342 people across southern states.

28   **Japan:** the Bank of Japan reduced its growth forecast for 2011 from 1.6 per cent to 0.6 per cent because of the tsunami disaster.

Morocco: a nail bomb exploded in a cafe in Djma-el-Fna square in central Marrakesh, killing 13 foreign tourists and three Moroccans.

Uganda: the televised violent arrest of opposition leader Kizza Besigye during a protest against rising prices provoked anti-government riots in Kampala.

USA: Leon Panetta was nominated as defence secretary, replacing Robert Gates; Panetta's post as CIA director was given to General David Petraeus, who would be replaced as US commander in Afghanistan by General John Allen.

29   **UK:** Heir to the throne Prince William married Catherine (Kate) Middleton in Westminster Abbey.

30   **Libya:** Colonel Kadhafi's youngest son and three grandchildren were killed in NATO air strikes on Tripoli.

Laos: elections were held to the National Assembly; one of the five permitted independent candidates won a seat.

MAY

1   **China:** banned smoking in public places.

2   **Canada:** in federal elections the governing Conservative Party won a parliamentary majority (166 seats in the 308 seat Parliament), whilst the Liberals were replaced as the official opposition by the New Democratic Party (NDP).

USA: US special forces killed Osama bin Laden, the founder of al-Qaida, in a nighttime rid on a compound in Abbottabad, Pakistan.

3   **Bahrain:** the government announced that 47 doctors and nurses, who had treated protesters injured by security forces in anti-government demonstrations in March, would be tried by a military court.

Kyrgyzstan: the independent Kyrgyzstan Inquiry Commission (KIC), a Nordic initiative, delivered its report on the June 2010 ethnic violence; it blamed security forces for complicity.

Pakistan: the prime minister, Yusuf Raza Gillani, reacting to the US operation against Osama bin Laden, said that the "unilateral" act had violated Pakistan's sovereignty.

4   **EU:** the European Commission allowed Schengen area countries to reimpose temporary border controls in the light of the arrival of a large number of North African migrants to Italy, and thence to France.

Palestine: Fatah and Hamas signed an agreement in Cairo backing the formation of a government of national unity.

5   **Scotland:** the pro-independence Scottish National Party won a majority in elections to the Scottish Parliament.

UK: a referendum on switching to the alternative vote (AV) system for parliamentary elections, as supported by the junior coalition partner the Liberal Democrats, was decisively defeated; local elections the same day also saw heavy defeats for the LibDems.

6   **Syria:** protesters gathering in a "Friday of defiance" were met with violent repression from security forces, and several were killed.

7   **Ecuador:** a referendum was held on a package of 10 constitutional amendments that
        would expand the power of the president; results released on 19 May showed that
        all had been passed.
        Niue: there were elections to the unicameral legislature, the Fono.
        Singapore: in a general election, the People's Action Party was re-elected, winning 60
        per cent of the vote, a significant drop in support compared with its victories in
        2006 and 2001.

8   **Bahrain:** the government announced that the state of emergency imposed in March
        would be lifted in June.

9   **Guatemala:** a court acquitted Alfonso Portillo, a former president, of embezzlement
        charges in a ruling condemned by the UN-sponsored International Commission
        Against Impunity in Guatemala.

10   **China:** there were protests in inner Mongolia, after a Chinese lorry driver killed a
        Mongolian herder attempting to protest against the coal mining industry.
        Japan: Naoto Kan, the prime minister, apologised during a televised news conference
        for "failing to prevent the nuclear accident".

11   **Libya:** rebels claimed to have captured the airport in Misrata.
        Syria: the government sent tanks into Homs, where scores of demonstrators were
        killed.
        Uganda: Parliament suspended a bill that called for the death penalty for homosexuals.

12   **Andorra:** a new government was formed under Democrats for Andorra leader, Antoni
        Marti, following the party's victory in the 3 April elections.
        Bangladesh: relaxing the ban on fatwas (Islamic religious edicts), the Supreme Court
        ruled that Muslim clerics could issue fatwas but that they could not be legally
        enforced by Bangladesh's secular legal system.
        Japan: TEPCO admitted that reactor No. 1 at the Fukushima nuclear plant had suf-
        fered meltdown soon after the tsunami of 11 March; subsequently, TEPCO con-
        firmed that meltdown had also occurred at reactors 2 and 3.

13   **India:** the results were released of four regional elections; they included the heavy
        defeat of the communists in West Bengal.
        Pakistan: a double suicide bombing killed more than 80 paramilitaries at their training
        camp in KPK province (which included Abbottabad); the Pakistani Taliban (TTP)
        organisation said the attack was revenge for the killing of Osama bin Laden.
        Vanuatu: a ruling by the court of appeal restored the government of Sato Kilman,
        which had been brought down in a no-confidence vote on 24 April.

14   **Belarus:** among various trials relating to the December 2010 post-election demonstra-
        tions, opposition presidential candidate Andrei Sannikov was sentenced to five
        years in prison.
        France: Dominique Strauss-Kahn, the managing director of the IMF and likely Social-
        ist Party candidate in France's 2012 presidential elections, was arrested in New
        York over his alleged sexual assault on a hotel maid, shocking the French political
        world.
        Haiti: in the first peaceful transition of power to an opposition party in Haiti's post-
        independence history, Michel Martelly was inaugurated president.
        Oman: the army arrested several protesters in Muscat.
        Singapore: Lee Kuan Yew, the founding father of Singapore and prime minister from
        1959 to 1990, resigned from the cabinet.
        Syria: a security operation began in Tel Kalakh, near the border with Lebanon, consist-
        ing of scores of arrests and the shelling of the town.

15 **Arab League:** a meeting elected Nabil al-Araby, Egypt's foreign minister, as the
League's new secretary general, replacing Amr Moussa.

Palestine: to mark the Nakba [catastrophe]—the fleeing or forced expulsion of hundreds of thousands of Palestinian Arabs during the creation of the state of Israel in
1948—protesters attempted to cross into Israel from Egypt, Jordan, Lebanon, Syria,
the West Bank and Gaza Strip; at least 14 were shot and killed.

16 **Italy:** the ruling People of Freedom grouping and the Northern League, its coalition
partner, were heavily defeated in local elections held over two days, further undermining the position of the prime minister, Silvio Berlusconi.

Libya: the prosecutor of the International Criminal Court requested arrest warrants for
Colonel Kadhafi, his son Saif al-Islam Kadhafi, and his chief of intelligence,
Abdullah al-Senussi.

17 **Ireland:** Queen Elizabeth II began the first visit by a reigning British monarch since
1922.

Libya: the oil minister, Shukri Mohammed Ghanem, fled to Tunisia.

Portugal: the terms of a €78 billion rescue package of emergency loans from the EU
and IMF were agreed.

Russia: the share swap and Arctic exploration deal between Rosneft and the British oil
group, BP, collapsed over objections from BP's existing Russian partner, TNK-BP.

Rwanda: the International Criminal Tribunal for Rwanda (ICTR) sentenced the former
head of Rwanda's army, General Augustin Bizimungu, to 30 years in prison on
charges relating to the Hutu massacre of Tutsis in 1994.

18 **IMF:** Dominique Strauss-Kahn, the managing director, sent his letter of resignation to
the board.

North Korea: media organisations reported the findings of a UN report which claimed
that North Korea was exporting ballistic missile technology to Iran via a third country that diplomats identified as China.

South Africa: the ruling African National Congress won municipal elections but faced
the strongest opposition since it came to power in 1994.

19 **China:** the State Council (cabinet) admitted "urgent problems" affecting the Three
Gorges Dam; unprecedented amounts of water were released to cope with drought
conditions in the Yangtze delta.

USA: in a major speech on the Middle East, President Barack Obama celebrated the
"Arab Spring", and called upon Israel to accept the 1967 borders as the basis for
peace with a Palestinian state.

20 **North Korea:** the leader, Kim Jong Il, started a seven-day visit to China.

Syria: attacks were launched on rallies gathering after Friday prayers across the country.

21 **Côte d'Ivoire:** Alassane Ouattara was inaugurated as president at the end of the power
struggle that had followed the November 2010 elections.

Iceland: the Griimsvotn volcano began erupting, affecting air traffic in Iceland and
northern Europe until 26 May.

Iraq: the UK's military operation in Iraq officially ended.

Seychelles: presidential elections ended with the re-election of the incumbent, James
Michel of the ruling Parti Lepep.

Sudan: troops from the (northern) Sudan Armed Forces occupied the disputed town of
Abyei on the border with South Sudan.

22 **Cyprus;** legislative elections were won by the opposition Democratic Rally (DISY).

Pakistan: a small group of Pakistani Taliban attacked the naval air base at Karachi, holding it for 18 hours, in apparent retaliation for the assassination of Osama bin Laden.

Spain: in local elections, the ruling Socialist Party lost heavily to the opposition People's Party, following youth demonstrations in Madrid and other cities.

Vietnam: elections were held to the National Assembly.

23   **Libya:** in the NATO operation against Kadhafi's forces, the UK and France deployed ground attack helicopter gunships, operating from warships off the Libyan coast.

Yemen: the Hashid tribal group defected to the opposition, leading to a situation approaching civil war.

26   **Georgia:** police action ended five days of opposition protest in Tbilisi, with violent scenes.

North Korea: under the provisions of UNSC Resolution 1874 (2009), a US warship intercepted a North Korean ship, thought to be carrying missile technology and bound for Burma.

Serbia: Ratko Mladic, the commander of Bosnian Serbs during the Balkan wars, was arrested in Serbia and flown on 31 May to The Hague to stand trial for war crimes.

27   **Afghanistan:** following several incidents involving civilian casualties, a NATO air strike killed 14 people, including 11 children in Helmand province. NATO apologised.

Syria: the release on YouTube of footage of the mutilated body of 13-year old Hamza al-Khatib, apparently tortured to death by the security services, inflamed the continuing anti-government protests.

Uganda: the president, Yoweri Museveni, named a new cabinet under Amama Mbabazi as prime minister.

28   **Benin:** President Yayi Boni named a new cabinet under Pascal Irénée Koupaki as prime minister.

Honduras: Manuel Zelaya, the former president, returned from exile in the Dominican Republic.

Nigeria: Goodluck Jonathan was inaugurated president, but the event provoked a series of bomb attacks in northern Nigeria blamed on the Boko Haram sect.

30   **Germany:** Chancellor Angela Merkel confirmed that all Germany's 17 nuclear power stations would be phased out by 2022.

Greece: EU officials held emergency talks with the Greek government, in preparation for drafting a new bailout package.

Libya: there was a mass defection to the rebels of 120 officers, including eight senior figures.

Yemen: as fighting continued in Sana'a between security forces and tribal fighters, at least 50 people were killed in Taiz, the second city, by the army's bulldozing of an opposition camp.

31   **Germany:** admitted that Spanish cucumbers had not been to blame for the outbreak of E coli in northern Germany that had killed at least 17 people to date.

JUNE

1   **Syria:** as opposition pro-democracy protests continued regularly after Friday prayers, Human Rights Watch issued a report detailing systematic killings and torture by Syria's security forces in the southern city of Deraa.

2   **Chile:** a judge announced an investigation into claims that the death of the poet, Pablo Neruda, in 1973, had been caused by agents of the Pinochet regime.

Latvia: the Saeima (parliament) elected Andris Berzins of the Union of Greens and Farmers as president of the republic, replacing Valdis Zatlers who had failed to secure a second term.

3 **China:** the US state department raised with China's foreign ministry allegations from Google that a recent cyber attack against its Gmail accounts had arisen from Jinan, Shandong province.

India: Baba Ramdev, a popular yogi, began a fast in protest against corruption and led 40,000 followers in a demonstration in Delhi that was broken up by police on 5 June.

Pakistan: a US drone attack was believed to have killed senior al-Qaida commander Ilyas Kashmiri.

Syria: more than 30 people were killed by security forces during a demonstration in Hama in memory of the murdered boy, Hamza al-Khatib.

Yemen: a mortar attack on the presidential compound in Sana'a wounded the president, Ali Abdullah Saleh, who left the country for Saudi Arabia.

4 **Belarus:** won a $3 billion loan from a regional fund, the Russian-dominated EurAsEC; IMF aid to rescue the economy was not forthcoming.

Chile: a volcano in southern Chile erupted, disrupting air traffic across the south of the globe.

5 **Nigeria:** Dimeji Bankole was arrested to face corruption charges; the former speaker of the House of Representatives was accused of having secured $65 million in loans using public assets.

Peru: the second round of presidential elections saw left-wing former general, Ollanta Humala Tasso, defeat Keiko Fujimori.

Portugal: the centre-right Social Democrats, led by Pedro Passos Coelho, won an early election; his new government would have to implement austerity measures imposed as a condition of the €78 billion EU-IMF bailout.

Syria: at least eight Palestinians were killed when they tried to breach the Israeli border on the Golan Heights.

6 **USA:** a long-term adviser to the president, the chairman of the Council of Economic Advisers, Austan Goolsbee, announced his resignation.

7 **Brazil:** Antonio Palocci resigned as presidency minister (presidential chief of staff) over media reports accusing him of corruption.

Japan: the authorities issued a revised estimate of how much radiation had escaped from the Fukushima plant that was double the previous figure.

Somalia: Somali soldiers shot dead Fazul Abdullah Mohammed, al-Qaida's leader in East Africa.

UK: following an independent review into a bill to reform the National Health Service, the government watered down its proposals.

8 **Afghanistan:** the US Senate foreign relations committee published a comprehensive report, criticising the uses to which $18.8 billion in US aid to Afghanistan had been put over 10 years.

Burma: fighting broke out in the north-east between the army and rebel Kachin militias.

Syria: many thousands of people fled the town of Jisr al-Shughour after Turkey opened its border, with reports of army reprisals against civilians and defecting soldiers.

Tunisia: elections scheduled for July were postponed until 23 October.

9 **Kenya:** Médecins sans frontières (MSF) warned that the Dadaab refugee camp in northern Kenya—the world's largest—was full. Other aid agencies raised fears of a humanitarian catastrophe caused by the drought in the Horn of Africa.

10   **China:** in one of the most serious examples of an estimated 200,000 disturbances per
          year, rioting began in Zenzheng, a manufacturing city in Guangdong province,
          which had to be put down by police.

          Germany: the authorities identified an organic bean sprout farm in Lower Saxony as
          the source of the outbreak of E coli that by the end of June had produced a death
          toll of 46 in Germany and one in Sweden.

11   **Somalia:** pirates released the *MV Zirku*, a Kuwaiti-owned oil tanker, after receiving a
          reported record $12 million in ransom.

12   **Jordan:** making a significant concession to protesters, King Abdullah II promised to
          relinquish his right to appoint ministers.

          Spain: protesters in Madrid—the "indignados"—began dismantling the tent city that
          had occupied Puerta del Sol square since 15 May.

          Turkey: the ruling Justice and Development (AK) Party won a third consecutive gen-
          eral election, although it failed to achieve a two-thirds majority of seats.

13   **Greece:** Standard & Poor's again downgraded the country's long-term sovereign debt
          to just above default status, giving Greece the lowest credit-rating of any country
          covered by the rating agency.

          Italy: a legally-binding referendum was held over two days on four items of legislation
          sponsored by the Berlusconi government. The government lost in each case.

          Lebanon: Najib Mikati, a Sunni supported by Hezbullah (the Shia party), was formally
          voted into office at the head of a new government, five months after having been
          nominated as prime minister.

          USA: seven contenders for the Republican presidential nomination took part in a tele-
          vised debate in New Hampshire.

16   **al-Qaida:** a website reported that Ayman al-Zawahiri was named the organisation's
          leader.

          Indonesia: a court found radical cleric Abu Bakar Bashir guilty of terrorism-related
          charges and sentenced him to 15 years' imprisonment.

          Philippines: the warship, *BRP Rajah Humabon* was despatched to patrol the Spratly
          Islands as tensions grew with China over alleged territorial infringements in the
          area of the South China Sea, which was claimed by a number of countries.

17   **China:** a leaked report from 2008 by the People's Bank of China said that some
          17,000 government officials had smuggled ¥800 billion out of the country in the 15
          years prior to 2008.

          Finland: a "rainbow" six-party coalition government was formed, following April's
          elections, under Jyrki Katainen of the National Coalition Party (KOK).

          Greece: the prime minister, George Papandreou, reshuffled his cabinet, appointing
          Evangelos Venizelos as finance minister and deputy prime minister.

          Saudi Arabia: in the first collective protest against the ban on women driving, several
          dozen women drove cars in Riyadh and Jeddah.

19   **Azerbaijan:** a pro-democracy rally went ahead in Baku, defying a ban by the authorities.

          Somalia: the president, Sheikh Sharif Ahmed, appointed Abdiweli Mohamed Ali as
          prime minister to replace the widely respected Mohamed Abdullahi Mohamed, who
          had been forced to resign as part of a 9 June deal struck between Sheikh Ahmed
          and the transitional federal government.

          Vietnam: began a joint naval patrol with China in disputed waters of the South China
          Sea, despite ongoing tensions between the two countries.

20   **Sudan:** and South Sudan agreed to create a demilitarised zone in their disputed border
          region of Abyei, to be policed by Ethiopian troops under the UN banner.

Tunisia: the former president, Zine el-Abidine Ben Ali, and his wife, Leila Trabelsi, were sentenced in absentia to 35 years' imprisonment for embezzlement of state assets.

21 **Northern Ireland:** two days of violence in east Belfast occurred when loyalist youths went on the rampage.

Pakistan: it was announced that a senior officer, Brigadier-General Ali Khan, had been arrested in May on suspicion of links to Hezb-ut-Tahrir, a banned Islamist group.

USA: Anthony Weiner, Democratic member of the House of Representatives from New York, resigned over a scandal involving the online exchange with young women of "inappropriate" photographs of himself.

22 **Bahrain:** eight pro-democracy campaigners (all Shia) were given life sentences for plotting against the government.

China: artist and dissident Ai Weiwei was released from detention.

USA: in a televised address, President Barack Obama outlined a timetable for the withdrawal of all US troops from Afghanistan by 2014.

Yemen: about 40 al-Qaida members escaped from a prison in the southern city of Mukalla, one of a number of advances made in June by al-Qaida in the Arabian Peninsula (AQAP).

23 **Bangladesh:** the younger son of opposition leader Khaleda Zia, Arafat Rahman Koko, was convicted in absentia of laundering money derived from bribes paid by foreign companies, and sentenced to six years' imprisonment.

Netherlands: in a test for freedom of speech laws, a court cleared far-right leader Geert Wilders of charges of inciting hatred against Muslims.

24 **Rwanda:** the International Criminal Tribunal for Rwanda sentenced former minister for family and women's development, Pauline Nyiramasuhuko, to life imprisonment for crimes relating to the 1994 genocide, including rape.

Spain: as part of its austerity drive, the government imposed a 3.8 per cent cut in the 2012 budget; this followed a 7.7 per cent cut approved for fiscal 2011.

USA: New York became the sixth and largest state to legalise same-sex marriage when governor Andrew Cuomo signed the bill into law.

26 **Libya:** NATO marked 100 days of action in Libya, committing the organisation to continued support of the rebel forces who in June made limited advances against the forces of Colonel Kadhafi.

27 **Afghanistan:** the head of the central bank, Abdul Qadir Fitrat, announced that he had resigned and fled to Washington DC in fear of his life, after giving evidence against the corrupt loans being offered by the Kabul Bank amounting to more than US$900 million.

Cambodia: preliminary hearings were conducted at the Extraordinary Chambers in the Courts of Cambodia in Case 002 against four surviving senior Khmer Rouge leaders.

28 **Afghanistan:** suicide bombers and gunmen staged an attack on the Inter-Continental Hotel in Kabul.

IMF: France's finance minister, Christine Lagarde, was named the new managing director of the IMF, from 5 July.

Senegal: the army was deployed to end anti-government riots in Dakar, the capital, exacerbated by prolonged power cuts.

29 **Egypt:** protests in Cairo's Tahrir square against the slow pace of reforms ended after three days; more than 1,000 people were injured in clashes with the police.

Libya: France confirmed that it had supplied arms to rebel forces south of Tripoli.

Pakistan: the defence minister, Chaudhry Ahmed Mukhtar, announced that the USA must end operations at the Shamsi airfield in Baluchistan from which drone attacks were launched against Taliban targets in the north-west border region.

Syria: the army withdrew from Hama, where at least 73 people were reported killed in June.

30   **Greece:** after two days of voting, legislators adopted further austerity measures essential to ensure the release of a €12 billion tranche of aid from the EU-IMF financial rescue package of May 2010; the votes were accompanied by strikes, protests and rioting.

JULY

1   **Morocco:** in a referendum proposed by King Mohammed VI, 98.5 per cent of voters approved constitutional changes that would move Morocco towards a constitutional monarchy.

3   **Belarus:** silent protests across the country marked Independence Day.

Mexico: three governor's contests, including that for Mexico State, were won by candidates of the PRI (Institutional Revolutionary Party), raising the likelihood of its taking the presidency in the 2012 elections.

Thailand: the opposition Pheu Thai party, led by Yingluck Shanawatra, sister of the deposed former prime minister Thaksin Shinawatra, won legislative elections.

5   **Japan:** Ryu Matsumoto, minister of reconstruction, resigned only eight days after assuming the newly created post after the broadcasting of his arrogant remarks to the governor of Miyagi province (that worst affected by the tsunami).

6   **Brazil:** in the second resignation in a month over corruption allegations, the transport minister, Alfredo Nascimento, quit his post.

7   **Turkmenistan:** a series of explosions at a munitions depot outside Abadan, around 20 km from Ashgabat, caused many deaths; the extent of the disaster was publicised in online media by opposition groups.

UK: after it emerged that private investigators working for *News of the World* had hacked into mobile telephones belonging to a young murder victim, and people killed in the 2005 terrorist attacks in London, Rupert Murdoch's News Corporation, announced the paper's closure.

USA: Texas executed Leal García, a Mexican national resident in the USA, who had been denied consular assistance when arrested.

8   **Egypt:** a large demonstration was staged in Tahrir Square.

Syria: the US and French ambassadors visited Hama to protest against the crackdown on protesters; their embassies in Damascus were attacked in retaliation during pro-government demonstrations on 10-11 July.

9   **Malaysia:** thousands marched in Kuala Lumpur in support of electoral reform.

South Sudan: celebrated independence following its official secession from Sudan, the culmination of the comprehensive peace agreement signed in 2005.

10   **Australia:** the government announced plans for a controversial carbon tax.

Bangladesh: the opposition called a general strike in protest at a constitutional amendment restoring the state principle of secularism.

Russia: a tourist boat capsized and sank on the river Volga, with over 120 deaths, including around 50 children.

11 **Cyprus:** the power station at Vasilikos was destroyed in a massive explosion caused when confiscated Iranian munitions, poorly stored at a naval base, exploded in a bush fire; 13 people were killed, power cuts followed and on 28 July the cabinet resigned pending a reshuffle.

Dominican Republic: there was a 24-hour general strike for higher pay and lower prices; some protests became violent.

Israel: adopted legislation that made a punishable offence any public call for a boycott against the state of Israel or Israeli settlements in the West Bank.

12 **Afghanistan:** Ahmed Wali Karzai, the half-brother of President Hamid Karzai and his key ally in Kandahar, was assassinated by a member of his own security staff.

India: a cabinet reshuffle followed the resignation of the textiles minister over corruption charges.

Ireland: the country's credit rating was reduced to junk status. It was the third eurozone country to be so tagged (after Greece and, on 5 July, Portugal).

13 **India:** three bombs exploded in Mumbai, killing 25 people, in the worst terrorist attack since 2008.

UK: News Corporation withdrew its bid for full ownership of BSkyB, the television satellite station.

14 **IWC:** the annual meeting of the International Whaling Commission, held in Jersey, broke up in procedural dispute and antagonism between pro- and anti-whaling nations.

15 **Egypt:** thousands marched in Cairo and other cities to demand faster political reform.

Italy: approval was given to an emergency €48 billion austerity package designed to rein in borrowing costs; on 12 July 10-year government bond-yields had risen above 6 per cent.

Libya: the USA formally recognised the rebel National Transitional Council, which thus gained access to $30 billion in frozen assets.

17 **Venezuela:** President Hugo Chávez returned to Cuba for further treatment for abdominal cancer; he delegated some powers to the vice president and finance minister, though neither was sworn in as interim president.

Afghanistan: Jan Muhammad Khan, a close aide and mentor of President Hamid Karzai, was assassinated in Kabul.

UK: Metropolitan Police commissioner Sir Paul Stephenson resigned in connection with the News International phone hacking scandal; the resignation of his deputy John Yates followed on 18 July.

18 **Afghanistan:** General David Petraeus stepped down as commander of US and NATO forces.

Canada: the combat mission of Canadian troops in Afghanistan ended; 161 Canadian lives had been lost since the mission's launch in 2001.

Chile: President Sebastian Piñera reshuffled his cabinet after protests against education and energy policies.

China: rioters in Xinjiang province stormed a police station in what was apparently a fresh outbreak of ethnic violence.

19 **Chile:** an autopsy confirmed that the socialist former president, Salvador Allende, had committed suicide and not been murdered in the 1973 coup that deposed him.

UK: Rupert Murdoch, owner of News International, and his son James, faced questioning from a parliamentary committee over the telephone hacking scandal.

20 **Côte d'Ivoire:** a "dialogue truth and reconciliation commission" was formed to investigate crimes committed during the conflict that had followed the presidential elections of November 2010.

Ireland: the prime minister, Enda Kenny, in the Dáil, accused the Vatican of attempting to minimise the scale of sexual abuse of children by Catholic clergy in Ireland. The Vatican recalled its envoy on 25 July.

Serbia: Croatian Serb Goran Hadzic, the last fugitive war crimes suspect sought by the ICTY, was arrested.

Somalia: the UN declared a famine in two southern regions of Somalia and appealed for $300 million in aid.

21   **Egypt:** responding to popular protests, the military government announced a cabinet reshuffle in which around half the ministers were replaced.

Greece: the EU agreed a second bailout for Greece; private bondholders would be asked to accept a voluntary reduction in the value of their holdings of Greek debt.

Malawi: after two days of rioting, security forces had killed at least 18 people who had joined anti-government protests in several cities organised by civil society groups and NGOs.

Space: the 135th and final NASA space shuttle mission ended with the return of *Atlantis*.

22   **Canada:** deported Chinese businessman Lai Changxing to China, where he faced charges of running a smuggling ring in Fujian province that had also involved hundreds of regional officials.

Norway: a right-wing extremist shot dead 69 people at a youth camp on the island of Utoya, after having detonated a car bomb in Oslo that killed eight.

USA: the repeal of the "Don't Ask, Don't Tell" policy that prohibited homosexuals from serving in the US military was finally enacted.

23   **China:** two bullet trains collided on a viaduct near Wenzhou, killing 40 people. Information about the accident, the first on China's rapidly expanding high-speed rail network, was initially suppressed by the authorities.

Sri Lanka: in local elections, Tamil parties won 80 per cent of the seats they contested in the north and east; elsewhere the ruling United People's Freedom Alliance (UPFA) won all councils.

25   **Norway:** some 100,000 people gathered in Oslo for a vigil commemorating those killed in the Utoya atrocity.

Vietnam: the National Assembly elected Truong Tan Sang to the largely ceremonial post of president.

26   **India:** the foreign ministers of India and Pakistan met in Delhi.

Australia: signed an agreement with Malaysia on the resettlement of asylum seekers.

27   **Afghanistan:** the mayor of Kandahar, Ghulam Haider Hamidi, a childhood friend of President Hamid Karzai, was killed by a suicide bomber.

Brazil: imposed a 1 per cent tax on futures contracts that betted on further strengthening of the real against the US dollar.

28   **Egypt:** pro-democracy marchers were attacked by vigilantes loyal to the military leadership.

Eritrea: a UN report accused the Eritrean government of organising a failed plot to attack an African Union summit in Addis Ababa on 30-31 January.

Libya: the death was announced of rebel commander Abdul Fatah Younis, in murky circumstances.

29   **Mexico:** police captured, José Antonio Acosta ("El Diego"), the suspected leader of the La Linea drug gang leader in Ciudad Juárez.

Poland: the defence minister resigned after a report into the 2010 air crash at Smolensk that killed the Polish president and 95 others blamed inadequate pilot training.

31   **India:** the chief minister of Karnataka state, B.S. Yeddyurappa, resigned after being named in a report on a mining scam that cost the state a reported $3.6 billion.

Nigeria: following an upsurge in Boko Haram attacks, and criticism of the government by Amnesty International for the military crackdown against the sect, the government announced the creation of a committee to open negotiations.

Syria: tanks and troops were sent into Hama on the eve of Ramadan, as Friday pro-democracy protests continued, and killed up to 80 people.

USA: shortly before the deadline of 2 August when the US government would have defaulted on its obligations, Democrats and Republicans reached a deal to raise the limit on the debt ceiling.

AUGUST

2   **Guatemala:** a court sentenced—to 6,060 years in prison, each—four soldiers for their part in a 1982 massacre during the country's civil war.

Papua New Guinea: veteran prime minister Sir Michael Somare was formally removed from office; he had been absent since heart surgery in April. Peter O'Neill became prime minister.

Tajikistan: new legislation to control religious observance was enacted amid fears of Islamic extremism.

USA: Congress approved the Budget Control Act of 2011, seen as a significant defeat for President Obama at the hands of the Tea Party wing of the Republican Party; it involved $917 billion in spending cuts over 10 years, plus a further $1,500 billion deficit reduction to be found by a new Congressional committee in return for an increase of the debt limit by $900 billion.

3   **Brazil:** the government announced a new industrial policy to boost domestic industry facing a strong currency and cheap imports.

Somalia: the UN extended to three more areas the declaration of famine made on 20 July.

South Africa: lent 2.4 billion rand to Swaziland; international donors had refused to bail out the absolutist monarchy.

4   **Brazil:** President Dilma Rousseff sacked the defence minister after he said that he had voted for her opponent in the 2010 election.

Syria: troops in Hama killed more than 100 people; the military withdrew from the city on 11 August.

Turkey: the four senior commanders in the Turkish military were replaced; their predecessors had resigned on 29 July in protest at government rules blocking promotion for officers accused of involvement in a coup plot.

5   **Thailand:** Yingluck Shinawatra was elected prime minister by the House of Representatives and formed a new cabinet, dominated by her Pheu Thai party and including associates of her brother, deposed former prime minister Thaksin Shinawatra, but not Red Shirt activists.

Ukraine: Yuliya Tymoshenko, the opposition leader and former prime minister, who was on trial in Kiev, was sent to prison for contempt of court.

USA: Standard & Poor's downgraded the USA's long-term credit rating, for the first time, to AA+.

6   **Afghanistan:** the Taliban shot down a NATO transport helicopter, killing all 38 people on board, including 22 Navy SEALS.

Israel: there were large protests in Tel Aviv, for the third consecutive Saturday, over economic hardships. Other cities saw smaller protests.

Somalia: the al-Shabaab militia withdrew from Mogadishu "for tactical purposes"; the Transitional Federal Government claimed military victory.

UK: rioting and looting broke out in a number of cities after a peaceful protest over the police shooting of a black suspect in London on 4 August. Five people were killed in the violence, which subsided after 10 August following a massive police deployment.

7 **Bahrain:** two Shia opposition former members of the House of Representatives, who had been detained after protesting at the violent suppression of opposition demonstrations, were freed from prison.

São Tomé and Príncipe: in the second round of the presidential election, Manuel Pinto da Costa, a former president standing as an independent, defeated the ruling party candidate.

8 **Bangladesh:** the corruption commission accused the former prime minister, Khaleda Zia, leader of the opposition BNP, of corruption.

Brazil: the deputy tourism minister and other officials were arrested on suspicion of corruption.

Global economy: stock markets worldwide plunged on the first day of trading after Standard & Poor's downgrade of the US government's credit rating. The ECB intervened to buy €22 billion of Spanish and Italian bonds and halt the rise in those country's bond yields.

Guatemala: the Constitutional Court upheld a ban on Sandra Torres's participation in September's presidential election; she had been married to President Alvaro Colom until divorcing him in March to circumvent a ban on relatives of the incumbent from standing for election.

Tibet: the government-in-exile, in Dharamsala, India, swore in a new prime minister, Lobsang Sangay, who denounced Chinese rule in Tibet as "unjust and untenable".

9 **Uganda:** Kizza Besigye, the opposition leader, was acquitted of all charges in connection with violent protests in April.

10 **China:** the country's first aircraft carrier—a refitted Soviet vessel—began its maiden sea trial.

North and South Korea: exchanged artillery fire along their disputed maritime border.

11 **Global economy:** the price of gold rose above $1,800 a troy ounce.

12 **Italy:** the government approved an emergency austerity package, parts of which were then excised by the prime minister, Silvio Berlusconi, on 29 August.

14 **Afghanistan:** a Taliban attack on the compound of the governor of Parwan—a hitherto relatively peaceful area—was driven back.

USA: Warren Buffet criticised "a billionaire-friendly Congress" for having "coddled" the wealthy; he urged tax rises for the rich (including himself).

15 **India:** the government arrested elderly activist Anna Hazare at an anti-corruption rally in Delhi, together with over 1,000 supporters, prompting national protests. Hazare, released on 18 August, went on hunger strike.

Iraq: several dozen bomb attacks killed at least 89 people in largely Shia Muslim areas.

16 **Eurozone:** at a bilateral summit in Paris, France's President Nicolas Sarkozy and Germany's Chancellor Angela Merkel agreed proposals for radical reform of the eurozone, improving its collective governance and economic management.

17 **Brazil:** the agriculture minister resigned amid corruption accusations.

18 **Israel:** co-ordinated attacks in the south by Palestinian militants who had crossed the Egyptian border killed eight Israelis.

Spain: Pope Benedict XVI arrived for a four-day celebration of the Roman Catholic Church's World Youth Day; the cost of his visit, as Spain struggled with austerity measures, caused controversy.

Syria: the USA and European countries called for the departure of President Bashar Assad.

19 **Afghanistan:** Taliban fighters stormed the British Council compound in Kabul and killed 12 people.

Burma: an apparent softening in attitude by the new, ostensibly civilian government towards the pro-democracy leader Aung San Suu Kyi included an invitation to meet ministers in the capital, Naypyidaw.

Pakistan: a suicide bombing at a mosque in north-west Pakistan was claimed by the Pakistani Taliban (TTP) to have been directed against tribal elders opposed to the Taliban.

21 **Cape Verde:** the presidential elections were won in the second round by opposition candidate Jorge Carlos Fonseca of the MPD.

22 **Canada:** the leader of the New Democratic Party (NDP), Jack Layton, who had led the party to a position as the country's main opposition, died of cancer.

Libya: rebels took control of the capital, Tripoli, but did not find Colonel Moamar Kadhafi.

23 **France:** a judge in New York dropped all charges of sexual assault against Dominique Strauss-Kahn, former managing director of the IMF, after the credibility of his accuser collapsed.

Pakistan: the MQM, the biggest political party in Karachi, called a strike in protest at continuing ethnic violence that had caused over 800 deaths in 2011, including 300 in August.

Thailand: exiled former prime minister Thaksin Shinawatra entered Japan, despite Japan's policy of denying visas to foreigners with outstanding prison sentences. The Thai government denied having exerted pressure on behalf of Thaksin.

Turkey: ended six days of air strikes and artillery fire on separatist Kurdish (PKK) bases in northern Iraq, claiming to have killed 100 PKK rebels.

25 **Chile:** a two-day general strike began, in which trade union members joined student protesters, demanding economic and education reforms.

Mexico: 52 people, including 42 women, were killed in a fire in Monterrey, in a casino which apparently had not paid protection money to gangsters. The government declared three days of mourning.

26 **Algeria:** al-Qaida in the Islamic Maghreb militants were believed to have committed a double suicide bomb attack on a military academy.

Nigeria: a suicide bomb attack on the UN building in Abuja, the capital, killed at least 23 people; the Boko Haram sect claimed responsibility.

Syria: the last Friday of Ramadan again saw protests throughout the country.

27 **Singapore:** Tony Tan, who had the support of the ruling PAP, narrowly won the presidential election.

28 **India:** Anna Hazare broke his hunger strike after 13 days, claiming victory in having forced Parliament to incorporate his proposals into an anti-corruption bill.

Nepal: Baburam Bhattarai replaced Jhalanath Khanal, who had resigned as prime minister on 14 August. They belonged to rival parties, whose inability to forge consensus had caused deadlock in the parliamentary system.

29   **Japan:** the ruling Democratic Party of Japan held a leadership election to replace the prime minister, Naoto Kan, who had resigned on 26 August. Yoshihiko Noda duly became Japan's sixth premier in five years.

30   **Bolivia:** the Supreme Court sentenced five military officers and two former ministers to prison sentences for their role in the deaths of civilians during the protests of "Black October", 2003.

       Russia: Rosneft signed a deal with ExxonMobil to explore three blocks in the Arctic; an earlier deal between Rosneft and BP had collapsed over a challenge from BP's Russian partner, TNK-BP.

31   **Australia:** the High Court ruled illegal government proposals to send asylum seekers to Malaysia.

       Colombia: the defence minister, Rodrigo Rivera Salazar, resigned because of increased attacks by FARC guerrillas upon civilians.

       Portugal: the government laid out further painful austerity measures, as international lenders praised its progress in reducing the country's debt.

SEPTEMBER

2   **Greece:** officials from the "troika"—the EU, IMF, and ECB—suspended their fifth quarterly review of Greece's compliance with the terms of the May 2010 bailout, accusing the government of delays in implementing the austerity plan.

       Syria: the EU announced a ban on importing Syrian oil.

       Turkey: ordered the Israeli ambassador to leave, and suspended all defence links with Israel, after publication of the UN report on Israel's attack on the aid flotilla to Gaza in May 2010, in which nine Turkish activists had been killed.

3   **Israel:** huge demonstrations were held for lower prices, cheaper housing, and better social services.

4   **Afghanistan:** the US commander of Western forces, General John Allen, ordered a halt to the transfer of detainees to nine Afghan jails, after reports of abuse and torture there.

       Japan: the country's west coast suffered widespread destruction from Typhoon Talas, with more than 50 deaths.

       Germany: the ruling CDU and allied FDP lost heavily in state elections in Mecklenburg-West Pomerania.

       Zimbabwe: WikiLeaks released a report from 2008 that claimed President Robert Mugabe had prostate cancer, which, according to doctors, could kill him by 2013.

5   **Colombia:** in response to the recent rise in guerrilla attacks, Juan Carlos Pinzón was sworn in as defence minister, new military commanders were appointed and an additional 1,500 billion pesos was allocated to the ministry.

       Somalia: the UN extended to six the number of areas affected by famine. The Bay region, controlled by the al-Shabaab militia, had the worst malnutrition rates ever recorded in Somalia.

6   **Italy:** a national strike against the austerity measures being debated in Parliament was observed by 3 million public employees.

       Somalia: pirates released a Danish family of five, the Johansens, and two crew, after the payment of a ransom believed to be $4 million; they had been captured in February.

       Switzerland: the central bank pegged the Swiss franc to the euro, setting an upper limit of €1.00=SFr1.20, in an attempt to halt the rising value of the Swiss franc, seen as a safe haven during the eurozone crisis.

7   **Bangladesh:** India's prime minister, Manmohan Singh, ended a two day visit—the first such exchange since 1999—without breakthrough agreements.

India: the high court in New Delhi suffered a bomb explosion that killed at least 13 people; an al-Qaida-linked Pakistani group claimed responsibility.

Pakistan: the Pakistani Taliban claimed responsibility for a twin suicide bombing in Quetta directed against the Frontier Corps.

Syria: further attacks on the city of Homs by the Syrian forces caused France's foreign minister, Alain Juppé, to accuse the Syrian government of crimes against humanity.

8   **Libya:** in an audio message, Colonel Moamar Kadhafi denied that he had left the country.

USA: President Barack Obama delivered a speech to Congress in which he outlined a $447 billion plan to stimulate the economy and create jobs.

9   **Egypt:** protesters broke into the building housing the Israeli embassy in Cairo; the following day, Egypt's military rulers revived the emergency laws of the Mubarak era.

European Central Bank: Jürgen Stark, the ECB's chief economist, resigned protesting at the bank's interventions to support weaker eurozone countries; Germany nominated Jörg Asmussen, the deputy finance minister, to be its senior official at the ECB.

10   **Japan:** the new government, announced on 2 September, lost its industry minister, who had to resign after making a joke about radiation.

11   **Kenya:** Somali pirates abducted a British tourist, Judith Tebbutt, after shooting dead her husband, David Tebbutt. They had been staying at a coastal resort close to the border with Somalia.

12   **Kenya:** an explosion near a leaking oil pipeline in a Nairobi slum killed around 100 people.

Nigeria: President Goodluck Jonathan ordered the military to take "all necessary actions" to end the ethnic and religious violence between Muslims and Christian groups in Plateau state.

Turkey: Prime Minister Recep Tayyip Erdogan was warmly welcomed in Cairo at the start of an "Arab Spring" tour of Egypt, Tunisia, and Libya.

UK: the Vickers commission (the Independent Commission on Banking) released its final report; it called for a separation between banks' retail and investment banking operations.

13   **Afghanistan:** the Taliban launched an attack on the centre of Kabul, focusing on the US embassy and NATO headquarters; they were driven back after 20 hours of fighting; there were 27 deaths.

Algeria: President Abdelaziz Bouteflika announced plans to allow independent radio and television stations, ending the state's monopoly of broadcasting that had lasted since 1962.

China: an investigation into the production and sale of reprocessed cooking oil, salvaged from sewage and restaurant waste, led to the arrest of 32 people.

Pakistan: monsoon flooding reached Karachi.

USA: the traditionally Democrat New York district House of Representatives seat that had been left vacant by the resignation of Anthony Weiner was won by a Republican.

14   **Brazil:** another minister (the tourism minister) resigned over corruption allegations.

Colombia: Jorge Noguera , a former head of the intelligence services, was sentenced to 25 years in prison for collaborating with right-wing paramilitaries.

Italy: Parliament finally passed a much revised €54.2 billion emergency austerity budget.

15   **Denmark:** a general election was narrowly won by the centre-left "Red Bloc", ending
        a decade of centre-right government.

        Syria: the Syrian National Council, a coalition of exile and opposition groups,
        announced in Istanbul its role as the main co-ordinating centre for the opposition to
        President Bashar al-Assad.

16   **Haiti:** Garry Conille, the president's third nominee to the post of prime minister, was
        finally accepted by the legislature.

17   **Latvia:** early elections to parliament returned the Harmony Centre—a largely ethnic
        Russian party—as the largest group.

        USA: the first "Occupy Wall Street" protests began with a march through the Lower
        Manhattan financial district of New York and a tent camp in Zuccotti Park.

18   **Italy:** there were calls for Silvio Berlusconi's resignation after the release of tran-
        scripts of telephone calls, in which the prime minister boasted of his sexual stam-
        ina and made an obscene reference to German Chancellor Angela Merkel. Stan-
        dard & Poor's put Italy on a negative outlook, downgrading its credit rating from
        A+ to A.

19   **Japan:** a rare mass protest was held in Tokyo, demanding an end to nuclear power
        generation in Japan.

        USA: President Obama released a deficit reduction plan that included proposals to
        raise taxes on those earning in excess of $1 million per year—the "Buffet rule".
        Republicans called it "class warfare".

20   **Afghanistan:** Burhanuddin Rabbani, a former president, and the chief negotiator
        between the government and the Taliban, was assassinated in Kabul.

        Zambia: opposition Patriotic Front candidate Michael Sata won presidential elections,
        defeating the incumbent, Rupiah Banda of the ruling Movement for Multiparty
        Democracy. The PF also won the legislative elections, held the same day.

21   **Greece:** the cabinet approved further austerity measures, demanded by creditors before
        the next tranche of bailout money was received.

        Kazakhstan: legislation was approved to restrict religious practice in Kazakhstan.

        Taiwan: the USA announced a $6 billion arms package for Taiwan that would upgrade
        its F-16 fighter jets rather than supply the new model of F-16s.

22   **Pakistan:** Mike Mullen, chairman of the US joint chiefs of staff, accused Pakistan's
        security services of having close links with the Haqqani network Islamist militia
        fighting in Afghanistan.

23   **Bulgaria:** anti-Roma protests erupted after a young man was killed in a traffic accident
        involving a notorious Roma figure.

        Palestine: lodged an application for admission as a full member of the UN on the basis
        of the 1967 borders.

        Yemen: President Ali Abdullah Saleh returned from Saudi Arabia, where he had been
        treated for injuries sustained during the insurgency; an escalation in fighting
        between government supporters and insurgents followed.

24   **Russia:** Vladimir Putin announced his intention to stand in the 2012 presidential elec-
        tions and make President Dmitry Medvedev his prime minister; the finance minster,
        Aleksei Kudrin, resigned in protest.

        Switzerland: the chief executive of UBS resigned after the bank admitted that losses
        from an alleged rogue trader amounted to $2.3 billion.

25   **France:** following indirect elections, left-wing parties took control of the Senate for the
        first time under the Fifth Republic.

26 **Bolivia:** the defence minister resigned, followed a day later by the interior minister, over criticism of police violence against Amerindian demonstrators who were protesting at the building of a new road through an indigenous reserve. President Evo Morales promised a referendum.

27 **Israel:** was rebuked by the US administration for proceeding with plans to build another 1,100 homes for Jewish settlers in East Jerusalem.

Kosovo: the EU postponed talks between Kosovo and Serbia, as violence flared on the border between the two countries.

28 **EU:** the European Commission set out proposals for a "Tobin tax" on financial transactions to take effect in 2014 and raise €57 billion a year.

Greece: troika officials returned to Greece to resume their audit of the government's compliance with the austerity plan, but striking civil servants prevented them from entering government offices.

29 **Germany:** the Bundestag approved Germany's participation in the expanded European Financial Stability Facility (EFSF), agreed by eurozone states in July.

Pakistan: an "all-parties conference" in Islamabad, convened by Prime Minister Yusuf Raza Gillani, produced a 13-point resolution refuting US allegations that Pakistan was doing too little in the fight against Islamic militancy, both domestically and in Afghanistan.

30 **Burma:** President Thein Sein announced a halt to work on the controversial hydroelectric dam at the headwaters of the Irrawaddy river.

Rwanda: the International Criminal Tribunal for Rwanda convicted two former ministers for their part in the 1994 genocide of ethnic Tutsis and moderate Hutus.

Yemen: a US drone air strike killed Anwar al-Awlaki, the leader of al-Qaida in the Arabian Peninsula (AQAP).

OCTOBER

1 **Seychelles:** legislative elections that began on 29 September ended with the ruling People's Party (PL) taking all 31 seats in the National Assembly.

Tokelau: followed Tuvalu in declaring a state of emergency caused by a shortage of fresh water.

2 **Environment:** a report in *Nature* said that ozone depletion over the Arctic could, for the first time, be described as an "ozone hole", matching ozone loss in the southern hemisphere.

Greece: the government announced that it would fail to reach its budget deficit targets for 2011 and 2012; later, eurozone finance ministers delayed payment of a tranche of bailout funding.

Syria; the Syrian National Council established a government-in-exile in Turkey and called for the overthrow of President Bashar al-Assad.

3 **Denmark:** Helle Thorning-Schmidt of the Social Democratic Party became Denmark's first female prime minister at the head of a centre-left coalition following September's elections.

4 **Afghanistan:** President Hamid Karzai signed a strategic pact with India, causing alarm in Pakistan.

Russia: in an article for *Izvestiya* that indicated his foreign policy if, as expected, he was elected president in 2012, the prime minister, Vladimir Putin, called for a "Eurasian Union" to group former Soviet republics.

Somalia: a truck bomb exploded in Mogadishu killing over 100 people; the al-Shabaab militias claimed responsibility.

South Africa: Archbishop Desmond Tutu denounced the ruling African National Congress after the Dalai Lama was refused an entry visa and was therefore unable to attend Tutu's 80th birthday celebrations; the government denied that it had denied entry to the Dalai Lama under pressure from China.

Syria: at the UN Security Council, Russia and China vetoed a resolution condemning the suppression of the pro-democracy movement.

5   **Information technology:** the world's cheapest tablet computer—the Aakash ("sky"), costing $35 for school students—was unveiled in India.

6   **EU:** the ECB offered to buy €40 billion in bonds issued by eurozone banks in an attempt to forestall a banking liquidity crisis.

Japan: to huge publicity, the trial opened in Tokyo of Ichiro Ozawa, a senior politician, on charges of violating political funding laws.

UK: the Bank of England added £75 billion to its quantitative easing programme, bringing the asset purchasing scheme to a total of £275 billion.

7   **Rwanda:** President Paul Kagame appointed Pierre Habumuremyi as prime minister, succeeding Bernard Makuza.

Syria: fresh protests broke out in Homs and other cities; according to the UN almost 3,000 people had been killed since the protests began in March.

9   **Belgium:** the governments of Belgium, France and Luxembourg agreed to break up Dexia, a Franco-Belgian bank, and separate out its toxic assets.

Cameroon: presidential elections were held; the results, ratified on 21 October, showed victory for incumbent President Paul Biya.

Poland: the ruling party, Civic Platform, easily won re-election.

10   **Egypt:** clashes between Coptic Christians and security forces in Cairo caused at least 25 deaths; the finance minister resigned over the government handling of the Christians' protests.

Peru: Ollanta Humala Tasso, the new president, dismissed 30 of the country's 45 police generals as part of an anti-corruption drive.

11   **Slovakia:** the legislature rejected a bill designed to strengthen the EFSF, the eurozone bailout fund, prompting the collapse of the coalition government.

Ukraine: opposition leader and former prime minister Yuliya Tymoshenko was sentenced to seven years in prison at the end of a trial that was widely viewed as politically motivated.

USA: the authorities accused Iran of plotting to assassinate the Saudi ambassador and bomb the Saudi and Israeli embassies in Washington, DC.

USA: the president's proposed $447 billion economic stimulus package failed its first legislative test in a procedural vote in the Senate.

12   **Australia:** the House of Representatives narrowly passed the controversial Clean Energy Bill that imposed a carbon tax on the 500 biggest polluters.

Burma: amnesty was granted to more than 6,300 prisoners, only around 220 of them political detainees.

Uganda: the foreign minister and two other members of the ruling party resigned to face corruption charges relating to the 2007 Commonwealth meeting in Kampala.

USA: on the second day of his trial in Detroit, Umar Farouk Abdulmutallab pleaded guilty to all eight charges relating to his failed attempt to blow up a flight to Detroit on Christmas Day 2009 with a bomb hidden in his underpants.

USA: Congress ratified a free trade agreement (FTA) with South Korea; FTAs with Colombia and Panama were also adopted. The agreements had long been stalled over the question of aid to US workers who lost their jobs because of cheaper labour abroad.

13 **China:** publicity surrounding a road accident in Guangdong province, in which toddler Yue Yue had been run over by a truck and lain, critically injured but unassisted, in the road, caused national unease at the apparent callousness of Chinese society.

India: the EU announced €3 million emergency funding for victims of monsoon flooding in northern and eastern states, where up to 300,000 people had been displaced and over 300 killed.

USA Raj Rajaratnam, a former hedge-fund executive, was sentenced to 11 years in prison for fraud, the longest term imposed for insider trading.

14 **Italy:** Prime Minister Silvio Berlusconi won a vote of confidence in the lower house, but by only 15 votes.

UK: Liam Fox resigned as defence secretary after allegations of conflict of interest involving his close friend, Adam Werrity.

15 **Economy:** anti-capitalist protesters staged large demonstrations in cities around the world, including New York, London, Madrid and Rome, as part of the "Occupy" movement.

Oman: contested elections were held to the 84-member Consultative Council.

16 **France:** François Hollande won the Socialist Party (PS) nomination to challenge President Nicolas Sarkozy in the 2012 presidential elections.

Somalia: Kenya sent 1,600 troops into southern Somalia in pursuit of al-Shabaab insurgents who were blamed for a spate of kidnappings in Kenya.

17 **Jordan:** Awn Khasawneh, a former judge at the ICJ, was appointed prime minister by King Abdullah, replacing Marouf Bakhit.

18 **Israel:** Gilad Shalit, the Israeli soldier captured by Hamas in 2006, was returned to Israel in exchange for the liberation of 1,027 Palestinian prisoners held by Israel.

19 **Afghanistan:** a high-level US delegation began a visit to Afghanistan and Pakistan amid concerns about the level of support from within Pakistan to Afghan insurgents.

20 **Greece:** a 48-hour general strike, accompanied by demonstrations that became violent in Athens, began in protest against fresh austerity measures.

Libya: Colonel Moamar Kadhafi was killed as rebel forces captured Sirte, his hometown and the final bastion of his fallen regime.

Spain: the Basque separatist group ETA made a ceasefire declaration that for the first time included a promise of a "definitive cessation" to violence.

Turkey: after the outlawed separatist Kurdistan Workers' Party (PKK) carried out a series of co-ordinated attacks on Turkish soldiers, Turkish troops entered northern Iraq to hunt down PKK fighters.

21 **Greece:** officials from the "troika" (the EU, IMF, and ECB) said that Greece could receive the next tranche of bailout money, amounting to €8 billion; the Greek government had warned that it would run out of funds in November without the subvention.

UK: St Paul's Cathedral shut its doors to visitors for the first time since World War II as anti-capitalist protesters refused to move their camp from the cathedral's precincts.

22   **Saudi Arabia:** Crown Prince Sultan ibn Abdul Aziz died, raising questions about the
        Saudi succession.
23   **Argentina:** President Cristina Fernández de Kirchner took nearly 54 per cent of the
        vote to win a second term.
        EU: leaders began meeting in Brussels to discuss the eurozone sovereign debt crisis;
        the 17 eurozone members held a parallel summit; the meetings resumed on 26
        October.
        Jamaica: Andrew Holness was selected by the ruling Labour Party to replace the
        prime minister, Bruce Golding, who had announced his resignation in September.
        Libya: the National Transitional Council (the rebel government) declared the coun-
        try's liberation, following the capture and killing of Moamar Kadhafi.
        Switzerland: a general election saw a fall in support for the anti-immigration Swiss
        People's Party.
        Tunisia: elections for a constituent assembly saw Ennahda, the main Islamist party,
        win 41 per cent of the seats.
        Turkey: an earthquake in the eastern province of Van killed several hundred people.
24   **Kenya:** two grenade attacks in Nairobi were blamed on the Islamist al-Shabaab mili-
        tia from neighbouring Somalia.
26   **Brazil:** the sports minister resigned over corruption allegations, becoming the fifth
        minister in the government of President Dilma Rousseff to do so.
        China: the authorities announced their intention to strengthen Internet censorship.
27   **EU:** a summit of eurozone leaders reached agreement to expand the European
        Financial Stability Facility (EFSF), recapitalise eurozone banks, and persuade
        private sector holders of Greek debt to accept a 50 per cent cut in the value of
        their bonds.
        Ireland: Michael Higgins, candidate of the junior coalition Labour Party, was elected
        president, succeeding Mary McAleese.
28   **Madagascar:** Andry Rajoelina, head of the High Authority of Transition, named
        Omer Beriziky as the new prime minister, as part of the "roadmap" agreement
        signed in September.
        Kiribati: a second round of elections completed the process, begun on 21 October, of
        electing the 44 seats in the legislature.
        Commonwealth: the Commonwealth heads of government meeting (CHOGM) was
        opened in Perth, Australia, by Queen Elizabeth II.
30   **Bulgaria:** the second round of presidential elections was won by Rosen Plevneliev.
        Colombia: local elections were held; in Bogota, the post of mayor was won by the
        former M-19 rebel group member Gustavo Petro.
        Kyrgyzstan: presidential elections were won by prime minister Almazbek Atam-
        bayev.
        Thailand: as the flooding that had inundated most of the centre of the country moved
        towards Bangkok, officials reported that the disaster had killed over 380 people.
        The monsoon rains had also caused deaths in Cambodia and Burma.
31   **Greece:** Prime Minister George Papandreou announced he would seek approval in a
        referendum for the eurozone package of rescue measures agreed on 27 October,
        jeopardising the new bailout.
        Libya: Abdurrahim El-Keib was selected as chairman of the National Transitional
        Council, effectively prime minister.
        Palestine: was admitted to UNESCO.
        UN: the organisation marked the world's population reaching the 7 billion mark.

NOVEMBER

2   **Greece:** summoned to Cannes ahead of a G-20 summit meeting, the prime minister, George Papandreou, was told by EU leaders that Greece must approve the rescue package drafted in October before receiving any more bailout funds.

3   **European Central Bank:** the ECB cut its main interest rate from 1.5 to 1.25 per cent.

4   **Colombia:** the army killed FARC guerrilla leader, Alfonso Cano, during an attack against a rebel camp.

    Germany: a hitherto unknown neo-Nazi group was discovered in eastern Germany; its members were believed to have committed several murders and other attacks on immigrants.

    Nigeria: the Islamist Boko Haram sect killed over 60 people in a series of attacks in the north-east of the country.

6   **Greece:** George Papandreou confirmed that he would step down as prime minister rather than attempt to lead a new consensus government.

    Guatemala: Otto Pérez Molina, a former military general, won the second round of voting in the presidential election.

    Nicaragua: Daniel Ortega was re-elected as president for a third, and second consecutive, term in office.

7   **British Virgin Islands:** in legislative elections, the opposition National Democratic Party, led by former chief minister Orlando Smith, was returned to power.

    France: a series of austerity measures amounting to €7 billion was announced, supplementing the €12 billion package announced in August to reduce the budget deficit and ensure France's retention of its AAA credit rating.

8   **Iran:** the International Atomic Energy Agency published a report expressing concern about the probable military aspects of Iran's nuclear programme.

    Liberia: in a runoff second round, the incumbent president, Ellen Johnson Sirleaf, defeated opposition candidate Winston Tubman.

10   **Greece:** Lucas Papademos, a former vice-president of the ECB, was mandated to form a government of national unity to implement the EU's new €130 billion bailout plan for Greece.

    South Africa: the ruling African National Congress dismissed Julius Malema, an outspoken critic of President Jacob Zuma, as head of its youth wing and suspended him from the ANC for five years.

12   **Iran:** in an explosion at a base for the Iranian Revolutionary Guard Corps near Teheran, 17 members of the corps died, including Hassan Moghaddam, described as the "architect" of Iran's missile programme.

    Italy: Silvio Berlusconi resigned as prime minister after he had lost his parliamentary majority on 8 November and following the passage of crucial austerity measures demanded by the EU; the following day, Mario Monti became prime minister at the head of a technocratic government.

13   **Equatorial Guinea:** constitutional changes were overwhelmingly approved in a national referendum.

14   **China:** dissident artist Ai Weiwei posted a bond for half of the ¥15 million demanded by the tax authorities; having been given just two weeks to pay the sum, Ai Weiwei had received over ¥8 million in donations from 30,000 supporters after an online campaign.

15   **Nauru:** Sprent Dabwido was elected president, replacing Marcus Stephen who had resigned on 9 November to pre-empt a vote of no-confidence.

USA: police cleared protesters from the symbolic heart of the Occupy Wall Street movement—the camp at Zuccotti Park, New York city; "Occupy" protests in other cities were also cleared.

16   **Solomon Islands:** Gordon Darcy Lilo became prime minister after the resignation of Danny Philip.

17   **Australia:** US President Barack Obama announced that the USA would station marines near Darwin to strengthen the US presence around the South China Sea.

18   **Afghanistan:** a loya jirga (grand council of elders and tribal leaders) closed in Kabul, having endorsed the plan of President Hamid Karzai to negotiate a long-term US presence beyond 2014.

     Burma: the opposition National League for Democracy said it would re-register as a political party and participate in forthcoming by-elections.

19   **Egypt:** large-scale protests began in Cairo and other cities against continued rule by the military.

     Libya: Saif al-Islam Kadhafi, the son and probable heir of Colonel Moamer Kadhafi, was captured in southern Libya.

20   **Bangladesh:** the first trial opened under the Bangladesh International Crimes Tribunal, a court established to investigate crimes against humanity committed in the war of independence from Pakistan in 1971.

     Russia: Prime Minister Vladimir Putin was jeered at a martial arts event as disillusion grew with Russia's leaders.

     Spain: in the general election, the opposition People's Party, under Mariano Rajoy Brey, defeated the ruling Socialists.

21   **USA:** the joint select committee on deficit reduction—the "supercommittee"—failed to reach a bipartisan agreement to reduce the budget deficit, triggering automatic spending cuts of $1,200 billion under the terms of the Budget Control Act of 2011.

22   **Pakistan:** the ambassador to the USA was forced to resign after it was alleged that he had requested US help to forestall a military coup against President Asif Ali Zardari following the US raid on Abbottabad in May and the killing of Osama bin Laden.

23   **Australia:** the lower house of Parliament passed a controversial bill to tax mining companies' profits; on 8 November the Senate (the upper house) had passed the carbon tax legislation adopted in October by the House of Representatives.

     Bahrain: a report by an independent commission said that the authorities had used "excessive force", including systematic torture, in suppressing demonstrations earlier in the year.

     Yemen: President Ali Abdullah Saleh signed an agreement brokered by the Gulf Co-operation Council that committed him to handing power to his vice president.

24   **Egypt:** Kamal Ganzoury became prime minister following the resignation of Essam Sharaf and his cabinet on 22 November in light of the mass protests.

     The Gambia: President Yahya Jammeh was re-elected for a fourth consecutive term.

     Portugal: a 24-hour general strike against austerity measures was staged; the same day, Portugal's sovereign debt rating was downgraded to junk status.

25   **Morocco:** elections were held to the House of Representatives (the lower house), in accordance with a decision by King Mohammed in August to expedite democratic change.

26   **New Zealand:** the National Party was returned to power for a second consecutive term, though without an overall majority.

Pakistan: US aircraft operating under ISAF in Afghanistan launched attacks on two military frontier posts on the border with Afghanistan that killed at least 24 Pakistani troops, further straining relations between Pakistan and the USA.

27 **Syria:** the Arab League voted to apply sanctions to Syria; the UN had said on 8 November that more than 3,500 people had been killed since the uprising began in March.

28 **Democratic Republic of Congo:** presidential and legislative elections were held, the first DRC-organised polls.

Guyana: the ruling People's Progressive Party/Civic won legislative elections and its leader, Donald Ramotar, became president-elect.

Kuwait: the prime minister and cabinet resigned over corruption allegations, following several weeks of protest.

Somalia: the al-Shabaab militia banned 16 UN and international aid agencies from central and southern Somalia.

St Lucia: the opposition St Lucia Labour party won legislative elections, returning former prime minister, Kenny Anthony, to power.

29 **EU:** finance ministers decided to release the sixth tranche of bailout money for Greece, but failed to agree measures to allow the ECB to purchase unlimited sovereign debt from countries in trouble.

Iran: protestors stormed the British embassy in Tehran in response to tighter economic sanctions imposed on Iran on 22 November by the UK (as well as the USA and Canada).

30 **Belarus:** a court sentenced two young men to death for bombing the Minsk metro system in April.

China: the People's Bank of China announced a loosening of monetary policy, reversing the previous policy of tighter monetary control to combat inflation.

Côte d'Ivoire: Laurent Gbagbo, the former president, was sent to face trial at the International Criminal Court at The Hague. It was the first time that a former head of state had been held in custody by the ICC.

Egypt: early results in the elections allowed Islamists to claim victory, with the Muslim Brotherhood taking around 40 per cent of the vote and a strong showing by conservative Salafi groups.

UK: public sector workers went on strike from midnight as more than 30 unions staged protests against changes to pension provision and austerity measures for the public sector.

Global economy: central banks (the US Federal Reserve, the Bank of Japan, the ECB, the Bank of Canada, the Swiss National Bank and the Bank of England) announced co-ordinated emergency measures to increase liquidity in the global banking system.

DECEMBER

1 **Burma:** US Secretary of State Hillary Clinton, on an historic visit to Burma, met pro-democracy campaigner Aung San Suu Kyi in Rangoon.

Japan: TEPCO said that fuel rods inside reactor No 1 at the Fukushima power plant may have melted, penetrated the concrete floor, and dropped into the outer steel containment vessel.

France: in a major speech, President Nicolas Sarkozy called for a new European treaty to save the euro and prevent the EU from fragmenting.

Iran: EU foreign ministers expanded sanctions against Iran because of concerns over its nuclear programme.

2   **CELAC:** the Community of Latin American and Caribbean States (CELAC) held its inaugural meeting, in Caracas, Venezuela, attended by the leaders of 33 countries.

Germany: in a speech to the Bundestag, Chancellor Angela Merkel laid out her proposals for new regulations for the eurozone.

4   **Croatia:** legislative elections resulted in a victory for the opposition left-wing coalition, led by the Social Democratic Party under Zoran Milanovic.

Iran: the armed forces shot down an unmanned US spy plane that had entered Iranian airspace.

Italy: the cabinet approved a €30 billion austerity package, dubbed "save Italy" by Prime Minister Mario Monti.

Russia: in elections for the State Duma (the lower chamber of the legislature), the ruling United Russia party saw its majority cut.

Slovenia: early elections to the National Assembly were won by the opposition Positive Slovenia.

5   **Afghanistan:** an international conference on Afghanistan's future opened in Bonn, Germany.

Brazil: Labour Minister Carlos Lupi resigned after corruption allegations against him had been raised in the media.

Syria: opposition activists reported that 34 bodies had been found on the streets of Homs. The victims had apparently been abducted by the Shabiha militia.

6   **Afghanistan:** a suicide bomber killed 59 people in an attack on a Shia Muslim shrine in Kabul on the festival of Ashura; a second attack on pilgrims was carried out in the northern city of Mazar-i-Sharif. The Taliban condemned the attacks; Lashkar-e-Jhangvi al-Alami, a Pakistani militant group linked to al-Qaida claimed responsibility.

Belgium: finally formed a government, a six-party coalition under Elio di Rupo.

Kuwait: the emir dissolved the National Assembly over corruption allegations.

USA: President Barack Obama made a major speech in Kansas, attacking Republican economic policy.

7   **Yemen:** a new government was formed, under the premiership of Mohammed Salim Basundwa, following the signature of an agreement in November providing for the removal of Ali Abdullah Saleh from the presidency.

8   **Gibraltar:** the opposition won a narrow majority in legislative elections. Fabian Picardo became chief minister.

Japan: TEPCO reversed plans to release radioactive water into the sea after protests from fishermen's groups. The water had been used to cool the nuclear reactors at Fukushima, damaged in March's tsunami.

9   **DRC:** Joseph Kabila, the incumbent president, was declared the winner of presidential elections held on 28 November; he defeated opposition leader Etienne Tshisekedi.

EU: at a Brussels summit, 23 European leaders agreed a new intergovernmental pact for greater oversight of government spending and a stronger European rescue fund. The UK vetoed a revision of the Lisbon Treaty, because there was no provision for exemptions for the UK's financial services sector.

Serbia: opposition by Germany, based on the unrest in Kosovo, meant that Serbia failed to obtain EU candidate status at the EU summit in Brussels.

10   **Russia:** following smaller protests earlier in the week, there were large demonstrations in Moscow and 50 other cities protesting at the conduct of the 4 December legislative elections and demanding a "Russia without Putin".

Peru: President Ollanta Humala Tasso reshuffled his cabinet after the prime minister, Salomón Lerner Ghitis, resigned. Oscar Valdés, the interior minister, was named as Ghitis's replacement.

11 **Côte d'Ivoire:** held the first elections to the National Assembly in a decade. The results put President Alassane Ouattara's Rally of Republicans (RDR) in first place.

Environment: UN climate change talks in Durban, South Africa, ended with agreement to work on a new climate change deal that would have legal force and affect both developed and developing countries.

Panama: former dictator Manuel Noriega returned to the country from France to serve out his sentence for crimes committed during his presidency, 1983-89.

12 **Papua New Guinea:** the political crisis deepened when the Constitutional Court declared illegal Parliament's attempt in August to install Peter O'Neill as prime minister.

Russia: billionaire Mikhail Prokhorov, who had failed to take the leadership of the Right Cause opposition party in the summer, announced that he would stand in the March 2012 presidential elections as a challenger to Vladimir Putin.

ICC: Fatou Bensouda was named the new chief prosecutor of the International Criminal Court in The Hague. The Gambian lawyer would take over from Luis Moreno Ocampo (Argentia), whose term would expire in June 2012.

13 **Belgium:** a man threw grenades and fired an assault rifle into crowds of shoppers in Liège, killing six and injuring over 100. The perpetrator, Nordine Amrani, died at the scene.

Iran: refused US requests to return a surveillance aircraft (drone) that had come down over eastern Iran.

Palestine: the Hamas-Israel prisoner exchange that had involved the release of Gilad Shalit in October was completed with the release of 450 Palestinian prisoners.

Tunisia: Moncef Marzouki was sworn in as interim president.

14 **USA:** President Barack Obama at a ceremony in Fort Bragg, North Carolina, marked the end of the war in Iraq.

15 **France:** former President Jacques Chirac received a suspended two-year prison sentence for the misuse of public funds when he was mayor of Paris (1977-95).

16 **Japan:** Prime Minister Yoshihiko Noda announced that a "cold shutdown" had been achieved at the Fukushima nuclear power plant, meaning that radioactive emissions and the temperature of the nuclear fuel were under control.

Kazakhstan: demonstrations in the Mangistau region, relating to a labour dispute by oil workers, were violently put down, with the death of at least 15 people.

Philippines: Typhoon Washi caused 1,200 deaths on the southern island of Mindanao.

USA: Bradley Manning, accused of leaking footage and documents relating to the USA's conduct in the Afghan and Iraq wars to WikiLeaks, appeared in court for the first time at a pre-trial hearing.

17 **Gabon:** the Gabonese Democratic Party (PDG) of President Ali Ben Bongo Ondimba won legislative elections by a large majority.

18 **Czech Republic:** Vaclav Havel, playwright, dissident, and former Czech president, died.

Iraq: the last contingent of US troops left Iraq.

Russia: an oil drilling rig capsized and sank in a storm, 200 km off Sakhalin island. Fourteen crew members were rescued; the rest of the 67 crew were feared dead.

19 **North Korea:** announced the death, on 17 December, of Kim Jong Il, the "dear leader". His third son, Kim Jung Un, was named as "successor".

Syria: signed an agreement to allow Arab League observers to monitor its implementation of a peace plan drafted by the Arab League. The first group of monitors arrived on 22 December.

20   **Egypt:** a march by several thousand women in Cairo, demanding the end of military rule, was provoked apparently by images broadcast on the Internet of soldiers beating and disrobing female protesters during marches on 17-18 December.

Spain: Mariano Rajoy Brey took office as prime minister; he split the finance ministry in two and put Luis de Guindos Jurado in charge of economic reform.

21   **China:** a rebellion in the village of Wukan, in Guangdong province, came to an end after provincial officials agreed to return illegally confiscated land and allow free local elections.

European Central Bank: the ECB made available €489 billion at low interest rates to more than 500 eurozone banks.

22   **France:** the National Assembly (the lower house) adopted a bill criminalising denial that the killing of Armenians in the Ottoman Empire during World War I had amounted to genocide.

Iraq: at least 12 explosions occurred in Baghdad, their co-ordinated timing suggesting that al-Qaida in Iraq was responsible.

Tunisia: a coalition government was formed under Prime Minister Hamadi Jebali of the Ennahda party.

23   **USA:** President Barack Obama signed into law measures extending a payroll tax cut and unemployment-insurance benefits for employees, a key component in his economic strategy, after Republicans in the House of Representatives dropped opposition to the legislation.

24   **Russia:** the largest demonstrations so far against alleged fraud in the 4 December Duma elections were held in Moscow and other cities.

25   **Nigeria:** a series of bombs exploded near churches across the country; Boko Haram, an Islamist sect, claimed responsibility.

26   **Guinea-Bissau:** an attempted coup, led by navy commander Bubo Na Tchuto, failed.

27   **Japan:** relaxed its policy banning the export of weapons-related items and technologies.

28   **Bosnia & Herzegovina:** in apparent resolution of a 15-month hiatus, the composition of a new government was agreed, under Vjekoslav Bevanda.

India: the lower house of Parliament passed a bill establishing the post of an anti-corruption ombudsman; arguments over the bill were at the heart of recent anti-government protests. The bill did not pass the upper house, however.

Turkey: a Turkish air strike killed 34 Kurdish civilians, in northern Iraq, after mistaking them for PKK fighters. The prime minister apologised.

29   **Jamaica:** the opposition People's National Party (PNP) under Portia Simpson Miller won legislative elections.

30   **Pakistan:** the Supreme Court announced an inquiry into the scandal that had led to the resignation of the ambassador to the USA in November.

Wendy Slater

INDEX

Page references in bold indicate location of main coverage.